WORKS OF MODERN ART

●●● YOU MUST KNOW
●● YOU SHOULD KNOW
● & YOU REALLY IMPRESS IF YOU KNOW

KUNSTWERKE DER MODERNE

●●● DIE MAN KENNEN MUSS
●● DIE MAN KENNEN SOLLTE
● & DEREN KENNTNIS BEEINDRUCKT

777

MODERNE KUNSTWERKEN

●●● DIE JE MOET KENNEN
●● DIE JE ZOU MOETEN KENNEN
● & WAARMEE JE INDRUK MAAKT ALS JE ZE KENT

OBRAS DE ARTE MODERNO

●●● QUE DEBE CONOCER
●● QUE TENDRÍA QUE CONOCER
● Y DE CUYO CONOCIMIENTO PODRÁ PRESUMIR

Text and picture research: Violetta Maria Farina
Phrases: Anne Muraro

Printed in China 2010

ISBN (English): 978-88-8117-558-1
ISBN (German): 978-88-8117-559-8
ISBN (Dutch): 978-88-8117-557-4

Created and distributed in cooperation with Frechmann Kolón GmbH
www.frechmann.com

Contents

Inhalt

Inhoudsopgave

Índice

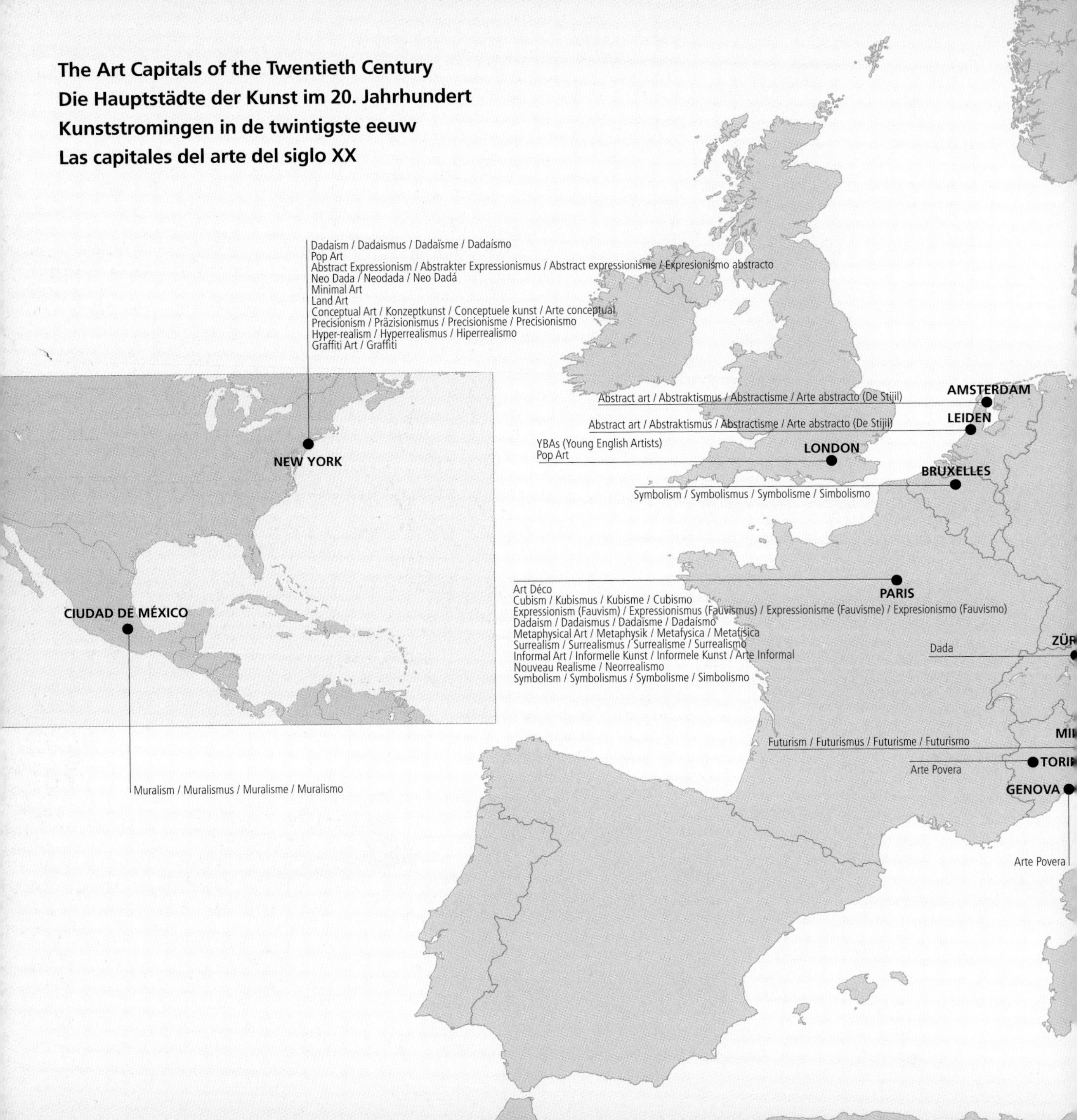

The Art Capitals of the Twentieth Century
Die Hauptstädte der Kunst im 20. Jahrhundert
Kunststromingen in de twintigste eeuw
Las capitales del arte del siglo XX

Dadaism / Dadaismus / Dadaïsme / Dadaísmo
Pop Art
Abstract Expressionism / Abstrakter Expressionismus / Abstract expressionisme / Expresionismo abstracto
Neo Dada / Neodada / Neo Dadá
Minimal Art
Land Art
Conceptual Art / Konzeptkunst / Conceptuele kunst / Arte conceptual
Precisionism / Präzisionismus / Precisionisme / Precisionismo
Hyper-realism / Hyperrealismus / Hiperrealismo
Graffiti Art / Graffiti

NEW YORK

Abstract art / Abstraktismus / Abstractisme / Arte abstracto (De Stijl)
AMSTERDAM
Abstract art / Abstraktismus / Abstractisme / Arte abstracto (De Stijl)
LEIDEN
YBAs (Young English Artists)
Pop Art
LONDON
BRUXELLES
Symbolism / Symbolismus / Symbolisme / Simbolismo

CIUDAD DE MÉXICO
Muralism / Muralismus / Muralisme / Muralismo

Art Déco
Cubism / Kubismus / Kubisme / Cubismo
Expressionism (Fauvism) / Expressionismus (Fauvismus) / Expressionisme (Fauvisme) / Expresionismo (Fauvismo)
Dadaism / Dadaismus / Dadaisme / Dadaísmo
Metaphysical Art / Metaphysik / Metafysica / Metafisica
Surrealism / Surrealismus / Surrealisme / Surrealismo
Informal Art / Informelle Kunst / Informele Kunst / Arte Informal
Nouveau Realisme / Neorrealismo
Symbolism / Symbolismus / Symbolisme / Simbolismo
PARIS

Dada
ZÜR

Futurism / Futurismus / Futurisme / Futurismo
MI
Arte Povera
TORI
GENOVA
Arte Povera

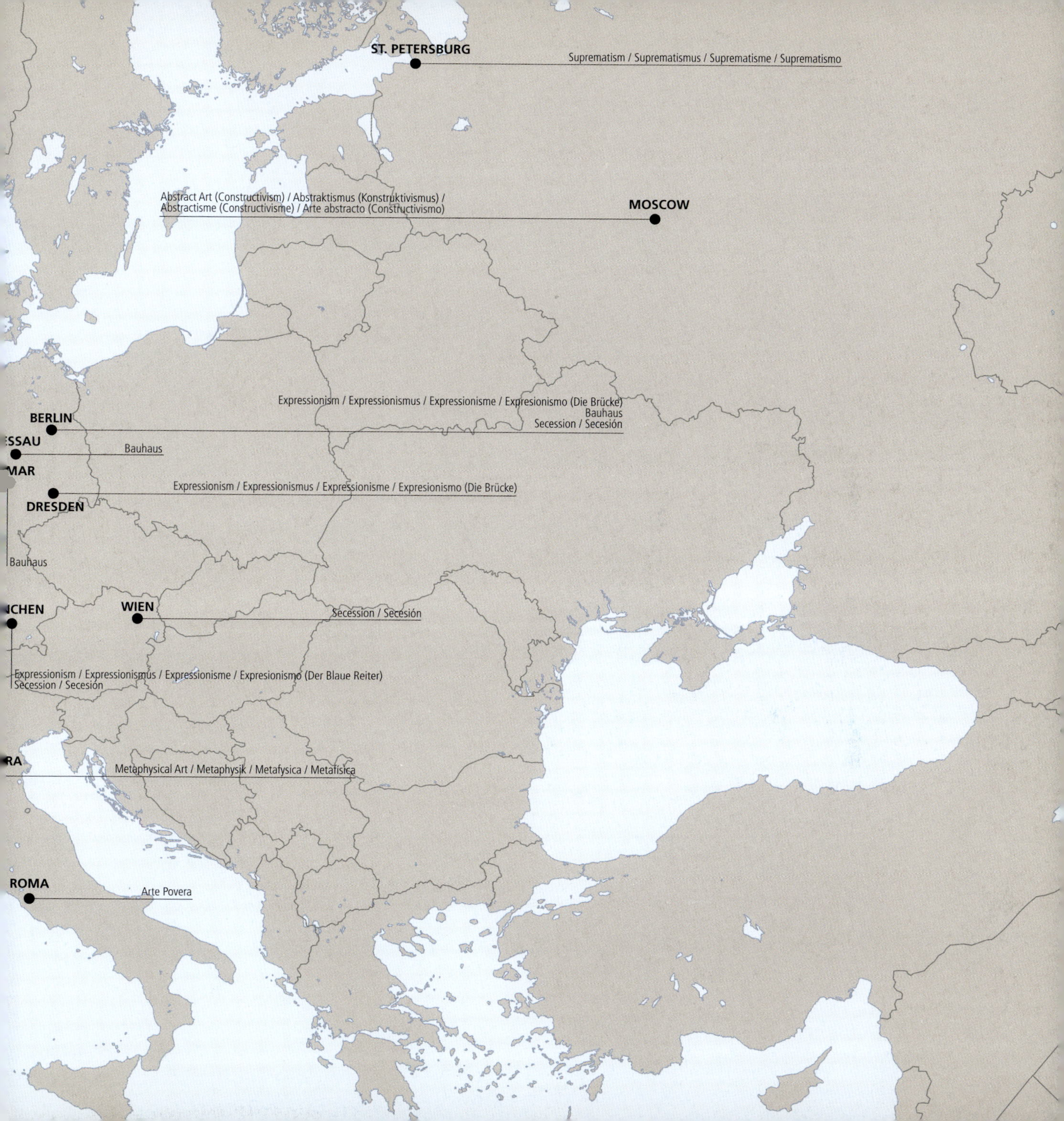

ST. PETERSBURG
Suprematism / Suprematismus / Suprematisme / Suprematismo
Abstract Art (Constructivism) / Abstraktismus (Konstruktivismus) /
Abstractisme (Constructivisme) / Arte abstracto (Constructivismo)
MOSCOW
Expressionism / Expressionismus / Expressionisme / Expresionismo (Die Brücke)
Bauhaus
Secession / Secesión
BERLIN
ESSAU
Bauhaus
MAR
Expressionism / Expressionismus / Expressionisme / Expresionismo (Die Brücke)
DRESDEN
Bauhaus
NCHEN
WIEN
Secession / Secesión
Expressionism / Expressionismus / Expressionisme / Expresionismo (Der Blaue Reiter)
Secession / Secesión
RA
Metaphysical Art / Metaphysik / Metafysica / Metafisica
ROMA
Arte Povera

Style chart
Stilschaubild
Stijlkaart
Tabla de estilos

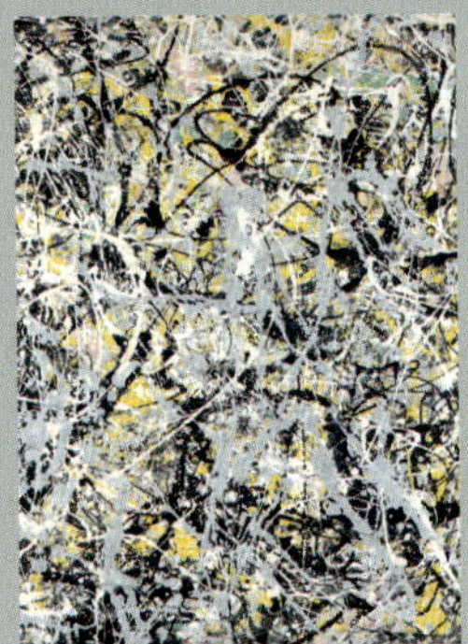

Action painting

Expression coined by the critic Harold Rosenberg in 1952 to define a type of painting whose goal is no longer that of depicting a subject but to suggest the idea of the physical and mental action of the artist. The main representatives of this trend are the United States artists Jackson Pollock, Mark Tobey, Willem de Kooning.

Action painting

Ein vom Kritiker Harold Rosenberg 1952 geprägter Ausdruck, um eine Art der Malerei zu bestimmen, deren Ziel es nicht mehr ist, ein Sujet darzustellen, sondern eine Vorstellung der physischen und mentalen Aktion des Künstlers zu vermitteln. Die Hauptvertreter dieser Tendenz sind die US-amerikanischen Künstler Jackson Pollock, Mark Tobey, Willem de Kooning.

Action painting

Deze uitdrukking is in 1952 uitgevonden door de criticus Harold Rosenberg. Het gaat bij deze schildersoort niet om het uitbeelden van een onderwerp maar om een idee te geven van de fysieke en mentale actie van de artiest. De belangrijkste vertegenwoordigers van deze stroming zijn de Amerikaanse kunstenaars Jackson Pollock, Mark Tobey en Willem de Kooning.

Action painting

Expresión acuñada por el crítico Harold Rosenberg en 1952 para definir un tipo de pintura cuyo objetivo no es ya el de representar un sujeto, sino sugerir la idea de la acción física y mental del artista. Los principales exponentes de esta tendencia son los artistas estadounidenses Jackson Pollock, Mark Tobey, Willem de Kooning.

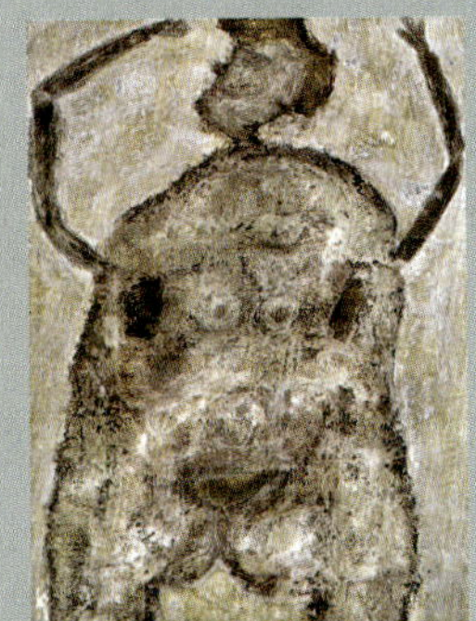

Art brut (*Outside Art*)

Expression ("raw art, spontaneous") used by the painter Jean Dubuffet in 1945 to indicate the works done by children, amateurs, the mentally ill and all those who are not part of the cultural and commercial system of mainstream art.

Art Brut

Ein Ausdruck ("rohe, spontane Kunst"), der vom Maler Jean Dubuffet 1945 verwendet wurde, um die von Kindern, Dilettanten, Geisteskranken und all denjenigen, die nicht Teil des kulturellen und gewerblichen Systems der offiziellen Kunst sind, hergestellten Werke zu bezeichnen.

Art Brut

Met deze uitdrukking ("instinctieve, spontane kunst") verwijst de schilder Jean Dubuffet in 1945 naar werken van kinderen, amateurs, geesteszieken en iedereen die geen deel uitmaakt van het culturele en commerciële systeem van de officiële kunst.

Art brut (*Arte marginal*)

Expresión ("arte bruto, espontáneo") usada por el pintor Jean Dubuffet en 1945 para referirse a las obras realizadas por niños, amateurs, enfermos mentales y todos aquellos que no forman parte del sistema cultural y comercial del arte oficial.

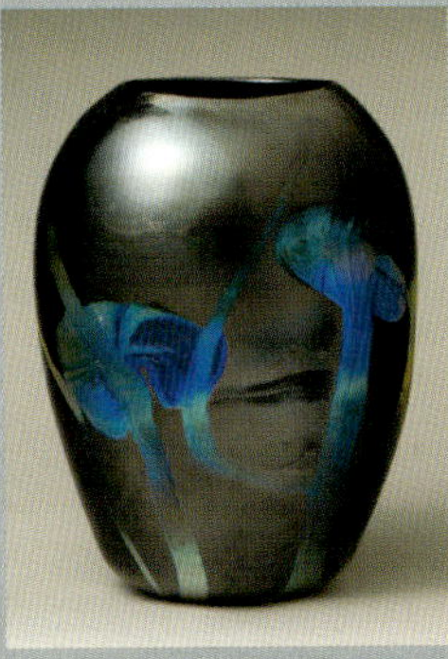

Art Nouveau and Art Déco

Art Nouveau is an artistic movement which developed between about 1890 and 1915. It is a polemic reaction to academic art of the 19th Century, marked by the abandonment of the styles of the past. From the stylistic features of Art Nouveau develops Art Deco, which rejects the sinuous and naturalistic lines for a more rational and geometric style.

Art Nouveau und Art Déco

Art Nouveau ist eine zwischen 1890 und 1915 entstandene künstlerische Bewegung, die als polemische Reaktion gegen den Akademismus des 19. Jahrhunderts auf den Gebrauch historischer Stile verzichtet. Aus Stilelementen des Art Nouveau entsteht die Art Déco, welche anstelle der kurvenreichen und naturalistischen Linien ihrer Vorgängerin einen rationaleren und geometrischen Stil entwickelt.

Art Nouveau en Art Déco

Art Nouveau is een kunstbeweging die zich tussen 1890 en 1915 circa ontwikkelt. Het is een reactie op het 19de-eeuwse academisme die de stijlen van het verleden achter zich gelaten heeft. Art Deco bouwt op de eigenschappen van de Art Nouveau en neemt afstand van de vloeiende en naturalistische lijnen ervan. De stijl is rationeler en meer geometrisch.

Art Nouveau y Art Déco

El Art Nouveau es un movimiento artístico, desarrollado entre 1890 y 1915 ca. Es una reacción polémica al academicismo decimonónico, marcada por el abandono de los estilos del pasado. A partir de los estilemas del Art Nouveau, se desarrolla el Art Déco, que rechaza las líneas sinuosas y naturalistas de dicho movimiento, optando por un estilo más racional y geométrico.

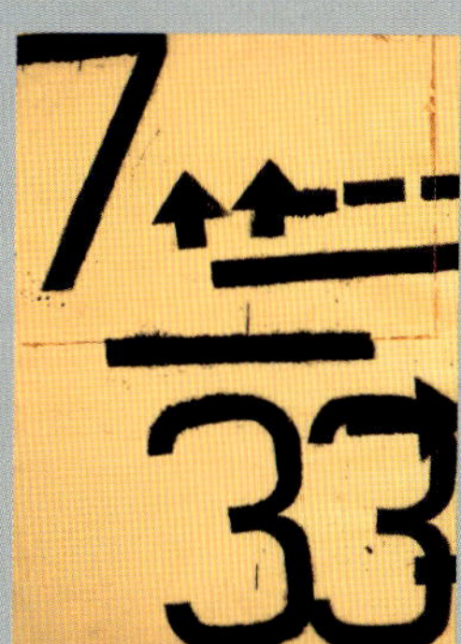

Conceptual Art

We owe the definition of Conceptual Art to Joseph Kosuth who used it around the middle of the 1960s to explain his objective of an art based on thought and no longer on now misunderstood and equivocal aesthetic pleasure.

Konzeptkunst

Der Begriff Konzeptkunst stammt von Joseph Kosuth, der ihn in der Mitte der 60er Jahre verwendete, mit dem Ziel eine Kunst zu etablieren, die auf Gedanken und nicht mehr auf missverstandenen und falschen ästhetischen Vorlieben basiert.

Conceptuele kunst

De definitie van conceptuele kunst komt van Joseph Kosuth die deze term halverwege de jaren zestig gebruikte om het streven naar een op ideeën gebaseerde kunst uit te leggen die niet langer leunt op een inmiddels verkeerd begrepen esthetisch genoegen.

Arte conceptual

La definición de arte conceptual se debe a Joseph Kosuth, que utilizó el término hacia la mitad de los años '60 para explicar su objetivo de lograr un arte basado en el pensamiento y ya no sobre un implícito y equívoco placer estético.

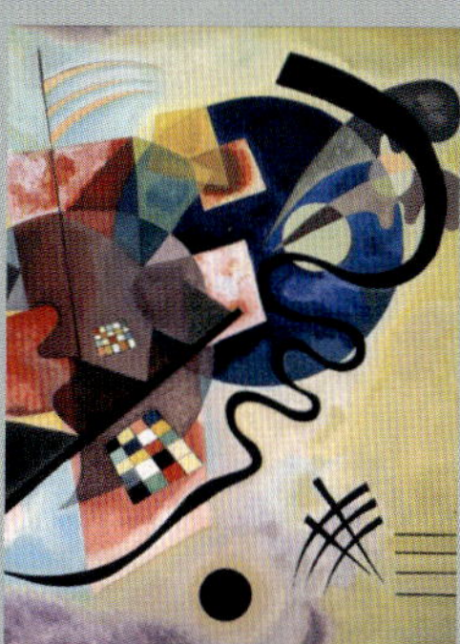

Arte Povera

Definition used for the first time by the critic Germano Celant in 1967 to indicate works created by using common materials such as newspapers, wood, sand and stones.

Arte povera (Arme Kunst)

Ein Begriff, der erstmals 1967 von dem Kritiker Germano Celant verwendet wurde, um Werke zu bezeichnen, die aus alltäglich verwendeten Materialien wie Zeitung, Holz, Sand und Stein hergestellt werden.

Arte Povera

Deze definitie wordt voor het eerst in 1967 door de criticus Germano Celant gebruikt. Hij doelde hiermee op werken die met gewone materialen gemaakt zijn zoals kranten, hout, zand en stenen.

Arte povera (Arte pobre)

Definición usada por primera vez por el crítico Germano Celant en 1967 para referirse a obras creadas utilizando materiales de uso común, como periódicos, madera, arena y piedras.

Bauhaus

School of architecture founded by Walter Gropius in Weimar in 1919, moved to Dessau in 1925 and suppressed by Nazism in 1933. The school aimed at a close collaboration between art and crafts to reach aesthetics that would improve industrial products and a renewal of society.

Bauhaus

Eine von Walter Gropius 1919 in Weimar gegründete Architekturschule, die 1925 umzog und ab 1933 von den Nationalsozialisten unterdrückt wurde. Erklärtes Ziel der Schule war die enge Zusammenarbeit zwischen Kunst und Handwerk, sowie die Begründung einer Ästhetik, die beansprucht, die Industrieprodukte zu veredeln und die Gesellschaft zu erneuern.

Bauhaus

Het Bauhaus was een architectenopleiding die in 1919 door Walter Gropius te Weimar is gesticht. In 1925 verhuist het naar Dessau en in 1933 wordt het door het nazisme verboden. De school had een nauwe samenwerking tussen kunst en ambacht voor ogen die door middel van de esthetica de industriële producten moest verbeteren en de maatschappij moest vernieuwen.

Bauhaus

Escuela de arquitectura fundada por Walter Gropius en Weimar en el año 1919, trasladada luego a Dessau en 1925, clausurada por el nazismo en 1933. La escuela aspiraba a una estrecha colaboración entre arte y artesanado para lograr una estética que mejorara los productos industriales y una renovación de la sociedad.

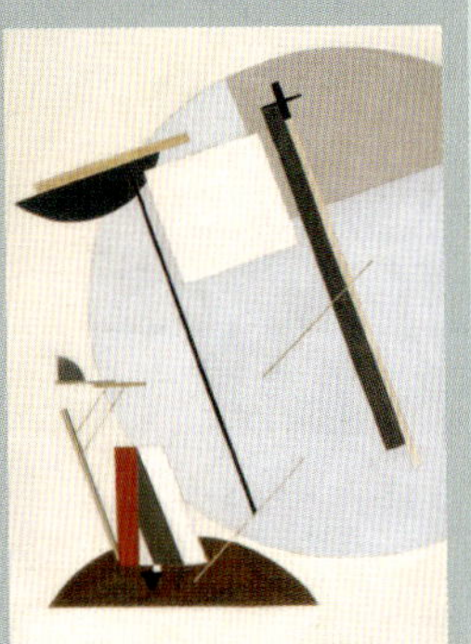

Constructivism
Avant-garde artistic movement started by Aleksej Gan with the goal of actively inserting art in the profound process of renewal started in Russia by the October Revolution. Art must have a political role so that the revolution reaches the people also in visual terms.

Konstruktivismus
Künstlerische Avantgarde-Bewegung, die von Aleksej Gan mit dem Ziel gegründet wurde, die Kunst als aktives Element des durch die Oktoberrevolution in Russland eingeleiteten, tiefgreifenden Erneuerungsprozesses einzugliedern. Demzufolge soll die Kunst eine eminent politische Rolle haben, sodass die Revolution dem Volk auch auf sichtbare Weise begreifbar werden kann.

Constructivisme
Avant-gardistische kunstbeweging opgezet door Aleksej Gan met het doel de kunst actief in te zetten in het grondige vernieuwingsproces dat in Rusland door de Oktoberrevolutie op gang is gebracht. De kunst moet een politieke rol krijgen waarmee de revolutie het volk ook visueel kan bereiken.

Constructivismo
Movimiento artístico de vanguardia iniciado por Aleksej Gan con el objetivo de introducir activamente al arte en el profundo proceso de renovación impulsado en Rusia por la Revolución de Octubre. El arte debe tener un rol político, para lograr que la revolución llegue al pueblo también en términos visuales.

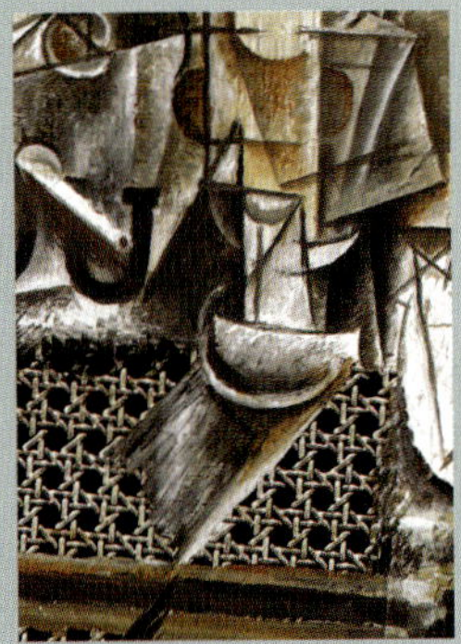

Cubism
The term was first used by the critic Louis Vauxcelles in 1908 in reference to the work of Braque. Rejection of perspective leads to a new organization of space in which viewpoints multiply producing a fragmentation of the object that renders the predilection for form over the content of the representation obvious.

Kubismus
Der Begriff wurde erstmals 1908 vom Kritiker Louis Vauxcelles in Bezug auf ein Werk von Braque verwendet. Der Verzicht auf die Perspektive führt zu einer neuen Raumorganisation, denn die Blickpunkte vermehren sich, das Objekt erscheint zersplittert und der Form fällt im Gegensatz zum Inhalt der Darstellung eine vorrangige Bedeutung zu.

Kubisme
De term werd voor het eerst in 1908 door de criticus Louis Vauxcelles in relatie tot het werk van Braque gebruikt. Het afwijzen van perspectief leidt tot een nieuwe organisatie van de ruimte waarin gezichtspunten zich vermenigvuldigen waardoor objecten gefragmenteerd worden. De vorm is duidelijk belangrijker dan de inhoud van de afbeelding .

Cubismo
El término fue usado por primera vez por el crítico Louis Vauxcelles en 1908 haciendo referencia a la obra de Braque. El rechazo de la perspectiva conduce a una nueva organización del espacio en el cual los puntos de vista se multiplican, produciendo una fragmentación del objeto que pone en evidencia la predilección por la forma respecto al contenido de la representación.

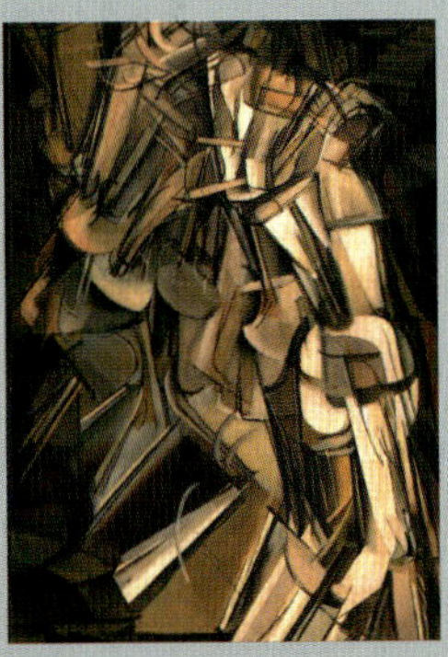

Dadaism
Movement that began with the founding in 1916 of the Cabaret Voltaire. The name dada (which in French means "hobby-horse") was given casually and illustrates well the irreverent attitude of the movement whose artistic research is based on provocation, on irony and on a strong creativity that is manifested in the intuitions of the artist.

Dadaismus
Eine Bewegung, die im Jahr 1916 im Cabaret Voltaire gegründet wurde. Der Name Dada (französisch für "Steckenpferd") wurde zufällig gefunden. Er veranschaulicht sehr gut die respektlose Haltung einer Bewegung, deren künstlerische Suche auf Provokation, Ironie und einer stark ausgeprägten, sich vor allem in der künstlerischen Intuition äußernden, Kreativität beruht.

Dadaïsme
Deze beweging kwam in 1916 in het Cabaret Voltaire van de grond. De naam dada (het Franse woord voor "hobbelpaard") werd bij toeval gevonden en benadrukt het schaamteloze gedrag van de beweging die door middel van kunst op zoek is naar provocatie, ironie en naar een grote creativiteit die tot uitdrukking komt in de intuïtie van de kunstenaar.

Dadaísmo
Movimiento nacido en 1916 con la fundación del Cabaret Voltaire. El nombre dada (que en francés significa "caballito balancín") fue encontrado casualmente, y pone en evidencia el comportamiento irreverente del movimiento cuya indagación artística se basa en la provocación, en la ironía y en una fuerte creatividad que se manifiesta en las intuiciones del artista.

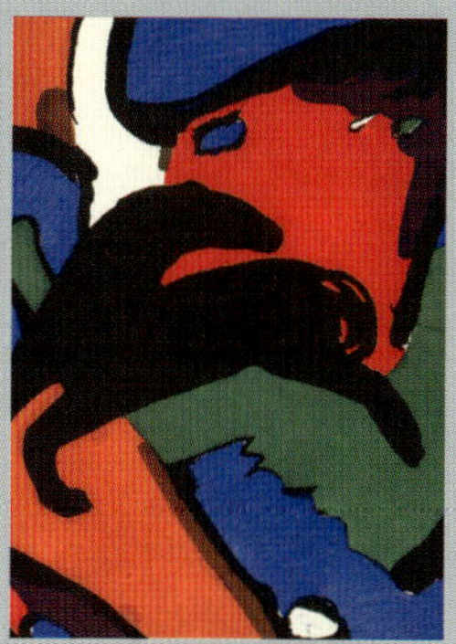

Der Blaue Reiter

Artistic movement founded in München in 1911 by the painters Vassily Kandinsky and Franz Marc. Through the *Der Blaue Reiter* (The Blue Rider) and *The Spiritual in Art* theoretical texts, the movement tries to support the spiritual and abstract trends in art.

Der Blaue Reiter

Eine 1911 in München von den Malern Vassily Kandinsky und Franz Marc gegründete künstlerische Bewegung. Mittels ihrer theoretischen Schriften *Der Blaue Reiter* und *Über das Geistige in der Kunst* versucht diese Bewegung die geistigen und abstrakten Strömungen der Kunst zu betonen.

Der Blaue Reiter

Deze kunstbeweging werd in 1911 door de schilders Vassily Kandinsky en Franz Marc in München opgericht. Door middel van de theoretische teksten *Der Blaue Reiter* en *Über das Geistige in der Kunst* insbesondere in der Malerei probeert de beweging de spirituele en abstracte stromingen te ondersteunen.

Der Blaue Reiter (El jinete azul)

Movimiento artístico fundado en Múnich en 1911 por los pintores Vassily Kandinsky y Franz Marc. A través de los textos teóricos *El jinete azul* (*Der Blaue Reiter*) y *De lo espiritual en el arte*, el movimiento busca sostener las corrientes espiritualistas y abstractas del arte.

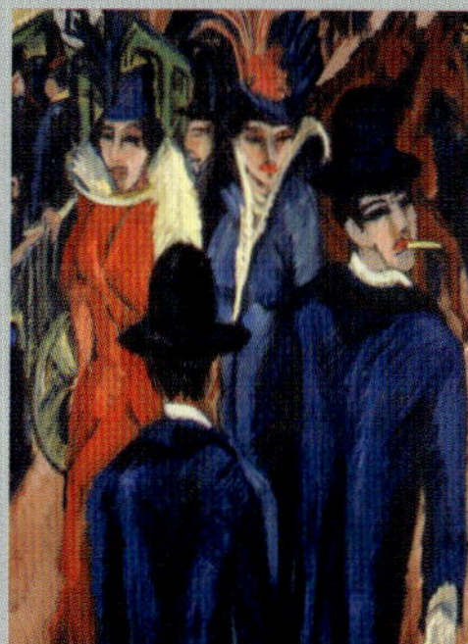

Die Brücke

Artistic group which was founded in Dresden in 1905 by Ernst Ludwig Kitchner and then moved to Berlin in 1911. It is based on a strong union between art and life and on a critique of the industrial society which materializes in the depiction of the city as a place of loneliness and alienation, in contrast to a primitive and uncontaminated nature.

Die Brücke

Eine 1905 in Dresden von Ernst Ludwig Kirchner gegründete und 1911 nach Berlin verlegte künstlerische Gruppe. Sie beruht auf einem engen Bund von Kunst und Leben und auf einer Kritik gegenüber der Industriegesellschaft, die sich in der Darstellung der Stadt als Ort der Einsamkeit und Entfremdung im Vergleich zu einer primitiven und unbeschmutzten Natur äußert.

Die Brücke

Deze kunstgroep werd in 1905 door Ernst Ludwig Kirchner in Dresden opgericht en is in 1911 naar Berlijn overgeplaatst. De groep baseert zich op een sterke relatie tussen kunst en leven en levert kritiek op de industriële maatschappij waarin de stad, in tegenstelling tot de primitieve en ongerepte natuur, een beeld geeft van eenzaamheid en vervreemding.

Die Brücke (El puente)

Grupo artístico fundado en Dresde en 1905 por Ernst Ludwig Kirchner y que luego se trasladó a Berlín en 1911. Se basa en una fuerte unión entre el arte y la vida real y en una crítica hacia la sociedad industrial que se materializa en la representación de la ciudad como lugar de soledad y alienación, en oposición a una naturaleza primitiva e incontaminada.

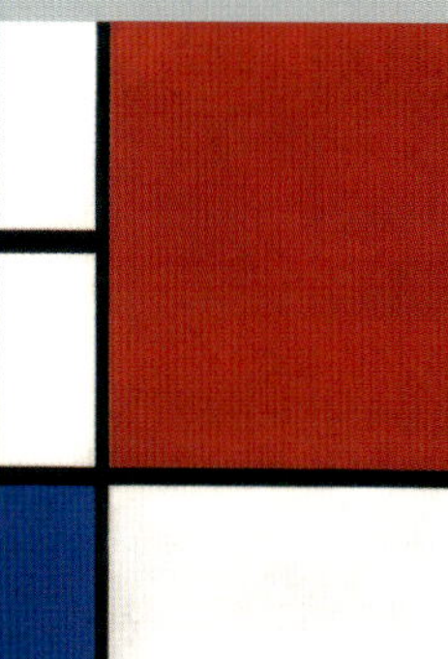

De Stijl

Dutch artistic movement that developed around the *"De Stijl"* magazine in 1918. The main theorist is Piet Mondrian for whom painting is a spiritual act that is expressed with a language that is non-figurative, based on horizontal and vertical lines that cross forming pure geometric areas, which contain primary colors.

De Stijl

Eine künstlerische Bewegung aus Holland, die sich 1918 um die Zeitschrift "De Stijl" entwickelte. Ihr Haupttheoretiker ist Piet Mondrian, für den die Malerei ein geistiger Akt darstellt, der sich mit einer nicht figürlichen Sprache ausdrückt und der auf sich kreuzenden, horizontalen und vertikalen Linien basiert, welche so reine, geometrische Flächen bilden.

De Stijl

De Stijl is een Nederlandse kunstbeweging die zich in 1918 rond het gelijknamige tijdschrift "De Stijl" heeft ontwikkeld. De belangrijkste theoreticus is Piet Mondriaan die vindt dat de schilderkunst een spirituele handeling is die door middel van een niet-figuratieve expressievorm tot uitdrukking moet komen. Als basis worden door elkaar lopende horizontale en verticale lijnen gebruikt waardoor geometrische ruimtes gevormd worden.

De Stijl (El estilo)

Movimiento artístico holandés desarrollado en torno a la revista "De Stijl" en 1918. Su principal teórico es Piet Mondrian, para quien la pintura es un acto espiritual que se expresa con un lenguaje no figurativo, basado en líneas horizontales y verticales que se entrecruzan formando áreas geométricas que encierran colores primarios.

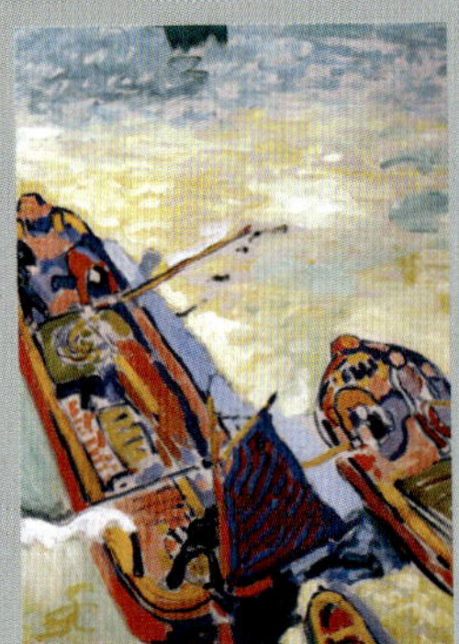

Fauvism

Term coined by the critic Louis Vauxcelles in 1905 to define the style of a group of French artists among which Matisse, Derain, and Van Donghen stand out. The style is associated with the experience of expressionism from which it differs however because of the absence of polemics against society.

Fauvismus

Ein 1905 vom Kritiker Louis Vauxcelles geprägter Begriff, mit dem der Stil einer Gruppe französischer Künstler um Matisse, Derain und Van Donghen bezeichnet wird. Ihr Stil wird gemeinhin mit der Erfahrung des Expressionismus assoziiert, allerdings sind sie frei von jeglicher Gesellschaftskritik.

Fauvisme

Deze term is in 1905 bedacht door de criticus Louis Vauxcelles en hiermee doelde hij op de stijl van een groep Franse kunstenaars onder wie Matisse, Derain, Van Donghen. De stijl wordt in verband gebracht met de ervaring van het expressionisme waar deze zich van onderscheidt door het ontbreken van kritiek op de maatschappij.

Fauvismo

Término acuñado por el crítico Louis Vauxcelles en 1905 para definir el estilo de un grupo de artistas franceses entre los cuales destacan Matisse, Derain y Van Donghen. El estilo se puede relacionar con la experiencia del expresionismo, del cual se diferencia sin embargo por la ausencia de polémica con la sociedad.

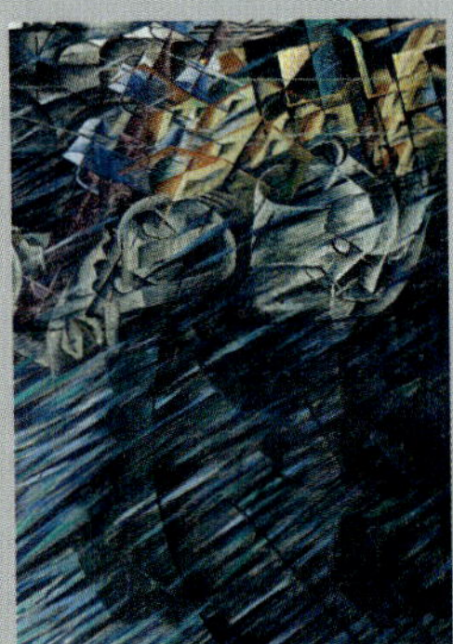

Futurism

Italian movement that involves various artistic fields, whose founder and theorist was Filippo Tommaso Marinetti. On 20 February 1909 the Futurist manifesto was published in the French newspaper "Le Figaro", it expressed a programme with a strong ideological imprint that railed against the rules of tradition and bourgeois values with a celebration of the progress and dynamism of modern civilization.

Futurismus

Eine italienische Bewegung, die verschiedene Felder der Kunst betrifft und in Filippo Tommaso Marinetti ihren Begründer und Theoretiker hat. Am 20. Februar 1909 wird in der französischen Zeitung "Le Figaro" das futuristische Manifest veröffentlicht, ein ausgesprochen ideologisch geprägtes Programm, das anstelle der Regeln der Tradition, sowie der bürgerlichen Werte, den Fortschritt und die Dynamik der modernen Kultur verherrlicht.

Futurisme

Italiaanse beweging die verscheidene kunstvlakken beslaat en waar Filippo Tommaso Marinetti de oprichter en theoreticus van is. Op 20 februari 1909 wordt in de Franse krant "Le Figaro" het futuristische manifest gepubliceerd, een programma met een sterke ideologie dat zich door middel van hulde aan de vooruitgang en aan het dynamisme van de moderne beschaving afzet tegen de regels van de traditie en burgerlijke waarden.

Futurismo

Movimiento italiano que involucra distintos campos artísticos, y tiene a Filippo Tommaso Marinetti como fundador y teórico. El 20 de febrero de 1909 se publica en el periódico francés "Le Figaro" el manifiesto futurista, un programa de fuerte impronta ideológica que arremete contra las reglas de la tradición y los valores burgueses con una celebración del progreso y del dinamismo de la civilización moderna.

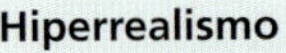

Hyper-realism

Artistic trend that started in the 1960s in the United States. It is characterized by works that reproduce objects and persons with almost obsessive clarity and precision, like the sculptures of John deAndrea, created with casts made of real people, which give the impression that a living being is in front of you. In paintings, the most constant reference is to photography.

Hyperrealismus

Eine künstlerische Tendenz, die in den USA der 60er Jahre entstanden ist. Charakteristisch dafür sind Arbeiten, die Objekte und Personen nahezu Detail-und Präzisionsversessen wiedergibt, was besonders an den Skulpturen von John de Andrea zum Ausdruck kommt. Sie werden aus Abdrücken nach realen Personen gefertigt und vermitteln dem Betrachter den Eindruck, er hätte eine lebendige Menschengestalt vor sich. In der Malerei zeigt sich hingegen ein konstanter Verweis auf die Photographie.

Hyperrealismus

In de Verenigde Staten ontstaat vanaf de jaren zestig een kunsttendens die zich kenmerkt door werken waarin objecten en personen met een bijna maniakale scherpte en precisie worden weergegeven, zoals bijvoorbeeld de sculpturen van John de Andrea. Deze zijn vervaardigd met op mensen toegepaste gietvormen en geven het idee een levend wezen voor je te hebben. De schilderkunstwerken worden vaak vergeleken met de fotografie.

Hiperrealismo

Corriente artística que se afirma a partir de los años '60 en los Estados Unidos. Está caracterizada por obras que reproducen objetos y personas con nitidez y precisión casi maníaca, como las esculturas de John de Andrea, realizadas a través de moldes tomados de personas reales, que dan la impresión de estar frente a un ser vivo. En las obras pictóricas, existe una referencia constante a la fotografía.

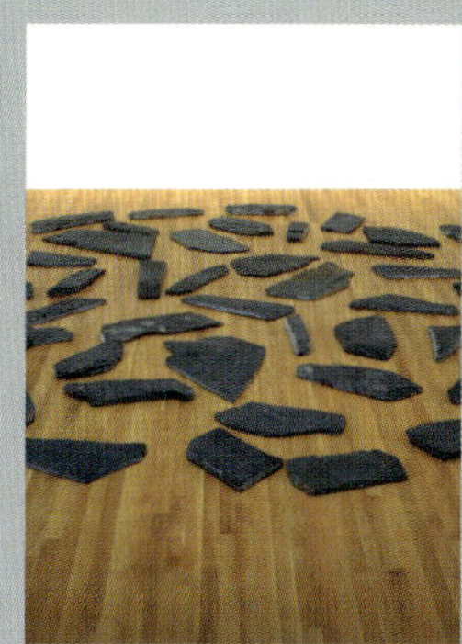

Land Art

Artistic trend of the Sixties whose objective is to participate in the landscape: wide geographic spaces on which large scale projects are created, such as excavations, piles of earth or large tracts outlined by stones or furrows that can extend over entire plateaux or cover whole islands, to produce results that often can only be fully seen in their entirety from up high. Major representatives of this trend are Richard Long and Christo.

Land Art

Eine künstlerische Tendenz aus den 60er Jahren, deren Ziel es ist, auf die Landschaft einzuwirken: es handelt sich dabei um breit angelegte geografische Räume, in denen in großem Maßstab Eingriffe ausgeführt werden, wie Ausgrabungen, Erdanhäufungen oder große, von Steinen oder Furchen gezeichnete Trassen, die sich auf ganze Hochebenen ausweiten und ganze Inseln bedecken können, so dass die Ergebnisse meist in ihrer Gesamtheit nur aus der Höhe zu betrachten sind. Bedeutende Vertreter dieser Richtung sind Richard Long und Christo.

Land Art

Kunsttendens van de jaren zestig met het doel om in het landschap ingrepen aan te brengen: op grote geografische oppervlaktes worden bijvoorbeeld op brede scala kuilen gegraven, land opgehoogd of lange tracé's met stenen en groeven gemaakt die zich kunnen uitstrekken tot hele hoogvlaktes of hele eilanden, die alleen vanuit de lucht in zijn geheel gezien kunnen worden. Belangrijke vertegenwoordigers van deze tendens zijn Richard Long en Christo.

Land Art

Corriente artística de los años '60 cuyo objetivo es intervenir en el paisaje: amplios espacios geográficos sobre los cuales se realizan intervenciones de gran escala, como excavaciones, acumulaciones de tierra o grandes trazados marcados con piedras o surcos que pueden extenderse sobre enteros altiplanos o cubrir toda una isla, de modo que produzcan resultados que a menudo se pueden observar en toda su extensión solamente desde lo alto. Exponentes significativos de esta tendencia son Richard Long y Christo.

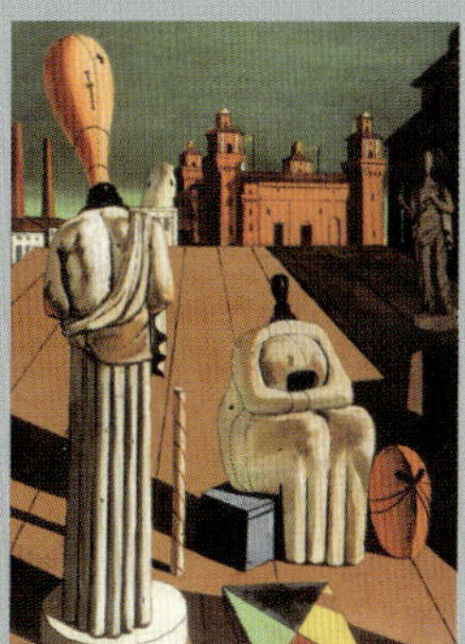

Metaphysical Art

Art movement whose most famous representatives are Giorgio De Chirico, along with his brother Alberto Savinio, Carlo Carrà and Giorgio Morandi. It is a type of painting characterized by immobile spaces formally well defined, in which the human presence, virtually absent, arouses feelings of loneliness and melancholy.

Metaphysische Malerei

Eine Bewegung in der Malerei, deren bekannteste Vertreter Giorgio de Chirico und sein Bruder Alberto Savinio, Carlo Carrà und Giorgio Morandi sind. Es handelt sich um eine Malerei, die von statisch anmutenden, formal gut definierten Räumen bestimmt ist, in denen eine praktisch nicht vorhandene, menschliche Präsenz Gefühle von Einsamkeit und Melancholie hervorruft.

Metafysica

Schildertendens waarvan Giorgio De Chirico, samen met zijn broer Alberto Savinio, Carlo Carrà en Giorgio Morandi de beroemdste vertegenwoordigers zijn. Kenmerken van deze schilderstijl zijn onbeweeglijke formeel goed afgebakende ruimtes waarin de mens meestal afwezig is waardoor gevoelens van eenzaamheid en weemoed opgewekt worden.

Metafísica

Corriente pictórica cuyos exponentes más célebres son Giorgio De Chirico, junto a su hermano Alberto Savinio, Carlo Carrà y Giorgio Morandi. Se trata de una pintura caracterizada por espacios inmóviles formalmente bien definidos, donde la presencia humana, prácticamente inexistente, suscita sentimientos de soledad y melancolía.

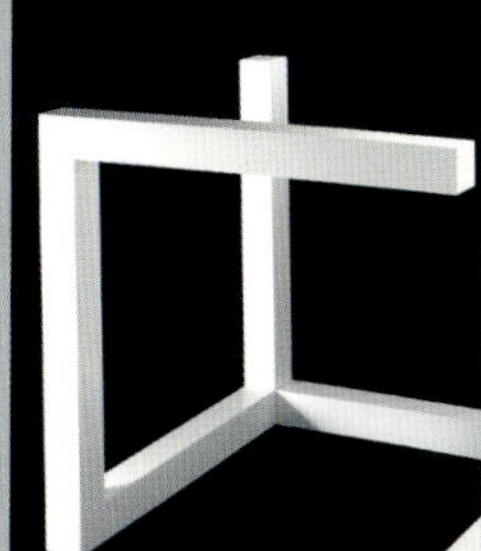

Minimal Art

Along with Pop Art it is one of the most widespread art movements in the United States starting from the 1960s. It is characterized by the essence of language, both in painting and sculpture, reduced to just a few elements and leaning towards abstraction and conceptualism. Sol Lewitt is an artist representative of this movement.

Minimalismus

Zusammen mit der Pop Art stellt er die in den USA am weitesten verbreitete Richtung seit den 60er Jahren dar. Sein Markenzeichen ist die Einfachheit sprachlicher Mittel in Malerei und Skulptur, welche jeweils auf wenige Elemente reduziert werden und sich zunehmend der Abstraktion und Konzeptualisierung annähern. Der wohl repräsentativste Vertreter dieser Richtung ist Sol Lewitt.

Minimal Art

Samen met pop art vormt deze stroming vanaf de jaren zestig van de 20ste eeuw de meest verspreide kunsttendens in de Verenigde Staten. Kenmerk van deze tendens is de eenvoud van de expressievorm, zowel in de schilder- en beeldhouwkunst, waarbij de weinige elementen tot een minimum gebracht zijn en die neigt naar abstractie en conceptualisme. Vertegenwoordiger van deze tendens is Sol Lewitt.

Minimal Art

Junto al Pop Art es una de las tendencias artísticas más difundidas en los Estados Unidos a partir de los años '60 del siglo XX. Se caracteriza por la esencialidad del lenguaje, tanto pictórico como escultórico, reducido a pocos elementos y tendente a la abstracción y al conceptualismo. Exponente representativo de esta tendencia es Sol Lewitt.

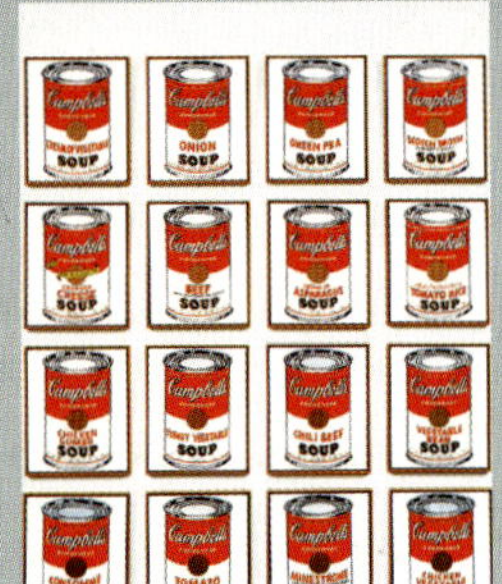

Pop Art

Form of artistic expression that emerged in England in the middle of the 1900s which reuses representations typical of mass communication (therefore popular, the term in fact comes from "popular art"), such as the comic strip, advertising posters and company logos. Lichtenstein, Rauschenberg, Warhol are just some of the most famous artists that dominated this movement.

Pop Art

Eine in England in der Mitte des 20. Jahrhunderts entstandene künstlerische Ausdrucksform, die typische Darstellungen der Massenkommunikation (also populäre Themen, woher auch der Begriff "popular art" stammt) wieder aufgreift, wie beispielsweise das Comic, Werbeplakate oder Firmenembleme. Lichtenstein, Rauschenberg, Warhol sind nur einige der bekanntesten Künstler, die die Szene der Bewegung beherrschten.

Pop-art

Pop-art is een kunstvorm die halverwege de 20ste eeuw ontstaan is en die typische afbeeldingen uit de massacommunicatie herbruikt (dus populair, "popular art", waar de term dan ook van afgeleid is), zoals stripverhalen, reclameposters of commerciële uithangborden. Lichtenstein, Rauschenberg en Warhol zijn slechts enkele onder de bekendste kunstenaars van deze beweging.

Pop Art

Forma de expresión artística surgida en Inglaterra a mediados del siglo XX que reutiliza representaciones típicas de la comunicación de masas (o sea, populares, de ahí el término, que deriva de hecho de "popular art"), como la historieta, los carteles publicitarios o los letreros comerciales. Lichtenstein, Rauschenberg o Warhol son sólo algunos de los más famosos artistas que dominaron el escenario de este movimiento.

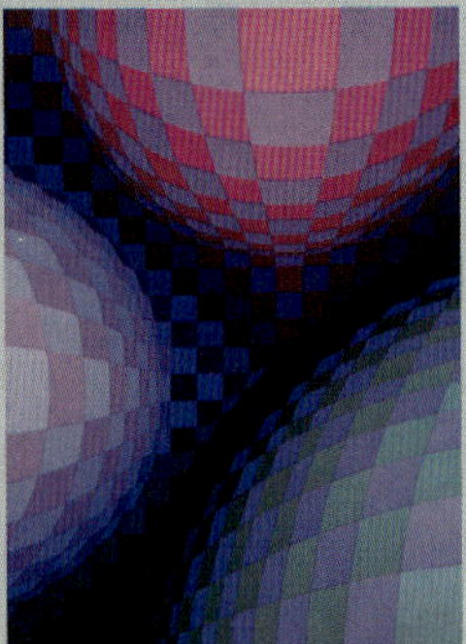

Op Art

Optical Art or Op Art is an artistic movement which emerged around the Sixties around the French painter, Vasarely and which then developed in the 1970s. It centres on creating optical illusions, typically of movement, by the opportune combination of particular abstract subject or by juxtaposition of colors.

Op Art

Die Optical Art oder Op Art ist eine in den 60er Jahren um den französischen Maler Vasarely entstandene, künstlerische Bewegung, die sich dann in den 70er Jahren des 20. Jahrhunderts entwickelt hat. Zentraler Aspekt ist es, optische Illusionen, die typisch für die Bewegung sind, hervorzurufen, indem besondere abstrakte Sujets günstig kombiniert oder die Farben nebeneinander gestellt werden.

Op-art

Optical Art of Op-Art is een kunstbeweging die rond de jaren zestig rond de Franse schilder Vasarely ontstaan is en die zich in de jaren zeventig verder ontwikkeld heeft. Deze beweging richt zich op optische illusies van bewegingen door abstracte voorwerpen op gepaste wijze te combineren of door gebruik te maken van kleuroverlappingen.

Op Art

El Optical Art u Op Art, es un movimiento artístico nacido en torno a los años '60 alrededor de la figura del pintor francés Vasarely y que evolucionó luego en los años '70 del siglo XX. Se basa en provocar ilusiones ópticas, por lo general de movimiento, a través de la unión oportuna de particulares sujetos abstractos o aprovechando la yuxtaposición de los colores.

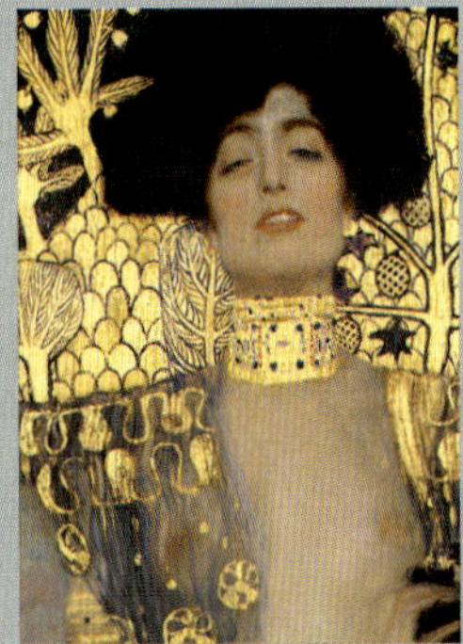

Secession

Term which indicates, in the second half of the XIX Century and the beginning of the XX Century, a series of movements or groups of artist that oppose the traditional art of the academies. The Secessions become established especially in Austria and Germany: among the most famous are those of München, Berlin and that of Vienna, led by Gustav Klimt.

Secession

Ein Begriff, mit dem in der zweiten Hälfte des 19. Jahrhunderts und zu Beginn des 20. Jahrhunderts eine Reihe von Künstlergruppen bezeichnet werden, die sich der traditionellen Kunst der Akademien Entgegenstellen. Die Secessionen behaupten sich vor allem in Österreich und in Deutschland: Zu den bekanntesten zählen die von München, Berlin, sowie die von Gustav Klimt angeführte in Wien.

Secession

Term waarmee in de tweede helft van de 19de en aan het begin van de 20ste eeuw gedoeld wordt op een reeks kunstbewegingen of kunstgroepen die zich afzetten tegen de traditionele kunst van de academies. De secessiebewegingen breken vooral in Oostenrijk en Duitsland door: de bekendste zijn die van München, Berlijn en Wenen, aangevoerd door Gustav Klimt.

Secesión

Término con el cual se denominan, en la segunda mitad del siglo XIX y comienzos del XX, una serie de movimientos o grupos de artistas que se oponen al arte tradicional de las academias. Las secesiones se afirman sobre todo en Austria y en Alemania: entre las más conocidas, las de Múnich, Berlín y la de Viena, liderada por Gustav Klimt.

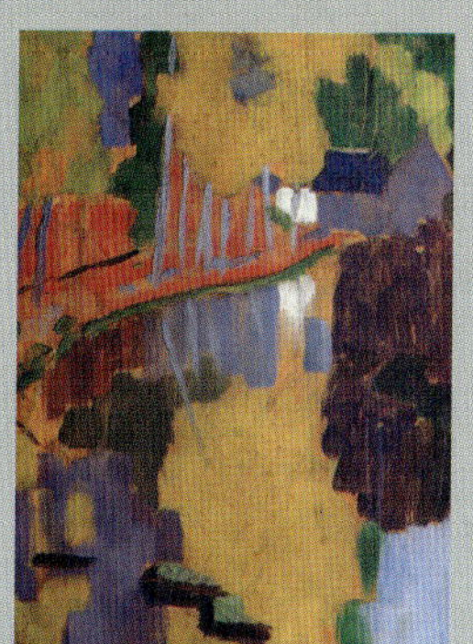

Symbolism

The first manifesto of Symbolism (1886) heralds an art that is not banally descriptive but evocative and capable of penetrating reality even in its most mysterious and profound elements through a synthesis of sensory and spiritual perceptions open to the world of dreams and fantasy.

Symbolismus

Das erste Manifest des Symbolismus (1886) Fordert anstelle der banal Beschreibenden eine suggestive Kunst, die in der Lage ist, die Wirklichkeit auch in ihren mysteriösesten und tiefsinnigsten Elementen zu durchdringen. Dies geschieht vor allem durch die Verarbeitung von Sinnes- und Geisteseindrücken, sowie durch die Einbeziehung von Träumen und Phantasien.

Symbolisme

Het eerste symbolische manifest (1886) heeft het over een kunstvorm met niet alleen een beschrijvend maar ook een evocatief doeleinde die de mysterieuze en diepste kanten van de werkelijkheid kan binnendringen door middel van zintuiglijke en spirituele waarnemingen die open staan voor een droom- en fantasiewereld.

Simbolismo

El primer manifiesto del Simbolismo (1886) brega por un arte no banalmente descriptivo, sino evocativo y capaz de penetrar la realidad incluso en sus elementos más misteriosos y profundos a través de percepciones sensoriales y espirituales abiertas al mundo del sueño y de la fantasía.

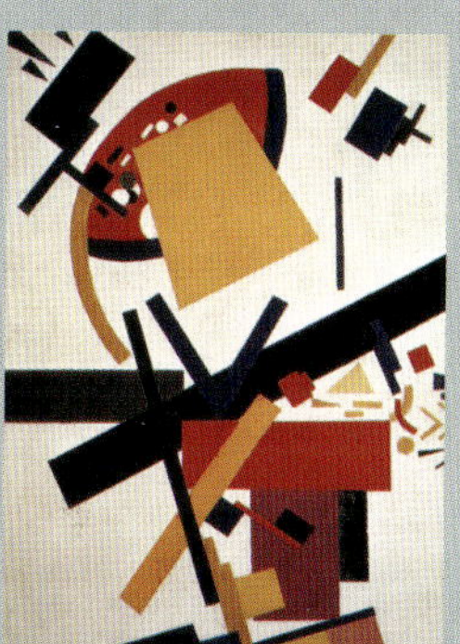

Suprematism

Russian art movement created by Kazimir Malevic which aspires to the *"supremacy of pure sensitivity"* which must be expressed in an art that rejects material reality in favor of the spirit. It is characterized by an extremely simplified language made of pure geometric shapes and conceptual images.

Suprematismus

Eine von Kazimir Malević geschaffene künstlerische Bewegung. Ihr erklärtes Ziel ist die *Vorherrschaft des reinen Gefühls"* in einer Kunst, die die materielle Wirklichkeit zugunsten des Geistes zurückweist. Markenzeichen ist eine extrem vereinfachende Bildsprache, die aus klaren geometrischen Formen und konzeptionellen Bildern besteht.

Suprematisme

Russische kunstbeweging opgericht door Kazimir Malevitsj die de "suprematie van de zuivere ervaring van de beeldende kunst" nastreeft hetgeen tot uitdrukking komt in een kunstvorm die de materiële werkelijkheid afwijst en die zich richt op de geest. Kenmerkend voor deze beweging is de extreem simpele expressievorm middels puur geometrische vormen en conceptuele afbeeldingen.

Suprematismo

Movimiento artístico ruso creado por Kazimir Malevic que aspira a la *supremacía de la sensibilidad pura"*, que se debe expresar en un arte que rechaza la realidad material a favor del espíritu. Está caracterizado por un lenguaje simplificado al máximo, compuesto de formas puras geométricas e imágenes conceptuales.

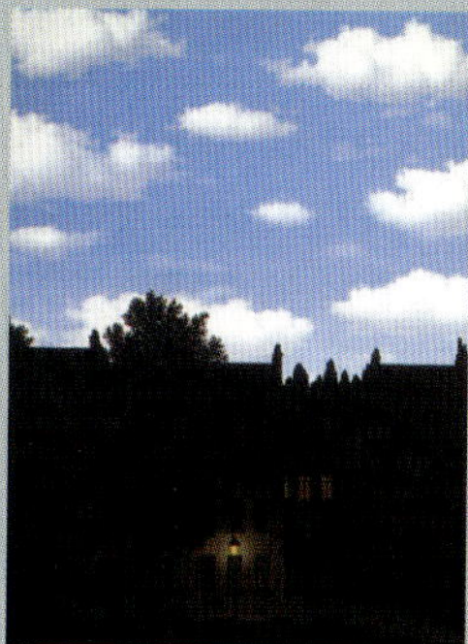

Surrealism

Its inception goes back to the *Surrealist Manifesto* written by Andre Breton in Paris in 1924. It establishes itself as a new attitude towards life which, starting from Freud's theories, re-evaluates the unconscious, dreams and the imagination. Chance is the principal regulator of life and art, beyond reason and logic. Magritte and Dali are among the most famous representatives of this movement.

Surrealismus

Seine Entstehung beruht auf dem *Manifest des Surrealismus*, das von André Breton 1924 in Paris herausgegeben wurde. Er versteht sich als neue Lebensauffassung, die, ausgehend von den Theorien Freuds, das Unbewusste, den Traum und die Vorstellungskraft neu bewertet. Der Zufall ist von nun an das bestimmende Prinzip des Lebens und der Kunst, jenseits von Vernunft und Logik. Magritte und Dalì gehören zu den bekanntesten Vertretern dieser Bewegung.

Surrealisme

Deze stroming ontstaat met het *Manifest van het Surrealisme* dat in 1924 door André Breton in Parijs wordt uitgegeven. Het gaat om een nieuwe levenshouding, waarbij, geïnspireerd door de theorieën van Freud, het onderbewustzijn, de droom en de verbeelding centraal staan. Het toeval regelt het leven en de kunst, en gaat het verstand en de logica voorbij. Magritte en Dalì zijn enkele van de bekendste vertegenwoordigers van deze beweging.

Surrealismo

Su acta de nacimiento se remonta al *Manifiesto del Surrealismo* redactado por André Breton en París en 1924. Se plantea como una actitud frente a la vida, que, partiendo de las teorías freudianas, reevalúa el inconsciente, el sueño y la imaginación. El azar es el principio regulador de la vida y del arte, más allá de la razón y de la lógica. Magritte y Dalí están entre los más famosos representantes de este movimiento.

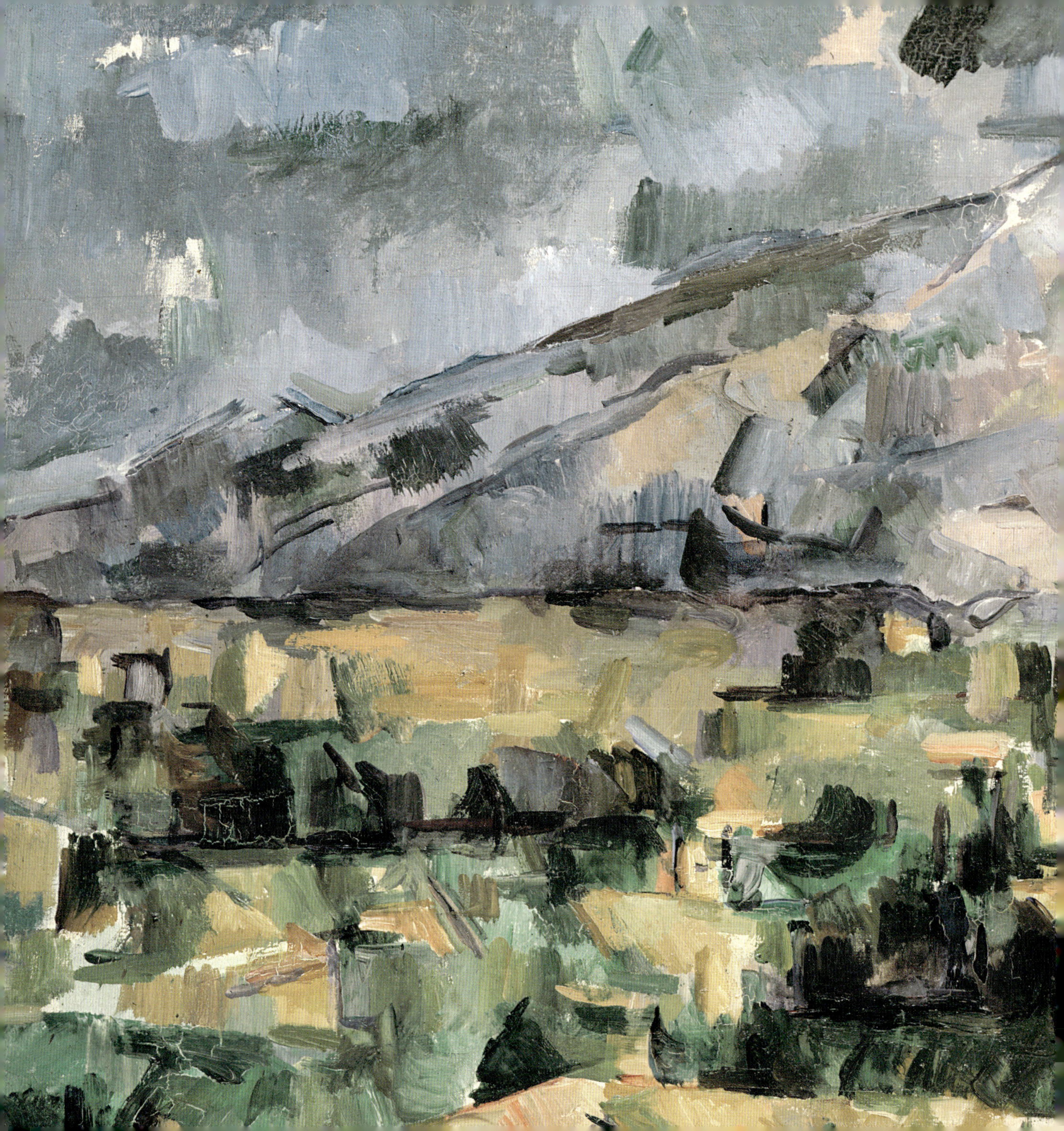

The dawn of the Twentieth Century • Das frühe 20. Jahrhundert
Het begin van de twintigste eeuw • Los albores del siglo XX

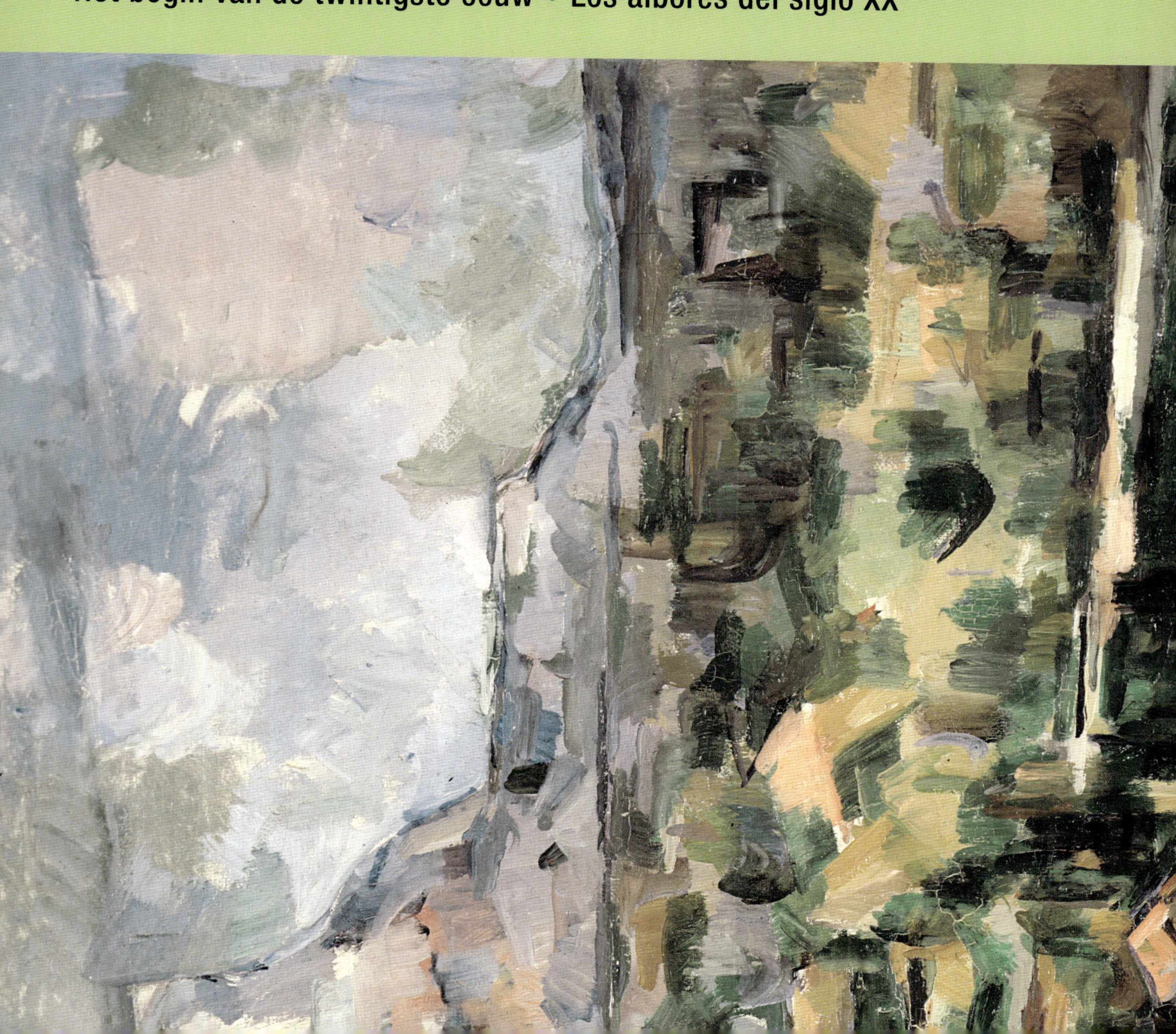

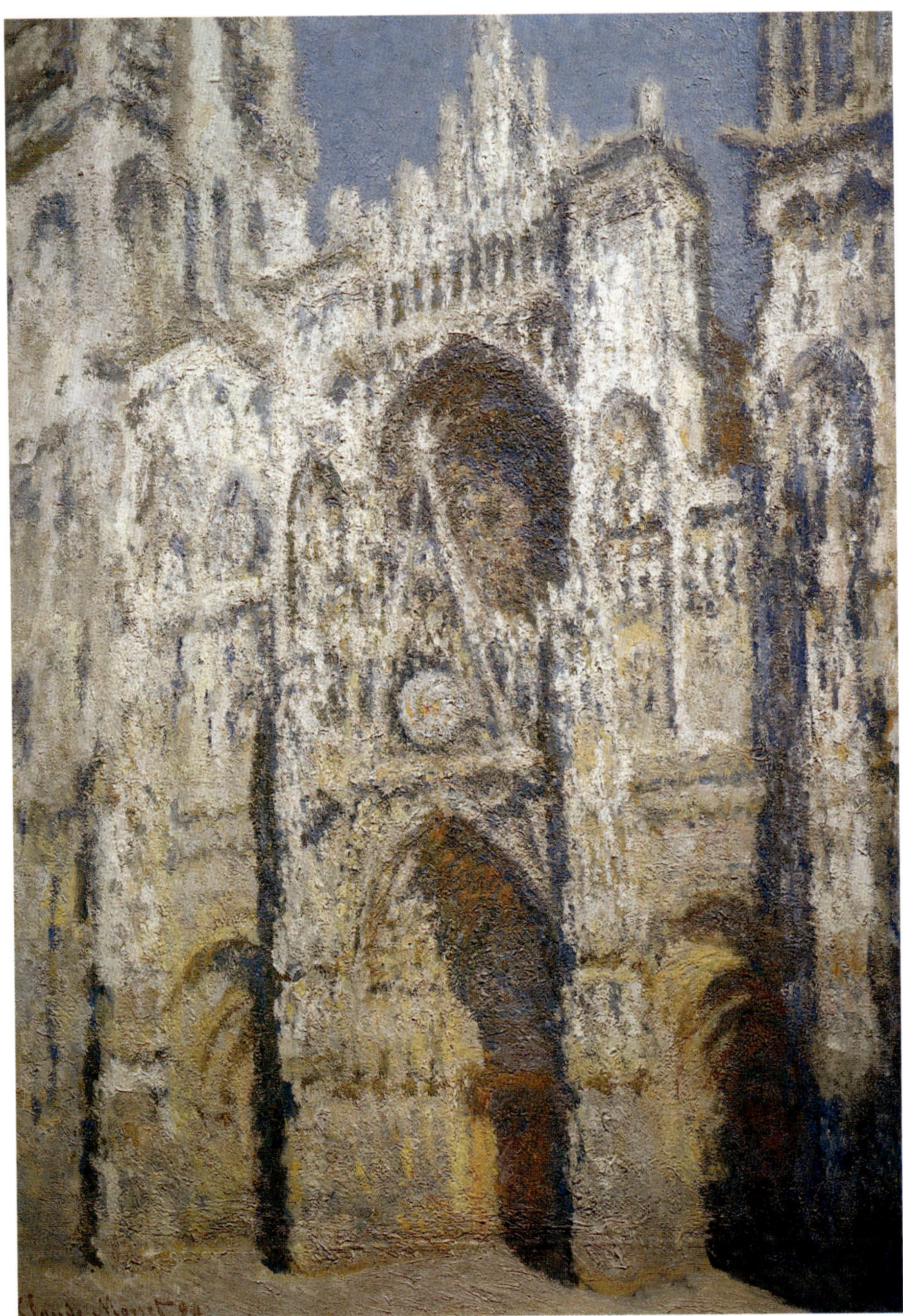

16

Claude Monet
(Paris 1840 - Giverny 1926)
**Rouen Cathedral,
Full sunlight
Kathedrale von Rouen
bei strahlender Sonne
Kathedraal van Rouen
in het volle zonlicht
La Catedral de Rouen
a pleno sol**
● ●

1893
107 x 73 cm / 42.1 x 28.7 in.
Musée d'Orsay, Paris

oil on canvas / Öl auf Leinwand
olieverf op doek / óleo sobre lienzo

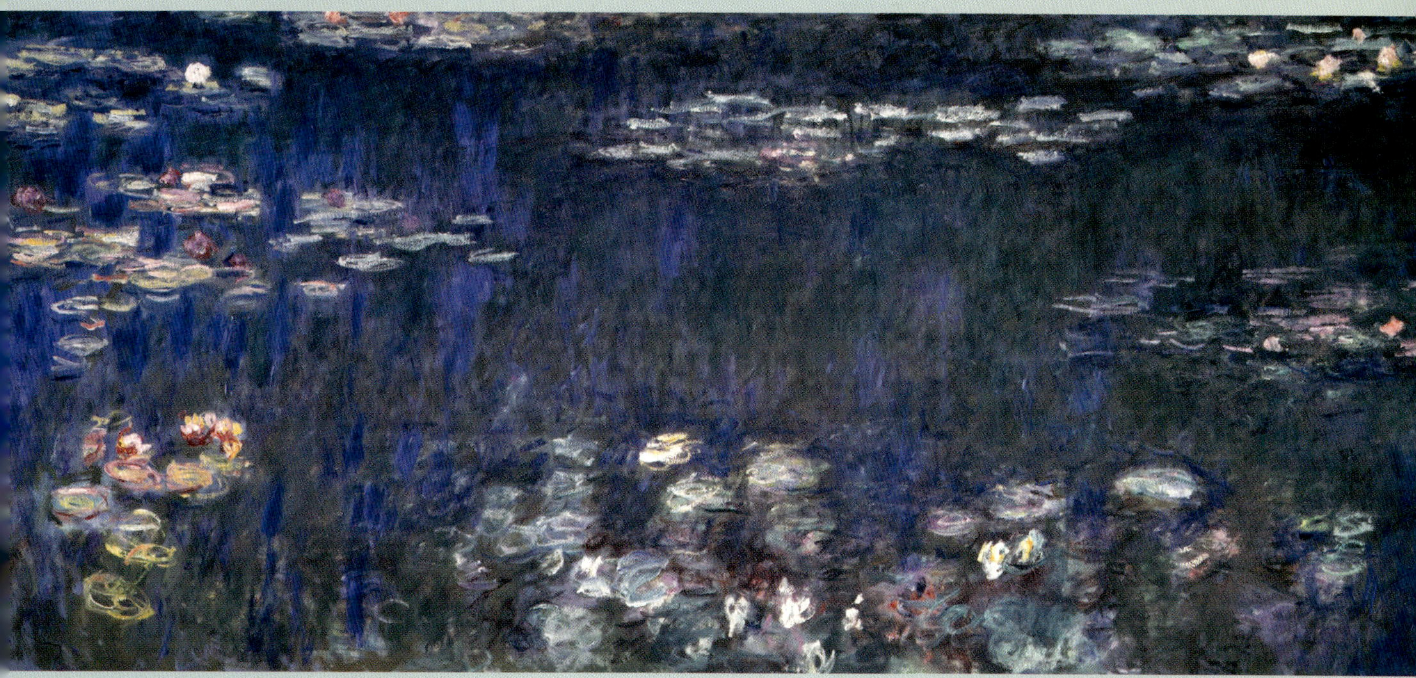

Claude Monet
(Paris 1840 - Giverny 1926)

Water-Lilies, green reflections
Seerosen, Grüne Reflektionen
De waterlelies, groene weerspiegelingen
Ninfeas (reflejos verdes)

●●

1914-1926
200 x 425 cm / 78,8 x 167.4 in.
Musée de l'Orangerie, Paris

oil on canvas / Öl auf Leinwand
olieverf op doek / óleo sobre lienzo

Surpassing Impressionism, the *Water Lilies* are a pure pictorial and chromatic experience.

Die *Seerosen* stellen eine Art Überwindung des Impressionismus, eine rein malerische und farbliche Erfahrung dar.

De *Waterlelies* ontstijgen het impressionisme en vormen een ware beeld- en kleurbeleving.

Superando el Impresionismo, las *Ninfeas* constituyen una pura experiencia pictórica y cromática.

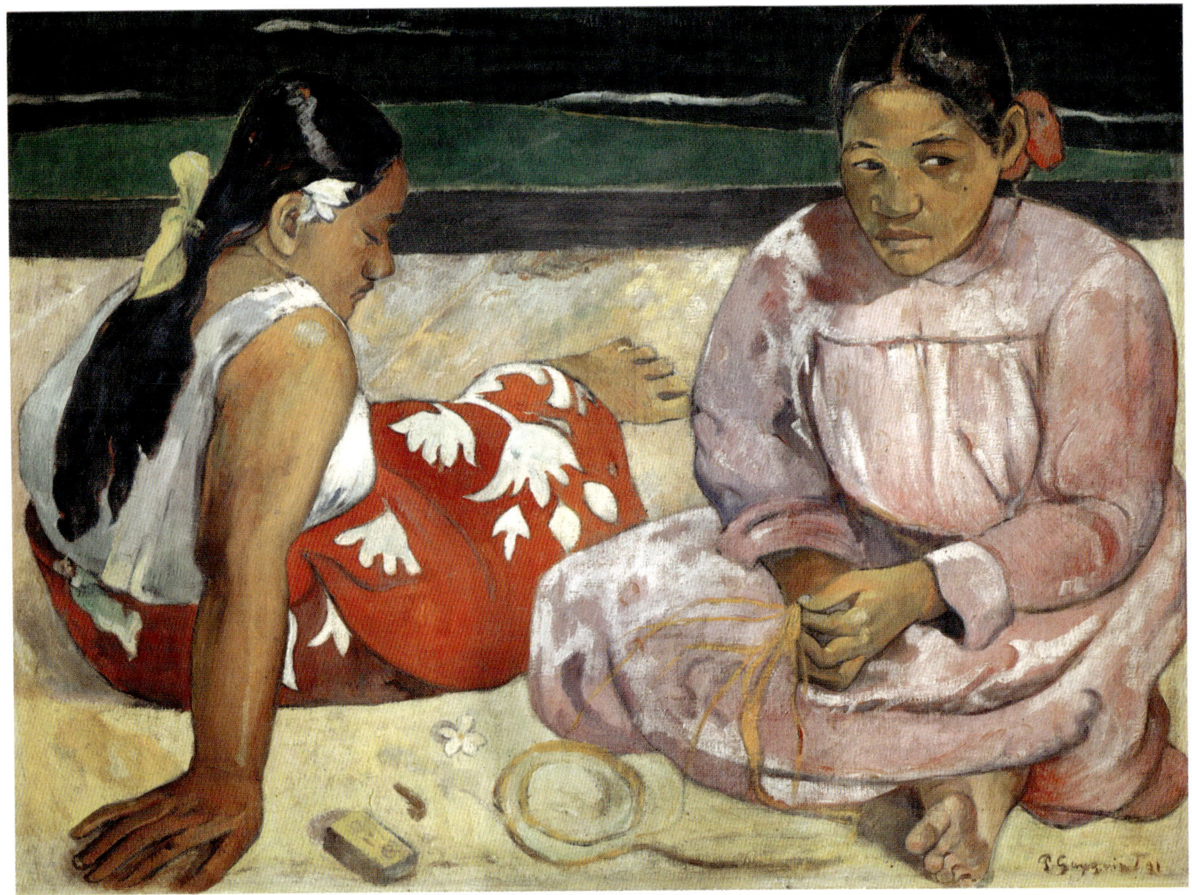

Paul Gauguin
(Paris 1848 - Hiva-Oa 1903)

Tahitian Women
Frauen aus Tahiti
Tahitiaanse vrouwen
Mujeres de Tahití

●●●

1891
69 x 91 cm / 27.2 x 35.8 in.
Musée d'Orsay, Paris

oil on canvas / Öl auf Leinwand
olieverf op doek / óleo sobre lienzo

"How is it possible to put so much
mystery into so much brilliance?"

"Wie ist es möglich, so viele Mysterien
in solch einer Pracht auszudrücken?"

"Hoe is het mogelijk dat er zoveel
mysterie in zoveel schittering zit?"

"¿Cómo es posible que se pueda poner
tanto misterio en tanto fulgor?"
Stephane Mallarmé

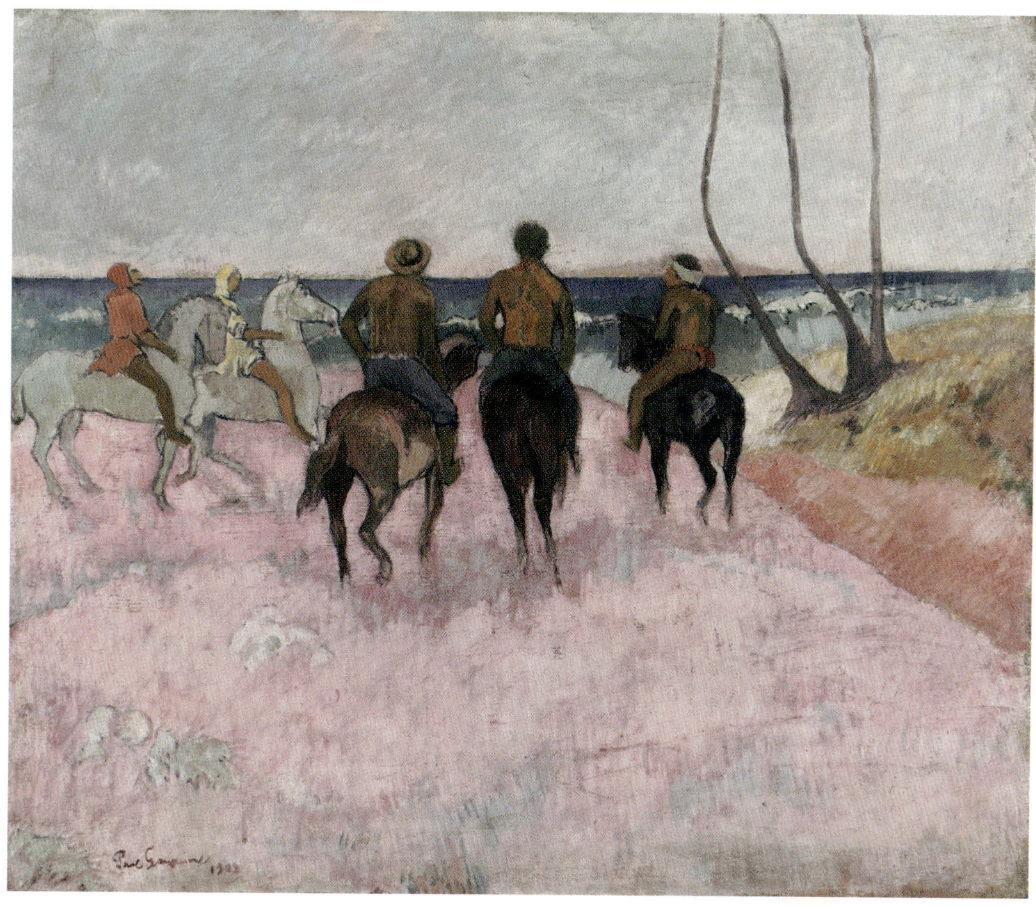

Paul Gauguin
(Paris 1848 - Hiva-Oa 1903)

Riders on the Beach
Reiter am Strand
Ruiters op het strand
Jinetes en la playa

●

1902
65,6 x 75,9 cm / 25.8 x 29.9 in.
Museum Folkwang, Essen

oil on canvas / Öl auf Leinwand
olieverf op doek / óleo sobre lienzo

Henri de Toulouse-Lautrec

(Albi 1864 - Saint-André-du-Bois 1901)

Woman of the house
Femme de maison
Huisvrouwen
El salón de la Rue des Moulins

1894
111,5 x 132,5 cm / 43.9 x 52.2 in
Musée Toulouse-Lautrec, Albi

tempera and oil on canvas / Tempera und Öl auf Leinwand
tempera en olieverf op doek / temple y óleo sobre lienzo

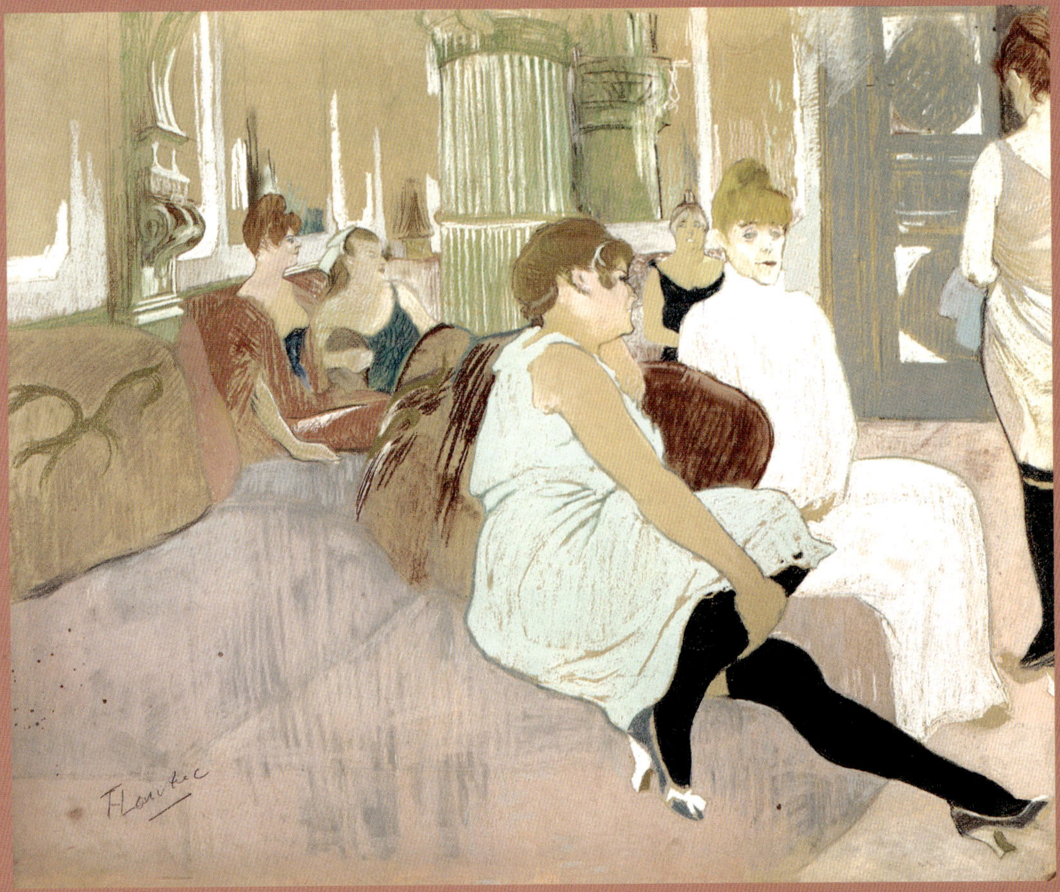

Henri de Toulouse-Lautrec
(Albi 1864 - Saint André du Bois 1901)

Yvette Guilbert

●

1894
186 x 93 cm / 73.2 x 36.6 in.
Musée Toulouse-Lautrec, Albi

oil on paper / Öl auf Papier
olieverf op papier / óleo sobre papel

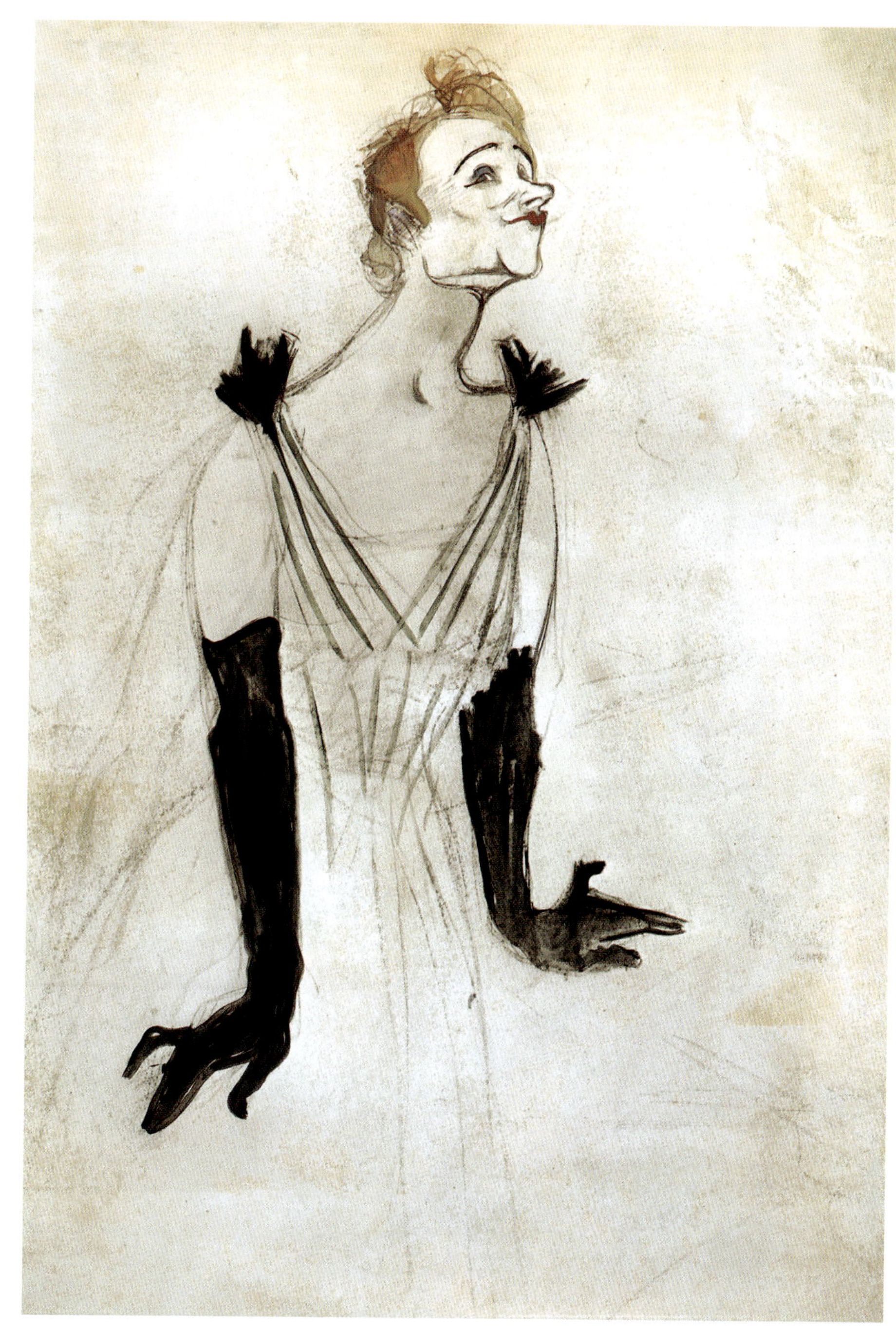

With his synthetic painting,
Lautrec achieves great
expressiveness.

Mit seiner synthetischen Malerei
erreicht Lautrec eine große
Expressivität.

De synthetische schilderijen van
Lautrec zijn één en al expressiviteit.

Con su pintura sintética, Lautrec
logra una gran expresividad.

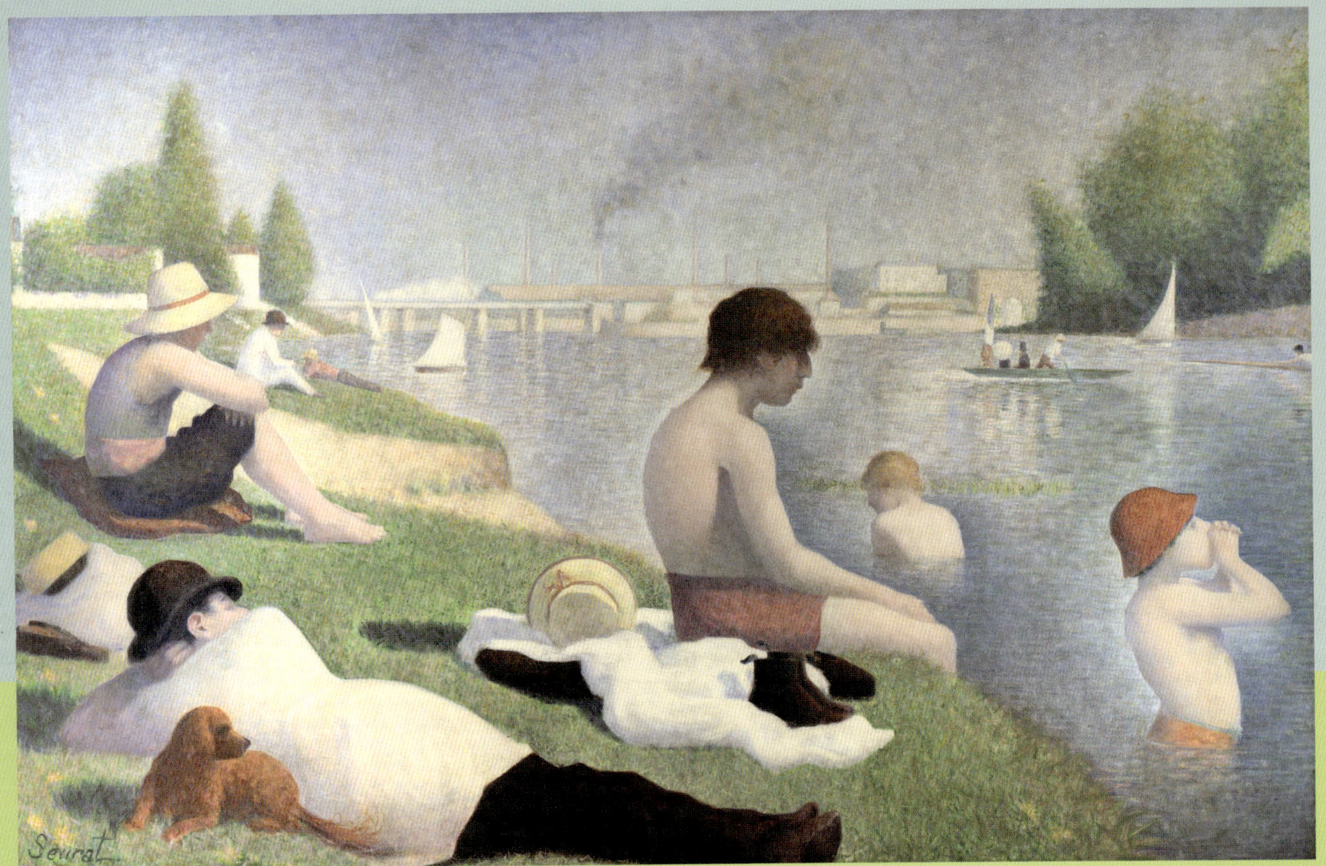

Georges Seurat
(Paris 1859 - Gravelines 1891)

Bathers at Asnières
Badende bei Asnieres
Badgasten in Asnières
Baño en Asnières

●●●

1884
201 x 300 cm / 79.1 x 118.1 in.
National Gallery, London

oil on canvas / Öl auf Leinwand
olieverf op doek / óleo sobre lienzo

▶ Georges Seurat
(Paris 1859 - Gravelines 1891)

The Circus
Der Zirkus
Het circus
El circo

●●●

1890-1891
185 x 152 cm / 72.9 x 59.9 in.
Musée d'Orsay, Paris

oil on canvas / Öl auf Leinwand
olieverf op doek / óleo sobre lienzo

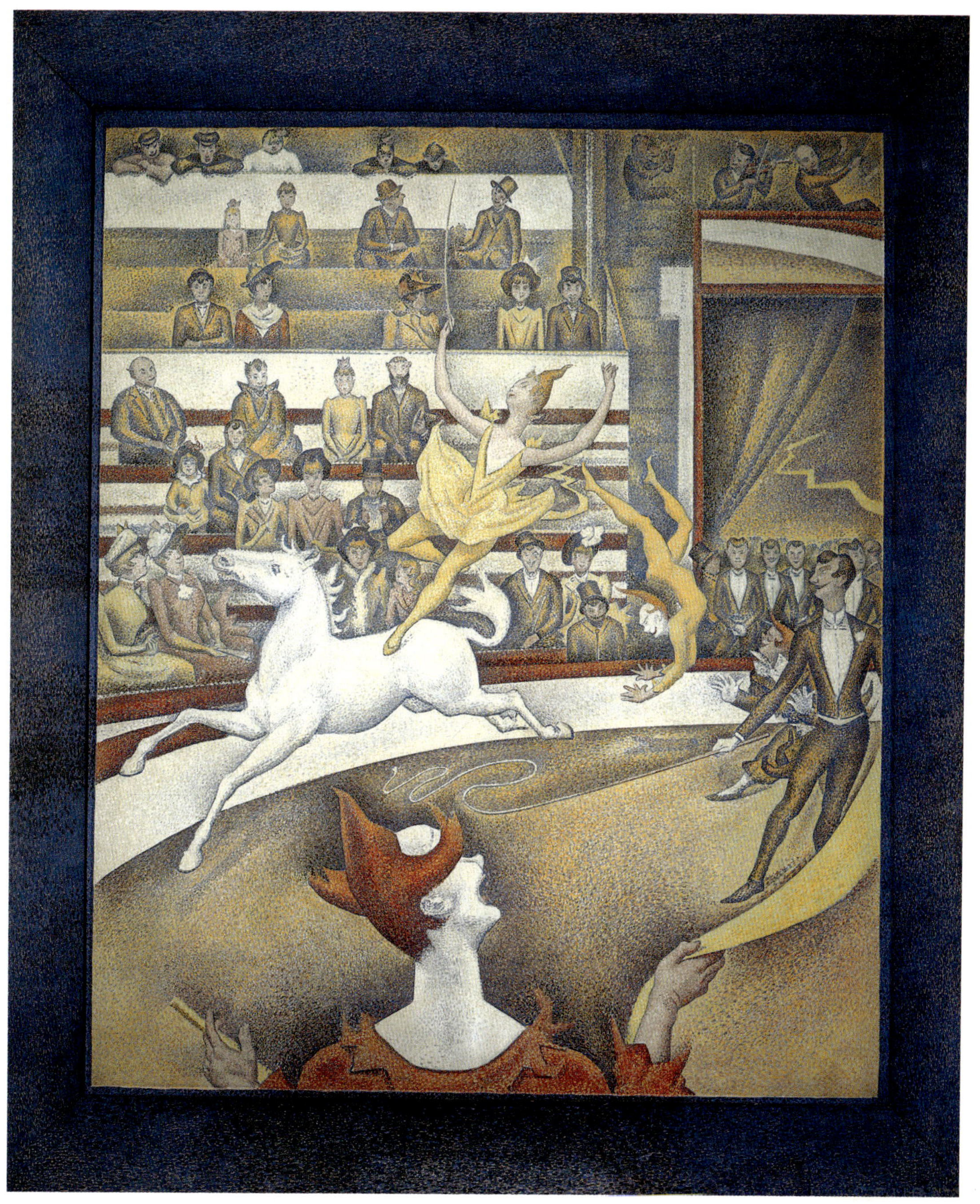

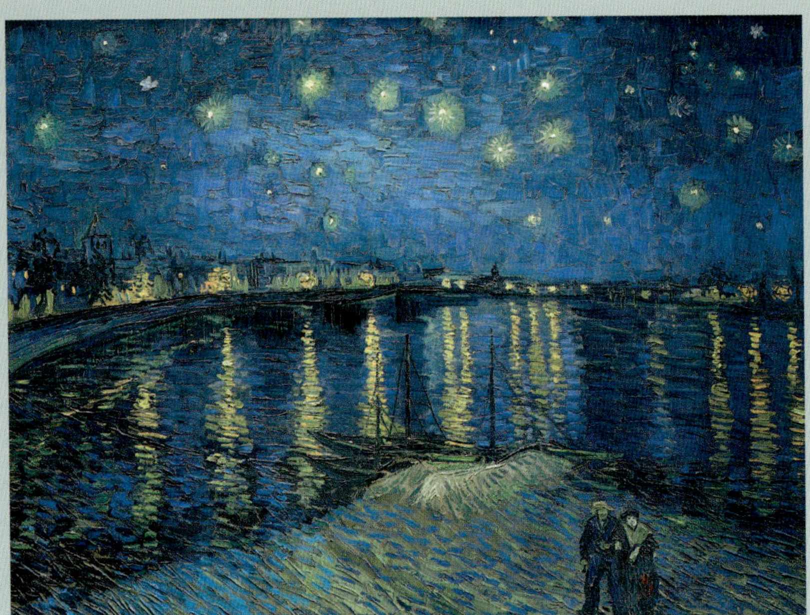

Vincent Van Gogh
(Zundert 1853 - Auvers-sur-Oise 1890)

The Starry Night
Sternennacht
De sterrennacht
La noche estrellada
● ●

1888
72,5 x 92 cm / 28.5 x 36.2 in.
Musée d'Orsay, Paris

oil on canvas / Öl auf Leinwand
olieverf op doek / óleo sobre lienzo

Vincent Van Gogh
(Zundert 1853 - Auvers-sur-Oise 1890)

Van Gogh's Room at Arles
Van Goghs Schlafzimmer in Arles
Van Goghs kamer in Arles
El dormitorio de Van Gogh en Arles
● ● ●

1889
72 x 90 cm / 28.3 x 35.4 in.
Musée d'Orsay, Paris

oil on canvas / Öl auf Leinwand
olieverf op doek / óleo sobre lienzo

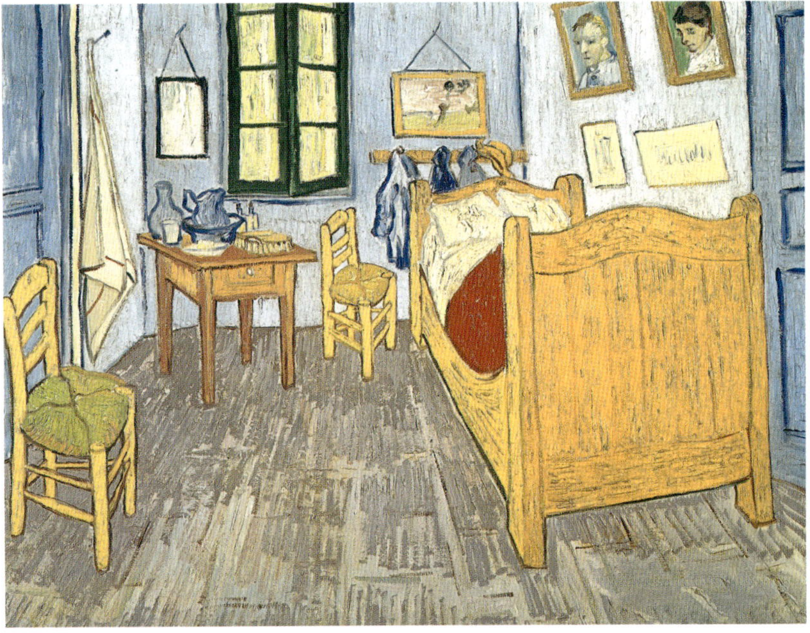

"If I use color arbitrarily,
it is so that I can express
myself with more force."

"Wenn ich mich beliebig
der Farbe bediene, ist es,
um mich mit mehr Kraft
auszudrücken."

"Als ik kleuren willekeurig
gebruik, dan is dat om mij
krachtiger uit te drukken."

"Si me sirvo del color
arbitrariamente, es para
poder expresarme con más
fuerza."
Vincent Van Gogh

Vincent Van Gogh
(Zundert 1853 -
Auvers-sur-Oise 1890)

**Sunflowers
Sonnenblumen
Zonnebloemen
Girasoles**

● ● ●

1888
92,1 x 73 cm / 36.3 x 28.7 in.
National Gallery, London

oil on canvas
Öl auf Leinwand
olieverf op doek
óleo sobre lienzo

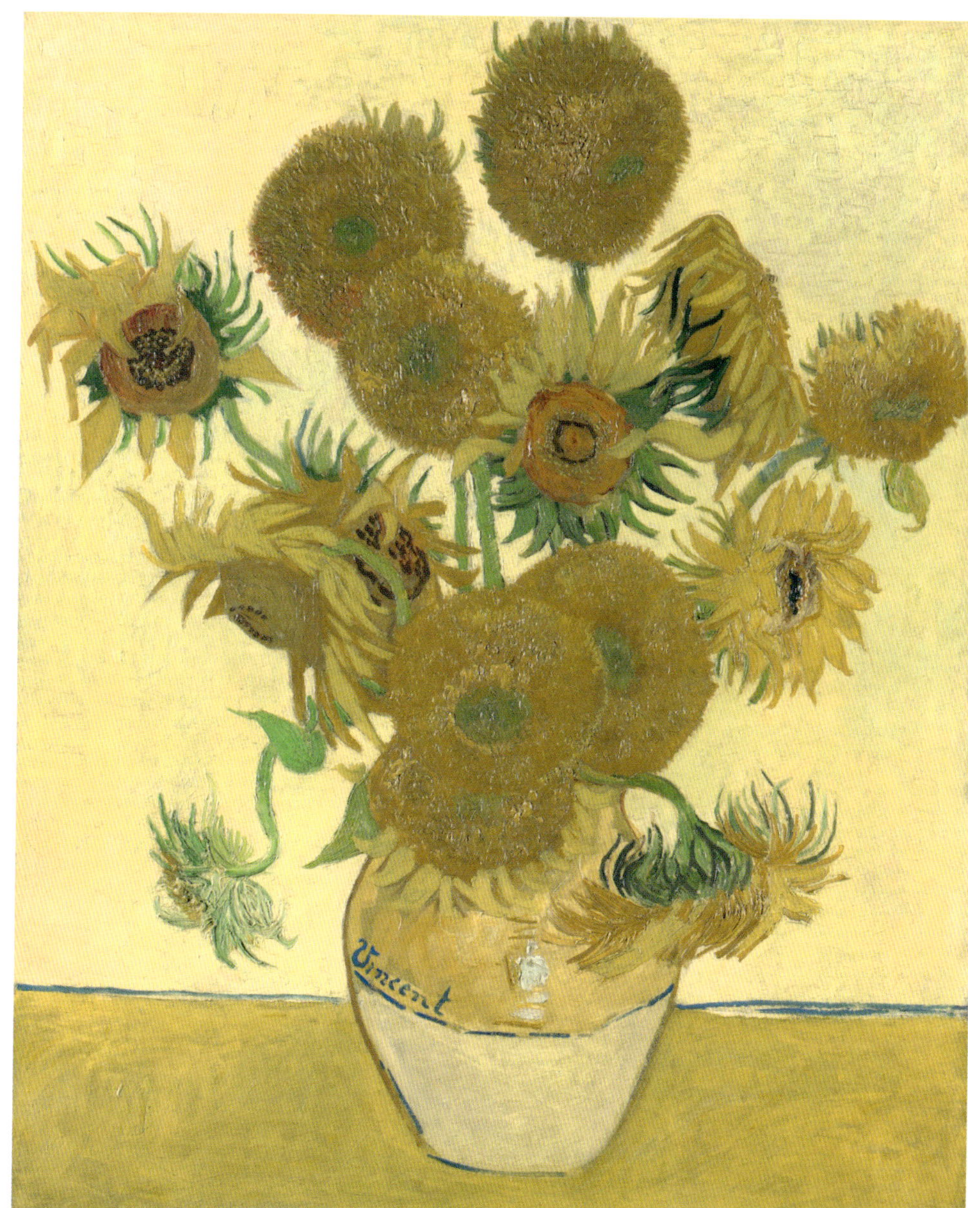

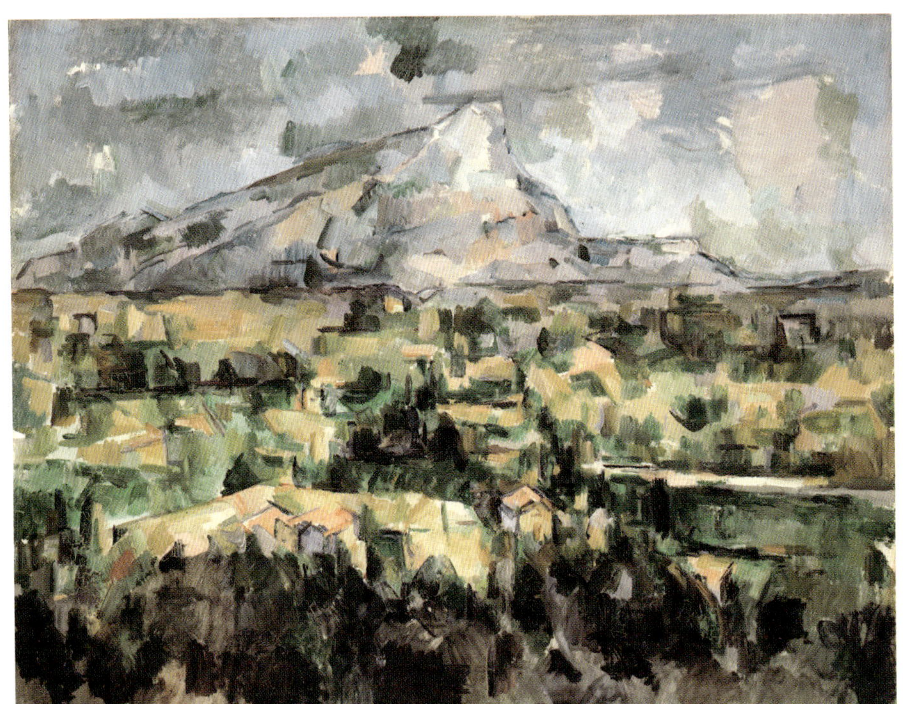

Paul Cézanne
(Aix-en-Provence 1839 - 1906)

**Mont Saint-Victoire
Der Berg Sainte-Victoire
Sainte-Victoire berg
La montaña de Sainte-Victoire**

●

1902-1904
73 x 91,9 cm / 28.7 x 36.2 in.
Philadelphia Museum of Art,
Philadelphia

oil on canvas / Öl auf Leinwand
olieverf op doek / óleo sobre lienzo

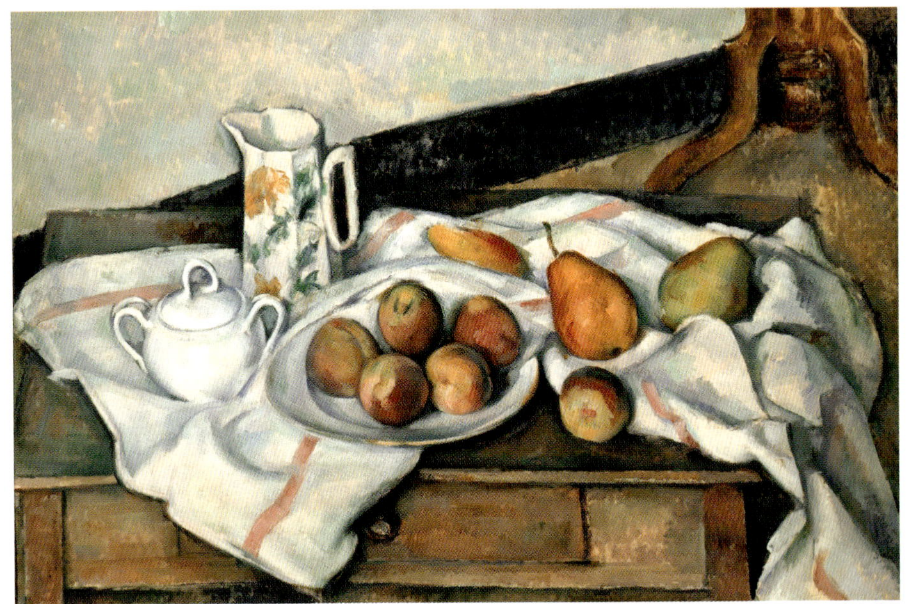

Paul Cézanne
(Aix-en-Provence 1839 - 1906)

**Sugar bowl, jug and plate with fruit
Stillleben mit Zuckerdose
Suikerpot, karaf en fruitschaal
Azucarera, jarra y plato de fruta**

●

Pushkin State Museum of Fine Arts,
Moscow
ca. 1890
61 × 90 cm / 24.3 x 35.46 in.

oil on canvas / Öl auf Leinwand
olieverf op doek / óleo sobre lienzo

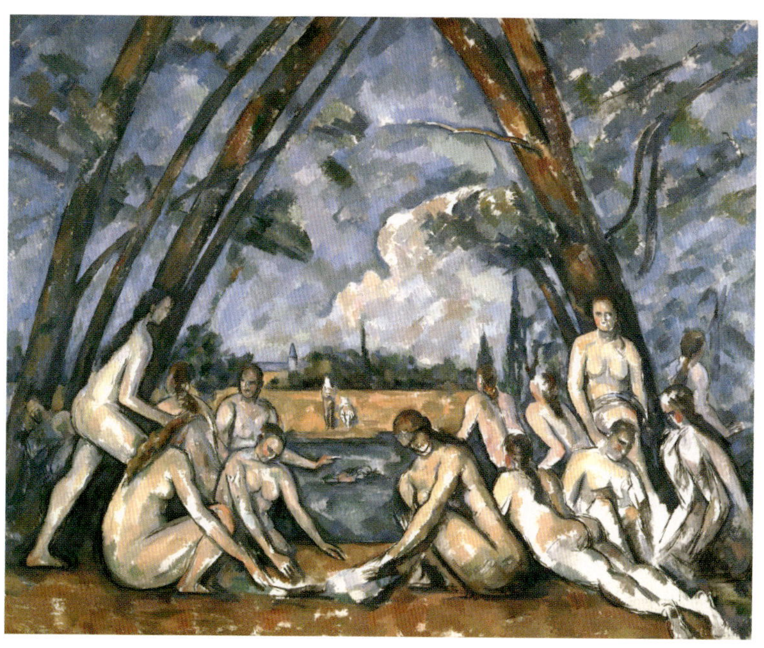

Cézanne surpasses the immediacy
of Impressionism by synthesizing, structuring,
and giving nature architecture.

Cézanne überwindet das Momentartige
des Impressionismus, indem er die Natur
synthetisiert, strukturiert,
sie wie eine Architektur gestaltet.

Cézanne laat de directheid van het
impressionisme achter zich en richt zich
op het samenvatten, indelen en opbouwen
van de natuur.

Cézanne supera la inmediatez del Impresionismo
sintetizando, estructurando, *arquitecturando* la
naturaleza.

Paul Cézanne
(Aix-en-Provence 1839 - 1906)

The Large Bathers
Die Großen Badenden
Grote baadsters
Las grandes bañistas

●●

1906
210,5 x 250,8 cm / 82.6 x 98.4 in.
Philadelphia Museum of Art,
Philadelphia

oil on canvas / Öl auf Leinwand
olieverf op doek / óleo sobre lienzo

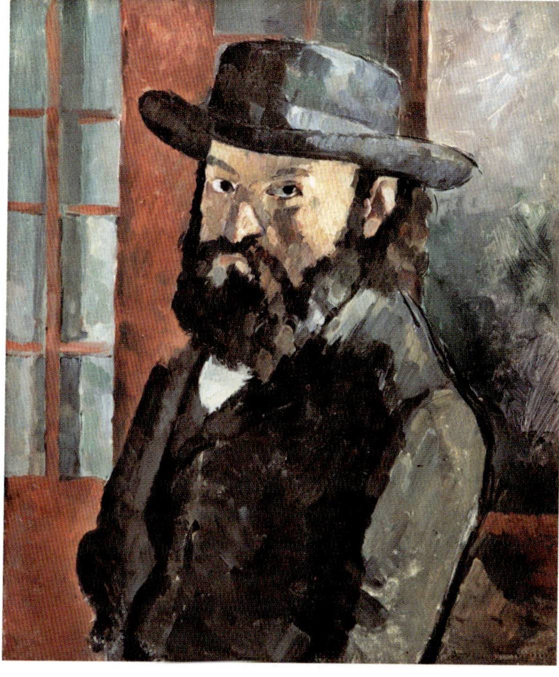

Paul Cézanne
(Aix-en-Provence 1839 - 1906)

Self-Portrait with Hat
Selbstporträt mit Hut
Zelfportret met hoed
Autorretrato con sombrero

●

ca. 1880
Kunstmuseum, Bern

oil on canvas / Öl auf Leinwand
olieverf op doek / óleo sobre lienzo

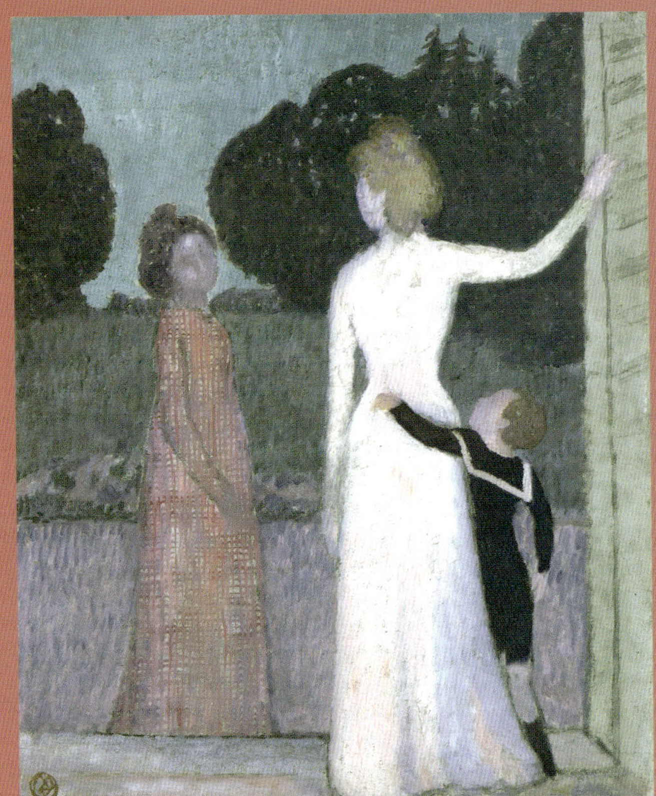

Maurice Denis
(Gramville 1870 - Paris 1943)

Madame Adrien Mithouard and her son Jacques
Madame Adrien Mithouard und ihr Sohn Jacques
Madame Adrien Mithouard en haar zoon Jacques
Madame Adrien Mithouard y su hijo Jacques

●

ca. 1903
51 x 40,2 cm / 20 x 15.8 in.
Hamburger Kunsthalle, Hamburg

oil on cardboard / Öl auf Karton
olieverf op karton / óleo sobre cartón

28

Maurice Denis
(Gramville 1870 - Paris 1943)

Rays of sun on the terrace
Sonnenflecken auf der Terrasse
Zonlicht op het terras
Manchas de sol en la terraza

●

1890
24 x 20 cm / 28.7 x 7.8 in.
Musée d'Orsay, Paris

oil on cardboard / Öl auf Karton
olieverf op karton / óleo sobre cartón

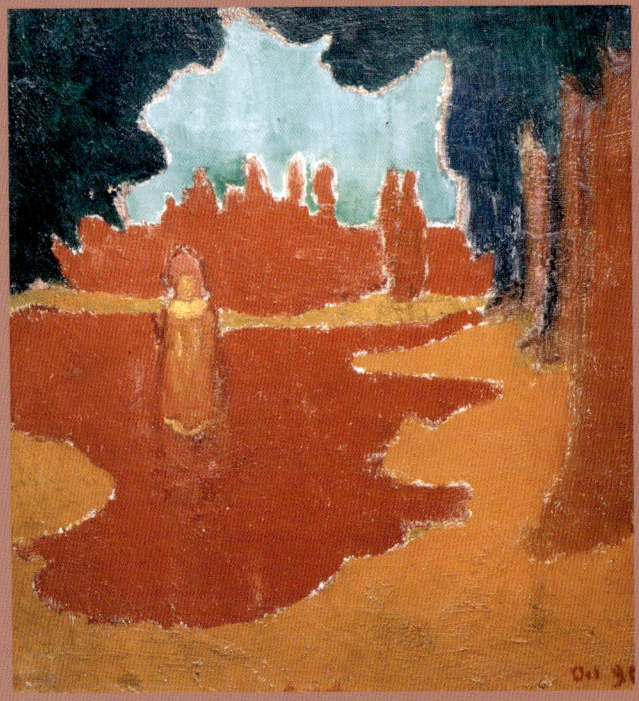

Paul Serusier
(Paris 1864 - Molraix 1927)

The Talisman
Der Talisman
De talisman
El talismán

1898
27 x 21,5 cm / 10.6 x 8.4 in.
Musée d'Orsay, Paris

oil on panel / Öl auf Tafel
olieverf op paneel / óleo sobre tabla

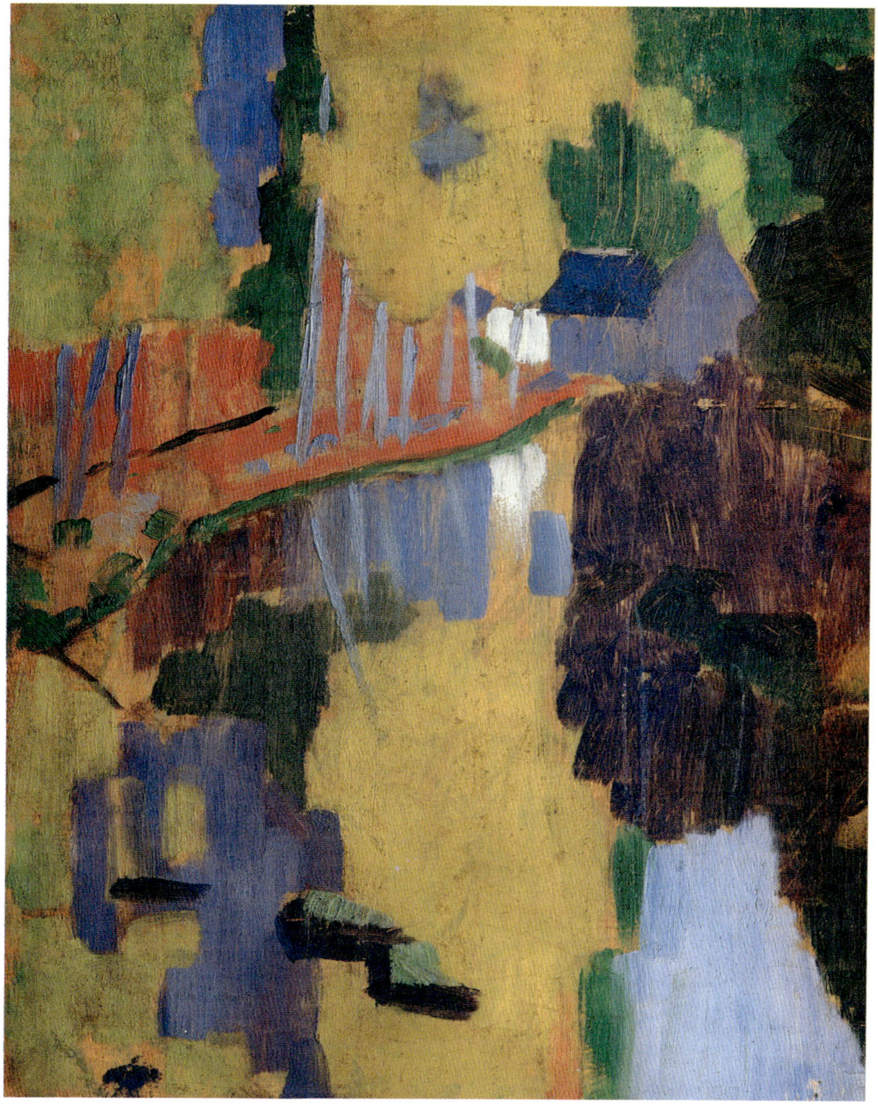

This small landscape was
a full-blown talisman for that new
generation that was reclaiming
subjectivity in painting.

Diese kleine Landschaft war
ein wirklicher Talisman
für eine neue Generation, die sich für
Subjektivität in der Malerei einsetzt.

Dit kleine landschap is een echte
talisman geweest voor die nieuwe
generatie voor wie subjectiviteit
in de schilderkunst centraal stond.

Este pequeño paisaje ha sido un
auténtico talismán para aquella nueva
generación que reivindicaba
la subjetividad en la pintura.

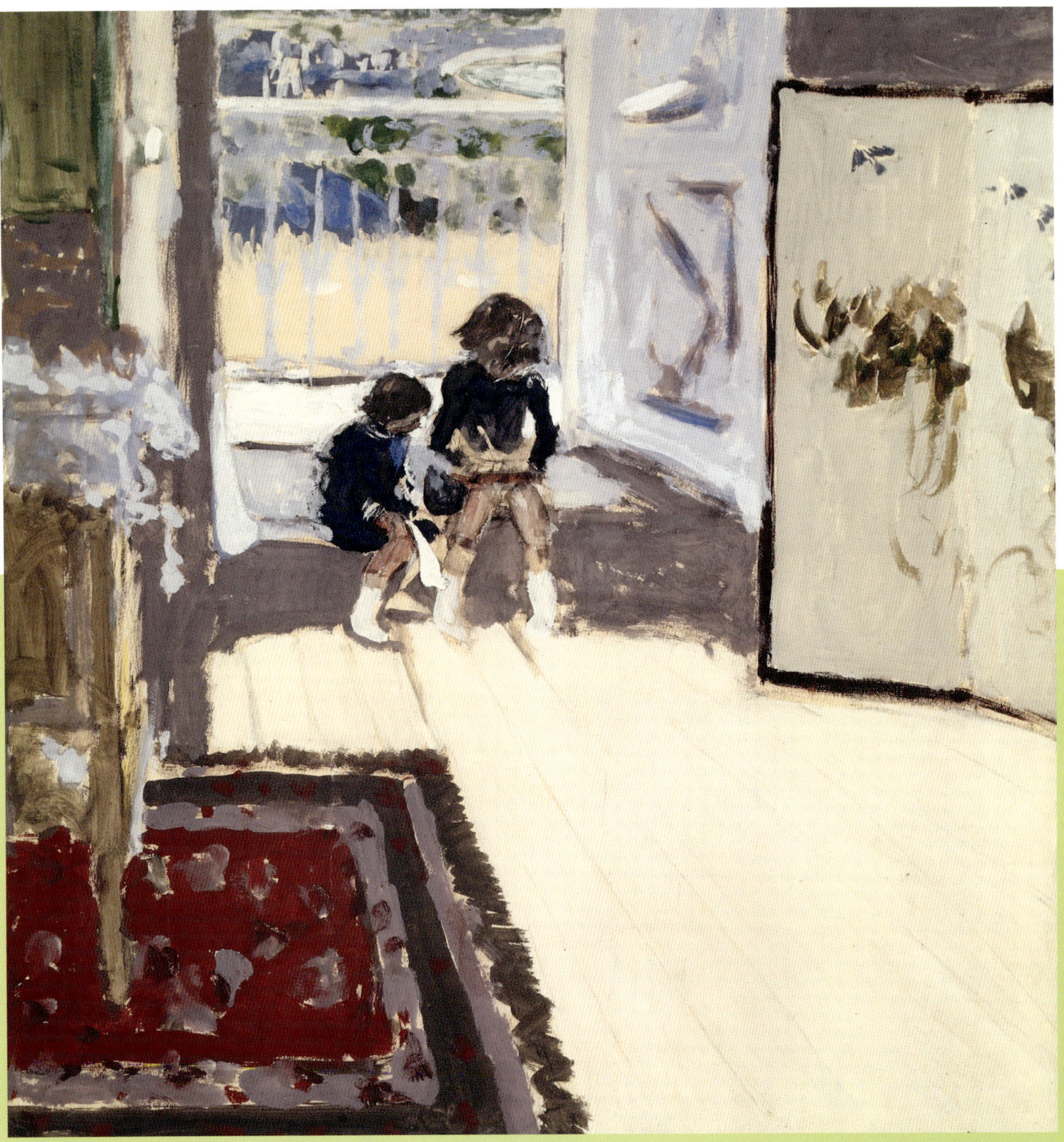

► **Édouard Vuillard**
(Cuiseaux 1868 - La Baule 1940)

**Public Gardens
(central panel)
Öffentliche Gärten
(Mitteltafel)
Openbaar park
(middenpaneel)
Jardines públicos
(panel central)**

● ●

1894
213,5 x 73 cm / 84.1 x 28.7 in.
Musée d'Orsay, Paris

painting with glue on canvas
Leimfarbe auf Leinwand
lijmverf op doek
pintura a la cola sobre lienzo

◄ **Édouard Vuillard**
(Cuiseaux 1868 - La Baule 1940)

**The Children
Die Kinder
De kinderen
Los niños**

●

1909
84,5 x 77,7 cm / 33.2 x 30.6 in.
The State Hermitage Museum,
St. Petersburg

gouache on paper glued
to canvas
Gouache auf Papier,
auf Leinwand aufgeklebt
op doek geplakte gouache
gouache sobre papel encolado
sobre lienzo

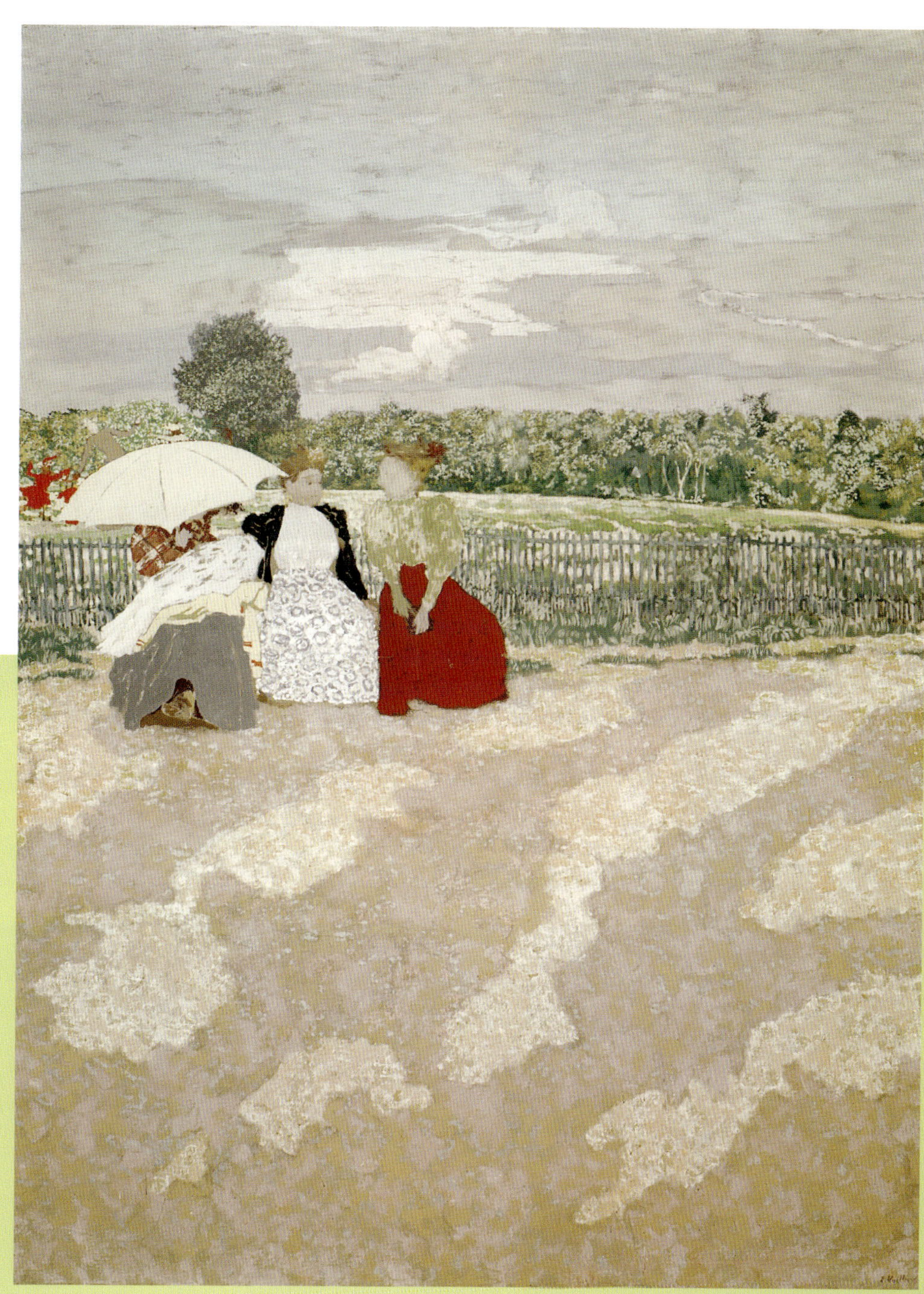

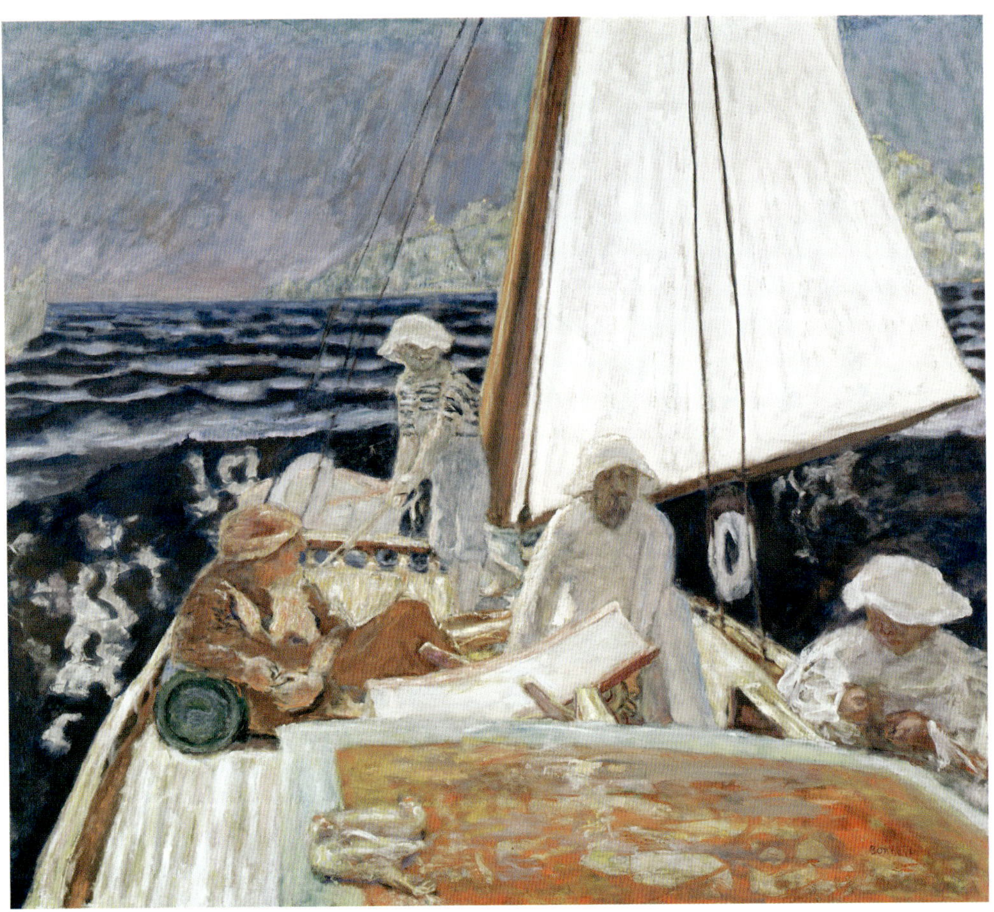

Pierre Bonnard
(Fontenay-aux-Roses 1867 - Le Cannet 1947)

Signac and his friends in a sailboat
Signac und seine Freunde im Segelboot
Signac en zijn vrienden op de zeilboot
Signac y sus amigos en velero

●

ca. 1924
124,5 x 139 cm / 49 x 54.7 in.
Kunsthaus, Zurich

oil on canvas / Öl auf Leinwand
olieverf op doek / óleo sobre lienzo

Pierre Bonnard
(Fontenay-aux-Roses 1867 - Le Cannet 1947)

The Croquet Match
Krocketpartie
Croquet
El partido de croquet

●

1892
130 x 162,5 cm / 51.2 x 64 in.
Musée d'Orsay, Paris

oil on canvas / Öl auf Leinwand
olieverf op doek / óleo sobre lienzo

Bonnard shares with the other nabis a passion for decorative arts, fabrics and Japonism.

Bonnard teilt mir den anderen Nabis die Leidenschaft für die dekorativen Künste, die Stoffe und den Japonismus.

Bonnard deelt met de andere nabis zijn passie voor decoratieve kunsten, stoffen en het Japonisme.

Bonnard comparte con los otros nabis la pasión por las artes decorativas, las telas y el japonismo.

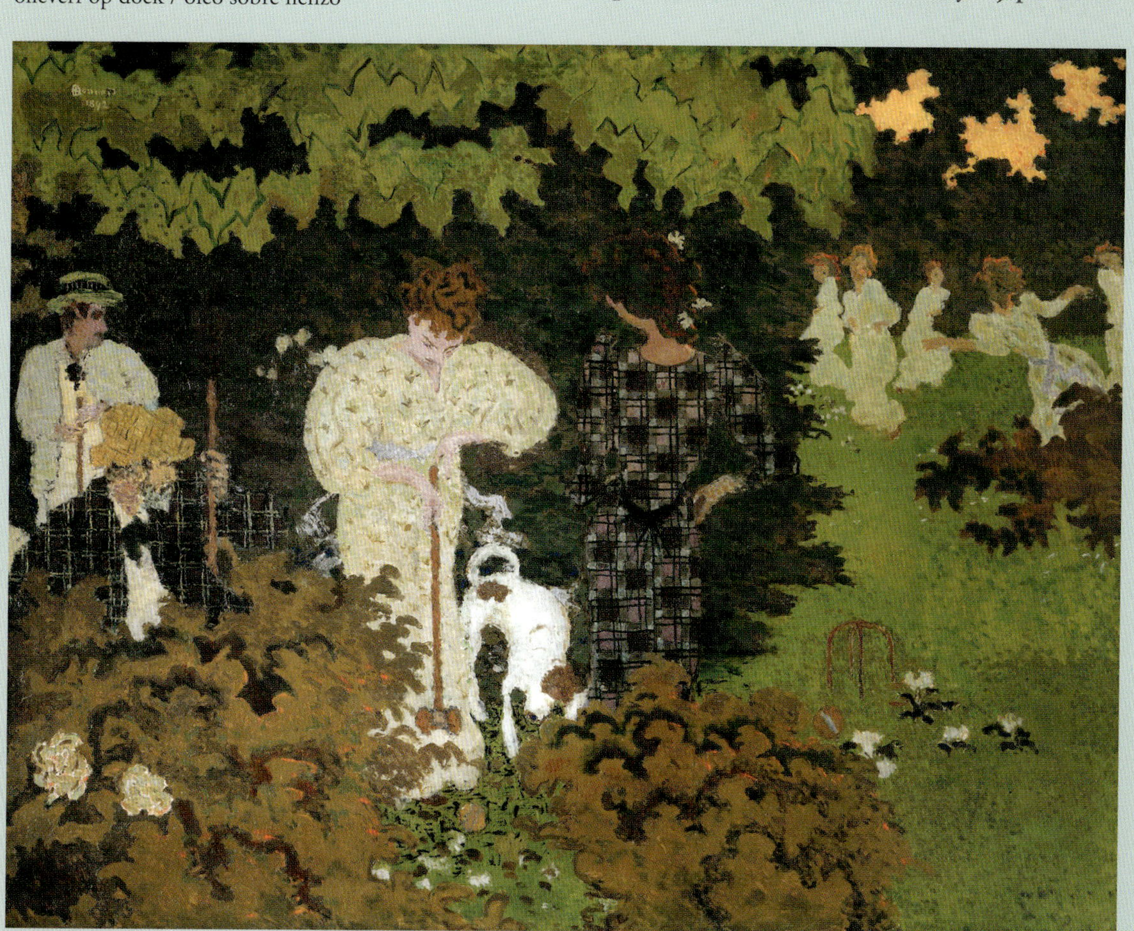

Henri Rousseau
(Laval 1844 - Paris 1910)

**Portrait
of Pierre Loti
Porträt
von Pierre Loti
Portret
van Pierre Loti
Retrato
de Pierre Loti**

●

ca. 1891
62 x 50 cm
24.4 x 19.7 in.
Kunsthaus, Zurich

oil on canvas
Öl auf Leinwand
olieverf op doek
óleo sobre lienzo

34

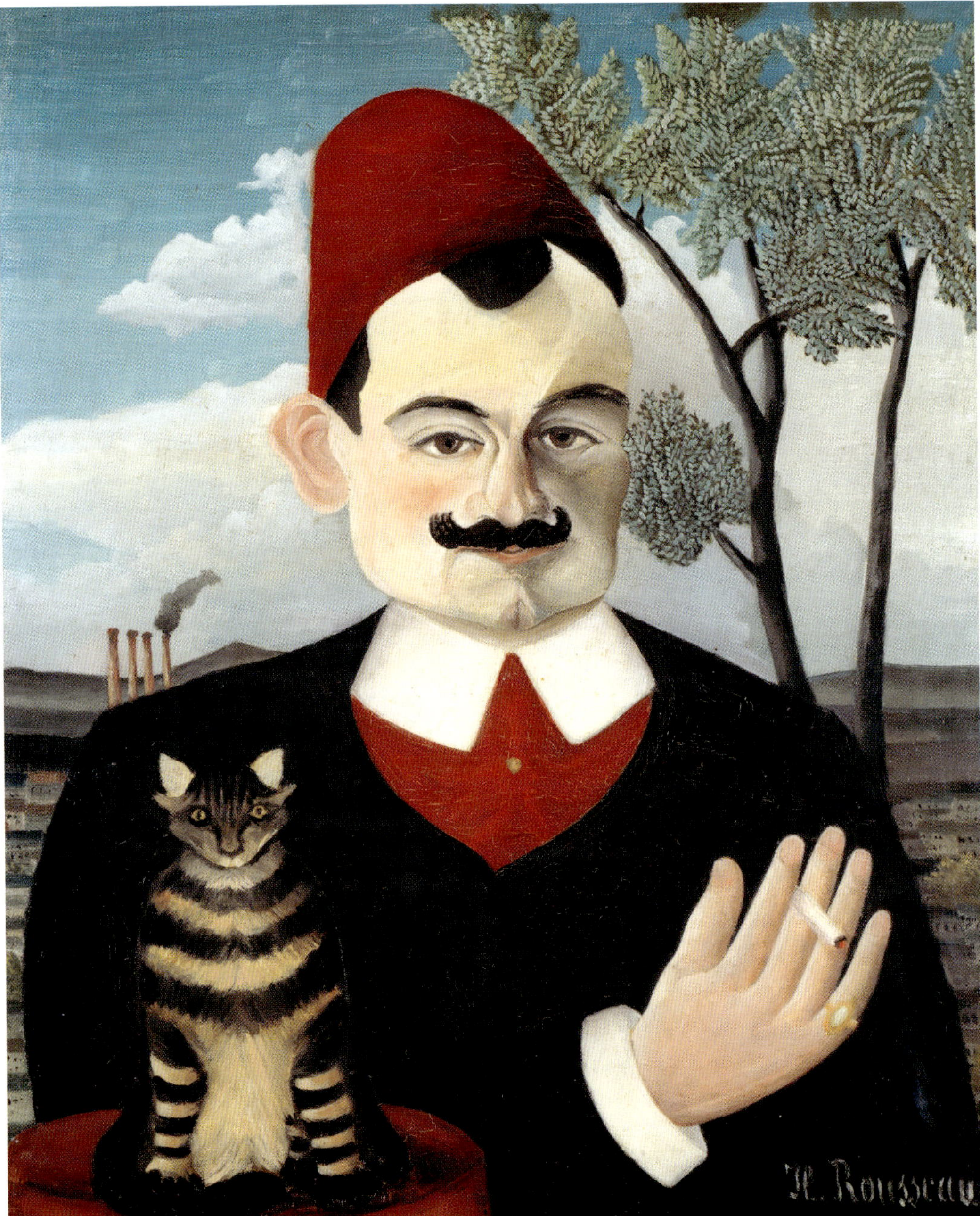

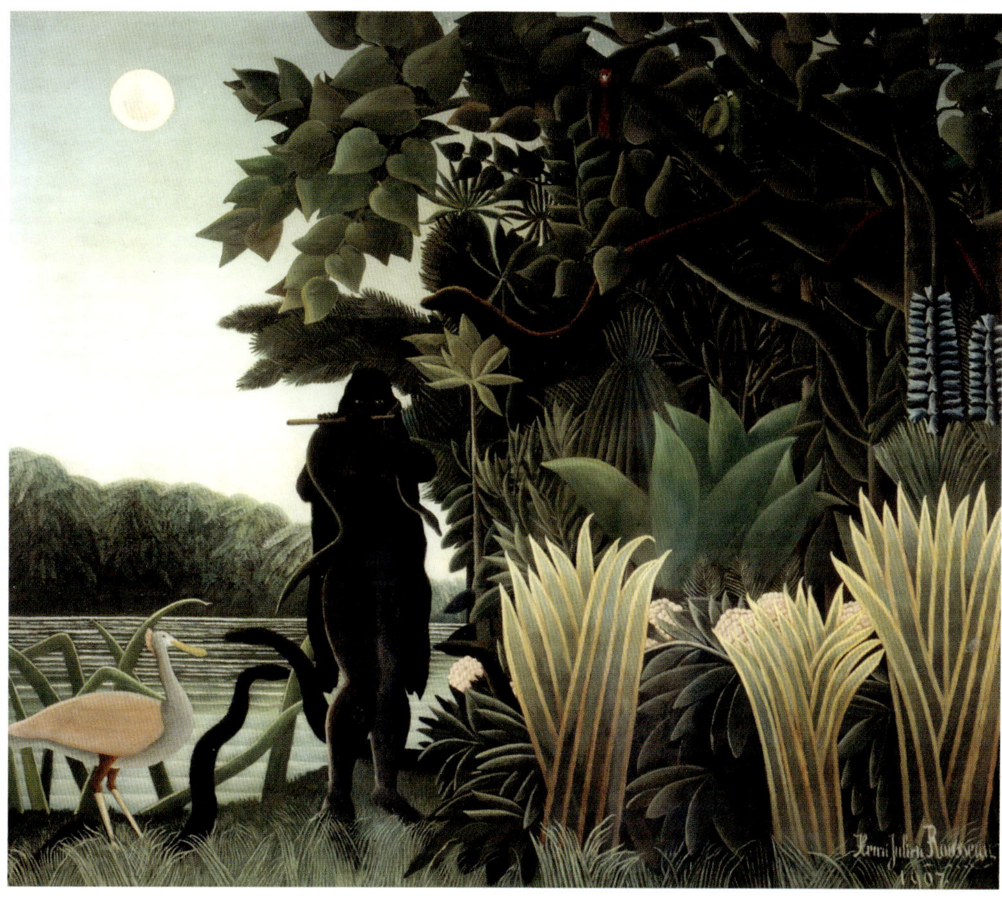

Henri Rousseau
(Laval 1844 - Paris 1910)

The Snake Charmer
Die Schlangenbeschwörerin
De slangenbezweerster
La encantadora de serpientes

●●●

1907
169 x 189 cm / 66.6 x 74.4 in.
Musée d'Orsay, Paris

oil on canvas / Öl auf Leinwand
olieverf op doek / óleo sobre lienzo

Rousseau only knew the vegetation in gardens and had only visited the universal exhibitions of Paris...

Rousseau kannte nur die Vegetation der Gärten und hatte nur die Weltausstellungen in Paris besucht...

Rousseau kende alleen de vegetatie van de tuinen en had alleen de wereldtentoonstellingen van Parijs bezocht...

Rousseau conocía sólo la vegetación de los jardines y había visitando sólo las exposiciones universales de París…

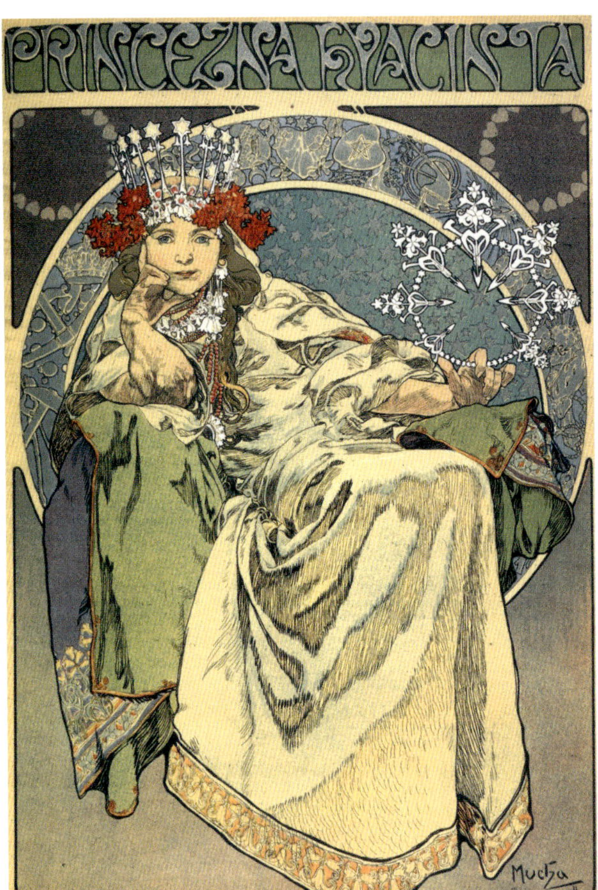

Alphonse Mucha
(Ivancice 1860 - Prague 1939)

Princezna Hyacinta

● ●

British Library, London

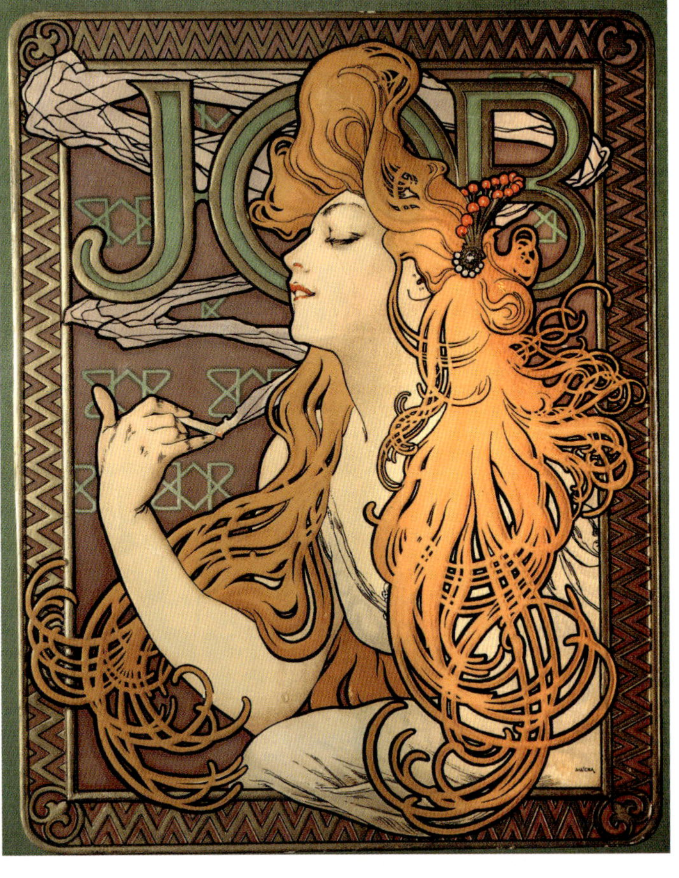

Alphonse Mucha
(Ivancice 1860 - Prague 1939)

Advertising for 'Job' cigarette papers
Werbung für das Zigarettenpapier 'Job'
Reclame voor sigarettenpapier 'Job'
Publicidad para el papel de cigarrillo 'Job'

●

ca. 1900-1930
Musée des Arts Decoratifs, Paris

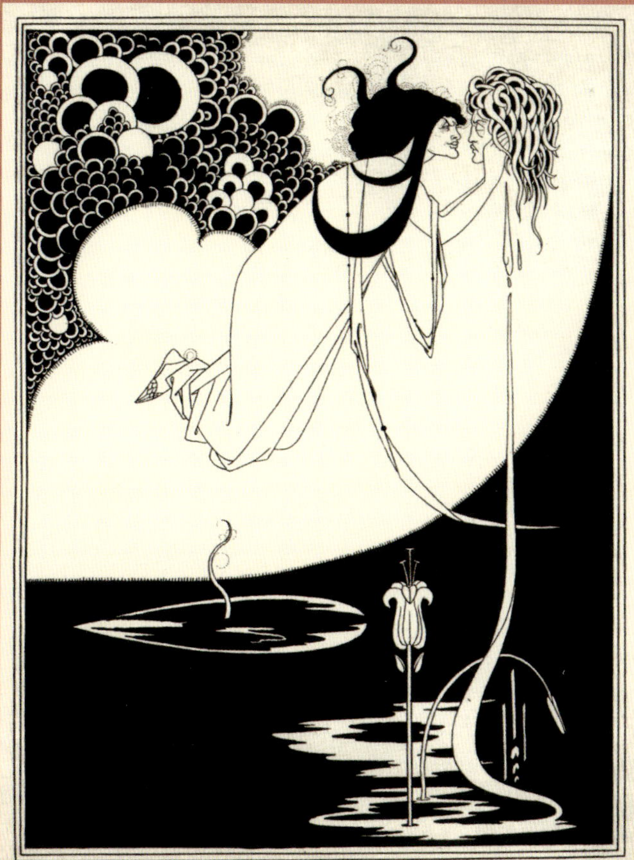

Aubrey Beardsley
(Brighton 1872 - Mentone 1898)

Salomè's Toilette
Die Toilette der Salomè
Het toilet van Salomè
La toilette de Salomé

●

1907
34,2 x 27,2 cm / 13.4 x 10.7 in.
Victoria & Albert Museum, London

line block print, ink on paper / Zinkotypie
lijn- blokprint, inkt op papier / cincotipia (cliché de zinc), tinta sobre papel

Aubrey Beardsley
(Brighton 1872 - Mentone 1898)

Climax
El clímax

● ● ●

1893
22,8 x 12,7 cm / 9 x 5 in.
Victoria & Albert Museum, London

line-block print / Zinkotypie
lijn- blokprint / cincotipia (cliché de zinc)

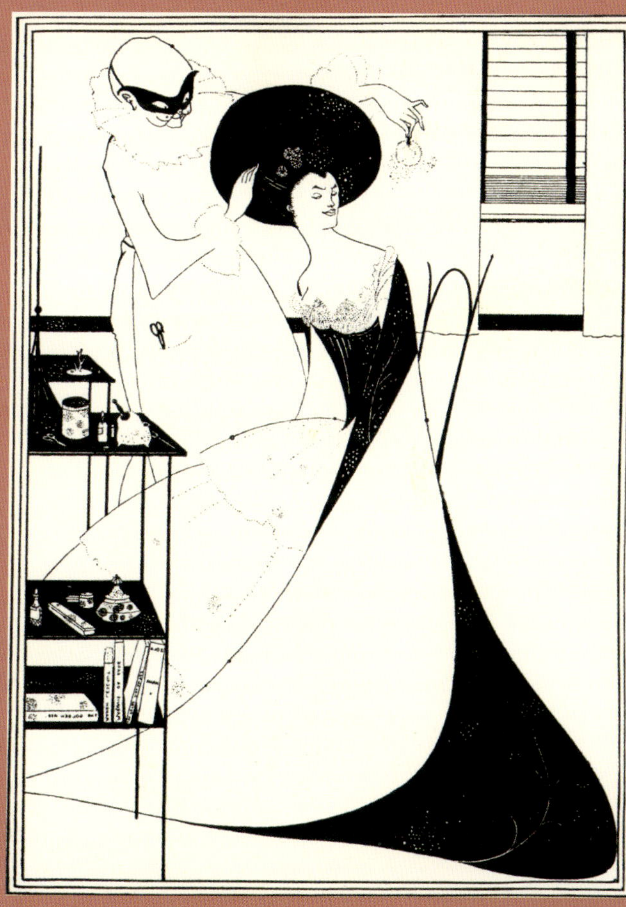

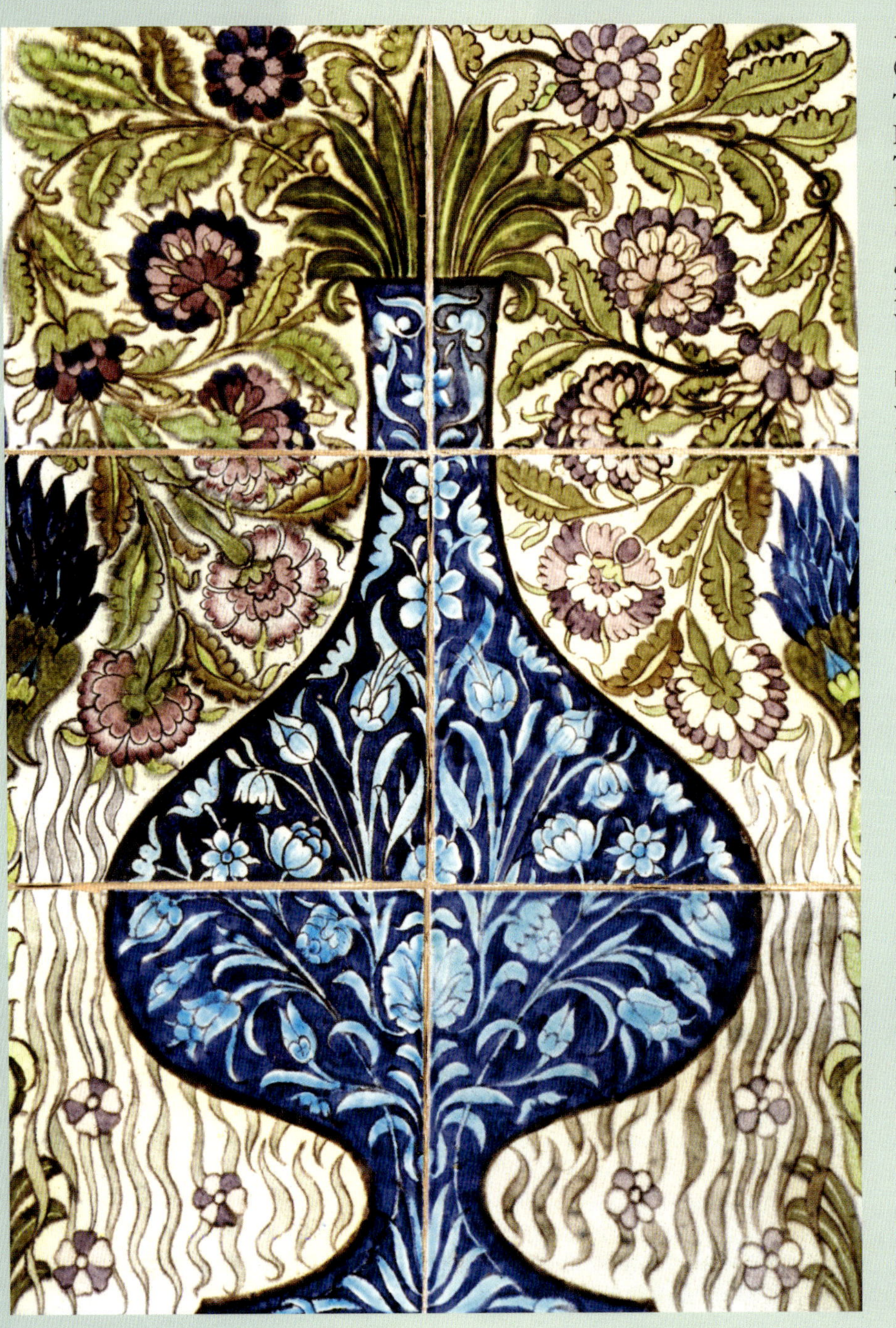

◄ William De Morgan
(London 1839 - 1917)

Tile panel
Kacheltafel
Tegelpaneel
Panel de azulejos
●
*ca.*1888-1897
20,6 x 20,6 x 1,9 cm / 8.1 x 8.1 x 0.7 in.
Victoria & Albert Museum, London

buff-colored earthenware,
with painting over a white slip
Dunkelgelbes Terrakotta
mit Zeichungen auf weißem Grund
vaaggeel aardewerk,
met schilderingen op een witte kleilaag
terracota de color ocre
con dibujos en engobe blanco

► John La Farge
(New York 1835 - Providence 1910)

The Fish
Der Fisch
Vis
El pez
●
*ca.*1890
76,8 x 76,8 x 3,2 cm / 30.2 x 30.2 x 1.2 in.
Museum of Fine Arts, Boston

painted leaded glass
Bemaltes Bleiglas
geverfd glas in lood
vidriera emplomada pintada

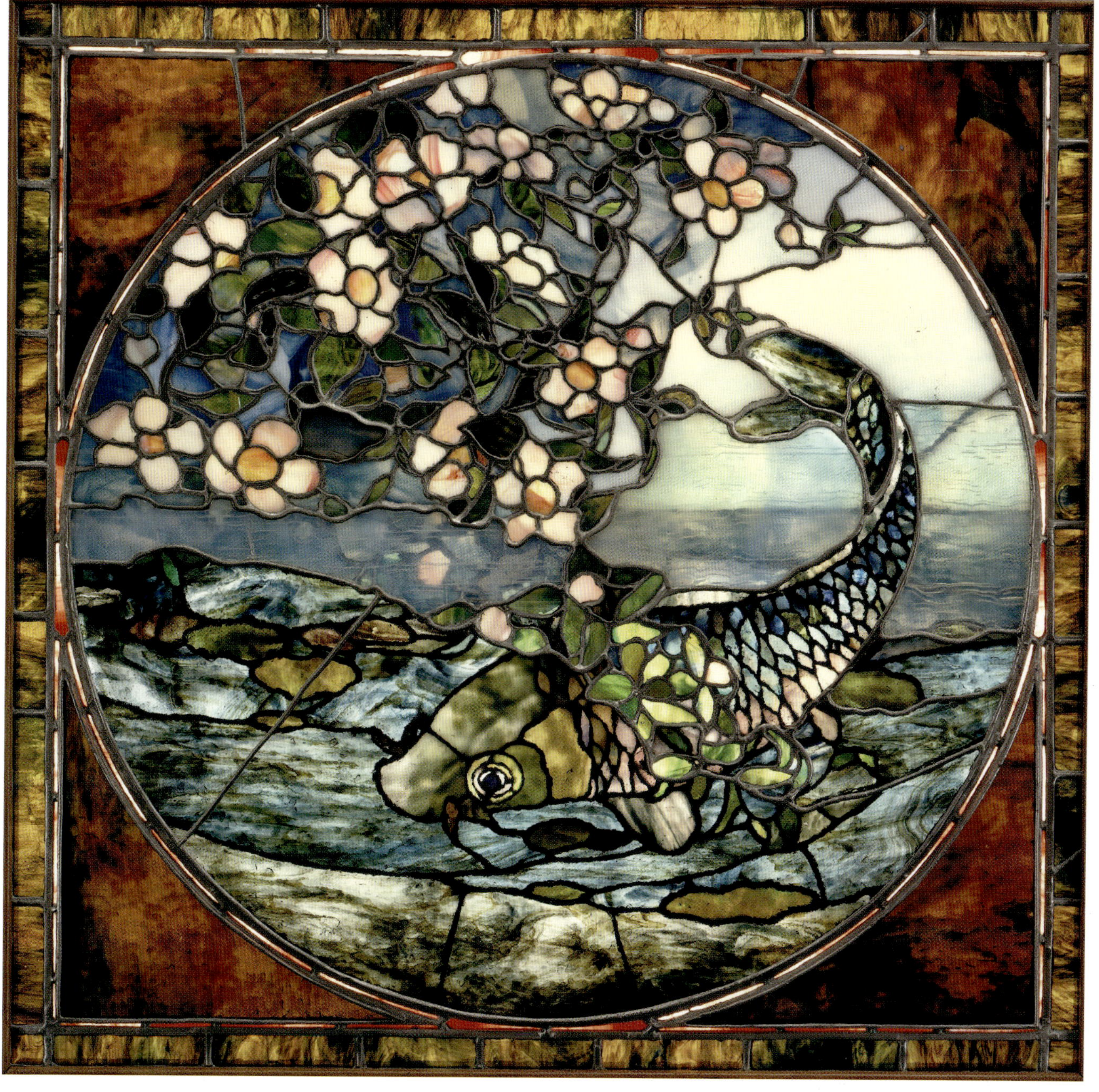

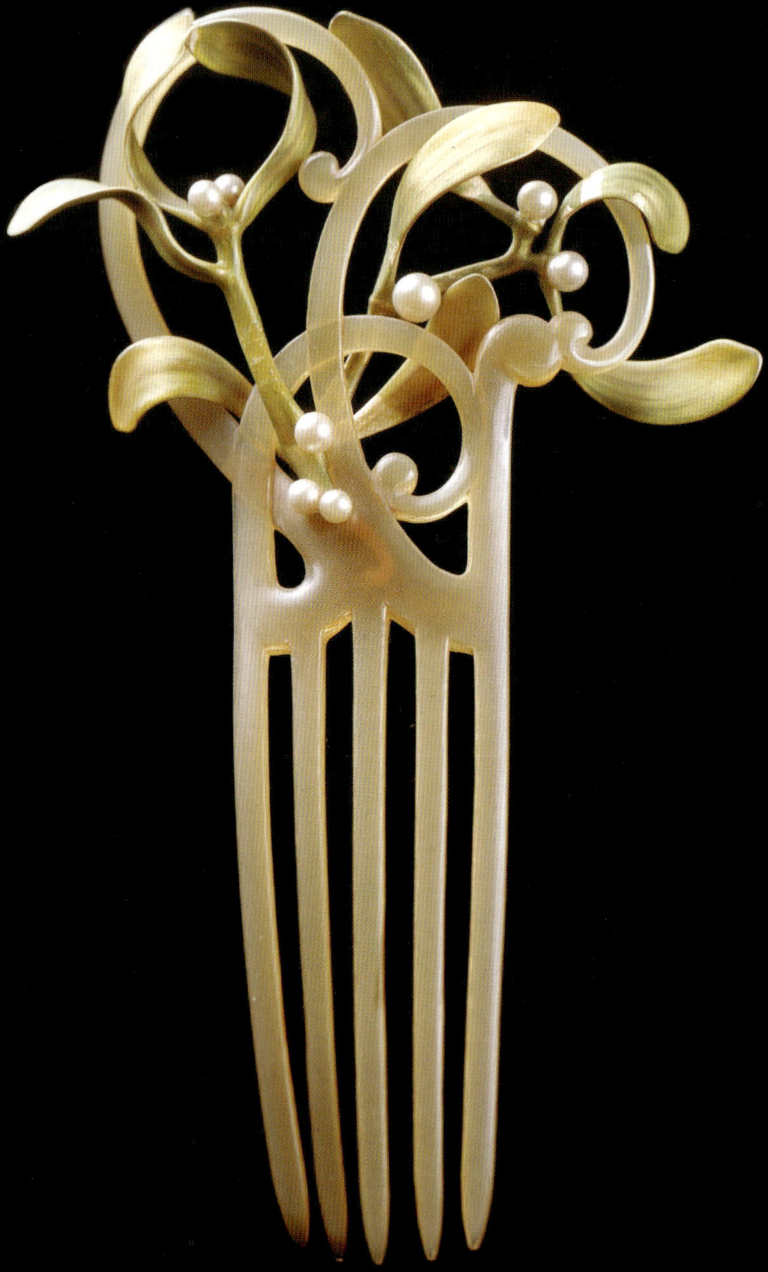

Lalique was originally famous for his Art Nouveau jewellery, in which he preferred to use translucent enamel and opal.

Lalique wurde bekannt durch seine Art Nouveau-Schmuckstücke, die er vornehmlich aus transparentem Email und Opale anfertigte.

Lalique was aanvankelijk beroemd om zijn art nouveau sieraden, waarvoor hij bij voorkeur doorschijnend email en opaal gebruikte.

Lalique fue inicialmente célebre por sus joyas Art Nouveau, donde usaba preferentemente el esmalte traslúcido y el opalino.

Paul Vever
(1851 - 1915);
Henri Vever
(1854 - 1942)

Comb
Kamm
Kam
Peine ornamental

1900
Musée des Arts Decoratifs, Paris

gold, tortoise shell, pearls and enamel
Gold, Schildkröte, Perlen und Email
goud, schildpad, parels en glazuur
oro, caparazón de tortuga, perlas y esmalte

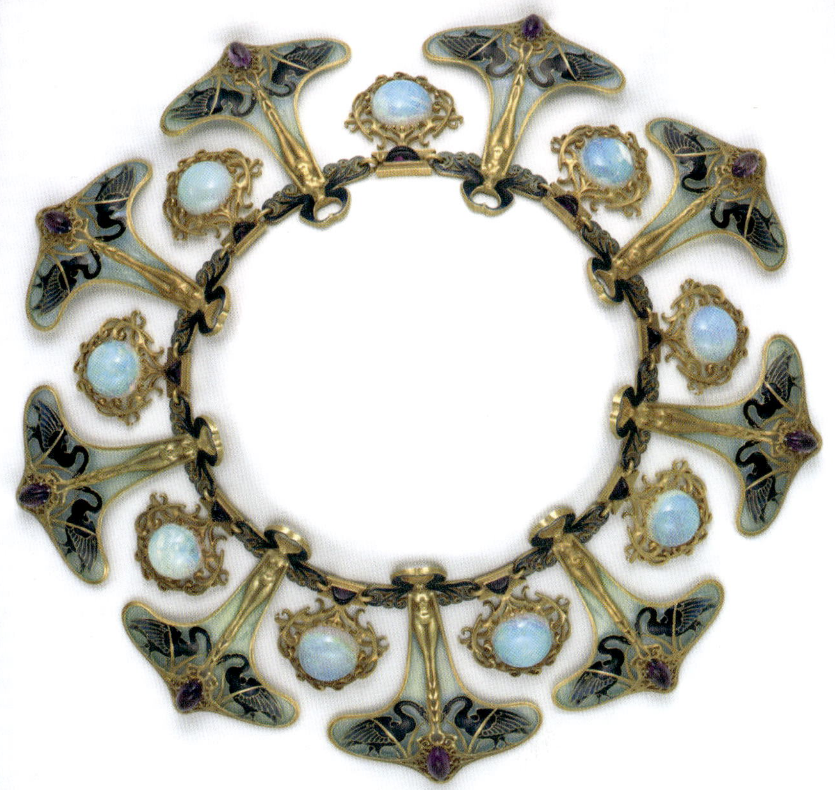

René Lalique
(Ay 1860 - Paris 1945)

Necklace
Kette
Ketting
Collar

ca. 1900
ø 24,1 cm / 9.5 in.
The Metropolitan Museum of Art, New York

gold, enamel, Australian opal, Siberian amethyst
Gold, Email, australischer Opal, sibirischer Amethyst
goud, glazuur, Australische opaalstenen, Siberische amethist
oro, esmalte, ópalo australiano, amatista siberiana

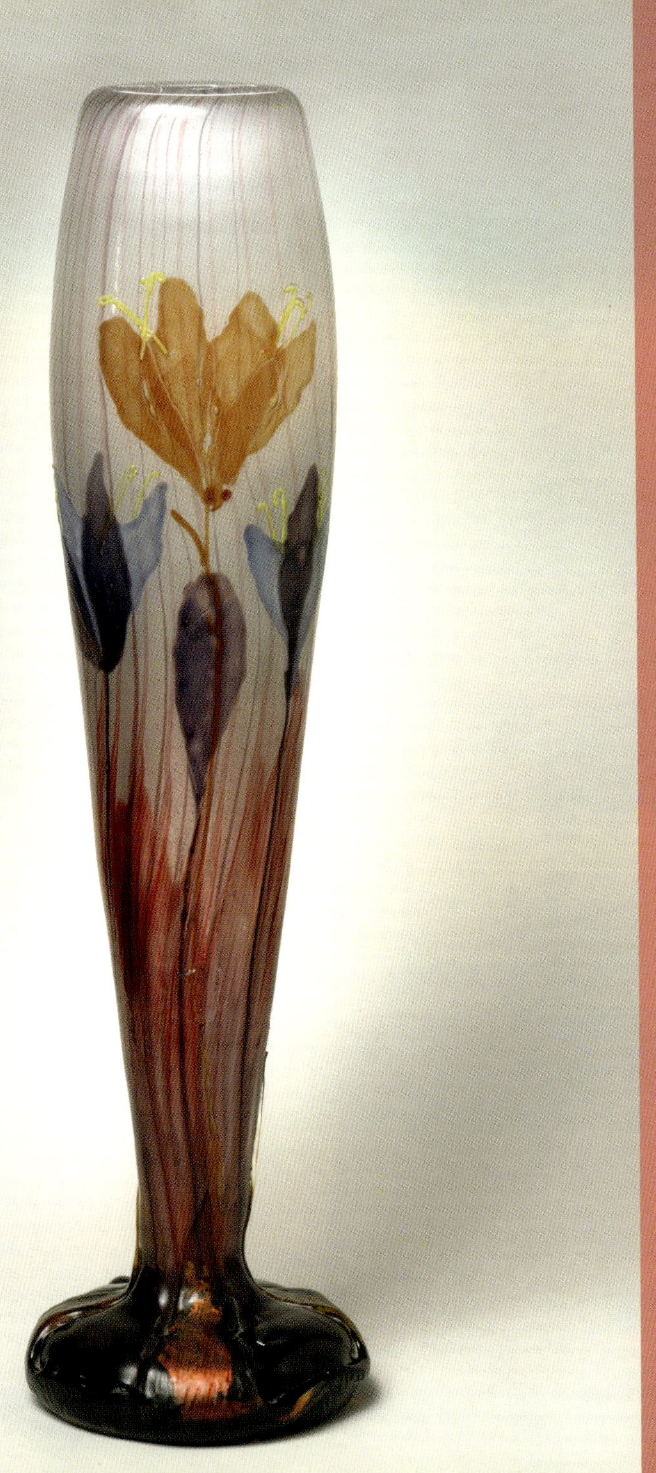

Emile Gallé
(Nancy 1846 - 1904)

Vase with Autumn Crocus
Vase mit Herbstkrokus
Vaas met herfstkrokus
Jarrón con crocus otoñal

●●

ca. 1900
44,1 x 9,5 cm / 17.3 x 3.7 in.
The Metropolitan Museum of Art, New York

glass / Glas / glas / vidrio

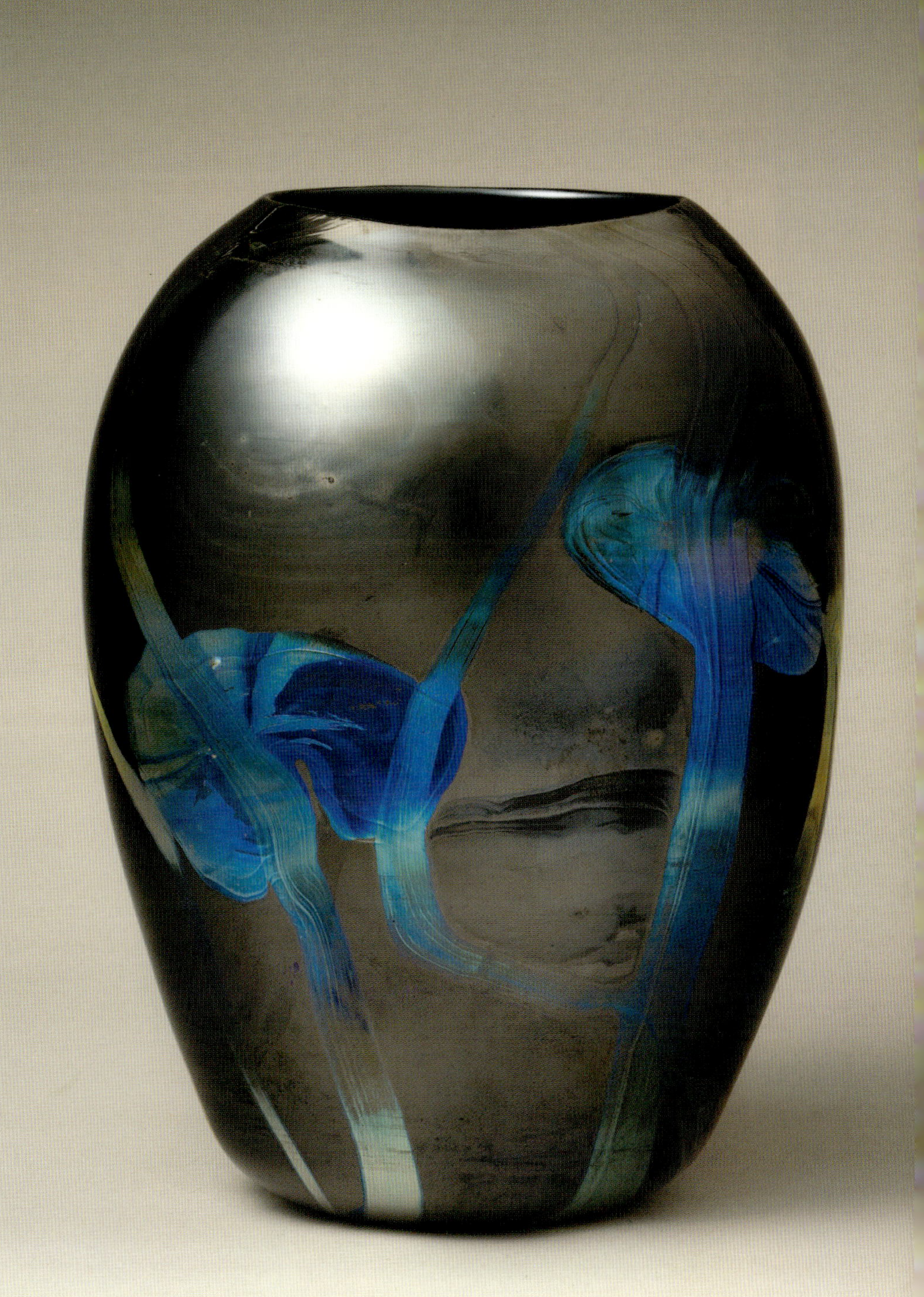

The term "favrile", coined
by Tiffany, comes from the
contraction of the Latin word
"fabrile" (hand-wrought,
handcrafted) and the English
"favourite".

Der von Tiffany geprägte
Begriff Favrile ist
eine Verbindung des
Lateinischen "fabrile"
(Handarbeit) mit dem
englischen Wort für Liebling
("favourite").

De door Tiffany
bedachte term favril is
de samenvoeging van het
Latijnse "fabrile" (handwerk)
en het Engelse "favoriet"
("favourite").

El término "favrile" acuñado
por Tiffany resulta de la
contracción del latín "fabrile"
(echo a mano) y del inglés
"preferido" ("favourite").

Louis Comfort Tiffany
(New York 1848 - 1933)

Vase
Vaas
Jarrón
● ●

ca. 1903
28,4 cm / 11.2 in.
The Metropolitan Museum of
Art, New York

vetro favrile / Favrile-Glas
favrile glas / vidrio favrile

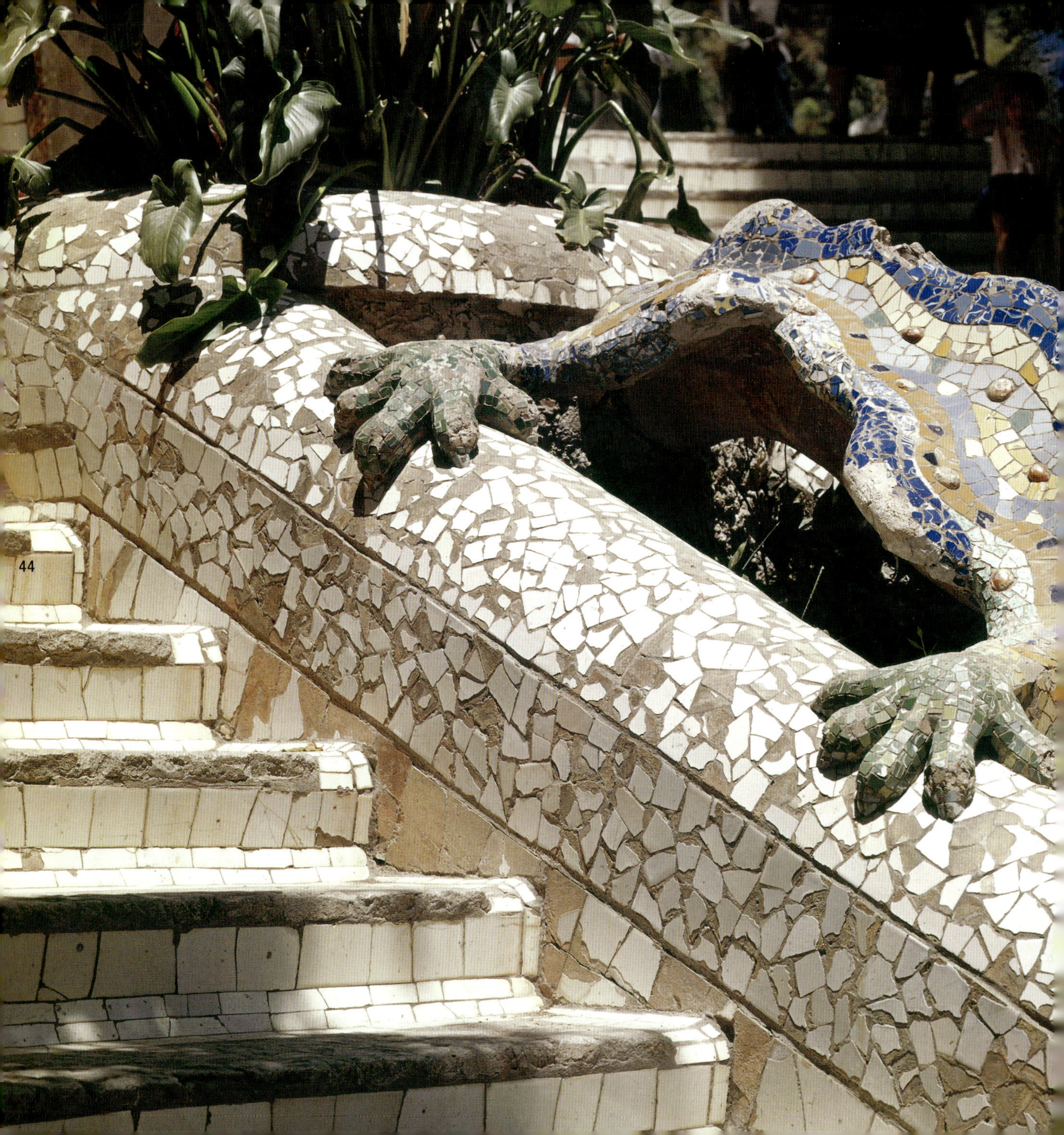
44

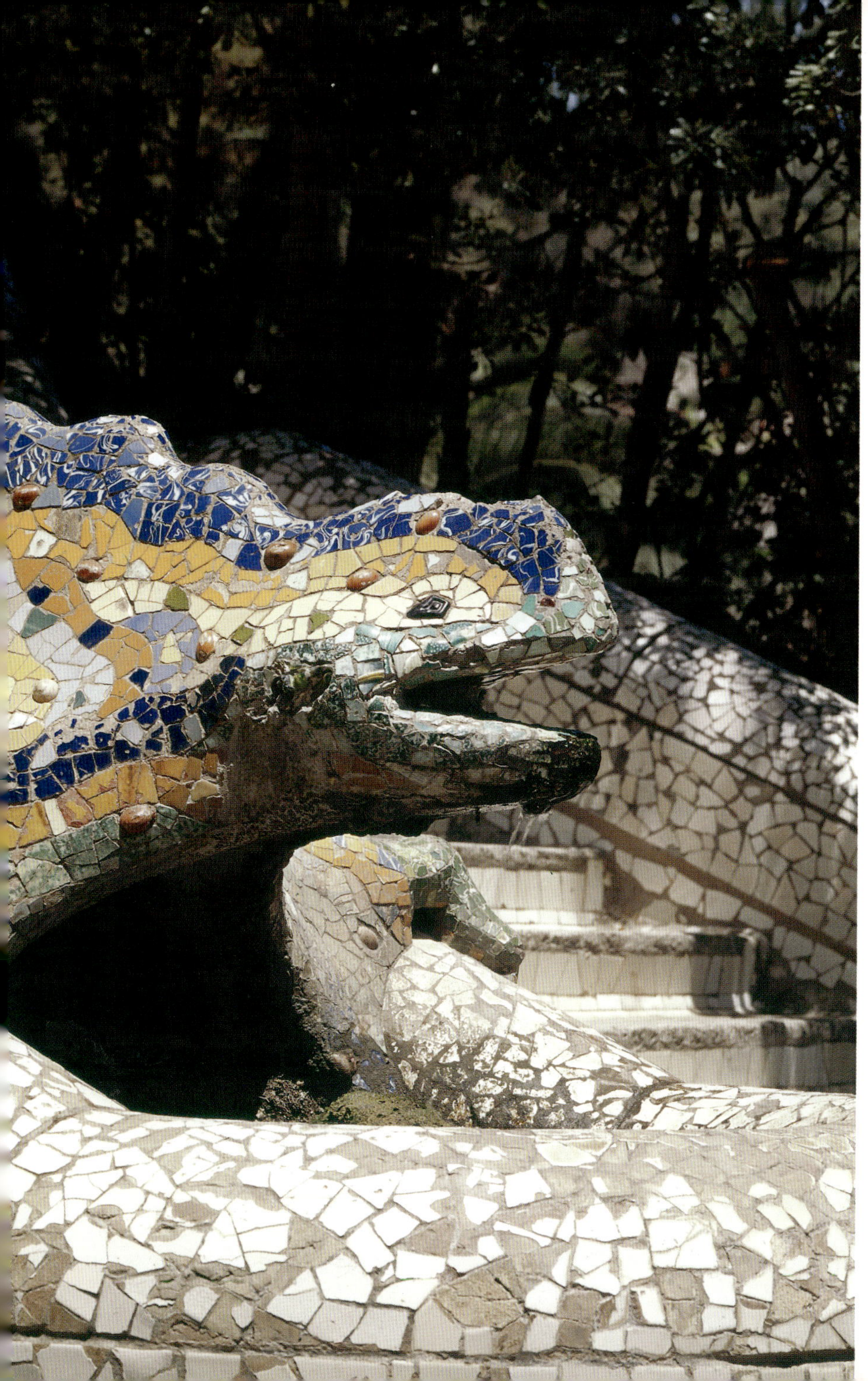

Anton Gaudí

(Reus, Cataluña 1852 - Barcelona 1926)

**Salamander
Salamandra**

●●●

1909-1914
Parque Güell, Barcelona

Antoni Gaudí, the master of catalan Art Nouveau, achieved excellent results in the technique called Trencadis, which consists in integrating ceramics into the architecture.

Antoni Gaudí, der Meister des katalanischen Art Nouveau, erzielte herausragende Ergebnisse in der Trencadis-Technik, der Integration von Keramik in den Baukörper.

Antoni Gaudí, meester van de catalaanse Art Nouveau, bereikte buitengewone resultaten met de trencadis-techniek, die bestond uit het integreren van keramiek in architectuur.

Antoni Gaudí, el maestro del Art Nouveau catalán, logró excelentes resultados en la técnica llamada trencadís, que consiste en integrar la cerámica a la arquitectura.

45

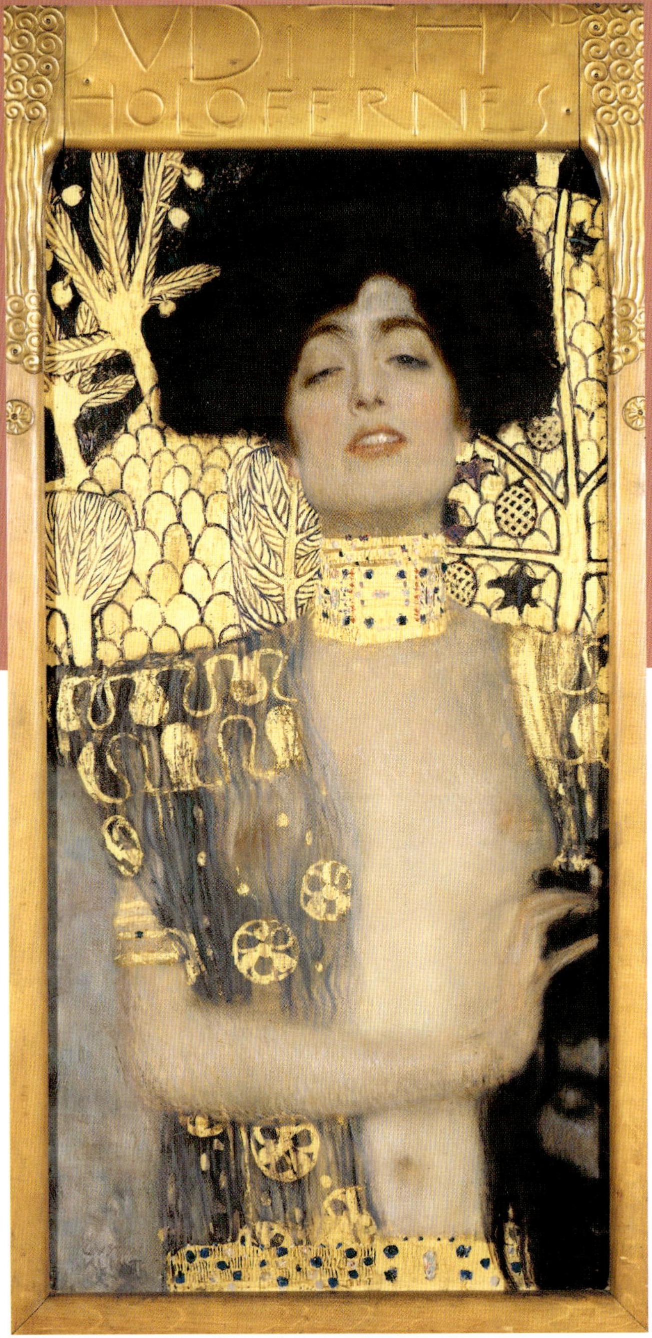

Gustav Klimt
(Wien 1862 - 1918)

Judith
Judit

● ●

1901
84 x 42 cm / 33 x 16.5 in.
Österreichische Galerie
Belvedere, Wien

oil on canvas
Öl auf Leinwand
olieverf op doek
óleo sobre lienzo

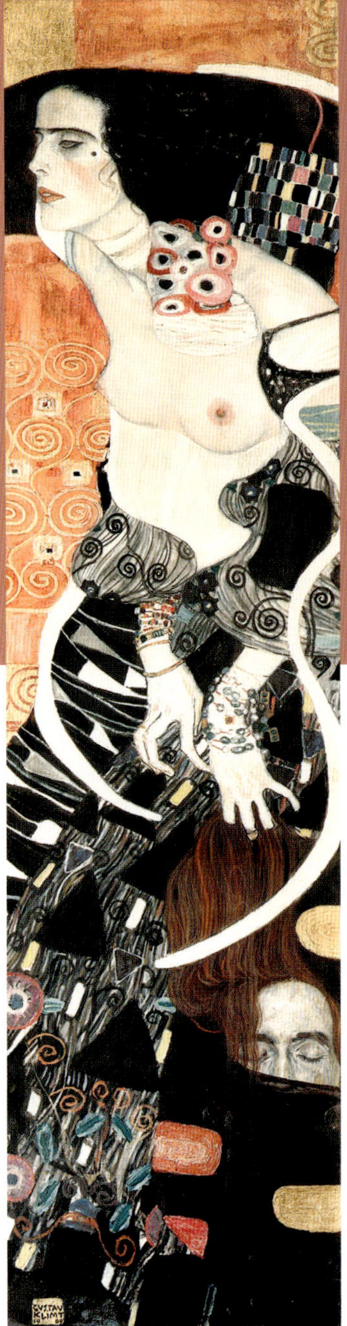

◀ Gustav Klimt
(Wien 1862 - 1918)

Judith II
Judit II

●●●

1909
178 x 46 cm
70.1 x 18.1 in.
Ca' Pesaro Galleria
d'Arte Moderna, Venezia

oil on canvas
Öl auf Leinwand
olieverf op doek
óleo sobre lienzo

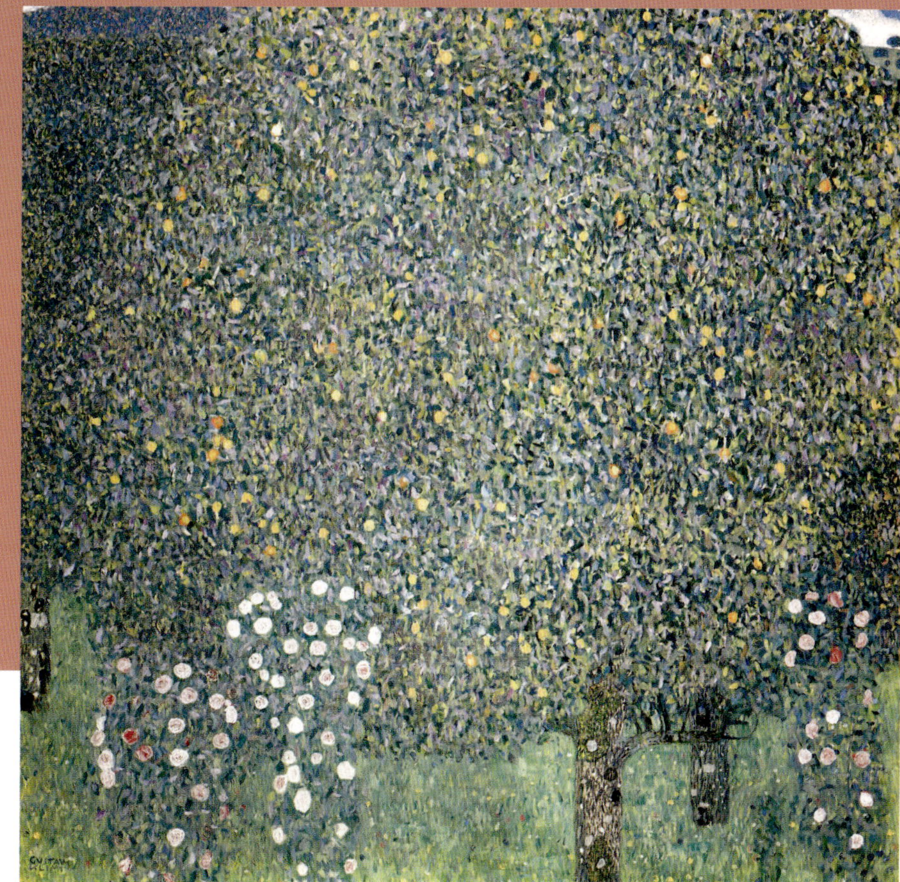

Gustav Klimt
(Wien 1862 - 1918)

Roses under the Trees
Rosen unter Bäumen
Rozen onder de bomen
Rosales bajo los árboles

●

ca. 1905
110 x 110 cm / 43.3 x 43.3 in.
Musée d'Orsay, Paris

oil on canvas / Öl auf Leinwand
olieverf op doek / óleo sobre lienzo

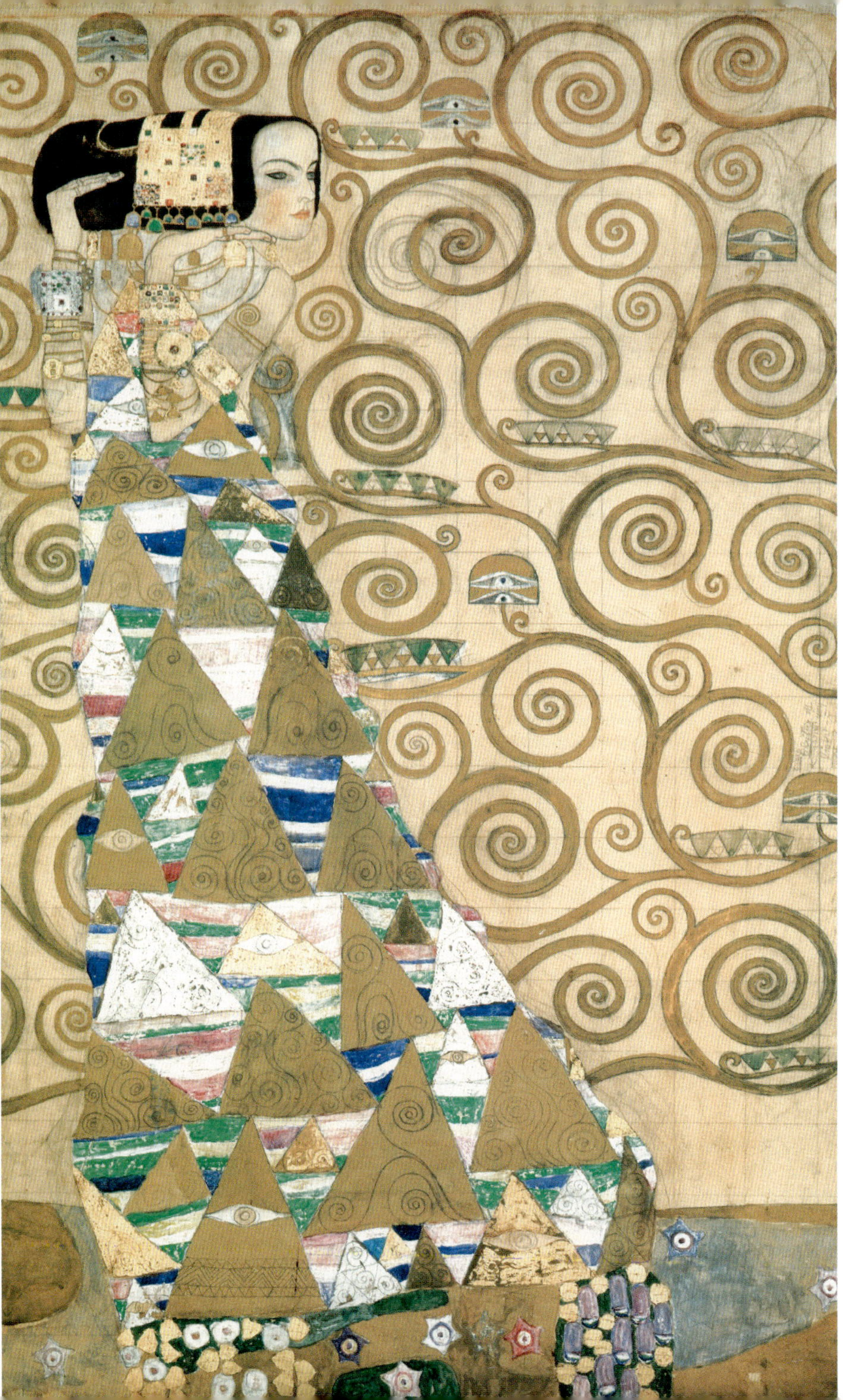

◄ Gustav Klimt
(Wien 1862 - 1918)
**Sketches for the frieze
with the Tree of Life
at the Stoclet Palace
Skizzen für den Fries
mit dem Baum des Lebens
im Palais Stoclet
Schetsen voor de fries
met de Levensboom
in het Stocletpaleis
Bocetos para el friso
con el Árbol de la vida
del Palacio Stoclet**
●

1905-1909
Museum für Angewandte Kunst,
Wien

watercolor and pencil
Aquarell und Bleistift
aquarel en potlood
acuarela y lápiz

► Gustav Klimt
(Wien 1862 - 1918)
**The Kiss
Der Kuss
De kus
El beso**
●●●

1907-1908
180 x 180 cm / 70.8 x 70.8 in.
Österreichische Galerie Belvedere,
Wien

oil on canvas / Öl auf Leinwand
olieverf op doek / óleo sobre lienzo

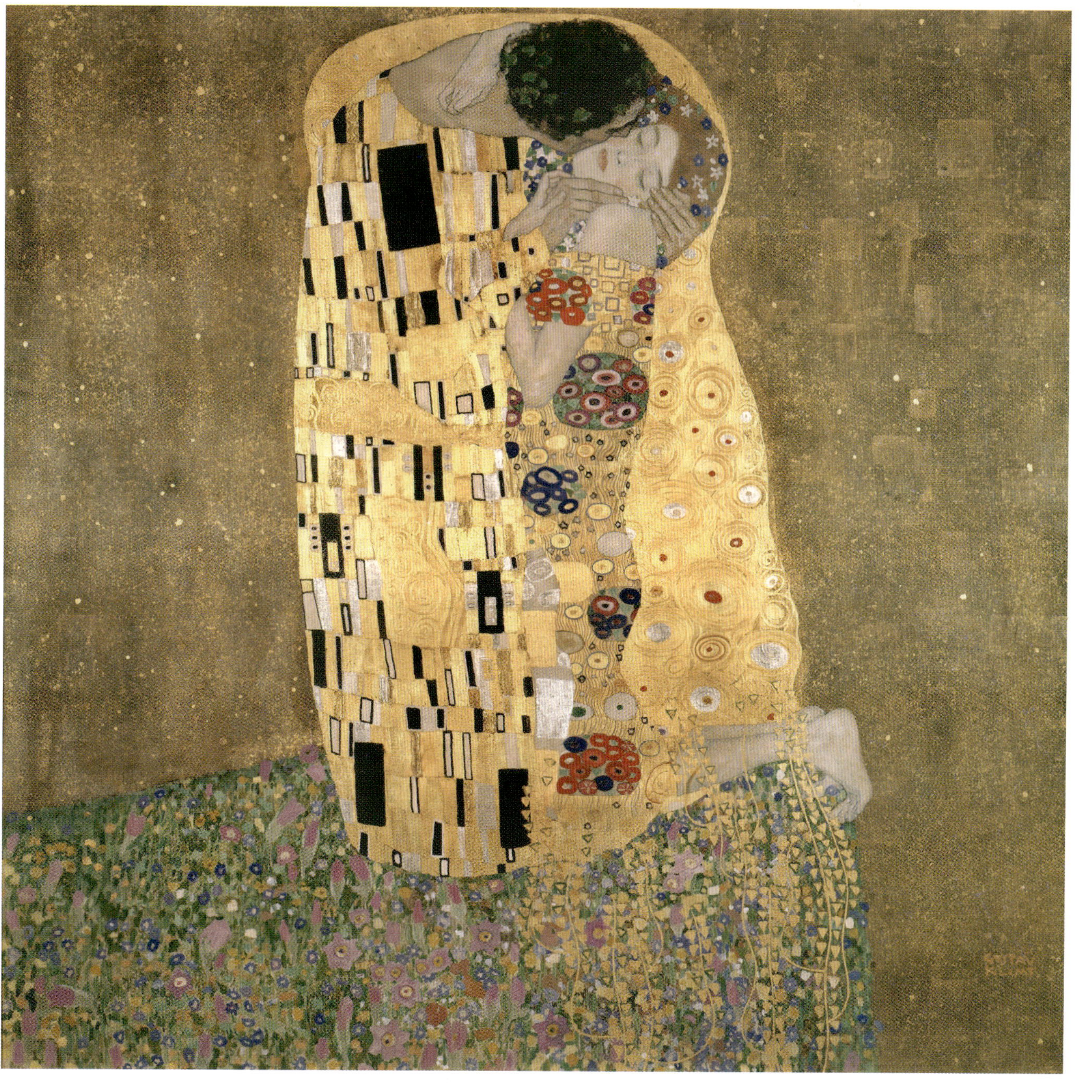

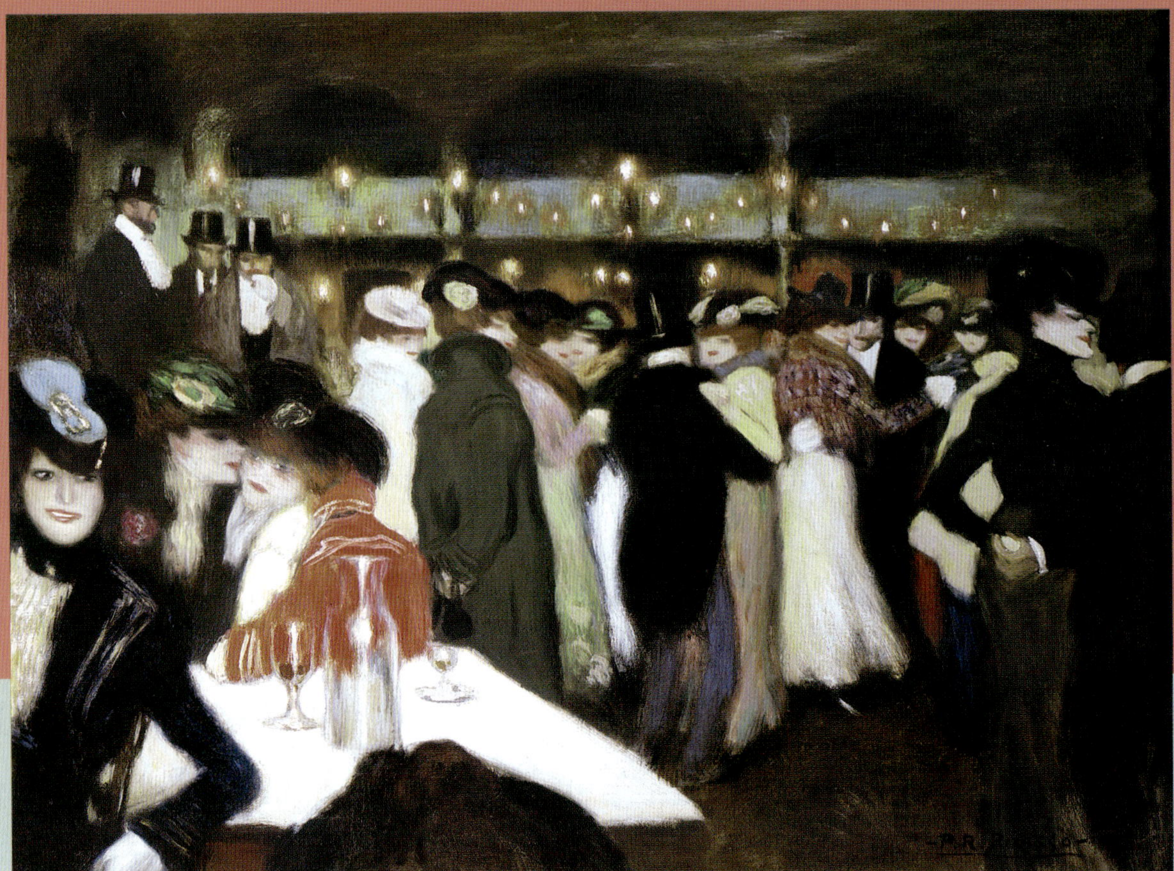

Pablo Picasso
(Málaga 1881 - Mougins 1973)

Le Moulin de la Galette
El molino de la Galette

●

1900
88,2 x 115,5 cm / 34.7 x 45.4 in.
Solomon R. Guggenheim Museum, New York

oil on canvas / Öl auf Leinwand
olieverf op doek / óleo sobre lienzo

Picasso is 19 years old, and feels the influence of Lautrec, the clubs of the Butte, of Paris of the Belle Époque.

Picasso ist 19 Jahre alt und spürt den Einfluss von Lautrec, der Lokale der Butte, des Paris der Belle Époque.

Picasso is 19 jaar als hij door Lautrec , de lokalen van La Butte, en door Parijs en haar Belle Époque beïnvloed wordt.

Picasso tiene 19 años, y se notan en él las influencias de Lautrec, de los locales de la Butte, de la París de la Belle Époque.

Pablo Picasso
(Málaga 1881 - Mougins 1973)

The Old Guitarist
Der alte Gitarrenspieler
Oude gitarist
El viejo guitarrista ciego

••

1903
121 x 82 cm / 47.6 x 32.3 in.
Art Institute of Chicago, Chicago

oil on panel / Öl auf Tafel
olieverf op paneel / óleo sobre tabla

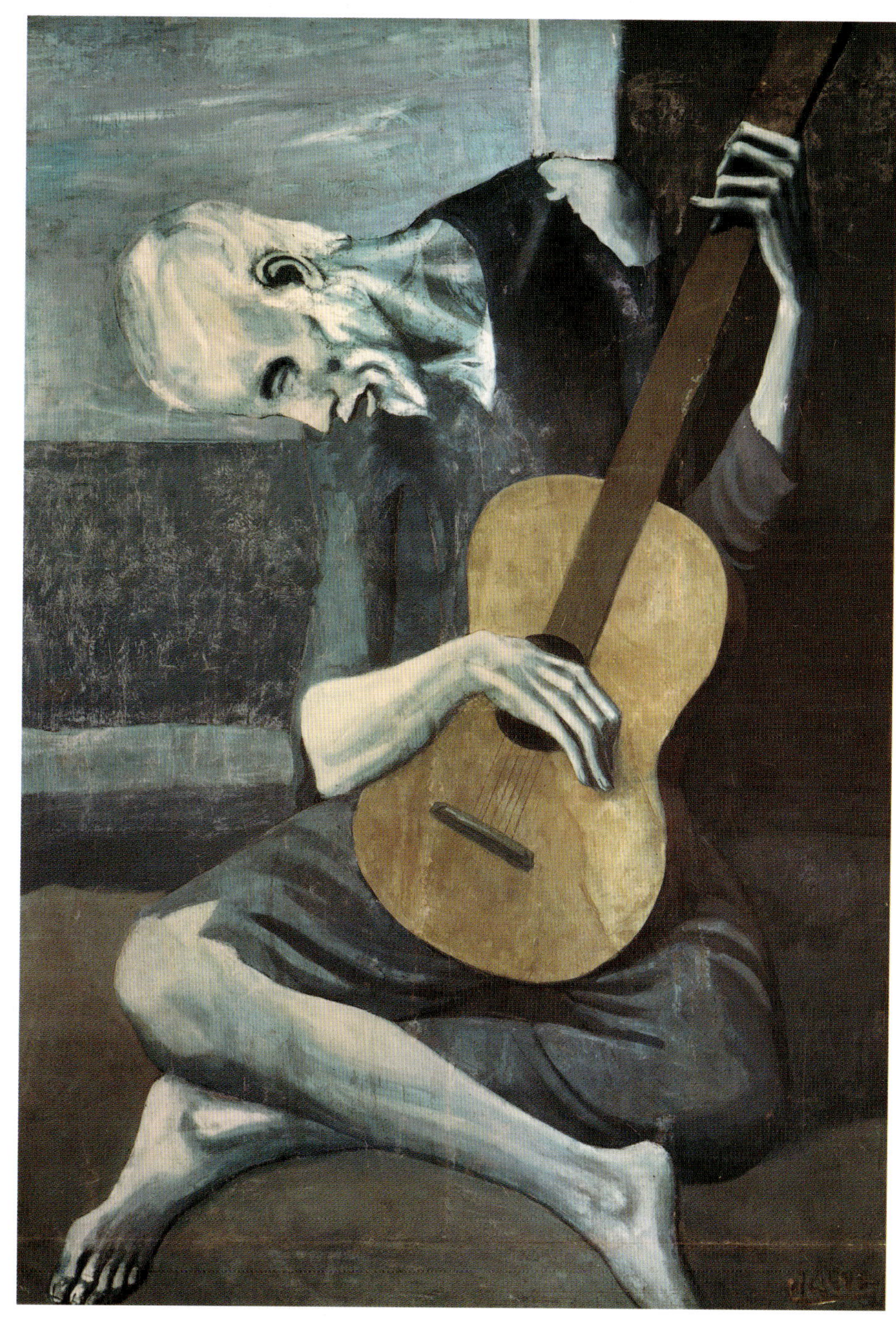

**Blue as the night, as pain, like the
skies of the paintings by El Greco.**

**Blau wie die Nacht, wie der
Schmerz, wie der Himmel
in den Bildern von El Greco.**

**Blauw als de nacht, als de pijn,
als de luchten van de schilderijen
van El Greco.**

**Azul como la noche, como
el dolor, como los cielos de
los cuadros de El Greco.**

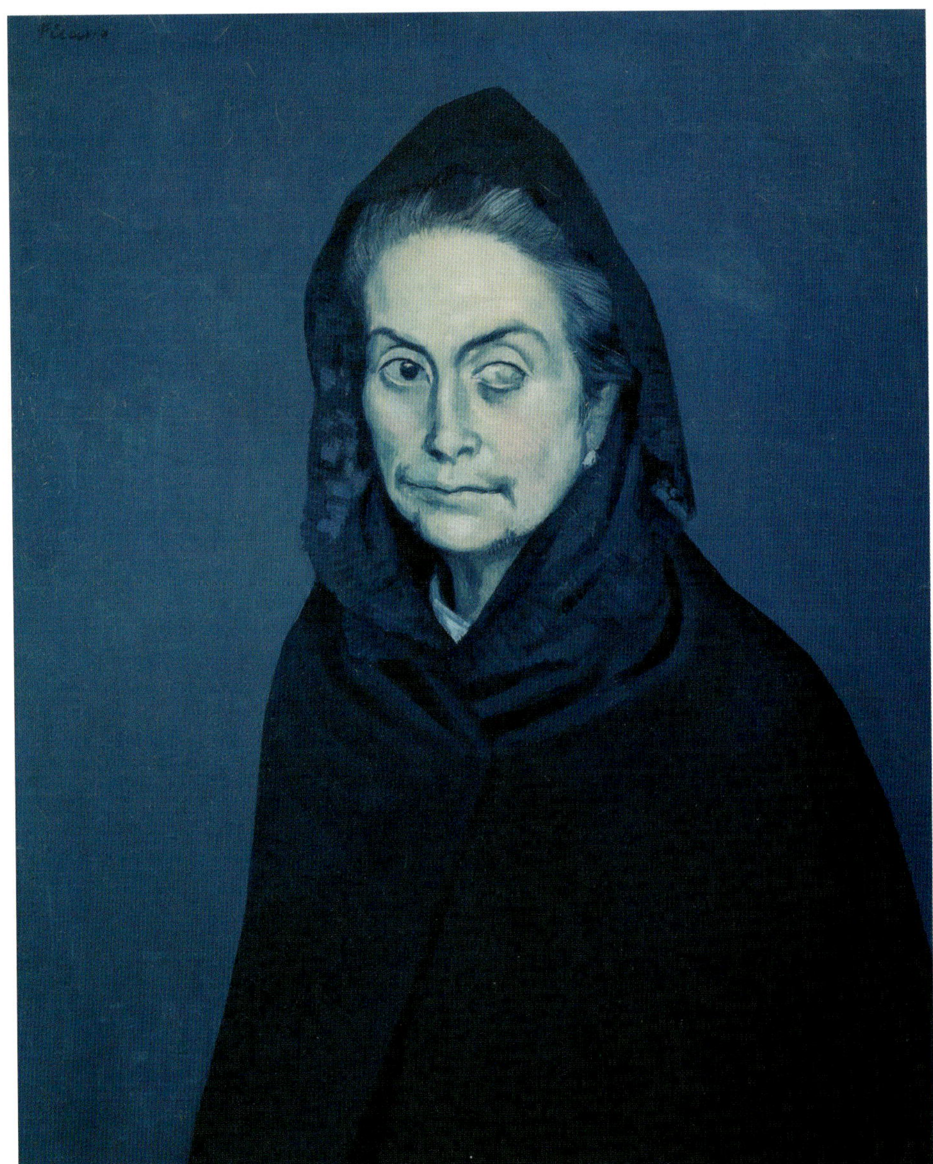

◀ Pablo Picasso
(Málaga 1881 - Mougins 1973)
**La Celestine
La Célestine
Celestina
La Celestina**
● ● ●
1904
74,5 x 58,5 cm / 29.5 x 23 in.
Musée Picasso, Paris

oil on canvas / Öl auf Leinwand
olieverf op doek / óleo sobre lienzo

▶ Pablo Picasso
(Málaga 1881 - Mougins 1973)
**Les Trois Hollandaises
Die drei Holländerinnen
De drie Nederlandsen
Las tres holandesas**
●
1905
77 x 67 cm / 30.3 x 26.3 in.
Centre Georges Pompidou,
Musée National d'Art Moderne, Paris

gouache on cardboard
Gouache auf Karton
gouache op karton
gouache sobre cartón

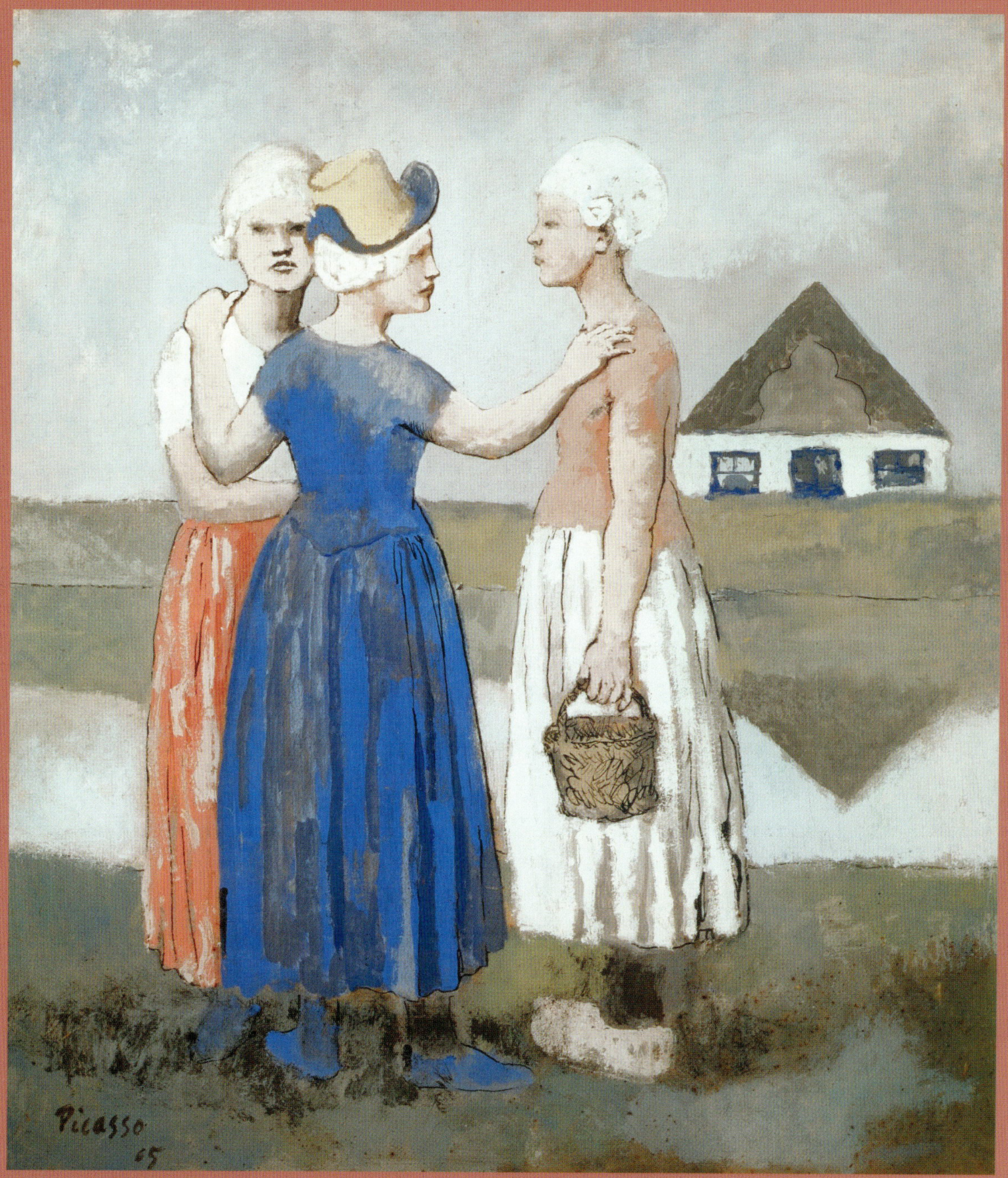

Edvard Munch
(Løten 1863 - Ekely 1944)

Girls on the Bridge
Mädchen auf der Brücke
Meisjes op de brug
Muchachas en el puente

ca. 1901
136 x 125 cm / 53.5 x 49.2 in.
Nasjonalgalleriet, Oslo

oil on canvas / Öl auf Leinwand
olieverf op doek / óleo sobre lienzo

Edvard Munch
(Løten 1863 - Ekely 1944)

Puberty
Pubertät
Puberteit
Pubertad

1894
151,5 x 110 cm / 59.7 x 43.3 in.
Nasjonalgalleriet, Oslo

oil on canvas / Öl auf Leinwand
olieverf op doek / óleo sobre lienzo

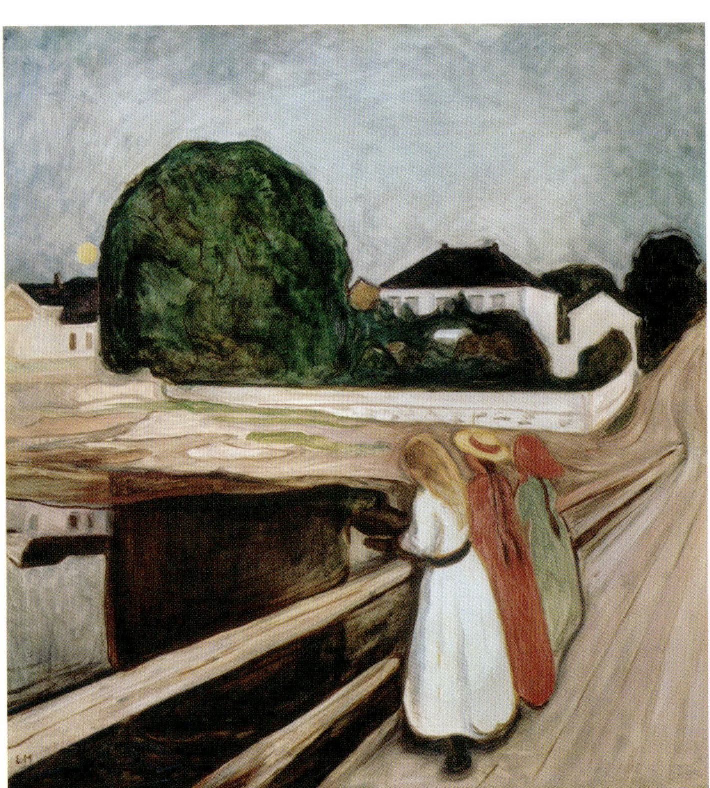

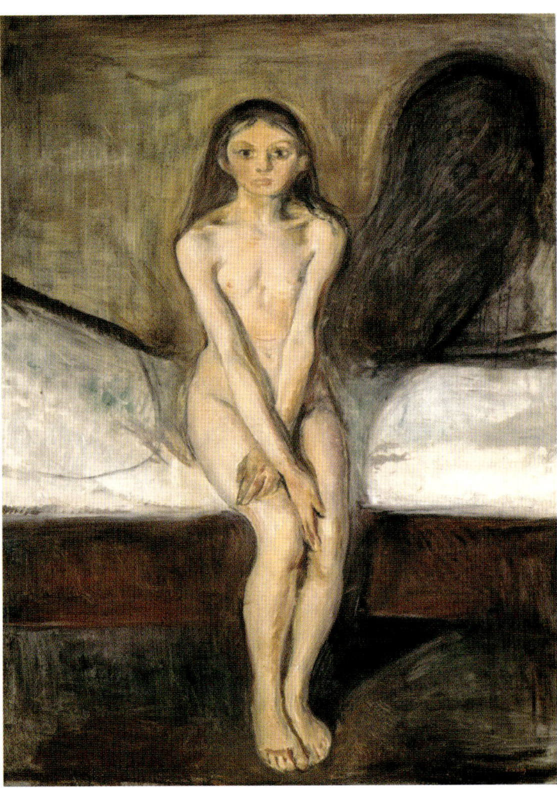

With this work, Munch
knew how to translate
visually a vibration
perceived in nature,
both visual and acoustic.

Mit diesem Werk gelang
es Munch eine in der
Natur wahrgenommene,
visuelle und akustische
Vibration bildlich
umzusetzen.

Met dit werk heeft Munch
de vibratie die hij in de
natuur voelde en hoorde
op plastische wijze weten
te vertalen.

Con esta obra, Munch
ha sabido traducir
plásticamente una
vibración percibida en
la naturaleza, tanto visual
como sonora.

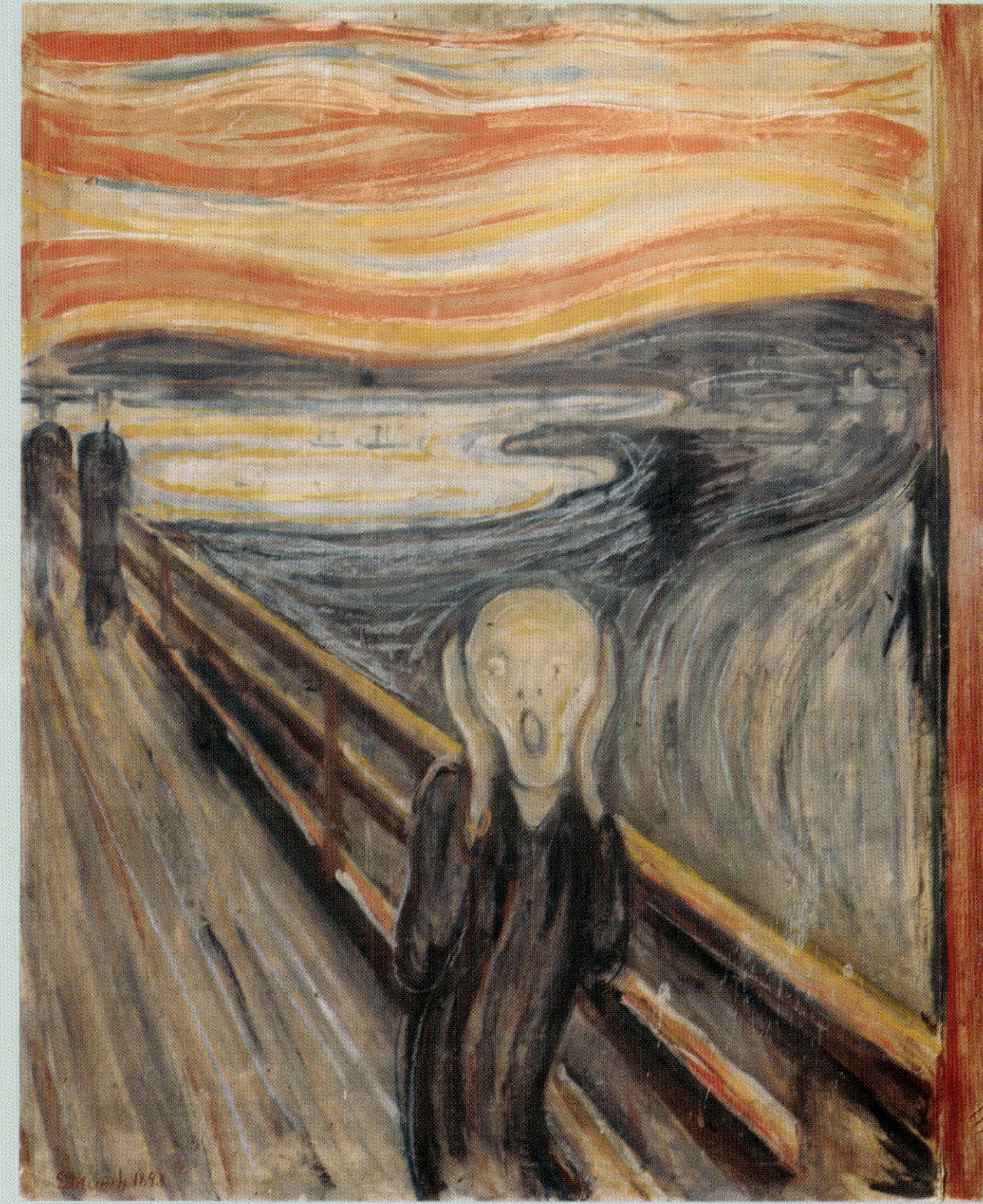

Edvard Munch
(Løten 1863 - Ekely 1944)

**The Scream
Der Schrei
De schreeuw
El grito**

●●●
1893
91 x 73 cm / 35.8 x 28.7 in.
Nasjonalgalleriet, Oslo

oil on canvas
Öl auf Leinwand
olieverf op doek
óleo sobre lienzo

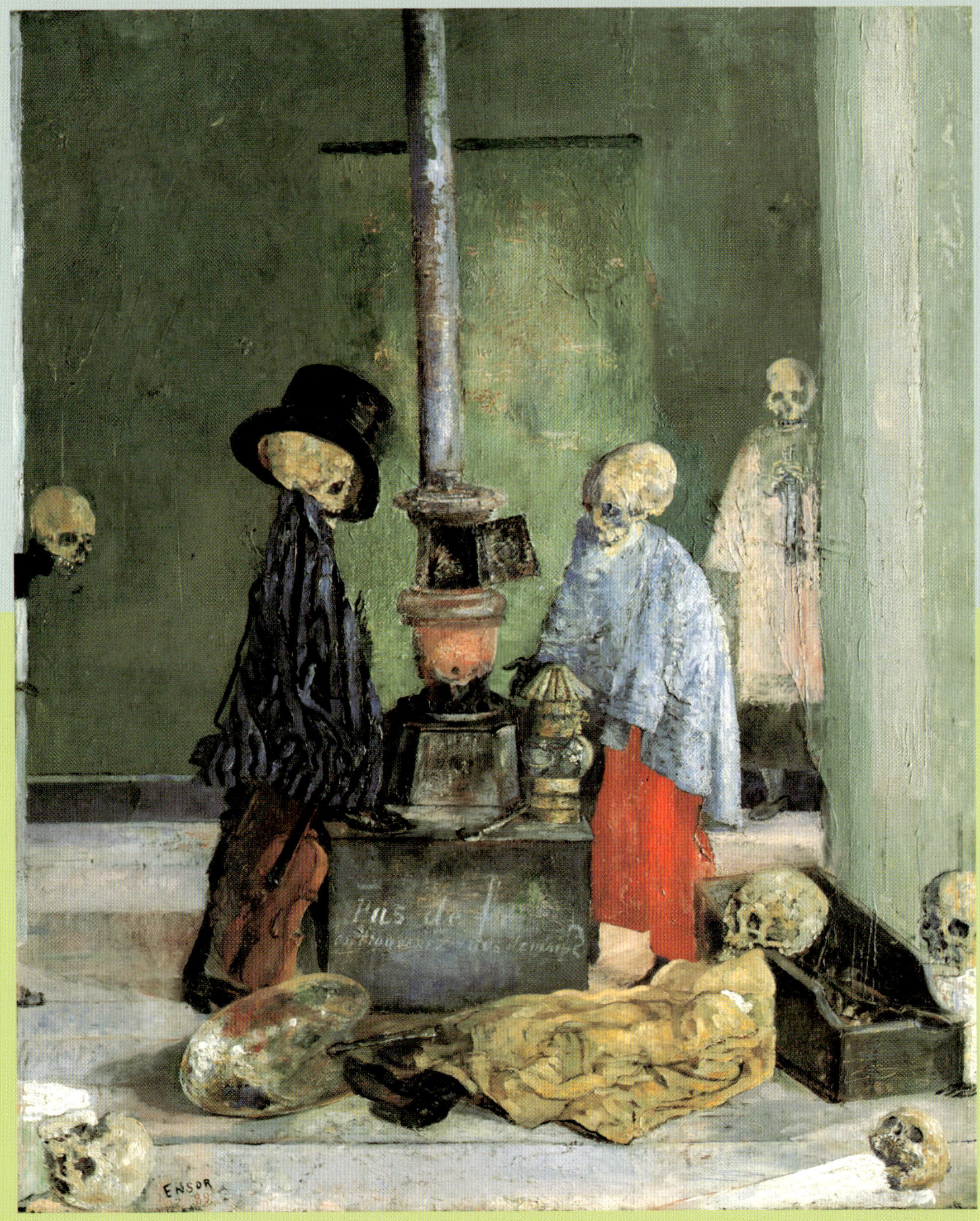

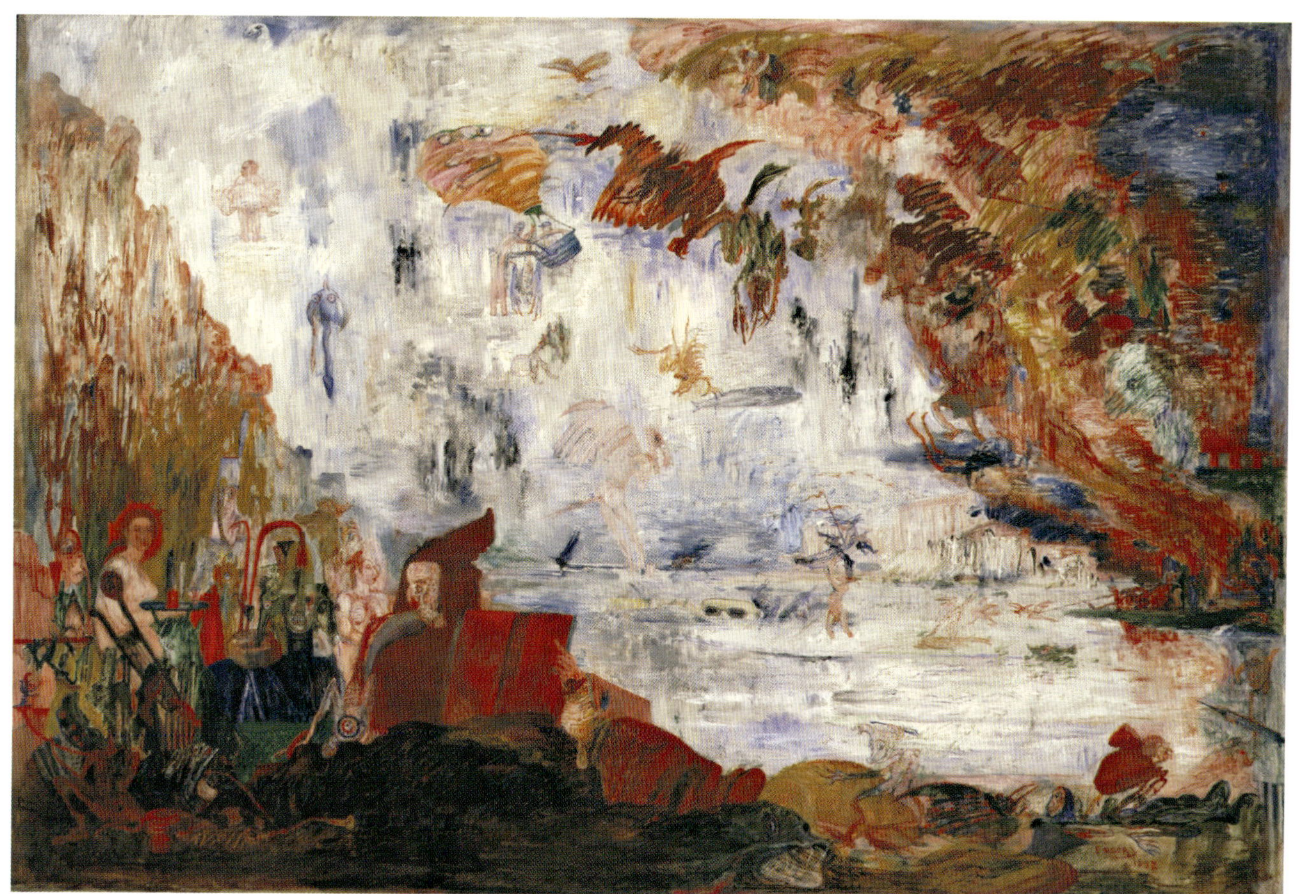

◄ James Ensor
(Oostende 1860 - 1949)

Skeletons warming themselves
Sich wärmende Skelette
Skeletten die zich aan het opwarmen zijn
Esqueletos intentando calentarse

●●

1889
74,8 x 60 cm / 29.5 x 23.6 in.
Kimbell Art Museum, Fort Worth (TX)

oil on canvas / Öl auf Leinwand
olieverf op doek / óleo sobre lienzo

James Ensor
(Oostende 1860 - 1949)

Tribulations of Saint Anthony
Die Versuchung des hl. Antonius
De verzoeking van de heilige Antonius
Las tentaciones de San Antonio

●

1887
117,8 x 167,6 cm / 46.4 x 66 in.
Museum of Modern Art (MoMA), New York

oil on canvas / Öl auf Leinwand
olieverf op doek / óleo sobre lienzo

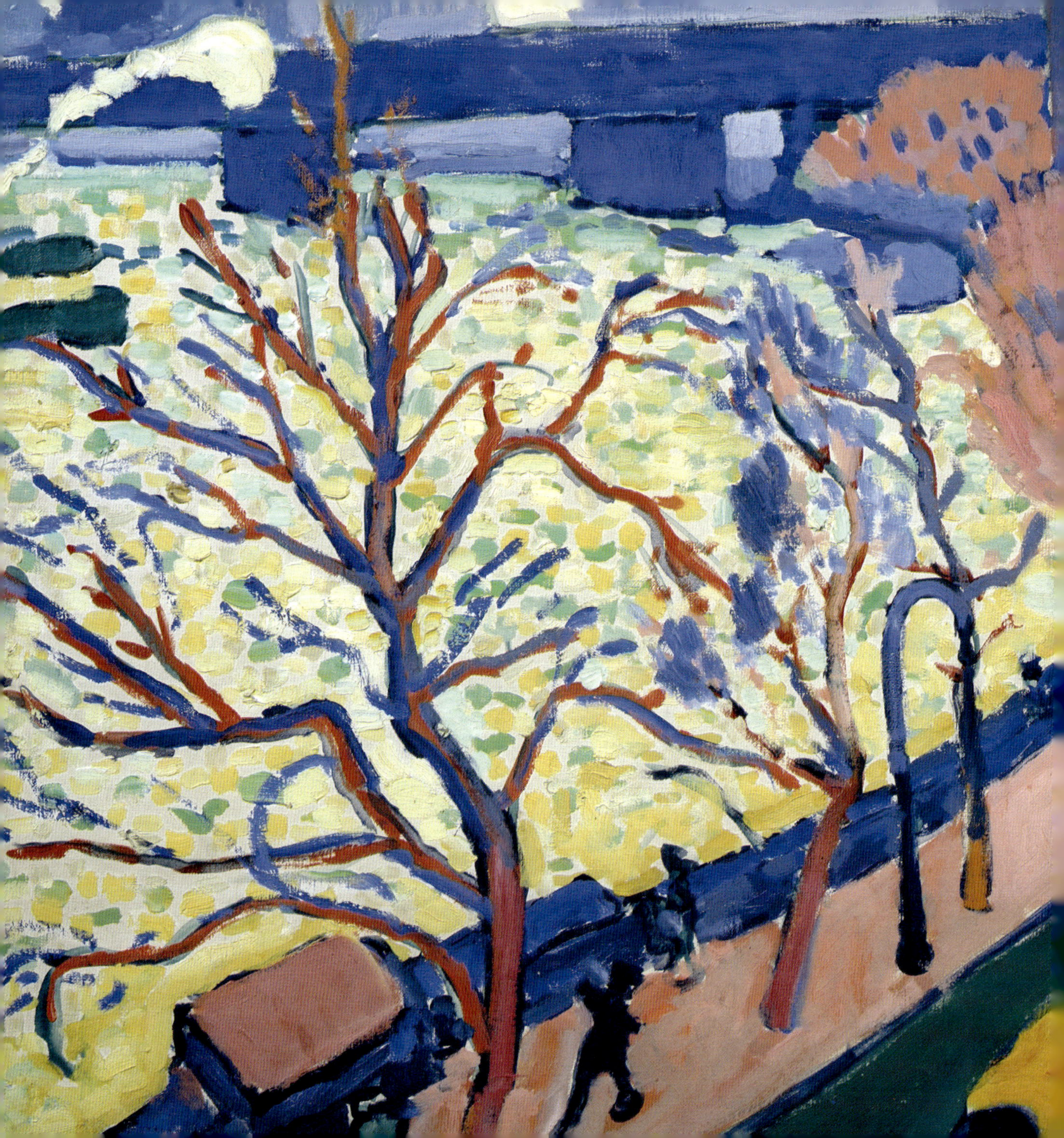

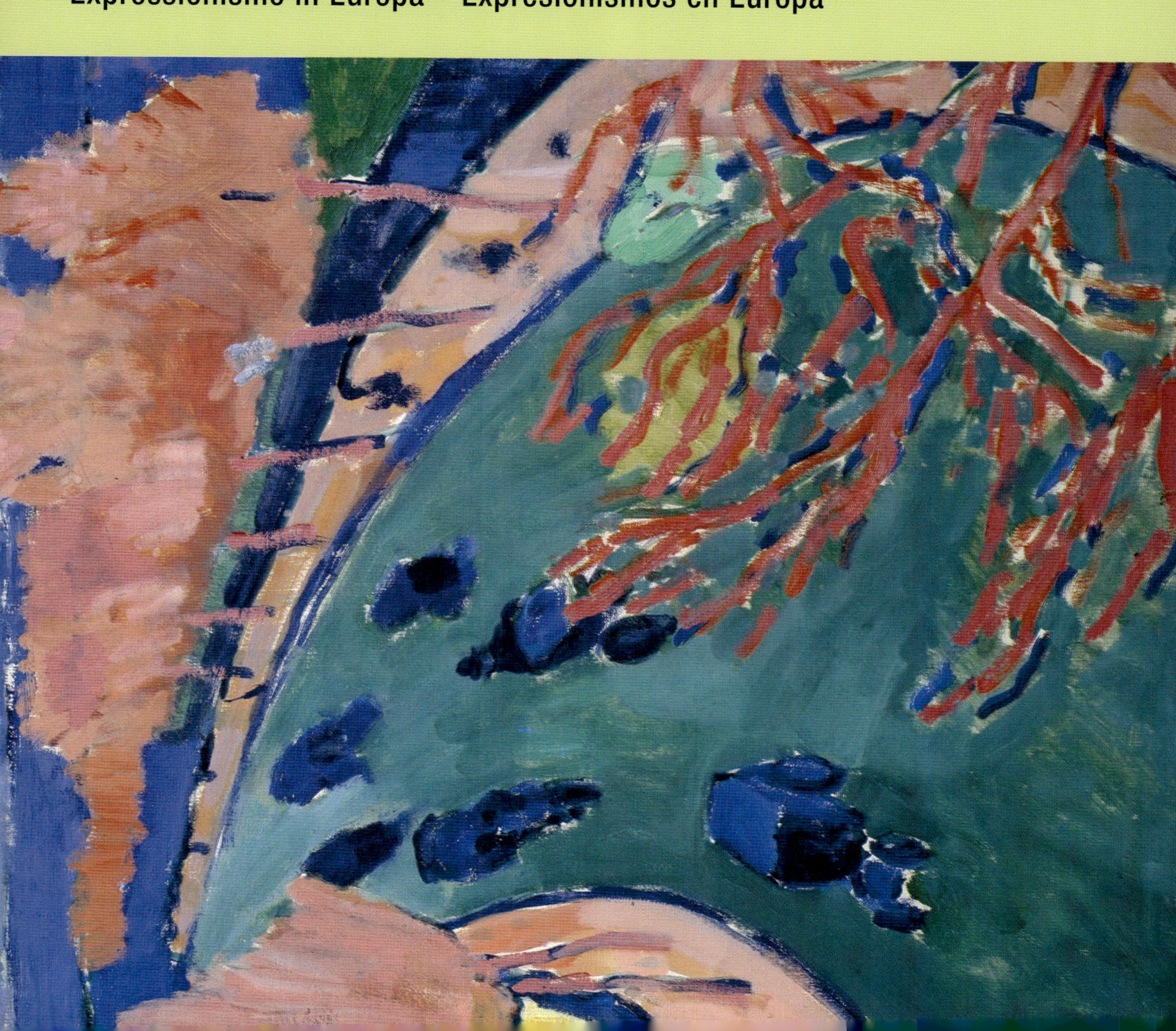

Expressionism in Europe • Expressionismen in Europa
Expressionisme in Europa • Expresionismos en Europa

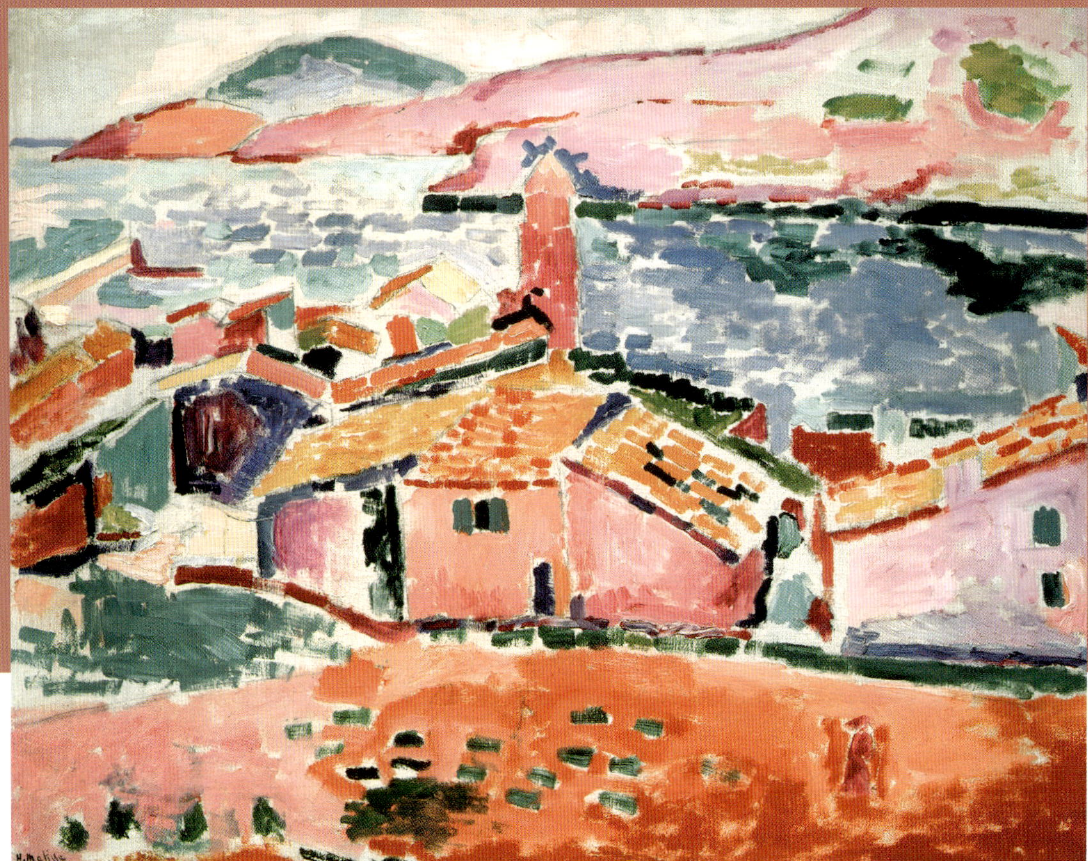

Henri Matisse
(Le Cateau-Cambrésis 1869 - Nice 1954)

View of Collioure
Die Dächer von Collioure
De daken van Collioure
Los techos de Collioure

●●

1905
59,5 x 73 cm / 23.4 x 28.7 in.
The State Hermitage Museum, St. Petersburg

oil on canvas / Öl auf Leinwand
olieverf op doek / óleo sobre lienzo

▶ Henri Matisse
(Le Cateau-Cambrésis 1869 - Nice 1954)

Gypsy
Zigeunerin
Zigeuner
La gitana

●

1905
55 x 46 cm / 21.6 x 18.1 in.
Musée de l'Annonciade, Saint-Tropez

oil on canvas / Öl auf Leinwand
olieverf op doek / óleo sobre lienzo

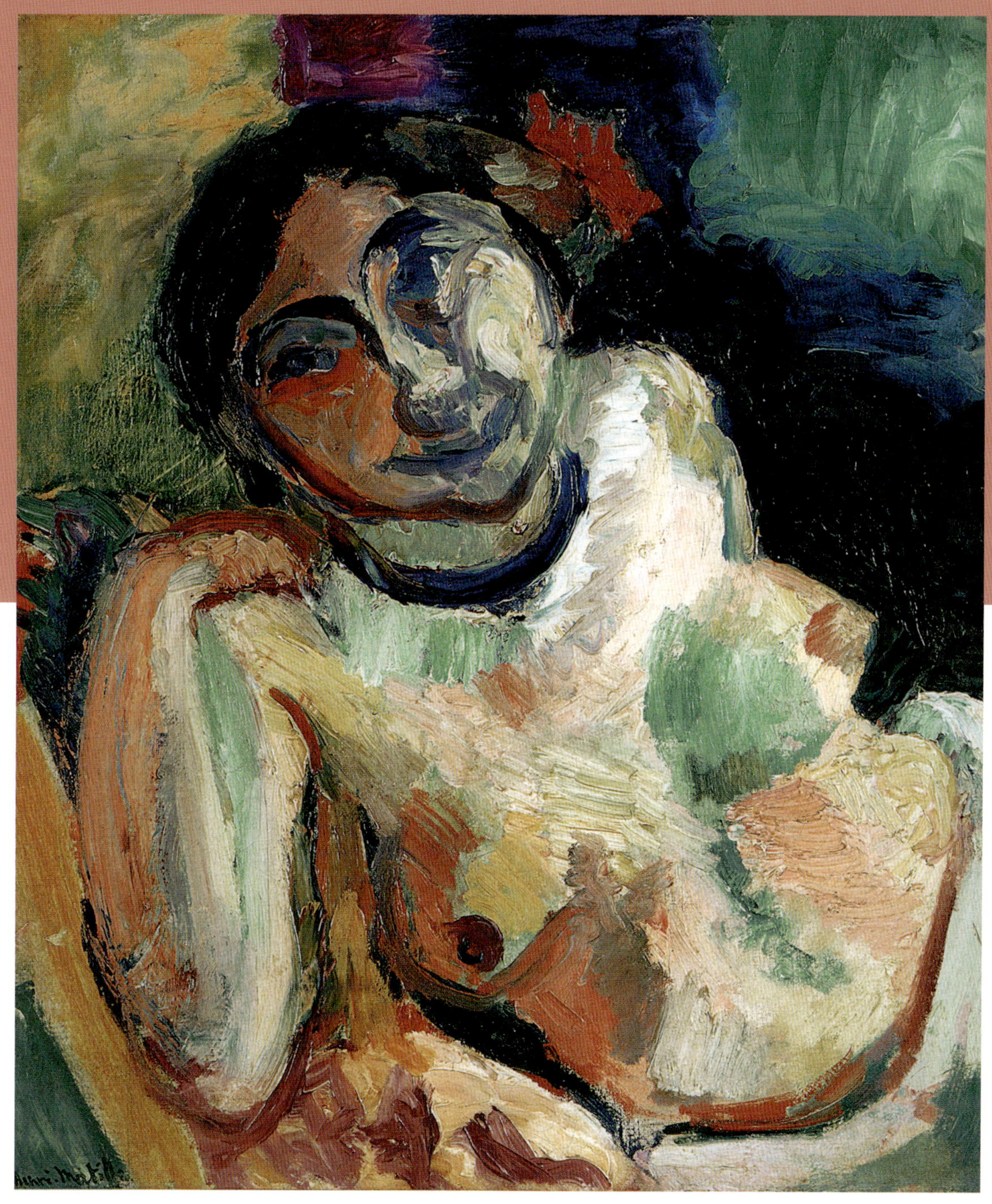

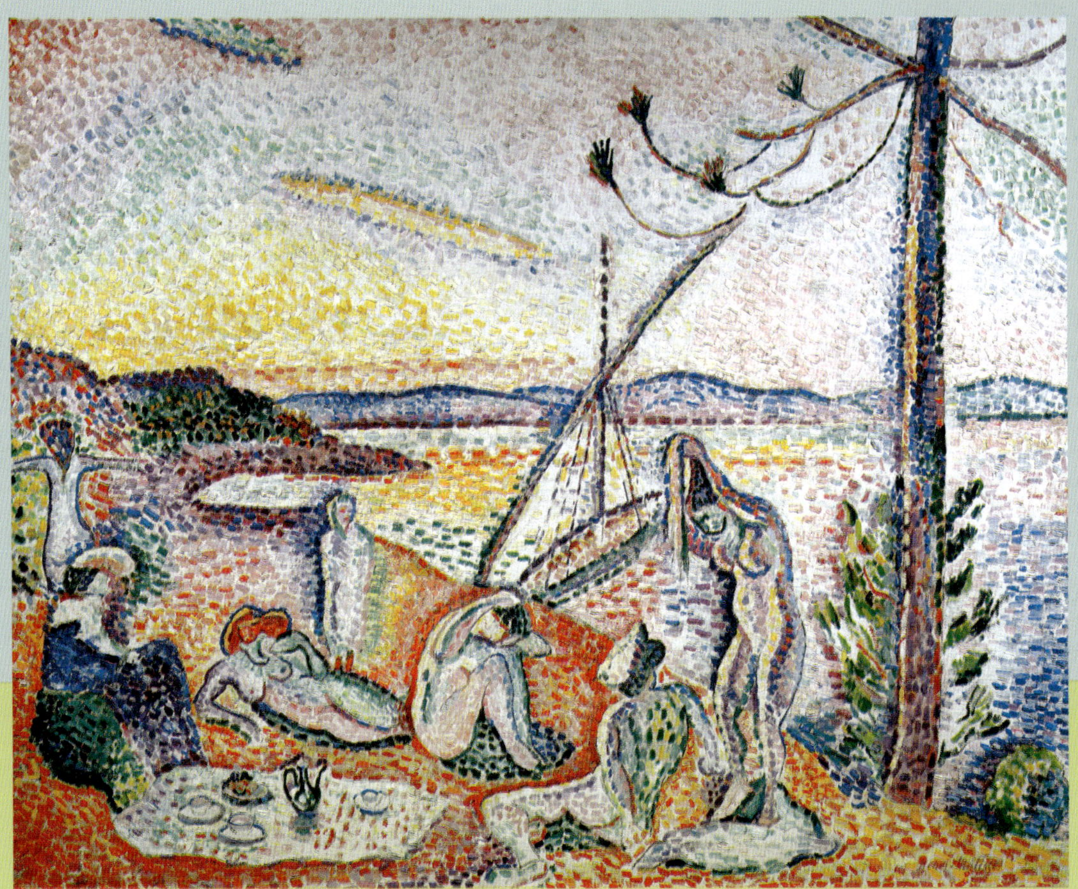

Henri Matisse
(Le Cateau-Cambrésis 1869 - Nice 1954)

Luxe, Calme et Volupté
Luxus, Stille und Begierde
Luxe, kalmte en genoegen
Lujo, calma y voluptuosidad

●●

1904
99 x 118 cm / 39 x 46.4 in.
Musée d'Orsay, Paris

oil on canvas / Öl auf Leinwand
olieverf op doek / óleo sobre lienzo

An invitation to travel, in a universe of perfect harmony between man and nature, the colors and the lines.

Eine Einladung zu einer Reise in ein Universum vollkommener Harmonie zwischen Mensch und Natur, Farben und Linien.

Een uitnodiging tot reizen, in een universum waar de mens en de natuur, kleuren en lijnen in perfecte harmonie leven.

Una invitación al viaje, en un universo de perfecta armonía entre el hombre y la naturaleza, los colores y las líneas.

Henri Matisse

(Le Cateau-Cambrésis 1869 - Nice 1954)

Harmony in Red
Harmonie in rot
Rode harmonie
Armonía en rojo

●●●

1908
180,5 x 221 cm / 71 x 87 in.
The State Hermitage Museum,
St. Petersburg

oil on canvas / Öl auf Leinwand
olieverf op doek / óleo sobre lienzo

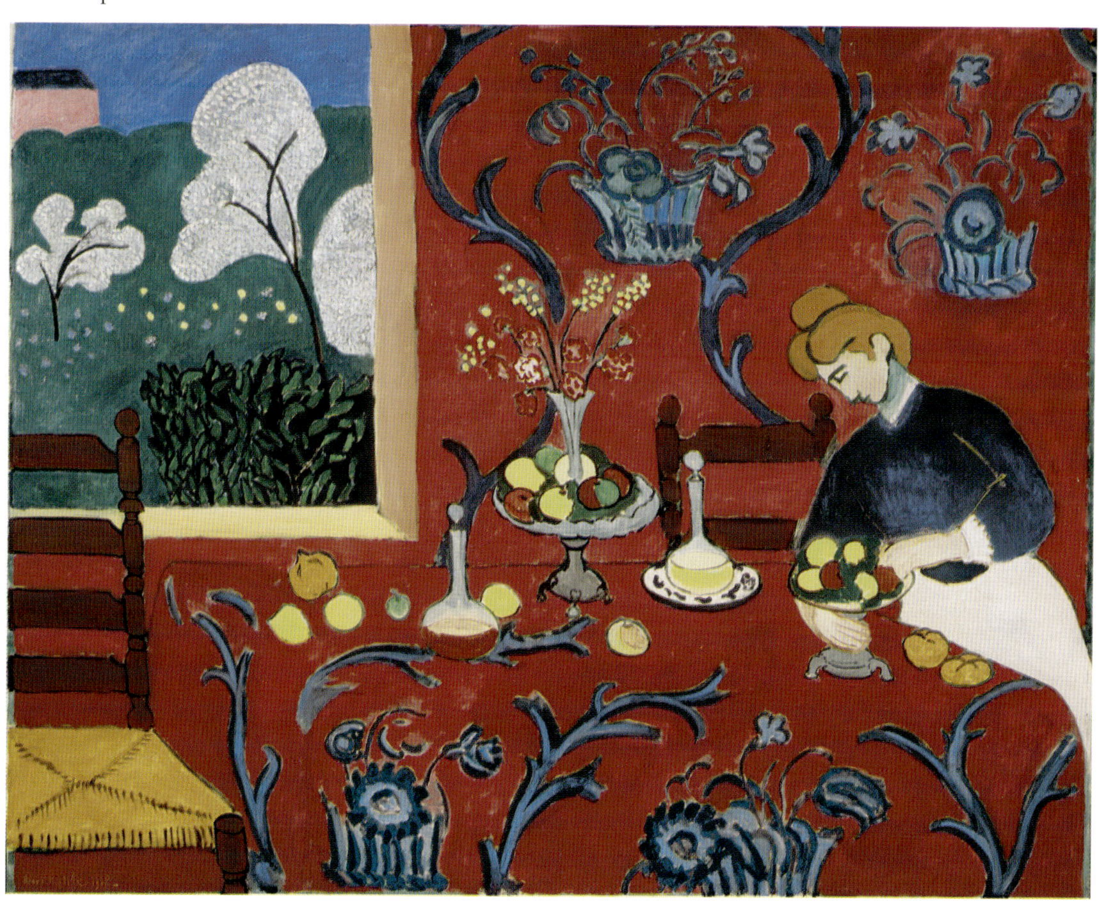

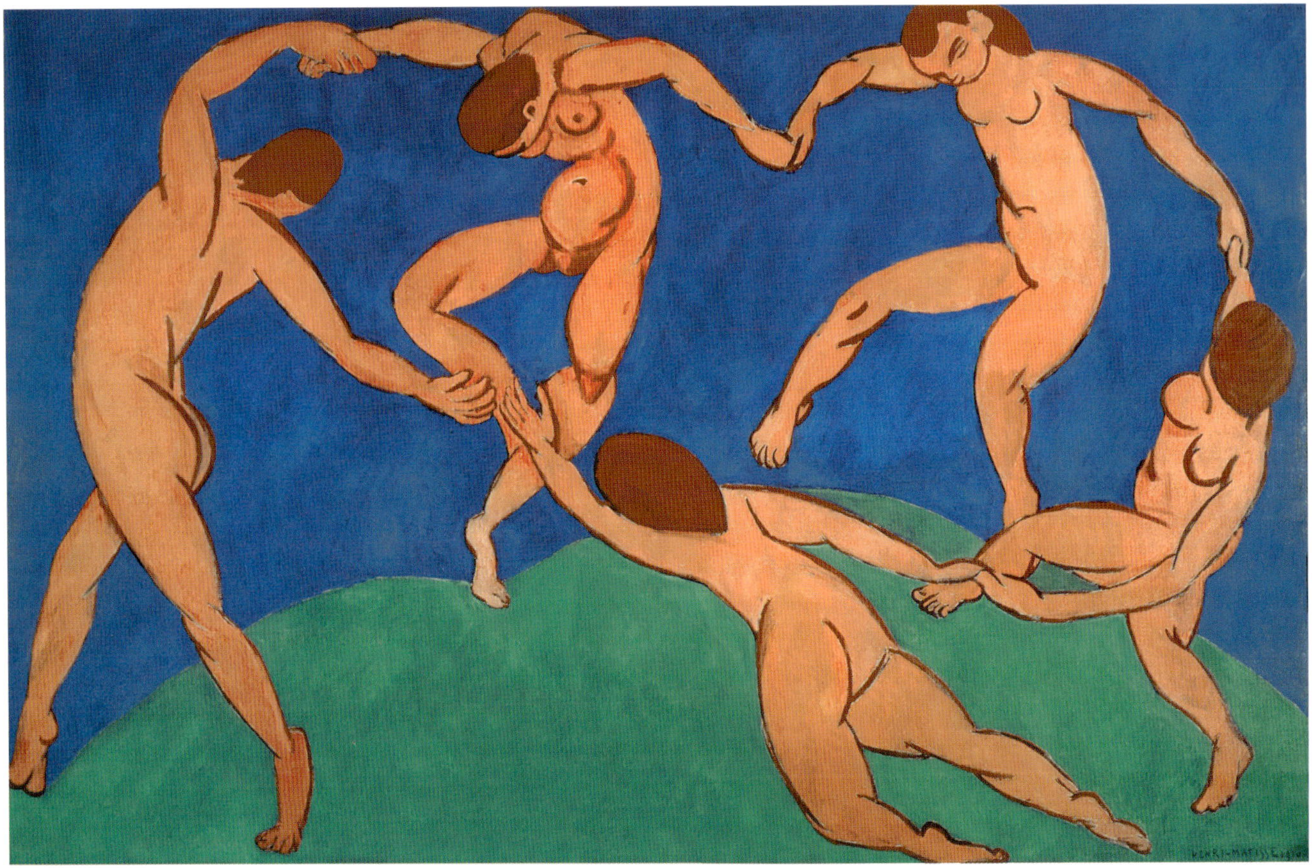

Henri Matisse
(Le Cateau-Cambrésis 1869 - Nice 1954)

The Dance II
Der Tanz II
De dans II
La danza II

●●●

1910
260 x 391 cm / 102.3 x 153.9 in.
The State Hermitage Museum, St. Petersburg

oil on canvas / Öl auf Leinwand
olieverf op doek / óleo sobre lienzo

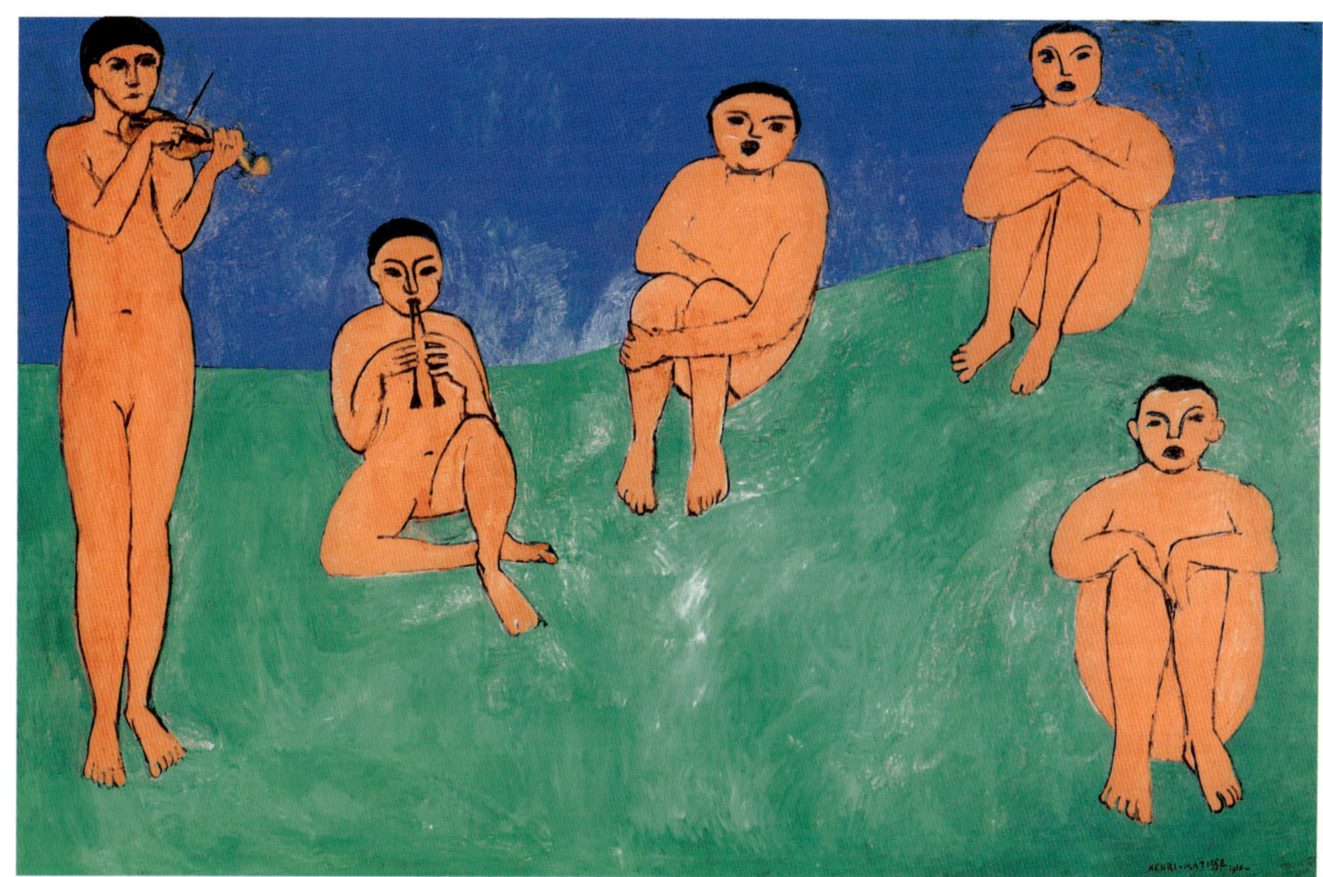

Henri Matisse
(Le Cateau-Cambrésis 1869 - Nice 1954)

Music
Die Musik
De muziek
La música

●

1910
260 x 389 cm / 102.3 x 153.1 in.
The State Hermitage Museum,
St. Petersburg

oil on canvas / Öl auf Leinwand
olieverf op doek / óleo sobre lienzo

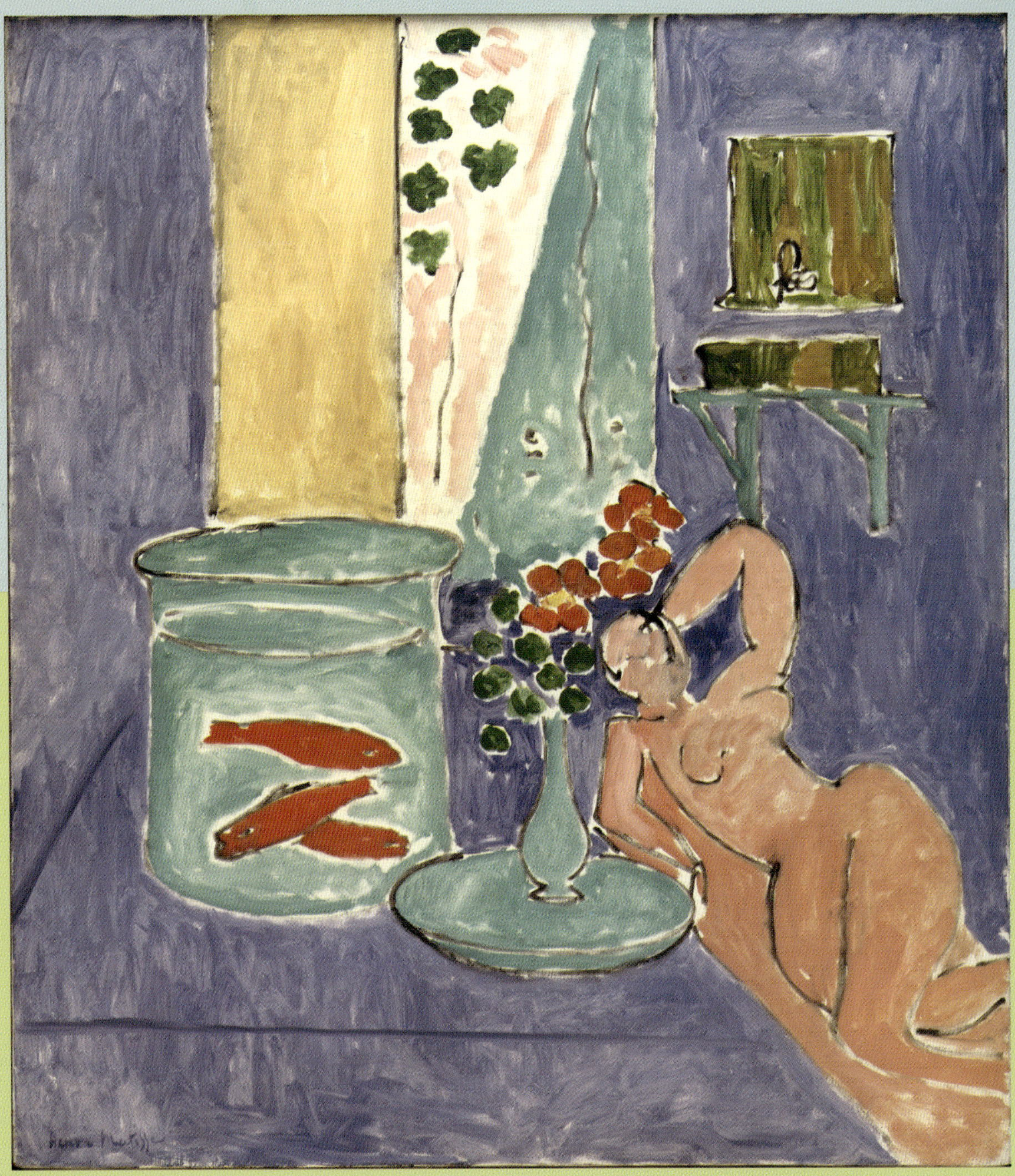

Henri Matisse
(Le Cateau-Cambrésis
1869 - Nice 1954)

**Moroccan Woman
Marokkanerin
Marokkaanse
La marroquí**

●

1912
36 x 28 cm / 14.1 x 11 in.
Musée de Grenoble,
Grenoble
oil on canvas
Öl auf Leinwand
olieverf op doek
óleo sobre lienzo

◄ Henri Matisse
(Le Cateau-Cambrésis
1869 - Nice 1954)

**Goldfish with
sculpture. Issy-les
Moulineaux
Goldfische und
Skulptur. Issy-les
Moulineaux
Goudvissen met
sculptuur. Issy-les
Moulineaux
Peces rojos y
escultura. Issy-les
Moulineaux**

●●

1912
116,2 x 100,5 cm
46 x 39.5 in.
Museum of Modern Art
(MoMA), New York
oil on canvas
Öl auf Leinwand
olieverf op doek
óleo sobre lienzo

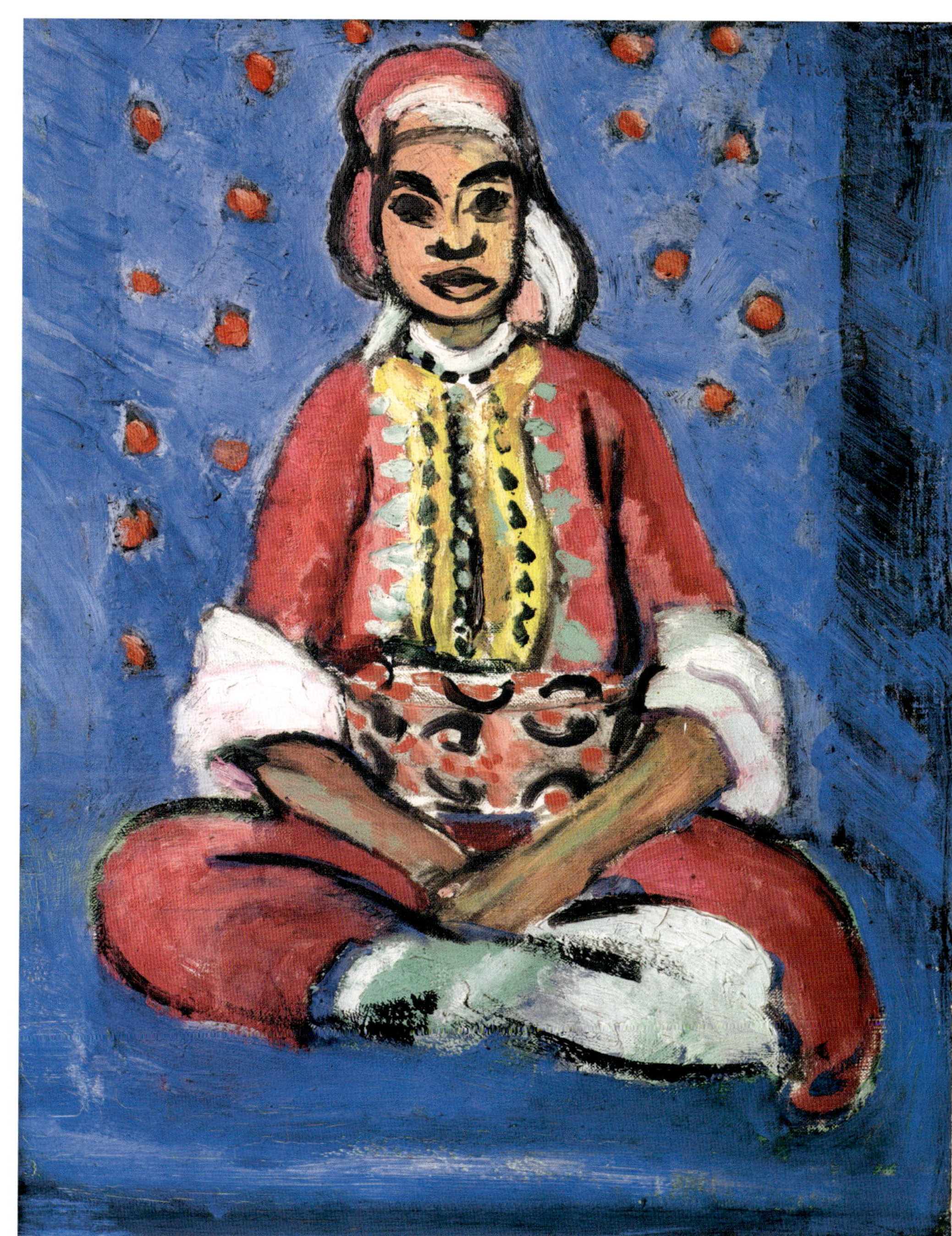

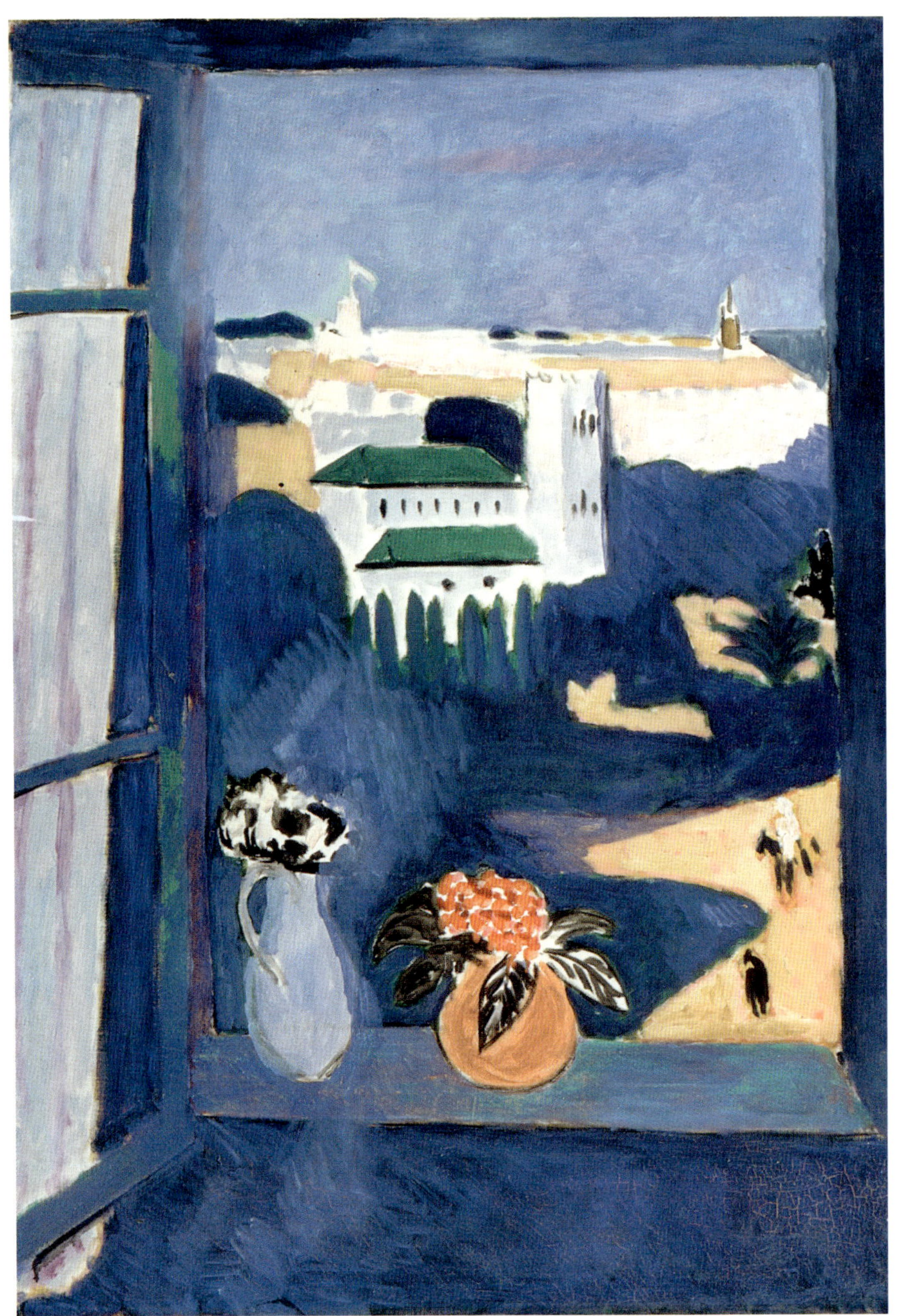

Henri Matisse
(Le Cateau-Cambrésis 1869 - Nice 1954)

Window at Tangier
Tanger, Blick aus einem Fenster
Tanger, uitzicht vanuit een raam
Tánger: paisaje visto desde una
ventana

●

1912
120 x 80 cm / 47.2 x 31.5 in.
Pushkin State Museum of Fine Arts,
Moscow

oil on canvas / Öl auf Leinwand
olieverf op doek / óleo sobre lienzo

68

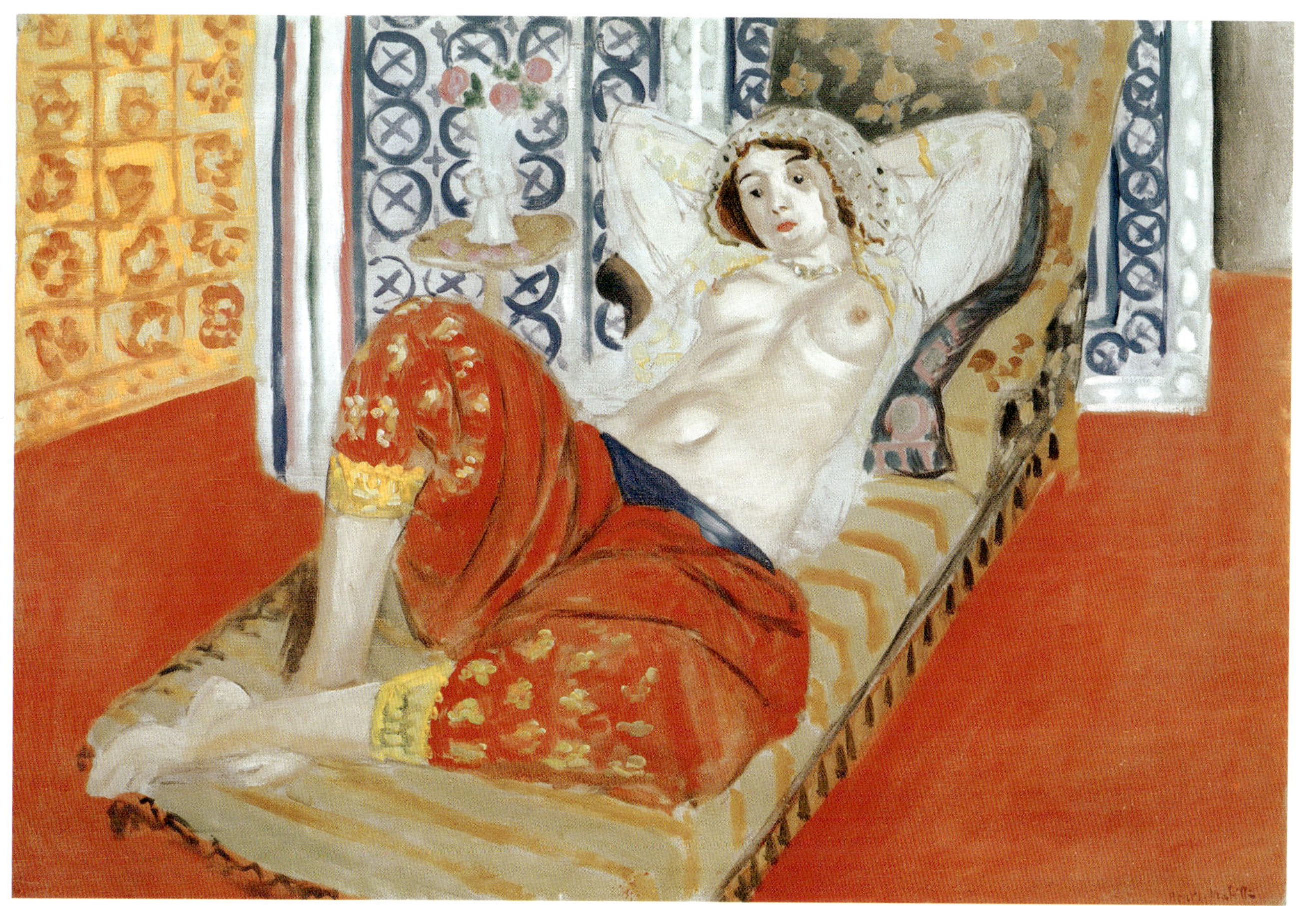

Henri Matisse
(Le Cateau-Cambrésis 1869 - Nice 1954)

Odalisque in red trousers
Odaliske mit roten Hosen
Odalisk met rode broek
Odalisca en pantalones rojos

●●

1921
65 x 90 cm / 25.6 x 35.4 in.
Centre Georges Pompidou, Musée National d'Art Moderne, Paris

oil on canvas / Öl auf Leinwand
olieverf op doek / óleo sobre lienzo

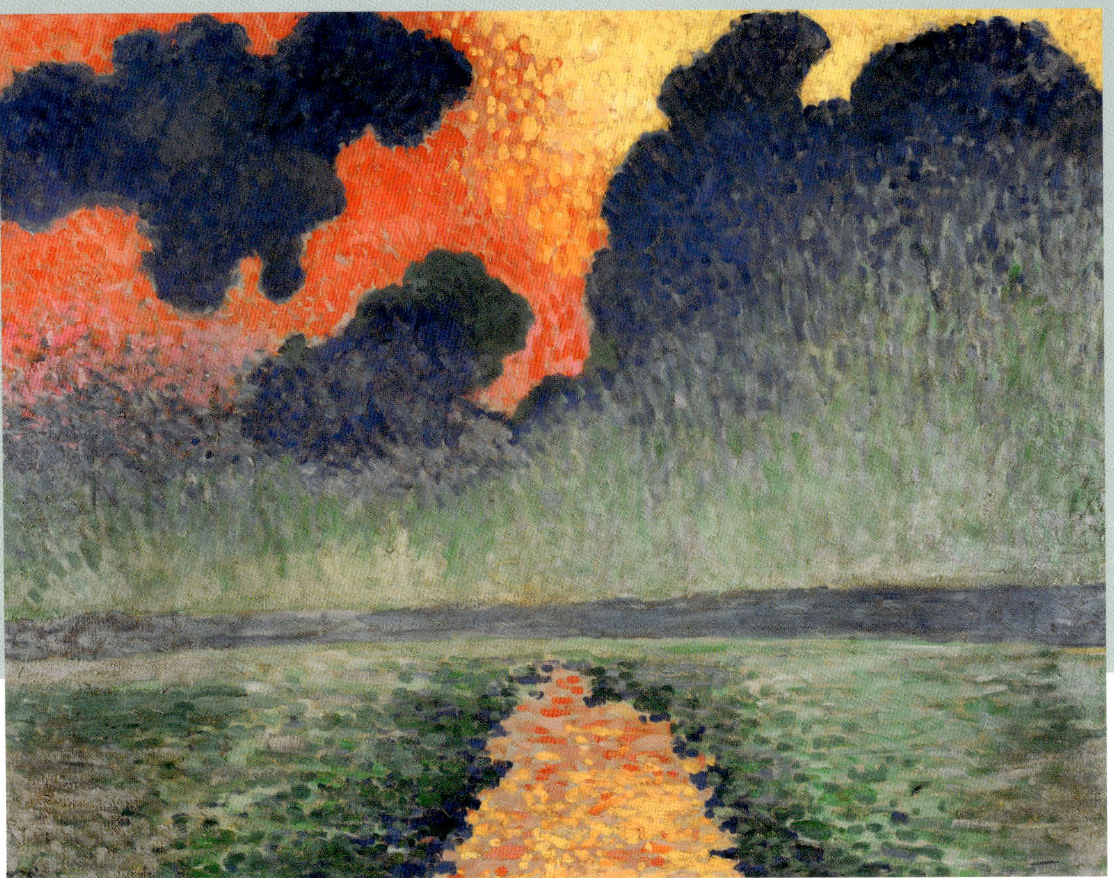

André Derain
(Chatou 1880 - Garches 1954)

**Effects of the sun on water
Spiegelung der Sonne im Wasser
Weerspiegeling van de zon op het water
Efectos del sol sobre el agua**

●

1905
80,5 x 100 cm / 31.7 x 39.3 in.
Musée de l'Annonciade, Saint-Tropez

oil on canvas / Öl auf Leinwand
olieverf op doek / óleo sobre lienzo

"The colors became cartridges of dynamite.
They had to discharge the lights…"

"Die Farben wurden zu Dynamitpatronen.
Sie müssen das Licht entladen…"

"Kleuren veranderden in patronen vol
dynamiet. Ze moesten het licht ontladen…"

"Los colores se transformaban en cartuchos
de dinamita. Debían descargar las luces…"
André Derain

André Derain
(Chatou 1880 - Garches 1954)

The Two Barges
Die zwei Kähne
De twee aken
Las dos barcazas

●

1906
80 x 97,5 cm / 31.5 x 38.4 in.
Centre Georges Pompidou, Musée National d'Art Moderne, Paris

oil on canvas / Öl auf Leinwand
olieverf op doek / óleo sobre lienzo

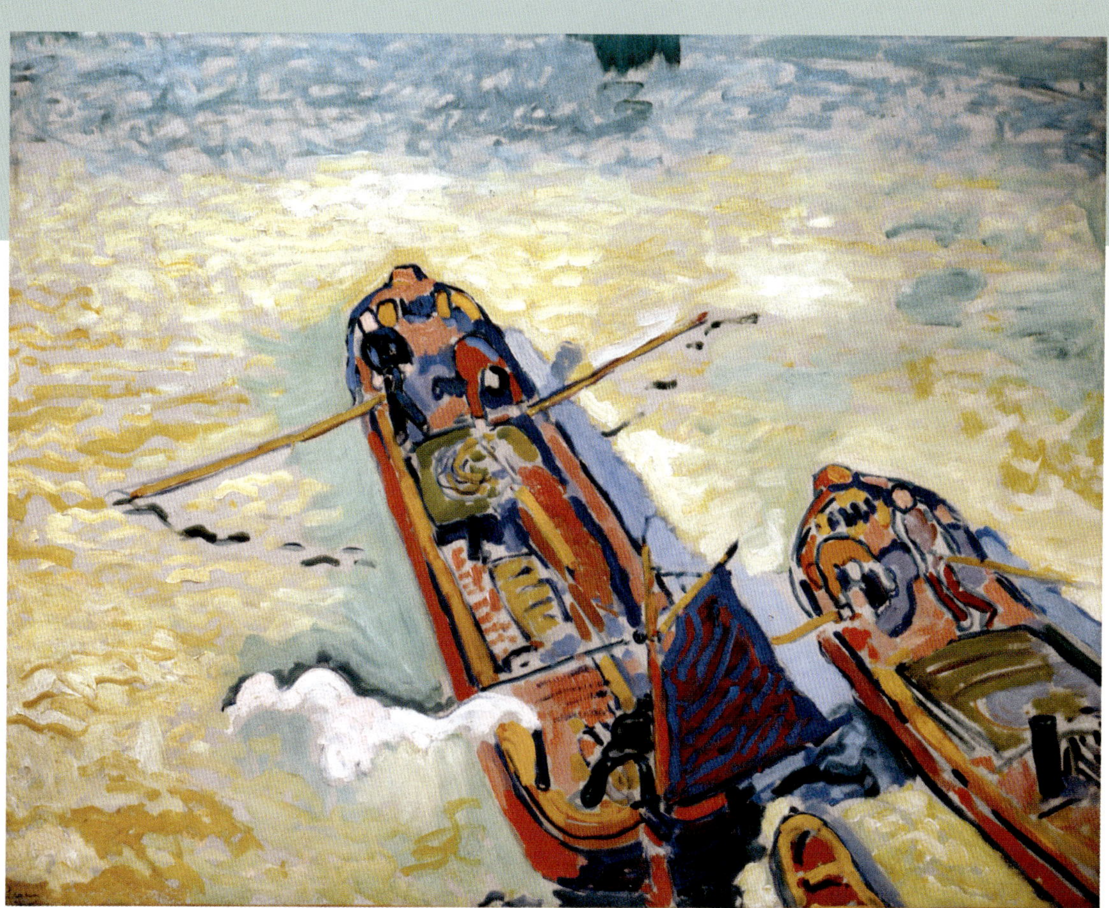

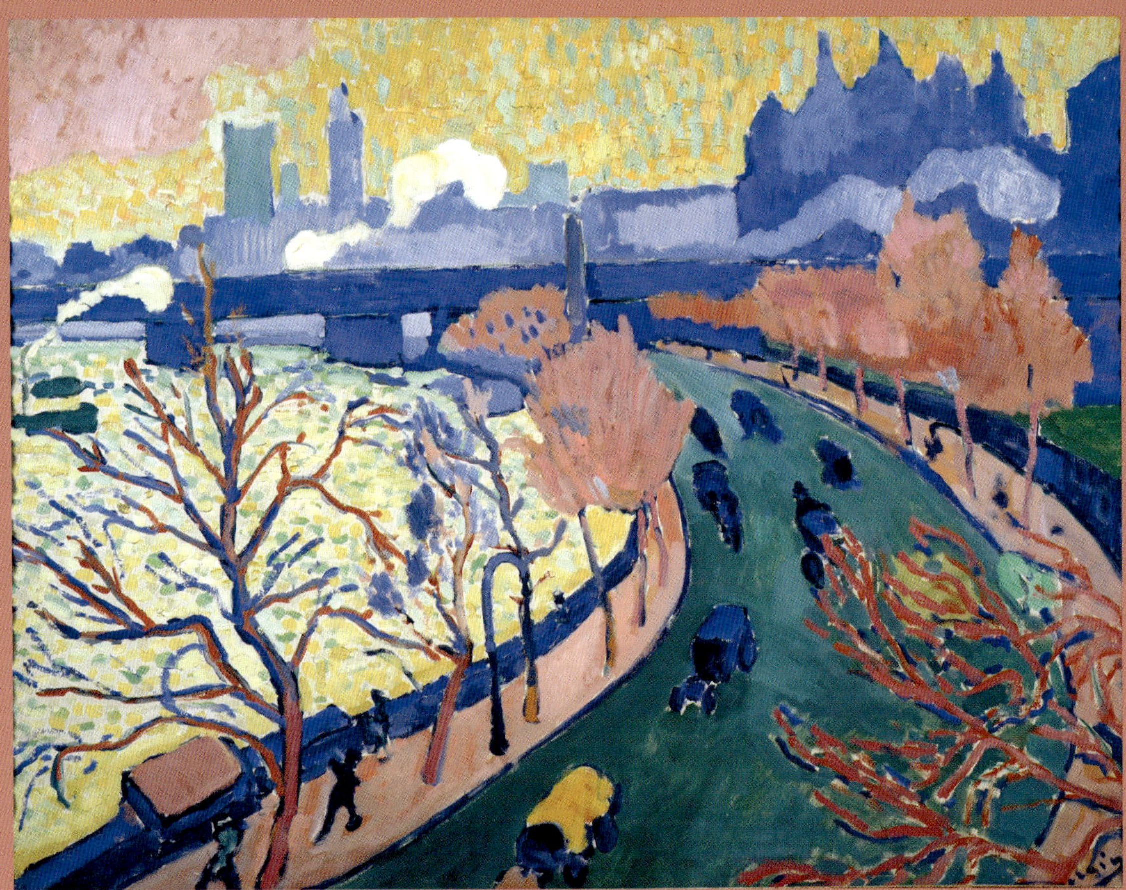

André Derain
(Chatou 1880 - Garches 1954)

Charing Cross Bridge
Brücke von Charing Cross
El puente de Charing Cross

●●

1906
81 x 100 cm / 31.9 x 39.3 in.
Musée d'Orsay, Paris

oil on canvas / Öl auf Leinwand
olieverf op doek / óleo sobre lienzo

André Derain
(Chatou 1880 - Garches 1954)

Mountain road
Bergstraße
Bergweg
Camino de montaña

●

1907
81 x 100 cm / 31.9 x 39.3 in.
The State Hermitage Museum,
St. Petersburg

oil on canvas / Öl auf Leinwand
olieverf op doek / óleo sobre lienzo

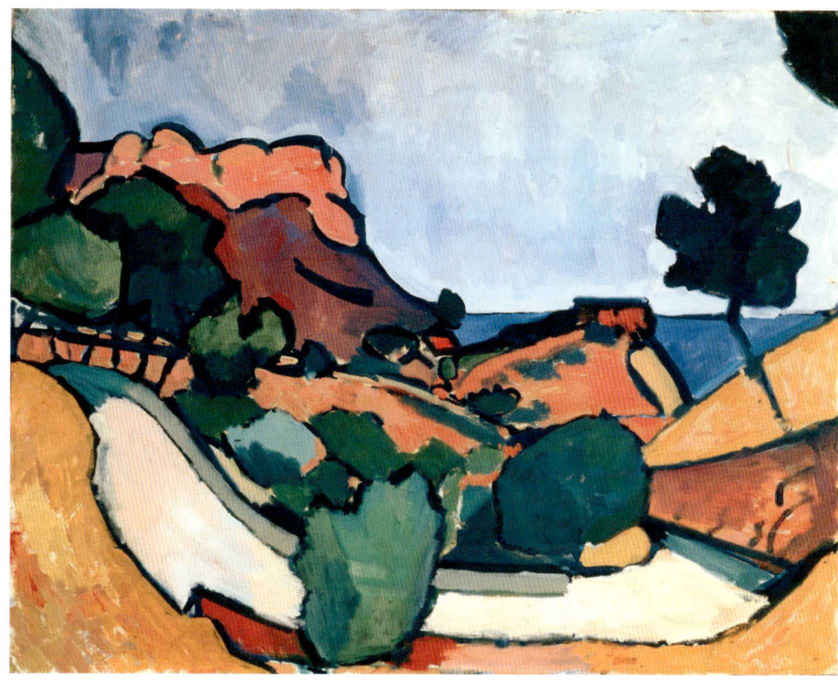

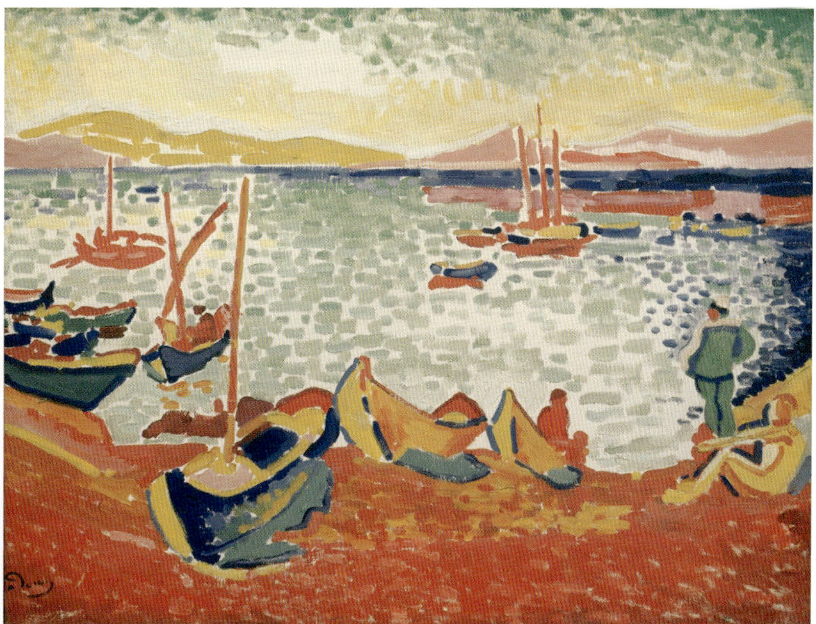

André Derain
(Chatou 1880 - Garches 1954)

Ships in port
Schiffe im Hafen
Boten in de haven
Barcos en el puerto

●

1905
Private collection / Private Sammlung
Privécollectie / Colección privada

oil on canvas / Öl auf Leinwand
olieverf op doek / óleo sobre lienzo

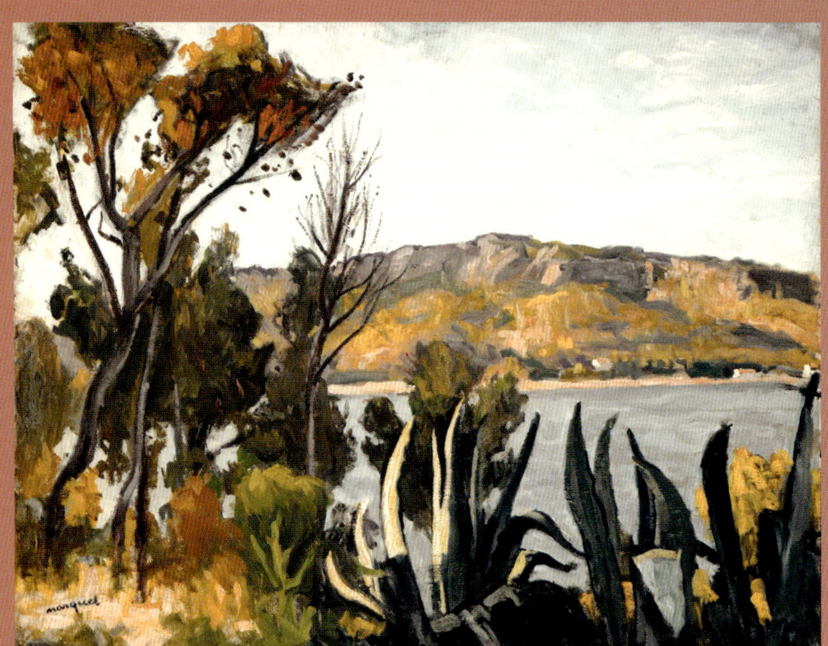

Albert Marquet
(Bordeaux 1875 - Paris 1947)
View of Agay
Ansicht von Agay
Zicht op Agay
Vista de Agay
●
ca. 1905
64,5 x 80,7 cm / 25.4 x 31.7 in.
Centre Georges Pompidou, Musée
National d'Art Moderne, Paris

oil on canvas / Öl auf Leinwand
olieverf op doek / óleo sobre lienzo

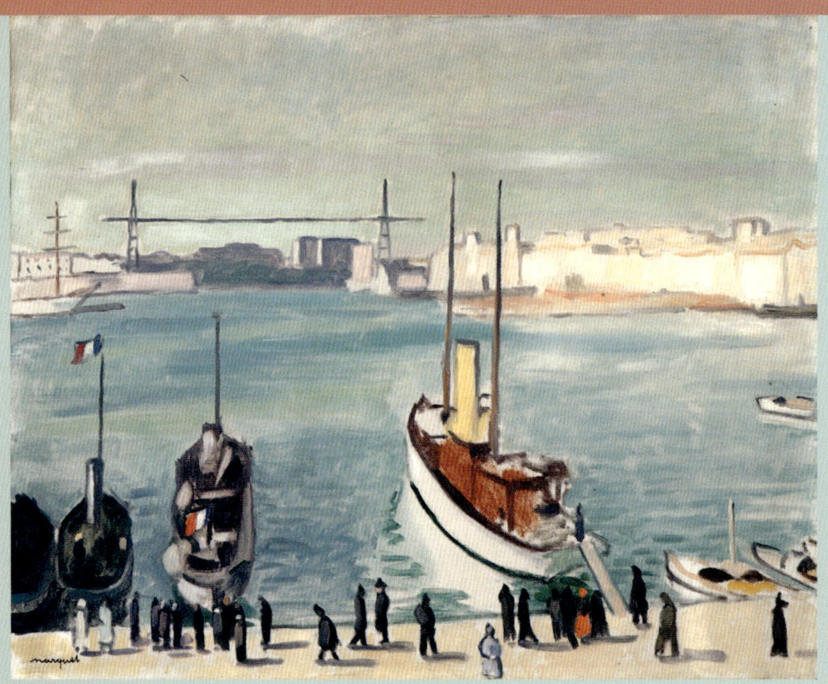

Albert Marquet
(Bordeaux 1875 - Paris 1947)
The Port of Marseilles
Der Hafen von Marseille
De haven van Marseille
El puerto de Marsella
●●
1916
60 x 73 cm / 23.6 x 28.7 in.
Musée Cantini, Marseille

oil on canvas / Öl auf Leinwand
olieverf op doek / óleo sobre lienzo

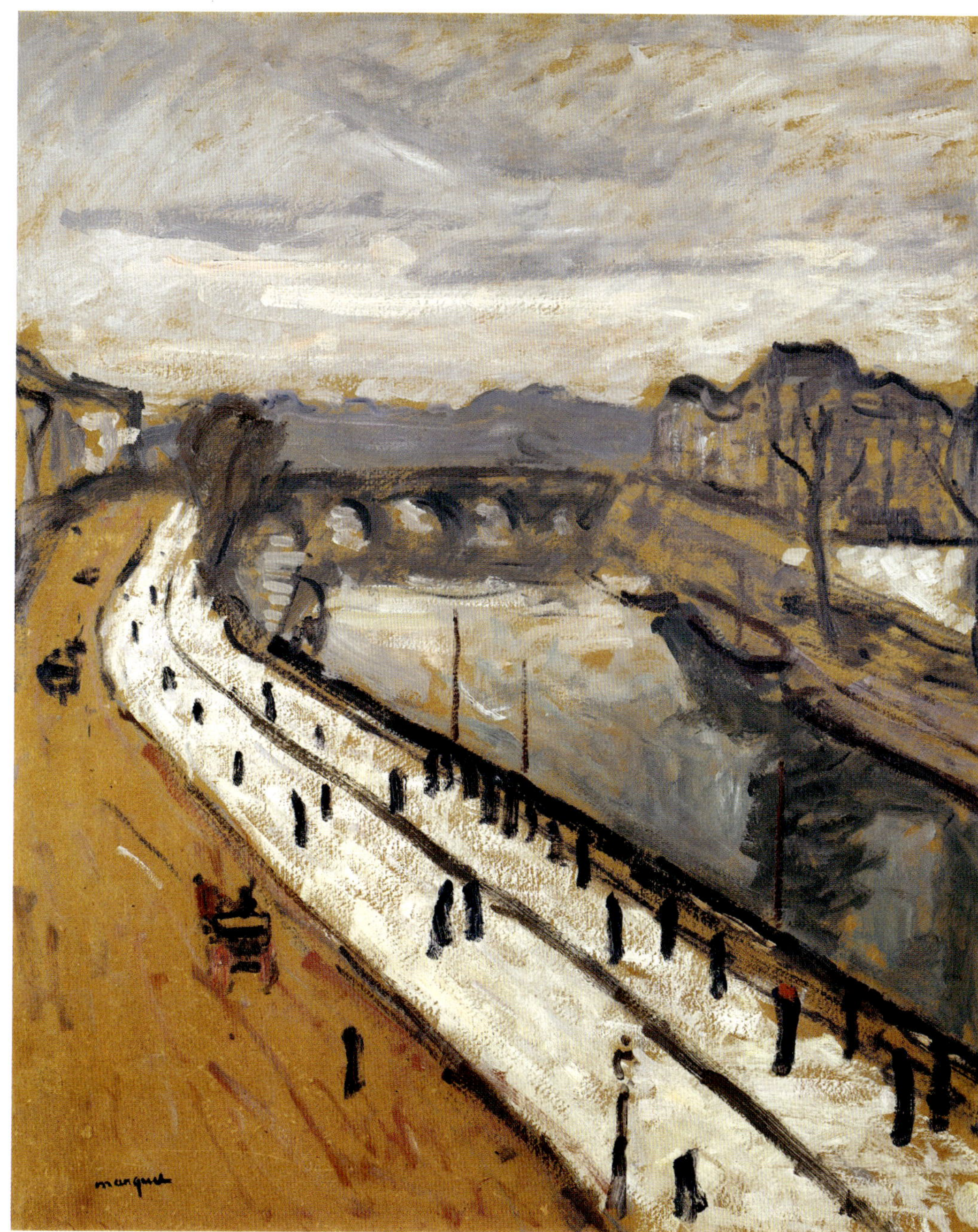

Albert Marquet
(Bordeaux 1875 -
Paris 1947)

**Le Quai des
Grands Augustins
in Paris in 1905
Der Kai der
Grands Augustins
in Paris 1905
Le quai des Grands
Augustins in Parijs
in 1905
El muelle de
Grands Augustins
en París en 1905**

•

1905
80 x 65 cm
31.5 x 25.6 in.
Centre Georges
Pompidou, Musée
National d'Art Moderne,
Paris

oil on paperboard
Öl auf Karton
olieverf op karton
óleo sobre cartón

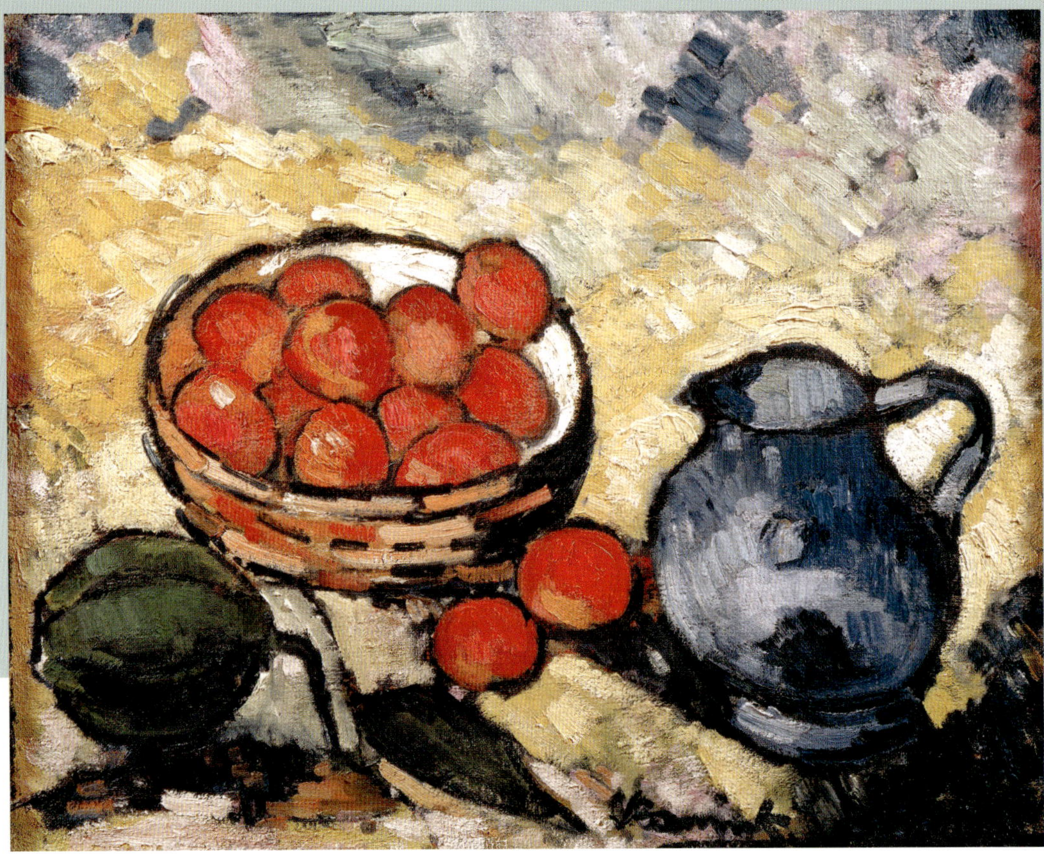

Maurice de Vlaminck
(Paris 1876 - Rueil-la-Gadelière 1958)

Still life
Stillleben
Stilleven
Bodegón

●

ca. 1907
60 x 73 cm / 23.6 x 28.7 in.
Musée de l'Annonciade, Saint-Tropez

oil on canvas / Öl auf Leinwand
olieverf op doek / óleo sobre lienzo

Self-educated artist strongly influenced by Van Gogh and by the rejection of artistic convention, painting by instinct, Vlaminck establishes himself quickly among the Fauves.

Als Autodidakt, der stark von Van Gogh und von der Ablehnung künstlerischer Konventionen geprägt war, konnte Vlaminck sich mit seiner instinktiven Malweise rasch bei den Fauves durchsetzen.

Vlaminck was een autodidact en werd sterk beïnvloed door Van Gogh, hij weigerde alle artistieke conventies en schilderde instinctief. Hij zou zich snel opwerken tussen de fauves.

Autodidacta fuertemente influenciado por Van Gogh y por el rechazo a las convenciones artísticas, pintando instintivamente, Vlaminck se impondrá rápidamente entre los fauves.

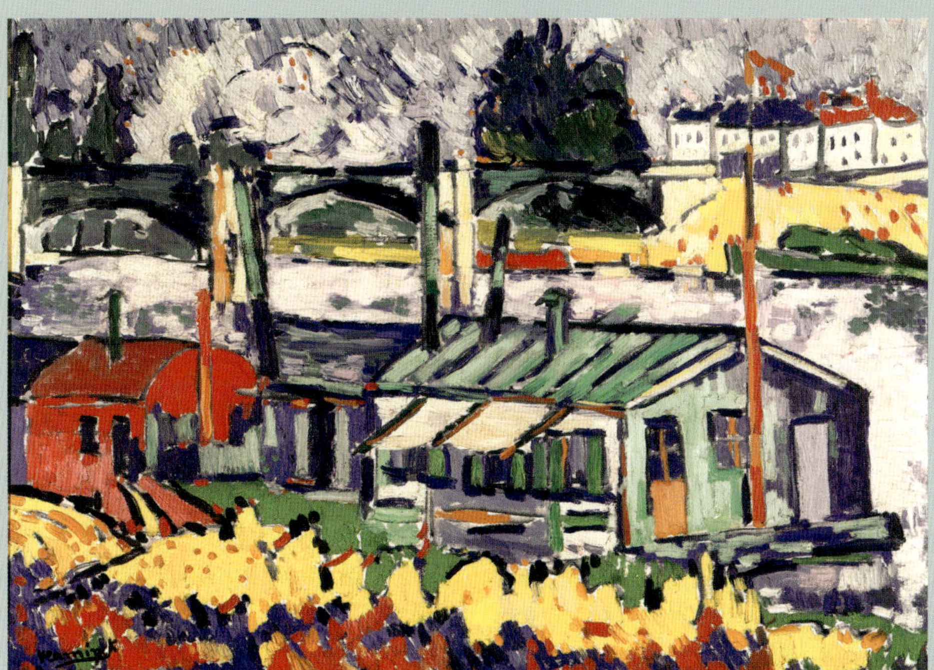

Maurice de Vlaminck
(Paris 1876 - Rueil-la-Gadelière 1958)

Bridge of Chatou
Die Brücke von Chatou
Brug van Chatou
Puente de Chatou

1906
54 x 73 cm / 21.2 x 28.7 in.
Musée de l'Annonciade, Saint-Tropez

oil on canvas / Öl auf Leinwand
olieverf op doek / óleo sobre lienzo

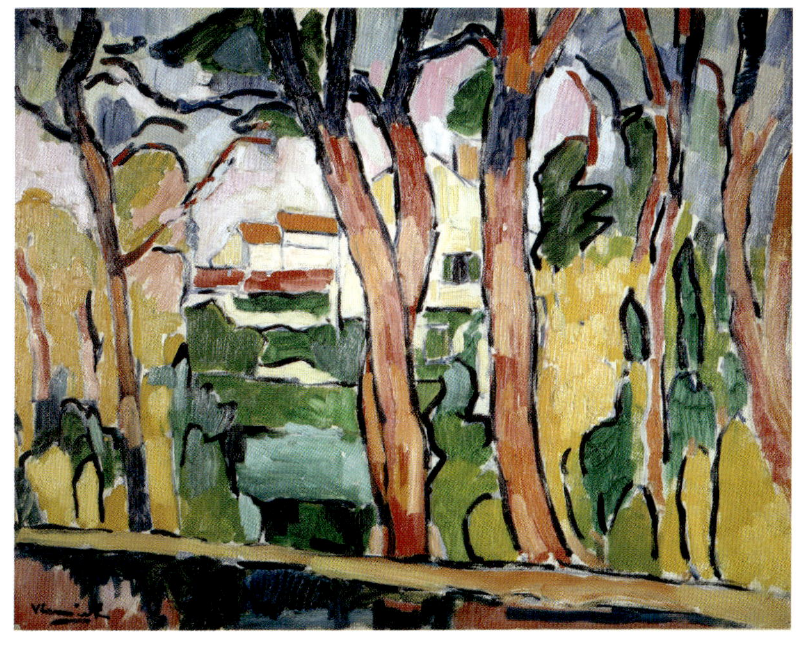

Maurice de Vlaminck
(Paris 1876 - Rueil-la-Gadelière 1958)

The Red Trees
Die roten Bäume
De rode bomen
Los árboles rojos

1906
65 x 81 cm / 25.6 x 31.9 in.
Centre Georges Pompidou, Musée
National d'Art Moderne, Paris

oil on canvas / Öl auf Leinwand
olieverf op doek / óleo sobre lienzo

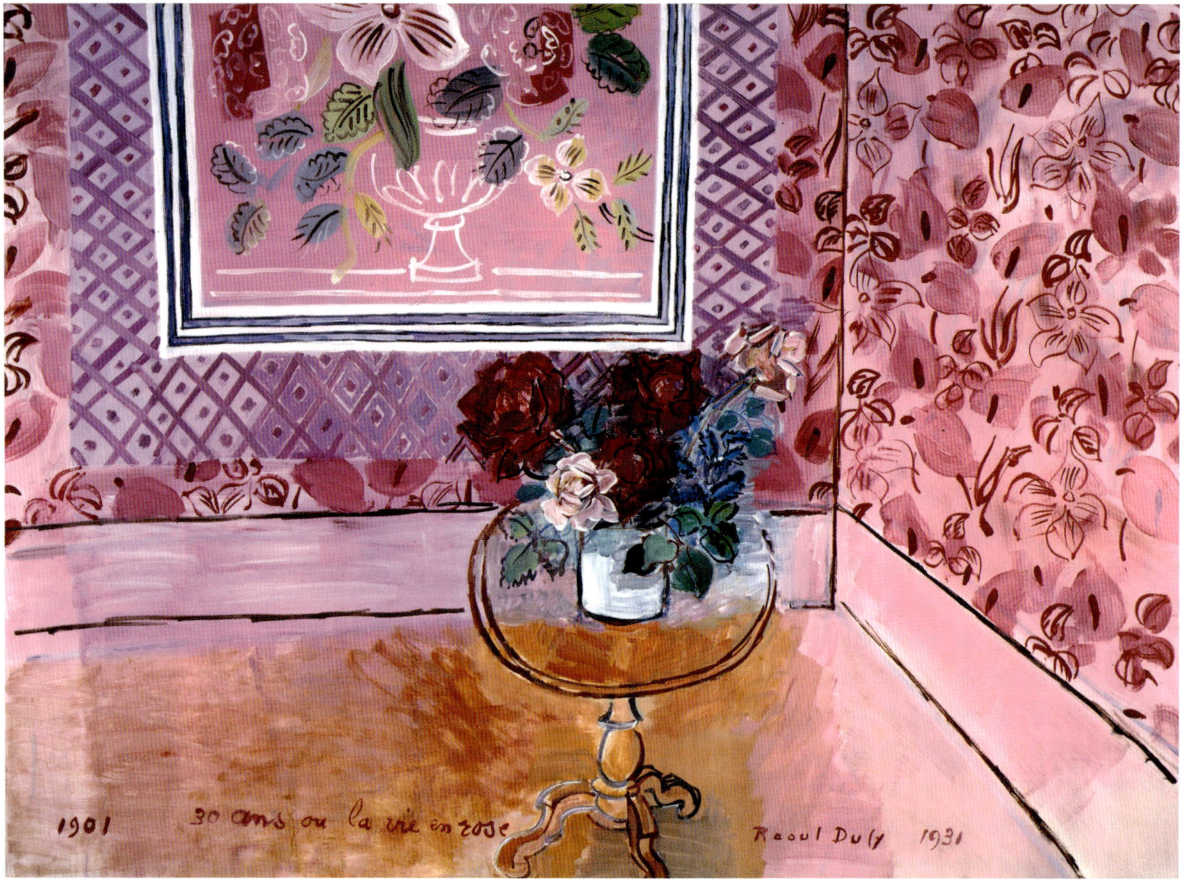

78

Raoul Dufy
(Le Havre 1877 - Forcalquier 1953)

Trente ans ou la vie en rose

●●

1931
98 x 128 cm / 38.6 x 59.4 in.
Musée d'Art Moderne de la Ville de Paris, Paris

oil on canvas / Öl auf Leinwand
olieverf op doek / óleo sobre lienzo

Everything in *La vie en rose* is lightness, transparency and translates into a play of balance between decorative motifs.

Alles in *La vie en rose* ist Leichtigkeit und Transparenz und das äußert sich in einem verspielten Gegensatz aus dekorativen Motiven.

Alles in *La vie en rose* is licht en transparant, wat vertaald wordt in een samenspel van decoratieve motieven.

Todo en *La vie en rose* es liviandad y transparencia que se traduce en un juego de correspondencias entre motivos decorativos.

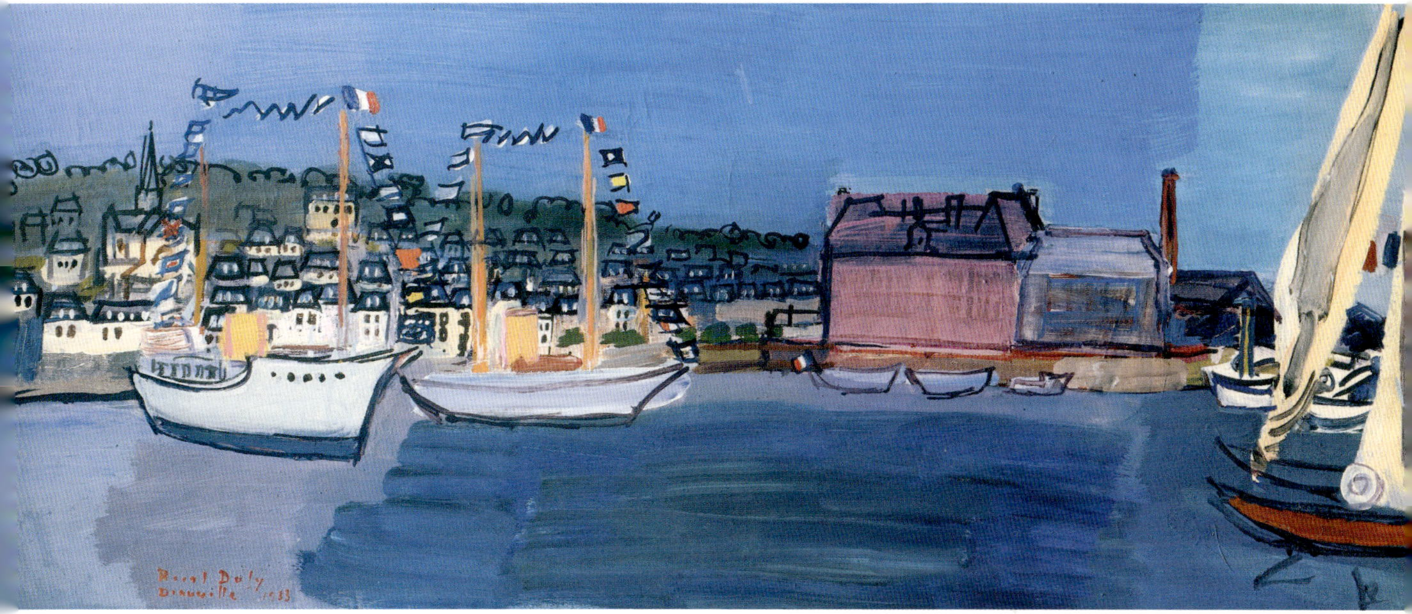

Raoul Dufy
(Le Havre 1877 - Forcalquier 1953)

14 July in Deauville
Der 14. Juli in Deauville
14 juli in Deauville
El 14 de julio en Deauville

1933
Pushkin State Museum of Fine Arts,
Moscow

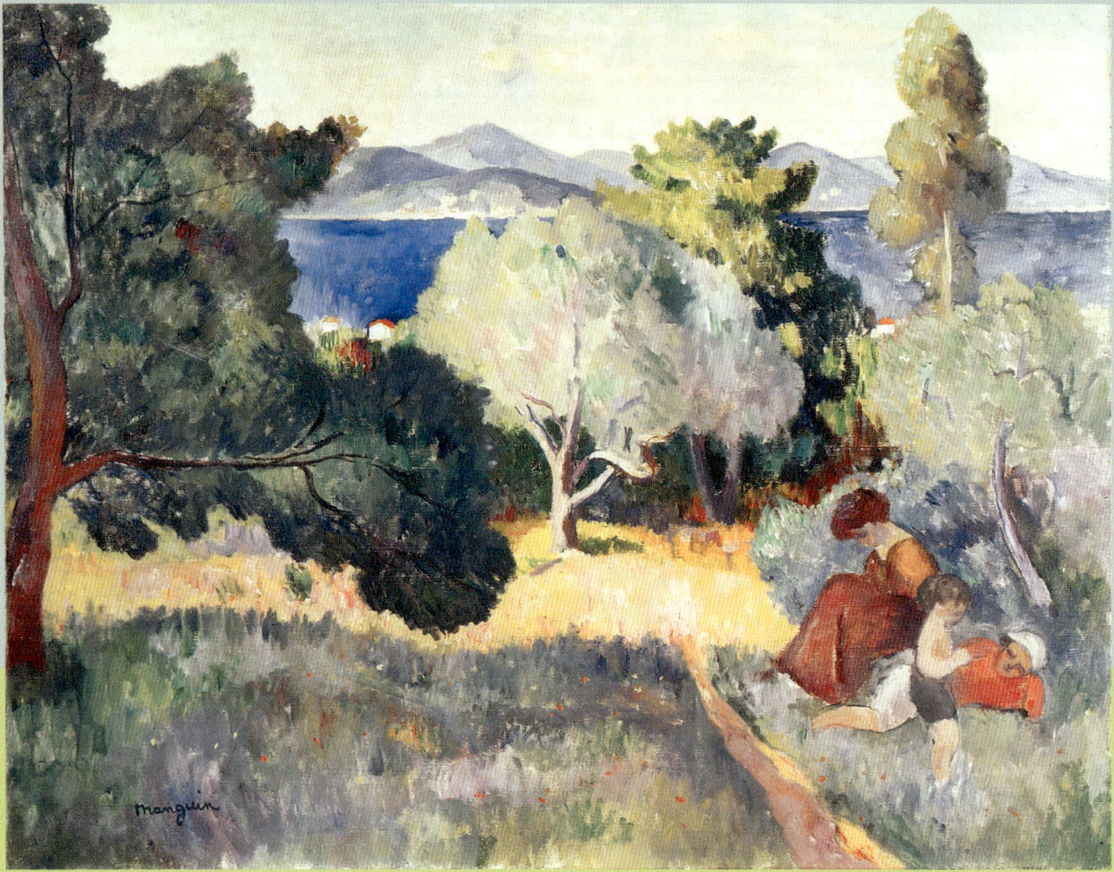

Henri Charles Manguin
(Paris 1874 - Saint-Tropez 1949)

Path at Saint-Tropez
Pfad in Saint-Tropez
Pad in Saint-Tropez
Sendero en Saint-Tropez

●

1905
50,5 x 60,5 cm / 19.9 x 23.8 in.
The State Hermitage Museum, St. Petersburg

oil on canvas / Öl auf Leinwand
olieverf op doek / óleo sobre lienzo

▶ Henri Charles Manguin
(Paris 1874 - Saint-Tropez 1949)

14 July in Saint-Tropez
Der 14. Juli in Saint-Tropez
14 juli in Saint-Tropez
El 14 de julio en Saint-Tropez

●

1905
Private collection / Private Sammlung
Privécollectie / Colección privada

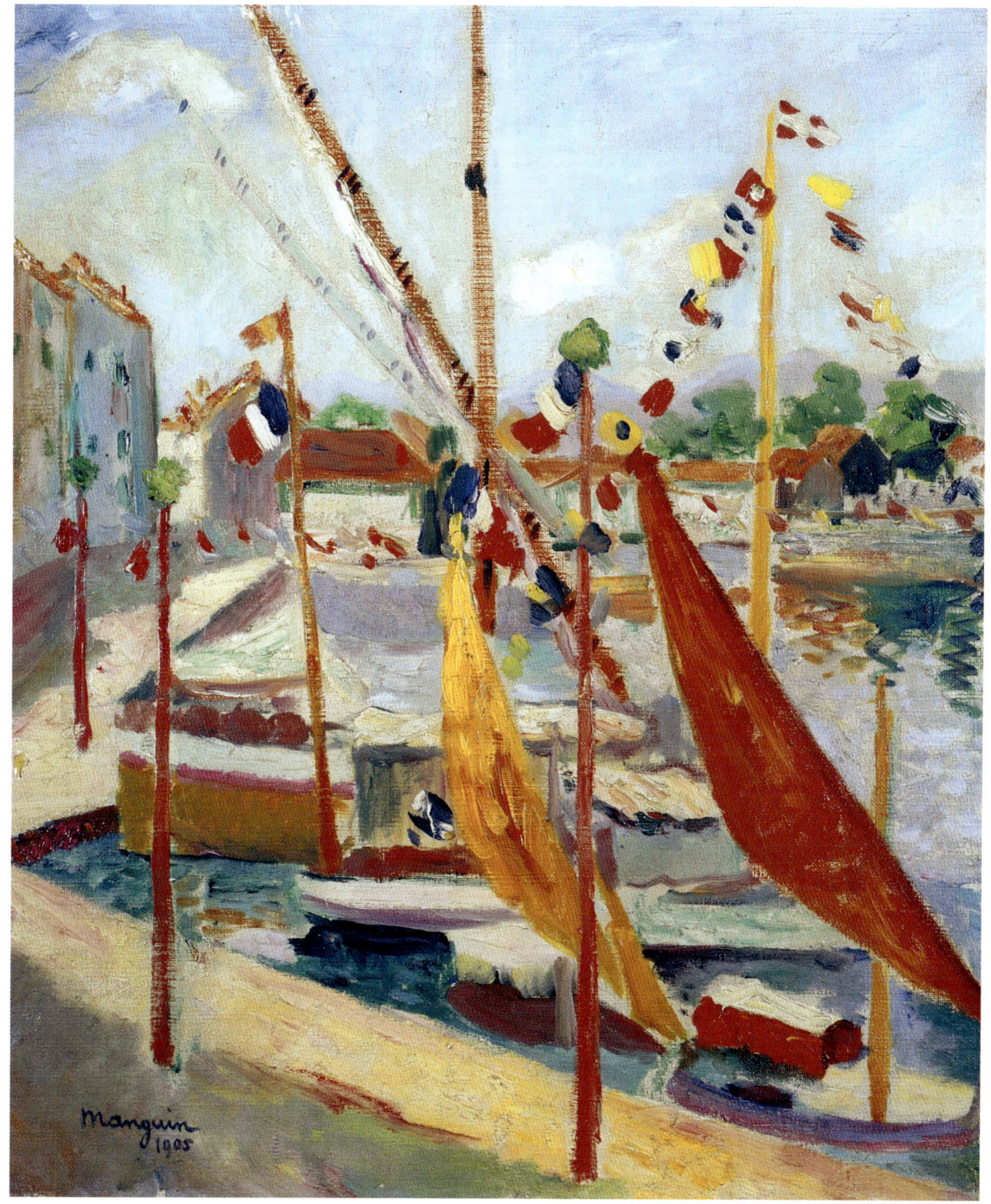

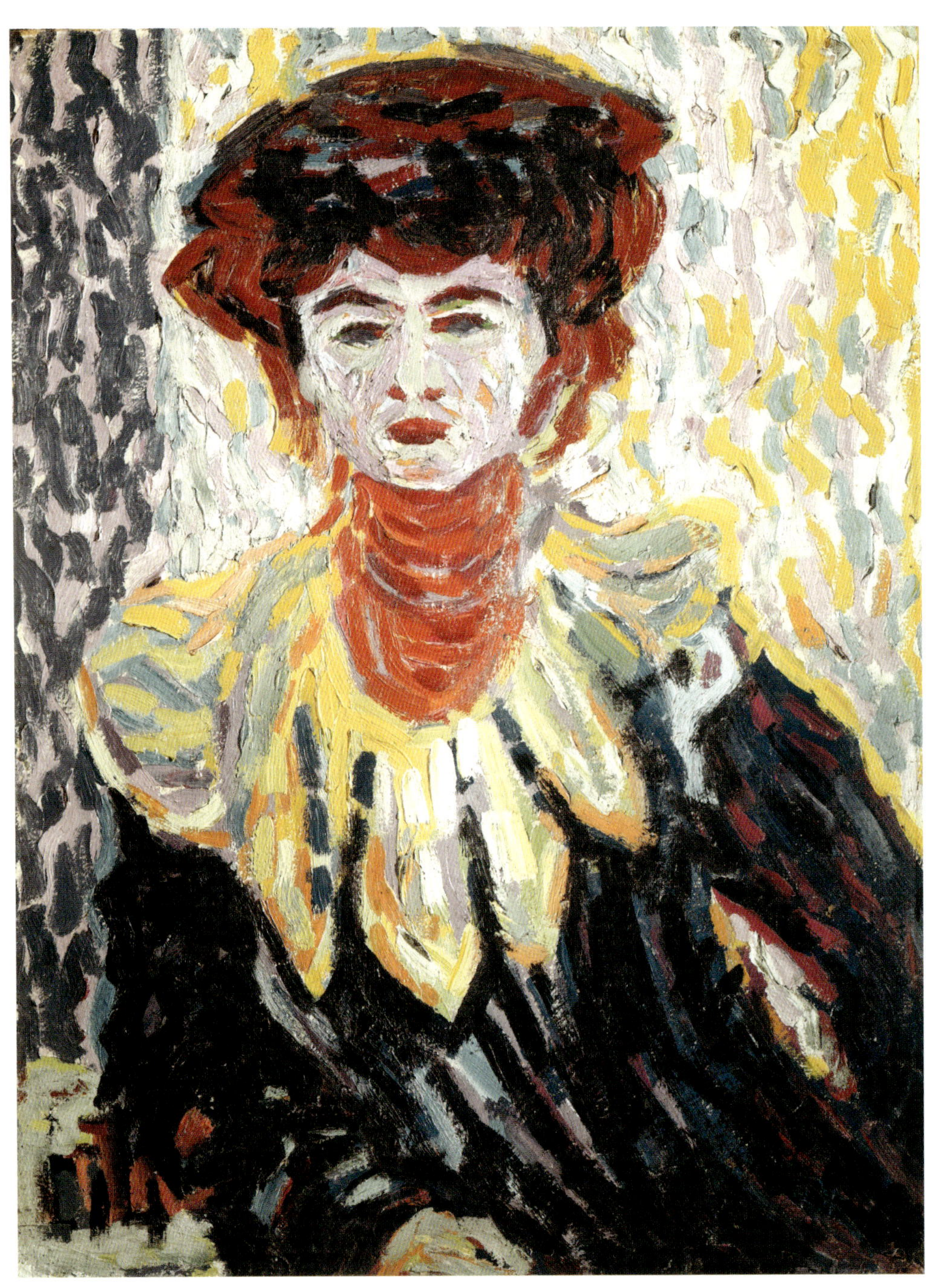

Ernst Ludwig Kirchner
(Aschaffenburg 1880 - Davos 1938

Doris with high ruffled colla
Doris mit der Halskrause
Doris met een hoge
geplooide kraag
Doris con cuello alto

●

1906
70,5 x 51 cm / 27.7 x 20.1 in.
Museo Thyssen-Bornemisza, Madrid

oil on paperboard
Öl auf Karton
olieverf op karton
óleo sobre cartón

Ernst Ludwig Kirchner
(Aschaffenburg 1880 -
Davos 1938)

Franzi in a carved chair
Fränzi vor einem
geschnitztem Stuhl
Franzi in een uitgehouwen
stoel
Fränzi ante una silla tallada

●●●

1908-1909
71 x 49,5 cm / 27.9 x 19.5 in.
Museo Thyssen-Bornemisza,
Madrid

oil on canvas / Öl auf Leinwand
olieverf op doek / óleo sobre lienzo

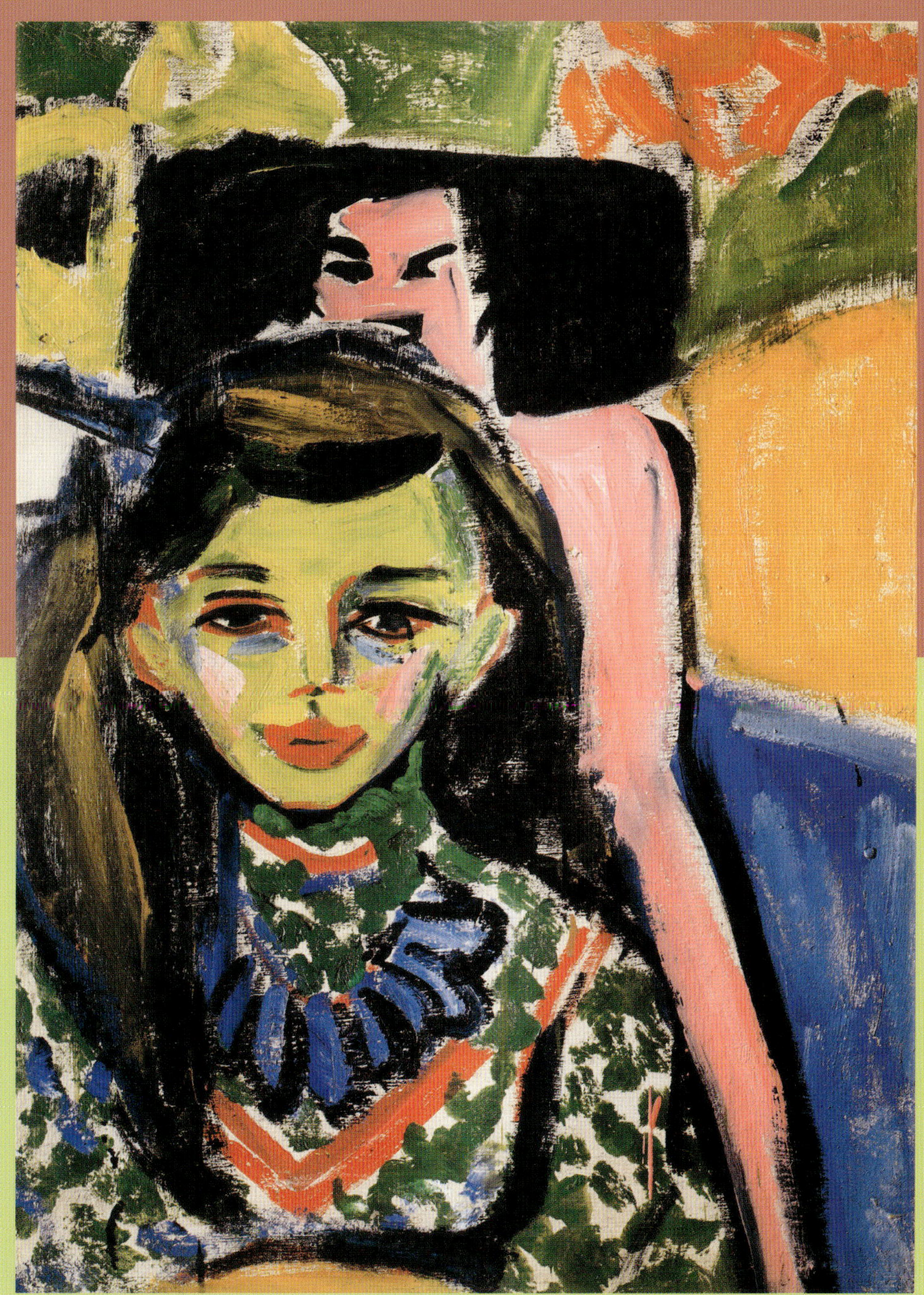

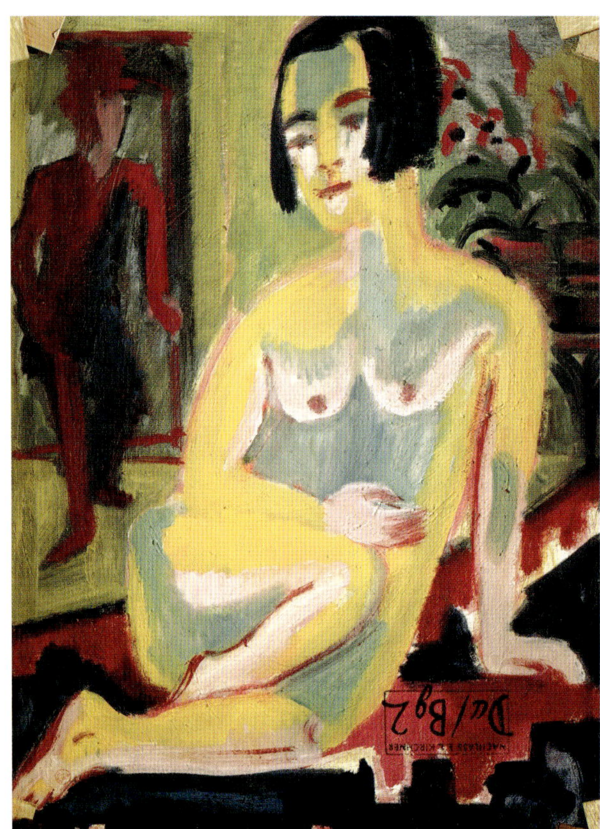

▲ Ernst Ludwig Kirchner
(Aschaffenburg 1880 - Davos 1938)
**Study of nude woman seated
Studie eines sitzenden weiblichen Akts
Studie van een zittend vrouwelijk naakt
Desnudo femenino sentado. Estudio (reverso)**
●

1921-1923
Museo Thyssen-Bornemisza, Madrid

oil on canvas / Öl auf Leinwand
olieverf op doek / óleo sobre lienzo

▼ Ernst Ludwig Kirchner
(Aschaffenburg 1880 - Davos 1938)
**Portrait of Erna Schilling
(Sick Woman or Lady with Hat)
Porträt von Erna Schilling
(Kranke Frau oder Dame mit Hut),
Portret van Erna Schilling
(Zieke vrouw of Dame met hoed)
Retrato de Erna Schilling
(Mujer enferma o Dama con sombrero)**
●●

1913
71,5 x 60,5 cm / 8.1 x 23.8 in.
Nationalgalerie, Staatliche Museen, Berlin

oil on canvas / Öl auf Leinwand olieverf op doek / óleo sobre lienzo

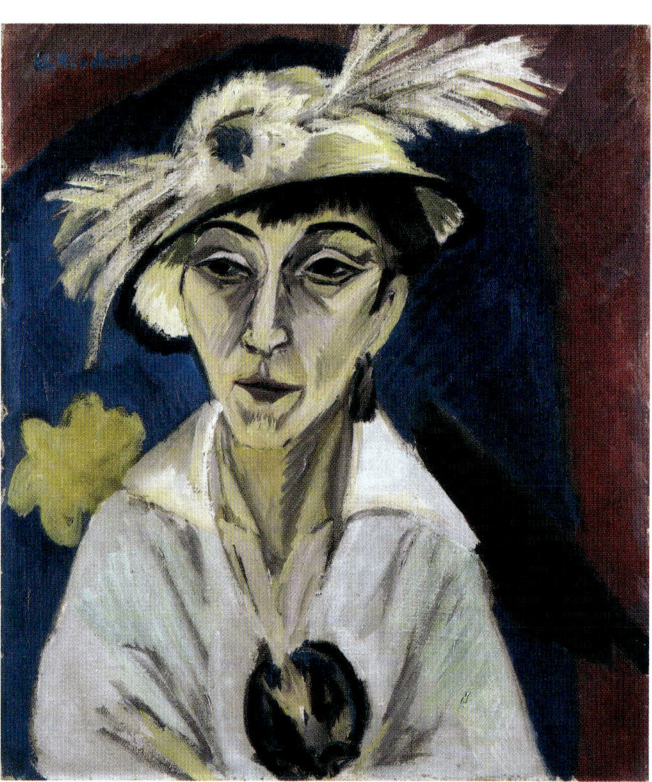

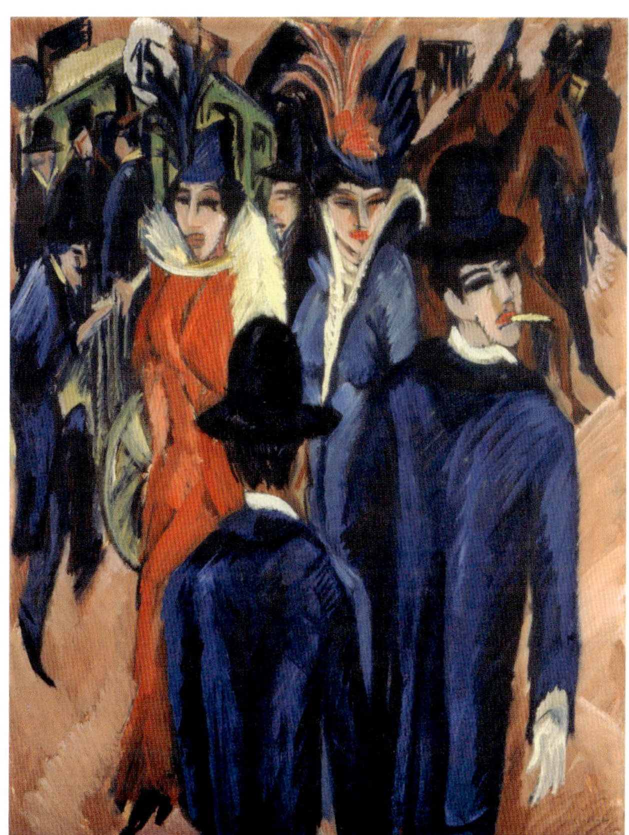

Ernst Ludwig Kirchner
(Aschaffenburg 1880 - Davos 1938)

**Berlin Street Scene
Berliner Straßenszene
Berlijnse straatscène
Escena callejera en Berlín**

●●

1913-1914
121 x 95 cm / 47.6 x 37.4 in.
Neue Galerie, New York

oil on canvas / Öl auf Leinwand
olieverf op doek / óleo sobre lienzo

Ernst Ludwig Kirchner
(Aschaffenburg 1880 - Davos 1938)
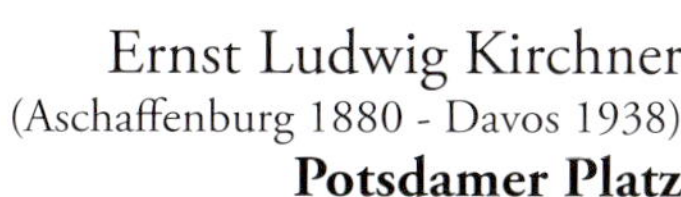

Potsdamer Platz

●

1914
200 x 150 cm / 78.8 x 59 in.
Nationalgalerie, Staatliche Museen,
Berlin

oil on canvas / Öl auf Leinwand
olieverf op doek / óleo sobre lienzo

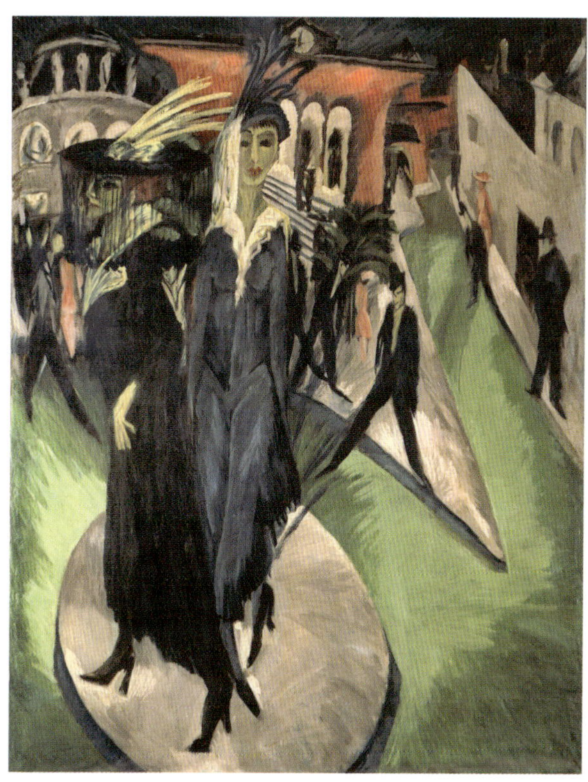

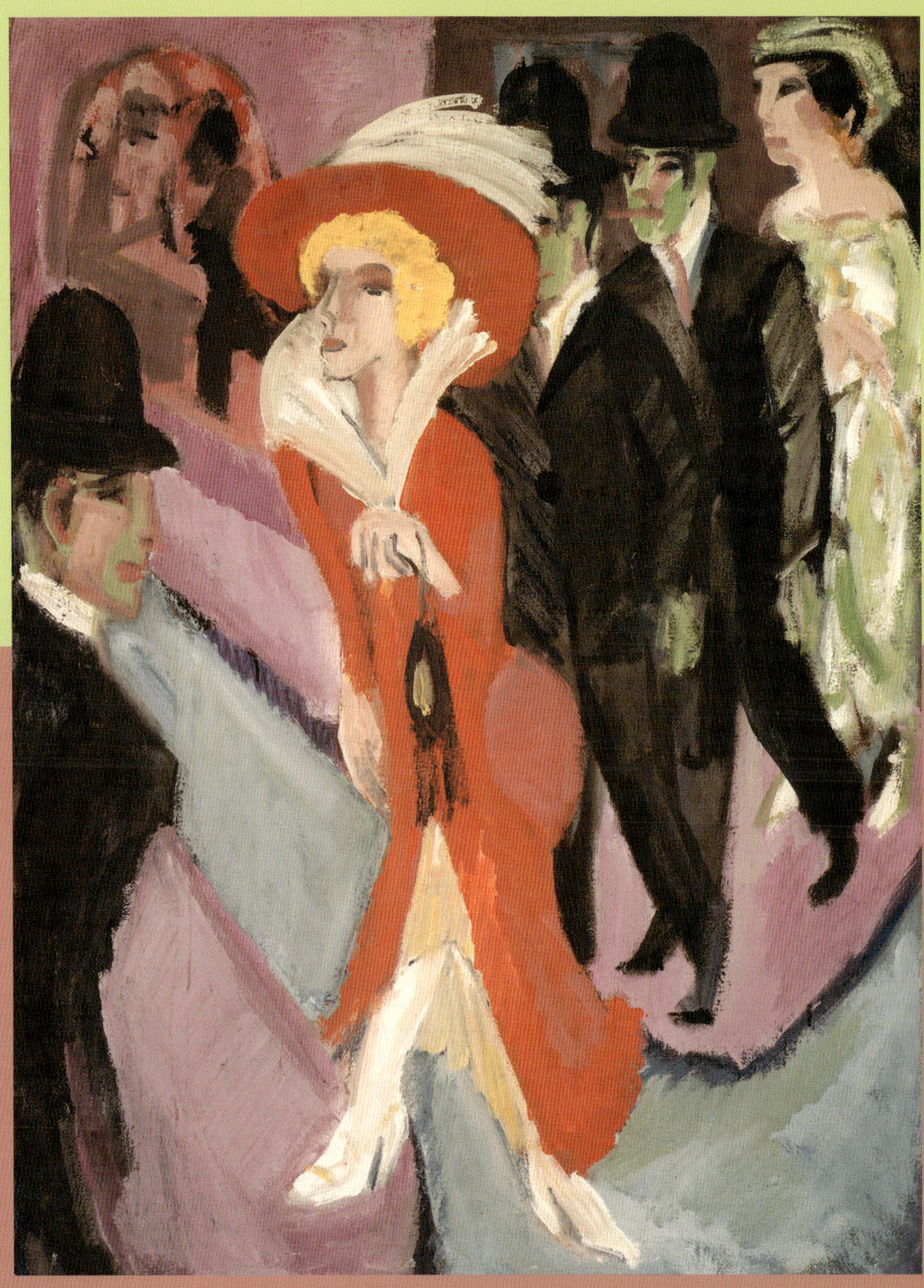

Ernst Ludwig Kirchner
(Aschaffenburg 1880 -
Davos 1938)

**Berlin Street Scene with
Tart in Red
Berliner Straßenszene mit
roter Kokotte
Berlijnse straatscène met
prostituee in het rood
Escena callejera berlinesa**

●●

1914-1925
125 x 90,5 cm / 49.2 x 35.6 in.
Museo Thyssen-Bornemisza,
Madrid

oil on canvas
Öl auf Leinwand
olieverf op doek
óleo sobre lienzo

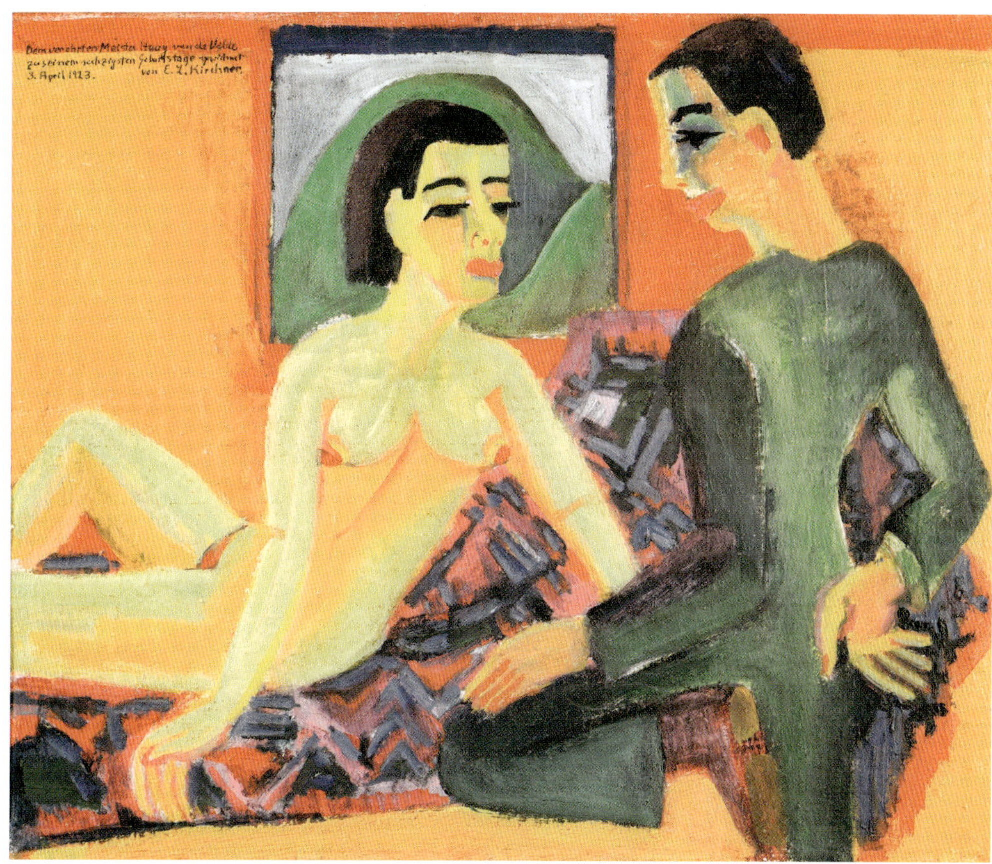

Ernst Ludwig Kirchner
(Aschaffenburg 1880 - Davos 1938)

The couple
Das Paar
Het stel
La pareja

●●●

1923
59 x 69 cm / 23.2 x 27.1 in.
Centre Georges Pompidou, Musée
National d'Art Moderne, Paris

oil on canvas / Öl auf Leinwand
olieverf op doek / óleo sobre lienzo

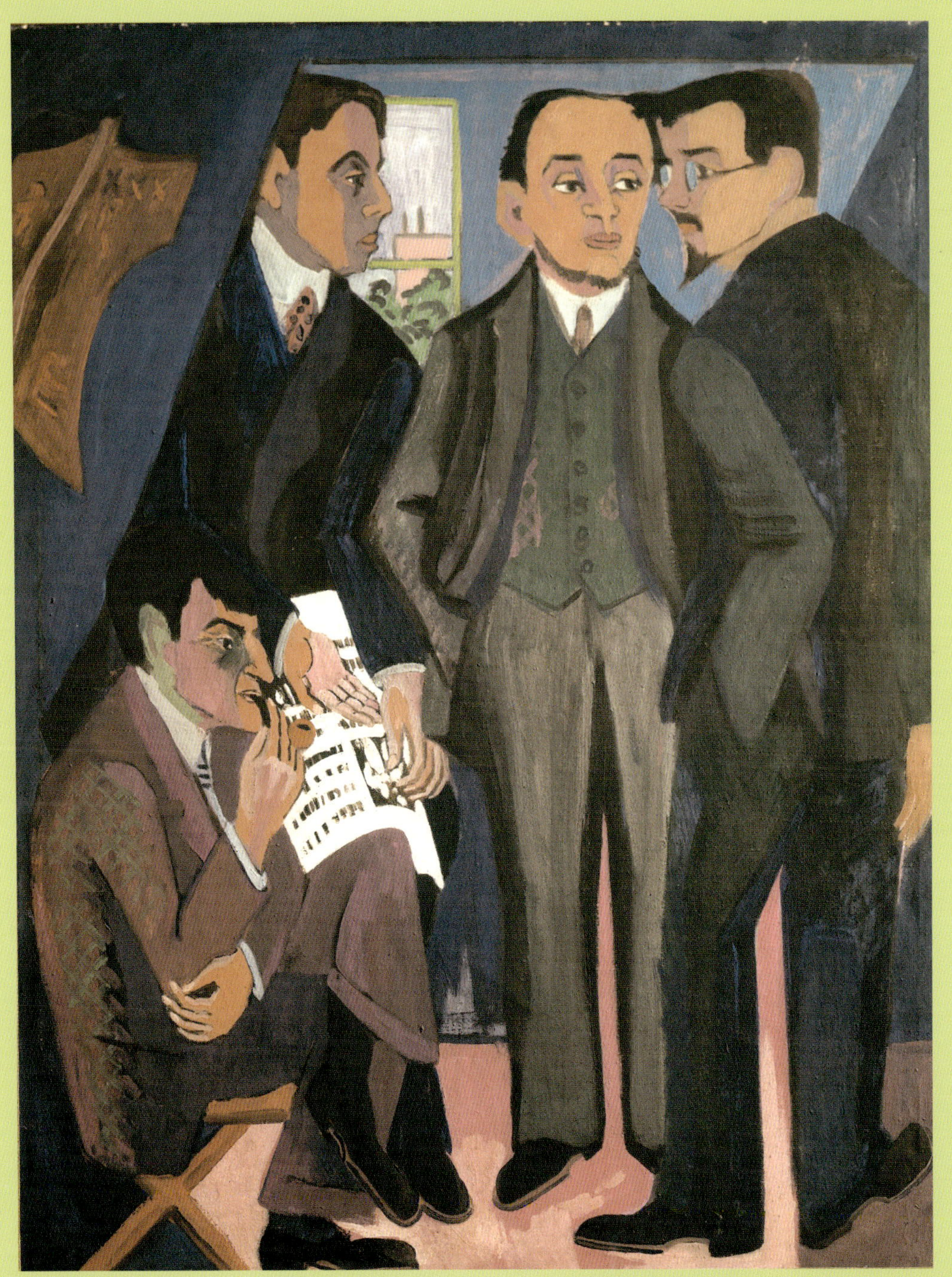

Ernst Ludwig Kirchner

(Aschaffenburg 1880 -
Davos 1938)

**Painters of the Bruecke
Group
Maler der Gruppe
Brücke
Schilders van de groep
'die Brücke'
Pintores del grupo
Bruecke**

●

1925
125 x 167 cm / 49.2 x 65.8 in.
Wallraf-Richartz Museum, Köln

oil on canvas
Öl auf Leinwand
olieverf op doek
óleo sobre lienzo

**Kirchner founded in 1905
in Dresden the Expressionist
Group, Die Brücke
(The Bridge) with Heckel
and Schmidt Rotluff.**

**Gemeinsam mit Heckel und
Schmidt-Rotluff gründete
Kirchner 1905 in Dresden
die expressionistische Gruppe
Die Brücke.**

**Kirchner stichtte in 1905
in Dresden samen met Heckel
en Schmidt Rotluff
de expressionistische groep
Die Brücke.**

**Kirchner fundó en 1905 en
Dresde el grupo Expresionista
Die Brücke (El Puente) con
Heckel y Schmidt Rotluff.**

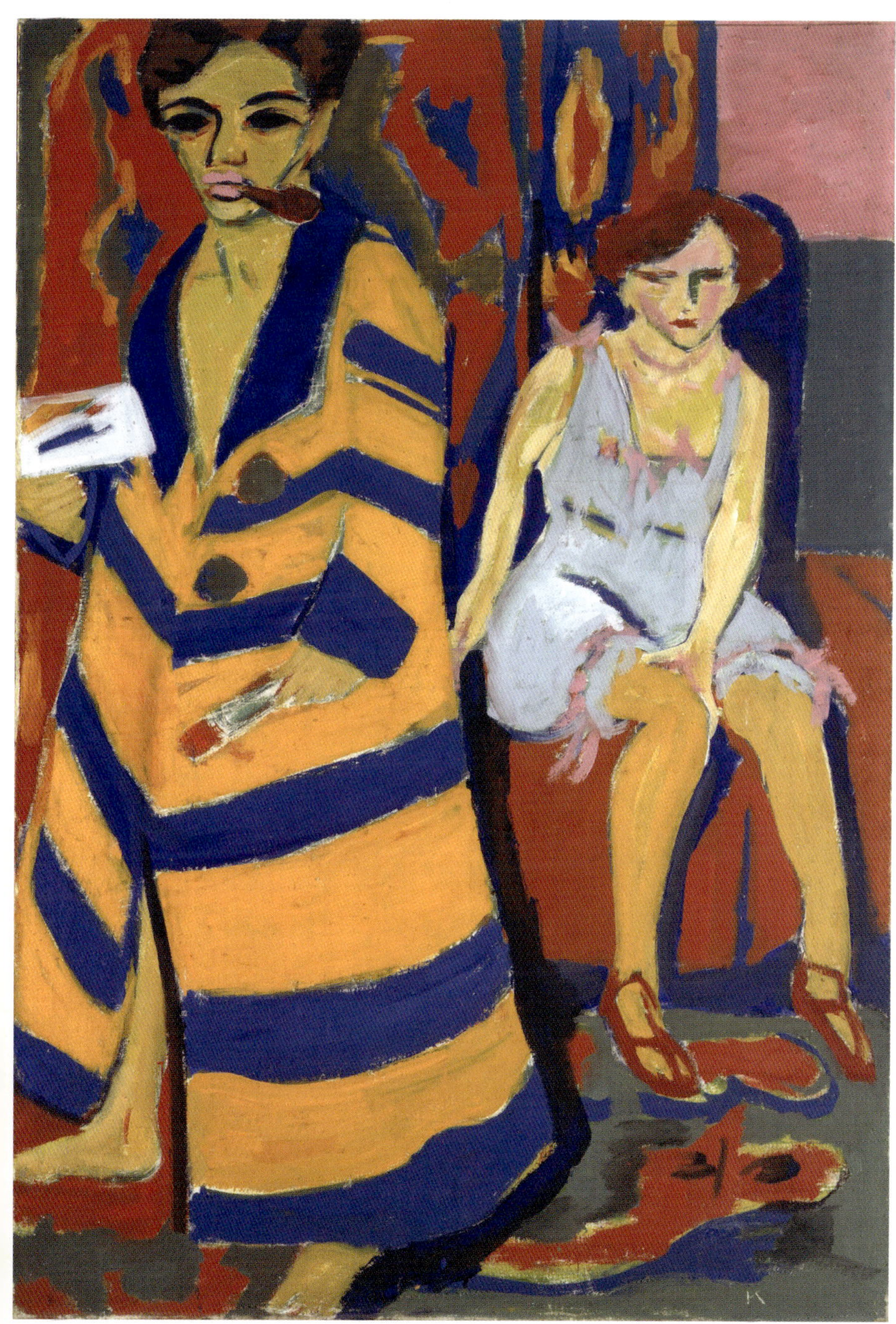

Ernst Ludwig Kirchner
(Aschaffenburg 1880 -
Davos 1938)

**Self-Portrait with Model
Selbstbildnis mit Modell
Zelfportret met model
Autorretrato con modelo**

● ●

1910
150,4 x 100 cm / 59.2 x 39.4 in.
Hamburger Kunsthalle, Hamburg

oil on canvas
Öl auf Leinwand
olieverf op doek
óleo sobre lienzo

A simplified and fast drawing,
flat strokes of bright colors and
a feeling of unease characterize
Kirchner's works.

Ein vereinfachter und schneller
Entwurf, flaches Auftragen lebhafter
Farben und ein Gefühl der Unruhe
charakterisieren die Werke von
Kirchner.

Een eenvoudige en snelle tekening,
platte streken met levendige kleuren
en een onrustgevoel kenmerken de
werken van Kirchner.

Un dibujo simplificado y rápido,
pinceladas planas de colores vivaces
y un cierto sentimiento de inquietud
caracterizan las obras de Kirchner.

89

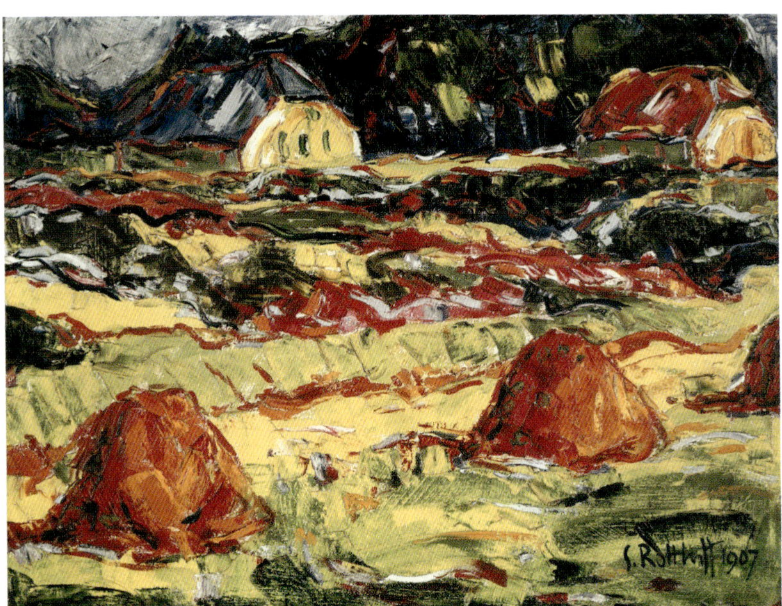

Karl Schmidt-Rottluff
(Rottluff 1884 - Berlin 1976)

Autumn Landscape in Oldenburg
Herbstlandschaft in Oldenburg
Herfstlandschap van Oldenburg
Paisaje de otoño en Oldenburg

●●

1907
76 x 97,5 cm / 29.9 x 38.4 in.
Museo Thyssen-Bornemisza, Madrid

oil on canvas / Öl auf Leinwand
olieverf op doek / óleo sobre lienzo

Karl Schmidt-Rottluff
(Rottluff 1884 - Berlin 1976)

Repose in the Artist's Studio
Atelierpause
De rustpauze in de studio
van de kunstenaar
Descanso de la modelo en el
estudio del artista

●

1910
76 x 84 cm / 29.9 x 33 in.
Hamburger Kunsthalle, Hamburg

oil on canvas / Öl auf Leinwand
olieverf op doek / óleo sobre lienzo

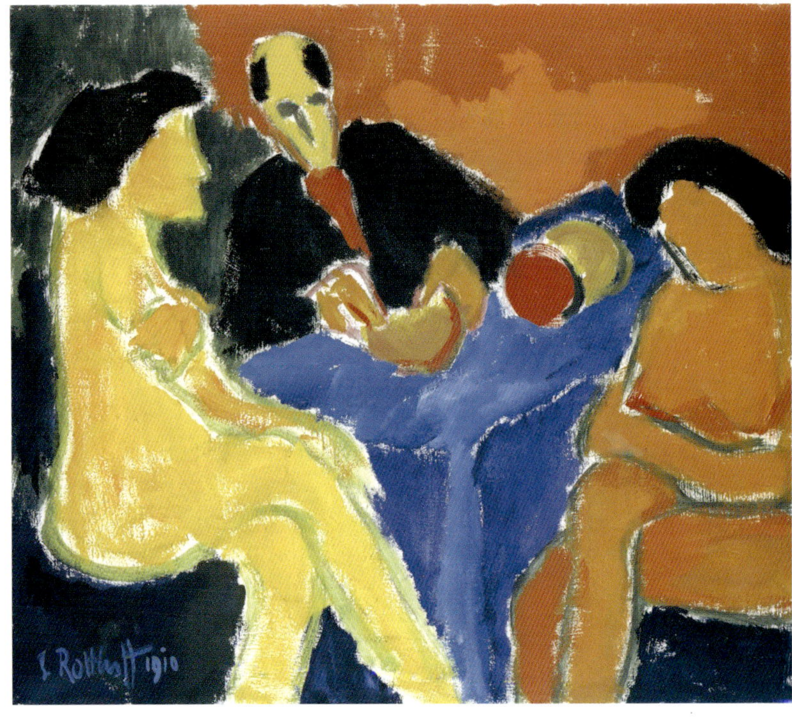

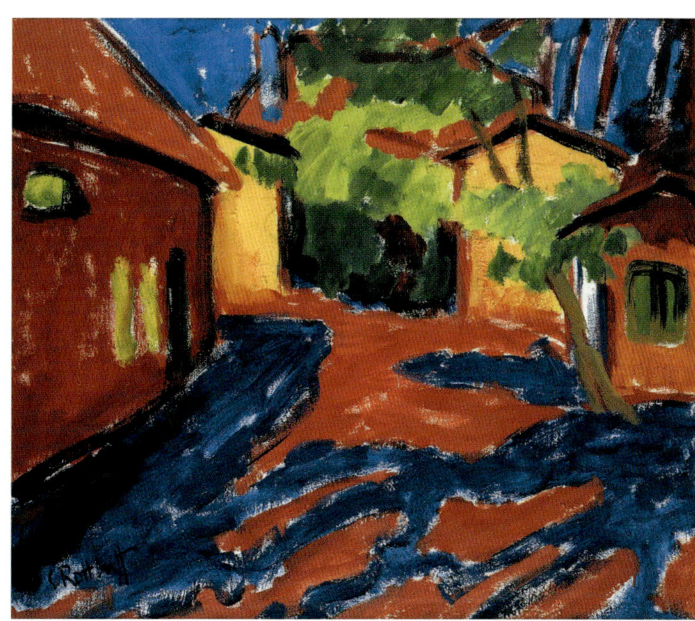

Karl Schmidt-Rottluff
(Rottluff 1884 - Berlin 1976)

The Villa at Dangast. Gramberg homes
Gutshof in Dangast. Grambergsche Häuser
De villa in Dangast. Gramberg huizen
La casa en Dangast. Casas Gramberg

●

1910
86 x 94 cm / 33.8 x 37 in.
Nationalgalerie, Staatliche Museen, Berlin

oil on canvas / Öl auf Leinwand
olieverf op doek / óleo sobre lienzo

With the force of the pure colors and
the rejection of an illusionist process
in *The Villa at Dangast*, German
Expressionism approaches Fauvism.

Durch die Kraft reiner Farben und
den Verzicht auf eine illusionistische
Malweise nähert sich der deutsche
Expressionismus in *Gutshof in Dangast*
dem Fauvismus.

Door de kracht van pure kleuren en
het weigeren van een illusionistische
benadering in *De villa in Dangast*
komt het Duitse expressionisme
dichter bij het fauvisme.

Por la fuerza de los colores puros
y el rechazo de un tratamiento
ilusionista, en *La casa en Dangast* el
Expresionismo alemán se acerca al
Fauvismo.

Karl Schmidt-Rottluff
(Rottluff 1884 - Berlin 1976)

**Portrait
of Dr. Paul Rauert
Porträt
Dr. Paul Rauert
Portret
van Dr. Paul Rauert
Retrato
del Dr. Paul Rauert**

●

1911
84 x 66 cm / 33 x 26 in.
Hamburger Kunsthalle,
Hamburg

oil on canvas
Öl auf Leinwand
olieverf op doek
óleo sobre lienzo

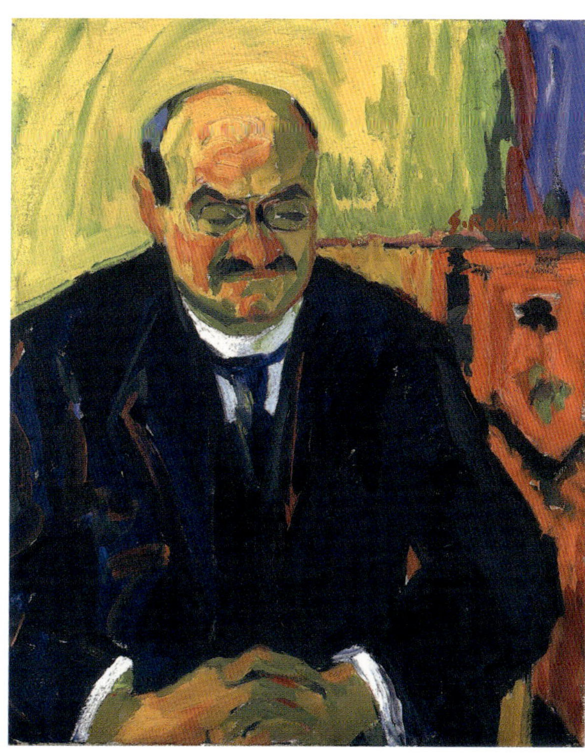

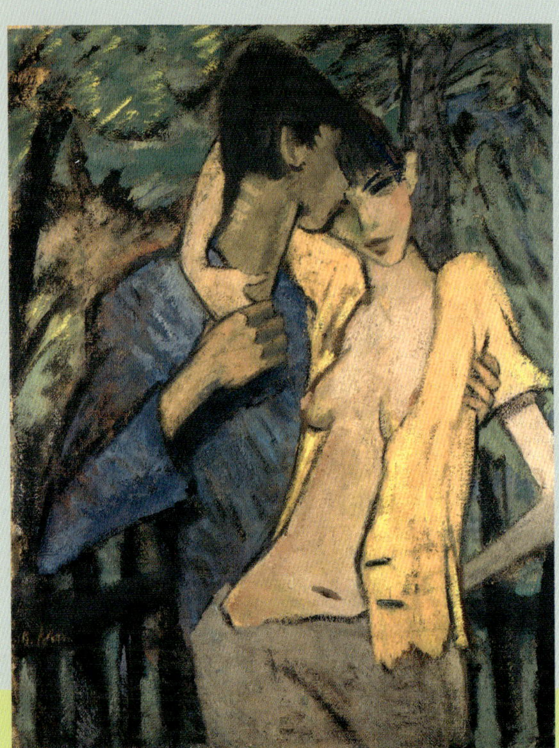

Otto Mueller
(Lubawka 1874 - Breaslau 1930)

Lovers
Liebespaar
Geliefden
Amantes

●

1919
106 x 80 cm / 41.7 x 31.5 in.
Museum der bildenden Künste,
Leipzig

oil on coarse canvas
Öl auf grober Leinwand
olieverf op ruw doek
óleo sobre lienzo texturizado

Otto Mueller
(Lubawka 1874 - Breaslau 1930)

Two female nudes in a landscape
Zwei weibliche Akte im Grünen
Twee vrouwelijke naakten
in een landschap
Dos desnudos femeninos
en un paisaje

●●

ca. 1922
100 x 138 cm / 39.4 x 54.3 in.
Museo Thyssen-Bornemisza, Madrid

oil on canvas / Öl auf Leinwand
olieverf op doek / óleo sobre lienzo

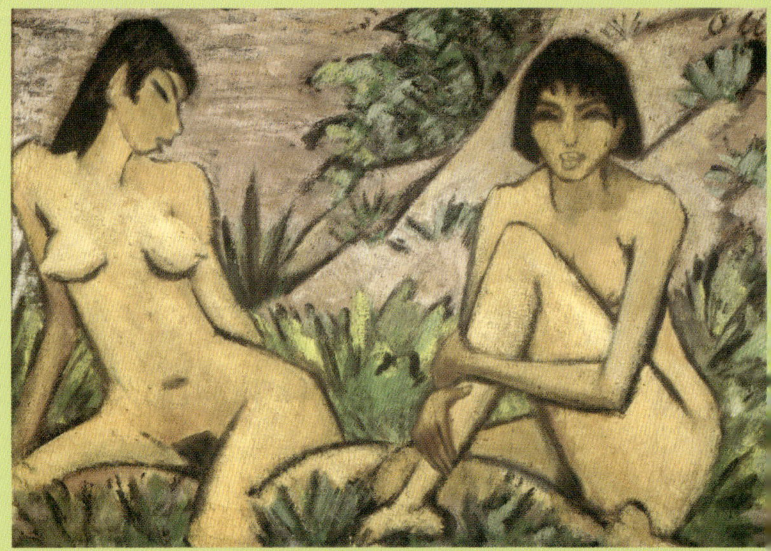

Erich Heckel
(Döbeln 1883 - Radolfzell 1970)

Furnaces at Dangast
Ziegelei in Dangast
Steenfabriek in Dangast
Fábrica de ladrillos en Dangast
●●
1907
68 x 86 cm / 26.7 x 37 in.
Museo Thyssen-Bornemisza, Madrid

oil on canvas / Öl auf Leinwand
olieverf op doek / óleo sobre lienzo

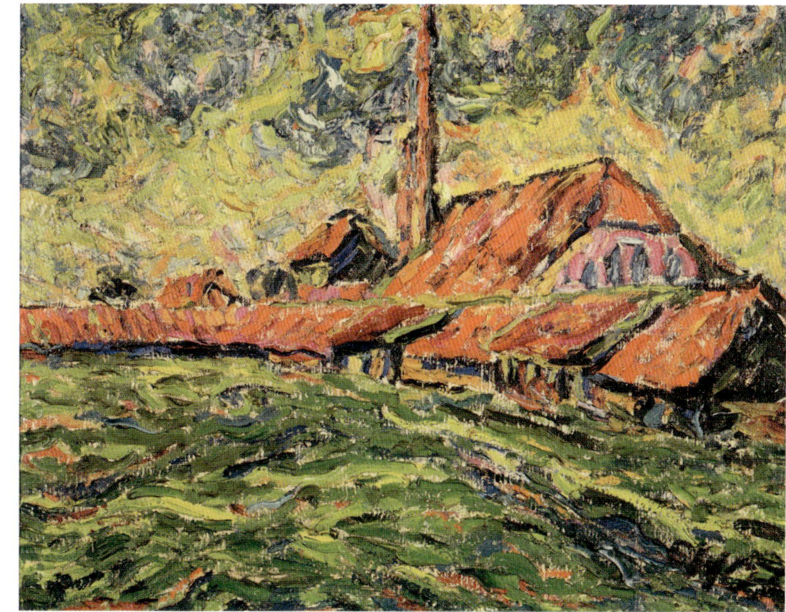

Erich Heckel
(Döbeln 1883 - Radolfzell 1970)

Country dance
Dorftanz
Dorpsbal
Baile de pueblo
●
1908
Nationalgalerie, Staatliche Museen, Berlin

oil on canvas / Öl auf Leinwand
olieverf op doek / óleo sobre lienzo

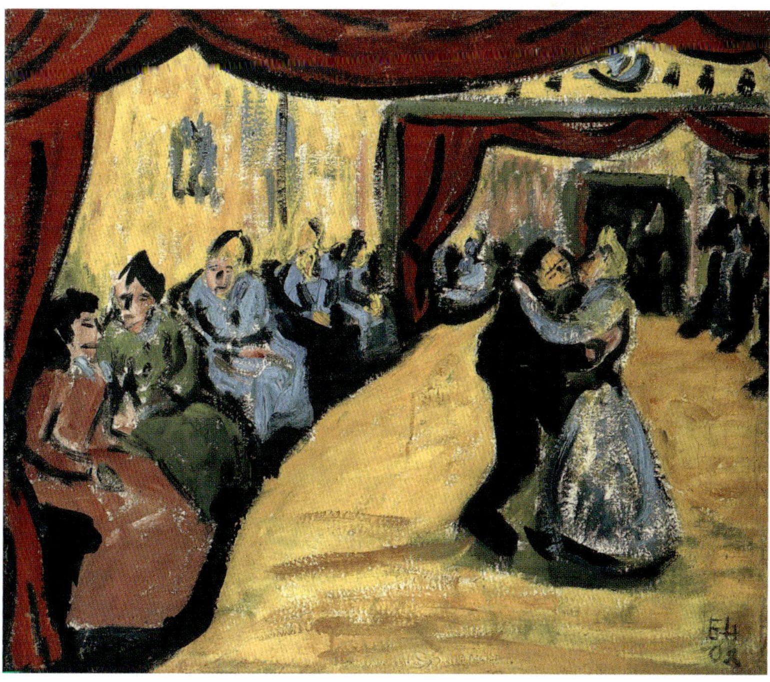

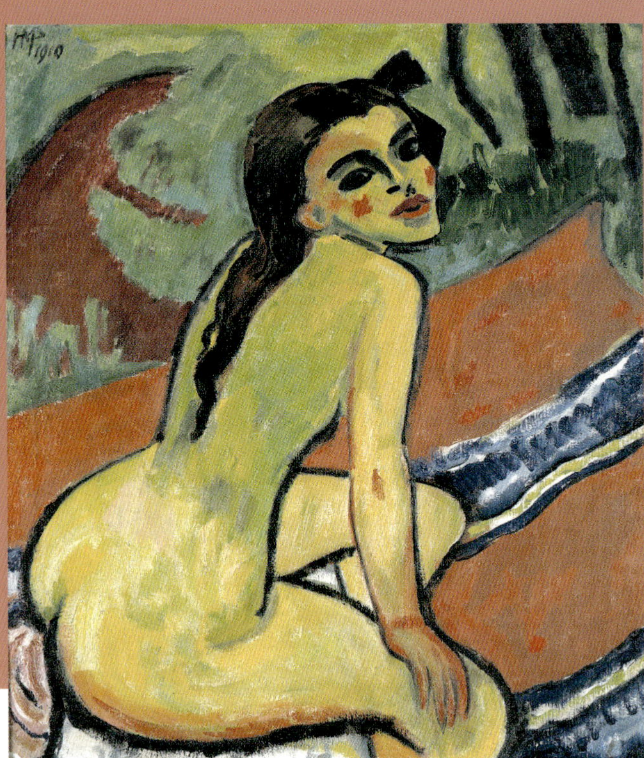

Max Pechstein
(Zwickau 1881 - Berlin 1955)

Girl seated. Moritzburg
Sitzendes Mädchen.
Moritzburg
Zittend meisje. Moritzburg
Muchacha sentada.
Moritzburg

●

1910
80 x 70 cm / 32 x 27.5 in.
Nationalgalerie, Staatliche Museen,
Berlin

oil on canvas / Öl auf Leinwand
olieverf op doek / óleo sobre lienzo

Max Pechstein
(Zwickau 1881 - Berlin 1955)

Summer at Nidden
Sommer in Nidden
Zomer in Nidden
Verano en Nidden

●●

ca. 1919
81,3 x 101 cm / 32 x 39.8 in.
Museo Thyssen-Bornemisza, Madrid

oil on canvas / Öl auf Leinwand
olieverf op doek / óleo sobre lienzo

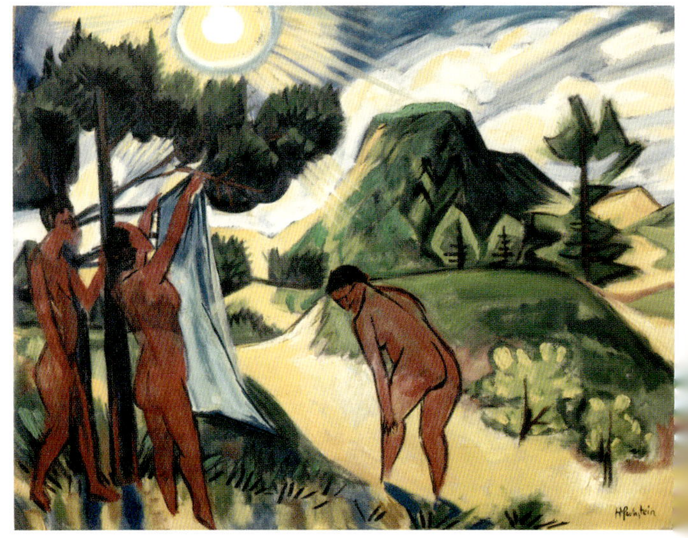

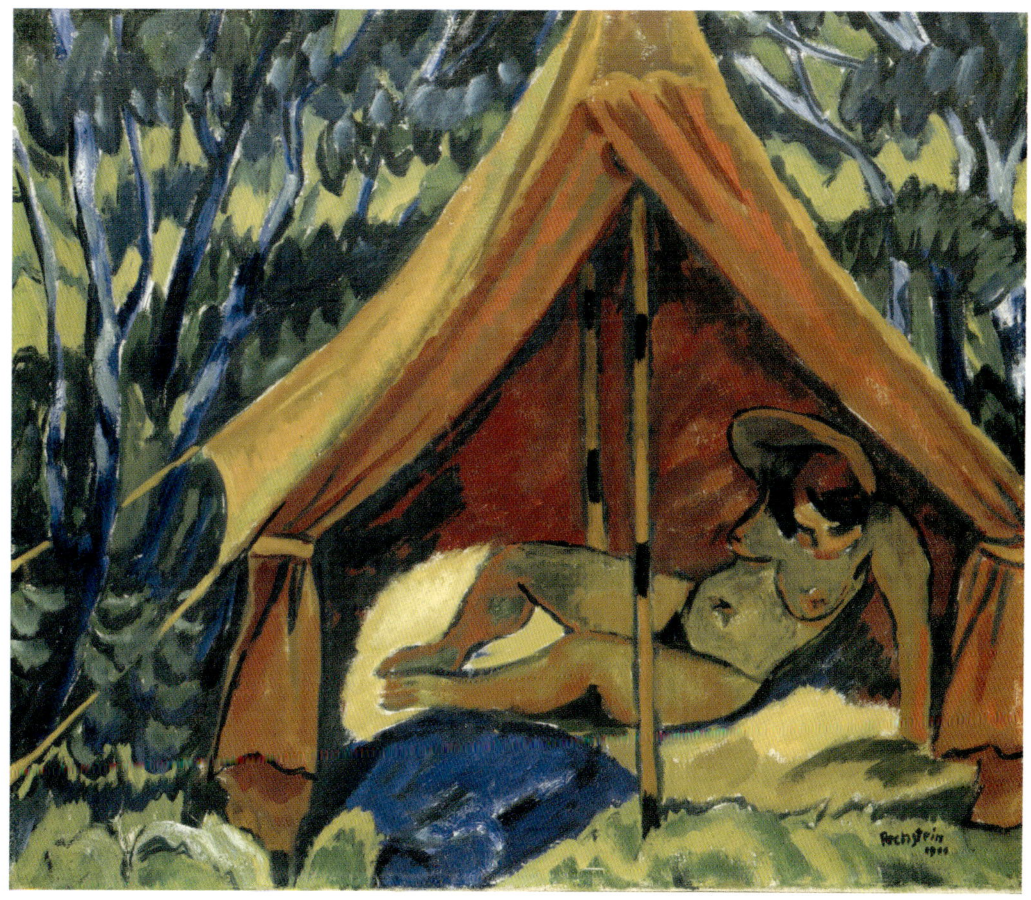

Max Pechstein
(Zwickau 1881 - Berlin 1955)

Nude under the tent
Akt im Zelt
Naakt onder de tent
Desnudo bajo la tienda

1911
70,5 x 80,5 cm / 27.7 x 31.7 in.
Pinakothek der Moderne, München

oil on canvas / Öl auf Leinwand
olieverf op doek / óleo sobre lienzo

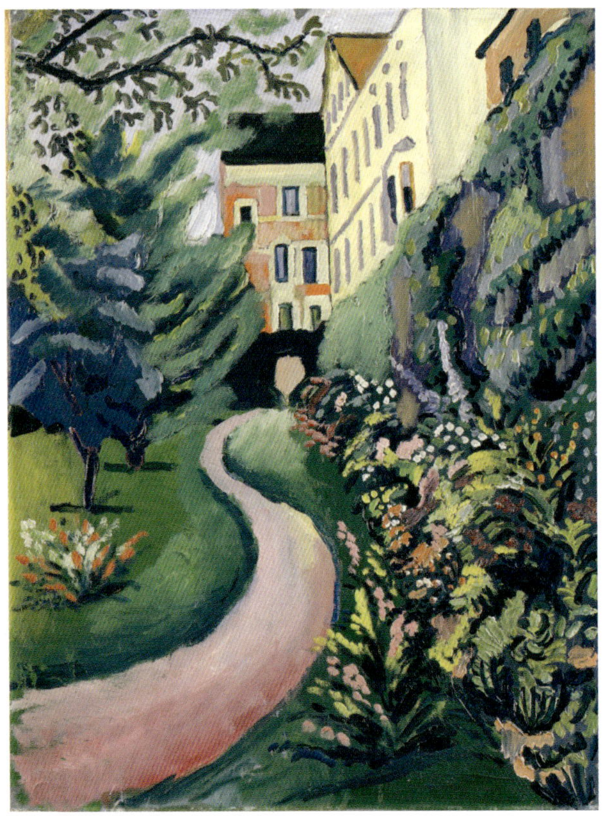

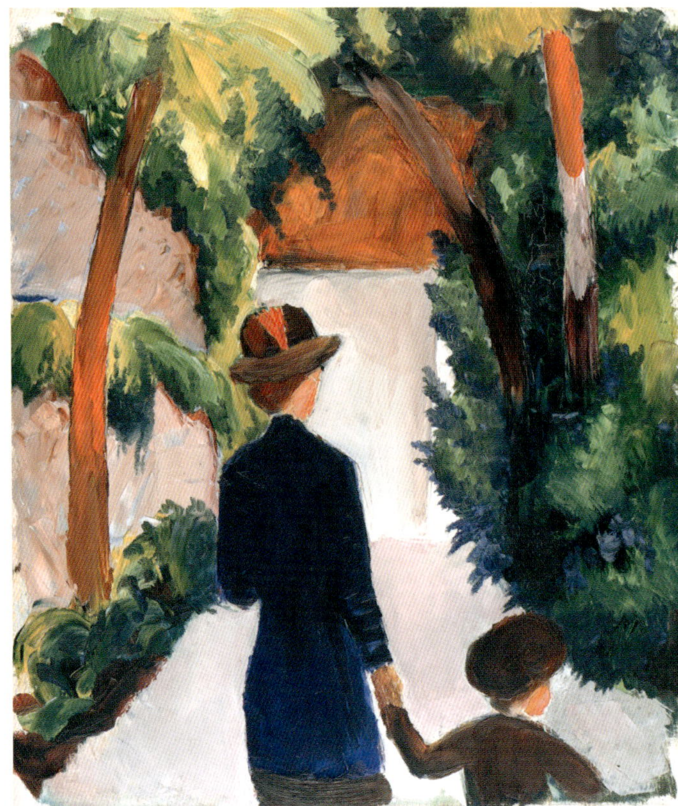

August Macke
(Meschede 1887 - Perthes-lès-Hurlus 1914)

Our garden with the flower beds
Unser Garten mit blühenden Rabatten
Onze tuin met bloemenperken in bloei
Nuestro jardín con los parterres en flor

●●

1911
64 x 47,5 cm / 25.2 x 18.7 in.
Hamburger Kunsthalle, Hamburg

oil on canvas / Öl auf Leinwand
olieverf op doek / óleo sobre lienzo

August Macke
(Meschede 1887 - Perthes-lès-Hurlus 1914)

Mother and son in the park
Mutter und Kind im Park
Moeder en zoon in het park
Madre e hijo en el jardín

●

1914
56,3 x 46 cm / 22.1 x 18.1 in.
Hamburger Kunsthalle, Hamburg

oil on canvas / Öl auf Leinwand
olieverf op doek / óleo sobre lienzo

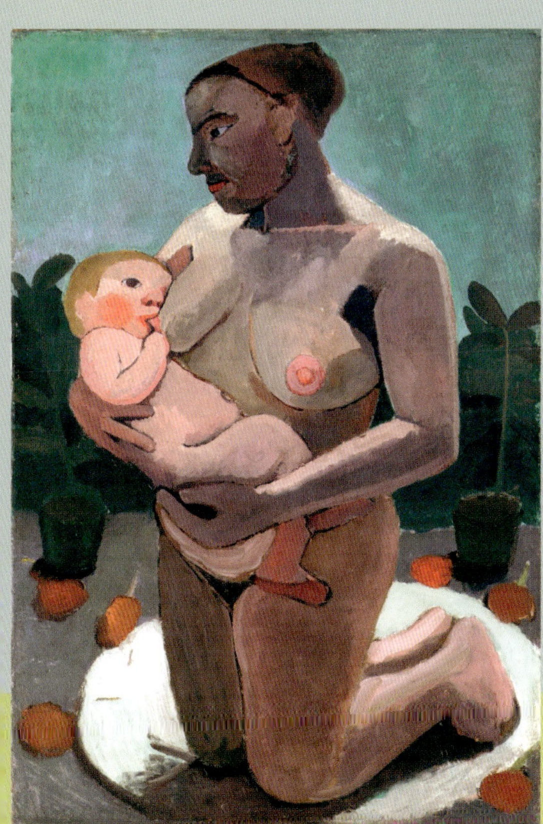

Paula Modersohn-Becker
(Dresden-Friedrichstadt 1876 - Worpswede 1907)

Mother nursing her son
Kniende Mutter mit Kind an der Brust
Moeder die haar kind de borst geeft
Madre amamantando a su hijo

●

1907
113 x 74 cm / 44.5 x 29.1 in.
Nationalgalerie, Staatliche Museen, Berlin

oil on canvas / Öl auf Leinwand
olieverf op doek / óleo sobre lienzo

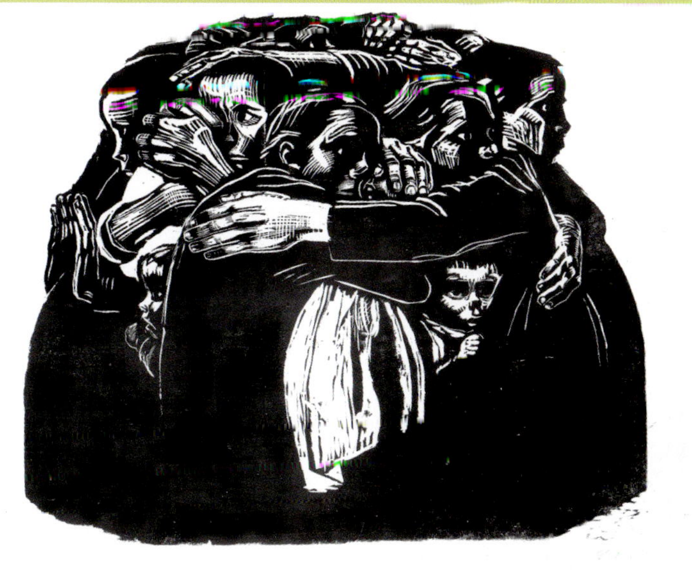

Kaethe Kollwitz
(Königsberg 1867 - Moritzburg 1945)

The mothers
Die Mütter
De moeders
Las madres

●

ca. 1923
Philadelphia Museum of Art, Philadelphia

xylography / Holzschnitt / xylografie / xilografía

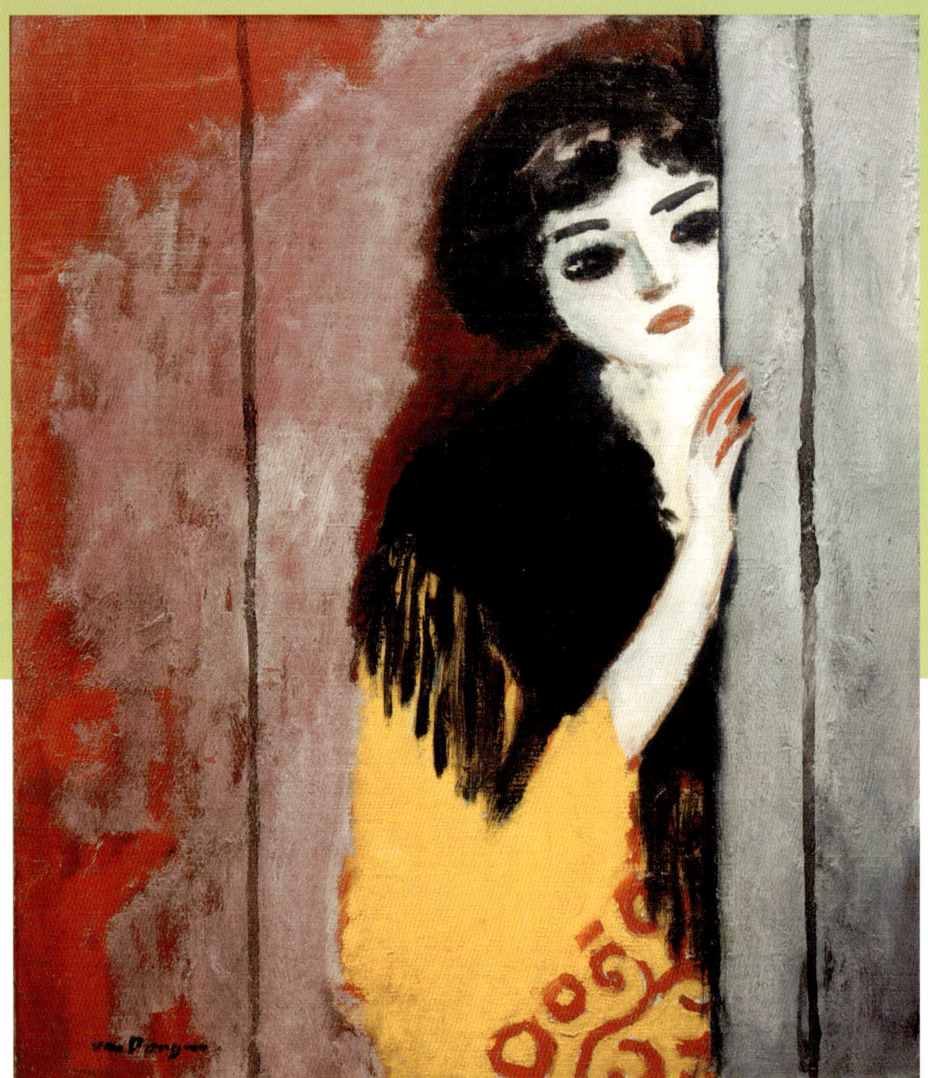

Kees van Dongen
(Delfshaven 1877 - Monte Carlo 1968)
Gypsy
Zigeunerin
De zigeunerin
Retrato de una gitana
●
Musée de l'Annonciade, Saint-Tropez

oil on canvas / Öl auf Leinwand
olieverf op doek / óleo sobre lienzo

98

Kees van Dongen
(Delfshaven 1877 - Monte Carlo 1968)

Portrait of Paul Guillaume
Porträt von Paul Guillaume
Portret van Paul Guillaume
Retrato de Paul Guillaume

••

ca. 1930
100 x 74 cm / 39.4 x 29.1 in.
Musée de l'Orangerie, Paris

oil on canvas / Öl auf Leinwand
olieverf op doek / óleo sobre lienzo

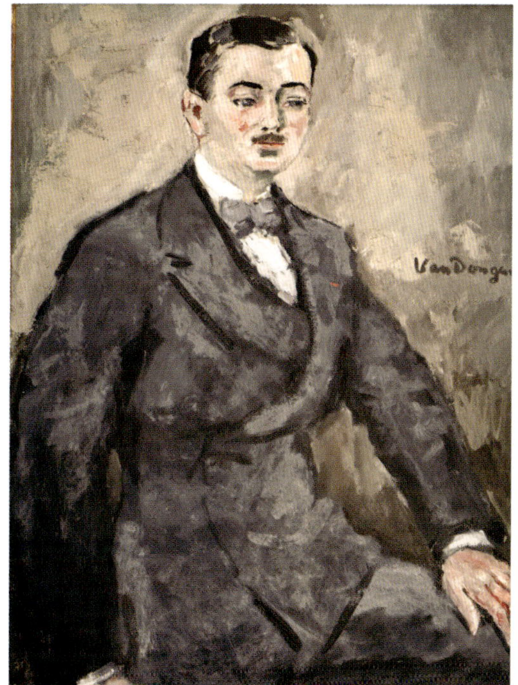

Self-taught, Paul Guillaume quickly became a famous art dealer in Paris and a great collector of Modern and African art.

Der Autodidakt Paul Guillaume wurde schnell ein bekannter Gallerist in Paris und ein großer Sammler von moderner und afrikanischer Kunst.

Paul Guillaume, een autodidact, werd in Parijs al snel een beroemde galeriehouder en een groot verzamelaar van moderne en Afrikaanse kunst.

Autodidacta, Paul Guillaume se volvió rápidamente un galerista famoso en París y un gran coleccionista de arte moderno y africano.

Kees van Dongen
(Delfshaven 1877 - Monte Carlo 1968)

In the square, two women on the balcony. Fauvism
Auf dem Platz. Zwei Frauen am Geländer. Fauvismus
Op het plein, twee vrouwen op het balkon. Fauvisme
En la plaza, dos mujeres en el balcón. Fauvismo

•

1911
81 x 100 cm / 31.9 x 39.4 in.
Musée de l'Annonciade, Saint-Tropez

oil on canvas / Öl auf Leinwand
olieverf op doek / óleo sobre lienzo

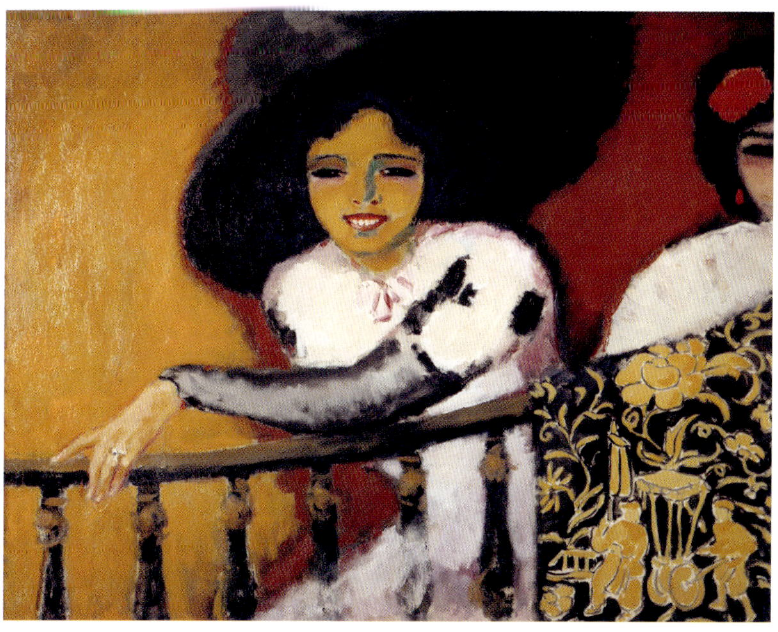

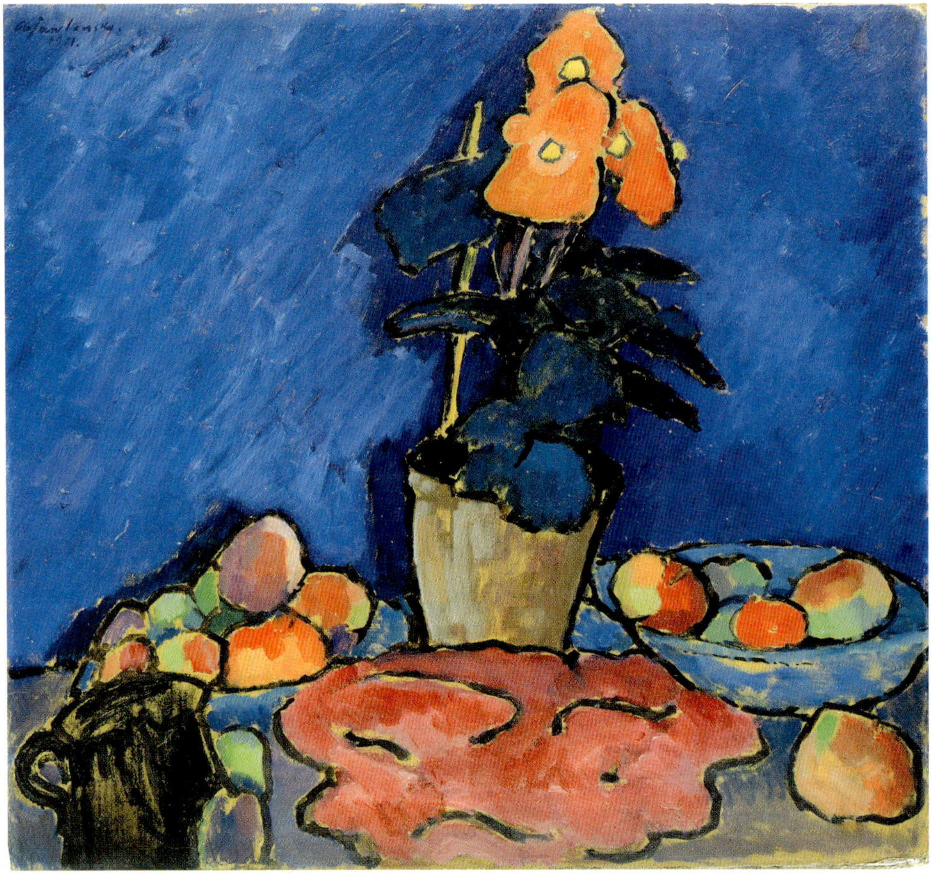

Alexei von Jawlensky
(Torzhok 1864 - Wiesbaden 1941)

Still life with begonia
Stillleben mit Begonie
Stilleven met een begonia
Bodegón con begonia

●

1911
71 x 75,5 cm / 28 x 29.7 in.
Hamburger Kunsthalle, Hamburg

oil on paperboard / Öl auf Karton
olieverf op karton / óleo sobre cartón

▶ Alexei von Jawlensky
(Torzhok 1864 - Wiesbaden 1941)

Meditating woman
Nachdenkende Frau
Mediterende vrouw
Mujer meditando

● ●

1912
Museo Thyssen-Bornemisza, Madrid

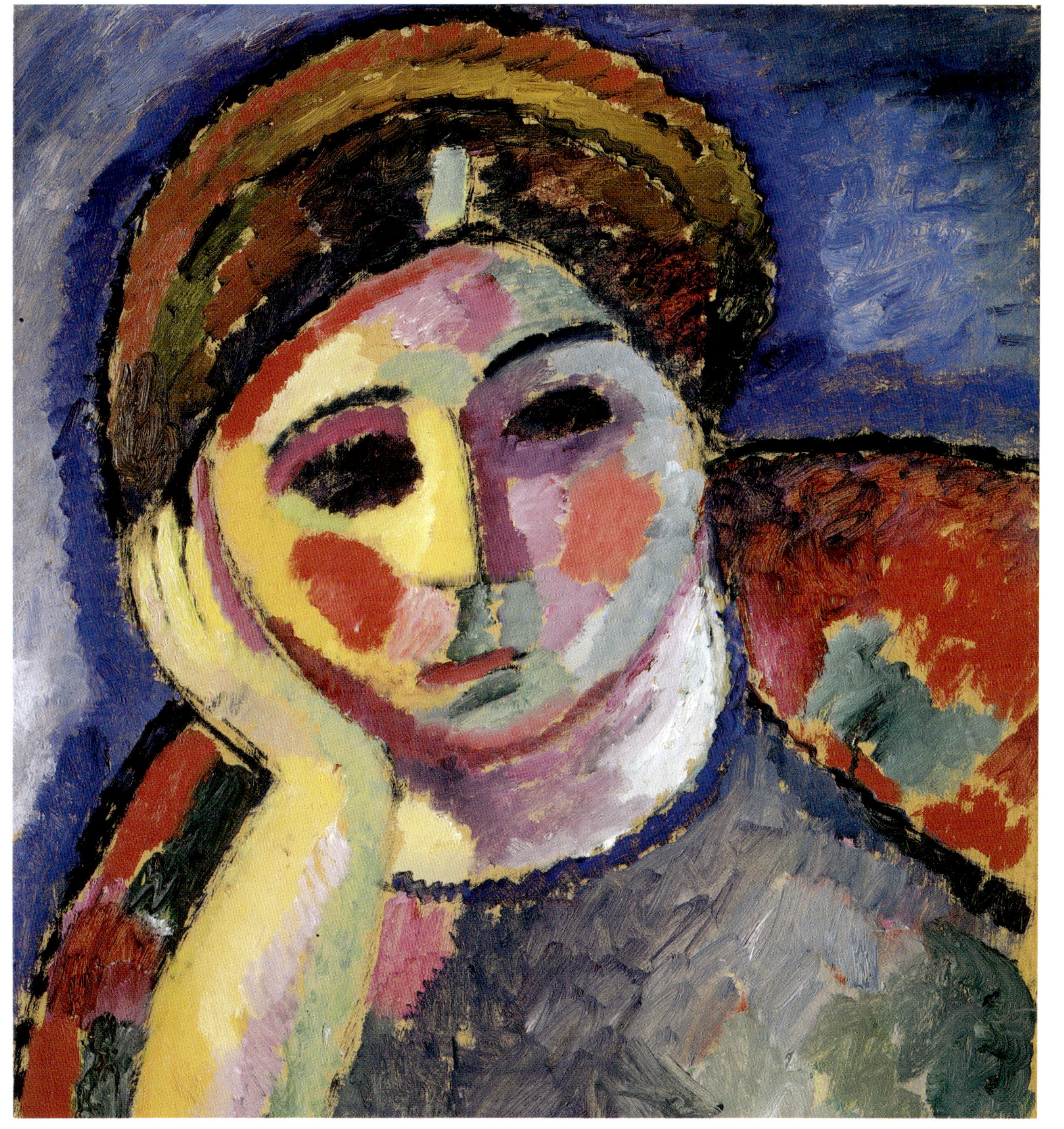

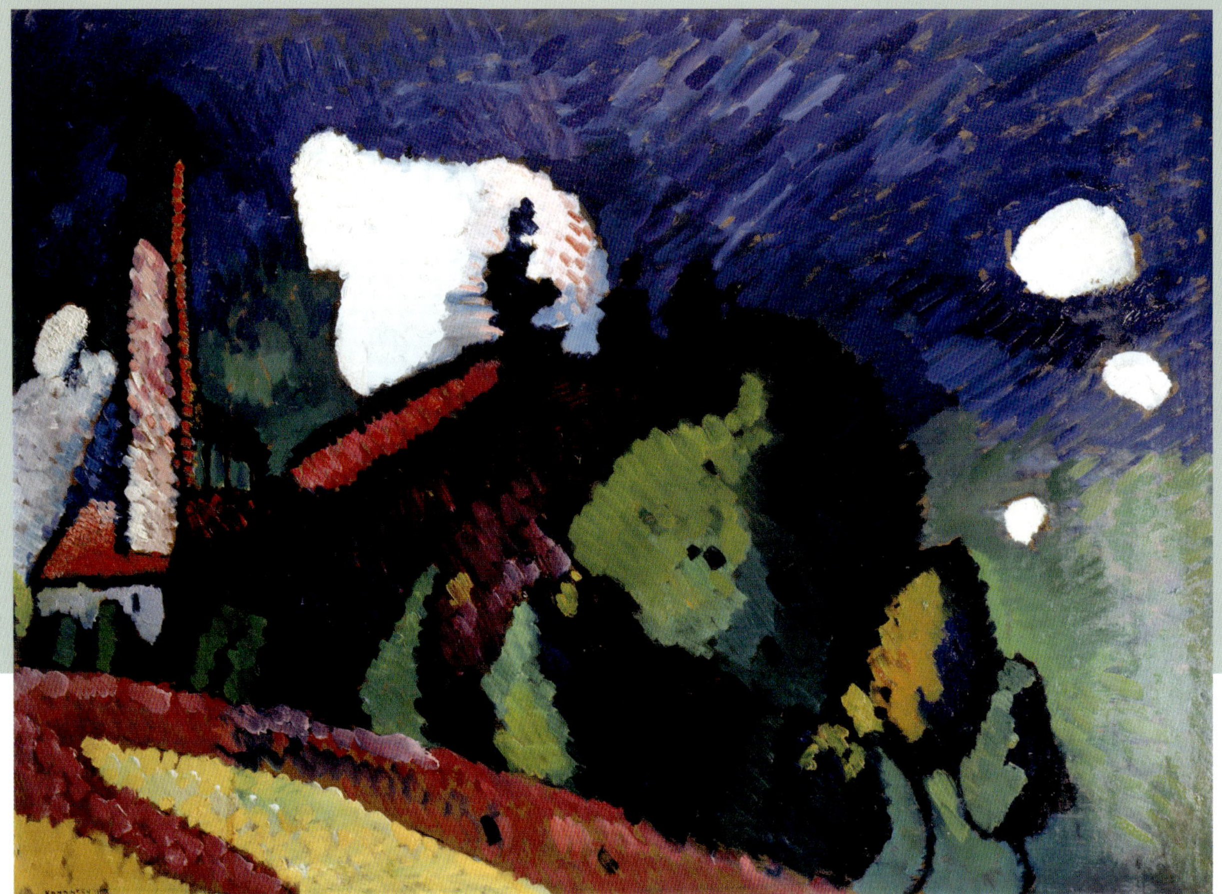

Vassily Kandinsky
(Moscow 1866 - Neuilly-sur-Seine 1944)

Paysage à la tour
Landschaft mit Turm
Paisaje con torre
●

1908
74 x 98 cm / 29.5 x 38.6 in.
Centre Georges Pompidou,
Musée National d'Art Moderne, Paris

oil on paperboard / Öl auf Karton
olieverf op karton / óleo sobre cartón

Slowly Kandinsky moves towards autonomy of color and design,
released from the steadfast representation of reality.

Zunehmend nähert sich Kandinsky der Autonomie
von Farbe und Zeichnung, die von der treuen Darstellung
des Wirklichen befreit sind.

Langzaam gaat Kandinsky richting een autonomie van kleur en
ontwerp, die bevrijd worden van de trouwe voorstelling van de
werkelijkheid

Poco a poco, Kandinsky se dirige hacia una independencia del color
y del dibujo, liberados de la fiel representación de lo real.

Vassily Kandinsky
(Moscow 1866 - Neuilly-sur-Seine 1944)
**Summer landscape
(Houses at Murnau)
Sommerlandschaft
(Häuser in Murnau)
Zomerlandschap
(huizen in Murnau)
Paisaje de verano
(Casas en Murnau)**
●●
1909
33 x 45 cm / 13 x 17.7 in.
The State Hermitage Museum,
St. Petersburg

oil on paperboard / Öl auf Karton
olieverf op karton / óleo sobre cartón

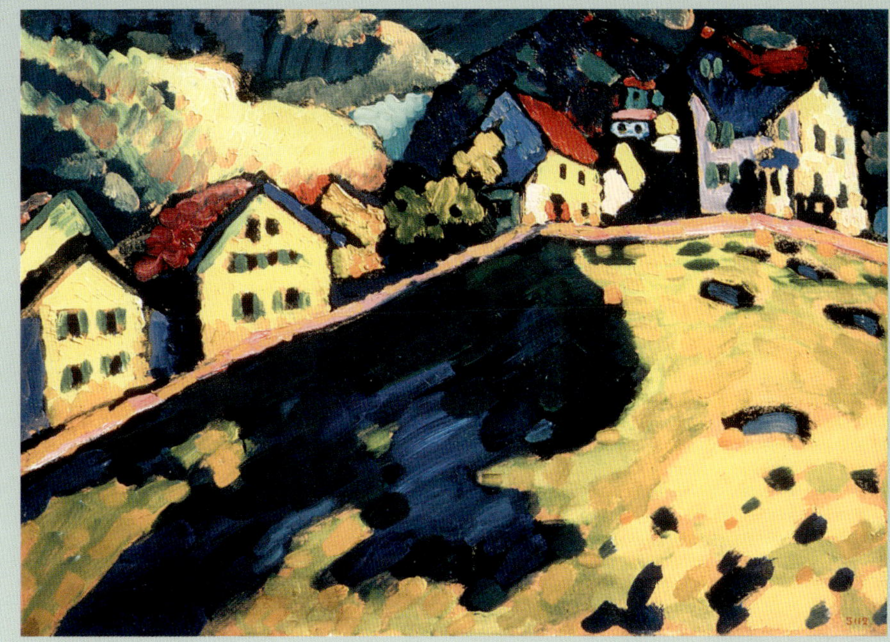

Vassily Kandinsky
(Moscow 1866 - Neuilly-sur-Seine 1944)
**Winter
Invierno**
●
1909
70 x 97 cm / 27.6 x 38.2 in.
The State Hermitage Museum, St.
Petersburg

oil on paperboard / Öl auf Karton
olieverf op karton / óleo sobre cartón

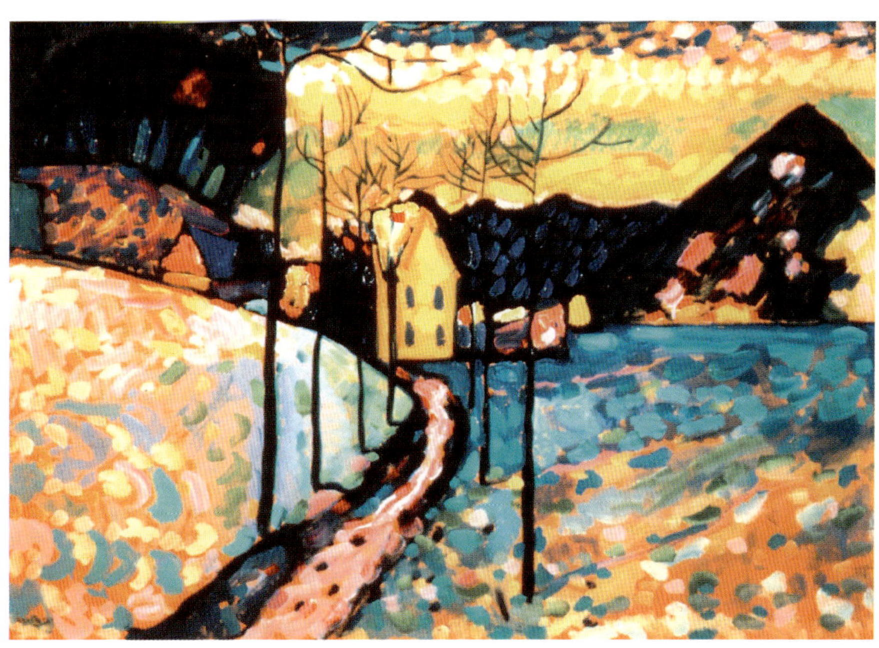

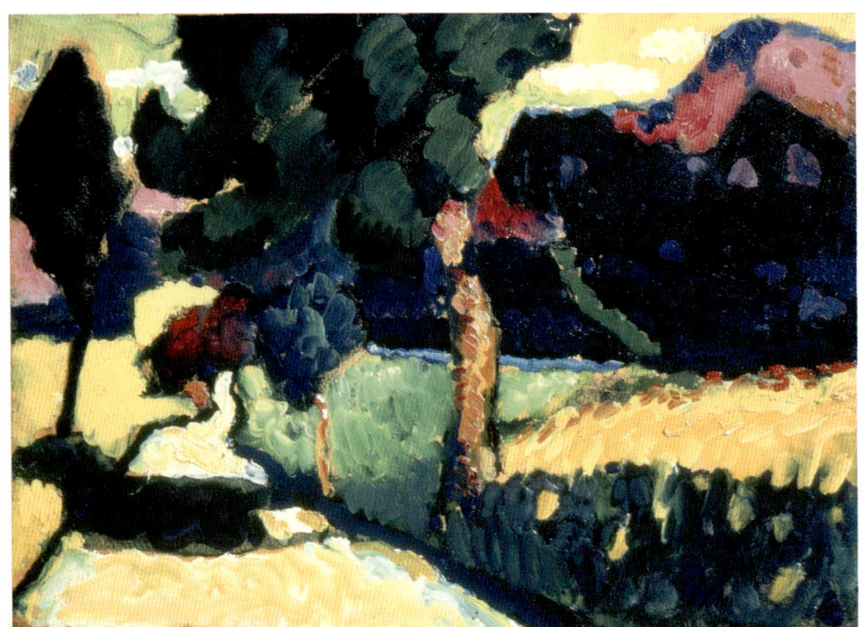

Vassily Kandinsky
(Moscow 1866 - Neuilly-sur-Seine 1944)

Fate
Das Schicksal
Het lot
El destino

●●

1909
Astrakhan Art Gallery, Astrakhan

104

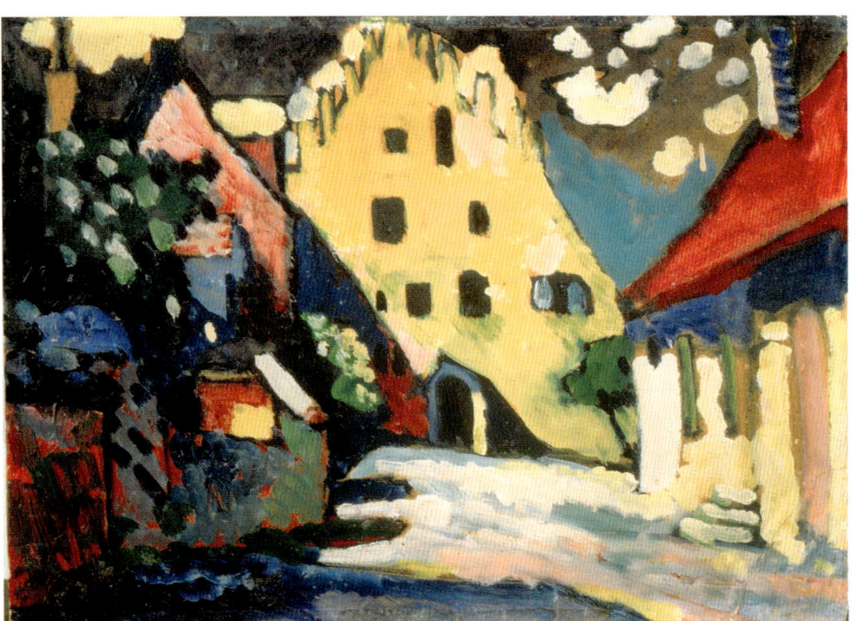

Vassily Kandinsky
(Moscow 1866 - Neuilly-sur-Seine 1944)

Landscape
Landschaft
Landschap
Paisaje

●

33 x 44,3 cm / 13 x 17.34 in.
State Tretyakov Gallery, Moscow

oil on cardboard / Öl auf Karton
olieverf op karton / óleo sobre cartón

Franz Marc
(München 1880 - Verdun 1916)

Vasily Kandinsky
(Moscow 1866 - Neuilly-sur-Seine 1944)

The Blue Rider
Der Blaue Reiter
De Blauwe Ruiter
El jinete azul

●●

1912
Museum of Fine Arts, Boston

illustrated book with two color xylographs,
colored by hand and photographic print reproductions
Illustriertes Buch mit zwei handgefärbten Farbholzschnitten
und photomechanischen Reproduktionen / Geïllustreerd
boek met twee kleuren xylografieën, met de hand ingekleurd
en reproducties van fotografische afdrukken / libro ilustrado
con dos xilografías a color, pintado a mano y reproducciones
por impresión fotográfica

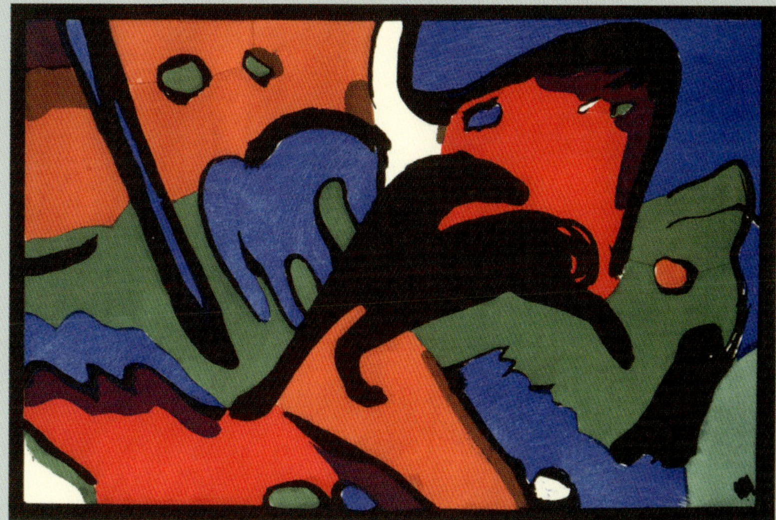

Franz Marc
(München 1880 - Verdun 1916)

Sleeping Shepherdess
Schlafende Hirtin
Slapende herderin
La pastorcilla adormecida

●

1912
27,5 x 39,2 cm / 10.8 x 15.4 in.
Victoria & Albert Museum, London

xylography / Holzschnitt
xylografie / xilografía

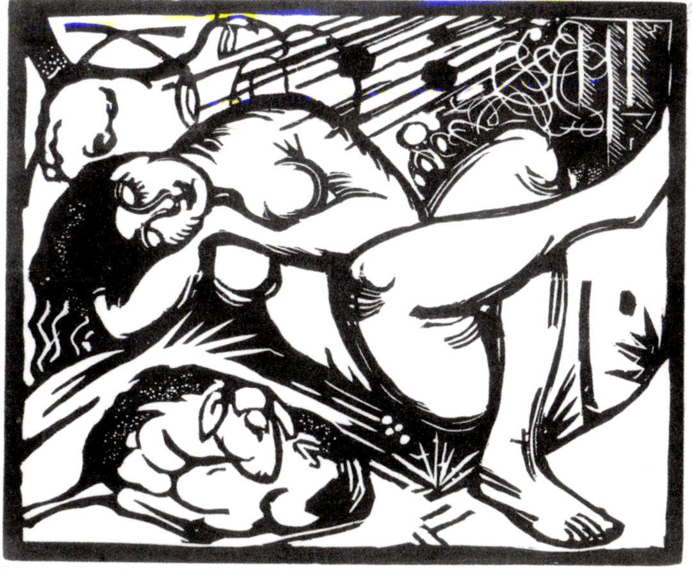

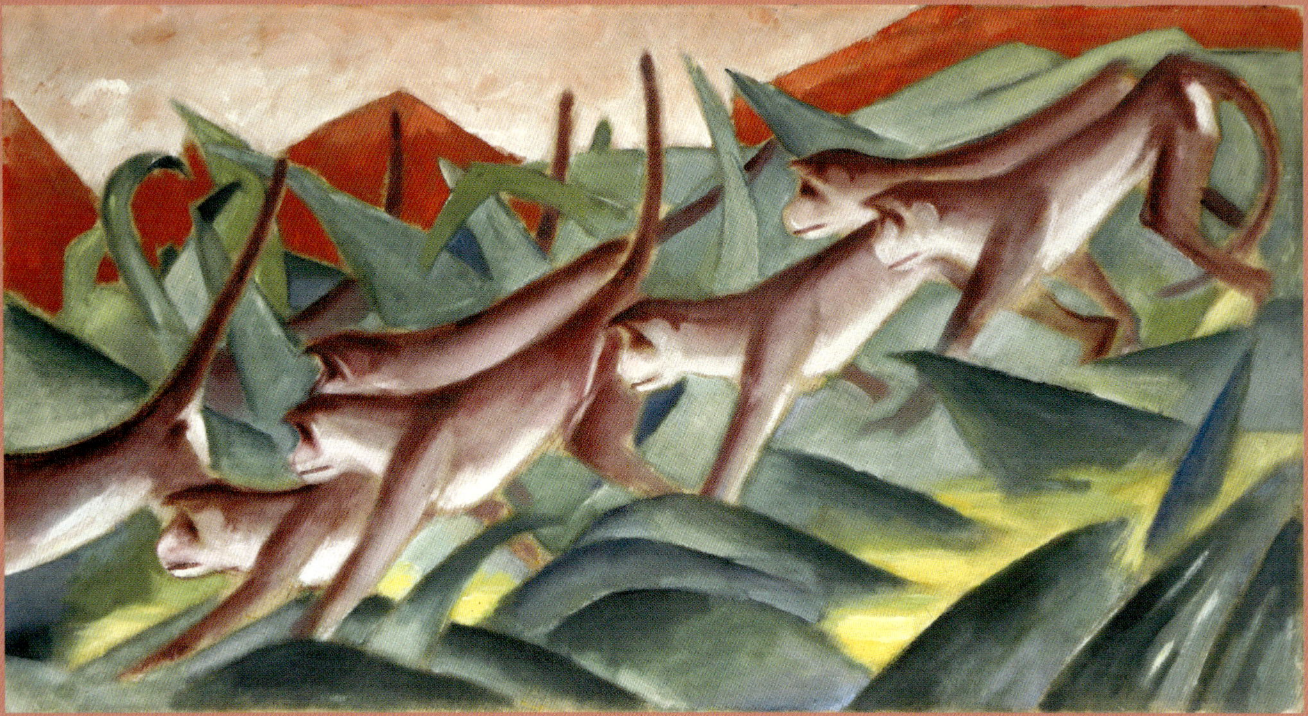

Franz Marc
(München 1880 - Verdun 1916)

Frieze with monkeys
Affenfries
Fries met apen
Friso de monos

1911
75,5 x 135,5 cm / 29.7 x 53.3 in.
Hamburger Kunsthalle, Hamburg

oil on canvas / Öl auf Leinwand
olieverf op doek / óleo sobre lienzo

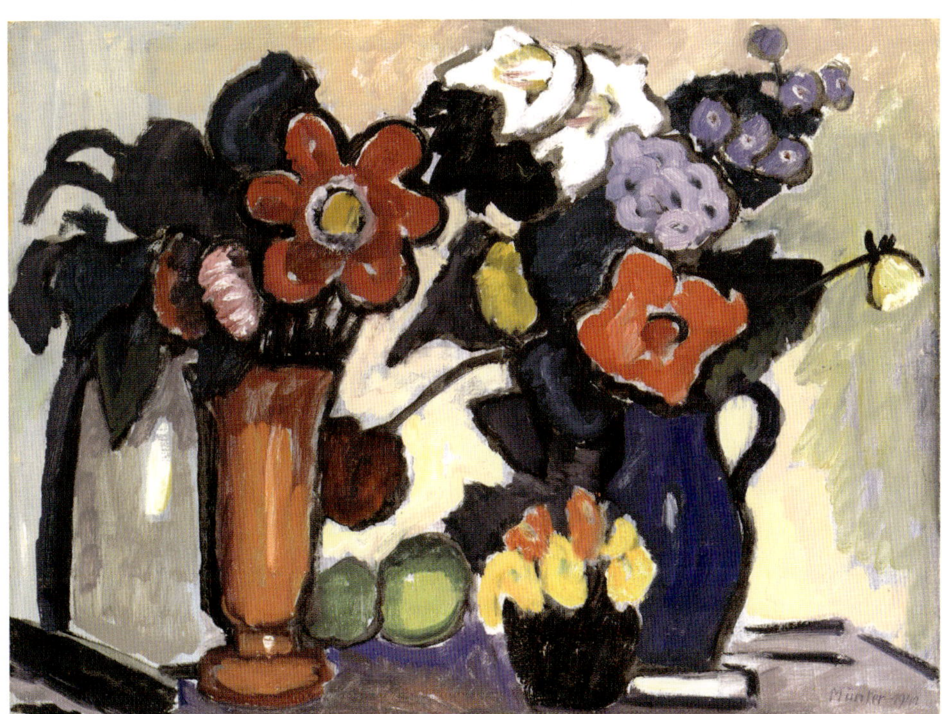

Gabriele Münter
(Berlin 1877 - Murnau am Staffelsee 1962)

Flowers of the night
Blumen in der Nacht
Bloemen in de nacht
Flores de noche

●

1941
50 x 65 cm / 19.7 x 25.6 in.
Hamburger Kunsthalle, Hamburg

oil on paperboard / Öl auf Karton
olieverf op karton / óleo sobre cartón

Gabriele Münter
(Berlin 1877 - Murnau am Staffelsee 1962)

Man on the chair (Paul Klee)
Mann im Sessel (Paul Klee)
De man op de stoel (Paul Klee)
El hombre en el sillón (Paul Klee)

●

1913
95 x 125,5 cm / 37.4 x 49.4 in.
Pinakothek der Moderne, München

oil on canvas / Öl auf Leinwand
olieverf op doek / óleo sobre lienzo

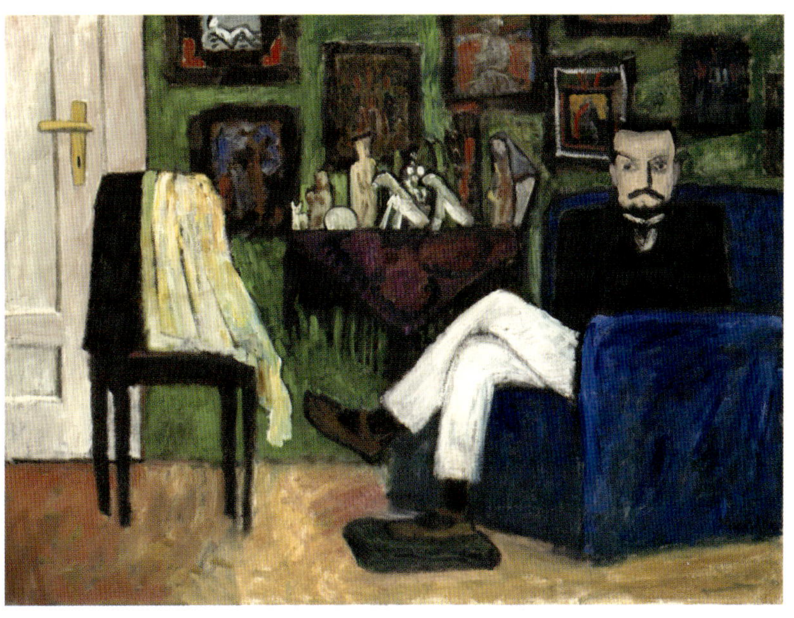

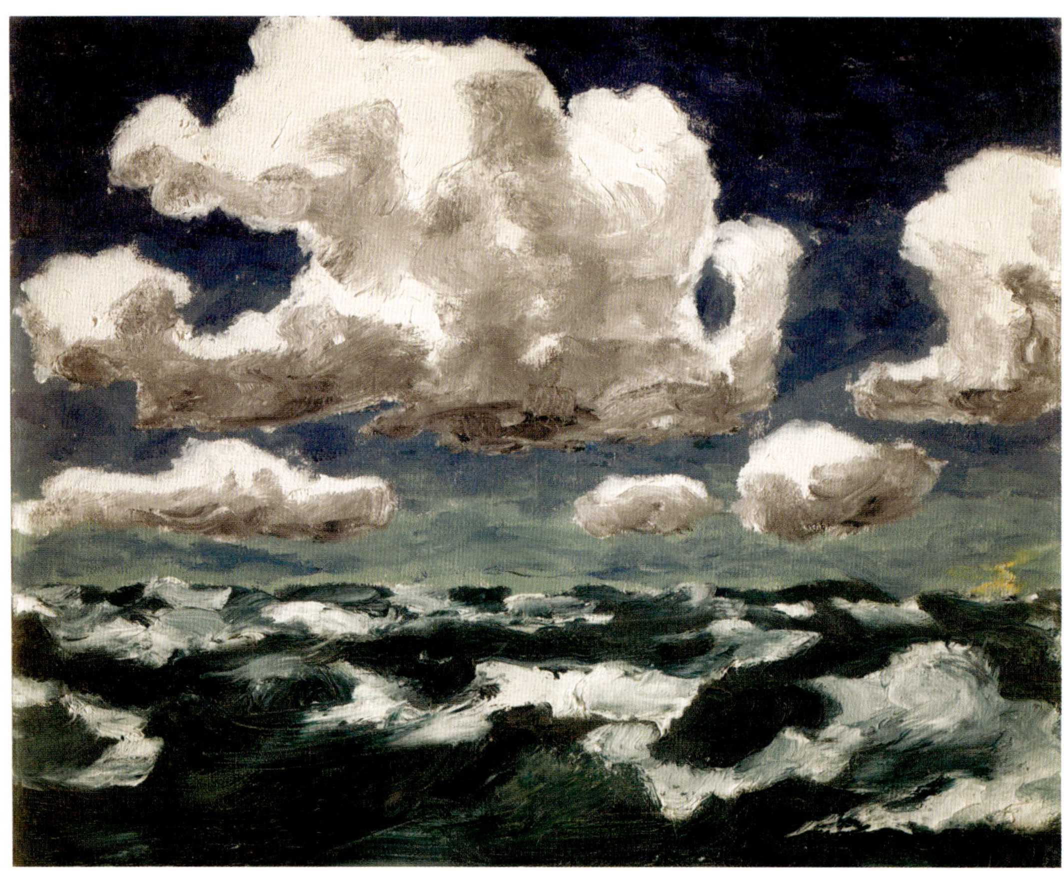

Emil Nolde
(Nolde 1867 - Seebüll 1956)

The clouds of summer
Sommerwolken
Zomerwolken
Nubes de verano

●●

1913
73 x 88 cm / 28.7 x 34.6 in.
Museo Thyssen-Bornemisza, Madrid

oil on canvas / Öl auf Leinwand
olieverf op doek / óleo sobre lienzo

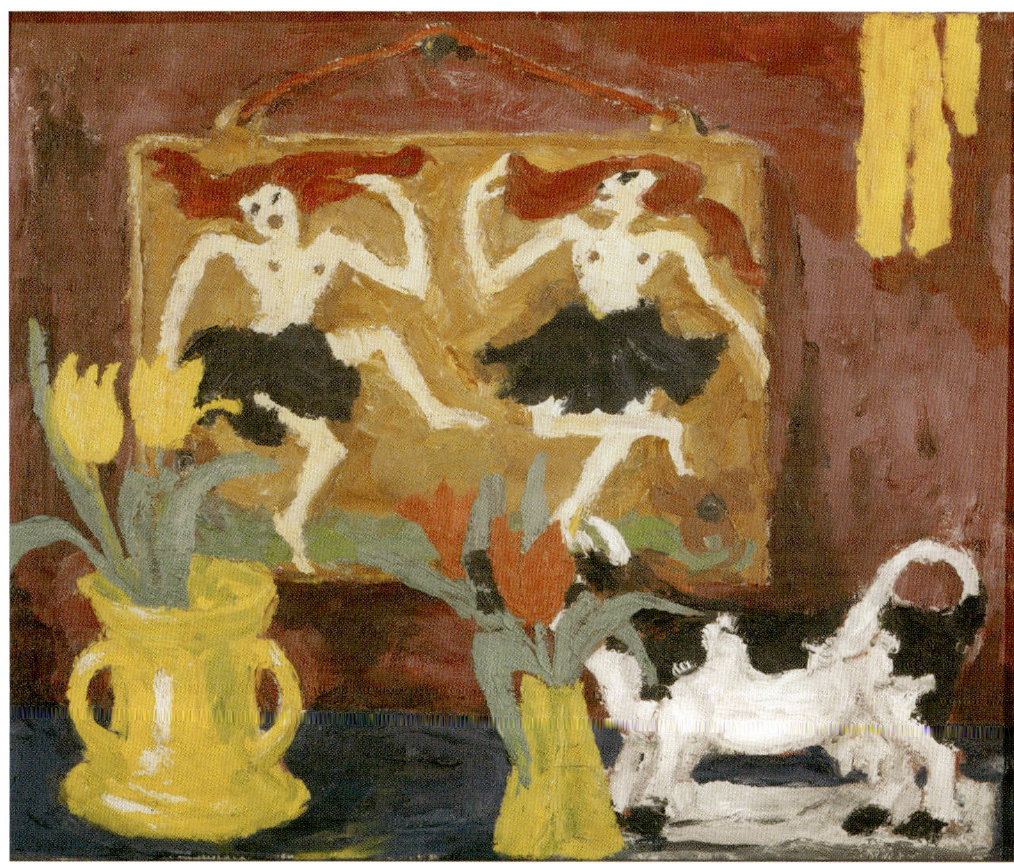

Emil Nolde
(Nolde 1867 - Seebüll 1956)

Still life with dancers
Stillleben mit Tänzerinnen
Stilleven met danseressen
Bodegón con bailarinas

●●●

1914
73 x 89 cm / 28.7 x 35 in.
Centre Georges Pompidou,
Musée National d'Art Moderne, Paris

oil on canvas / Öl auf Leinwand
olieverf op doek / óleo sobre lienzo

By mixing the fierceness of the primitives and the objects of popular art, *Still life with dancers* by Nolde compares the cultures of the world.

Indem es die Wildheit der Primitiven mit Objekten der volkstümlichen Kunst vereint, stellt Noldes *Stillleben mit Tänzerinnen* die Kulturen der Welt gegenüber.

Door de woestheid van de primitievelingen en de objecten van de volkskunst te mengen, vergelijkt Nolde in *Stilleven met danseressen* de culturen van de wereld.

Mezclando la ferocidad de los primitivos y los objetos del arte popular, *Bodegón con bailarinas*, de Nolde, compara las distintas culturas del mundo.

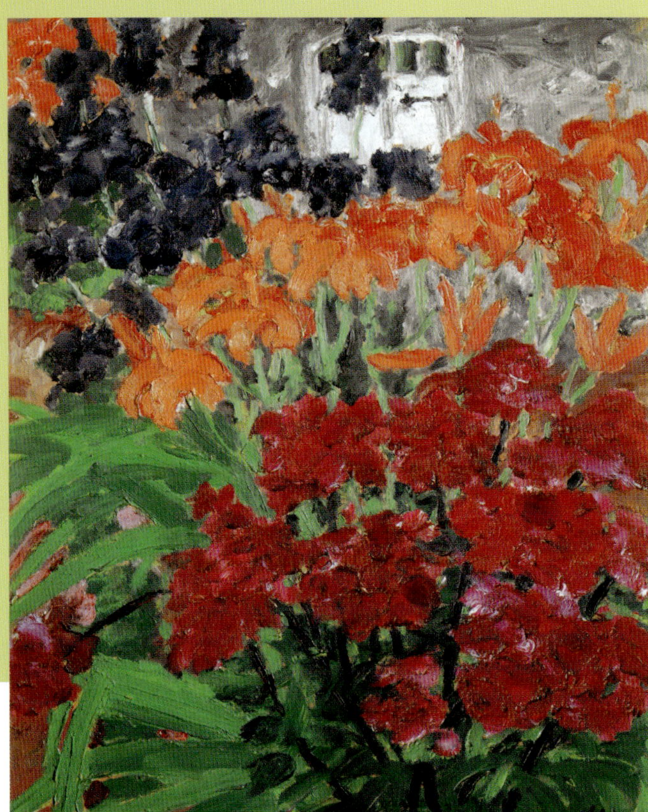

Emil Nolde
(Nolde 1867 - Seebüll 1956)
Roses, lilies and larkspur
Rosen, Lilien und Rittersporn
Rozen, lelies en wilde ridderspoor
Rosas, azucenas y espuelas de caballero
● ●

1917
Collezione Thyssen-Bornemisza, Lugano

oil on panel / Öl auf Tafel
olieverf op paneel / óleo sobre tabla

Emil Nolde
(Nolde 1867 - Seebüll 1956)
Poppies and fleurs-de-lis
Mohnblumen und Kornblumen
Klaprozen en korenbloemen
Amapolas y lirios
●

ca. 1930
45,6 x 34,1 cm / 14.9 x 13.4 in.
Museum der bildenden Künste, Leipzig

watercolor / Aquarell
aquarel / acuarela

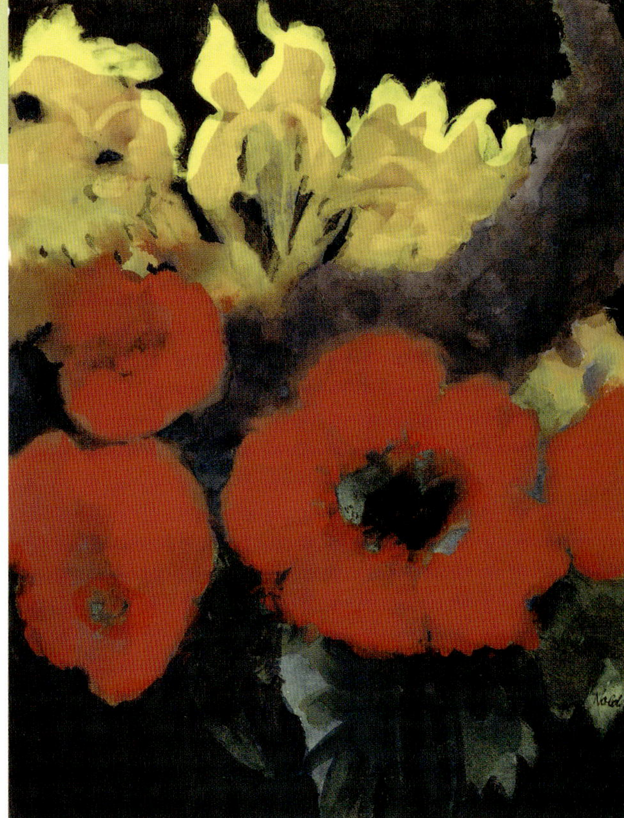

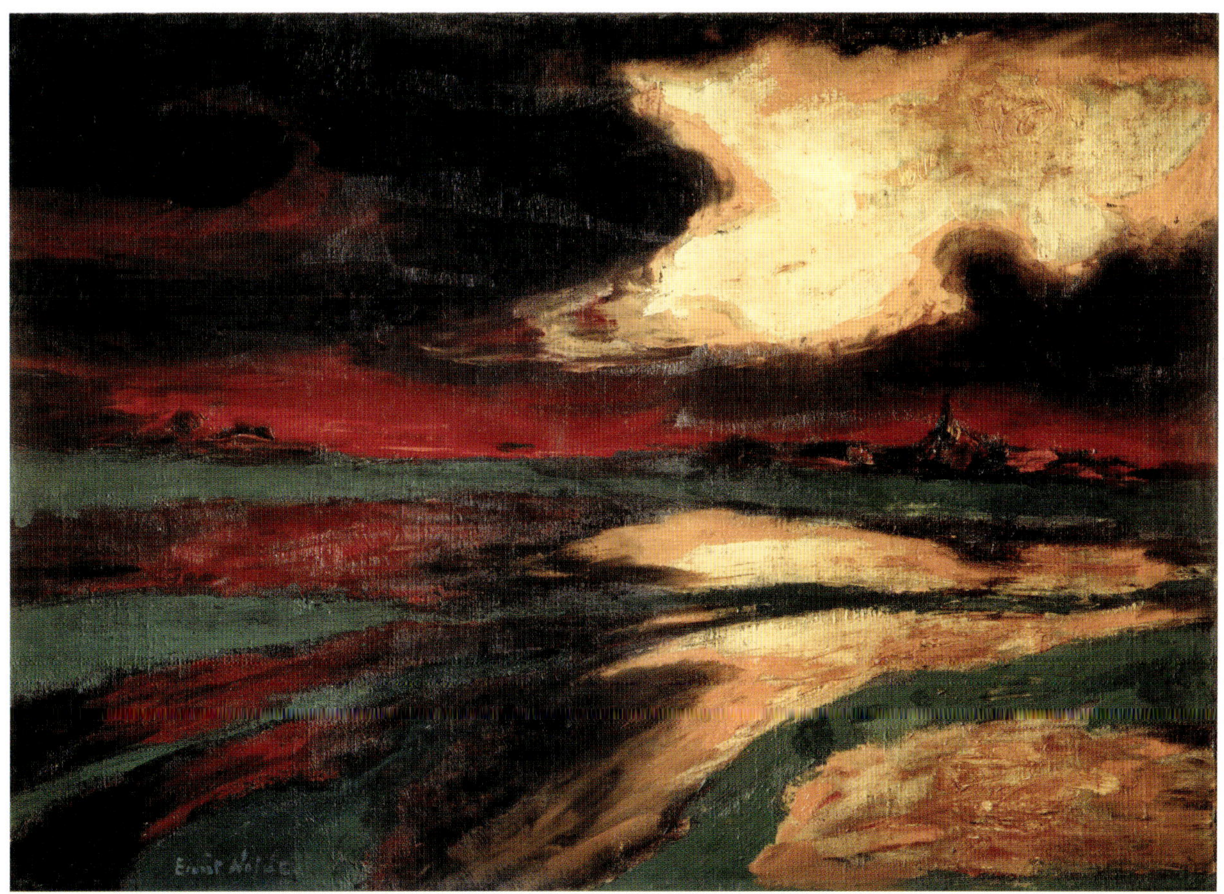

Emil Nolde
(Nolde 1867 - Seebüll 1956)

Autumn Evening
Herbstabend
Herfstavond
Atardecer de otoño

●

1924
73 x 100,5 cm / 28.7 x 39.5 in.
Museo Thyssen-Bornemisza, Madrid

oil on canvas / Öl auf Leinwand
olieverf op doek / óleo sobre lienzo

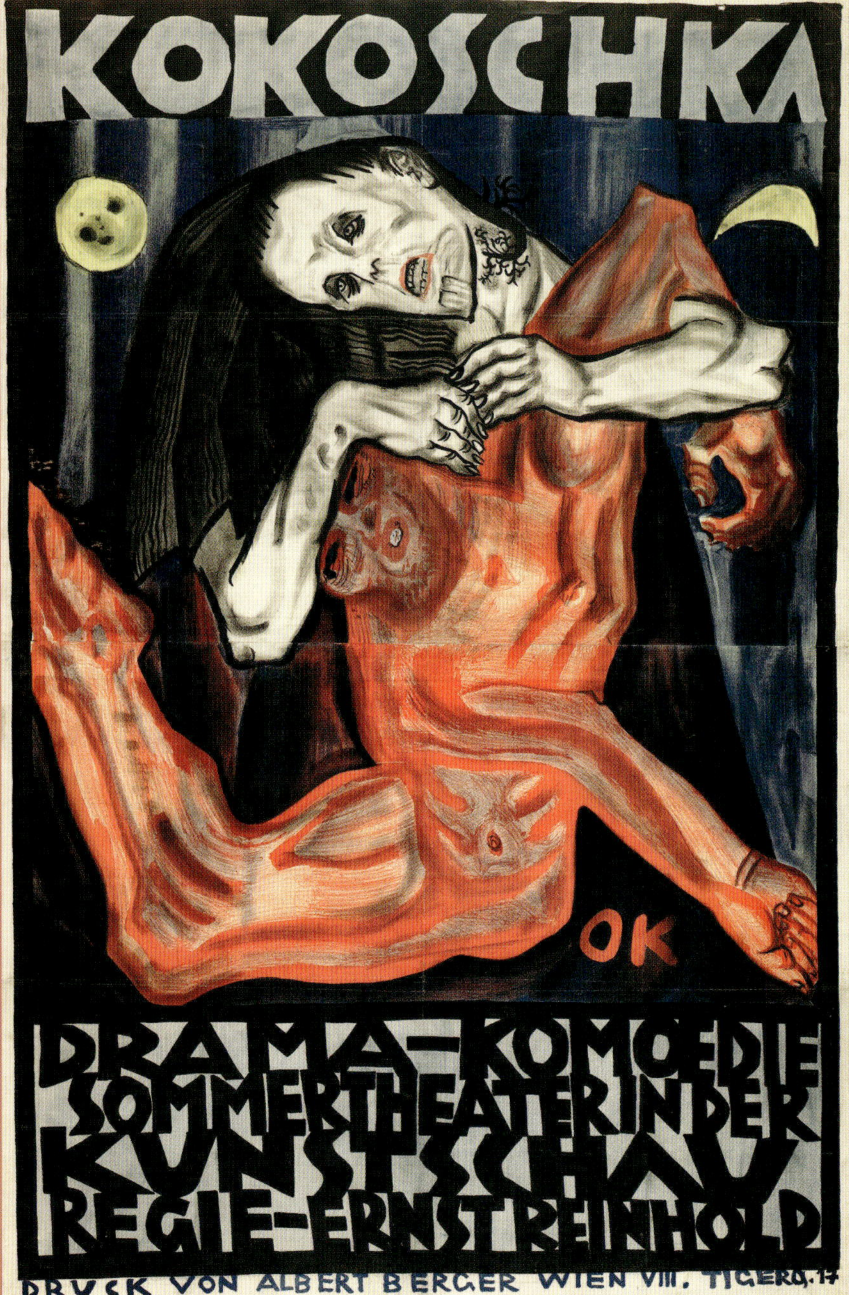

Oskar Kokoschka
(Pöchlarn 1886 - Montreux 1980)

Kokoschka, Drama-Komoedie

●●●

1907
118,1 x 76,2 cm / 46.5 x 30 in.
Museum of Modern Art (MoMA),
New York

lithography / Lithographie
lithografie / litografía

Oskar Kokoschka
(Pöchlarn 1886 - Montreux 1980)

Two nudes (The lovers)
Zwei Nackte (Die Liebenden)
Twee naakten (geliefden)
Dos desnudos (Los amantes)

●

1913
163,2 x 97,5 cm / 64.2 x 38.3 in.
Museum of Fine Arts, Boston

oil on canvas / Öl auf Leinwand
olieverf op doek / óleo sobre lienzo

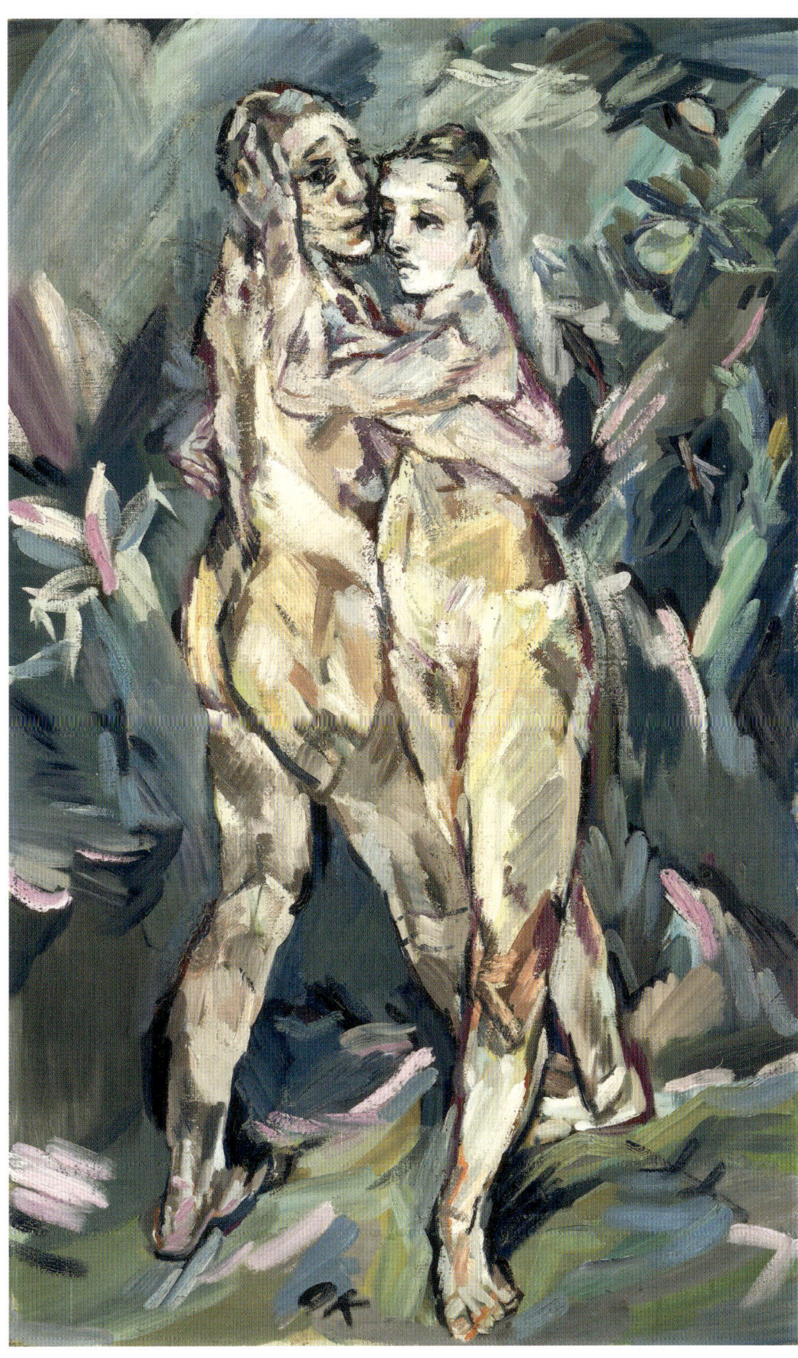

Tormented self-portrait by Kokoschka and his lover, Alma Malher, which attests to the complexity of their relationship.

Kokoschka und seine Geliebte Alma Mahler in einem qualvollen Selbstbildnis, das die Vielschichtigkeit ihrer Beziehung widerspiegelt.

Gekweld zelfportret van Kokoschka en zijn minnares Alma Malher, dat de gecompliceerdheid van hun relatie weergeeft.

Autorretrato atormentado de Kokoschka y de su amante Alma Malher, que testimonia la complejidad de su relación.

Oskar Kokoschka
(Pöchlarn 1886 - Montreux 1980)

**Self-Portrait with hand
on his face
Selbstbildnis, die Hand
ans Gesicht gelegt
Zelfportret met de hand op
het gezicht
Autorretrato con mano
sobre la cara**

●

1918-1919
83,6 x 62,7 cm / 32.9 x 24.7 in.
Leopold Museum, Wien

oil on canvas / Öl auf Leinwand
olieverf op doek / óleo sobre lienzo

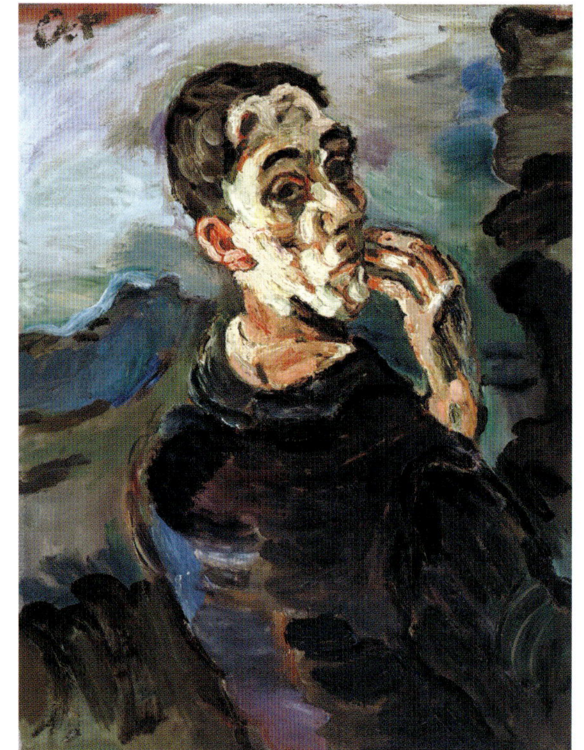

114

Oskar Kokoschka
(Pöchlarn 1886 - Montreux 1980)

**Lovers with cat
Liebespaar mit Katze
Geliefden met kat
Amantes con gato**

● ●

1917
93,5 x 130,5 cm / 36.84 x 51.42 in.
Kunsthaus, Zurich

oil on canvas / Öl auf Leinwand
olieverf op doek / óleo sobre lienzo

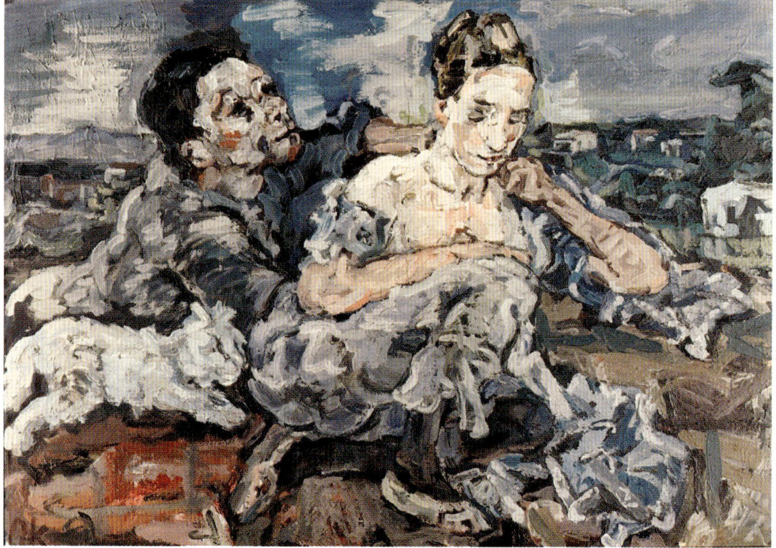

Oskar Kokoschka
(Pöchlarn 1886 - Montreux 1980)

Emil Loewenbach

●

1914

125 x 79 cm / 49.2 x 31.1 in.

Neue Galerie, New York

oil on canvas / Öl auf Leinwand
olieverf op doek / óleo sobre lienzo

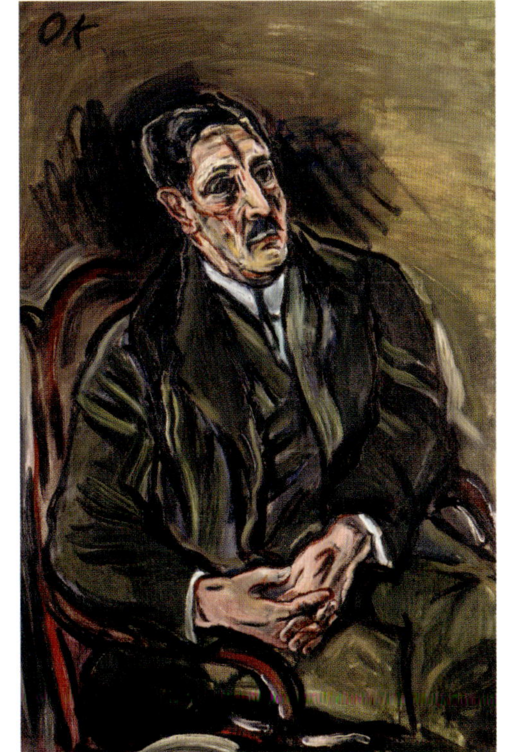

115

Oskar Kokoschka
(Pöchlarn 1886 - Montreux 1980)

**Landscape of the Dolomites
with the 'Cima Tre Croci'
Dolomitenlandschaft
mit der Cima Tre Croci
Dolomietenlandschap
met de bergtop 'Tre Croci'
Paisaje de los Dolomitas
con la 'Cima Tres Cruces'**

●●●

1913

79,5 x 120,3 cm / 31.3 x 47.4 in.

Leopold Museum, Wien

oil on canvas / Öl auf Leinwand
olieverf op doek / óleo sobre lienzo

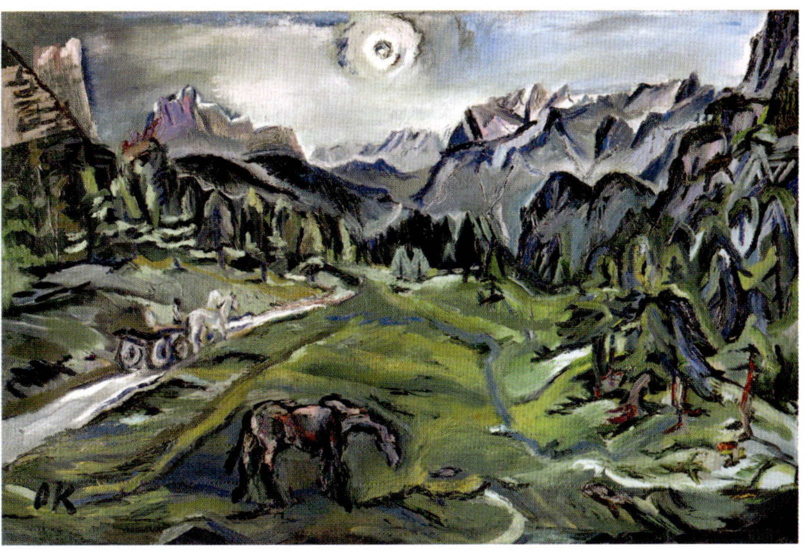

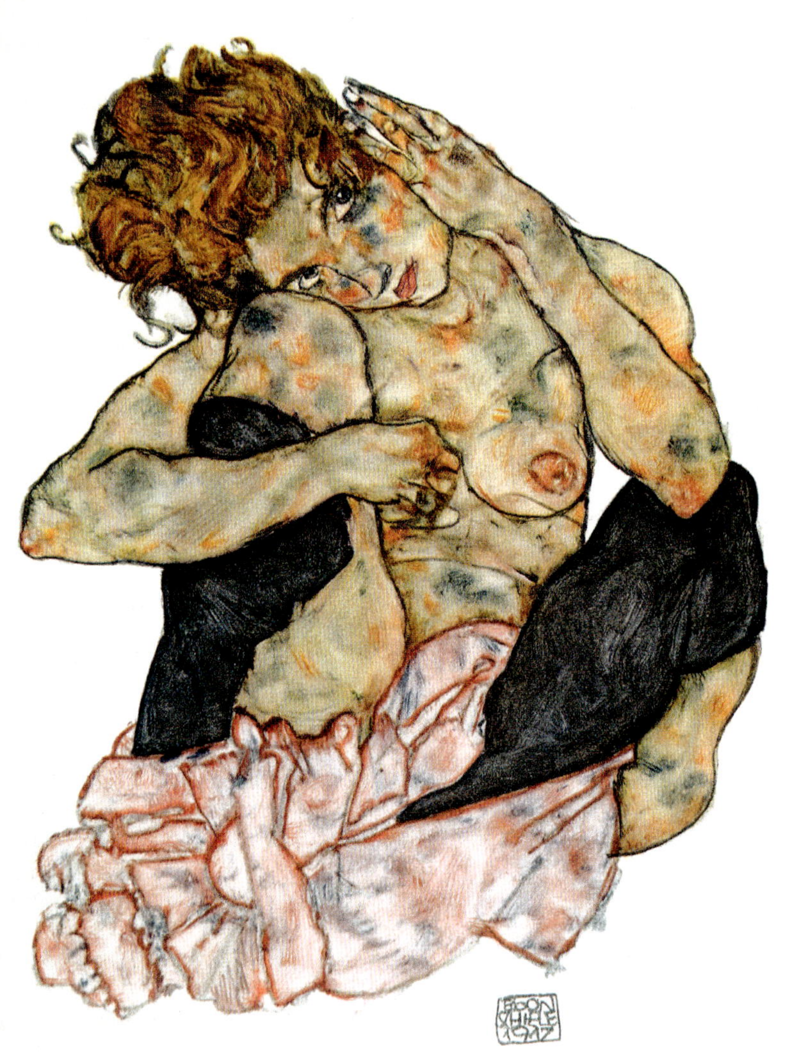

Egon Schiele
(Tulln 1890 - Wien 1918)

Female nude squatting, with neck bent over right knee
Kauernder Mädchenakt, die Wange auf das rechte Knie lehnend
Gehurkt vrouwelijk naakt met haar nek leunend op haar rechterknie
Desnudo femenino en cuclillas, con el cuello inclinado sobre la rodilla derecha

●●●

1917
95 x 60 cm / 37.4 x 23.6 in.
Private collection / Private Sammlung
Privécollectie / Colección privada

gouache, black pastel on paper
Gouache, schwarzes Pastell auf Papier
goauche, zwarte pastel op papier
gouache, pastel negro sobre papel

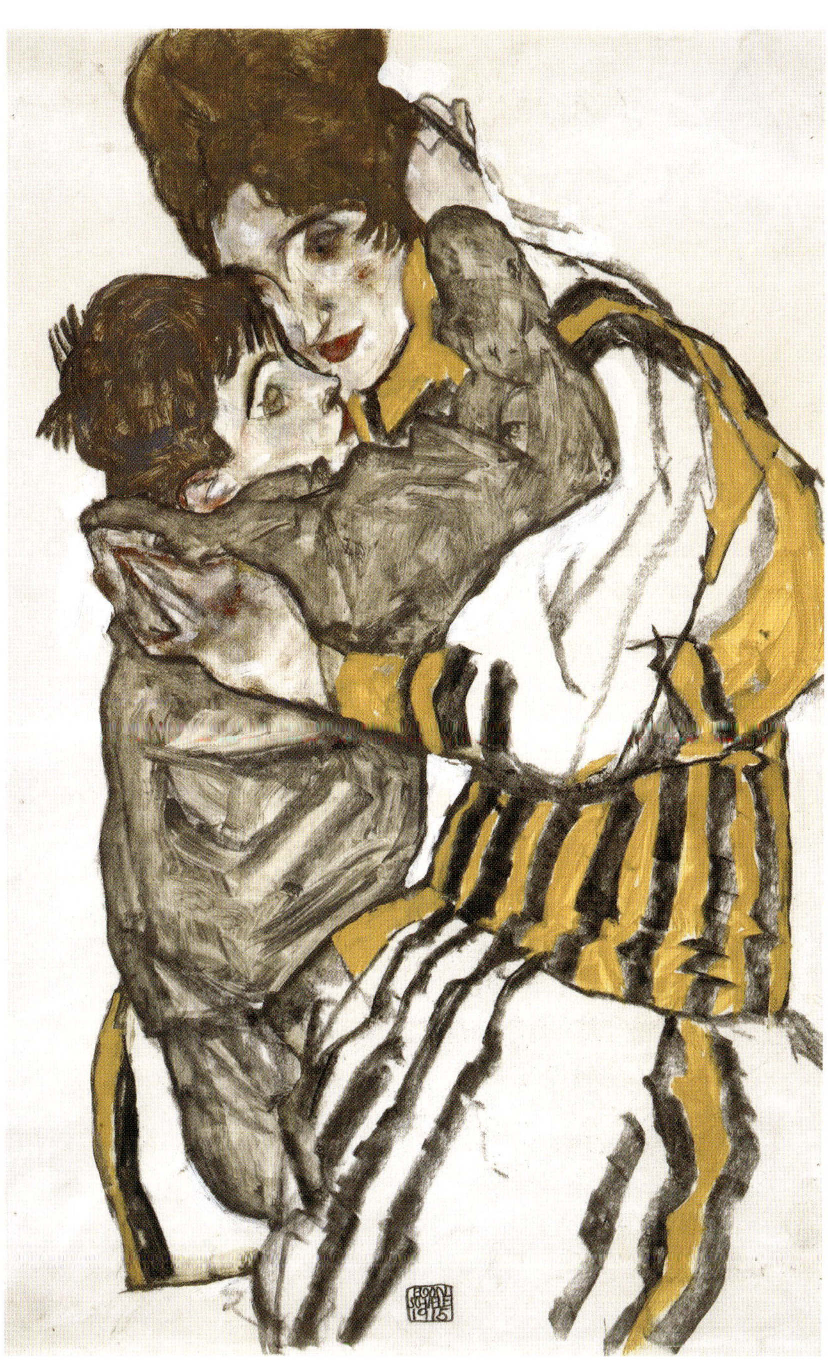

Egon Schiele
(Tulln 1890 - Wien 1918)
**Schiele's wife
and his nephew
Schieles Frau
mit seinem Neffen
De vrouw van Schiele
en zijn kleinkind
La mujer de Schiele
y su sobrinito**

●●

1915
48,3 x 31,8 cm / 19 x 12.5 in.
Museum of Fine Arts, Boston

charcoal and watercolor, opaque and
transparent on paper
Zeichenkohle und Aquarell, opak
und transparent auf Papier
houtskool en aquarel, ondoorzichtig
en doorzichtig op papier
carboncillo y acuarela, opaco
y transparente sobre papel

**Portrait of woman with
wide hat. Postcard of the
'Wiener Werkstaette'
(Nr. 289)**
**Rothaarige Dame mit
Hut. Karte der 'Wiener
Werkstaette' (Nr. 289)**
**Portret van een vrouw
met een brede hoed.
Ansichtkaart van de
'Wiener Werkstaette'
(Nr. 289)**
**Retrato de mujer con
sombrero ancho. Postal de
las 'Wiener Werkstaette'
(Nr. 289)**

●●

1910
Private collection
Private Sammlung
Privécollectie
Colección privada

118

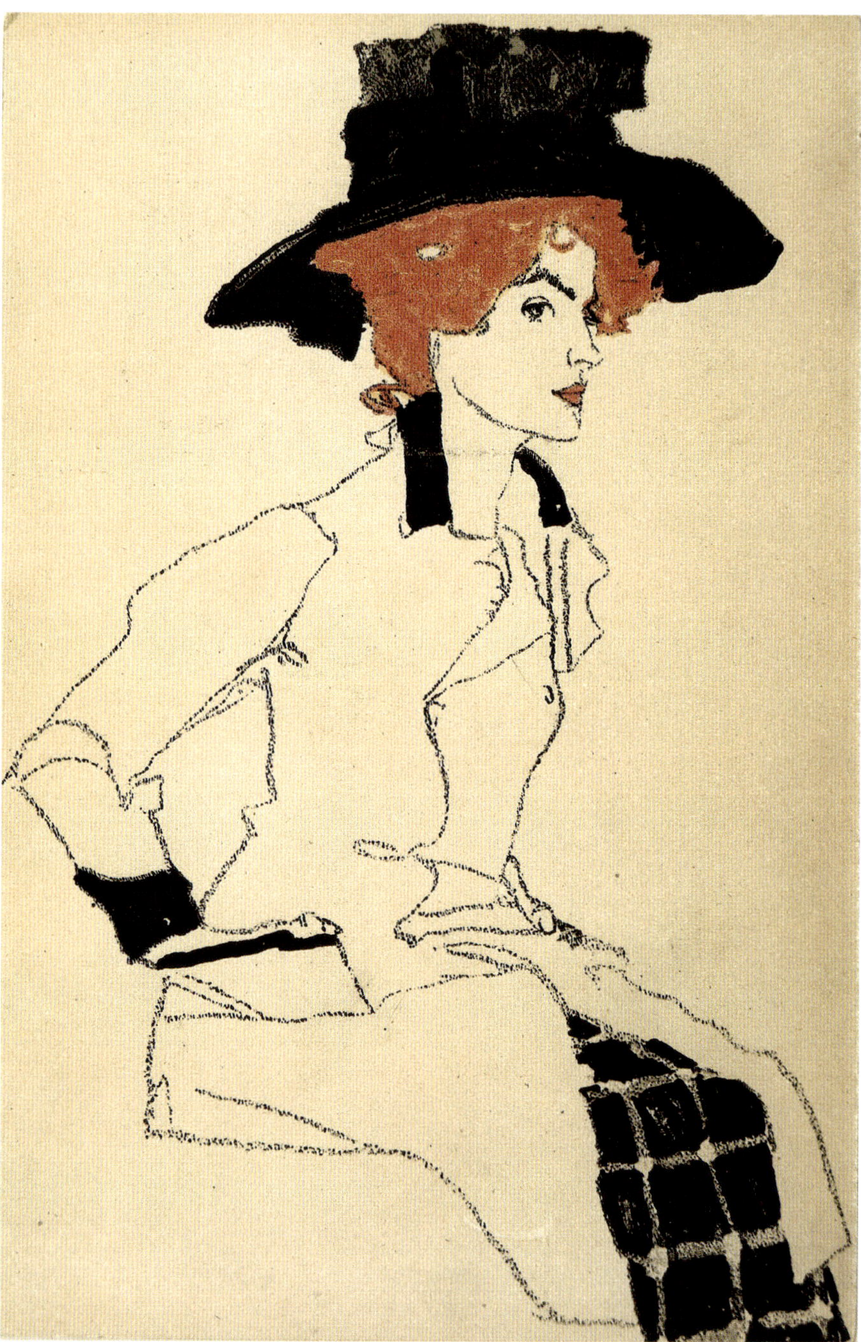

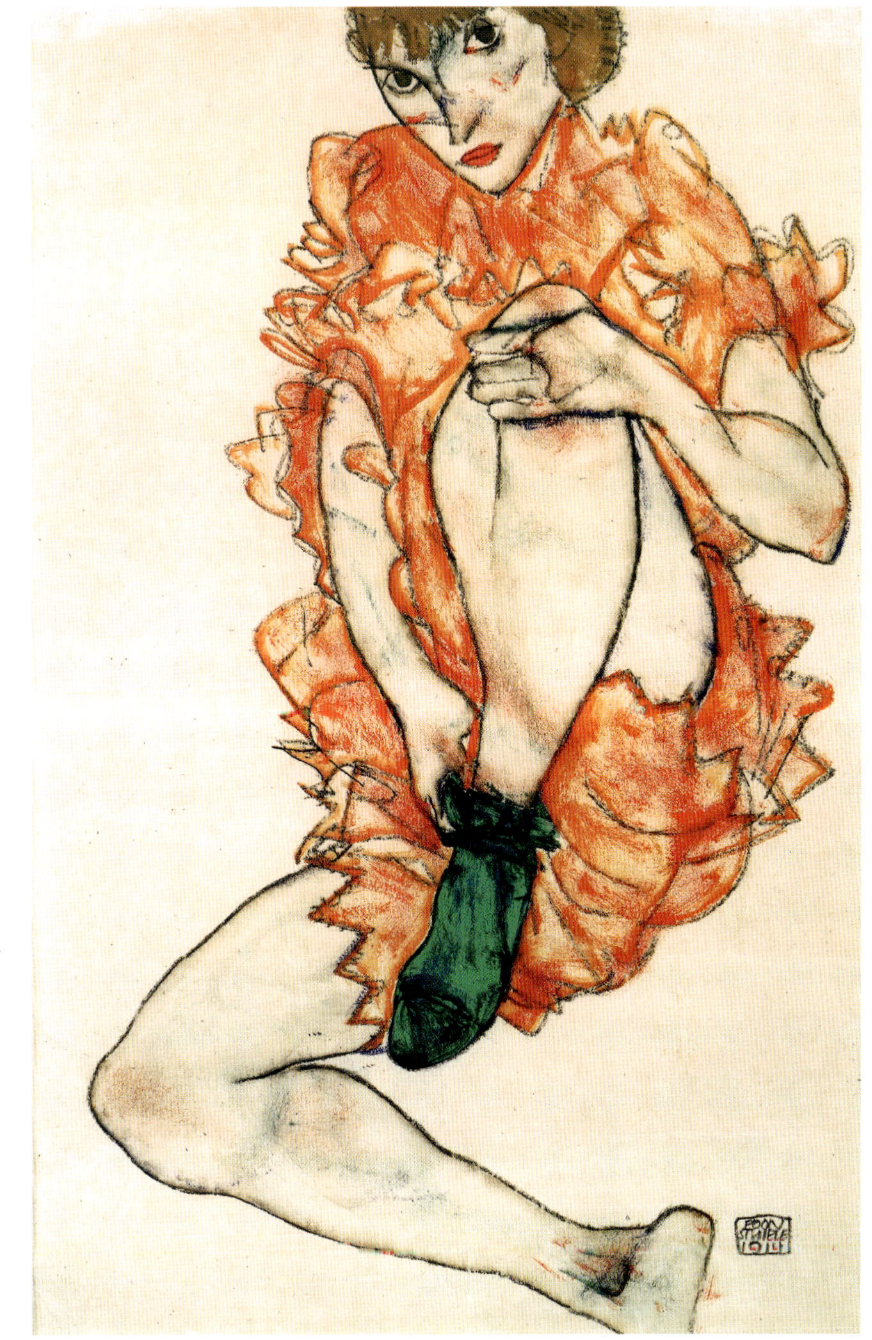

Egon Schiele
(Tulln 1890 - Wien 1918)
The green sock
Der grüne Strumpf
De groene kous
La media verde

●

1914
47 x 29,2 cm / 18.5 x 11.5 in.
rivate collection / Private Sammlung
Privécollectie / Colección privada

gouache and pencil on paper
Gouache und Bleistift auf Papier
gouache en potlood op papier
gouache y lápiz sobre papel

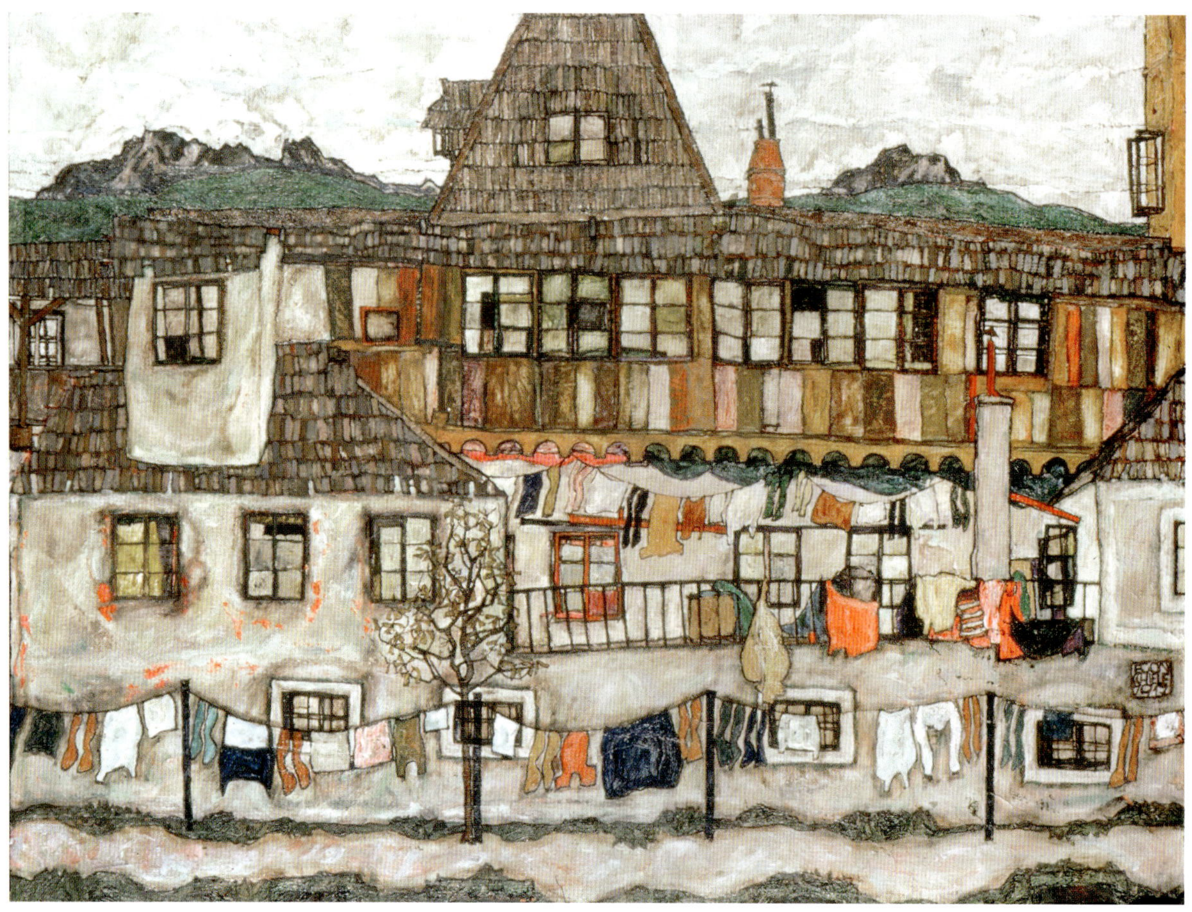

Egon Schiele
(Tulln 1890 - Wien 1918)

House with laundry drying
Hauswand am Fluss
Huis met wasgoed
Casa con ropa tendida

●●

1917
110 x 140,4 cm / 43.3 x 55.3 in.
Leopold Museum, Wien

canvas / Leinwand / doek / lienzo

This dance of sheets hung to dry in the foreground breaks the repetitive linearity of the facades and gives the composition rhythm and life.

Dieser Tanz von zum Trocknen aufgehängten Laken im Vordergrund bricht die eintönige Linearität der Fassaden und bringt Rhythmus und Leben in die Komposition.

Deze dans van te drogen gehangen lakens op de voorgrond breekt de herhaaldelijke rechtlijnigheid van de voorgevels en brengt ritme en leven in de compositie.

Esta danza de sábanas tendidas a secarse en primer plano rompe la linealidad repetitiva de las fachadas y da ritmo y vida a la composición.

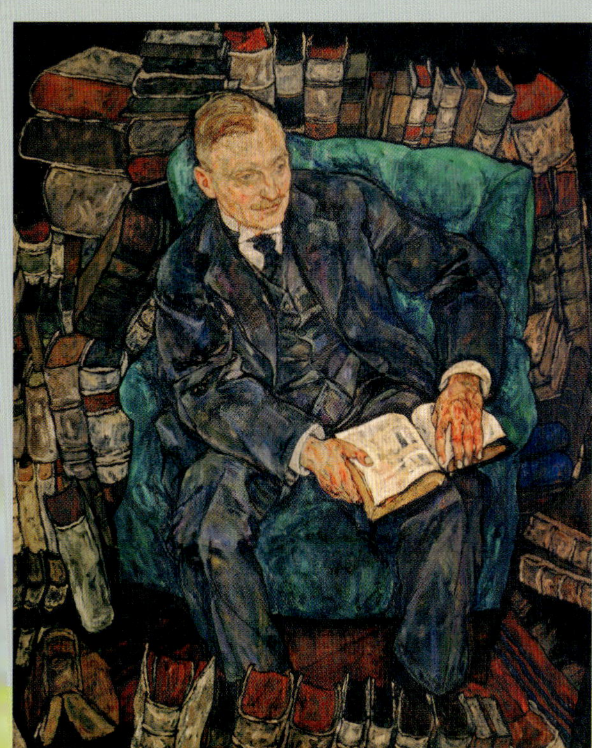

Egon Schiele
(Tulln 1890 - Wien 1918)

Portrait of Doctor Hugo Koller
Porträt des Hugo Koller
Portret van Dr. Hugo Koller
Retrato del doctor Hugo Koller

●●●

1919
140,3 x 109,6 cm / 55.2 x 75 in.
Österreichische Galerie Belvedere, Wien

oil on canvas / Öl auf Leinwand
olieverf op doek / óleo sobre lienzo

Egon Schiele
(Tulln 1890 - Wien 1918)

Self-portrait with fingers splayed
Selbstbildnis mit gespreizten Fingern
Zelfportret met gespreide vingers
Autorretrato con dedos abiertos

●●●

1911
27,5 x 34 cm / 10.8 x 13.4 in.
Historisches Museum der Stadt, Wien

oil on panel / Öl auf Tafel
olieverf op paneel / óleo sobre tabla

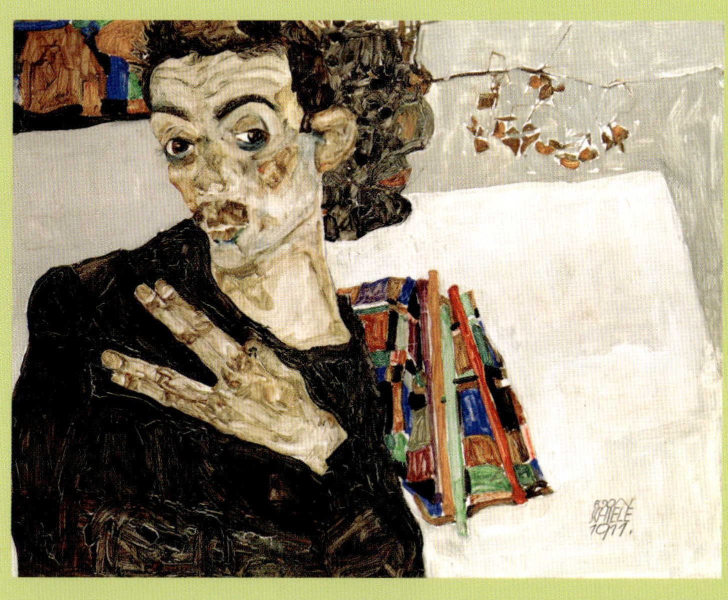

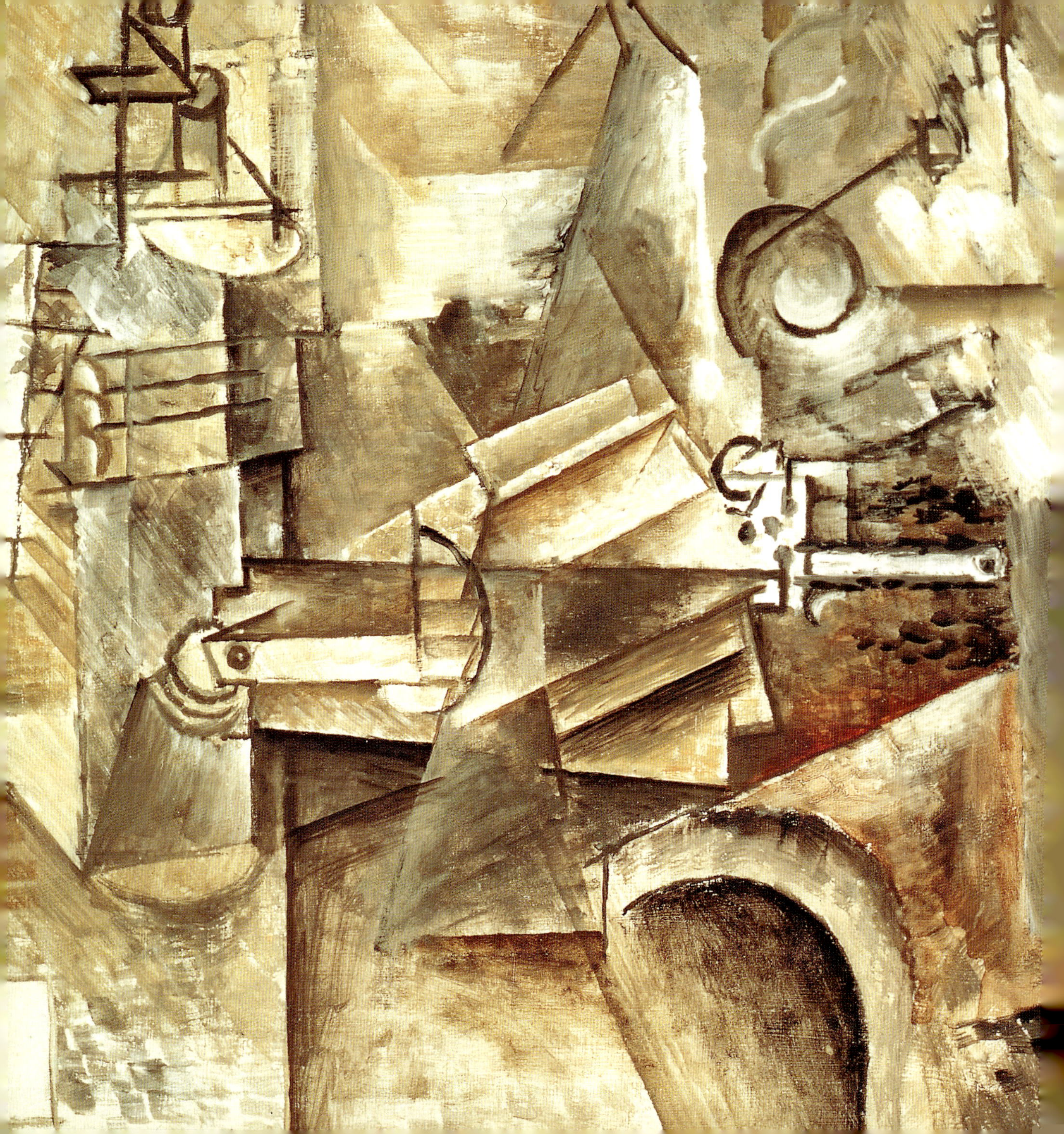

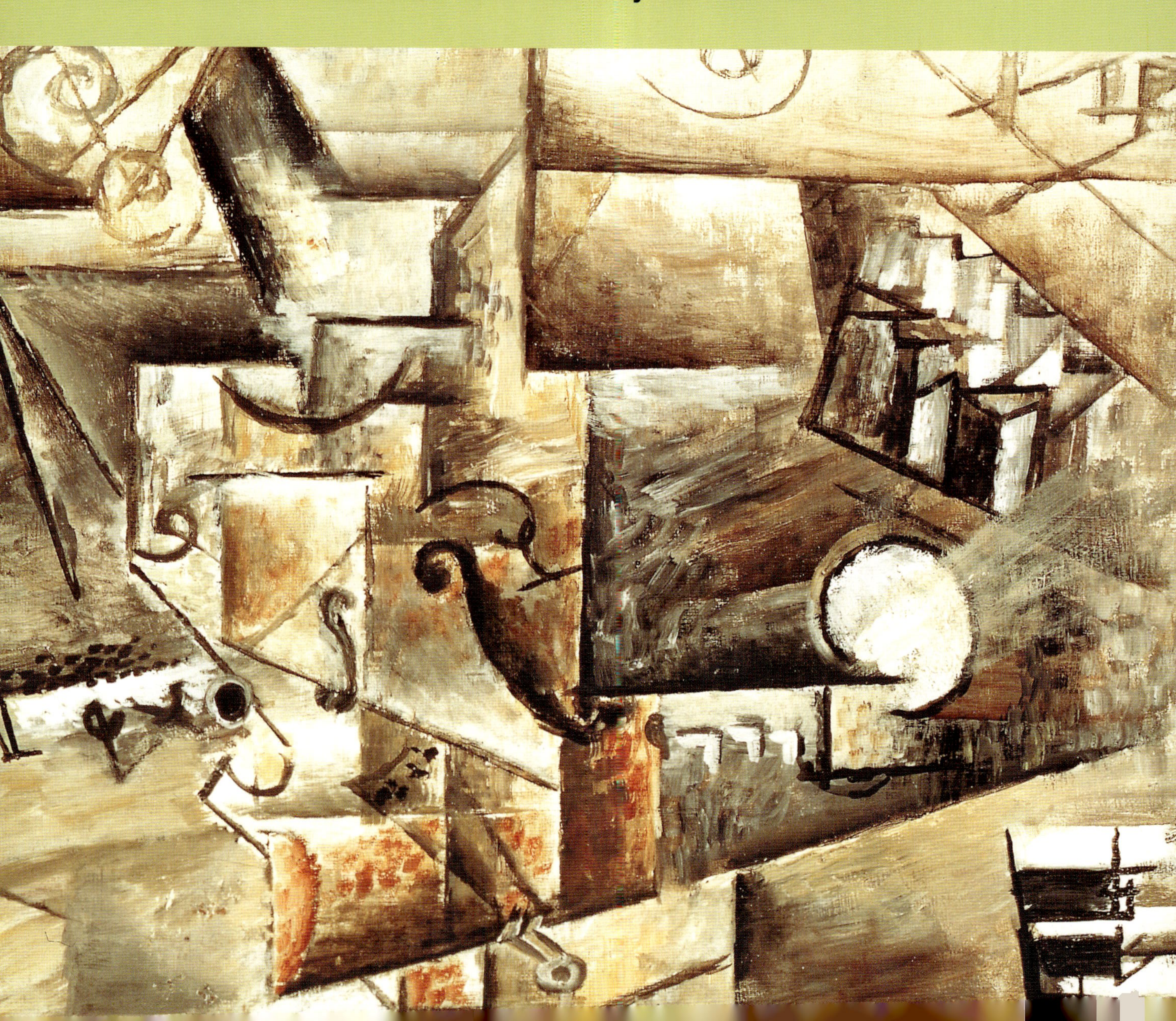
Cubism and Futurism • Der Kubismus und der Futurismus
Het Kubisme en Futurisme • El Cubismo y el Futurismo

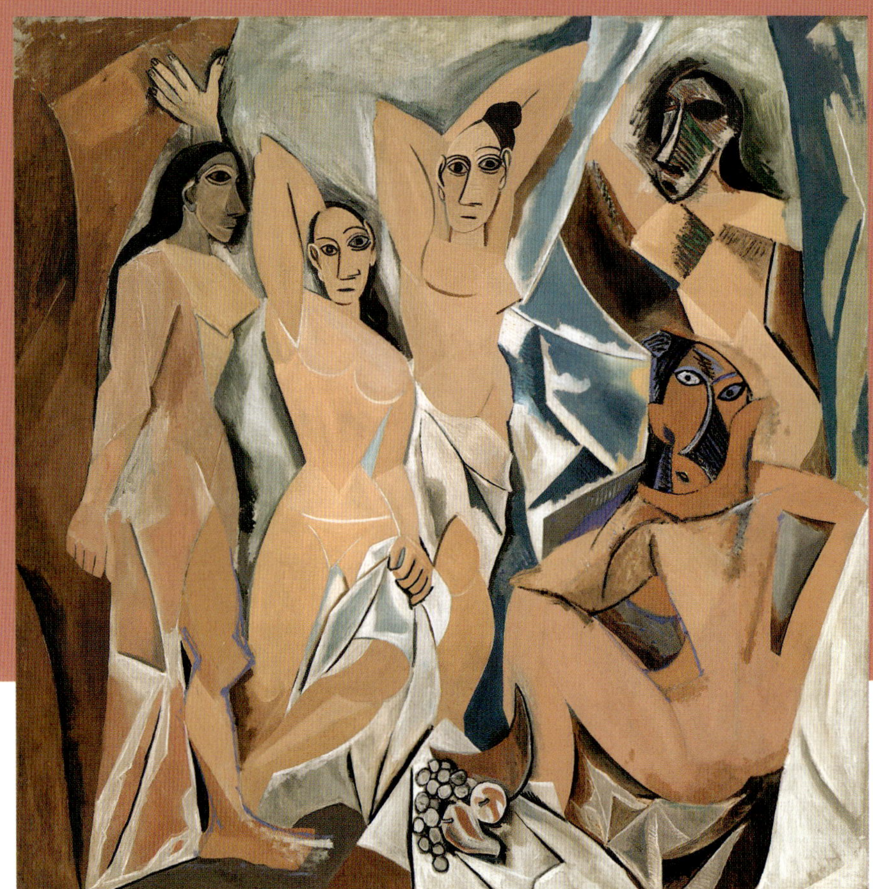

124

Pablo Picasso
(Málaga 1881 - Mougins 1973)
Les Demoiselles d'Avignon
●●●
1907
243,9 x 233,7 cm / 96 x 92 in.
Museum of Modern Art (MoMA),
New York

oil on canvas / Öl auf Leinwand
olieverf op doek / óleo sobre lienzo

**Geometrization of the forms, abandonment of
perspective and multiplication of the points of view,
cubism is born.**

**Geometrisierung der Formen, Verzicht auf Perspektive,
Multiplikation der Blickpunkte.
So entsteht der Kubismus.**

**Gegeometriseerde vormen, afgevlakt perspectief,
meerdere standpunten: het kubisme is uitgevonden.**

**Geometrización de las formas, abandono de la
perspectiva, multiplicación de los puntos de vista: nace
el cubismo.**

Pablo Picasso
(Málaga 1881 - Mougins 1973)

Woman with fan
Frau mit Fächer
Vrouw met waaier
Mujer con abanico

●●

1908
152 x 101 cm / 59.8 x 39.7 in.
The State Hermitage Museum,
St. Petersburg

oil on canvas / Öl auf Leinwand
olieverf op doek / óleo sobre lienzo

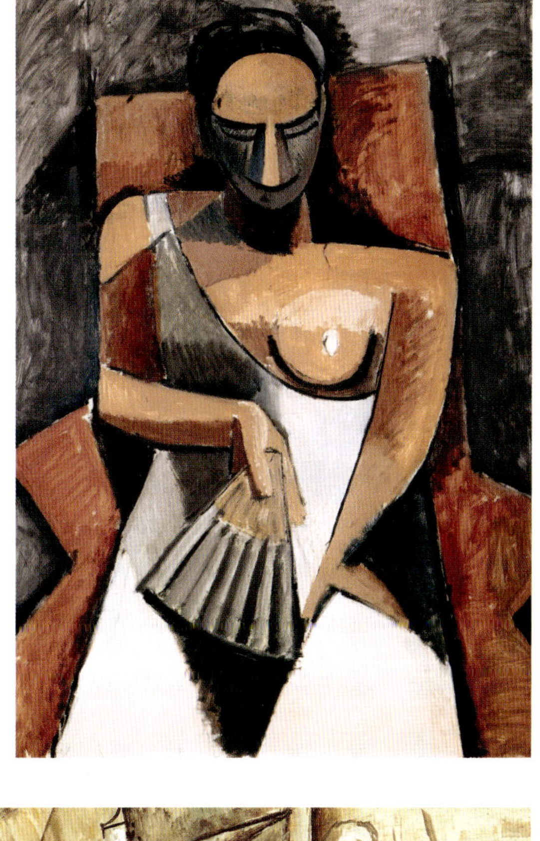

Pablo Picasso
(Málaga 1881 - Mougins 1973)

Still life on a piano
Stillleben auf einem Klavier
Stilleven op een piano
Naturaleza muerta sobre un piano

●

1911
50 x 130 cm / 19.7 x 51.2 in.
Gallerie Berggruen, Paris

oil on canvas / Öl auf Leinwand
olieverf op doek / óleo sobre lienzo

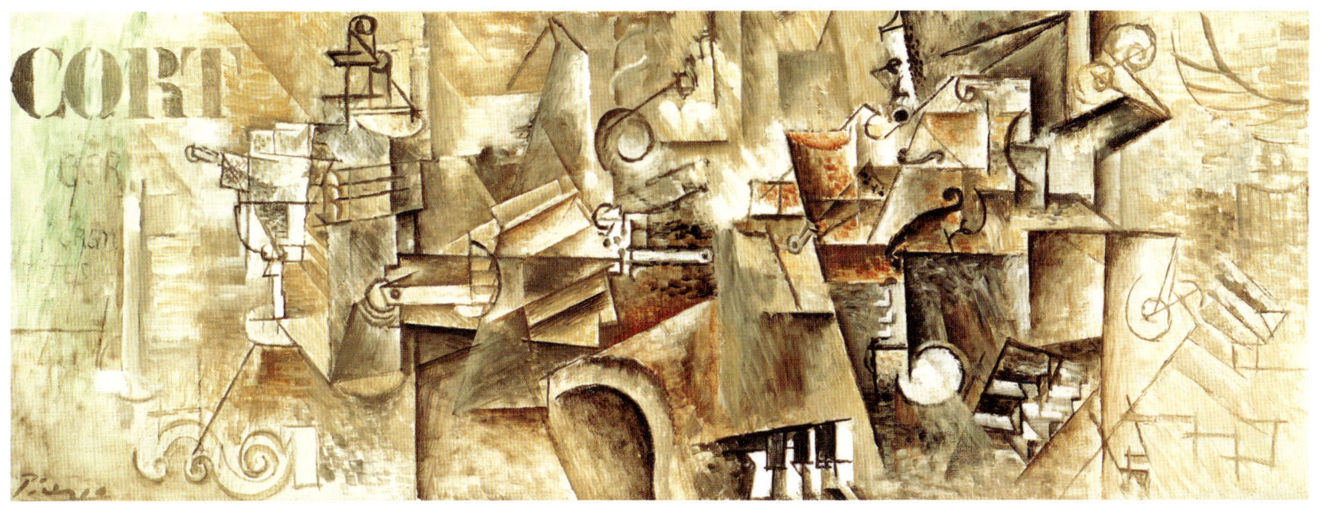

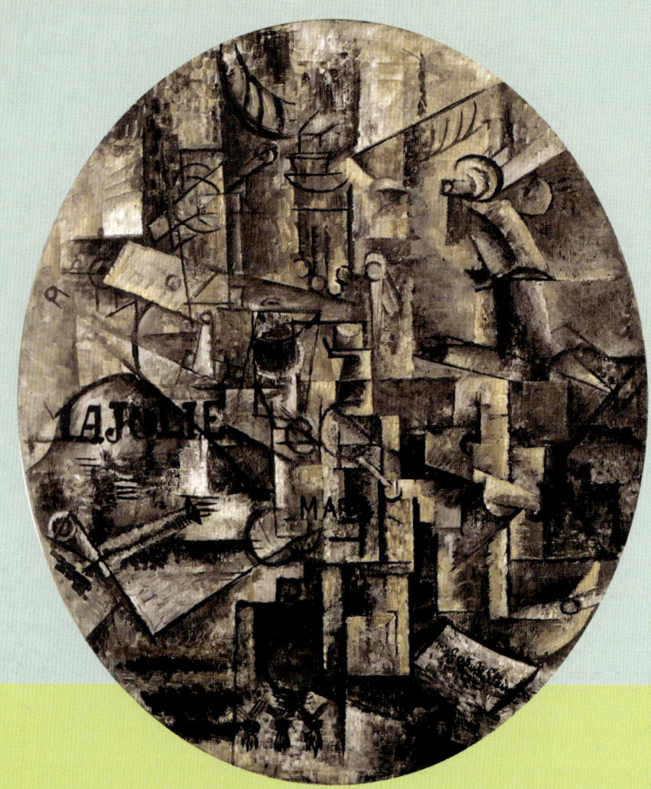

Pablo Picasso
(Málaga 1881 - Mougins 1973)

The Architect's Table
Tisch des Architekten
De tafel van de architect
La mesa del arquitecto

●

1912
72,6 x 59,7 cm / 28.6 x 23.5 in.
Museum of Modern Art (MoMA), New York

oil on canvas / Öl auf Leinwand
olieverf op doek / óleo sobre lienzo

126

Pablo Picasso
(Málaga 1881 - Mougins 1973)

Violin, glass, pipe and inkwell
Geige, Glas, Pfeife und Tintenfass
Viool, glas, pijp en inktpot
Violín, vaso, pipa y tintero

● ●

1912
81 x 54 cm / 31.9 x 9.2 in.
Národní Muzeum, Praha

oil on canvas / Öl auf Leinwand
olieverf op doek / óleo sobre lienzo

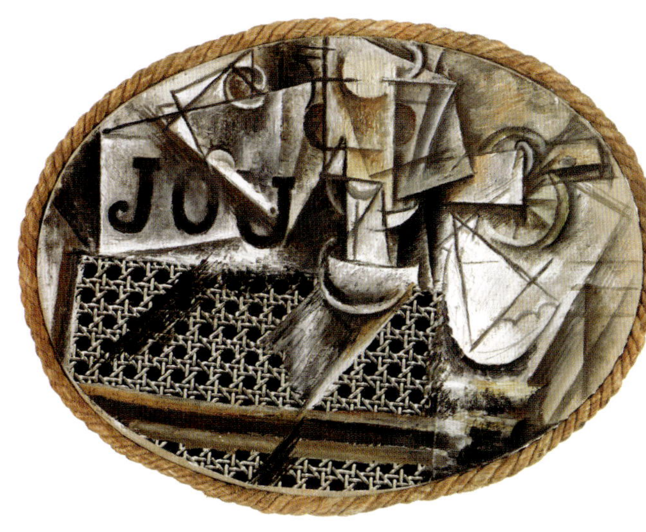

Pablo Picasso
(Málaga 1881 - Mougins 1973)

Still life with rush-covered chair
Stillleben mit Flechtstuhl
Stilleven met rieten stoel
Naturaleza muerta con silla de paja

●●●

1912
29 x 37 cm / 12.5 x 14.5 in.
Musée Picasso, Paris

oil on canvas, wax paper on canvas, strong
Öl auf Leinwand, Ölpapier auf Leinwand, Kordel
olieverf op doek, waspapier op doek, touw
óleo sobre lienzo, papel encerado sobre lienzo, cuerda

Pablo Picasso
(Málaga 1881 - Mougins 1973)

Tableau-relief: guitar and bottle of Bass
Tableau-Relief: Gitarre und Bass-Flasche
Tableaureliëf: gitaar en bass-fles
Cuadro-relieve: guitarra y botella de Bass

●

1913
89,5 x 80 x 14 cm / 35.2 x 31.5 x 5.5 in.
Musée Picasso, Paris

elements of fir partially painted and paper glued on wood
Tannenholzelemente teilweise bemalt und geleimtes Papier
delen van een spar gedeeltelijk geverfd en papier op hout geplakt
elementos de abeto parcialmente pintados y papel encolado
sobre madera

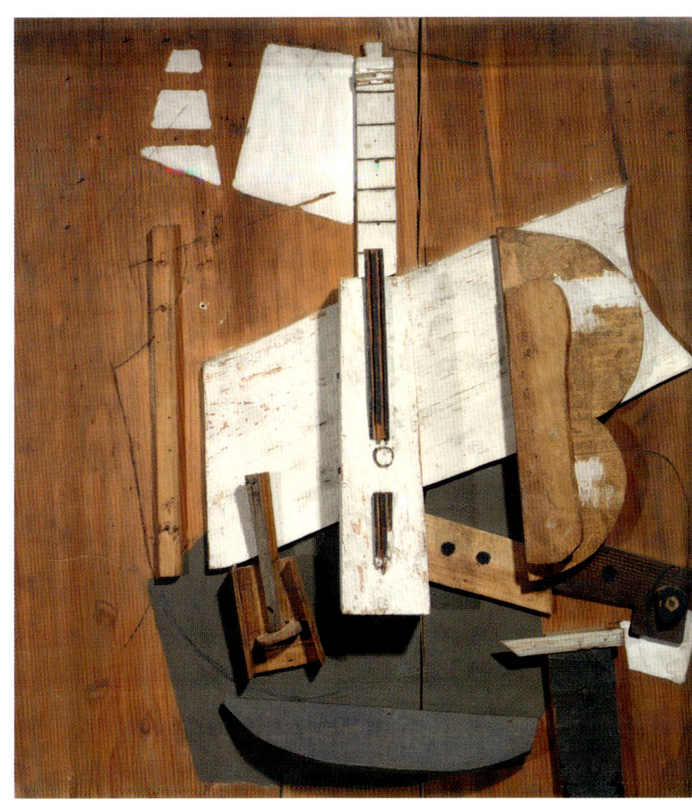

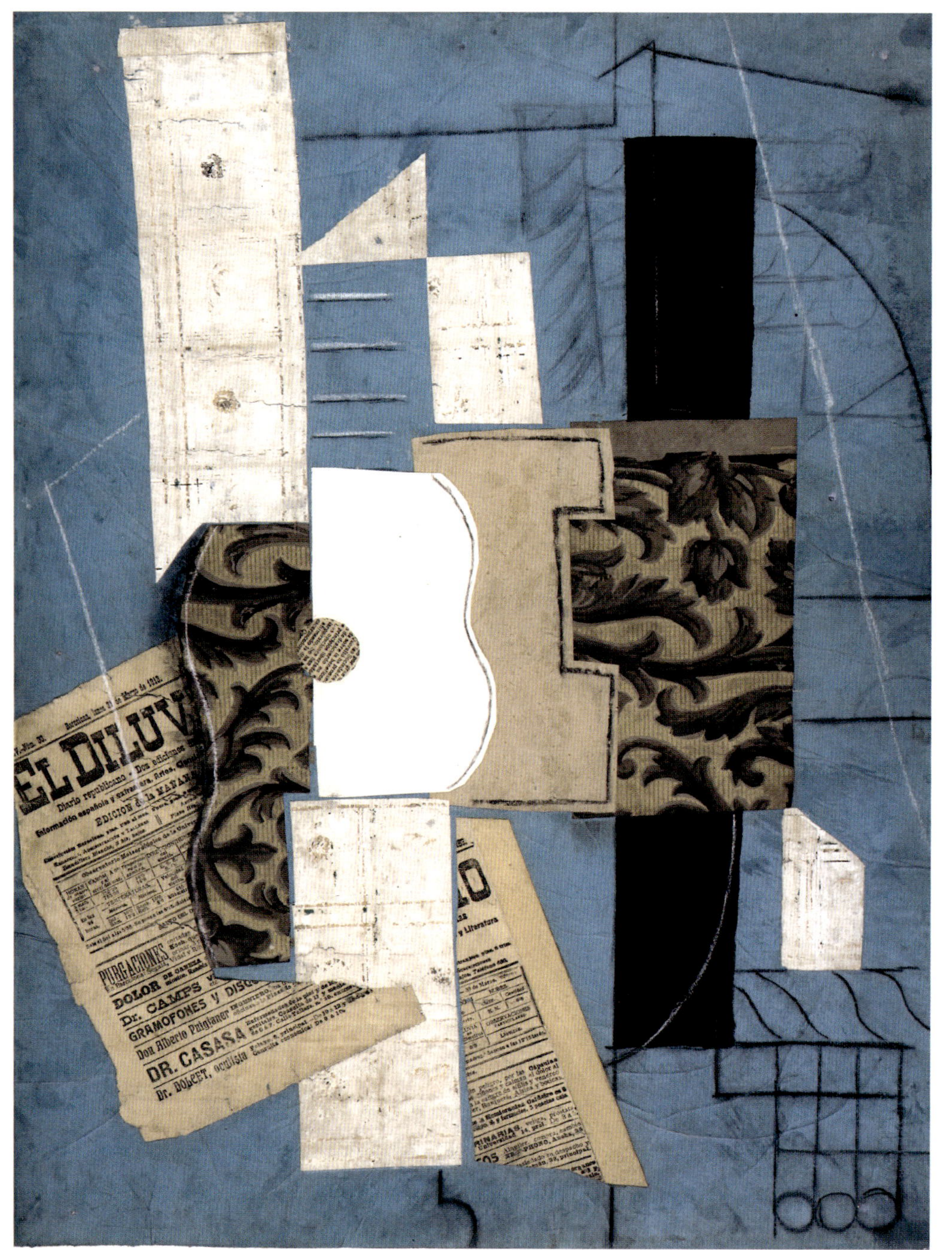

◀ **Pablo Picasso**
(Málaga 1881 - Mougins
1973)
Guitar
Gitarre
Gitaar
Guitarra
●●
1913
66,4 x 49,6 cm
26.1 x 19.5 in.
Museum of Modern Art
(MoMA), New York

glued paper, charcoal, ink,
chalk on blue paper mounted
on paperboard / geleimtes
Papier, Zeichenkohle, Tinte,
Kreide auf blauem Papier und
Kartonbasis / Gelijmd papier,
houtskool, inkt, krijt op blauw
papier geplakt op karton /
papel encolado, carboncillo,
tinta, tiza sobre papel azul
montado sobre cartón

▶ Pablo Picasso
(Málaga 1881 - Mougins 1973)
The violin
Die Violine
De viool
El violín
●
1914
81 x 75 cm / 31.9 x 29.5 in.
Centre Georges Pompidou,
Musée National d'Art Moderne,
Paris

oil on canvas / Öl auf Leinwand
olieverf op doek / óleo sobre
lienzo

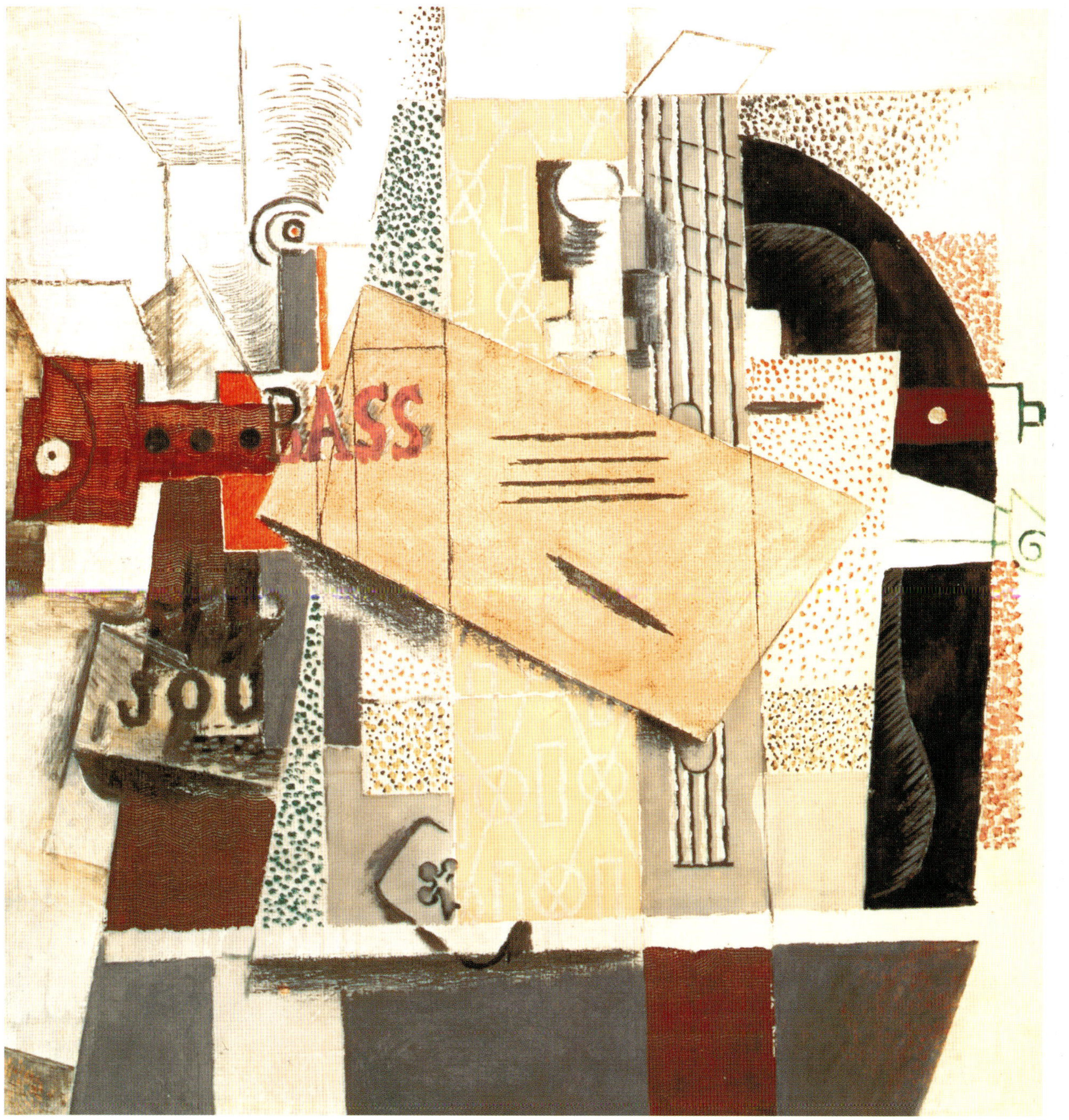

ASS
JOU

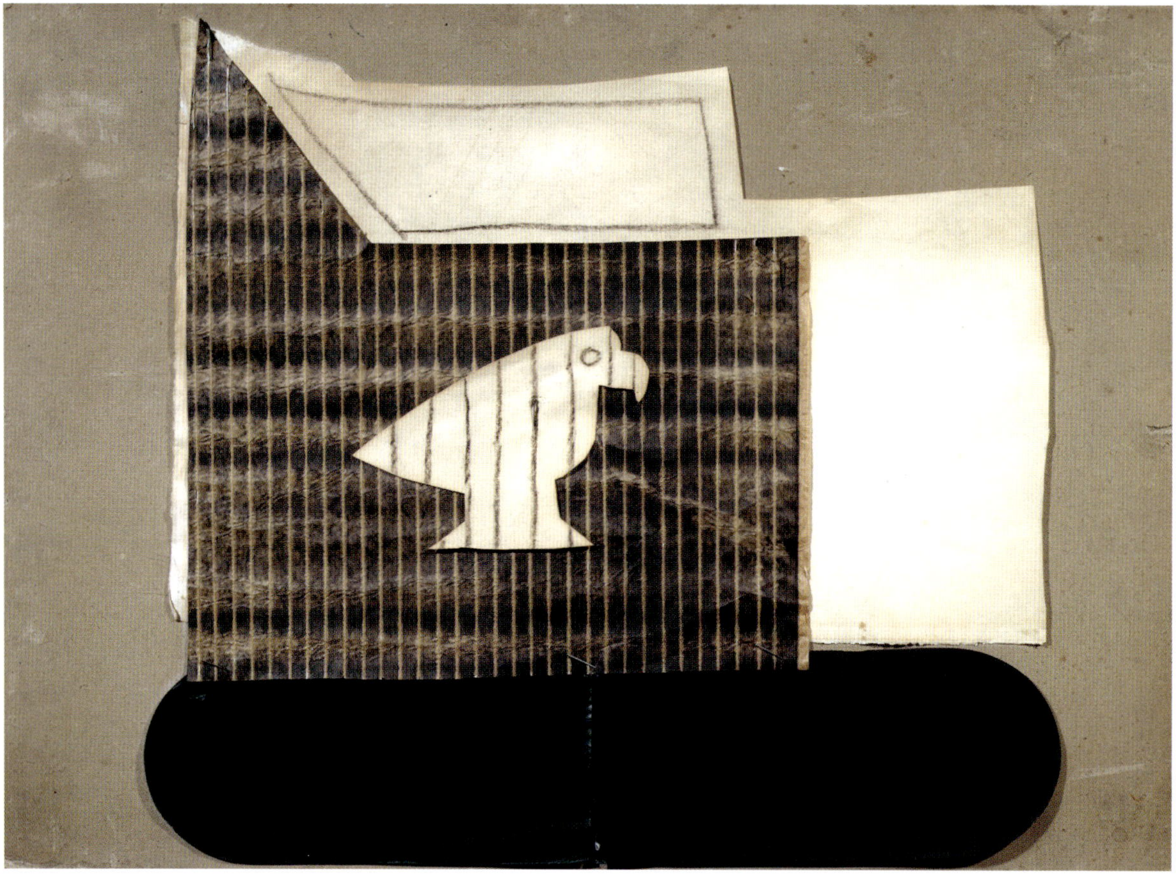

Pablo Picasso
(Málaga 1881 - Mougins 1973)

Bird in Cage / Vogel im Käfig
Vogel in kooi / Pájaro enjaulado

●

1919
41 x 59 cm / 16.1 x 23.2 in.
Musée Picasso, Paris

Glued paper. Tarred papers, pinned and charcoal on grey paperboard
Papiercollage. Kohlepapier, Stecknadeln und Zeichenkohle auf grauem Karton
Gelijmd papier. Vastgespeld asfaltpapier en houtskool op grijs karton
papel encolado. Papeles alquitranados sujetados con alfileres y carboncillo sobre cartón gris

▶ Pablo Picasso
(Málaga 1881 - Mougins 1973)

Portrait of Marie-Thérèse
Porträt von Marie-Thérèse
Portret van Marie-Thérèse
Retrato de Marie-Thérèse

●●

1937
100 x 81 cm / 39.3 x 31.9 in.
Musée Picasso, Paris

oil on canvas / Öl auf Leinwand
olieverf op doek / óleo sobre lienzo

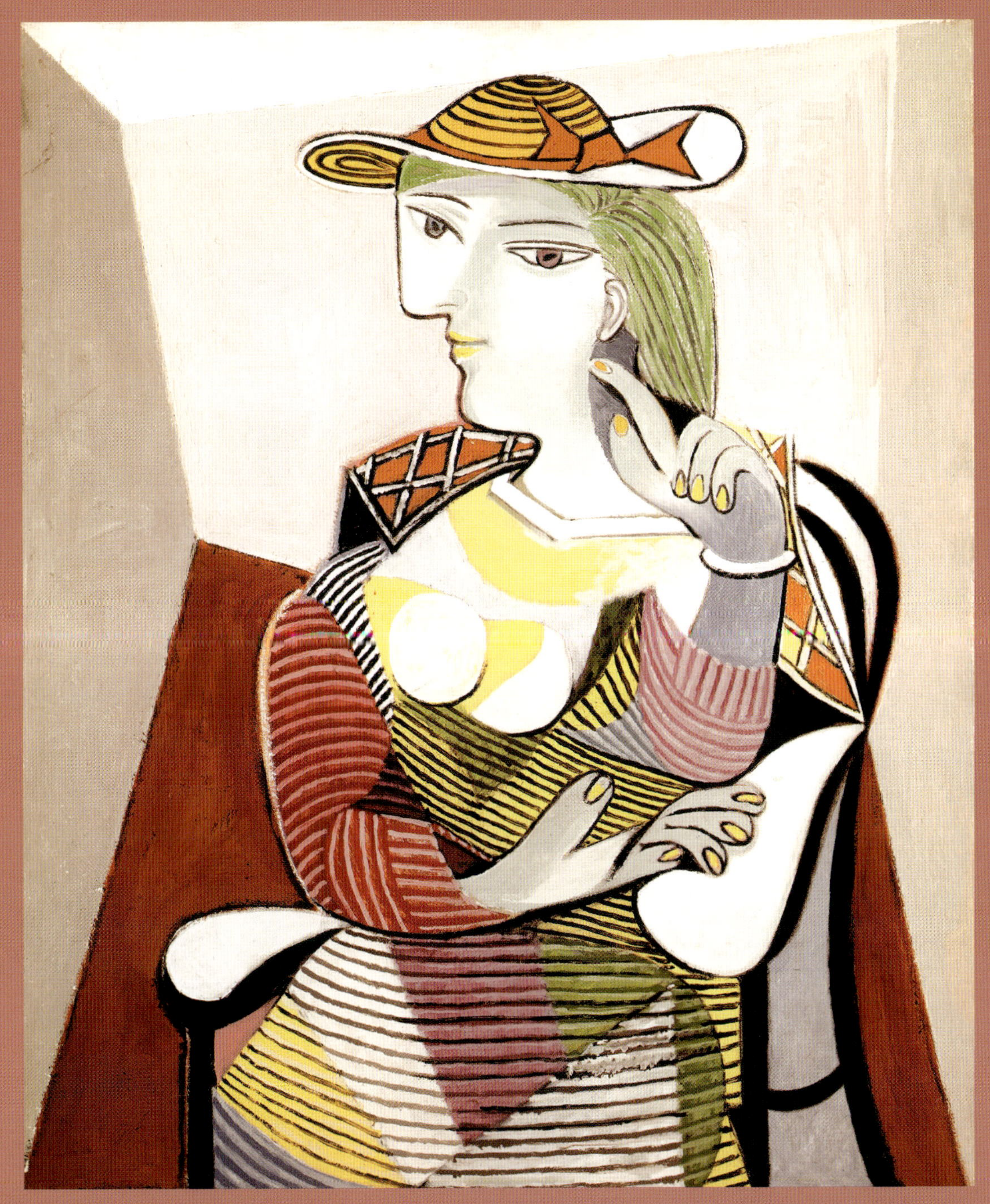

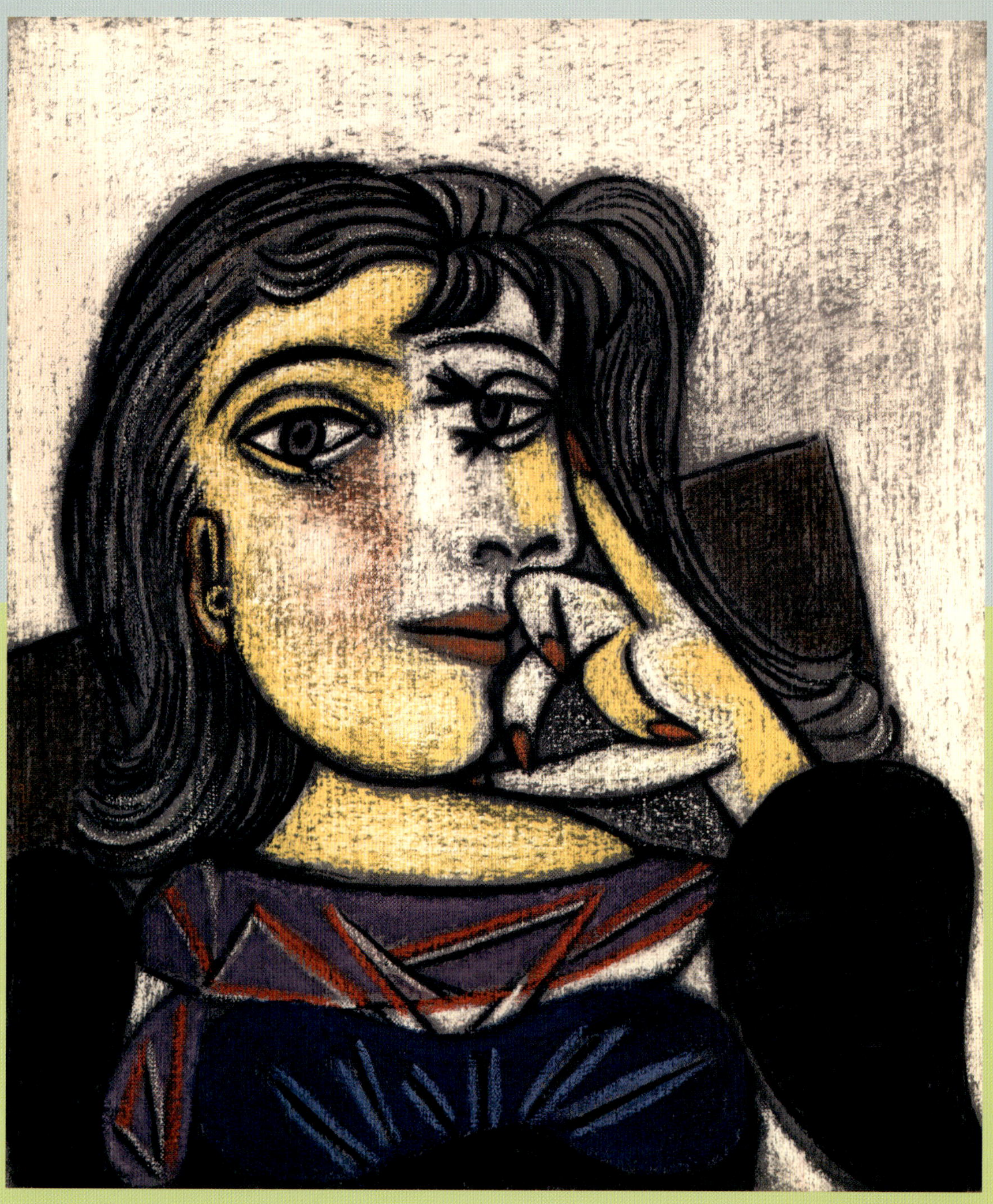

▶ Pablo Picasso
(Málaga 1881 - Mougins 1973)
Portrait of Marie Therese
Porträt von Marie-Thérèse
Portret van Marie-Thérèse
Retrato de Marie-Thérèse
●

1937
46 x 38 cm / 18.1 x 15 in.
Musée Picasso, Paris

oil and pencil on canvas
Öl und Bleistift auf Leinwand
olieverf en potlood op doek
óleo y lápiz sobre lienzo

◀ Pablo Picasso
(Málaga 1881 - Mougins 1973)
Portrait of Dora Maar
Porträt von Dora Maar
Portret van Dora Maar
Retrato de Dora Maar
●●

1937
55 x 45 cm / 21.6 x 17.7 in.
Musée Picasso, Paris

oil on canvas
Öl auf Leinwand
olieverf op doek
óleo sobre lienzo

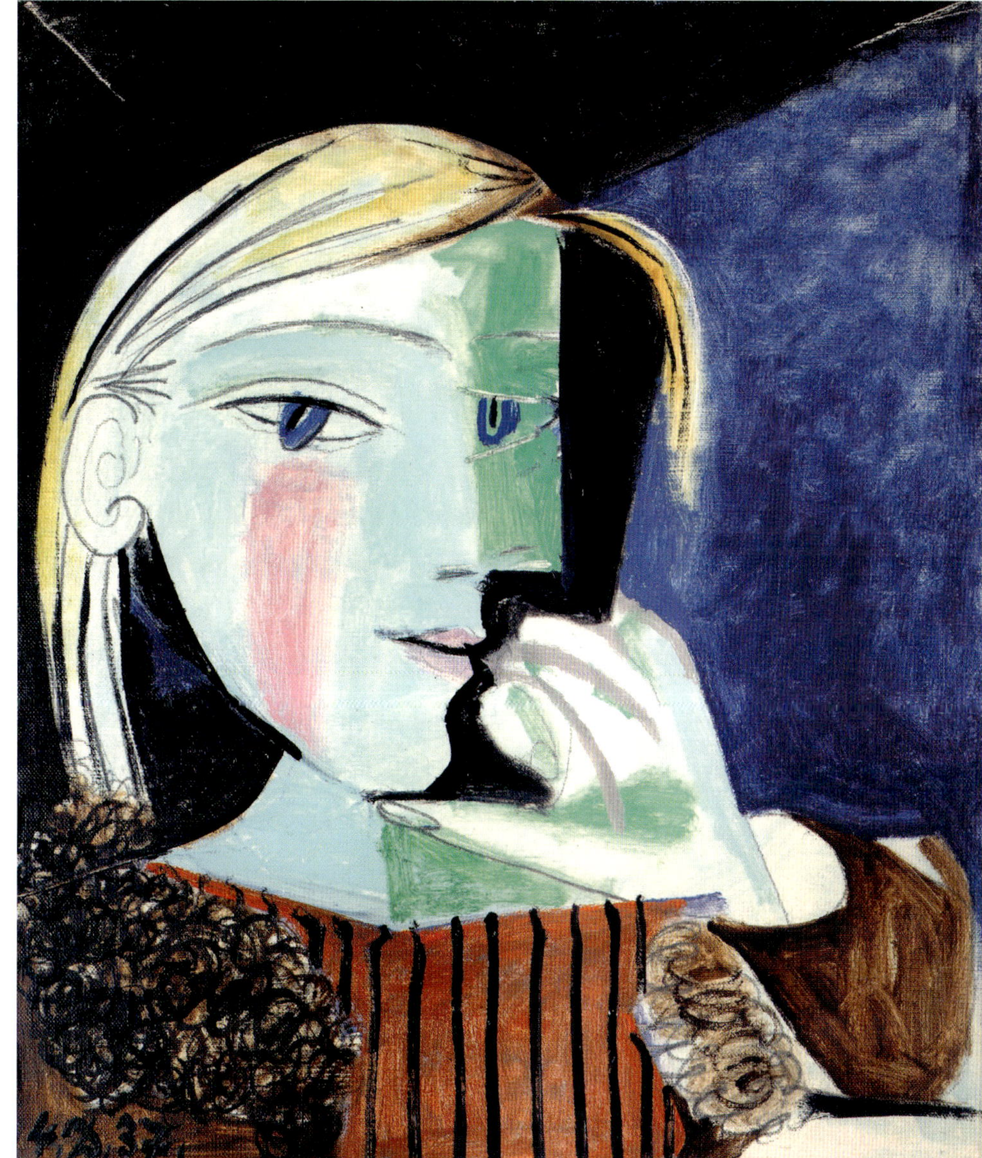

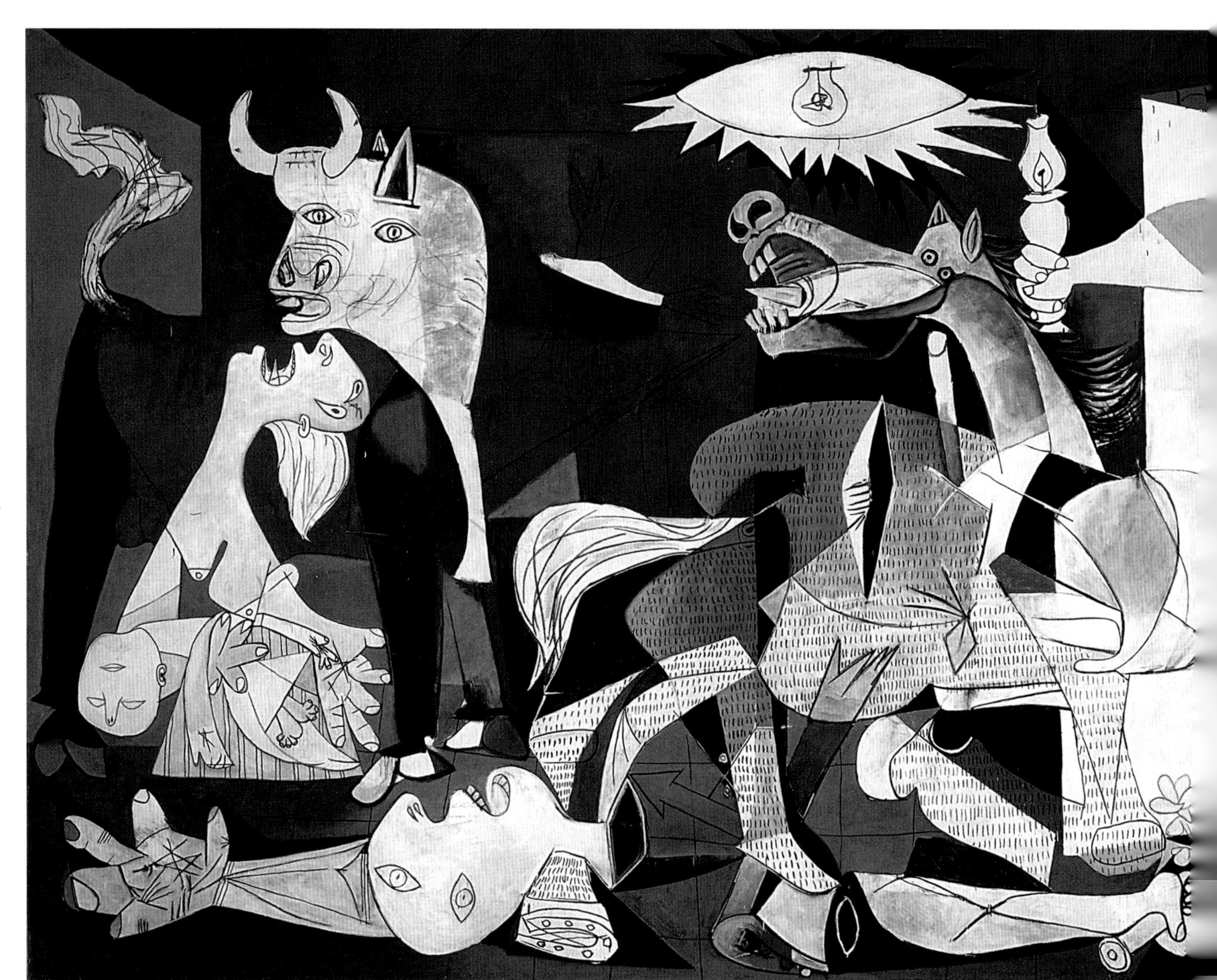

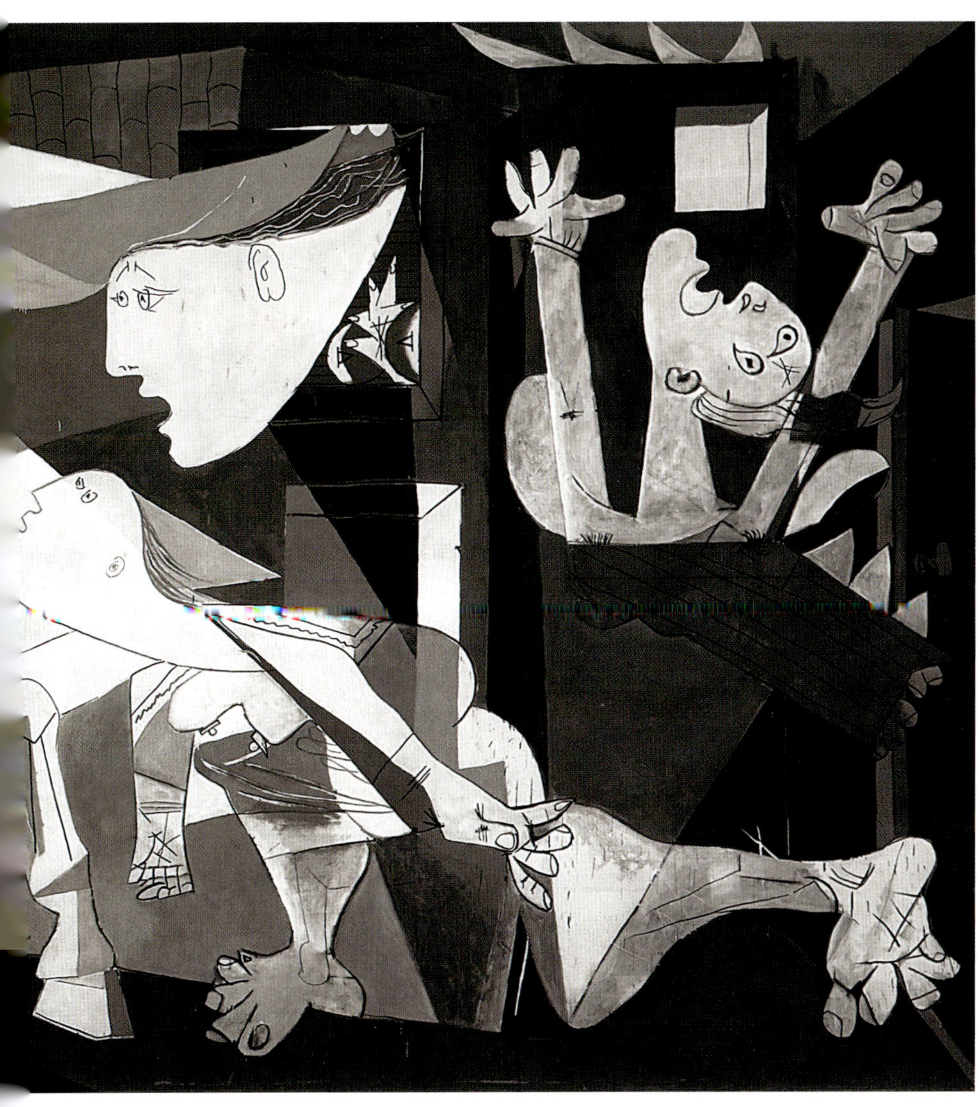

Pablo Picasso
(Málaga 1881 - Mougins 1973)

Guernica

●●●

1937
350 x 782 cm / 137.8 x 307.8 in.
Museo Nacional Centro de Arte
Reina Sofia, Madrid

oil on canvas / Öl auf Leinwand
olieverf op doek / óleo sobre lienzo

**What better style than cubism
to describe the horror of the
massacre and shout out one's
own pain?**

**Welcher Stil, wenn nicht der
Kubismus, ist geeigneter, die
Grauen des Massakers und die
Schmerzesschreie auszudrücken?**

**Welke stijl beter dan het
kubisme zou de gruwelijkheden
van het bloedbad en het
uitschreeuwen van pijn kunnen
uitbeelden?**

**¿Qué mejor estilo que el
cubismo para describir el
horror de la masacre y gritar el
propio dolor?**

135

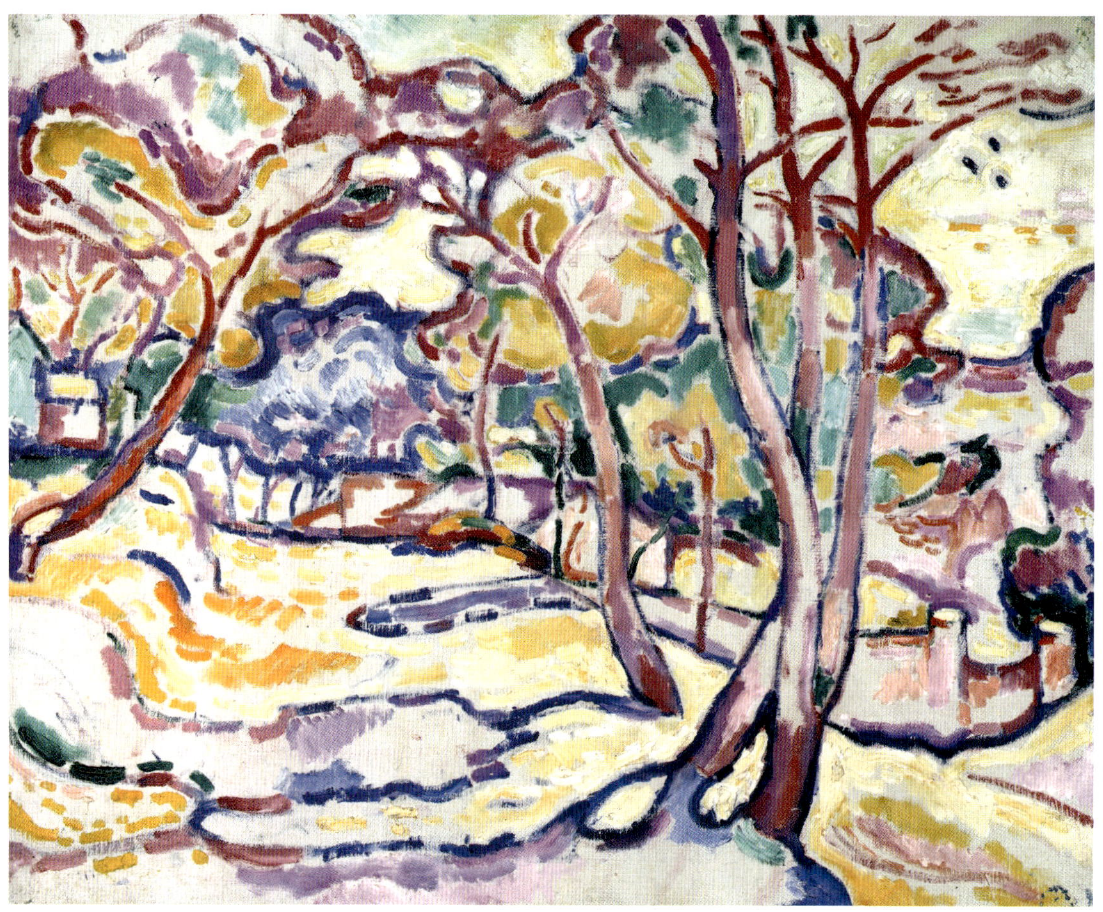

Georges Braque
(Argenteuil 1882 - Paris 1963)

**Landscape of L'Estaque
Landschaft bei L'Estaque
Landschap van L'Estaque
Paisaje de L'Estaque**

●●

1906
50 x 61 cm / 19.6 x 24 in.
Musée d'Orsay, Paris

oil on canvas / Öl auf Leinwand
olieverf op doek / óleo sobre lienzo

Braque, before meeting Picasso, had belonged to the Fauvist movement and exhibited in 1906 next to Matisse.

Bevor Braque Picasso kennen lernte, gehörte er der fauvistischen Bewegung an und hatte 1906 neben Matisse ausgestellt.

Braque had zich, nog voor hij Picasso ontmoette, aangesloten bij de fauvistische beweging en had in 1906 naast Matisse geëxposeerd.

Braque, antes de su encuentro con Picasso, había adherido al movimiento fauvista y expuesto en 1906 junto a Matisse.

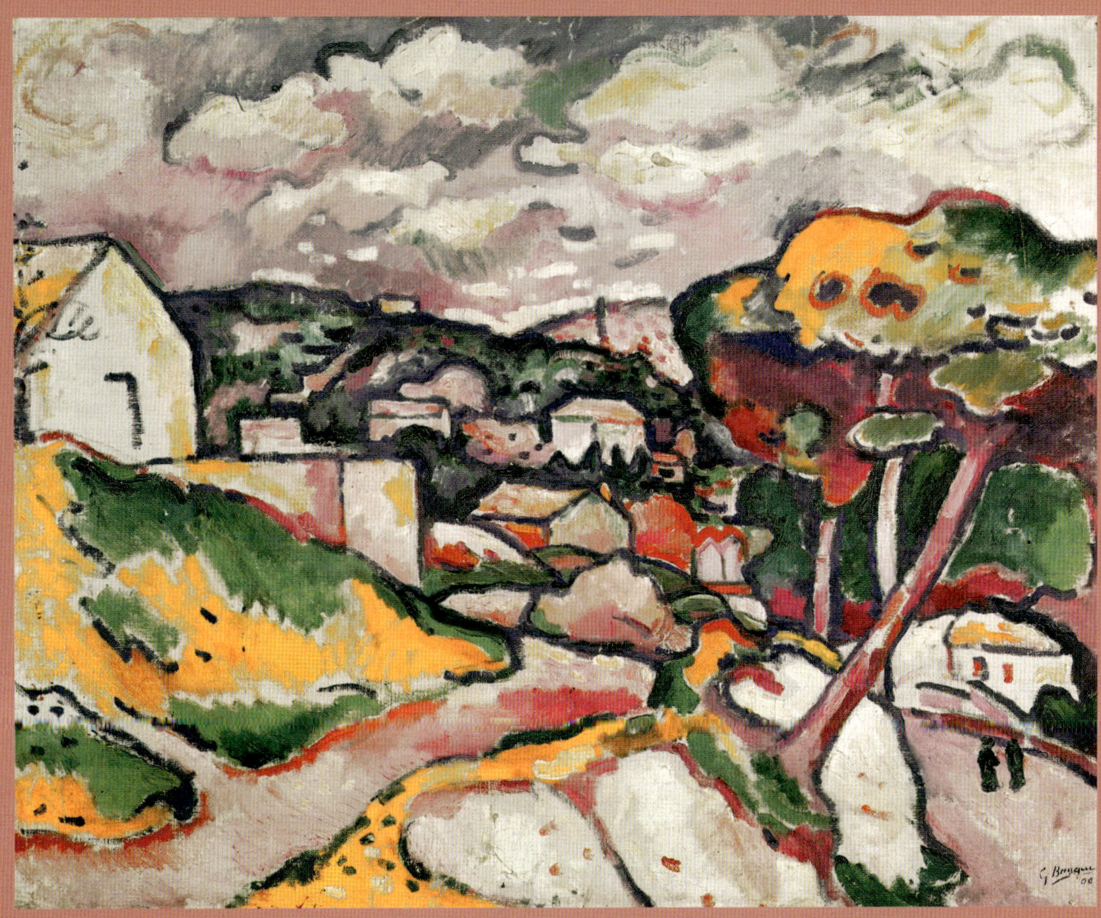

Georges Braque
(Argenteuil 1882 - Paris 1963)

L'Estaque

●

1906
60 x 73 cm / 23.6 x 28.7 in.
Musée de l'Annonciade, Saint-Tropez

oil on canvas / Öl auf Leinwand
olieverf op doek / óleo sobre lienzo

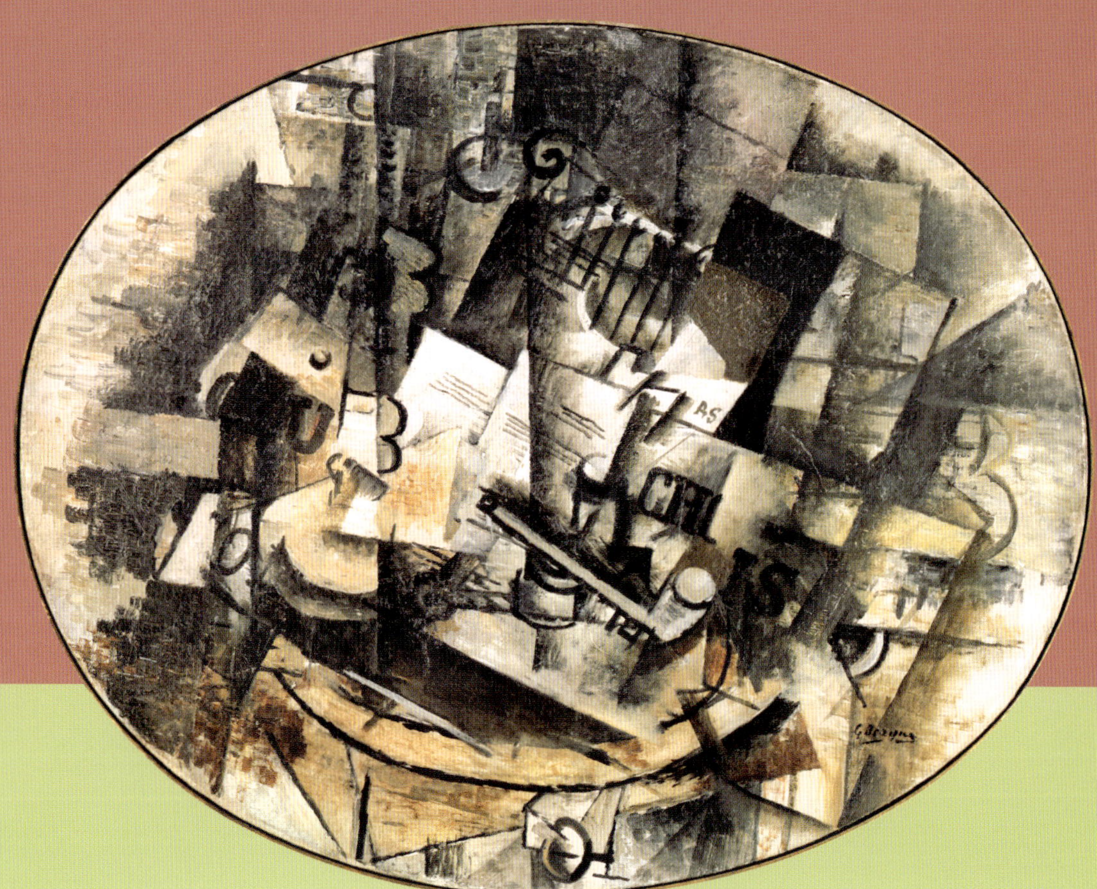

Georges Braque
(Argenteuil 1882 - Paris 1963)

Table with pipe
Tisch mit Pfeife
Tafel met pijp
Mesa con pipa

● ●

1912
23,4 x 73 cm / 23.6 x 28.7 in.
Stiftung Rosengart, Luzern

oil on canvas / Öl auf Leinwand
olieverf op doek / óleo sobre lienzo

Braque and Picasso acknowledged that if their works were not signed it was impossible for them to tell them apart.

Braque und Picasso erkannten, dass ihre jeweiligen Werke ohne Signatur nicht auseinander zu halten waren.

Braque en Picasso bekenden dat als zij hun werken niet zouden signeren, zij deze niet uit elkaar zouden kunnen houden.

Braque y Picasso reconocían que si sus obras no estaban firmadas, para ellos era imposible distinguirlas.

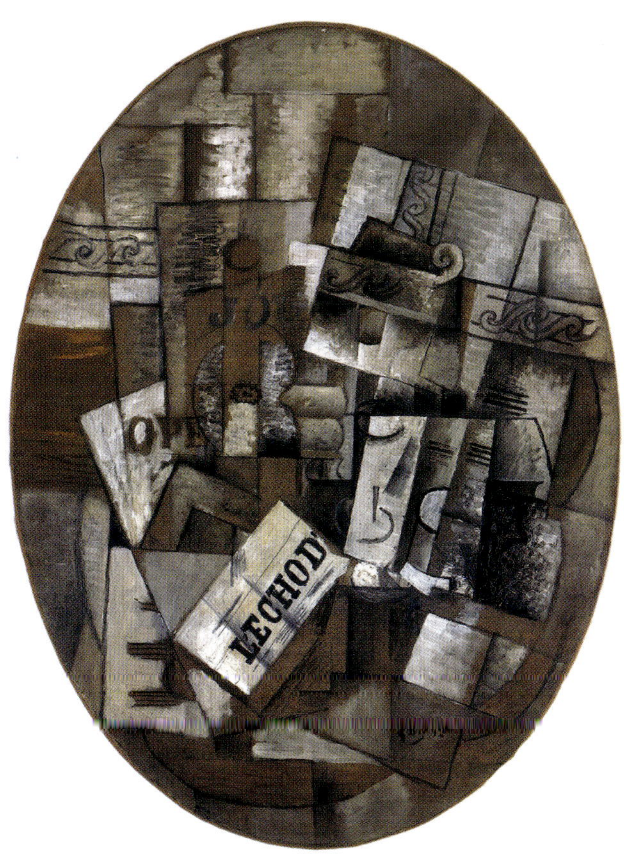

◀ Georges Braque
(Argenteuil 1882 - Paris 1963)

Still life with glass and newspaper (Le Guéridon)
Stillleben mit Weinglas und Zeitung (Le Guéridon)
Stilleven met glas en krant (Le Guéridon)
Naturaleza muerta con vaso y periódico (Le Guéridon)

●

1913
98,7 x 72,5 cm / 38.8 x 28.5 in.
Museum Berggruen, Staatliche Museen, Berlin

black chalk, charcoal and oil on canvas
Schwarze Kreide, Zeichenkohle und Öl auf Leinwand
zwart krijt, houtskool en olieverf op doek
tiza negra, carboncillo y óleo sobre lienzo

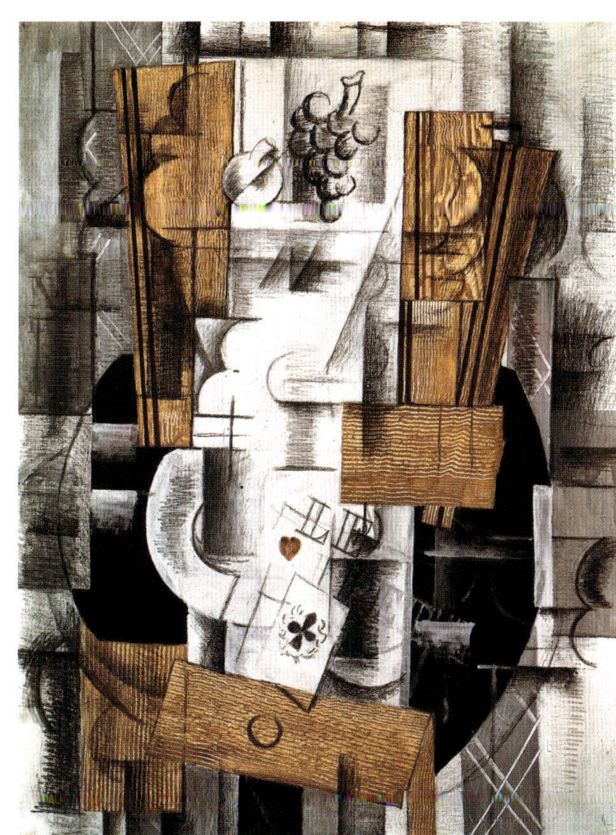

▶ Georges Braque
(Argenteuil 1882 - Paris 1963)

Still life with playing cards
Stillleben mit Pique As
Stillleven met speelkaarten
Naturaleza muerta con naipes

●●●

1913
81 x 60 cm / 31.9 x 23.6 in.
Centre Georges Pompidou, Musée National d'Art Moderne, Paris

oil, pencil and charcoal on canvas
Öl, Bleistift und Zeichenkohle auf Leinwand
olieverf, potlood en houtskool op doek
óleo, lápiz y carboncillo sobre lienzo

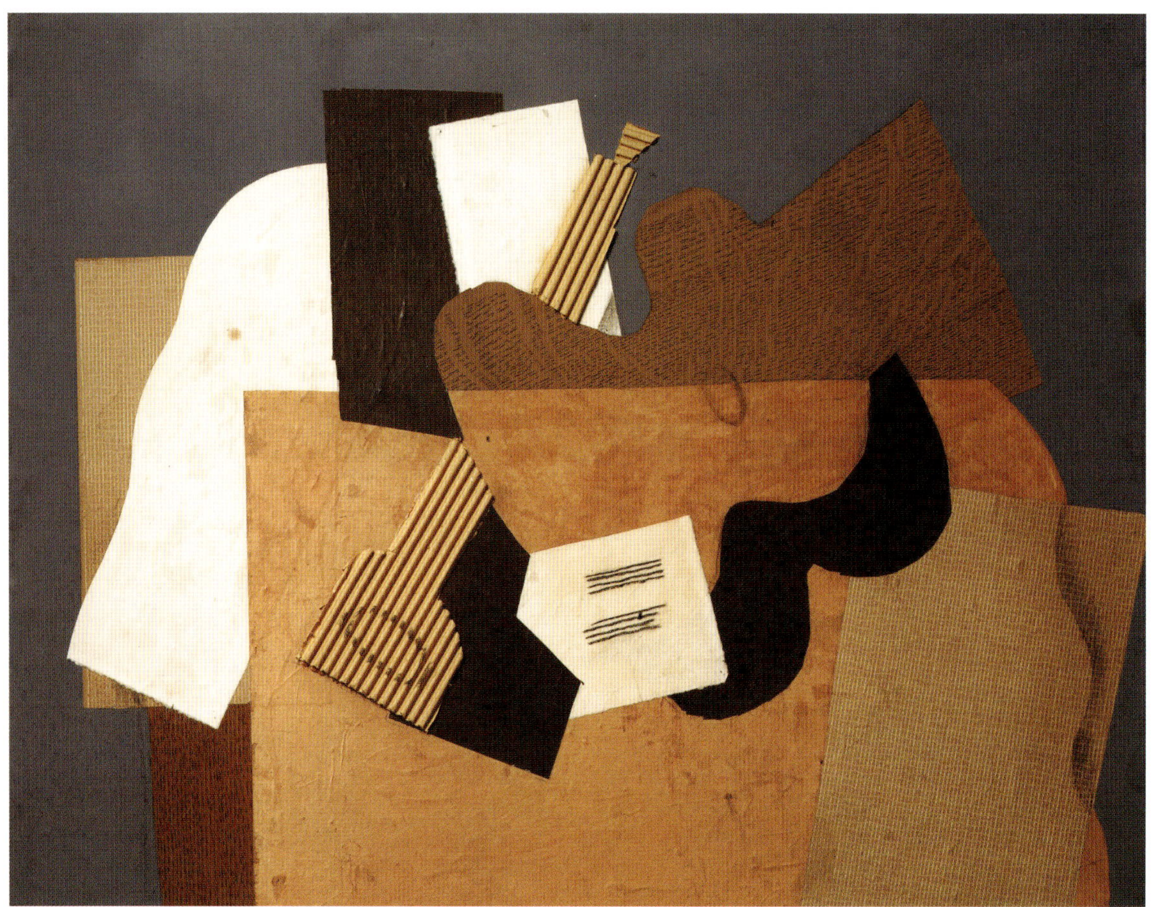

140

Georges Braque
(Argenteuil 1882 - Paris 1963)

Musical shapes / Musikalische Formen
Muzikale vormen / Formas musicales

●●

1918
77,5 x 95,3 cm / 30.5 x 37.5 in.
Philadelphia Museum of Art, Philadelphia

charcoal, cut paper, corrugated cardboard and traces of graphite on composition board
Zeichenkohle, geschnittenes Papier, plissierter Karton und Graphit auf Komposittafel
houtskool, afgeknipt papier, golfkarton en grafietstrepen op een compositiepaneel
carboncillo, papel cortado, cartón corrugado y trazos de grafito sobre la tabla de composición

Georges Braque
(Argenteuil 1882 - Paris 1963)
**Still life
with score of Satie
Stillleben
mit Partitur von Eric Satie
Stilleven
met een partituur van Satie
Naturaleza muerta
con partitura de Satie**

•

1921
43 x 73 cm / 16.9 x 28.7 in.
Centre Georges Pompidou, Musée
National d'Art Moderne, Paris

oil on canvas / Öl auf Leinwand
olieverf op doek / óleo sobre lienzo

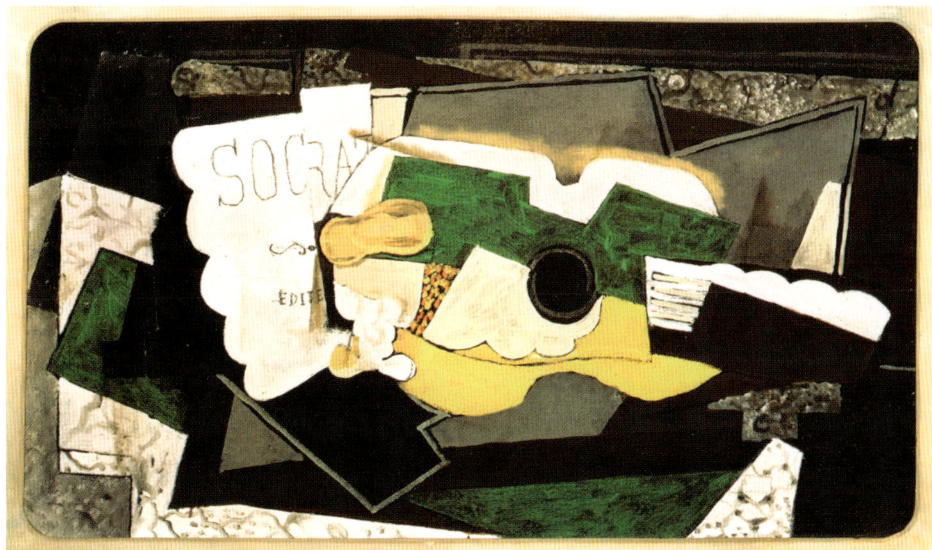

Georges Braque
(Argenteuil 1882 - Paris 1963)
**The Black Fish
Schwarzer Fisch
Zwarte vissen
Los peces negros**

•

1942
33 x 55 cm / 13 x 21.6 in.
Centre Georges Pompidou,
Musée National d'Art Moderne,
Paris

oil on canvas / Öl auf Leinwand
olieverf op doek / óleo sobre lienzo

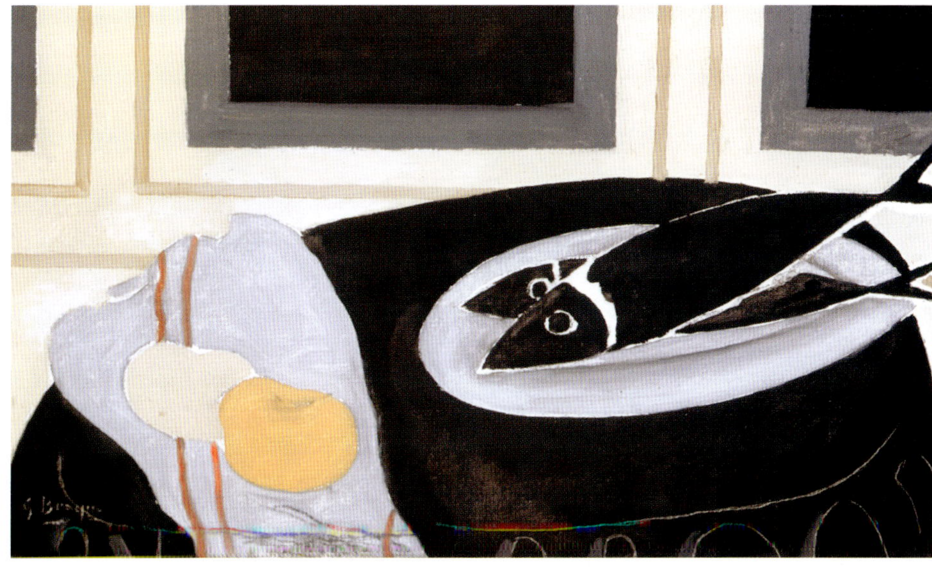

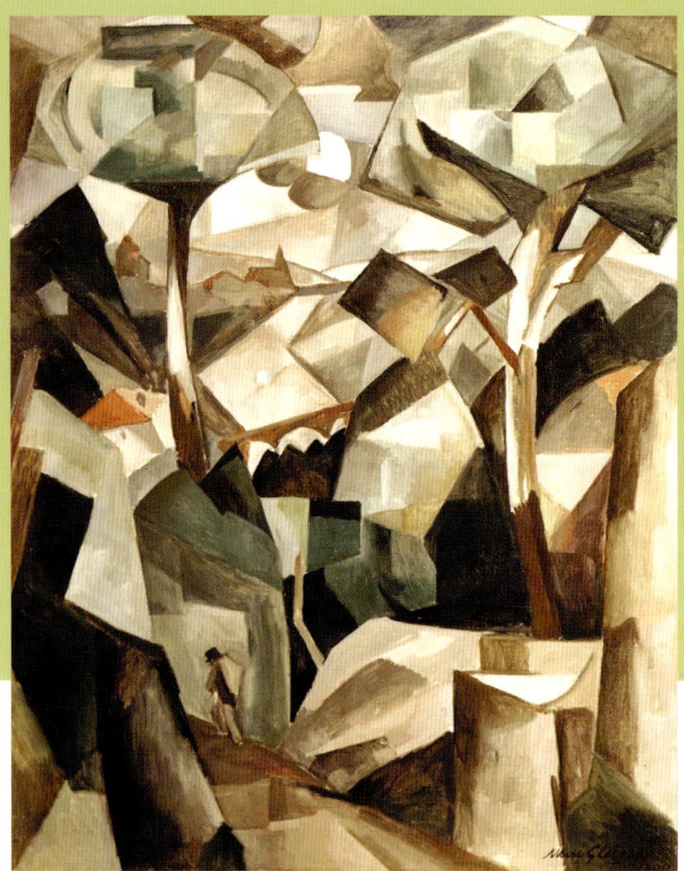

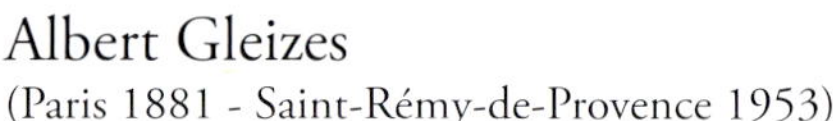

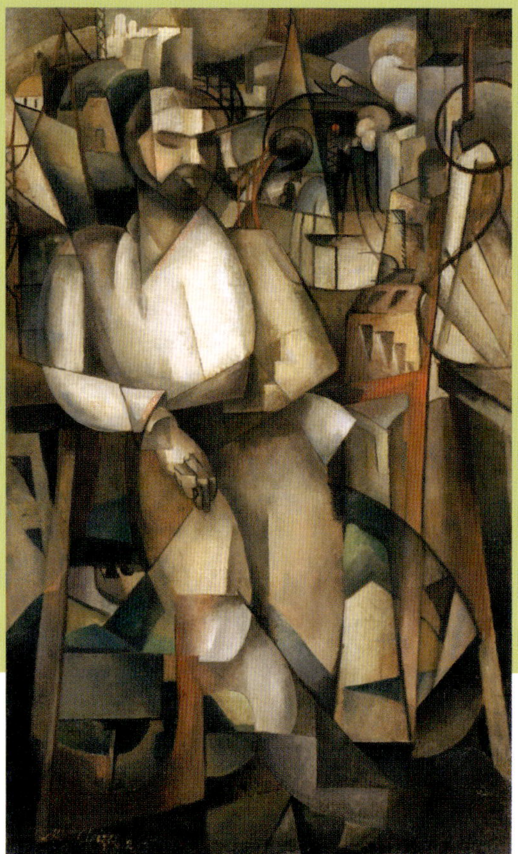

Albert Gleizes
(Paris 1881 - Saint-Rémy-de-Provence 1953)

Landscape with figure
Landschaft mit Figur
Landschap met persoon
Paisaje con personaje

●

1911
146 x 114 cm / 28.7 x 44.9 in.
Centre Georges Pompidou,
Musée National d'Art Moderne, Paris

oil on canvas / Öl auf Leinwand
olieverf op doek / óleo sobre lienzo

Albert Gleizes
(Paris 1881 - Saint-Rémy-de-Provence 1953)

Man on a balcony (Portrait of Dr. Morinaud)
Mann auf dem Balkon (Porträt von Dr. Morinaud)
Man op een balkon (Portret van dr. Morinaud)
Hombre en el balcón
(Retrato del doctor Morinaud)

●

1912
195,6 x 114,9 cm / 77 x 45.2 in.
Philadelphia Museum of Art, Philadelphia

oil on canvas / Öl auf Leinwand
olieverf op doek / óleo sobre lienzo

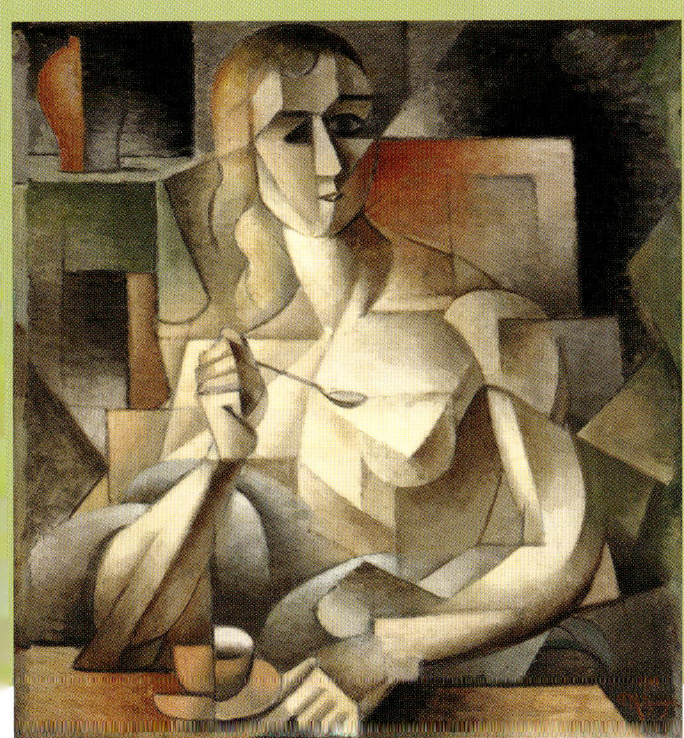

Jean Metzinger
(Nantes 1883 - Paris 1956)

Tea Time (Woman with a teaspoon)
Tea Time (Frau mit Teelöffel)
Thee-uurtje (vrouw met theelepel)
La hora del té (Mujer con cuchara)

●●

1911
75,9 x 70,2 cm / 29.9 x 27.6 in.
Philadelphia Museum of Art, Philadelphia

oil on paperboard / Öl auf Karton
olieverf op karton/óleo sobre cartón

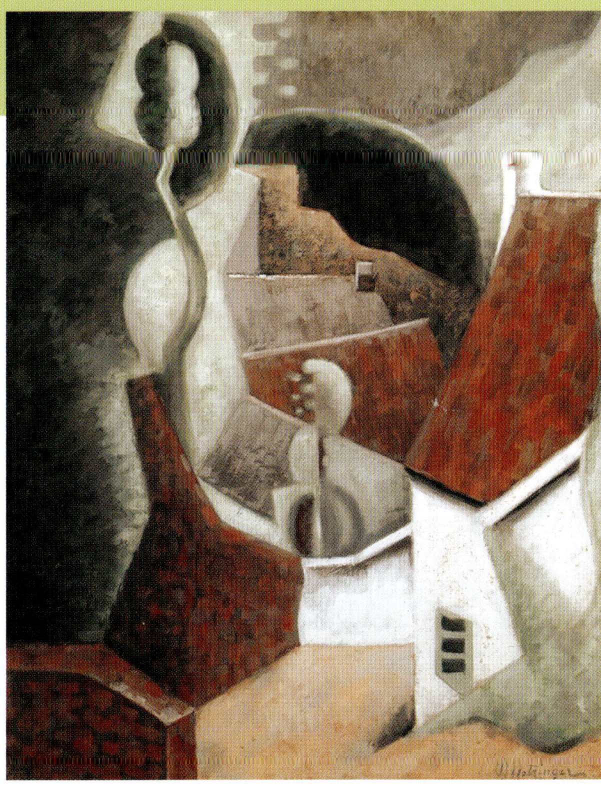

Jean Metzinger
(Nantes 1883 - Paris 1956)

Landscape
Landschaft
Landschap
Paisaje

●

1919
81 x 65 cm / 31.9 x 25.6 in.
Centre Georges Pompidou,
Musée National d'Art Moderne, Paris

oil on canvas / Öl auf Leinwand
olieverf op doek / óleo sobre lienzo

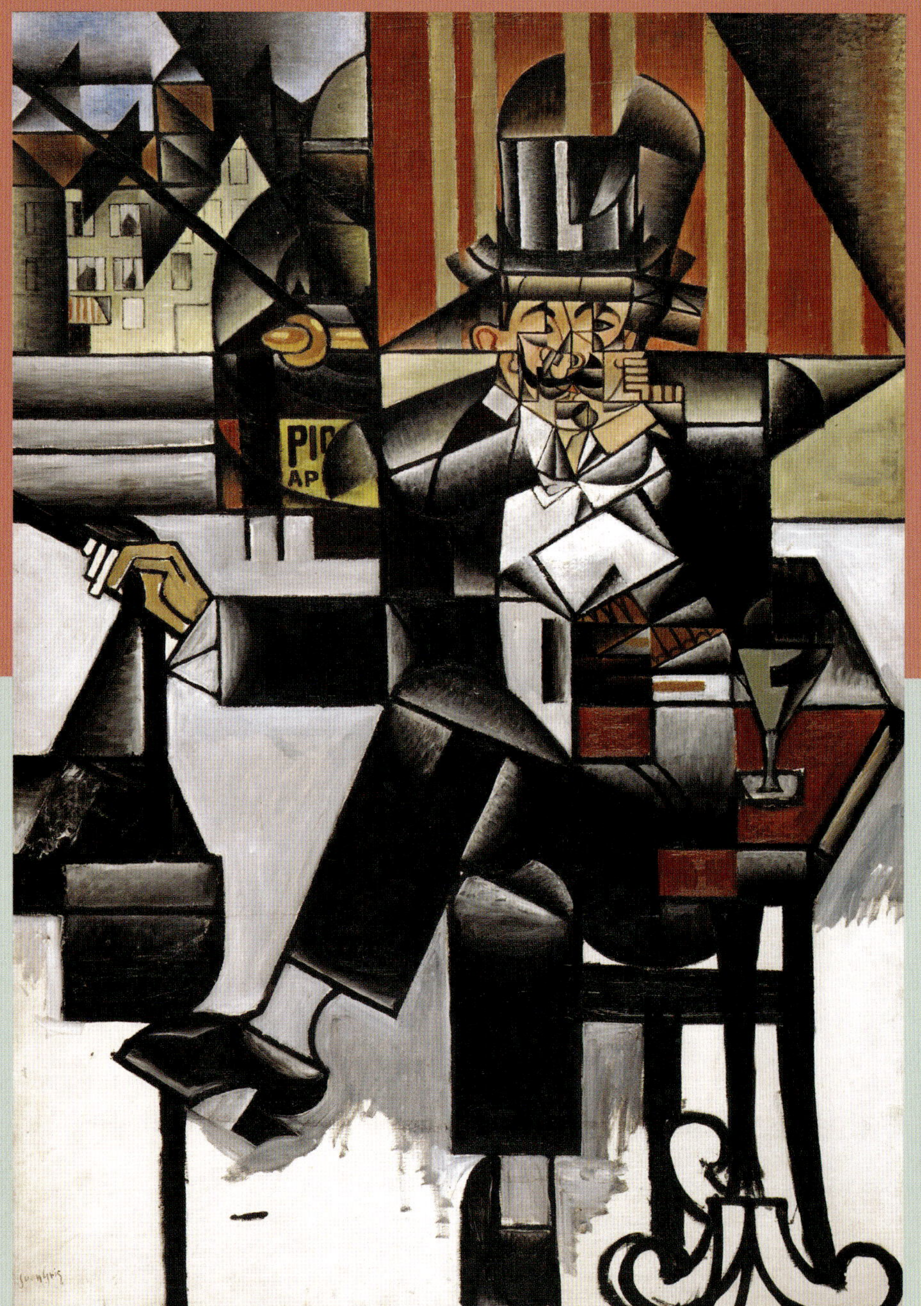

Juan Gris
(Madrid 1887 - Boulogne-sur-Seine 1927)

Man in a café
Mann im Café
Man in een café
El hombre en el café

●●

1912
127,6 x 88,3 cm / 50.2 x 34.7 in.
Philadelphia Museum of Art,
Philadelphia

oil on canvas / Öl auf Leinwand
olieverf op doek / óleo sobre lienzo

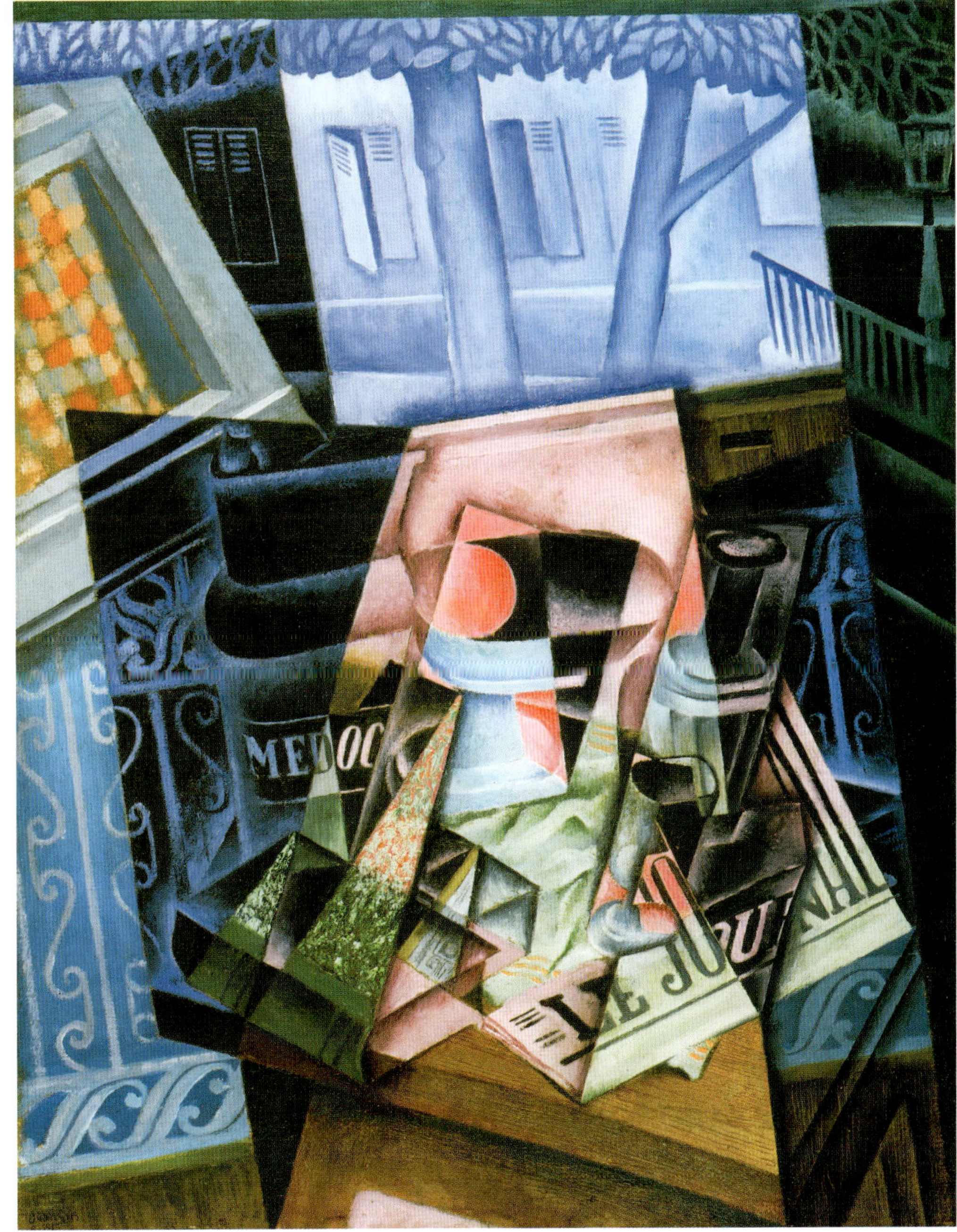

Juan Gris
(Madrid 1887 - Boulogne-
sur-Seine 1927)
**Still life in front
of an open window,
Place Ravignan
Stillleben
vor geöffnetem
Fenster an der Place
Ravignan
Stillleven
voor een open raam,
Place Ravignan
Naturaleza muerta
delante de una
ventana abierta:
la Plaza Ravignan**

●

1915
115,9 x 88,9 cm
45.6 x 35 in.
Philadelphia Museum of
Art, Philadelphia

oil on canvas
Öl auf Leinwand
olieverf op doek
óleo sobre lienzo

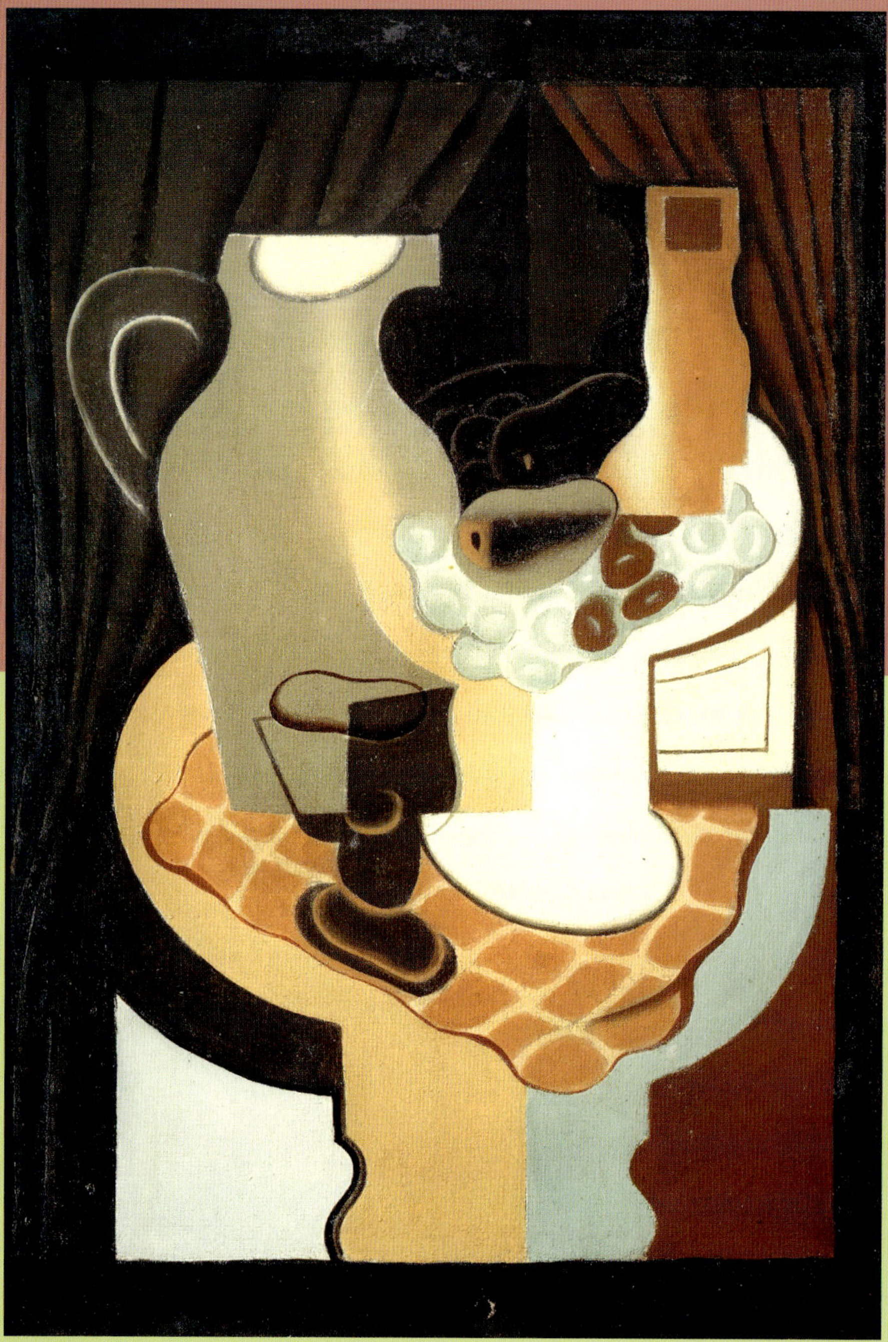

◀ **Juan Gris**
(Madrid 1887 - Boulogne-
sur-Seine 1927)

Broc et compotier
Stillleben mit Krug
und Obstschale
●
1921
61 x 38 cm / 24 x 14.9 in.
Centre Georges Pompidou, Musée
National d'Art Moderne, Paris

oil on canvas / Öl auf Leinwand
olieverf op doek / óleo sobre lienzo

▶ **Juan Gris**
(Madrid 1887 - Boulogne-
sur-Seine 1927)

The Guitar
Die Gitarre
De gitaar
La guitarra
●●
1913
61 x 50 cm / 24 x 19.7 in.
Centre Georges Pompidou,
Musée National d'Art Moderne, Paris

oil and paper glued on canvas
Öl und geleimtes Papier auf Leinwand
olieverf en papier op doek geplakt
óleo y papel encolado sobre lienzo

146

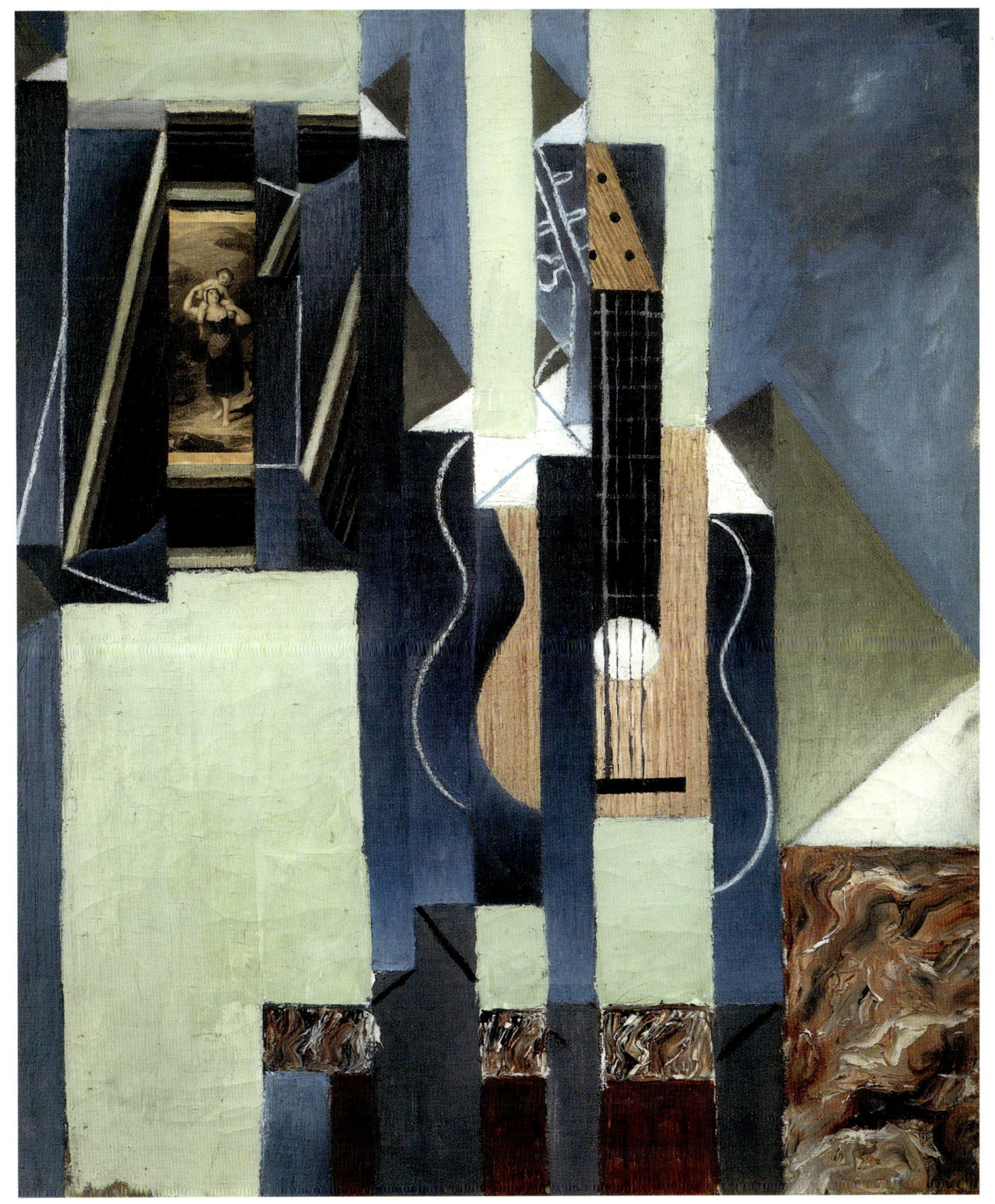

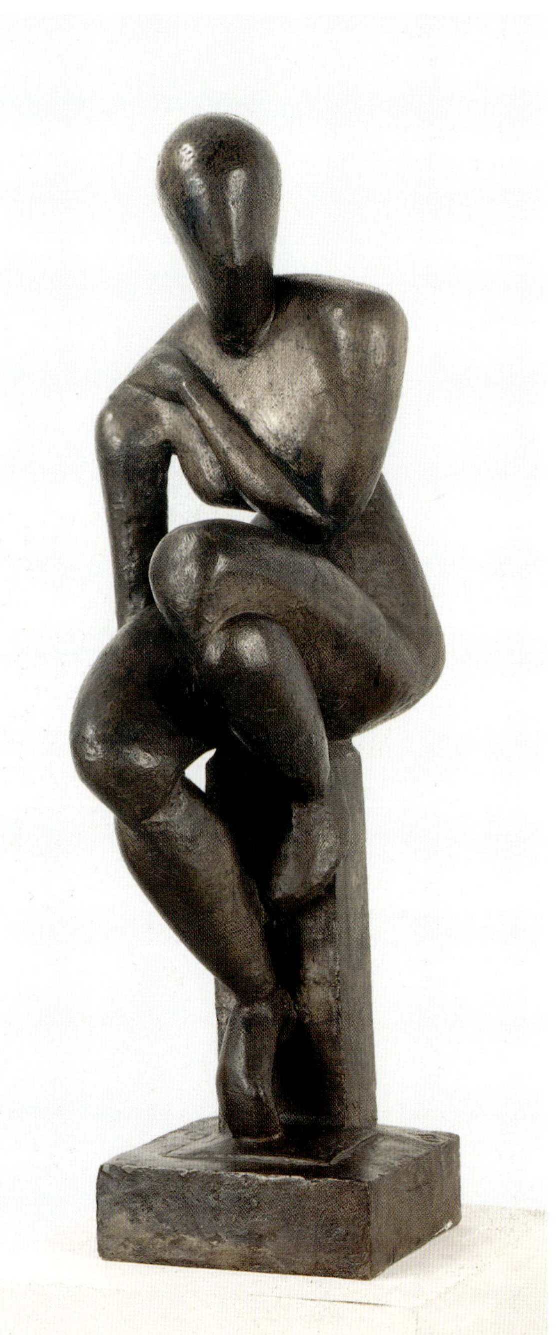

Raymond Duchamp-Villon
(Damville 1876 - Cannes 1918)

Woman seated
Sitzende Frau
Zittende vrouw
Mujer sentada

●

1914
71 x 22 x 28 cm
27.9 x 8.6 x 11 in.
Centre Georges Pompidou,
Musée National d'Art Moderne,
Paris

bronze / Bronze / brons / bronce

Raymond Duchamp-Villon
(Damville 1876 - Cannes 1918)

The Horse
Das Pferd
Het paard
El caballo

●●

1914-1976
44 x 44 x 26 cm
17.3 x 17.3 x 10.2 in.
Centre Georges Pompidou, Musée
National d'Art Moderne, Paris

bronze / Bronze / brons / bronce

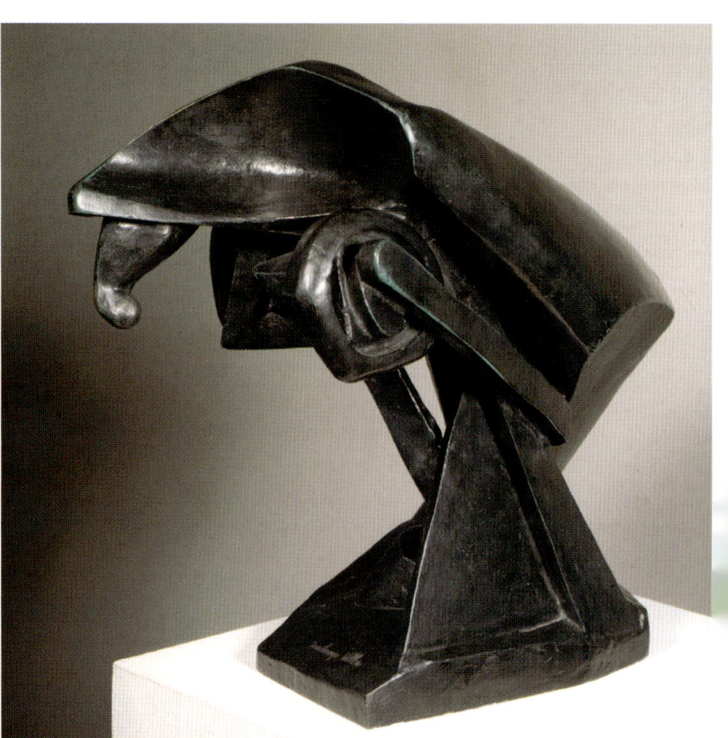

Jacques Villon
(Damville 1875 - Puteaux 1963)

Portrait of the artist's father
Porträt des Vaters des Künstlers
Portret van de kunstenaar's vader
Retrato del padre del artista

●

1913
Musée des Beaux-Arts, Rouen

Jacques Villon
(Damville 1875 - Puteaux 1963)

The Adventure
Das Abenteuer
Het avontuur
La aventura

●

1935
163 x 115 cm / 64.2 x 45.3 in.
Centre Georges Pompidou,
Musée National d'Art Moderne, Paris

oil on canvas / Öl auf Leinwand
olieverf op doek / óleo sobre lienzo

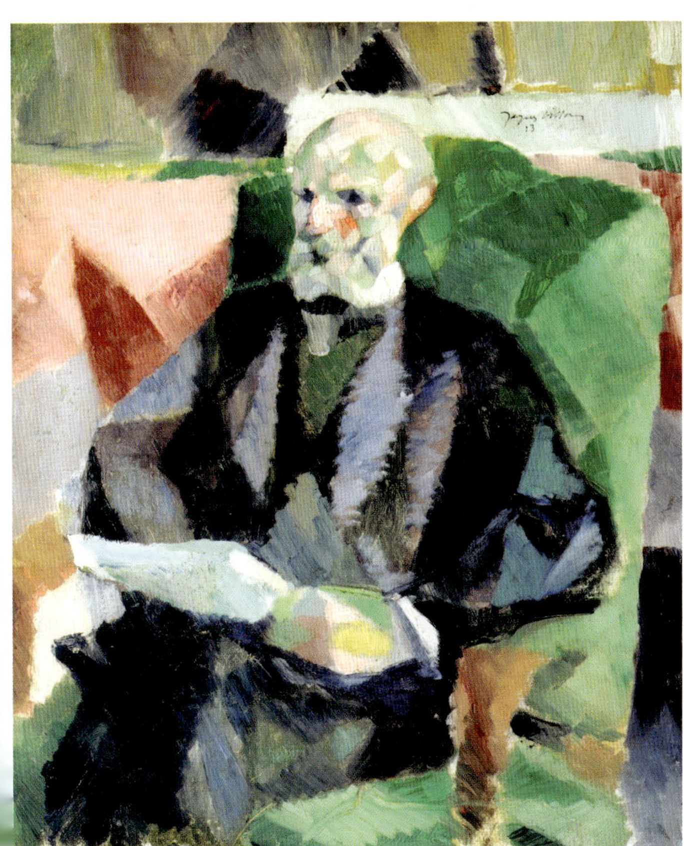

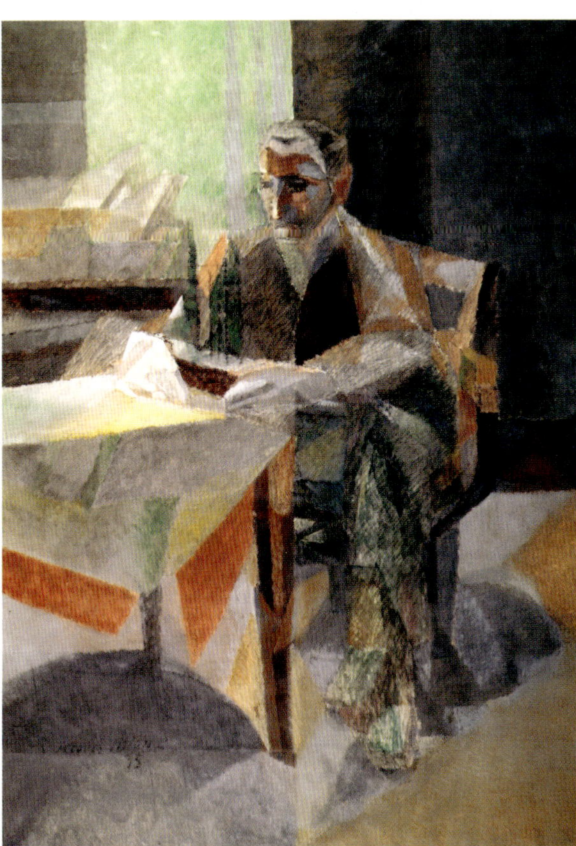

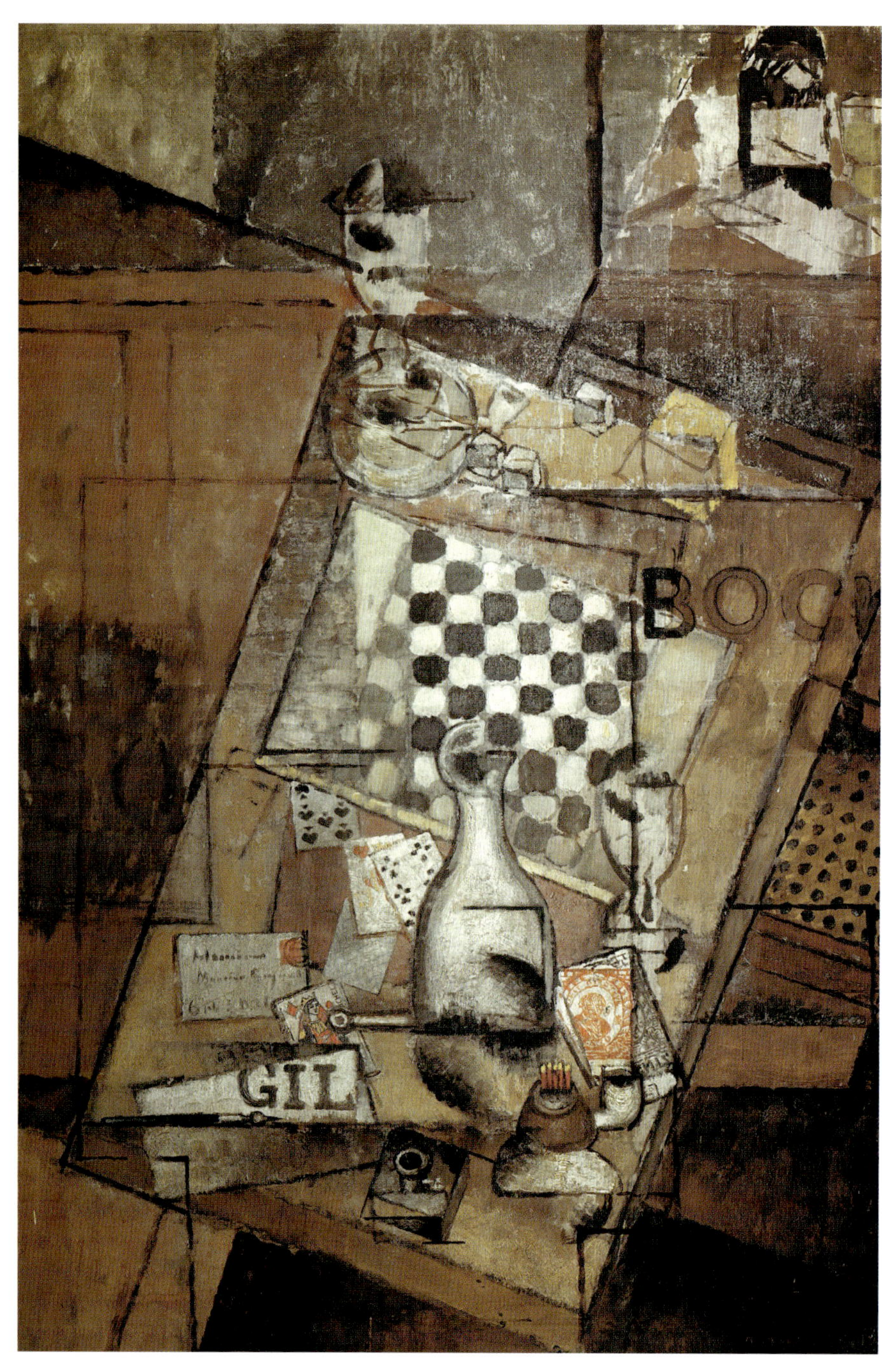

Louis Marcoussis
(Warsaw 1878 - Cusset 1941)
Still life with chessboard
Stillleben mit Schachbrett
Stilleven met schaakbord
Naturaleza muerta
con tablero de ajedrez

●

1912
143 x 97 cm / 56.3 x 38.2 in.
Centre Georges Pompidou,
Musée National d'Art Moderne, Paris

oil on canvas / Öl auf Leinwand
olieverf op doek / óleo sobre lienzo

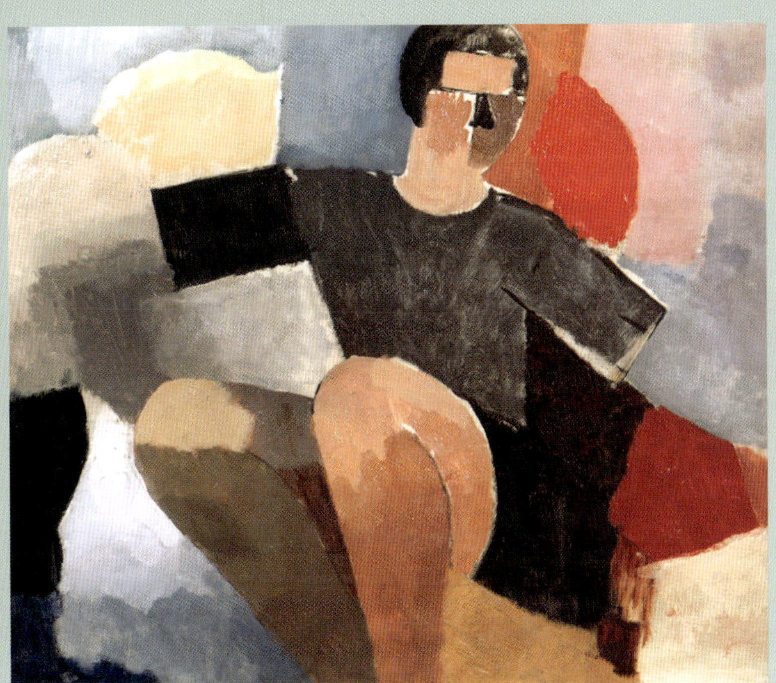

Roger de La Fresnaye
(Le Mans 1885 - Grasse 1925)

**Rower
Ruderer
Roeier
Remero**

●

1912
Musée de l'Annonciade, Saint-Tropez

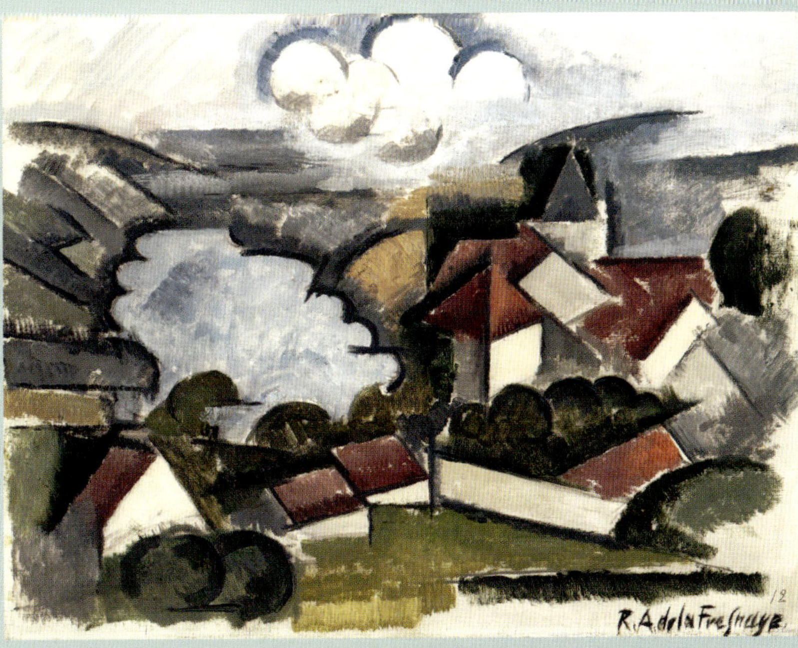

Roger de La Fresnaye
(Le Mans 1885 - Grasse 1925)

**Landscape
Landschft
Landschap
Paisaje**

●

1912
47,6 x 60,3 cm / 18.7 x 23.7 in.
Philadelphia Museum of Art,
Philadelphia

oil on canvas / Öl auf Leinwand
olieverf op doek / óleo sobre lienzo

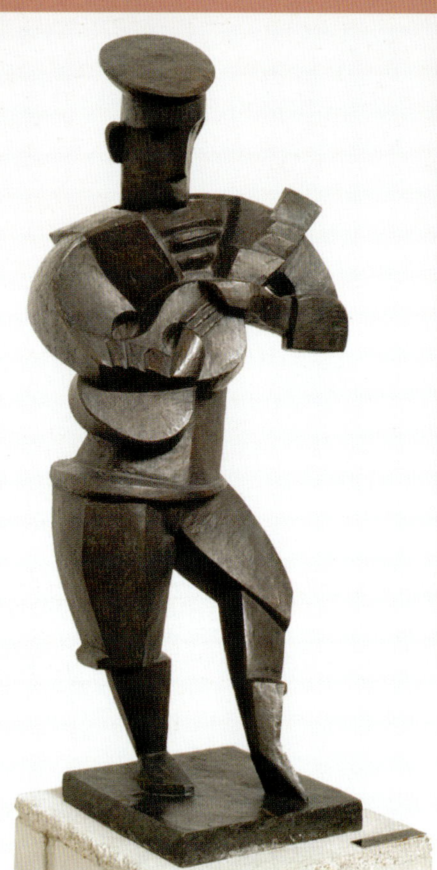

152

Jacques Lipchitz
(Druskininkai 1891 - Capri 1973)

Man with mandolin
Mann mit Mandoline
Man met mandoline
Hombre con mandolina

●

1916-1917
76,2 x 26 x 28,9 cm / 30 x 10.2 x 11.4 in.
Yale University Art Gallery, New Haven (CT)

limestone / Kalkstein / kalk / caliza

Jacques Lipchitz
(Druskininkai 1891 - Capri 1973)

Sailor with guitar
Matrose mit Gitarre
Zeeman met gitaar
Marinero con guitarra

●●

1914
77,5 x 29 x 24,5 cm / 30.5 x 11.4 x 9.6 in.
Centre Georges Pompidou, Musée National d'Art
Moderne, Paris

bronze / Bronze / brons / bronce

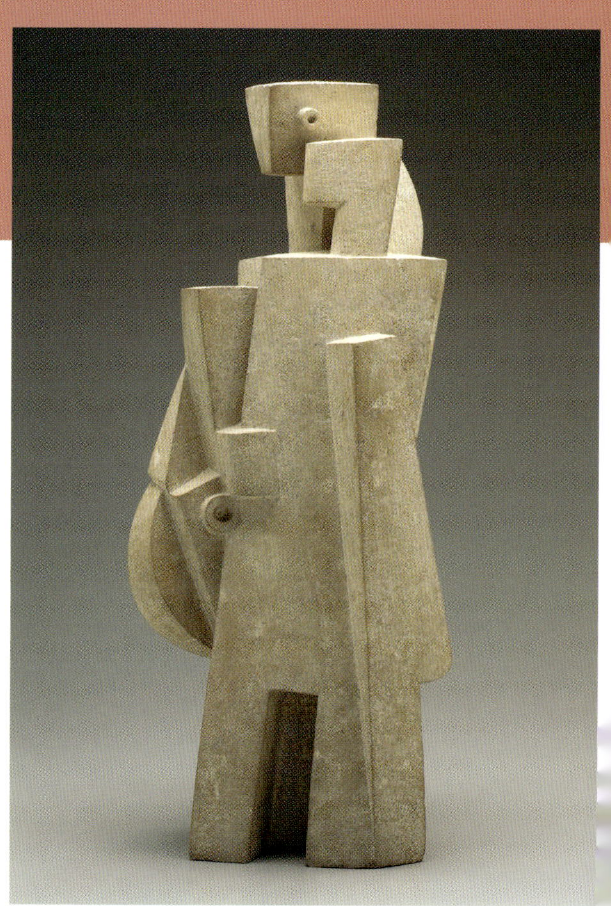

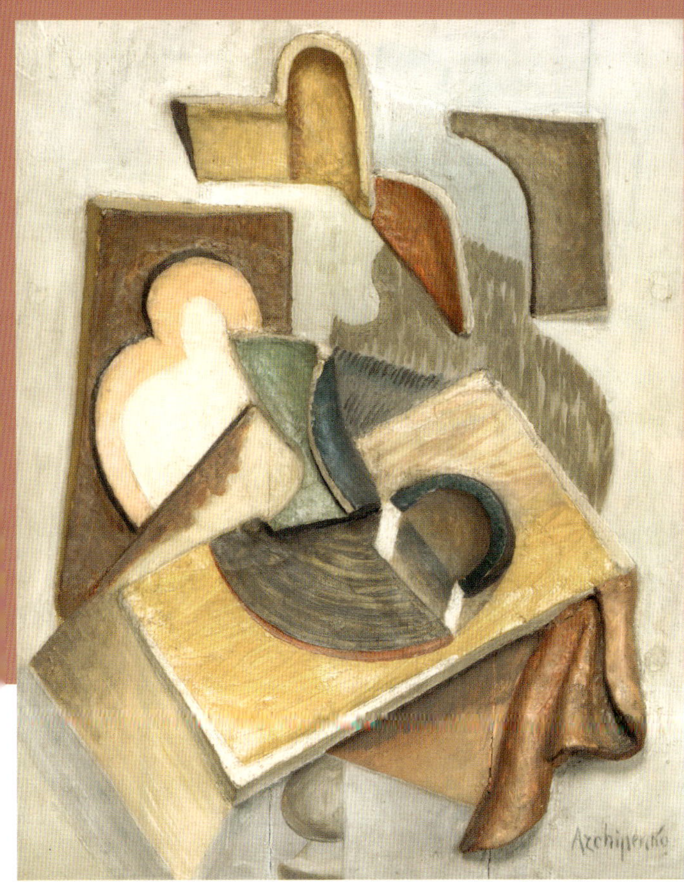

Aleksandr Archipenko
(Kiev 1887 - New York City 1964)

Glass on a table
Glas auf einem Tisch
Glas op een tafel
Vaso sobre una mesa

●

1920
41 x 33 x 3,2 cm / 16.1 x 13 x 1.2 in.
Museum of Modern Art (MoMA), New York

painted wood and chalk / bemaltes Holz und Kreide
beschilderd hout en krijt / madera pintada y tiza

153

Aleksandr Archipenko
(Kiev 1887 - New York City 1964)

Gondolier
Gondelfahrer
Gondelier
Gondolero

●●

1914 (1966)
83,8 x 30,1 x 25,5 cm / 33 x 11.8 x 10 in.
Museum of Modern Art (MoMA), New York

bronze / Bronze / brons / bronce

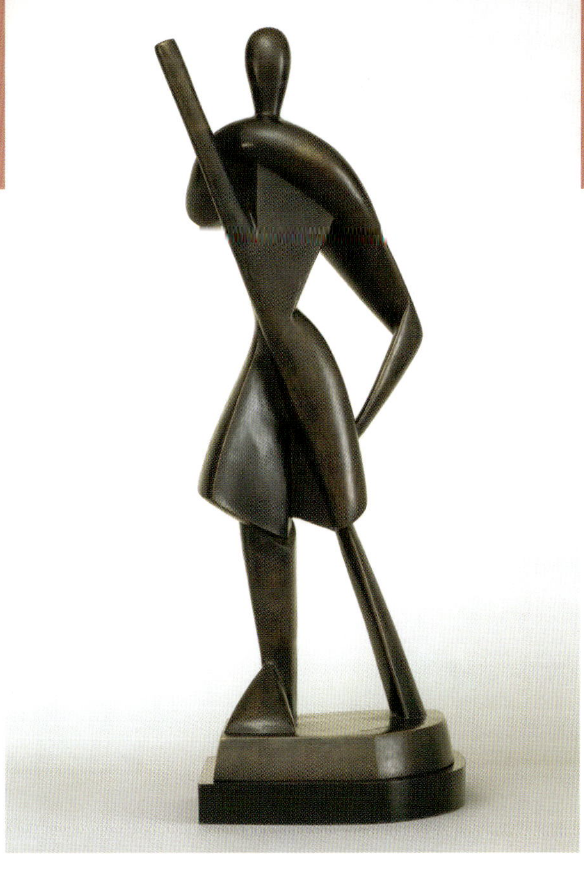

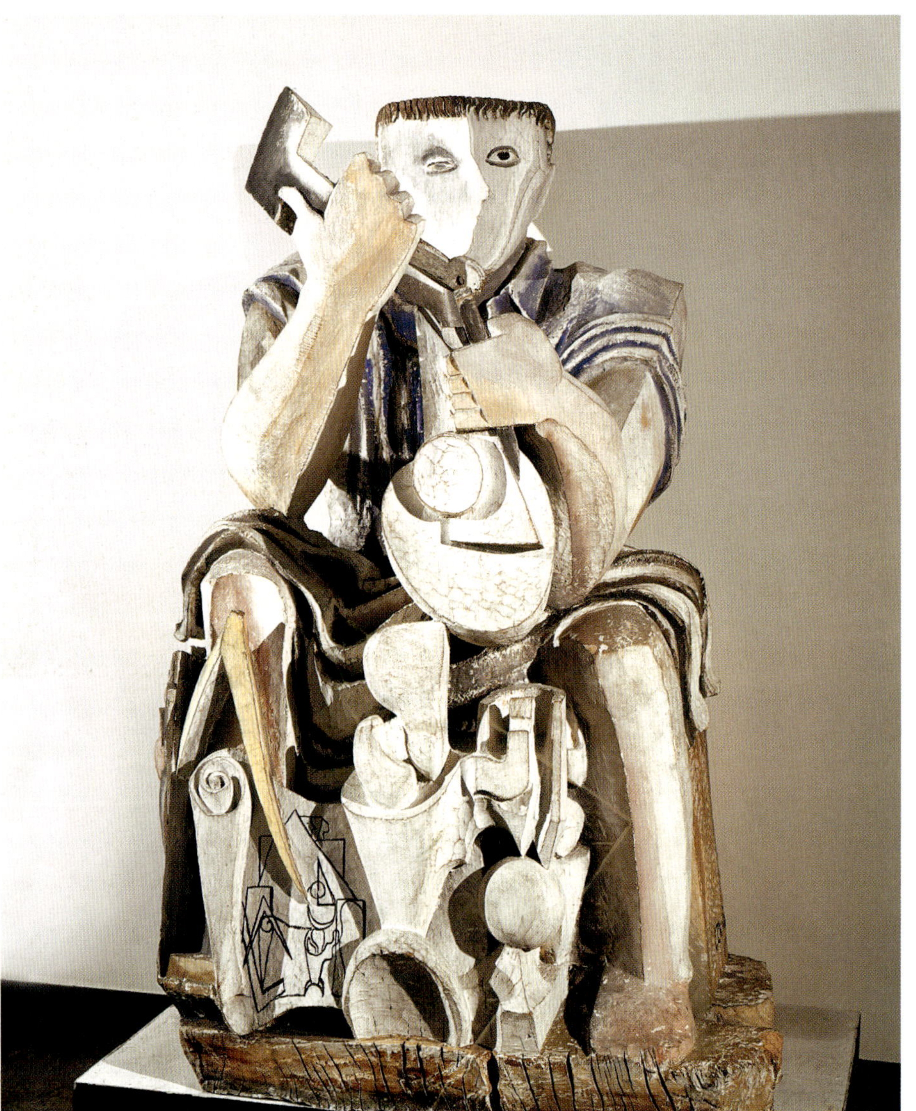

Ossip Zadkine
(Vitebsk 1890 - Neuilly-sur-Seine 1967)

The Sculptor
Der Bildhauer
De beeldhouwer
El escultor

●

1939
195 x 129 x 100 cm
76.8 x 50.8 x 39.4 in.
Centre Georges Pompidou,
Musée National d'Art Moderne, Paris

painted wood / Bemaltes Holz
beschilderd hout / madera pintada

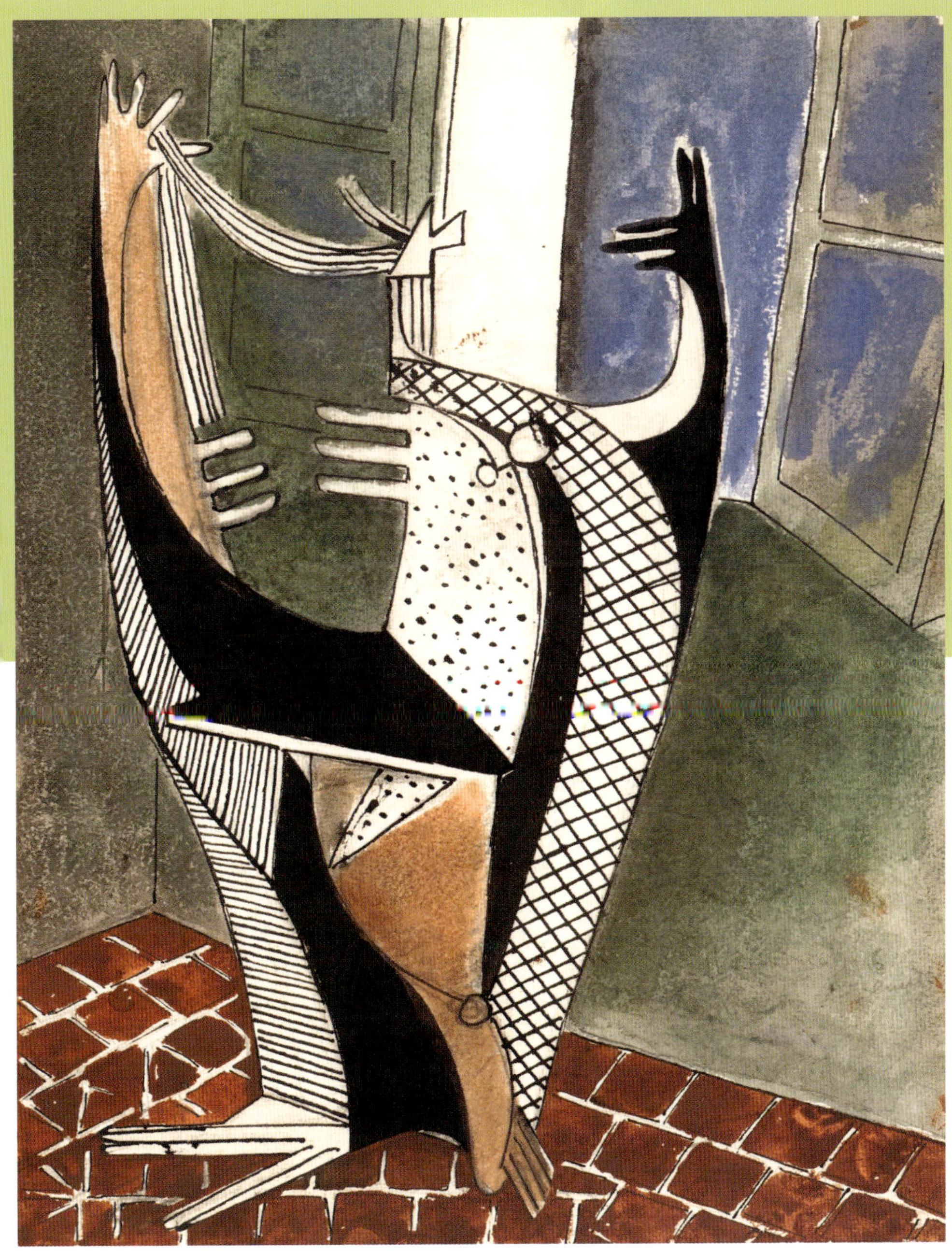

Julio González
(Barcelona 1876 - Arcueil 1942)

Standing Figure
Stehende Figur
Staande figuur
Figura de pie

●

ca. 1941
31,8 x 24,3 cm / 12.5 x 9.5 in.
Museum of Modern Art
(MoMA), New York

watercolor and ink on paper
Aquarell und Tinte auf Papier
aquarel en inkt op papier
acuarela y tinta sobre papel

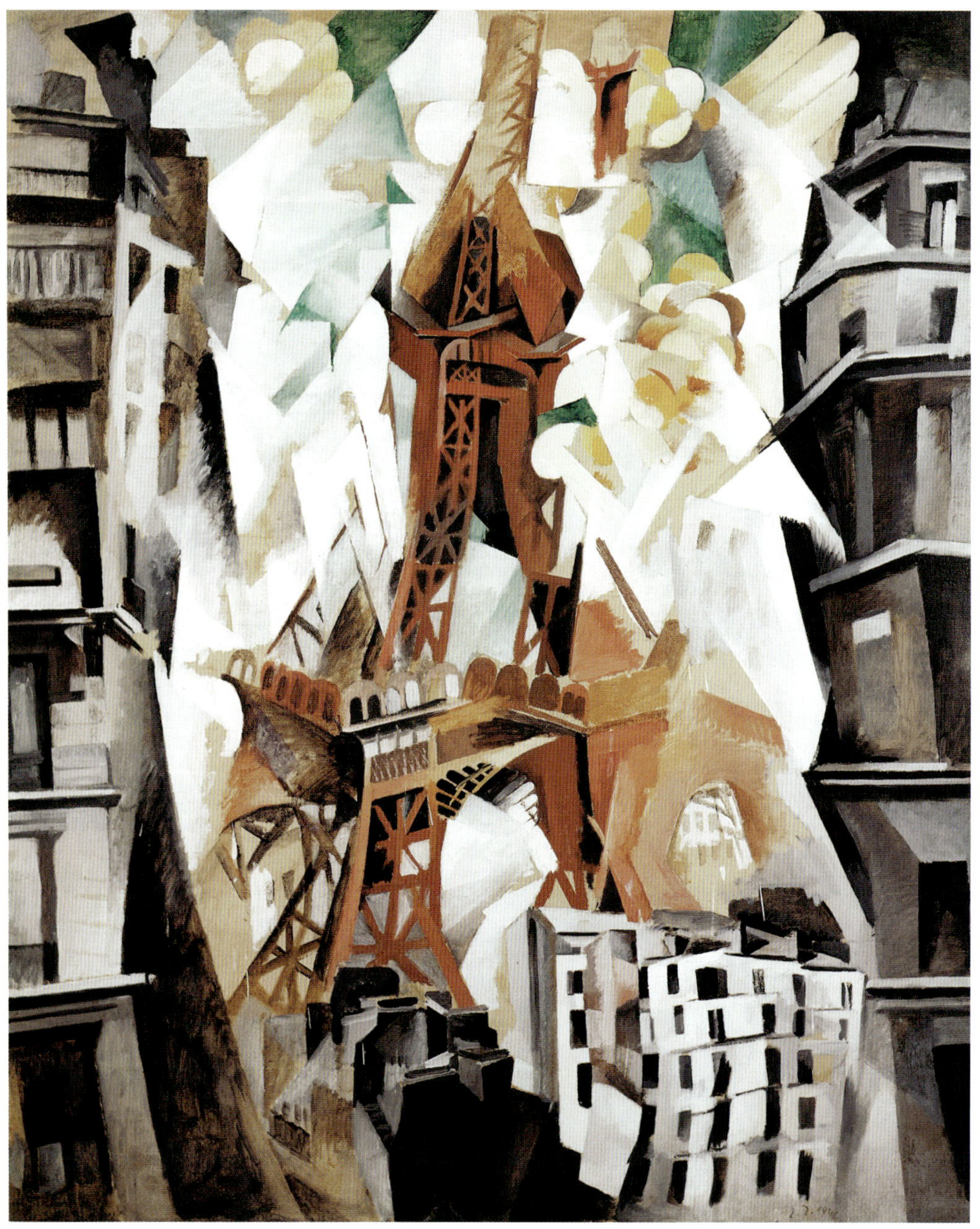

Robert Delaunay
(Paris 1885 -
Montpellier 1941)

**Campo di Marte,
the Red Tower
Marsfeld,
der rote Turm
Champ de Mars,
de rode toren
Campo de Marte,
la Torre Roja**

●●●

1911
160,7 x 128,6 cm
63.2 x 50.6 in.
Art Institute of Chicago,
Chicago

oil on canvas
Öl auf Leinwand
olieverf op doek
óleo sobre lienzo

156

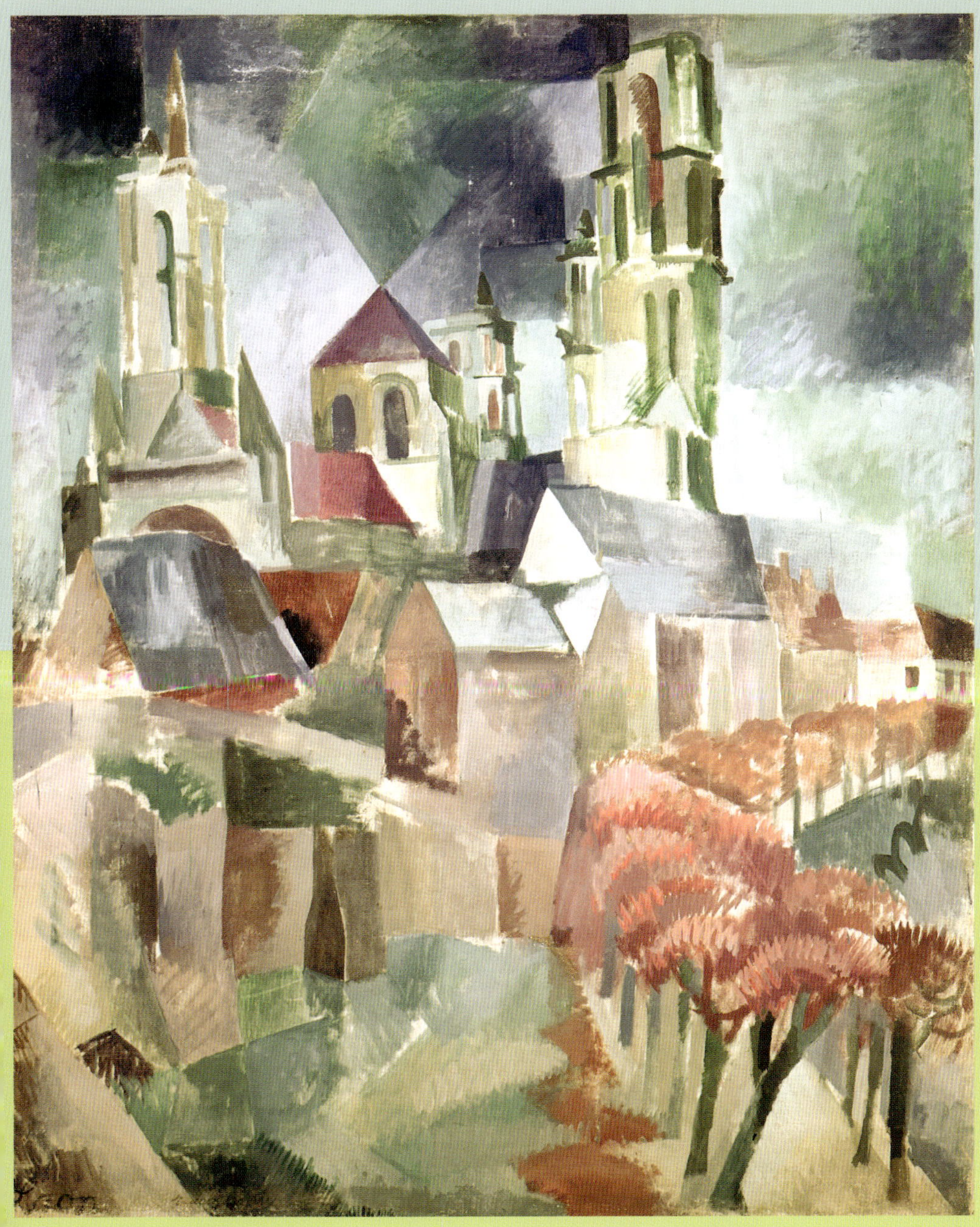

Robert Delaunay
(Paris 1885 -
Montpellier 1941)

The Tower of Laon
Die Türme von Laon
De toren van Laon
La torre de Laon

●●

1912
162 x 130 cm
63.8 x 58.2 in.
Centre Georges Pompidou,
Musée National d'Art Moderne,
Paris

oil on canvas
Öl auf Leinwand
olieverf op doek
óleo sobre lienzo

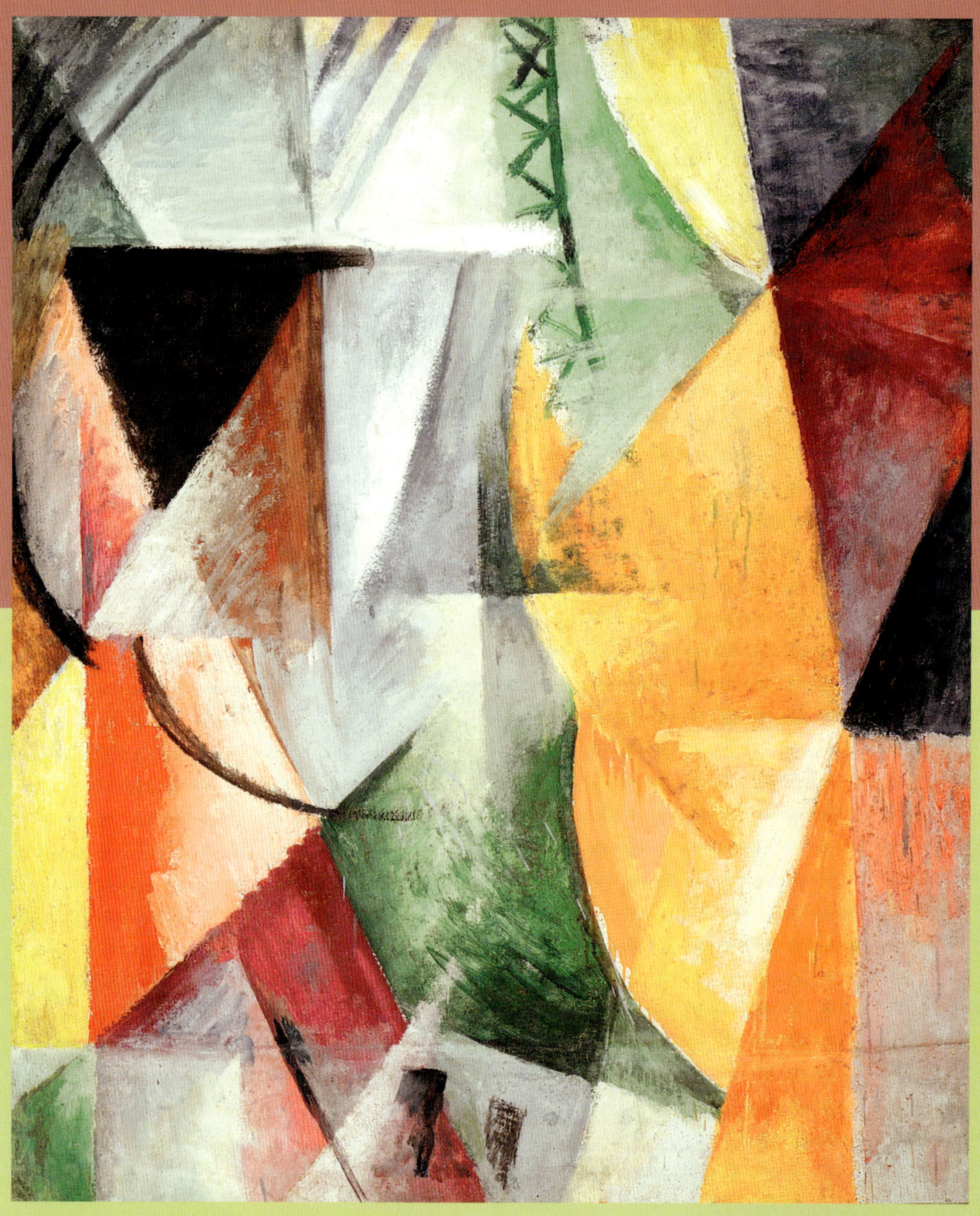

▶ Sonia Terk
Delaunay
(Hradyz'k 1885 - Paris 1979)

Electric prism
Elektrische Prismen
Elektrisch prisma
Prisma eléctrico

●●●

1914
250 x 250 cm
98.4 x 98.4 in.
Centre Georges Pompidou,
Musée National d'Art Moderne,
Paris

oil on canvas
Öl auf Leinwand
olieverf op doek
óleo sobre lienzo

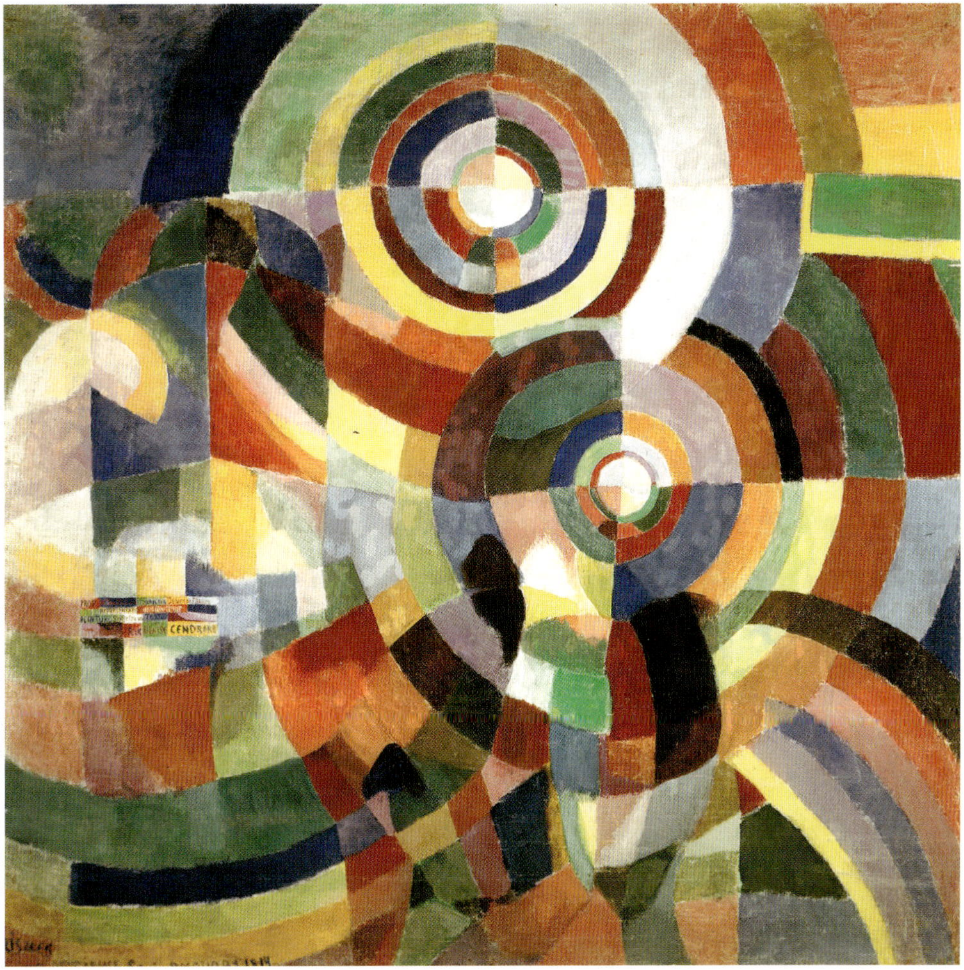

◀ Robert Delaunay
(Paris 1885 - Montpellier 1941)

Window
Fenster
Raam
Ventana a la ciudad

●

1912
111 x 90 cm
43.7 x 35.4 in.
Centre Georges Pompidou, Musée
National d'Art Moderne,
Paris

oil on canvas
Öl auf Leinwand
olieverf op doek
óleo sobre lienzo

159

Delauney was 4 years old when the Eiffel Tower, symbol of modernity which he will paint about thirty times, was inaugurated.

Delaunay war 4 Jahre alt, als der Eiffelturm, das Symbol der Moderne, das er an die 30 Mal reproduzieren würde, eingeweiht wurde.

Delaunay was 4 jaar toen de Eiffeltoren, symbool voor moderniteit, geopend werd. Hij zou deze wel dertig keer schilderen.

Delaunay tenía cuatro años cuando fue inaugurada la Torre Eiffel, símbolo de la modernidad que el artista reproducirá unas treinta veces.

Fernand Léger
(Argentan 1881 - Gif-sur-Yvette 1955)

The City
Die Stadt
De stad
La ciudad

●

1919
231,1 x 298,4 cm / 91 x 117.5 in.
Philadelphia Museum of Art, Philadelphia

oil on canvas / Öl auf Leinwand
olieverf op doek / óleo sobre lienzo

Fernand Léger
(Argentan 1881 - Gif-sur-Yvette 1955)

The Tugboat
Der Schlepper
De sleepboot
El remolcador

●

1920
104 x 132 cm / 40.9 x 52 in.
Musée de Grenoble, Grenoble

oil on canvas / Öl auf Leinwand
olieverf op doek / óleo sobre lienzo

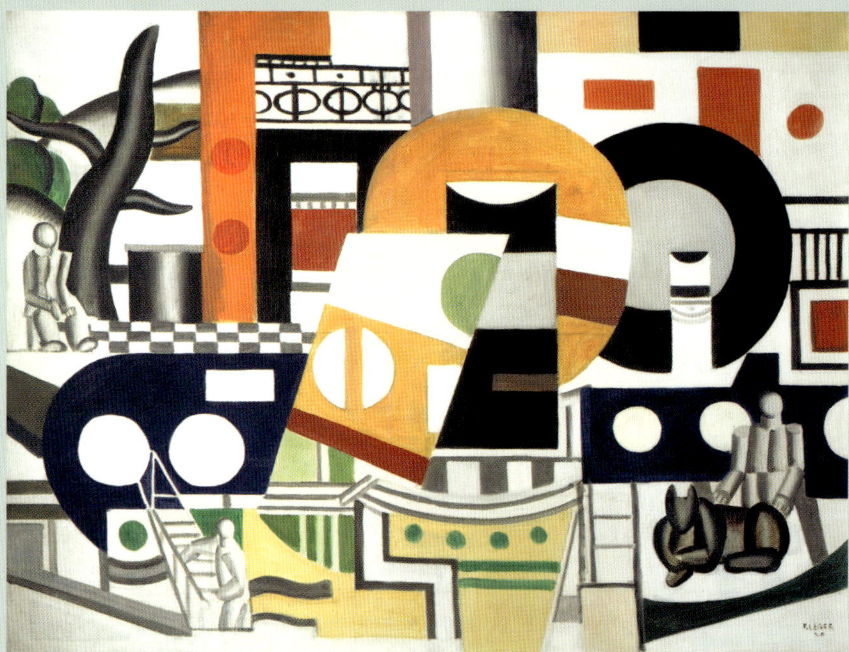

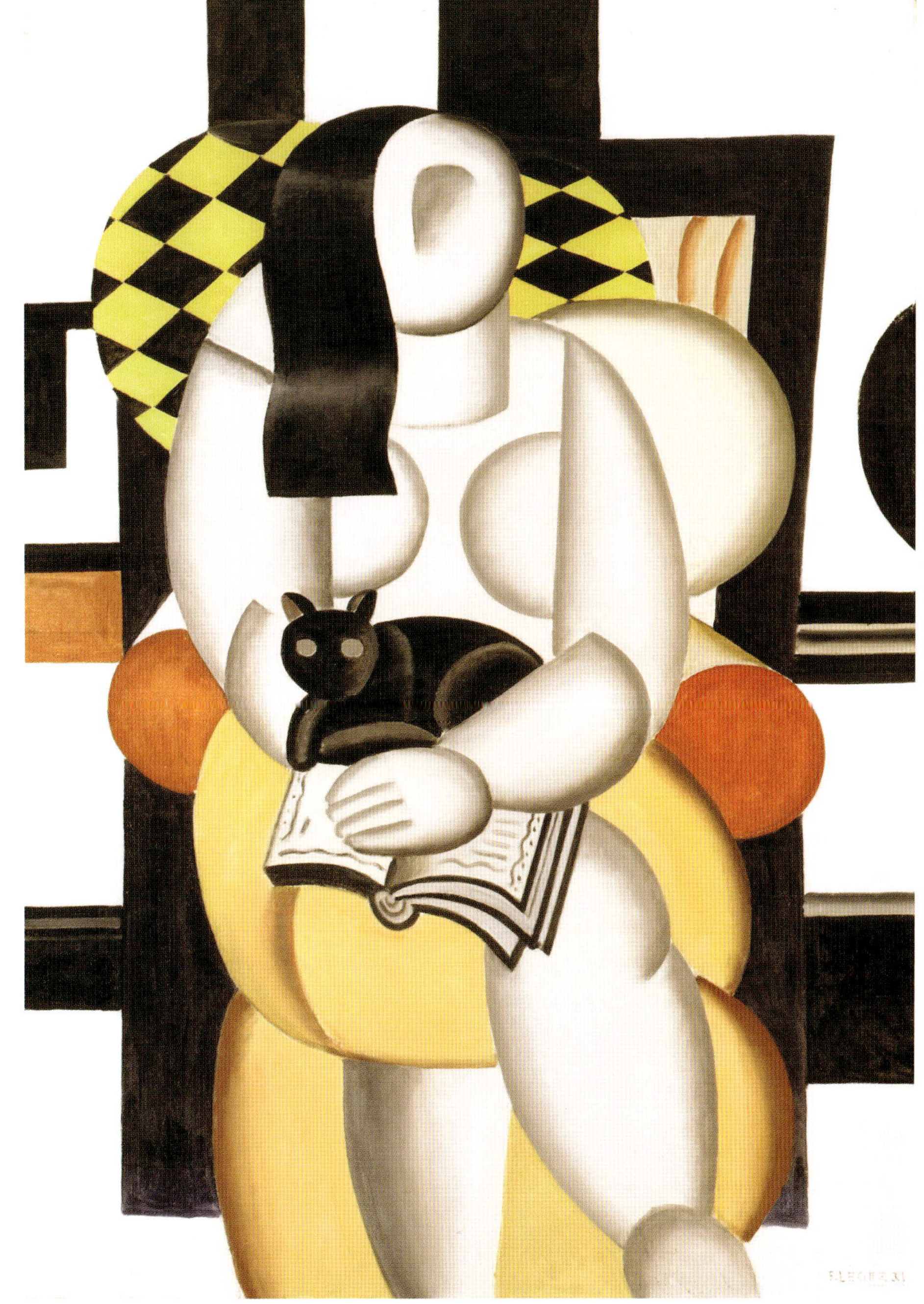

Fernand Léger
(Argentan 1881 - Gif-sur-Yvette 1955)

Woman with a cat
Frau mit einer Katze
Vrouw met een kat
Mujer con gato

●●

1921
130,5 x 89,5 cm / 51.3 x 35.2 in.
The Metropolitan Museum of Art,
New York

oil on canvas / Öl auf Leinwand
olieverf op doek / óleo sobre lienzo

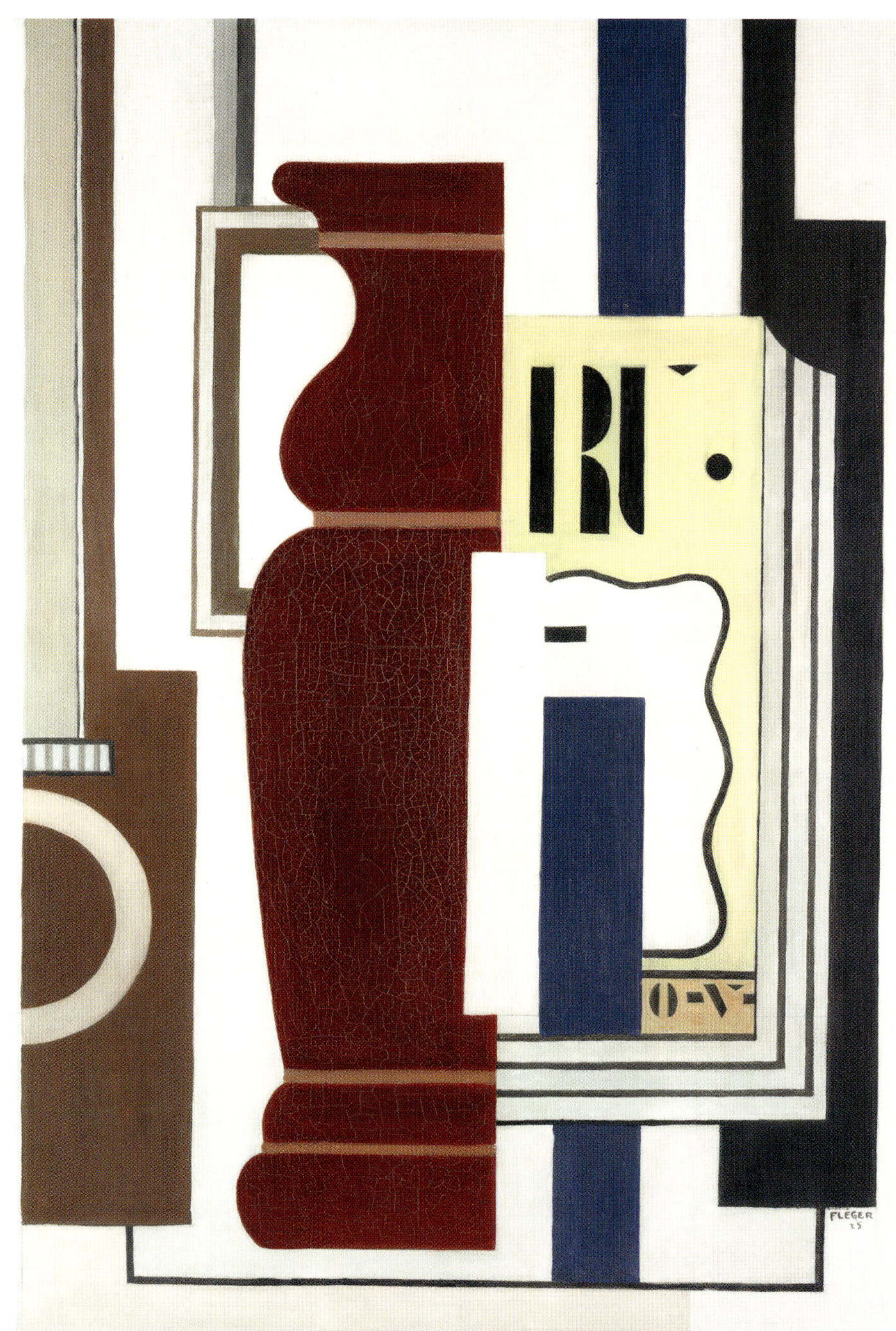

Fernand Léger
(Argentan 1881 - Gif-sur-Yvette 1955)
Composition No. VII
Komposition Nr. VII
Compositie n. VII
Composición Nº VII

●

1925
132 x 91 cm / 51.9 x 35.8 in.
Yale University Art Gallery,
New Haven (CT)

oil on canvas mounted on aluminium
Öl auf Leinwand
auf Aluminium angebracht
olieverf op doek
op aluminium gemonteerd
óleo sobre lienzo
montado sobre aluminio

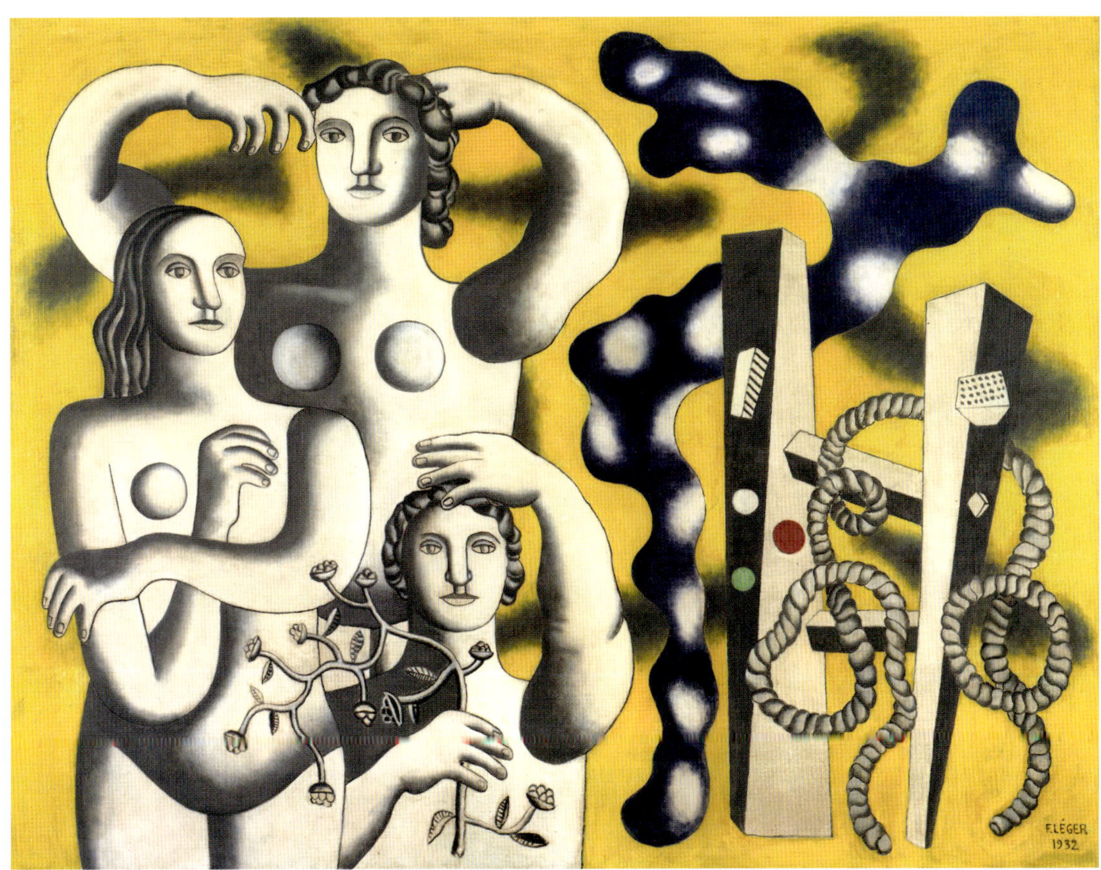

Fernand Léger
(Argentan 1881 - Gif-sur-Yvette 1955)

Composition with three figures
Komposition mit drei Figuren
Compositie met drie figuren
Composición con tres figuras

●●

1932
128 x 230 cm / 50.4 x 90.6 in.
Centre Georges Pompidou, Musée National
d'Art Moderne, Paris

oil on canvas / Öl auf Leinwand
olieverf op doek / óleo sobre lienzo

Starting in 1930, Léger abandons the pure geometric shapes
replacing them with nudes combined with organic shapes.

Nach 1930 gibt Léger die geometrischen Formen auf
und ersetzt sie durch Akte, die aus organischen Formen
zusammengesetzt sind.

Vanaf 1930 laat Léger de puur geometrische vormen achter
zich en vervangt deze door naakten in combinatie met
organische vormen.

A partir de 1930, Léger abandona las formas geométricas
puras reemplazándolas por desnudos unidos a formas
orgánicas.

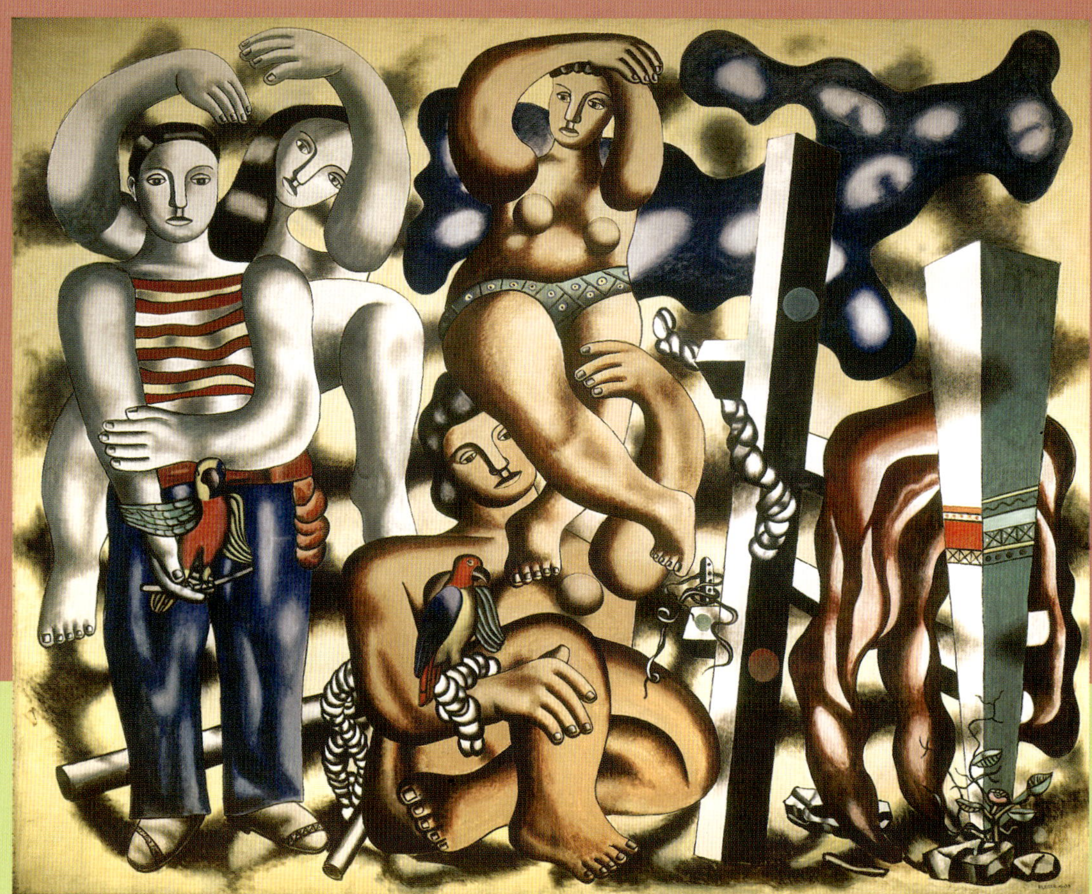

Fernand Léger
(Argentan 1881 - Gif-sur-Yvette 1955)

Composition with parrots
Komposition mit Papageien
Compositie met papegaaien
Composición con loros
● ● ●

1935-1939
400 x 480 cm / 157.5 x 189 in.
Centre Georges Pompidou,
Musée National d'Art Moderne, Paris

oil on canvas / Öl auf Leinwand / olieverf op doek / óleo sobre lienzo

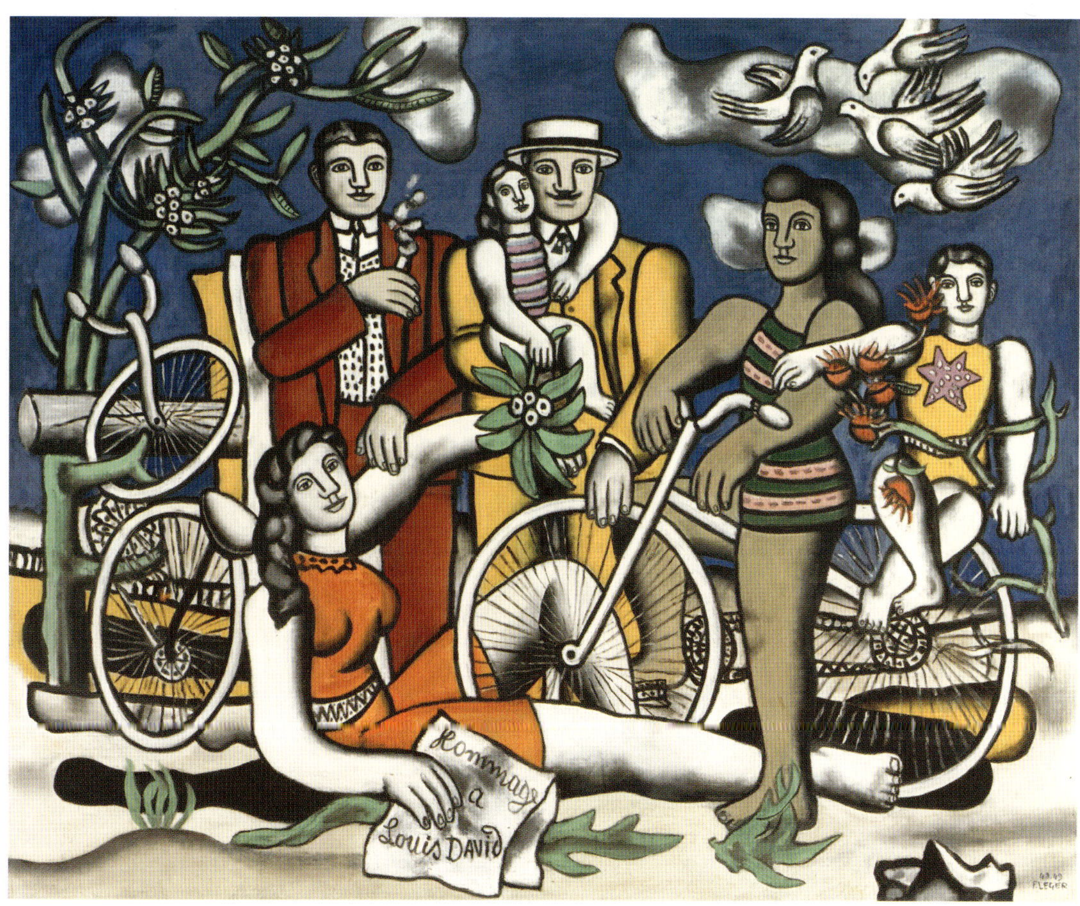

Fernand Léger
(Argentan 1881 - Gif-sur-Yvette 1955)

Les Loisirs:
Tribute to Louis David
Hommage an Louis David
Hulde aan Louis David
Homenaje a Louis David

●●●

1948-1949
154 x 185 cm / 60.6 x 72.8 in.
Centre Georges Pompidou, Musée National d'Art Moderne, Paris

oil on canvas / Öl auf Leinwand / olieverf op doek / óleo sobre lienzo

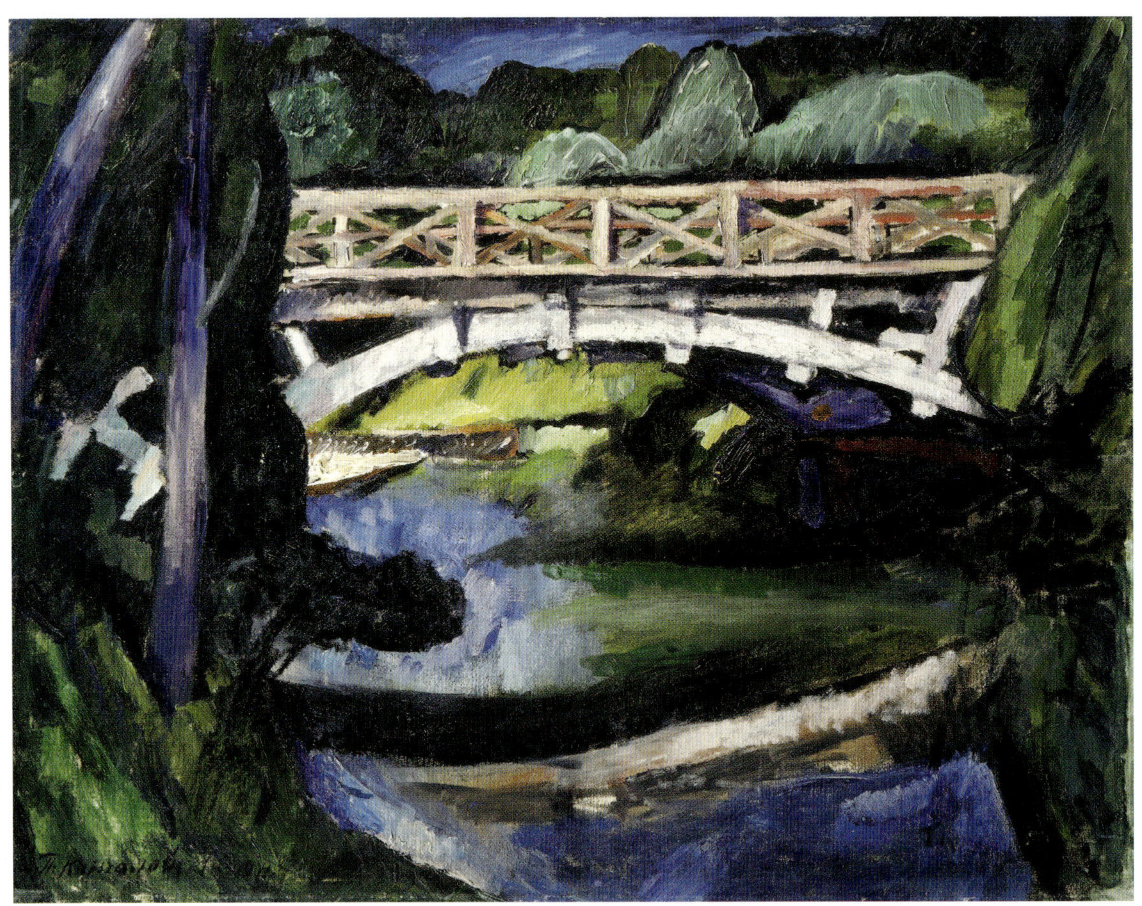

Piotr Konchalovskij
(Slaviansk 1876 - Moscow 1956)

Bridge
Brücke
Brug
Puente

●

1911
Vrubel Museum of Fine Arts, Omsk

oil on canvas / Öl auf Leinwand
olieverf op doek / óleo sobre lienzo

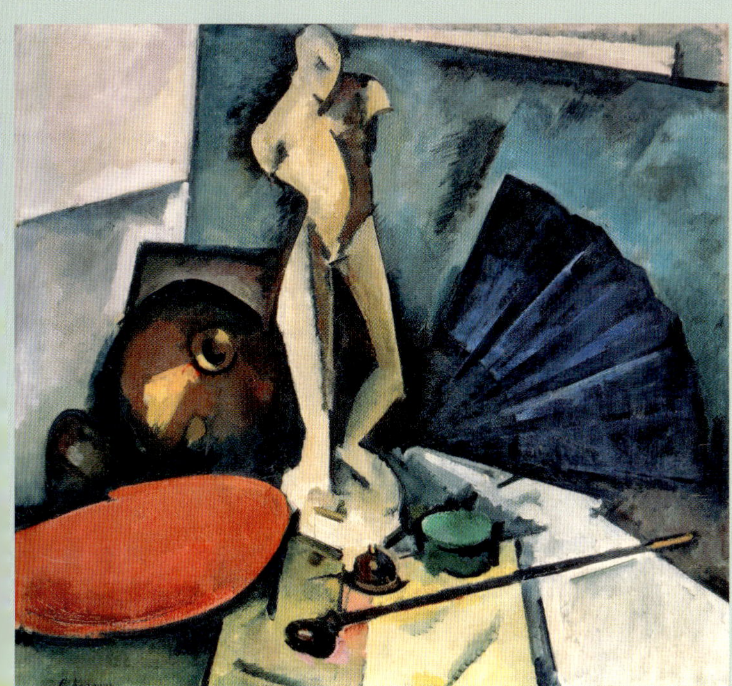

Aleksandr Kuprin
(Borisoglebsk 1880 - Moscow 1960)

Still life with fan and statuette
Stillleben mit Fächer und Statue
Stilleven met waaier en beeldje
Bodegón con abanico y estatuilla

●

1919
The State Tretyakov Gallery, Moscow

oil on canvas / Öl auf Leinwand
olieverf op doek / óleo sobre lienzo

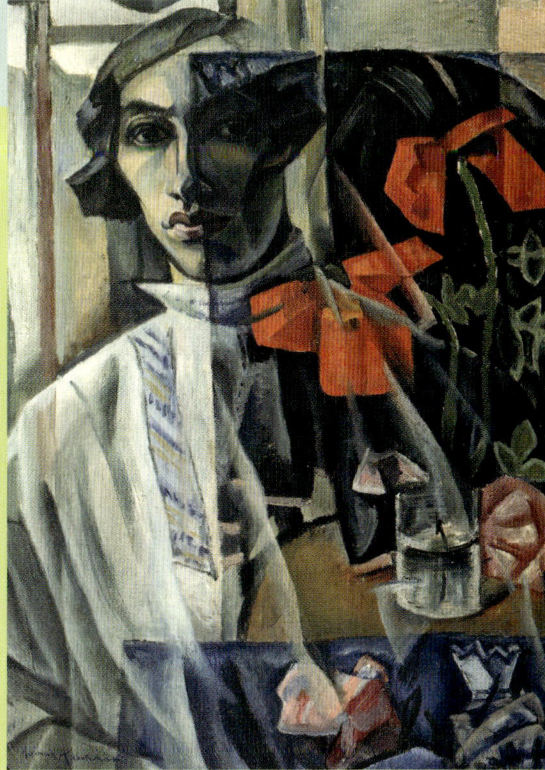

Altman Nathan
(Vinnytsia 1889 - St. Petersburg 1970)

Self-portrait
Selbstbildnis
Zelfportret
Autorretrato

●

1912
The State Tretyakov Gallery, Moscow

oil on canvas / Öl auf Leinwand
olieverf op doek / óleo sobre lienzo

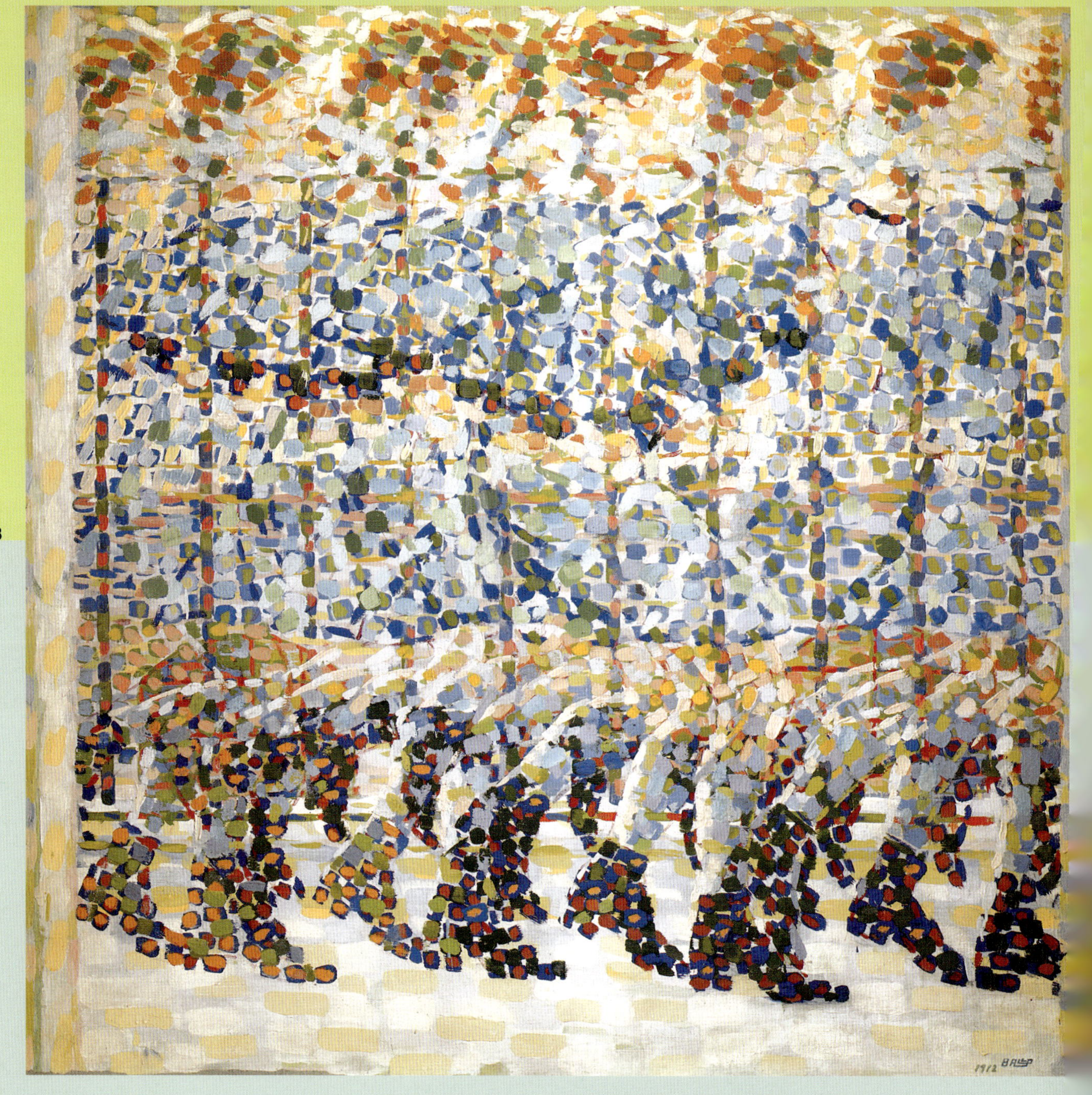

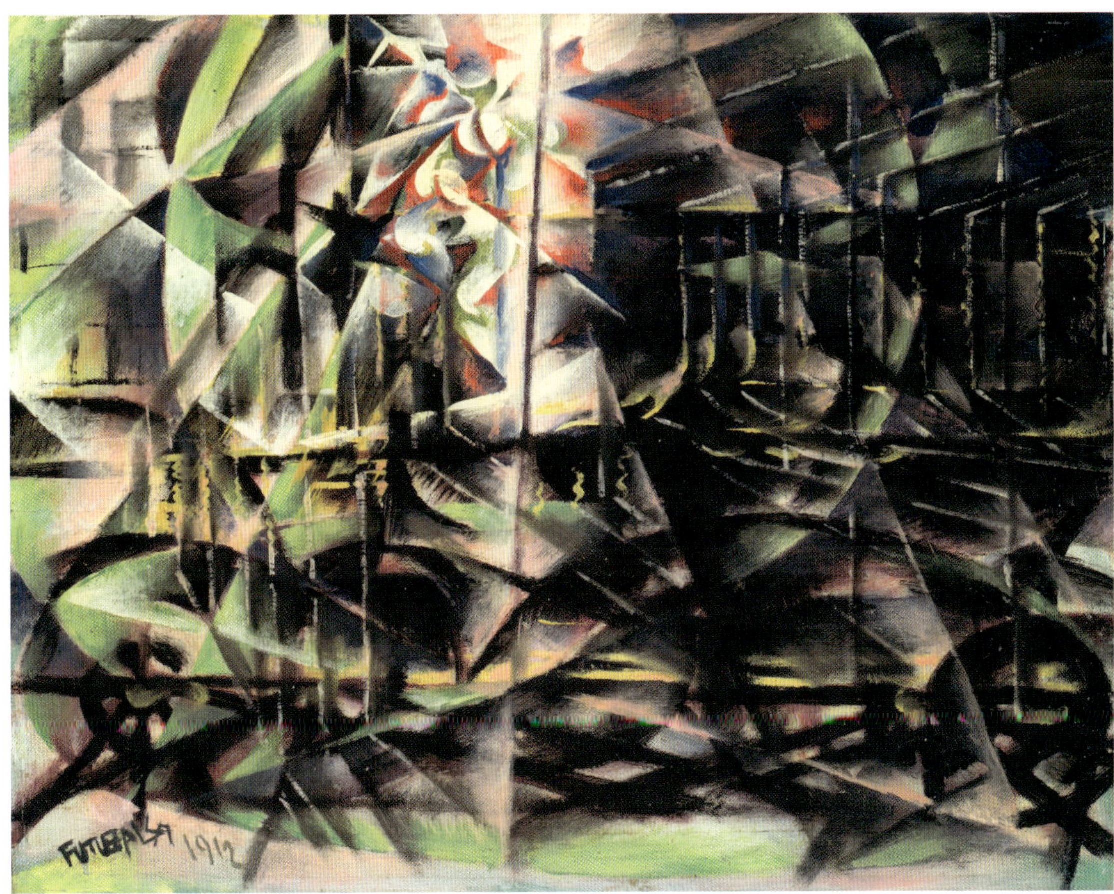

◀ Giacomo Balla
(Torino 1871 - Roma 1958)

Little girl running on the balcony
Ein Kind läuft über den Balkon
Meisje dat op het balkon rent
Niña corriendo en un balcón

●●●

1912
125 x 125 cm / 49.2 x 49.2 in.
Galleria d'Arte Moderna, Milano

oil on canvas / Öl auf Leinwand
olieverf op doek / óleo sobre lienzo

Giacomo Balla
(Torino 1871 - Roma 1958)

Automobile speed
Geschwindigkeit des Automobils
Snelheid van de automobiel
Velocidad de automóvil

●

1912
55,6 x 68,9 cm / 21.9 x 21.1 in.
Museum of Modern Art (MoMA), New York

oil on wood / Öl auf Holz
olieverf op hout/óleo sobre madera

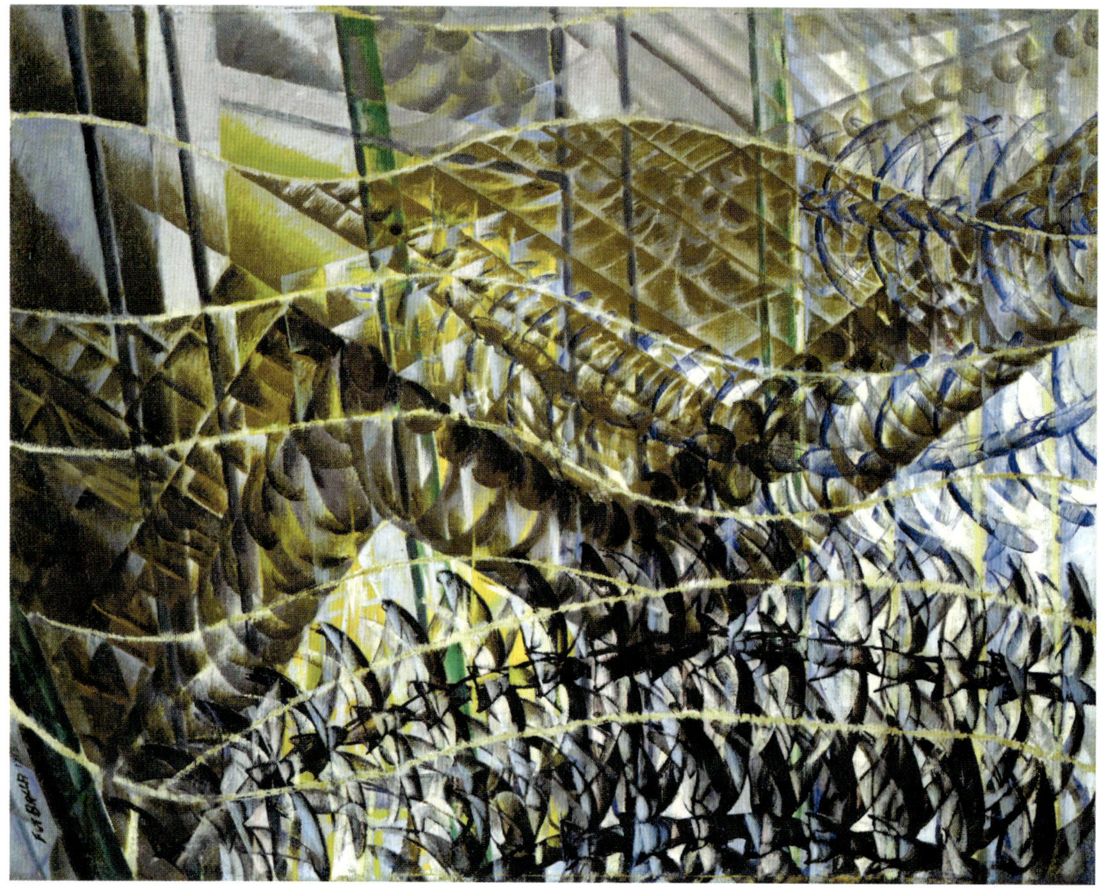

Giacomo Balla
(Torino 1871 - Roma 1958)

Swallows: lines of motion + dynamic sequences
Schwalben: Bewegungslinien + dynamische Sequenzen
Zwaluwen: bewegingslijnen + dynamische volgorde
Golondrinas: líneas de movimiento + secuencias dinámicas

●

1913
96,8 x 120 cm / 38.1 x 47.2 in.
Museum of Modern Art (MoMA), New York

oil on canvas / Öl auf Leinwand
olieverf op doek / óleo sobre lienzo

▶ Giacomo Balla
(Torino 1871 - Roma 1958)

Arc lamp
Bogenlampe
Booglamp
Lámpara de arco

●●●

1909
174,7 x 114,7 cm / 68.8 x 45.1 in.
Museum of Modern Art (MoMA), New York

oil on canvas / Öl auf Leinwand
olieverf op doek / óleo sobre lienzo

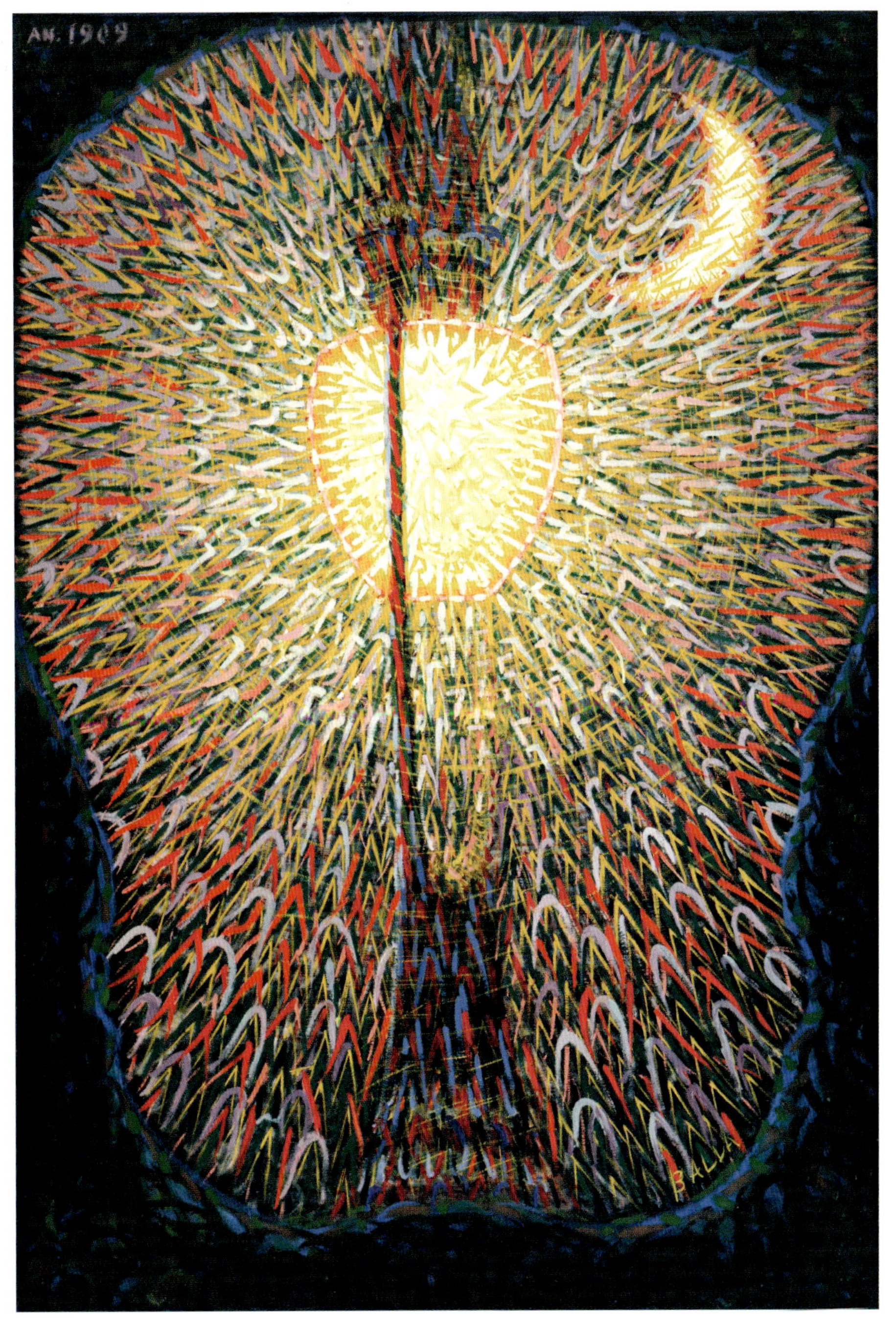

AN. 1909
BALLA

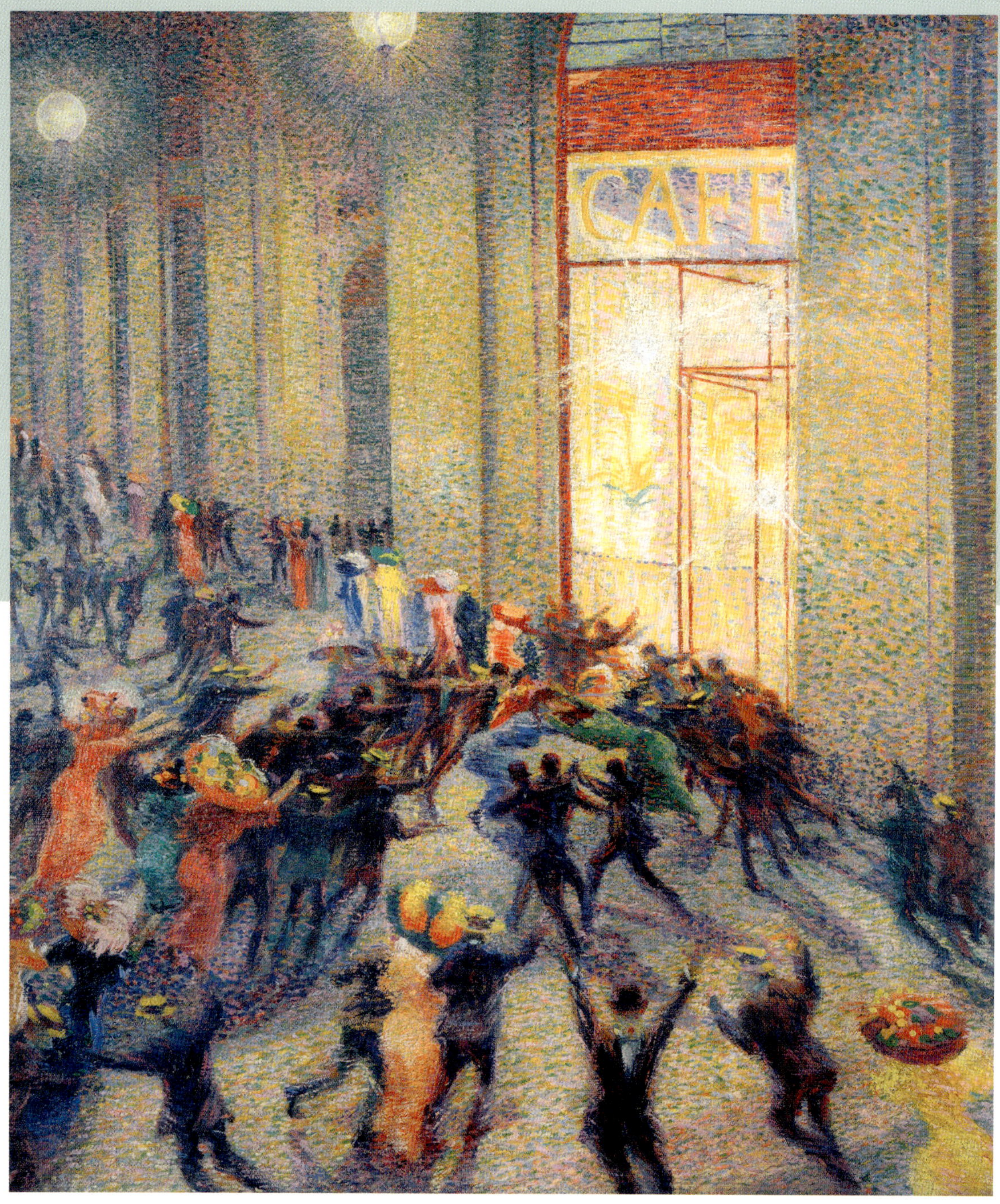
CAFE

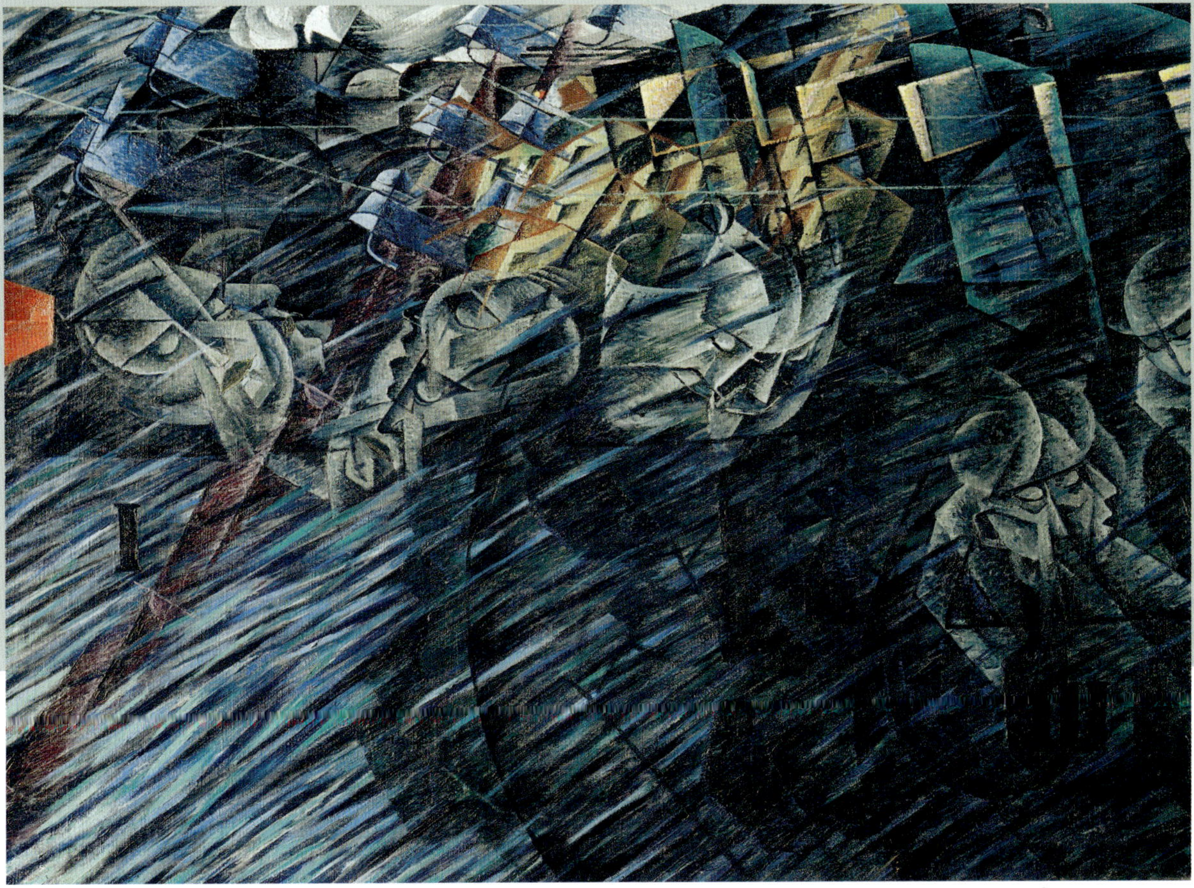

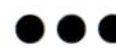

◀ Umberto Boccioni
(Reggio Calabria 1882 - Verona 1916)

Brawl in the tunnel
Schlägerei in der Galleria
Vechtpartij in de galerij
Pelea en la galería

●●●

1910
76 x 64 cm / 29.9 x 25.2 in.
Pinacoteca di Brera, Milano

oil on canvas / Öl auf Leinwand
olieverf op doek / óleo sobre lienzo

Umberto Boccioni
(Reggio Calabria 1882 - Verona 1916)

States of Mind: Those who go
Seelenzustände: Die Abschiede
Gemoedstoestand: vaarwel
Estados de ánimo: los que van

●

1911
70,3 x 96 / 27.6 x 37.7 in.
Galleria d'arte Moderna, Milano

oil on canvas / Öl auf Leinwand
olieverf op doek / óleo sobre lienzo

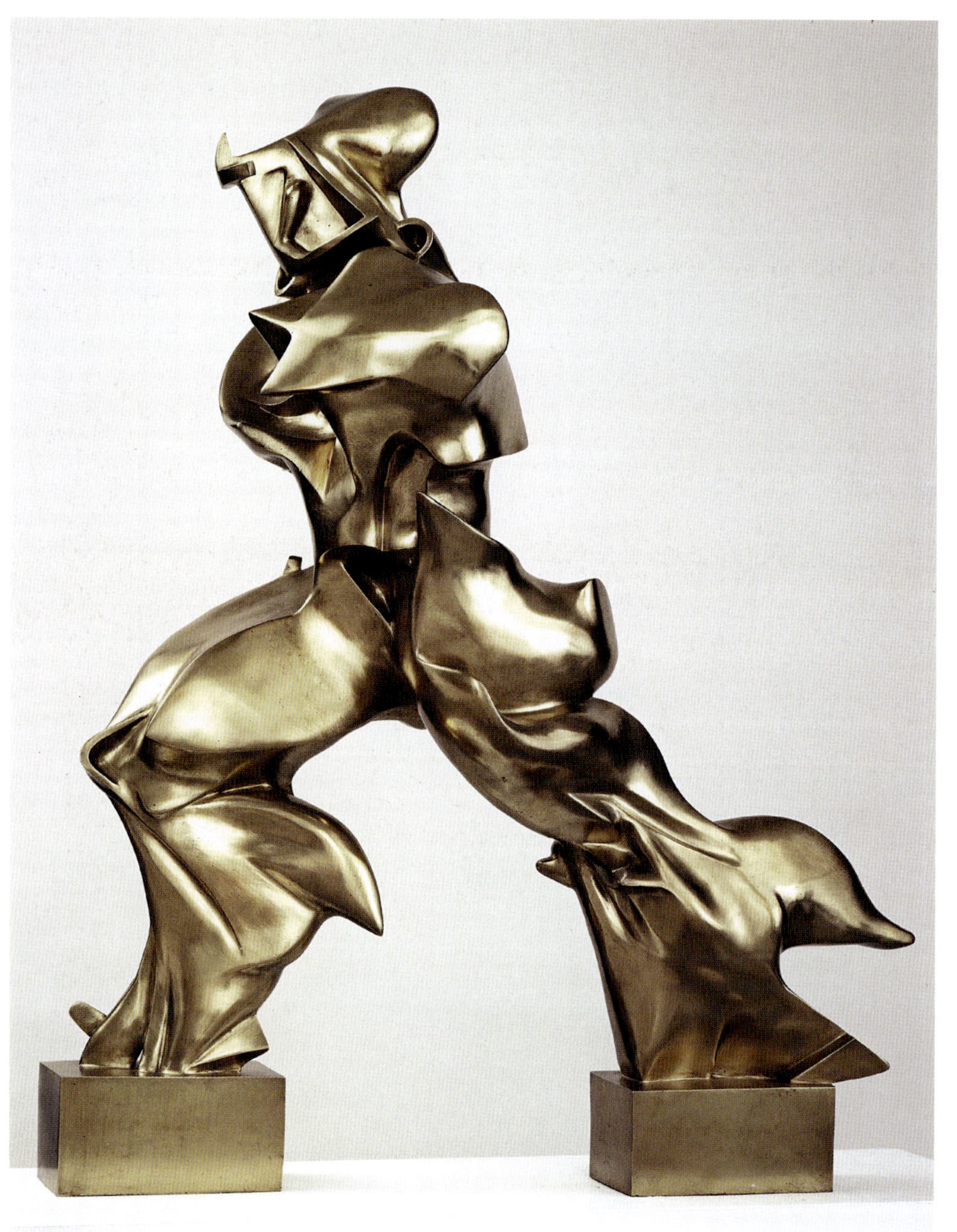

174

Umberto Boccioni
(Reggio Calabria 1882 -
Verona 1916)

**Unique forms of the
continuity of space
Einzigartige Formen
in der räumlichen
Kontinuität
Unieke vormen van de
continuïteit in de ruimte
Formas únicas de la
continuidad en el espacio**

●●●

1913
111,2 x 88,5 x 40 cm
43.8 x 34.8 x 15.7 in.
Museum of Modern Art
(MoMA), New York

bronze / Bronze / brons / bronce

**In sculpture as well, the
Futurists will try to convey
the feelings of movement,
speed and fluidity.**

**Auch in der Bildhauerei
versuchen die Futuristen,
das Gefühl von Bewegung,
Geschwindigkeit und
Flüssigkeit umzusetzen.**

**Ook in de beeldhouwkunst
proberen de futuristen
het gevoel van beweging,
snelheid en vloeibaarheid
over te brengen.**

**También en la escultura,
los futuristas tratarán de
transmitir las sensaciones
de movimiento, rapidez y
fluidez.**

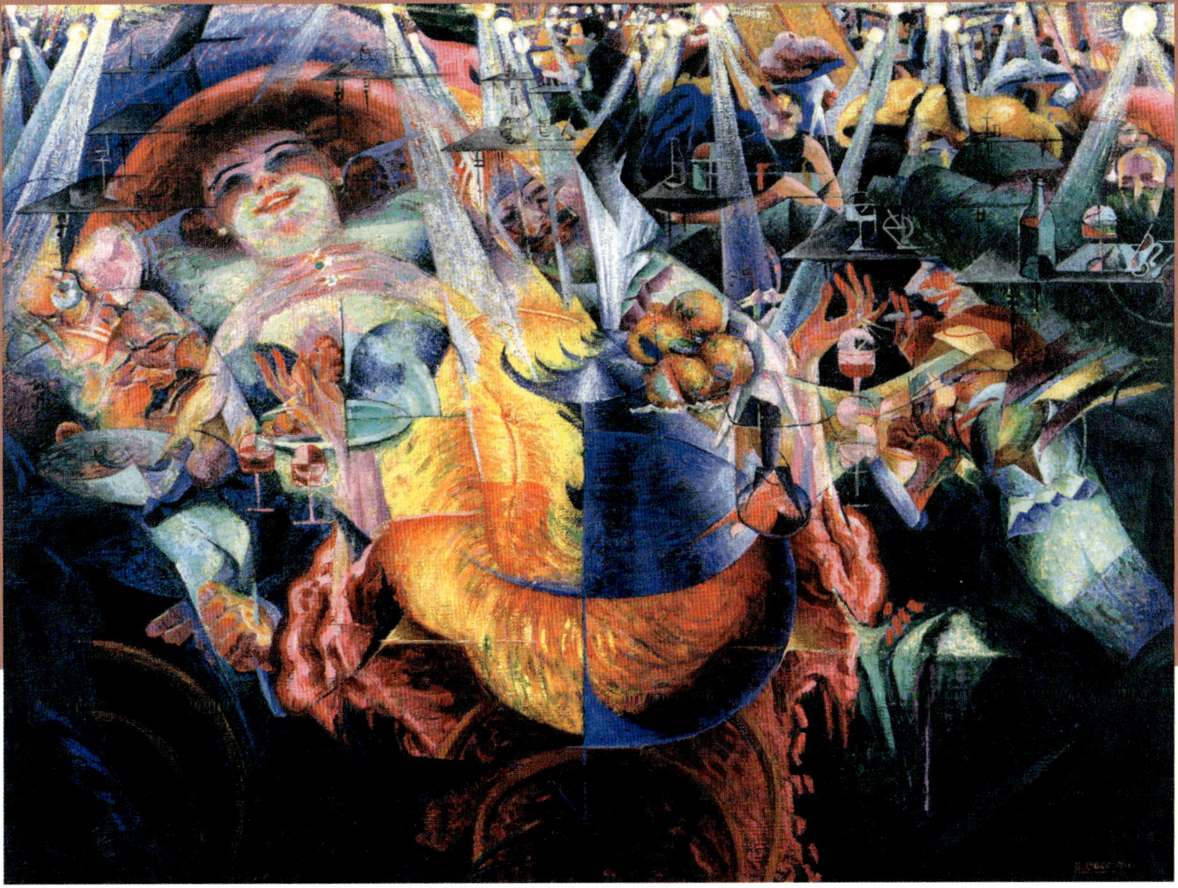

Umberto Boccioni
(Reggio Calabria 1882 - Verona 1916)

Laughter
Das Lachen
De lach
La carcajada

1911
110,2 x 145,4 cm / 43.4 x 57.3 in.
Museum of Modern Art (MoMA), New York

oil on canvas / Öl auf Leinwand / olieverf op doek / óleo sobre lienzo

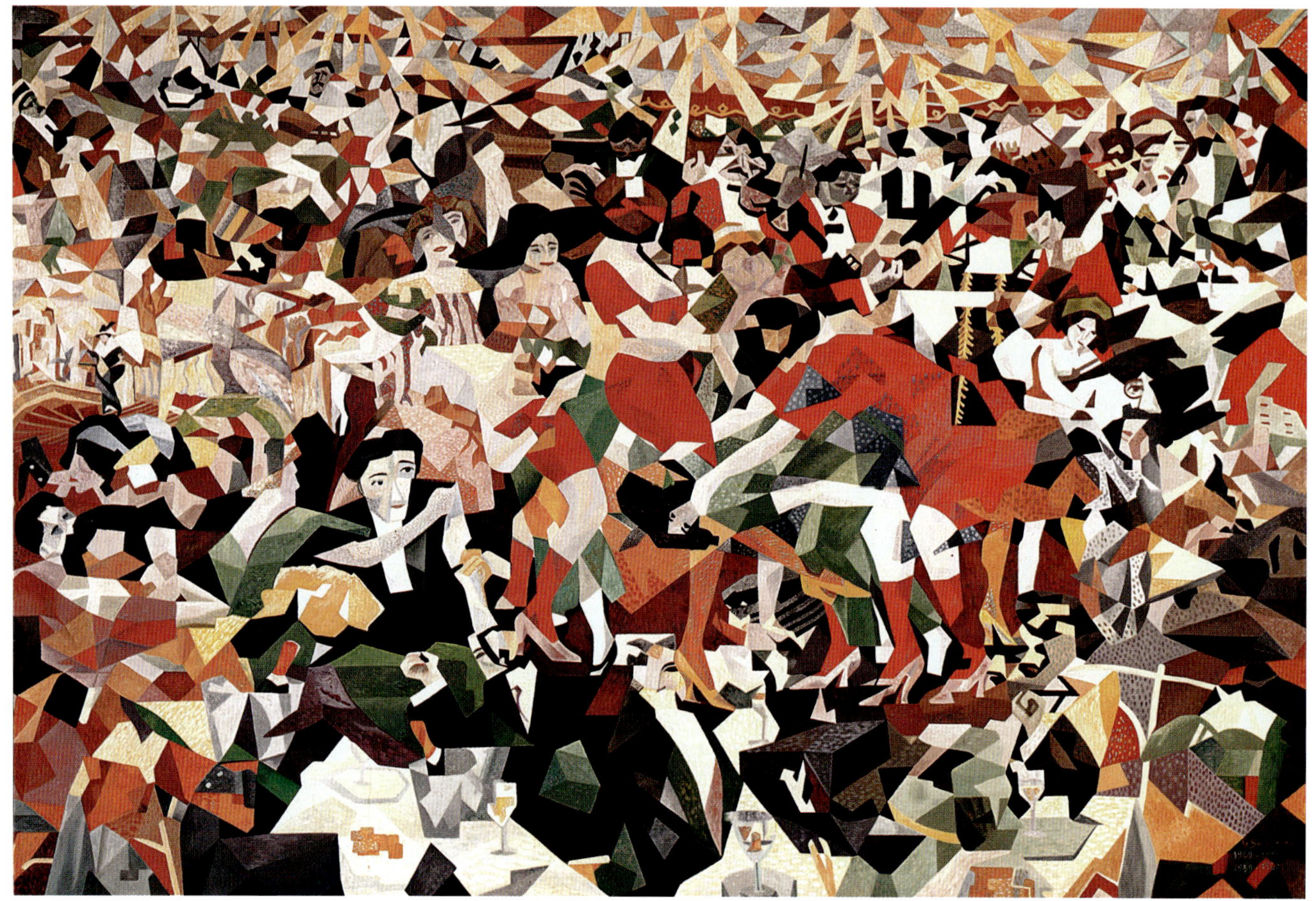

Gino Severini
(Cortona 1883 - Parigi 1966)

Pan-pan at the 'Monico'
Der Pan-Pan-Tanz im 'Monico'
Pan-pan in de 'Monico'
La danza del Pan-pan en el 'Monico'

●●

1909-1911 (1959-1960)
280 x 400 cm / 110.3 x 157.6 in.
Centre Georges Pompidou, Musée National d'Art Moderne, Paris

mixed medium on canvas/Mischtechnik auf Leinwand
gemengde techniek op doek/técnica mixta sobre lienzo

Dance is a theme much loved by artists fascinated with the notions of time and movement.

Der Tanz ist ein sehr beliebtes Motiv bei den Künstlern, die von Zeit- und Bewegungsbegriffen fasziniert sind.

De dans is een zeer geliefd motief van kunstenaars die gefascineerd raken door ritme en beweging.

La danza es un tema muy popular entre los artistas fascinados por las nociones del tiempo y del movimiento.

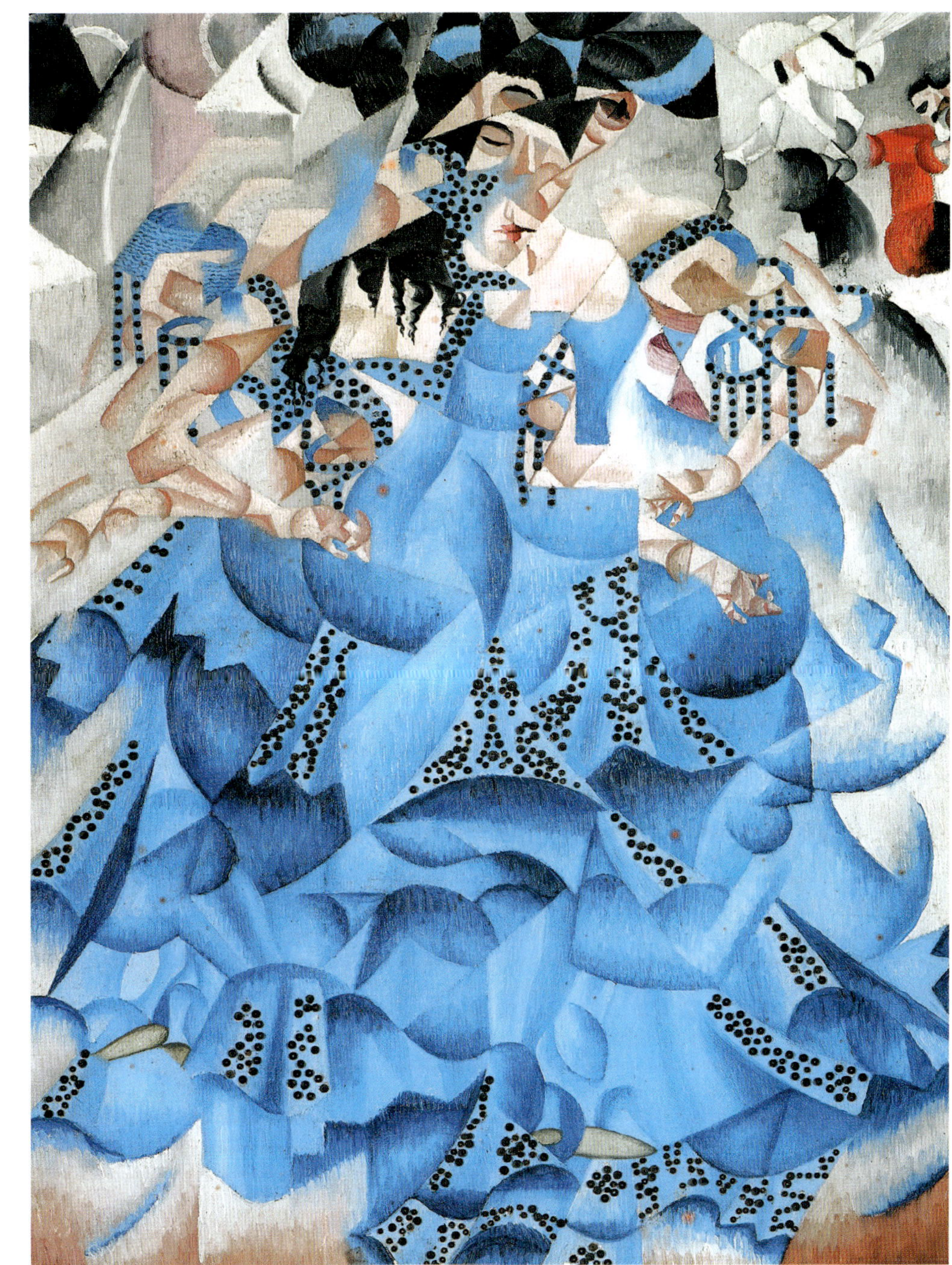

Gino Severini
(Cortona 1883 - Parigi 1966)

**Dancer in Blue
Blaue Tänzerin
In blauw geklede danseres
Bailarina azul**

●●●

1912
61 x 46 cm / 24 x 18.1 in.
Collezione Peggy Guggenheim,
Venezia (Collezione Mattioli,
Milano)

oil on canvas
Öl auf Leinwand
olieverf op doek
óleo sobre lienzo

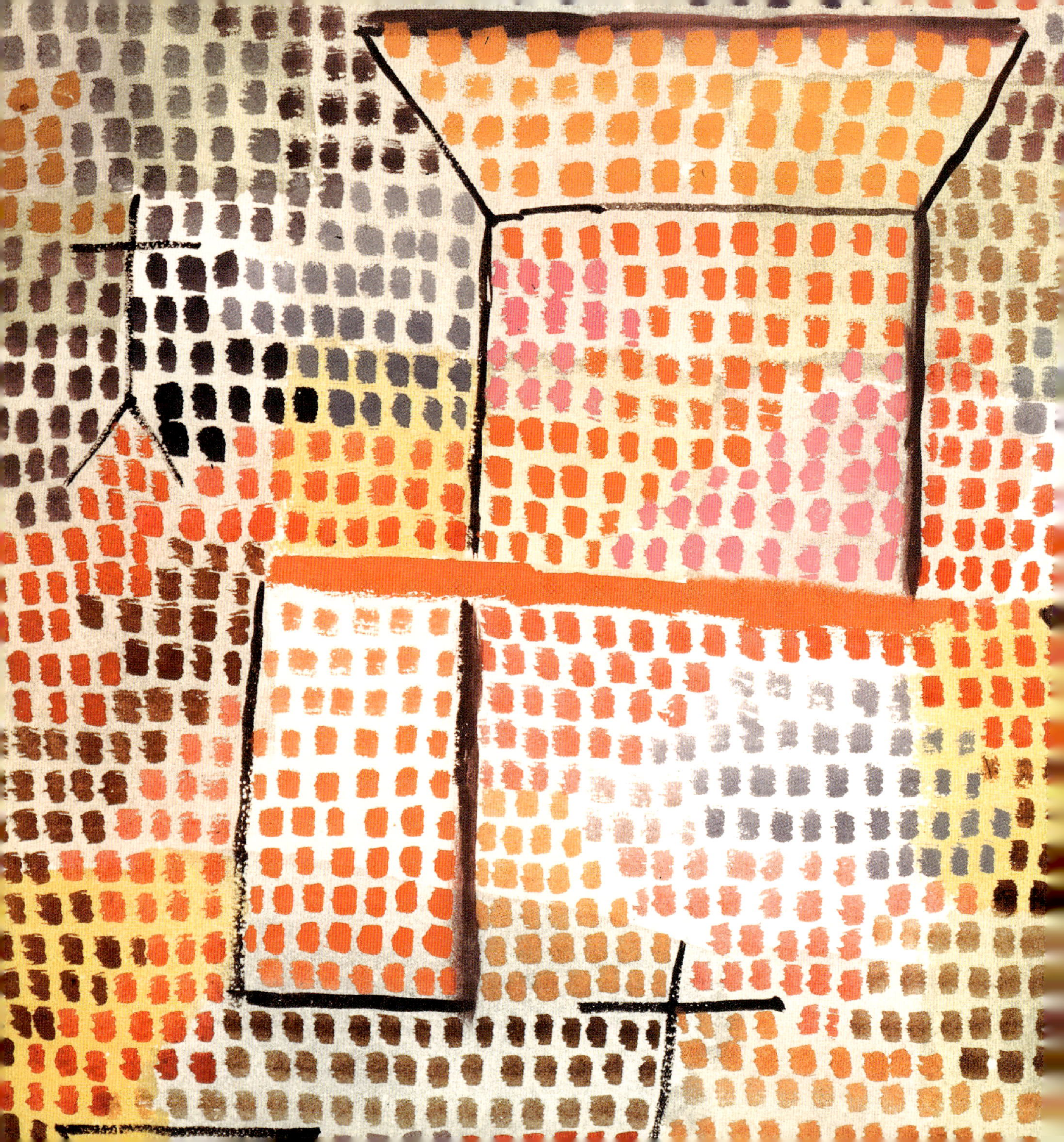

Abstract movements from Kandinsky to Mondrian • Die Strömungen des Abstraktismus von Kandinsky bis Mondrian • De abstracte stromingen van Kandinsky en Mondrian • Las corrientes abstractas, de Kandisky a Mondrian

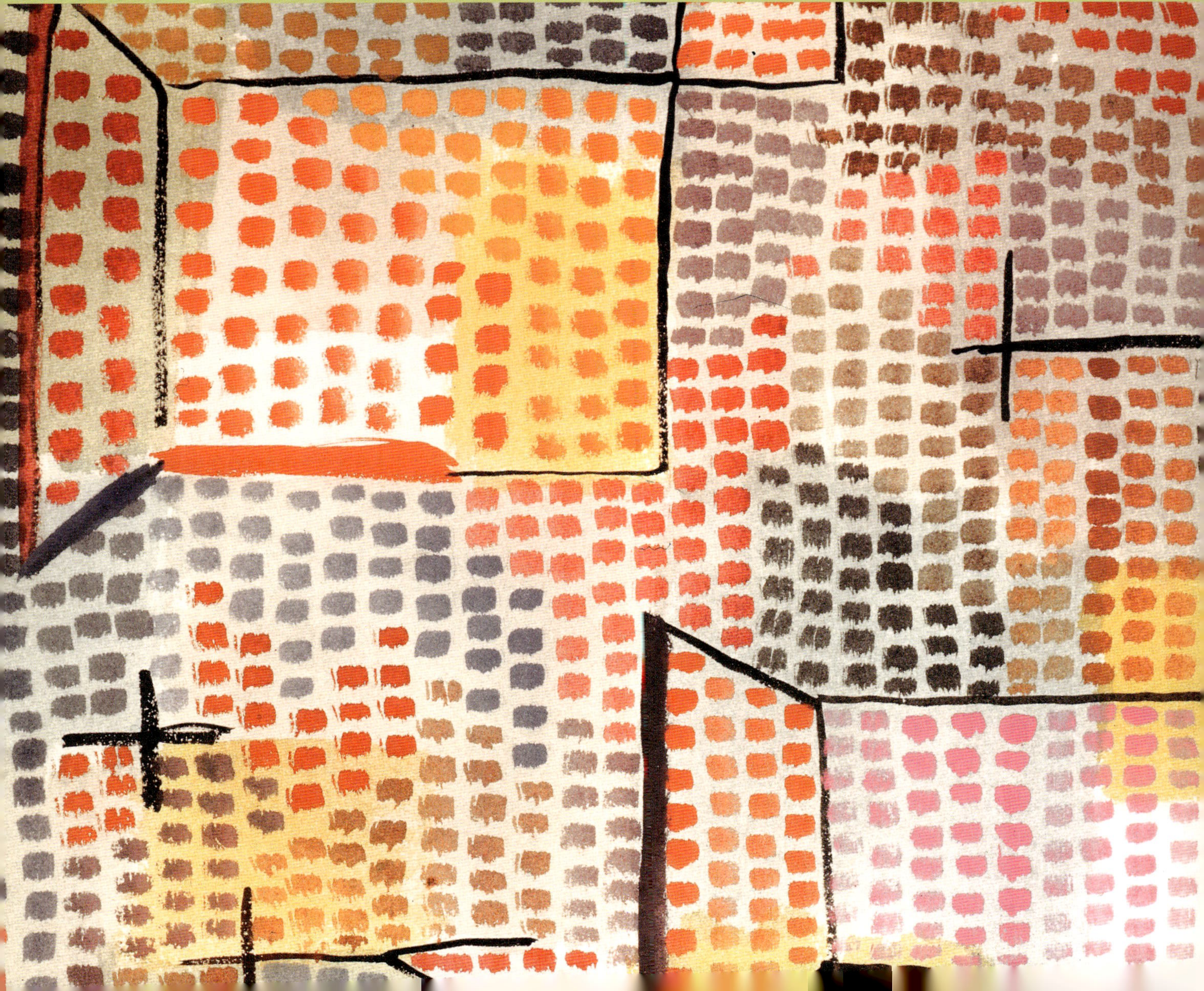

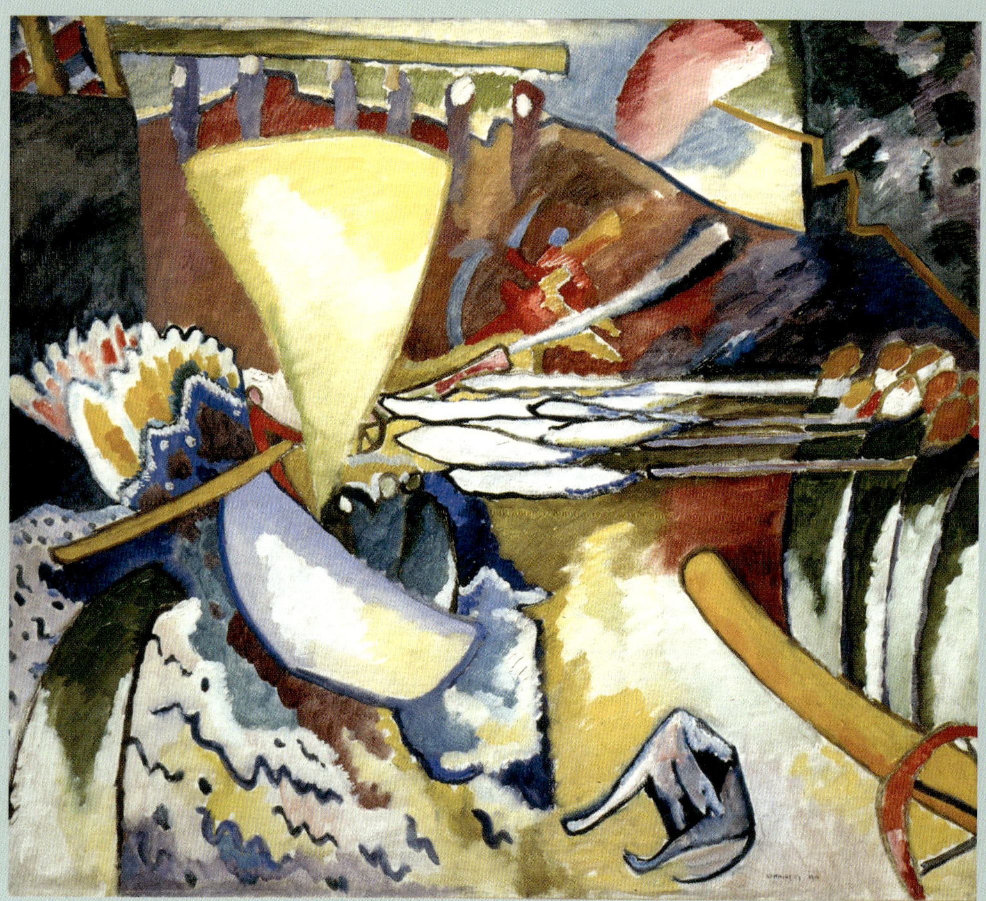

Vassily Kandinsky
(Moscow 1866 - Neuilly-sur-Seine 1944)

Improvisation 11
Improvisatie 11
Improvisación 11

●

1910
97,5 x 106,5 cm / 38.4 x 41.9 in.
The Russian Museum, St. Petersburg

oil on canvas / Öl auf Leinwand
olieverf op doek / óleo sobre lienzo

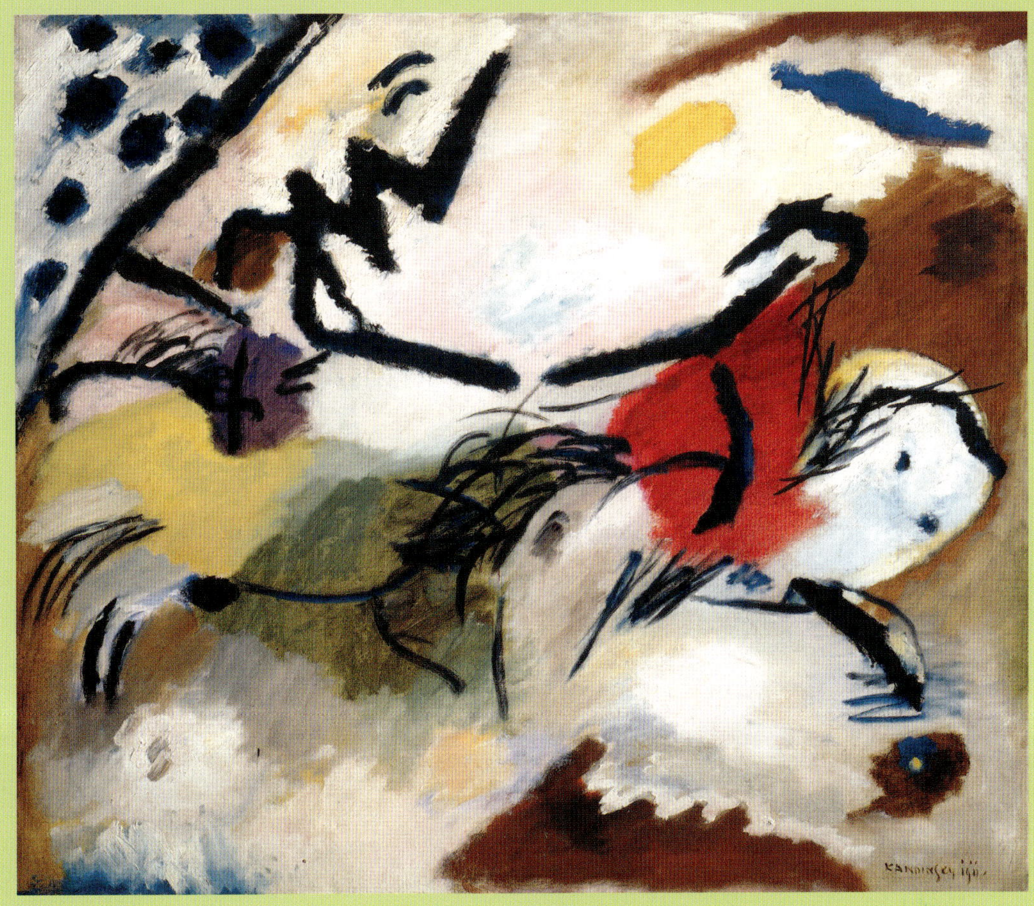

Vassily Kandinsky
(Moscow 1866 - Neuilly-sur-Seine 1944)

Improvisation 20
Improvisatie 20
Improvisación 20

●●

1911
94,5 x 108 cm / 37.2 x 42.5 in.
Pushkin State Museum of Fine Arts, Moscow

oil on canvas / Öl auf Leinwand
olieverf op doek / óleo sobre lienzo

In *Improvisations* Kandinsky translates only the
internal, spontaneous and unconscious impressions.

Bei den *Improvisationen* setzt Kandinsky nur die
inneren, spontanen und unbewussten Eindrücke um.

In de *Improvisaties* vertaalt Kandinsky alleen de
innerlijke, spontane en onderbewuste indrukken.

En las *Improvisaciones*, Kandinsky traduce solamente
las impresiones internas, espontáneas e inconscientes.

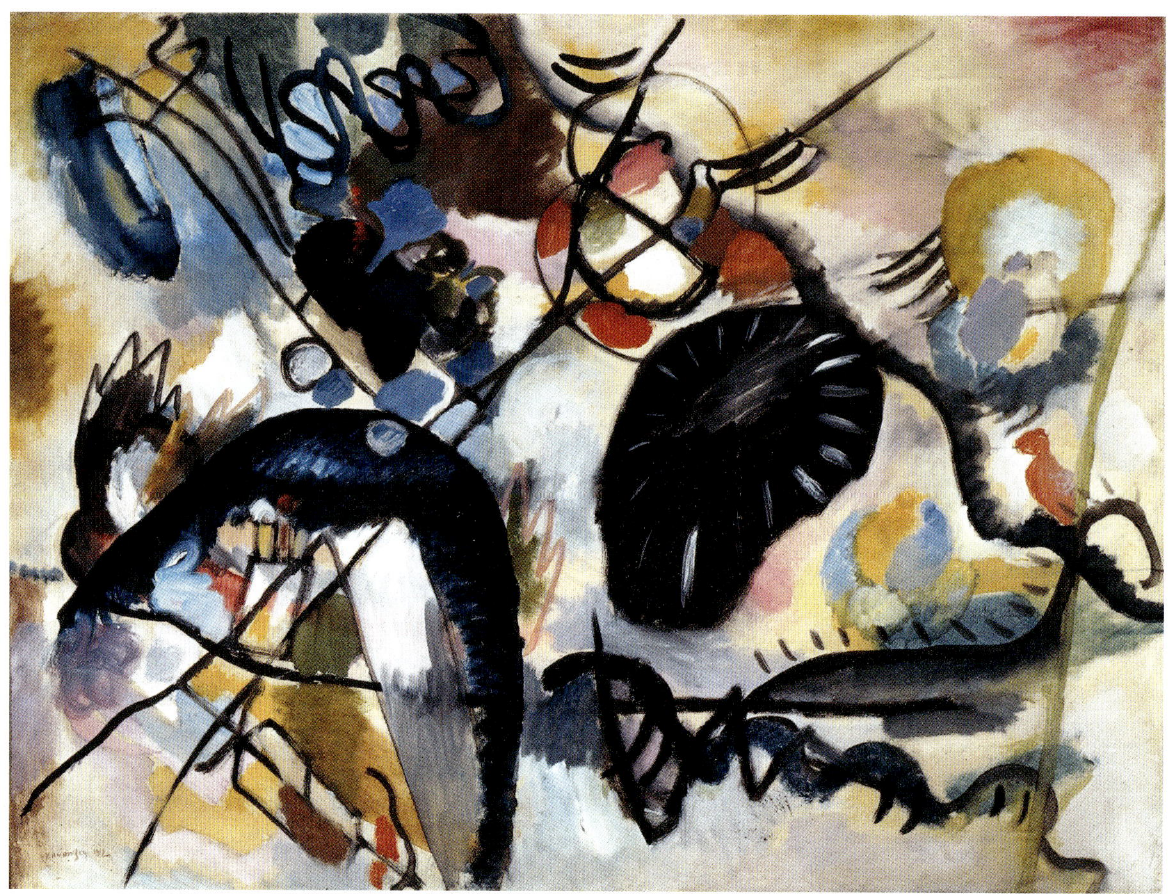

Vassily Kandinsky
(Moscow 1866 - Neuilly-sur-Seine 1944)

Black Mark I
Schwarzer Fleck I
Zwarte vlek I
Mancha negra I

●

1912
100 x 130 cm / 39.3 x 51.1 in.
The Russian Museum, St. Petersburg

oil on canvas / Öl auf Leinwand
olieverf op doek / óleo sobre lienzo

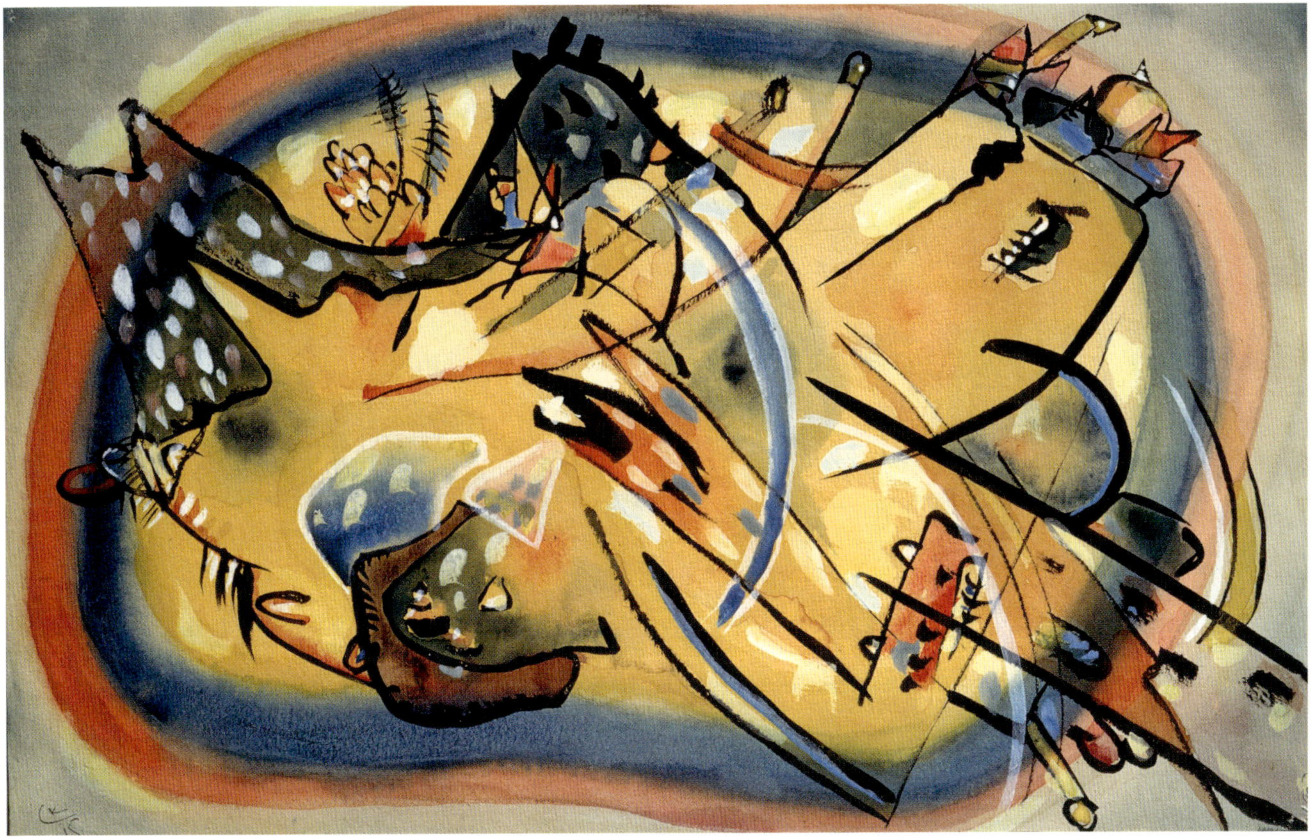

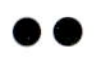

Vassily Kandinsky
(Moscow 1866 - Neuilly-sur-Seine 1944)

Composition (Landscape)
Komposition (Landschaft)
Compositie (Landschap)
Composición (Paisaje)

●●

1915
22,5 x 33,8 cm / 8.8 x 13.3 in.
The Russian Museum, St. Petersburg

watercolor and India ink with touches of white on paper / Aquarell und Tusche mit weißen Strichen auf Papier
acquarel en Oost-Indische inkt met wit bijgewerkt op papier / acuarela y tinta china con retoques de blanco sobre papel

Vassily Kandinsky
(Moscow 1866 -
Neuilly-sur-Seine 1944)

**On white
Auf weiss
Op wit
Sobre el blanco**
●●●
1920
The Russian Museum,
St. Petersburg

oil on canvas
Öl auf Leinwand
olieverf op doek
óleo sobre lienzo

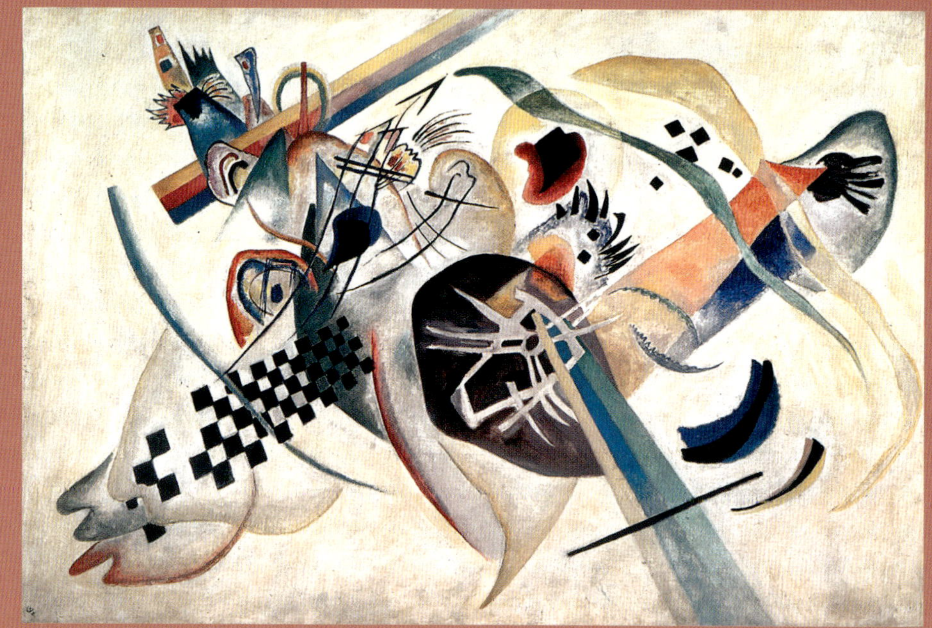

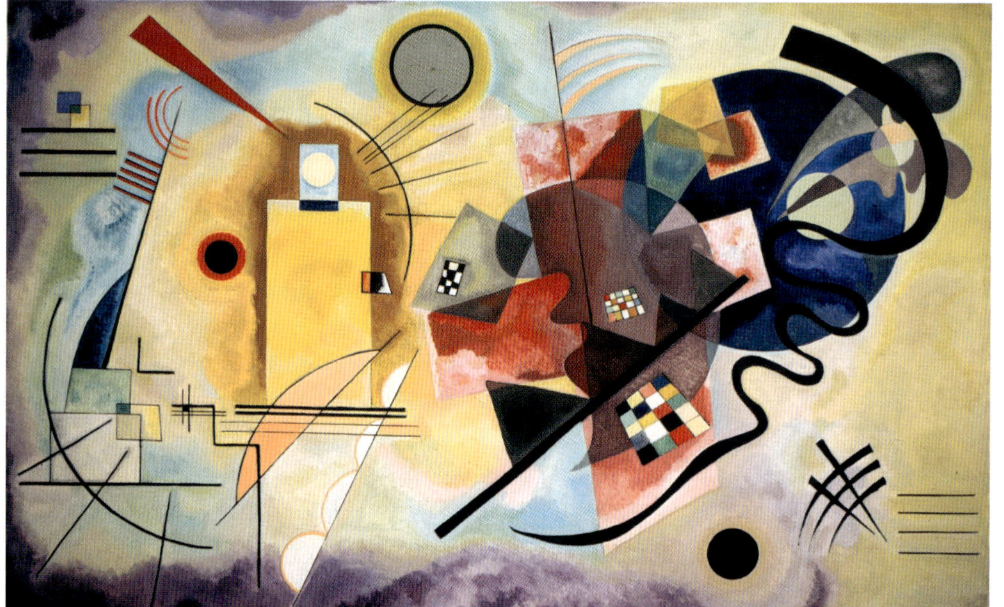

Vassily Kandinsky
(Moscow 1866 -
Neuilly-sur-Seine 1944)

**Yellow, red, blue
Gelb, Rot, Blau
Geel, rood, blauw
Amarillo, rojo, azul**
●●
1925
128 x 210 cm / 50.4 x 82.7 in
Centre Georges Pompidou,
Musée National d'Art Moderr
Paris

oil on canvas
Öl auf Leinwand
olieverf op doek
óleo sobre lienzo

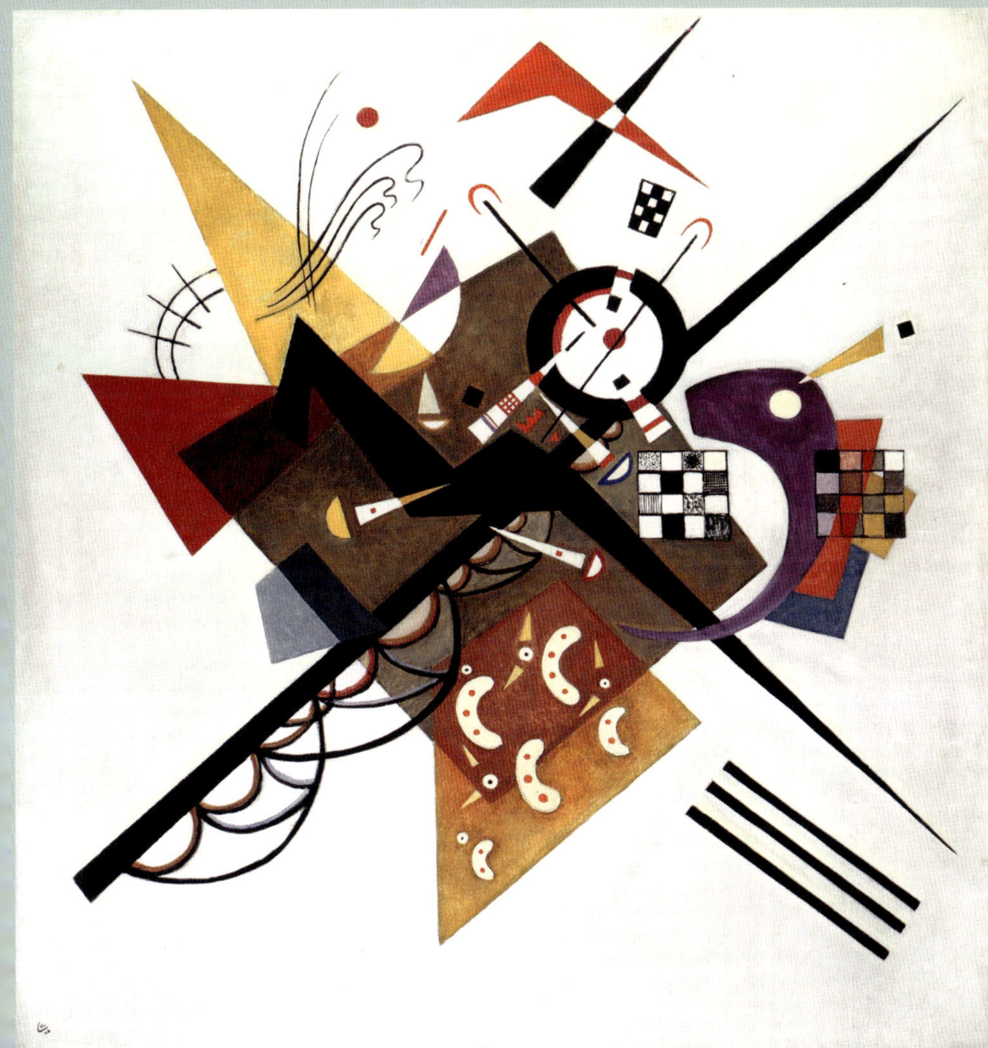

Vassily Kandinsky
(Moscow 1866 -
Neuilly-sur-Seine 1944)

On white II
Auf weiss II
Op wit II
Sobre el blanco II

●●

1923
105 x 98 cm / 41.3 x 38.6 in.
Centre Georges Pompidou,
Musée National d'Art Moderne,
Paris

oil on canvas
Öl auf Leinwand
olieverf op doek
óleo sobre lienzo

185

Starting in 1922, while he was teaching at the Bauhaus, Kandinsky points his style towards a more pronounced geometrization.

Nach 1922, während seiner Lehrtätigkeit am Bauhaus, neigt Kandinskys Stil zunehmend zur Geometrisierung.

Vanaf 1922, toen hij aan het Bauhaus lesgaf, oriënteerde Kandinsky zijn stijl op een meer uitgesproken geometrisering van vormen.

A partir de 1922, mientras enseñaba en la Bauhaus, Kandinsky orienta su estilo hacia una geometrización más marcada.

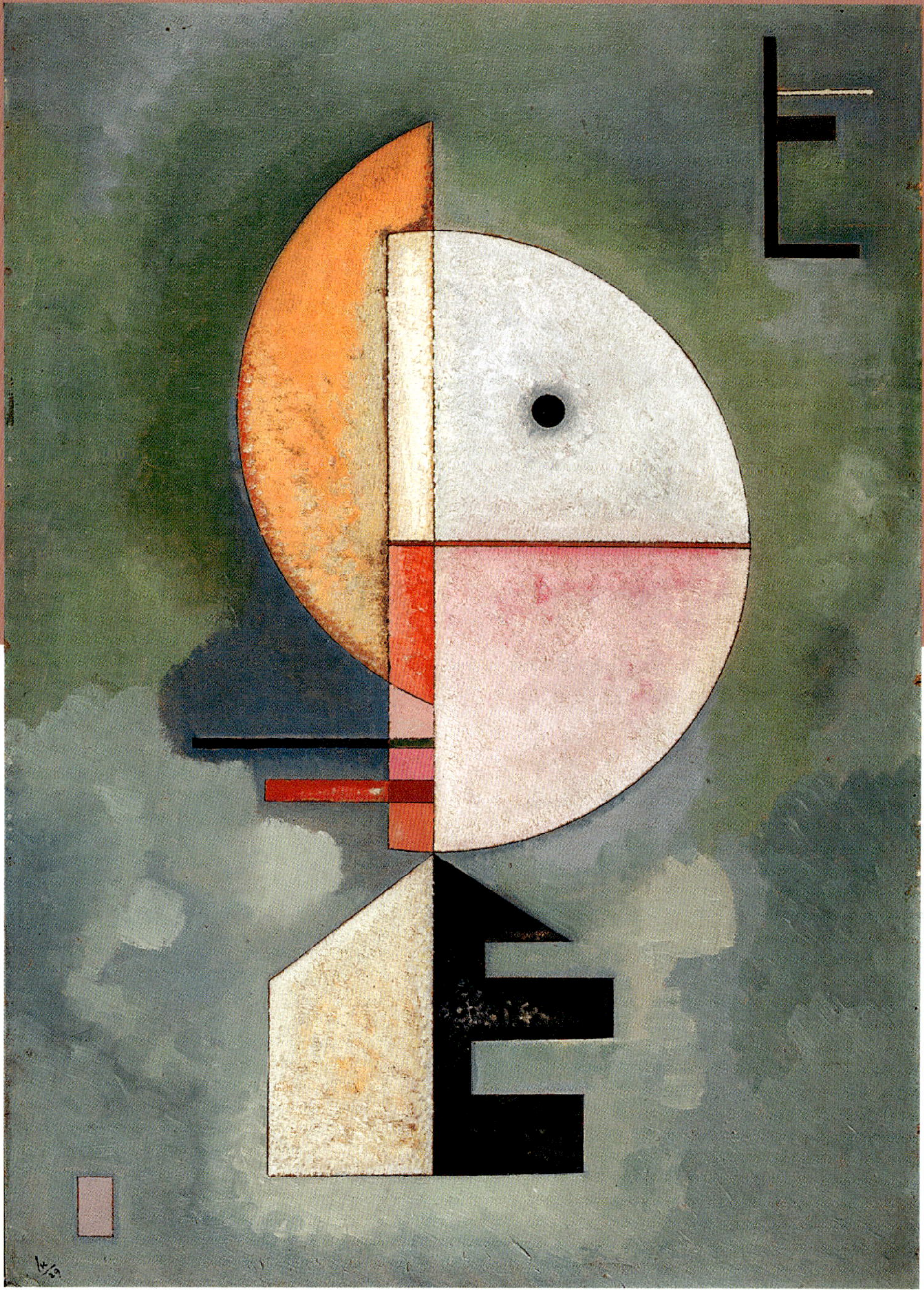

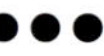

Vassily Kandinsky
(Moscow 1866 -
Neuilly-sur-Seine 1944)

Upwards (Empor)
Empor
Omhoog (Empor)
Hacia arriba (Empor)
● ● ●
1929
70 x 49 cm / 27.5 x 19.3 in.
Collezione Peggy Guggenheim,
Venezia

oil on paperboard
Öl auf Karton
olieverf op karton
óleo sobre cartón

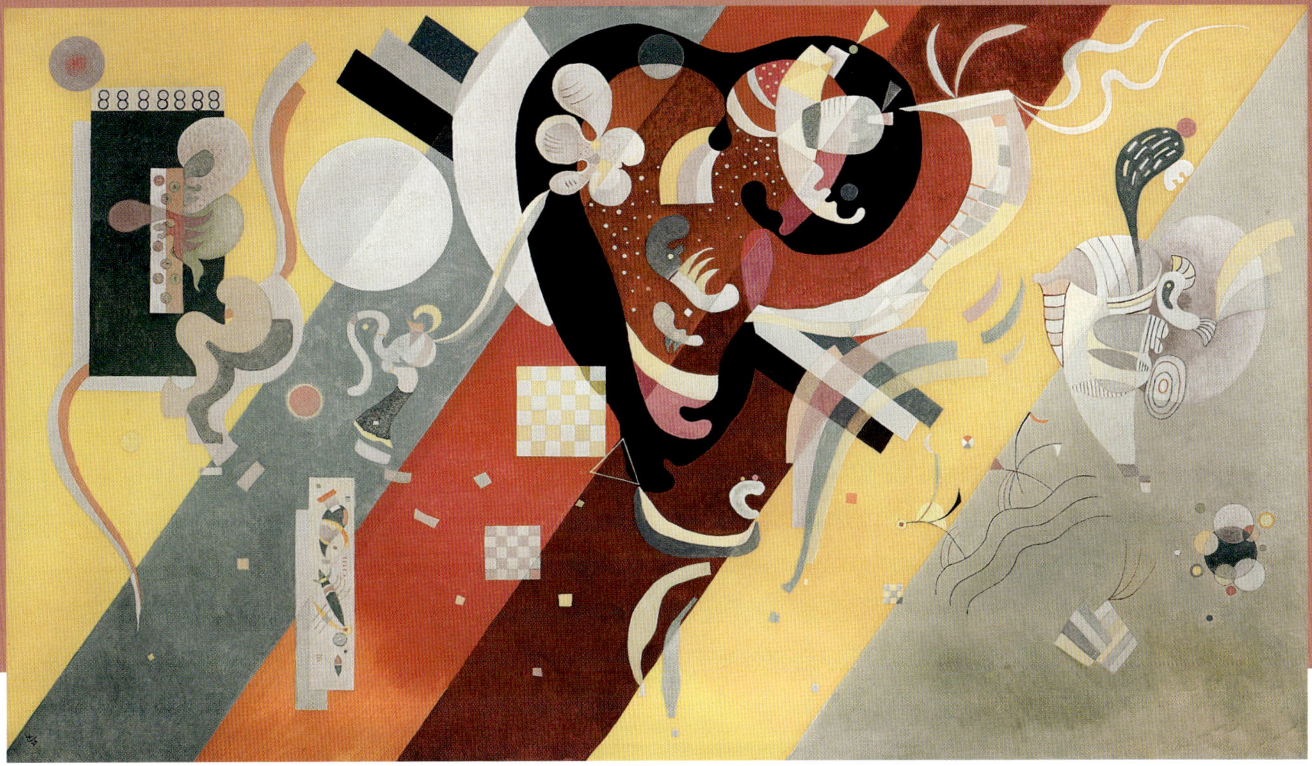

Vassily Kandinsky
(Moscow 1866 - Neuilly-sur-Seine 1944)

Composition IX
Komposition IX
Compositie IX
Composición IX

●●

1936
113,5 x 195 cm / 44.7 x 76.7 in.
Centre Georges Pompidou, Musée National d'Art Moderne, Paris

oil on canvas / Öl auf Leinwand / olieverf op doek / óleo sobre lienzo

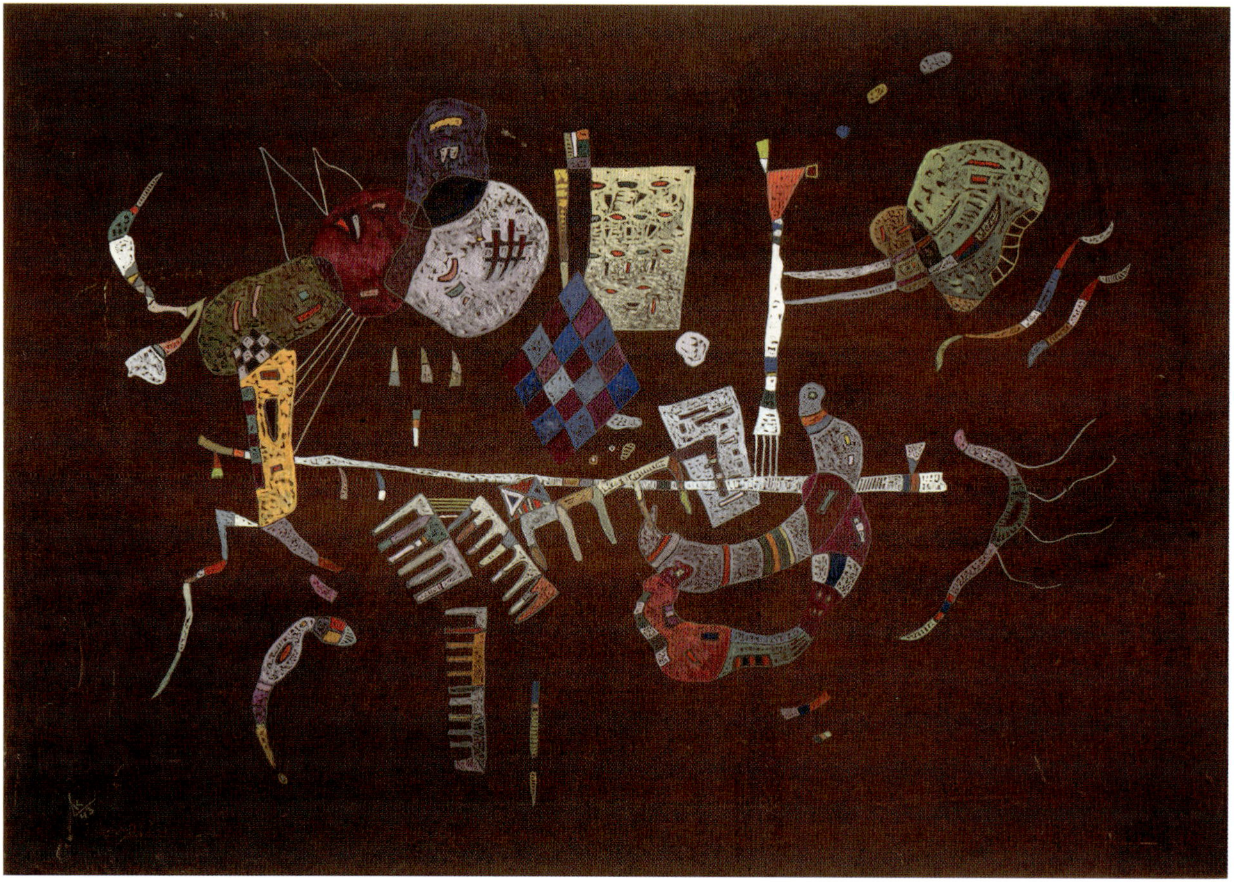

Vassily Kandinsky
(Moscow 1866 - Neuilly-sur-Seine 1944)

Around the line
Um die Linie herum
Rondom de lijn
Alrededor de la línea

●

1943
42 x 57,8 cm / 16.5 x 22.7 in.
Museo Thyssen-Bornemisza, Madrid

oil on paperboard / Öl auf Karton / olieverf op karton / óleo sobre cartón

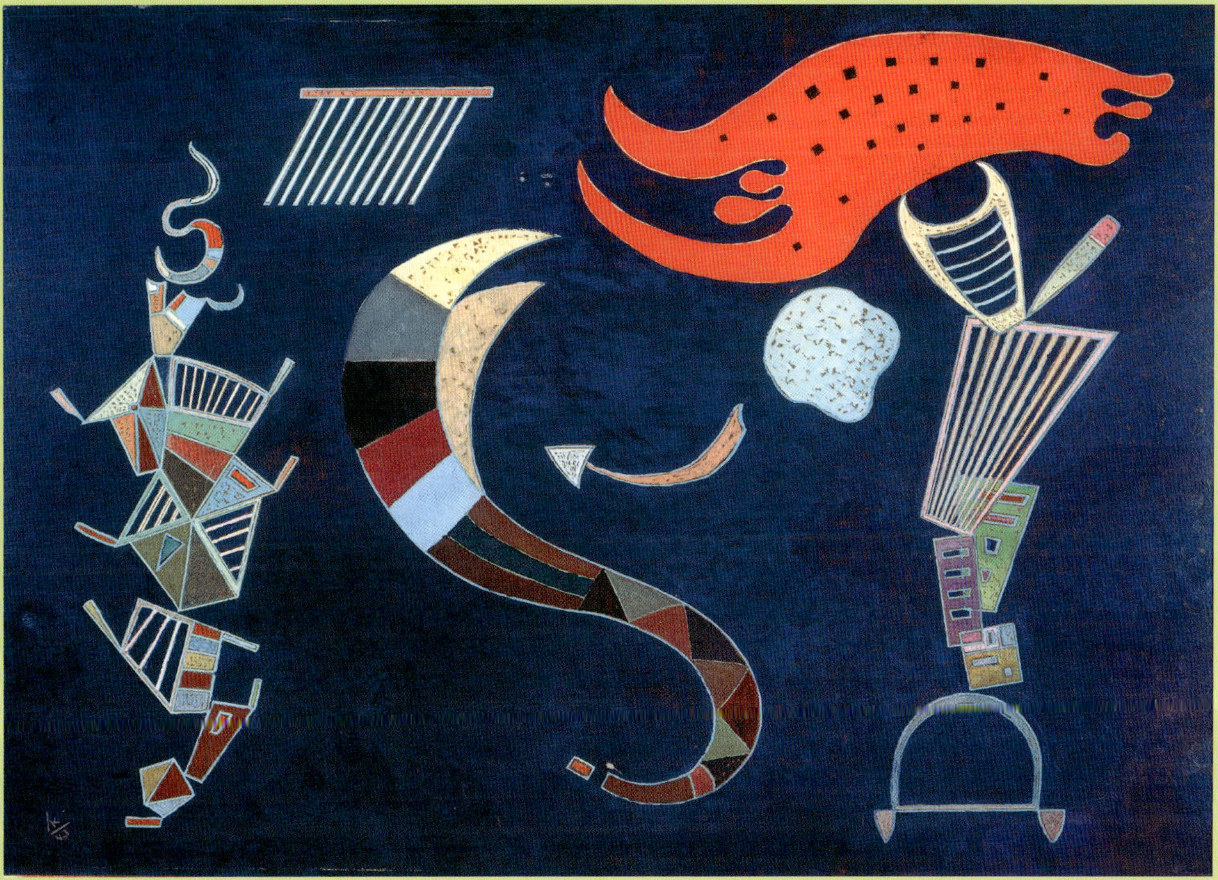

Vassily Kandinsky
(Moscow 1866 - Neuilly-sur-Seine 1944)

The Arrow
Der Pfeil
De pijl
La flecha

●

1943
42 x 58 cm / 16.5 x 22.8 in.
Kunstmuseum, Basel

oil on paperboard / Öl auf Karton / olieverf op karton / óleo sobre cartón

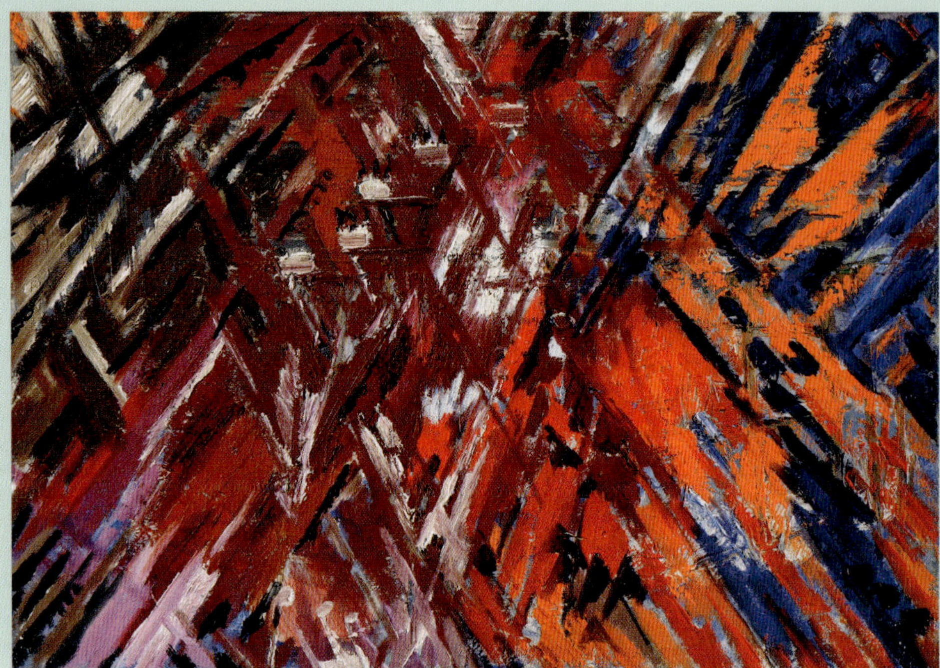

Mikhail Larionov
(Tiraspol, Odessa 1881 -
Fontenay-aux-Roses 1964)

**Rayonist composition: red
and yellow
Strahlenkomposition:
vorherrschend rot
Rayonistische compositie:
overheersing van rood
Composición rayonista:
dominación del rojo**

●●

1911-1913
52,7 x 72,4 cm / 20.7 x 28.5 in.
Museum of Modern Art (MoMA),
New York

oil on canvas / Öl auf Leinwand
olieverf op doek / óleo sobre lienzo

Mikhail Larionov
(Tiraspol, Odessa 1881 -
Fontenay-aux-Roses 1964)

**Sketch of backcloth for
Baba-Jaga
Entwurf eines Vorhangs
für Baba-Jaga
Schets van beschilderd
toneelgordijn
voor Baba-Jaga
El bosque (dibujo para
cuadro escénico
de Baba Yaga)**

●

1916
The State Tretyakov Gallery,
Moscow

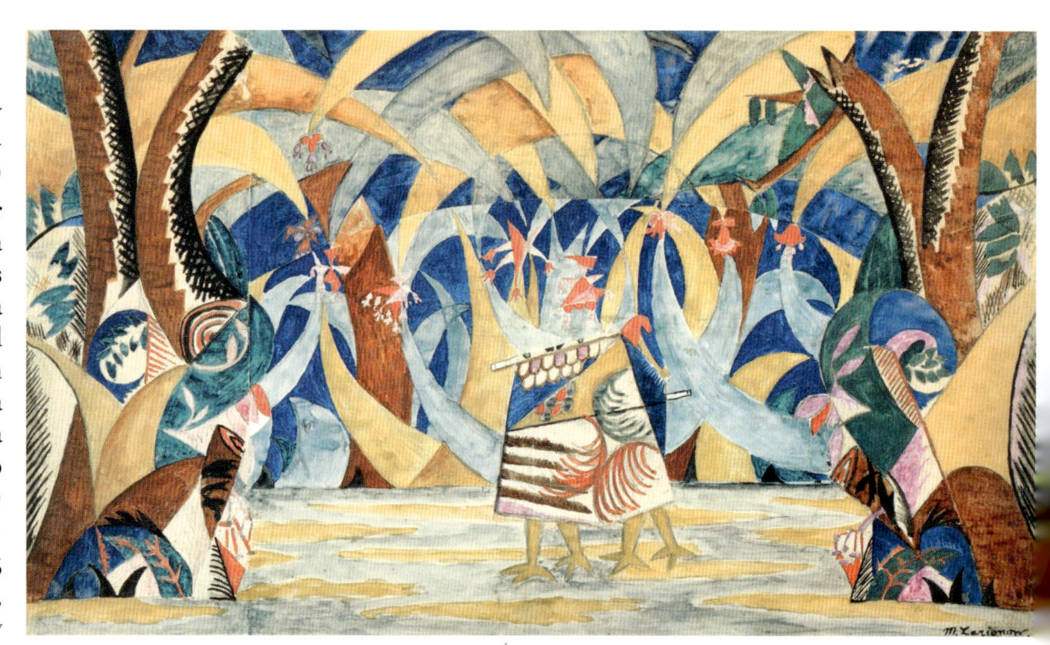

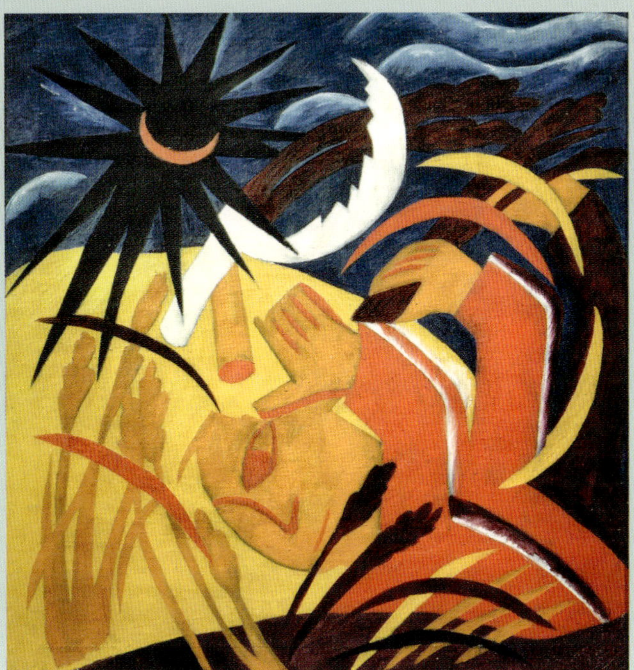

Natalija Goncharova
(Ladyskino, Tula 1881
- Paris 1962)

**The Harvest
Die Ernte
De graanoogst
La cosecha**

●

1911
100 x 93 cm / 39.3 x 36.6 in.
Vrubel Museum of Fine Arts,
Omsk

oil on canvas
Öl auf Leinwand
olieverf op doek
óleo sobre lienzo

Natalija Goncharova
(Ladyskino, Tula 1881 -
Paris 1962)

**The Frost
Der Raureif
Rijp
La escarcha**

●

1910-1911
101 x 132 cm / 39.7 x 51.9 in.
The Russian Museum,
St. Petersburg

oil on canvas
Öl auf Leinwand
olieverf op doek
óleo sobre lienzo

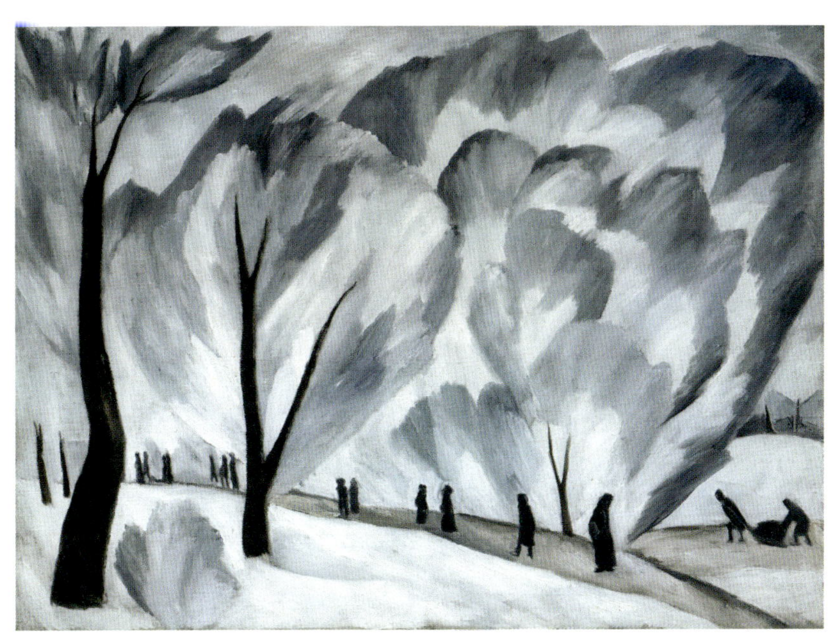

El Lissitzky
(Počinok 1890 -
Moscow 1941)

Proun 3A

ca. 1920
71,12 x 58,42 cm / 28 x 23 in.
Los Angeles County Museum
of Art, Los Angeles

oil on canvas
Öl auf Leinwand
olieverf op doek
óleo sobre lienzo

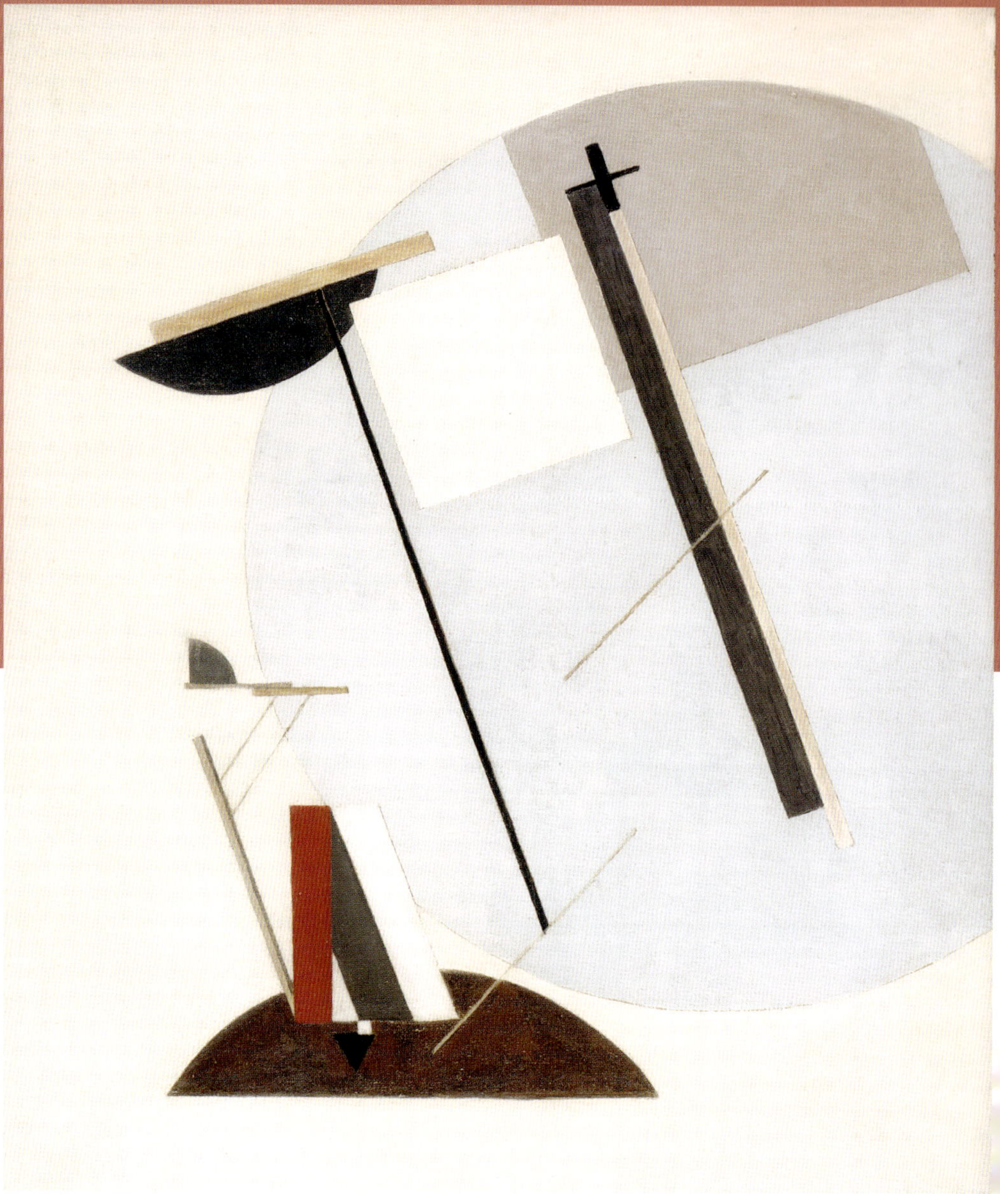

Proun is an acronym
for "design for the
affirmation of the new".

Proun ist die Abkürzung
von "Projekt für
die Behauptung des
Neuen".

Proun is een acroniem
voor "ontwerp voor
de bevestiging van het
nieuwe".

Proun es un acrónimo
para "proyecto de
afirmación de lo nuevo".

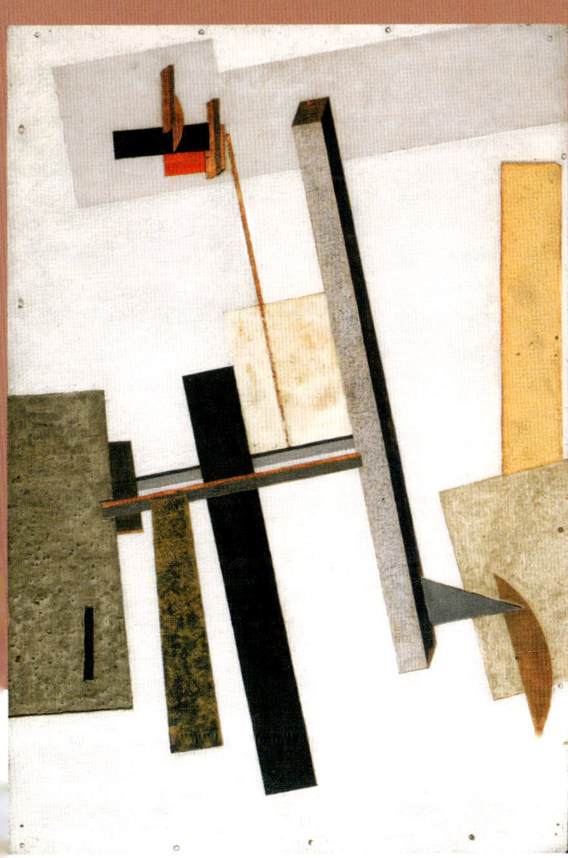

▼ El Lissitzky
(Počinok 1890 - Moscow 1941)

**The new man, plate 10 from the portfolio
'Victory over the sun'
Der neue Mensch, Tafel 10 des Portfolio
'Sieg über die Sonne'
De nieuwe mens, paneel 10 van het portfolie
'overwinning op de zon'
El hombre nuevo, tabla 10 del portafolio
para 'Victoria sobre el sol'**

●

1923
53,3 x 45,7 cm / 21 x 18 in.
Philadelphia Museum of Art, Philadelphia

color lithograph / Farblithographie
kleurenlithografie / litografía a color

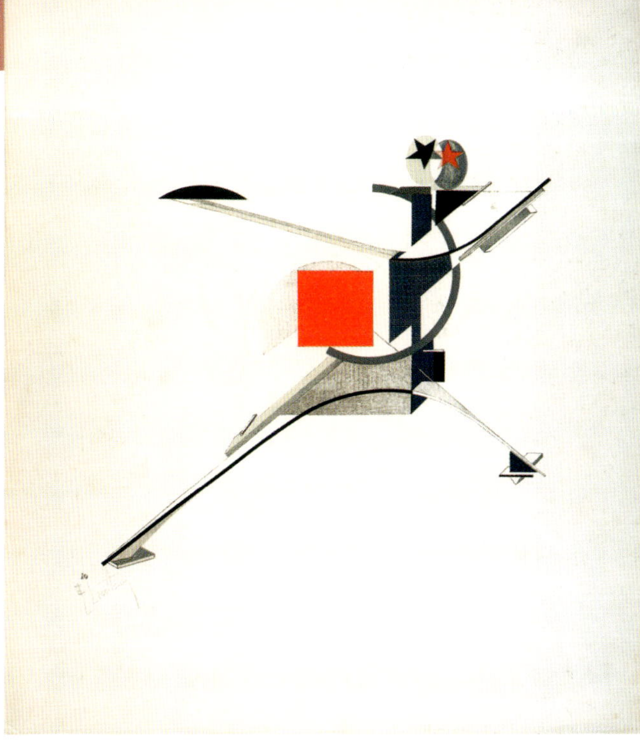

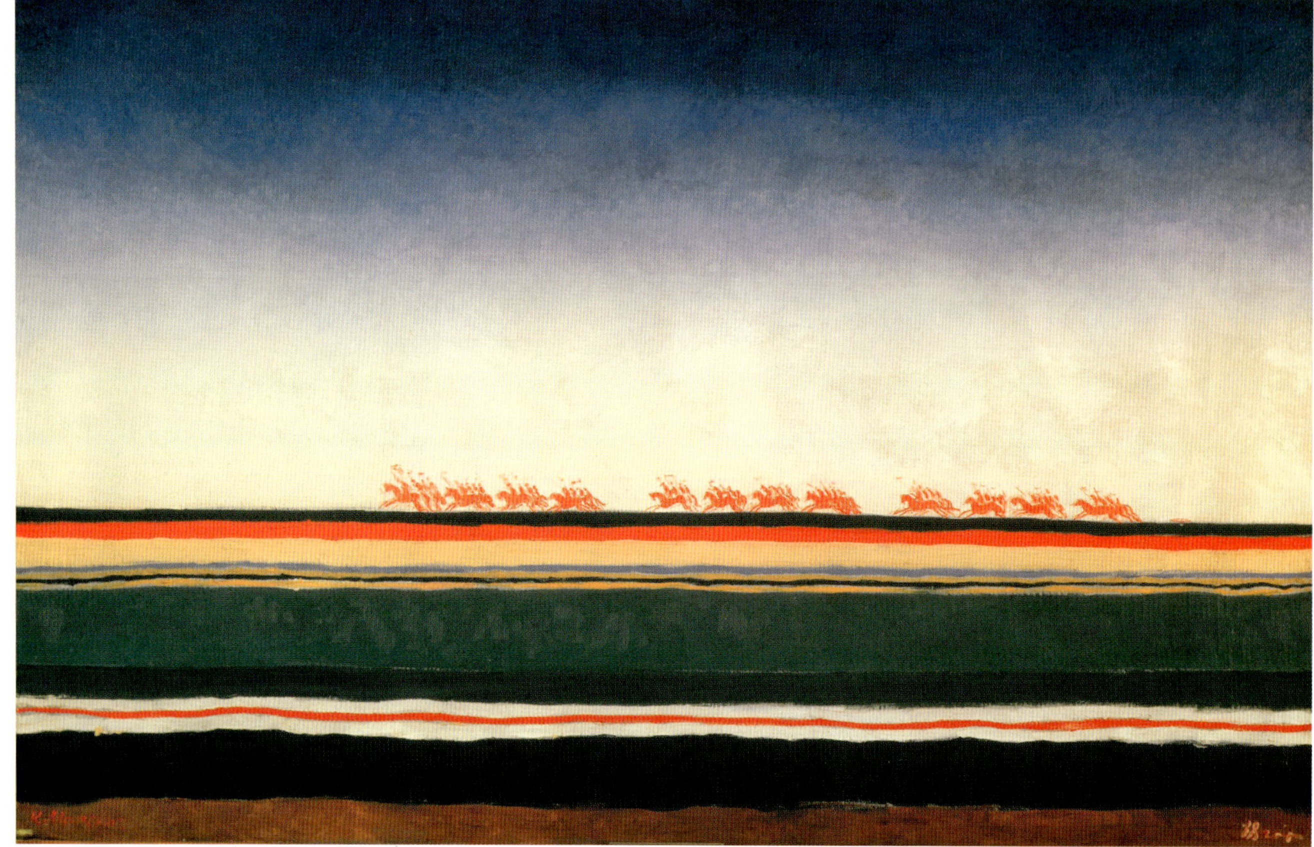

194

Kasimir Malevich
(Kiev 1878 - St. Petersburg 1935)

Advance of the Red Cavalry
Die rote Kavallerie
Het voortschrijden van de rode cavalerie
Caballería roja

●●

ca. 1930
91 x 140 cm / 35.8 x 55.1 in.
The Russian Museum, St. Petersburg

oil on canvas / Öl auf Leinwand
olieverf op doek / óleo sobre lienzo

Some Cossacks riding on a ground whose colors
are inspired by the motifs of Ukrainian fabrics.

Einige Kosaken reiten über einen Boden, dessen
Farben von den Motiven ukrainischer Stoffe
inspiriert sind.

Enkele Kozakken galopperen over een stuk
land waarvan de kleuren inspiratie vinden in de
Oekraïense stofmotieven.

Algunos cosacos cabalgan sobre una tierra cuyos
colores se inspiran en los motivos de las telas
ucranianas.

Kasimir Malevich
(Kiev 1878 - St. Petersburg 1935)

Bust of woman
Frauenbüste
Vrouwelijke buste
Busto de mujer

●

1920
73 x 52,5 cm / 28.7 x 20.6 in
The Russian Museum, St. Petersburg

oil on canvas / Öl auf Leinwand
olieverf op doek / óleo sobre lienzo

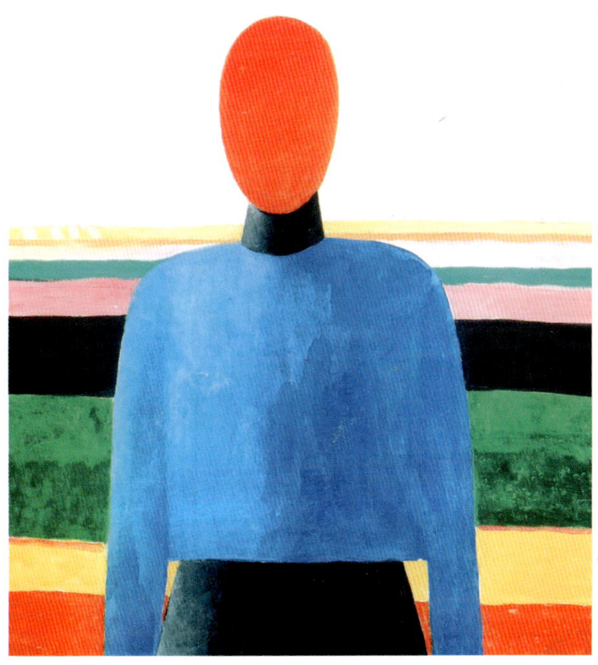

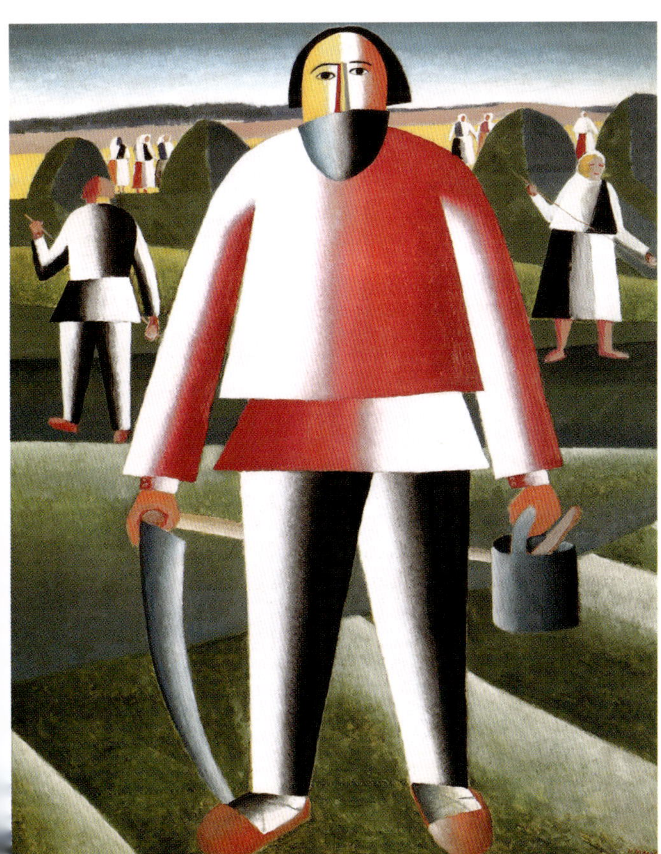

Kasimir Malevich
(Kiev 1878 - St. Petersburg 1935)

Haymaking
Heuernte
Hooitijd
El segador

● ●

ca. 1912
85,8 x 65,6 cm / 33.8 x 25.8 in.
The State Tretyakov Gallery, Moscow

oil on canvas / Öl auf Leinwand
olieverf op doek / óleo sobre lienzo

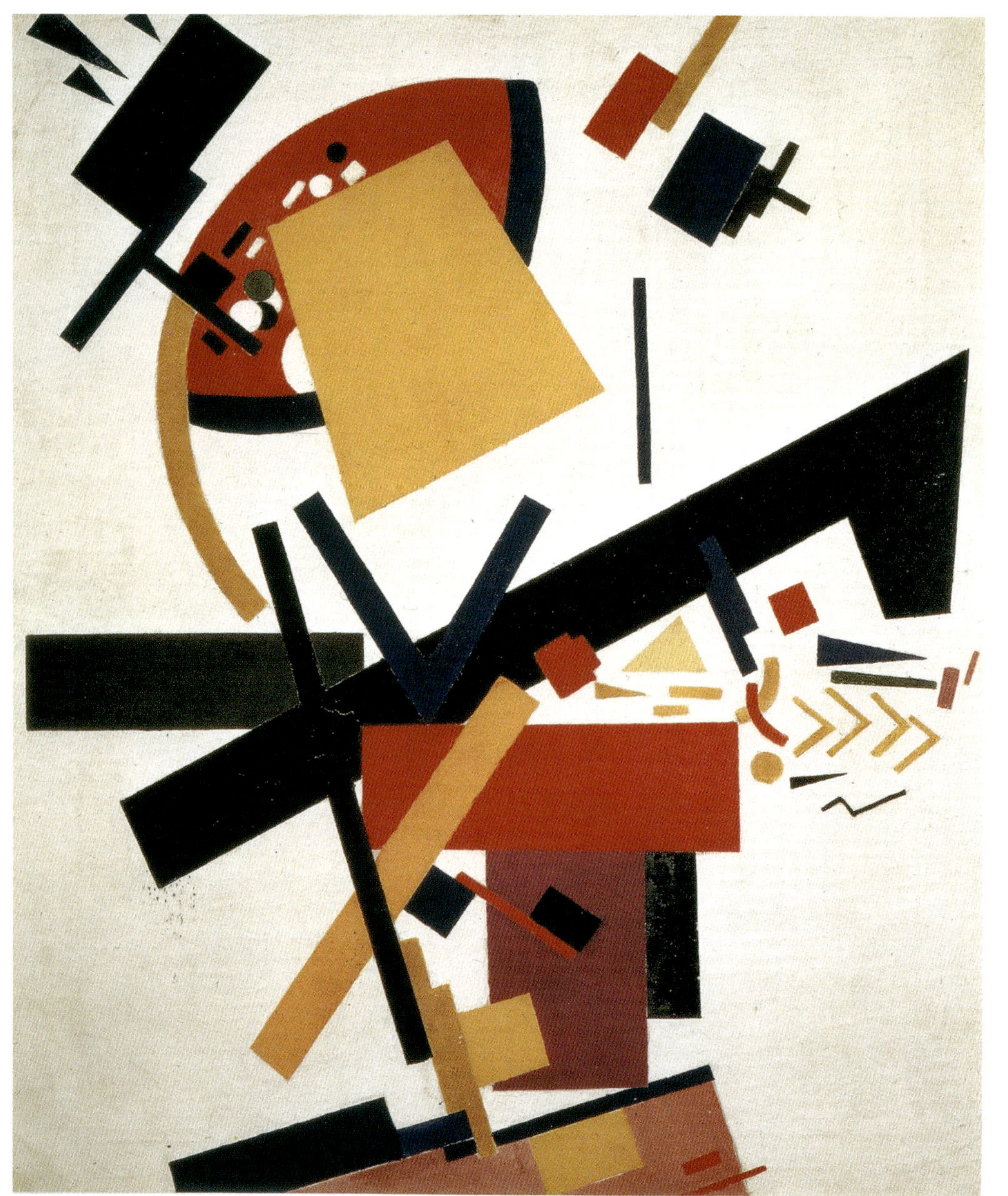

Kasimir Malevich
(Kiev 1878 -
St. Petersburg 1935)

**Suprematism
Suprematismus
Suprematisme
Suprematismo**

●

1915
87 x 72 cm / 34.2 x 28.3 in.
The Russian Museum,
St. Petersburg

oil on canvas
Öl auf Leinwand
olieverf op doek
oleo sobre lienzo

"The supreme goal of
art is the non objective
representation", this is the
motto of Suprematism.

"Das höchste Ziel der
Kunst ist die nicht
gegenständliche
Darstellung": dies ist das
Motto des Suprematismus.

"Het sublieme doel
van kunst is de niet-
objectieve voorstelling",
dit is het motto van het
suprematisme.

"El objetivo supremo del
arte es la representación no
objetiva", éste es el lema
del Suprematismo.

Kasimir Malevich
(Kiev 1878 - St. Petersburg 1935)

Suprematism (Supremus n° 56)
Suprematismus (Supremus Nr. 56)
Suprematisme (Supremus n° 56)
Suprematismo (Supremus n° 56)

●

1916
cm 80,5 x 71 / 31.6 x 27.9 in.
The Russian Museum, St. Petersburg

oil on canvas / Öl auf Leinwand
olieverf op doek / óleo sobre lienzo

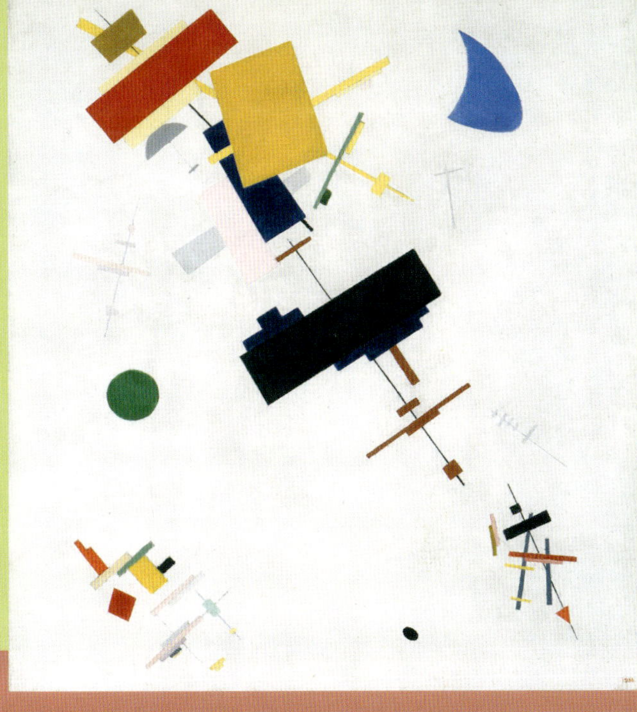

197

Kasimir Malevich
(Kiev 1878 - St. Petersburg 1935)

Suprematist composition: white on white
Suprematistische Komposition: weiß auf weiß
Suprematistische compositie: wit op wit
Composición suprematista: blanco sobre blanco

●●●

1918
79,4 x 79,4 cm / 31.2 x 31.2 in.
Museum of Modern Art (MoMA), New York

oil on canvas / Öl auf Leinwand / olieverf op doek / óleo sobre lienzo

Kasimir Malevich
(Kiev 1878 - St. Petersburg 1935)

Red square
Rotes Quadrat
Rood vierkant
Cuadrado rojo

 ●●

1915
53 x 53 / 20.8 x 20.8 in.
The Russian Museum, St. Petersburg

oil on canvas / Öl auf Leinwand
olieverf op doek / óleo sobre lienzo

Kasimir Malevich
(Kiev 1878 - St. Petersburg 1935)

Black square
Schwarzes Quadrat
Zwart vierkant
Cuadrado negro

●●

ca. 1923
106 x 106 cm / 41.7 x 41.7 in.
The Russian Museum, St. Petersburg

oil on canvas / Öl auf Leinwand
olieverf op doek / óleo sobre lienzo

Kasimir Malevich
(Kiev 1878 - St. Petersburg 1935)
Black circle
Schwarzer Kreis
Zwarte cirkel
Círculo negro
●
105 x 105 cm / 41.3 x 41.3 in.
ca. 1923
The Russian Museum,
St. Petersburg

oil on canvas
Öl auf Leinwand
olieverf op doek
óleo sobre lienzo

199

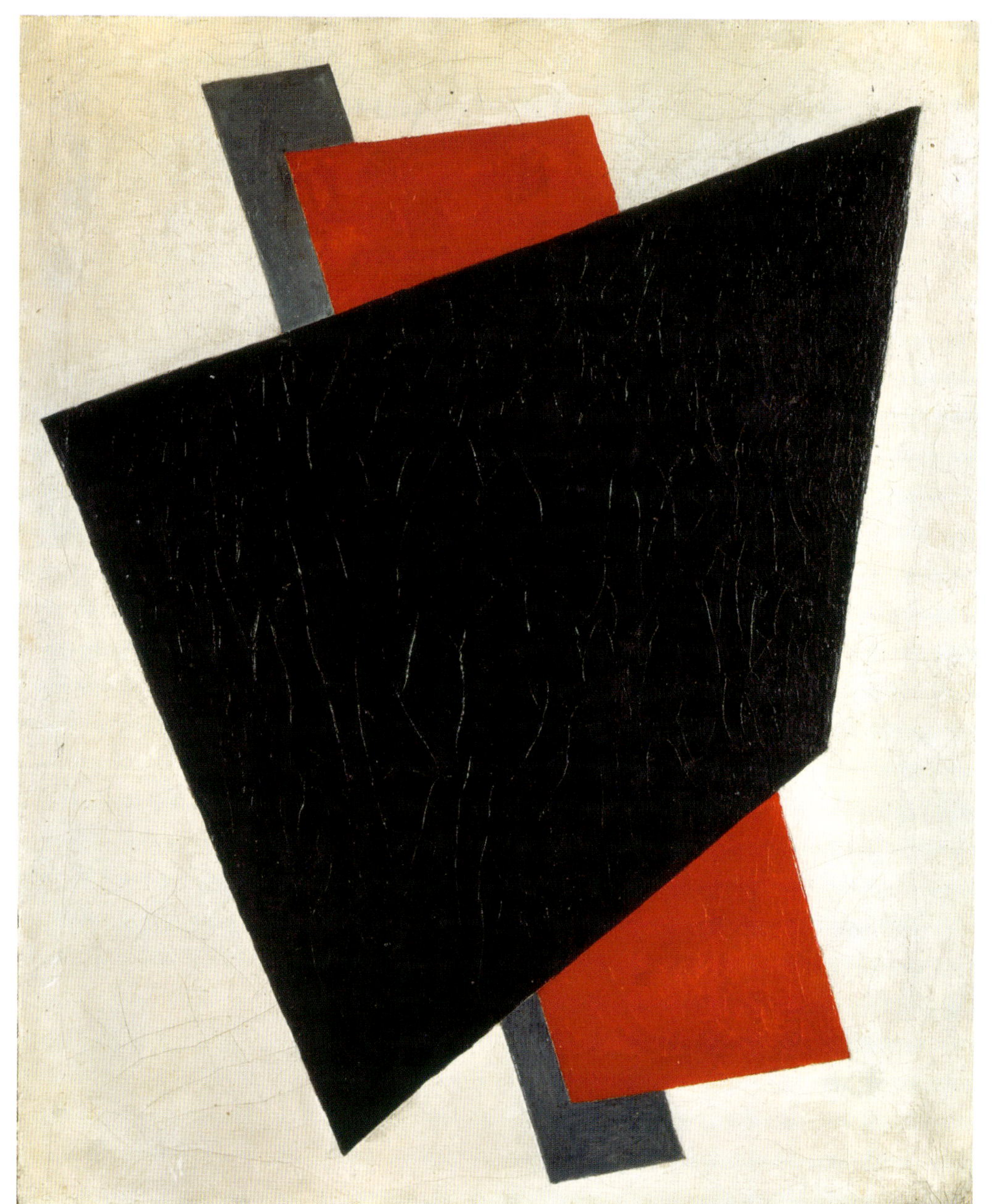

Lyubov Sergeievna
Popova
(Moscow 1889 - 1924)

**Pictorially architectural
with black triangle
Malerisch architektonis‹
mit schwarzem Dreieck
Schilderachtig
architectonisch met
zwarte driehoek
Pictóricamente
arquitectónico con
triángulo negro**

●

1916
89 x 71 cm / 35 x 27.9 in.
The State Tretyakov Gallery,
Moscow

oil on canvas
Öl auf Leinwand
olieverf op doek
óleo sobre lienzo

200

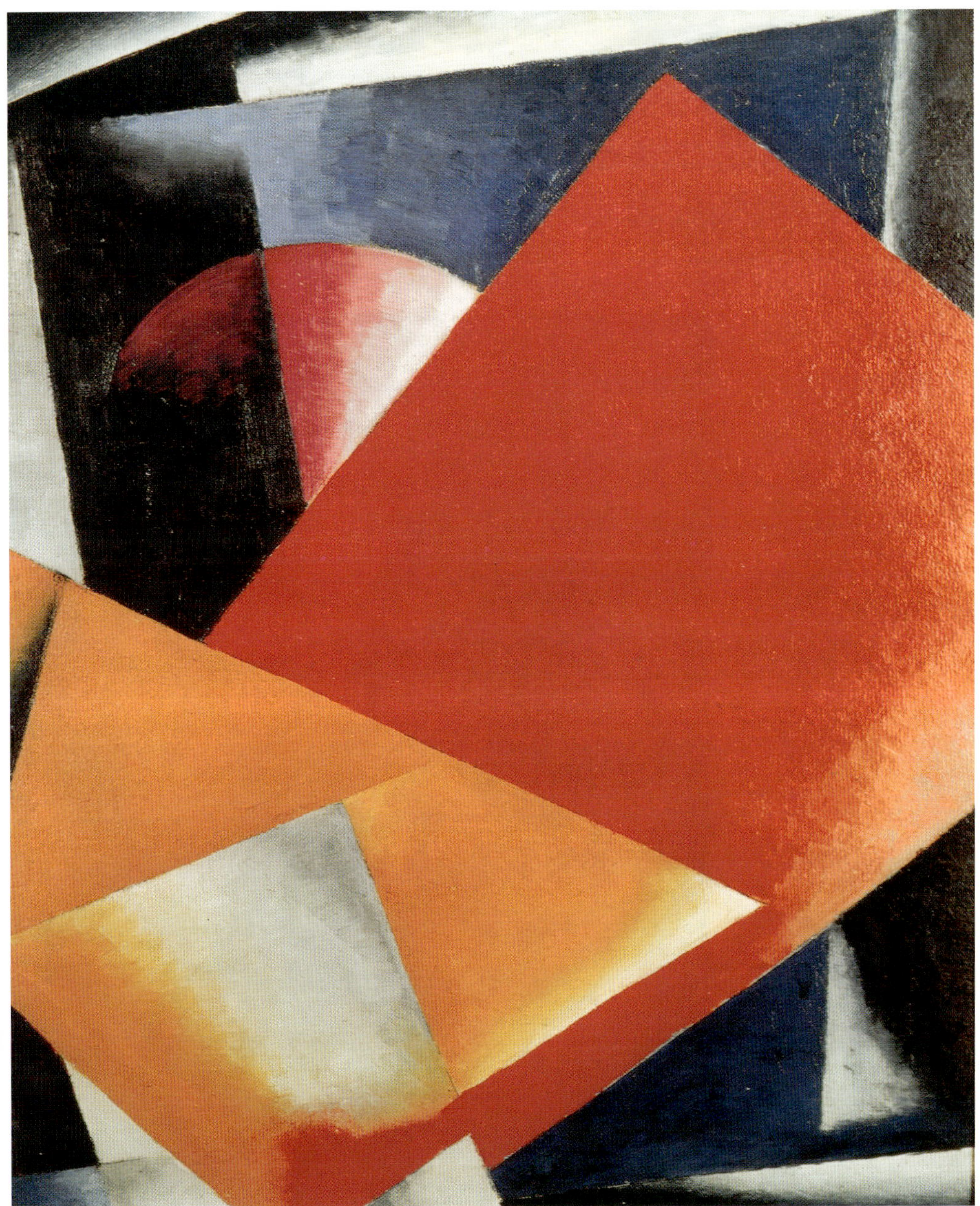

Lyubov Sergeievna
Popova
(Moscow 1889 - 1924)

**Pictorially architectural
with red semicircle
Malerisch
architektonisch mit
rotem Halbkreis
Schilderachtig
architectonisch met
rode halve cirkel
Pictóricamente
arquitectónico con
semicírculo rosado**

●

1918
59,5 x 48,4 cm / 23.4 x 19 in.
The State Tretyakov Gallery,
Moscow

oil on paperboard
Öl auf Karton
olieverf op karton
óleo sobre cartón

201

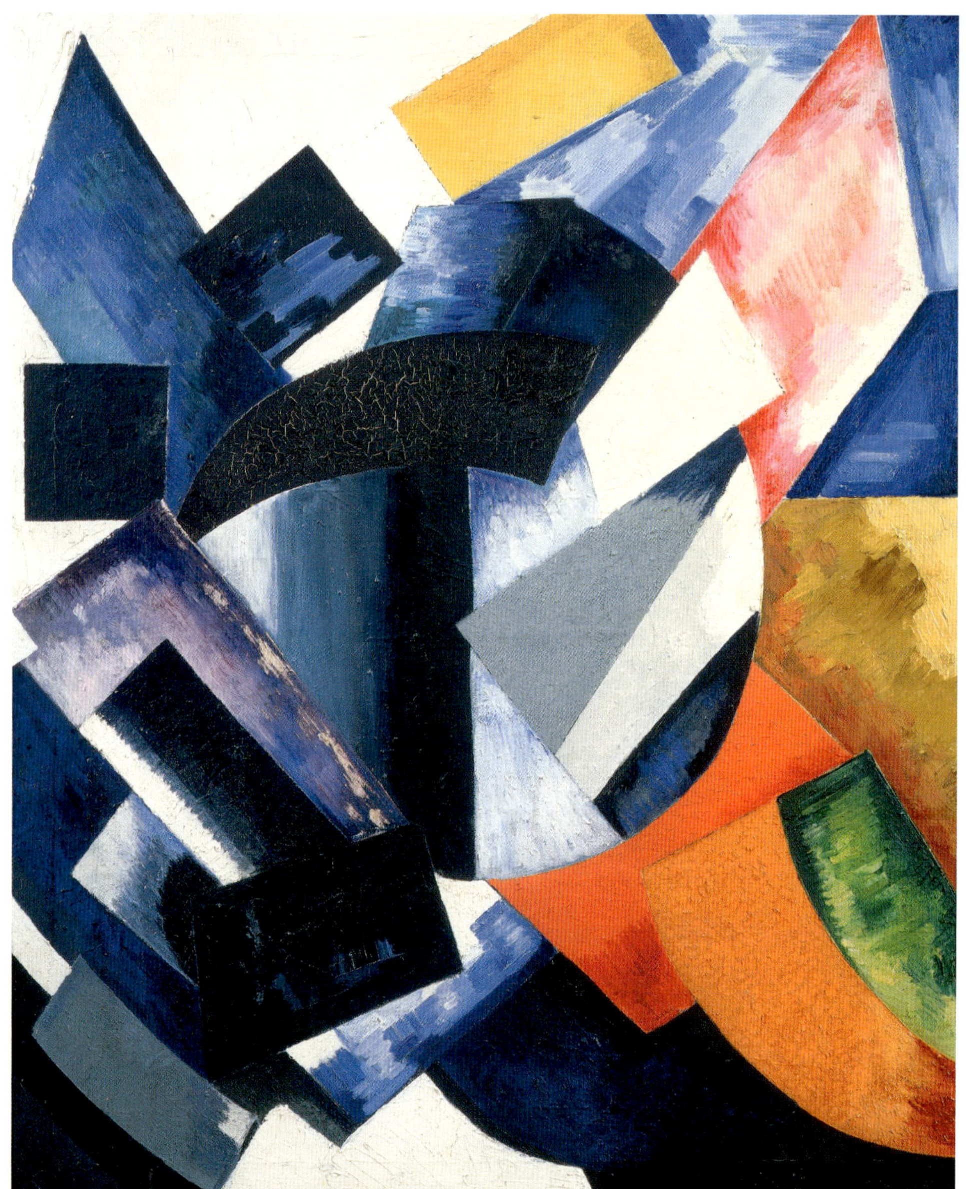

Aleksandra Ekster
(Białystok 1884 -
Fontenay-aux-Roses 1949)

Abstract composition
Abstrakte Komposition
Abstracte compositie
Composición abstracta

●

1917
121 x 109 / 47.6 x 42.9 in.
The Russian Museum, St.
Petersburg

oil on paperboard
Öl auf Karton
olieverf op karton
óleo sobre cartón

Aleksandra Ekster reclaims a non-objective art, based on the constructions of the shapes and the dynamic interaction of the colors.

Aleksandra Ekster fordert eine nicht gegenständliche Kunst, die auf der Konstruktion von Formen und der dynamischen Interaktion von Farben basiert.

Aleksandra Ekster maakt niet-objectieve kunst, gebaseerd op het bouwen van vormen en de dynamische interactie van kleuren.

Aleksandra Ekster reivindica un arte no objetivo, basado en la construcción de las formas y la interacción dinámica de los colores.

Alexander Rodchenko
(St. Petersburg 1891 - Moscow 1956)

Red and yellow
Rot und Gelb
Rood en geel
Rojo y amarillo

••

The Russian Museum, St. Petersburg

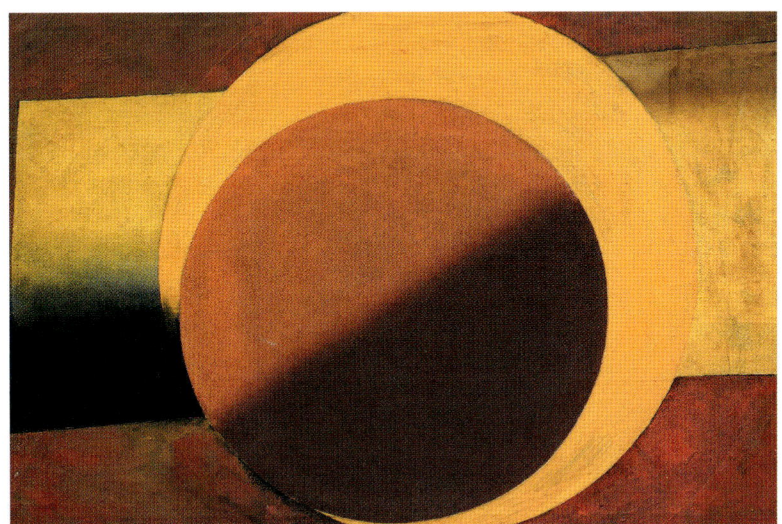

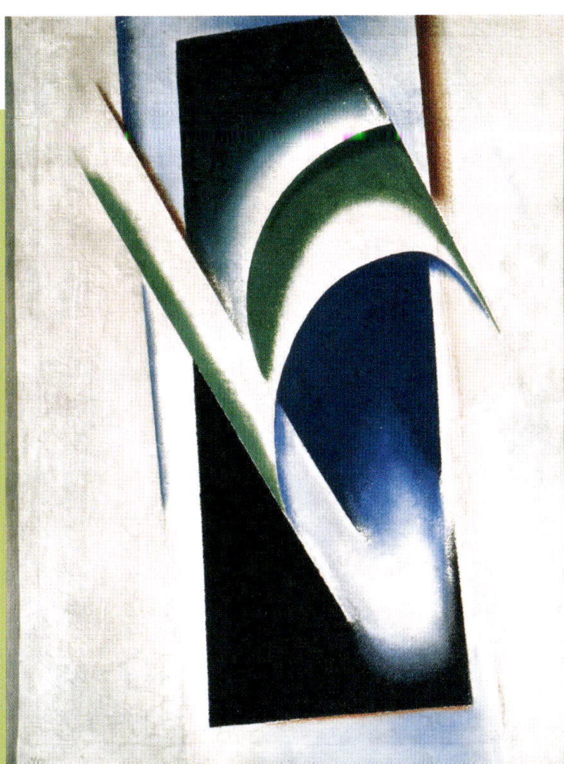

Alexander Rodchenko
(St. Petersburg 1891 - Moscow 1956)

Abstract composition
Abstrakt
Abstract
Abstracto

•

The Russian Museum, St. Petersburg

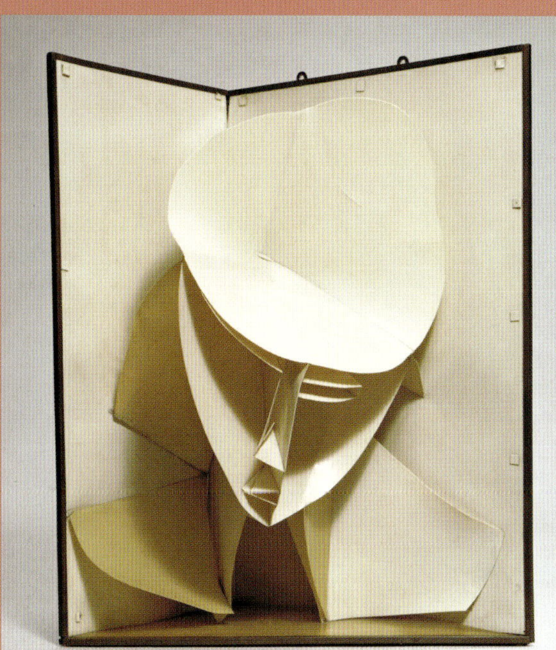

Naum Gabo
(Briansk 1890 - Waterbury, Connecticut 1977)

Head of woman
Frauenkopf
Hoofd van een vrouw
Cabeza de mujer

●●

ca. 1917-1920
62,2 x 48,9 x 35,4 cm / 24.5 x 19.2 x 14 in.
Museum of Modern Art (MoMA), New York

celluloid and metal / Zelluloid und Metall
celluloïde en metaal / celuloide y metal

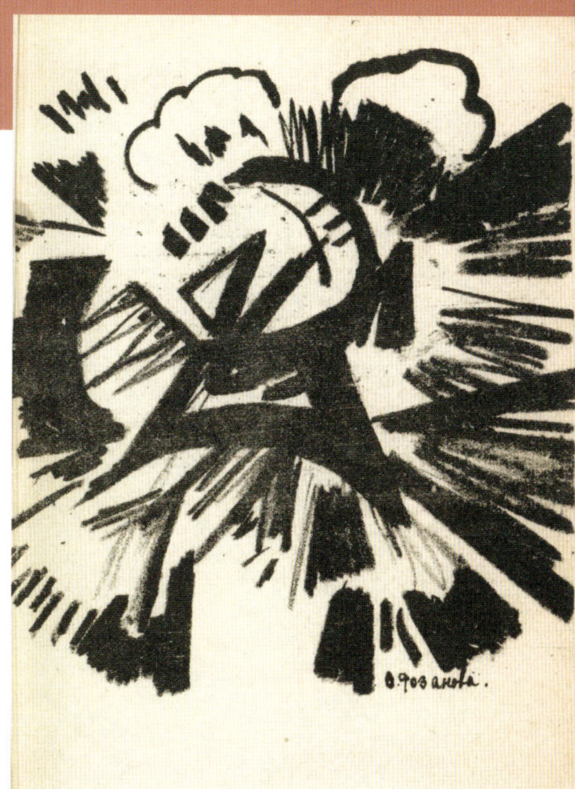

Olga Rozanova
(Melenki 1886 - Moscow 1918)

Vzorval'
(Explosion), illustration from the book of Aleksei
Kruchenykh
(Explosion), Illustration des Buches von Aleksei
Kruchenykh
(Explosie), illustratie van het boek van Aleksei
Kruchenykh
(Explosión), ilustración del libro de Aleksei Kruchenykh

●

1913
17,4 x 11,7 cm / 6.8 x 4.6 in.
Museum of Modern Art (MoMA), New York

illustrated book with 17 litographed illustrations
Illustriertes Buch mit 17 Lithographien
boek geillustreerd met 17 lithografieen
libro ilustrado con 17 litografías

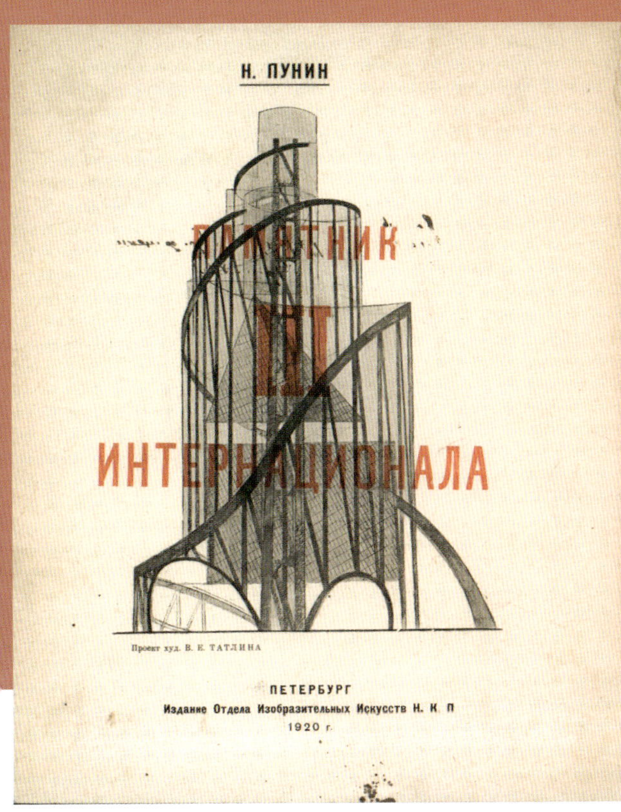

Vladimir Tatlin
(Charkiv 1885 - Moscow 1953)

Pamiatnik III Internatsionala
(Monument to the Third International)
(Denkmal der Dritten Internationalen)
(Monument op de Derde Internationale)
(Monumento a la Tercera Internacional)

●●●

1920
28 x 21.9 cm / 11 x 8.6 in.
Museum of Modern Art (MoMA), New York

cover with letterpress illustration on front;
Einband mit Reliefdruck-Illustration auf der ersten Seite
omslag met boekdrukillustratie op de voorpagina
tapa con ilustración hecha con impresión tipográfica sobre la primera
página

Vladimir Tatlin
(Charkiv 1885 - Moscow 1953)

Composition
Komposition
Compositie
Composición

●

1916
52 x 39 cm / 20.4 x 15.3 in.
Nationalgalerie, Staatliche Museen, Berlin

mixed media on plate
Mischtechnik auf Tafel
Gemengde technieken op paneel
técnica mixta sobre tabla

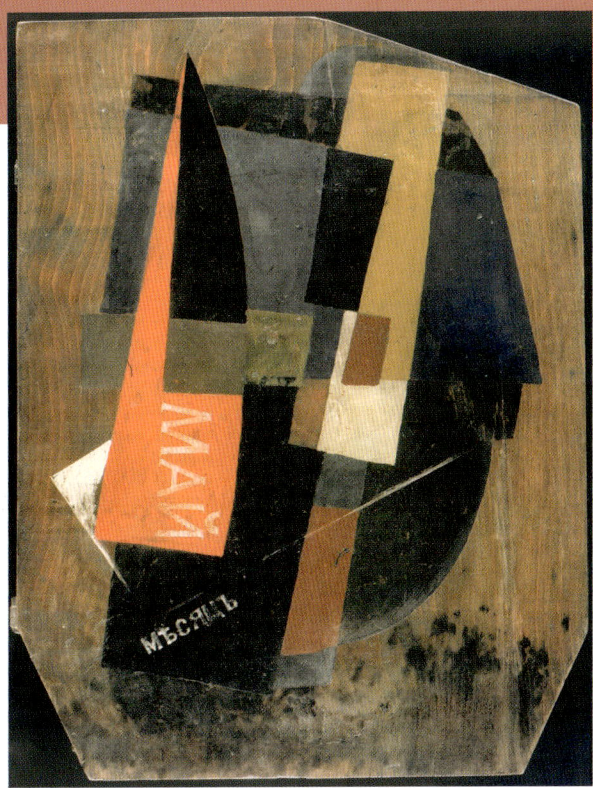

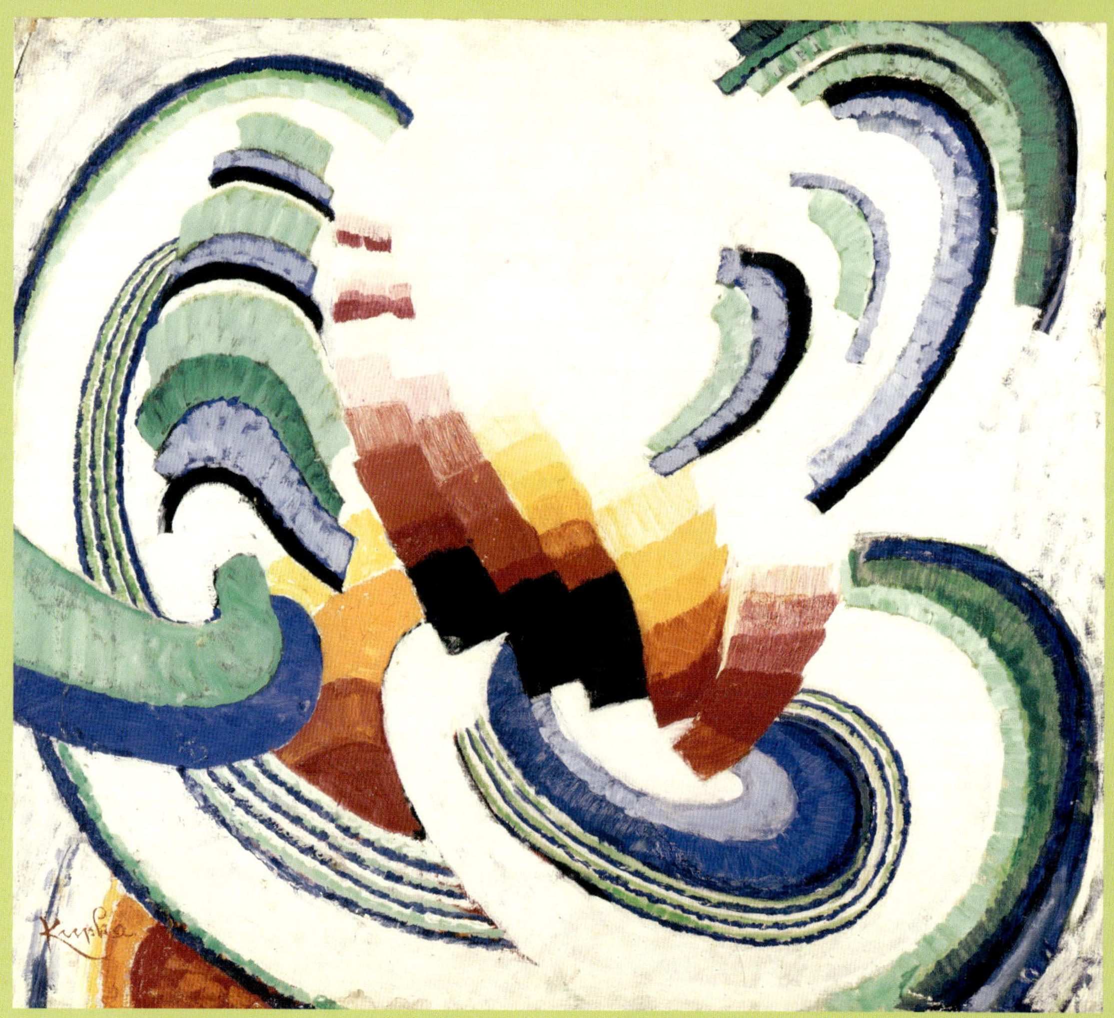

Frantisek Kupka
(Opočno 1871 - Puteaux 1957)

The Eddy
Der Wirbel
De werveling
El remolino

●

Musée de Grenoble, Grenoble

Frantisek Kupka
(Opočno 1871 - Puteaux 1957)
**Discs of Newton
(Study for the 'Fugue
in two colors')
Newtons Ringe (Studie zur
'Fuge in zwei Farben')
De schijven van Newton (studie
voor 'Fuga in twee kleuren')
Discos de Newton (Estudio
para 'Fuga a dos colores')**

●●

1912
100,3 x 73,7 cm / 39.5 x 29 in.
Philadelphia Museum of Art,
Philadelphia

oil on canvas / Öl auf Leinwand
olieverf op doek / óleo sobre lienzo

Kupka is part of the group of
pioneers of Abstract Art, for
whom color becomes subject and
not just simple effect.

Kupka gehört einer Gruppe von
Pionieren der abstrakten Kunst
an, für die die Farbe selbst zum
Bildgegenstand wird und nicht
allein ein Effekt ist.

Kupka maakt deel uit van de
pioniersgroep van de abstracte
kunst, voor wie kleur als
onderwerp wordt gezien en niet
langer als effect.

Kupka forma parte del grupo de
pioneros del arte abstracto, para
quienes el color se convierte en
sujeto y ya no en un simple efecto.

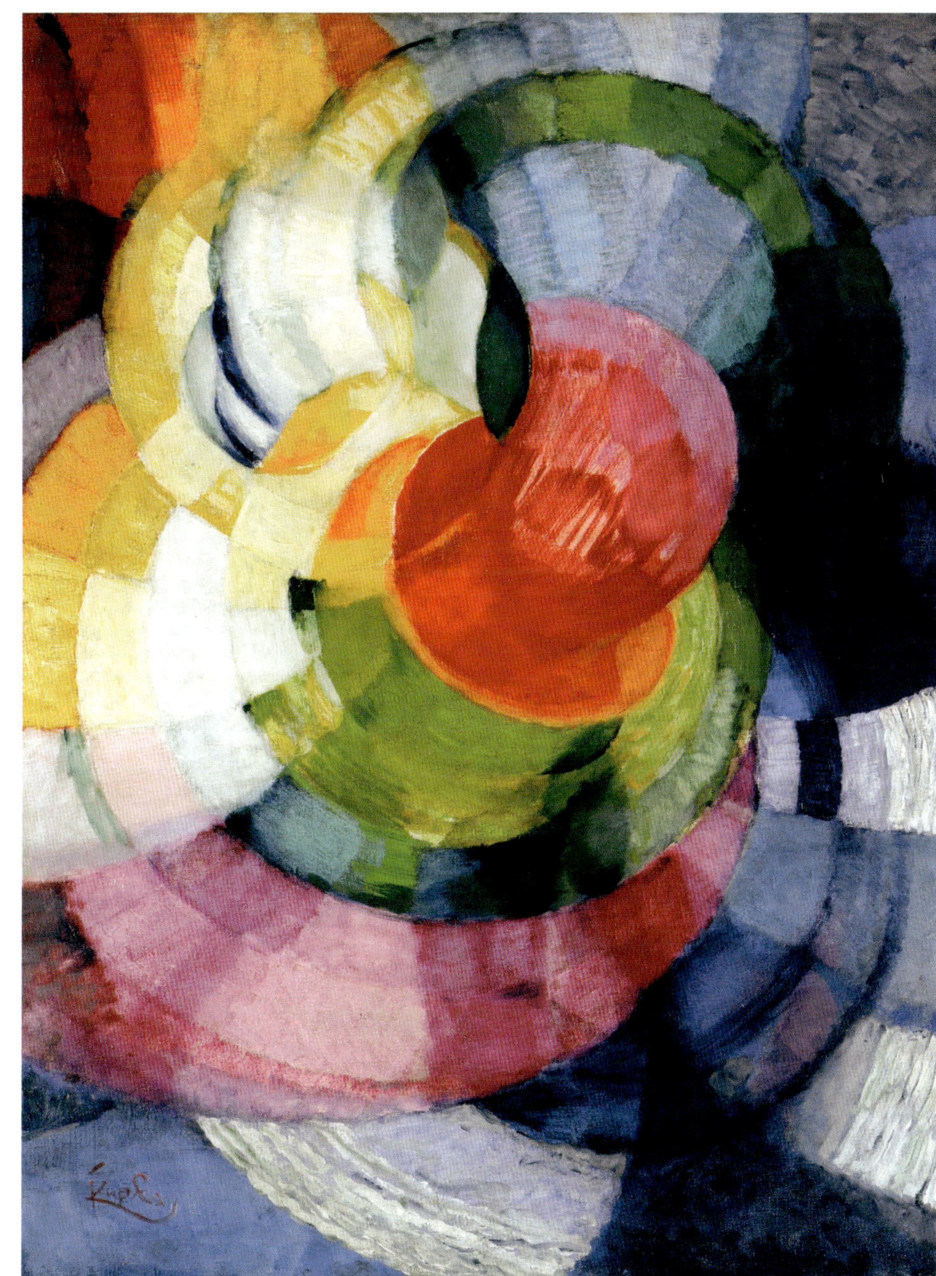

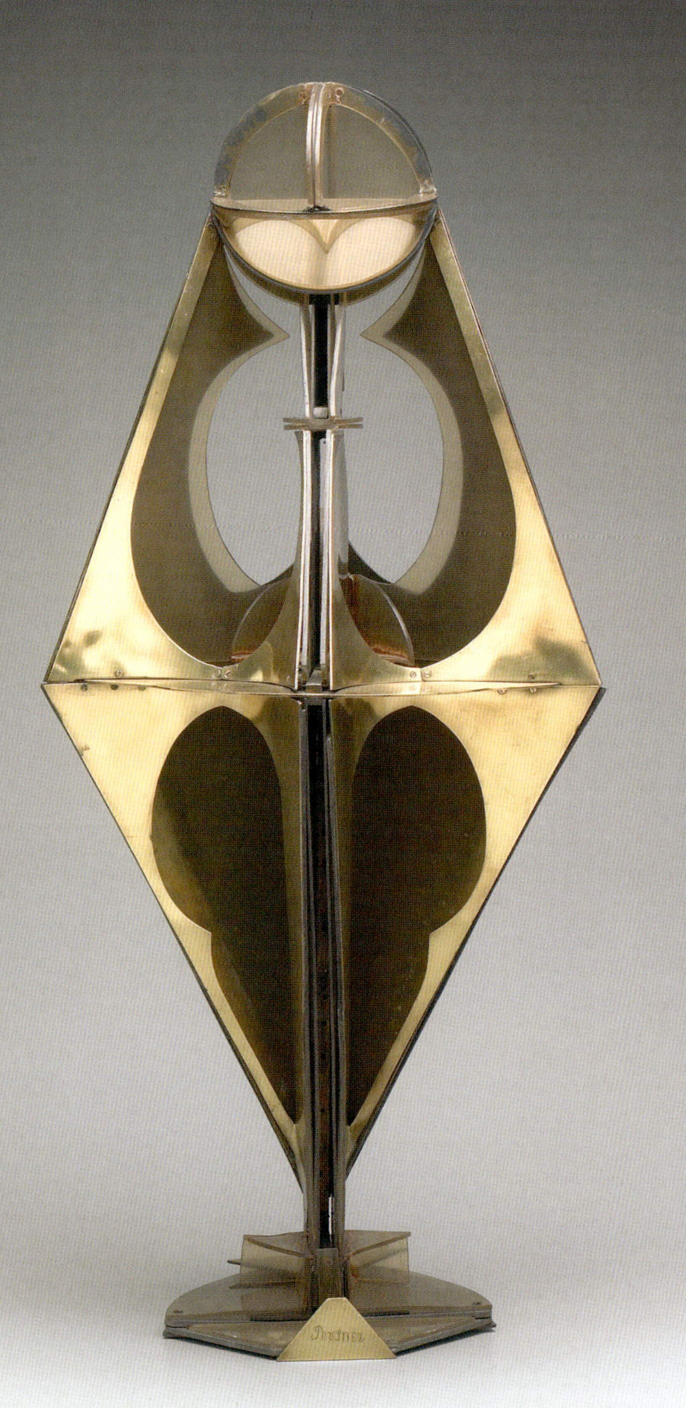

208

Antoine Pevsner
(Orel 1884 - Paris 1962)

The Dancer
Die Tänzerin
De danseres
La bailarina

●●

1927-1928
81 x 34,3 x 27,9 cm
31.9 x 13.5 x 11 in.
Yale University Art Gallery,
New Haven (CT)

brass and celluloid
Messing und Zelluloid
messing en celluloïde
latón y celuloide

Antoine Pevsner
(Orel 1884 - Paris 1962)

Meeting of planets
Treffen der Planeten
Ontmoeting tussen planeten
Encuentro de dos planetas

●●

1961
80,8 x 53,6 cm / 31.8 x 21.1 in.
Centre Georges Pompidou,
Musée National d'Art Moderne, Paris

oil on plywood / Öl auf Sperrholz
olieverf op multiplex / óleo sobre aglomerado

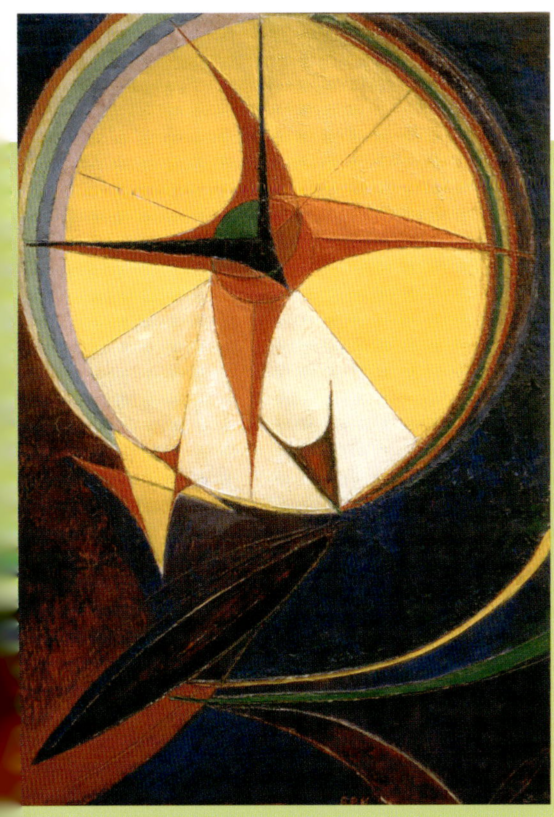

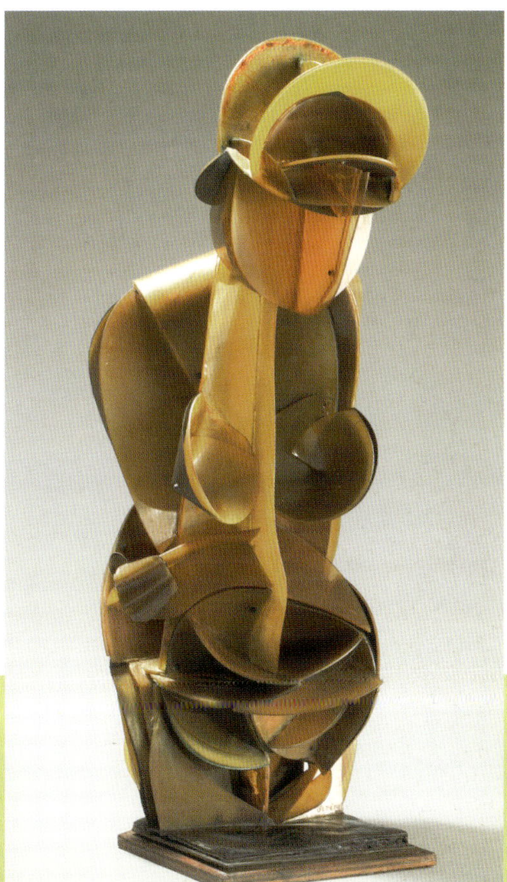

209

Antoine Pevsner
(Orel 1884 - Paris 1962)

Torso / Torso
Bovenlijf / Torso

●●●

1924-1926
74,9 x 29,4 x 38,7 cm / 29.5 x 11.5 x 15.2 in.
Museum of Modern Art (MoMA), New York

construction in plastic and copper
Kupfer- und Plastikkonstruktion
constructie van plastic en koper
construcción en plástico y cobre

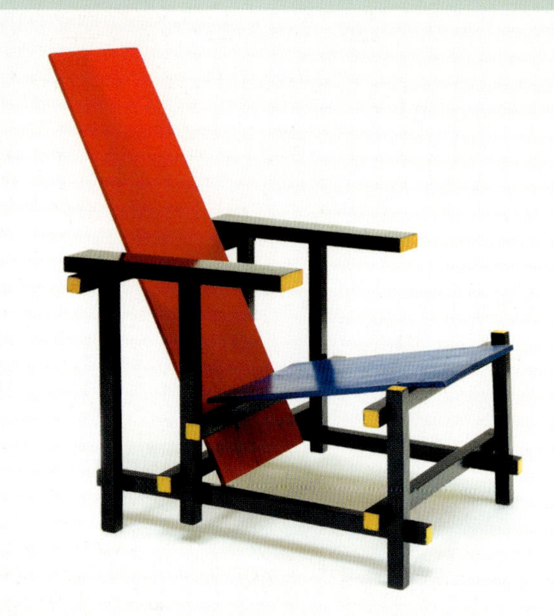

Gerrit Rietveld
(Utrecht 1888 - 1964)

Red and blue chair
Der Rot-Blaue Stuhl
Rood-blauwe stoel
Silla en rojo y azul

●●●

ca. 1918
86,5 x 66 x 83,8 cm / 34 x 26 x 33 in.
Museum of Modern Art (MoMA), New York

painted wood / Bemaltes Holz
beschilderd hout / madera pintada

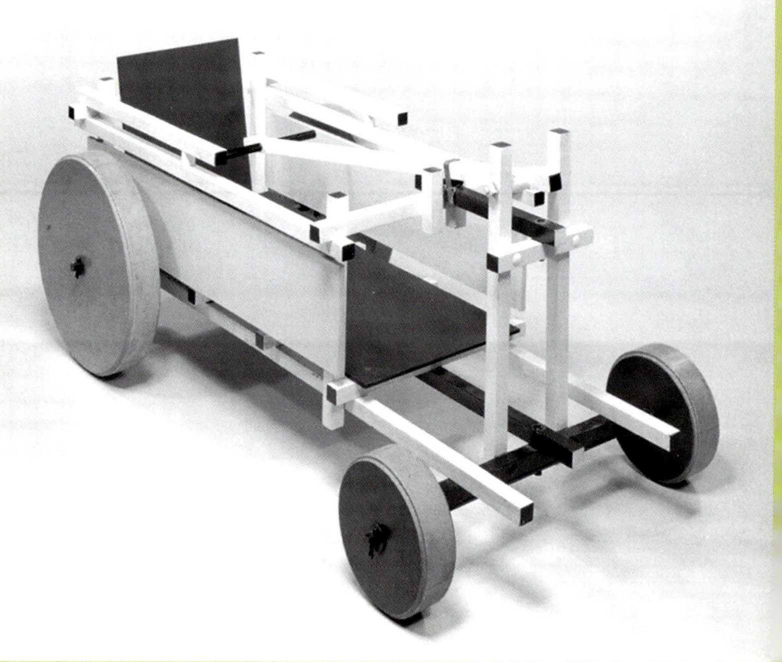

Gerrit Rietveld
(Utrecht 1888 - 1964)

Go-kart

●

1918 (1968)
Victoria & Albert Museum, London

wood / Holz / hout / madera

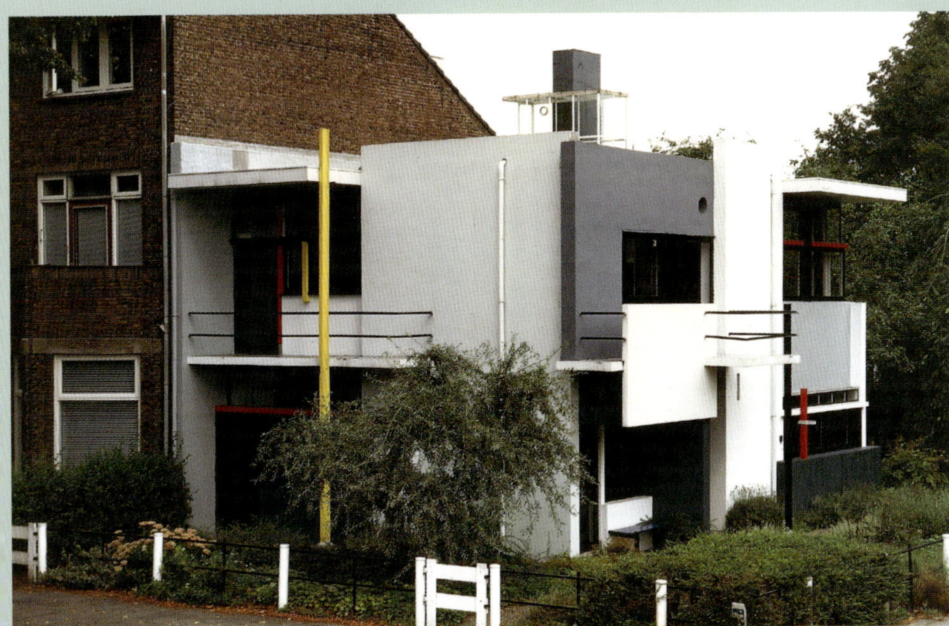

Gerrit Rietveld
(Utrecht 1888 - 1964)

**Schroder House
Das Rietveld-Schröder-
Haus / Schroder Huis
Rietveld Schröderhuis
Casa Schroder**
●●

1923
Utrecht

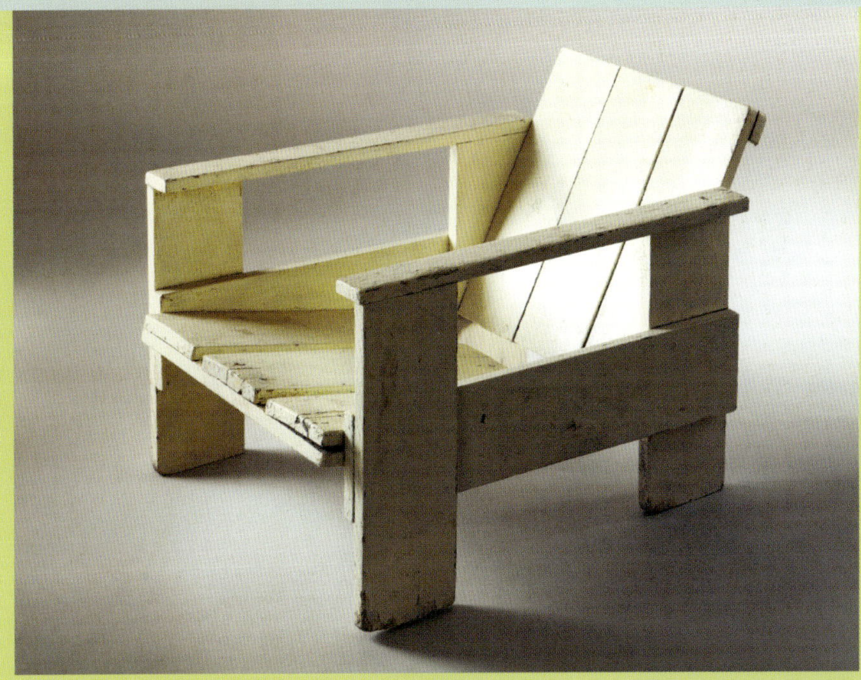

Gerrit Rietveld
(Utrecht 1888 - 1964)

**Crate Chair
Kistenstuhl**
●●●

ca. 1938
55,3 x 57,5 x 79 cm / 21.7 x 22.6 x 31.1 in.
Victoria & Albert Museum, London

painted wood / Bemaltes Holz
beschilderd hout / madera pintada

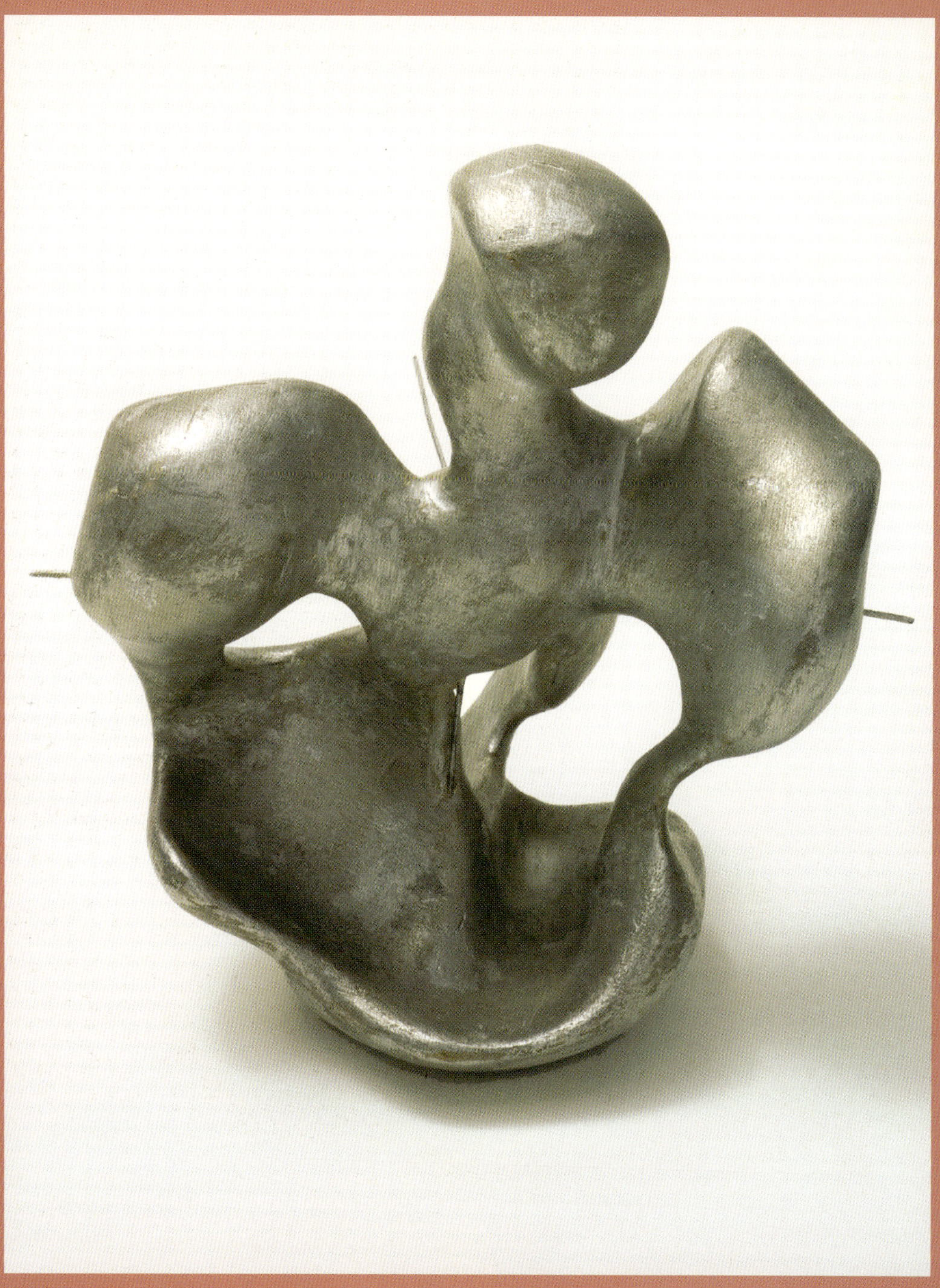

◀ Georges
Vantongerloo
(Antwerp 1886 - Paris 1965)
**Construction inside
a sphere
Konstruktion innerhalb
einer Sphäre
Constructie in een sfeer
Construcción dentro
de una esfera**
●
1917
17,8 x 14 x 17,2 cm
7 x 5.5 x 6.7 in.
Museum of Modern Art
(MoMA), New York

silvered plaster / Versilberter Gips
zilverkrijt / yeso plateado

▶ Theo van Doesburg
(Utrecht 1883 - Davos 1931)
**Simultaneous
counter-composition
Simultane
Gegenkomposition
Simultane
contra-compositie
Contra-composición
simultánea**
●
1929-1930
50,1 x 49,8 cm / 19.7 x 19.6
Museum of Modern Art
(MoMA), New York

oil on canvas
Öl auf Leinwand
olieverf op doek
óleo sobre lienzo

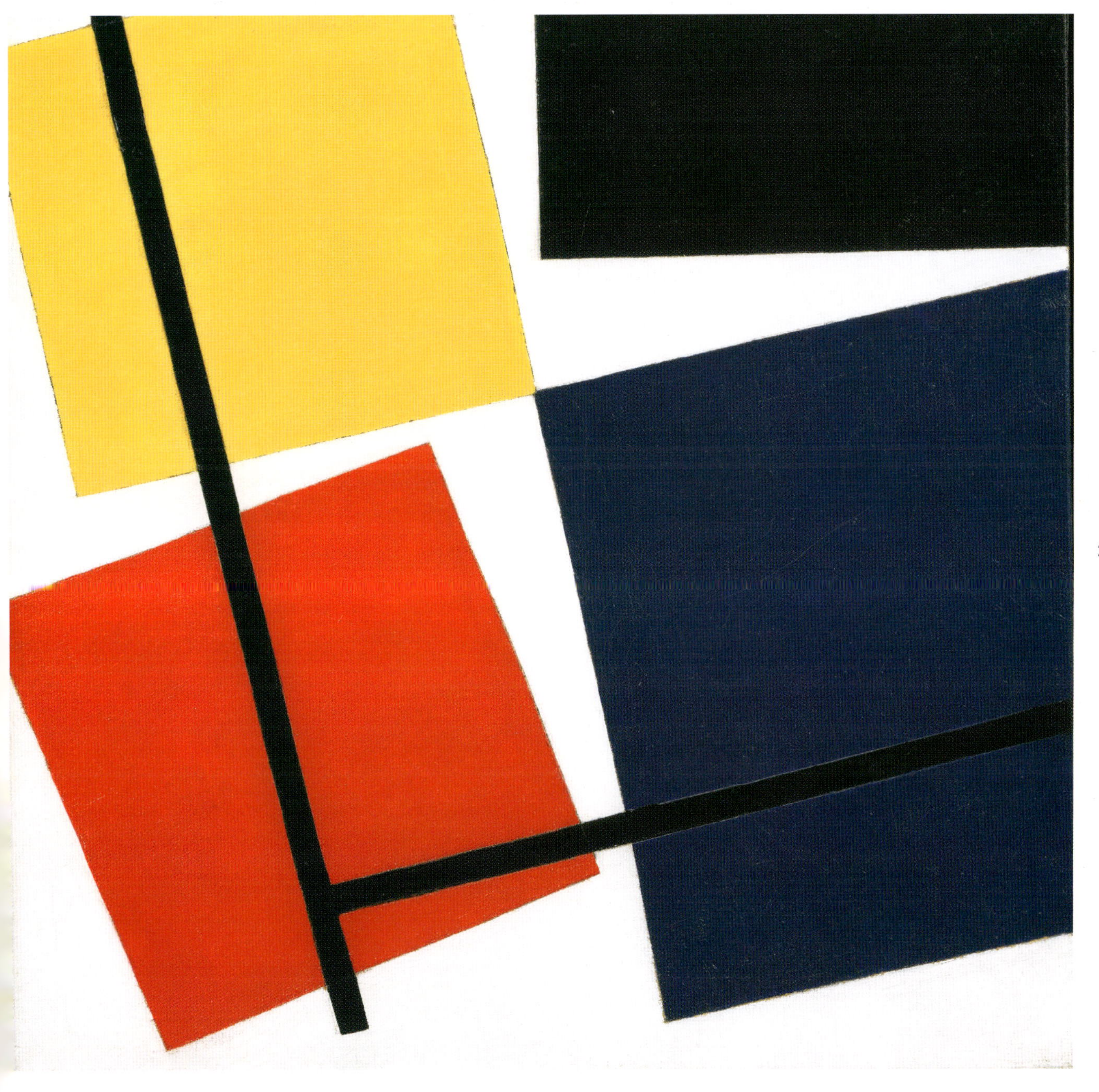

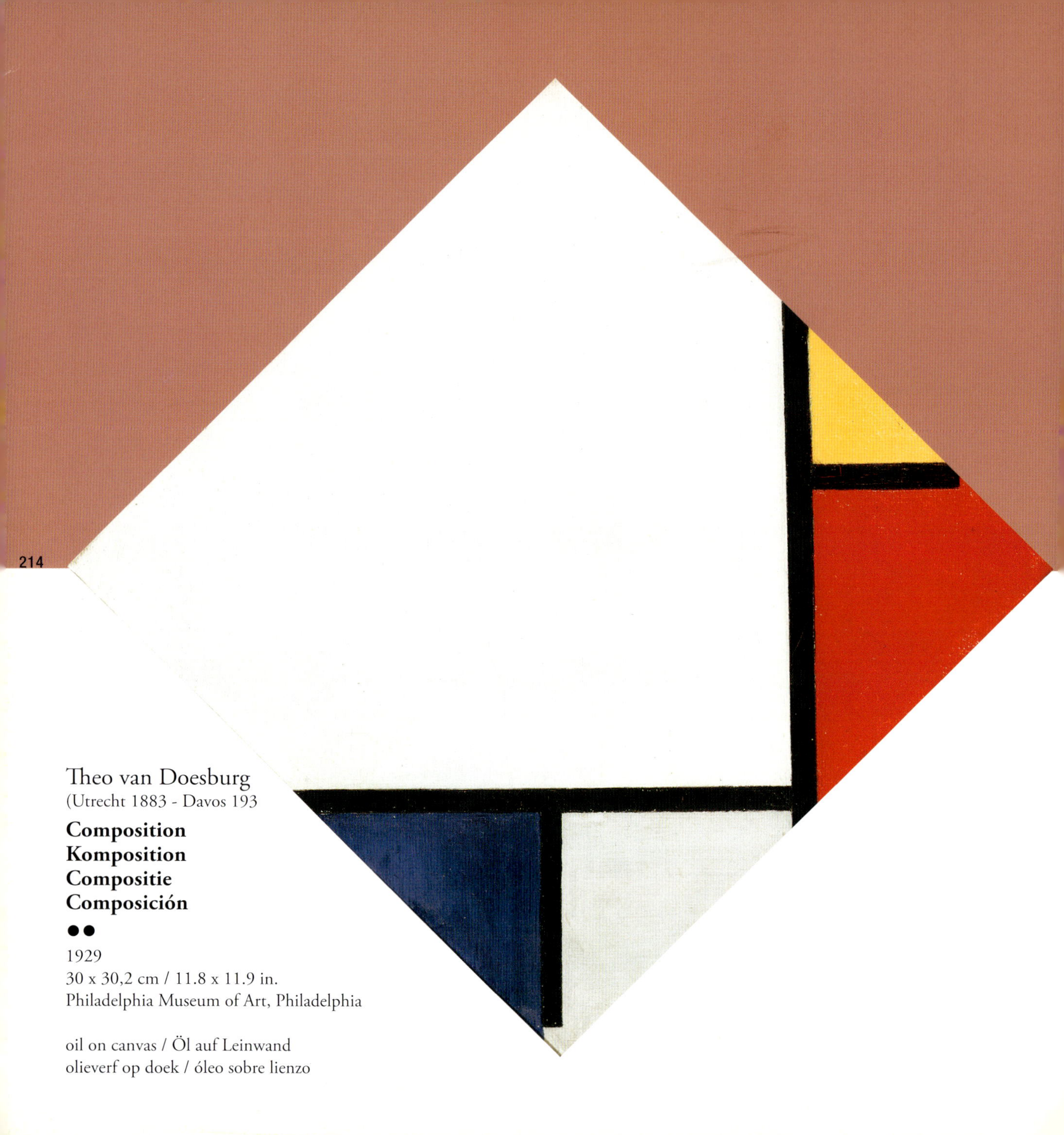

Theo van Doesburg
(Utrecht 1883 - Davos 193

Composition
Komposition
Compositie
Composición

●●

1929
30 x 30,2 cm / 11.8 x 11.9 in.
Philadelphia Museum of Art, Philadelphia

oil on canvas / Öl auf Leinwand
olieverf op doek / óleo sobre lienzo

Mondrian's painting shows extreme radicality: neither curved lines nor oblique lines but the use of just three primary colors and two non colors.

Mondrians Malerei weist eine extreme Radikalität auf: weder geschwungene, noch schräge Linien, nur drei Primärfarben und zwei unbunte Farben verwendet er.

De schilderijen van Mondriaan zijn extreem radicaal: er zijn geen kromme noch schuine lijnen en hij gebruikt slechts drie primaire kleuren en twee niet-kleuren.

La pintura de Mondrian muestra una radicalidad extrema: ni líneas curvas ni líneas oblicuas, y el uso de sólo tres colores primarios y dos no-colores.

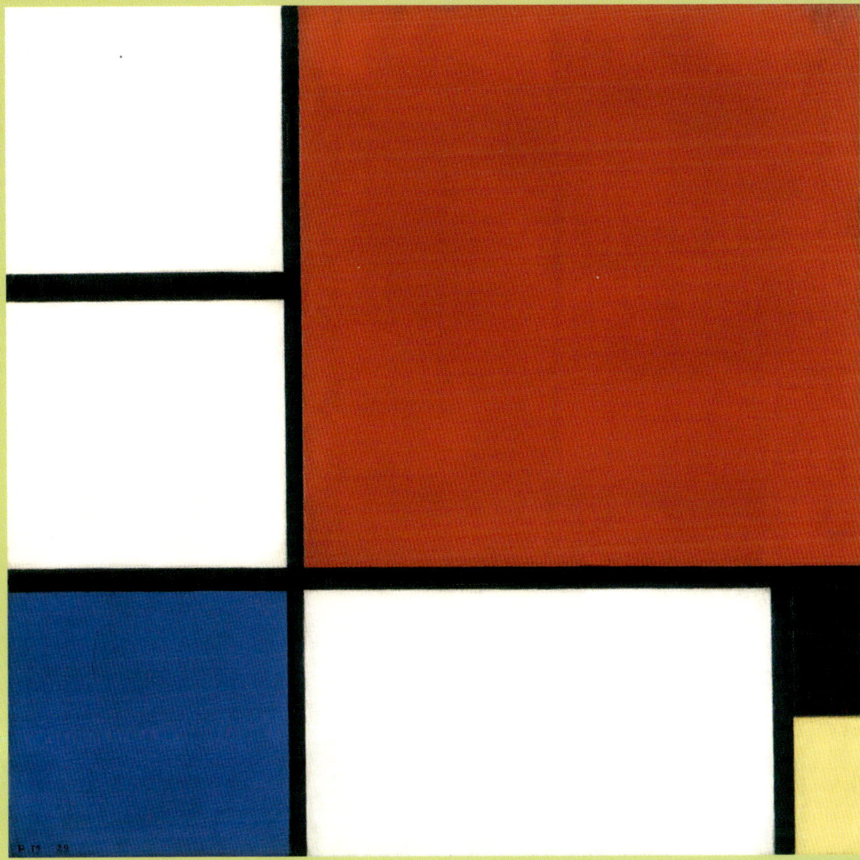

Piet Mondrian
(Amersfoort 1872 - New York 1944)

Composition
Komposition
Compositie
Composición

●●●

1929
45 x 45 cm / 17.7 x 17.7 in.
National Museum, Belgrade

oil on canvas / Öl auf Leinwand
olieverf op doek / óleo sobre lienzo

Laszlo Moholy Nagy
(Bácsbórsod 1895 - Chicago 1946)

**Telephone figure EM 2
(Telefonbild)
Telefonbild EM 2
Telefoonbeeld EM 2
(Telefonbild)
Figura telefónica EM 2
(Telefonbild)**

••

1922
47,5 x 30,1 cm / 18.7 x 11.8 in.
Museum of Modern Art (MoMA),
New York

porcelain enamel on steel
emailliertes Porzellan auf Stahl
porseleinemaille op staal
esmalte de porcelana sobre acero

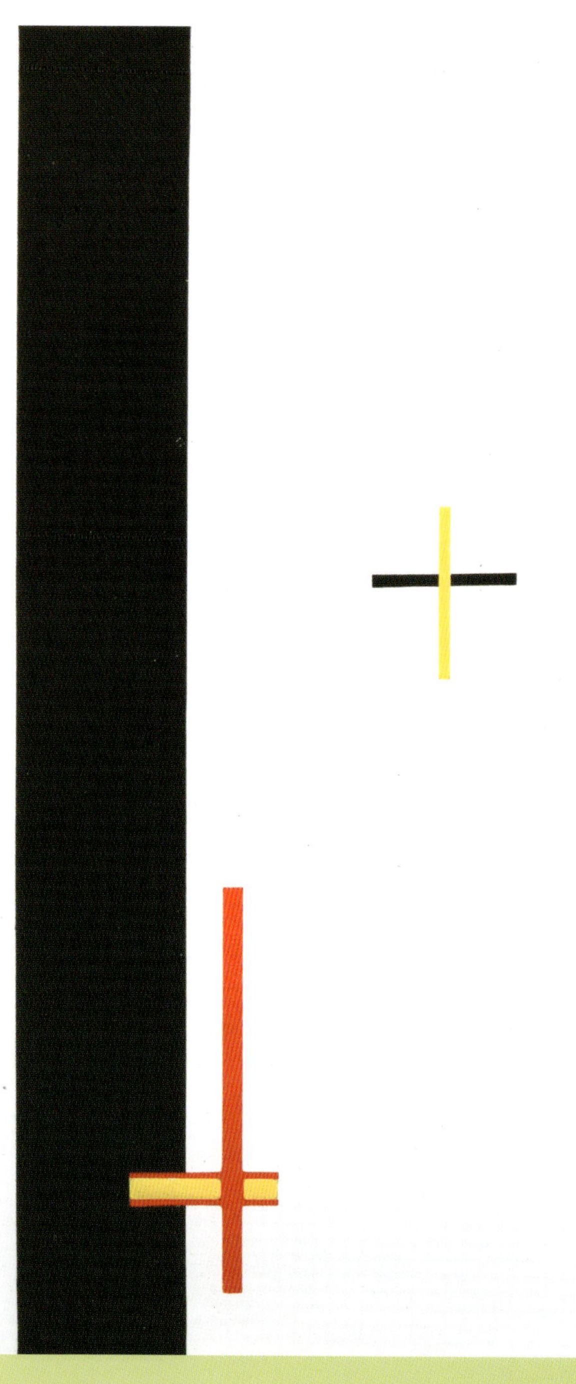

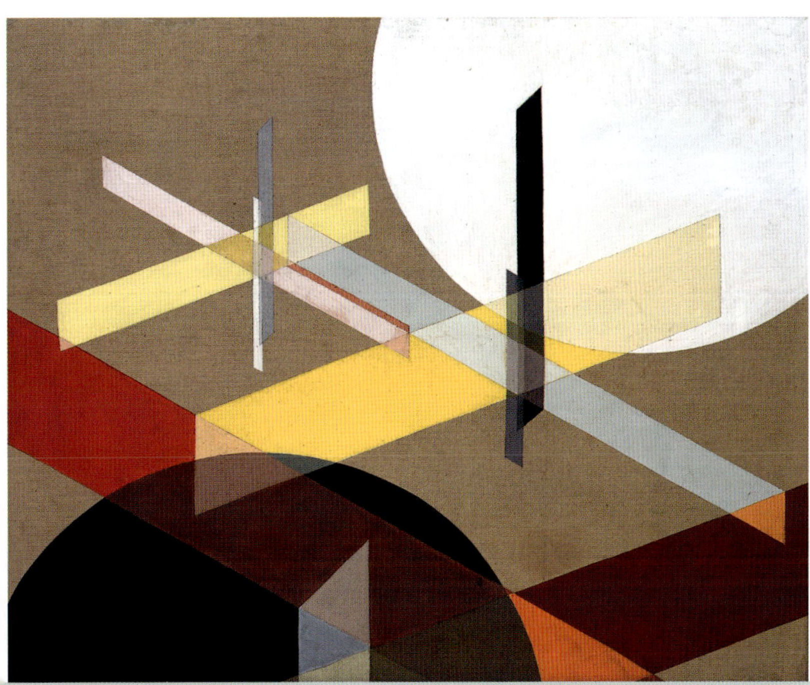

Laszlo Moholy Nagy
(Bácsbórsod 1895 - Chicago 1946)

Composition Z VIII
Komposition Z VIII
Compositie Z VIII
Composición Z VIII

●

1924
114 x 132 cm / 44.9 x 52 in.
Nationalgalerie, Staatliche Museen,
Berlin

glued color on canvas
Leimfarbe auf Leinwand
lijmverf op doek
colores a la cola sobre lienzo

Laszlo Moholy Nagy
(Bácsbórsod 1895 - Chicago 1946)

Bauhausbücher 11

●

1931
13,3 x 10,3 cm / 5.2 x 4 in.
Museum of Modern Art (MoMA), New York

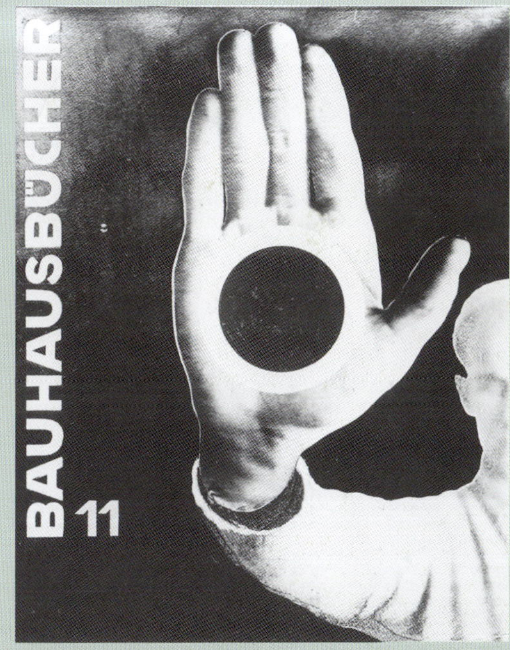

Ludwig Mies van der Rohe
(Aachen 1886 - Chicago 1969)

Glass skyscraper
Glashochhaus
Glazen wolkenkrabber
Rascacielos de vidrio
● ●

1922
Museum of Modern Art (MoMA),
New York

model (lost) / Modell (verloren)
model (verloren) / modelo (perdido)

Ludwig Mies van der Rohe
(Aachen 1886 - Chicago 1969)

German Pavilion. Barcelona,
International Exposition
Deutscher Pavillon auf der
Weltausstellung in Barcelona
Duits paviljoen. Barcelona,
Internationale Expositie
Pabellón alemán. Barcelona,
Exposición Internacional
● ● ●

1928-1929
Museum of Modern Art (MoMA),
New York

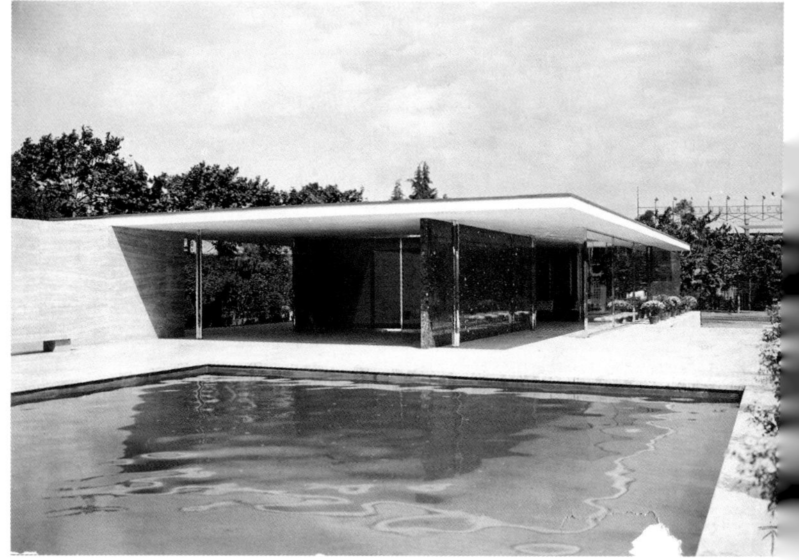

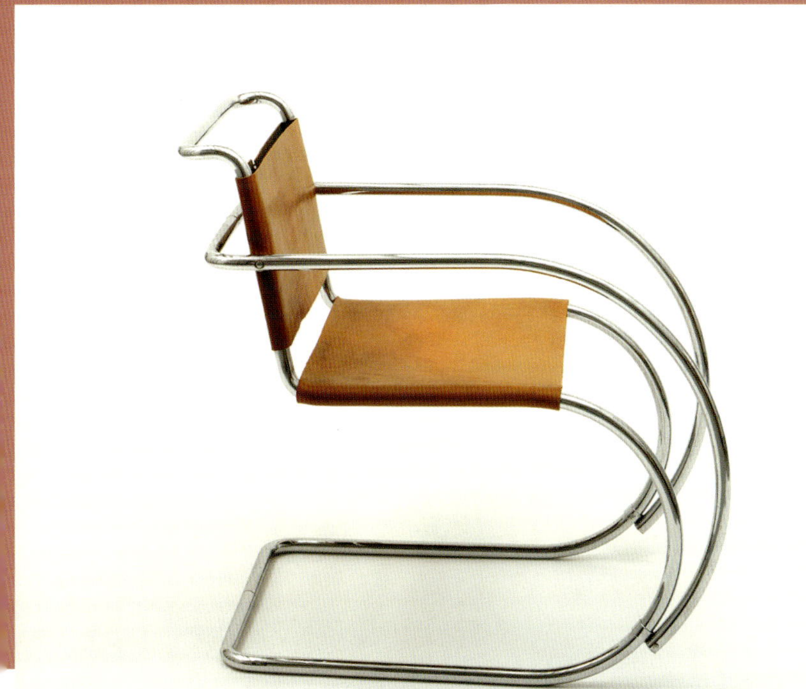

Ludwig Mies van der Rohe
(Aachen 1886 - Chicago 1969)

MR Armchair

●●●

1927
78,7 x 51,9 x 81,9 cm / 31 x 20.4 x 32.2 in.
Museum of Modern Art (MoMA),
New York

chrome-plated steel tubing and leather
Stahlröhren mit Farben plattiert und Leder
Verchroomde staalbuizen met lederen zitting
tubos de acero cromado y cuero

Ludwig Mies van der Rohe
(Aachen 1886 - Chicago 1969)

Table for the Barcelona Pavilion
Tisch für den Barcelona-Pavillon
Tafel voor het Barcelona Paviljoen
**Mesa para el pabellón de
Barcelona**

●

1928
79,8 x 75 x 59 cm / 31.5 x 29.5 x 23.5 in.
Neue Galerie, New York

chrome-plated metal, glass
mit Farben plattiertes Metall, Glas
Verchroomd staal, glas
metal cromado, vidrio

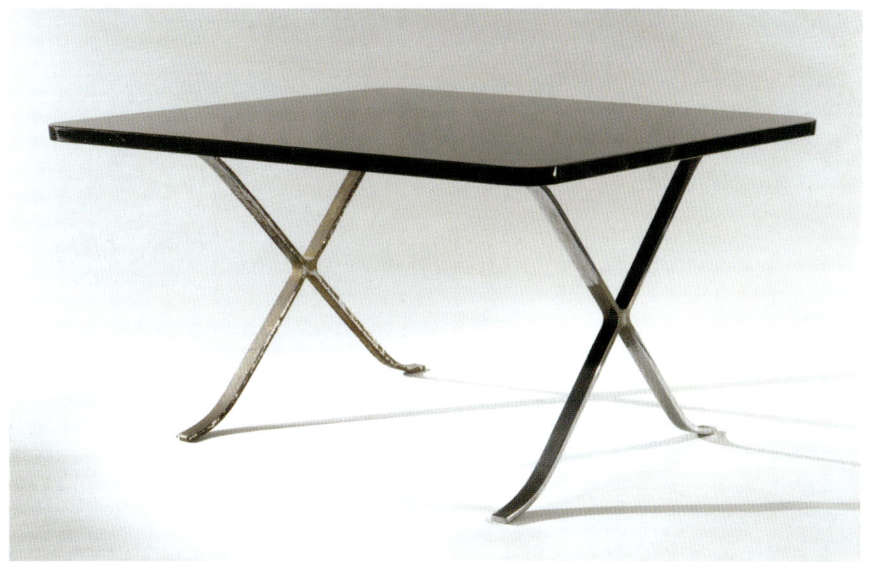

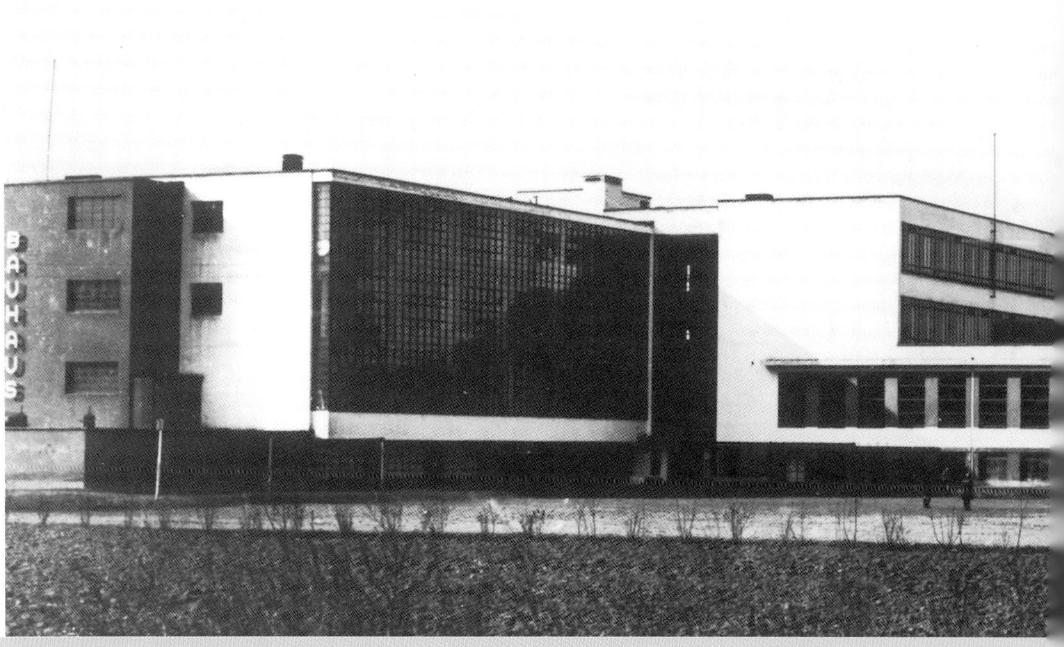

Walter Gropius
(Berlin 1883 - Boston 1969

Fagus workshops at Alfeld. Second building phase, view from Hannoverschen Strasse
Fagus-Werk in Alfeld. Zweite Bauphase, Ansicht von der Hannoverschen Strasse
Fagus-fabriek in Alfeld. Tweede constructiefase, gezien uit de Hannoverschen Strasse
Fábrica Fagus en Alfeld. Segunda fase constructiva, vista desde la Hannoverschen Strasse

●●●

1910-1925

Architect, Gropius is the founder in 1919 of the Bauhaus, which wanted to combine applied arts and the beaux arts.

Der Architekt Gropius gründete 1919 das Bauhaus, in dem er angewandte und schöne Künste vereinen wollte.

Gropius is architect en stichtte in 1919 het Bauhaus waarin hij toegepaste kunst en schone kunsten wilde verenigen.

Arquitecto, Gropius es el fundador en 1919 de la Bauhaus, que quiere conjugar las artes aplicadas con las bellas artes.

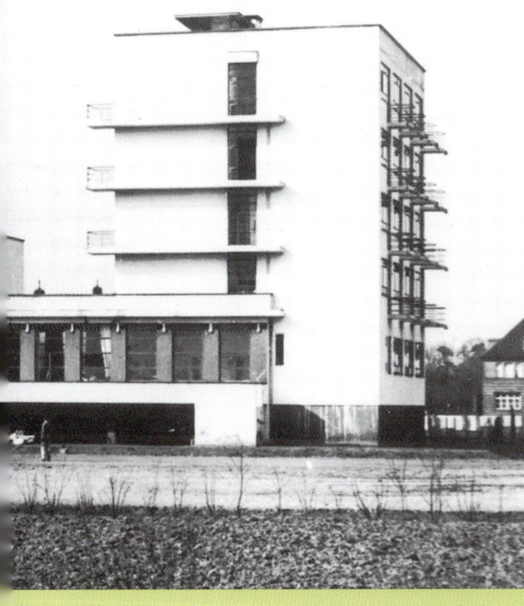

Walter Gropius
(Berlin 1883 - Boston 1969)

**Bauhaus building at Dessau in
a photo of 1928
Der Sitz des Bauhaus in Dessau
auf einem Photo von 1928
Het Bauhaus-gebouw in Dessau
op een foto uit 1928
La sede de la Bauhaus en
Dessau en una foto de 1928**

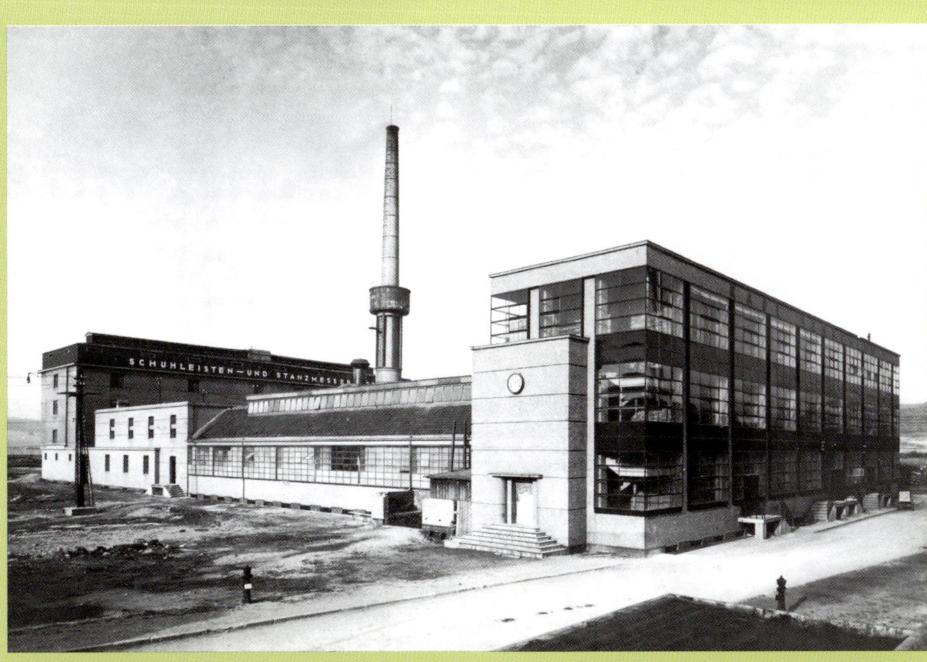

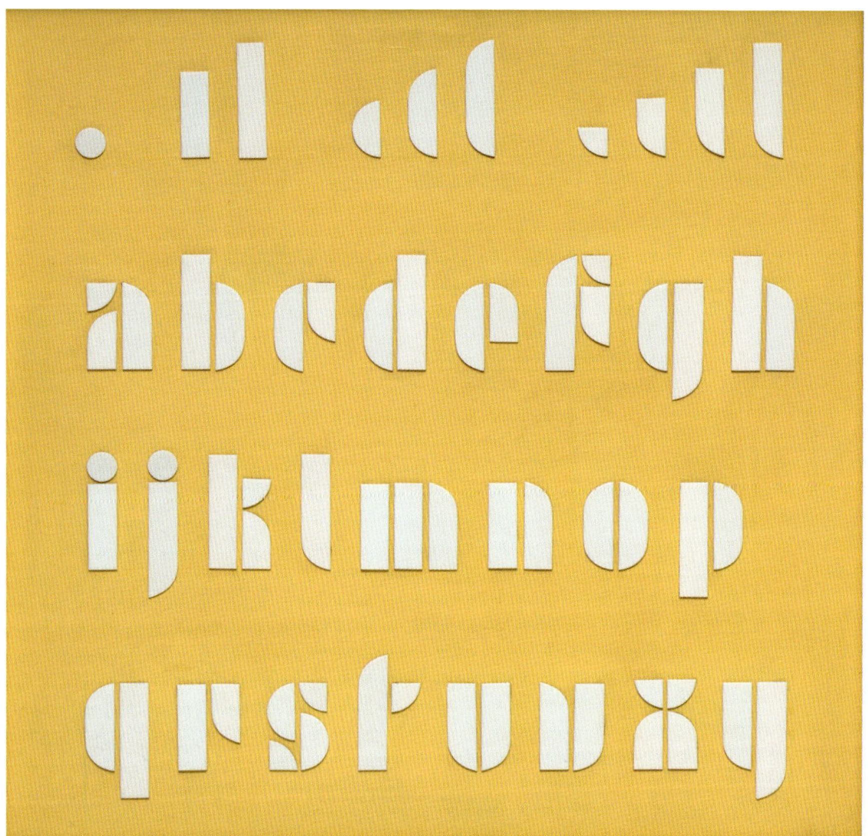

Josef Albers
(Bottrop 1888 - New Haven 1976)

Typographical characters
Typographische Schriftzeichen
Typografische karakters
Caracteres tipográficos
●

1926-1931
61,3 x 60,6 cm / 24.1 x 23.8 in.
Museum of Modern Art (MoMA), New York

white opaque glass and painted wood / Opakes, weißes
Glas und bemaltes Holz / mat wit glas en beschilderd
hout / vidrio blanco opaco y madera pintada

▶ Theodor Bogler
(Hofgeismar 1897 - Andernach 1968)

Teaset consisting
Teeset
Theeservies
Juego de té
●●●

1923
10,5 cm / 4.1 in.
Neue Galerie, New York

cast earthenware with black metallic
glaze / Terrakottaguss mit metallischer
und schwarzer Lasur / aardewerk met
zwarte metaalglazuurlaag / moldeado de
terracota con esmalte metálico negro

▶ Marianne Brandt
(Chemnitz 1893 - Kirchberg, Sachsen 1983)

Tea infuser Model MT 49
Tee-Extraktkännchen MT 49
Theepot met zeef Model MT 49
Tetera modelo MT 49
●●

1927
7,8 cm x 15,1 cm x 10,1 cm / 3 x 5.9 x 3.9 in.
Neue Galerie, New York

tombac, ebony, silver
Tombak, Ebenholz, Silber
rood koper, ebbenhout, zilver
tombac, ébano, plata

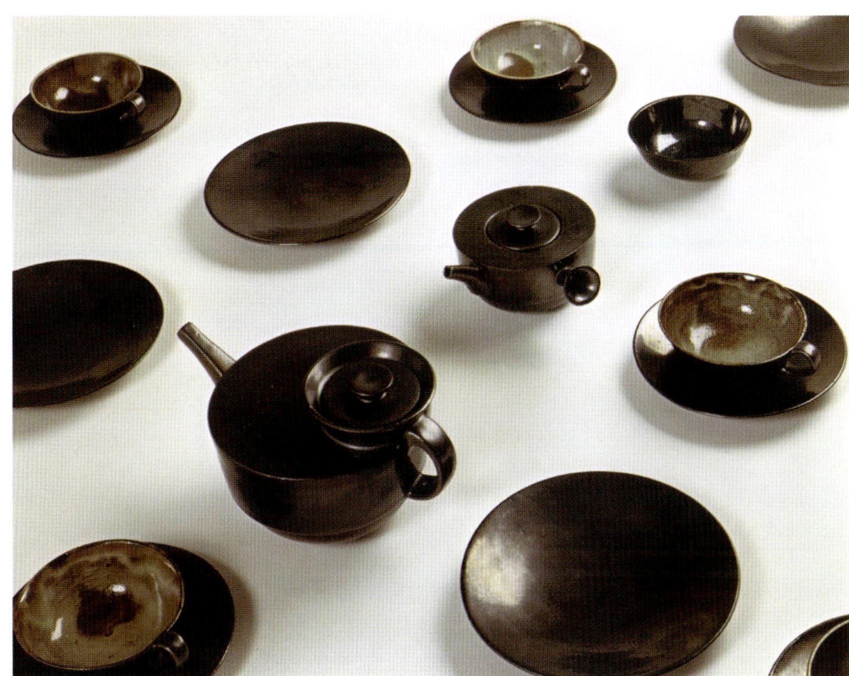

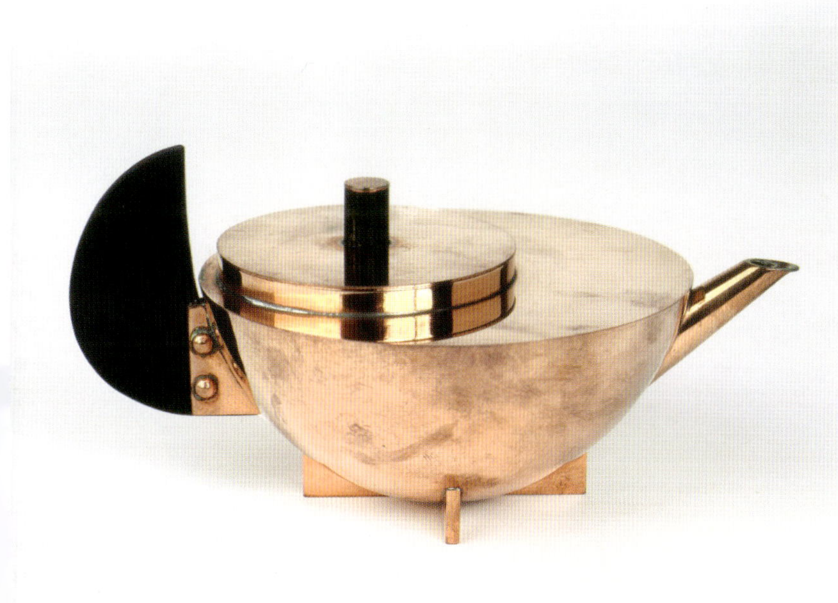

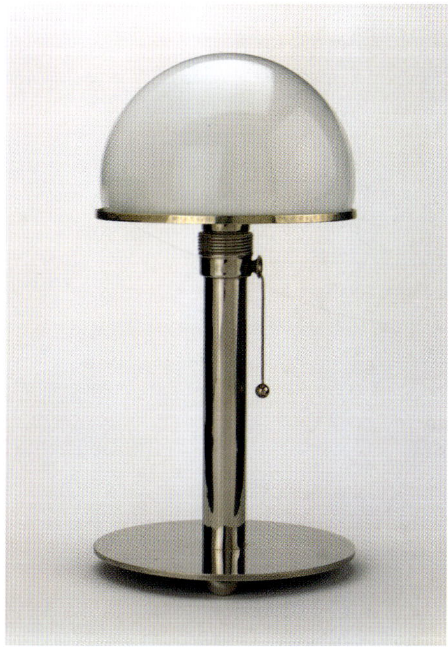

Wilhelm Wagenfeld
(Bremen 1900 - Stuttgart 1990)

Table lamp
Tischlampe
Tafellamp
Lámpara de mesa

●

1924
h. 35,5 cm / 13.9 in.
Victoria & Albert Museum, London

nickel plated brass and milk colored
glass / Mit Nickel plattiertes Messing
und Milchglas / vernikkeld koper en
wit opaalglas / latón plateado, níquel
y vidrio opalino blanco

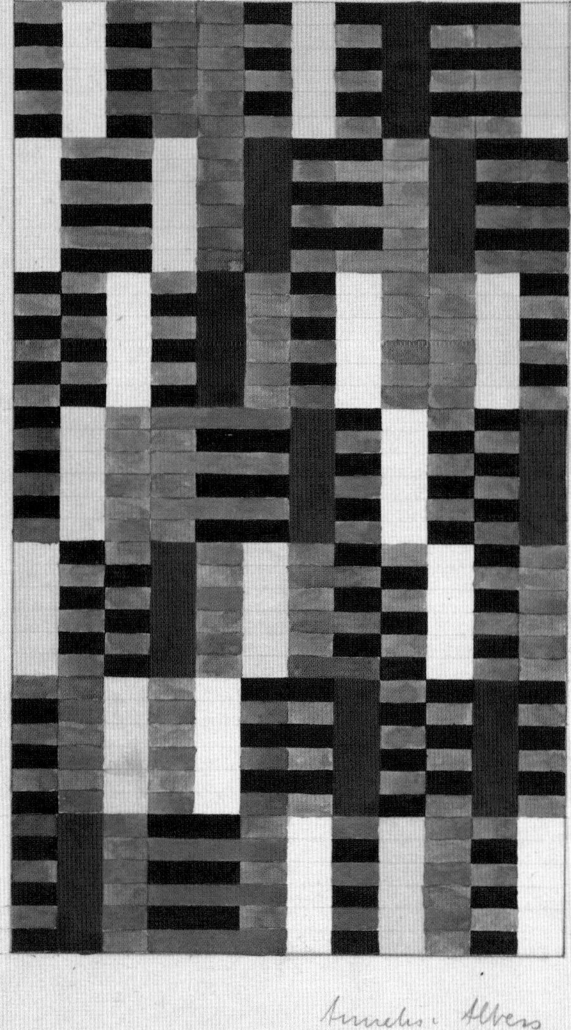

Anni Albers
(Berlin 1899 - Orange, Connecticut 1994)

Design for wall tapestry
Projekt für Wandteppich
Ontwerp voor een wandtapijt
Estudio para tapiz de pared

●

1926
34,9 x 23,8 cm / 13.7 x 9.3 in.
Museum of Modern Art (MoMA), New York

gouache and pencil on paper
Gouache und Bleistift auf Papier
gouache en potlood op papier
gouache y lápiz sobre papel

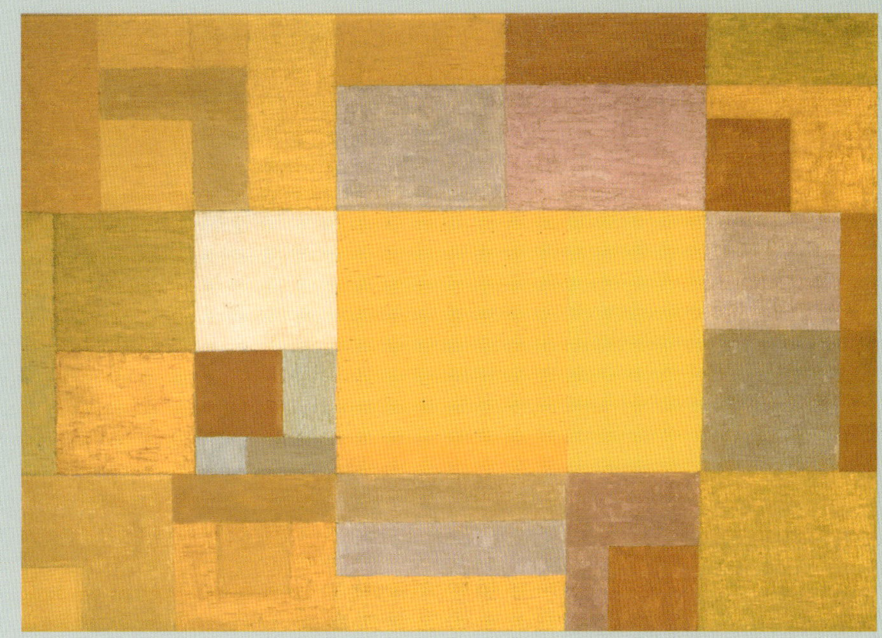

Johannes Itten
(Süderen-Linden 1888 -
Zurich 1967)
Benign light
Gutes Licht
Gunstig licht
Luz benigna
•
1920-1921
Collezione Thyssen-Bornemisza,
Lugano

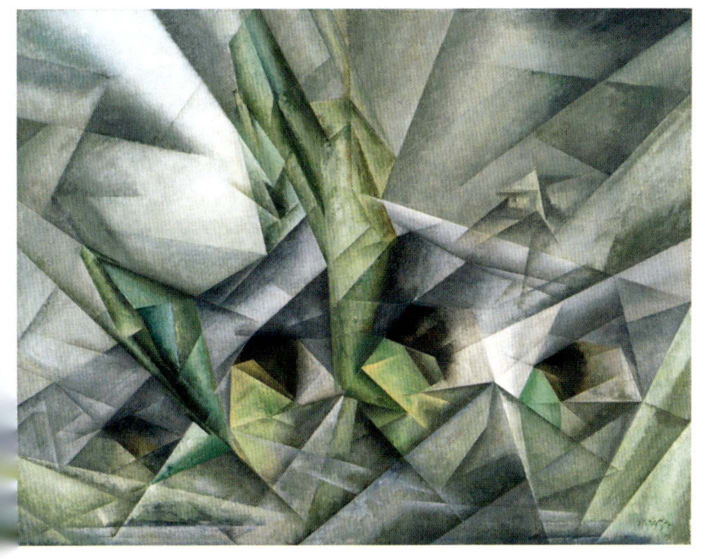

Lyonel Feininger
(New York 1871 - 1956)

Bridge V
Brücke V
Brug V
Puente V
●●
1919
80,3 x 100,3 cm / 31.6 x 39.5 in.
Philadelphia Museum of Art,
Philadelphia

oil on canvas / Öl auf Leinwand
olieverf op doek / óleo sobre lienzo

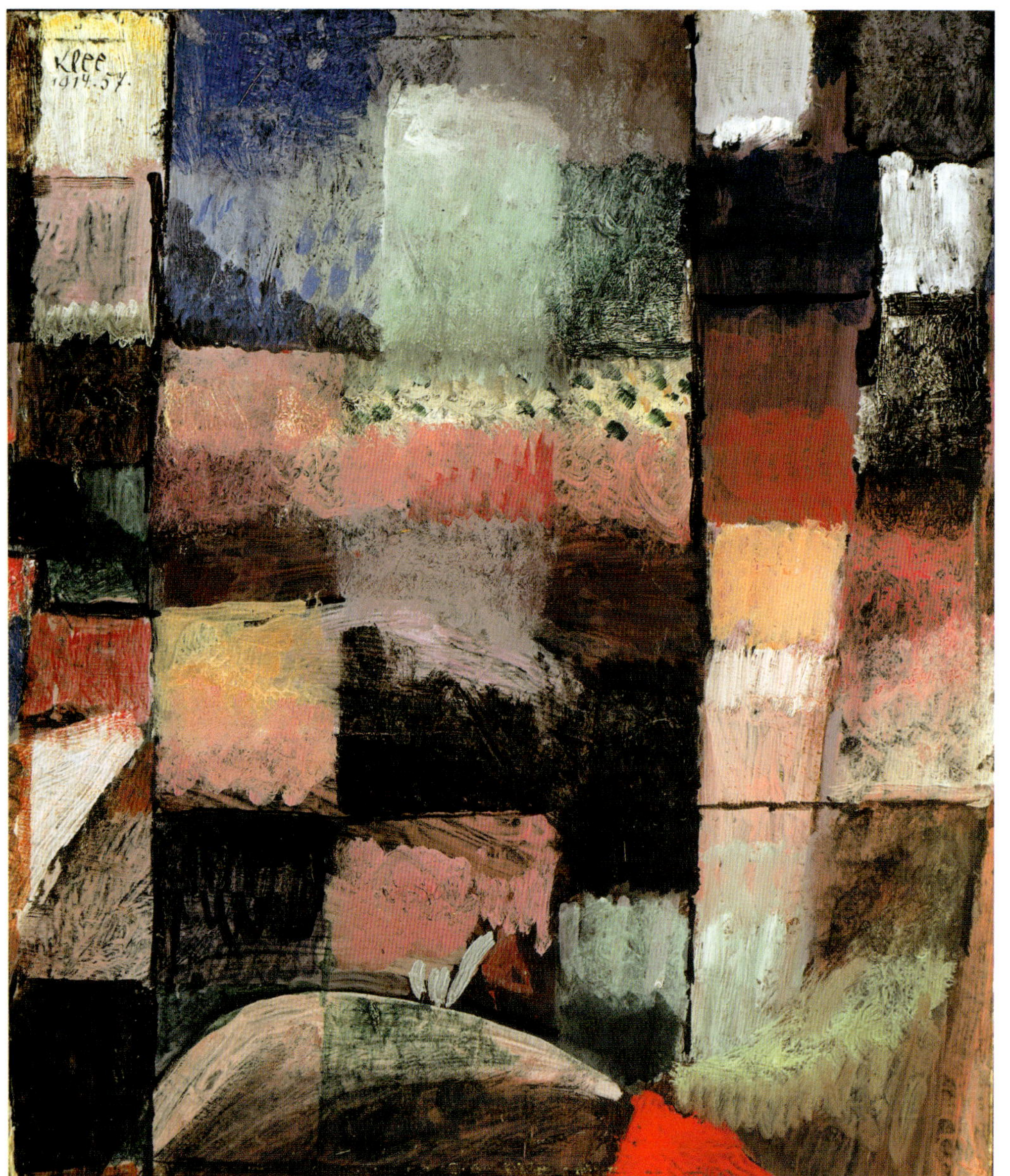

◄ Paul Klee
(Münchenbuchsee 1879 -
Muralto 1940)

**Composition or On a motif of Hammamet
Komposition oder Ein Motiv aus Hammamet
Compositie of een motif uit Hammamet
Composición o En base a un motivo de Hammamet**

●●

1914
27 x 22,5 cm / 10.6 x 8.6 in.
Kunstmuseum, Basel

tempera / Tempera
tempera / temple

► Paul Klee
(Münchenbuchsee 1879 -
Muralto 1940)

**Hammamet with its mosque
Hammamet mit seiner Moschee
Hammamet en de moskee
Hammamet con su mezquita**

●

1914
20,6 x 19,4 cm / 8.1 x 7.6 in
The Metropolitan Museum o
Art, New York

watercolor and pencil on pape
Aquarell e Bleistift auf Papier
aquarel en potlood op papier
acuarela y lápiz sobre papel

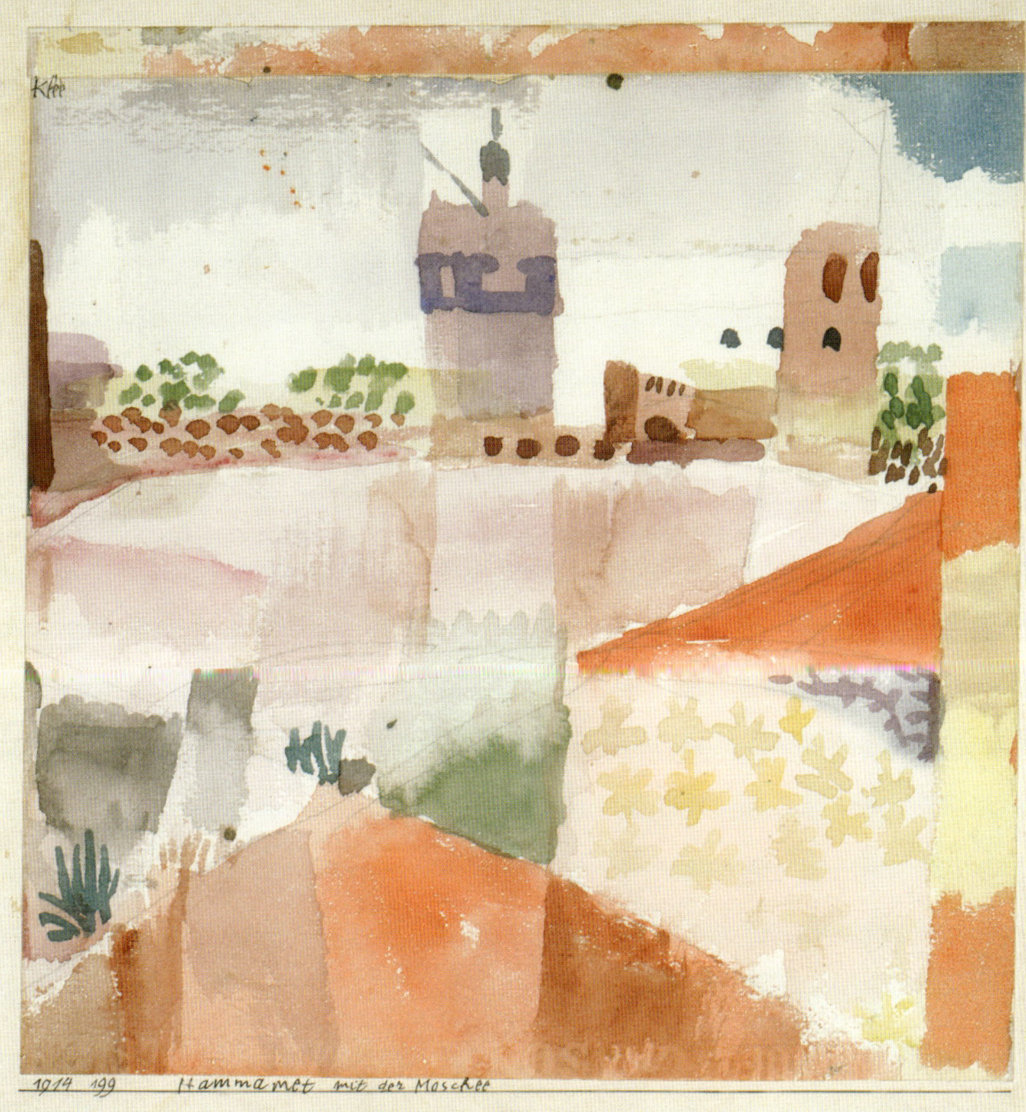

Klee
1914 199   Hammamet mit der Moschee

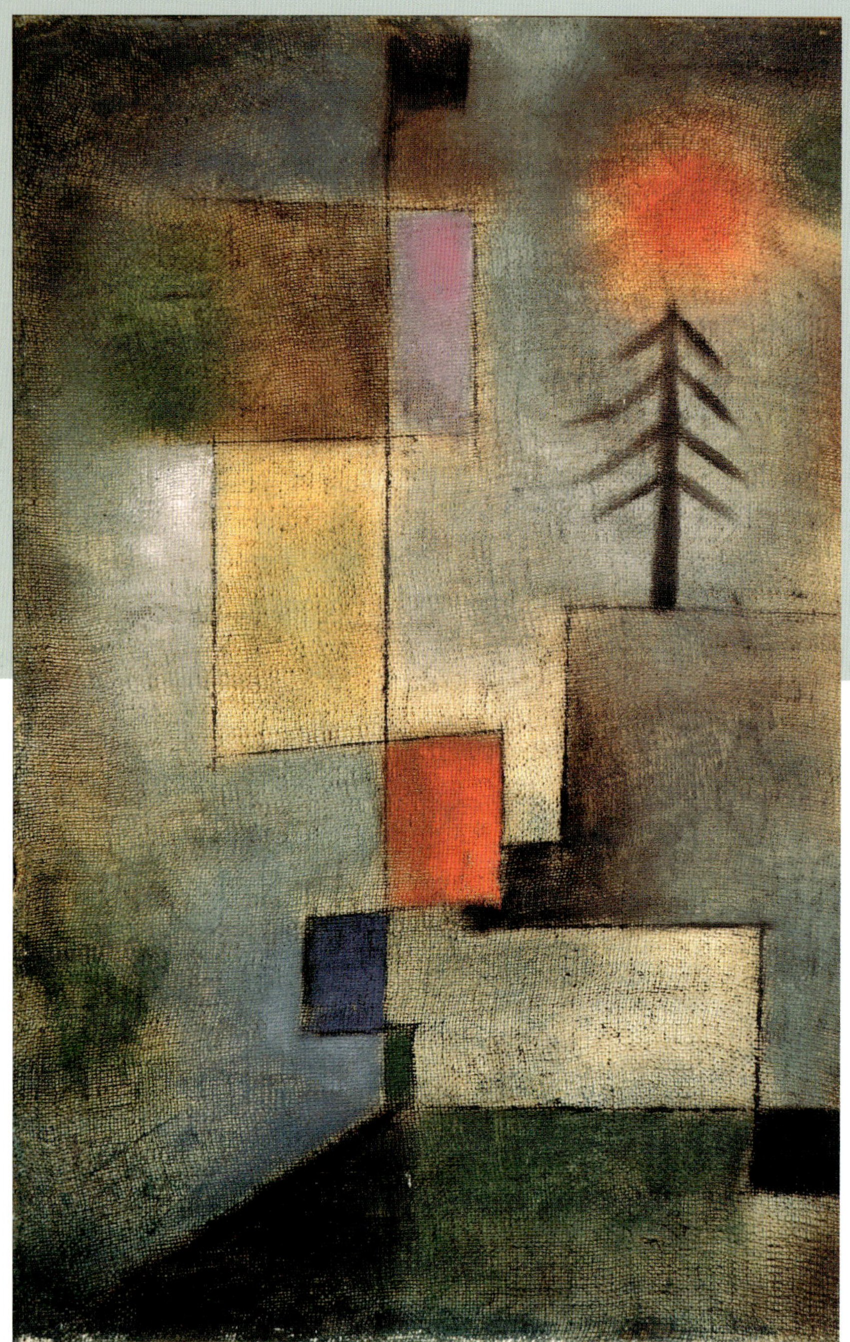

Paul Klee
(Münchenbuchsee 1879 - Muralto 1940)

Small painting of pine tree
Kleines Tannenbild
Klein schilderij met pijnboom
Pequeño cuadro de abeto

••

1922
31,5 x 20 cm / 12.4 x 7.8 in.
Kunstmuseum, Basel

Klee explores here the relations of colors amongst themselves: from the dark exterior of the composition – therefore static – to the more lively and dynamic center.

Klee ergründet die Beziehungen der Farben untereinander: vom dunklen, eher statischen Äußeren der Komposition bis zum lebendigeren und dynamischeren Mittelpunkt.

Klee onderzoekt hier de relatie tussen kleuren: van de donkere buitenkant van de compositie – statisch dus – tot de levendiger en dynamischer kern.

Klee explora aquí las relaciones de los colores entre sí: desde el exterior oscuro de la composición – por ende, estático – hasta el centro, más vivaz y dinámico.

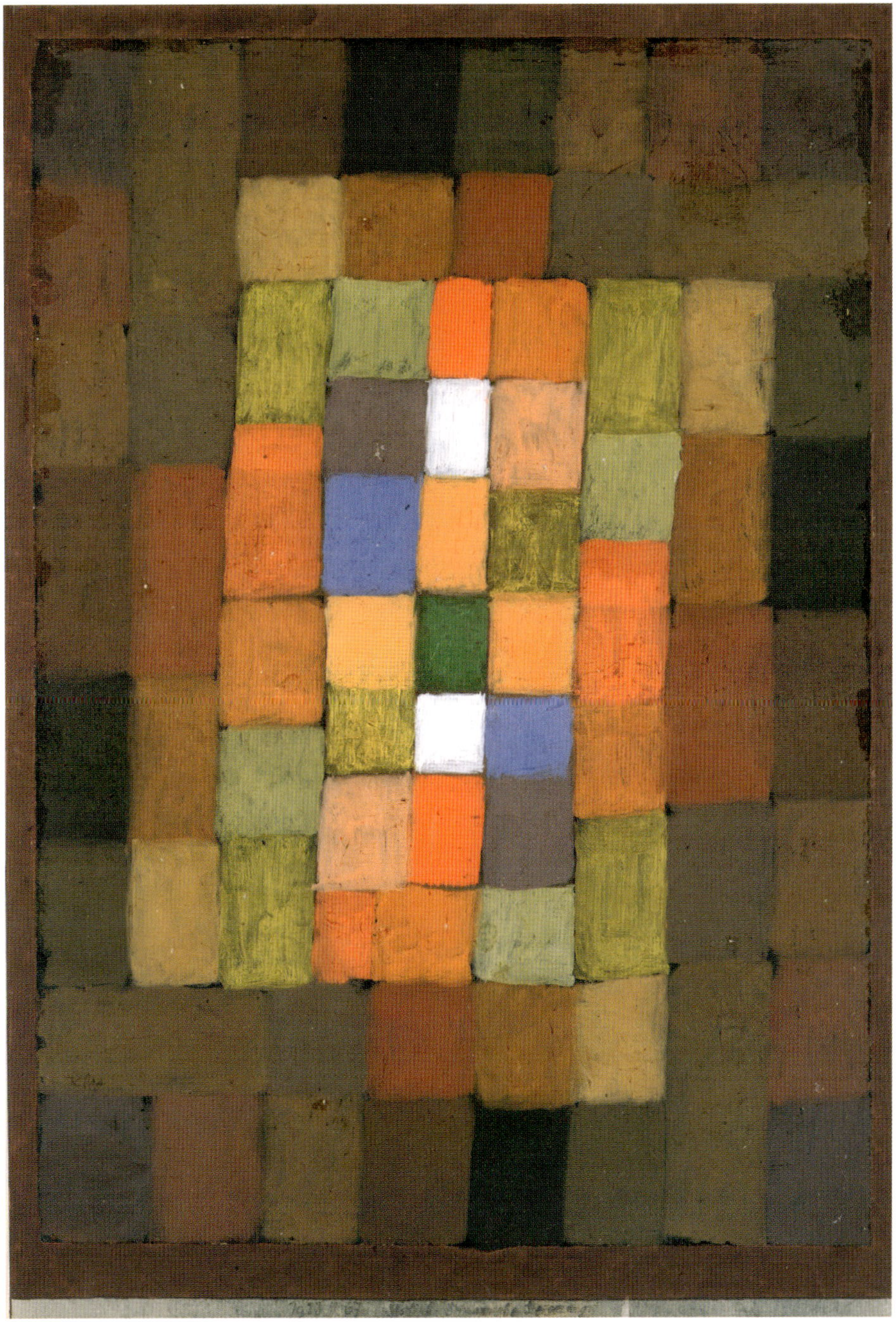

Paul Klee
(Münchenbuchsee 1879 - Muralto 1940)

Static-dynamic gradation
Statisch-dynamische Abstufung
Statisch-dynamische gradatie
Gradación estática-dinámica

●●

1923
38,1 x 26,1 cm / 15 x 10.3 in.
The Metropolitan Museum of Art, New York

oil and gouache on paper, edged with gouache, watercolor and ink / Öl und Gouache auf Papier, umrahmt mit Gouache, Aquarell und Tinte / olieverf en gouache op papier, afgezet met gouache, aquarel en inkt / óleo y gouache sobre papel, con borde en gouache, acuarela y tinta

229

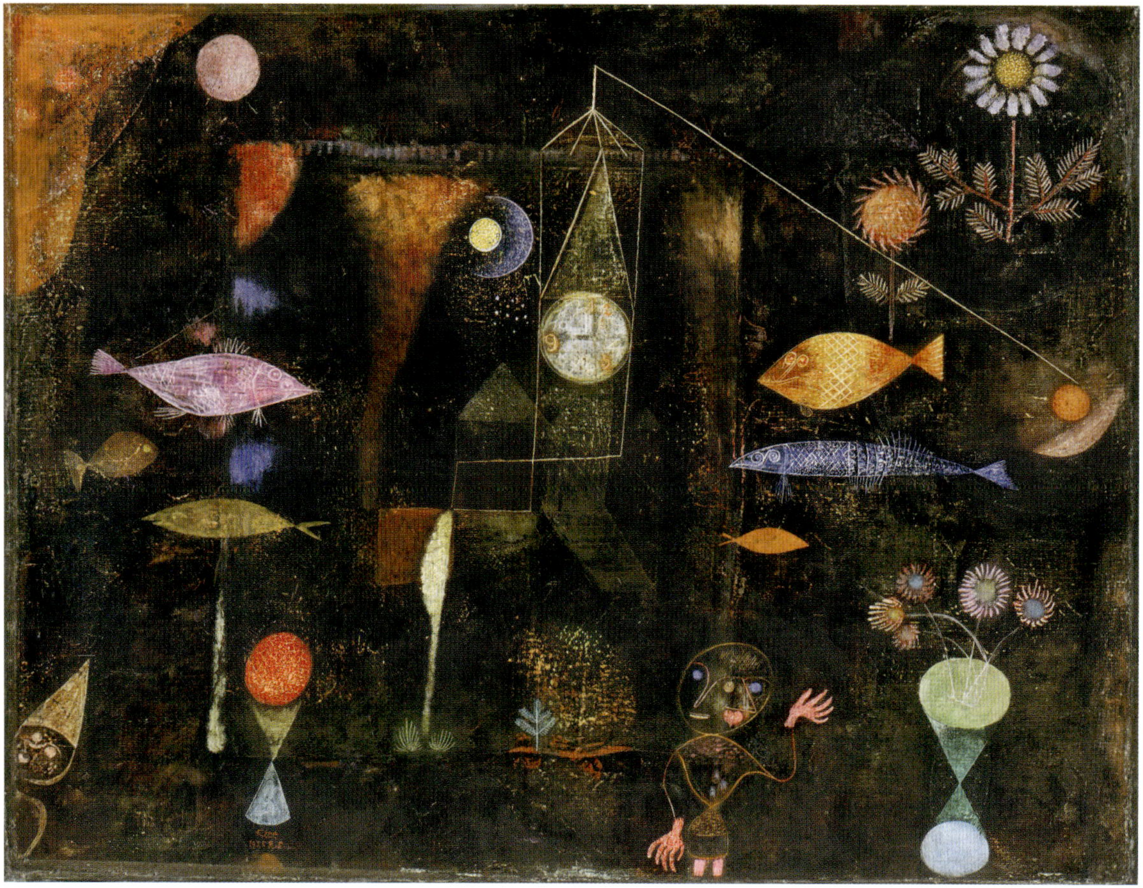

Paul Klee
(Münchenbuchsee 1879 - Muralto 1940)

Magical fish
Magische Fische
Wondervissen
Magia de peces

●●

1925
77,1 x 98,4 cm / 30.3 x 38.7 in.
Philadelphia Museum of Art, Philadelphia

oil and watercolor on canvas on panel / Öl und Aquarell auf Leinwand auf Tafel
olieverf en aquarel op doek op paneel / óleo y acuarela sobre lienzo sobre panel

230

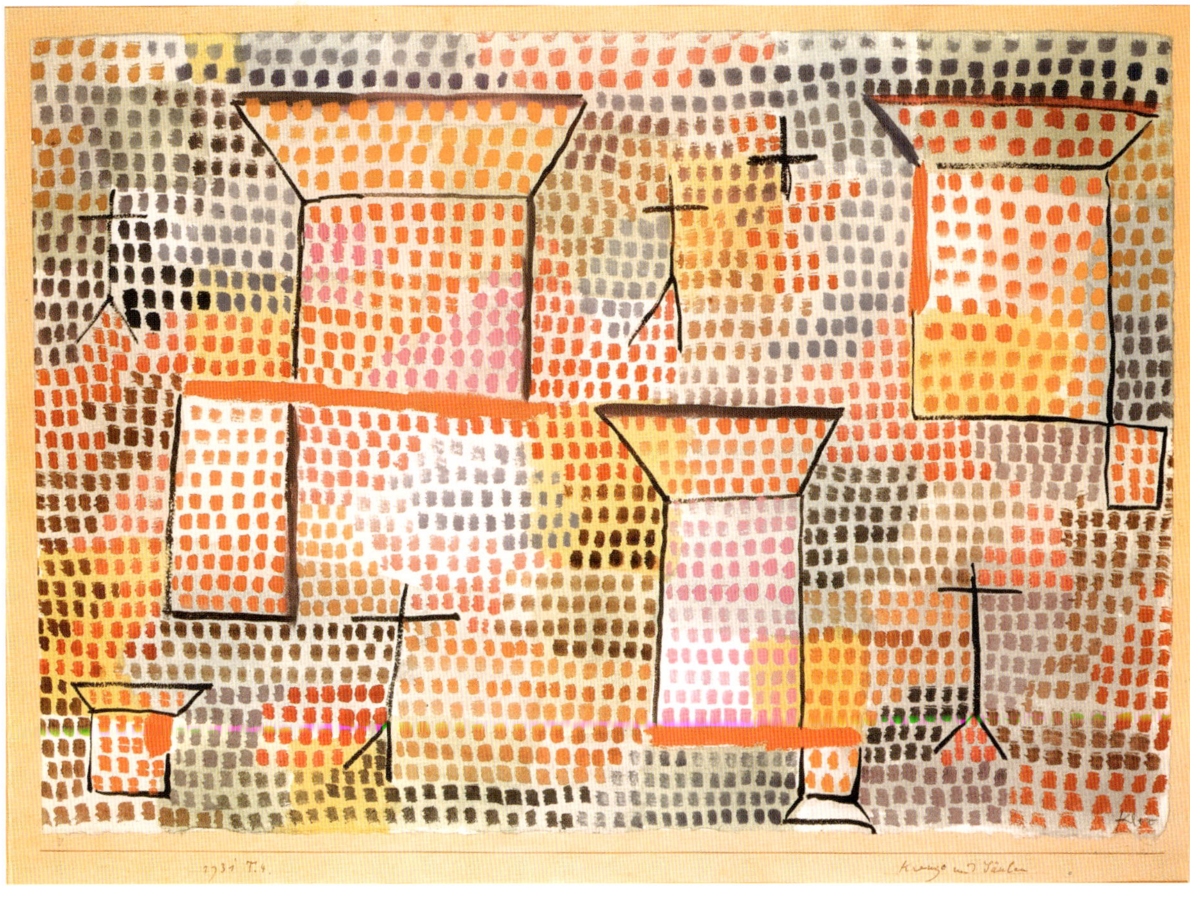

Paul Klee
(Münchenbuchsee 1879 - Muralto 1940)

Crosses and columns
Kreuze und Säulen
Kruizen en zuilen
Cruces y columnas

●●●

1931
49 x 68,2 cm / 19.3 x 26.8 in.
Neue Pinakothek, München

tempera on paper / Tempera auf Papier
tempera op papier / temple sobre papel

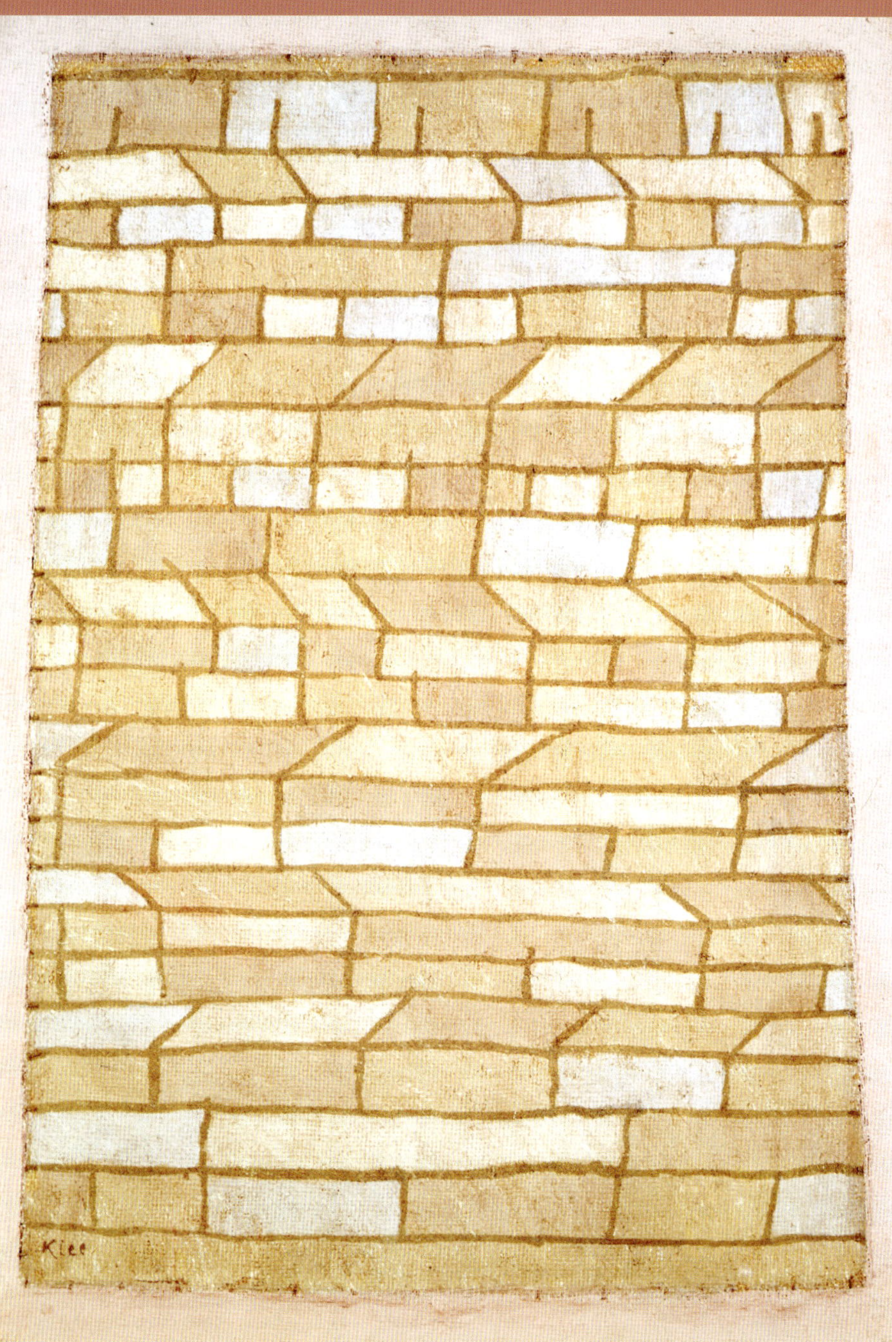

Paul Klee
(Münchenbuchsee 1879 -
Muralto 1940)

**Area of huts
Scheunenviertel
Sloppenwijk
Barrio de chozas**

●●●

1932
77 x 58 cm / 30.3 x 22.8 in.
Kunstmuseum, Basel

tempera on bale
Tempera auf Ballen
tempera op baal
temple sobre bala

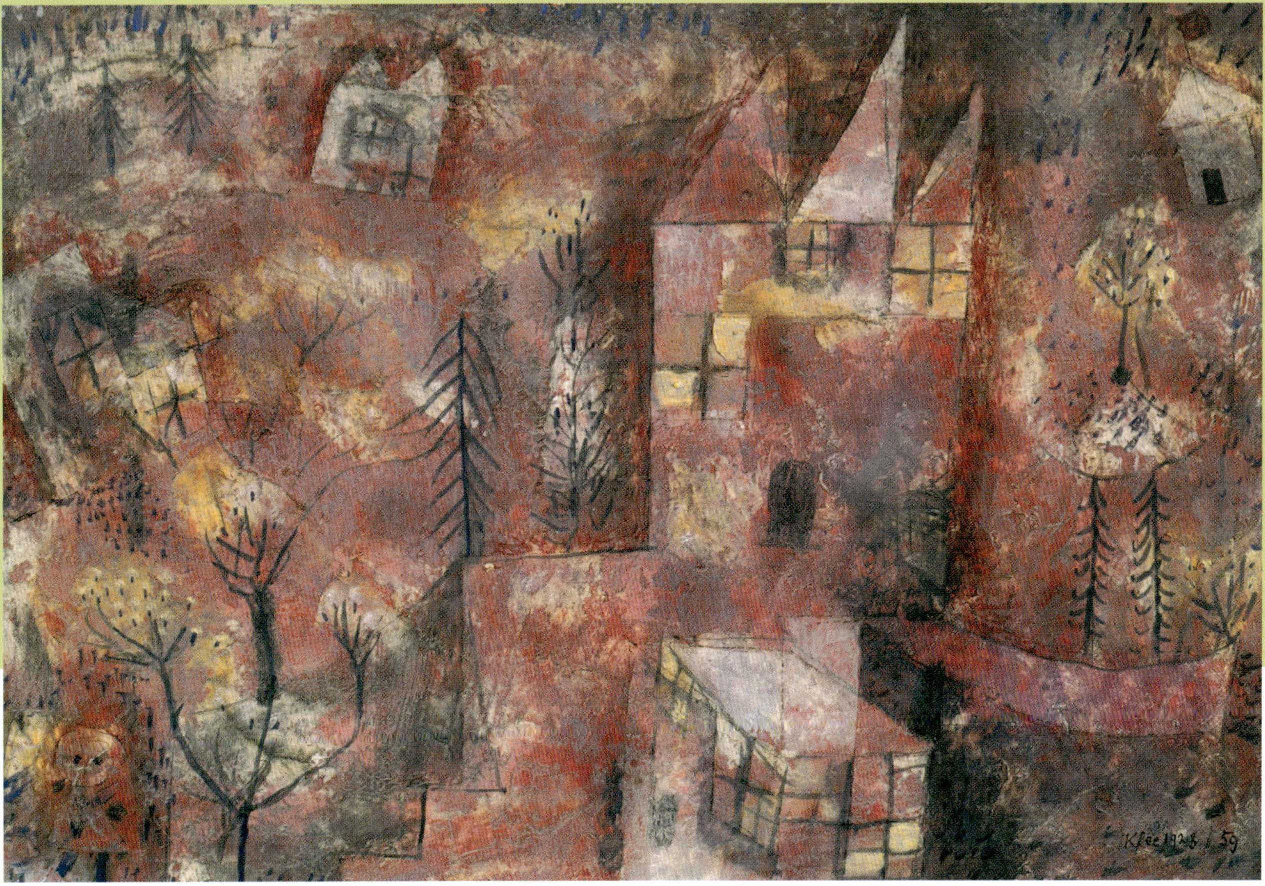

Paul Klee
(Münchenbuchsee 1879 - Muralto 1940)

The child from the landscape
Das Kind in der Landschaft
Een kind uit het landschap
El niño del paisaje

●●

Musée de Grenoble, Grenoble

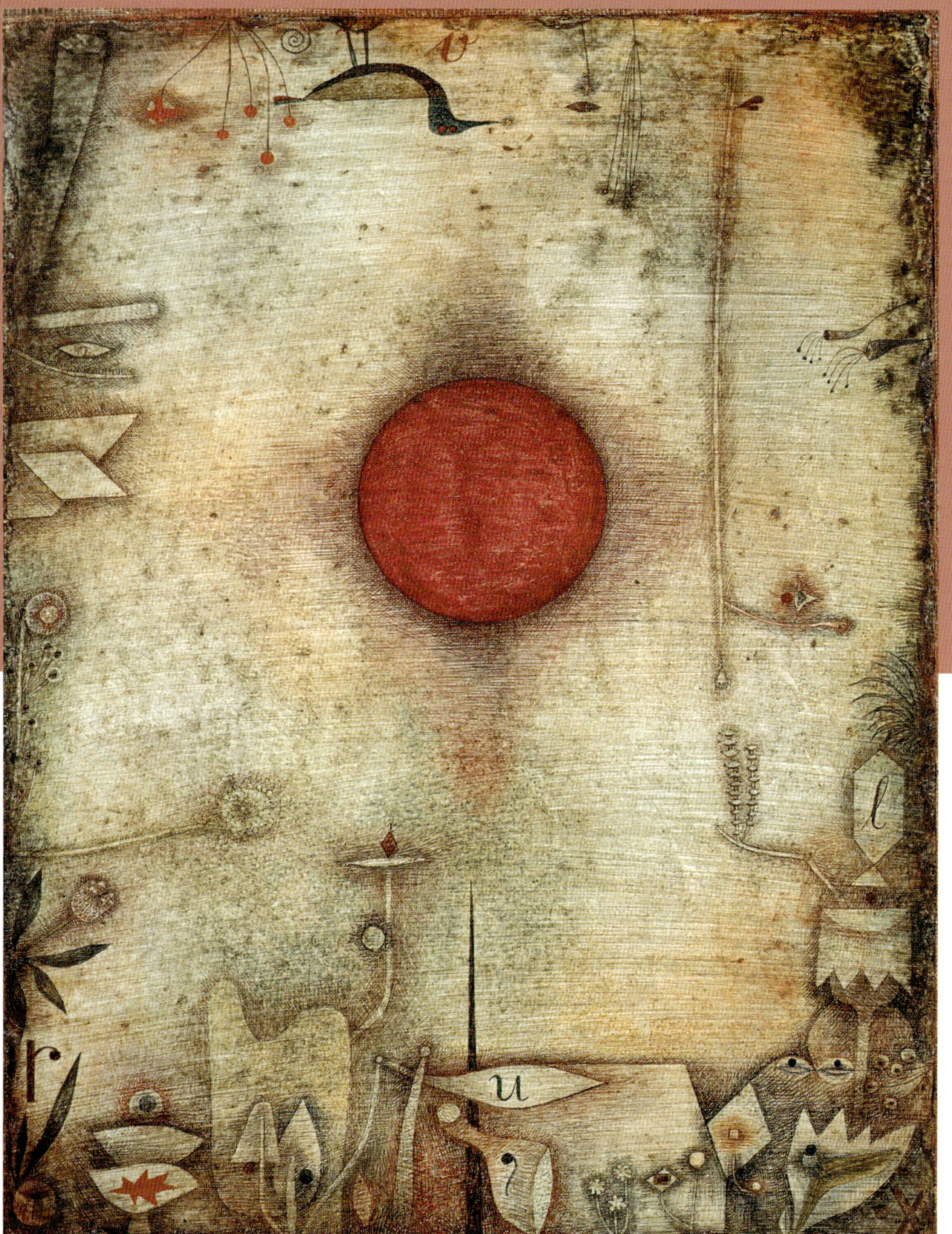

Paul Klee
(Münchenbuchsee 1879 -
Muralto 1940)

**Ad marginem 1930
a 1935-36**
●●

ca. 1930
43,5 x 33 cm / 17.1 x 12.9
Kunstmuseum, Basel

watercolor and pen
Aquarell und Tinte
aquarel en pen
acuarela y pluma

On the aerial background,
Klee inserts ships, people and
shores reduced to plastic signs
of great poetry.

In den luftigen Hintergrund
setzt Klee Schiffe, Personen
und Ufer, die er mit großer
Poesie in plastische Zeichen
verwandelt.

Op de lichte achtergrond
plaatst Klee schepen,
personages en oevers die
gereduceerd zijn tot grote
poëtische plastische tekens.

Sobre el fondo aéreo, Klee
coloca barcos, personajes
y costas reducidas a trazos
plásticos de gran poesía.

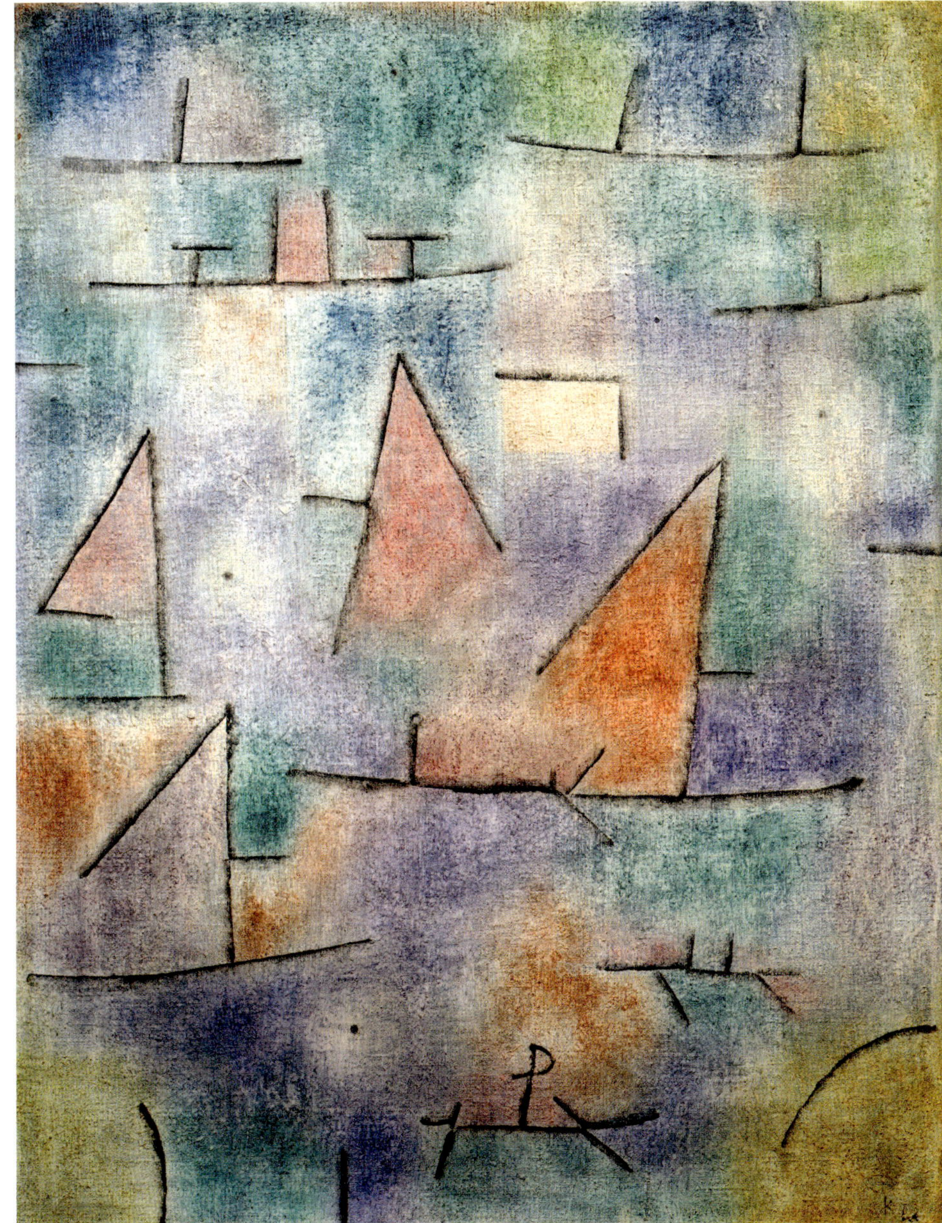

Paul Klee
(Münchenbuchsee 1879 -
Muralto 1940)
**Port and sailboats
Hafen mit Segelschiffen
Haven en zeilen
Puerto y velas**
●
1937
80 x 60,5 cm / 31.5 x 23.8 in.
Centre Georges Pompidou, Musée
National d'Art Moderne, Paris

oil on canvas / Öl auf Leinwand
ieverf op doek / óleo sobre lienzo

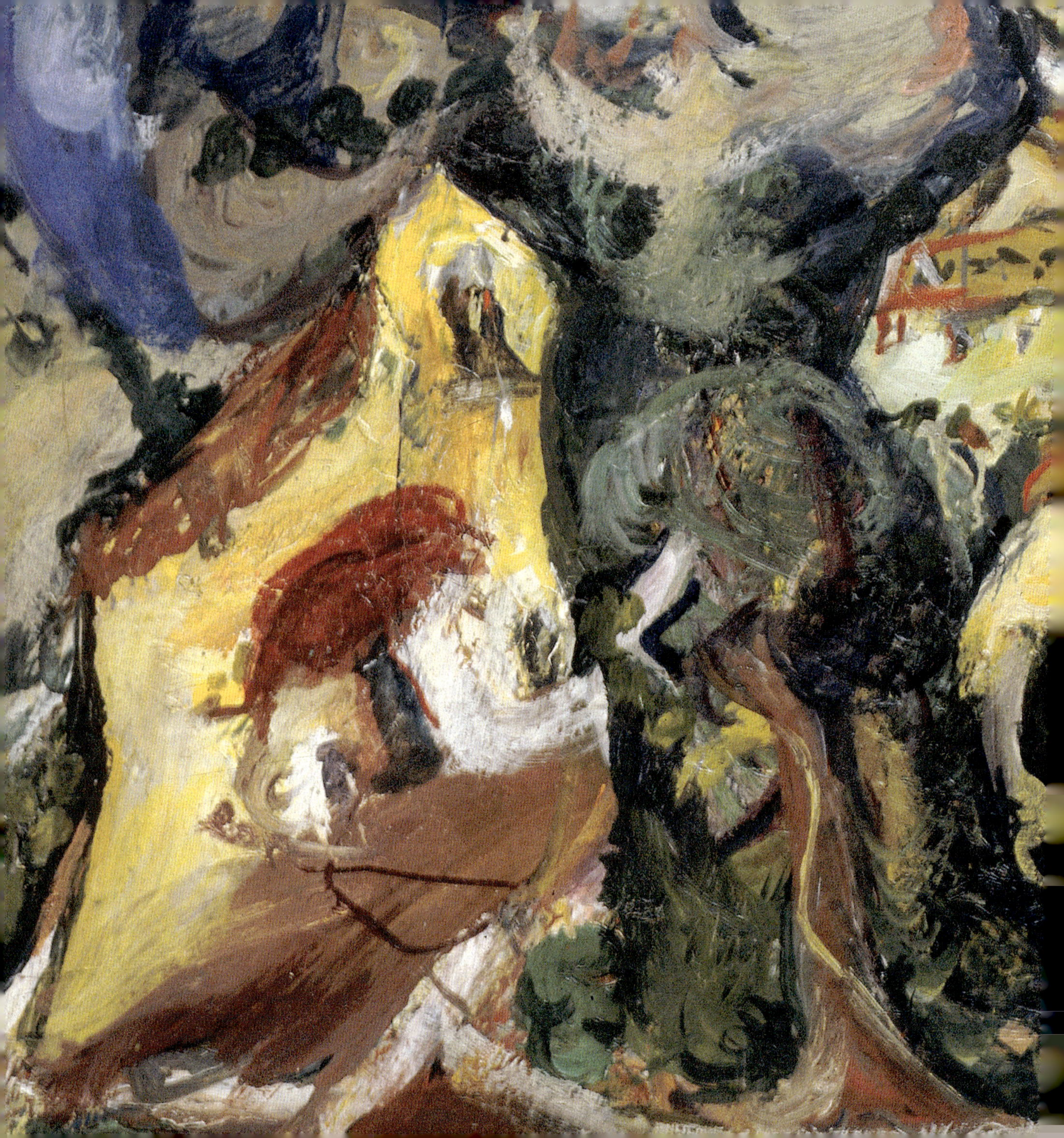

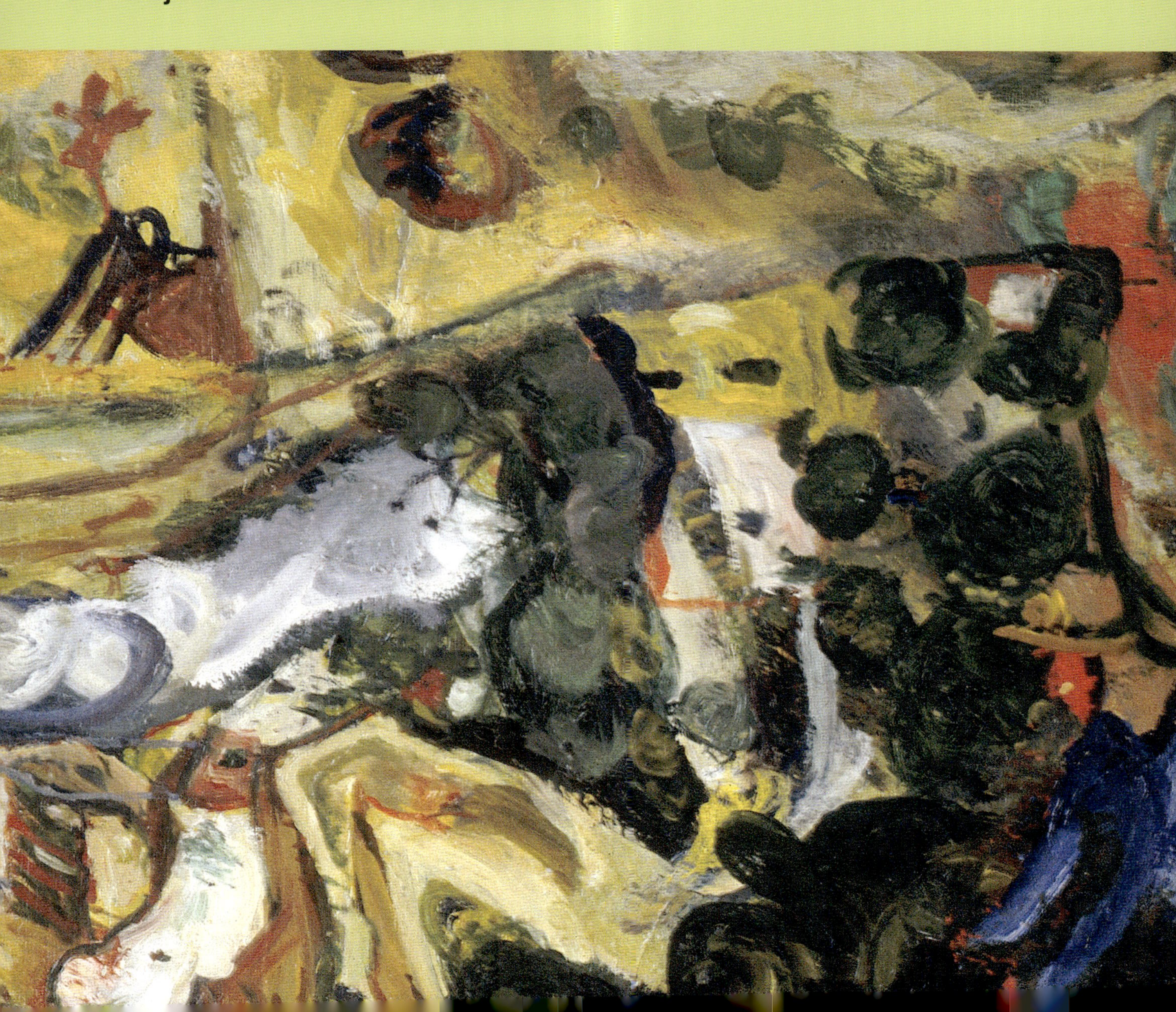

The Paris School • Die Pariser Schule
De Parijse school • La escuela de París

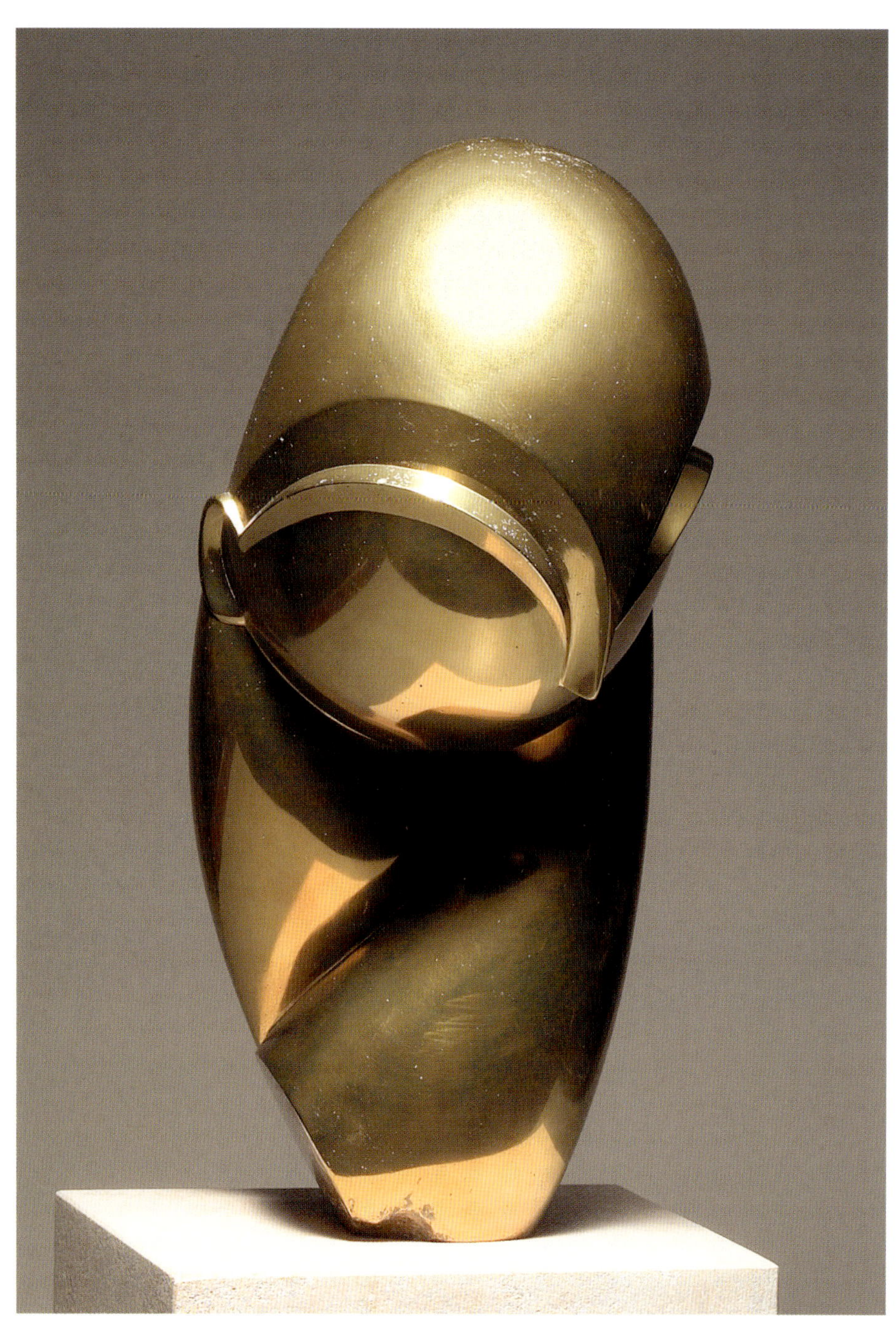

Constantin Brancusi
(Peştişani Gorj 1876 - Paris 1957)
Mademoiselle Pogany II
●●●
1919
43,5 x 18 x 28,5 cm
17.1 x 7 x 11.2 in.
Yale University Art Gallery,
New Haven (CT)

polished bronze / Polierte Bronze
gepoleist brons / bronce pulido

For Brancusi the base has the same
importance as the sculpture and is an
integral part of the work.

Für Brancusi hat die Basis der Skulptur die
gleiche Bedeutung wie die Skulptur selbst
und ist daher Bestandteil des Werkes.

Het voetstuk is van even groot belang
als de sculptuur zelf en maakt deel uit van
het kunstwerk.

Para Brancusi, la base tiene la misma
importancia que la escultura y es parte
integrante de la obra.

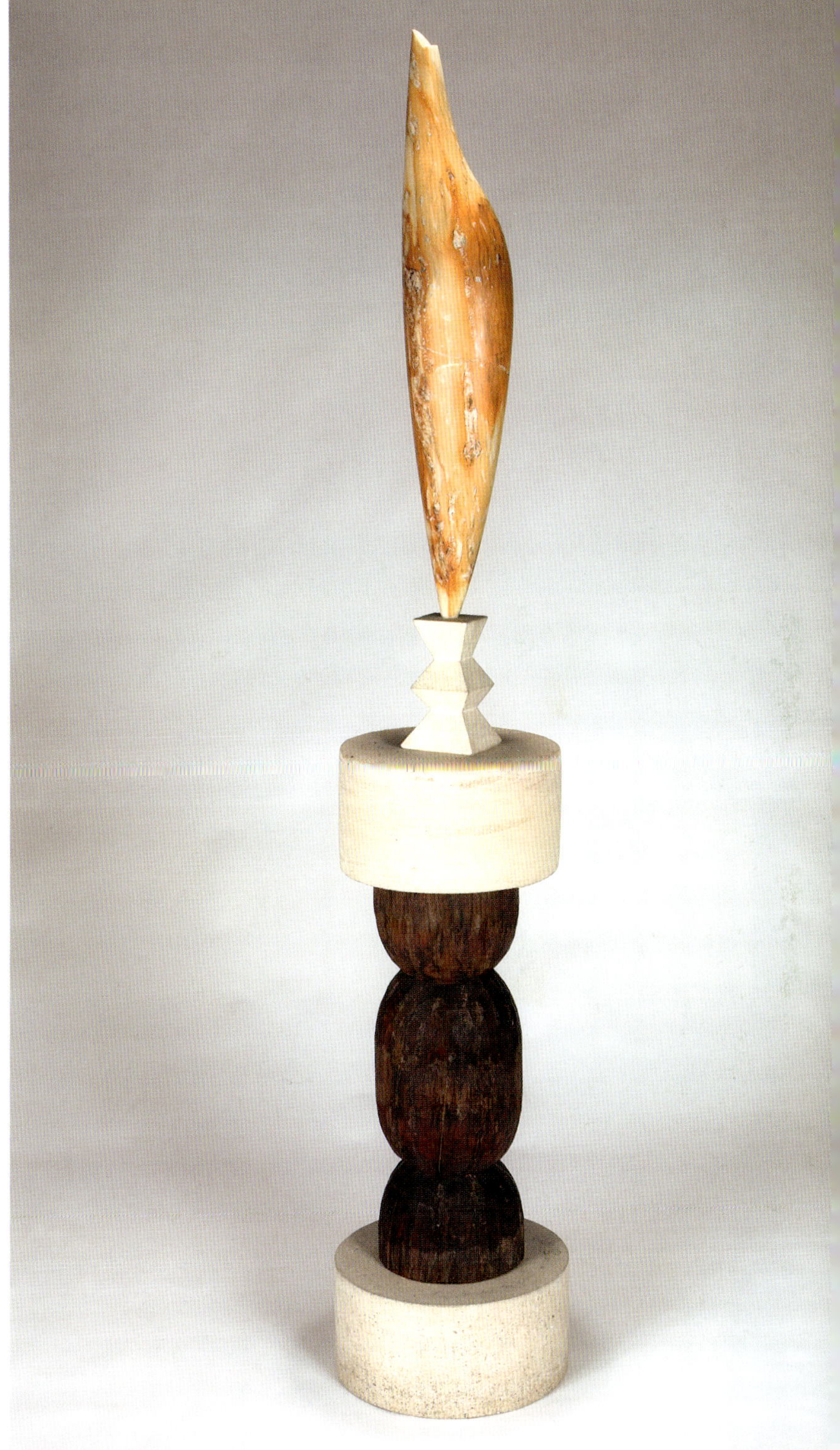

Constantin Brancusi
(Peştişani Gorj 1876 - Paris 1957)

Yellow bird
Der gelbe Vogel
Gele vogel
Pájaro amarillo

●●

1919
h. 221,6 cm / 87.2 in.
Yale University Art Gallery, New Haven (CT)

yellow marble, limestone and wooden base
Gelber Marmor, Kalkstein und Holzbasis
geel marmer, kalksteen en houten basis
mármol amarillo, caliza y base en madera

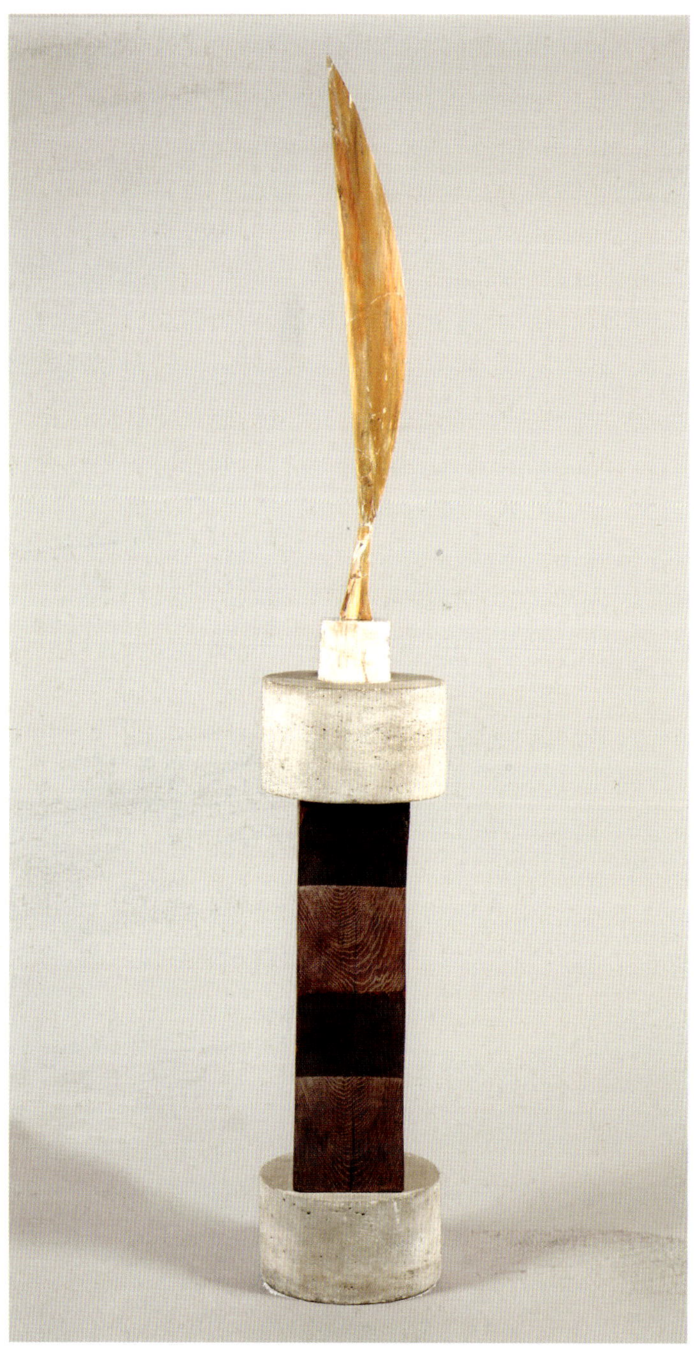

◄ Constantin Brancusi
(Peştişani Gorj 1876 - Paris 1957)

Bird in space
Vogel im Raum
Vogel in de ruimte
Pájaro en el espacio
●●
1924
h. 261,6 cm / 103 in.
Philadelphia Museum of Art, Philadelphia

marble with marble base, sandstone
and oak wood
Marmor auf Marmorbasis, Sandstein und
Eichenholz
marmer met basis gemaakt van marmer,
zandsteen en eikenhout
mármol con base en mármol, arenaria
y madera de roble

► Constantin Brancusi
(Peştişani Gorj 1876 - Paris 1957)

The Kiss
Der Kuss
De kus
El beso
●●●
ca. 1940
h. 71 cm / 27.9 in.
Centre Georges Pompidou,
Musée National d'Art Moderne, Paris

chalky yellow stone / gelber Kalkstein
Geel kalksteen / piedra caliza amarilla

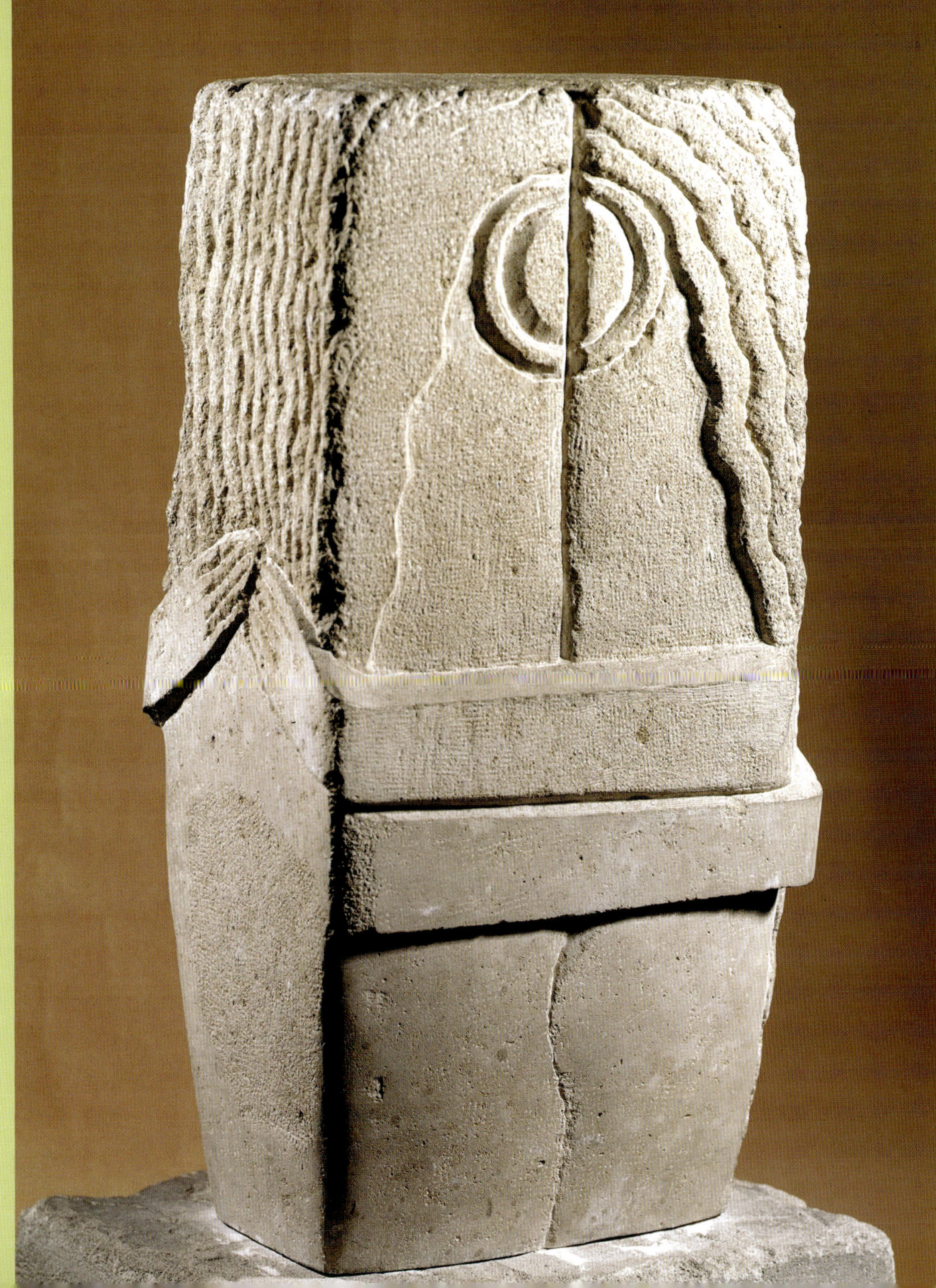

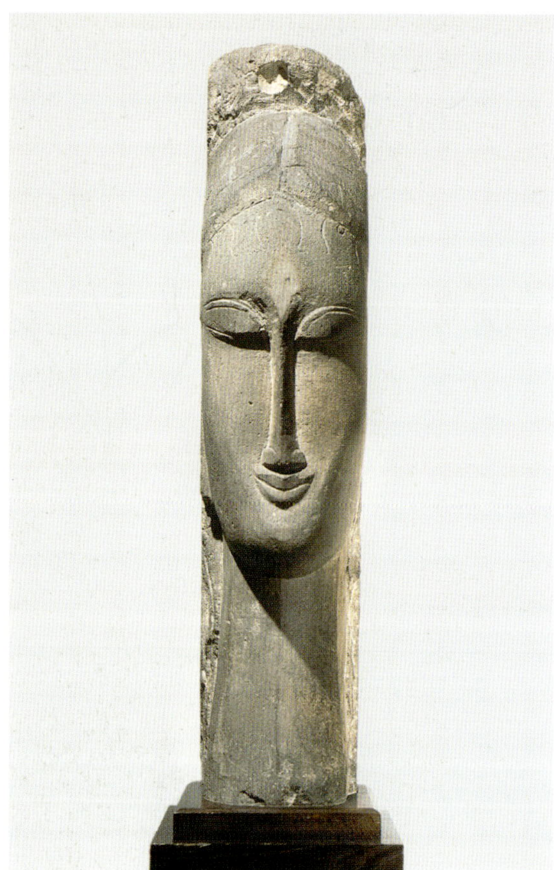

242

Amedeo Modigliani
(Livorno 1884 - Paris 1920)

Woman's head
Frauenkopf
Hoofd van een vrouw
Cabeza de mujer

●●

1912
h. 58 cm / 22.8 in.
Centre Georges Pompidou, Musée
National d'Art Moderne, Paris

stone / Stein / steen / piedra

Amedeo Modigliani
(Livorno 1884 - Paris 1920)

Portrait of Paul Guillaume
Porträt des Paul Guillaume
Portret van Paul Guillaume
Retrato de Paul Guillaume

●●●

1915
105 x 75 cm / 41.3 x 29.5 in.
Musée de l'Orangerie, Paris

oil on glued paperboard on parquet plywood
Öl auf Karton auf geleimtem Sperrholz
olieverf op karton op multiplex hout geplakt
óleo sobre cartón encolado sobre aglomerado símil parqué

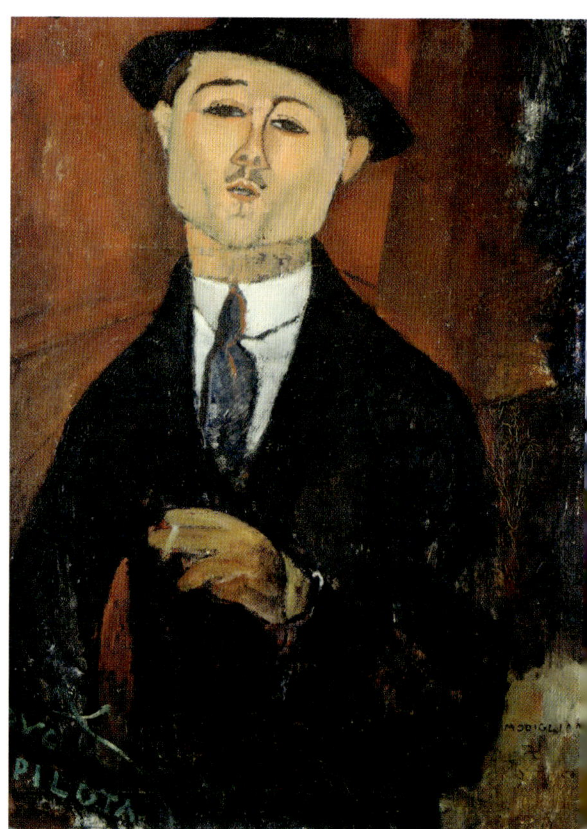

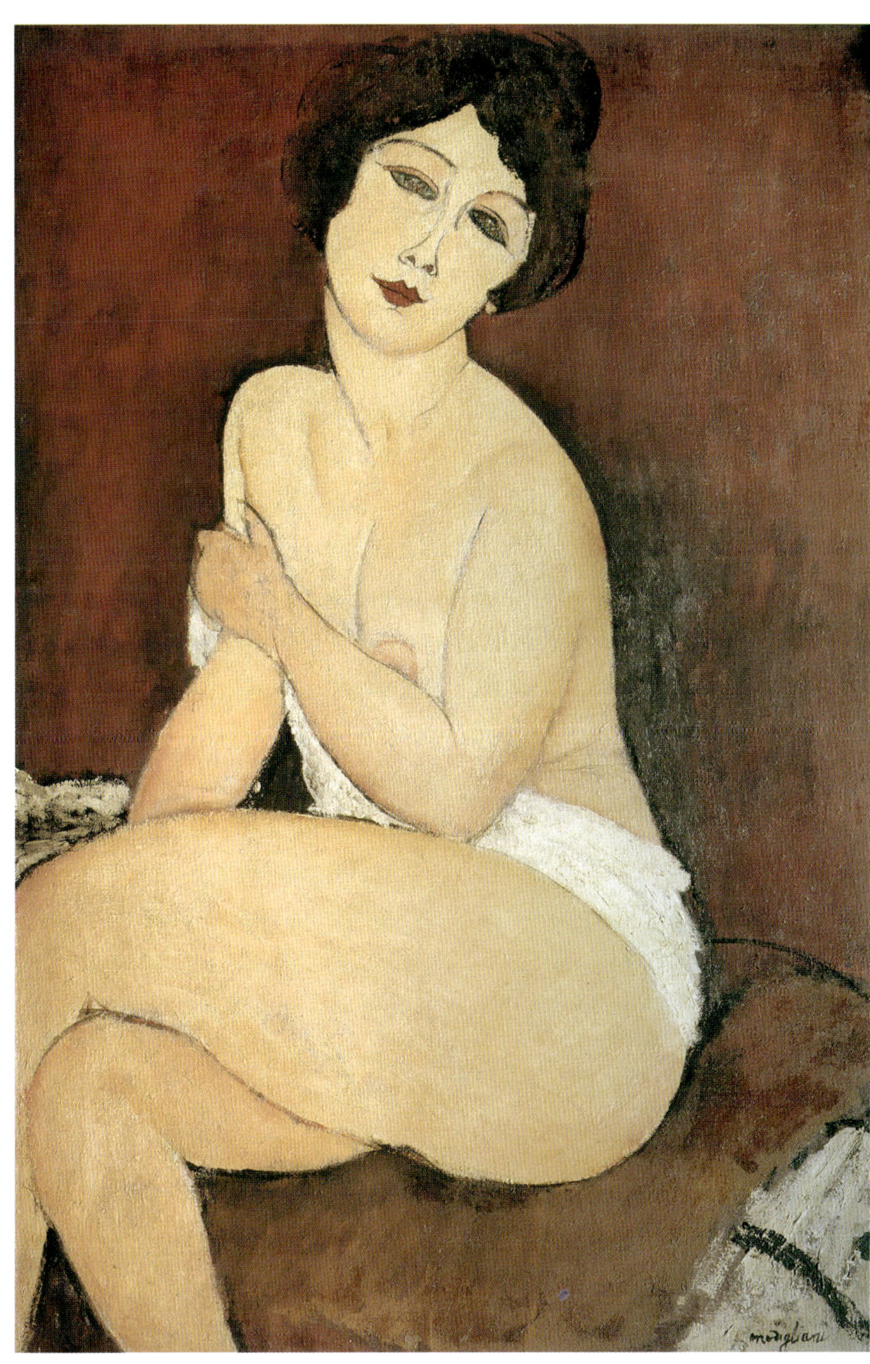

Modigliani was first a sculptor then,
for health reasons, also encouraged
by his dealer, Paul Guillaume,
he started painting.

Modigliani war zunächst Bildhauer
und später, aus gesundheitlichen
Gründen und auf Drängen seines
Händlers Paul Guillaume, widmete er
sich auch der Malerei.

Modigliani was eerst beeldhouwer
waarna hij om gezondheidsredenen en
op aandringen van zijn kunsthandelaar
Paul Guillaume zich op de
schilderkunst heeft gestort.

Modigliani ha sido en un primer
momento escultor y luego, por razones
de salud, inducido también por su
marchante Paul Guillaume, se ha
dedicado a la pintura.

Amedeo Modigliani
(Livorno 1884 - Paris 1920

Nude woman seated
Sitzender weiblicher Akt
Zittende naakte vrouw
Mujer desnuda sentada

●

1917
100 x 65 cm / 39.4 x 25.6 in.
Private collection / Private Sammlung
Privécollectie / Colección privada

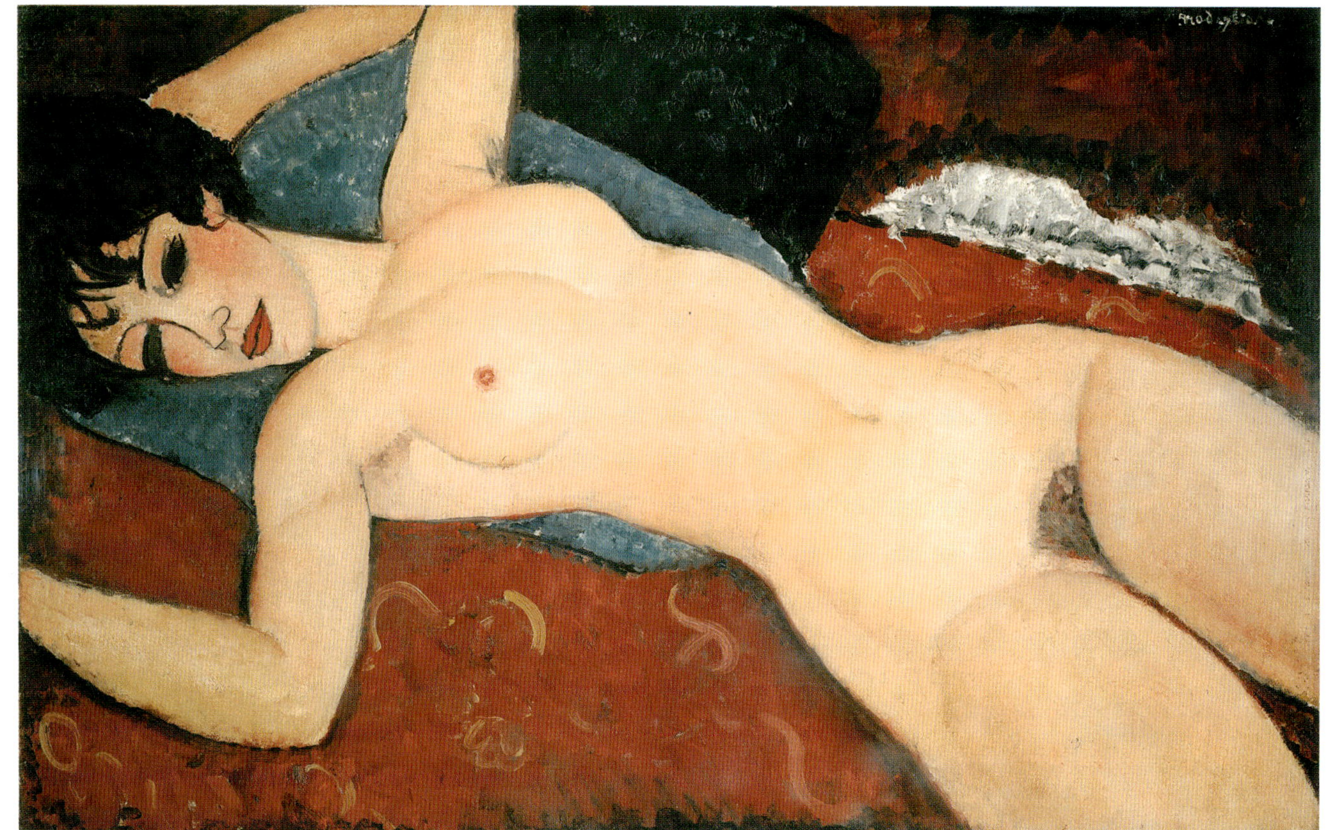

Amedeo Modigliani
(Livorno 1884 - Paris 1920)

Nude lying down with arms open (Red Nude)
Schlafender Akt mit geöffneten Armen (Akt in Rot)
Liggend naakt met open armen (rood naakt)
Desnudo acostado con los brazos abiertos (Desnudo rojo)

●●●

1917
60 x 92 cm / 23.6 x 36.2 in.
Private collection / Private Sammlung
Privécollectie / Colección privada

oil on canvas / Öl auf Leinwand
olieverf op doek / óleo sobre lienzo

Amedeo Modigliani
(Livorno 1884 - Paris 1920)

Portrait of Dedie
Porträt von Dedie
Portret van Dedie
Retrato de Dédie
(Odette Hayden)

●

1918
92 x 60 cm / 36.2 x 23.6 in.
Centre Georges Pompidou, Musée
National d'Art Moderne, Paris

oil on canvas / Öl auf Leinwand
olieverf op doek / óleo sobre lienzo

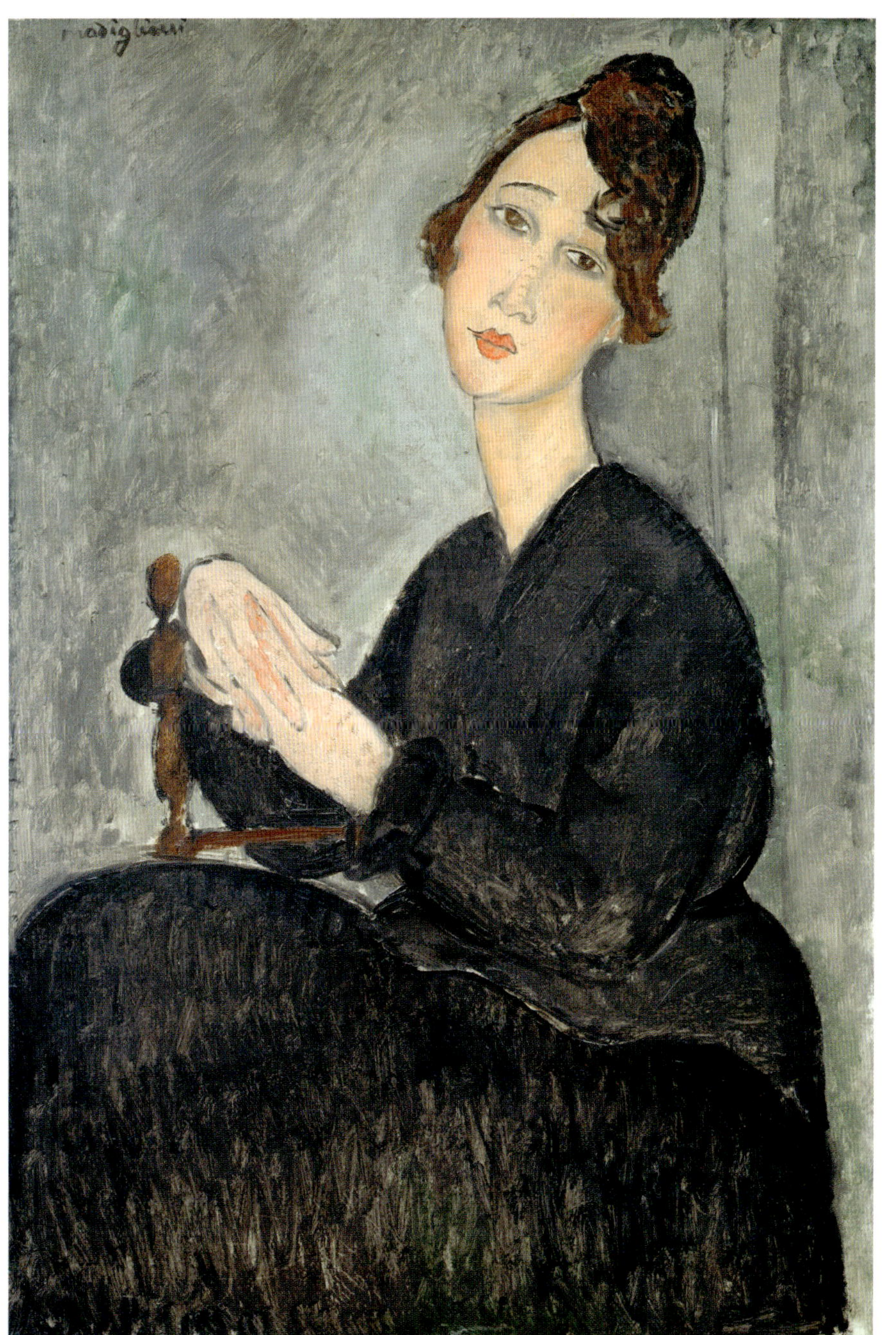

245

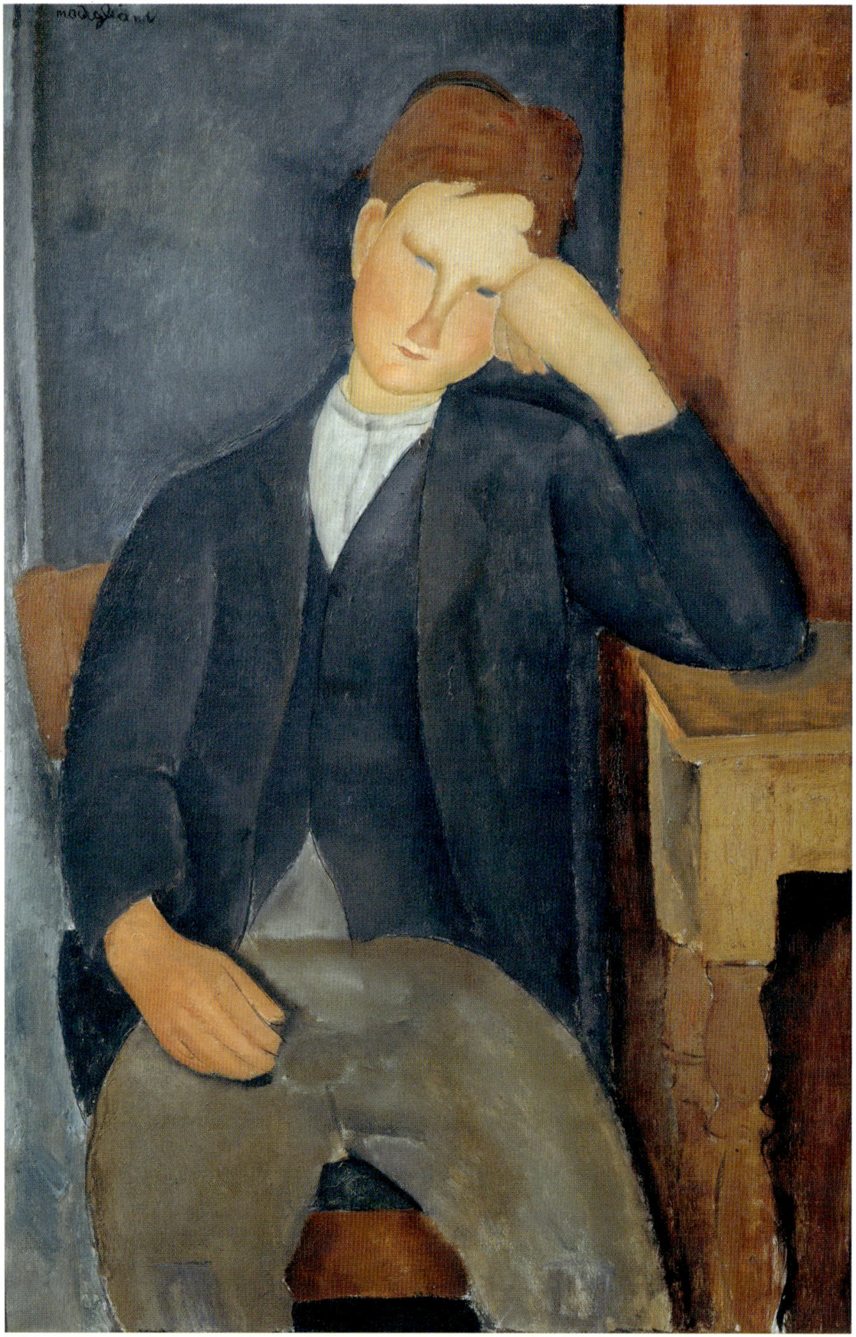

They nicknamed him the *Black Botticelli* since it was inspired both by the grace of the Florentine master and African art.

Man hat ihn auch den *schwarzen Botticelli* genannt, da er sich am florentinischen Meister und an der afrikanischen Kunst inspirierte.

Het had de bijnaam *zwarte Botticelli* daar hij zich zowel door de gratie van de Florentijnse meester als door de Afrikaanse kunst liet inspireren.

Le habían apodado el *Botticelli negro*, ya que se inspiraba tanto en la gracia del maestro florentino como en el arte africano.

Amedeo Modigliani
(Livorno 1884 - Paris 1920

Young workman
Bauernjunge
Jonge arbeider
Joven obrero

● ●

1918-1919
100 x 65 cm / 39.3 x 25.6 in.
Musée de l'Orangerie, Paris

oil on canvas / Öl auf Leinwand
olieverf op doek / óleo sobre lienzo

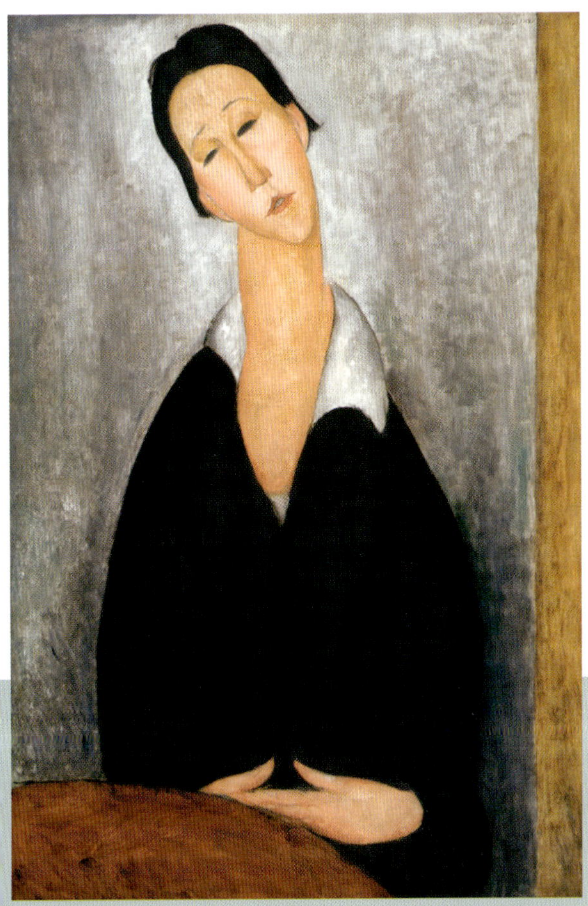

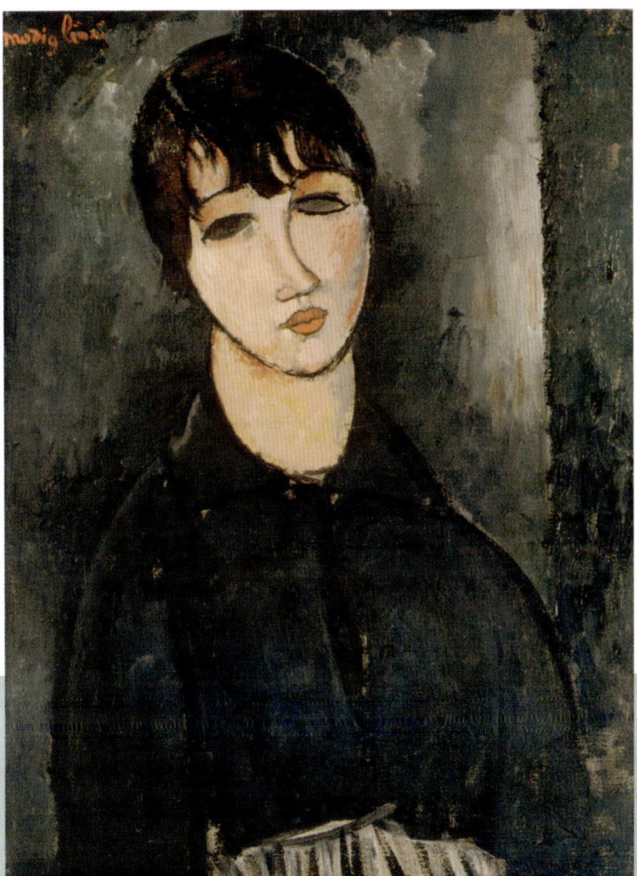

Amedeo Modigliani
(Livorno 1884 - Paris 1920

Portrait of a Polish woman
Porträt einer Polin
Portret van een Poolse vrouw
Retrato de mujer polaca

●●

1919
100,3 x 64,8 cm / 39.5 x 25.5 in.
Philadelphia Museum of Art, Philadelphia

oil on canvas / Öl auf Leinwand
olieverf op doek / óleo sobre lienzo

Amedeo Modigliani
(Livorno 1884 - Paris 1920

The maid
Porträt einer Zofe
De serveerster
La camarera

●

1916
Kunsthaus, Zurich

oil on canvas / Öl auf Leinwand
olieverf op doek / óleo sobre lienzo

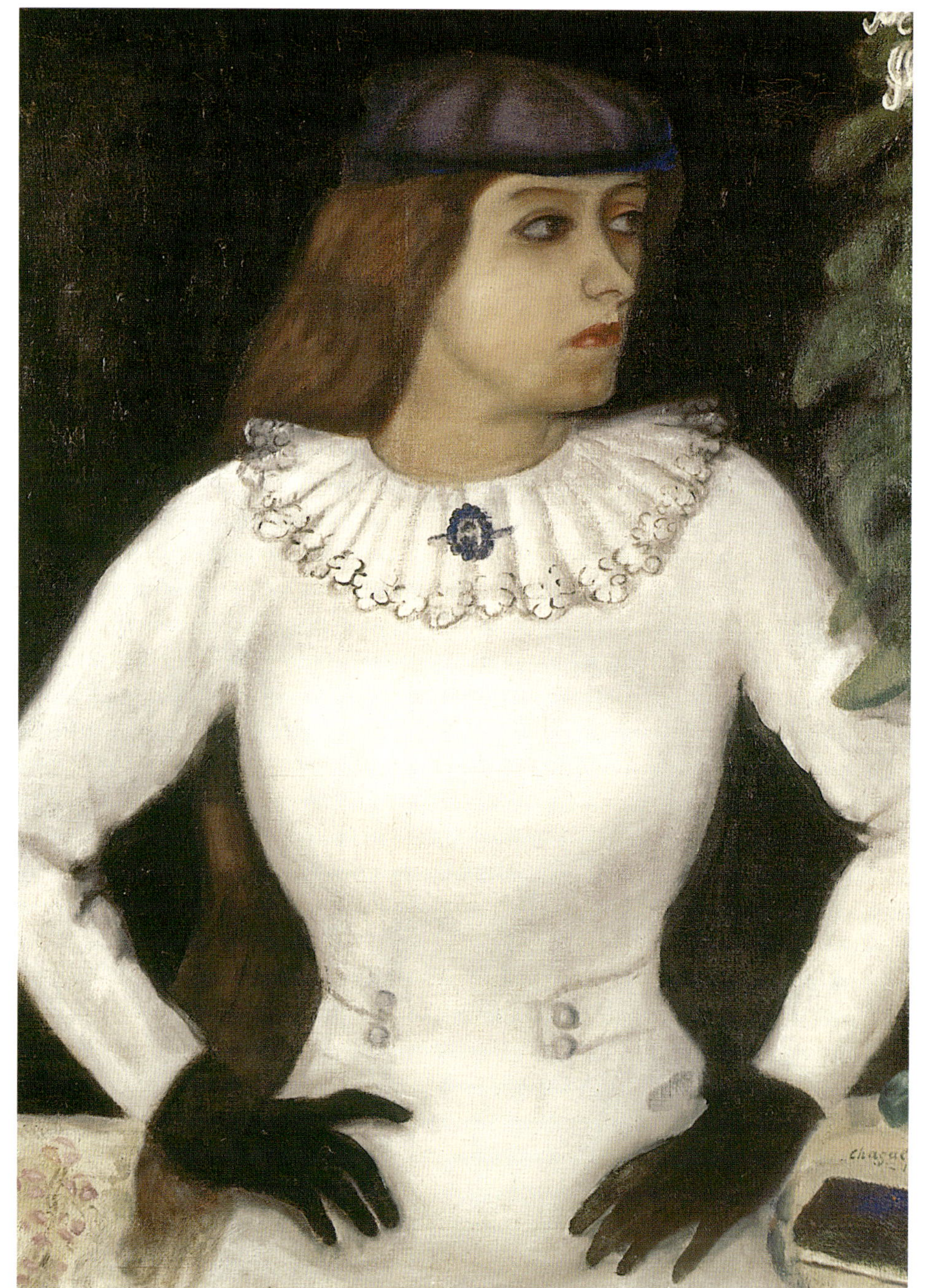

Marc Chagall

(Vitebsk 1887 - Saint-Paul-de-Vence 1985)

Portrait of my fiancée with black gloves
Meine Braut mit schwarzen Handschuhen
Portret van mijn verloofde met zwarte handschoenen
Retrato de mi prometida con guantes negros

●

1909
Kunstmuseum, Basel

oil on canvas / Öl auf Leinwand
olieverf op doek / óleo sobre lienzo

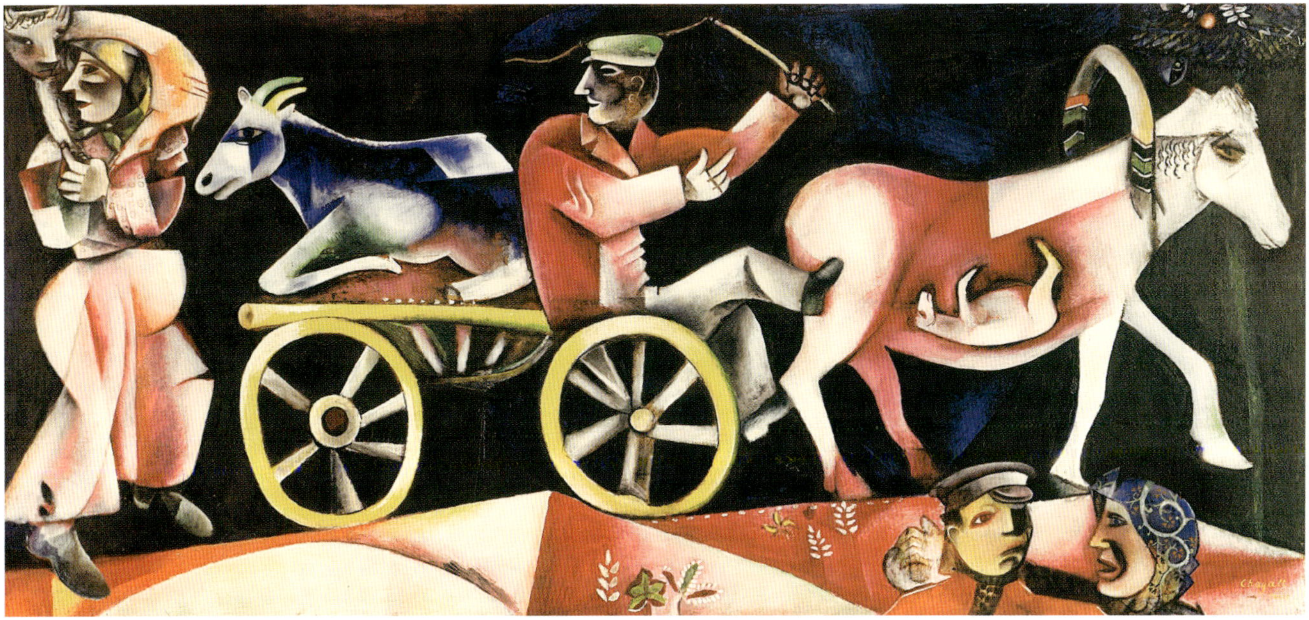

Marc Chagall
(Vitebsk 1887 - Saint-Paul-de-Vence 1985)

The livestock merchant
Der Viehhändler
De veemarkt
El comerciante de ganado

●●

1912
99,5 x 180 cm / 39.1 x 70.8 in.
Kunstmuseum, Basel

oil on canvas / Öl auf Leinwand
olieverf op doek / óleo sobre lienzo

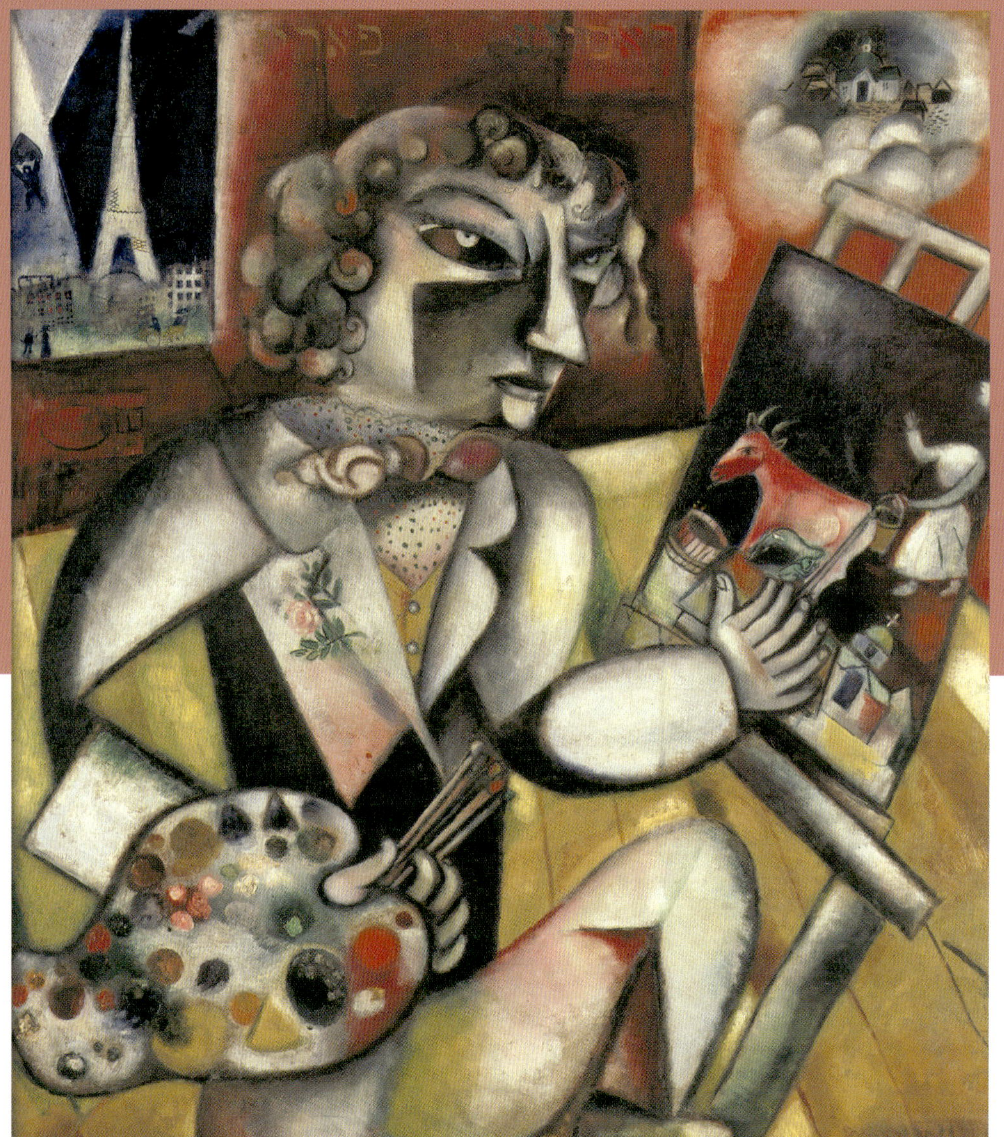

◀ Marc Chagall
(Vitebsk 1887 -
Saint-Paul-de-Vence 1985)
**Self-portrait with seven
fingers
Selbstporträt mit sieben
Fingern
Zelfportret met zeven
vingers
Autorretrato con siete
dedos**
●
1912
132 x 93 cm / 52 x 36.6 in.
Stedelijk Museum, Amsterdam

oil on canvas
Öl auf Leinwand
olieverf op doek
óleo sobre lienzo

▶ Marc Chagall
(Vitebsk 1887 -
Saint-Paul-de-Vence 1985)
**The violinist
Der Geiger
De violinist
El violinista**
●●
1912
188 x 158 cm / 74 x 62.2 in.
Stedelijk Museum, Amsterdam

oil on canvas
Öl auf Leinwand
olieverf op doek
óleo sobre lienzo

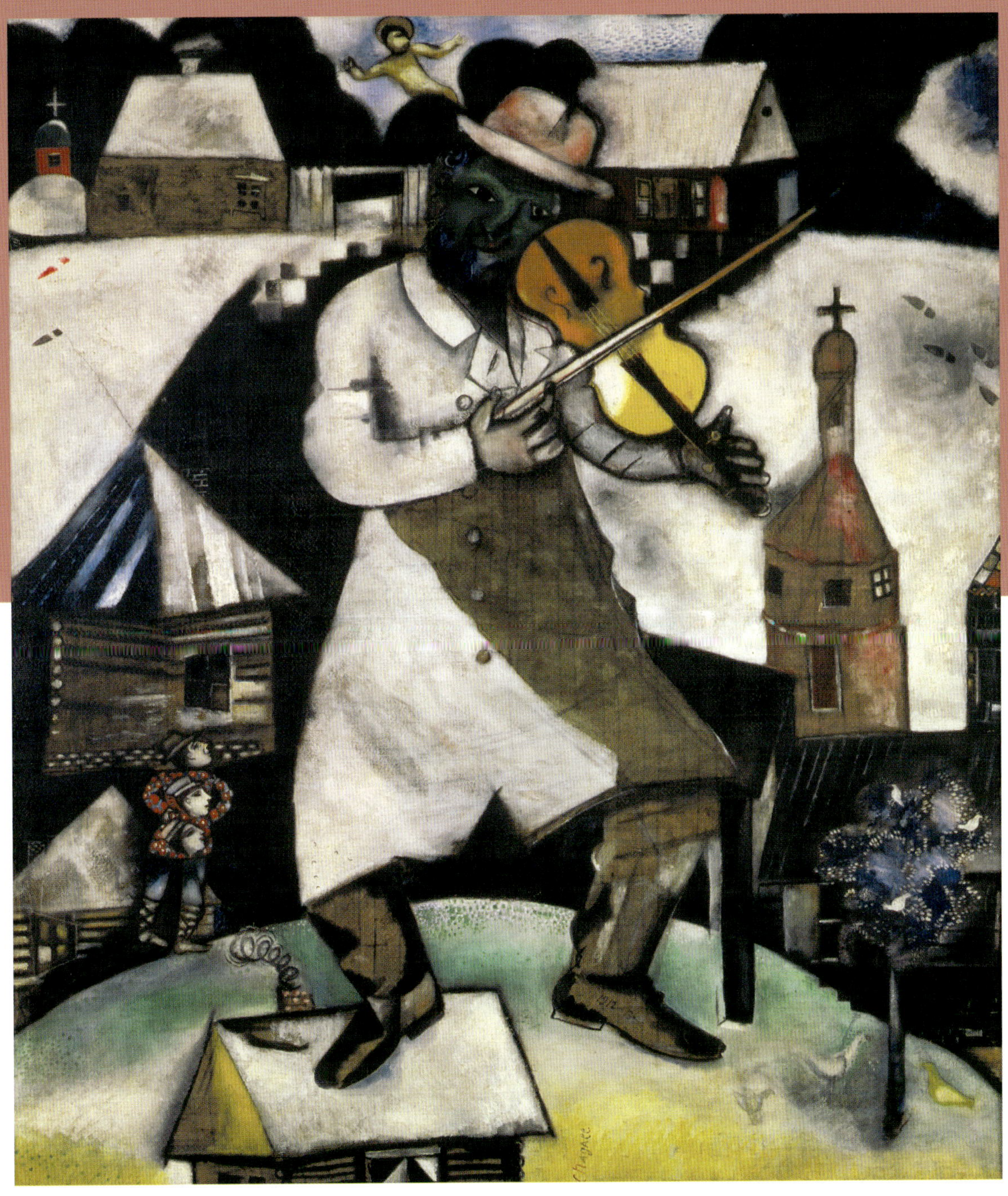

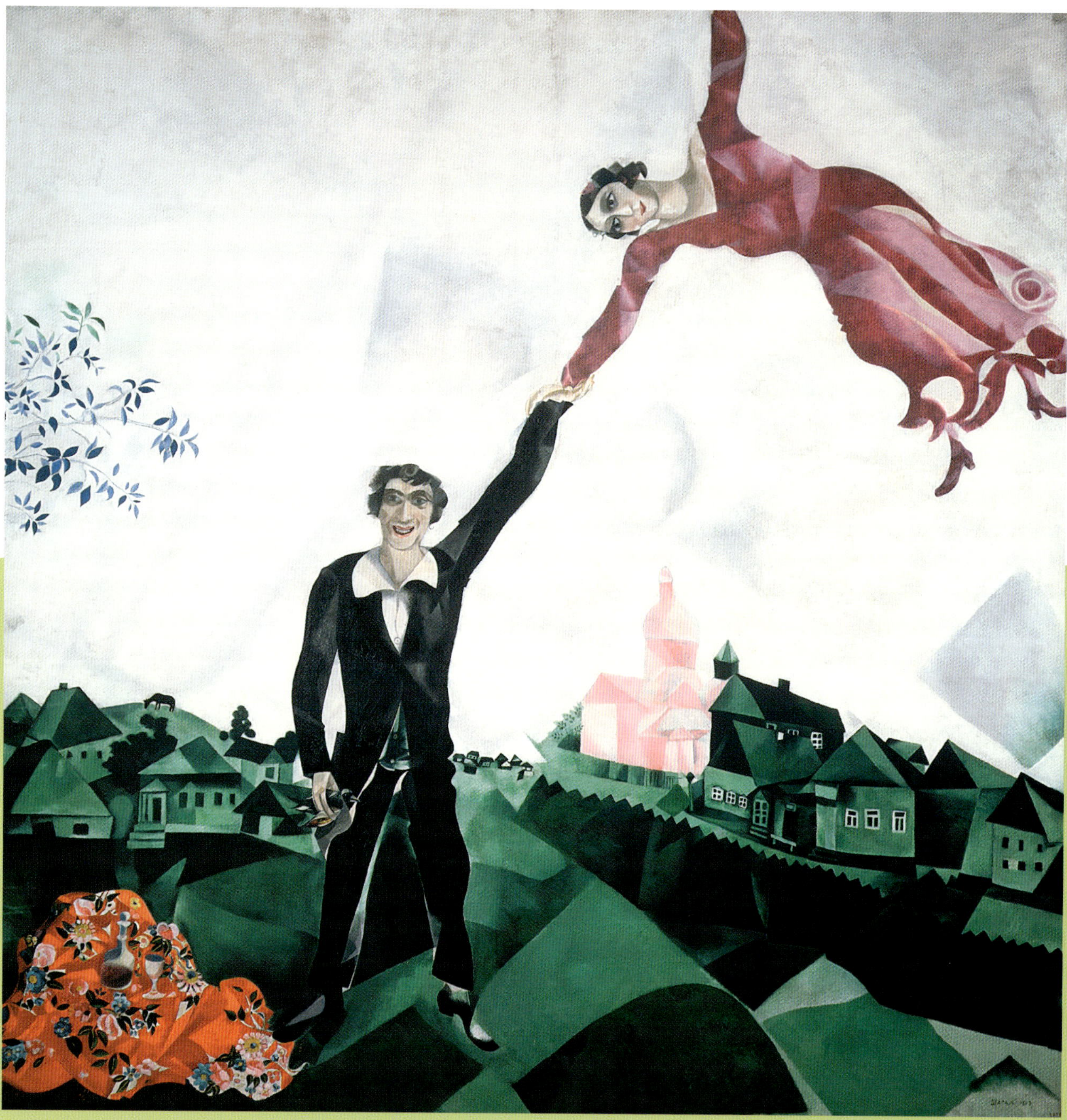

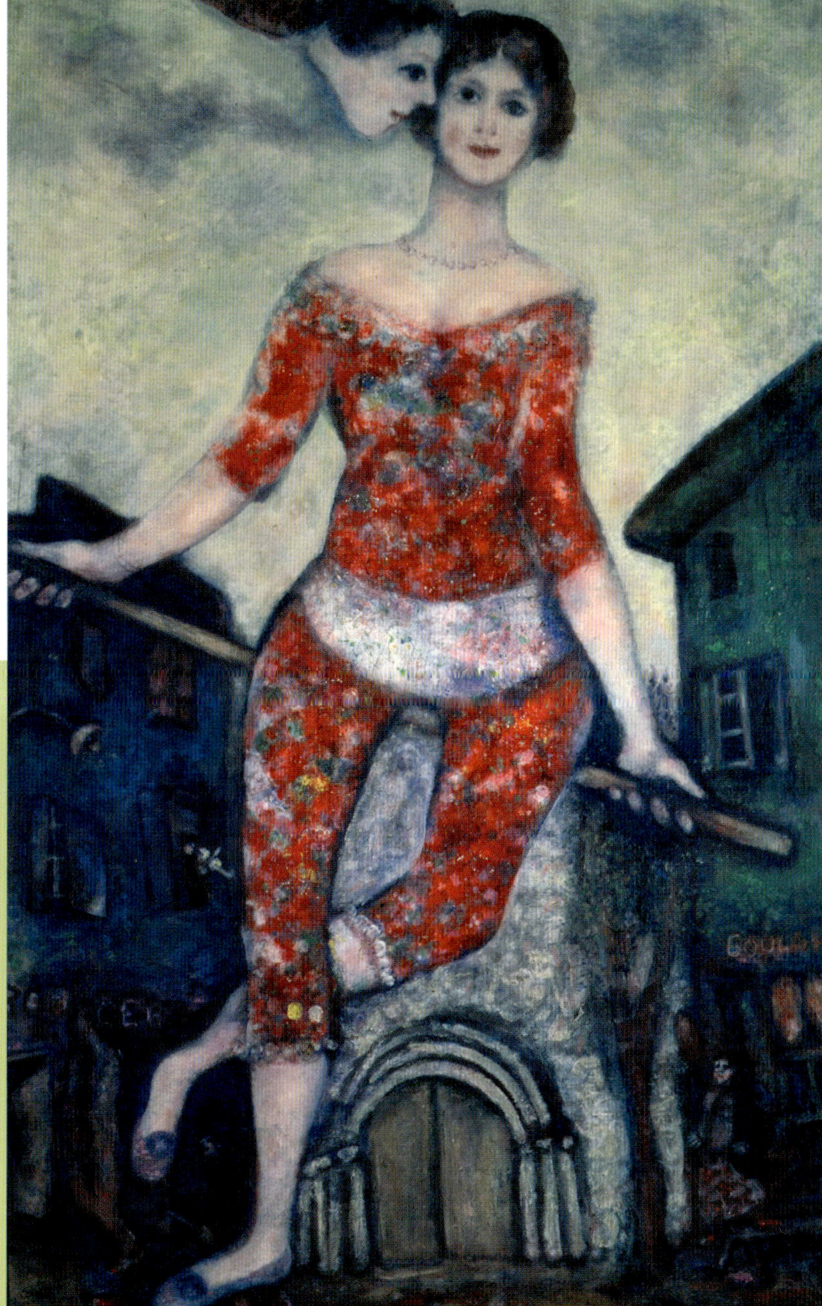

◄ Marc Chagall
(Vitebsk 1887 - Saint-Paul-de-Vence 1985)

The stroll
Der Spaziergang
De wandeling
El paseo
●●●
1917-1918
170 x 164 cm / 66.9 x 64.5 in.
The State Hermitage Museum,
St. Petersburg

oil on canvas / Öl auf Leinwand
olieverf op doek / óleo sobre lienzo

► Marc Chagall
(Vitebsk 1887 - Saint-Paul-de-Vence 1985)

The acrobat
Die Akrobatin
De acrobaat
La acróbata
●●
1930
65 x 52 cm / 25.6 x 20.4 in.
Centre Georges Pompidou,
Musée National d'Art Moderne, Paris

oil on canvas / Öl auf Leinwand
olieverf op doek / óleo sobre lienzo

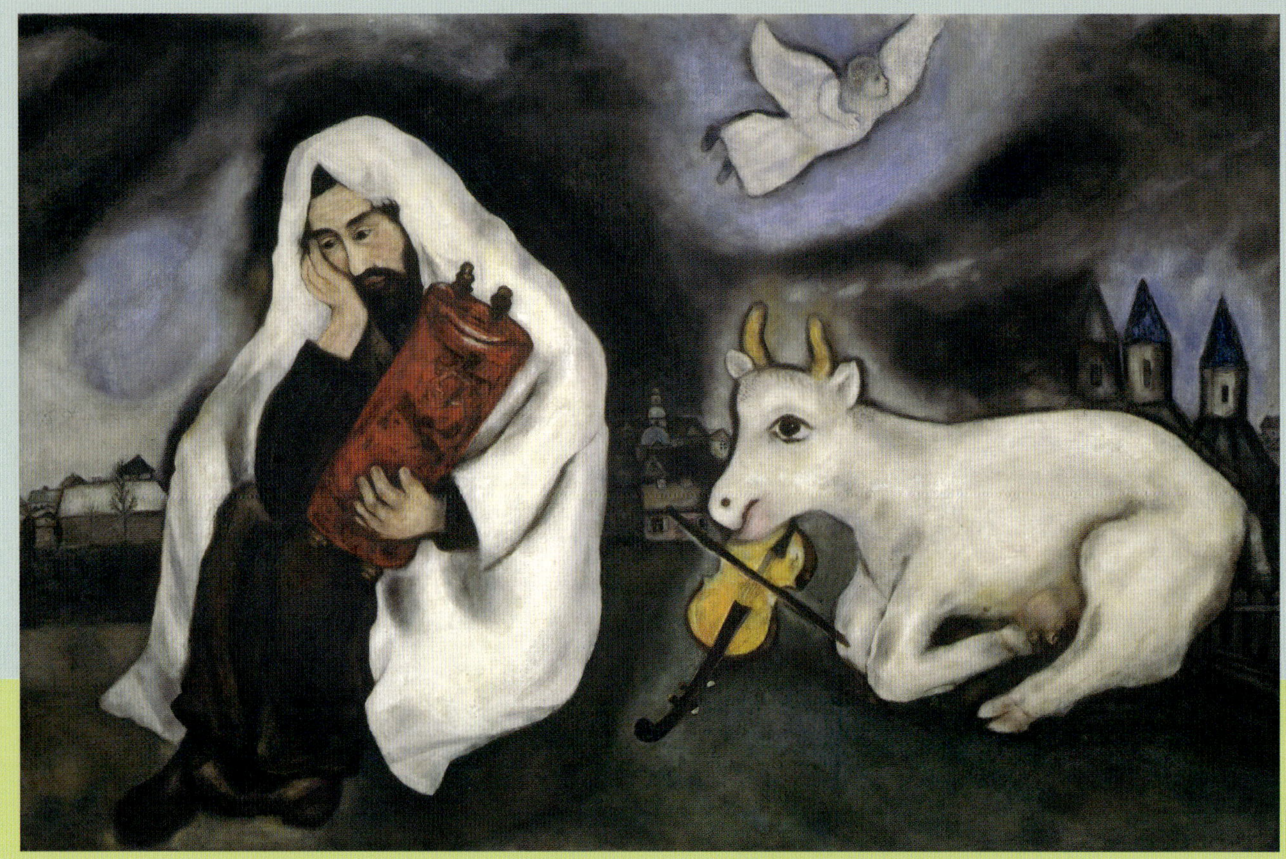

Marc Chagall
(Vitebsk 1887 - Saint-Paul-de-Vence 1985)

Solitude
Einsamkeit
Eenzaamheid
Soledad
●

1933
102 x 169 cm / 40.2 x 66.6 in.
Tel Aviv Museum of Arts, Tel Aviv

oil on canvas / Öl auf Leinwand
olieverf op doek / óleo sobre lienzo

▶ Marc Chagall
(Vitebsk 1887 - Saint-Paul-de-Vence 1985)

Newlyweds with Tour Eiffel
Brautpaar mit Eiffelturm
Huwelijkspaar met de Eiffeltoren
Los recién casados de la Torre Eiffel
●●●

1938
148 x 145 cm / 58.2 x 57.1 in
Centre Georges Pompidou,
Musée National d'Art Moderne, Paris

oil on canvas / Öl auf Leinwand
olieverf op doek / óleo sobre lienzo

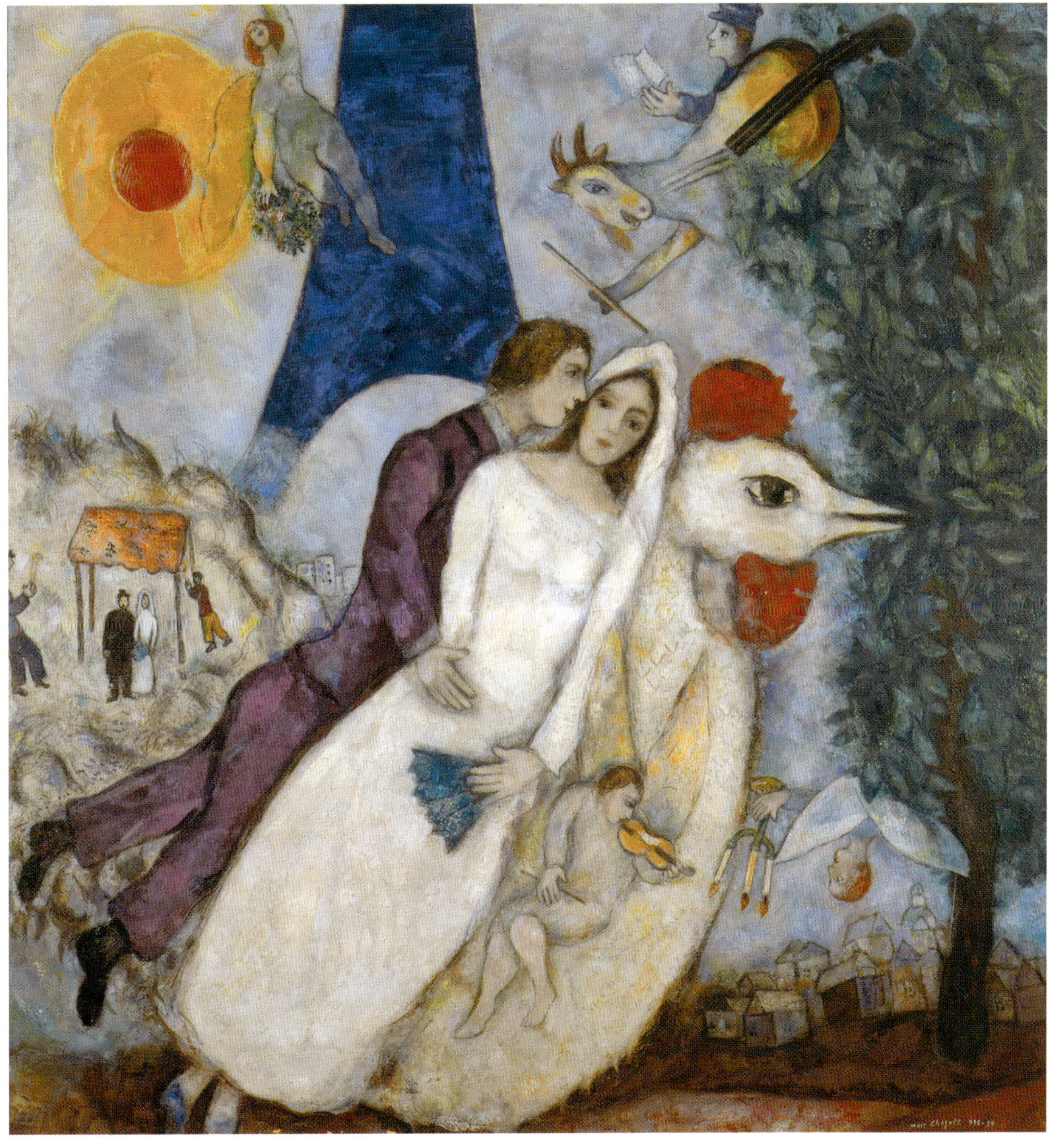

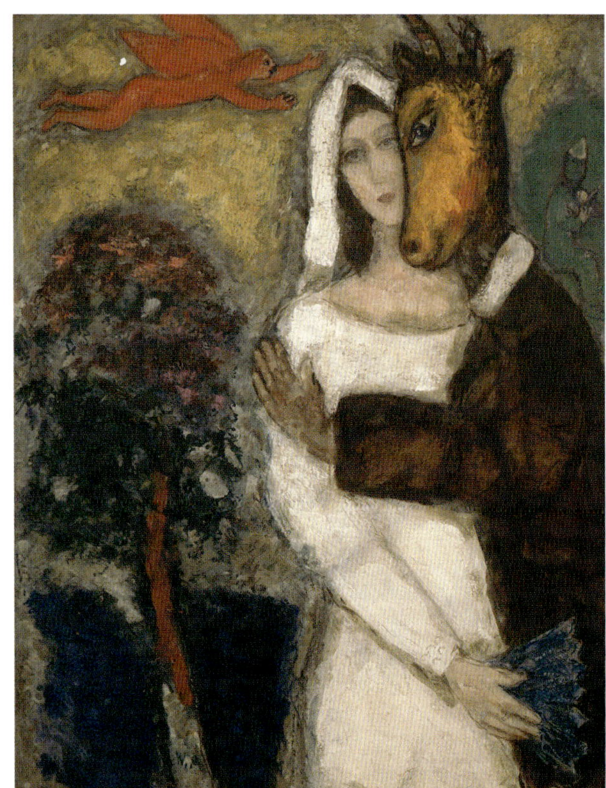

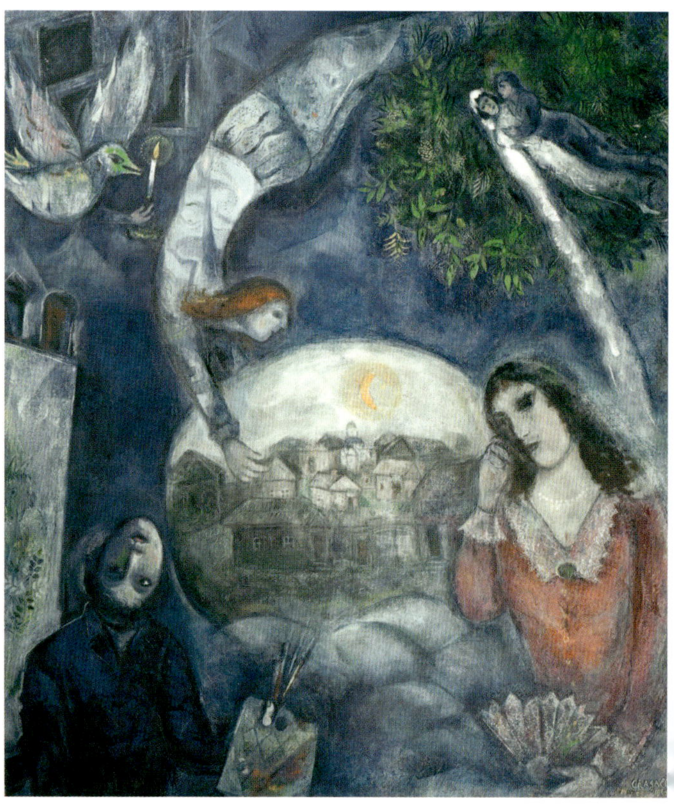

Marc Chagall
(Vitebsk 1887 - Saint-Paul-de-Vence 1985)

Summer Night's Dream
Der Sommernachtstraum
Droom van een zomernacht
Sueño de una noche de verano

●●

1939
117,1 x 88,6 cm / 46.1 x 34.8
Musée de Grenoble, Grenoble

oil on canvas / Öl auf Leinwand
olieverf op doek / óleo sobre lienzo

256

Marc Chagall
(Vitebsk 1887 - Saint-Paul-de-Vence 1985)

Around her
Um sie herum
Om haar heen
Alrededor de ella

●

1945
131 x 109,5 cm / 51.6 x 43.1 in.
Centre Georges Pompidou,
Musée National d'Art Moderne, Paris

oil on canvas / Öl auf Leinwand
olieverf op doek / óleo sobre lienzo

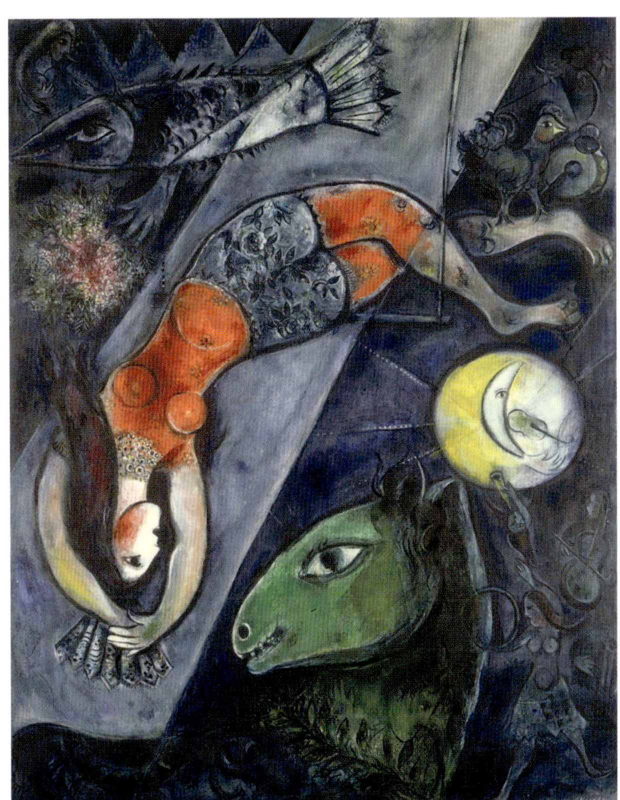

Marc Chagall
(Vitebsk 1887 - Saint-Paul-de-Vence 1985)

The Blue Circus
Blauer Zirkus
Het blauwe circus
El circo azul

●

1950
232 x 175 cm / 91.4 x 68.9 in.
Centre Georges Pompidou,
Musée National d'Art Moderne, Paris

oil on canvas / Öl auf Leinwand
olieverf op doek / óleo sobre lienzo

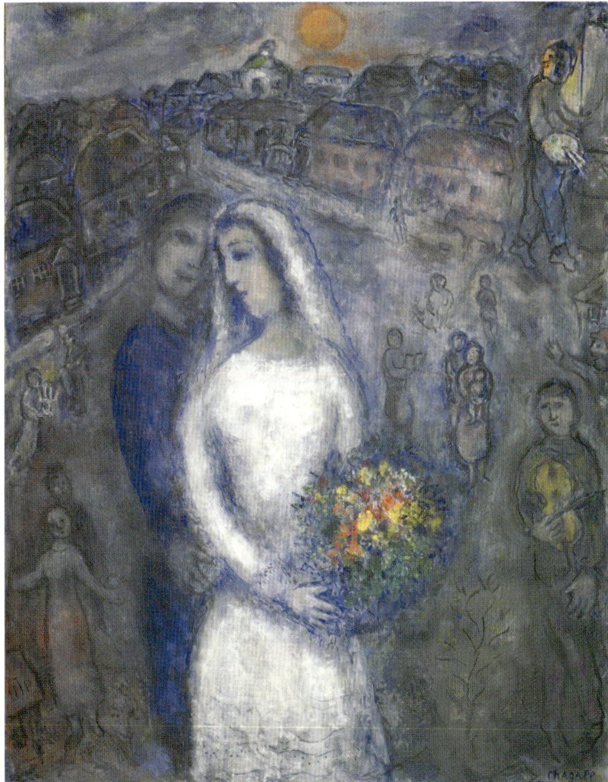

Marc Chagall
(Vitebsk 1887 - Saint-Paul-de-Vence 1985)

The Couple
Das Paar
Het stel
La pareja

● ● ●

1977
Private collection / Private Sammlung
Privécollectie / Colección privada

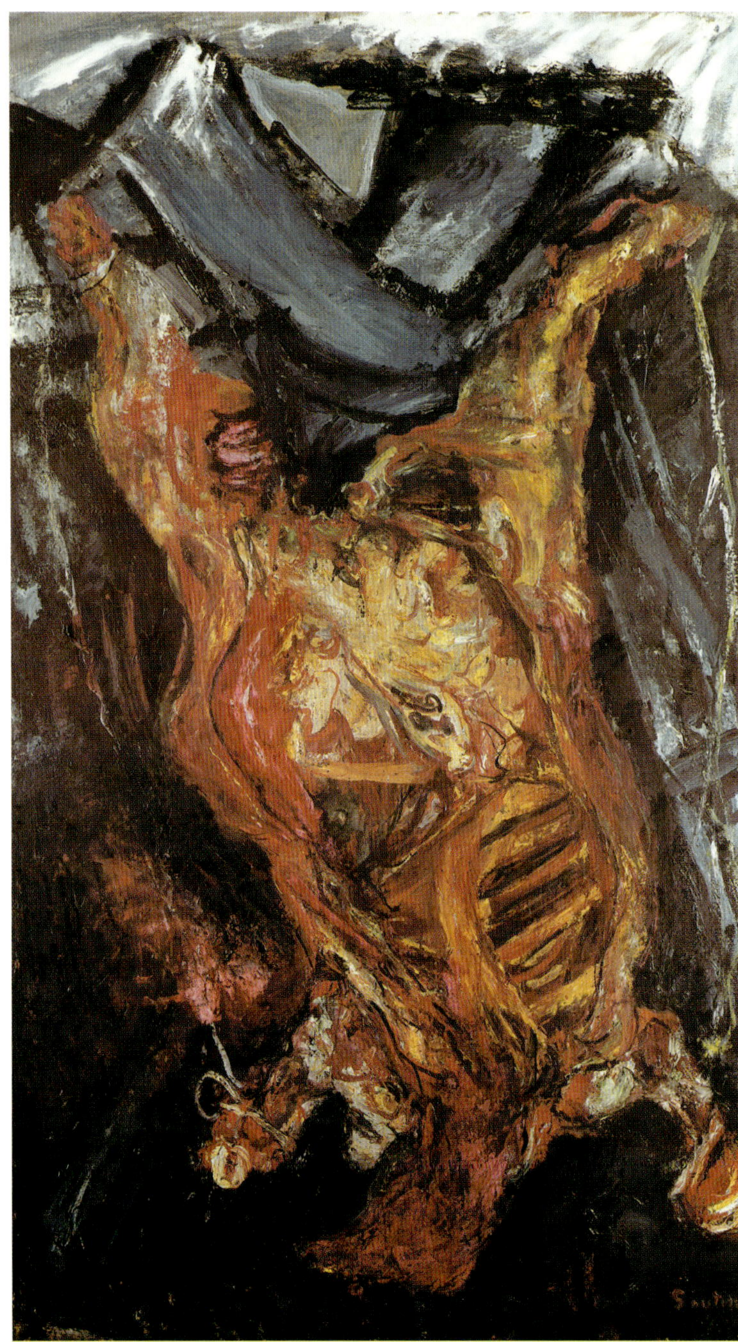

◄ Chaïm Soutine
(Smilavichy 1893 - Paris 1943)

The Skinned Ox
Geschlachteter Ochse
De gevilde os
La vaca desollada

●●●

1925
116,21 x 80,65 cm / 47.7 x 31.7 in.
Musée de Grenoble, Grenoble

oil on canvas / Öl auf Leinwand
olieverf op doek / óleo sobre lienzo

► Chaïm Soutine
(Smilavichy 1893 - Paris 1943)

The Bellboy
Der Hotelpage
Loopjongen in een hotel
El botones de hotel

●●

1925-1928
98 x 80,5 cm / 38.6 x 31.7 in.
Centre Georges Pompidou, Musée
National d'Art Moderne, Paris

oil on canvas / Öl auf Leinwand
olieverf op doek / óleo sobre lienzo

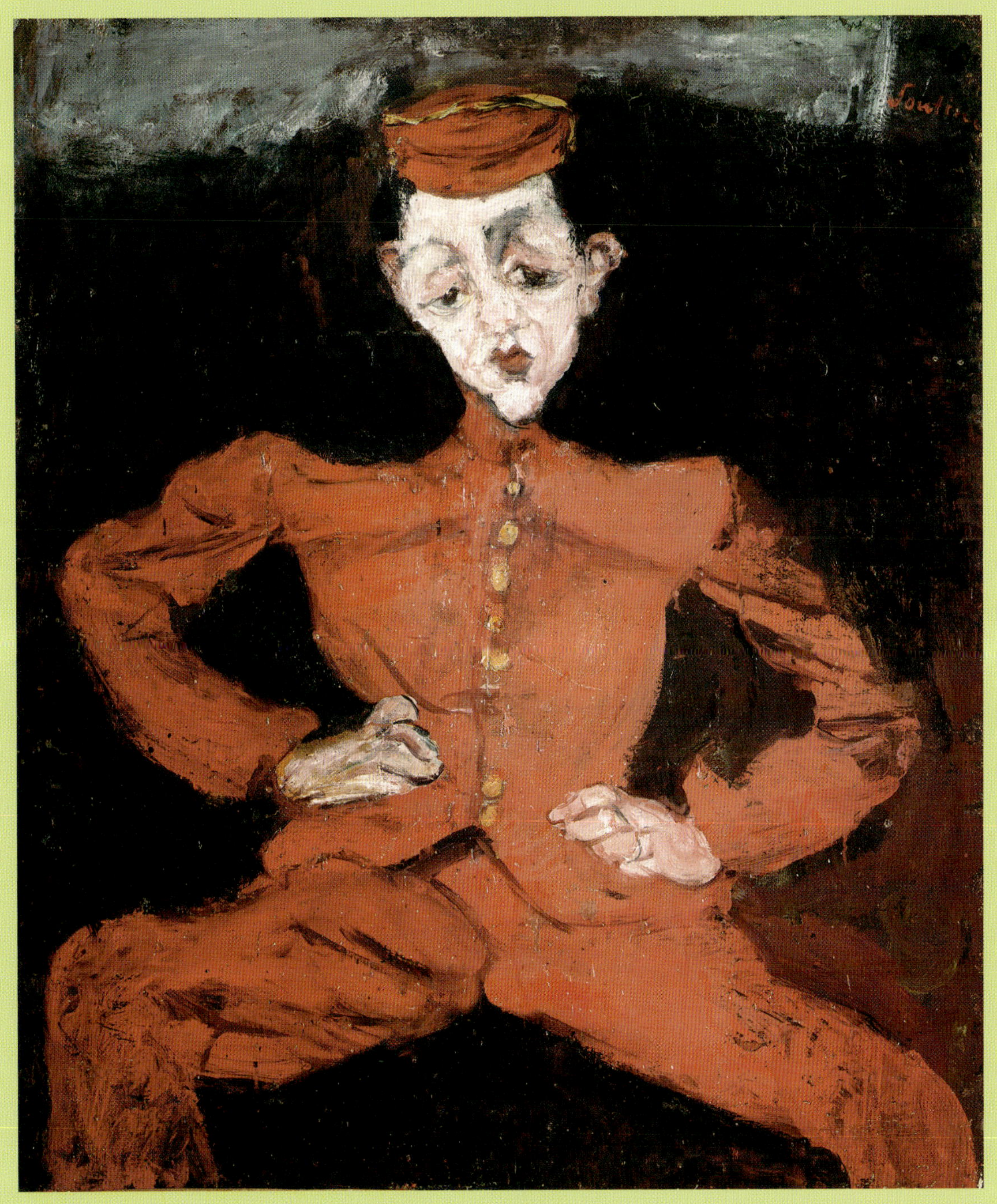

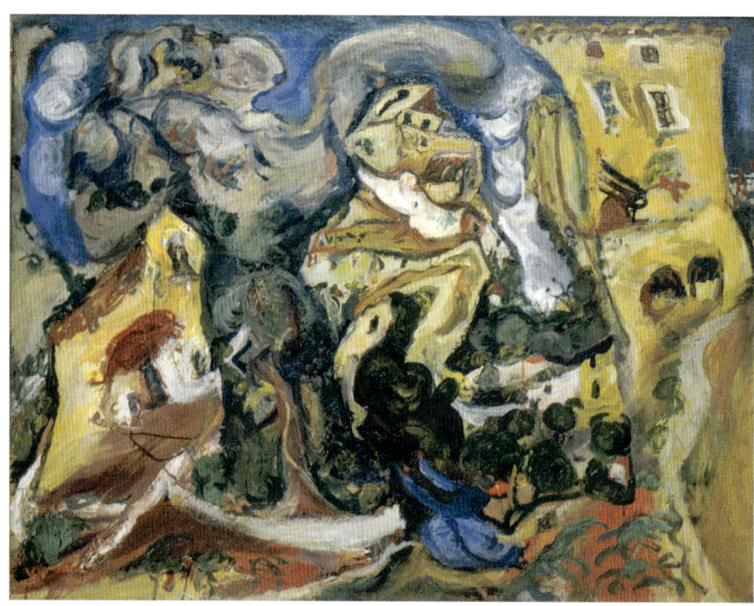

Influenced by Van Gogh and heralding Willem de Kooning, Soutine gives proof of an exacerbated Expressionism.

Zwischen Van Gogh, von dem er beeinflusst wurde, und Willem de Kooning, den er vorwegnimmt, liegt Soutines verschärfter Expressionismus.

Soutine was door Van Gogh beïnvloed en als voorganger van Willem de Kooning gaf hij blijk van een heviger wordend expressionisme.

Influenciado por Van Gogh y preanunciando a Willem de Kooning, Soutine da muestras de un Expresionismo exacerbado.

Chaïm Soutine
(Smilavichy 1893 - Paris 1943)

The Village
Das Dorf
Het dorp
La aldea

●

1922
75 x 93 cm / 29.5 x 36.6 in.
Musée de l'Orangerie, Paris

oil on canvas / Öl auf Leinwand
olieverf op doek / óleo sobre lienzo

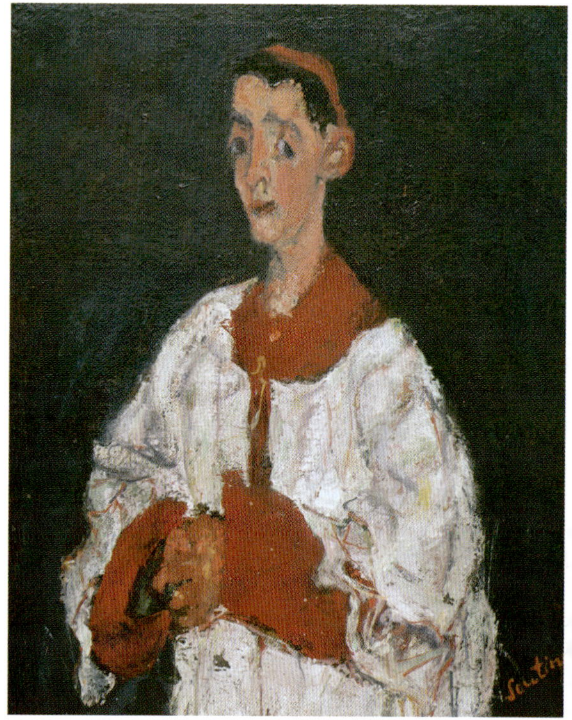

▶ **Chaïm Soutine**
(Smilavichy 1893 - Paris 1943)

Madeleine Castaing

●

ca. 1929
100 x 73.3 cm / 39.4 x 28.9 in.
The Metropolitan Museum of
Art, New York

oil on canvas
Öl auf Leinwand
olieverf op doek
óleo sobre lienzo

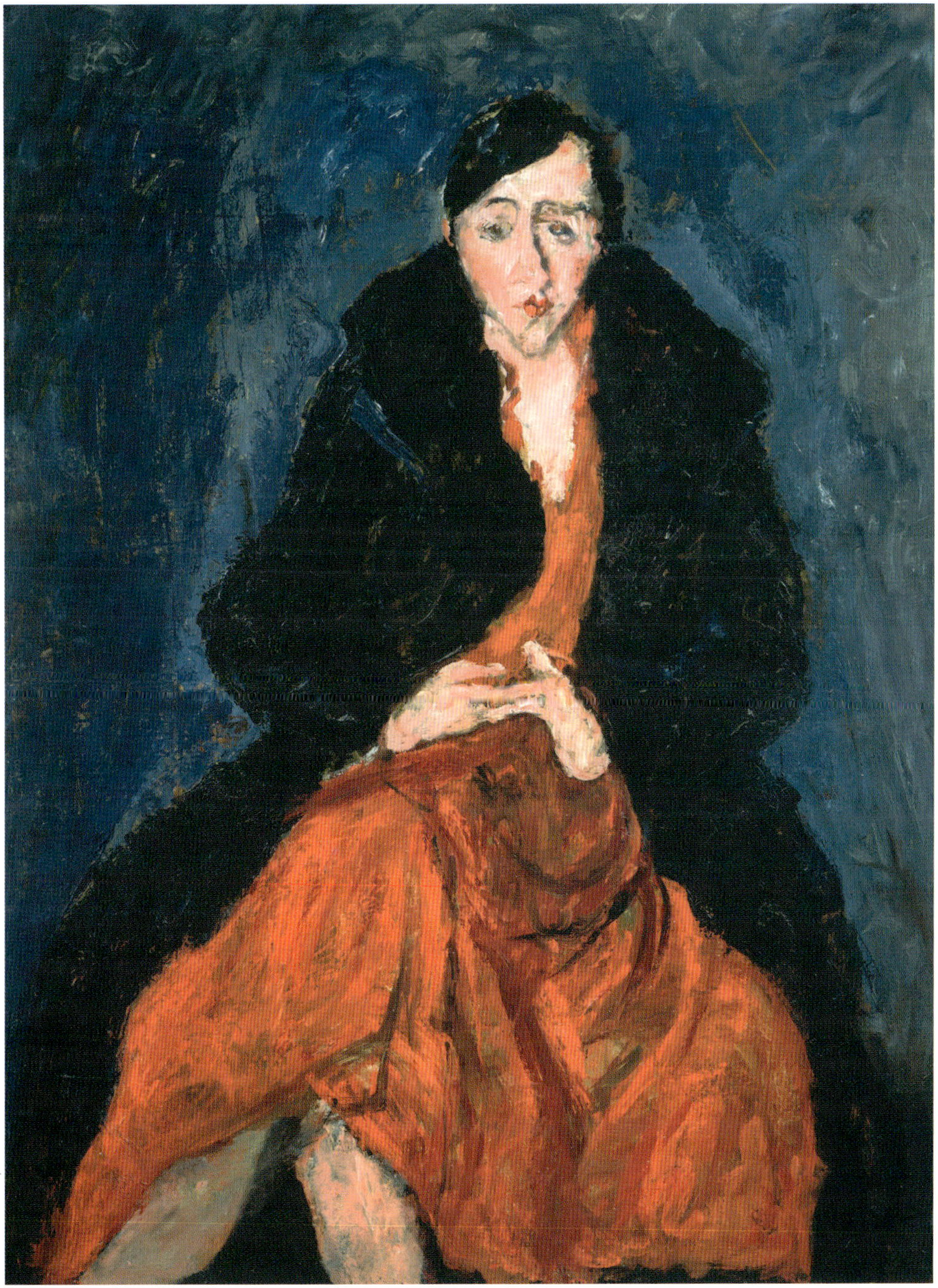

◀ Chaïm Soutine
(Smilavichy 1893 - Paris 1943)

Altar boy
Ministrant
Misdienaar
El monaguillo

● ●

1927-1928
69 x 49 cm / 27.2 x 19.3 in.
Musée de l'Orangerie, Paris

oil on canvas
Öl auf Leinwand
olieverf op doek
óleo sobre lienzo

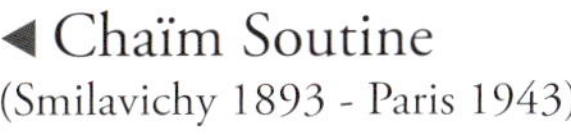

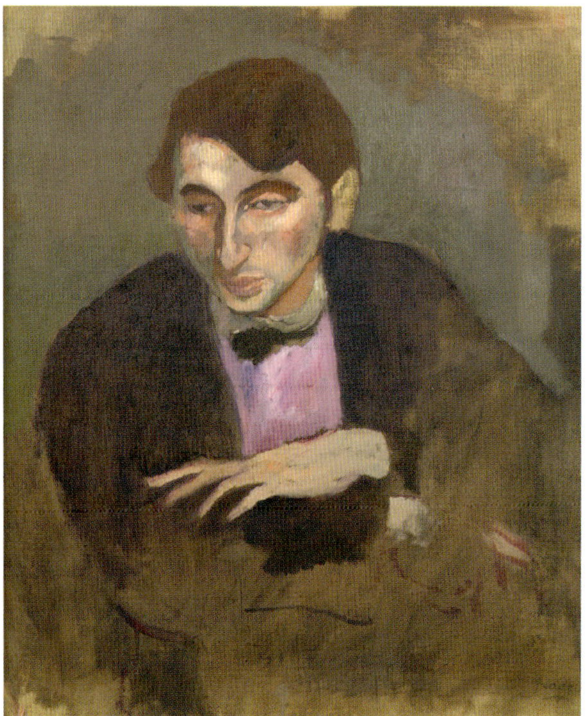

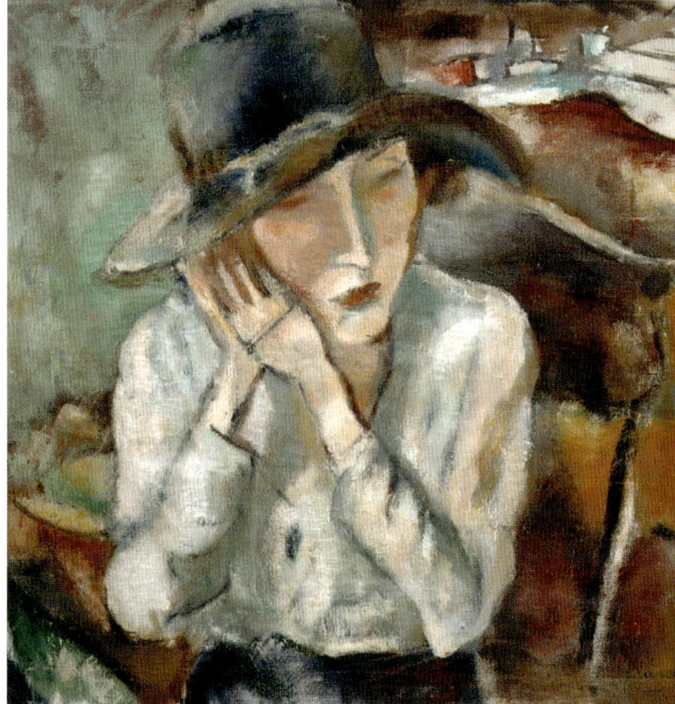

Jules Pascin
(Vidin 1885 - Paris 1930)

Portrait of Isaac Grunewald
Porträt von Isaac Grunewald
Portret van Isaac Grunewald
Retrato de Isaac Grunewald

●

1911
64,9 x 54 cm / 25.5 x 21.2 in.
The Jewish Museum, New York

oil on canvas
Öl auf Leinwand
olieverf op doek
óleo sobre lienzo

Jules Pascin
(Vidin 1885 - Paris 1930)

Portrait of Hermine with a wide hat
Porträt von Hermine mit einem großen Hut
Portret van Hermine met een grote hoed
Retrato de Hermine con un gran sombrero

●

1916
48 x 46 cm / 20 x 18.1 in.
Musée de Grenoble, Grenoble

oil on canvas
Öl auf Leinwand
olieverf op doek
óleo sobre lienzo

Jules Pascin
(Vidin 1885 - Paris 1930)

**Portrait of Andrée. Portrait of woman
seated
Porträt von Andrée. Porträt einer
sitzenden Frau
Portret van Andrée. Portret van een
zittende vrouw
Retrato de Andrée. Retrato de mujer
sentada**

•

1923
Musée de Grenoble, Grenoble

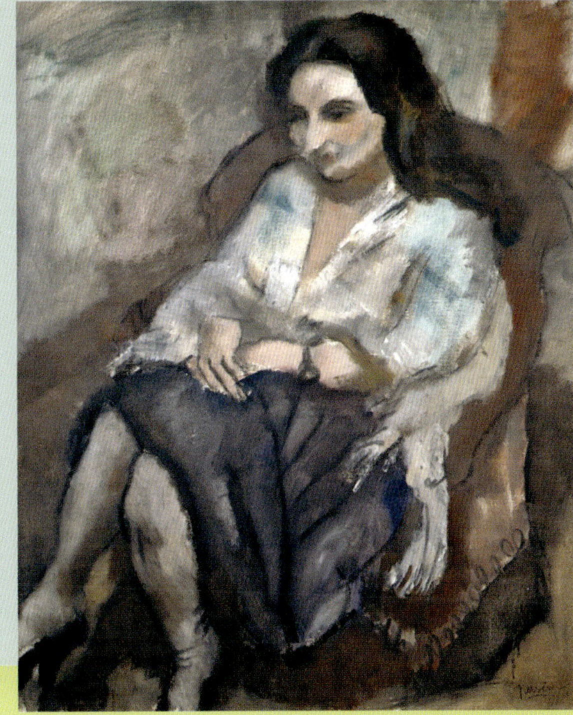

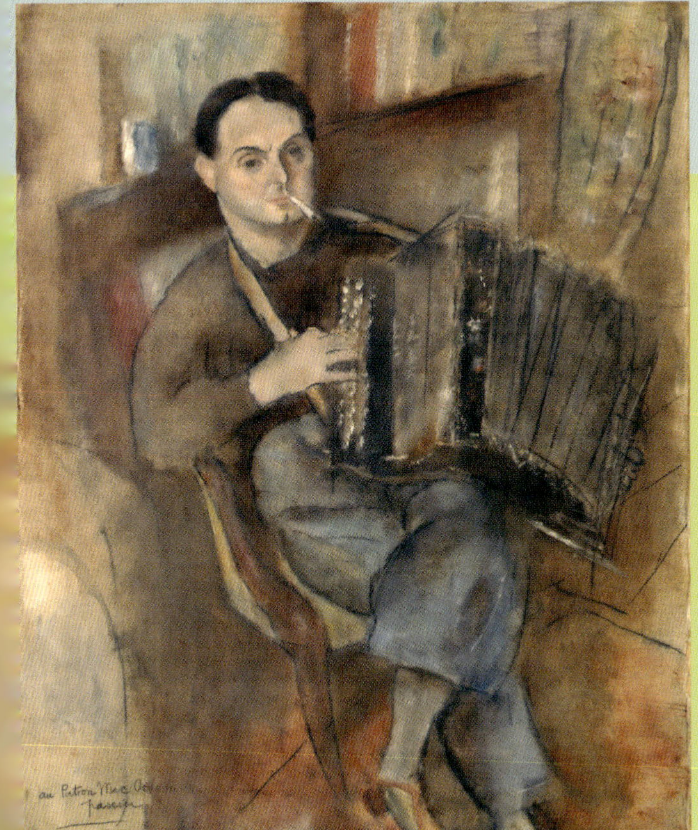

Jules Pascin
(Vidin 1885 - Paris 1930)

Pierre Mac Orlan

••

1924
92,1 x 73 cm / 36.2 x 28.7 in.
The Metropolitan Museum of Art,
New York

oil on canvas
Öl auf Leinwand
olieverf op doek
óleo sobre lienzo

Georges Rouault
(Paris 1871 - 1951)

Portrait of Carmencita
Porträt von Carmencita
Portret van Carmencita
Retrato de Carmencita

●●

1938
54 x 37 cm / 21.2 x 14.5 in.
Musée des Beaux-Arts, Lyon

oil on canvas / Öl auf Leinwand
olieverf op doek / óleo sobre lienzo

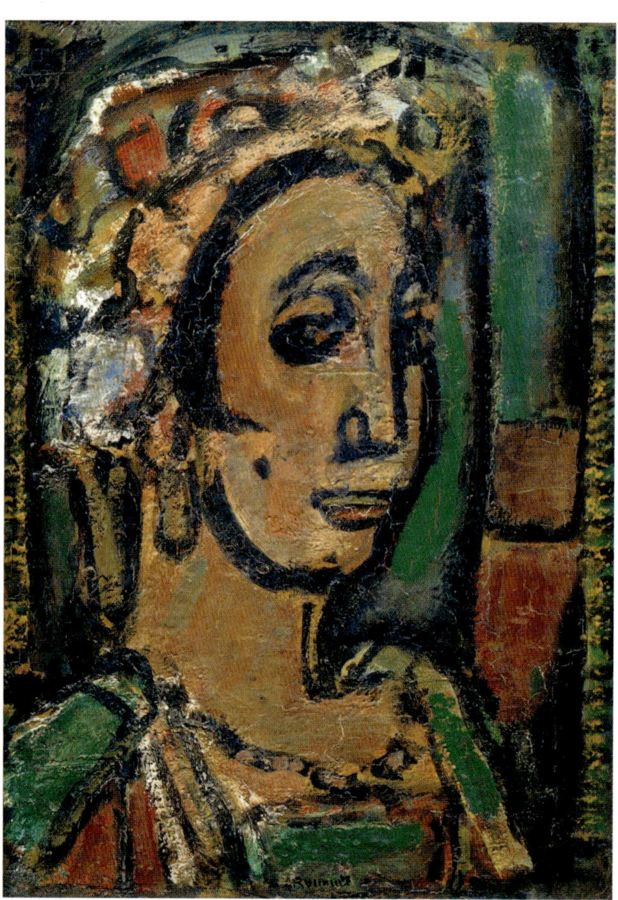

Georges Rouault
(Paris 1871 - 1951)

Pierrot with a rose
Pierrot mit einer Rose
Pierrot met een roos
Pierrot con una rosa

●●●

ca. 1936
92,7 x 61,7 cm / 36.5 x 24.3 in.
Philadelphia Museum of Art, Philadelphia

oil on canvas / Öl auf Leinwand
olieverf op doek / óleo sobre lienzo

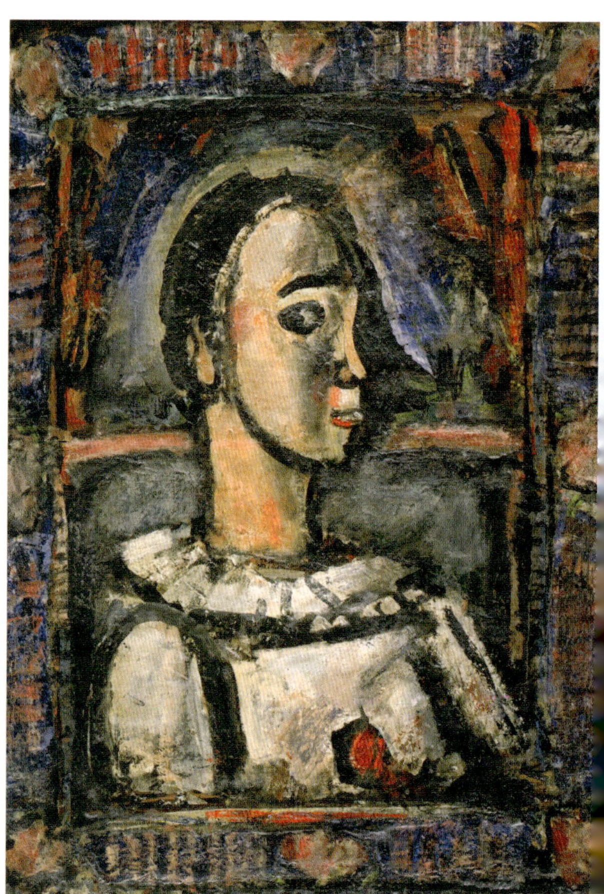

Georges Rouault
(Paris 1871 - 1951)

Nazareth

•

ca. 1948
Collezione d'Arte Religiosa
Moderna, Città del Vaticano

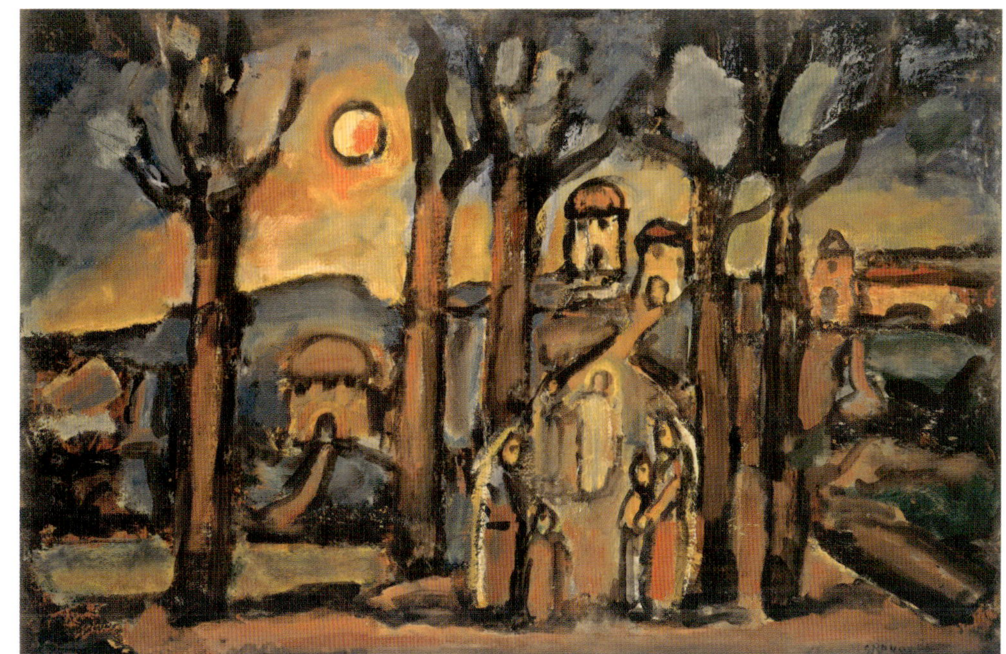

Georges Rouault
(Paris 1871 - 1951)

Tiberiade
Tiberias
Tiberíades

•

1948
39 x 63 cm / 15.3 x 24.8 in.
Ca' Pesaro Galleria d'Arte
Moderna, Venezia

oil on panel
Öl auf Tafel
olieverf op panee
óleo sobre tabla

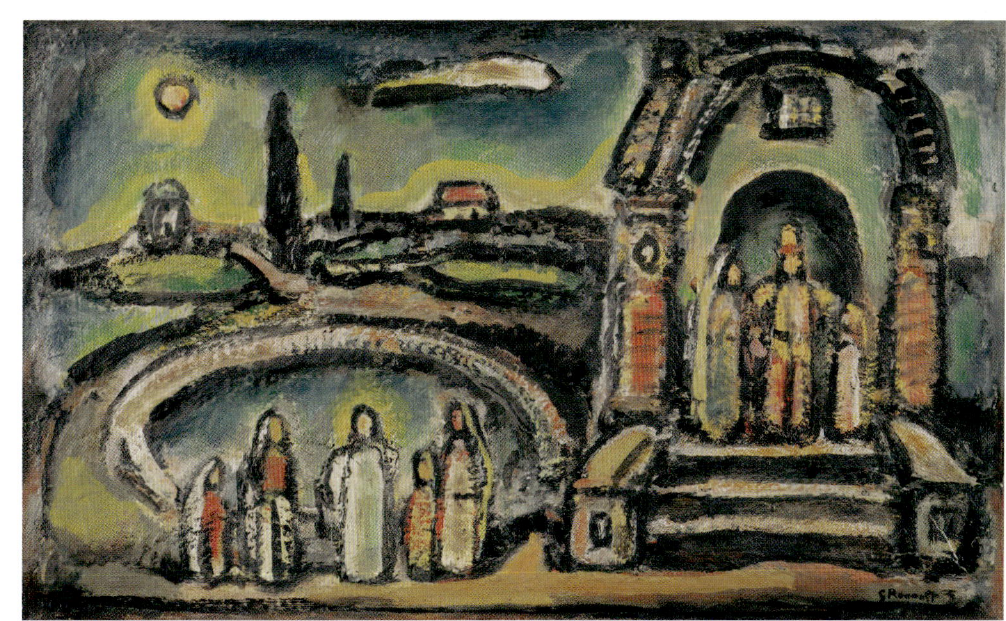

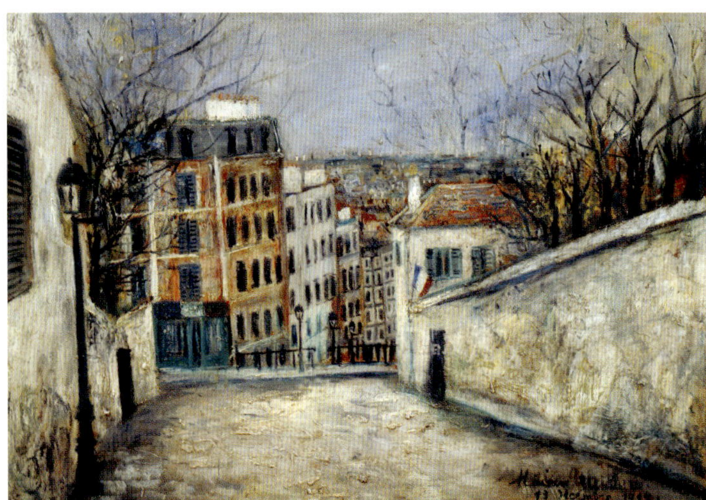

Maurice Utrillo
(Paris 1883 - Dax 1955)

The Mont-Cenis road to Montmartre
Rue Du Mont Cenis à Montmartre
De weg Mont-Cenis in Montmartre
La calle Mont-Cenis en Montmartre

●

1914
72 x 100 cm / 28.3 x 39.4 in.
Musée de l'Orangerie, Paris

oil on wood
Öl auf Holz
olieverf op hout
óleo sobre madera

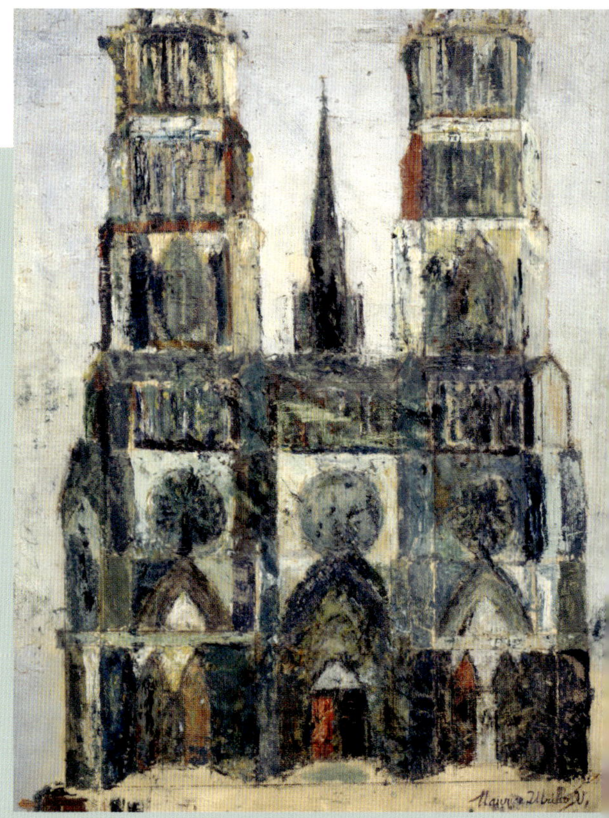

Maurice Utrillo
(Paris 1883 - Dax 1955)

The Cathedral of Notre Dame d'Amiens
Die Kathedrale von Notre Dame d'Amiens
De kathedraal van de Notre Dame d'Amiens
La catedral de Notre Dame de Amiens

●●

63 x 49 cm / 24.8 x 19.3 in.
Musée de l'Orangerie, Paris

oil on cardboard / Öl auf Karton
olieverf op karton / óleo sobre cartón

Maurice Utrillo
Paris 1883 - Dax 1955)

Saint Pierre de Montmartre, the Sacred Heart
Saint-Pierre de Montmartre, Sacré-Cœur
Saint Pierre de Montmartre en le Sacre Coeur
Saint Pierre de Montmartre, el Sagrado
Corazón

●●

931
1 x 61 cm / 20.1 x 24 in.
Musée Carnavalet, Paris

Self-taught, although his mother was the artist
Suzanne Valadon, Utrillo loved to paint his district:
Montmartre.

Der Autodidakt Utrillo, dessen Mutter die
Künstlerin Suzanne Valadon war, liebte es, sein
Viertel zu malen: Montmartre.

Utrillo was een autodidact, en ondanks dat zijn
moeder de kunstenares Suzanne Valadon was, hield
hij ervan zijn wijk te schilderen: Montmartre.

Autodidacta, a pesar de que su madre era la artista
Suzanne Valadon, Utrillo amaba pintar su barrio:
Montmartre.

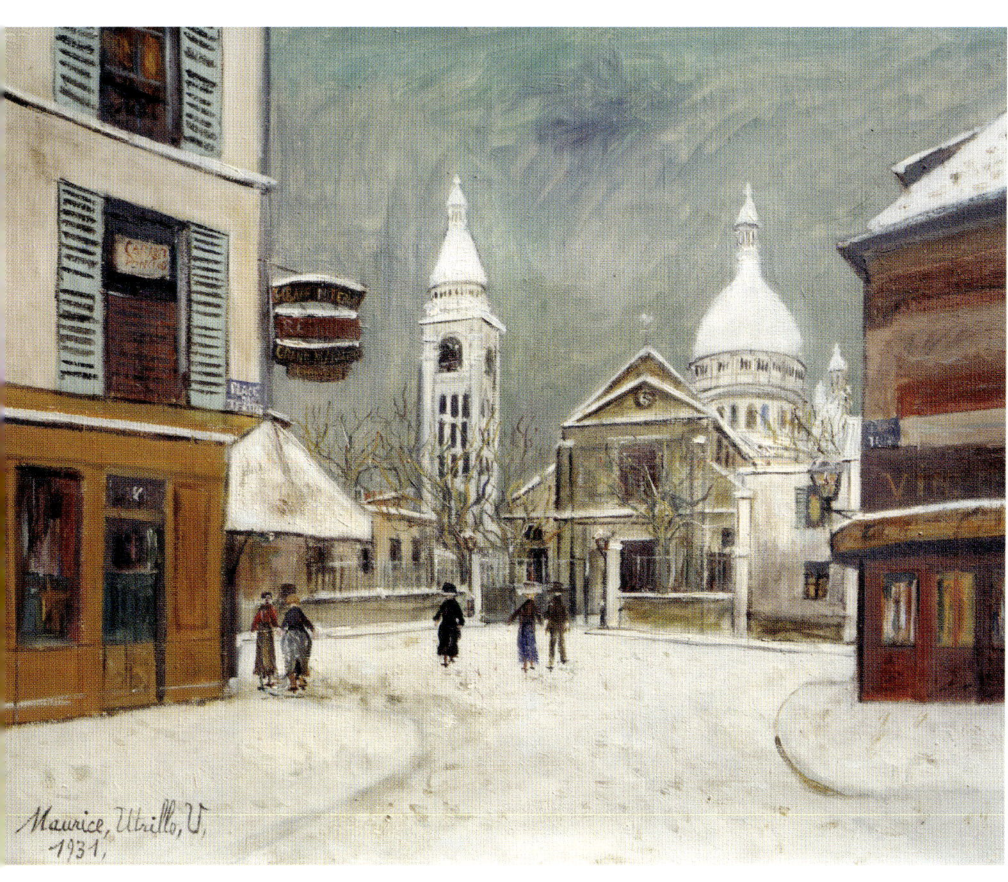

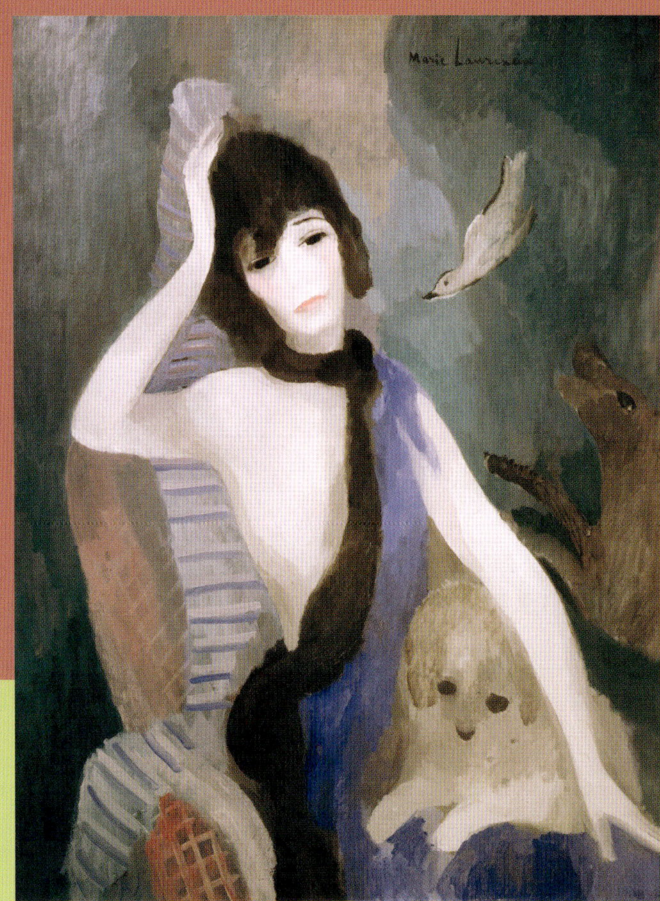

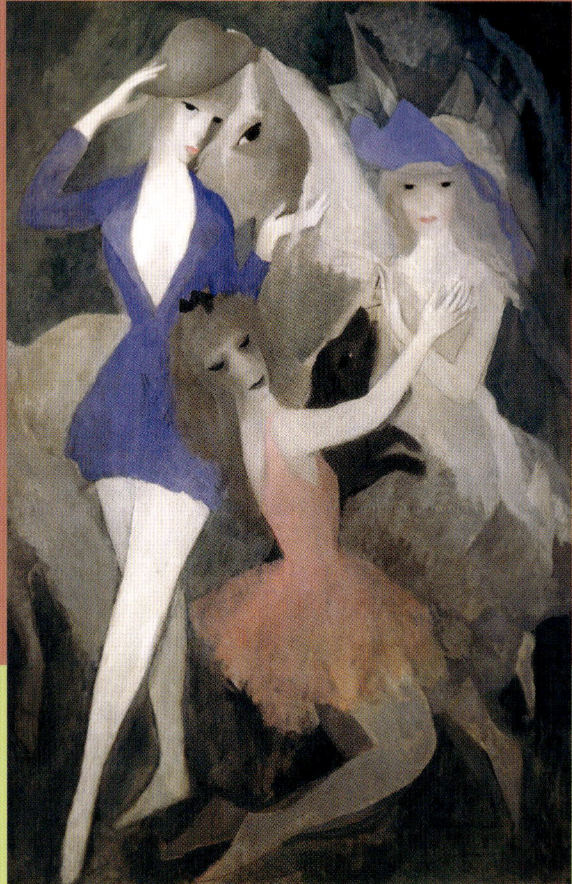

Marie Laurencin
(Paris 1885 - 1956)

Portrait of Mademoiselle Chanel
Porträt von Mademoiselle Chanel
Portret van Mademoiselle Chanel
Retrato de Mademoiselle Chanel

●●

1923
92 x 73 cm / 36.2 x 28.7 in.
Musée de l'Orangerie, Paris

oil on canvas / Öl auf Leinwand
olieverf op doek / óleo sobre lienzo

Marie Laurencin
(Paris 1885 - 1956)

Spanish Dancers
Spanische Tänzerinnen
Spaanse danseressen
Bailarinas españolas

●

1920-1921
150 x 95 cm / 59.1 x 37.4 in.
Musée de l'Orangerie, Paris

oil on canvas / Öl auf Leinwand
olieverf op doek / óleo sobre lienzo

Leonard Tsuguharu Foujita
(Tokyo 1886 - Zurich 1968)

**Portrait of the artist
in the studio
Porträt des Künstlers
im Atelier
Portret van de artiest
in zijn atelier
Retrato del artista
en su estudio**

●

1926
81 x 61 cm / 31.9 x 24 in.
Musée des Beaux Arts, Lyon

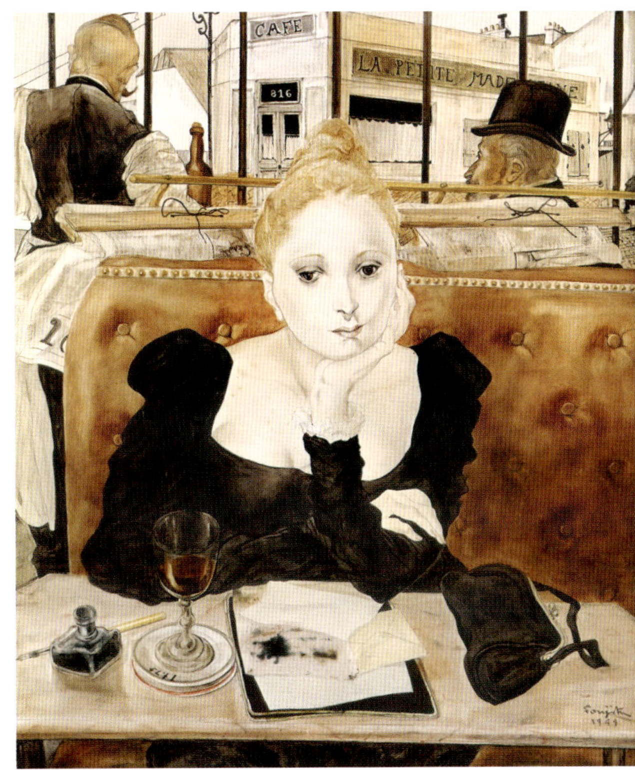

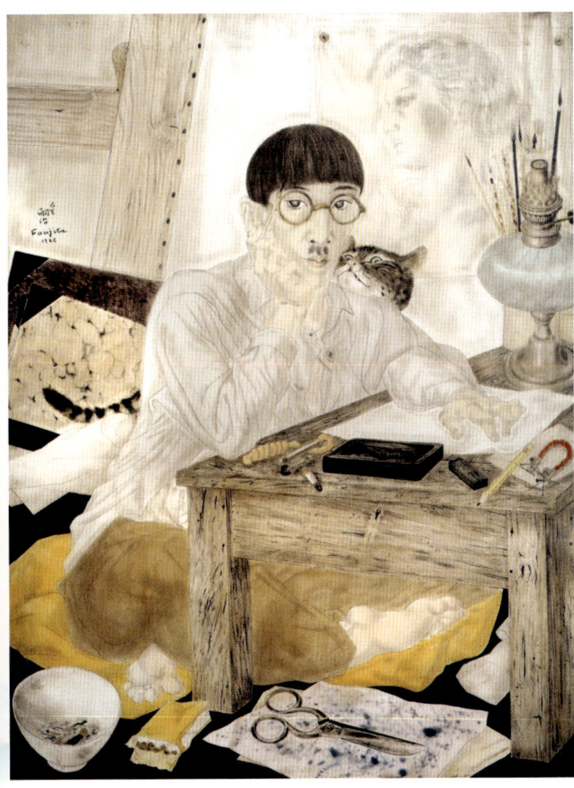

Leonard Tsuguharu Foujita
(Tokyo 1886 - Zurich 1968)

**At the caffè
Im Café
In het café
En el café**

●●

1949
76 x 64 cm / 29.9 x 25.2 in.
Centre Georges Pompidou,
Musée National d'Art Moderne, Paris

oil on canvas / Öl auf Leinwand
olieverf op doek / óleo sobre lienzo

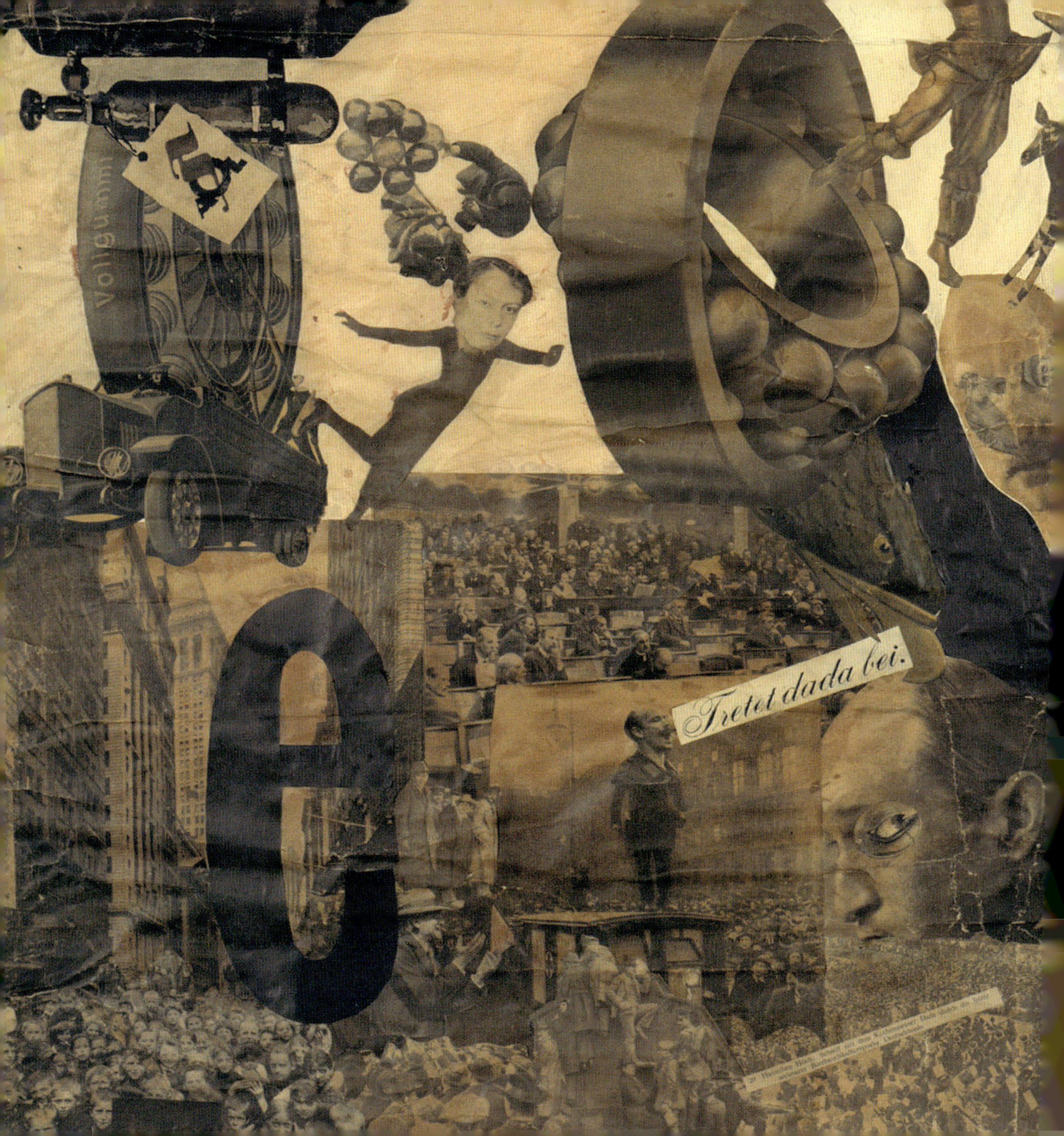

Vollgummi
Tretet dada bei.

Die große
WELT
dada
DADA i Sten
BALKANZUG

Art or play? Dada! • Kunst oder Spiel? Dada!
Kunst of spel? Dada! • ¿Arte o juego? ¡Dada!

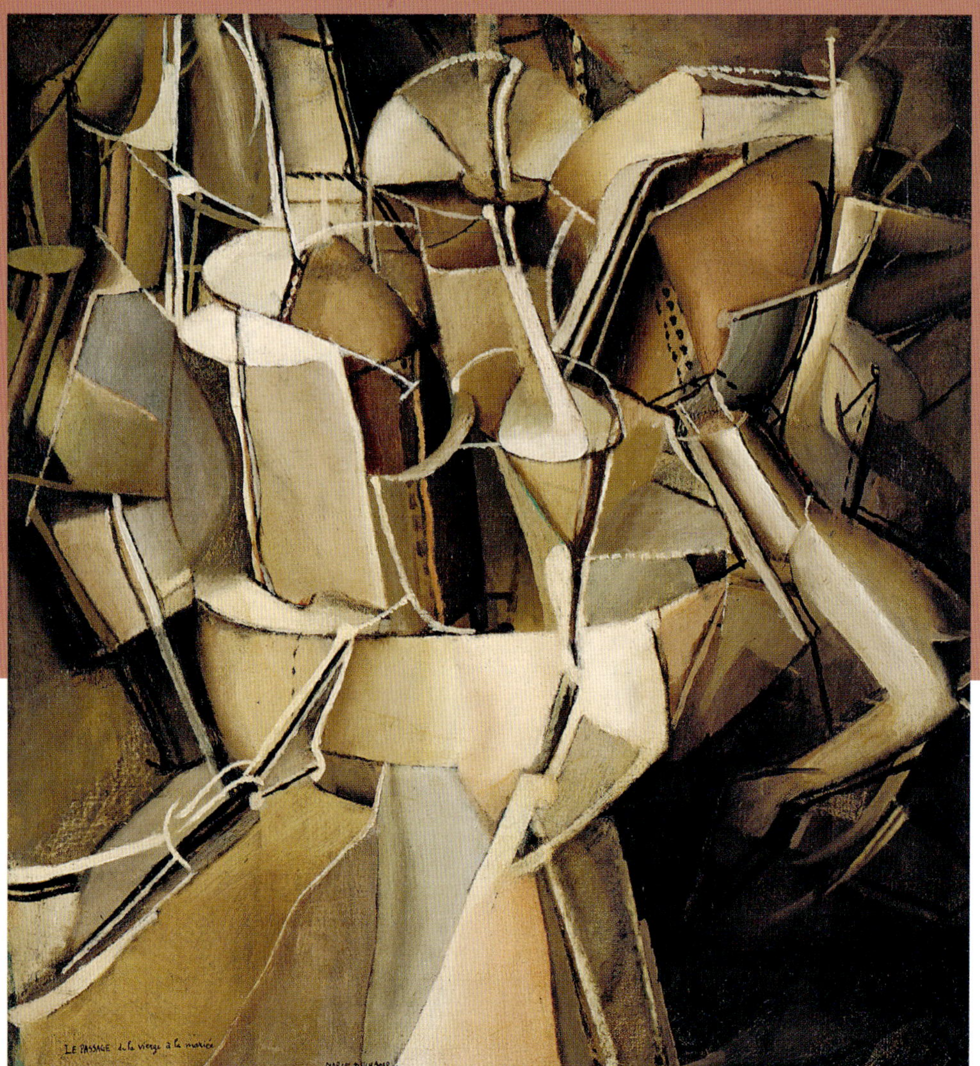

272

Marcel Duchamp
(Blainville-Crevon 1887 -
Neuilly-sur-Seine 1968)

**The passage from Virgin
to Bride
Der Übergang von der
Jungfrau zur Braut
Van maagd naar bruid
El pasaje de la Virgen
a la Novia**

●●

1912
59,4 x 54 cm / 23.4 x 21.2 in.
Museum of Modern Art
(MoMA), New York

oil on canvas
Öl auf Leinwand
olieverf op doek
óleo sobre lienzo

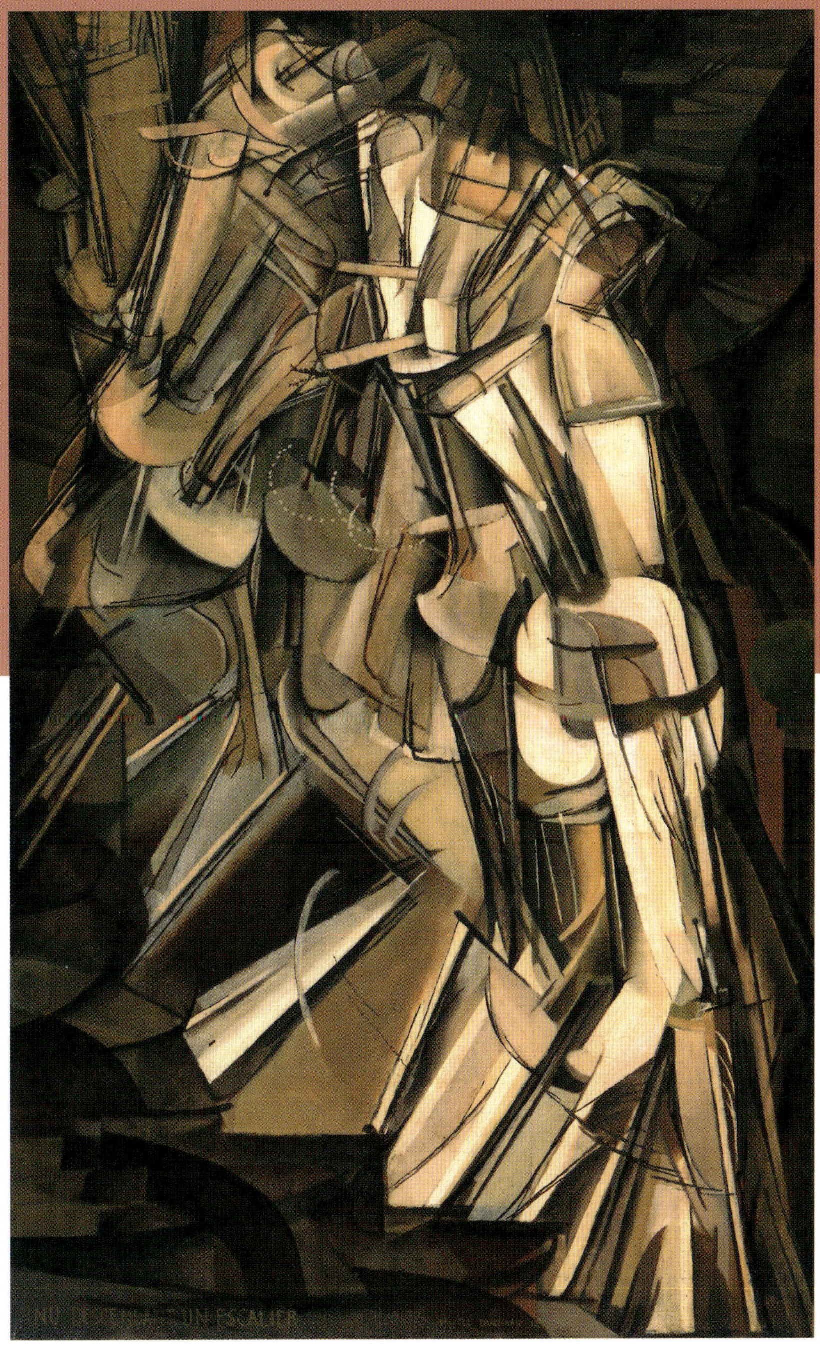

Marcel Duchamp

(Blainville-Crevon 1887 -
Neuilly-sur-Seine 1968)

Nude descending the stairs (n. 2)
Akt, eine Treppe herabsteigend (Nr. 2)
Naakt dat de trap afdaalt (n. 2)
Desnudo bajando una escalera (n. 2)

● ● ●

1912
147 x 89,2 cm / 57.9 x 35.1 in.
Philadelphia Museum of Art, Philadelphia

oil on canvas / Öl auf Leinwand
olieverf op doek / óleo sobre lienzo

A rather unorthodox nude because
of the antinaturalist and futurist treatment,
which caused a scandal when it was exhibited
in 1912 in New York.

Dieser antinaturalistisch und futuristisch
geprägte, ausgesprochen unorthodoxe Akt löste
zur Zeit seiner Ausstellung, 1912 in New York,
einen Skandal aus.

Een weinig orthodox naakt dat wegens de
antinaturalistische en futuristische benadering
ervan, in de periode van de expositie van 1912
in New York een schandaal veroorzaakte.

Un desnudo poco ortodoxo a causa
del tratamiento antinatural y futurista,
que causó escándalo en la época de su
exposición, en el año 1912 en Nueva York.

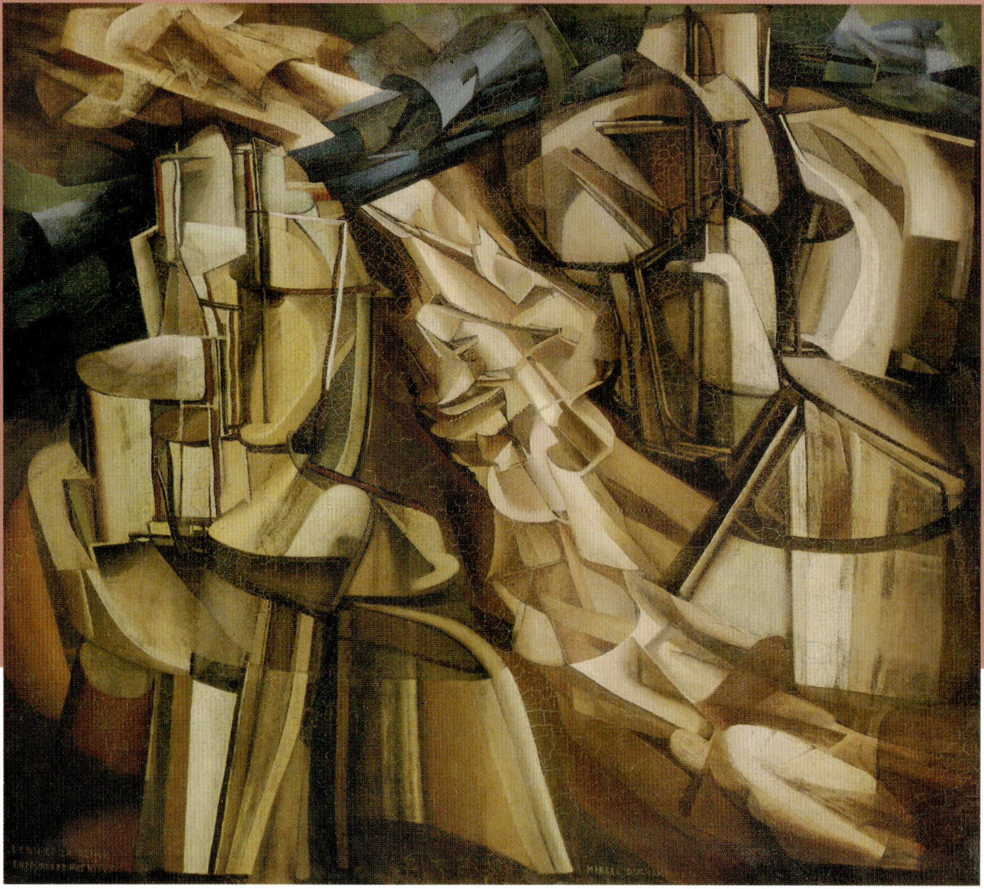

Marcel Duchamp
(Blainville-Crevon 1887 - Neuilly-sur-Seine 1968)

The king and queen surrounded by fast nudes
König und Königin, von schnellen Akten umgeben
De koning en de koningin omringd door schielijke naakten
El rey y la reina rodeados de desnudos veloces

●

1912
114,6 x 128,9 cm / 45.1 x 50.7 in.
Philadelphia Museum of Art, Philadelphia

oil on canvas / Öl auf Leinwand / olieverf op doek / óleo sobre lienzo

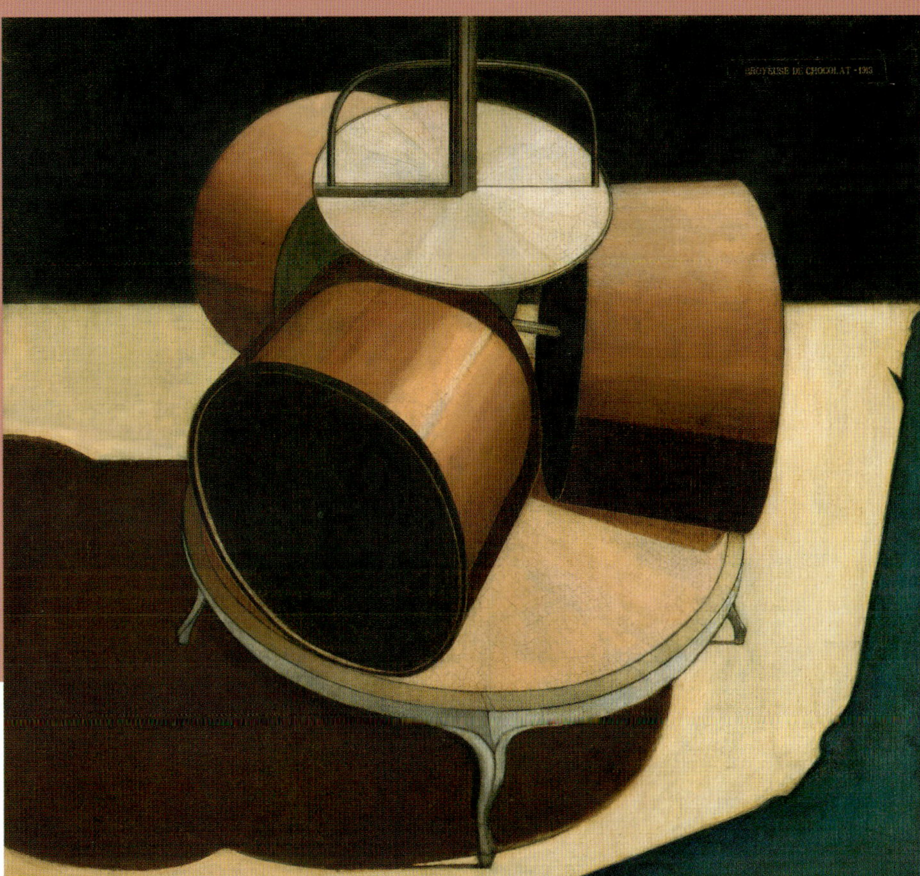

Marcel Duchamp
(Blainville-Crevon 1887 - Neuilly-sur-Seine 1968)

Chocolate grinder (n. 1)
Schokoladenreibe (Nr. 1)
Chocolademaalmachine (n. 1)
Molinillo de chocolate (n. 1)

●●●

1913
61,9 x 64,5 cm / 24.4 x 25.4 in.
Philadelphia Museum of Art, Philadelphia

oil on canvas / Öl auf Leinwand
olieverf op doek / óleo sobre lienzo

This machine, inspired by the memory of a shop of sweets in Rouen, symbolizes solitary pleasure for Duchamp.

Diese Maschine, die aus der Erinnerung an ein Süßigkeitengeschäft in Rouen entstand, wird für Duchamp zum Symbol des einsamen Vergnügens.

Deze machine, in zijn herinnering van een snoepwinkel in Rouen, staat voor Duchamp symbool voor stil genot.

Esta máquina, concebida a partir del recuerdo de un negocio de dulces de Rouen, simboliza para Duchamp el placer solitario.

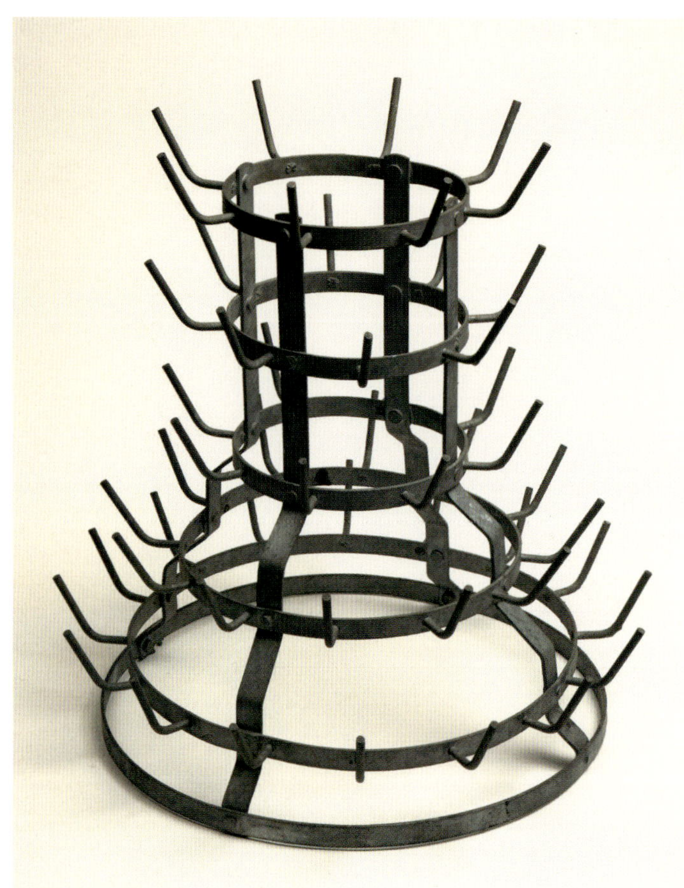

Marcel Duchamp
(Blainville-Crevon 1887 - Neuilly-sur-Seine 1968)

Bottle drainers
Der Flaschentrockner
Flessenrek
Botellero

●●

1914 (1961)
h. 49,8 cm / 19.6 in.
Philadelphia Museum of Art, Philadelphia

galvanized iron / Galvanisiertes Eisen
gegalvaniseerd ijzer / hierro galvanizado.

Marcel Duchamp
(Blainville-Crevon 1887 -
Neuilly-sur-Seine 1968)

Comb

●

1916
3,2 x 16,5 cm / 1.2 x 6.5 in.
Philadelphia Museum of Art,
Philadelphia

steel / Stahl / staal / acero

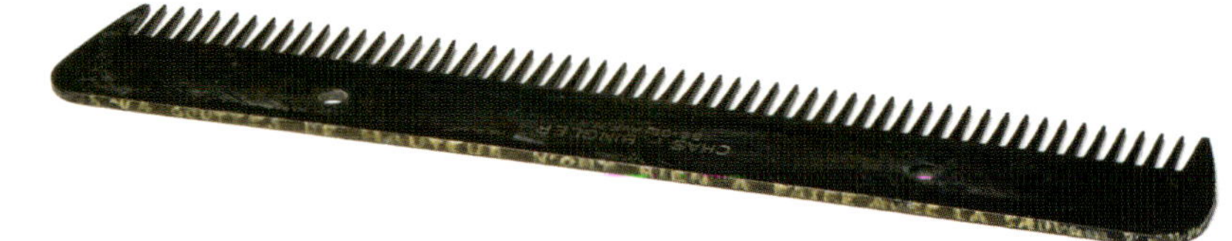

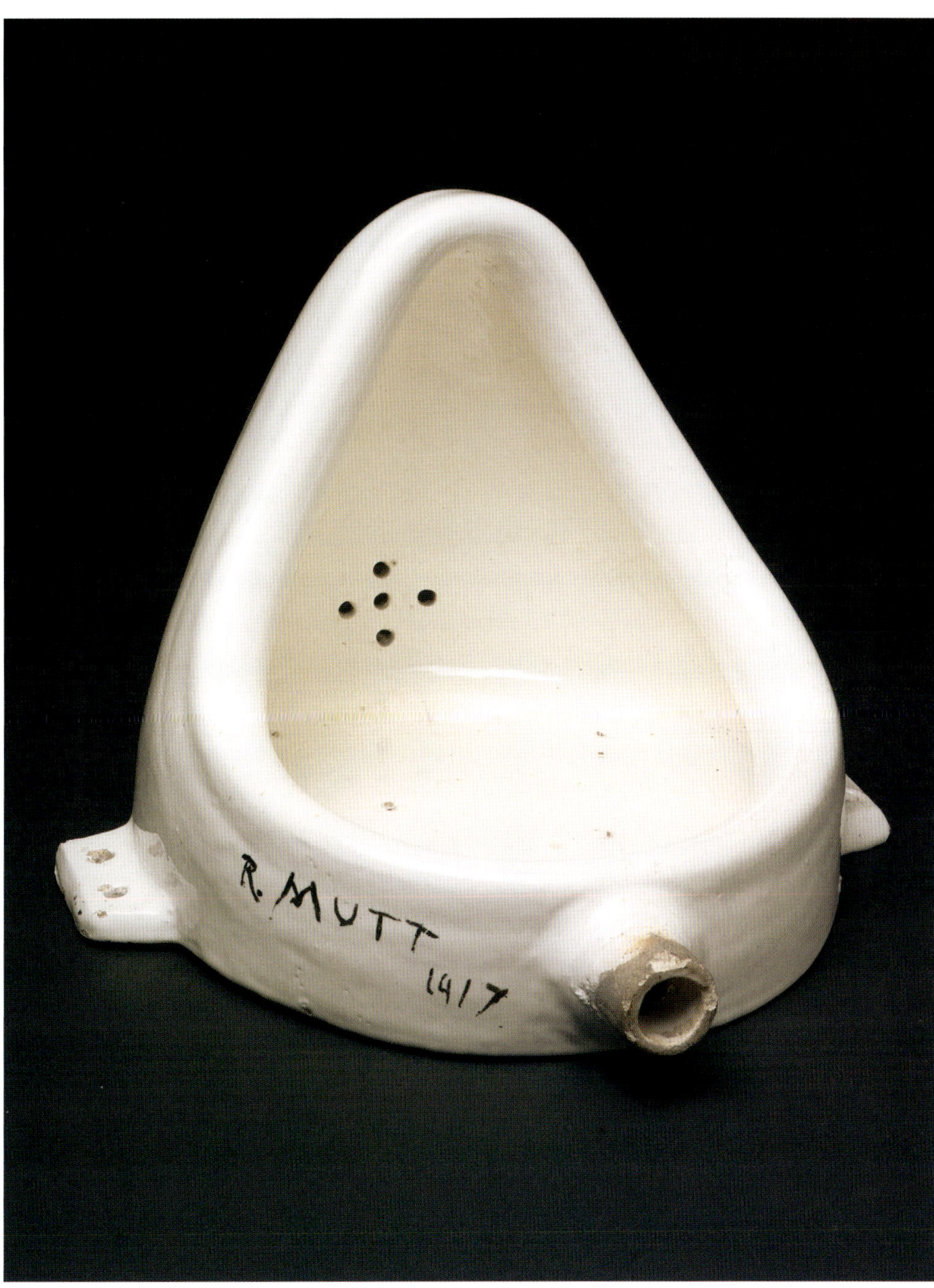

Marcel Duchamp
(Blainville-Crevon 1887 -
Neuilly-sur-Seine 1968)

The Fountain
Brunnen
De fontein
Fuente

●●●

1917 (1950)
30,5 x 38,1 x 45,7 cm
12 x 15 x 18 in.
Philadelphia Museum of Art,
Philadelphia

porcelain urinal
Pissoir aus Porzellan
porseleinen urinoir
orinal de porcelana

Following the choice of the
artist, with the addition of a
title and a signature, a simple
object is raised to the rank
of work of art.

Allein durch die Wahl des
Künstlers, das Hinzufügen
eines Titels und die Signatur,
wird ein einfacher Gegenstand
in den Stand eines eines
Kunstwerks erhoben.

Met de toevoeging van
een titel en een signering
krijgt een simpel, door de
kunstenaar uitgezocht object
de rang van een kunstwerk.

Siguiendo la elección del
artista, con el agregado
de un título y de una firma,
un simple objeto es elevado
al rango de obra de arte.

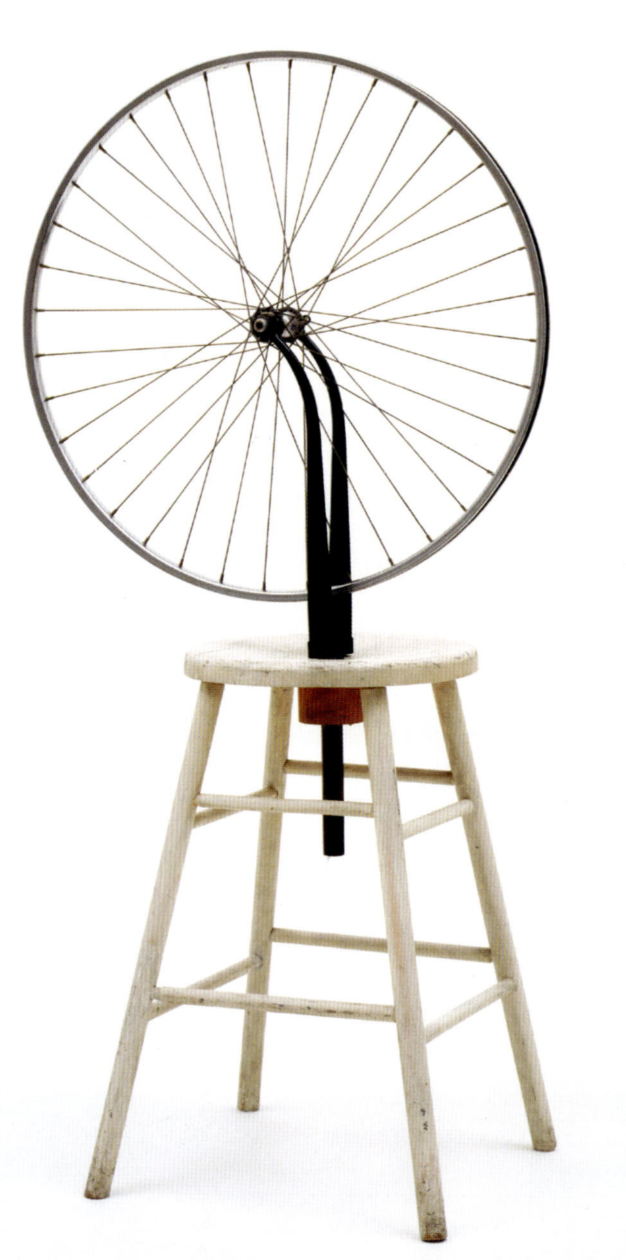

278

Marcel D
(Blainville-C
Neuilly-sur-

**Bicycle wh
Fahrrad-Ra
Fietswiel
Rueda de bicicleta**

●●●

1913 (1951)
h. 128,3 cm / 50.5 in.
Museum of Modern Art (MoMA),
New York

assembly of a metal wheel mounted
on a painted wood pedestal
Montage eines Metallrads auf einem Sockel
aus bemaltem Holz
assemblage van een metalen wiel gemonteerd
op een voetstuk van beschilderd hout
ensamblaje de una rueda de metal montada
sobre un pedestal de madera pintada

Marcel Duchamp
(Blainville-Crevon 1887
- Neuilly-sur-Seine 1968)

**Recently widowed
Seit Kurzem verwitwet
Sinds kort weduwe
Viuda reciente**

●●

1920
77,5 x 44,8 cm
30.5 x 17.6 in.
Museum of Modern Art
(MoMA), New York

assembly of a miniature
window with eight leather
plates
Montage eines
Mniniaturfensters mit acht
Lederplatten
assemblage van een raam in
miniatuur met acht met leer
beplakte vensterruiten
ensamblaje de una ventana
en miniatura con ocho
planchas de cuero

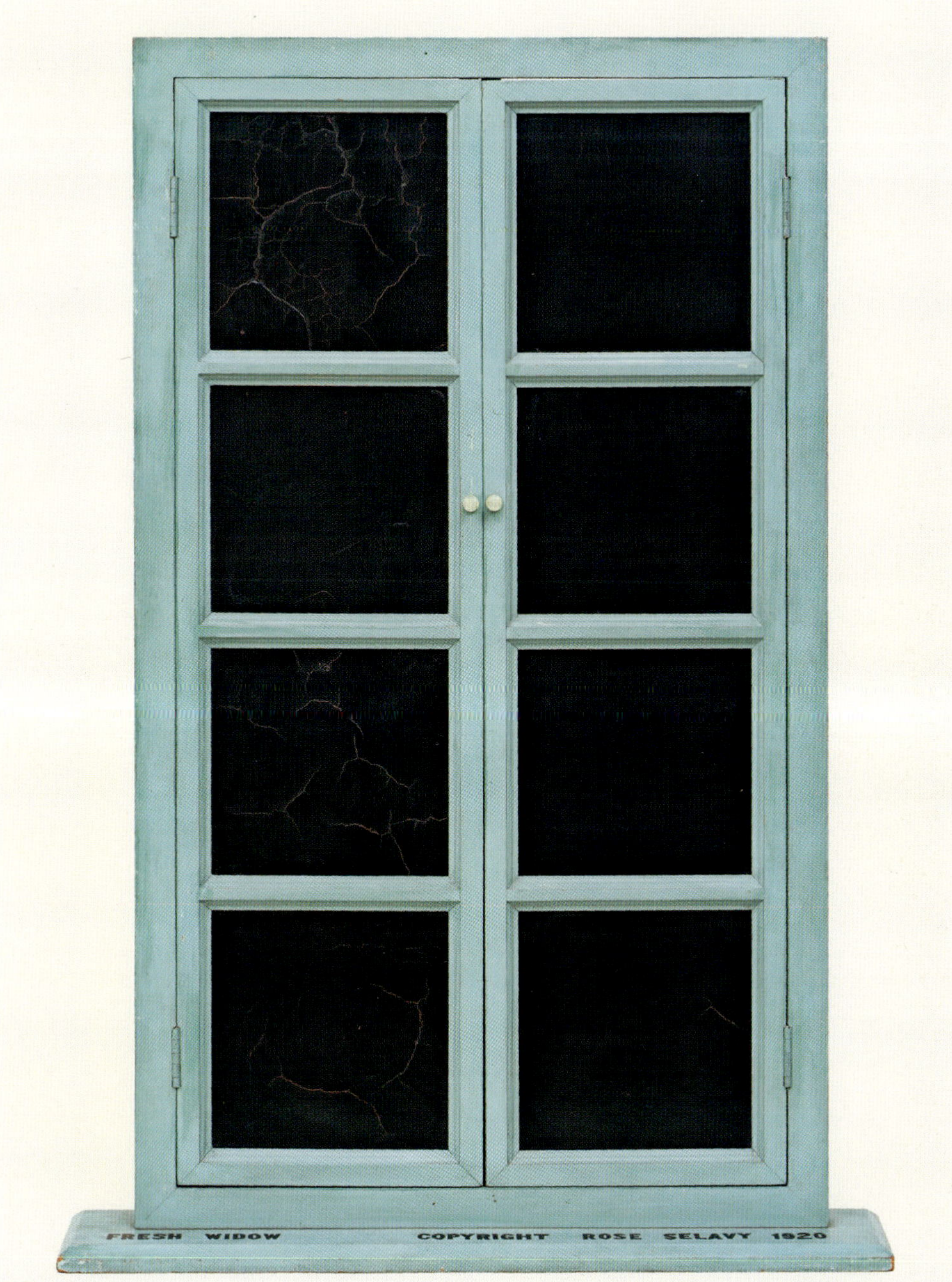

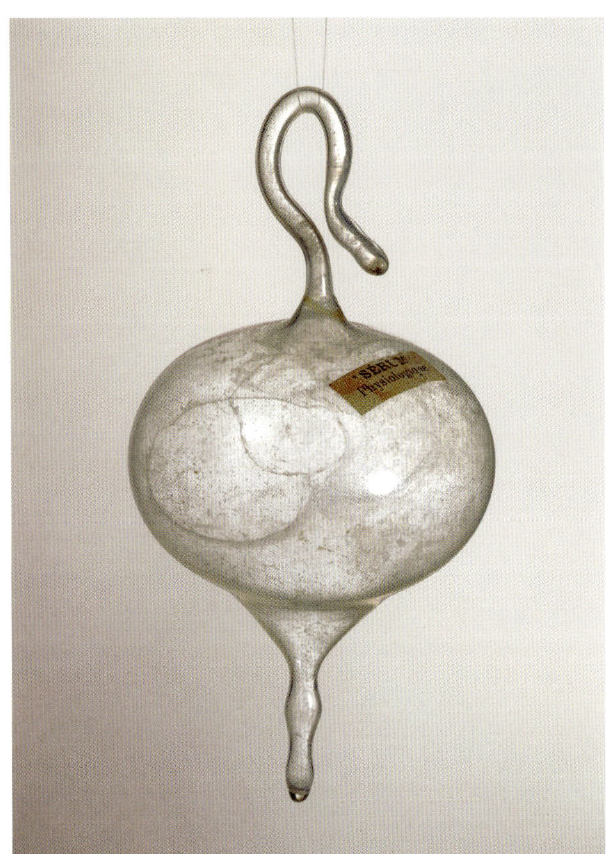

Marcel Duchamp
(Blainville-Crevon 1887 - Neuilly-sur-Seine 1968)

Sculpture (50 cc of Paris)
Skulptur (50 cc aus Paris)
Sculptuur (50 cc van Parijs)
Escultura (50 cc de París)

●

1919
h. 13,3 cm / 5.2 in.
Philadelphia Museum of Art, Philadelphia

glass beaker / Glasfläschchen
glazen flesje / ampolla de vidrio

Marcel Duchamp
(Blainville-Crevon 1887 - Neuilly-sur-Seine 1968)

Rotating hemisphere (optics of precision)
Rotierende Halbkugel (Präzisionsoptik)
Ronddraaiende halve bol (precisie-optiek)
Semisfera rotativa (óptica de precisión)

●

1925
148,6 x 64,2 x 60,9 cm / 58.5 x 25.2 x 23.9 in.
Museum of Modern Art (MoMA), New York

motor-driven construction / Motorengesteuerte Konstruktion
Motorbestuurde constructie / construcción moto-guiada

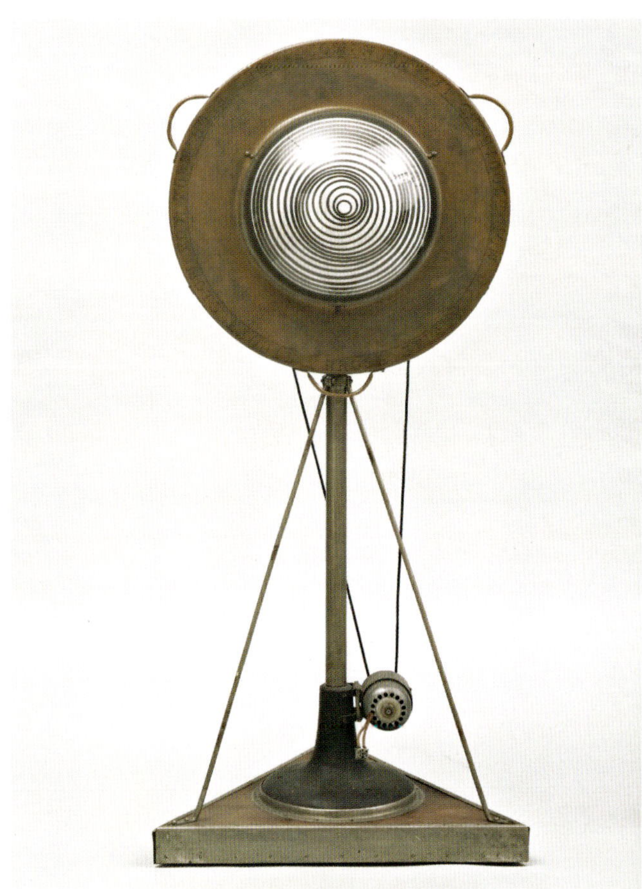

Mona Lisa, paradigm of the
masterpiece, is desecrated: Duchamp
here commits a sacrilegious act
by disguising her with mustache
and a subversive inscription.

Die Mona Lisa, das Paradigma
des Meisterwerks, wird entweiht:
Duchamp begeht hier eine frevelhafte
Tat, indem er einen Schnauzbart und
eine subversive Inschrift hinzufügt.

Mona Lisa, paradigma van alle
meesterwerken, wordt ontwijd:
Duchamp pleegt heiligschennis door
haar van een snor te voorzien
en een subversieve inscriptie.

La Mona Lisa, paradigma de la obra
de arte, es profanada: Duchamp
comete aquí un acto sacrílego
enmascarándola con bigotes
y una inscripción subversiva.

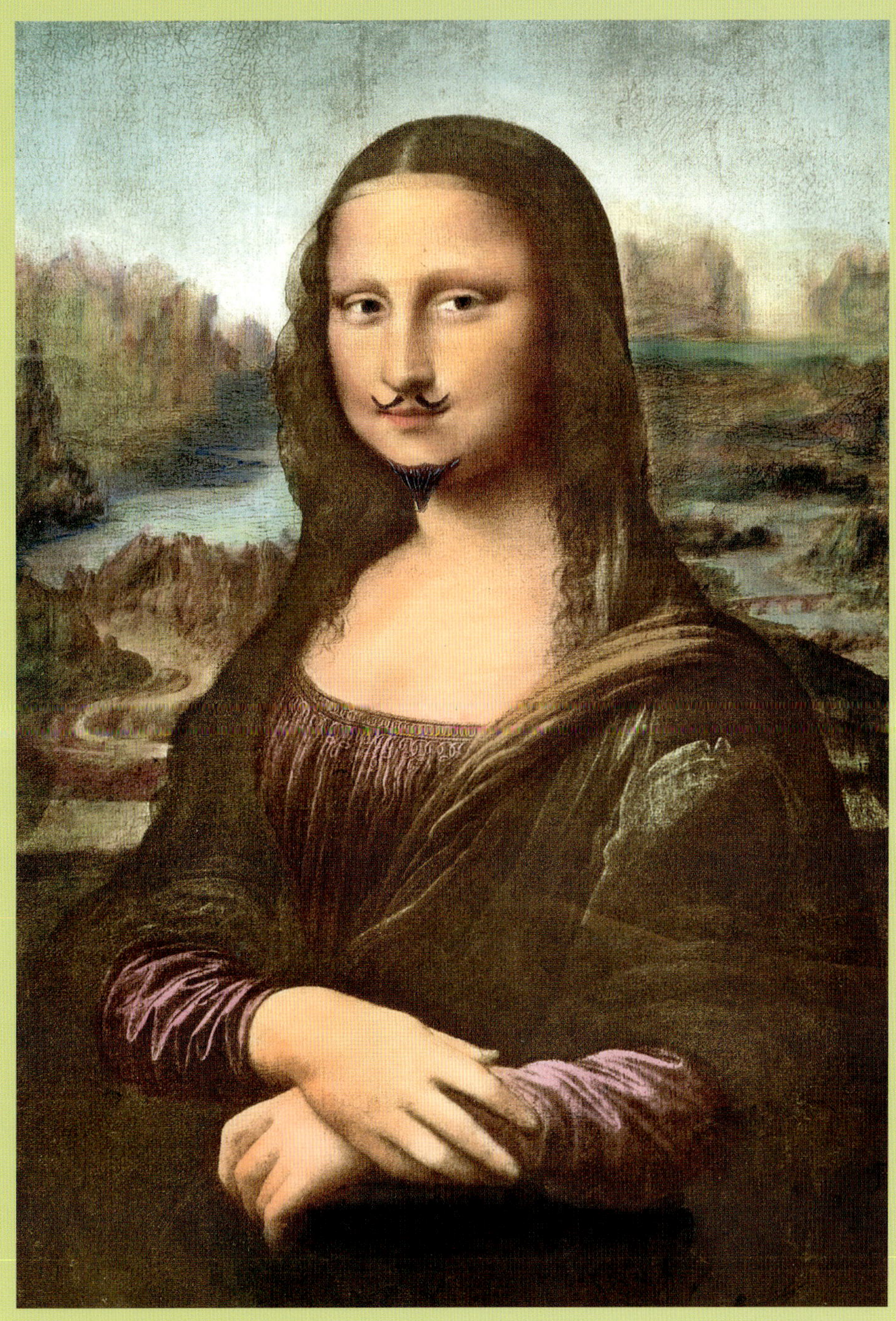

Marcel Duchamp
(Blainville-Crevon 1887 -
Neuilly-sur-Seine 1968)
**LHOOQ
Portrait of Mona Lisa
with beard and mustache
Porträt der Monna Lisa
mit Kinnbart und Schnurrbart
Portret van Mona Lisa met
baard en snor
Retrato de la Mona Lisa
con barba y bigotes**
•••

Private collection / Private Sammlung
Privécollectie / Colección privada

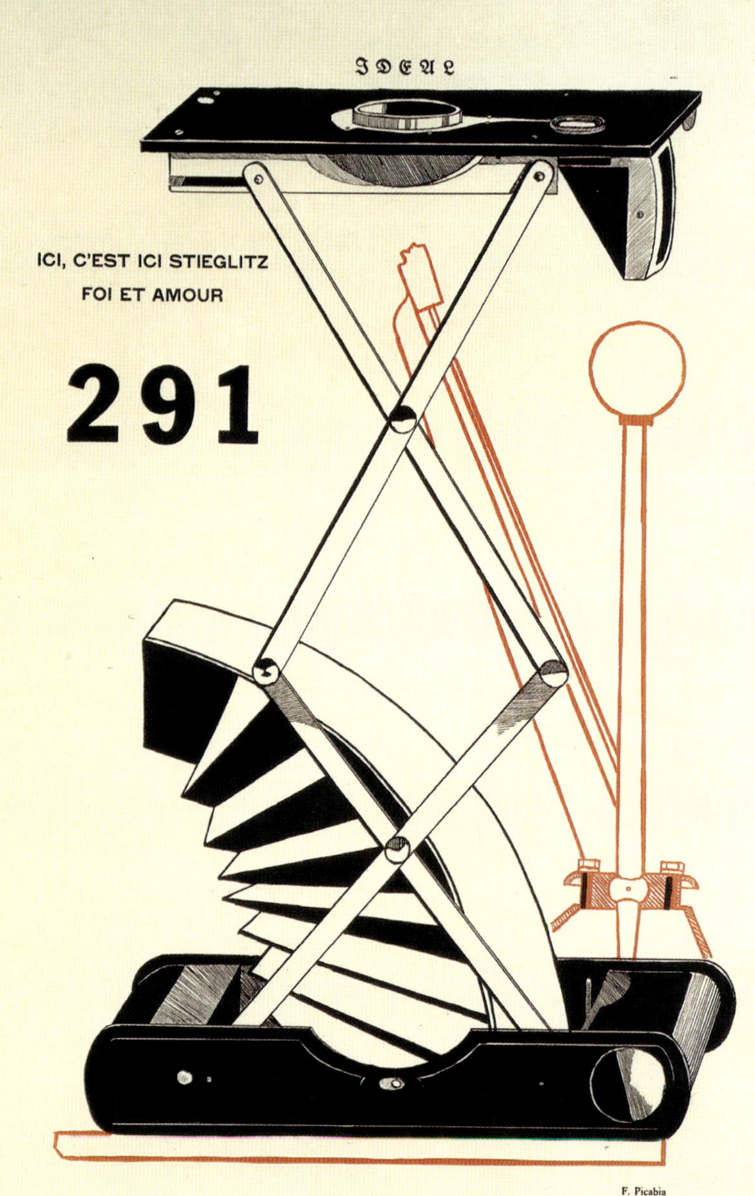

Francis Picabia
(Paris 1879 - 1953)

**Here, Stieglitz is here,
cover of «291»
Ici, c'est ici Stieglitz, Deckblatt
von «291»
Hier, hier is Stieglitz,
cover van «291»
Aquí, es aquí Stieglitz, portada
de «291»**

●

1915
38 x 22,8 cm / 14.2 x 8.9 in.
National Portrait Gallery, Smithsonian
Institution, Washington, DC

print on paper / Druck auf Papier
print op papier / impresión sobre papel

**Picabia pays tribute to Stieglitz, famous
American photographer who had
opened a gallery of modern art in New
York at 291 Fifth Avenue.**

**Picabia ehrt Stieglitz, den berühmten
amerikanischen Fotografen, der eine
Galerie für moderne Kunst in New York,
in der 5th Street 291, eröffnet hat.**

**Picabia brengt hulde aan Stieglitz, een
beroemde Amerikaanse fotograaf die
een galerie van moderne kunst had
geopend in 291 Fifth Street, New York.**

**Picabia rinde homenaje a Stieglitz,
célebre fotógrafo americano que había
abierto una galería de arte moderno
en Nueva York en el 291 de la Quinta
Avenida.**

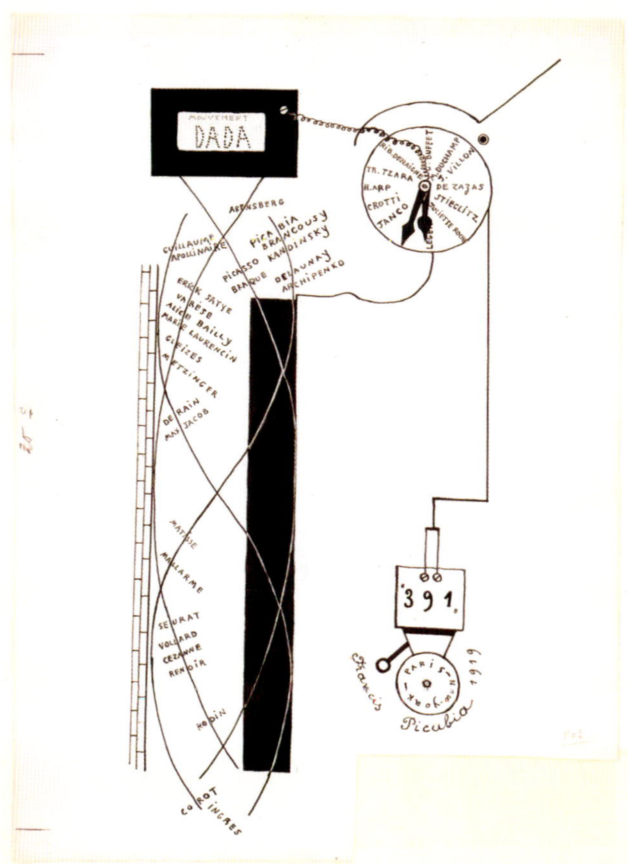

Francis Picabia
(Paris 1879 - 1953)

Dada Movement
Dada-Bewegung
Dada-beweging
Movimiento Dada

●

1919
51,1 x 36,2 cm / 20.1 x 14.2 in.
Museum of Modern Art (MoMA), New York

pen and ink on paper / Feder und Tinte auf Papier
pen en inkt op papier / pluma y tinta sobre papel

Francis Picabia
(Paris 1879 - 1953)

Take me there
Bringt mich dorthin
Breng me daar heen
Llevadme allí

●●

1919-1920
129,2 x 89,8 cm / 50.8 x 35.4 in.
Museum of Modern Art (MoMA), New York

oil on cardboard / Öl auf Karton
olieverf op karton / óleo sobre cartón

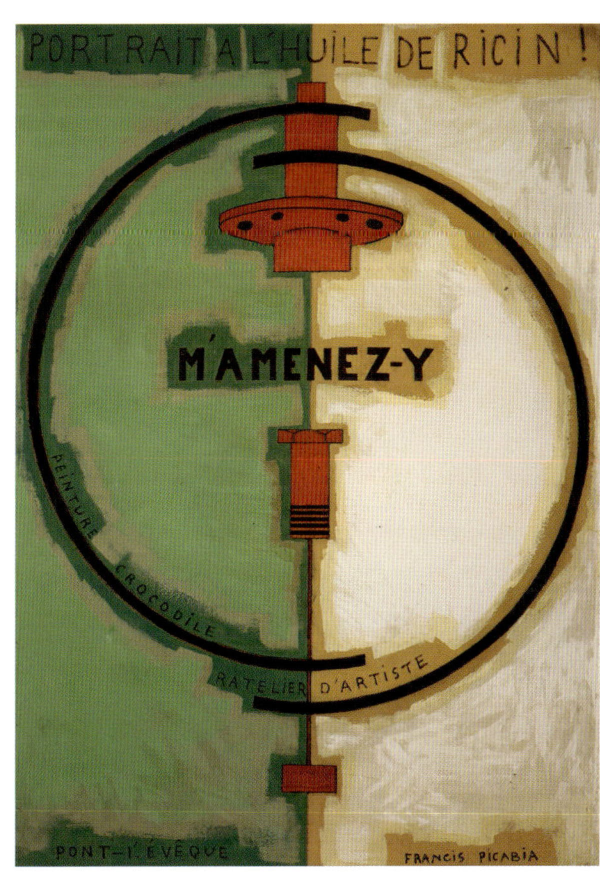

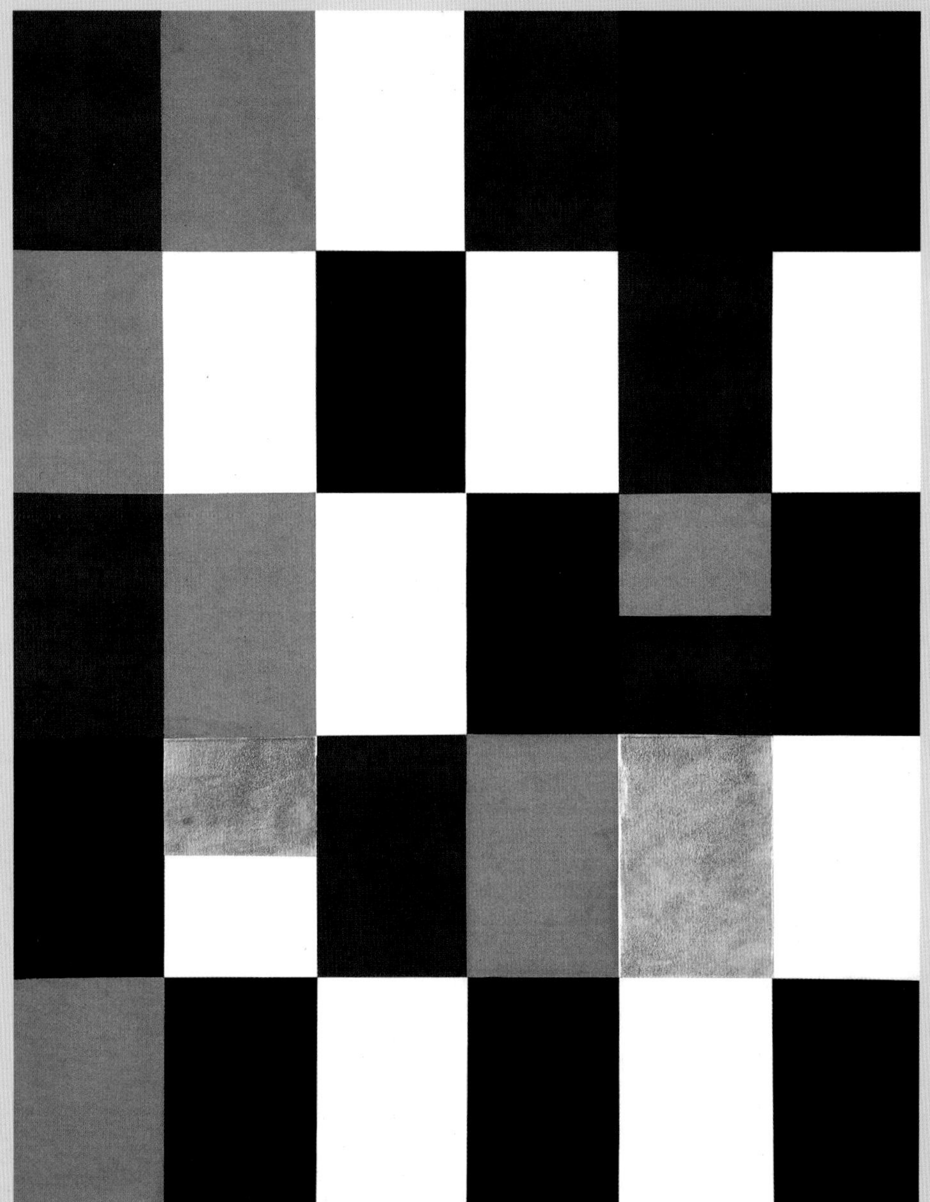

The reduction of the plastic
elements to geometric surfaces
cut out onto colored backgrounds
enters the artist into the stream of
pure geometric abstraction.

Die Reduktion der plastischen
Elemente auf geometrische
Oberflächen, die auf farbigen
Hintergründen ausgeschnitten
sind, schreibt die Künstlerin der
Strömung der puren geometrischen
Abstraktion zu.

Het verminderen van plastische
elementen op geometrische
oppervlakken tegen gekleurde
achtergronden brengt de
kunstenaar in de stroming van pure
geometrische abstractie.

La reducción de los elementos
plásticos a superficies geométricas
recortadas sobre fondos de colores
inscribe al artista en la corriente de
la abstracción geométrica pura.

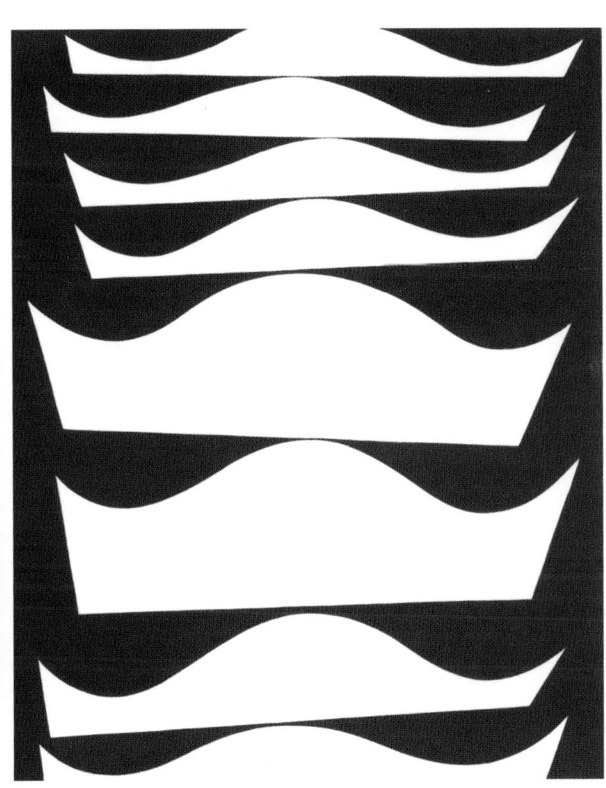

Sophie Taeuber-Arp
(Davos 1889 - Zürich 1943)

Unbalanced spacing
Unausgeglichene Verteilung
Ongebalanceerde verdeling
Escalonamiento fuera de eje

●

1934
35.2 x 27 cm / 13.8 x 10.6 in.
Museum of Modern Art (MoMA), New York

gouache on paper / Gouache auf Papier
gouache op papier / gouache sobre papel

Sophie Taeuber-Arp
(Davos 1889 - Zürich 1943)

Fluctuating shapes
Fluktuierende Formen
Fluctuerende vormen
Formas fluctuantes

●

1935
50 x 65 cm / 19.7 x 25.6 in.
Hamburger Kunsthalle, Hamburg

oil on canvas / Öl auf Leinwand
olieverf op doek / óleo sobre lienzo

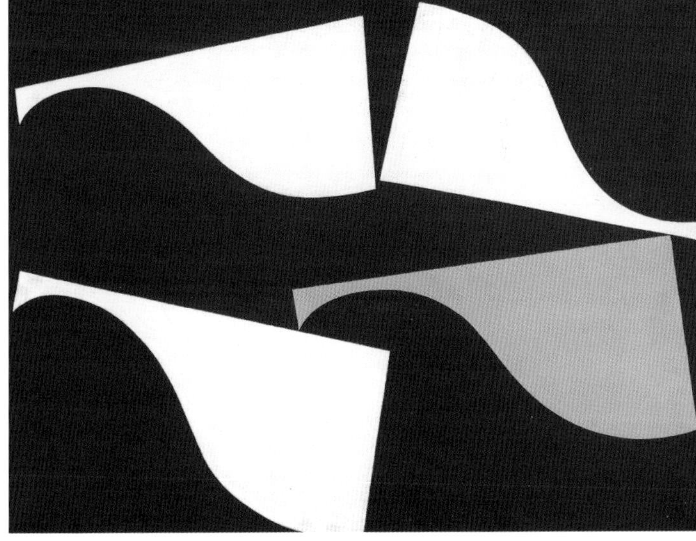

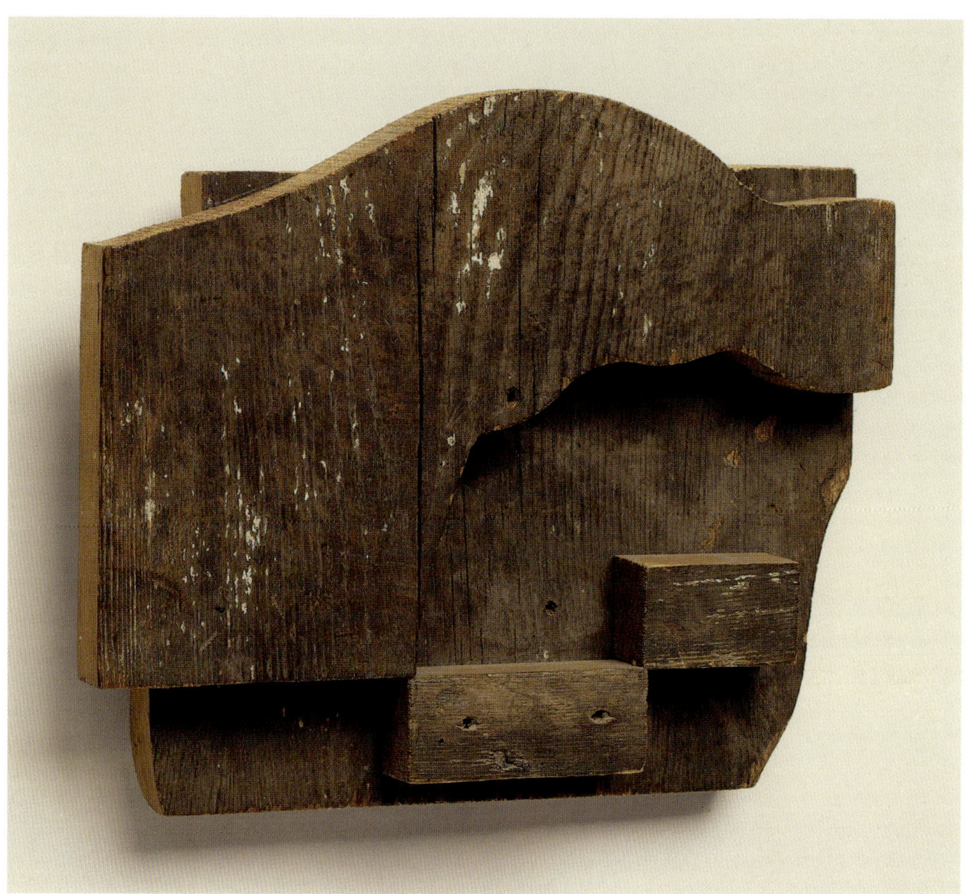

Jean Arp
(Strasbourg 1887 - Basel 1966)

Dada relief
Dada-Relief
Dada-reliëf
Relieve Dada

●●

1917
24,5 x 28 x 6 cm / 9.6 x 11 x 2.3 in.
Nationalgalerie, Staatliche Museen, Berlin

wood / Holz / hout / madera

Jean Arp
(Strasbourg 1887 - Basel 1966)
**Arabische Acht
(Eight, Arabic number). Panel 7
from "7 Arpaden von Hans Arp"
(Arabische Acht). Tafel 7 aus
"7 Arpaden von Hans Arp"
(Acht, Arabisch cijfer). Paneel 7 uit
"7 Arpaden von Hans Arp"
(Ocho en arábigo). Tabla 7 de
"7 Arpaden von Hans Arp"**
●
1923
45,1 x 34,9 cm / 17.7 x 13.7 in.
Museum of Modern Art (MoMA), New York

lithograph from an album of seven
Lithographie aus einem siebenteiligen Album
lithografie uit een zevendelig album
litografía de un álbum de siete

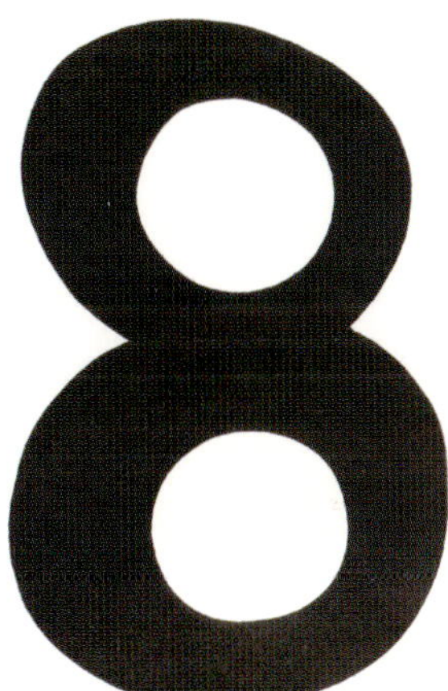

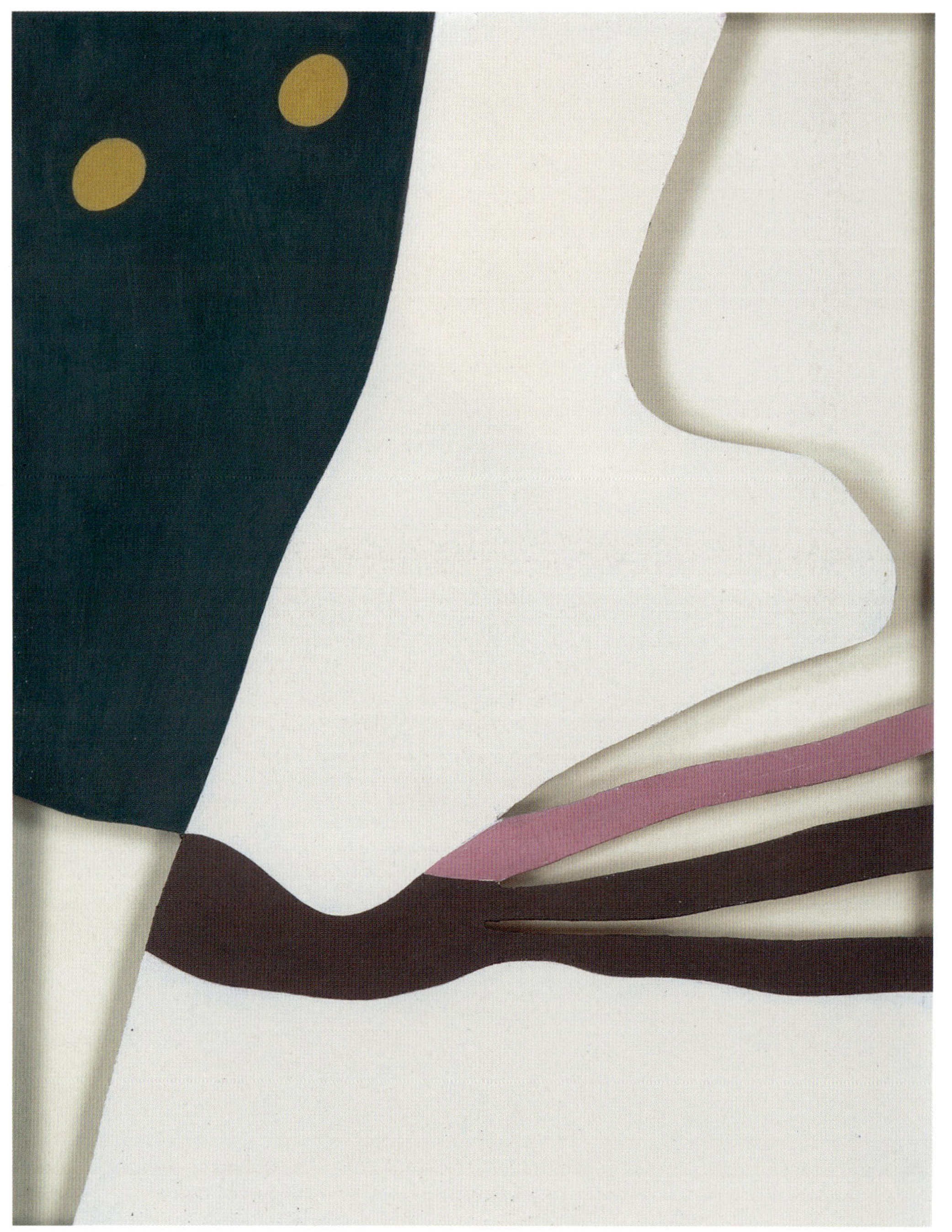

Jean Arp

(Strasbourg 1887 - Basel
1966)

**Eyes, nose, mustache
Augen, Nasen,
Schnurrbärte
Ogen, neus, snor
Ojos, nariz, bigotes**

●

1928
51 x 38,7 cm / 20 x 15.2 in.
Hamburger Kunsthalle,
Hamburg

painted cardboard, irregular
shape with glass plates and
grey frame
Bemalter Karton, in
unregelmäßiger Form, mit
Glastafeln und grauem
Rahmen
beschilderd karton, met
onregelmatige vorm en
glazen platen en grijze lijst
cartón pintado, de forma
irregular con losas de vidrio
y marco gris

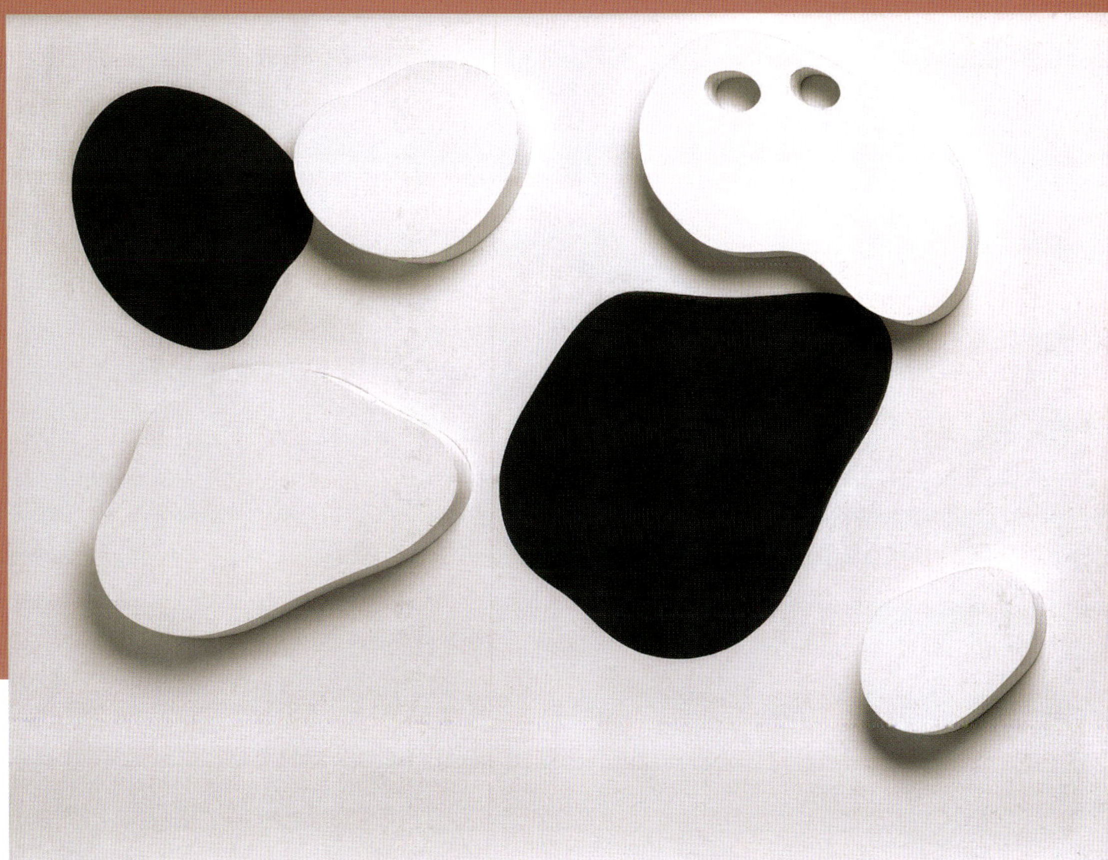

Jean Arp
(Strasbourg 1887 - Basel 1966)

Configuration with two dangerous points
Konfiguration mit zwei gefährlichen Punkten
Samenstelling met twee gevaarlijke punten
Configuración con dos puntos peligrosos

●●

ca. 1930
69,8 x 85,1 cm / 27.5 x 33.5 in.
Philadelphia Museum of Art, Philadelphia

wood / Holz / hout / madera

Arp created his semi-organic and semi-abstract compositions starting from shapes of paper that he let fall to the ground.

Arp schuf seine halborganischen und halbabstrakten Kompositionen mit Papierformen, die er auf den Boden fallen ließ.

Arp creëerde zijn semi-organische en semi-abstracte composities op basis van papiervormen die hij op de grond liet vallen.

Arp creaba sus composiciones semi-orgánicas y semi-abstractas a partir de formas de papel que dejaba caer al suelo.

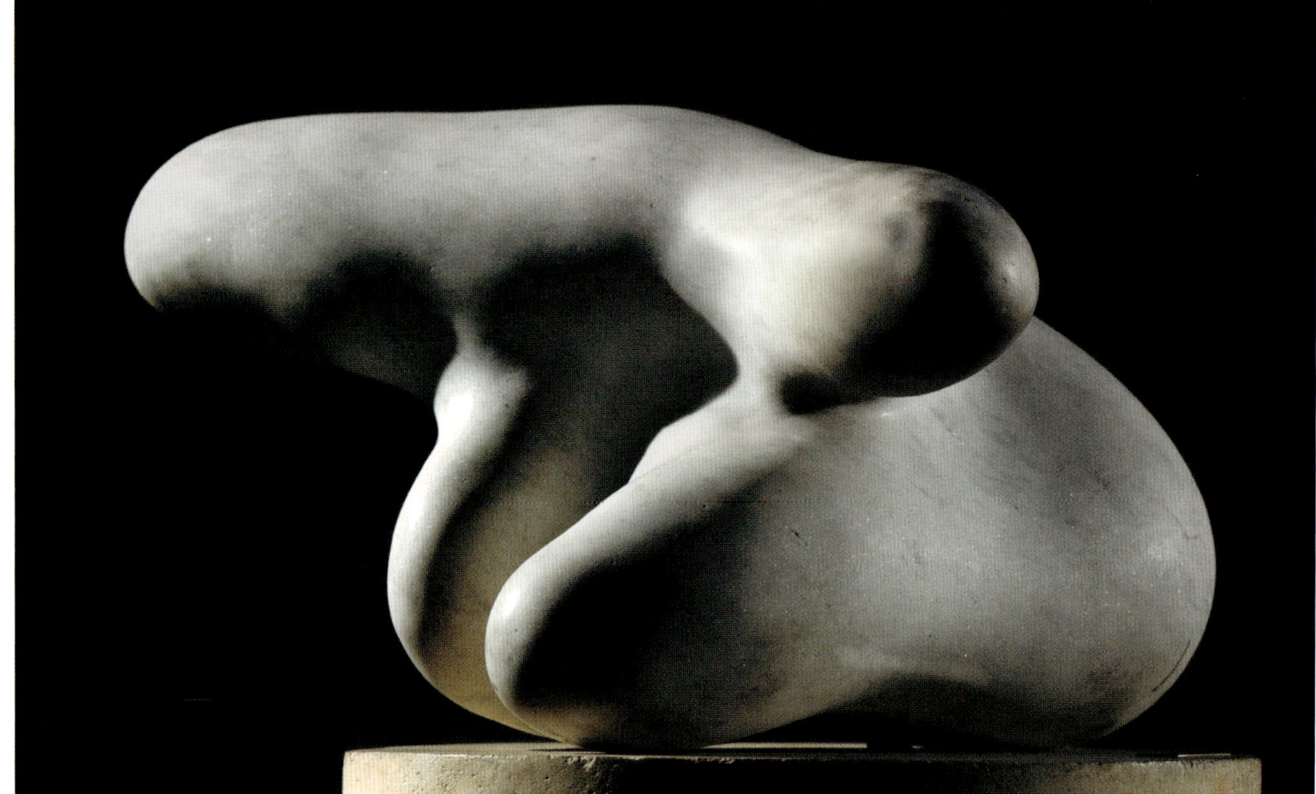

Jean Arp
(Strasbourg 1887 - Basel 1966)

Human concretion
Menschliche Konkretion
Menselijke concretie
Concreción humana

●●

1934
47 x 74 x 45,5 cm / 18.5 x 29.1 x 17.9 in.
Centre Georges Pompidou, Musée National d'Art Moderne, Paris

hollow plaster, pumice, white coating. Plaster coating
Hohle Gipsform, Bimsstein, weißer Anstrich, Gipsanstrich
holle pleister, puimsteen, witte deklaag. Pleister deklaag
yeso hueco, pulido, enduido blanco reciente. Yeso enduido

Jean Arp
(Strasbourg 1887 -
Basel 1966)

Giant seed
Pepin geant
Riesenkorn
Gigantische pit
Pepita gigante
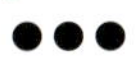
1937
162 x 125 x 77 cm
63.8 x 49.2 x 30.3 in.
Centre Georges Pompidou,
Musée National d'Art
Moderne, Paris

stone / Stein / steen / piedra

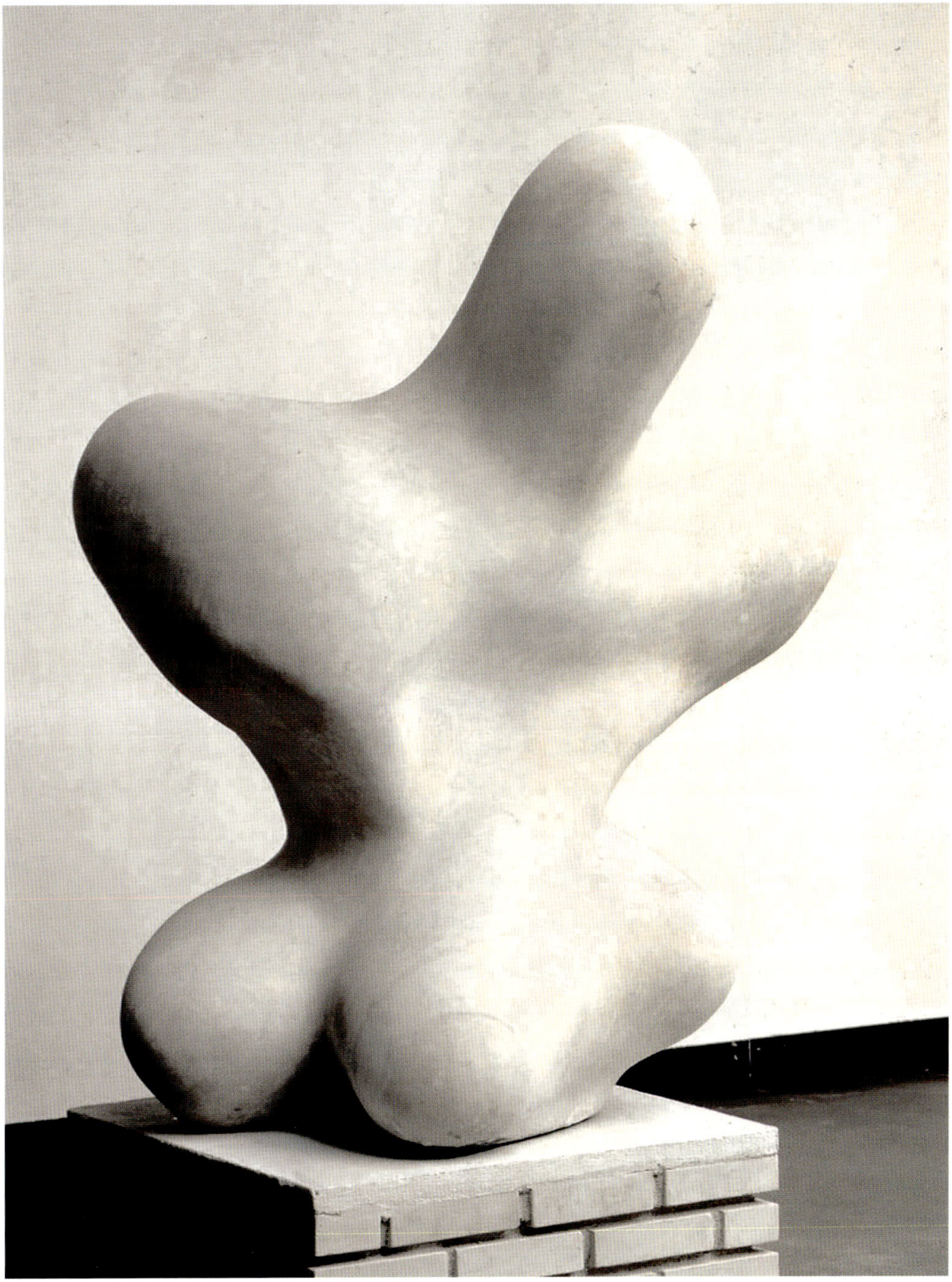

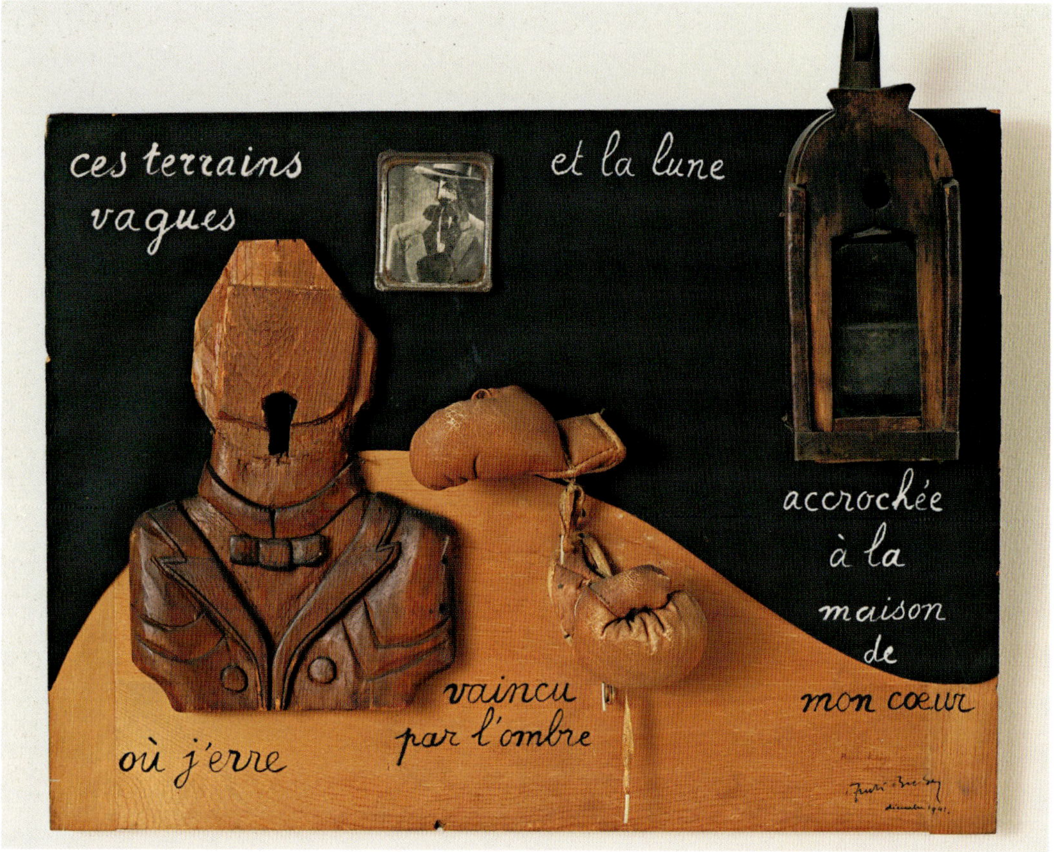

André Breton
(Tinchebray 1896 - Paris 1966)

Poetry-Object / Poesie-Gegenstand
Poëzie-Object / Poesía-objeto

●●

1941
45,8 x 53,2 x 10,9 cm / 18 x 20.9 x 4.3 in.
Museum of Modern Art (MoMA), New York

assemblage mounted on wood drawing board: carved wood bust of man, oil lantern, framed photograph, toy boxing gloves / Montage auf einer Zeichentafel aus Holz: Männerbüste aus geschnitztem Holz, Laternenöl, gerahmte Fotografie, Spielzeugboxhandschuhe / assemblage gemonteerd op een houten tekenbord uit hout gesneden mannelijke buste, lampenolie, ingelijste foto, speelgoed boxhandschoenen / ensamblaje montado sobre pizarra de dibujo de madera: busto de hombre de madera tallado, lámpara de aceite, fotografía enmarcada, guantes de box de juguete

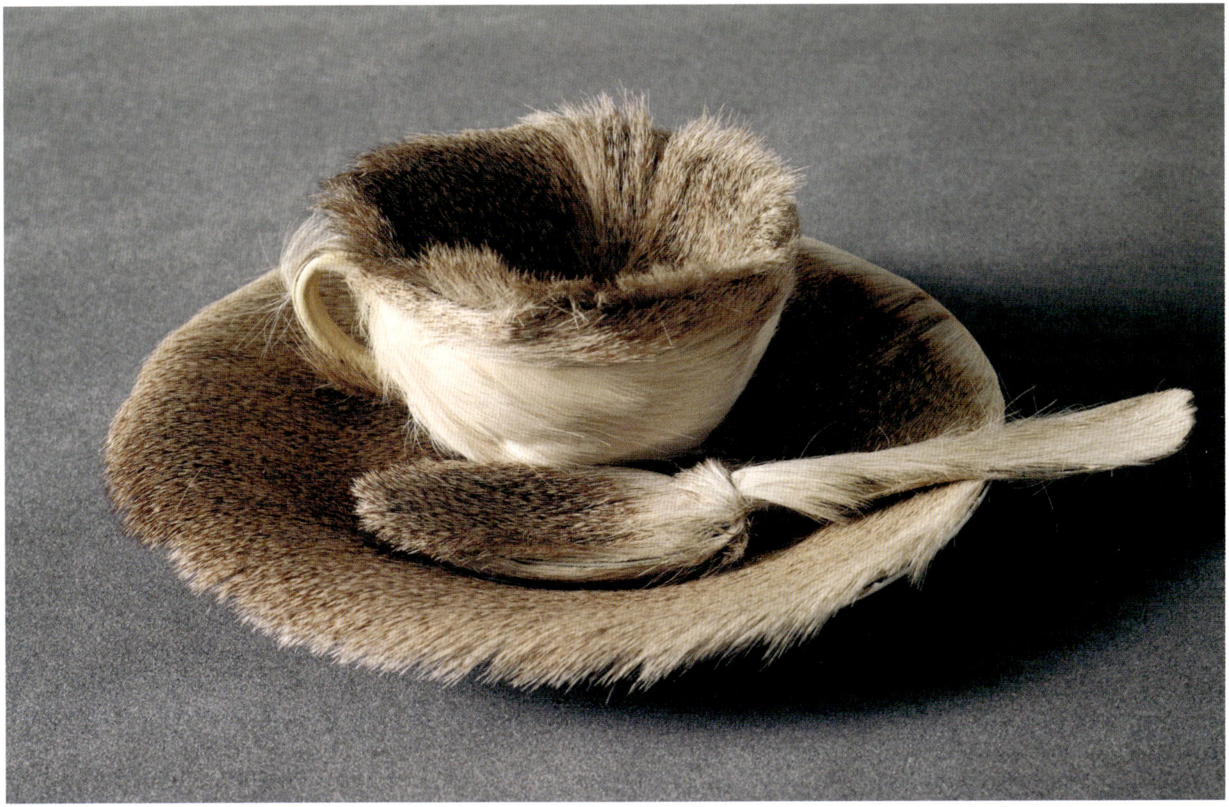

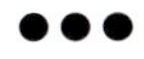

Meret Oppenheim
(Berlin 1913 - Basel 1985)

Object (Lunch in fur coat)
Objekt (Frühstück im Pelz)
Object (Het ontbijt in bontjas)
Juego de desayuno de piel

●●●

1936
h. 7,3 cm / 2.8 in.
Museum of Modern Art (MoMA), New York

cup, plate and spoon covered in fur
Tasse, Teller und Löffel, mit Pelz eingehüllt
kopje, bord en lepel met bont bekleed
taza, plato y cuchara revestidos de piel

Unexpected, incongruous, this estrangement of object causes the viewer to have strange associations of ideas.

Überraschend, unangebracht, diese Objektentfremdung ruft beim Betrachter seltsame Assoziationen von Ideen hervor.

Onverwacht, ontoereikend, de vervreemding van dit voorwerp veroorzaakt in de toeschouwer vreemde ideeënassociaties.

Inesperado, incoherente, este extrañamiento del objeto provoca en el espectador insólitas asociaciones de ideas.

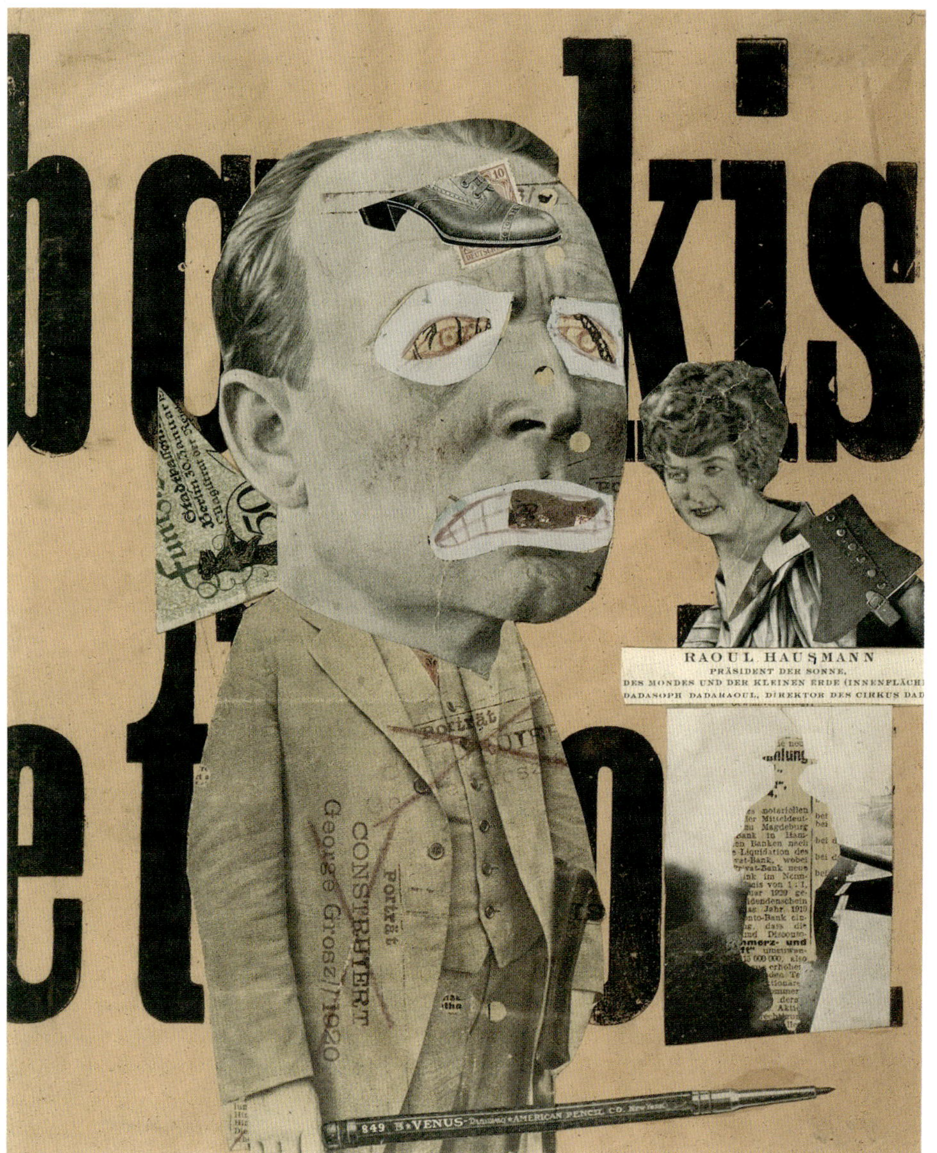

Raoul Hausmann
(Wien 1886 - Limoges 1971)

The art critic
Der Kunstkritiker
De kunstcriticus
El crítico de arte

●●●

1919
31,8 x 25,4 cm / 12.5 x 10 in.
Tate Gallery, London

collage / Collage

Fierce portrait of the art critic: armed with a pointed pen, a blind look, a banknote stuck in his collar, is he still capable of judging a work?

Erbarmungsloses Porträt eines Kunstkritikers: bewaffnet mit einer spitzen Feder, einem blinden Blick und einer Banknote am Kragen fragt sich nur, ob er noch in der Lage ist, ein Werk zu beurteilen?

Wreed portret van de kunstcriticus: gewapend met een pen, blik op oneindig en met een bankbiljet in zijn kraag, zou hij nog in staat zijn een werk te beoordelen?

Retrato feroz del crítico de arte: armado con un bolígrafo puntiagudo, la mirada ciega y un billete ensartado en el cuello, ¿es aún capaz de juzgar una obra?

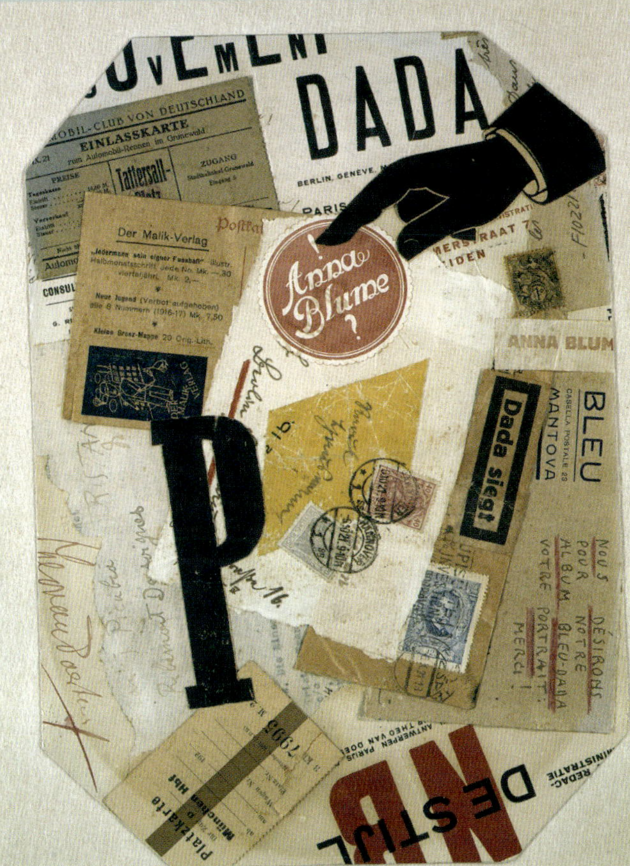

Raoul Hausmann
(Wien 1886 - Limoges 1971)

P'

●

1921
Hamburger Kunsthalle, Hamburg

collage / Collage

Raoul Hausmann
(Wien 1886 - Limoges 1971)

Conrad Felixmueller as mechanical head
Conrad Felixmüller als mechanischer Kopf
Conrad Felixmueller als mechanisch hoofd
Conrad Felixmueller como cabeza mecánica

●●

37 x 34,6 cm / 14.5 x 13.6 in.
Kupferstichkabinett, Staatliche Museen, Berlin

pencil / Bleistift / potlood / lápiz

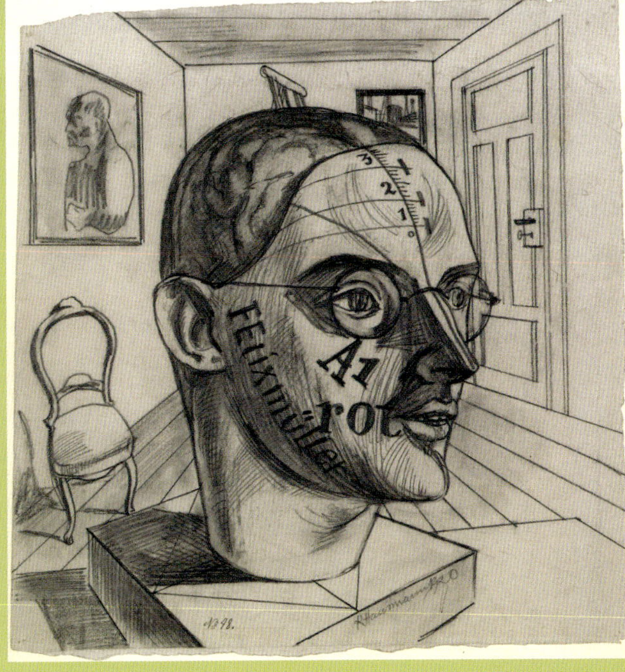

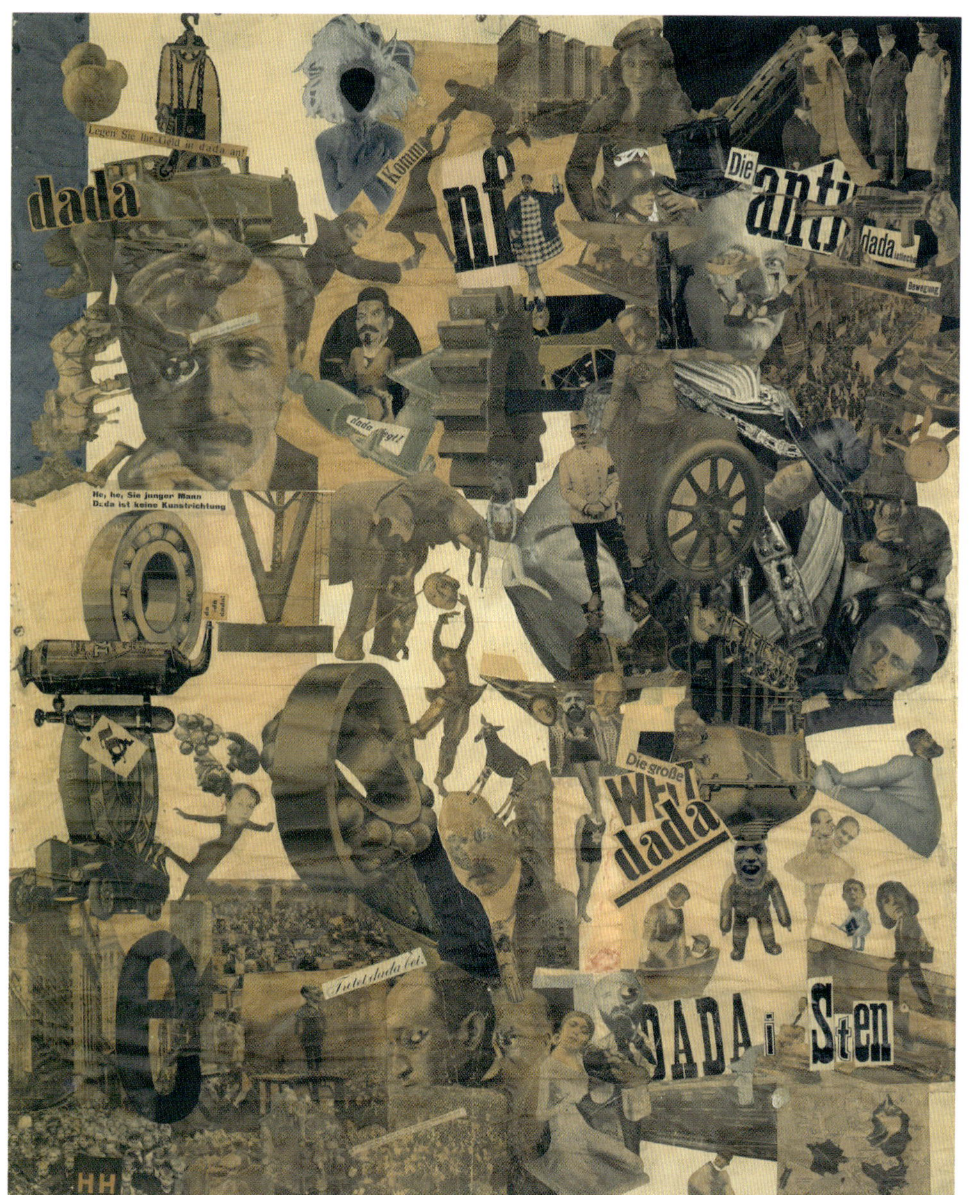

Hannah Hoech
(Gotha 1889 - Berlin 1978)

**Cut with the kitchen
knife Dada through
the last cultural "fat" era
of Weimar in Germany
Schnitt mit dem
Küchenmesser.
Dada während
der letzten Weimarer
Bierbauchkulturepoche
Gesneden met een
Dada-keukenmes door
de laatste Weimar
bierbuikige cultuurperiode
in Duitsland
Corte con el cuchillo
de cocina Dada
a través de la última epoca
cultural 'gorda'
de Weimar en Alemania**

●●

1919
114 x 90 cm / 44.9 x 35.4 in.
Nationalgalerie,
Staatliche Museen, Berlin

collage / Collage

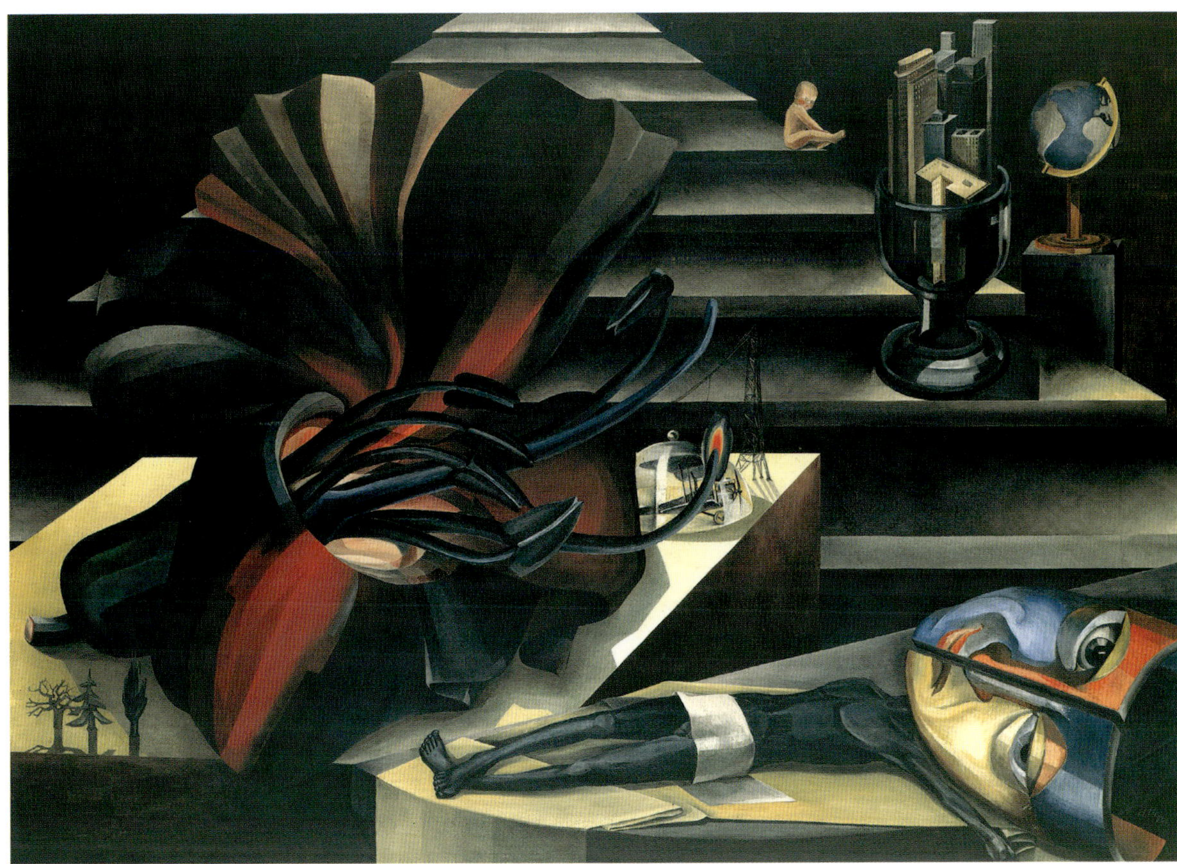

Hannah Hoech
(Gotha 1889 - Berlin 1978)

The staircas
Die Treppe
De trap
La escalinata

●

1923-1926
77 x 106 cm / 30.3 x 41.7 in.
Nationalgalerie,
Staatliche Museen, Berlin

oil on canvas / Öl auf Leinwand
olieverf op doek / óleo sobre lienzo

Rare female exponent of the Dada Avant-Garde movement, Hannah Hoech uses collage and photomontage as tools of social and political criticism.

Als seltene, weibliche Vertreterin der dadaistischen Avantgarde-Bewegung verwendet Hanna Hoech die Collage und die Fotomontage als Instrumente der gesellschaftlichen und politischen Kritik.

Hannah Hoech, zeldzame vrouwelijke vertegenwoordigster van de avant-gardistische dada-beweging, gebruikt collages en fotomontages om kritiek te leveren op maatschappij en politiek.

Rara exponente femenina del movimiento de vanguardia Dadá, Hannah Hoech utiliza el collage y el fotomontaje como herramientas de crítica social y política.

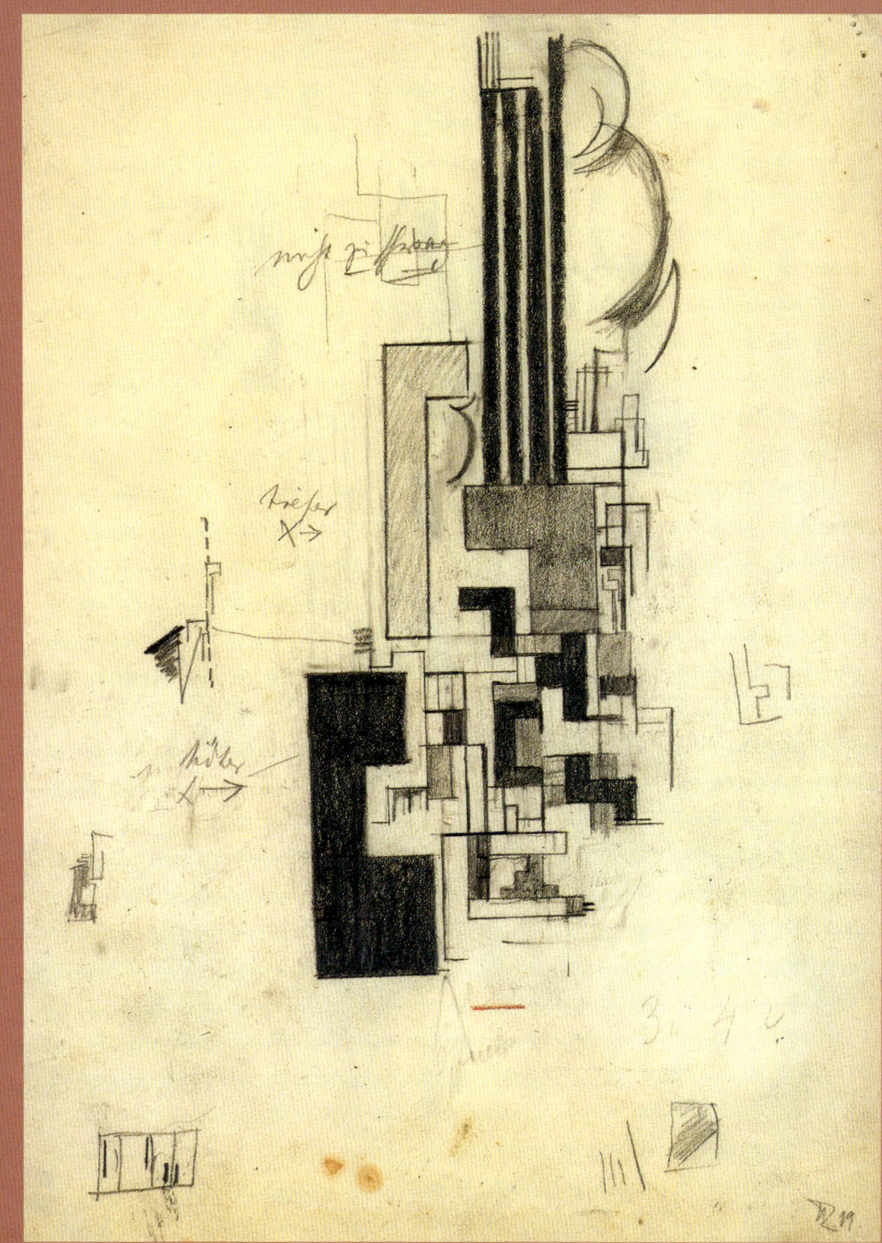

Hans Richter
(Berlin 1888 - Minusio, Schweiz 1976)
Study for "Praeludium"
Studie für "Praeludium"
Studie voor "Praeludium"
Estudio para "Preludio"
●
32,5 x 22,5 cm / 12.8 x 8.8 in.
Kupferstichkabinett, Staatliche Museen,
Berlin

pencil / Bleistift / potlood / lápiz

J.T. Baargeld
(Stettin 1892 -
Mont Blanc 1927)
Beetles
Käfer
Kevers
Sin título
(Escarabajos)

●

1920
29,2 x 23,2 cm
11.5 x 9.1 in.
Museum of Modern Art
(MoMA), New York

pen and ink on tissue paper
Feder und Tinte auf
Papiertaschentuch
pen en inkt op een papieren
zakdoekje
pluma y tinta sobre papel
de seda

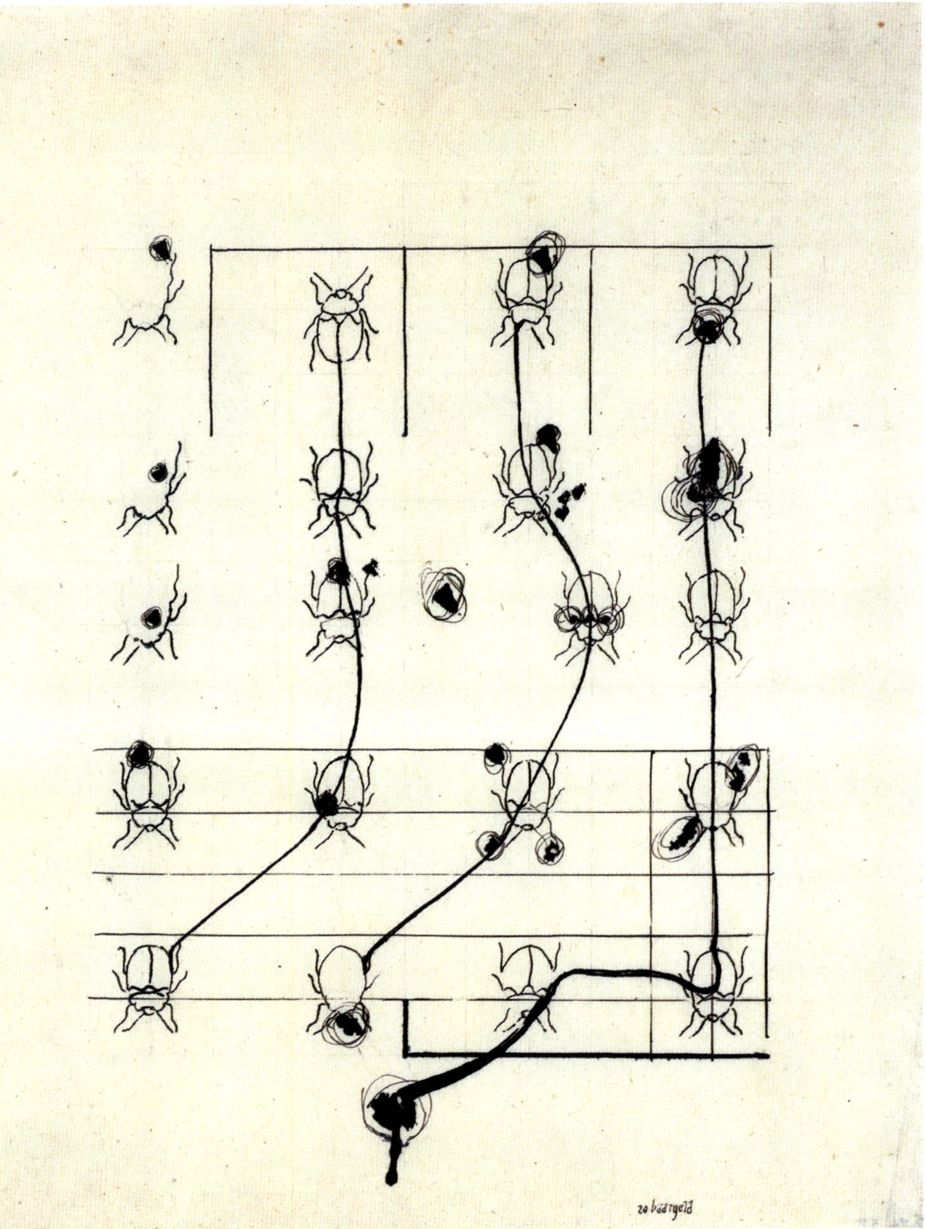

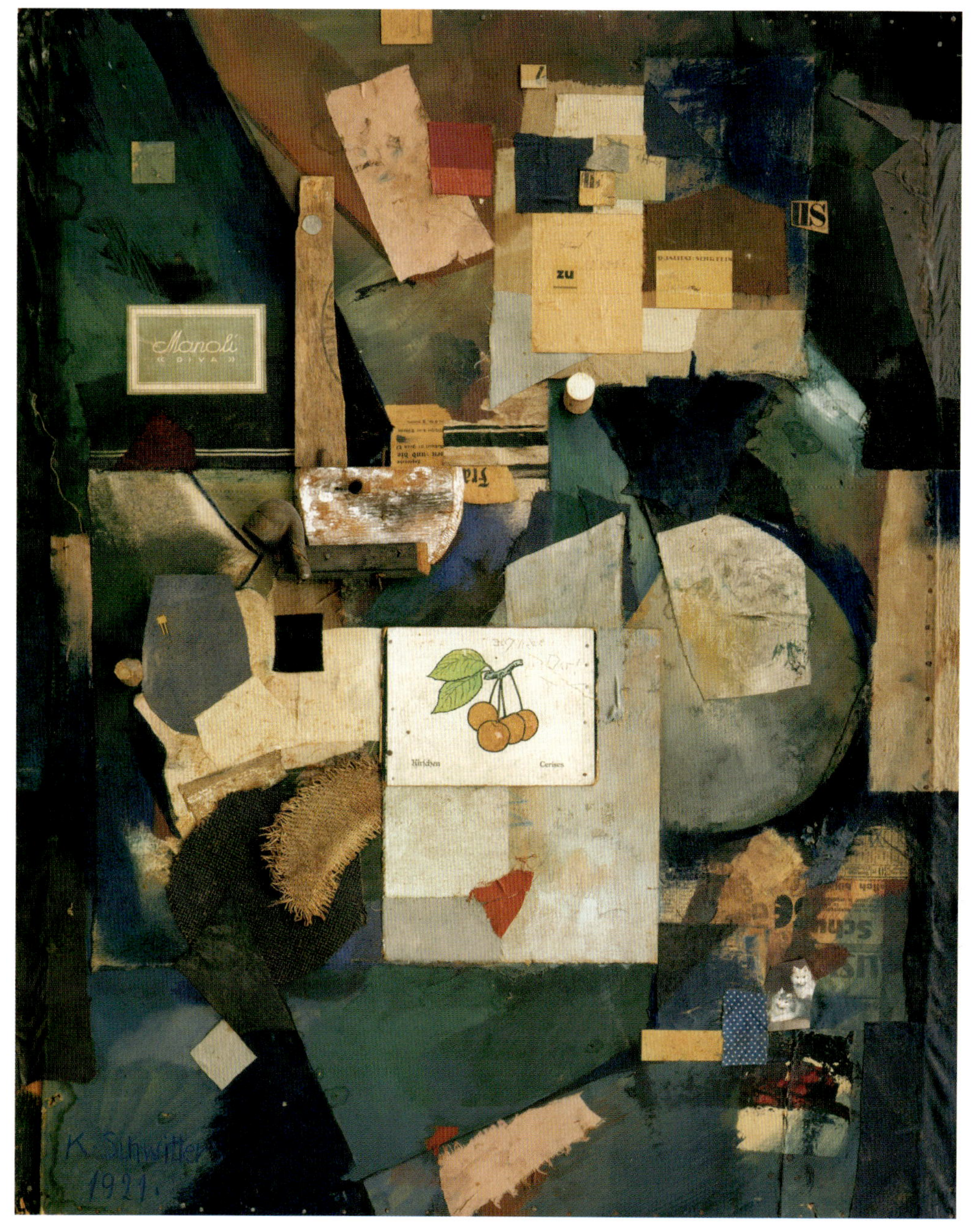

In his compositions *Merz*
Schwitters accumulates
discarded objects, paper
and various elements thus
pretending to make
the real enter Art.

In seinen *Merz-*
Kompositionen verarbeitet
Schwitters aussondierte
Gegenstände, Papier
sowie verschiedene andere
Elemente mit der Absicht,
die Wirklichkeit in die
Kunst einzuführen.

Schwitters verzamelt in
zijn composities rommel,
papier en verschillende
elementen en wil op deze
manier de realiteit
in de Kunst opnemen.

En sus composiciones
Merz Schwitters acumula
objetos de desecho,
papel y elementos varios,
pretendiendo así dar
cabida a lo real en el arte.

▶ **Kurt Schwitters**
(Hannover 1887 - Ambleside 1948)

Small columns (Kleine Saeule)
Kleine Säulen
Kleine zuilen
Pequeñas columnas (Kleine
Saeule)

●

ca. 1922
23 x 22 x 16 cm / 9 x 8.6 x 6.3 in.
Nationalgalerie, Staatliche Museen, Berlin

painted wood / Holz dipinto
beschilderd hout / madera pintada

◀ **Kurt Schwitters**
(Hannover 1887 - Ambleside 1948)

Merz 32 A.
Painting with cherries
Das Kirschenbild
Schilderij met kersen
Cuadro de las cerezas

●●

1921
91,8 x 70,5 cm / 36.1 x 27.7 in.
Museum of Modern Art (MoMA),
New York

collage of fabric, wood, metal, gouache, oil,
cut and glued on paper
Collage aus Stoff, Holz, Metall, Gouache
und Ölmalerei auf Papier geklebt
collage van uitgeknipt en op papier
geplakte stof, hout, metaal en goauche
collage de tela, madera, metal, gouache,
óleo, cortados y pegados sobre papel

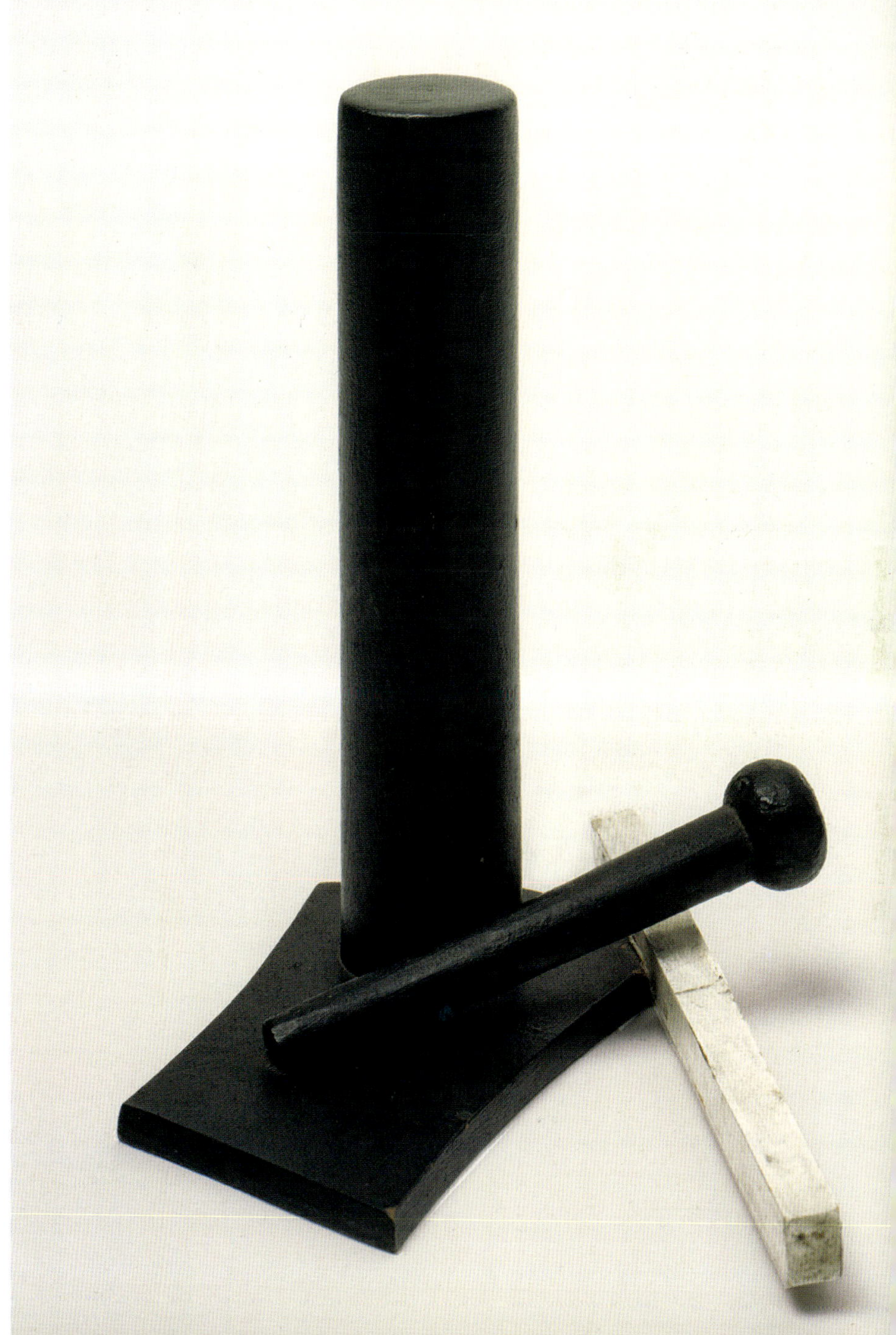

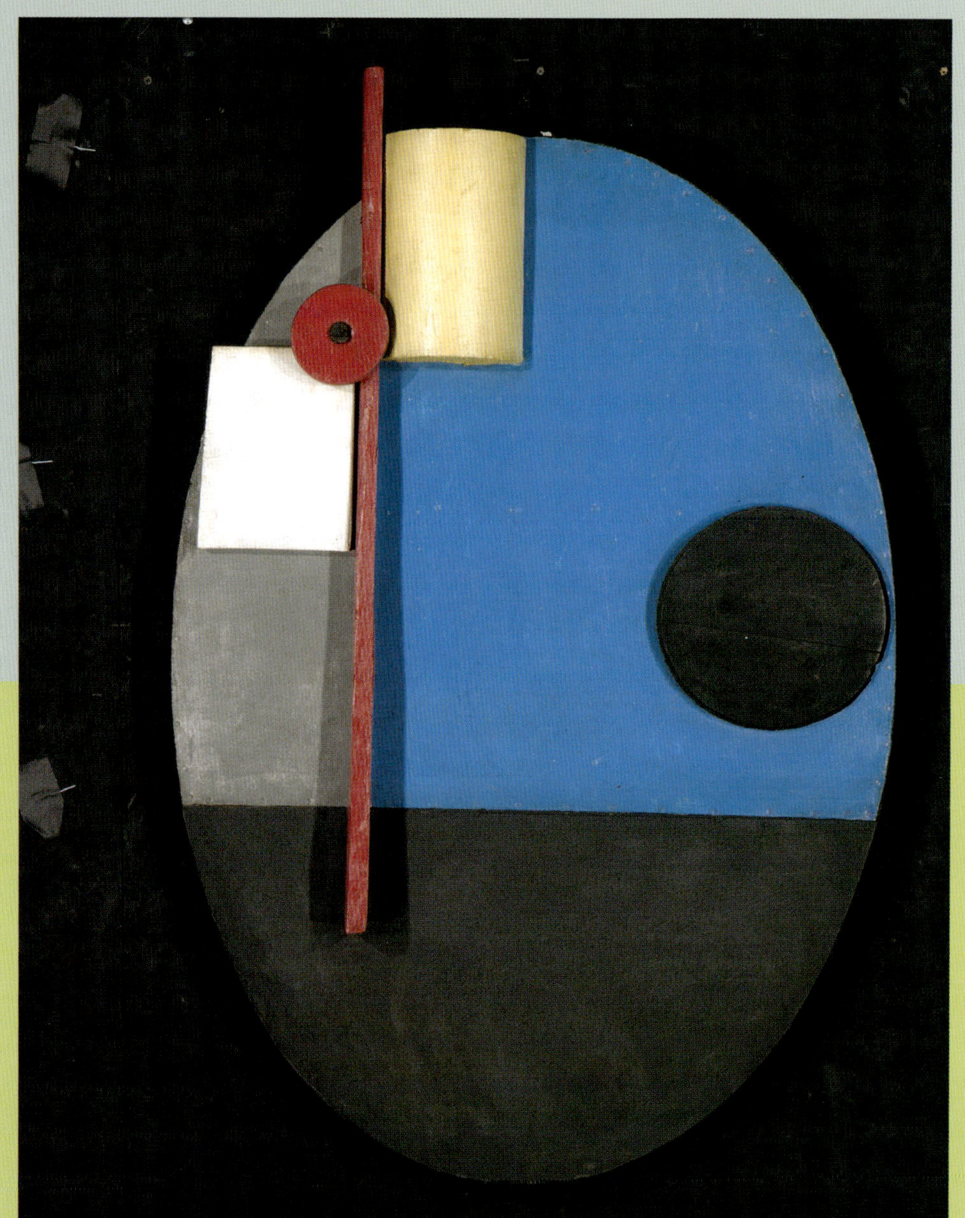

Kurt Schwitters
(Hannover 1887 - Ambleside 1948)

Oval Construction
Ovale Konstruktion
Ovale constructie
Construcción oval

●

1925
116,5 x 75 x 13,6 cm
45.8 x 29.5 x 5.3 in.
Yale University Art Gallery,
New Haven (CT)

Wood, plywood, nails, and paint
Holz, Sperrholz, Nägel, Malerei
hout, multiplex, spijkers en verf
madera, aglomerado, clavos, pintura

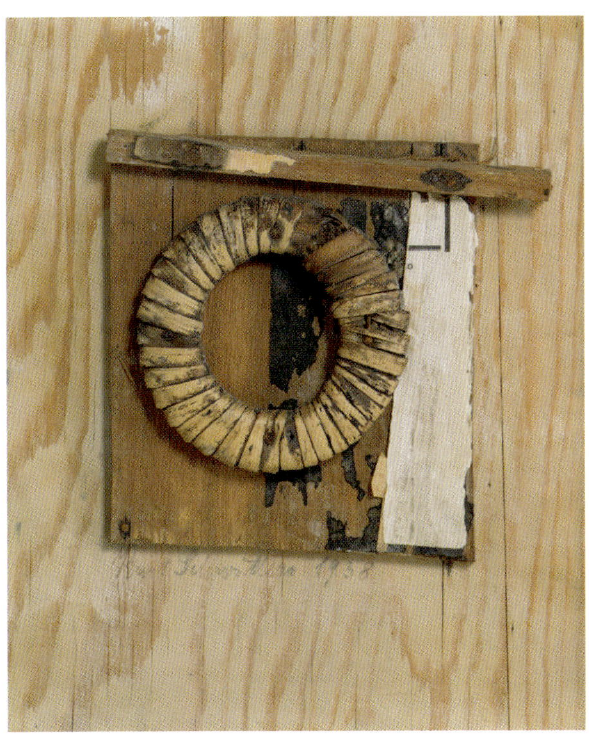

Kurt Schwitters

(Hannover 1887 - Ambleside 1948)

Painting with basket
Bild mit Korbring
Schilderij met korf
Cuadro con anillo de canasto

● ●

1938
38,1 x 29,8 cm / 15 x 11.7 in.
Museum of Modern Art (MoMA), New York

assemblage: wood, rattan ring, paper, iron and steel nails on wood
Montage: Holz, Rattanringe, Papier, Eisen, Stahl, Haken auf Holz
assemblage: hout, rotan ringen, papier, ijzer, staal, spijkers op hout
ensamblaje: madera, anillo de ratán, papel, hierro, acero, clavos de acero
sobre madera

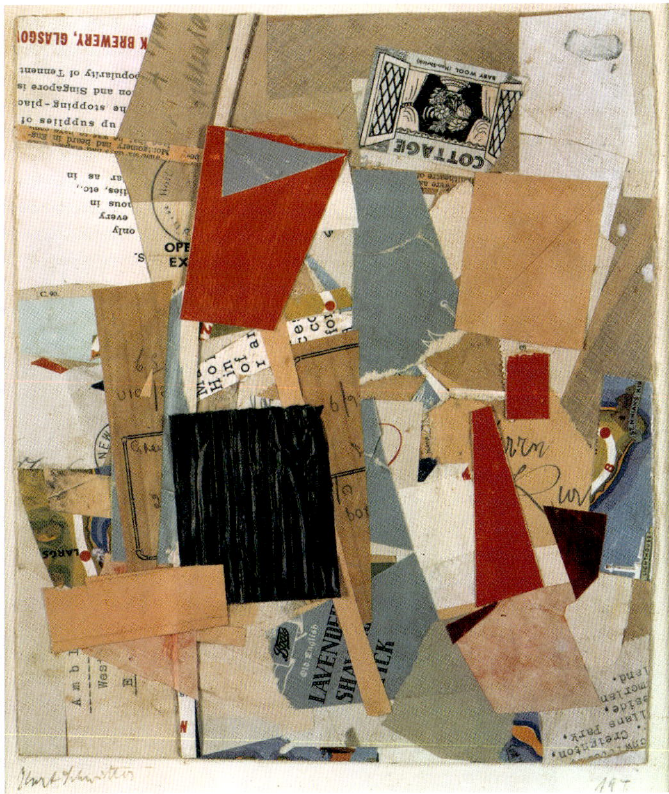

303

Kurt Schwitters

(Hannover 1887 - Ambleside 1948)

Cottage

●

1946
25,5 x 21,2 cm / 10 x 8.3 in.
Nationalgalerie, Staatliche Museen, Berlin

collage / Collage

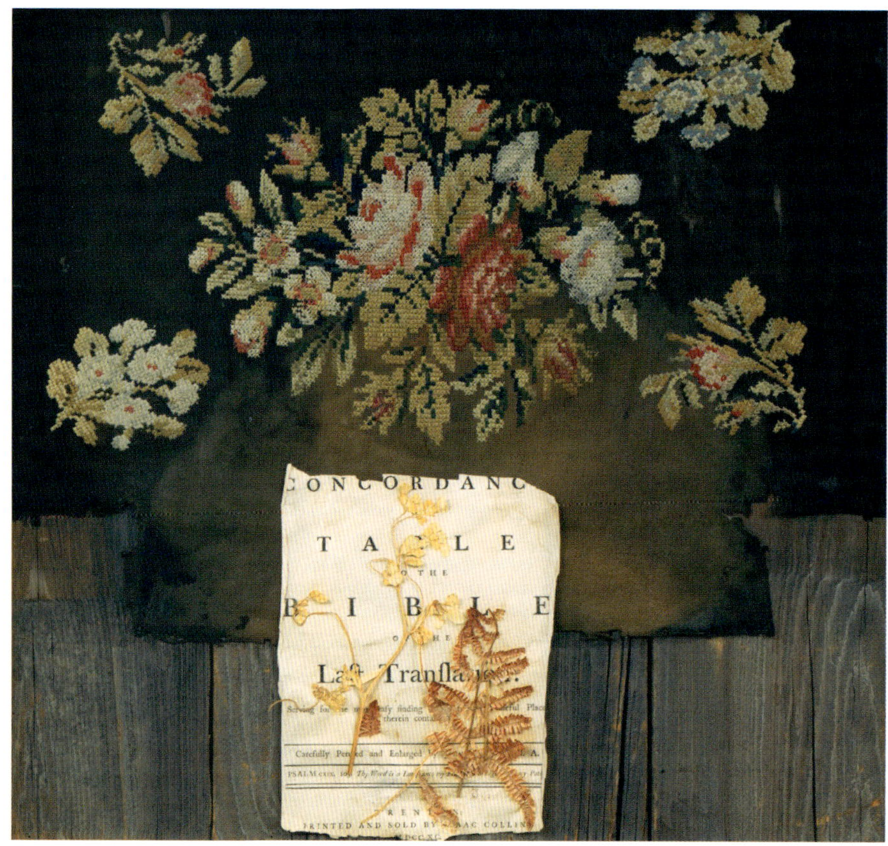

304

Arthur G. Dove
(Canandaigua, New York 1880 - Huntingdon, New York 1946)

Grandmother / Großmutter
Oma / Abuela

●

1925
50,8 x 54 cm / 20 x 21.2 in.
Museum of Modern Art (MoMA), New York

collage of shingles, needlepoint, page from the Concordance, pressed flowers, and ferns, mounted on cloth-covered wood / Collage aus Kies, Häkelarbeit, einer Seite aus der "Concordance", gepressten Blumen, Farn, auf bezogenem Holz montiert / collage van grind, haakwerk, pagina uit de "Concordance", gedroogde bloemen, varens, gemonteerd op met stof bekleed hout / collage de grava, trabajo de ganchillo, página del "Concordance", flores prensadas, helechos, montados sobre madera forrada en tela

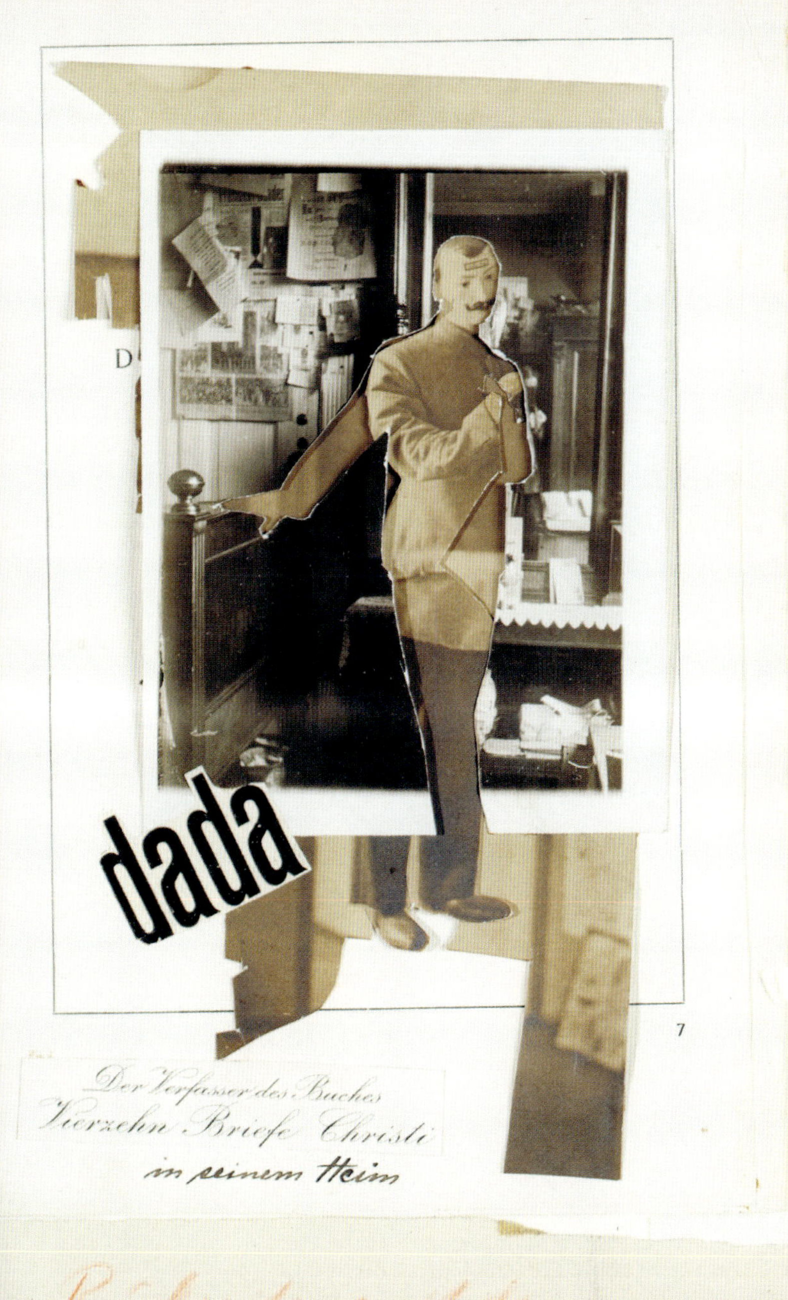

Dada is more than an artistic movement
that unhinges conventions, it is a shout
of revolt against a failed society

Dada ist mehr als eine künstlerische
Bewegung, die Konventionen überwirft.
Es ist ein Schrei der Revolte gegen eine
Gesellschaft, die im Scheitern begriffen ist.

Dada is meer dan een kunstbeweging
die de conventies uit zijn scharnieren rukt,
de beweging is een opstandige kreet tegen
een falende maatschappij.

Dadá es más que un movimiento artístico
que desquicia las convenciones, es un grito de
rebelión contra una sociedad en decadencia.

Johannes Baader
(Stuttgart 1876 - Adldorf 1955)

**The author of the book
"Fourteen Letters of Christ"
in his house
Der Autor des Buches
"Vierzehn Briefe Christi"
in seinem Haus
De schrijver van het boek
"Veertien brieven van Christus"
in zijn huis
El autor del libro
"Catorce cartas de Cristo" en su casa**

●

ca. 1920
21,6 x 14,6 cm / 8.5 x 5.7 in.
Museum of Modern Art (MoMA),
New York

collage of pasted photographs on book page
Collage aus Fotografien, auf einer Buchseite geklebt
collage van op boekpagina geplakte foto's
collage de fotografías pegadas sobre una
página de libro

John Heartfield
(Berlin 1891 - 1968)

**"Hurrah,
butter is everything!"**
**"Hurrah,
die Butter ist alle!"**
**"Hoera,
boter is het helemaal!"**
**"¡Hurra,
la mantequilla es todo!"**

●●

1935

photomontage / Fotomontage
fotomontage / fotomontaje

306

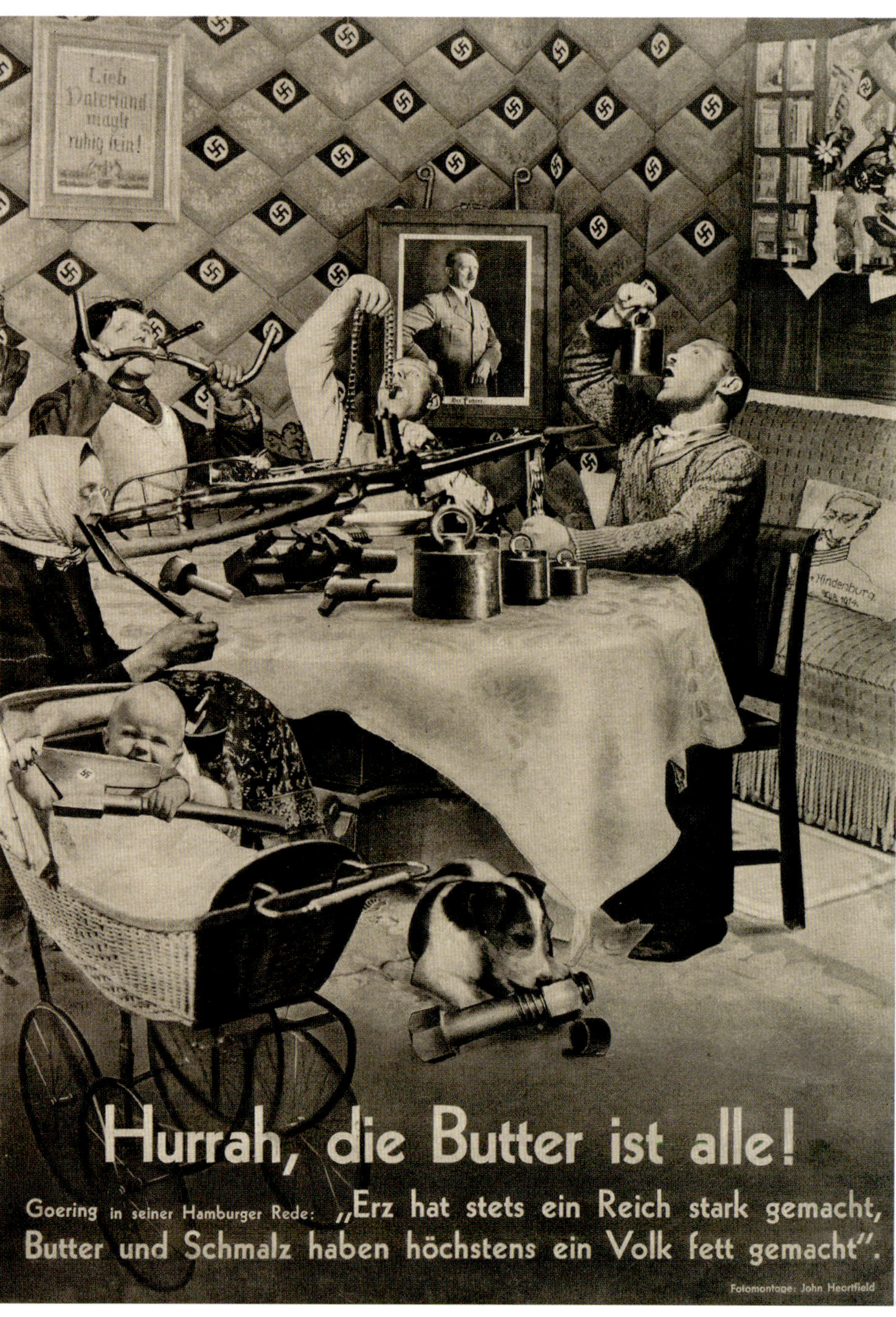

Tristan Tzara
(Moineşti 1896 - Paris 1963)

Portrait of Tristan Tzara
Porträt von Tristan Tzara
Portret van Tristan Tzara
Retrato de Tristan Tzara

●●

1928
Collezione Schwarz, Milano

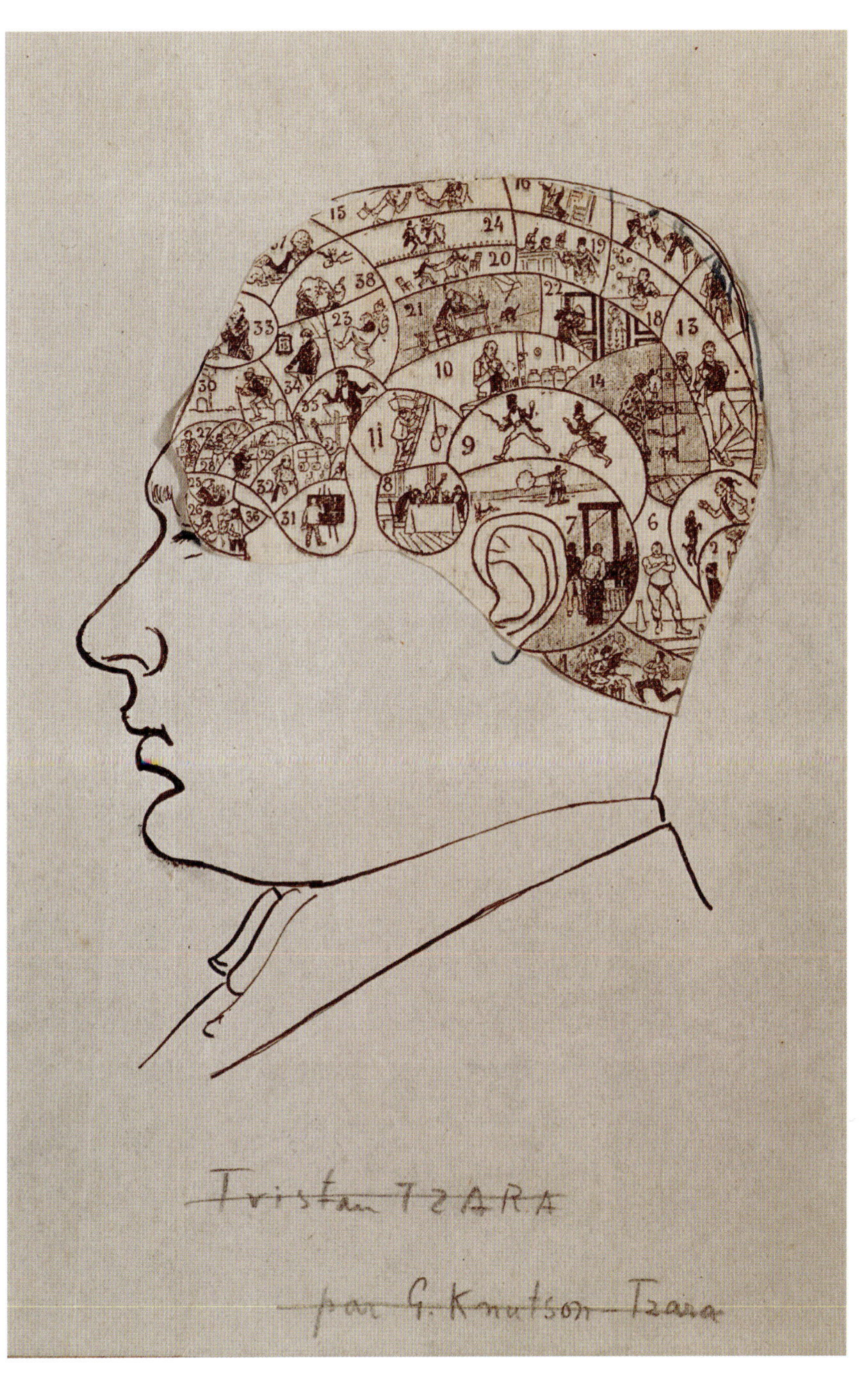

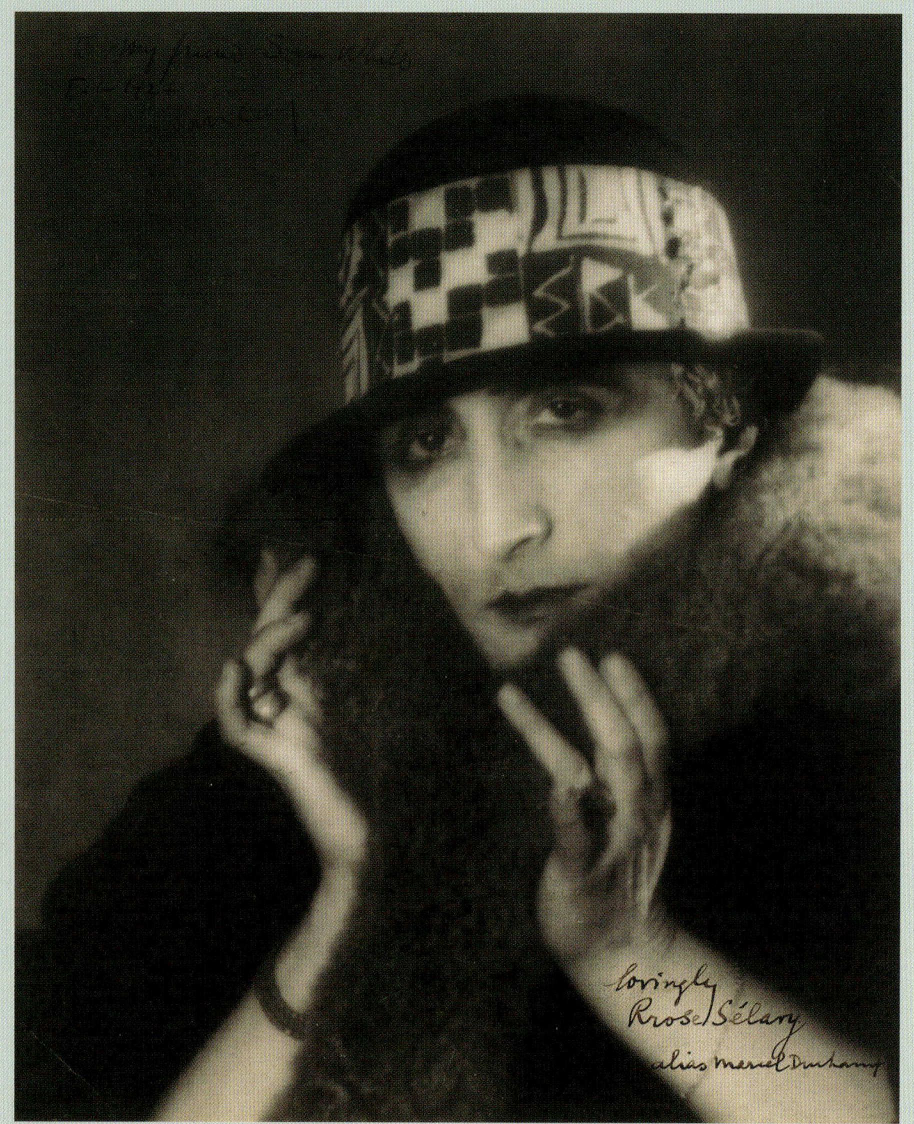

308

Man Ray
(Philadelphia 1890 - Paris 1976)

**Marcel Duchamp
as Rrose Selavy
Marcel Duchamp
als Rrose Selavy
Marcel Duchamp
als Rrose Selavy
Marcel Duchamp
como Rrose Selavy**

●●●

1920-1921
21,6 x 17,3 cm / 48.5 x 6.8 in.
Philadelphia Museum of Art,
Philadelphia

print with salts of silver
Druck mit Silbersalzen
zilverzouten print
impresión por sales de plata

Marcel disguised as *femme fatale*: his
double is an ode to love since Eros
is life. From this comes the phonetic
game of the name Rrose Sélavy.

Marcel Duchamp als *Femme Fatale*
verkleidet: sein Doppel ist eine Ode
an die Liebe, da Eros das Leben ist.
Daher auch das phonetische Spiel
mit dem Namen Rrose Sélavy.

Marcel Duchamp verkleed als *femme
fatale*: het is een ode aan de liefde in
zoverre dat Eros het leven is. Vandaar
de fonetische woordspeling Rrose
Sélavy.

Marcel Duchamp vestido de mujer
fatal: su doble es una oda al amor,
en tanto que Eros es la vida. He aquí
el porqué del juego fonético del
nombre Rrose Sélavy.

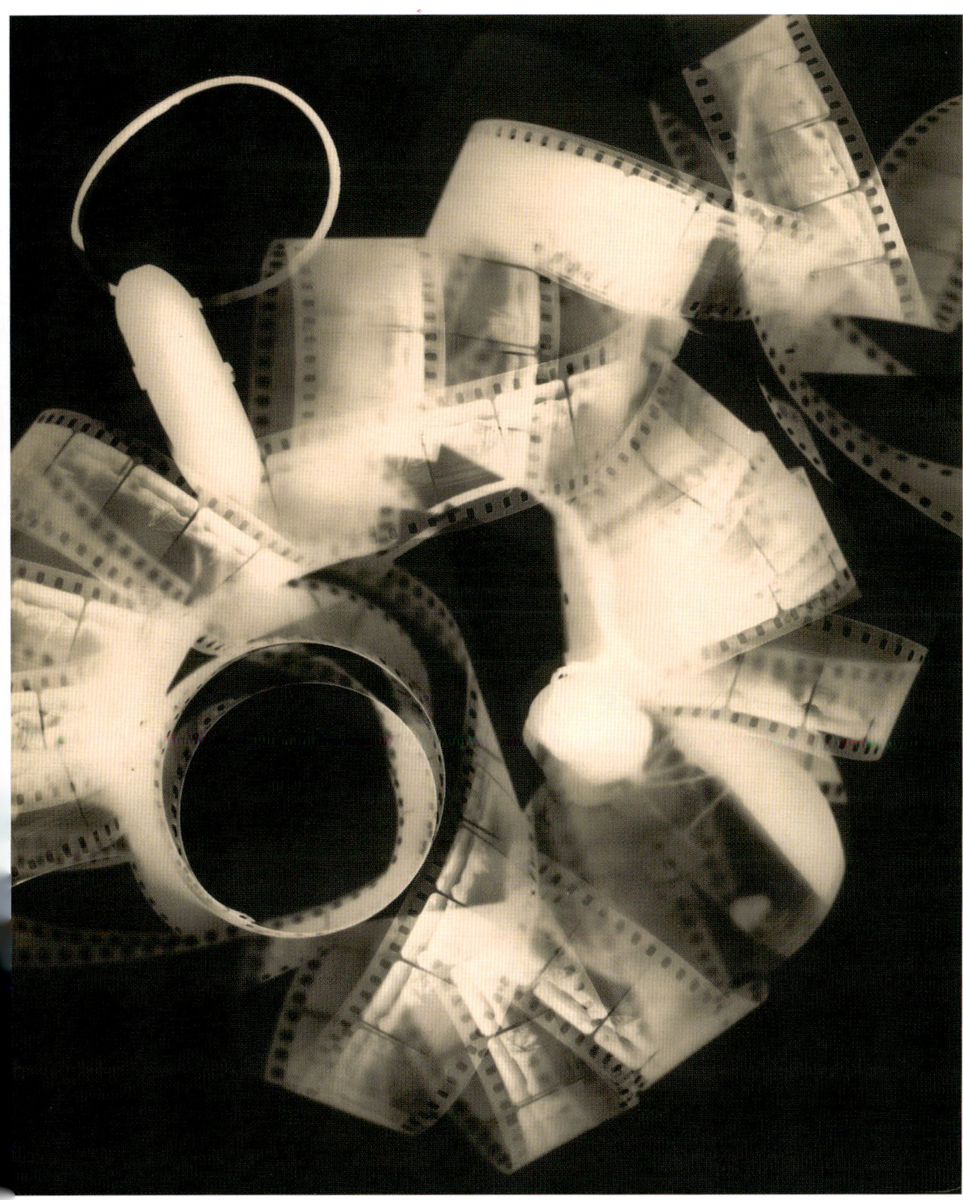

Man Ray
(Philadelphia 1890 - Paris 1976)

**Rayograph
(spirals of film)
Rayographie
(Filmspiralen)
Rayografie (filmspiralen)
Rayograma
(espirales de película)**

●●

1923
29,4 x 23,5 cm / 11.6 x 9.2 in.
Museum of Modern Art
(MoMA), New York

gelatin silver print
Silbergelatinedruck
gelatine-zilverprint
impresión en gelatina de plata

309

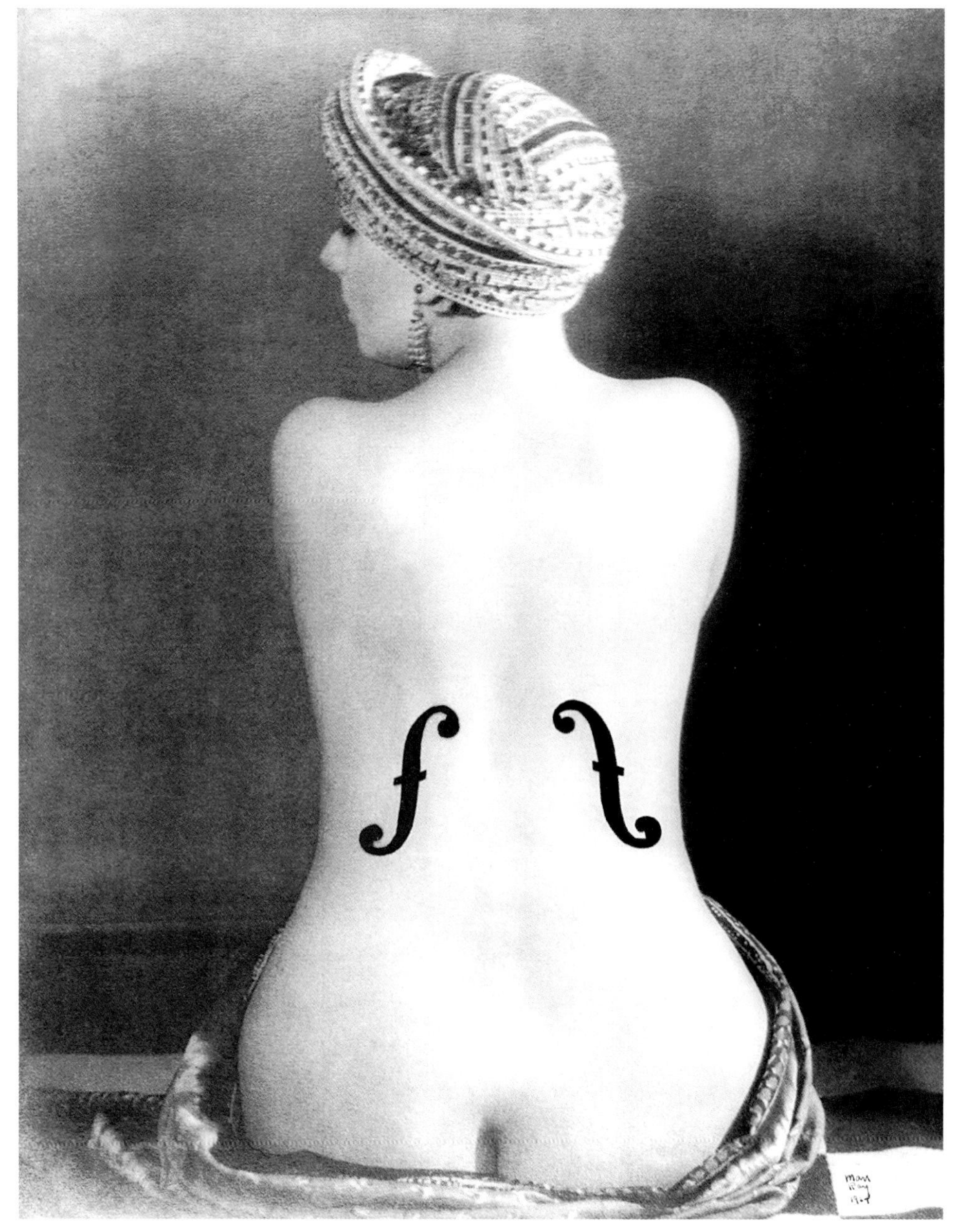

310

Game of visual and sensual balance between the famous painting by Ingres, *The Turkish Bath*, and the French expression *violon d'Ingres* which means pastime.

Ein auf visuellen und sinnlichen Doppeldeutigkeiten basierendes Spiel mit Ingres' berühmtem Gemälde *Das türkische Bad* und dem französischen Ausdruck *violon d'Ingres*, das Zeitvertreib bedeutet.

Visueel en sensueel samenspel tussen het beroemde schilderij van Ingres *Het Turkse bad* en de Franse uitdrukking *violon d'Ingres* wat hobby betekent.

Juego de correspondencias visuales y sensuales entre el célebre cuadro de Ingres *El baño turco* y la expresión francesa *violon d'Ingres* que significa pasatiempo.

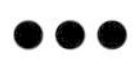

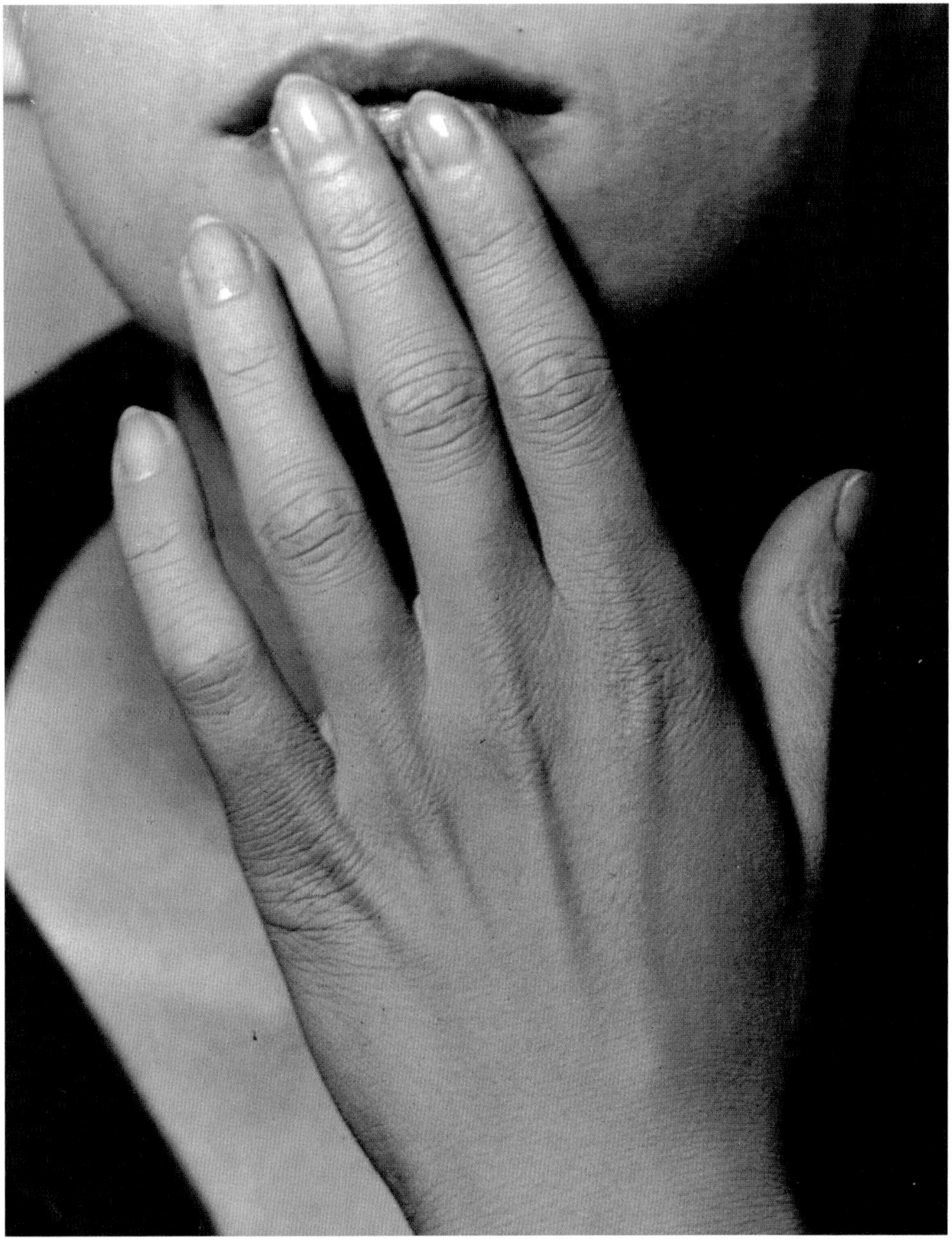

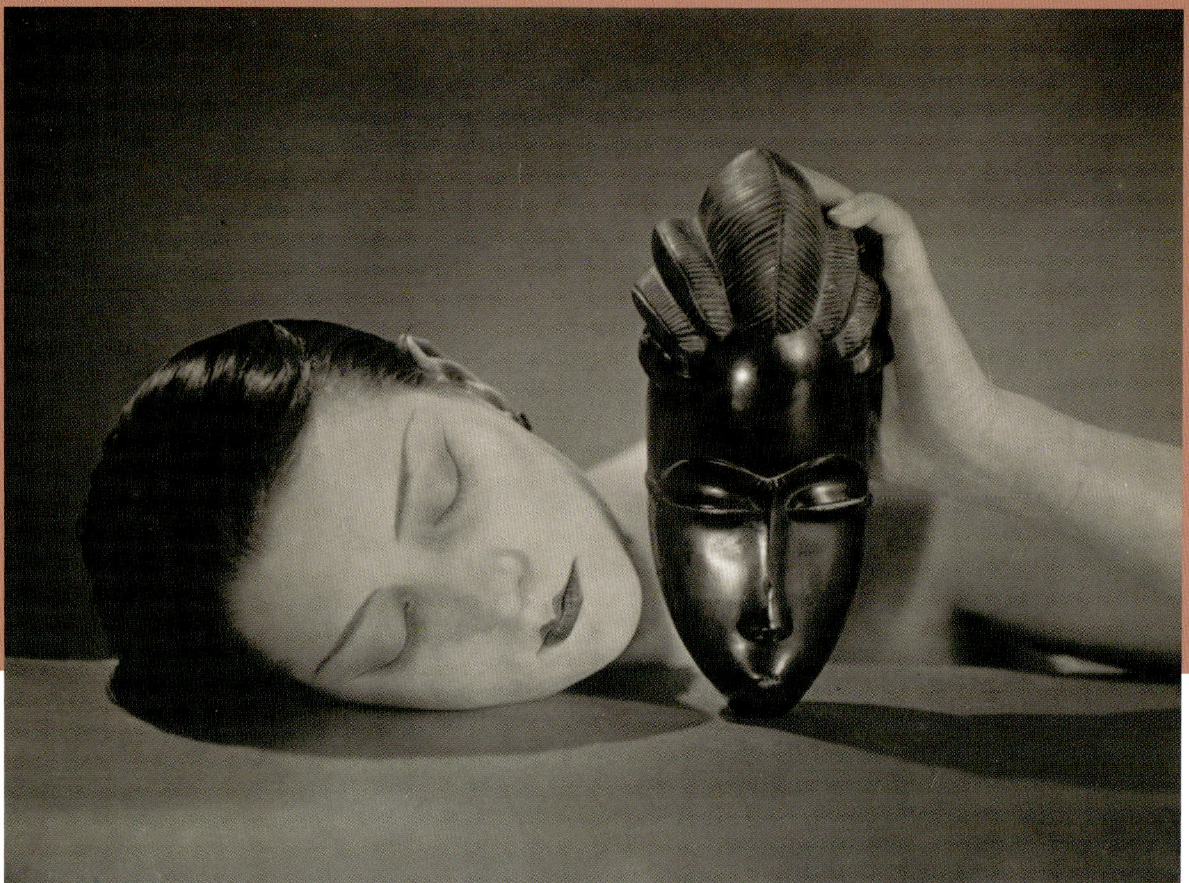

Man Ray
(Philadelphia 1890 - Paris 1976)

Black and White
Schwarz und weiß
Zwart en Wit
Negro y blanco

●●

1926
17,1 x 22,4 cm / 6.7 x 8.8 in.
Museum of Modern Art (MoMA), New York

gelatin silver print / Silbergelatinedruck
gelatine-zilverprint / impresión en gelatina de plata

▶ Man Ray
(Philadelphia 1890 - Paris 1976)

Erotique voilée

●●●

1933
Kupferstichkabinett, Staatliche Museen, Berlin

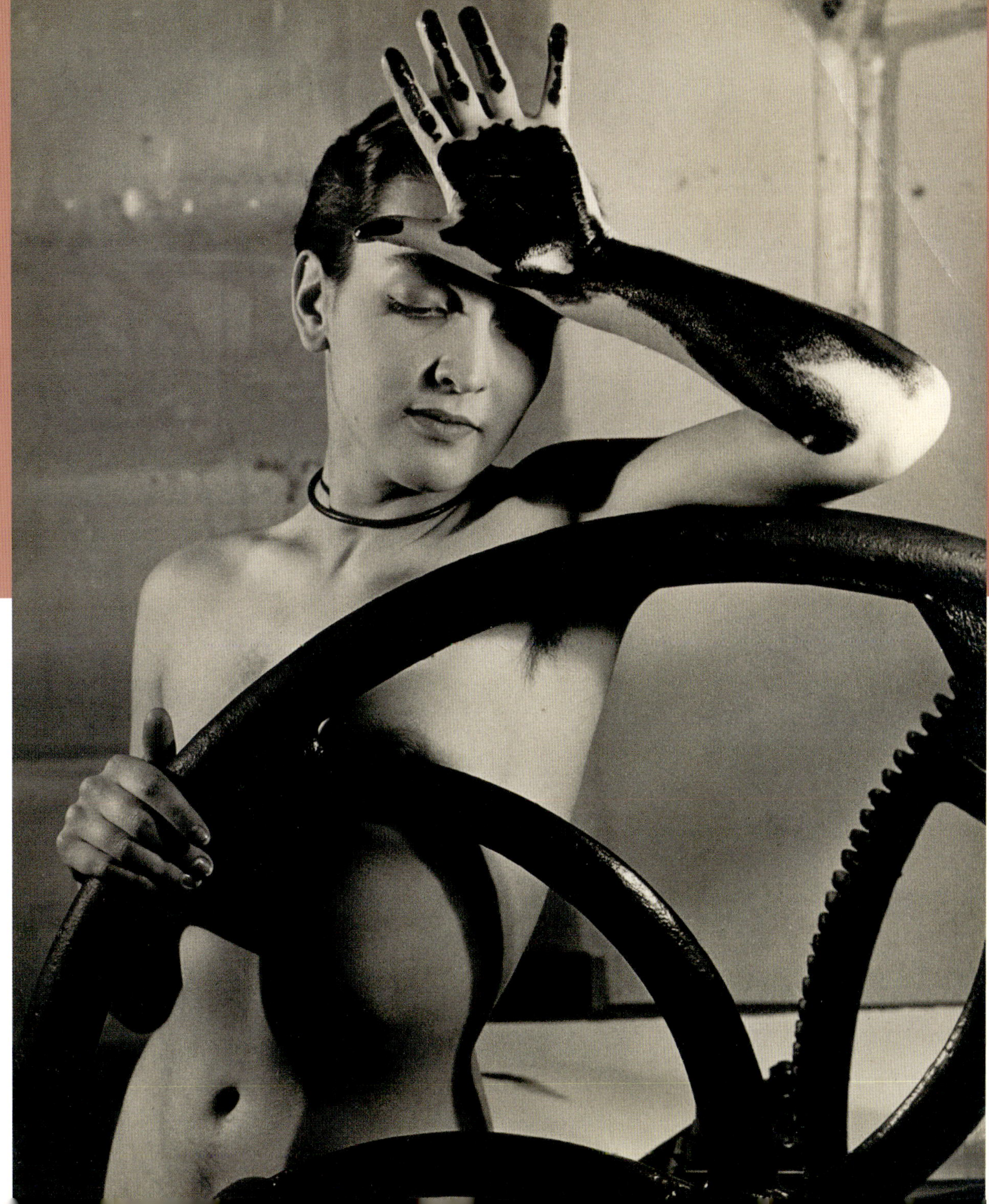

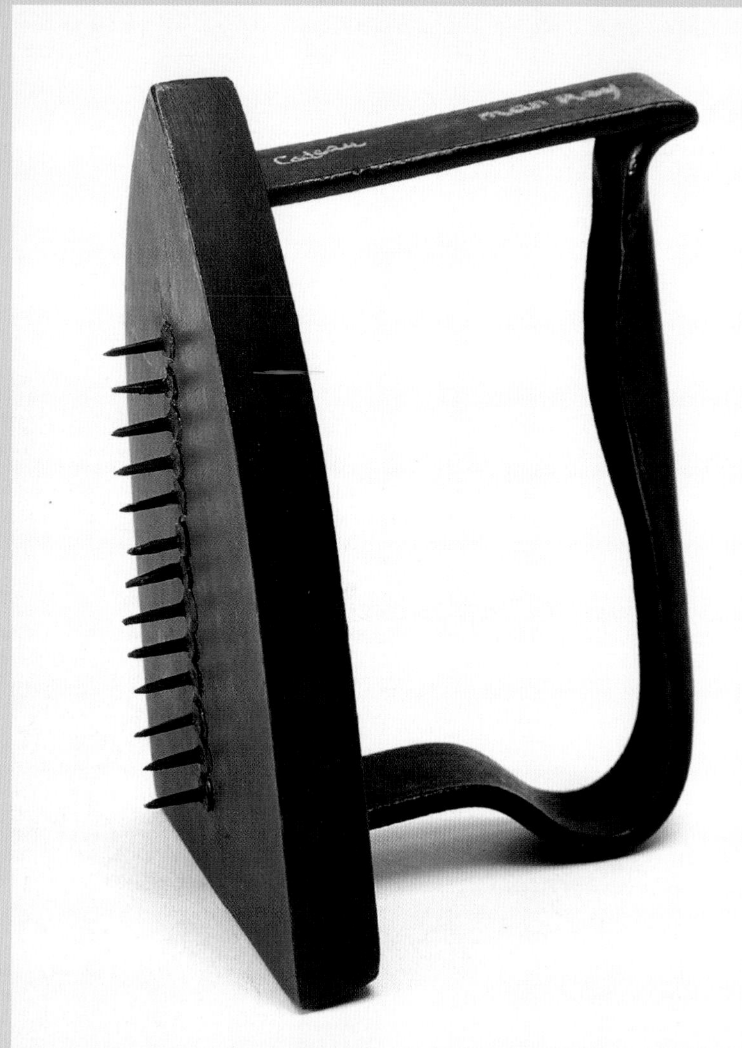

Man Ray
(Philadelphia 1890 - Paris 1976)

Gift
Geschenk
Cadeau
Regalo

●●

1921 (1958)
15,3 x 9 x 11,4 cm / 6 x 3.5 x 4.5 in.
Museum of Modern Art (MoMA), New York

iron painted with a row of thirteen nails glued
Bemaltes Bügeleisen mit einer Schnur von dreizehn
angehängten Haken / strijkijzer beschilderd met een
rij van 13 opgeplakte spijkers / plancha pintada con
una fila de trece clavos encolados

**Surprising gift which questions and challenges
the viewer with the unsettling strangeness of the
surrealist objects, whose function is more symbolic
than concrete.**

**Ein verrücktes Geschenk aus seltsamen
surrealistischen Objekten, die eher eine
symbolische als konkrete Funktion besitzen und
den Betrachter zu Fragen anregen.**

**Verbluffend cadeau waarvan de verontrustende
eigenaardigheid van deze surrealistische objecten,
die meer symbolisch dan concreet zijn, de
toeschouwer aan het denken zet.**

**Asombroso regalo donde la inquietante extrañeza
de estos objetos surrealistas, de funcionamiento
más simbólico que concreto, interroga al
espectador.**

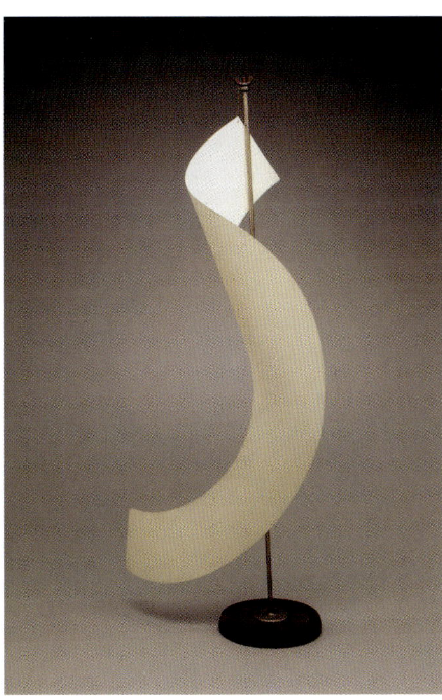

Man Ray
(Philadelphia 1890 - Paris 1976)

Lampshade
Lampenschirm
Lampenkap
Pantalla de lámpara

●

1921
115,3 x 7,7 cm / 45.4 x 3 in.
Yale University Art Gallery, New Haven (CT)

painted (white) tin, metal rod, wing bolt, square bolt,
round metal flange, screwed to round wood base
Bemaltes Zinn, Metallstange, Schutzblechbolzen, quadratischer Bolzen,
runder Flansch aus Metall, auf eine runde Holzbasis geschraubt
beschilderd tin, metalen staaf, schroef van spatbord, vierkante schroef,
ronde metalen kraag, vastgeschroefd op een ronde basis
estaño pintado, barra de metal, tornillo de oreja, tornillo cuadrado,
brida redonda de metal, atornillada sobre una base de madera redonda

Man Ray
(Philadelphia 1890 - Paris 1976)

Indestructible object
(or Object to be destroyed)
Unzerstörbares Objekt
(oder zu zerstörendes Objekt)
Onvernietigbaar object
(of Te vernietigen object)
Objeto indestructible
(u Objeto a destruir)

●●

1923 (1964)
22,5 x 11 x 11,6 cm / 8.8 x 4.3 x 4.5 in.
Museum of Modern Art (MoMA), New York

metronome in wood and photograph
Metronom aus Holz und Fotografie
houten metronoom met foto
metrónomo en madera y fotografía

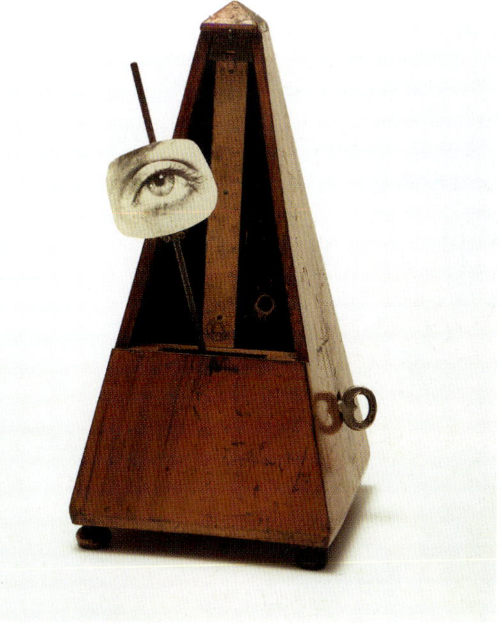

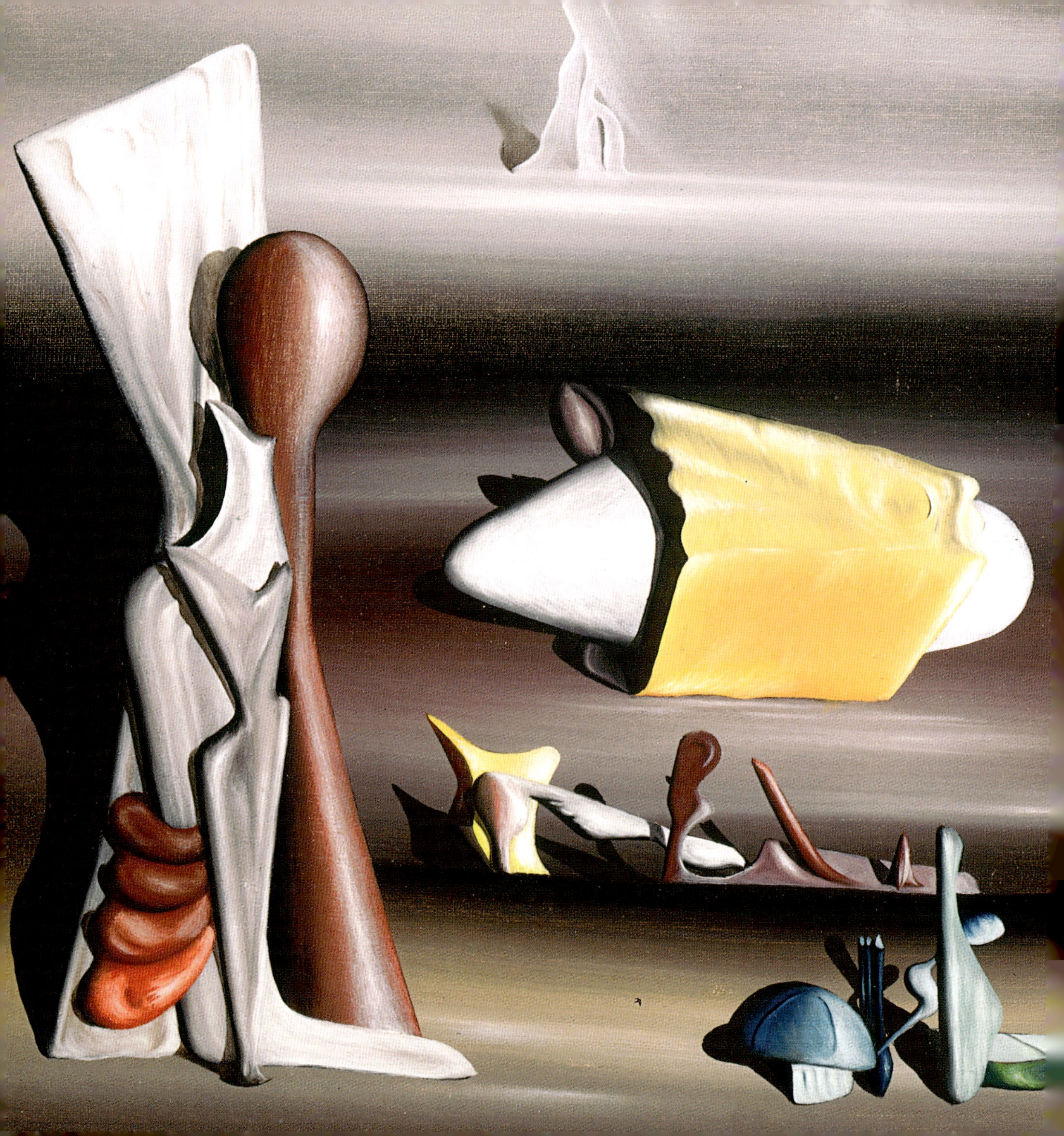

Traces of the unconscious. Metaphysics and Surrealism • Spuren des Unbewussten. Metaphysik und Surrealismus • Sporen van het onderbewustzijn. Metafysica en Surrealisme • Huellas del inconsciente. Metafísica y Surrealismo

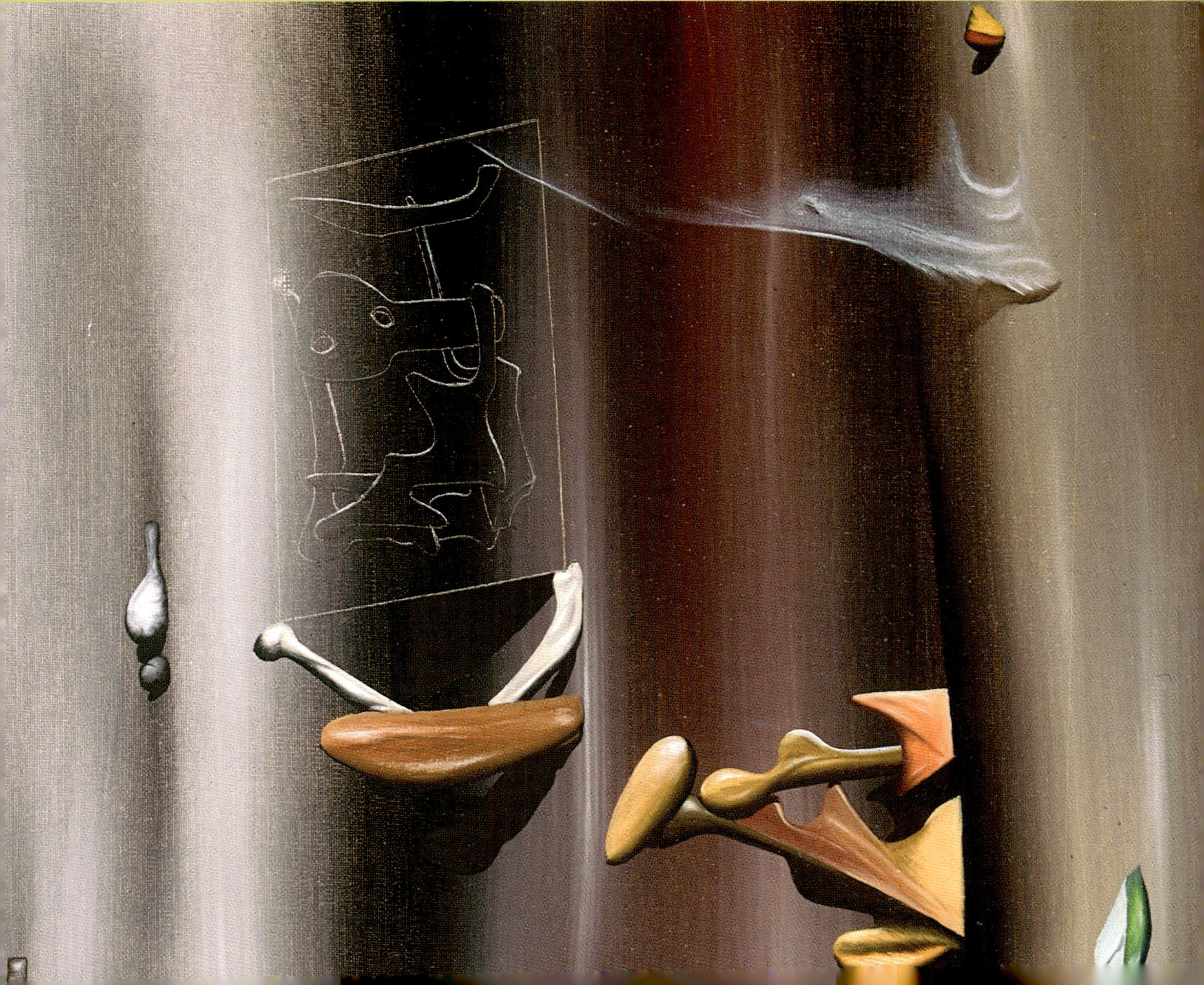

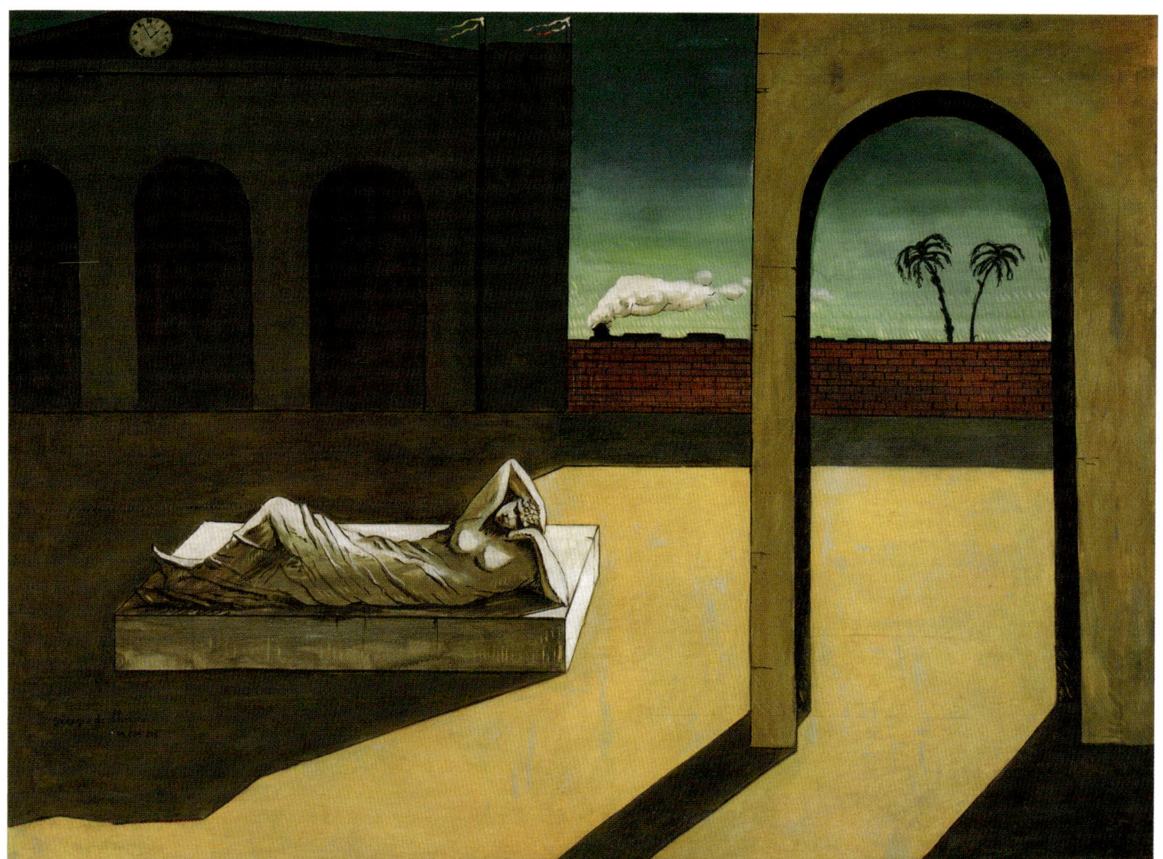

Giorgio de Chirico
(Volos 1888 - Roma 1978)

The Fortune-teller's Reward
Der Lohn des Hellsehers
De vergoeding van de waarzegger
La recompensa del adivino

●●

1913
135,6 x 180 cm / 53.4 x 70.9 in.
Philadelphia Museum of Art, Philadelphia

oil on canvas / Öl auf Leinwand
olieverf op doek / óleo sobre lienzo

▶ Giorgio de Chirico
(Volos 1888 - Roma 1978)

The Disquieting Muses
Die beunruhigenden Musen
De verontrustende muzen
Las musas inquietantes

●●●

1916
97 x 66 cm / 38.2 x 26 in.
Private collection / Private Sammlung
Privécollectie / Colección privada

oil on canvas / Öl auf Leinwand
olieverf op doek / óleo sobre lienzo

With his monumental architecture, uninhabited and silent, and with his strange sculptures, De Chirico was considered a precursor of Surrealism.

Mit seinen monumentalen, verlassenen und stillen Architekturen und mit seinen seltsamen Skulpturen galt De Chirico als Vorreiter des Surrealismus.

De Chirico werd met zijn monumentale, verlaten en stille architecturen en met zijn vreemde sculpturen, beschouwd als voorloper van het surrealisme.

Con sus obras arquitectónicas monumentales, desiertas y silenciosas, y con sus esculturas extrañas, De Chirico fue considerado un precursor del surrealismo.

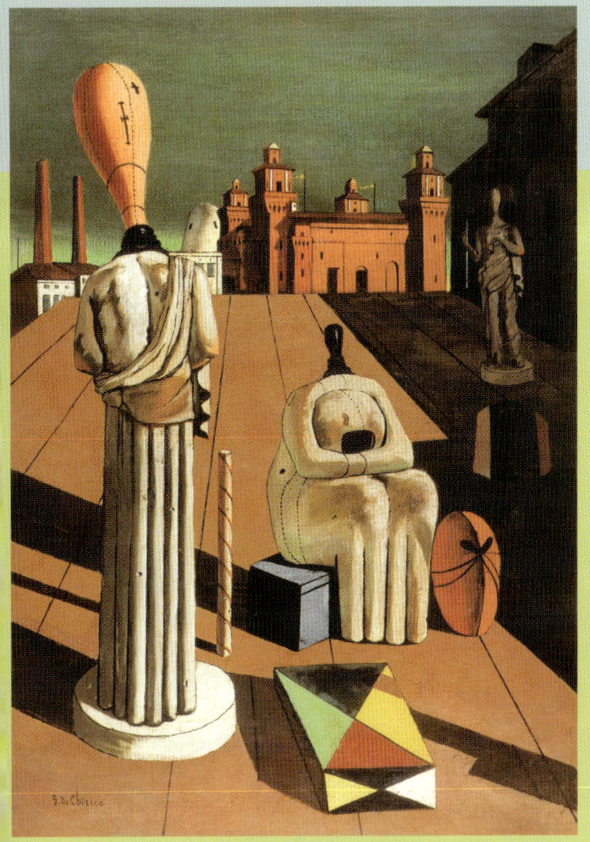

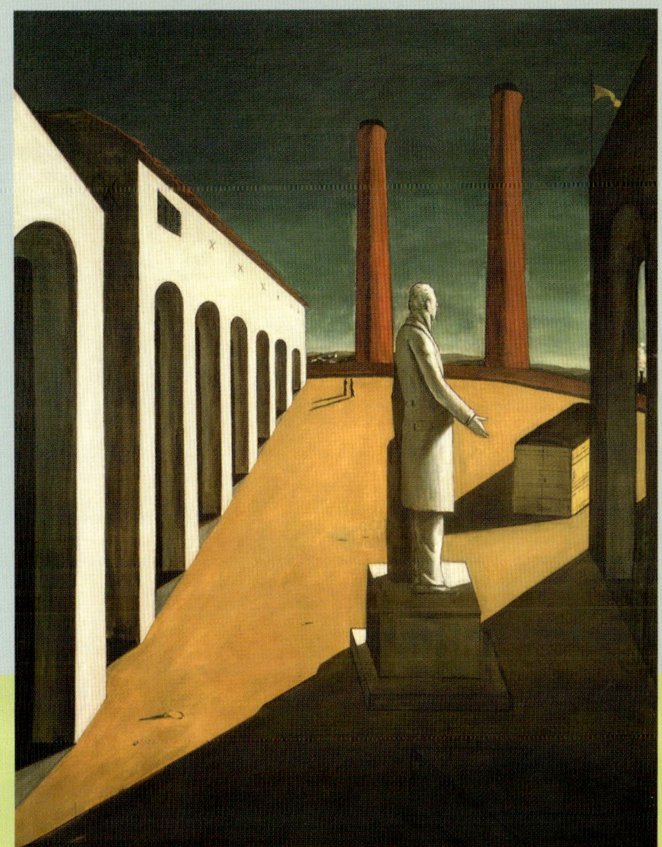

▲ Giorgio de Chirico
(Volos 1888 - Roma 1978)

The Enigma of a day
Das Rätsel eines Tages
Raadsel van een dag
El enigma de una jornada

●

1914
185,5 x 139,7 cm / 73 x 55 in.
Museum of Modern Art (MoMA),
New York

oil on canvas / Öl auf Leinwand
olieverf op doek / óleo sobre lienzo

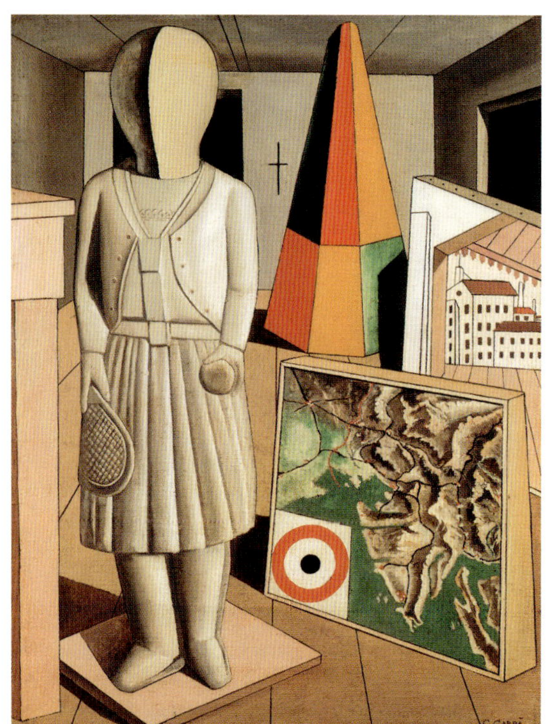

Carlo Carrà
(Quargnento 1881 - Milano 1966)

The Metaphysical Muse
Die metaphysische Muse
De metafysische muze
La musa metafísica

●●●

1917
90 x 66 cm / 35.4 x 26 in.
Pinacoteca di Brera, Milano

oil on canvas / Öl auf Leinwand
olieverf op doek / óleo sobre lienzo

320

Carlo Carrà
(Quargnento 1881 - Milano 1966)

Western Rider
Der Reiter aus dem Westen
Ruiter uit het westen
El caballero de Occidente

●●

1917
Private collection / Private Sammlung
Privécollectie / Colección privada

oil on canvas / Öl auf Leinwand
olieverf op doek / óleo sobre lienzo

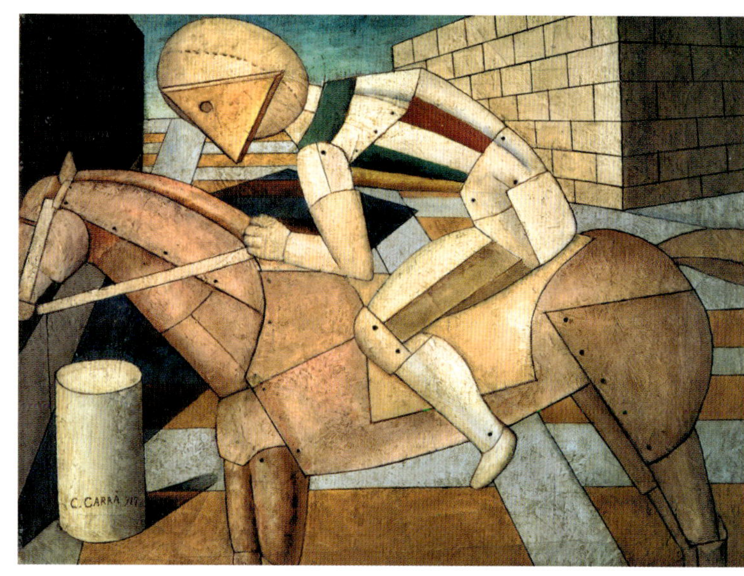

Giorgio Morandi
(Bologna 1890 - 1964)

Large Metaphysical Still Life
Großes metaphysisches Stillleben
Groot metafysisch stilleven
Gran naturaleza muerta metafísica

•

1918
68,5 x 72 cm / 26.9 x 28.3 in.
Pinacoteca di Brera, Milano

oil on canvas / Öl auf Leinwand
olieverf op doek / óleo sobre lienzo

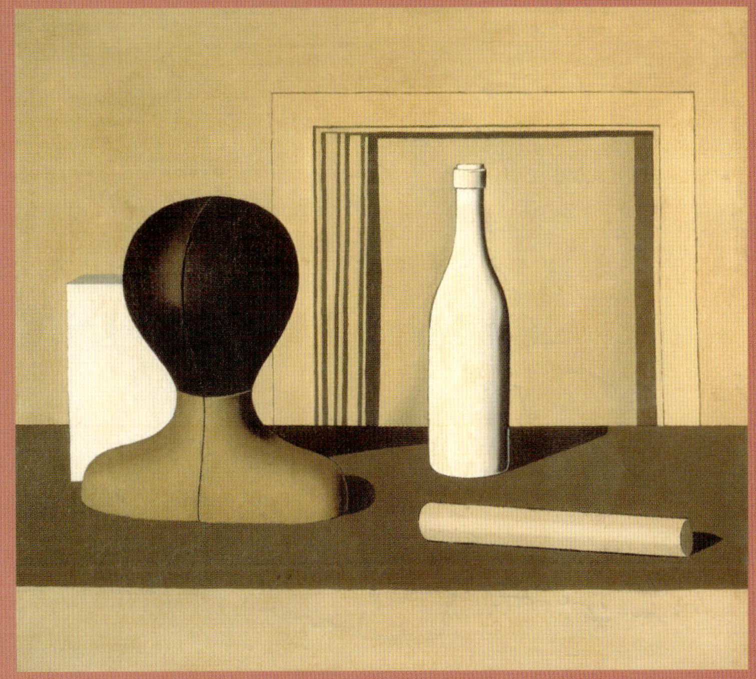

321

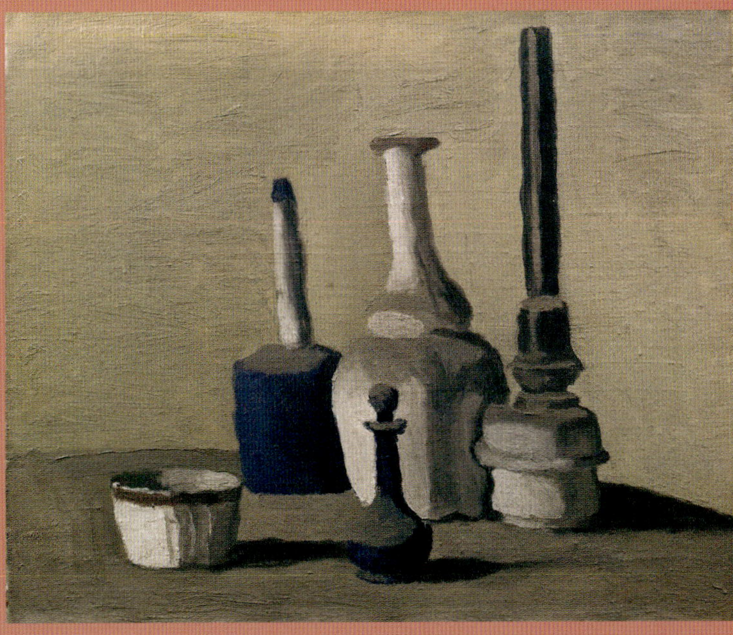

Giorgio Morandi
(Bologna 1890 - 1964)

Still life
Stillleben
Stilleven
Naturaleza muerta

•

Collezione Jucker, Milano

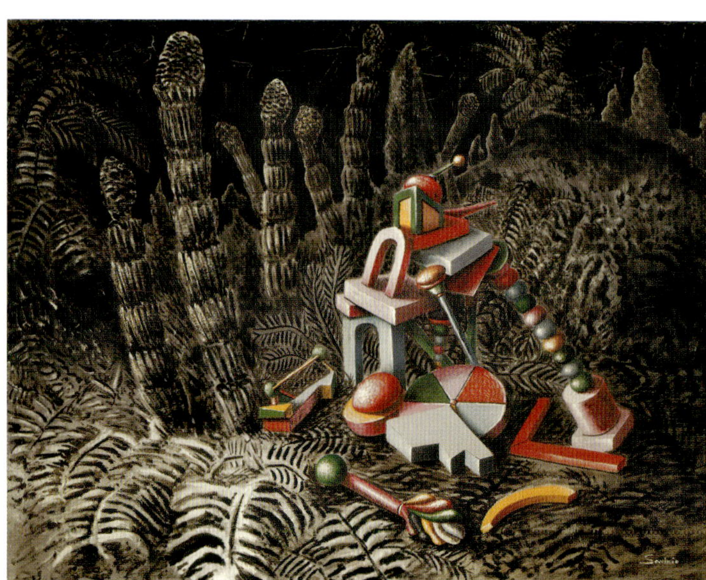

Alberto Savinio
(Athens 1891 - Roma 1952)

In the Forest
Im Wald
In het bos
En el bosque
● ●
1928
65 x 81 cm / 25.6 x 31.9 in.
Private collection / Private Sammlung
Privécollectie / Colección privada

oil on canvas / Öl auf Leinwand
olieverf op doek / óleo sobre lienzo

322

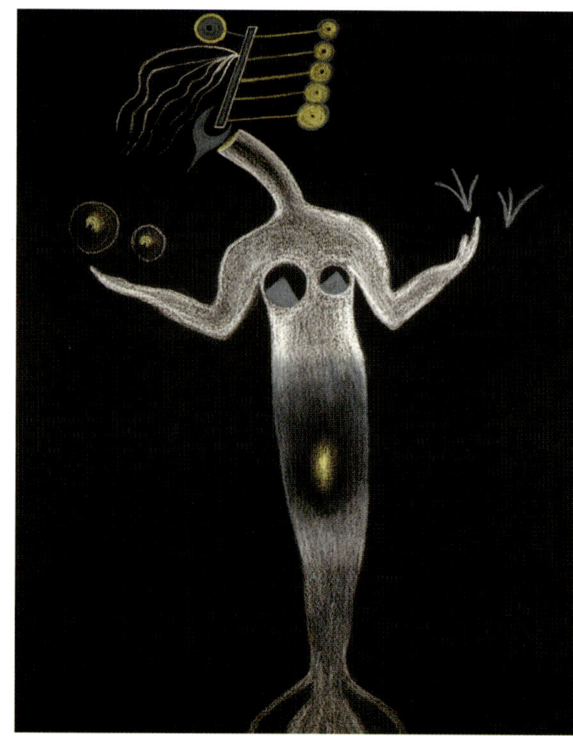

Paul Eluard,
(Saint-Denis 1895 - Charenton-le-Pont 1952)
Nush Eluard,
(Mühlhausen 1906 - Paris 1946)
Valentine Hugo,
(Boulogne-sur-Mer 1887 - Paris 1968)
Andre Breton
(Tinchebray 1896 - Paris 1966)

Cadavre exquis
●
1938
Musée d'Art et d'Histoire,
Saint-Denis

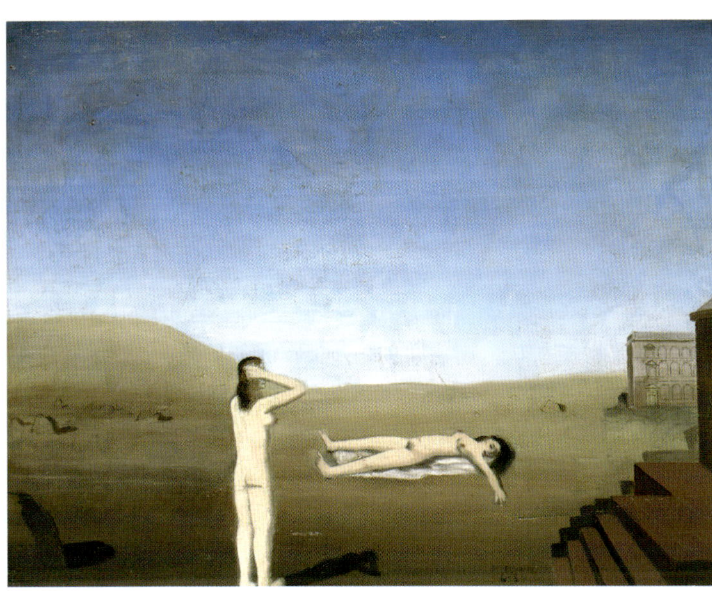

Paul Delvaux
(Antheit 1897 - Furnes 1994)

Women and stones
Frauen und Steine
Vrouwen en stenen
Mujeres y piedras

1934
80,5 x 100,5 cm / 31.7 x 39.59 in.
Hamburger Kunsthalle, Hamburg

oil on canvas / Öl auf Leinwand
olieverf op doek / óleo sobre lienzo

Paul Delvaux
(Antheit 1897 - Furnes 1994)

The Staircase
Die Treppe
De trap
La escalera

● ● ●

1946
122 x 152,5 cm / 48 x 60 in.
Museum voor Schone Kunsten, Gent

oil on canvas / Öl auf Leinwand
olieverf op doek / óleo sobre lienzo

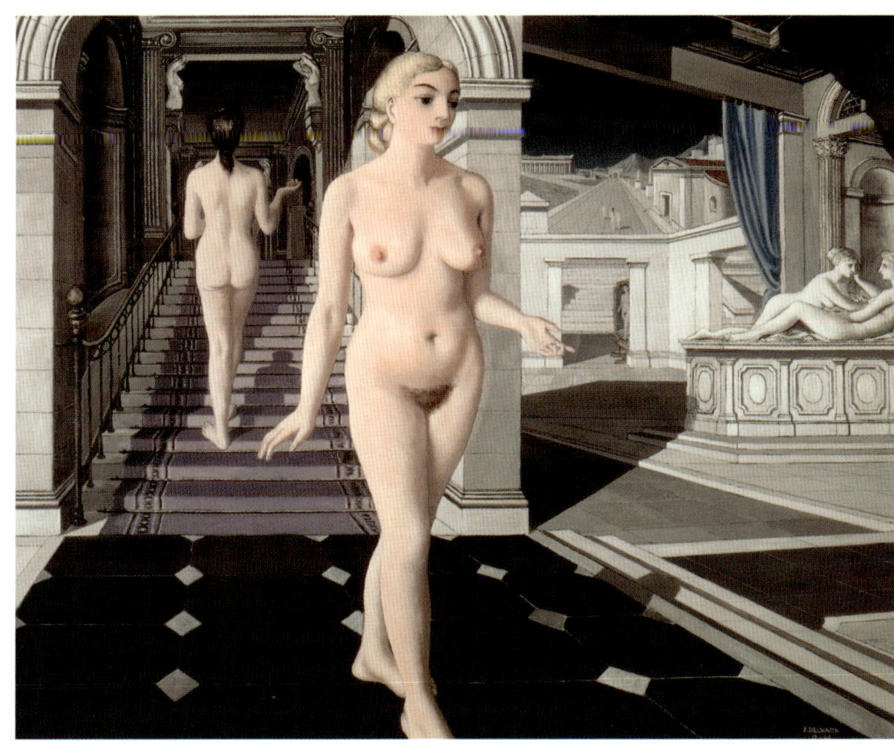

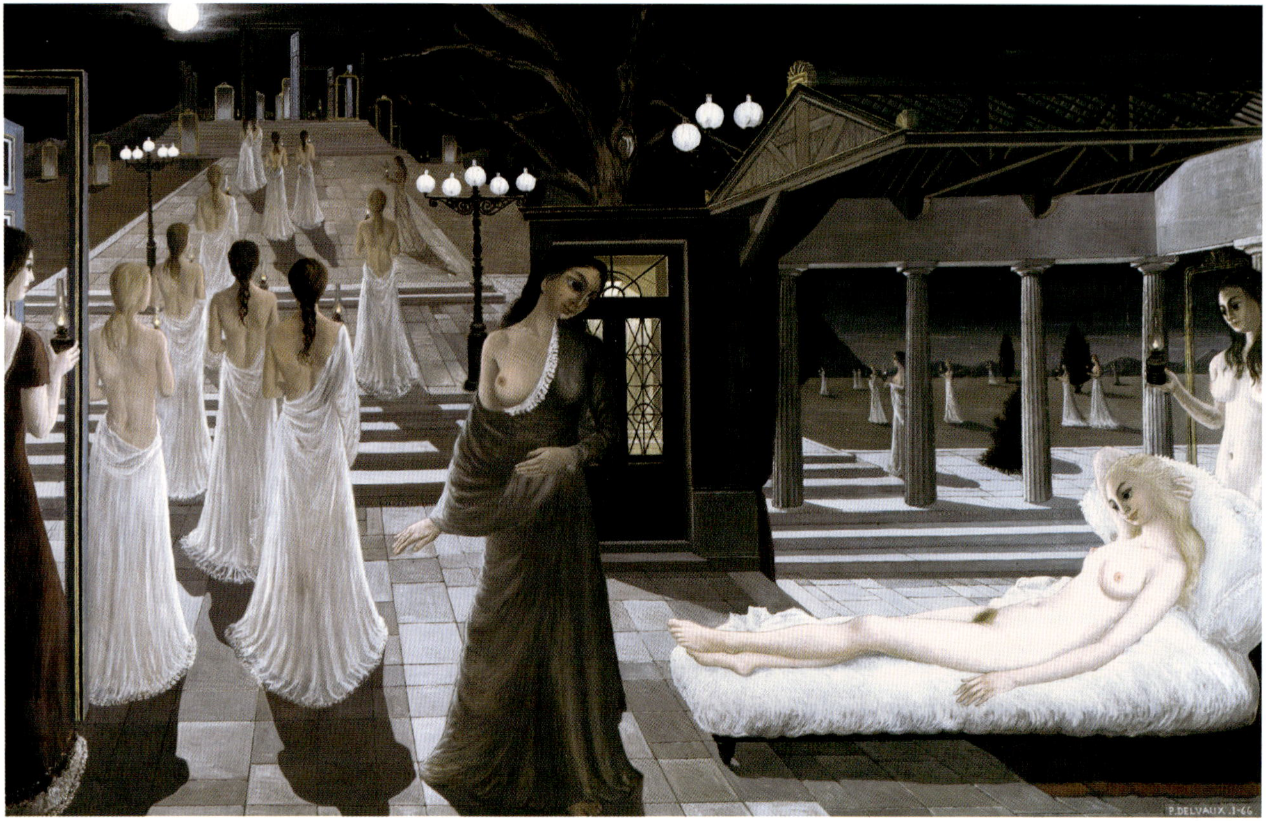

324

Paul Delvaux
(Antheit 1897 - Furnes 1994)

The Acropolis 1-66
Die Akropolis 1-66
De Akropolis 1-66
La Acrópolis 1-66

●●

1966
150 x 230 cm / 59.1 x 90.6 in.
Centre Georges Pompidou, Musée National d'Art Moderne, Paris

oil on canvas
Öl auf Leinwand
olieverf op doek
óleo sobre lienzo

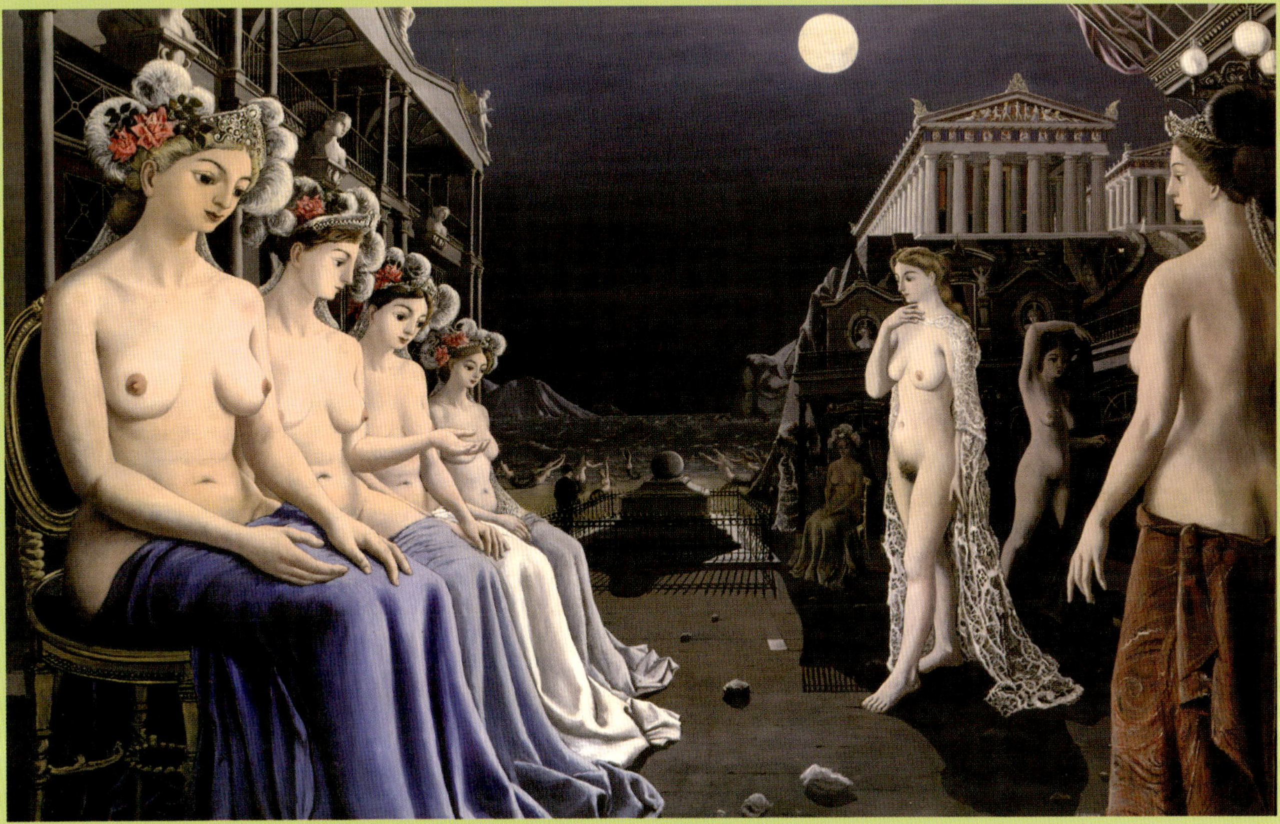

Paul Delvaux
(Antheit 1897 - Furnes 1994)

The Great Sirens
Die großen Verführerinnen
De grote zeemeerminnen
Las grandes sirenas

●●

1947
201,9 x 3099 cm / 79 x 122 in.
The Metropolitan Museum of Art, New York

oil on canvas
Öl auf Leinwand
olieverf op doek
óleo sobre lienzo

A woman – always the same one – repeated endlessly in an unknown urban night-time landscape, transports the viewer into a dream universe.

Eine Frau – immer die gleiche – ins Unendliche wiederholt in einer unbekannten städtischen Landschaft bei Nacht trägt den Betrachter in ein traumhaftes Universum.

Een vrouw – steeds dezelfde – oneindig vaak herhaald in een onbekend nachtelijk stadslandschap, voert de toeschouwer naar een droomuniversum.

Una mujer –siempre la misma– repetida hasta el infinito en un paisaje urbano nocturno desconocido, transporta al espectador hacia un universo onírico.

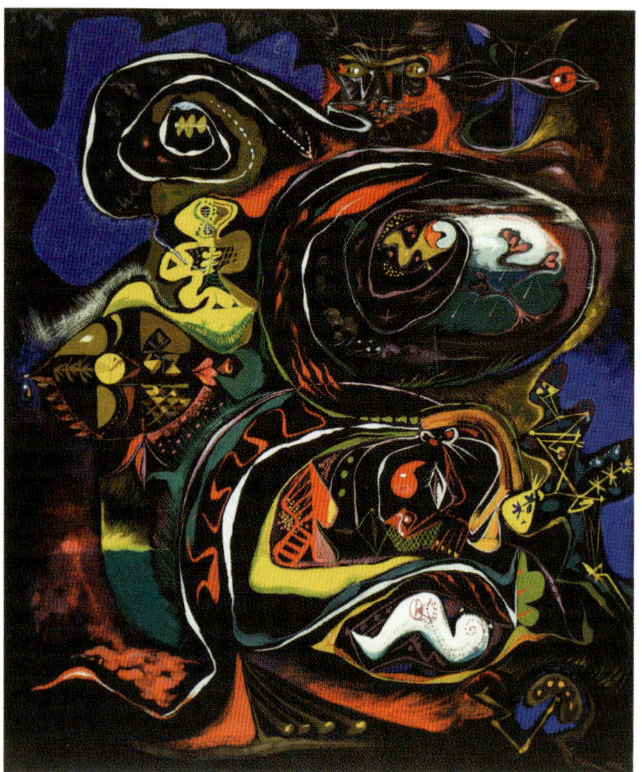

André Masson
(Balagny, Oise 1896 - Paris 1987)

Meditation on an oak leaf
Meditation über ein Eichenblatt
Meditatie op een eikenblad
Meditación sobre una hoja de roble

●●

1942
101,6 x 83,8 cm / 40 x 33 in.
Museum of Modern Art (MoMA), New York

tempera, 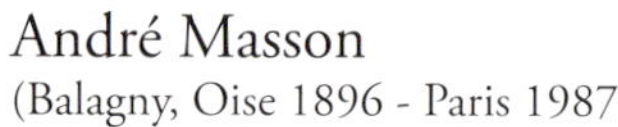pastel and sand on canvas
Tempera, Pastell und Sand auf Leinwand
tempera, pastel en zand op doek
temple, pastel y arena sobre lienzo

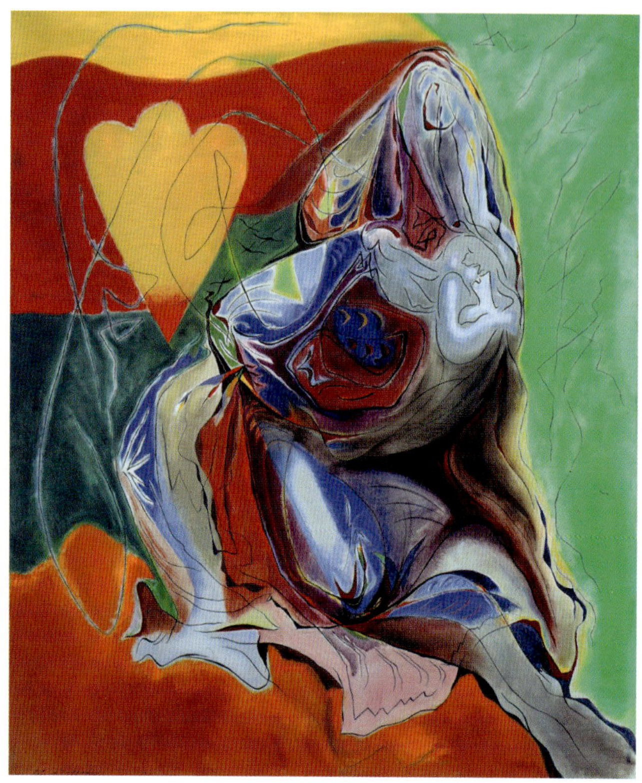

André Masson
(Balagny, Oise 1896 - Paris 1987)

Niobe
(tribute to pain)
(Hommage an den Schmerz)
(hulde aan pijn)
(homenaje al dolor)

●

1946
178 x 140 cm / 70.1 x 55.1 in.
Musée des Beaux Arts, Lyon

André Masson
(Balagny, Oise 1896 - Paris 1987)

Bird on the Camargue
Vogel über der Camargue
Vogel boven de Camargue
Pájaro en la Camarga

●●●

1949
65 x 49,5 cm / 25.6 x 19.5 in.
Hamburger Kunsthalle, Hamburg

oil on canvas / Öl auf Leinwand
olieverf op doek / óleo sobre lienzo

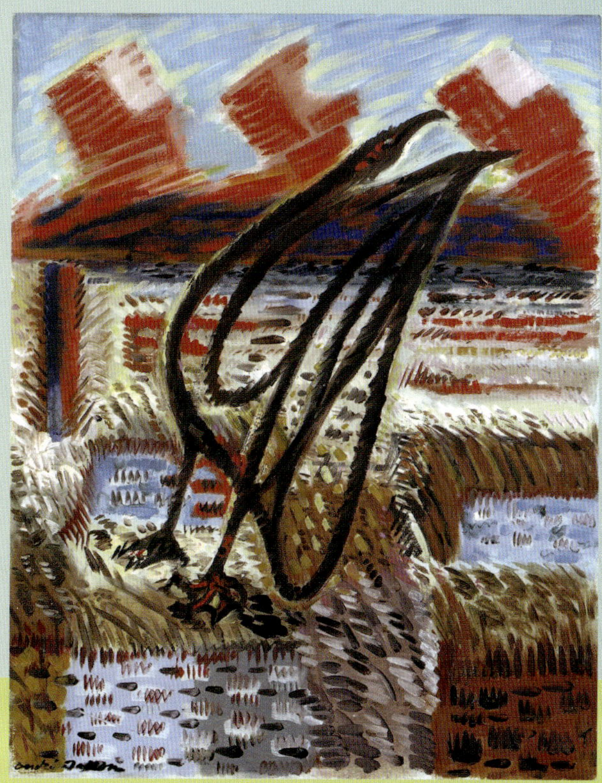

327

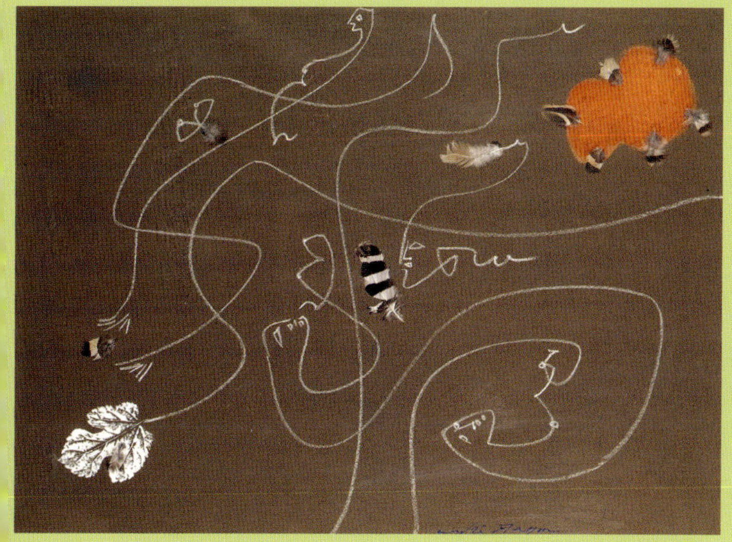

André Masson
(Balagny, Oise 1896 - Paris 1987)

Composition of feathers
Komposition aus Federn
Verencompositie
Composición de plumas

●●

Private collection
Private Sammlung
Privécollectie
Colección privada

Yves Tanguy
(Paris 1900 - Woodbury 1955)

Turning off useless lights
Auslöschen der nutzlosen Lichter
De nutteloze lampen uitdoen
La extinción de las luces inútiles

●

1927
92,1 x 65,4 cm / 36.2 x 25.7 in.
Museum of Modern Art (MoMA), New York

oil on canvas / Öl auf Leinwand
olieverf op doek / óleo sobre lienzo

Yves Tanguy
(Paris 1900 - Woodbury 1955)

Parallels
Parallelen
De parallellen
Los paralelos

●

1929
92,2 x 73 cm / 36.3 x 28.7 in.
Philadelphia Museum of Art, Philadelphia

oil on canvas / Öl auf Leinwand
olieverf op doek / óleo sobre lienzo

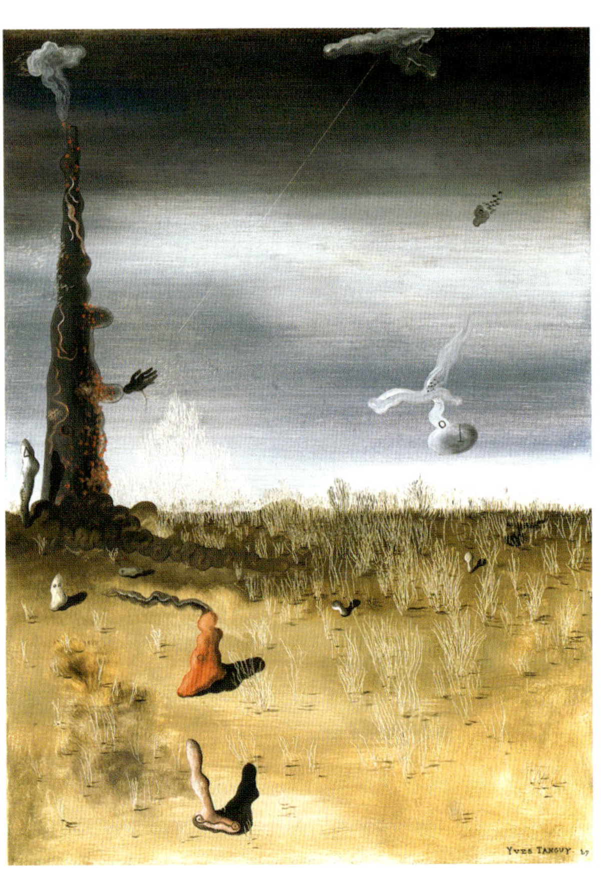

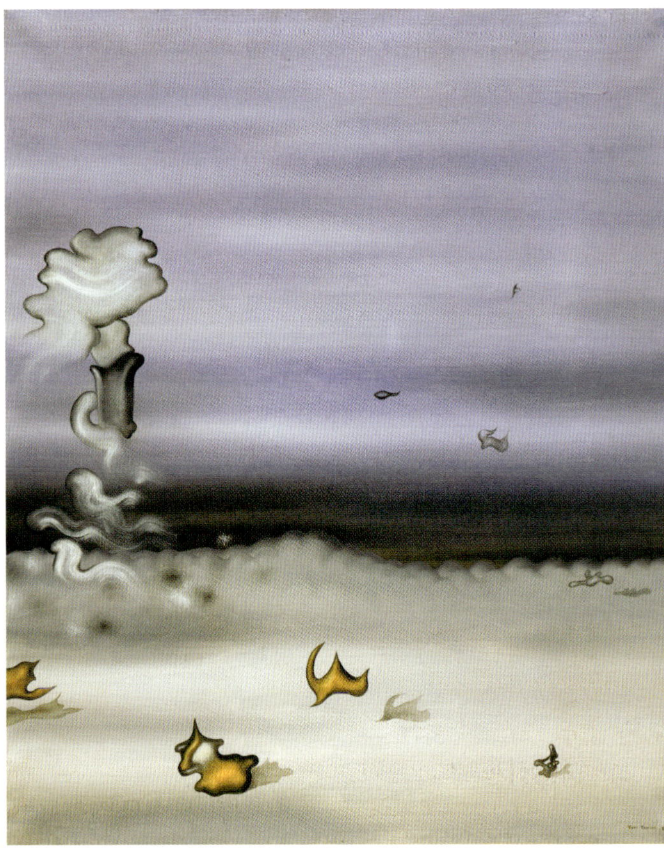

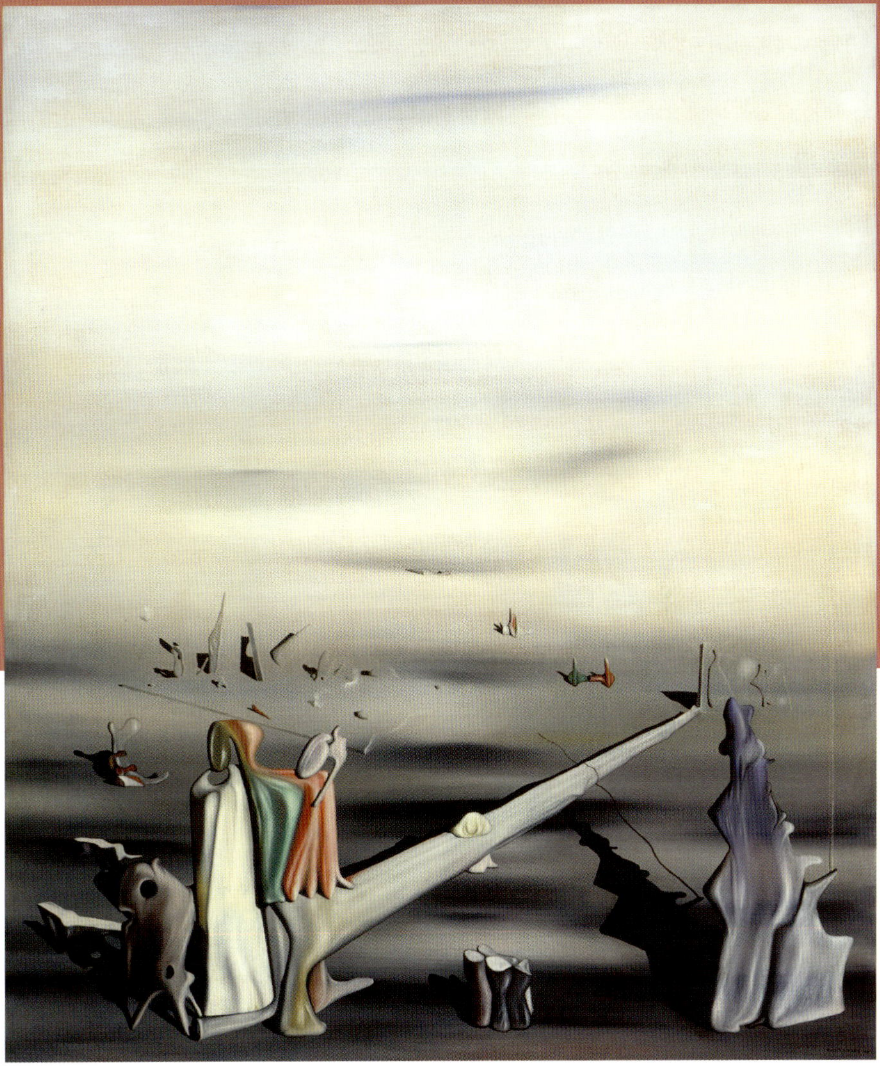

Yves Tanguy
(Paris 1900 - Woodbury 1955)

The Satin Tuning Fork
Die glatte Stimmgabel
De satijnen stemvork
El diapasón de raso

●●●

1940
99 x 81,3 cm / 38.9 x 32 in.
The Metropolitan Museum of Art,
New York

oil on canvas / Öl auf Leinwand
olieverf op doek / óleo sobre lienzo

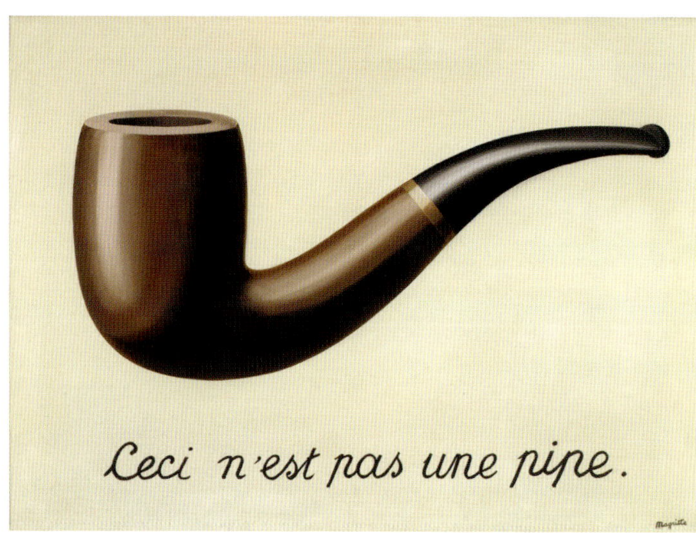

◀ René Magritte
(Lessines 1898 - Bruxelles 1967)

The Betrayal of the Images (This is not a pipe)
Die Illusion der Bilder (Dies ist keine Pfeife)
Het verraad van de beelden (Dit is geen pijp)
La traición de las imágenes (Esto no es una pipa)

●●●

1929
64,4 x 93,9 cm / 25.3 x 36.9 in.
Los Angeles County Museum of Art, Los Angeles

oil on canvas / Öl auf Leinwand
olieverf op doek / óleo sobre lienzo

No catch here, only means through which Magritte wants
to attract our attention to the difference between the object
and its depiction.

Hier gibt es keine Falle, Magrittes Absicht ist es lediglich, unsere
Aufmerksamkeit auf den Unterschied zwischen Objekten und
deren Darstellung zu lenken.

Dit is geen hinderlaag, Magritte wil hier alleen onze aandacht
vestigen op het verschil tussen het object en de voorstelling ervan.

Ninguna trampa aquí, sólo un medio a través del cual Magritte
quiere atraer nuestra atención sobre la diferencia entre el objeto
y su representación.

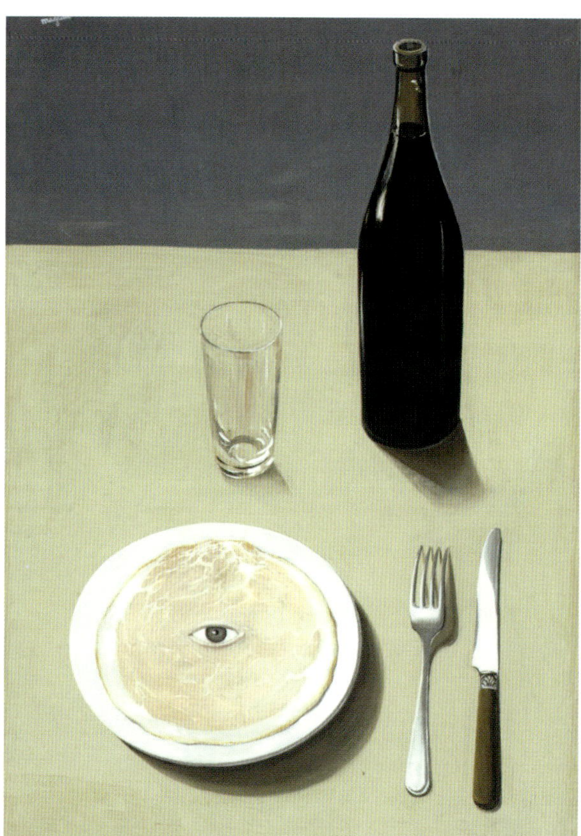

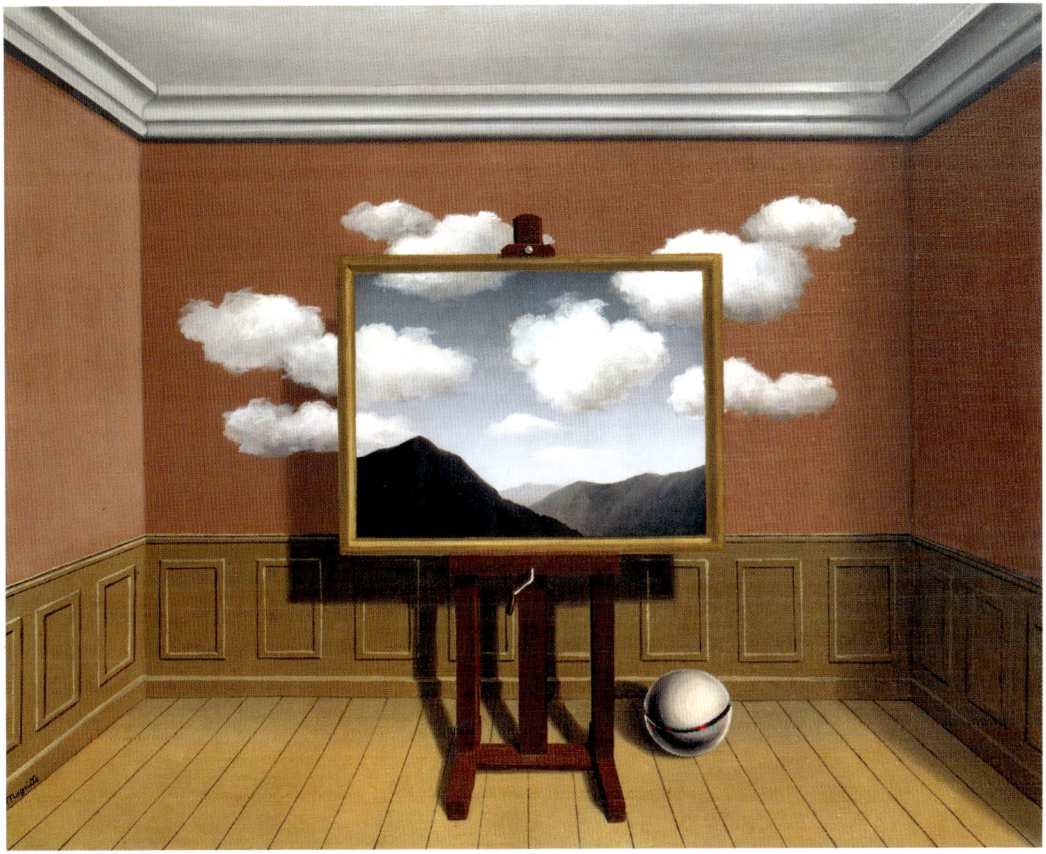

◀ René Magritte
(Lessines 1898 - Bruxelles 1967)

Portrait
Porträt
Portret
Retrato

●●●

1935
73,3 x 50,2 cm / 28.8 x 19.7 in.
Museum of Modern Art (MoMA),
New York

oil on canvas / Öl auf Leinwand
olieverf op doek / óleo sobre lienzo

René Magritte
(Lessines 1898 - Bruxelles 1967)

The Vengeance
Die Rache
De wraak
La venganza

●●

1936
54 x 65 cm / 21.2 x 25.6 in.
Private collection / Private Sammlung
Privécollectie / Colección privada

oil on canvas / Öl auf Leinwand
olieverf op doek / óleo sobre lienzo

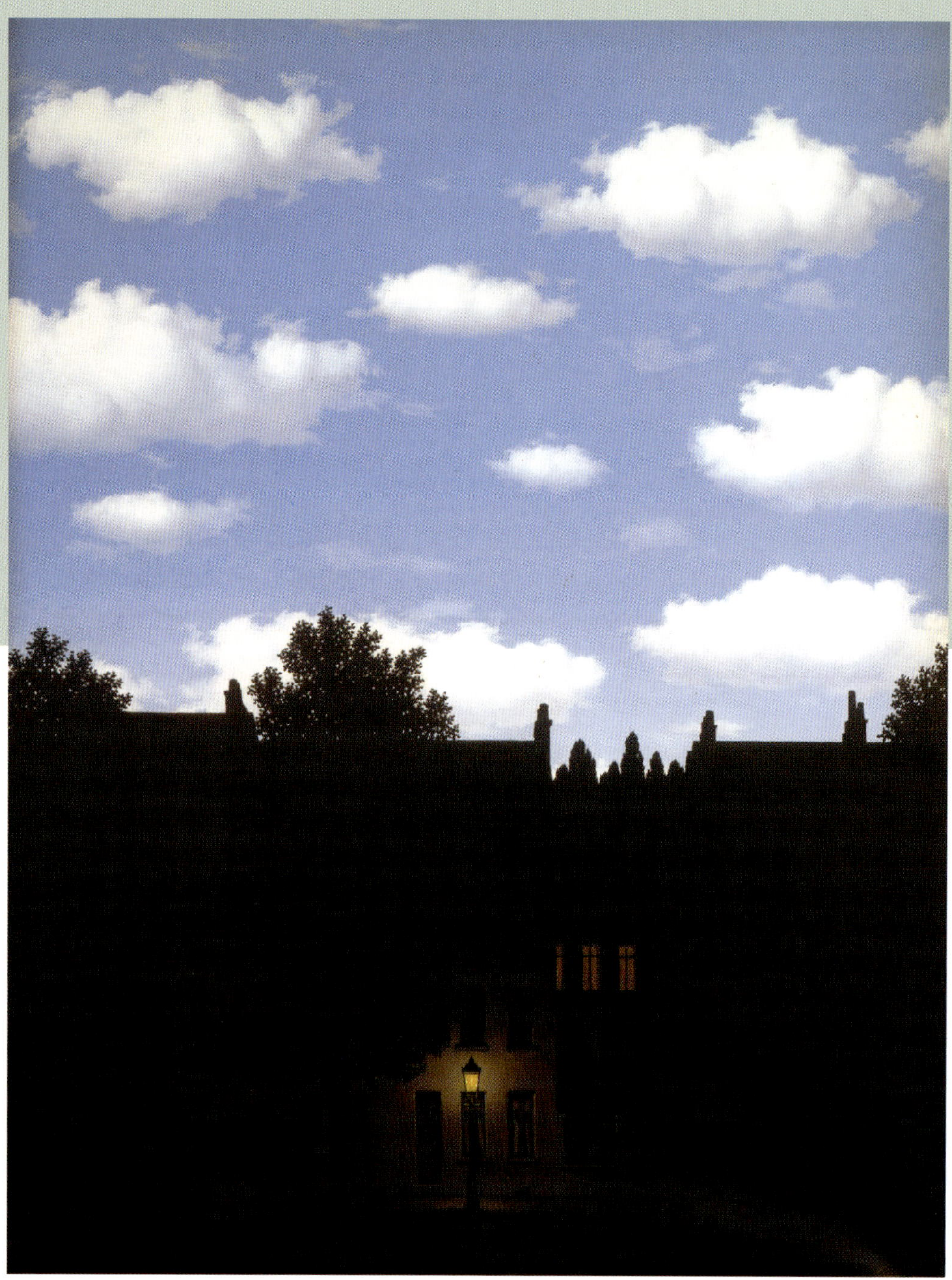

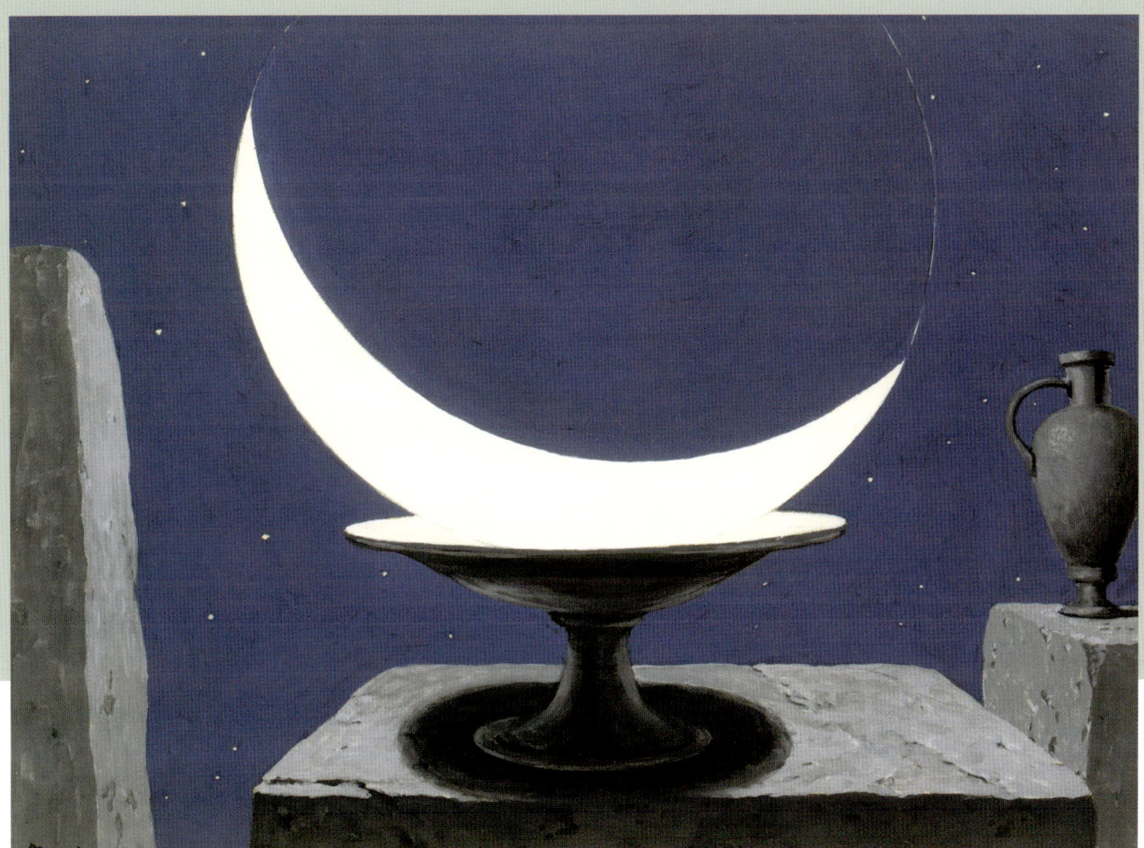

◀ René Magritte
(Lessines 1898 - Bruxelles 1967)

The Empire of the Lights
Das Reich der Lichter
Het rijk der lichten
El imperio de las luces

●●●

1952
100 x 80 cm / 39.3 x 31.5 in.
Private collection / Private Sammlung
Privécollectie / Colección privada

oil on canvas / Öl auf Leinwand
olieverf op doek / óleo sobre lienzo

René Magritte
(Lessines 1898 - Bruxelles 1967)

Melusine's Window
Das Fenster von Melusine
Het raam van Melusine
La ventana de Melusina

●

1953
26,4 x 34,7 cm / 10.4 x 13.6 in.
Yasaka Gallery, Nagoya

gouache on paper / Gouache auf Papier
gouache op papier / gouache sobre papel

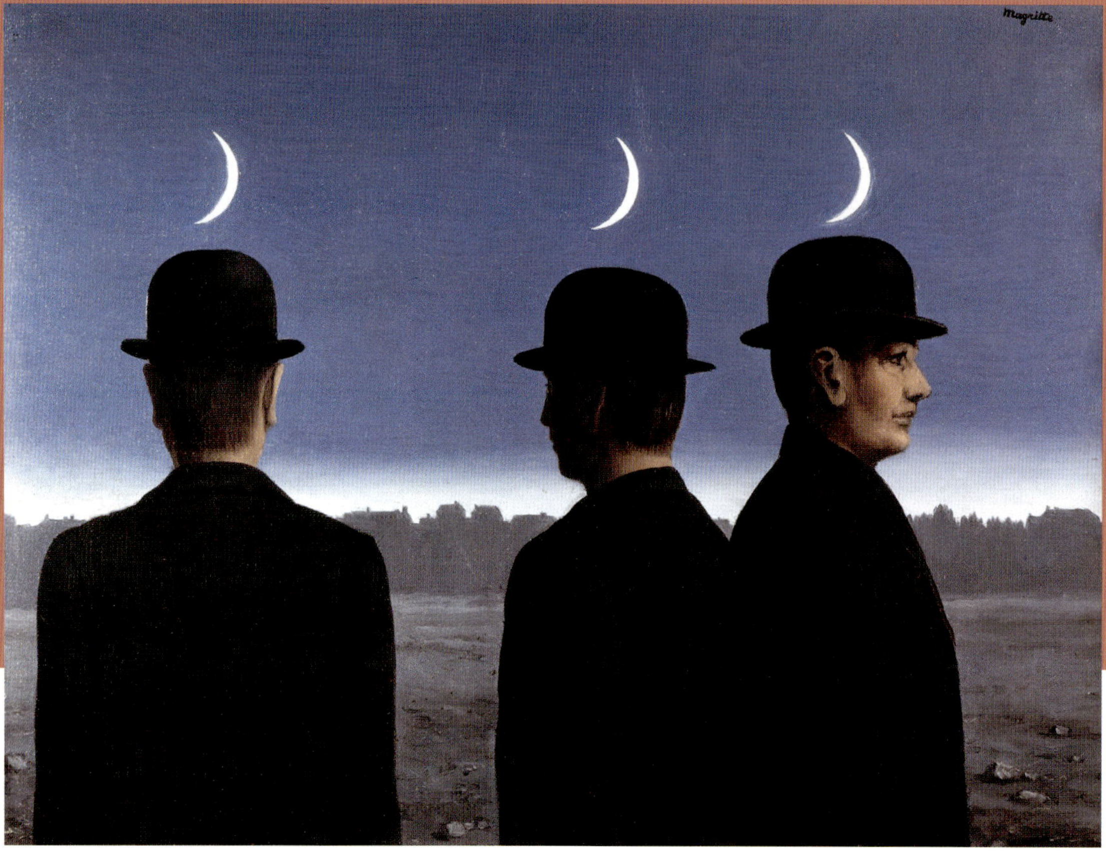

334

René Magritte
(Lessines 1898 - Bruxelles 1967)

The Masterpeice or the Mysteries of the Horizon
Das Meisterwerk oder die Mysterien des Horizonts
Het meesterwerk of de mysteries van de horizon
La obra maestra o Los misterios del horizonte

●●●

1955
50 x 65 cm / 19.7 x 25.6 in.
Frederick Weisman Company,
Los Angeles

oil on canvas / Öl auf Leinwand
olieverf op doek / óleo sobre lienzo

▶ René Magritte
(Lessines 1898 - Bruxelles 1967)

Trip Souvenir
Reiseerinnerung
Reisherinnering
Recuerdo de viaje

●

1963
81 x 100 cm / 31.9 x 39.4 in.
Private collection / Private Sammlung
Privécollectie / Colección privada

oil on canvas / Öl auf Leinwand
olieverf op doek / óleo sobre lienzo

René Magritte
(Lessines 1898 - Bruxelles 1967)

The Large Family
Die große Familie
De grote familie
La gran familia

••

1963
100 x 81 cm / 39.4 x 31.9 in.
Utsunomiya Museum of Art,
Utsunomiya

oil on canvas / Öl auf Leinwand
olieverf op doek / óleo sobre lienzo

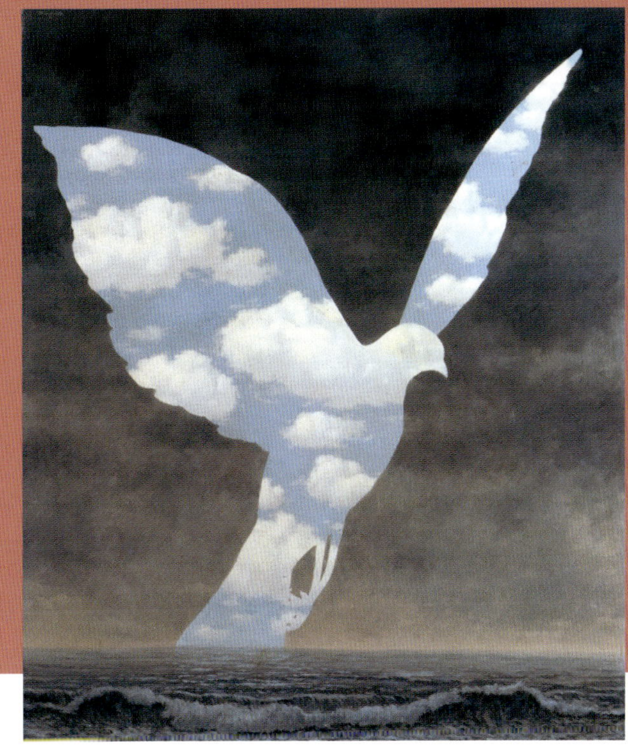

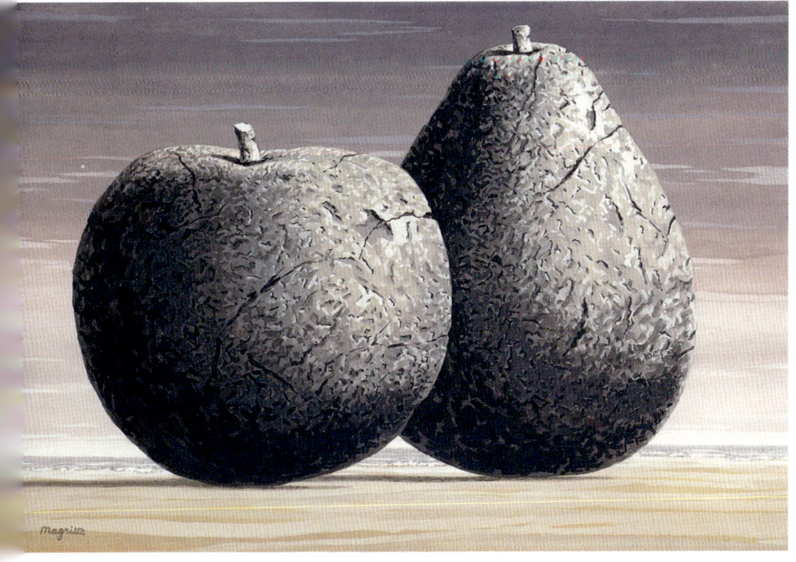

The change of scale, the transformation,
the repetition... expressly create a poetic
universe which moves the viewer.

Die Änderung des Maßstabs,
die Transformation, die Wiederholung...
sie schaffen bewusst ein poetisches
Universum, das den Betrachter bewegt.

De verandering van de trap,
de overschrijding, de herhaling...
creëren duidelijk een poëtisch universum
dat de toeschouwer in vervoering brengt.

El cambio de escala, la trasmutación,
la repetición... crean expresamente
un universo poético que emociona
al espectador.

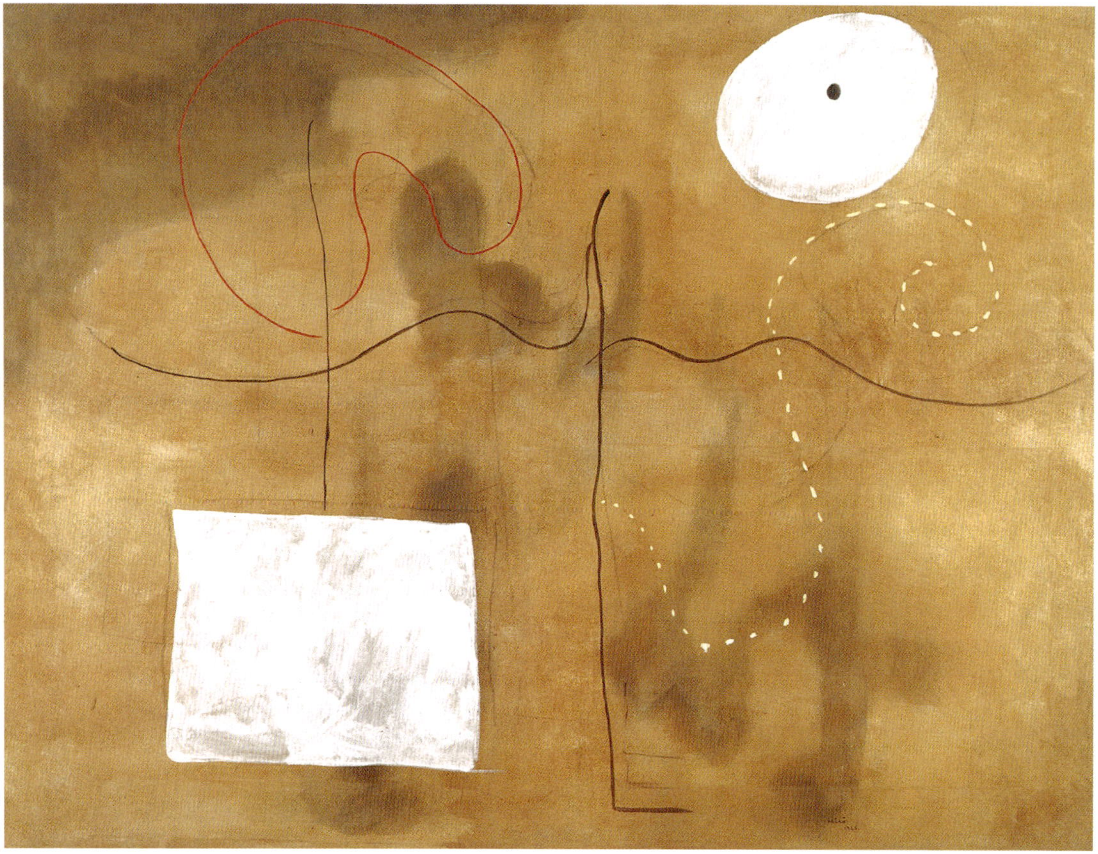

Joan Miró
(Barcelona 1893 - Palma de Mallorca 1983)

Dog howling to the moon
Hund, den Mond anbellend
Hond die naar de maan huilt
Perro ladrando a la luna

●

1926
73 x 92,1 cm / 28.7 x 36.2 in.
Philadelphia Museum of Art, Philadelphia

oil on canvas / Öl auf Leinwand
olieverf op doek / óleo sobre lienzo

▶ Joan Miró
(Barcelona 1893 - Palma de Mallorca 1983)

Dutch Interior II
Holländisches Interieur II
Hollands interieur II
Interior holandés II

● ●

1928
92 x 73cm / 36.2 x 28.7 in.
Collezione Peggy Guggenheim, Venezia

oil on canvas / Öl auf Leinwand
olieverf op doek / óleo sobre lienzo

Joan Miró
(Barcelona 1893 - Palma de Mallorca 1983)

Catalan peasant with guitar
Katalanischer Bauer mit Gitarre
Catalaanse boer met gitaar
Campesino catalán con guitarra

●●●

1924
147 x 114 cm / 57.9 x 44.9 in.
Museo Thyssen-Bornemisza, Madrid

oil on canvas
Öl auf Leinwand
olieverf op doek
óleo sobre lienzo

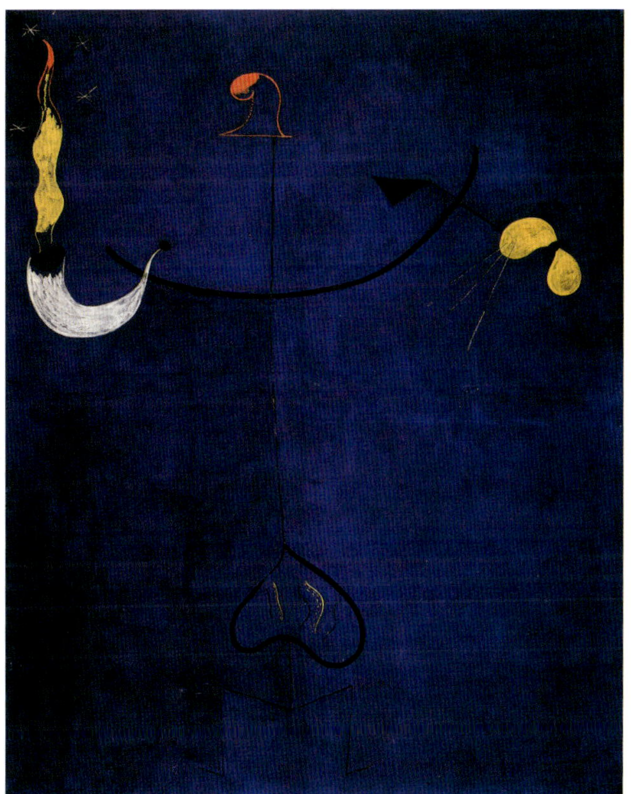

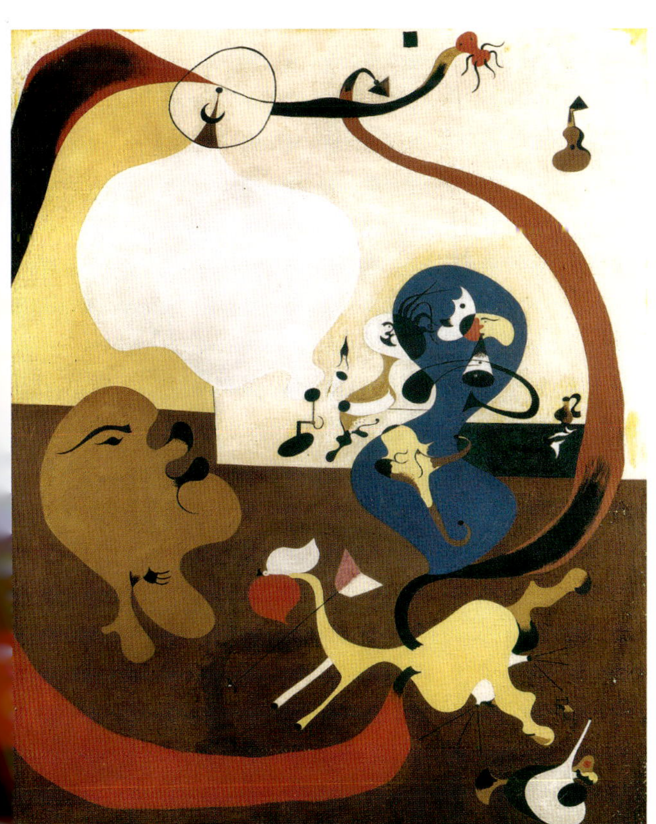

After a trip to Holland, Miró creates some paintings freely inspired by Dutch painters, all of surrealist fantasy and full of gaiety.

Infolge einer Reise nach Holland realisiert Miró einige frei nach niederländischen Malern inspirierte Gemälde, die allesamt der surrealistischen Fantasie entstammen und voller Freude sind.

Na een reis in Nederland maakt Miró enkele op Nederlandse schilders geïnspireerde schilderijen, vol surrealistische fantasie en vrolijkheid.

Después de un viaje a Holanda, Miró realiza algunas pinturas libremente inspiradas en pintores holandeses, todas cargadas de fantasía surrealista y llenas de alegría.

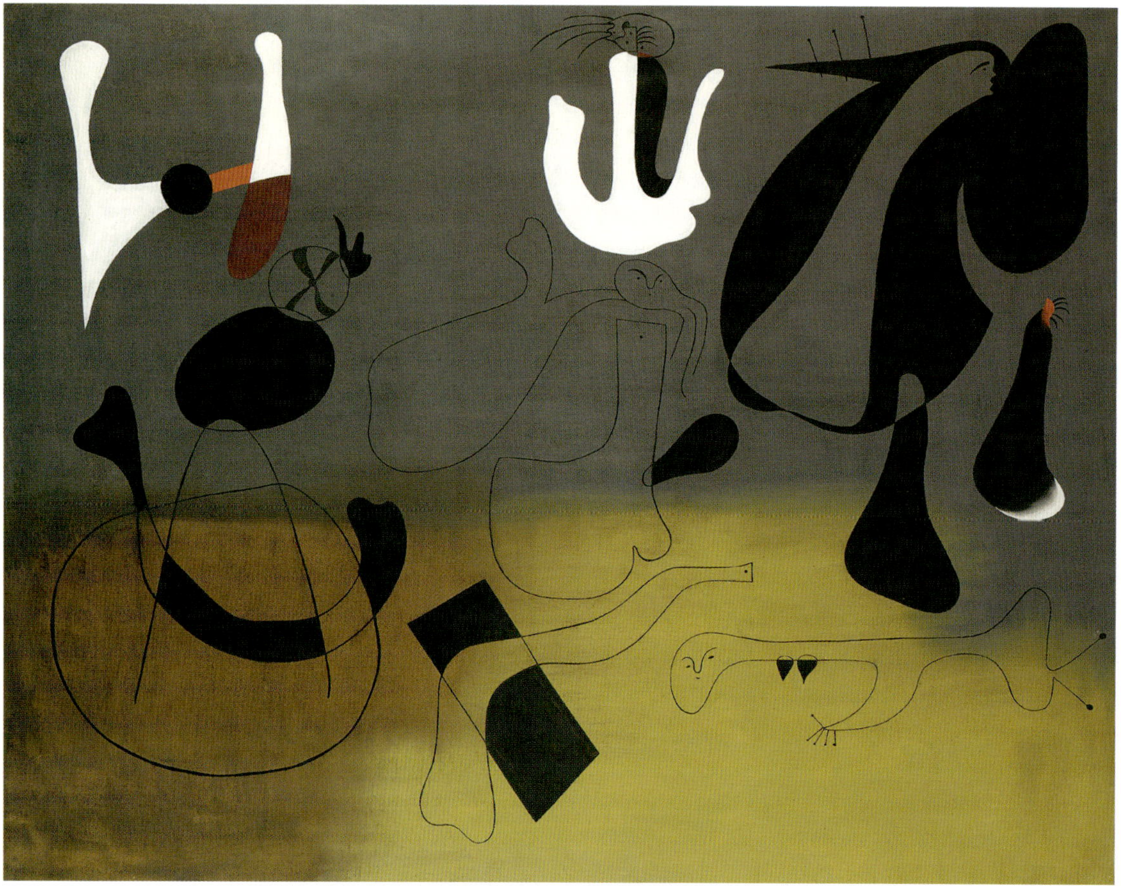

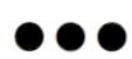

Joan Miró
(Barcelona 1893 - Palma de Mallorca 1983)

Painting
Gemälde
Schilderij
Pintura

●●●

1933
103,4 x 162,8 cm / 40.7 x 64.1 in.
Wadsworth Atheneum Museum of Art, Hartford (CT)

oil on canvas / Öl auf Leinwand
olieverf op doek / óleo sobre lienzo

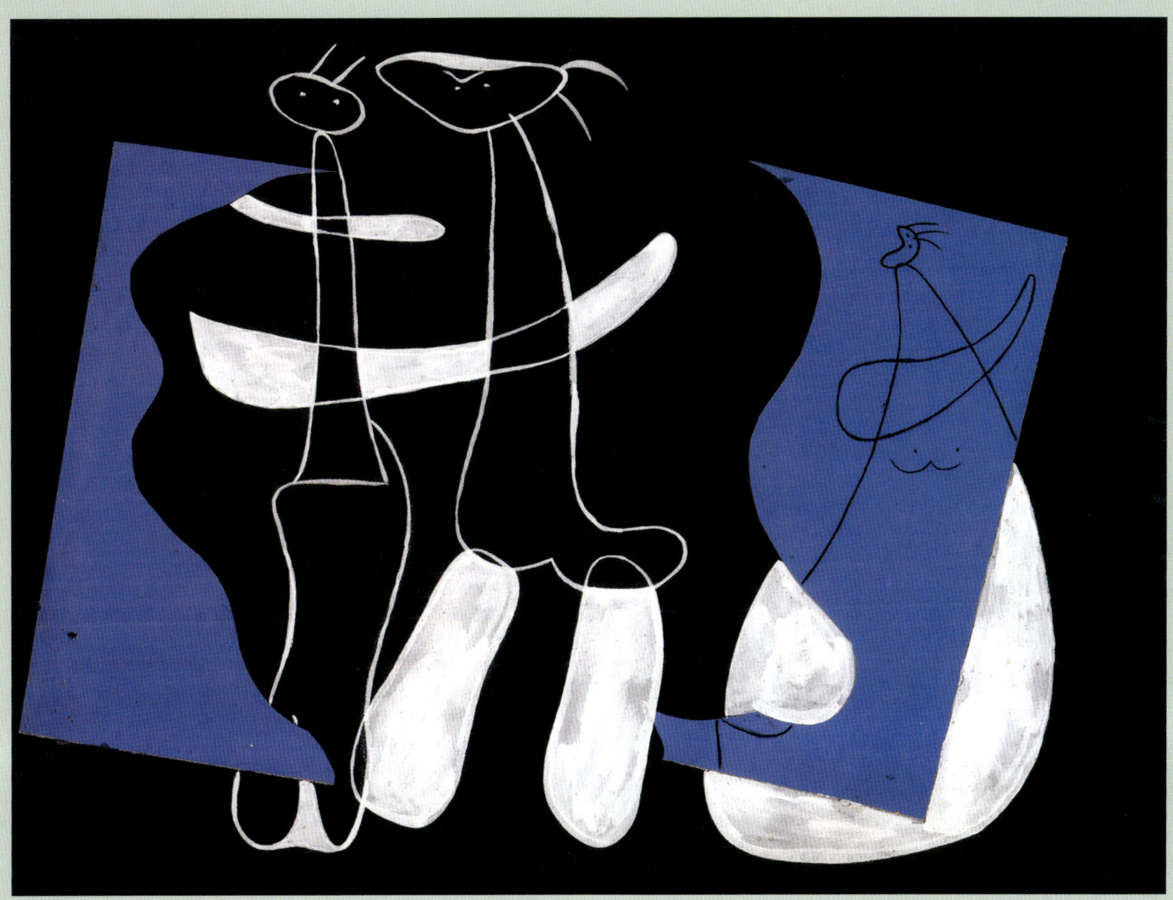

Joan Miró
(Barcelona 1893 - Palma de Mallorca 1983)

Three figures on a black background
Drei Personen auf schwarzem Grund
Drie personages op een zwarte achtergrond
Tres personajes sobre fondo negro

●

1934
49 x 64 cm / 19.3 x 25.2 in.
Musée des Beaux-Arts, Lille

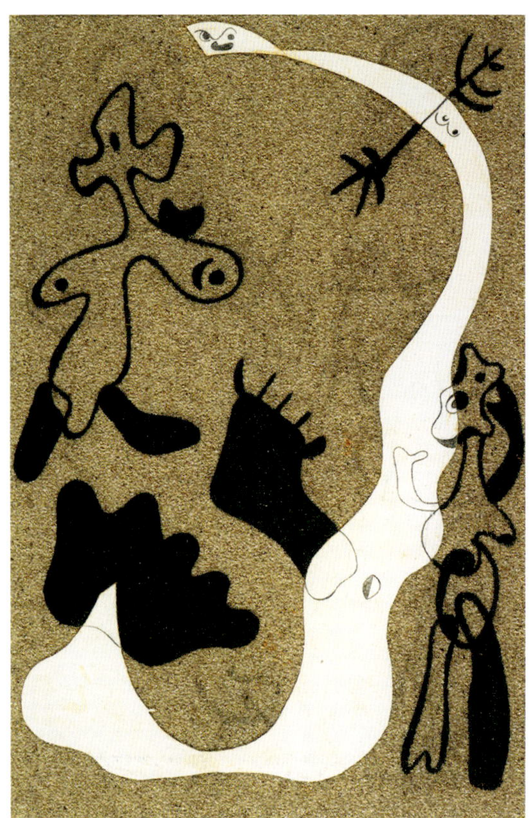

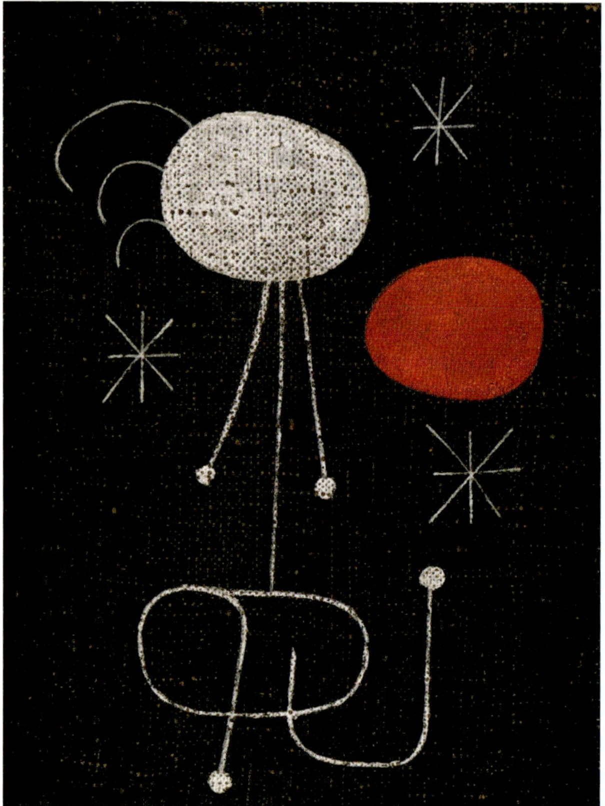

Joan Miró
(Barcelona 1893 - Palma de Mallorca 1983)

Painting
Gemälde
Schilderij
Pintura

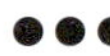

1934
36,2 x 23,5 cm / 14.2 x 9.2 in.
Philadelphia Museum of Art, Philadelphia

oil, lapis and paper on sandpaper, sheet
Öl, Bleistift und Papier auf Schmirgelpapier, Blatt
olieverf, lapis en papier op een blad schuurpapier
óleo, lápiz y papel sobre papel de lija, hoja

Joan Miró
(Barcelona 1893 - Palma de Mallorca 1983)

Woman in front of the sun
Frau vor Sonne
Vrouw voor de zon
Mujer ante el sol

● ● ●

1944
33,3 x 24,4 cm / 13.1 x 9.6 in.
Philadelphia Museum of Art, Philadelphia

oil and acqueous solvent on coarse canvas
Öl und wasserhaltiges Lösungsmittel auf rauher Leinwand
olieverf en oplosmiddel op ruw doek
óleo y solvente acuoso sobre lienzo

Joan Miró
(Barcelona 1893 -
Palma de Mallorca 1983)

Women, Birds and a Star
Frauen, Vögel und ein Stern
Vrouwen, vogels en sterren
Mujer, pájaro y estrella
●●●

1949
91,5 x 73,4 cm / 36 x 28.9 in.
The Metropolitan Museum of Art,
New York

oil on canvas / Öl auf Leinwand
olieverf op doek / óleo sobre lienzo

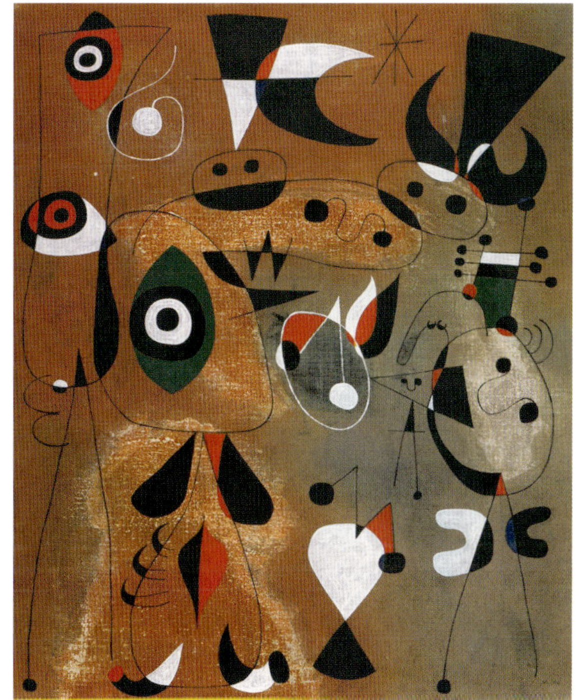

Joan Miró
(Barcelona 1893 -
Palma de Mallorca 1983)

Bleu II
●●

1961
270 x 355 cm / 10.6 x 14 in.
Centre Georges Pompidou, Musée
National d'Art Moderne, Paris

oil on canvas / Öl auf Leinwand
olieverf op doek / óleo sobre lienzo

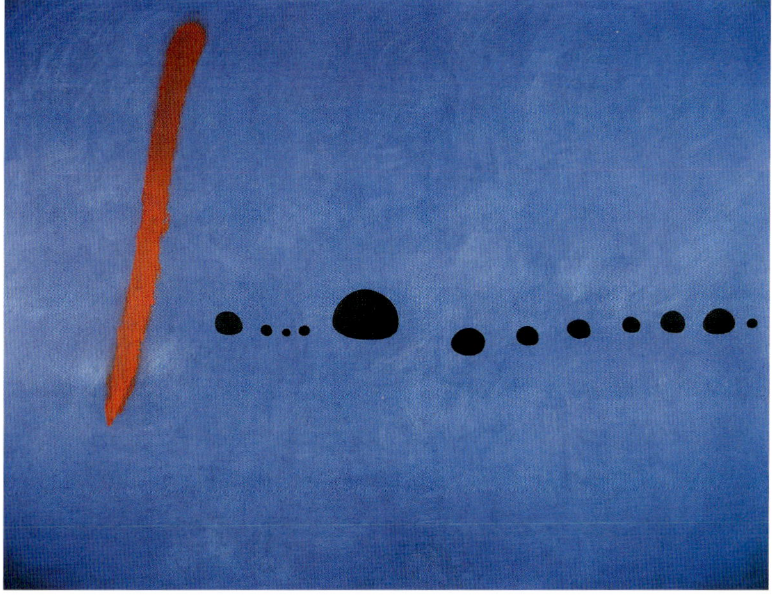

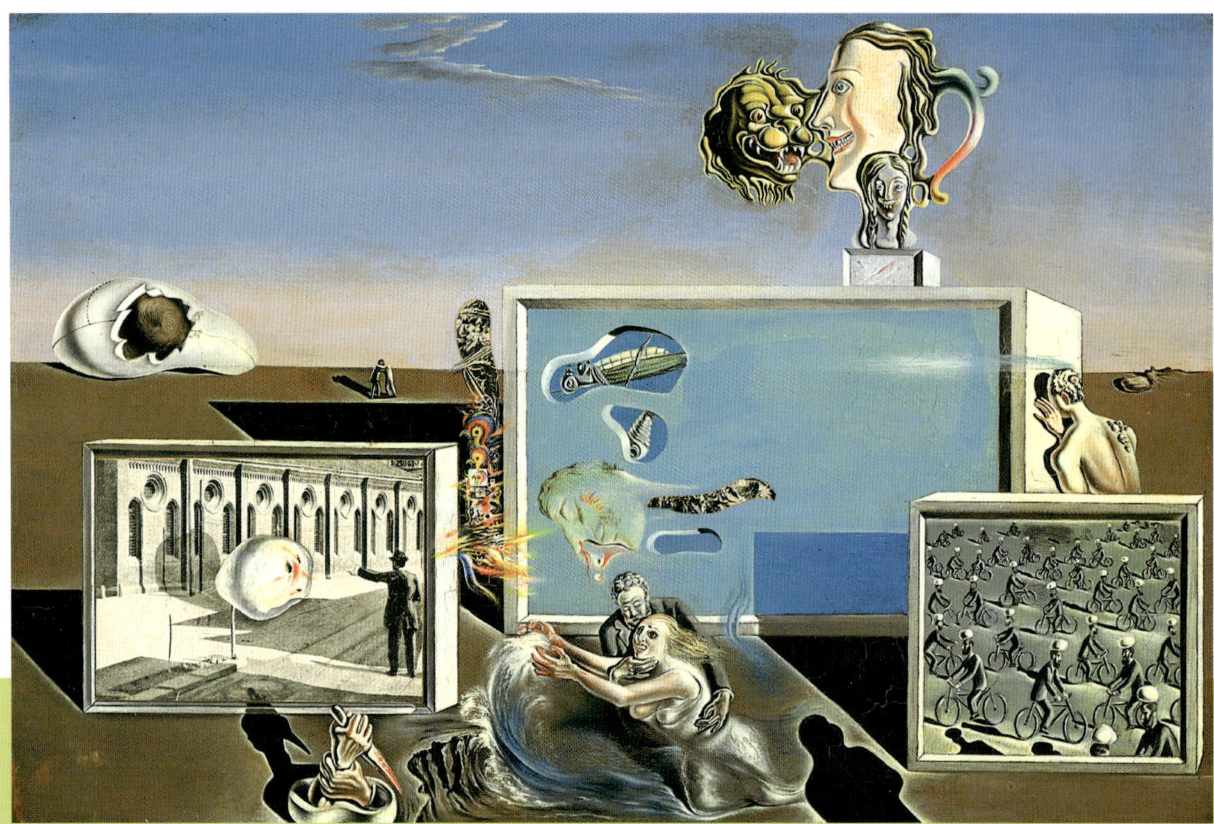

Salvador Dalí
(Figueras 1904 - 1989)

Illuminated Pleasures
Erleuchtete Lüste
Verlichte genoegens
Los placeres iluminados

●●●

1929
23,8 x 34,7 cm / 9.3 x 13.6 in.
Museum of Modern Art (MoMA), New York

oil and collage on panel
Öl und Collage auf Brett
olieverf en collage op paneel
óleo y collage sobre panel

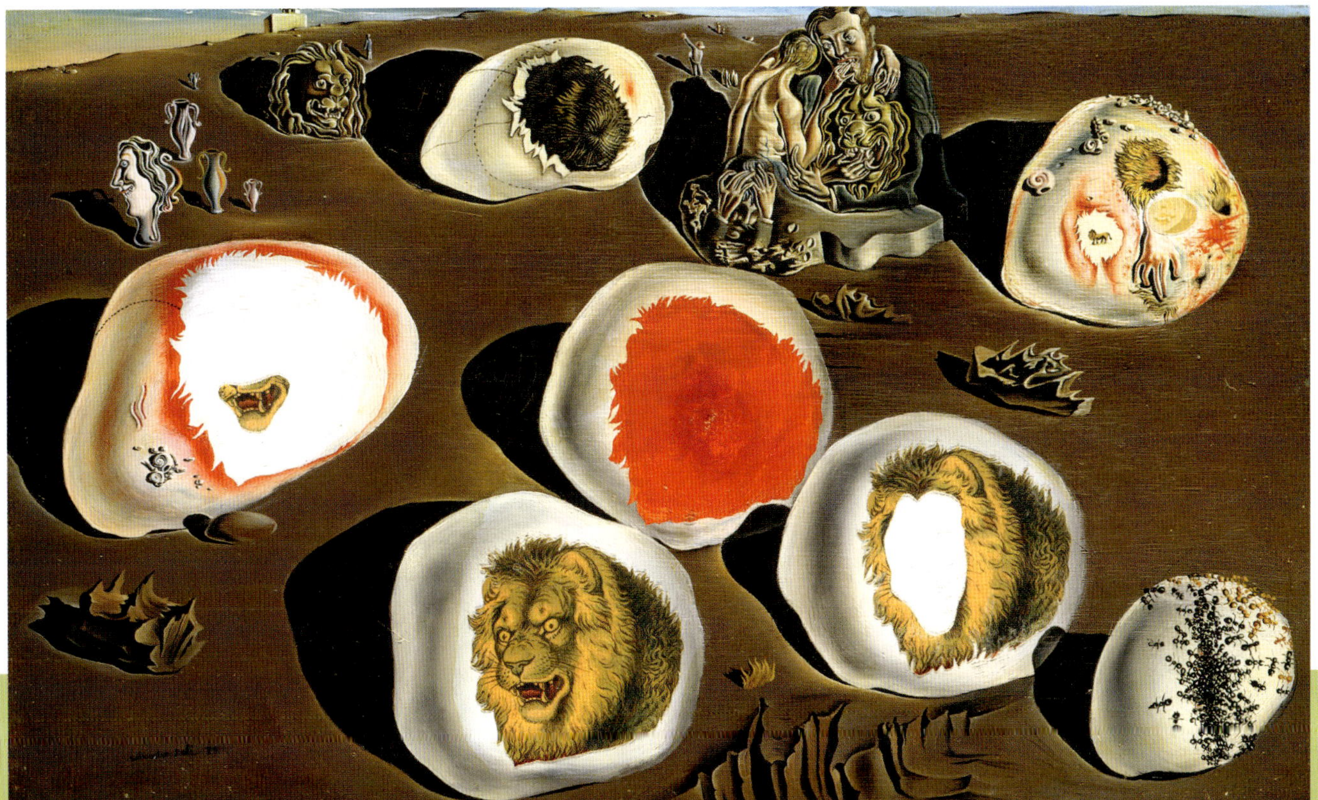

Salvador Dalí
(Figueras 1904 - 1989)

Arrangements of Desire
Zusammenstellung der Begierden
De verzoening van de wens
La acomodación de los deseos

●●●

1929
22,2 x 34,9 cm / 8.7 x 13.7 in.
The Metropolitan Museum of Art, New York

oil and printed paper cut and glued to cardboard
Öl und geschnittenes, bedrucktes und auf Karton geklebtes Papier
olieverf en gedrukt papier uitgeknipt en geplakt op karton
óleo y papel impreso recortado y encolado sobre cartón

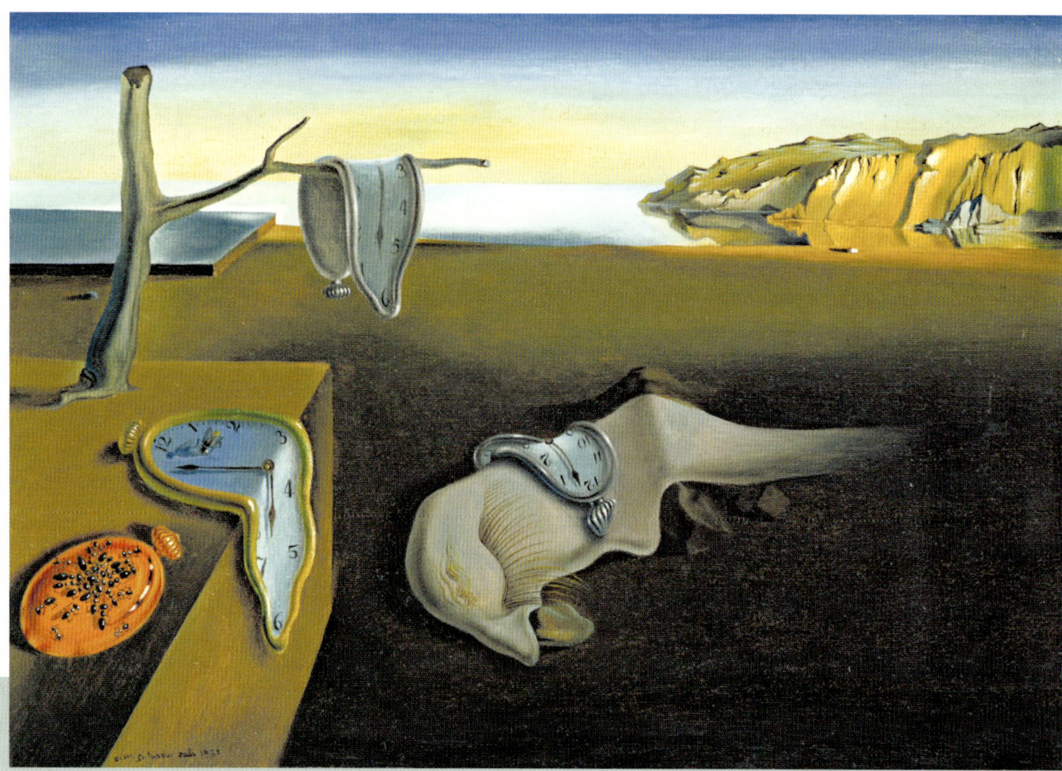

Salvador Dalí
(Figueras 1904 - 1989)

The Persistence of Memory
Die Beständigkeit der Erinnerung
De volharding der herinnering
La persistencia de la memoria

●●●

1931
24,1 x 33 cm / 9 x 13 in.
Museum of Modern Art (MoMA),
New York

oil on canvas / Öl auf Leinwand
olieverf op doek / óleo sobre lienzo

▶ Salvador Dalí
(Figueras 1904 - 1989)

Soft contructions with boiled beans
(Premonition of the Civil War)
Weiche Konstruktion mit gekochten Bohnen
(Vorahnung des Bürgerkriegs)
Zachte constructie met gekookte bonen
(Voorgevoel van de Burgeroorlog)
Construcción blanda con judías hervidas
(Premonición de la Guerra Civil)

●●●

1936
99,9 x 100 cm / 39.3 x 39.4 in.
Philadelphia Museum of Art, Philadelphia

oil on canvas / Öl auf Leinwand
olieverf op doek / óleo sobre lienzo

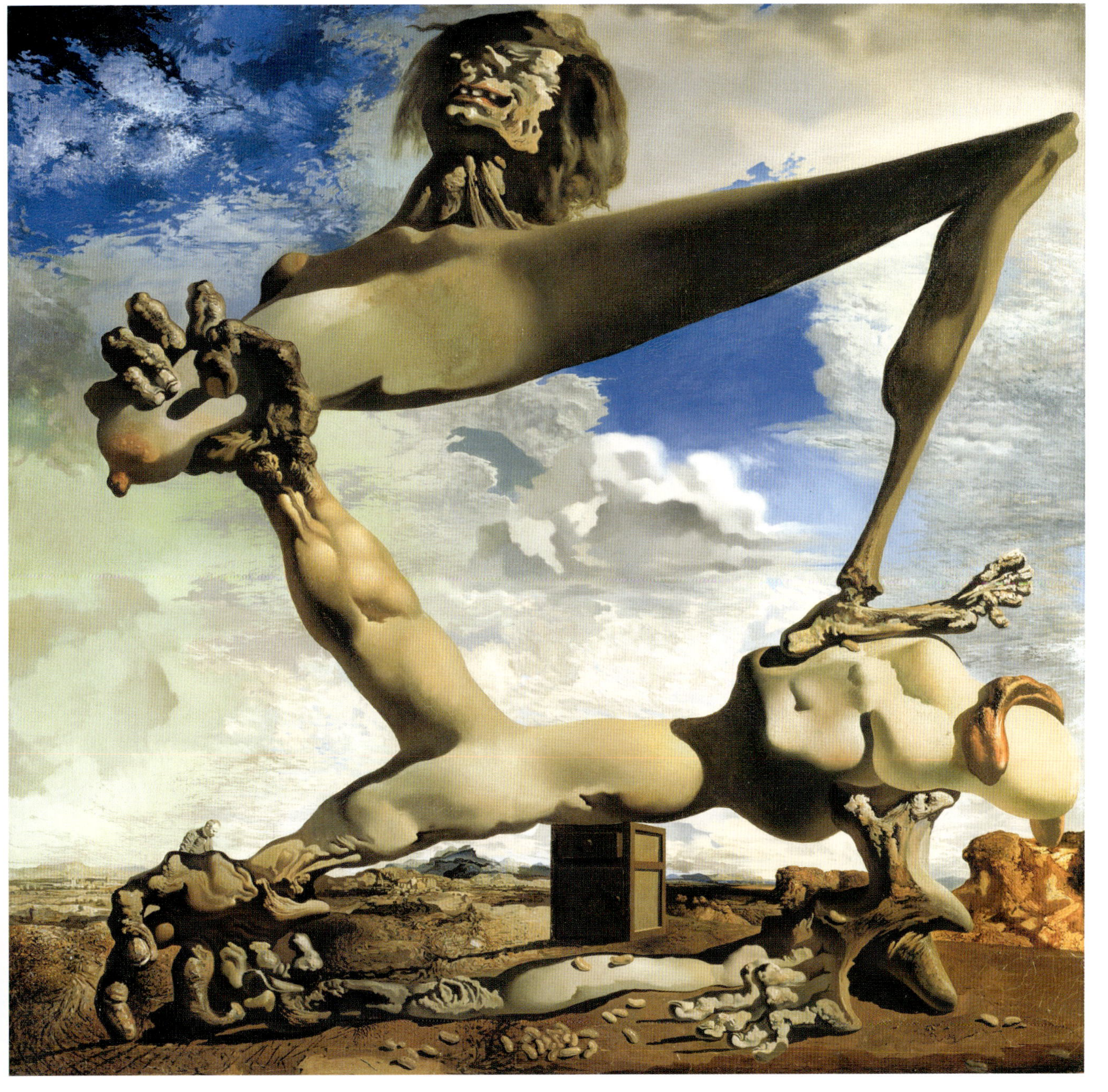

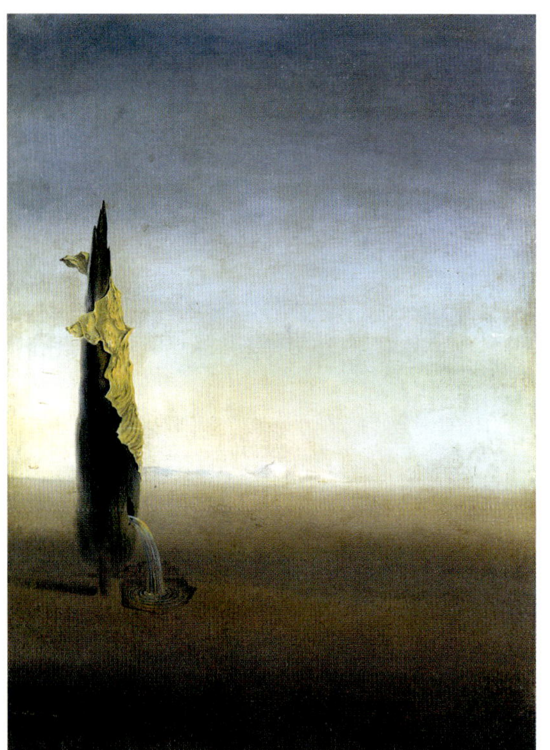

What the public often admires in Dalí is his craft, that savoir-faire worthy of the old masters, amplified by a powerful imagination.

Das, was die Betrachter oft an Dalí schätzen, ist seine Fertigkeit, dieses Savoir-faire, das den alten Meistern würdig ist und durch eine starke Vorstellungskraft angereichert wird.

Wat het publiek vaak in Dalí waardeert, is zijn vakkundigheid, zijn savoir-faire waarover oude meesters beschikten, vergroot door een sterke verbeelding.

Lo que el público aprecia a menudo en Dalí es su oficio, este savoir-faire digno de los viejos maestros, ampliado gracias a una poderosa imaginación.

346

▲ Salvador Dalí
(Figueras 1904 - 1989)

The Birth of Liquid Anxieties
Die Geburt des flüssigen Verlangens
De geboorte van vloeibare bezorgheid
El nacimiento de las angustias líquidas

●

1932
86,5 x 70 cm / 34 x 27.5 in.
Hamburger Kunsthalle, Hamburg

oil on canvas / Öl auf Leinwand
olieverf op doek / óleo sobre lienzo

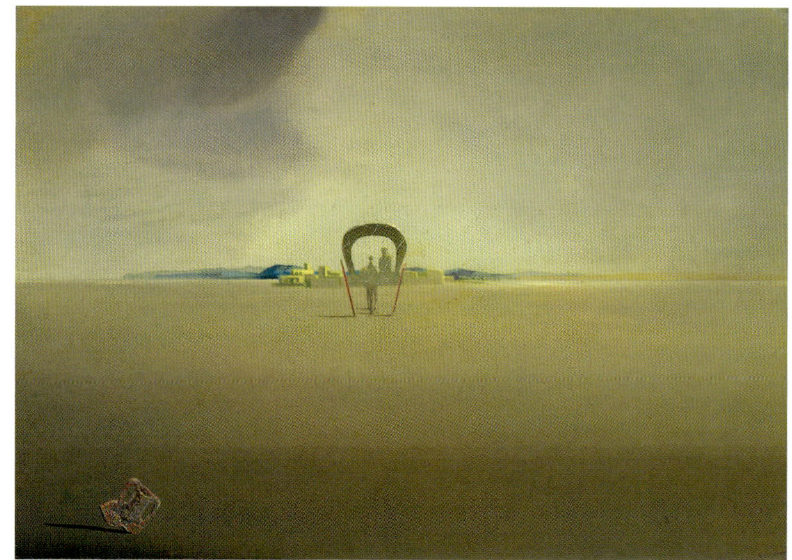

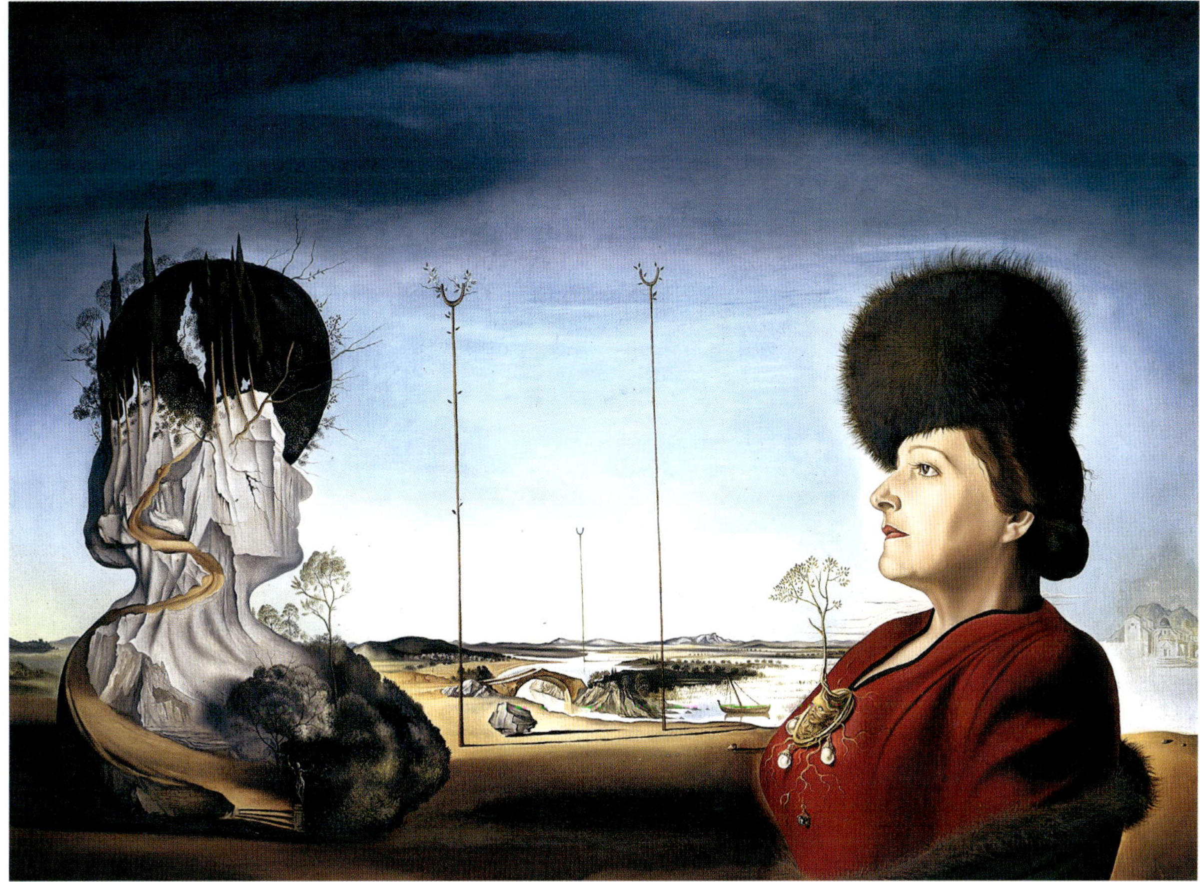

◄ Salvador Dalí
(Figueras 1904 - 1989)

The phantom cart
Der Phantomwagen
De spookkar
La carreta fantasma

●●

1933
5,9 x 21,9 cm / 2.3 x 8.6 in.
Yale University Art Gallery, New Haven (CT)

oil on wood / Öl auf Holz
olieverf op hout / óleo sobre madera

Salvador Dalí
(Figueras 1904 - 1989)

Portrait of Mrs. Isabel Styler-Tas (Melancholy)
Bildnis Isabel Styler-Tas (Melancolia)
Portret van Isabel Styler-Tas (Melancholie)
Retrato de la señora Isabel Styler-Tas (Melancolía)

●●●

1945
65,5 x 86 cm / 25.8 x 33.8 in.
Nationalgalerie, Staatliche Museen, Berlin

oil on canvas / Öl auf Leinwand
olieverf op doek / óleo sobre lienzo

Max Ernst
(Brühl 1891 - Paris 1976)

Ubu imperator

●●

1923
81 x 65 cm / 31.9 x 25.6 in.
Centre Georges Pompidou,
Musée National d'Art Moderne, Paris

oil on canvas
Öl auf Leinwand
olieverf op doek
óleo sobre lienzo

Max Ernst
(Brühl 1891 - Paris 1976)

Pietà or La Revolution la nuit
Pietà oder Die Revolution bei Nacht
Pietà of Nachtelijke revolutie
Piedad o La Revolution la nuit

●●●

1923
116,2 x 88,9 cm / 45.8 x 35 in.
Tate Modern, London

oil on canvas / Öl auf Leinwand
olieverf op doek / óleo sobre lienzo

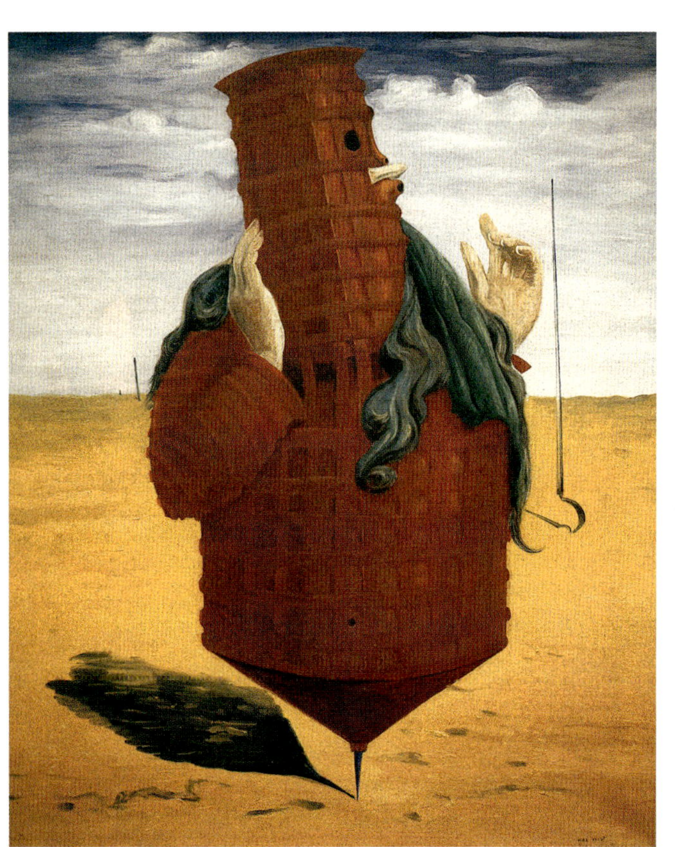

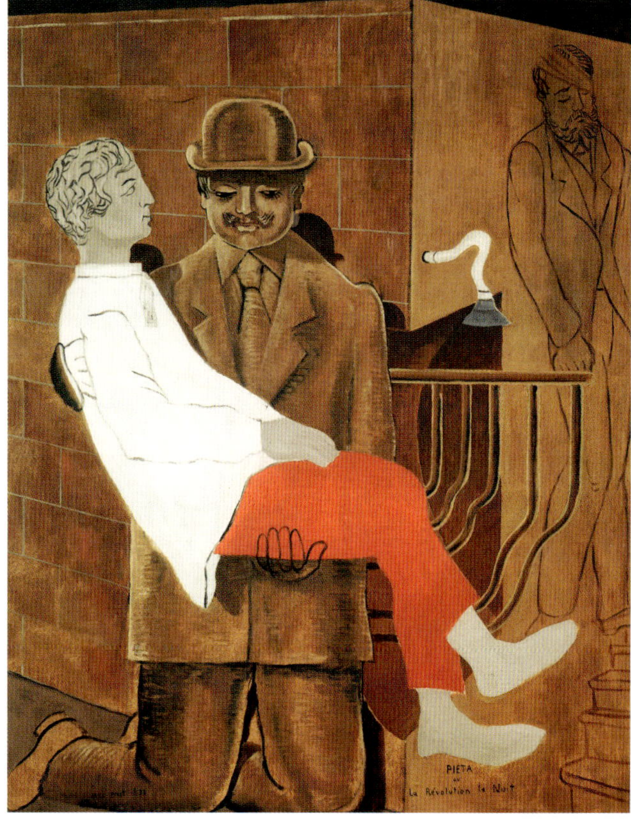

Max Ernst
(Brühl 1891 - Paris 1976)

Fleur coquille

•

1927
19 x 24 cm / 7.5 x 9.4 in.
Museo Thyssen-Bornemisza, Madrid

oil on canvas
Öl auf Leinwand
olieverf op doek
óleo sobre lienzo

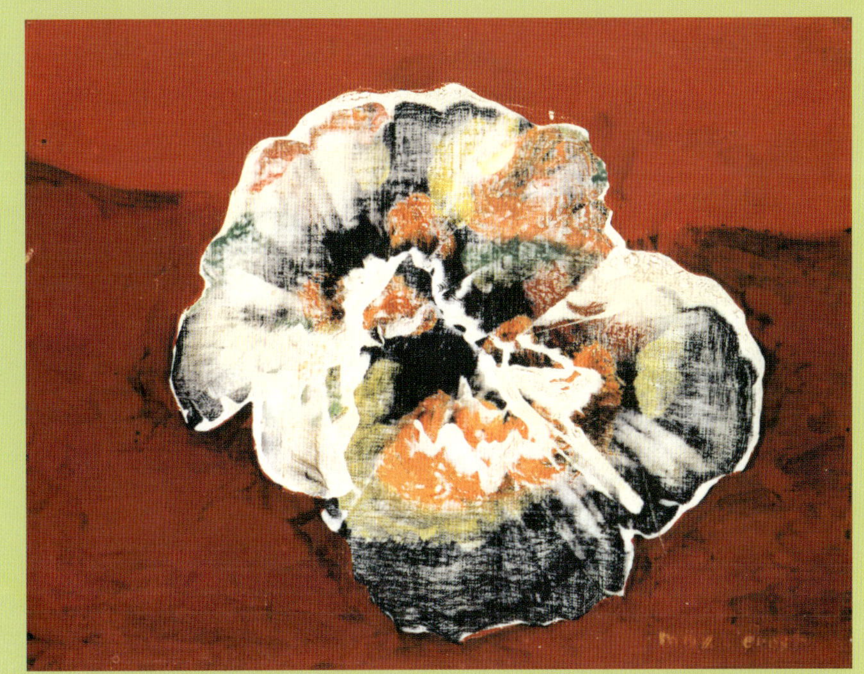

Max Ernst
(Brühl 1891 - Paris 1976)

Chimera
Mischwesen
Chimère
Quimera

••

1928
114 x 145,8 cm / 44.9 x 57.4 in.
Centre Georges Pompidou,
Musée National d'Art Moderne, Paris

oil on canvas
Öl auf Leinwand
olieverf op doek
óleo sobre lienzo

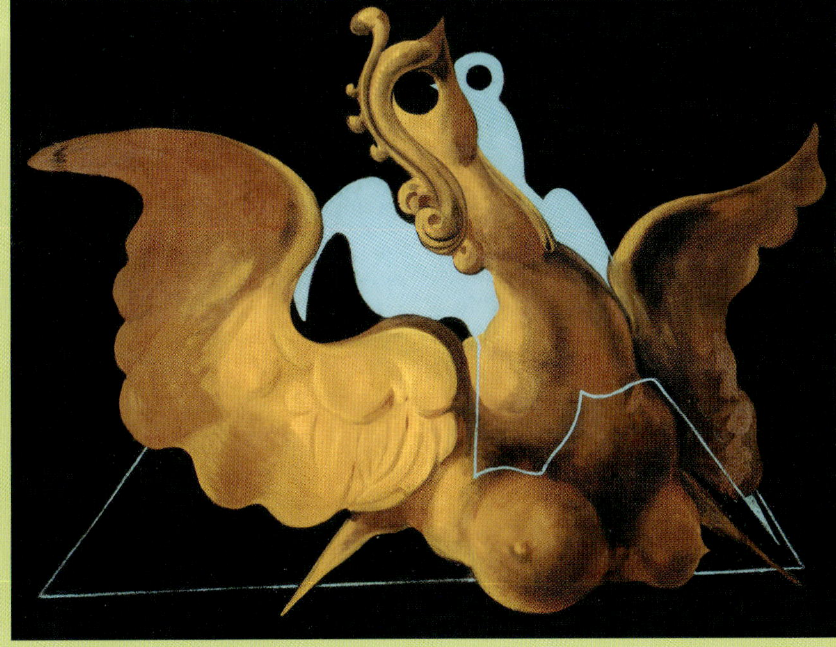

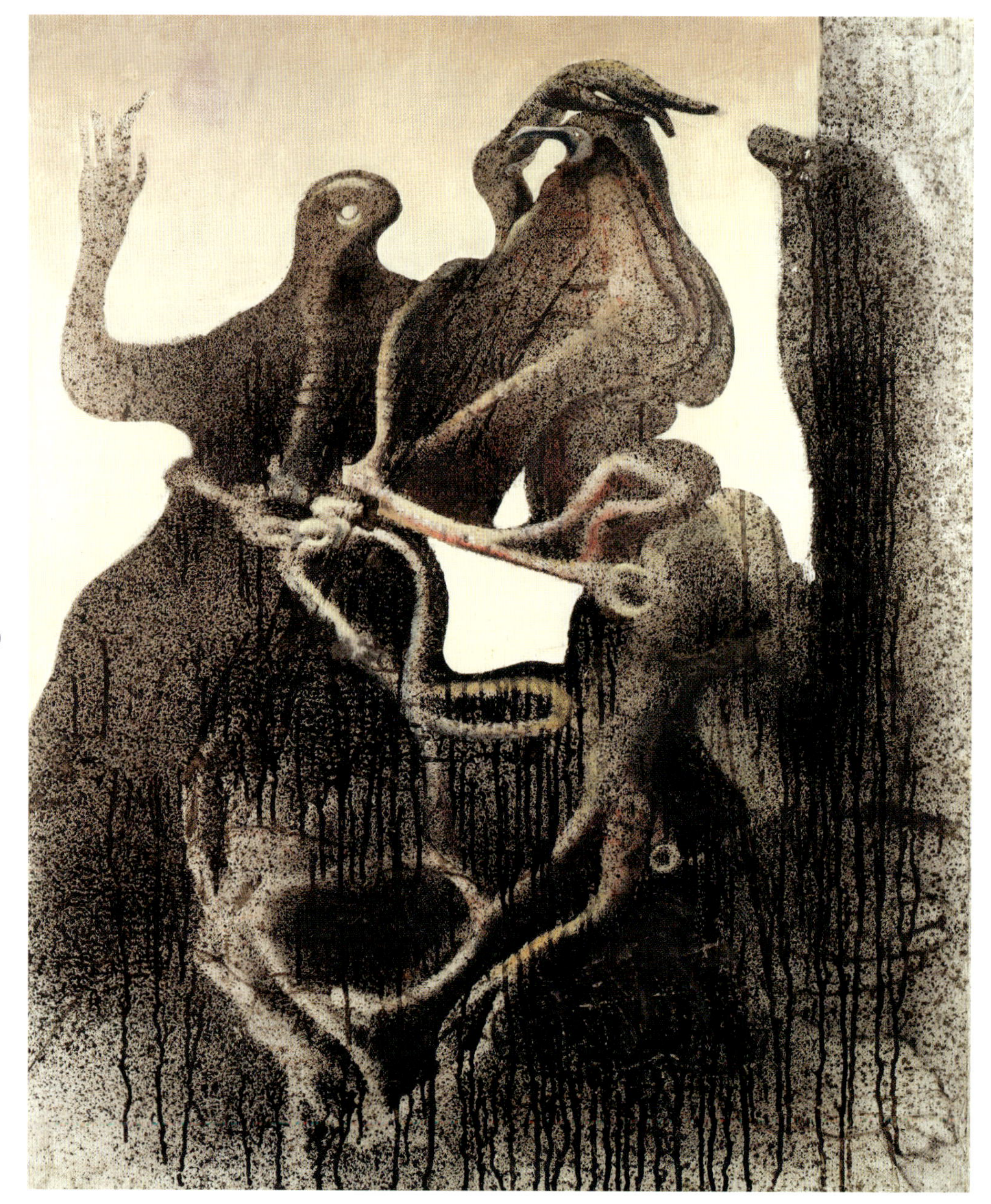

Max Ernst
(Brühl 1891 - Paris 1976)
**Zoomorphic couple
Zoomorphes Paar
Het zoömorfische stel
Pareja zoomorfa**

●

1933
91,9 x 73,3 cm
36.2 x 28.8 in.
Collezione Peggy Guggenheim,
Venezia

oil on canvas
Öl auf Leinwand
olieverf op doek
óleo sobre lienzo

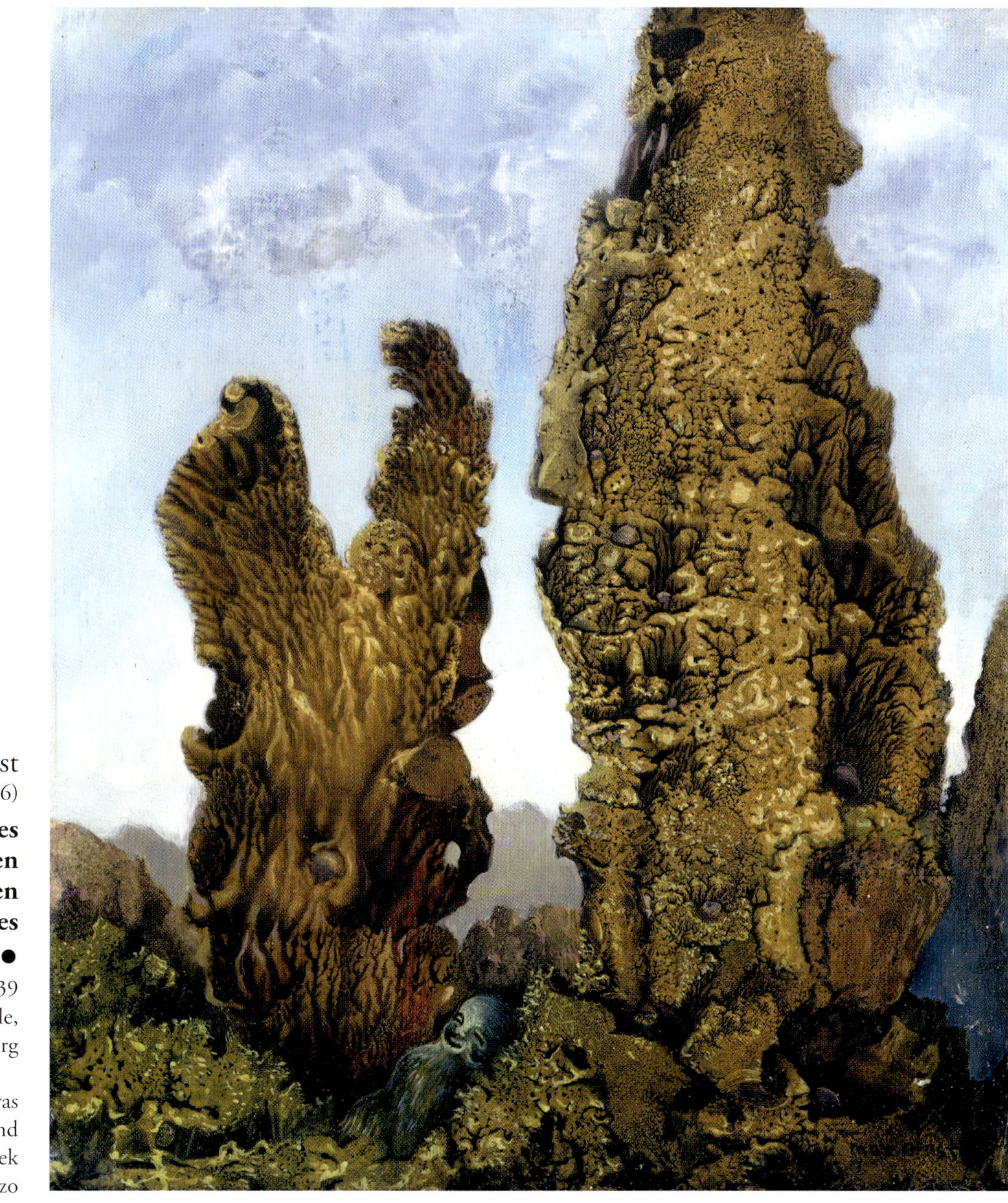

Max Ernst
(Brühl 1891 - Paris 1976)

**Cypresses
Zypressen
Cipressen
Cipreses**

● ●

1939
Hamburger Kunsthalle,
Hamburg

oil on canvas
Öl auf Leinwand
olieverf op doek
óleo sobre lienzo

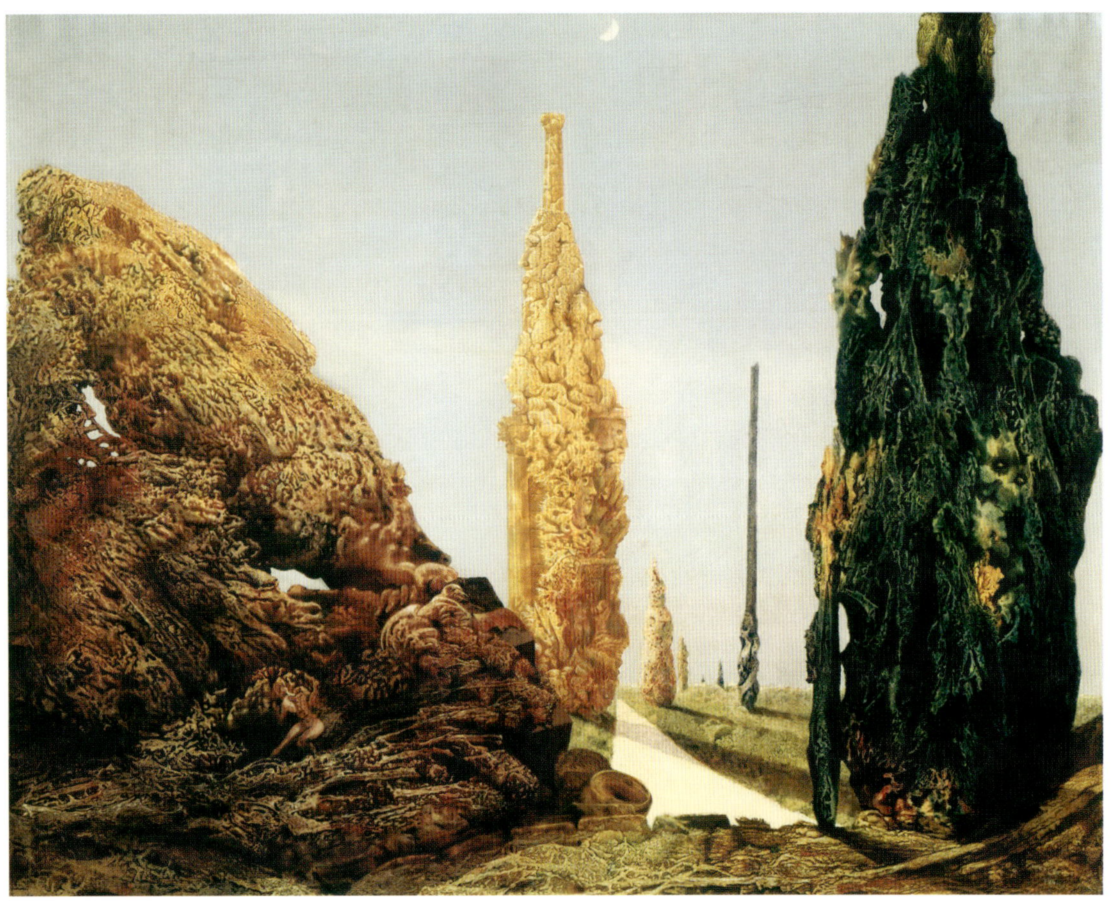

Max Ernst
(Brühl 1891 - Paris 1976)

Solitary Tree and and Conjugal Trees
Einsamer Baum und vermählte Bäume
Eenzame boom en gehuwde bomen
Árbol solitario y árboles conyugales

● ●

1940
81,5 x 100,5 cm / 32.1 x 39.5 in.
Museo Thyssen-Bornemisza, Madrid

oil on canvas / Öl auf Leinwand
olieverf op doek / óleo sobre lienzo

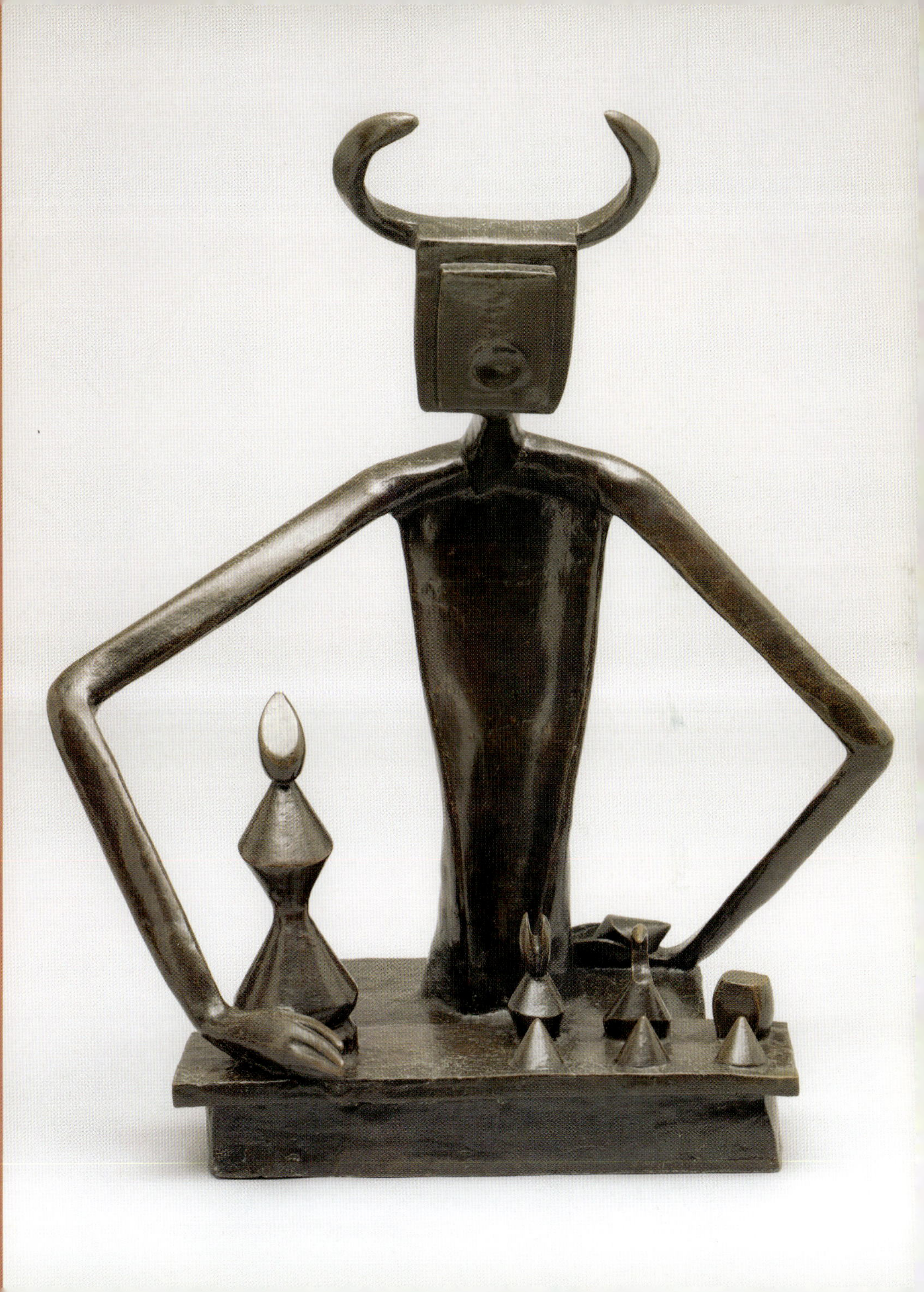

Max Ernst
(Brühl 1891 - Paris 1976)

**The King plays
with the Queen
Der König spielt
mit der Königin
De koning speelt
met de koningin
El rey juega
con la reina**

•••

1944 (1954)
h. 97,8 cm / 38.5 in.
Museum of Modern Art
(MoMA), New York

bronze
Bronz
brons
bronce

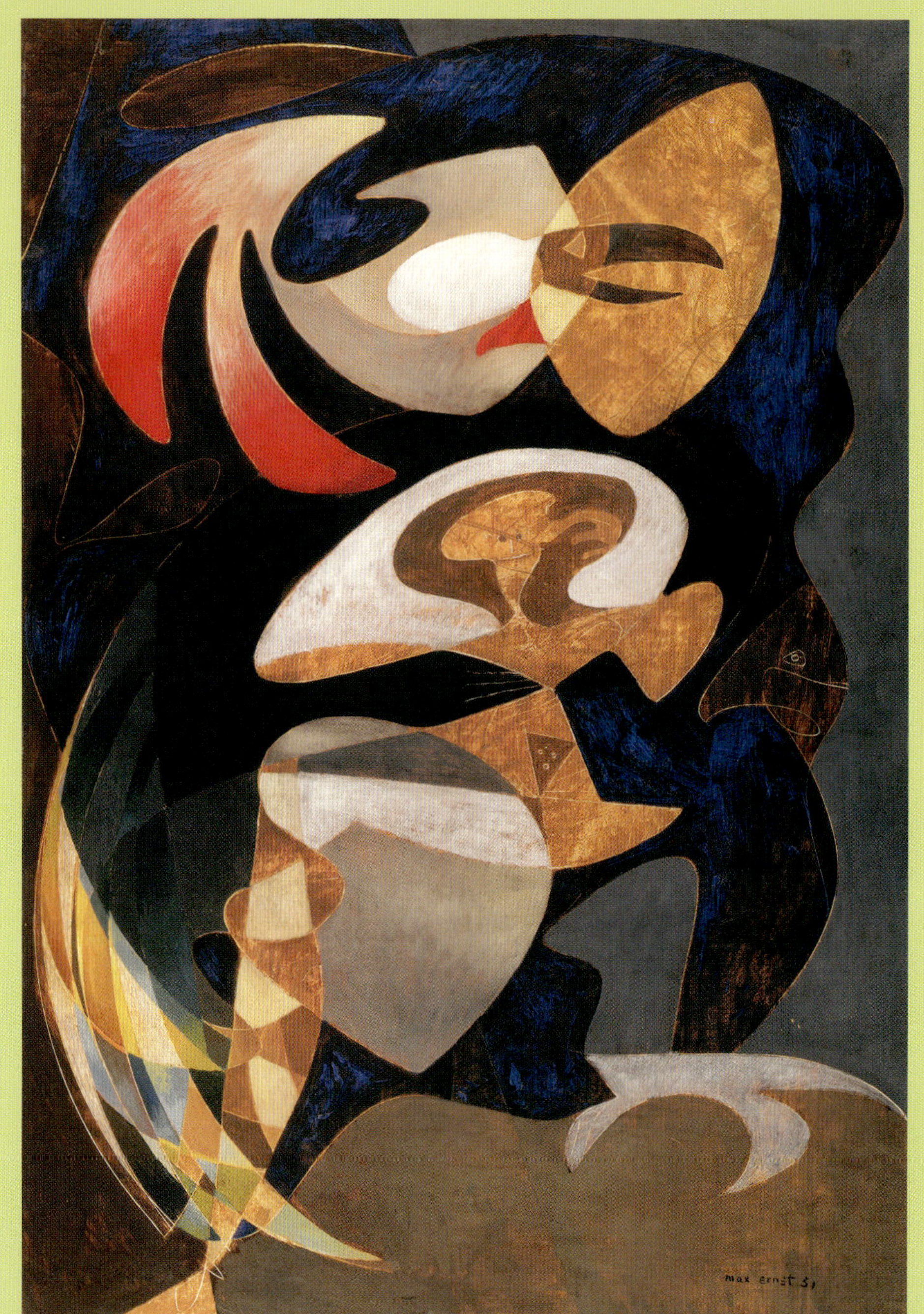

▶ Max Ernst
(Brühl 1891 - Paris 1976)

The Forest
Der Wald
Het woud
El bosque
● ● ●

Collezione Mazzotta, Milano

◀ Max Ernst
(Brühl 1891 - Paris 1976)

The weatherman
Der Wettermann
●

1951
92 x 62 cm / 36.2 x 24.4 in.
Ca' Pesaro Galleria d'Arte Moderna,
Venezia

oil on hardboards
Öl auf Hartfaserplatte
olieverf op masoniet
óleo sobre masonita

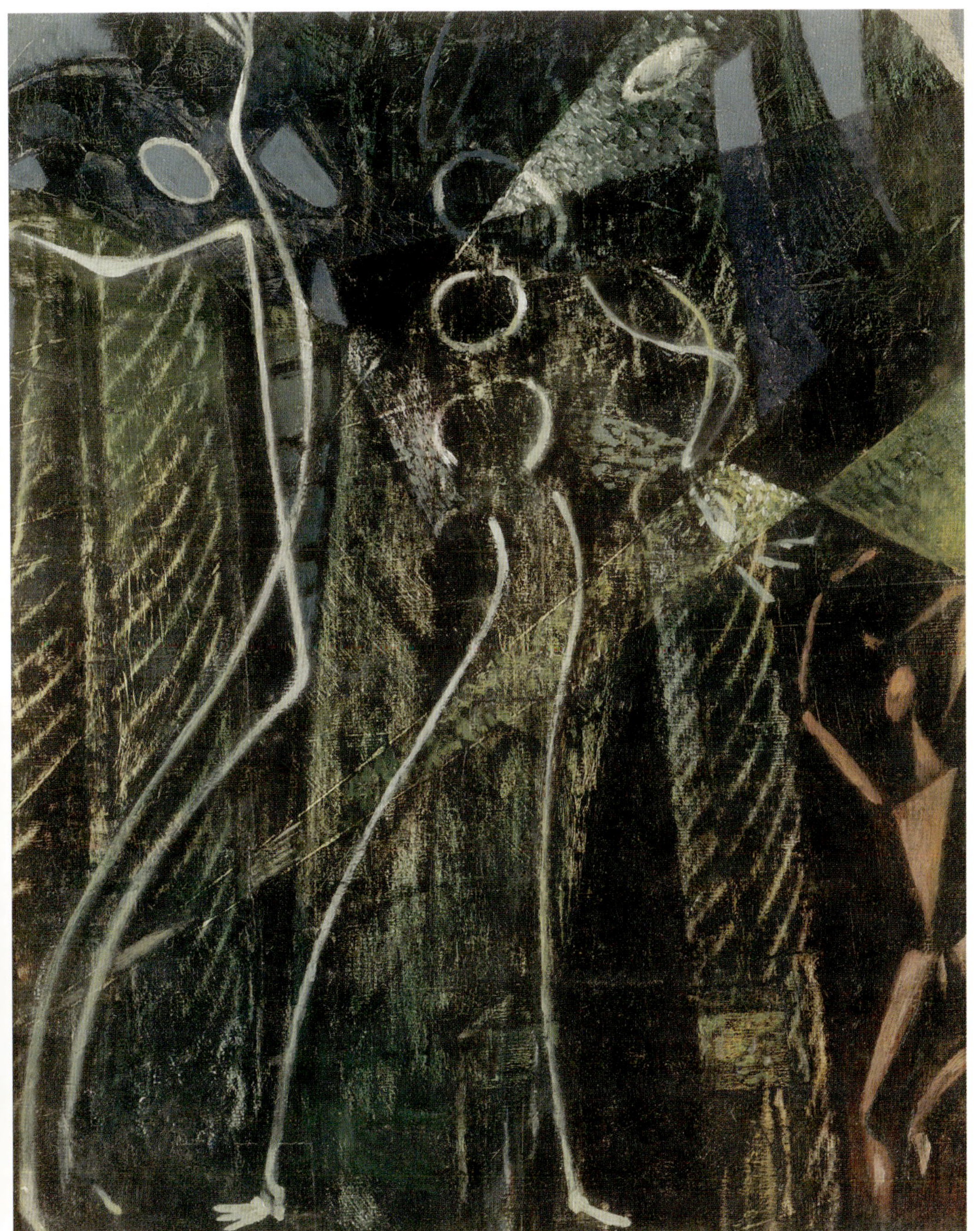

Through the technique
of rubbing and
scraping of the canvas,
the event reveals
unexpected shapes
that animate the
surfaces in an uneasy
manner.

Mittels der Technik
des Scheuerns
und Kratzens der
Leinwand, kommen
durch Zufall
unerwartete Formen
zum Vorschein, die
die Oberfläche auf
beunruhigende Weise
beleben.

Door het doek in te
wrijven of te schuren
worden onverwachte
vormen verkregen die
het oppervlak op een
verontrustende manier
verlevendigen.

A través de la técnica
del frotamiento o del
rasgado del lienzo,
el azar revela formas
inesperadas que
animan la superficie
de una manera
inquietante.

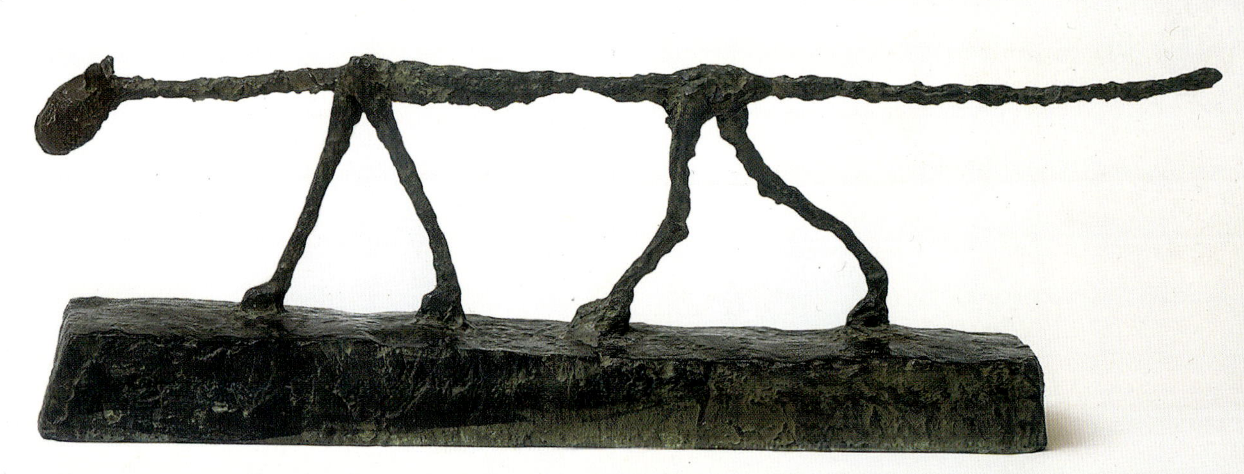

Alberto Giacometti

356

(Borgonovo di Stampa 1901 - Chur 1966)

The Cat
Die Katze
De kat
El gato
●●●

1951
81 x 25 cm / 31.9 x 9.8 in.
Museum Berggruen, Staatliche Museen, Berlin

bronze / Bronze / brons / bronce

▶ Hans Bellmer

(Katowice 1902 - Paris 1975)

The Immobile Hands
Die unbeweglichen Hände
De bewegingloze handen
Las manos inmóviles
●

28 x 27 x 17 cm / 11 x 10.6 x 6.7 in.
Private collection / Private Sammlung
Privécollectie / Colección privada

bronze / Bronze / brons / bronce

"In a fire, between a Rembrandt and a cat, I would save the cat."

"Aus einem brennenden Haus würde ich eher eine Katze als einen Rembrandt retten."

"Als ik bij brand of een Rembrandt of een kat moest redden, zou ik voor de kat kiezen."

"En un incendio, entre un Rembrandt y un gato, salvaría el gato."
Alberto Giacometti

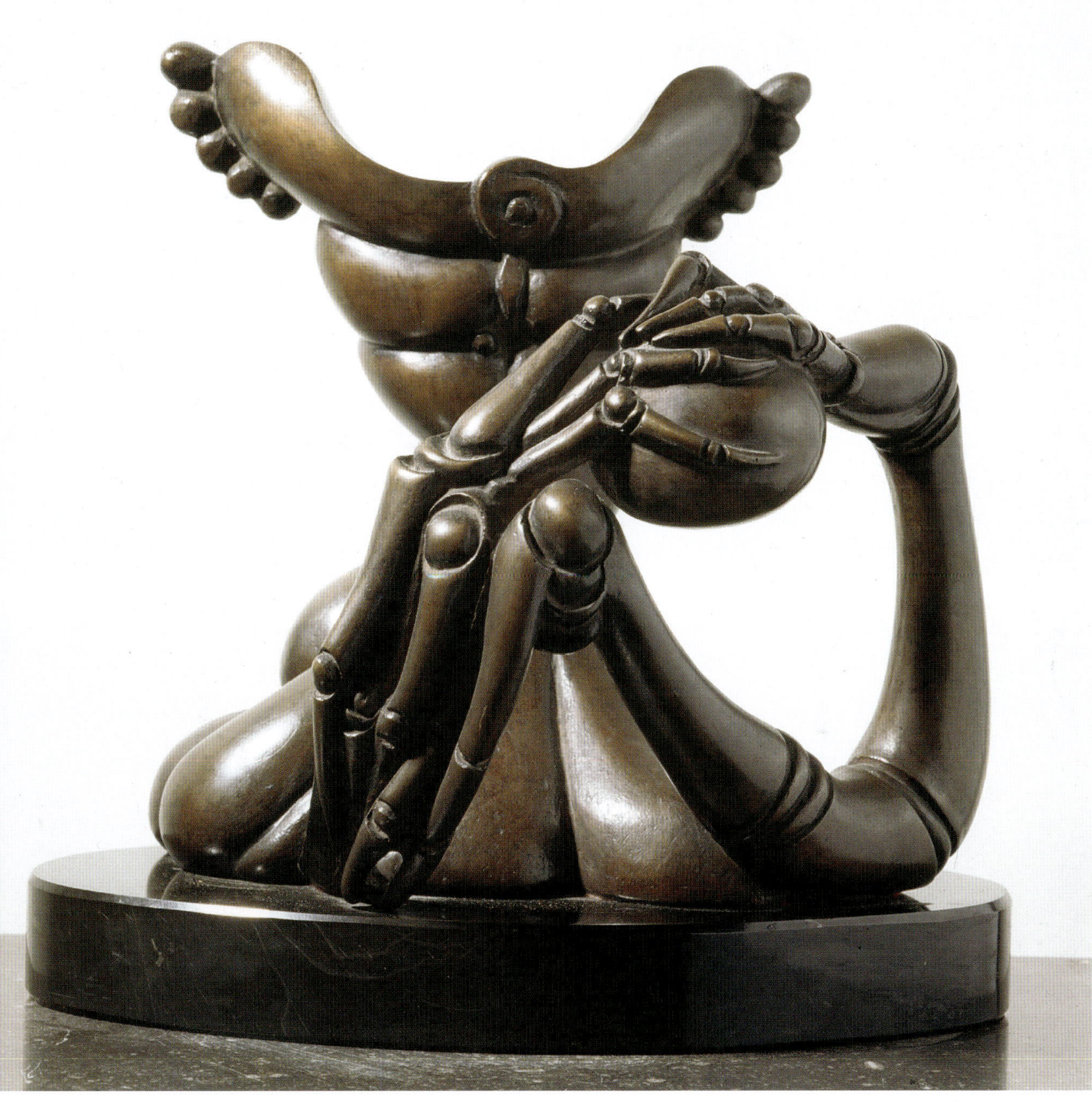

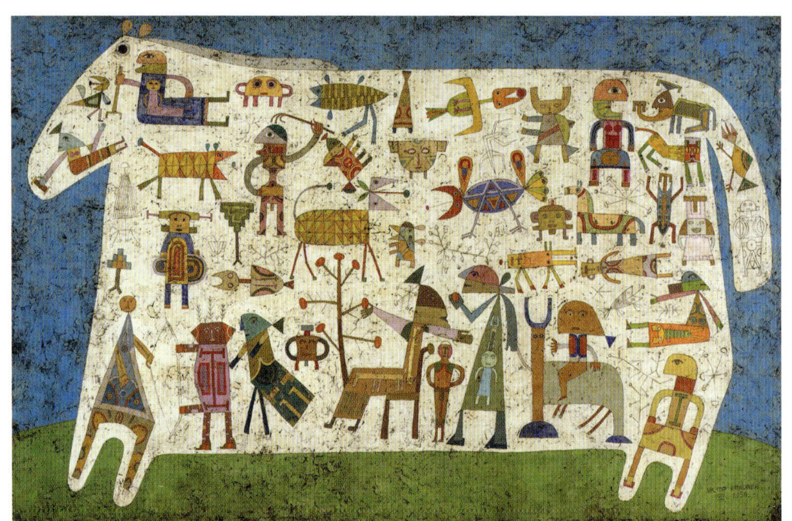

Victor Brauner
(Piatra-Neamt 1903 - Paris 1966)

Prelude to Civilisation
Präludium zur Zivilisation
Inleiding van de beschaving
Preludio de la civilización

● ●

1954
129,5 x 202,5 cm / 51 x 79.8 in.
The Metropolitan Museum of Art, New York

encaustic and pen and ink on masonite
Wachsmalerei, Feder und Tinte auf Holzfaserplatte
encaustiek en pen en inkt op masoniet
encáustica y pluma y tinta sobre masonita

Victor Brauner
(Piatra-Neamt 1903 - Paris 1966)

The woman and the Bird
Die Frau und der Vogel
De vrouw en de vogel
La mujer y el pájaro

●

1955
65 x 54 cm / 25.6 x 21.2 in.
Musée de Grenoble, Grenoble

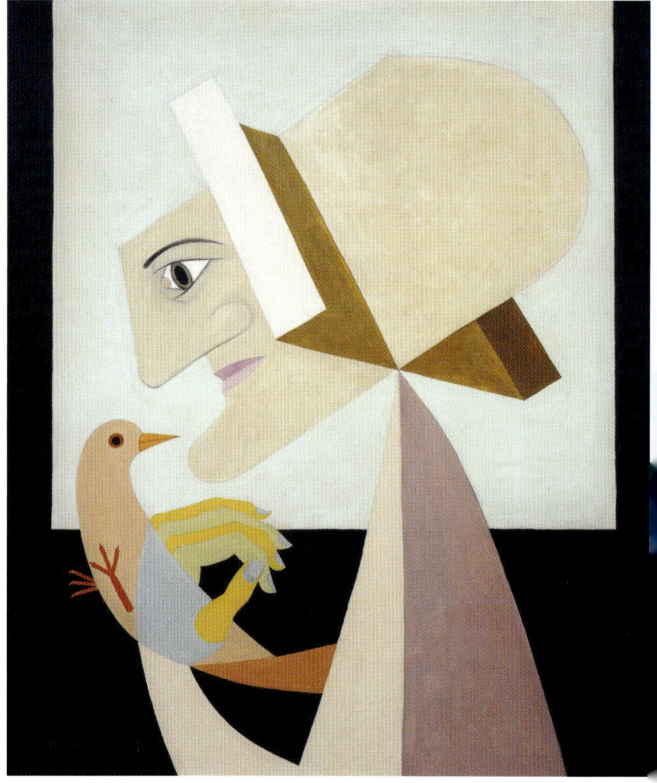

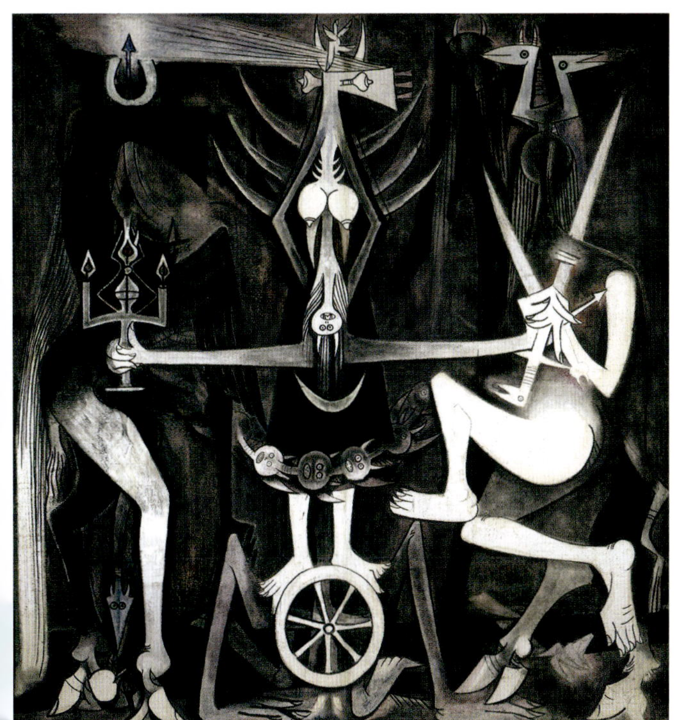

Wilfredo Lam
(Sagua la Grande 1902 - Paris 1982)

The Wedding
Die Hochzeit
De bruiloft
Las bodas

●

1947
215 x 197 cm / 84.7 x 77.6 in.
Nationalgalerie, Staatliche Museen, Berlin

oil on canvas
Öl auf Leinwand
olieverf op doek
óleo sobre lienzo

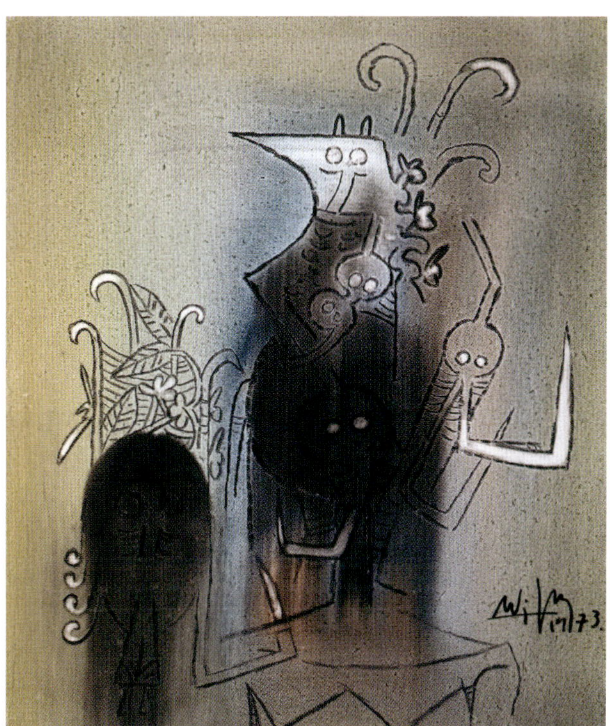

Wilfredo Lam
(Sagua la Grande 1902 - Paris 1982)

The Awakening of Spring
Das Wiedererwachen des Frühlings
Het ontwaken van de lente
El despertar de la primavera

● ● ●

1975
Musée des Beaux-Arts, Lyon

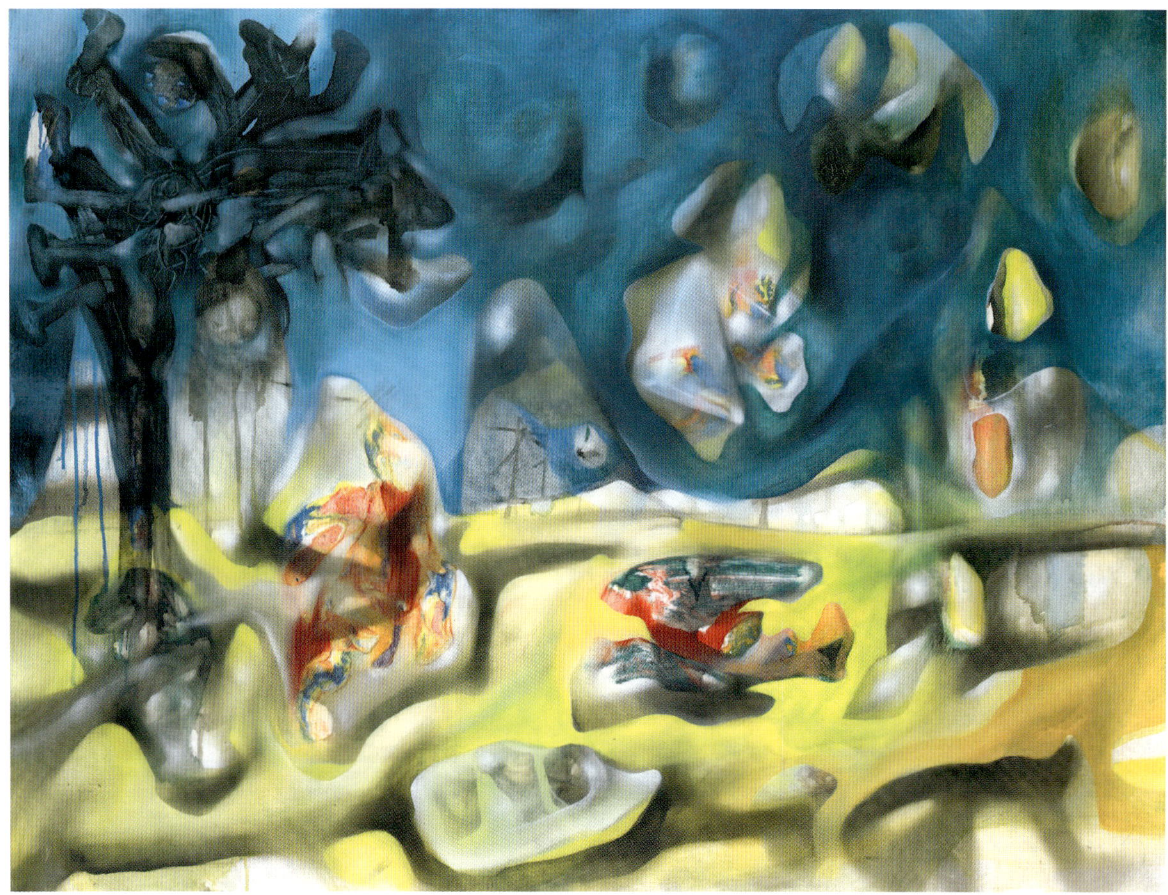

Roberto Sebastian Echaurren Matta
(Santiago de Chile 1911 - Civitavecchia 2002)

Fabulous Race Track of Death (Instrument very dangerous to the eye)
Fabelhafte Todesrennstrecke (Äußerst gefährliches Instrument für das Auge)
Ongelooflijk parcours van de dood (zeer gevaarlijk instrument voor het oog)
Pista fabulosa de la muerte (Instrumento muy peligroso para el ojo)

●●

ca. 1941
71,1 x 91,4 cm / 28 x 36 in.
Yale University Art Gallery, New Haven (CT)

oil on canvas / Öl auf Leinwand
olieverf op doek / óleo sobre lienzo

Roberto Sebastian Echaurren Matta

(Santiago de Chile 1911 - Civitavecchia 2002)

The Bachelors Twenty Years Later
Junggesellen 20 Jahre später
De vrijgezellen twintig jaar later
Los solteros veinte años después

●

1943
96,5 x 101,6 cm / 38 x 40 in.
Philadelphia Museum of Art, Philadelphia

oil on canvas / Öl auf Leinwand
olieverf op doek / óleo sobre lienzo

This painting, which appears to be the result of automatic gestures, refers to the work of Duchamp, *The Bride Stripped bare by her Bachelor*s.

Dieses Bild erscheint als Ergebnis von automatischen Gesten und es verweist Duchamps Werk *Die Braut wird von ihren Freiern entblößt*.

Dit schilderij, dat het resultaat lijkt van automatische gebaren, verwijst naar het werk van Duchamp *De bruid, ontbloot van haar vrijgezellen*.

Este cuadro, que parece el resultado de gestos automáticos, hace referencia a la obra de Duchamp *La novia desnudada por sus solteros*.

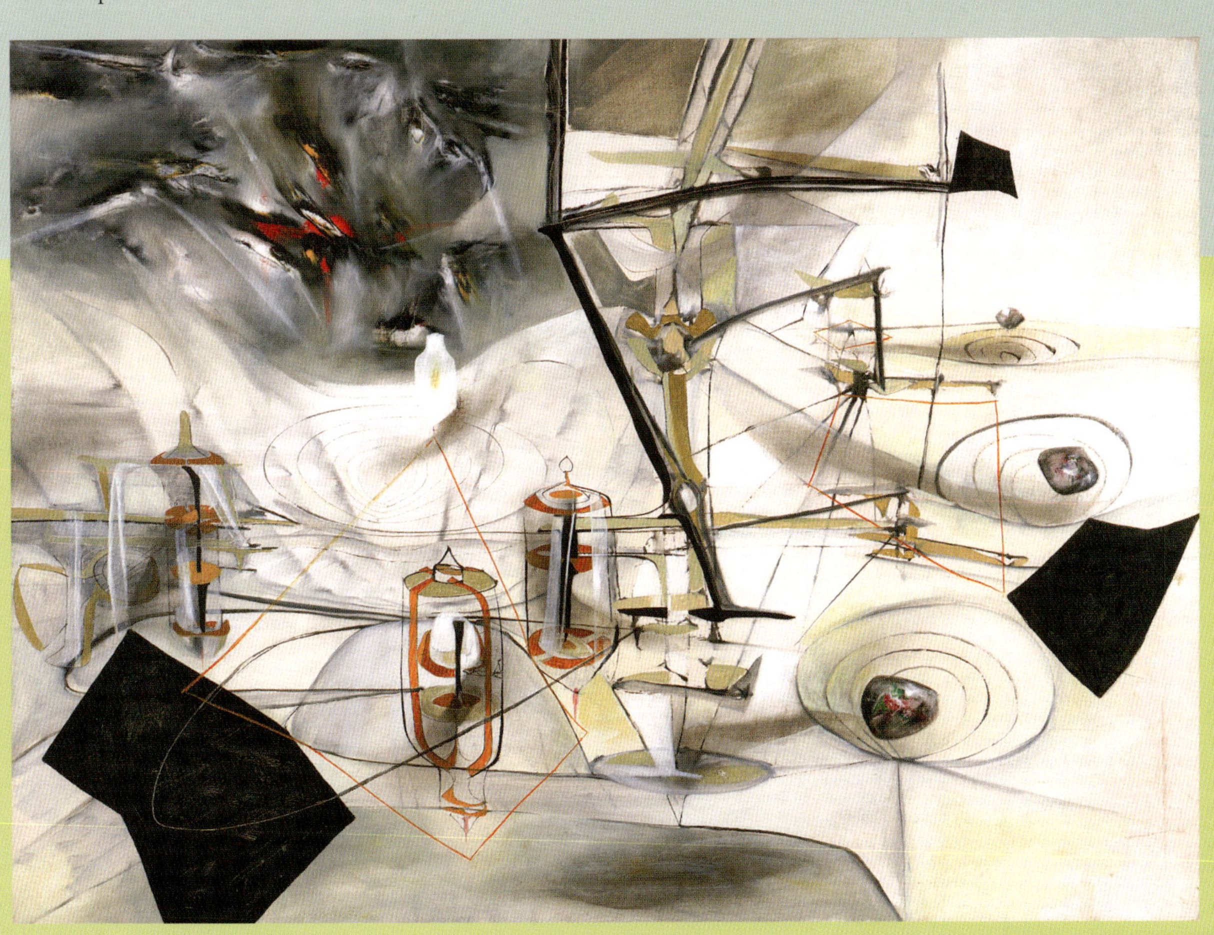

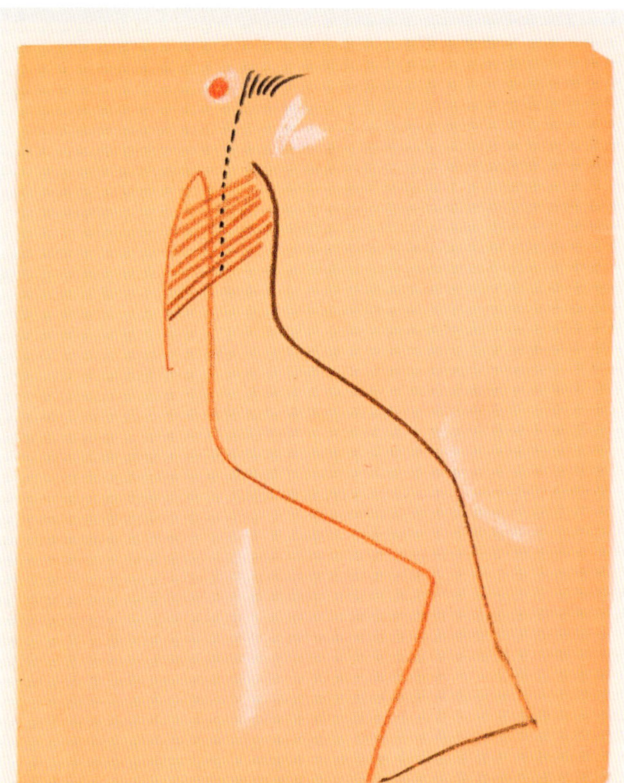

Georges Bataille
(Billom 1897 - Paris 1962)

Untitled drawing for Soleil Vitré
Zeichnung ohne Titel für Soleil Vitré
Tekening zonder titel voor Soleil Vitré
Dibujo sin título para Soleil Vitré

●●

29,2 x 22,2 cm / 11.5 x 8.7 in.
Museum of Modern Art (MoMA), New York

crayon and graphite on buff paper
Pastell und Graphit auf Pauspapier
pastel en grafiet op geel papier
pastel y grafito sobre papel beige

Georges Bataille
(Billom 1897 - Paris 1962)

Untitled drawing for Soleil Vitré
Zeichnung ohne Titel für Soleil Vitré
Tekening zonder titel voor Soleil Vitré
Dibujo sin título para Soleil Vitré

●●

29,2 x 22,2 cm / 11.5 x 8.7 in.
Museum of Modern Art (MoMA), New York

crayon and graphite on buff paper
Pastell und Graphit auf Papier lucida
pastel en grafiet op geel papier
pastel y grafito sobre papel beige

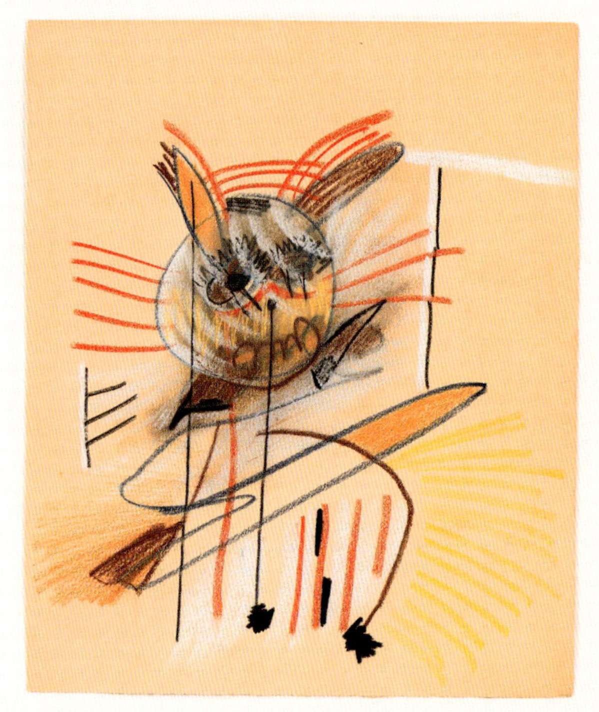

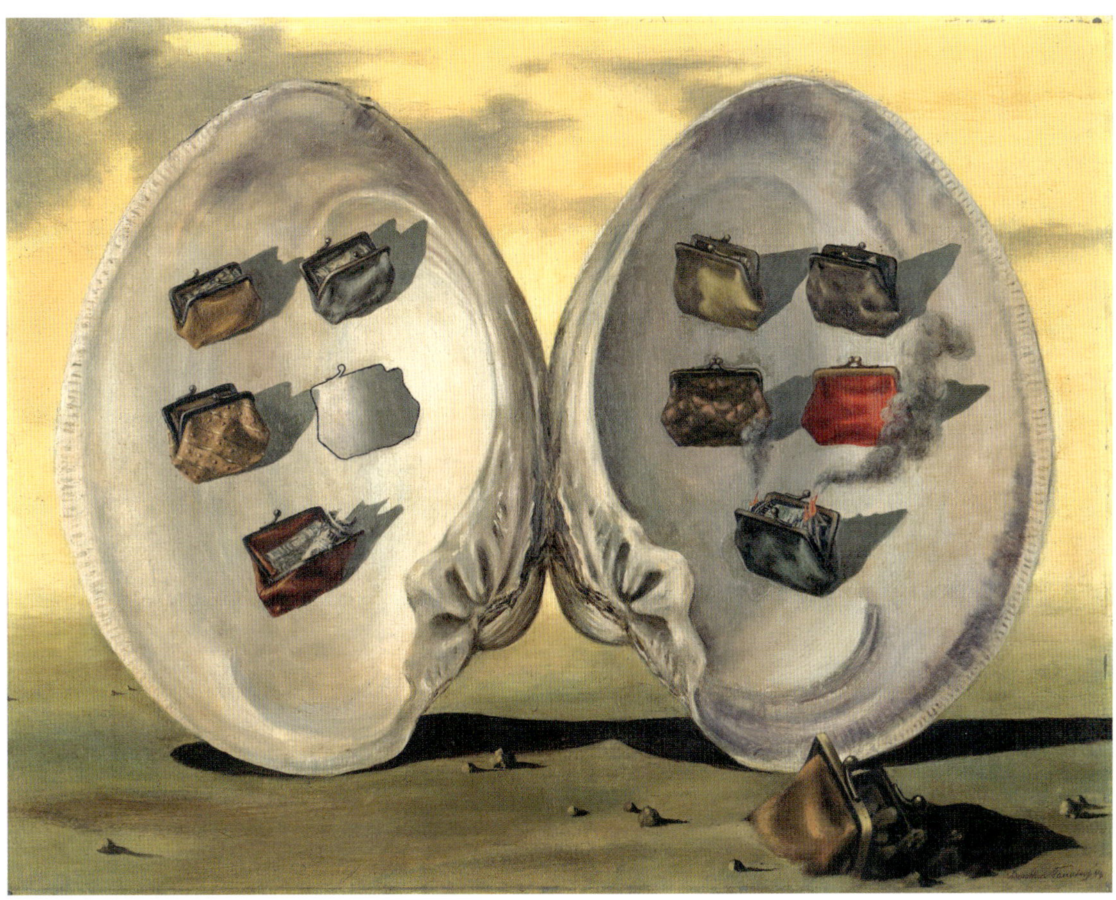

Dorothea Tanning
(Galesburg 1910)

Dream
Traum
Droom
Sueño

●

1944
40,6 x 50,8 cm / 16 x 20 in.
Yale University Art Gallery, New Haven (CT)

oil on canvas / Öl auf Leinwand
olieverf op doek / óleo sobre lienzo

Alexander Calder
(Lawnton 1898 - New York 1976)

Spider
Spinne
Spin
Araña

●●●

1939
203,5 x 224,5 x 92,6 cm / 80.1 x 88.4 x 36.4 in.
Museum of Modern Art (MoMA), New York

laminate of painted aluminium, reinforcing rod and steel cable
Lackierte Aluminiumplatte, Rundeisen und Stahlseil
geverniste aluminiumplaat, stang en stalen kabel
lámina de aluminio pintado, varilla y cable de acero

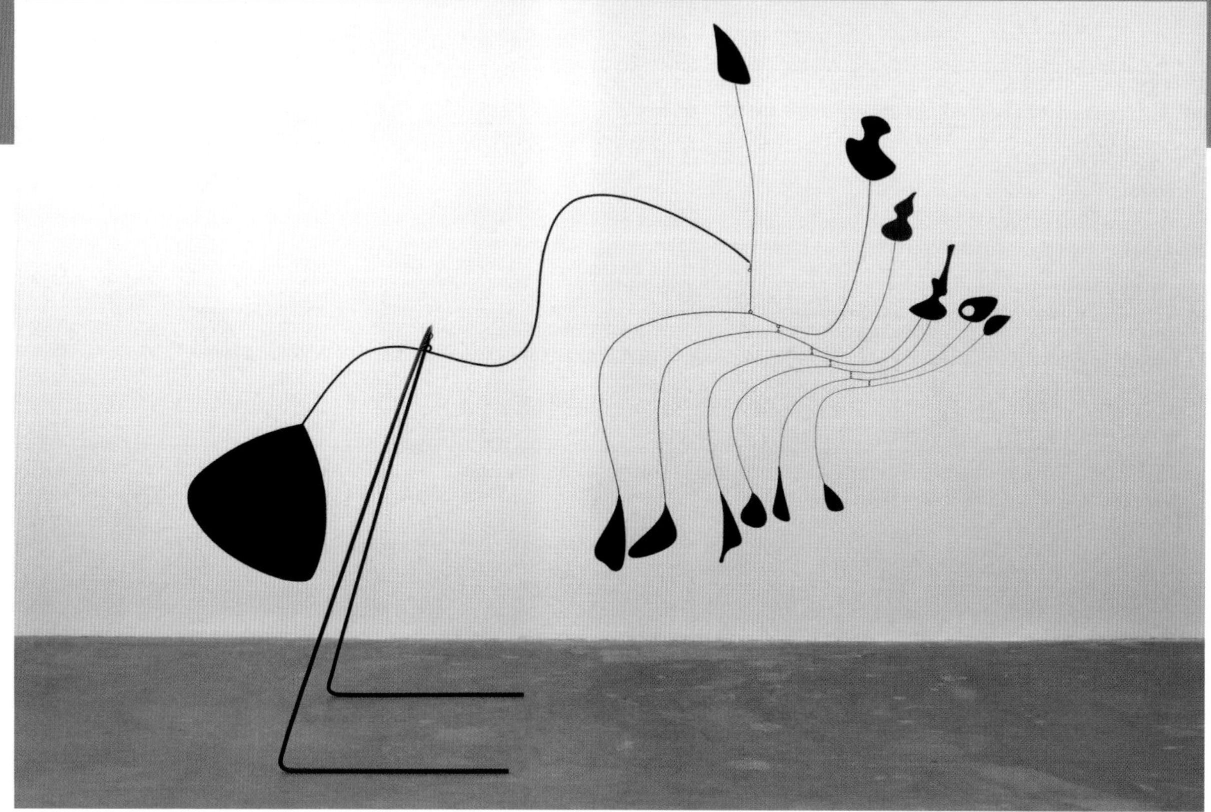

Alexander Calder
(Lawnton 1898 -
New York 1976)

**Untitled
Ohne Titel
Zonder titel
Sin título**

1939
37,1 x 22,8 x 27,5 cm / 14.6 x 8.9 x 10.8 in.
Museum of Modern Art (MoMA),
New York

painted aluminium laminate and steel cable
Bemalte Aluminiumplatte und Stahlseil
beschilderde aluminiumplaat en stalen kabel
lamina di aluminio pintada y cable de acero

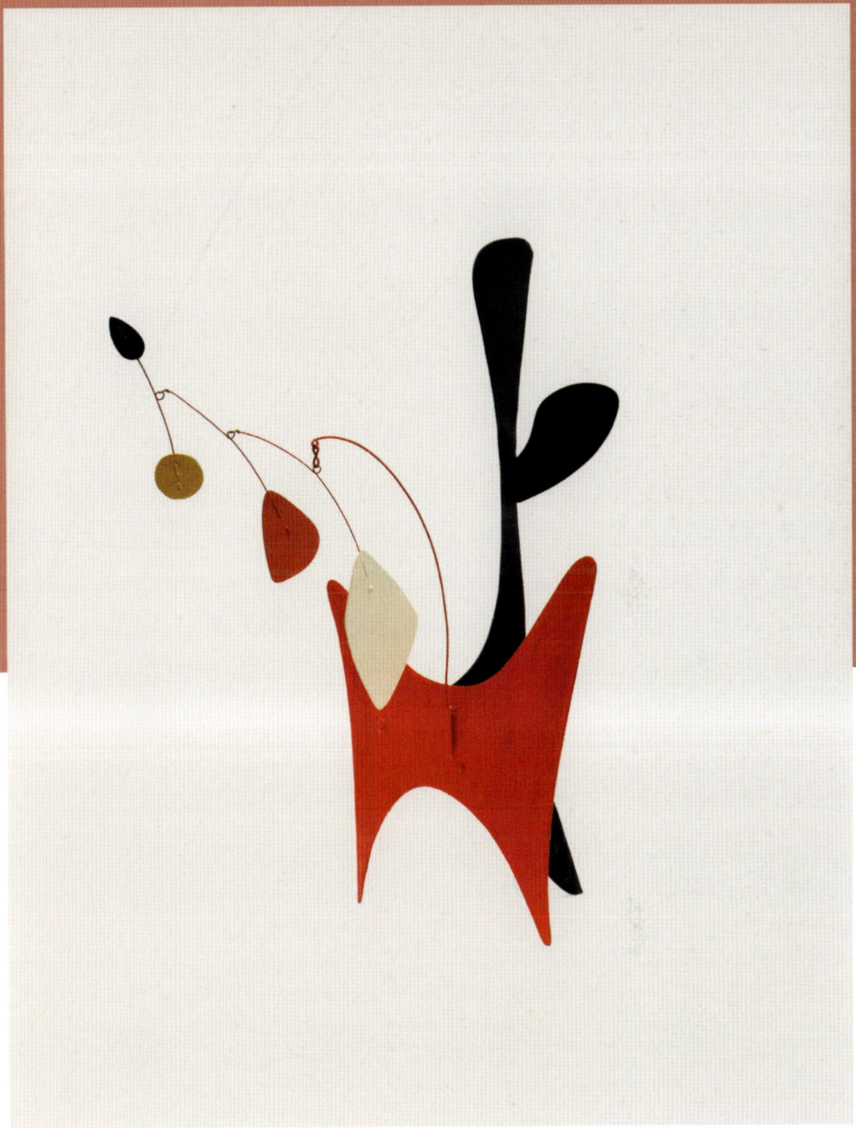

Calder wanted to sculpt shapes in
movement in space: thus the *mobiles*,
as Marcel Duchamp called them, were
born.

Calder wollte bewegliche Formen im
Raum schaffen: So entstanden die
mobiles, ein Name, der von Duchamp
stammt.

Calder wilde bewegende vormen in de
ruimte maken: zo zijn de door Marcel
Duchamp gedoopte *mobiles* ontstaan.

Calder quería esculpir formas en
movimiento en el espacio: de este modo
nacieron los *mobiles*, bautizados así por
Marcel Duchamp.

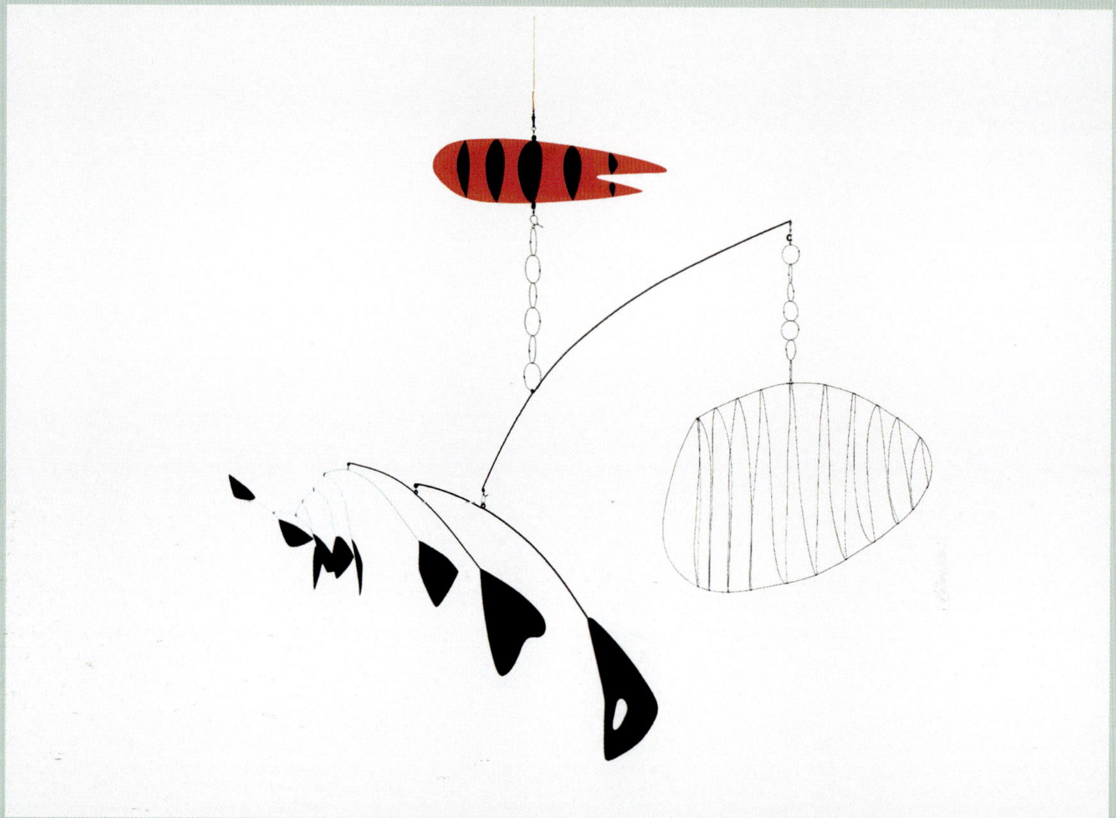

Alexander Calder
(Lawnton 1898 - New York 1976)

Lobster trap and fish tail
Falle für Langusten und Seeteufel
Kreeftenval en visstaart
Trampa para langostas y cola de pez

●●

1939
260 x 290 cm / 102.3 x 114.1 in.
Museum of Modern Art (MoMA), New York

steel wire, aluminium and painted sheet metal
Stahlschnur Aluminium und lackiertes Blech
staaldraad, gevernist aluminium en geverniste staalplaat
alambre, aluminio y chapa pintados

Alexander Calder
(Lawnton 1898 - New York 1976)

Pair of earrings
Ein Paar Ohrringe
Een paar oorbellen
Par de aros

●

15,2 x 7 x 1 cm / 6 x 2.7 x 0.4 in.
Museum of Fine Arts, Boston

silver, brass / Silber, Messing
goud, messing / plata, latón

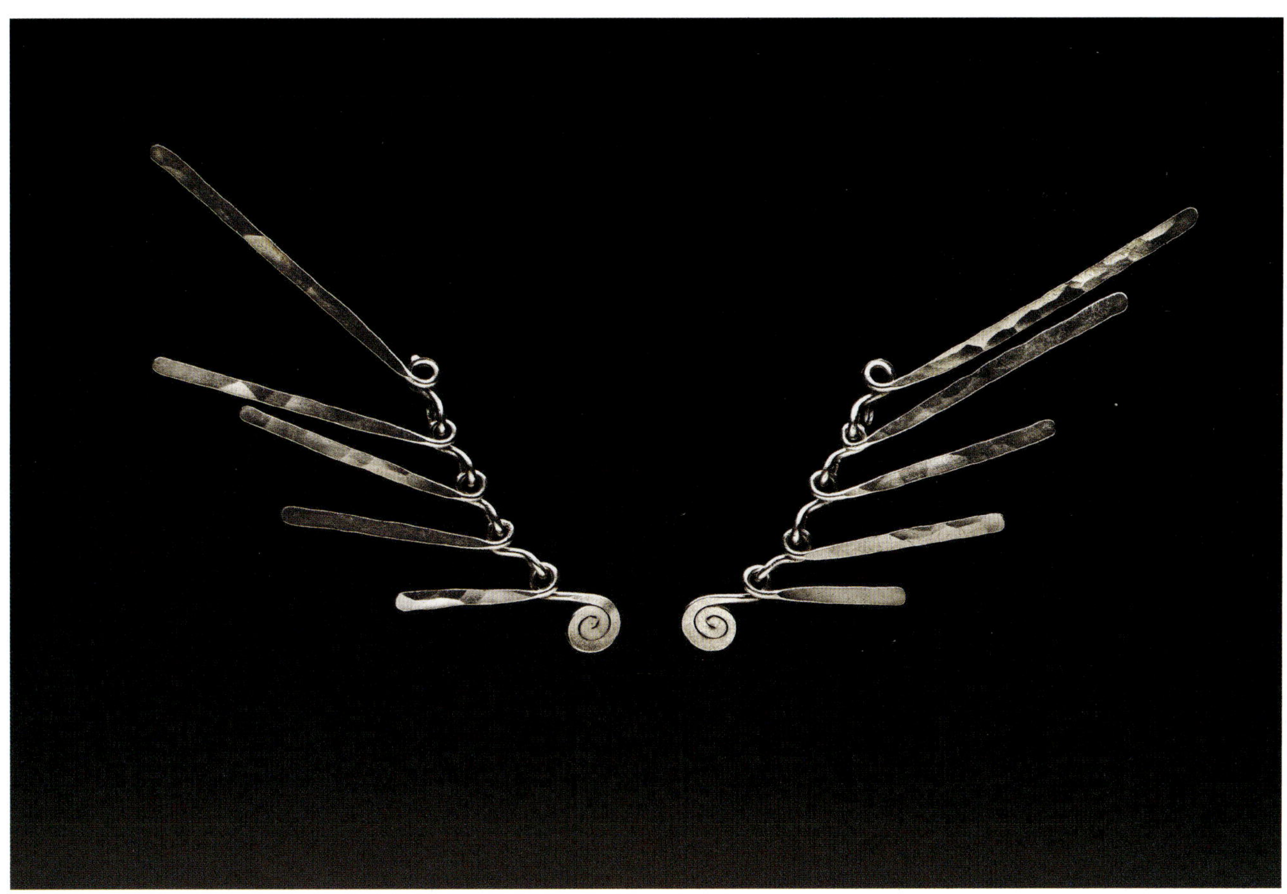

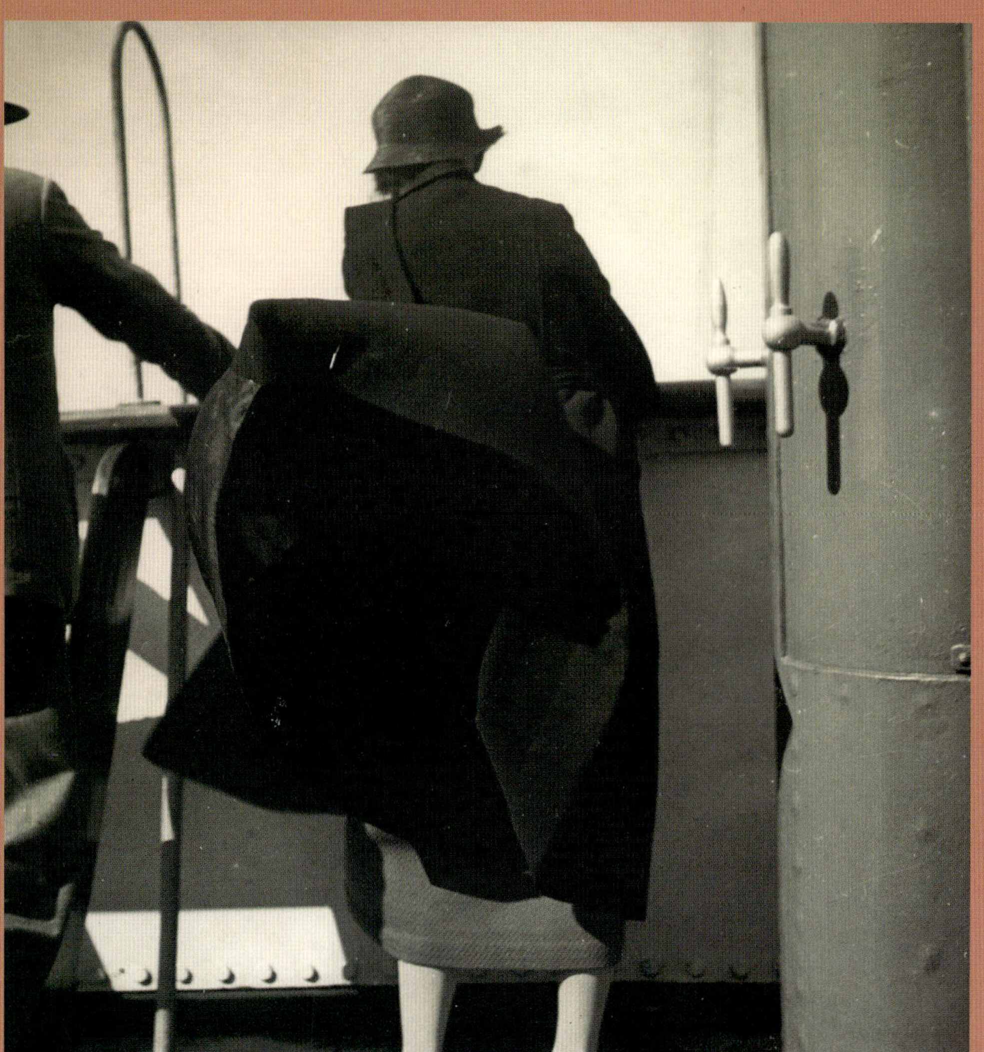

Dora Maar (Henriette
Theodora Markovitch)
(Tours 1907 - Paris 1997)

**Untitled (woman with coat
raised against the wind)
Ohne Titel
(Frau mit vom Wind
hochgewehtem Mantel)
Zonder titel
(vrouw met door de wind
opwaaiende jas)
Sin título
(mujer con tapado
levantado por el viento)**

•

ca. 1930
26,4 x 23,9 cm / 10.4 x 9.4 in.
Museum of Modern Art (MoMA)
New York

silver salts print
Druck mit Silbersalzen
zilverzouten print
impresión a las sales de plata

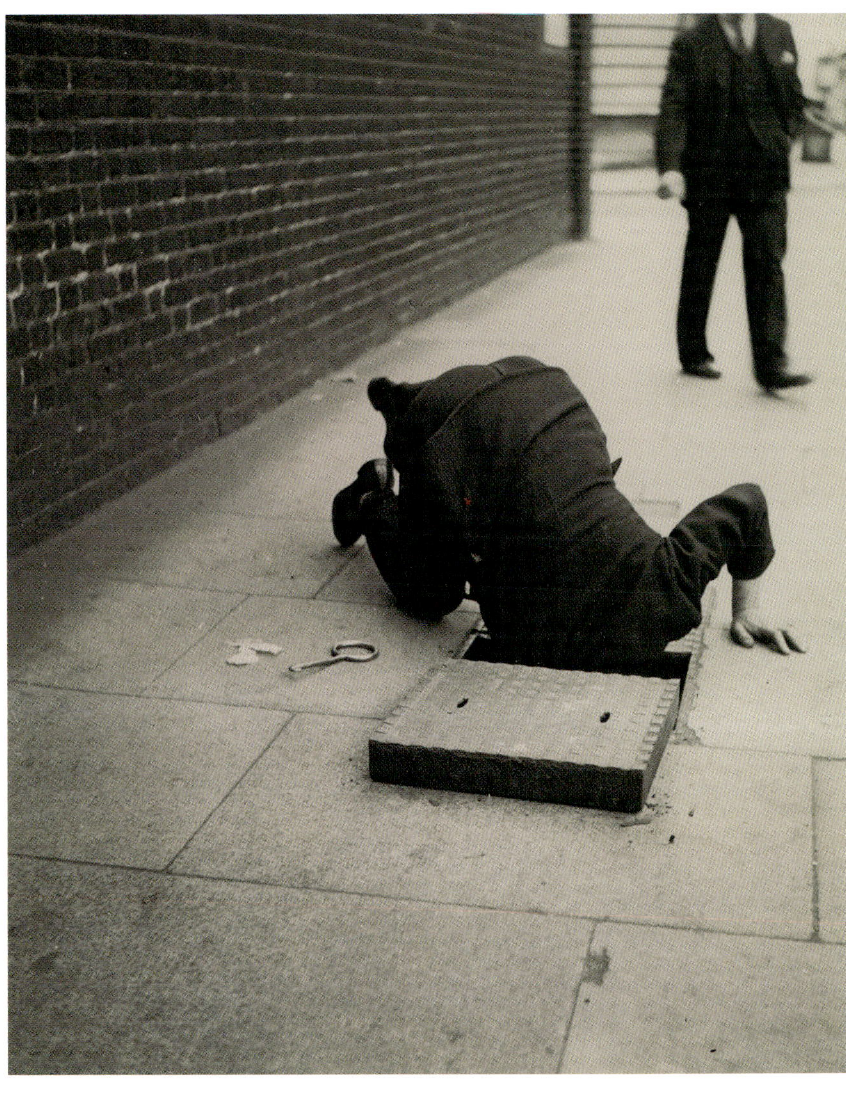

Dora Maar (Henriette Theodora Markovitch)
(Tours 1907 - Paris 1997)

Untitled (man with his head in a manhole)
Ohne Titel (Mann mit Kopf in einem Kanalschacht)
Zonder titel (man met hoofd in een afvoerput)
Sin título (hombre con la cabeza en una alcantarilla)

●●●

ca. 1935
29,8 x 23,4 cm / 11.7 x 9.2 in.
Museum of Modern Art (MoMA), New York

silver salts print
Druck mit Silbersalzen
zilverzouten print
impresión a las sales de plata

Before becoming Picasso's lover, Dora Maar was known as a surrealist photographer of deformed images.

Bevor sie die Geliebte von Picasso wurde, war Dora Maar als surrealistische Fotografin deformierter Bilder bekannt.

Dora Maar stond, voordat ze de minnares van Picasso werd, bekend als surrealistische fotografe van vervormde beelden.

Antes de ser la amante de Picasso, Dora Maar era conocida como fotógrafa surrealista, creadora de imágenes deformadas.

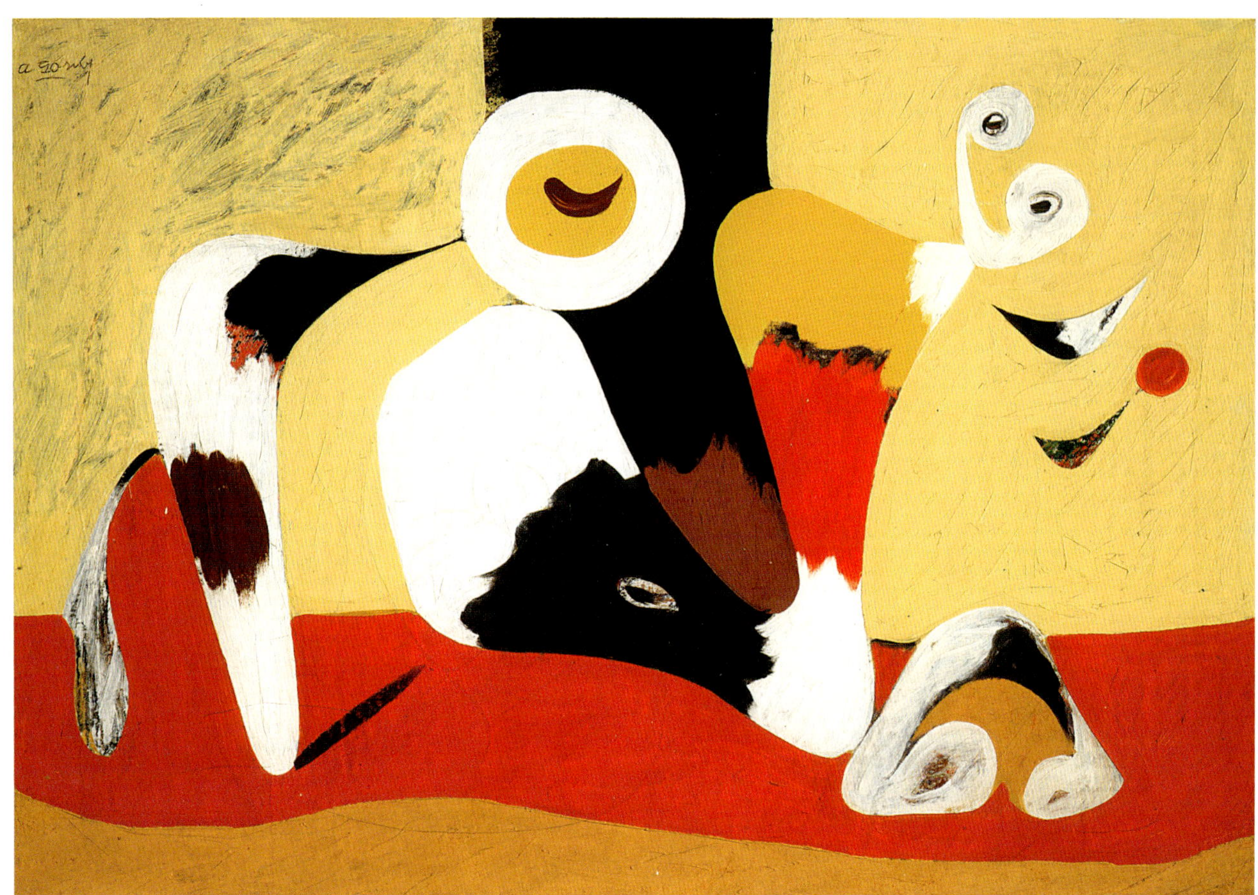

370

Arshile Gorky
(Vosdanig Adoian 1904 -
Sherman 1948)

Mojave

●●●

1941-1942
73 x 102,8 cm / 28.7 x 40.4 in.
Los Angeles County Museum of Art,
Los Angeles

oil on canvas / Öl auf Leinwand
olieverf op doek / óleo sobre lienzo

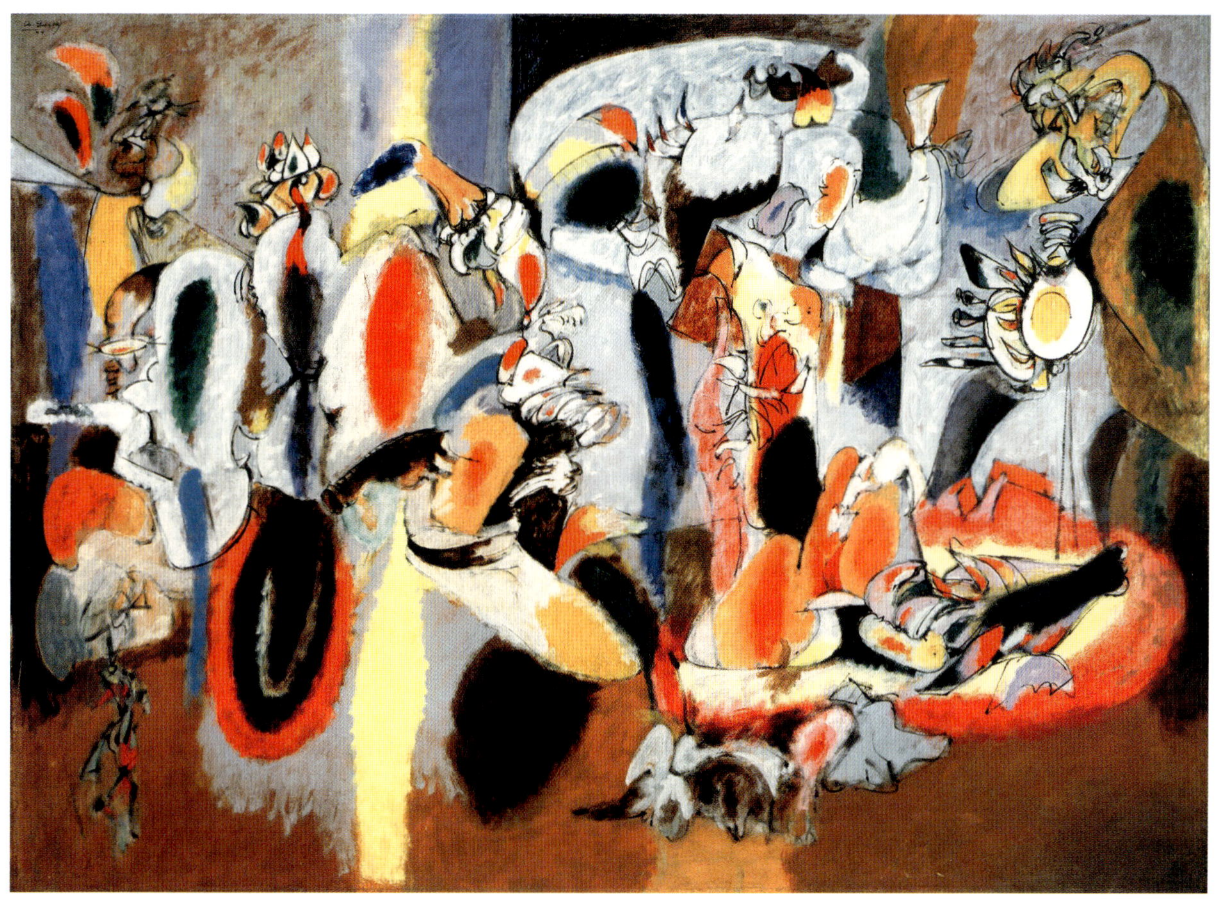

Arshile Gorky
(Vosdanig Adoian 1904 - Sherman 1948)

The Liver is the Cock's Comb
Die Leber ist der Hahnenkamm
De lever is de kam van de haan
El hígado es la cresta del gallo

●

1944
191,1 x 254,9 x 7 cm / 75.2 x 100.3 x 2.7 in.
Albright-Knox Art Gallery, Buffalo

oil on canvas / Öl auf Leinwand
olieverf op doek / óleo sobre lienzo

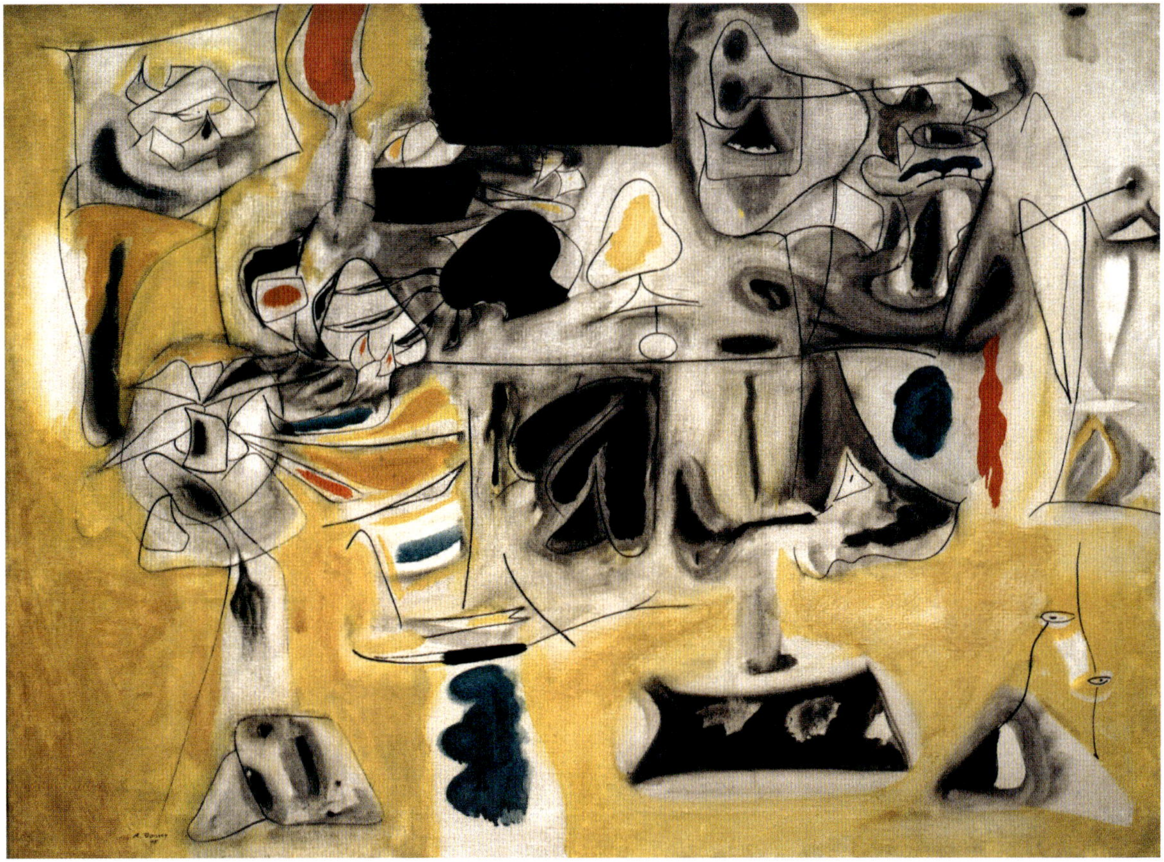

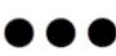

Arshile Gorky
(Vosdanig Adoian 1904 - Sherman 1948)

Landscape Table

●●●

1945
92 x 121 cm / 36.2 x 47.6 in.
Centre Georges Pompidou,
Musée National d'Art Moderne, Paris

oil on canvas
Öl auf Leinwand
olieverf op doek
óleo sobre lienzo

A landscape more mental than geographic in which one can see the influence of Picasso, Miró and the automatic writing of the surrealists.

Eine eher geistige, als geografische Landschaft, in der der Einfluss von Picasso, Miró und der automatischen Schrift der Surrealisten erkennbar ist.

Een meer mentaal dan geografisch landschap waarin de invloed van Picasso, Miró en de automatische stijl van de surrealisten is terug te vinden

Un paisaje más mental que geográfico, en el cual se lee la influencia de Picasso, Miró y la escritura automática de los surrealistas.

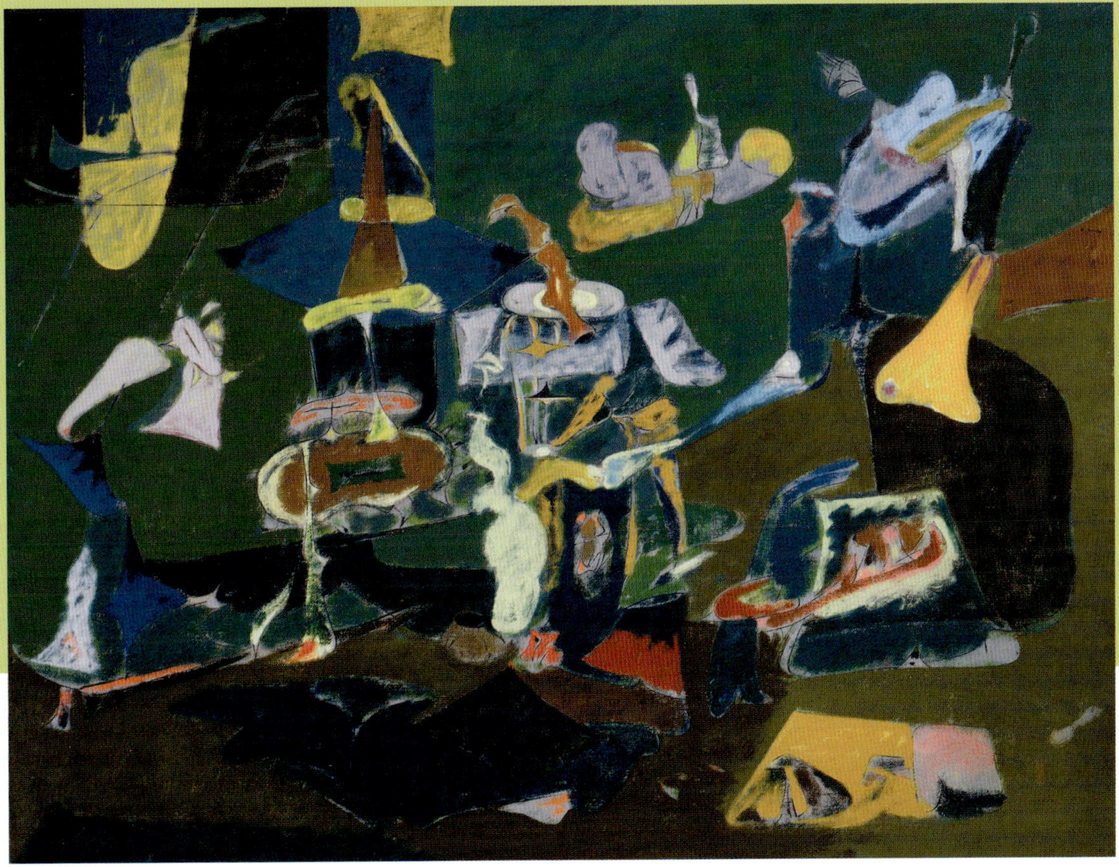

Arshile Gorky
(Vosdanig Adoian 1904 - Sherman 1948)

Dark green painting
Dunkelgrünes Gemälde
Donkergroen schilderij
Pintura verde oscura

●●

ca. 1948
111,1 x 141 cm / 43.7 x 55.5 in.
Philadelphia Museum of Art, Philadelphia

oil on canvas / Öl auf Leinwand
olieverf op doek / óleo sobre lienzo

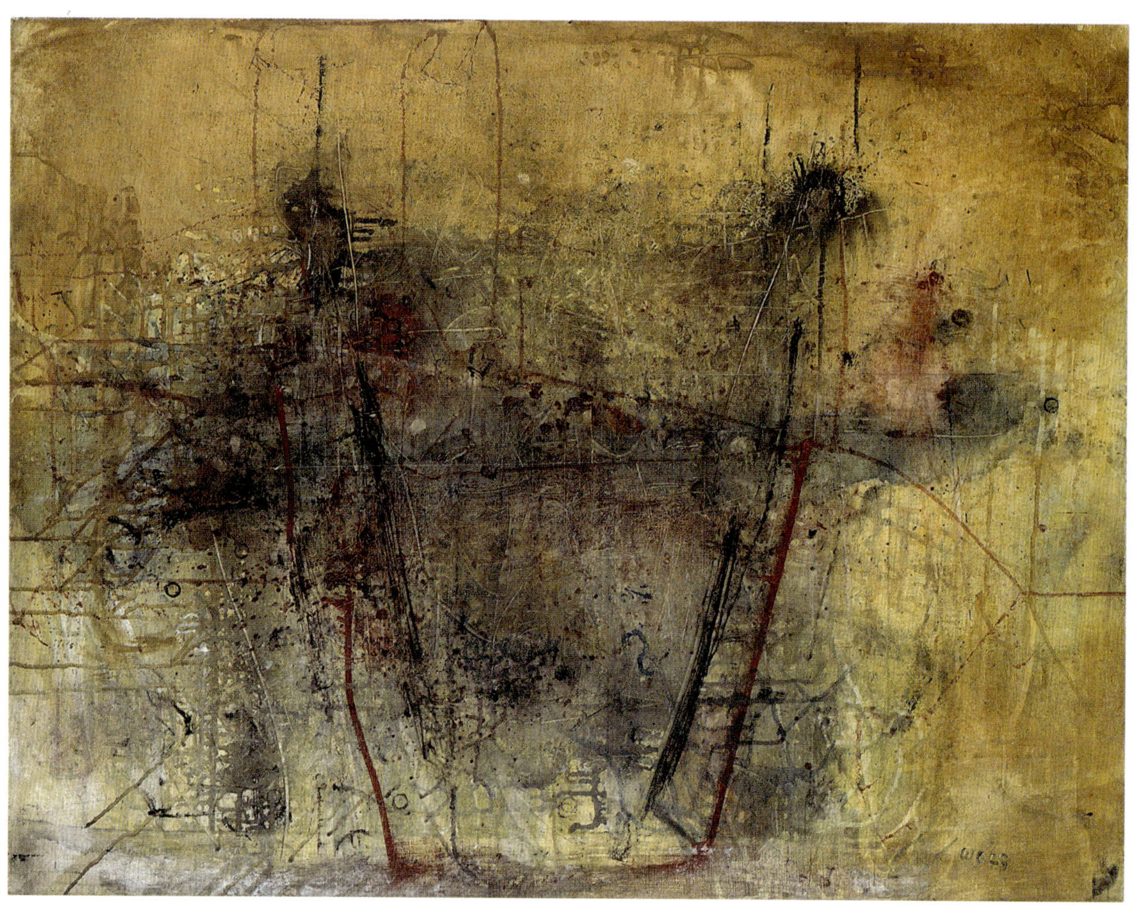

Wols
(Otto Alfred Wolfgang Schulze)
(Berlin 1913 - Paris 1951)

Yellow composition
Gelbe Komposition
Gele compositie
Composición amarilla

●

1947
73 x 92 cm / 28.7 x 36.2 in.
Nationalgalerie, Staatliche Museen, Berlin

oil on canvas / Öl auf Leinwand
olieverf op doek / óleo sobre lienzo

Wols canvases are torn, scratched; the finely chopped matter joins confused and spotted backgrounds: the painter opens the way to informal art.

Wols' Leinwände sind zerrissen, zerkratzt. Die zerkleinerte Materie vereint sich mit den verworrenen und fleckigen Hintergründen: Der Maler bereitet den Weg zur informellen Kunst.

De doeken van Wols zijn gescheurd, bekrast: met het verpulverde materiaal op verwarde en gevlekte achtergronden maakt de schilder de weg vrij voor de informele kunst.

Los lienzos de Wols están lacerados, rasgados, la materia triturada se inscribe sobre fondos confusos y manchados: el pintor abre camino al arte informal.

Wols (Otto Alfred Wolfgang Schulze)
(Berlin 1913 - Paris 1951)

Composition
Komposition
Compositie
Composición

●●●

1947
81 x 64,7 cm / 31.9 x 25.5 in.
Hamburger Kunsthalle, Hamburg

oil on canvas / Öl auf Leinwand
olieverf op doek / óleo sobre lienzo

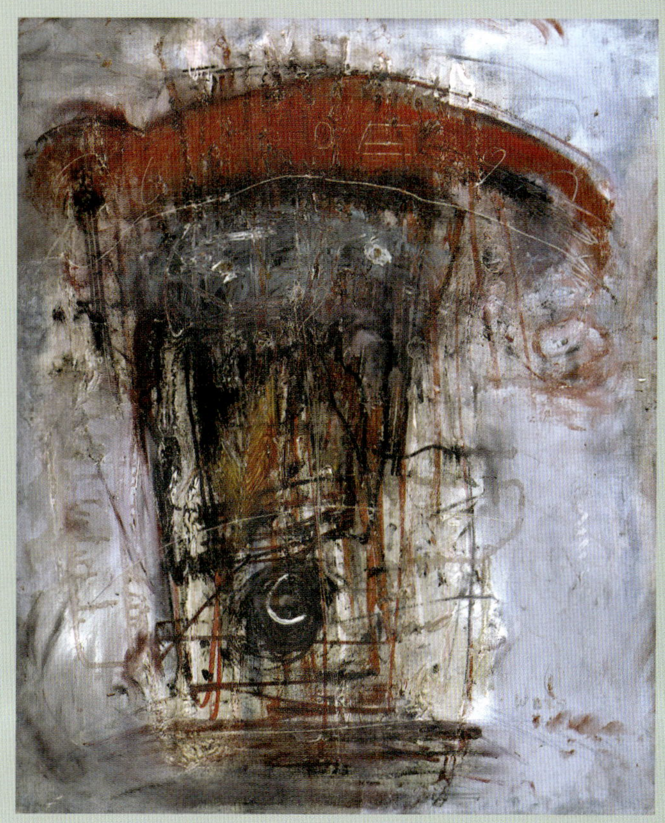

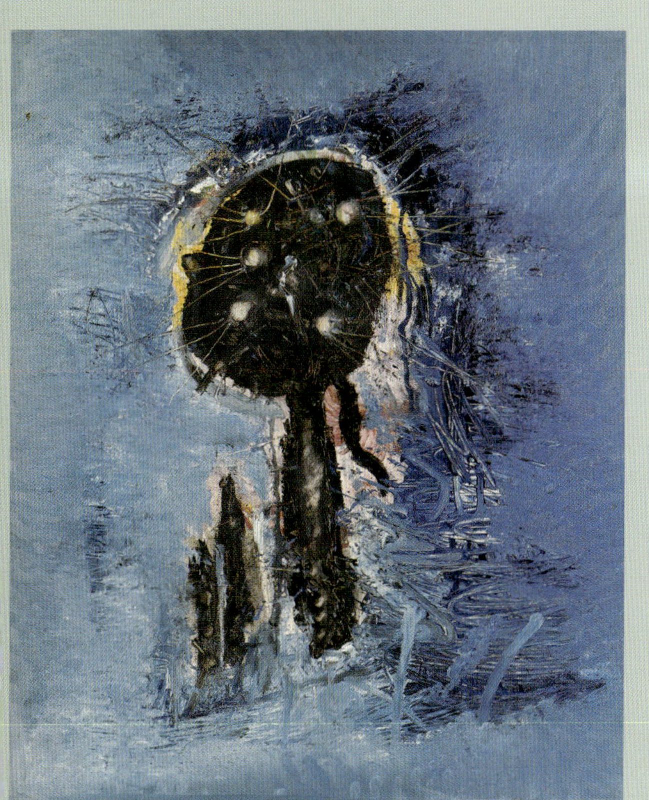

Wols (Otto Alfred Wolfgang Schulze)
(Berlin 1913 - Paris 1951)

The Blue Ghost
Das Blaue Phantom
Het blauwe spook
El fantasma azul

●●

1951
Collezione Jucker, Milano

oil on canvas / Öl auf Leinwand
olieverf op doek / óleo sobre lienzo

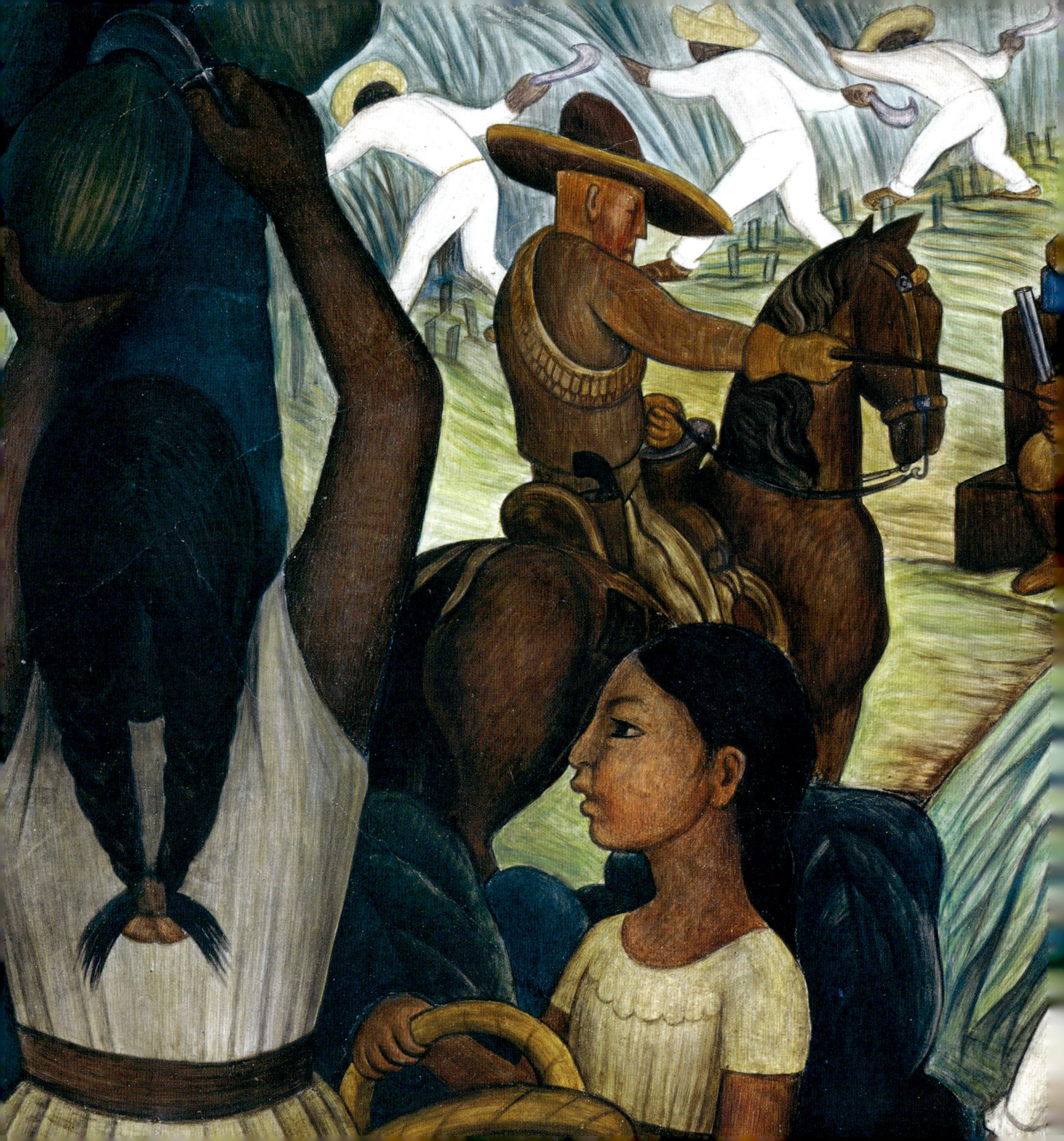

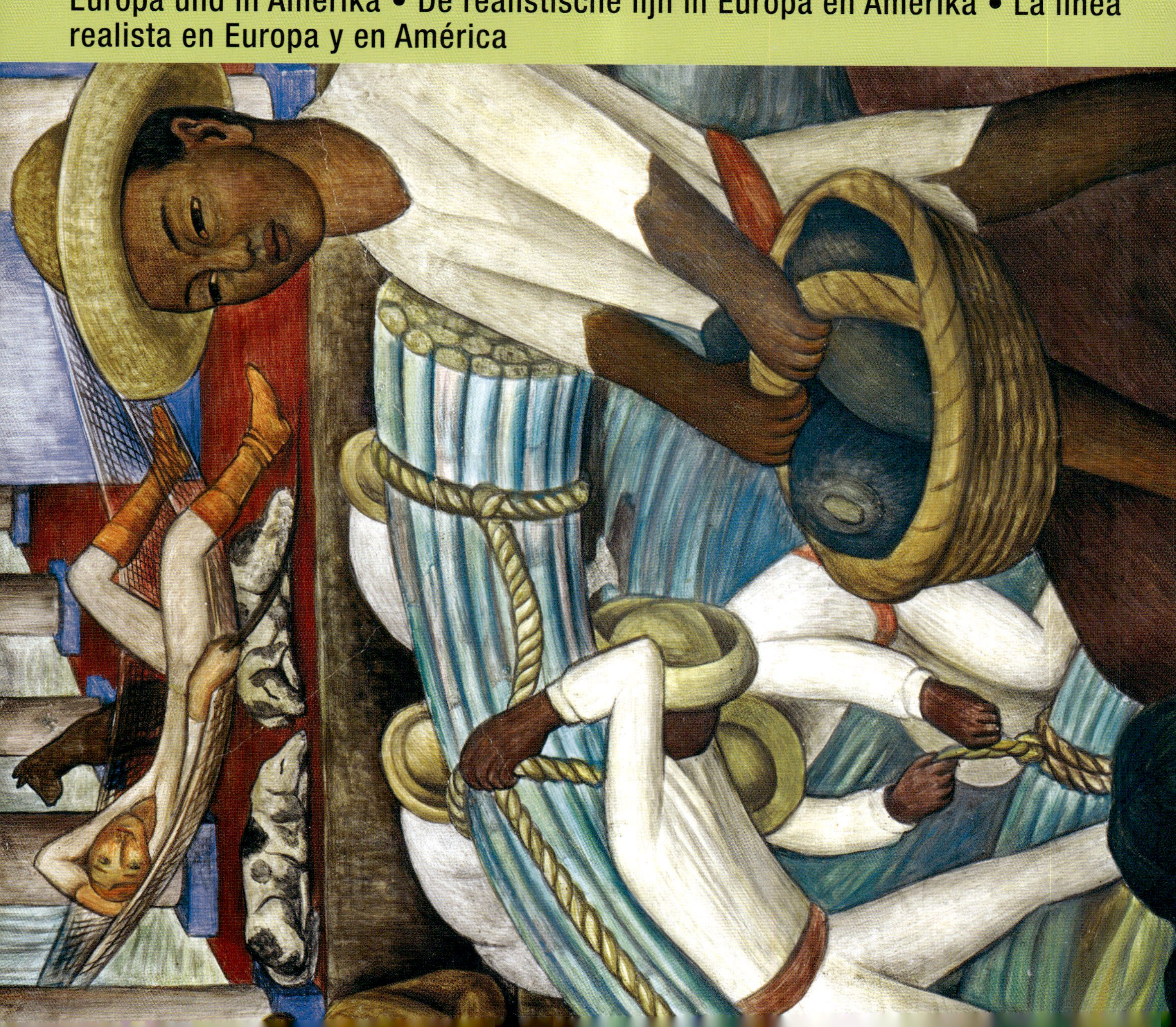

The realistic line in Europe and in America • Die realistische Strömung in Europa und in Amerika • De realistische lijn in Europa en Amerika • La línea realista en Europa y en América

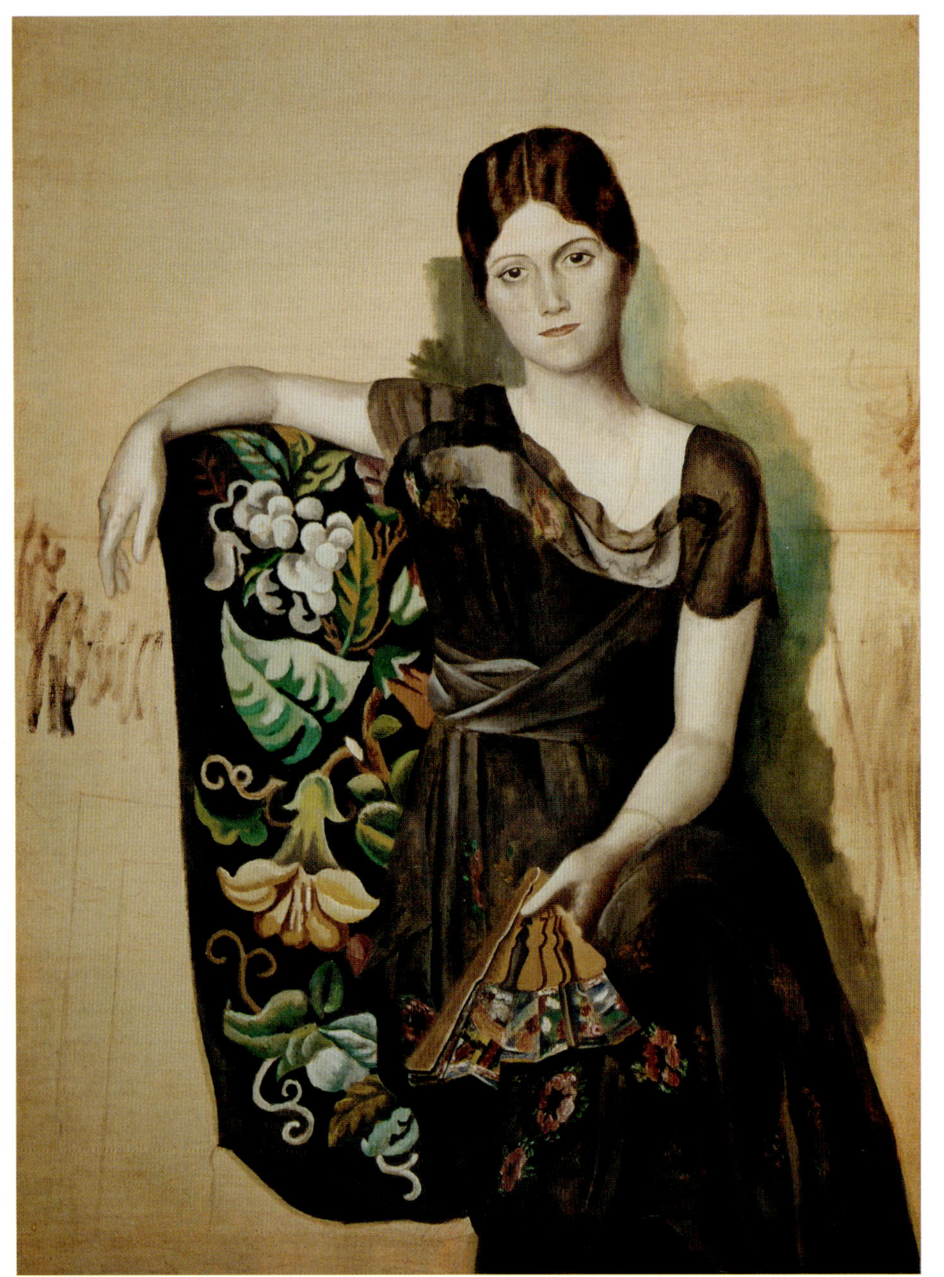

Pablo Picasso

(Málaga 1881 - Mougins 1973)

**Portrait of Olga in armchair
Bildnis von Olga in einem
Sessel
Portret van Olga in een stoel
Retrato de Olga en un sillón**

●●●

1917
130 x 88,8 cm / 51.2 x 34.9 in.
Musée Picasso, Paris

oil on canvas / Öl auf Leinwand
olieverf op doek / óleo sobre lienzo

A more classic Picasso who returns to depiction, inspired by the great French painter Ingres, to portray his wife, dancer with the Ballets Russes Company.

Ein klassischerer Picasso, der zur Darstellung zurückkehrt und sich am großen französischen Maler Ingres inspiriert, um seine Frau, die Tänzerin aus dem Ensemble Ballets Russes, zu porträtieren.

Een klassiekere Picasso die terugkeert naar de symbolische voorstelling, waarbij hij zich, om zijn vrouw te schilderen die bij de Ballets Russes danste, door de Franse Schilder Ingres laat inspireren.

Un Picasso más clásico que vuelve a la figuración, inspirándose en el gran pintor francés Ingres, para retratar a su mujer, bailarina de la compañía de los Ballets Russes.

378

Pablo Picasso
(Málaga 1881 -
Mougins 1973)

Pierrot
●●●
1918
92,7 x 73 cm / 36.5 x 28.7 in.
Museum of Modern Art
(MoMA), New York

oil on canvas
Öl auf Leinwand
olieverf op doek
óleo sobre lienzo

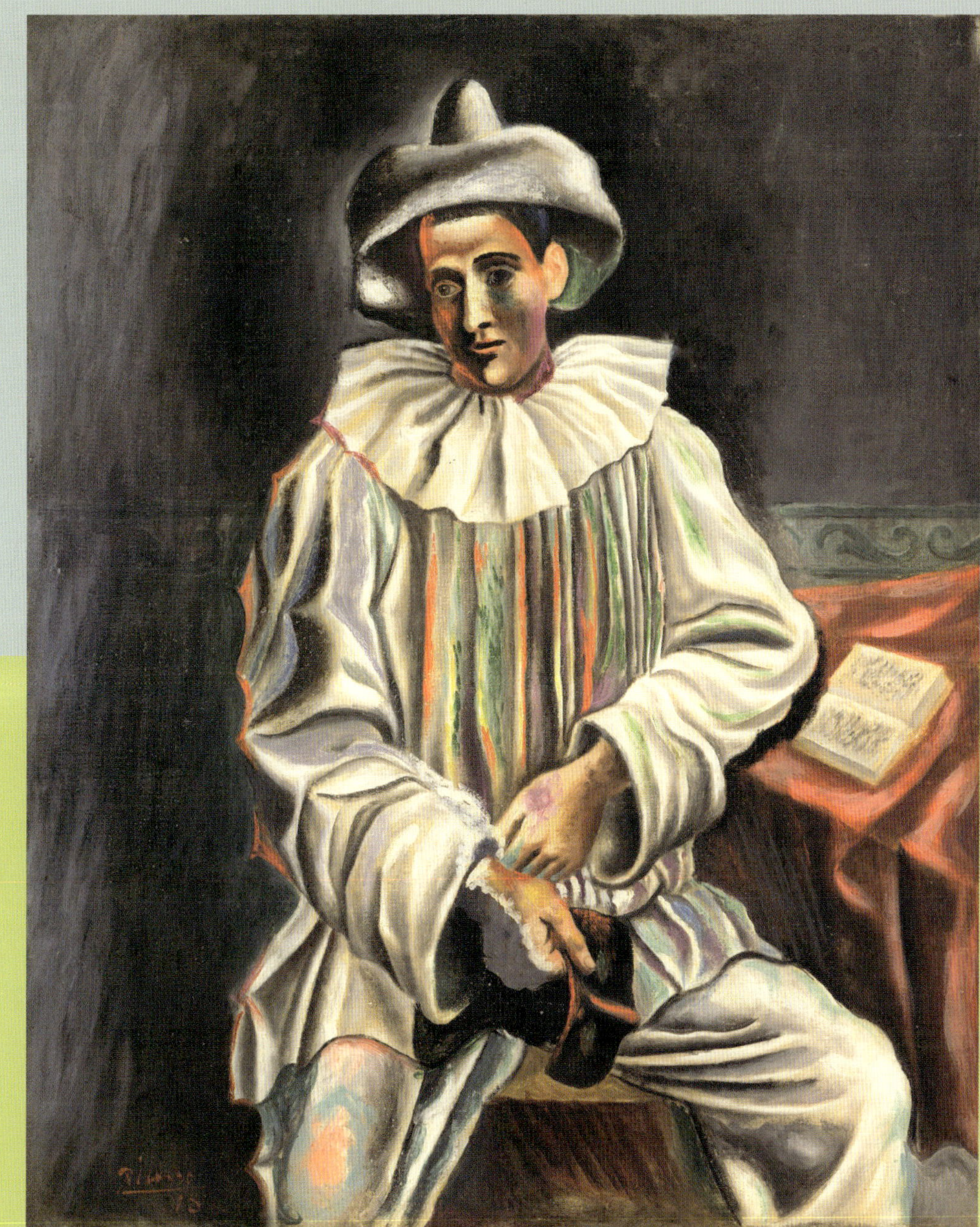

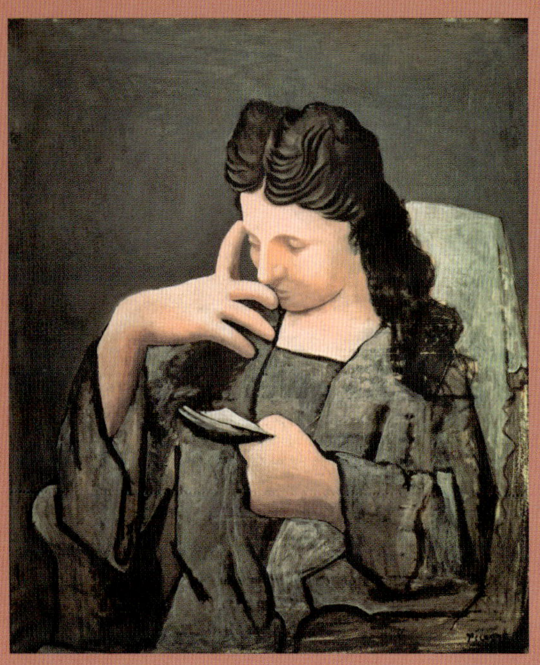

◀ Pablo Picasso
(Málaga 1881 - Mougins 1973)

Woman reading
Lesende Frau
Lezende vrouw
Mujer leyendo

●

1920
100 x 81 cm / 39.3 x 31.9 in.
Musée de Grenoble, Grenoble

oil on canvas
Öl auf Leinwand
olieverf op doek
óleo sobre lienzo

▶ Pablo Picasso
(Málaga 1881 - Mougins 1973)

Pan's flute
Die Panflöte
De panfluit
La flauta de Pan

● ●

1923
205 x 174 cm
80.7 x 68.5 in.
Musée Picasso, Paris

oil on canvas
Öl auf Leinwand
olieverf op doek
óleo sobre lienzo

Pablo Picasso
(Málaga 1881 - Mougins 1973)

Two women running on the beach
Laufende Frauen am Strand
Twee over het strand rennende vrouwen
Dos mujeres corriendo en la playa

● ● ●

1922
32,5 x 41,1 cm / 12.8 x 16.2 in.
Musée Picasso, Paris

gouache on plywood
Gouache auf Sperrholz
gouache op multiplex
gouache sobre aglomerado

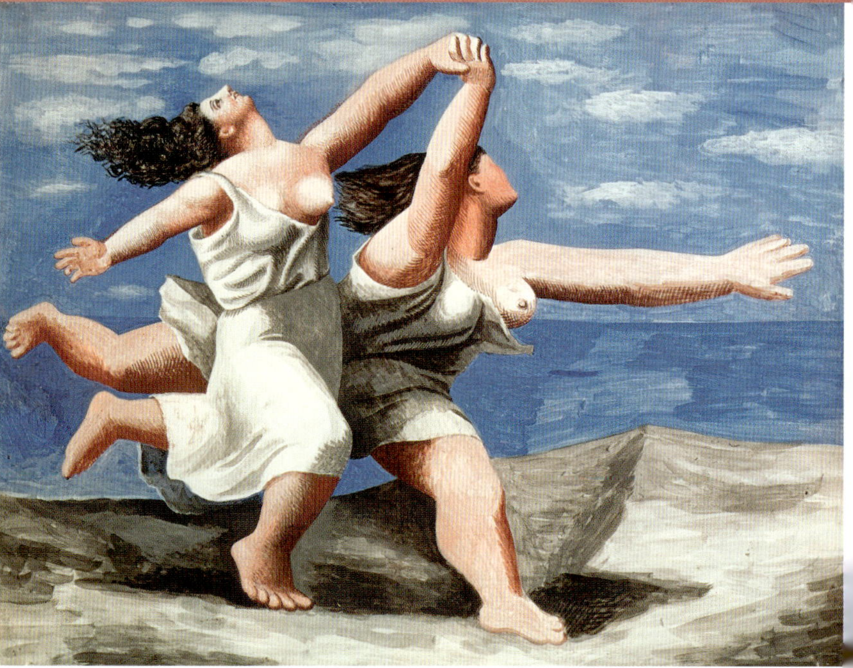

Pan's Flute with its ancient
feel is a mysterious subject
interwoven with a sweet
melancholy, which never left
Picasso's atelier.

Die Panflöte, ein misteriöses
Sujet mit antikem Flair,
ist von süßer Melancholie
durchwoben und hat niemals
Picassos Atelier verlassen.

Het antieke en mysterieus
aandoende en enigszins
melancholische schilderij
De panfluit, heeft nooit
Picasso's atelier verlaten.

La flauta de pan, obra de
atmósfera antigua y temática
misteriosa, pero entretejida
con una dulce melancolía,
no dejó nunca el taller
de Picasso.

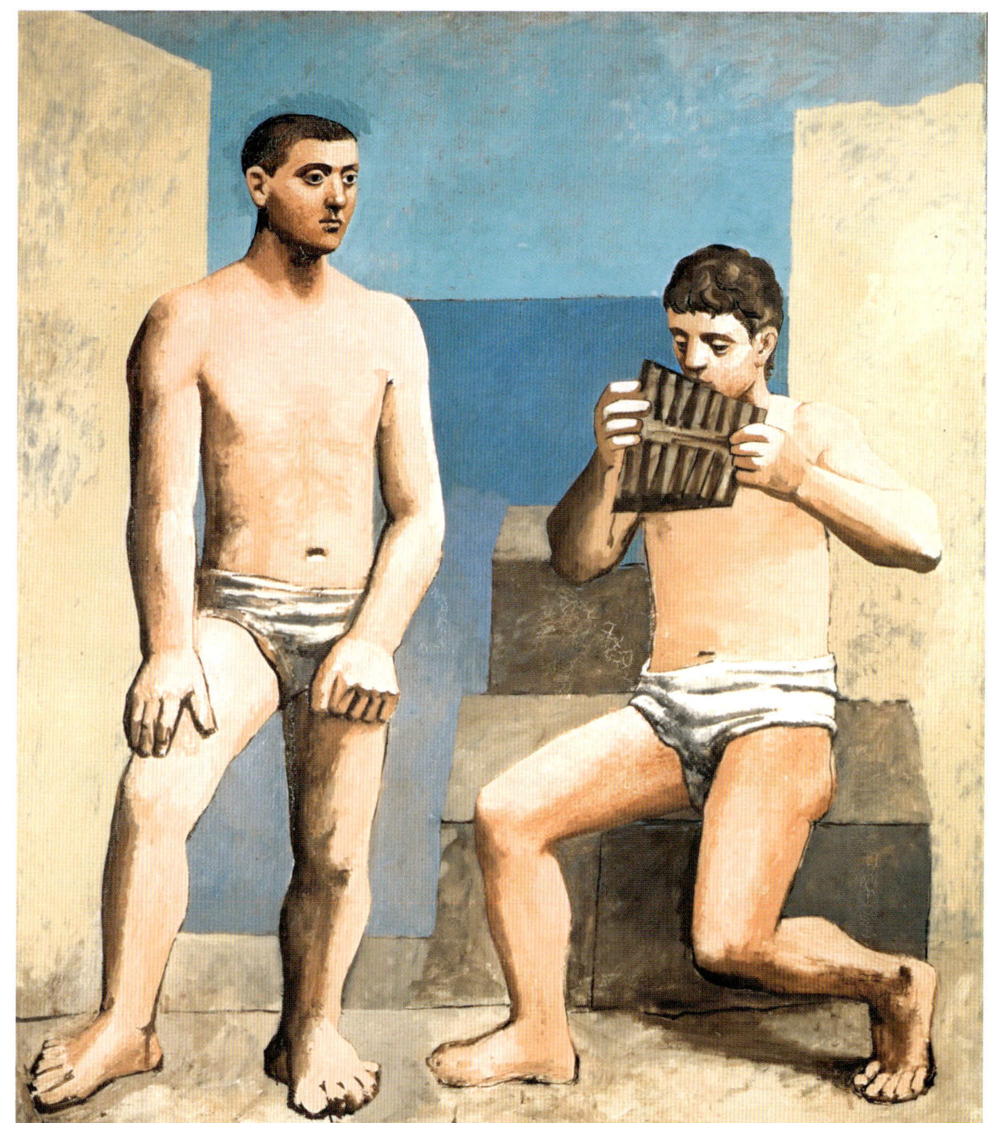

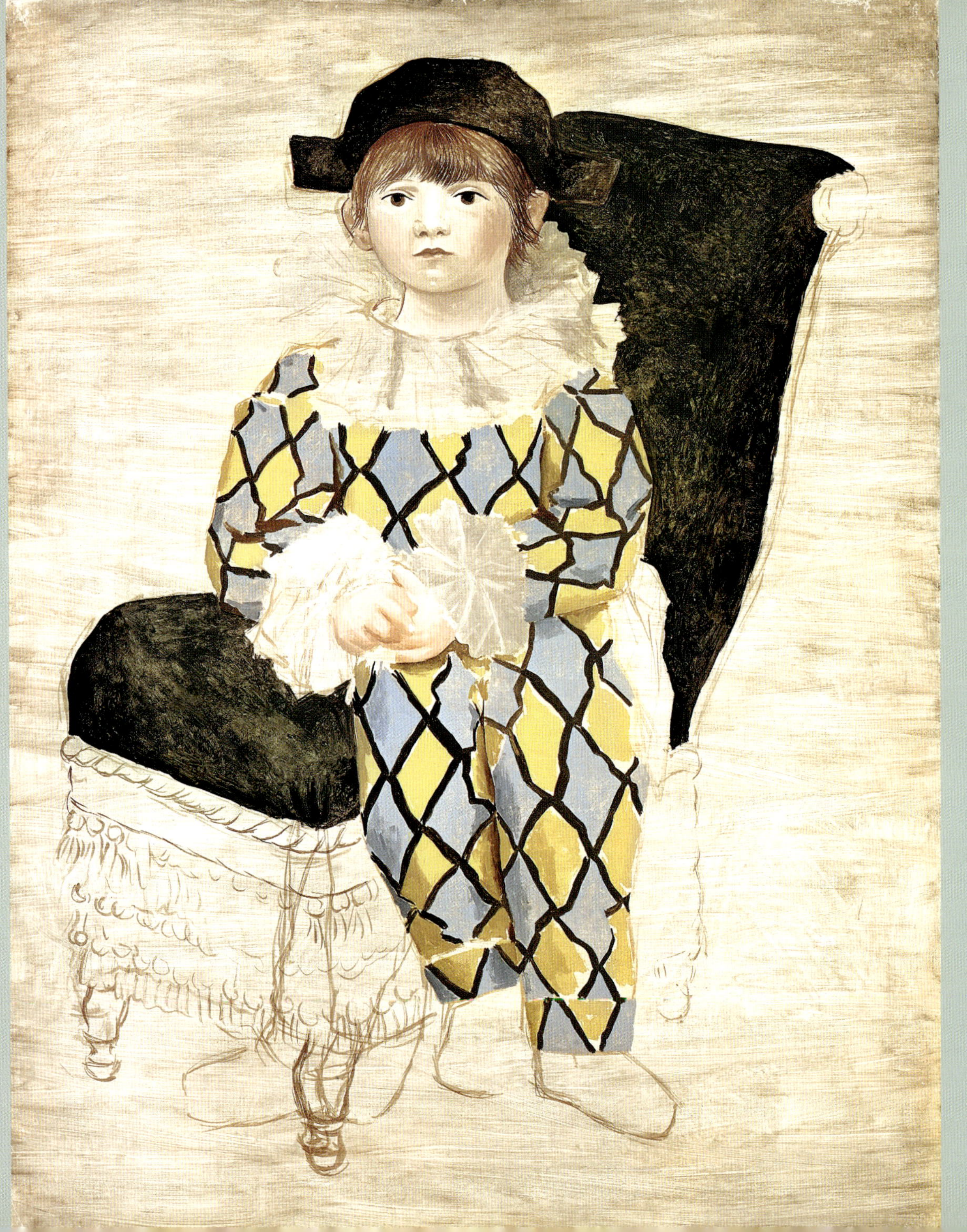

► Pablo Picasso
(Málaga 1881 - Mougins 1973)
Paul in Pierrot costume
Paul im Pierrotkostüm
Paul in Pierrotkostuum
Paul vestido de Pierrot
●●
1925
130 x 97 cm / 51.2 x 38.2 in.
Musée Picasso, Paris

oil on canvas
Öl auf Leinwand
olieverf op doek
óleo sobre lienzo

◄ Pablo Picasso
(Málaga 1881 - Mougins 1973)
Paul in Harlequin
costume
Paul als Harlekin
Paul in
Harlekijnskleding
Paul vestido
de Arlequín
●●
1924
130 x 97 cm / 51.2 x 38.2 in.
Musée Picasso, Paris

oil on canvas
Öl auf Leinwand
olieverf op doek
óleo sobre lienzo

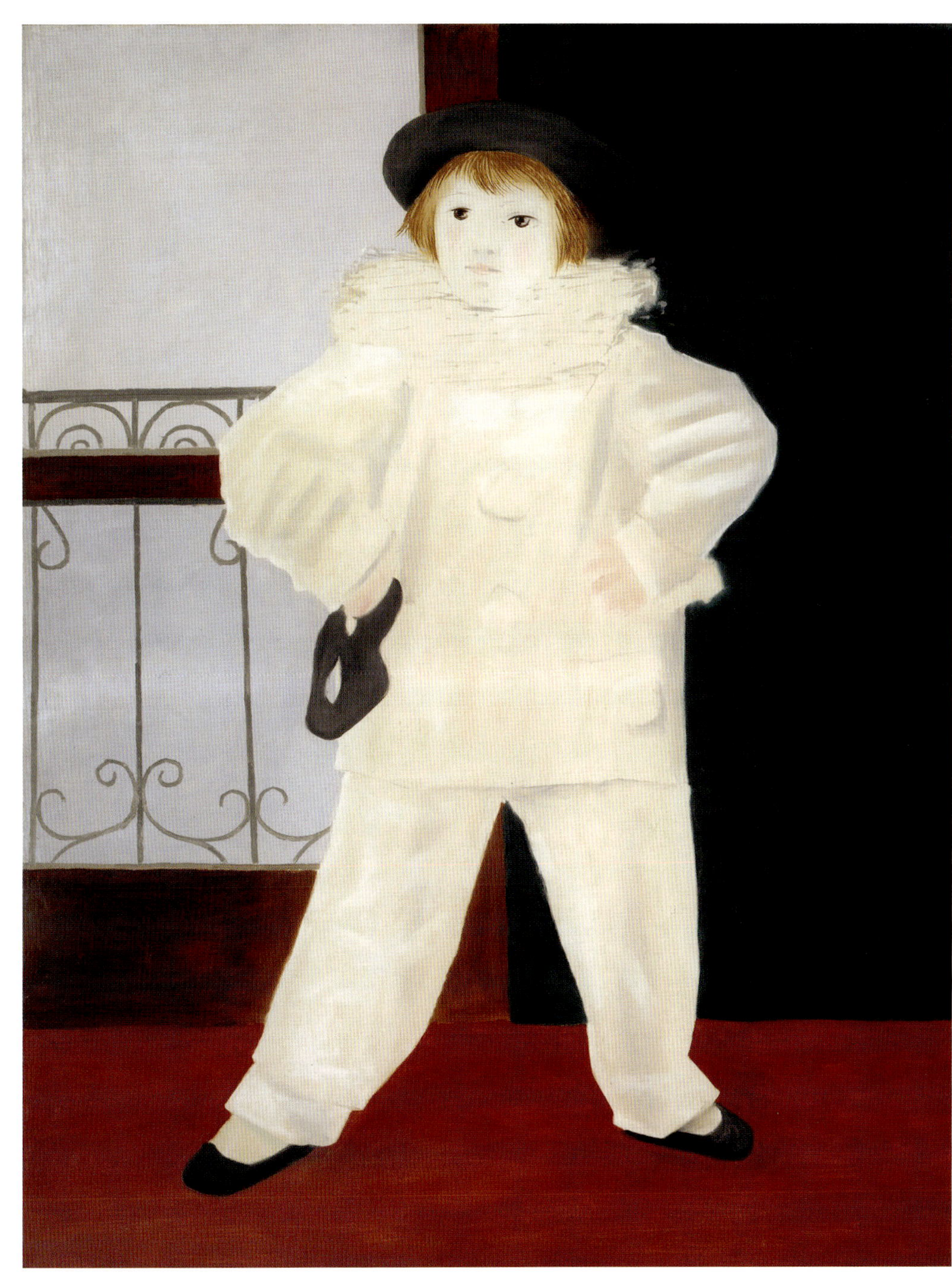

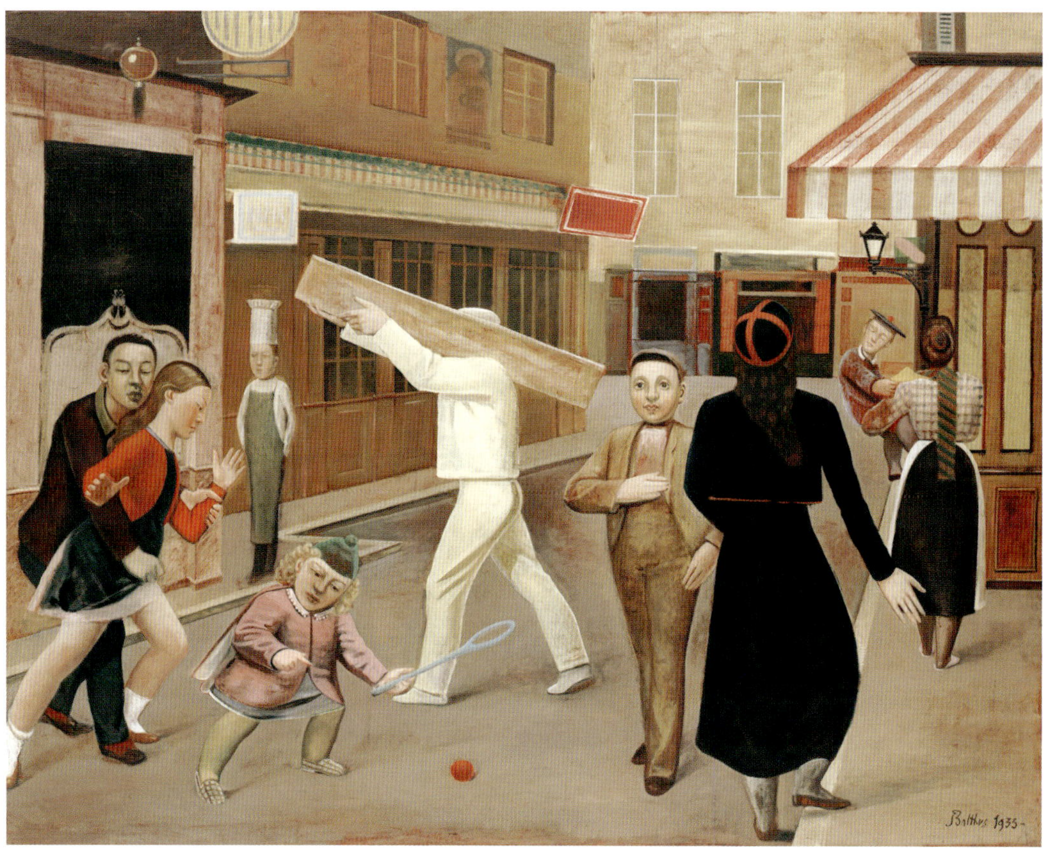

Balthus
(Klossowski de Rola Balthasar)
(Paris 1908 - Rossinière 2001)

**The Road / Die Strasse
De straat / La calle**

●

1933
195 x 240 cm / 76.7 x 94.5 in.
Museum of Modern Art (MoMA),
New York

oil on canvas / Öl auf Leinwand
olieverf op doek / óleo sobre lienzo

Here we witness a dream with our eyes open, in which the
gestures are suspended and the strangeness of the people
and their attitudes emerge slowly.

Wir sind Zeugen eines Traums mit offenen Augen, in dem die
Gesten wie eingefroren wirken, sodass die Eigenartigkeit der
Personen und ihrer Verhaltensweisen langsam zum Vorschein
komm.

Hier zijn we getuigen van een droom met onze ogen open,
waarin gebaren blijven hangen en de eigenaardigheid van
de personages en hun houding langzaam naar voren komt.

Henos aquí, testimonios de un sueño con ojos abiertos,
en el cual los gestos están suspendidos y emerge lentamente
la extrañeza de los personajes y de sus comportamientos.

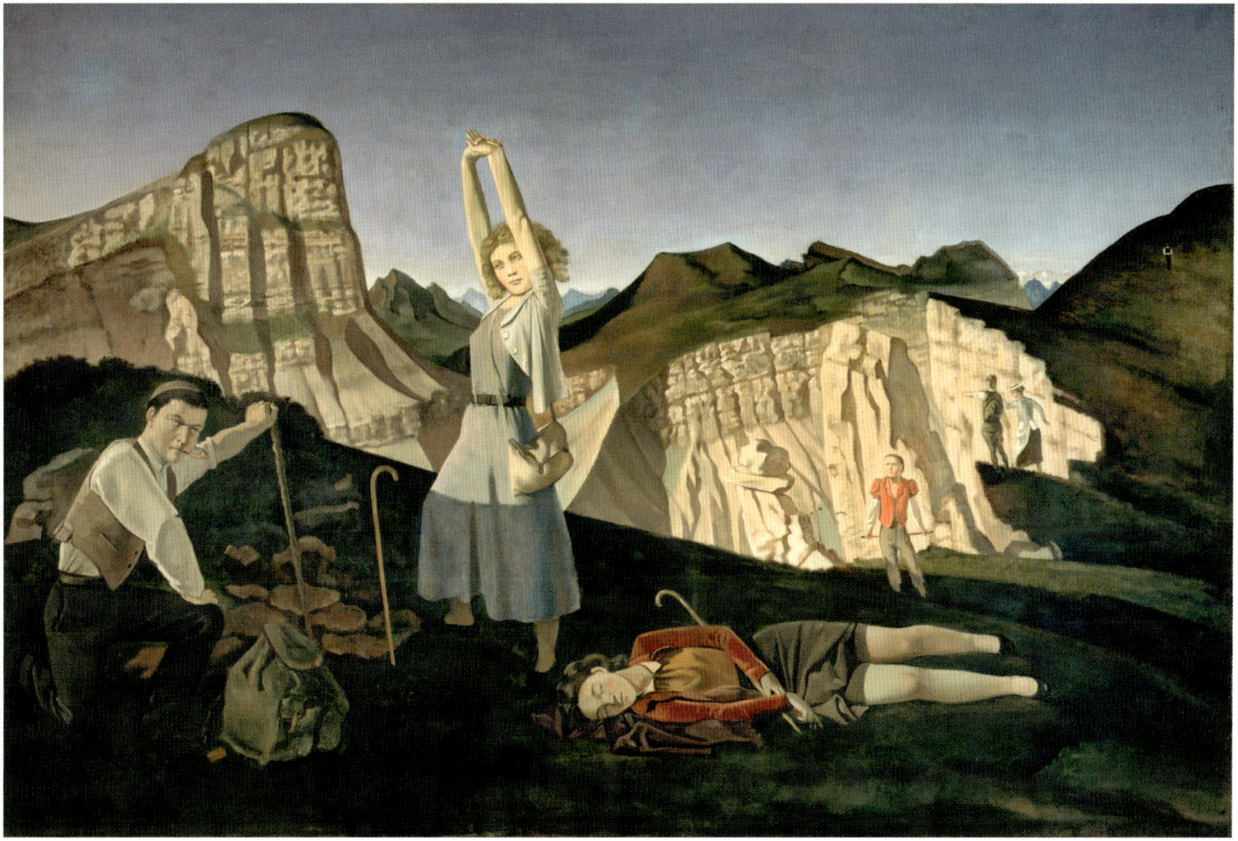

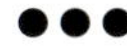

Balthus (Klossowski de Rola Balthasar)
(Paris 1908 - Rossinière 2001)

The Mountain
La Montagne (Das Gebirge)
De berg
La montaña

●●●

1937
248,9 x 365,8 cm / 98 x 144.1 in.
The Metropolitan Museum of Art, New York

oil on canvas / Öl auf Leinwand
olieverf op doek / óleo sobre lienzo

Otto Dix
(Gera 1892 - Singen 1969)

The businessman Max Roesberg, Dresden
Der Kaufmann Max Roesberg, Dresden
Zakenman Max Roesberg, Dresden
El hombre de negocios Max Roesberg, Dresde

●

1922
94 x 63,5 cm / 37 x 25 in.
The Metropolitan Museum of Art, New York

oil on canvas / Öl auf Leinwand
olieverf op doek / óleo sobre lienzo

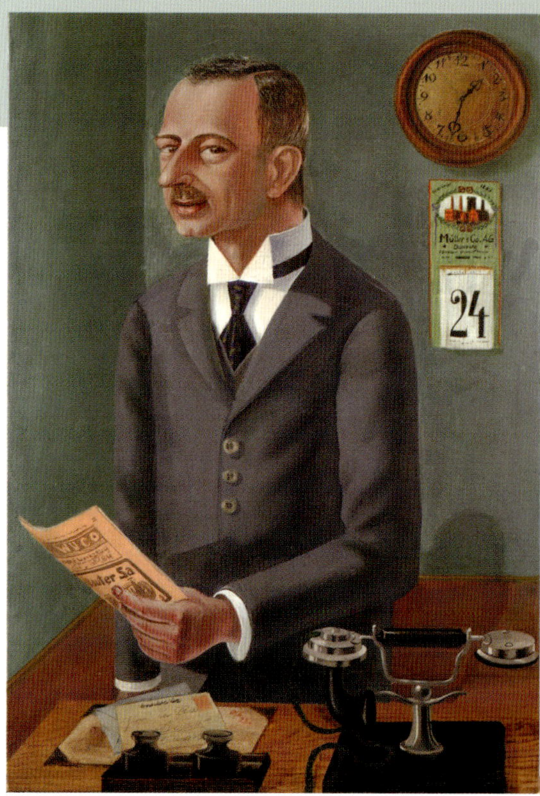

Otto Dix
(Gera 1892 - Singen 1969)

Dr. Mayer-Hermann

●●

1926
149,2 x 99,1 cm / 58.7 x 39 in.
Museum of Modern Art (MoMA),
New York

oil and tempera on wood / Öl und Tempera auf Holz
olieverf en tempera op hout / óleo y temple sobre madera

Otto Dix
(Gera 1892 - Singen 1969)

**Portrait of the journalist,
Sylvia von Harden**
*Bildnis der Journalistin
Sylvia von Harden*
*Portret van journalist
Sylvia von Harden*
**Retrato de la periodista
Sylvia von Harden**

●●●

1926
121 x 89 cm / 47.6 x 35 in.
Centre Georges Pompidou,
Musée National d'Art Moderne, Paris

oil and tempera on wood
Öl und Tempera auf Holz
olieverf en tempera op hout
óleo y temple sobre madera

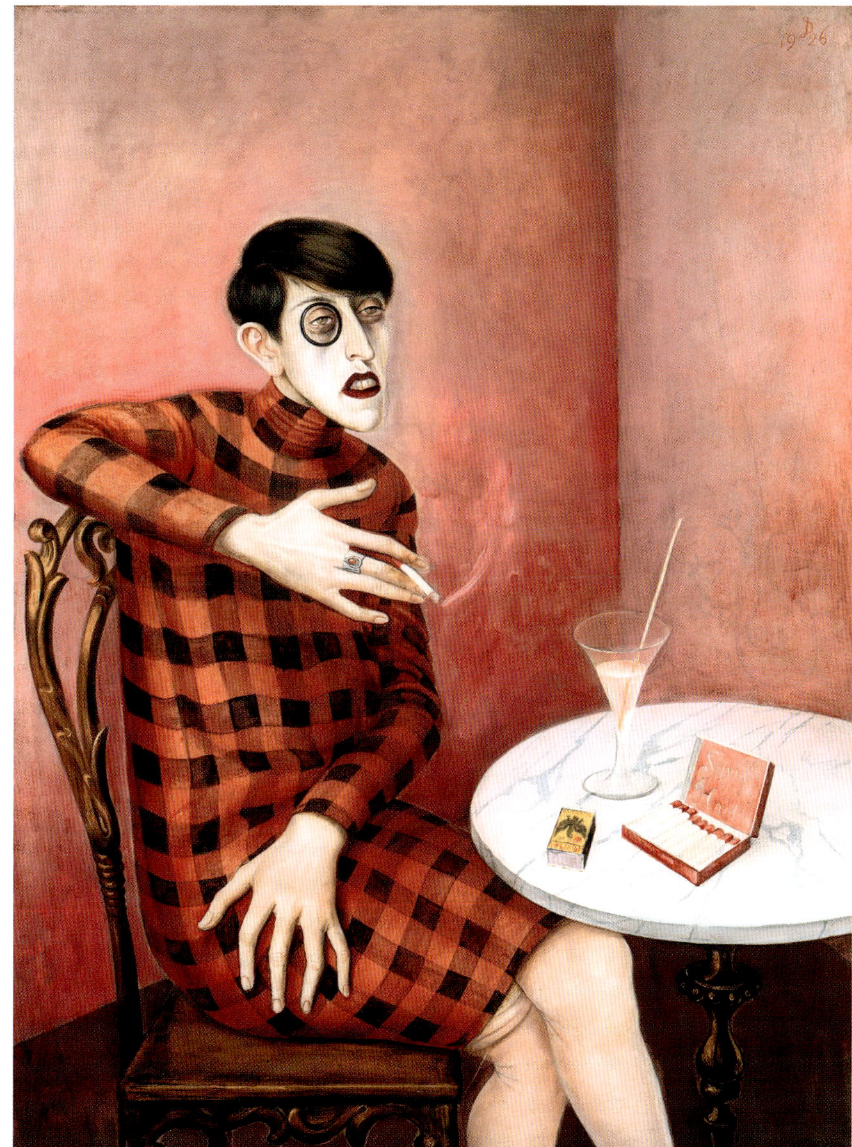

Sylvia von Harden, female journalist
in the Weimar Republic, independent,
indifferent to social conventions, is
portrayed here without embellishments.

Sylvia von Harden, eine Journalistin
zur Zeit der Weimarer Republik,
die unabhängig und unberührt von
gesellschaftlichen Konventionen war, wird
hier ohne Verschönerung porträtiert.

Sylvia von Harden, journaliste van de
republiek van Weimar, onafhankelijk
en onverschillig voor sociale conventies,
wordt hier zonder verfraaiing afgebeeld.

Sylvia von Harden, mujer periodista en
la república de Weimar, independiente,
indiferente a las convenciones sociales,
es retratada aquí sin realces ni
embellecimientos.

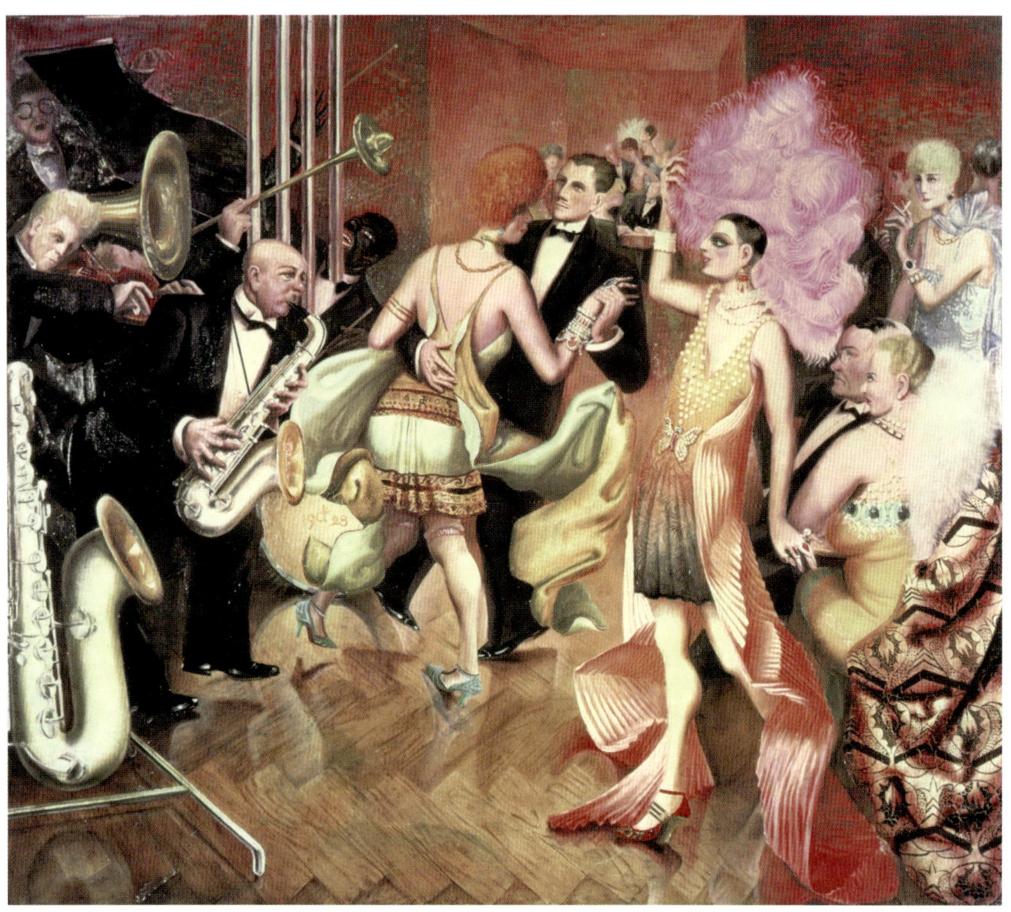

Otto Dix
(Gera 1892 - Singen 1969)

Tryptich: The big city
Tryptichon: Die Großstadt
Drieluik: De grote stad
Tríptico de la Gran Ciudad

●

1927-1928
181 x 201 cm / 71.3 x 82.7 in.
Staatsgalerie, Stuttgart

oil on panel / Öl auf Tafel
olieverf op paneel / óleo sobre tabla

George Grosz
(Berlin 1893 - 1959)

Grey Day
Grauer Tag
Grijze dag
Día gris

●●

1921
115 x 80 cm / 45.3 x 31.5 in.
Nationalgalerie, Staatliche Museen, Berlin

oil on canvas / Öl auf Leinwand
olieverf op doek / óleo sobre lienzo

George Grosz
(Berlin 1893 - 1959)

The gymnast
Der Athlet
De gymnast
El gimnasta

●●●

ca. 1922
104,1 x 80 cm / 41 x 31.5 in.
McNay Art Museum, San Antonio (TX)

oil on canvas / Öl auf Leinwand
olieverf op doek / óleo sobre lienzo

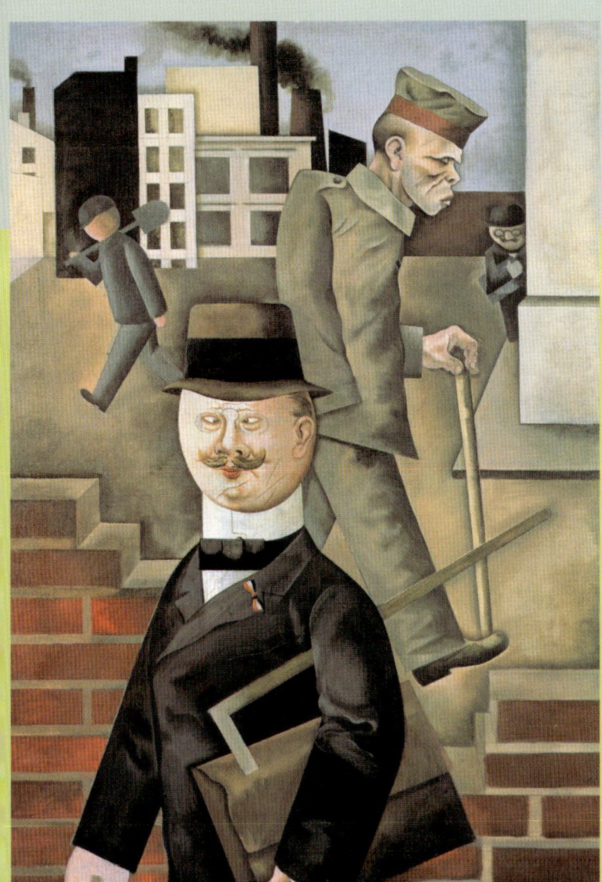

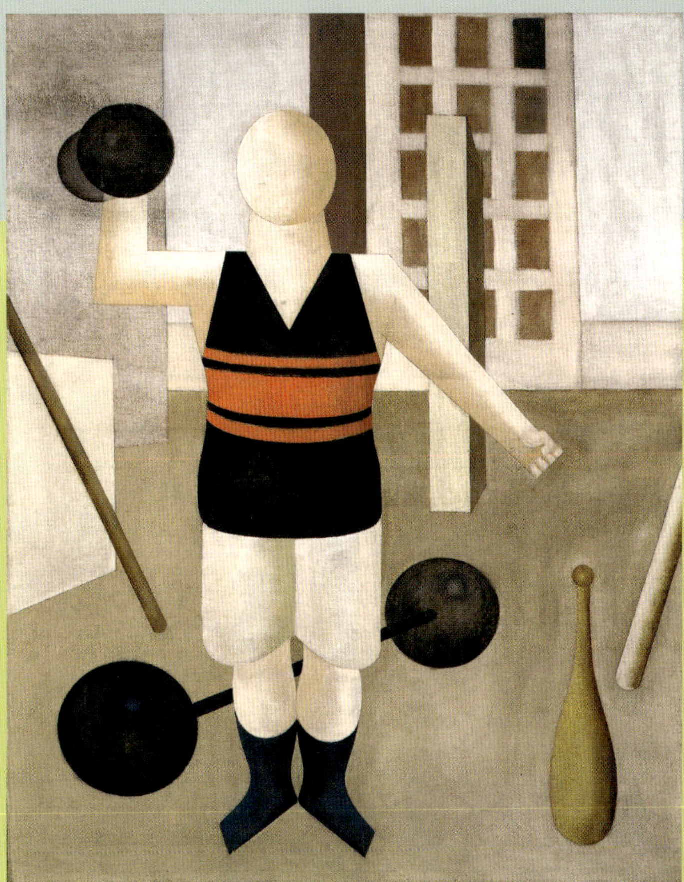

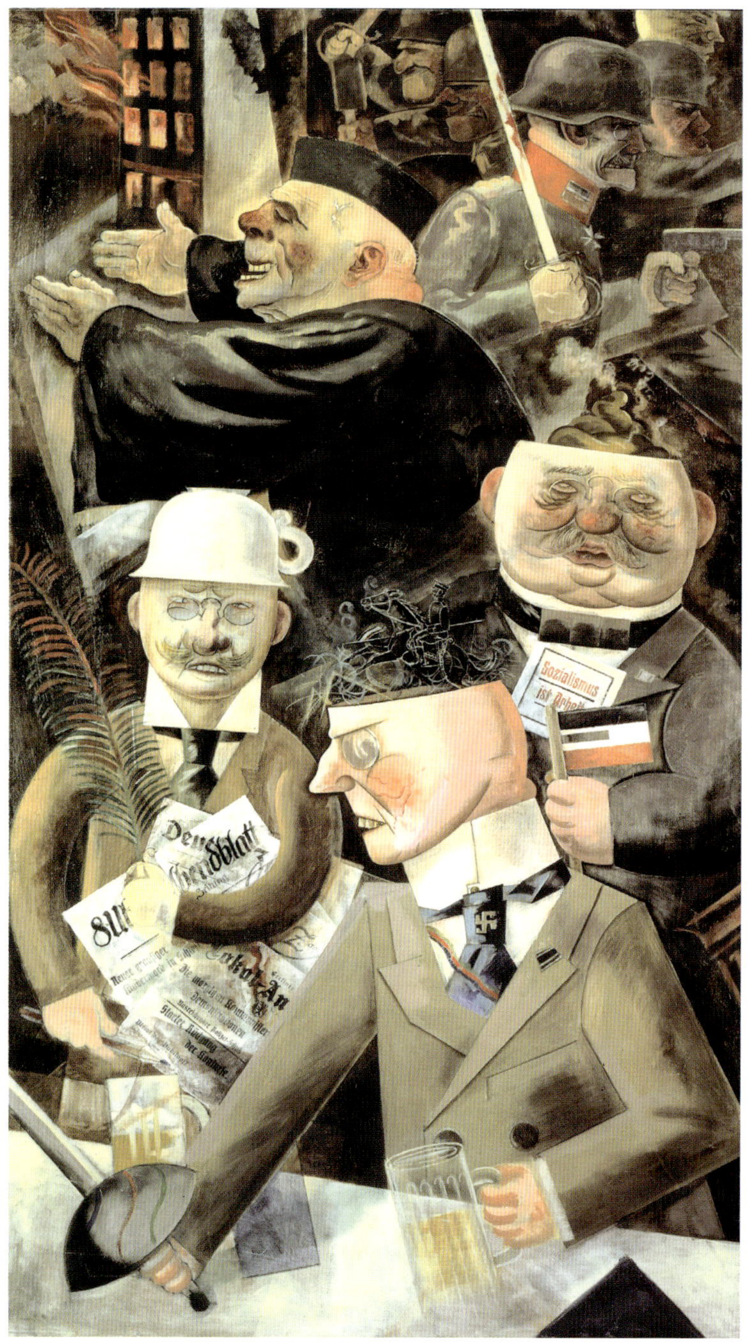

George Grosz
(Berlin 1893 - 1959)

The Pillars of Society
Die Stützen der Gesellschaft
De steunpilaren van de
maatschappij
Los pilares de la sociedad

●●●

1926
200 x 108 cm / 78.7 x 42.5 in.
Nationalgalerie,
Staatliche Museen, Berlin

oil on canvas / Öl auf Leinwand
olieverf op doek / óleo sobre lienzo

In the defeated Germany, Grosz leads a crude critique of the society and its representatives: The army, the Church, the intellectuals.

Im besiegten Deutschland kritisiert Grosz grausam die Gesellschaft und ihre Repräsentanten: das Heer, die Kirche und die Intellektuellen.

Grosz levert in het verslagen Duitsland rauwe kritiek op de maatschappij en haar vertegenwoordigers: het leger, de kerk en de intellectuelen.

En la Alemania derrotada, Grosz realiza una crítica cruda de la sociedad y de sus representantes: el ejército, la Iglesia y los intelectuales.

390

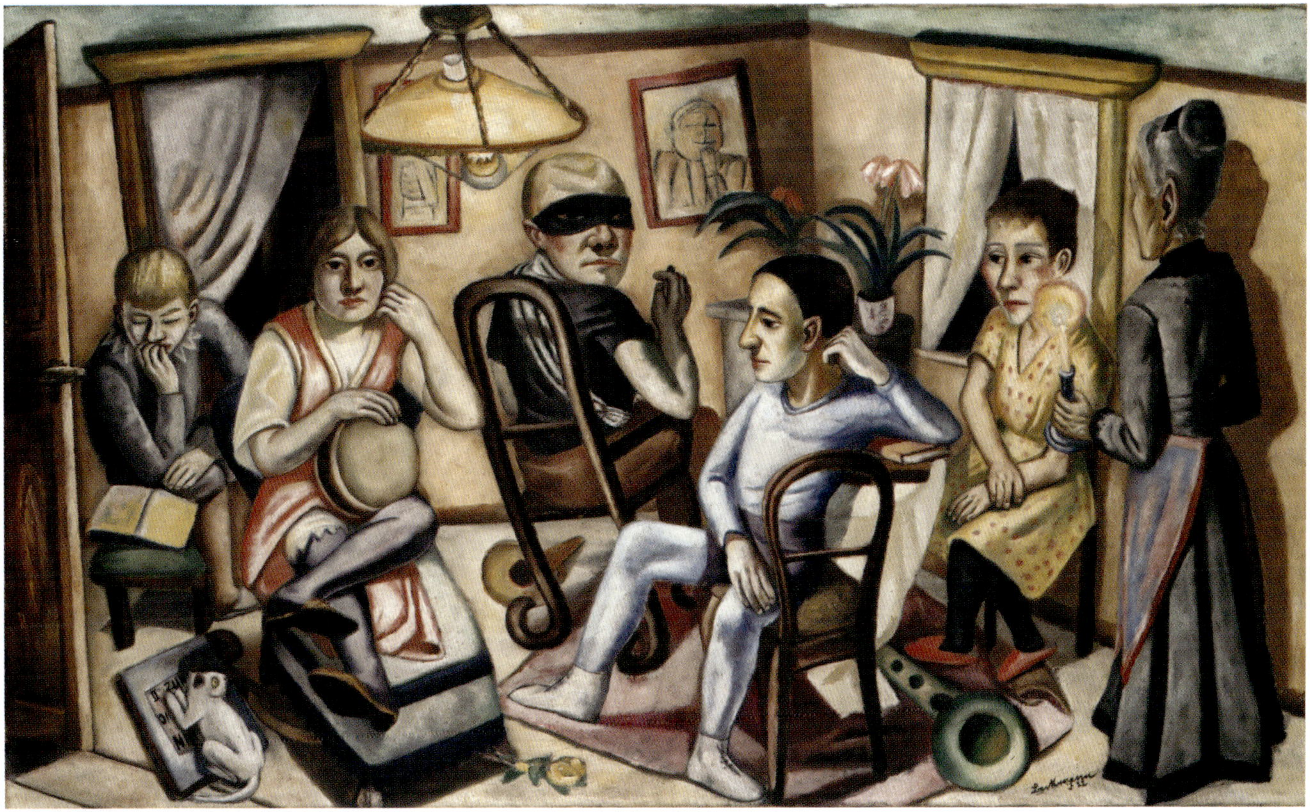

Max Beckmann
(Leipzig 1884 - New York 1950)

Vor dem Maskenball
Voor het gemaskerde bal
Vor dem Maskenball (Baile de máscaras)

●●●

1922
Pinakothek der Moderne, München

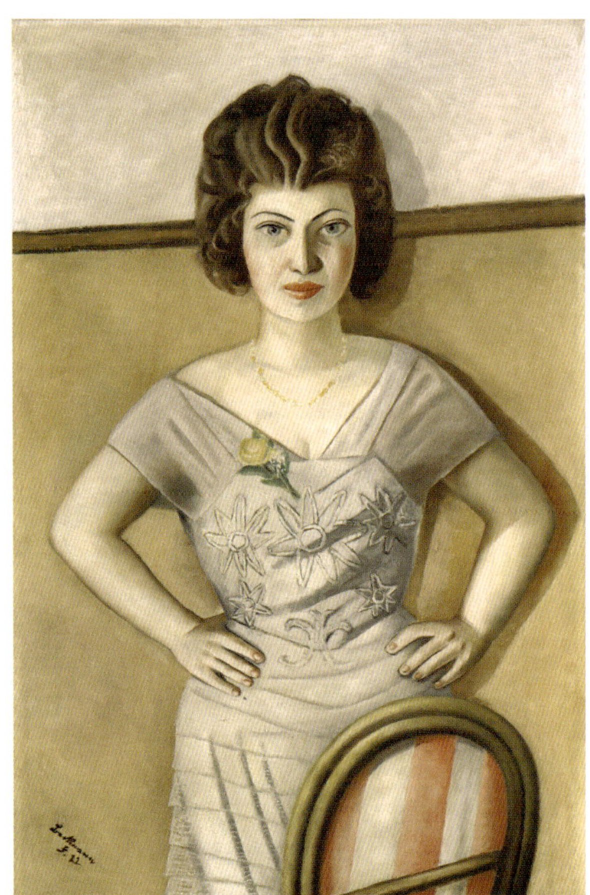

Max Beckmann
(Leipzig 1884 - New York 1950)

Romenian woman
Die Rumänin
Roemeense vrouw
Mujer rumana

●

1922
100 x 65 cm / 39.4 x 25.6 in.
Hamburger Kunsthalle, Hamburg

oil on canvas / Öl auf Leinwand
olieverf op doek / óleo sobre lienzo

Exiled to Holland where he awaits his visa for the United States,
Beckmann seems to be listening for messages
that the world is sending him.

In seinem holländischen Exil, wo er auf sein Visum für die USA
wartet, scheint Beckmann den Nachrichten Gehör zu schenken,
die ihm die ganze Welt zukommen lässt.

Terwijl de verbannen Beckman in Nederland op zijn visum voor
de Verenigde Staten wacht, lijkt hij zich te wijden aan het
beluisteren van alle berichten die hij uit de hele wereld ontvangt.

Exiliado en Holanda, donde espera su visa para los Estados Unidos,
Beckmann parece ponerse a la escucha de los mensajes
que el mundo le envía.

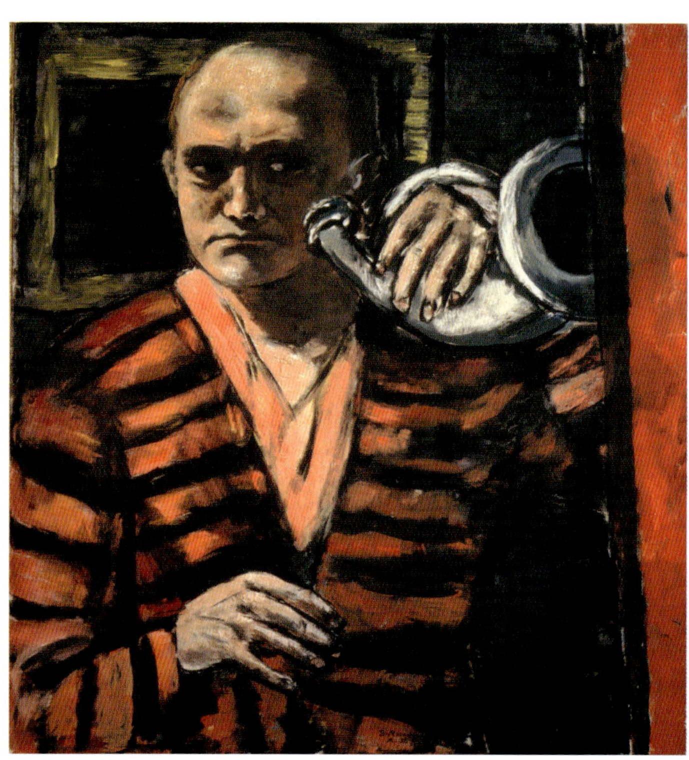

Alexander Kanoldt
(Karlsruhe 1881 - Berlin 1939)

View of Subiaco. Italy
Ansicht von Subiaco. Italien
Gezicht op Subiaco. Italië
Vista de Subiaco. Italia
●
1924
100 x 60 cm / 39.4 x 23.6 in.
Museum der bildenden Künste,
Leipzig

oil on canvas / Öl auf Leinwand
olieverf op doek / óleo sobre lienzo

◄ Max Beckmann
(Leipzig 1884 - New York 1950)

Self-Portrait with horn
Selbstbildnis mit Horn
Zelfportret met hoorn
Autorretrato con cuerno
●●
1938
110 x 101 cm / 43.3 x 39.7 in.
Neue Galerie, New York

oil on canvas / Öl auf Leinwand
olieverf op doek / óleo sobre lienzo

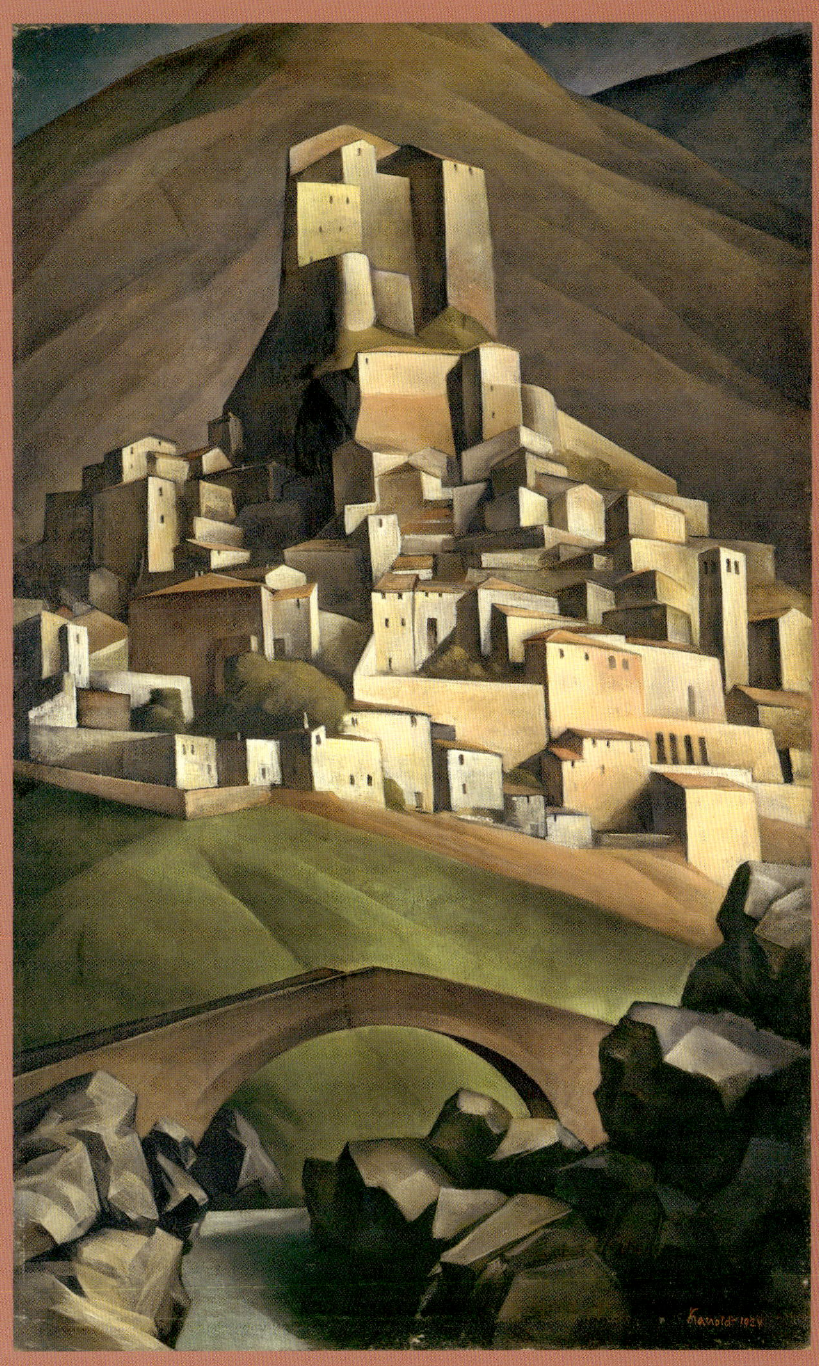

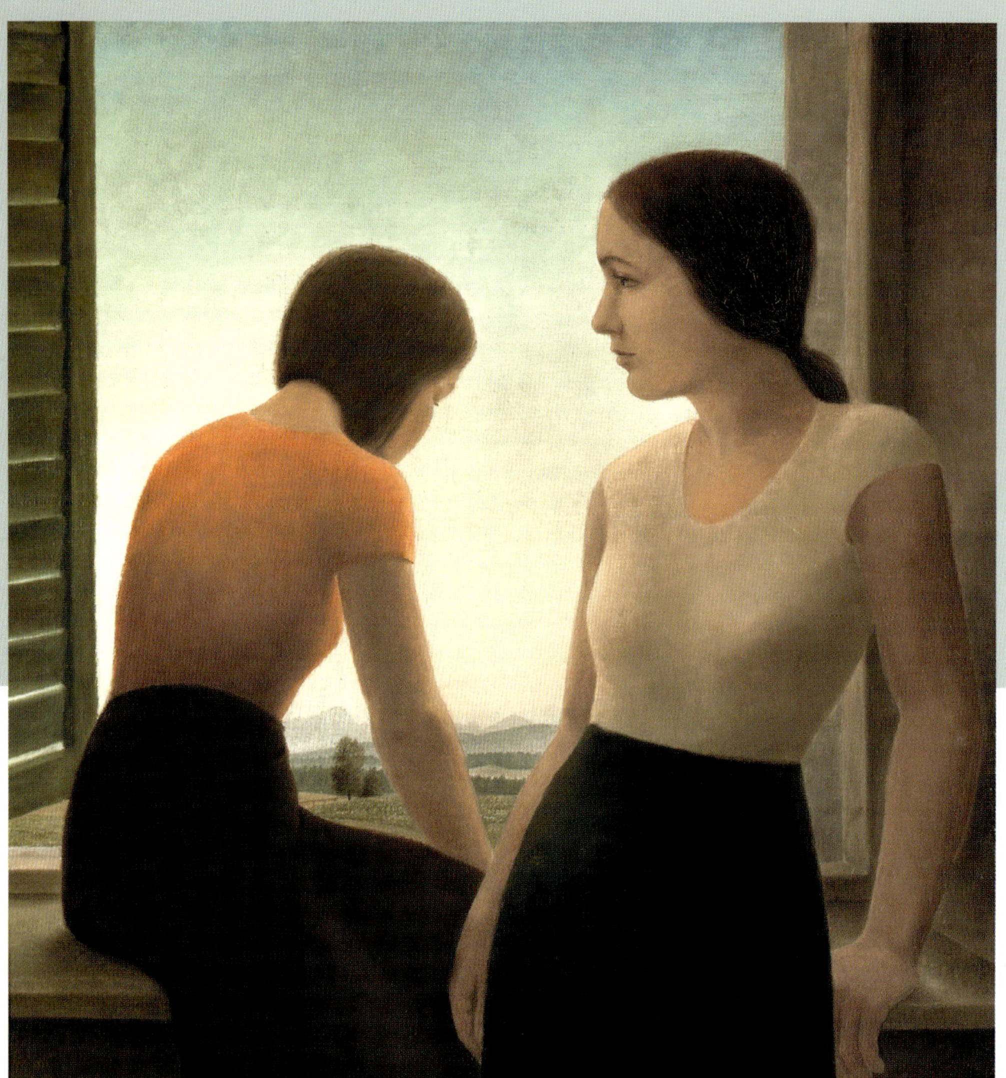

Georg Schrimpf
(München 1889 -
Berlin 1938)

**Two girls
at the window
Mädchen am Fenster
Twee meisjes
bij het raam
Dos muchachas
en la ventana**

●

1937
78,5 x 73 cm / 30.9 x 28.7 in.
Nationalgalerie,
Staatliche Museen, Berlin

oil on canvas
Öl auf Leinwand
olieverf op doek
óleo sobre lienzo

394

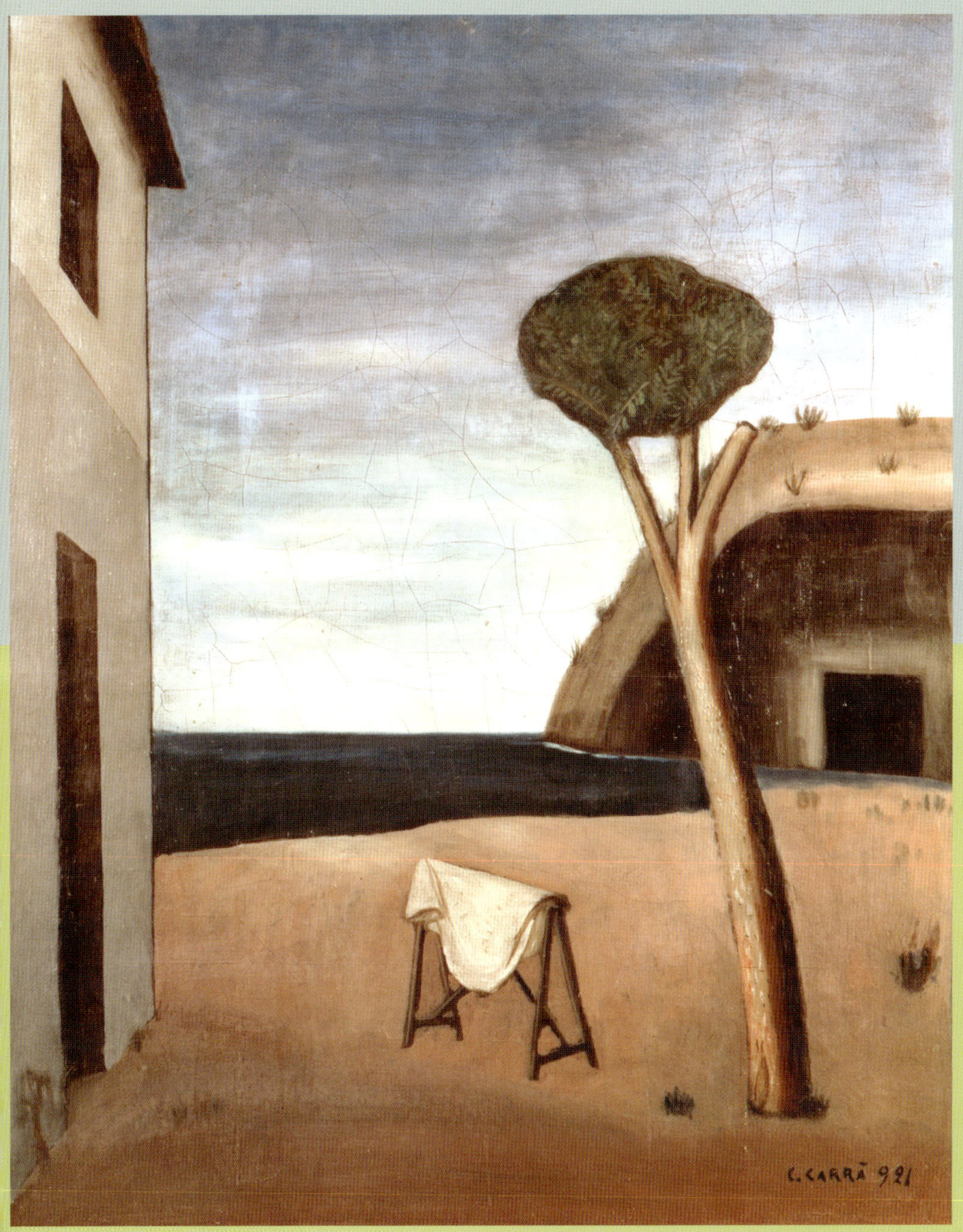

Carlo Carrà
(Quargnento 1881 -
Milano 1966)

Pine tree on the sea
Die Pinie am Meer
Pijnboom aan zee
Pino en el mar
●●●

1921
68 x 52,5 cm / 26.7 x 20.6 in.
Collezione Casella, Roma

oil on canvas
Öl auf Leinwand
olieverf op doek
óleo sobre lienzo

395

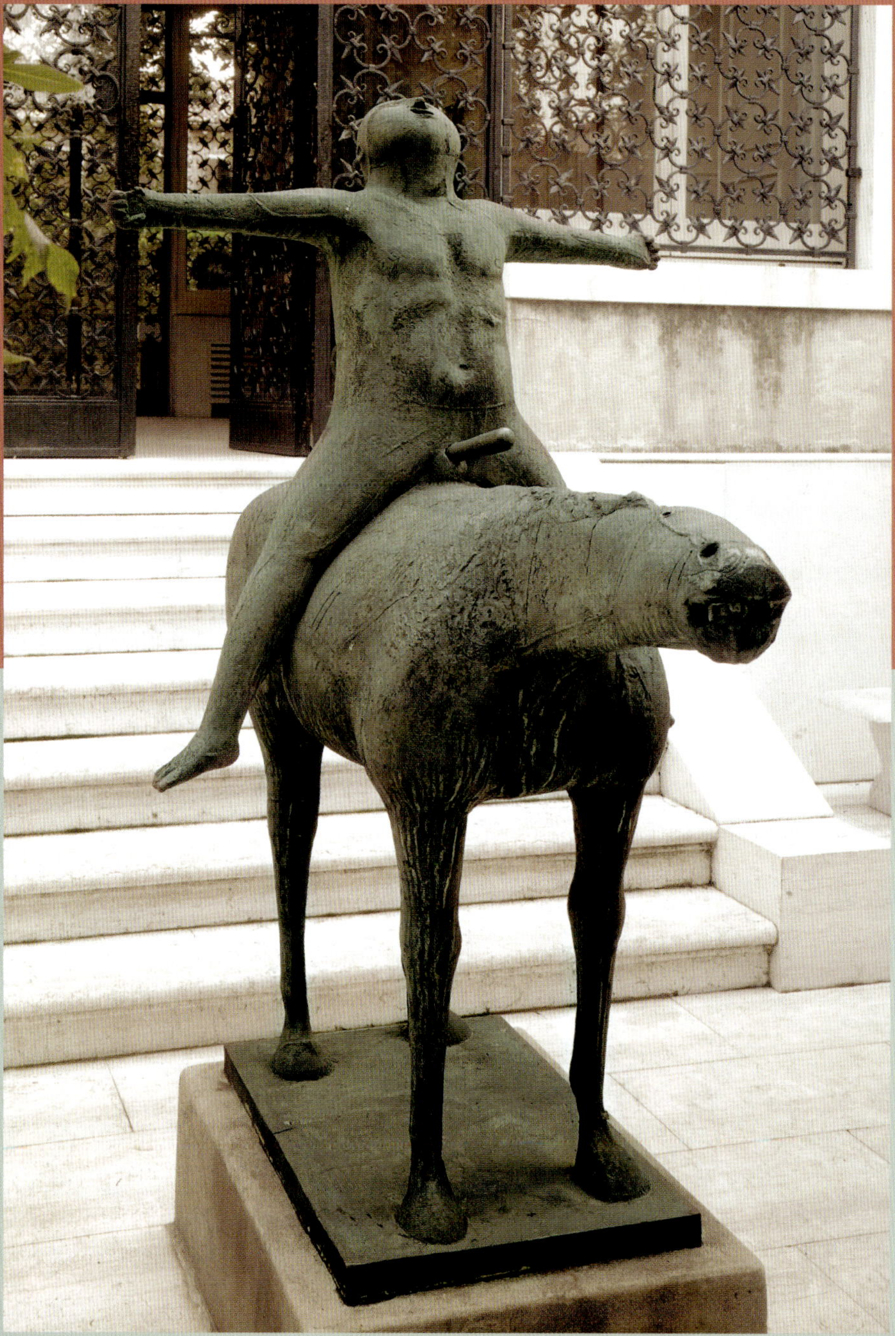

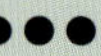

This *Rider* of Marini, archaically inspired and influenced by Etruscan sculpture, has a penis that can be dismantled.

Marinis archaisch inspirierter, von der etruskischen Plastik beeinflusster *Reiter* besitzt einen abnehmbaren Penis.

Deze archaïsche *Ruiter* van Marini, was beïnvloed door de Etruskische beeldhouwkunst en bezit een demonteerbare penis.

Este *Jinete* de Marini, de inspiración arcaica, e influenciado por la escultura etrusca, posee un pene desmontable.

Marino Marini
(Pistoia 1901 - Viareggio 1980)
Angel of the city
Engel der Stadt
Stadsengel
El ángel de la ciudad
●●●
1948
247,9 x 106 cm / 97.6 x 41.7 in.
Collezione Peggy Guggenheim, Venezia

bronze / Bronze / brons / bronce

Tamara de Lempicka
(Warsaw 1898 - Cuernavaca 1980)

Portrait of Marchese d'Afflitto
Porträt des Marquis D'Afflitto
Portret van markiezin d'Afflitto
Retrato del marqués de Afflitto

●●

1925
81 x 130 cm / 31.9 x 51.2 in.
Private collection, New York

oil on canvas / Öl auf Leinwand
olieverf op doek / óleo sobre lienzo

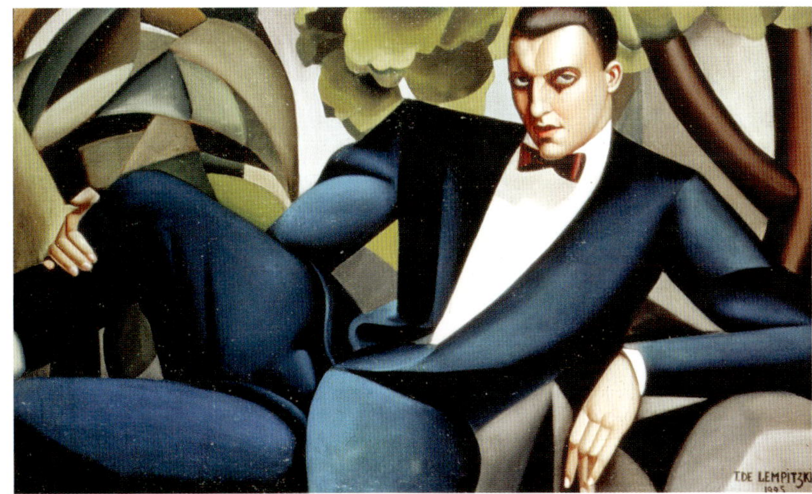

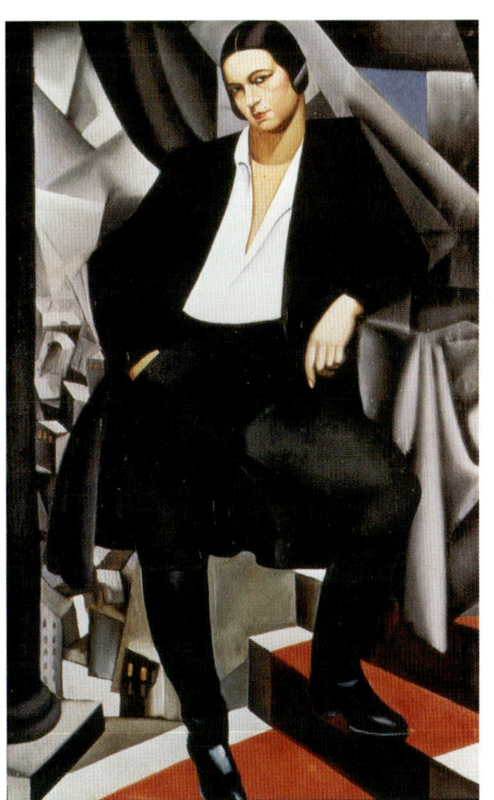

Tamara de Lempicka
(Warsaw 1898 - Cuernavaca 1980)

Portrait of Duchess de la Salle
Porträt der Duchesse de la Salle
Portret van gravin de la Salle
Retrato de la duquesa de La Salle

●●●

1925
162 x 97 cm / 63.8 x 38.2 in.
Private collection, New York

oil on canvas / Öl auf Leinwand
olieverf op doek / óleo sobre lienzo

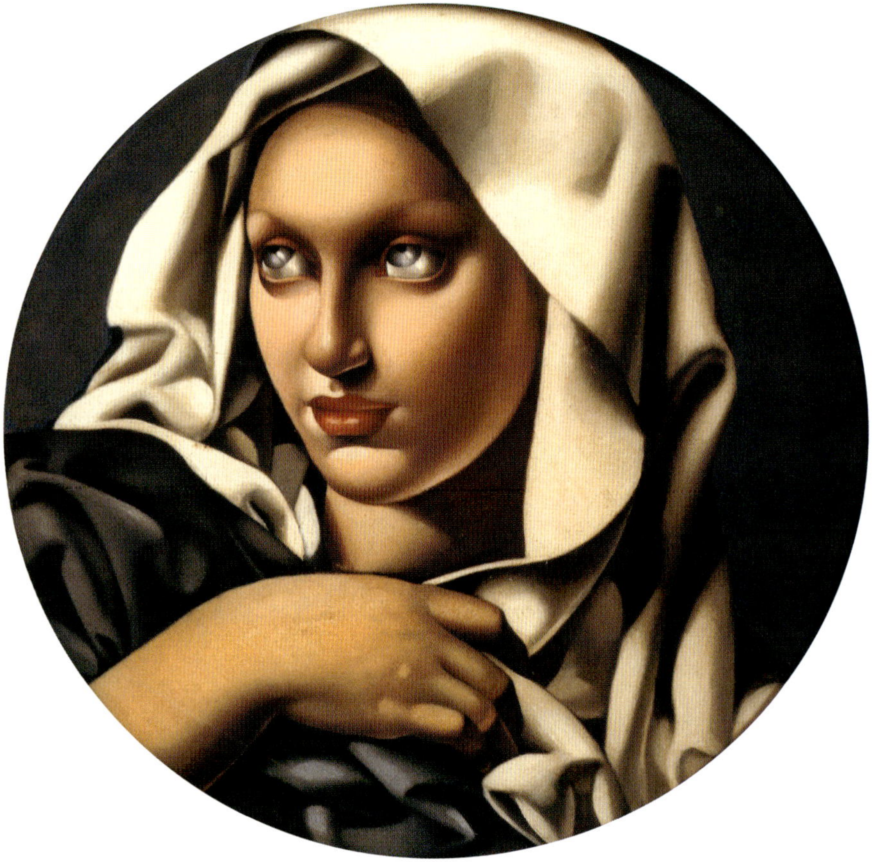

Tamara de Lempicka
(Warsaw 1898 - Cuernavaca 1980)

Madone ronde

●●

1935
33 x 33 cm / 12.9 x 12.9 in.
Musée Departemental de l'Oise,
Beauvais

oil on panel
Öl auf Tafel
olieverf op paneel
óleo sobre tabla

Icon of Art Deco and portrait painter, Lempicka also created religious works that demonstrate the influence of the Italian Renaissance and Michelangelo.

Als Ikone der Art Deco und Porträtistin hat Lempicka auch religiöse Werke geschaffen, die von der italienischen Renaissance und Michelangelo beeinflusst sind.

Lempicka is icoon van de art deco en portretschilder, maar heeft ook religieuze werken gemaakt die beïnvloed zijn door de Italiaanse renaissance en Michelangelo.

Ícono del Art Decó y del arte del retrato, Lempicka ha realizado también obras religiosas en las cuales se nota la influencia del Renacimiento italiano y de Miguel Ángel.

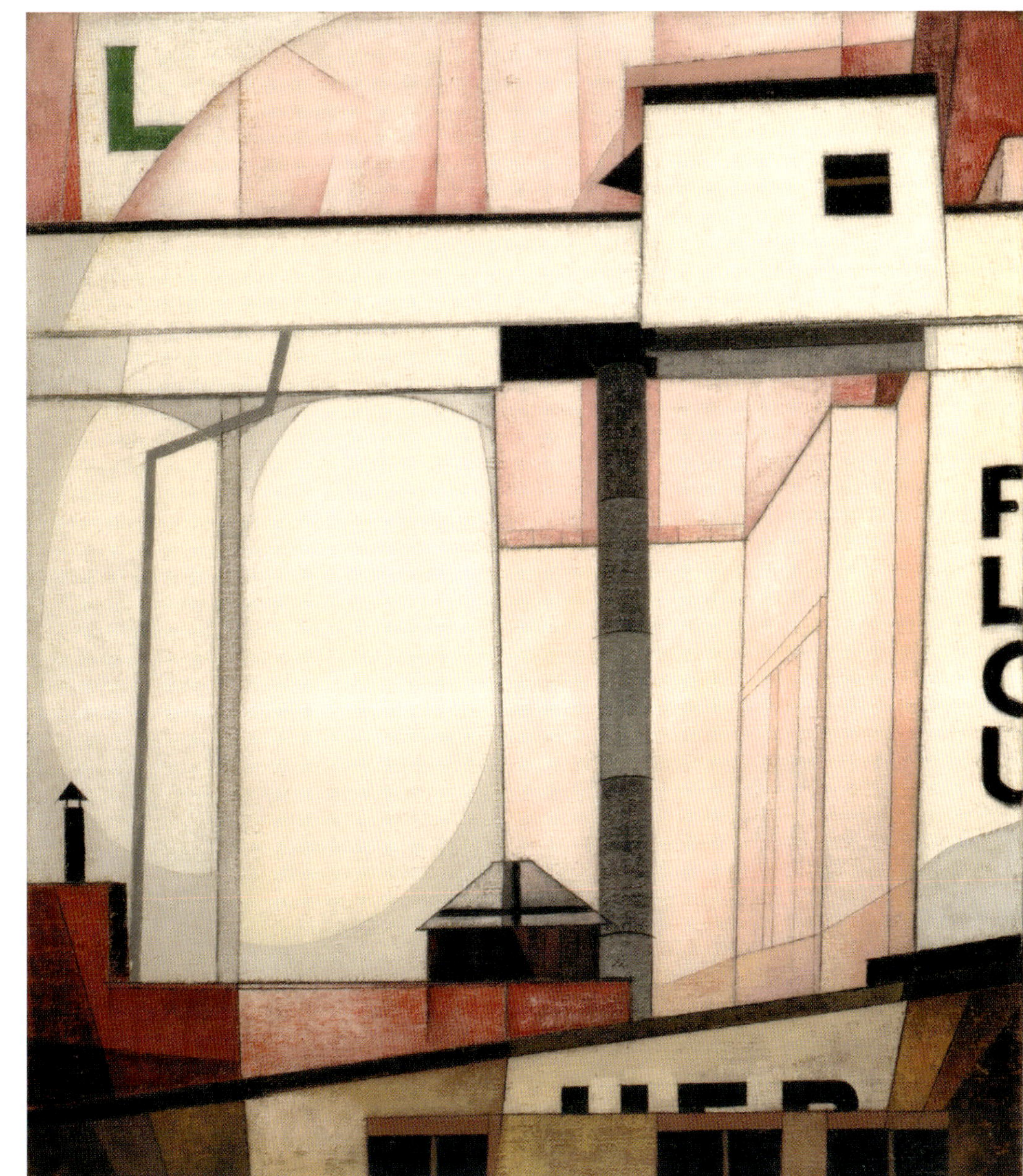

Charles Demuth
(Lancaster
1883- 1935)

Nospmas. M.
Egiap Nospmas. M.

●

1921
60,9 x 51,4 cm
23.9 x 20.2 in.
Munson-Williams-
Proctor Arts Institute,
Utica (NY)

oil on canvas
Öl auf Leinwand
olieverf op doek
óleo sobre lienzo

399

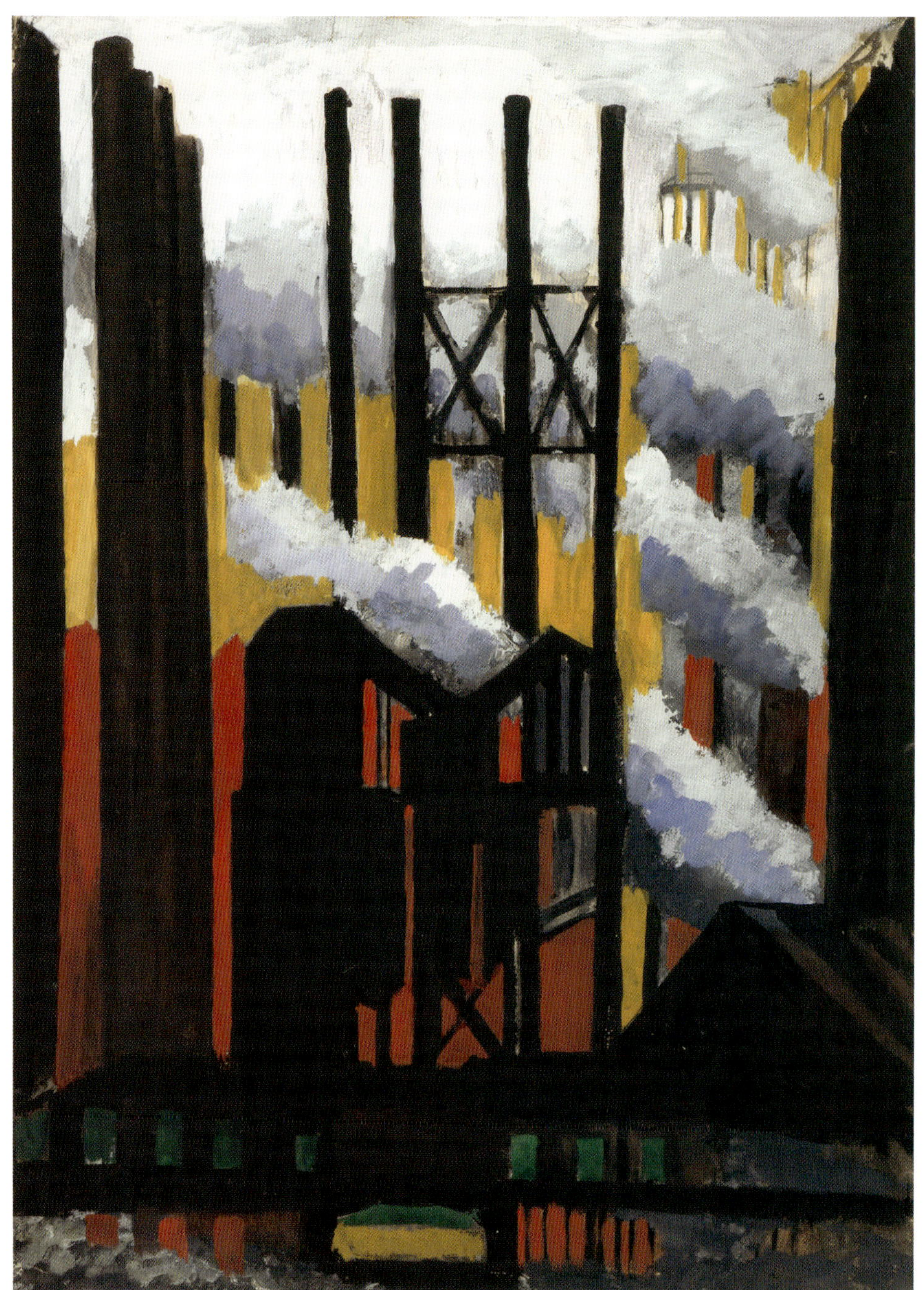

◄ Joseph Stella
(Muro Lucano 1877 -
New York 1946)

Rolling mill for steel
Stahlwalzwerk
Staalmolen
Fábrica de acero

●

1919-1920
44,8 x 31,5 cm / 17.6 x 12.4 in.
Smithsonian American Art
Museum, Washington DC

gouache on paper mounted on
paperboard
Gouache auf Papier, auf Karton
montiert
gouache op papier op karton
gouache sobre papel montado
sobre cartón

► Thomas Hart Benton
(Neosho 1889 -
Kansas City 1975)

Self-portrait with Rita
Selbstbildnis mit Rita
Zelfportret met Rita
Autorretrato con Rita

●

1922
125,7 x 101,6 cm / 49.5 x 40 in.
National Portrait Gallery,
Smithsonian Institution,
Washington DC

oil on canvas
Öl auf Leinwand
olieverf op doek
óleo sobre lienzo

Thomas Hart Benton
(Neosho 1889 - Kansas City 1975)

New England editor
Der Herausgeber von New England
Uitgever uit New England
Editor del New England
●

76,2 x 93,98 cm / 30 x 37 in.
Museum of Fine Arts, Boston

oil and tempera on panel treated with plaster
Öl und Tempera auf mit Gips behandeltem Brett
olieverf en tempera op met krijt bewerkt paneel
óleo y temple sobre panel tratado con yeso

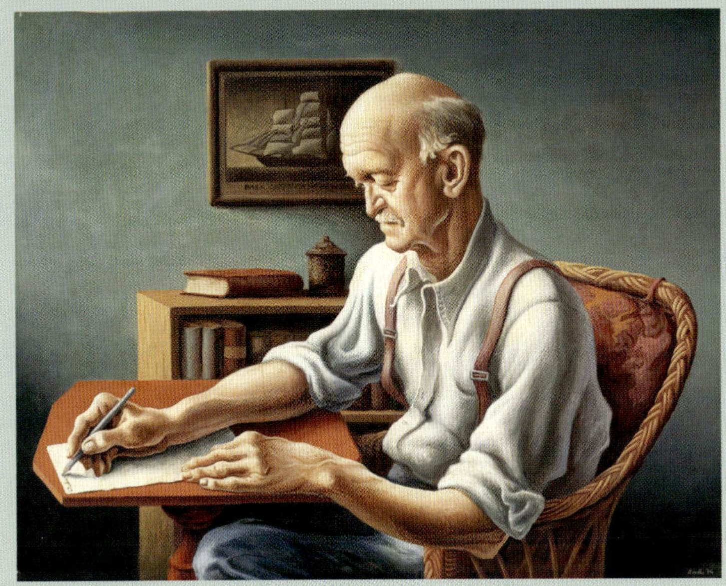

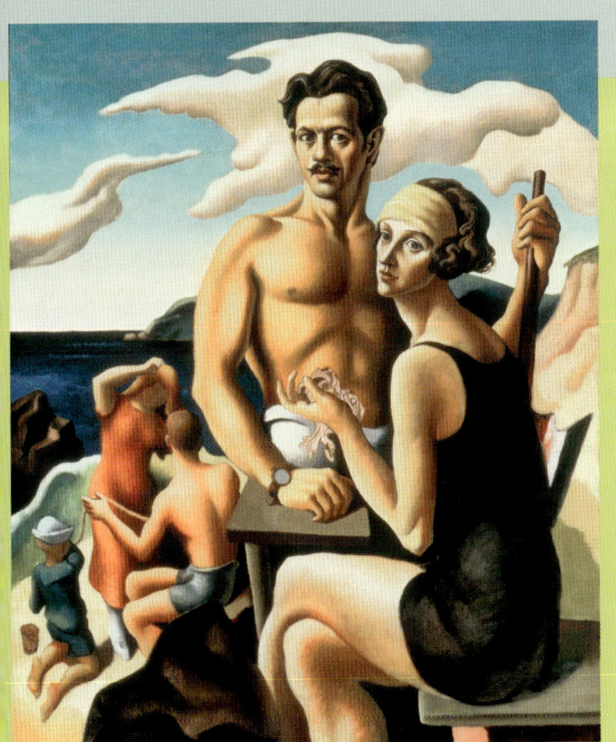

Thomas Hart Benton and his wife on a Massachusetts island, place of inspiration where the stylistic renewal of the painter took place and he then abandoned abstract art.

Thomas Hart Benton und seine Frau auf einer Insel in Massachusetts, einem Ort der Inspiration und der stilistischen Erneuerung des Künstlers, der zu jenem Zeitpunkt die abstrakte Kunst hinter sich ließ.

Thomas Hart Benton en zijn vrouw op een eiland van Massachussetts, waar hij inspiratie vond en zijn stijl vernieuwde, de abstracte kunst achter zich latend.

Thomas Hart Benton y su mujer, en una isla del Massachusetts, lugar de inspiración donde tuvo lugar la renovación estilística del pintor, que abandonó por entonces el arte abstracto.

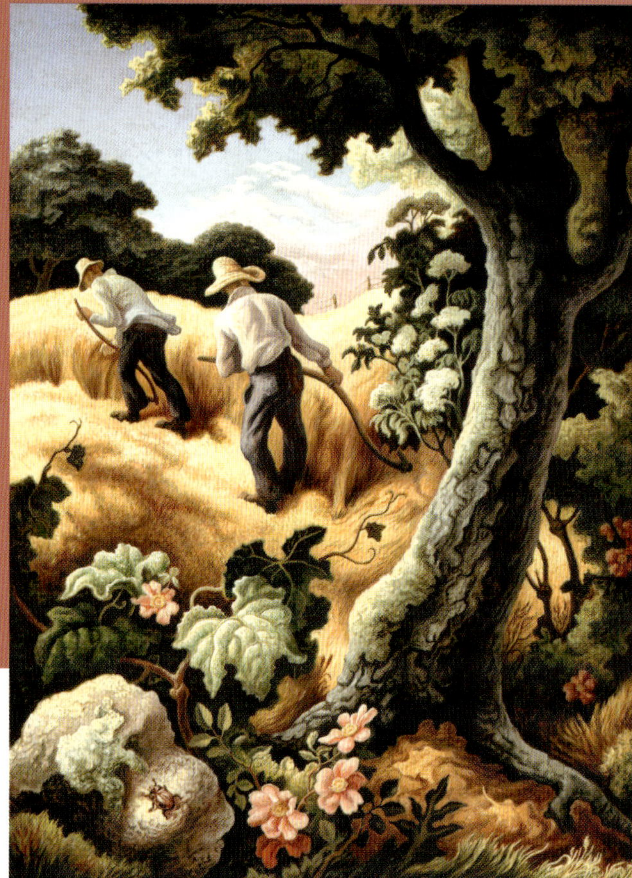

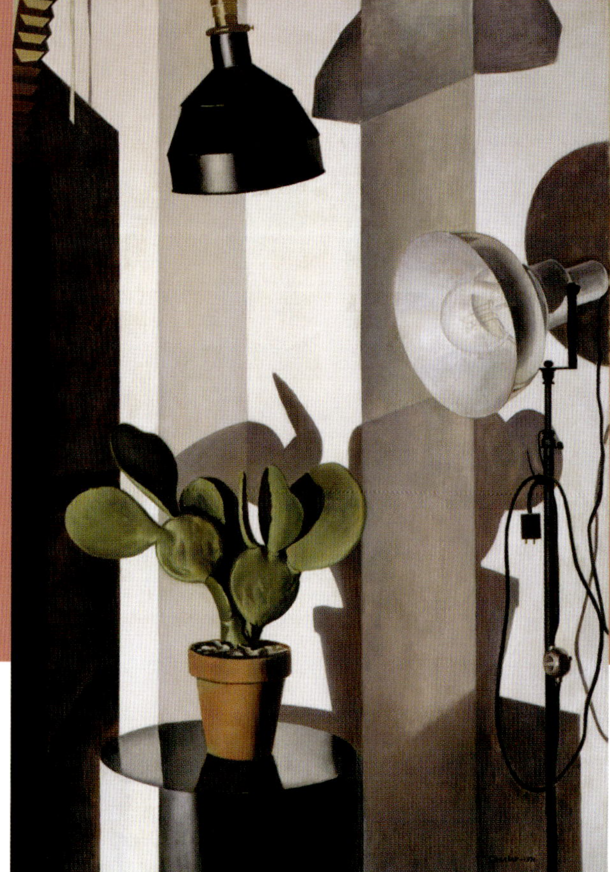

Thomas Hart Benton
(Neosho 1889 - Kansas City 1975)

Hay in July / Heu im Juli
Hooi in juli / Heno en julio

●

1943
96,5 x 67,9 cm / 38 x 26.7 in.
The Metropolitan Museum of Art, New York

tempera, wood cellulose and oil on masonite
Eitempera, Methylcellulose und Öl auf Holzfaserplatte
eitempera, methylcellulose en olieverf op masoniet
temple al huevo, celulosa metílica y óleo sobre masonita

Charles Sheeler
(Philadelphia 1883 - New York 1965)

Cactus
Kaktus

● ●

1931
114,6 x 76,4 cm / 45.1 x 30.1 in.
Philadelphia Museum of Art, Philadelphia

oil on canvas / Öl auf Leinwand
olieverf op doek / óleo sobre lienzo

Charles Sheeler

(Philadelphia 1883 - New York 1965)

**American Interior
Amerikanisches Interieur
Amerikaans interieur
Interior americano**

●●

1934
84,5 x 76,8 cm / 33.2 x 30.2 in.
Yale University Art Gallery,
New Haven (CT)

oil on canvas / Öl auf Leinwand
olieverf op doek / óleo sobre lienzo

Clarity and photographic
precision just like a love for
handcrafts and simplicity
characterize the work of Sheeler,
painter and photographer.

Fotografische Klarheit
und Präzision, sowie eine
Liebe für die Produkte des
Handwerks und die Einfachheit
charakterisieren die Arbeit
von Sheeler, einem Maler und
Fotografen.

Helderheid en nauwkeurigheid,
liefde voor ambachtelijke
producten en eenvoud zijn
kenmerkend voor het werk van
Sheeler, schilder en fotograaf.

La claridad y la precisión
fotográfica, así como el
amor por los productos del
artesanado y la simplicidad,
caracterizan el trabajo de
Sheeler, pintor y fotógrafo.

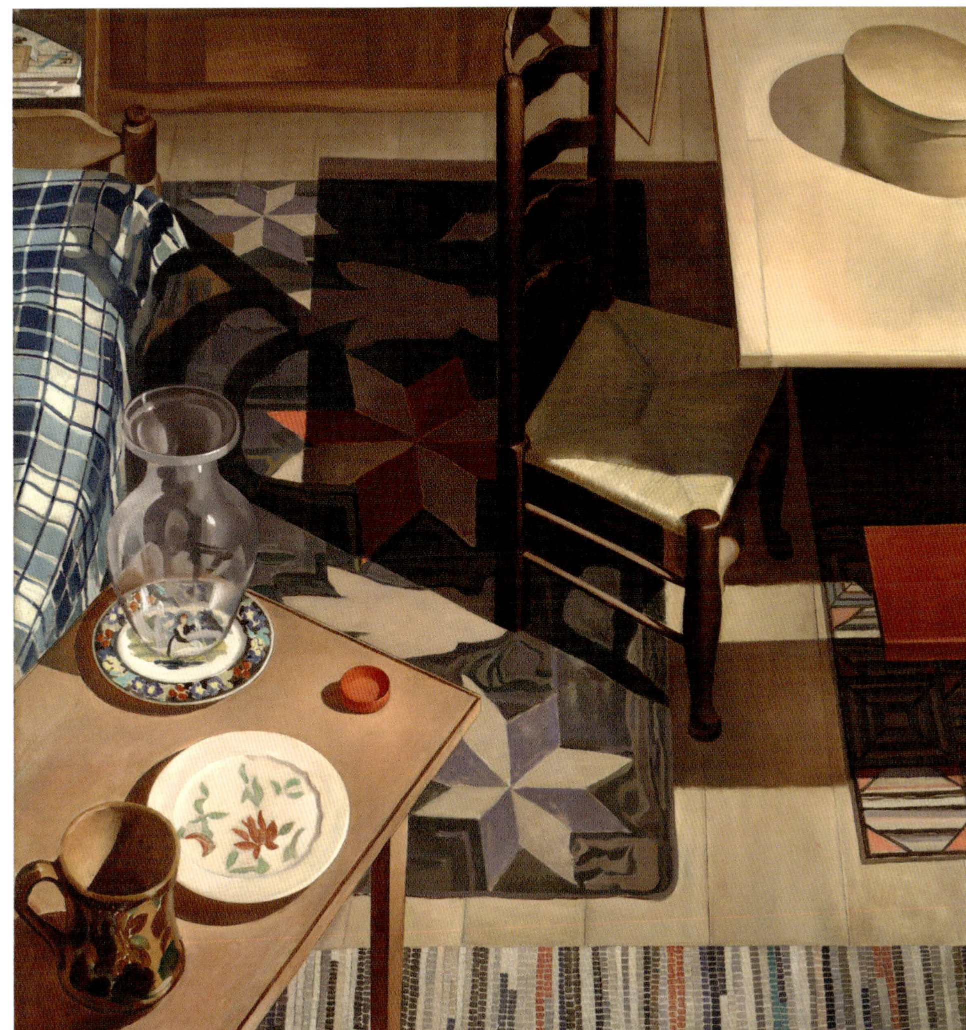

404

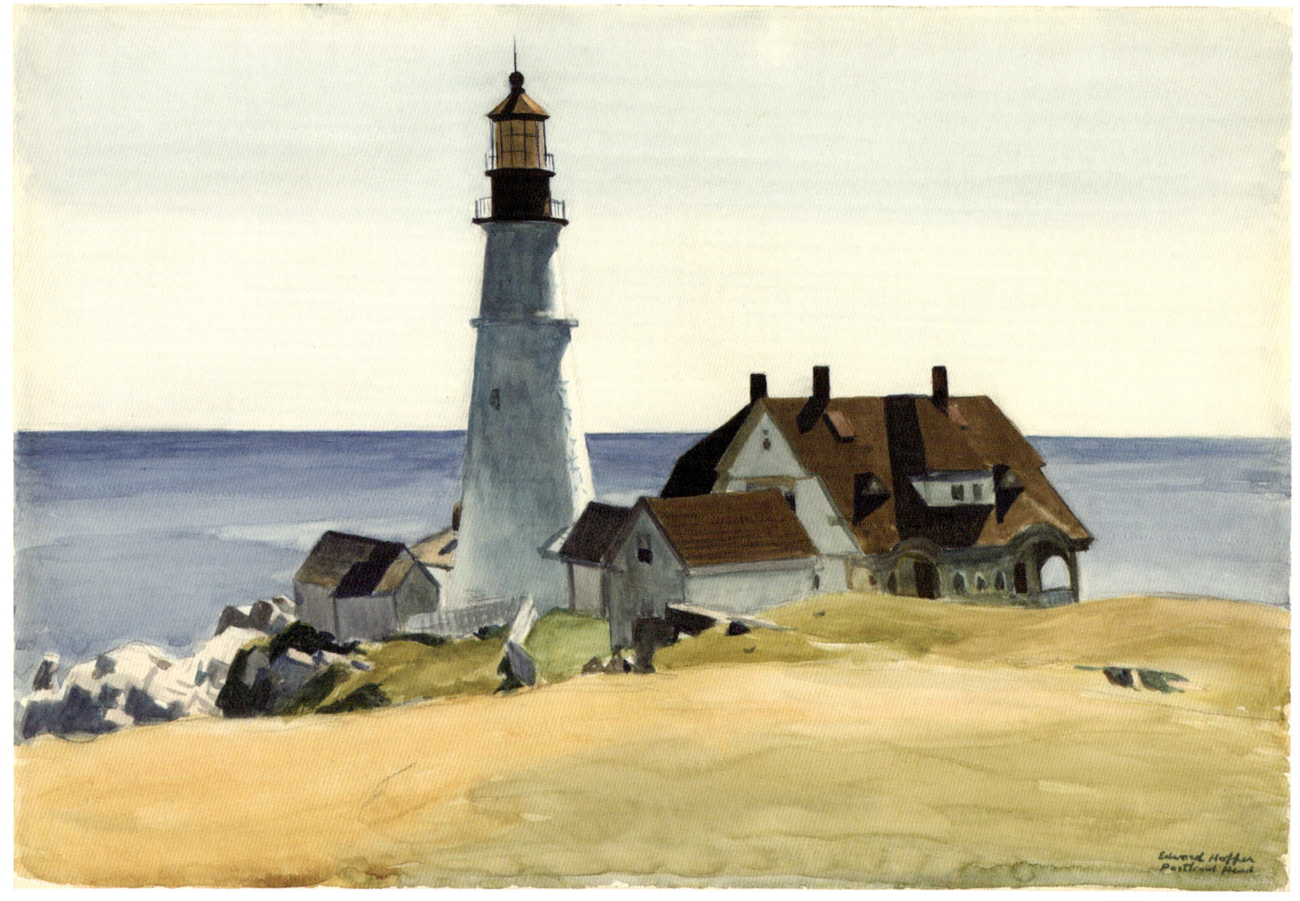

Edward Hopper
(Nyack 1882 - New York 1967)

Lighthouse and buildings, Portland Head, Cape Elizabeth, Maine
Leuchtturm und Gebäude, Portland Head, Cape Elizabeth, Maine
Vuurtoren en gebouwen, Portland Head, Cape Elizabeth, Maine
Faro y edificios, Portland Head, Cape Elizabeth, Maine

●●

1927
34,3 x 49,5 cm / 13.5 x 19.5 i
Museum of Fine Arts, B

watercolor on graphite o   harell über Graphit auf Papier
aquarel en grafiet op papi   sobre grafito sobre papel

Edward Hopper
(Nyack 1882 - New York 1967)

Martha McKean of Wellfleet
Die Martha McKean von Wellfleet
Martha McKean uit Wellfleet
El "Martha McKean" de Wellfleet

●

1944
81,3 x 167 cm / 32 x 65.8 in.
Museo Thyssen-Bornemisza, Madrid

oil on canvas / Öl auf Leinwand / olieverf op doek / óleo sobre lienzo

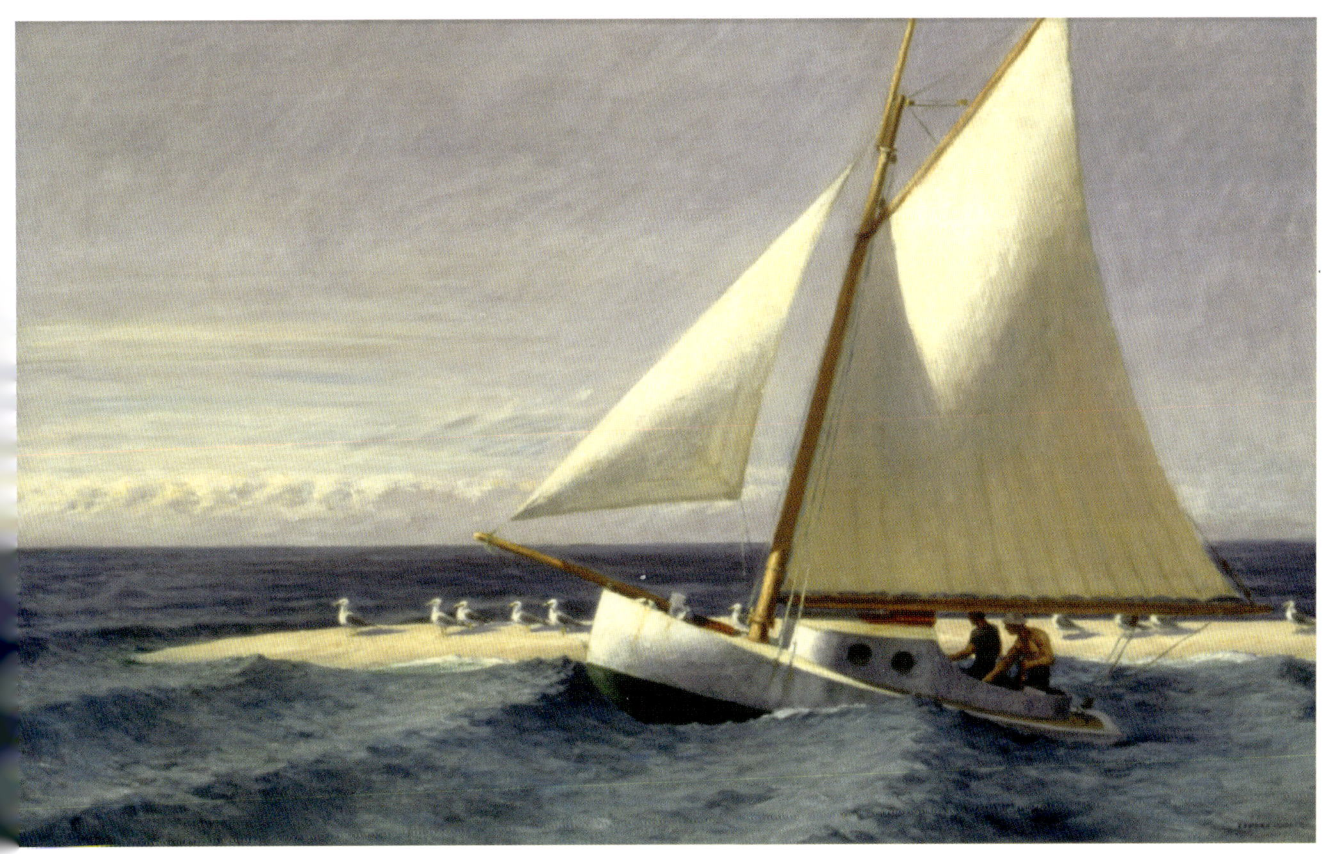

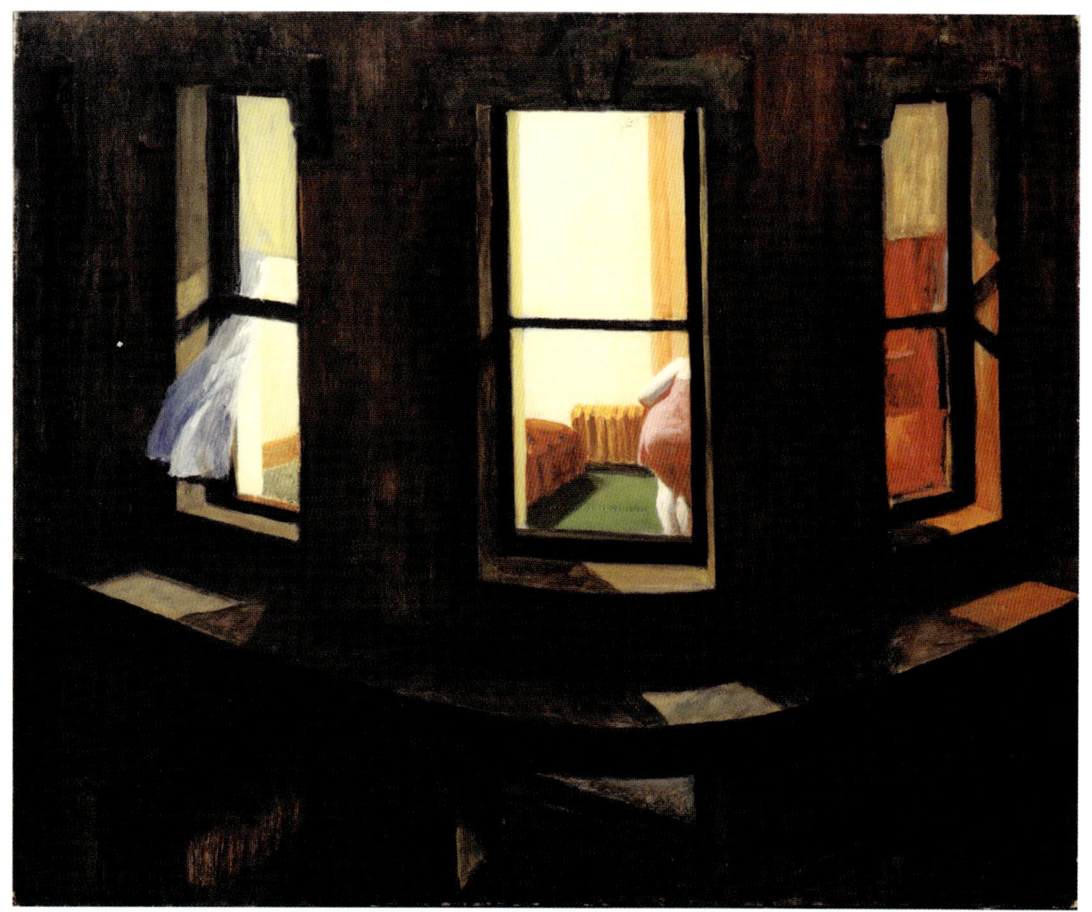

Edward Hopper
(Nyack 1882 - New York 1967)

Night window
Fenster bei Nacht
Raam bij nacht
Ventanas de noche

●●●

1928
73,7 x 86,4 cm / 29 x 34 in.
Museum of Modern Art (MoMA), New York

oil on canvas / Öl auf Leinwand / olieverf op doek / óleo sobre lienzo

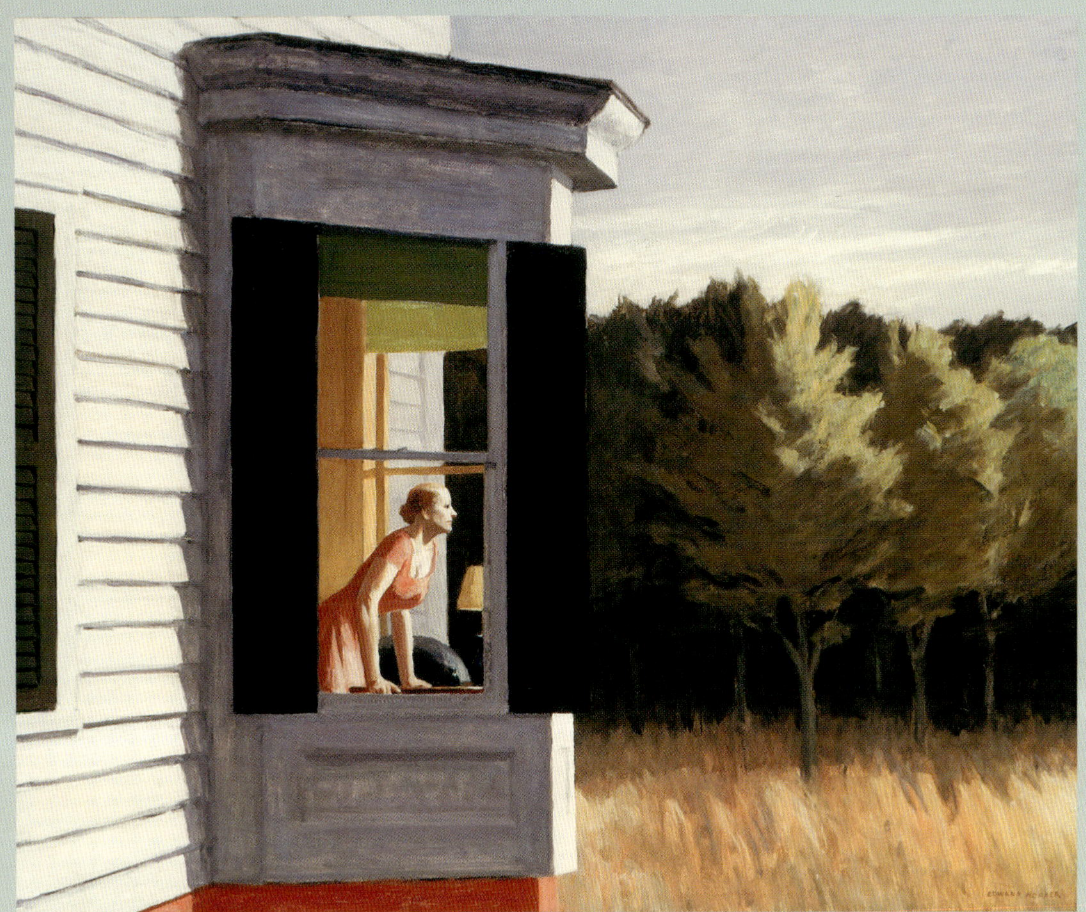

Edward Hopper
(Nyack 1882 - New York 1967)

Morning in Cape Cod
Morgens in Cape Cod
Ochtend in Cape Cod
Cabo Cod por la mañana

●●●

1950
86,7 x 102,3 cm / 34.1 x 40.2 in.
Smithsonian American Art Museum, Washington DC

oil on canvas / Öl auf Leinwand / olieverf op doek / óleo sobre lienzo

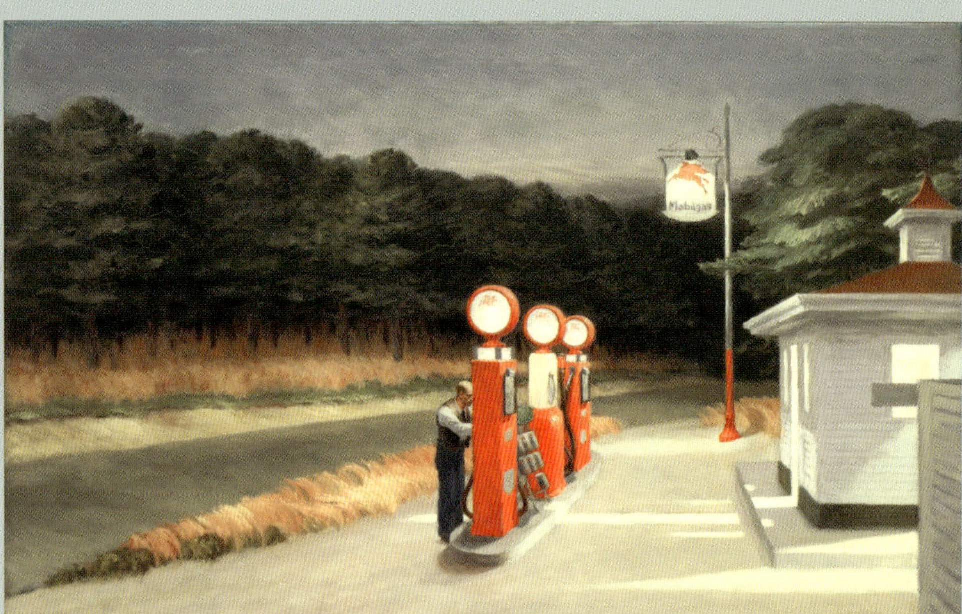

Edward Hopper
(Nyack 1882 - New York 1967)

Petrol Station
Tankstelle
Benzinepomp
Gasolinera
●●

1940
66,7 x 102,2 cm / 26.2 x 40.2 in.
Museum of Modern Art (MoMA
New York

oil on canvas / Öl auf Leinwand
olieverf op doek / óleo sobre lienz

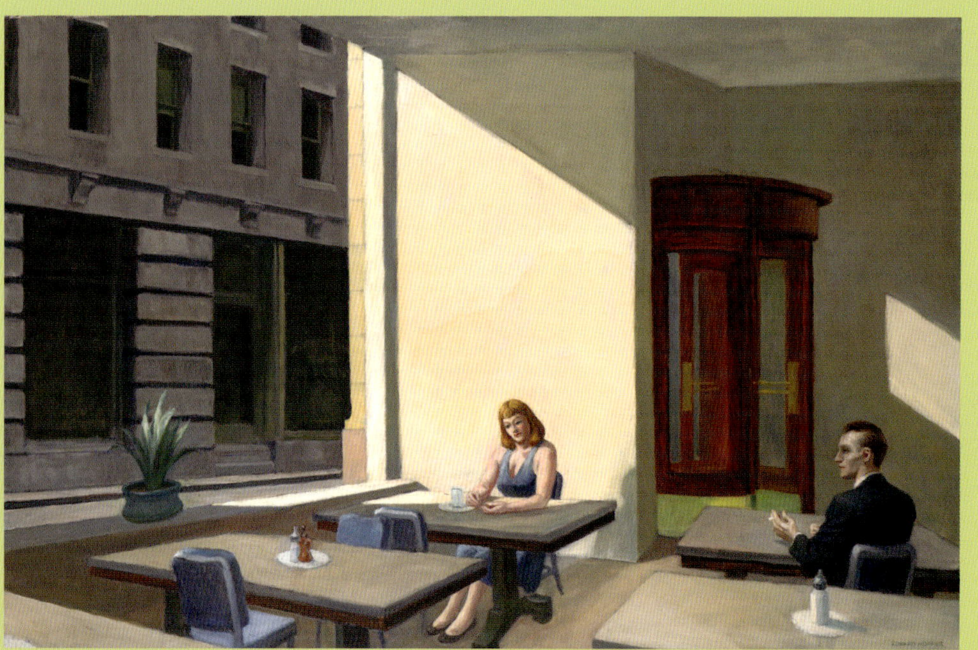

Edward Hopper
(Nyack 1882 - New York 1967)

Ray of sunshine in a caffè
Sonnenstrahl im Café
Zonnestraal in een café
Luz del sol en un café
●●

1958
102,1 x 152,7 cm / 40.2 x 60.1 in
Yale University Art Gallery,
New Haven (CT)

oil on canvas
Öl auf Leinwand
olieverf op doek
óleo sobre lienzo

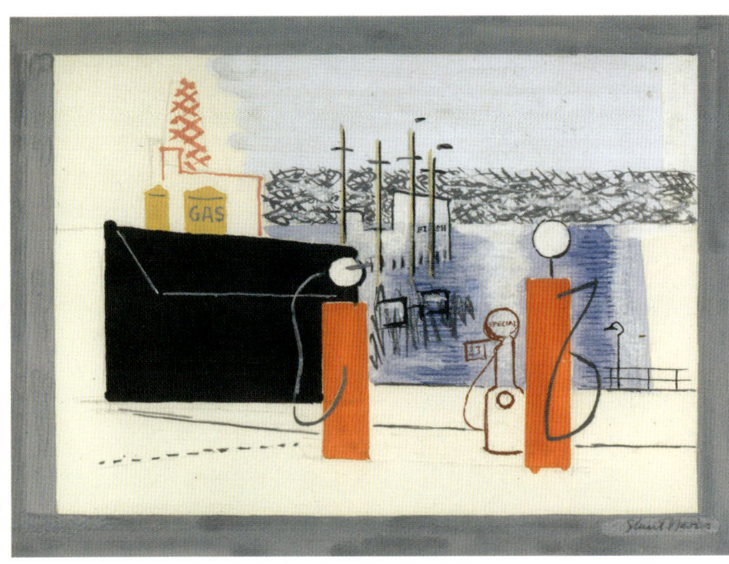

Stuart Davis
(Philadelphia 1892 - New York 1964)
Petrol tank (Petrol pumps)
Benzintank (Zapfsäule)
Benzinetank (benzinepompen)
Surtidores de gasolina

●

1930
40,3 x 53 cm / 15.8 x 20.9 in.
The Newark Museum, Newark

watercolor on paper / Aquarell auf Papier
aquarel op papier / acuarela sobre papel

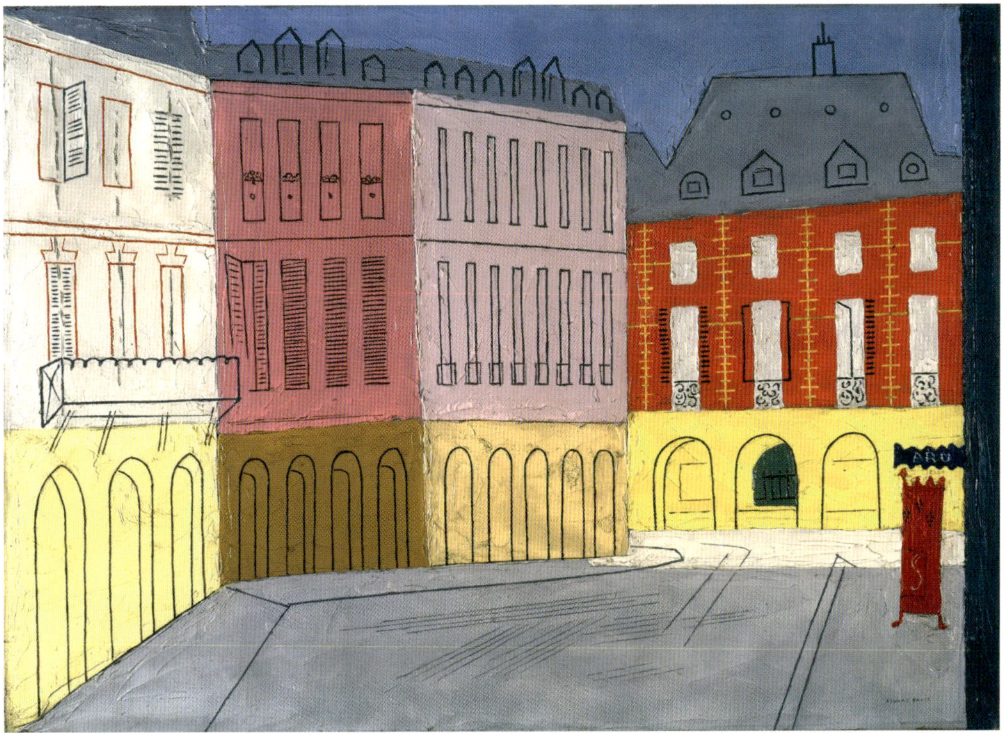

Stuart Davis
(Philadelphia 1892 -
New York 1964)
Place des Vosges No. 1
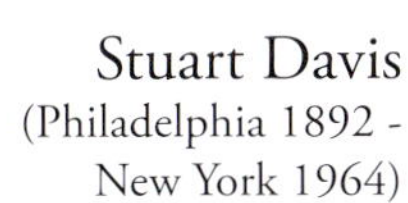
1928
53,3 x 73 cm / 21 x 28.7 in.
The Newark Museum,
Newark

oil on canvas
Öl auf Leinwand
olieverf op doek
óleo sobre lienzo

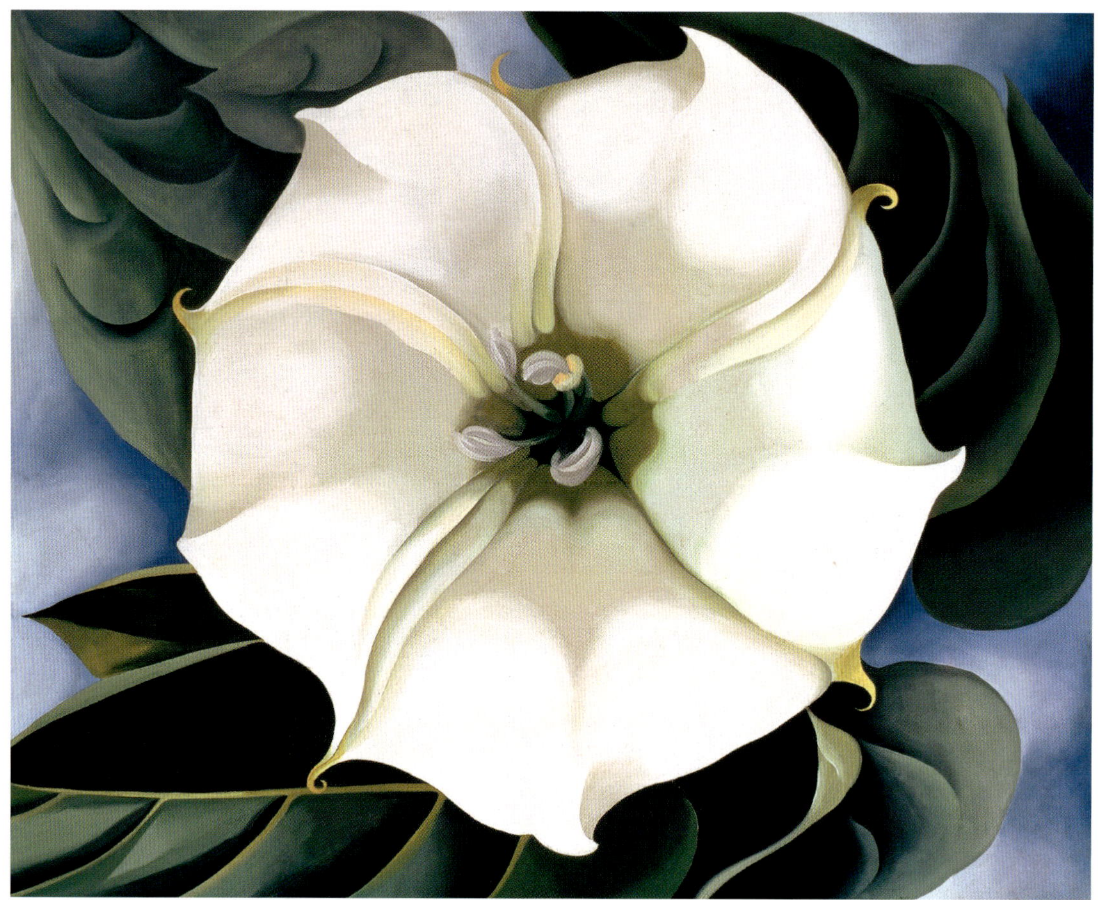

410

Georgia O'Keeffe
(Sun Prairie 1887 - Santa Fe 1986)

Thorn-apple flower
Weißer Stechapfel
Bloem van een doornappel
Flor de estramonio

●●●

1932
48 x 40 cm / 18.9 x 15.7 in.
The Georgia O'Keeffe Museum, Santa Fe

oil on canvas / Öl auf Leinwand / olieverf op doek / óleo sobre lienzo

Georgia O'Keeffe
(Sun Prairie 1887 - Santa Fe 1986)

White Flower on Red Earth n. 1
Weiße Blume auf Roter Erde Nr.1
Witte bloem op rode grond n. 1
Flor blanca sobre tierra roja No. 1

●●●

1943
66,7 x 76,8 cm / 26.2 x 30.2 in.
The Newark Museum, Newark

oil on canvas / Öl auf Leinwand
olieverf op doek / óleo sobre lienzo

Married to the photographer Stieglitz, O'Keeffe was inspired
by the close shots of the photos of flowers for her compositions
that she enriches with symbolic values.

O'Keefe, die Ehefrau des Fotografen Stieglitz, inspirierte sich
an den kleinen Bildausschnitten der Blumenfotos für ihre
Kompositionen, die sie mit symbolischen Werten anreicherte.

O'Keefe was getrouwd met fotograaf Stieglitz en liet zich voor
haar composities die zij verrijkte met symbolische waarden,
inspireren door de nauwe indeling van de bloemenfoto's.

Casada con el fotógrafo Stieglitz, O'Keefe se inspiraba en
los encuadres cercanos de las fotografías de flores para sus
composiciones, las cuales enriquece con valores simbólicos.

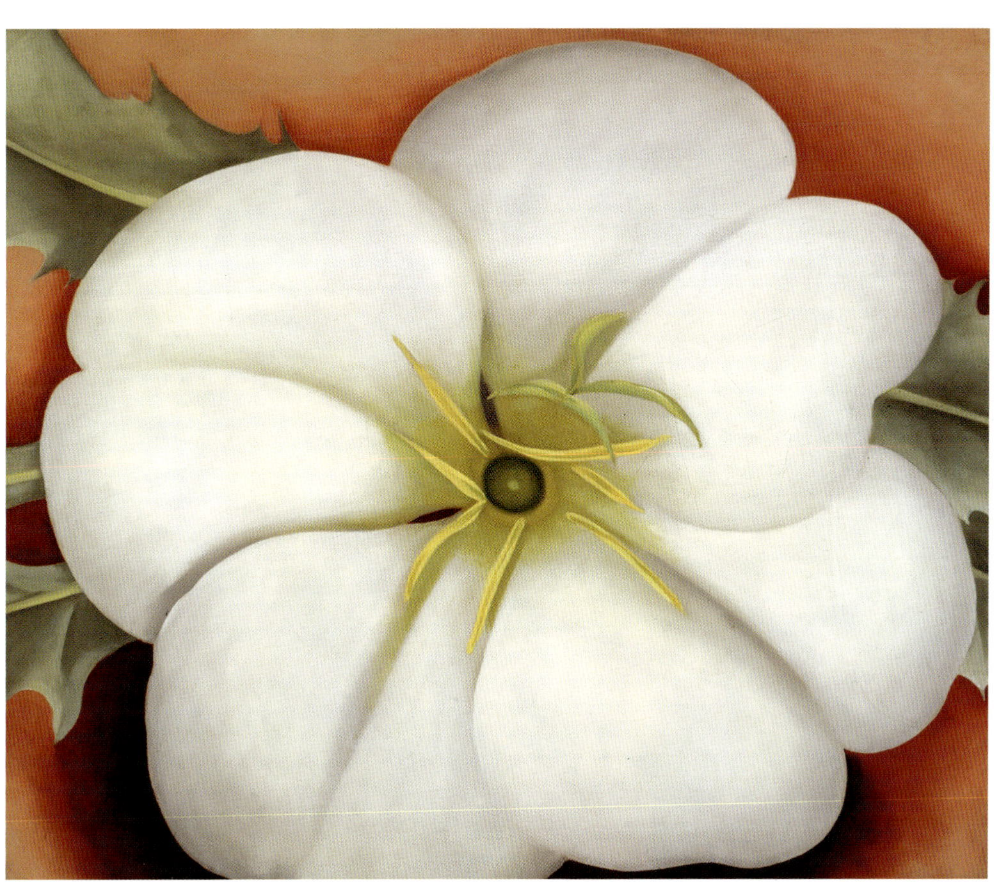

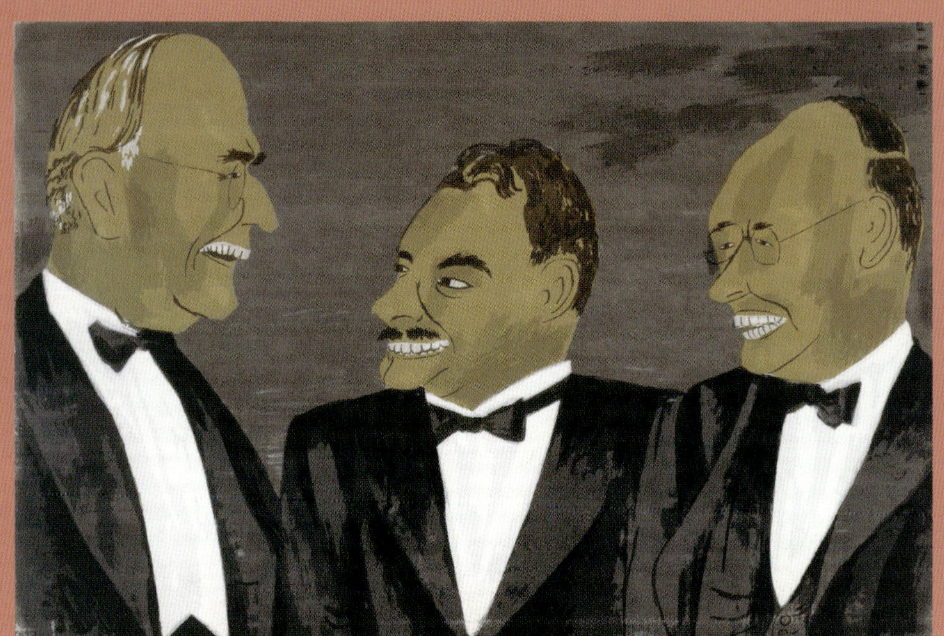

Ben Shahn
(Kovno 1898 - New York 1969)

Vanderbing, Dewey and Taft
Vanderbing, Dewey und Taft
Vanderbing, Dewey en Taft
Vanderbing, Dewey y Taft

●●

post 1945
Downtown Gallery, New York

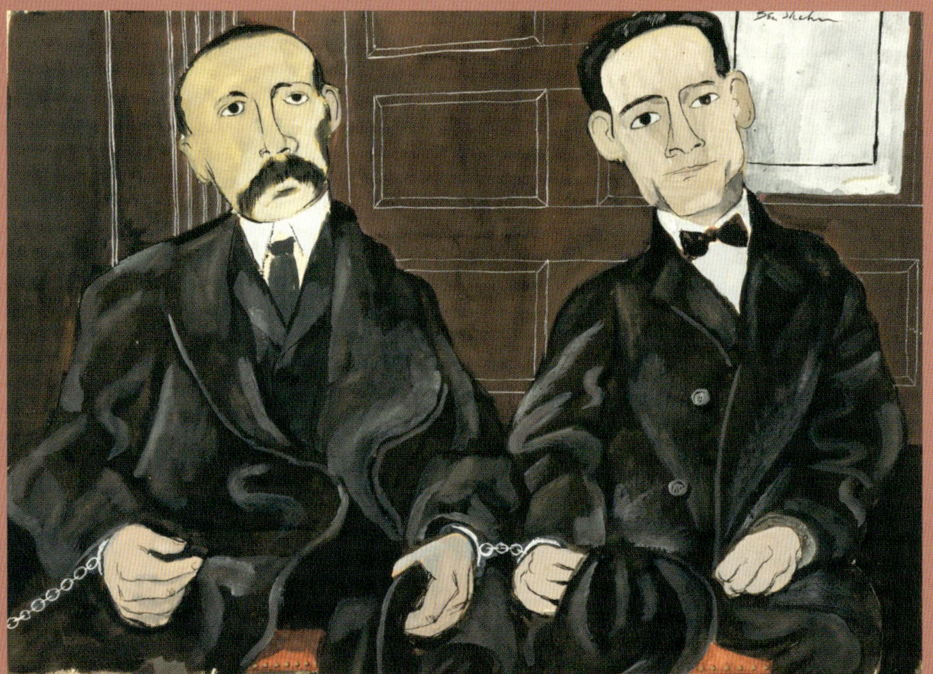

Ben Shahn
(Kovno 1898 - New York 1969)

**Bartolomeo Vanzetti
and Nicola Sacco
Bartolomeo Vanzetti
und Nicola Sacco
Bartolomeo Vanzetti
en Nicola Sacco
Bartolomeo Vanzetti
y Nicola Sacco**

●●●

1931-1932
26,7 x 36,8 cm / 10.5 x 14.5 in.
Museum of Modern Art (MoMA),
New York

tempera on paper over composition boa
Tempera auf Papier auf einer
Kompositionstafel
tempera op papier op een compositietaf
temple sobre papel sobre una tabla
de composición

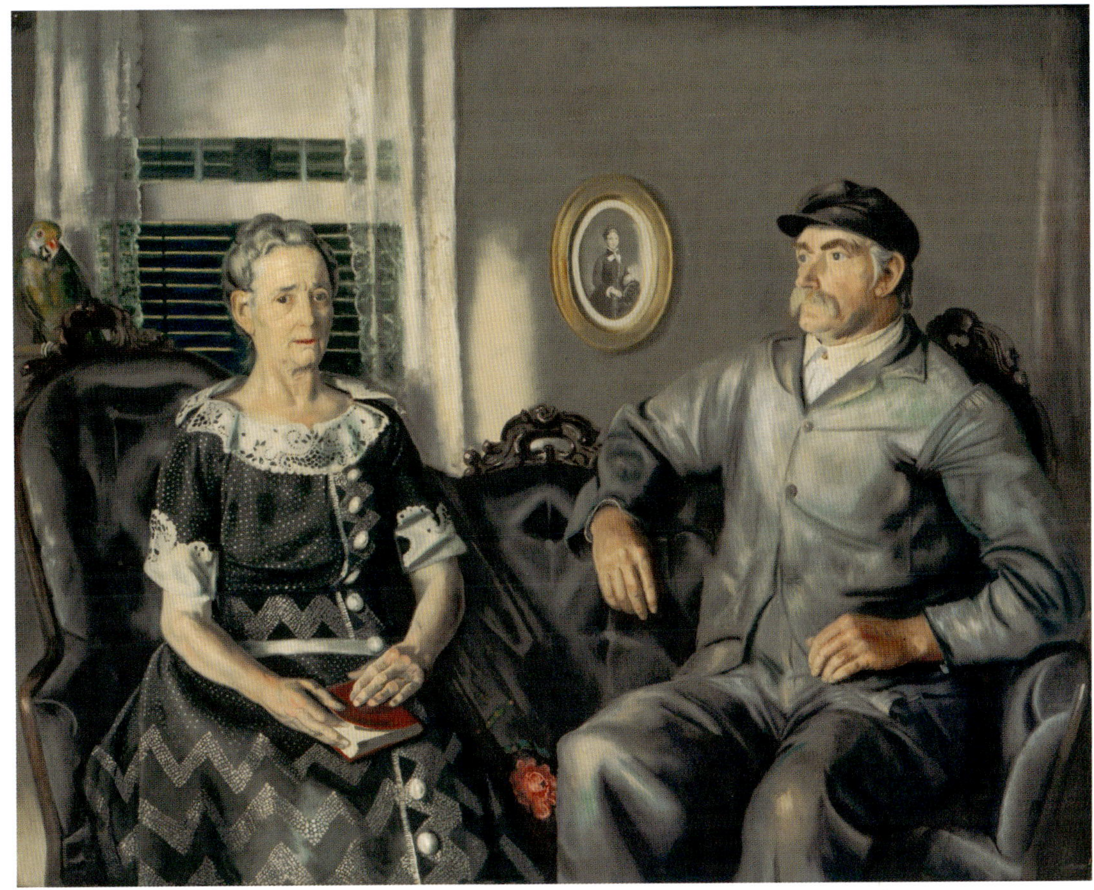

Ben Shahn created 30 works on paper inspired by the famous trial of the XX century: that of the anarchists, Sacco and Vanzetti.

Ben Shahn schuf 30 Werke auf Papier, die an dem bekanntesten Prozess des 20. Jahrhunderts inspiriert waren: dem der Anarchisten Sacco und Vanzetti.

Ben Shahn maakte 30 werken op papier die geïnspireerd zijn op het beroemdste proces van de twintigste eeuw: dat van de anarchisten Sacco en Vanzetti.

Ben Shahn realizó 30 obras sobre papel inspiradas en el proceso judicial más famoso del siglo XX: el de los anarquistas Sacco y Vanzetti.

George Bellows
(Columbus 1882 - New York 1925)

Mr. and Mrs. Phillip Wase
Mr. und Mrs. Phillip Wase
Dhr. en Mw. Phillip Wase
Mr. y Mrs. Phillip Wase

●

130,2 x 159,9 cm / 51.2 x 62.9 in.
Smithsonian American Art Museum,
Washington DC

oil on canvas / Öl auf Leinwand
olieverf op doek / óleo sobre lienzo

Ralston Crawford
(St. Catharines 1906 - Houston 1978)

Grain Silos in Buffalo
Getreidesilos in Buffalo
Graansilo's in Buffalo
Ascensores de grano de Buffalo

●●

1978
102,1 x 127,6 cm / 40.2 x 50.2 in.
Smithsonian American Art Museum,
Washington DC

oil on canvas
Öl auf Leinwand
olieverf op doek
óleo sobre lienzo

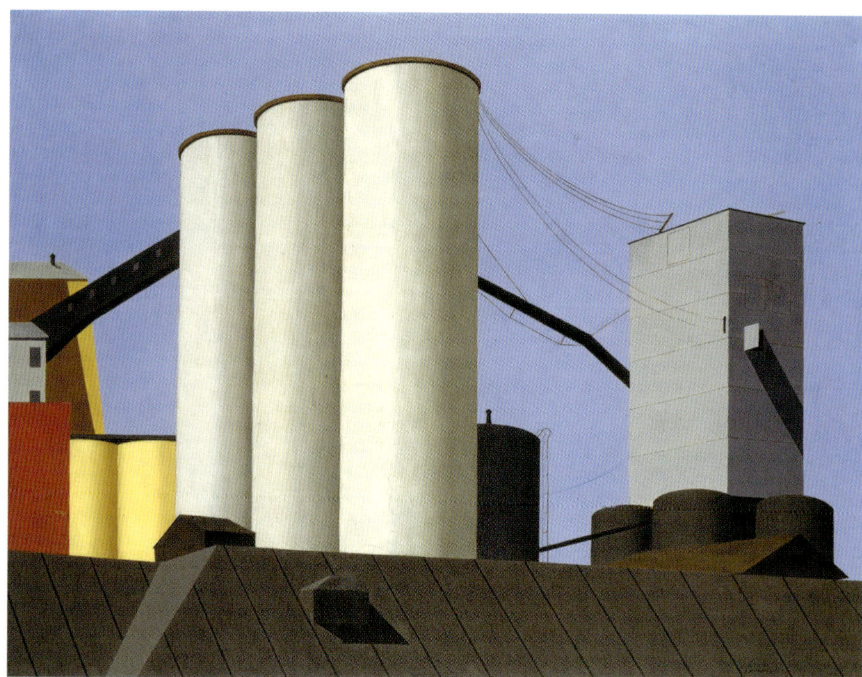

414

Reginald Marsh
(Paris 1898 - Dorset 1954)

Lower Manhattan

●

1930
60,9 x 121,9 cm / 23.9 x 48 in.
Munson-Williams-Proctor
Arts Institute, Utica (NY)

tempera on canvas mounted on
masonit / Tempera auf Leinwand,
auf Holzfaserplatte montiert
/ tempera op een op masoniet
gemonteerd doek / temple sobre
lienzo montado sobre masonita

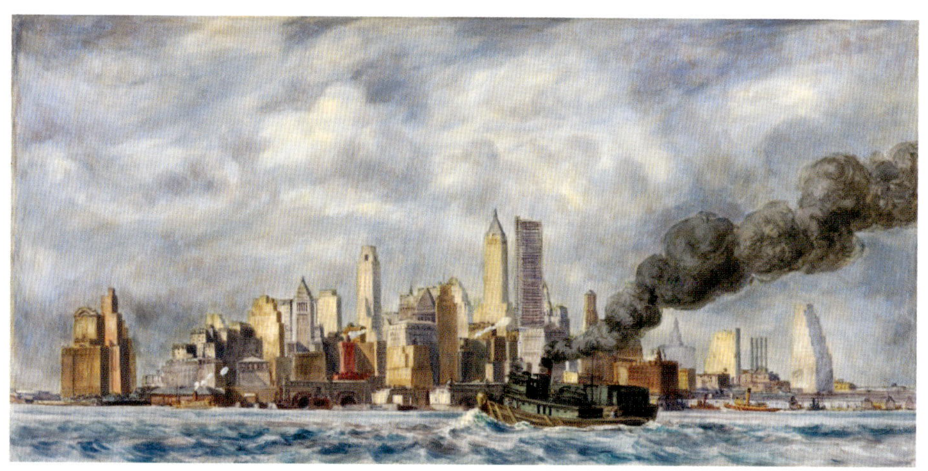

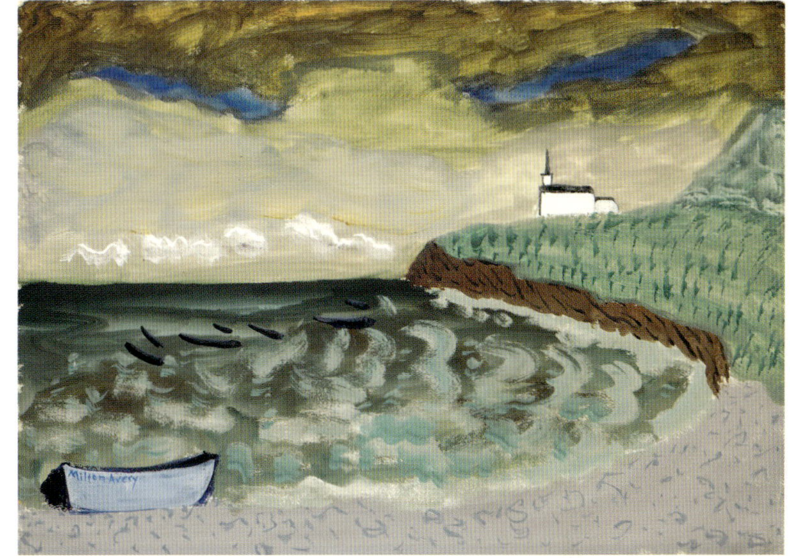

Milton Avery
(Altmar 1885 - New York 1965)

Church by the sea
Kirche am Meer
Kerk bij zee
Iglesia junto al mar

•

1939
54,7 x 75,7 cm / 21.5 x 29.8 in.
Wadsworth Atheneum Museum of Art,
Hartford (CT)

gouache on paper / Gouache auf Papier
gouache op papier / gouache sobre papel

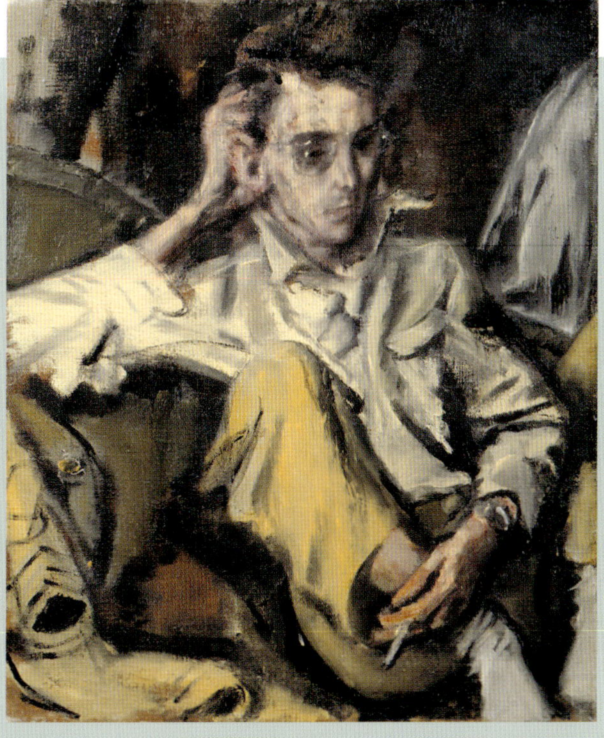

Jack Levine
(Boston 1915)

In the service
Beim Dienst
In dienst
En servicio

•

ca. 1940
50,8 x 40,6 cm / 20 x 16 in.
The Jewish Museum, New York

oil on canvas / Öl auf Leinwand
olieverf op doek / óleo sobre lienzo

Edward Steichen
(Bivange 1879 - West Redding 1973)

Willa Cather
●●
1926
42,5 x 34 cm / 16.7 x 13.4 in.
Museum of Modern Art (MoMA), New York

gelatin silver print / Gelatinedruck mit Silbersalzen
gelatine-zilverprint / impresión a la gelatina a las sales de plata

Edward Steichen
(Bivange 1879 - West Redding 1973)

Self-portrait with photographic equipment
Selbstporträt mit Fotoausrüstung
Zelfportret met fotoapparatuur
Autorretrato con equipo fotográfico
●●
1929
24,3 x 17,4 cm / 9.5 x 6.8 in.
Museum of Modern Art (MoMA), New York

gelatin silver print / Gelatinedruck mit Silbersalzen
gelatine-zilverprint / impresión a la gelatina a las sales de plata

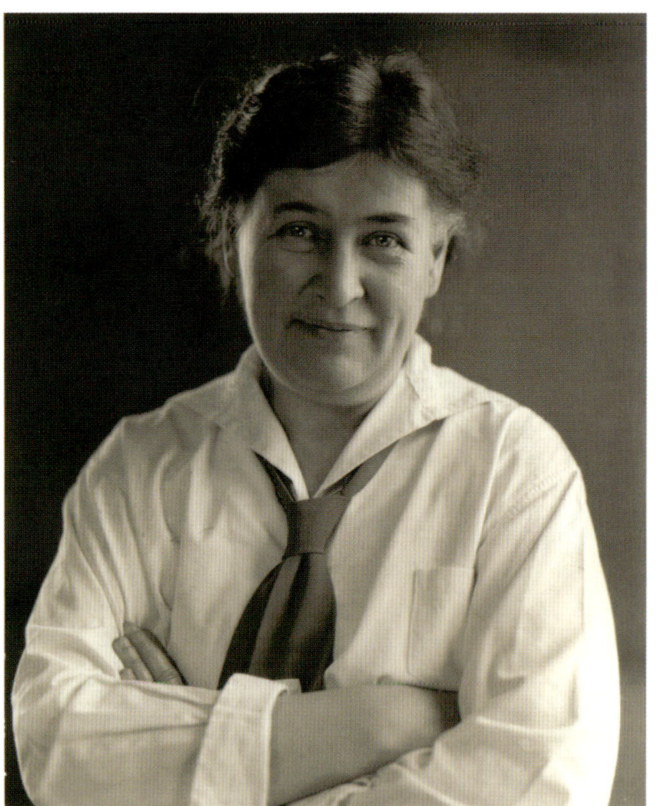

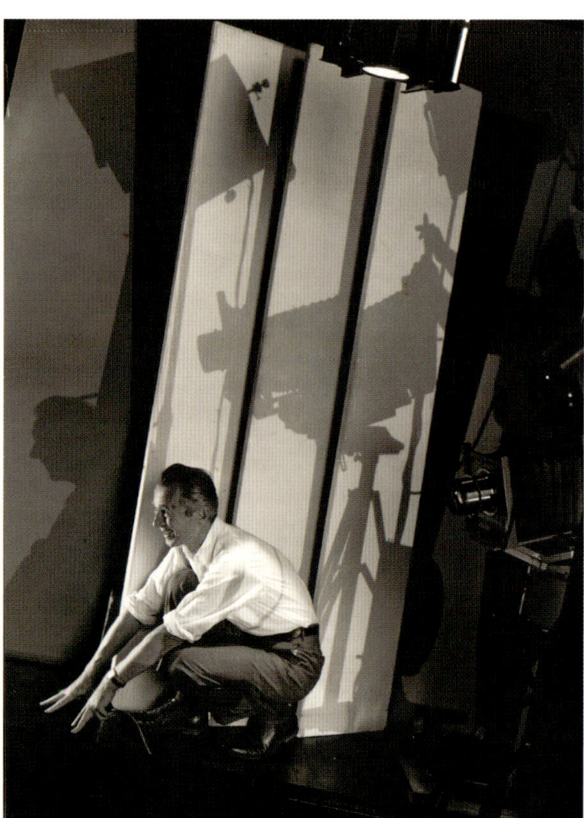

Dorothea Lange
(Hoboken 1895 - San Francisco 1965)

Emigrant mother, Nipomo, California
Emigrantenmutter, Nipomo, Kalifornien
Emigrerende moeder, Nipomo, California
Madre emigrante, Nipomo, California

●●●

1936
28,3 x 21,8 cm / 11.1 x 8.6 in.
Museum of Modern Art (MoMA),
New York

gelatin silver print
Gelatinedruck mit Silbersalzen
gelatine-zilverprint
impresión a la gelatina a las sales de plata

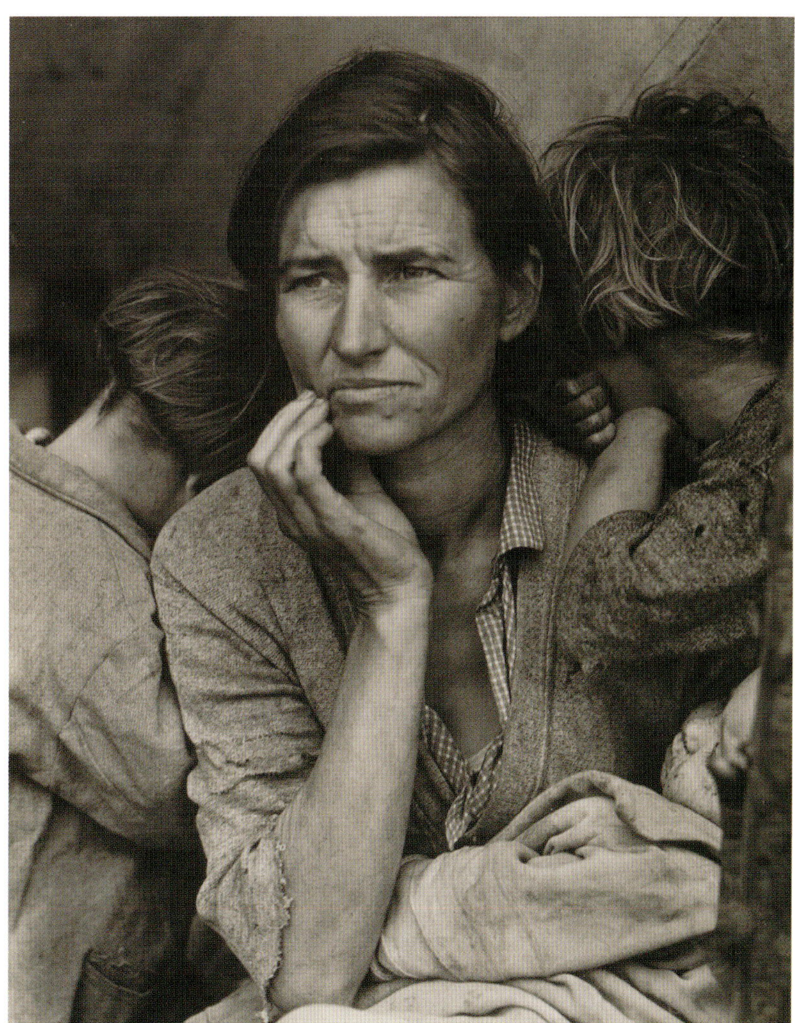

This photo of a worried woman, with her two
daughters hiding their faces and a sleeping
newborn, has become the symbol of the
American Great Depression.

Dieses Foto einer besorgten Mutter mit ihren
zwei Töchtern, die ihr Gesicht verbergen,
und dem schlafenden Neugeborenen ist zum
Symbol der großen amerikanischen Depression
geworden.

Deze foto van een bezorgde moeder met haar
twee dochters die hun gezicht verbergen en een
slapende baby, is het symbool geworden van de
Amerikaanse grote depressie.

Esta fotografía de una mujer preocupada, con
sus dos hijas ocultando el rostro y un bebé
dormido, se ha convertido en el símbolo de la
Gran Depresión estadounidense.

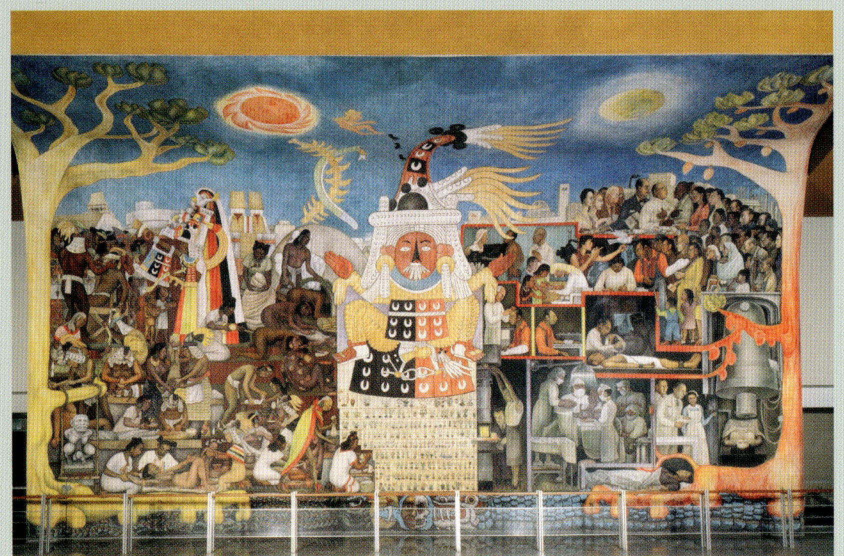

Diego Rivera
(Guanajuato 1886 - Ciudad de México 1957)

**The Story of Medicine in Mexico:
the people's request for better health
Geschichte der Medizin in Mexiko:
das Volk fordert eine bessere
Gesundheitsfürsorge
De geschiedenis van de geneeskunde
in Mexico: het verzoek van het volk
voor een betere gezondheid
Historia de la Medicina en México.
El pueblo en demanda de salud**

●●●

1935
740 x 1080 cm / 291.3 x 425.2 in.
Hospital de la Raza, Ciudad de México

mural painting / Wandgemälde
muurschildering / pintura mural

418

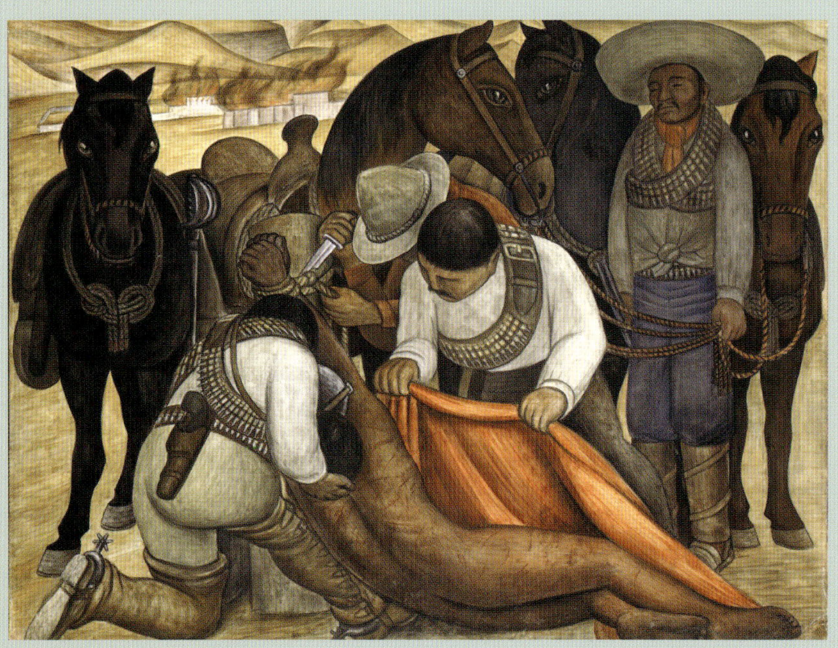

Diego Rivera
(Guanajuato 1886 - Ciudad de México 1957)

**Liberation of the peon
Die Befreiung des Peon
Bevrijding van de peon
La liberación del peón**

●●

1931
185,4 x 239,4 cm / 73 x 94.2 in.
Philadelphia Museum of Art, Philadelphia

fresco / Fresko / fresco / fresco

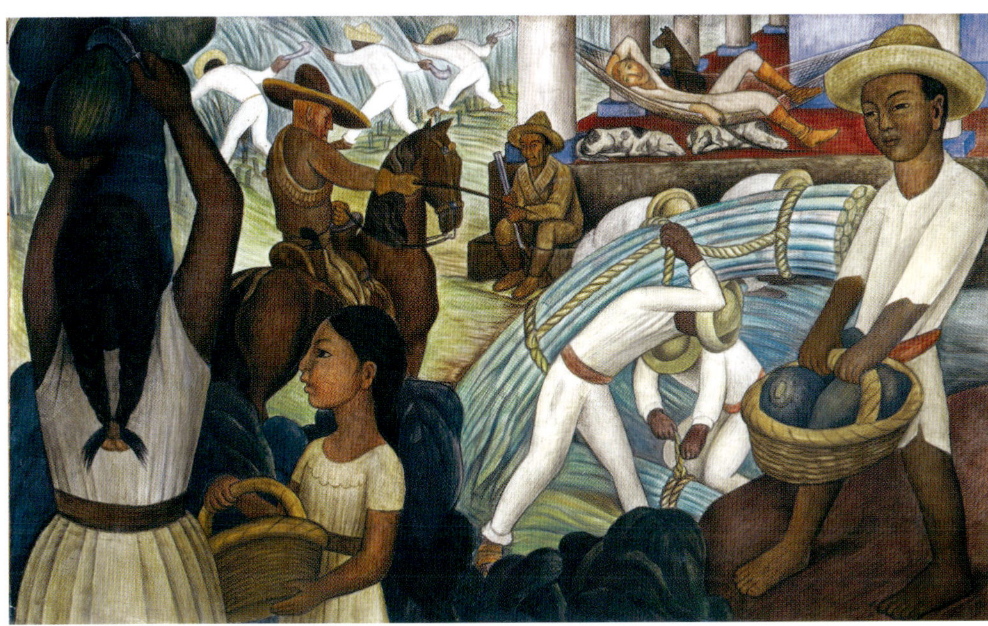

Diego Rivera
(Guanajuato 1886 -
Ciudad de México 1957)

Sugarcane
Zuckerrohr
Suikerriet
Caña de azúcar

●●●

1930
145,1 x 239,1 cm
57.1 x 94.1 in.
Philadelphia Museum of Art,
Philadelphia

mural painting
Wandbild
muurschildering
pintura mural

Diego Rivera
(Guanajuato 1886 -
Ciudad de México 1957)

The Miller's Wife
(La molendera)
Die Müllerin (La molendera)
De molenaarster
La molendera

●

1926
90 x 116,9 cm / 35.4 x 46 in.
Museo Nacional de Arte Moderno,
Ciudad de México

oil on canvas / Öl auf Leinwand
olieverf op doek / óleo sobre lienzo

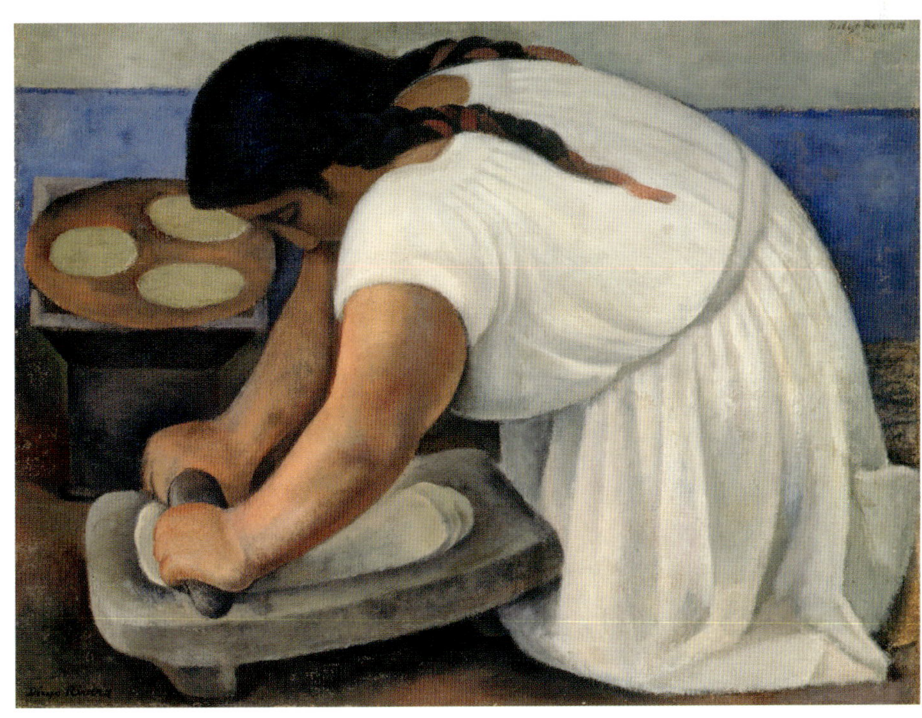
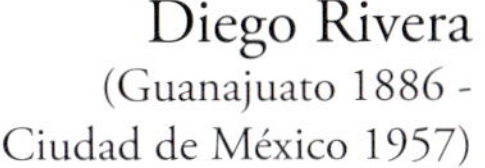

▼ José Clemente Orozco
(Ciudad Guzmàn 1883 - Ciudad de México 1949)

The Destruction of the Old Order
Die Zerstörung der alten Ordnung
De vernietiging van de oude orde
La destrucción del viejo orden

●●

Escuela Nacional Preparatoria San Ildefonso,
Ciudad de México

mural painting / Wandbild
muurschildering / pintura mural

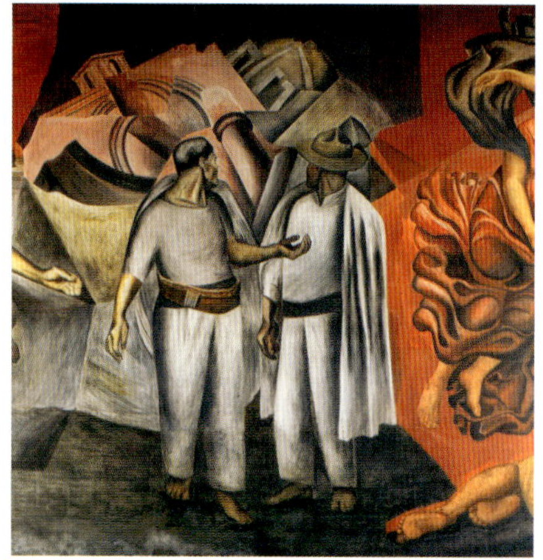

420

◄ José Clemente Orozco
(Ciudad Guzmàn 1883 -
Ciudad de México 1949)

Zapata

●●●

1930
198,8 x 122,6 cm / 78.2 x 48.2 in.
Art Institute of Chicago,
Chicago

oil on canvas
Öl auf Leinwand
olieverf op doek
óleo sobre lienzo

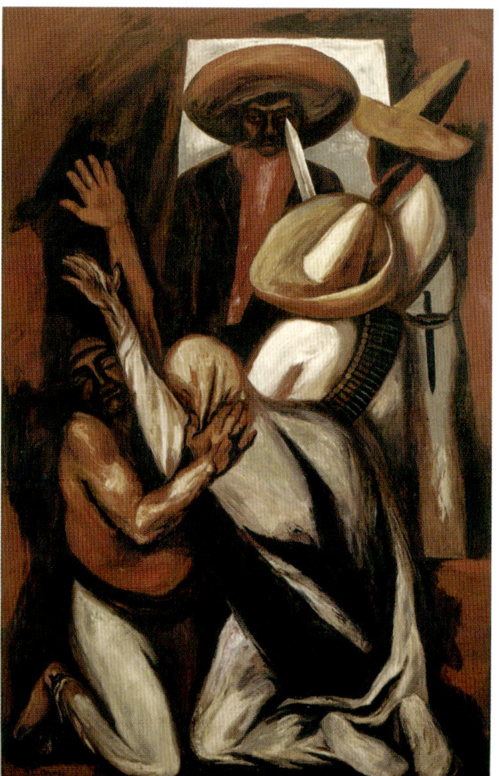

► José Clemente Orozco
(Ciudad Guzmàn 1883 - Ciudad de México 1949)

The Free Man
Der freie Mensch
De vrije mens
El hombre libre

●●

Hospicio Cabanas, Guadalajara

mural painting / Wandbild
muurschildering / pintura mural

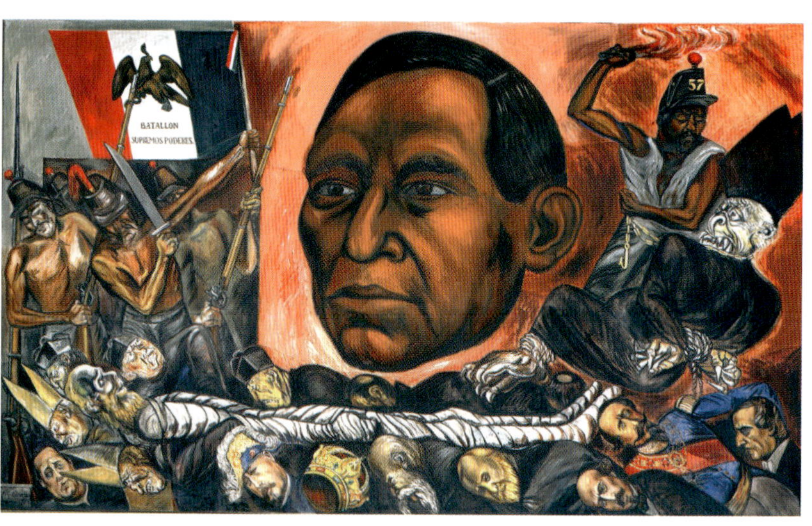

David Alfaro Siqueiros
(Camargo 1896 - Cuernavaca 1974)

Echo of a Shout
Echo eines Schreis
Echo van een gil
Eco de un grito

●●●

1937
121,9 x 91,4 cm / 48 x 36 in.
Museum of Modern Art (MoMA), New York

enamel on wood / Email auf Holz
glazuur op hout / esmalte sobre madera

David Alfaro Siqueiros
(Camargo 1896 - Cuernavaca 1974)

Victims of the War
Kriegsopfer
Oorlogsslachtoffers
Víctimas de la guerra

●●●

1945
368,5 x 246 cm / 145 x 96.8 in.
Palacio de Bellas Artes, Ciudad de México

mural painting / Wandbild
muurschildering / pintura mural

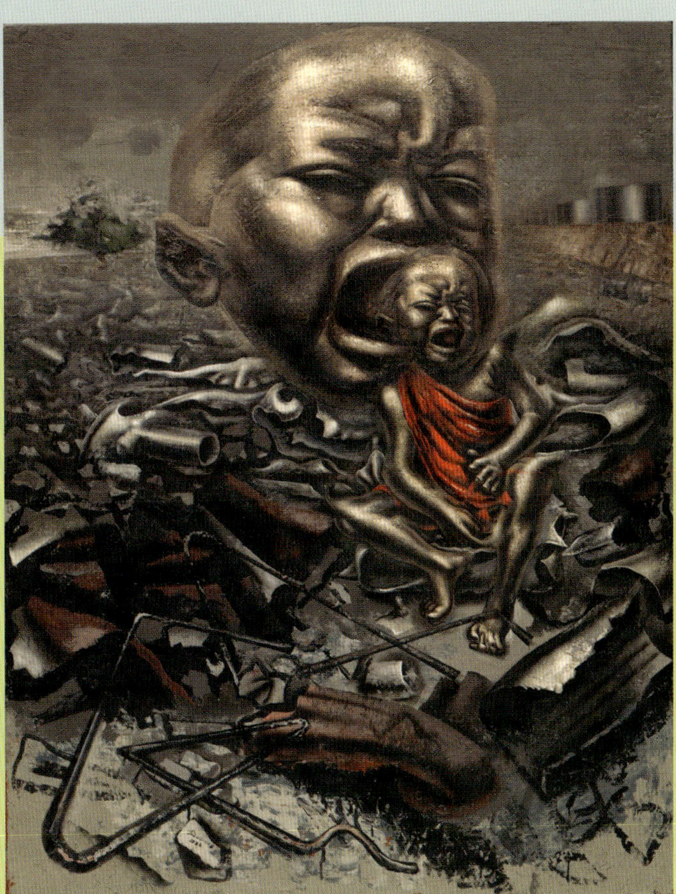

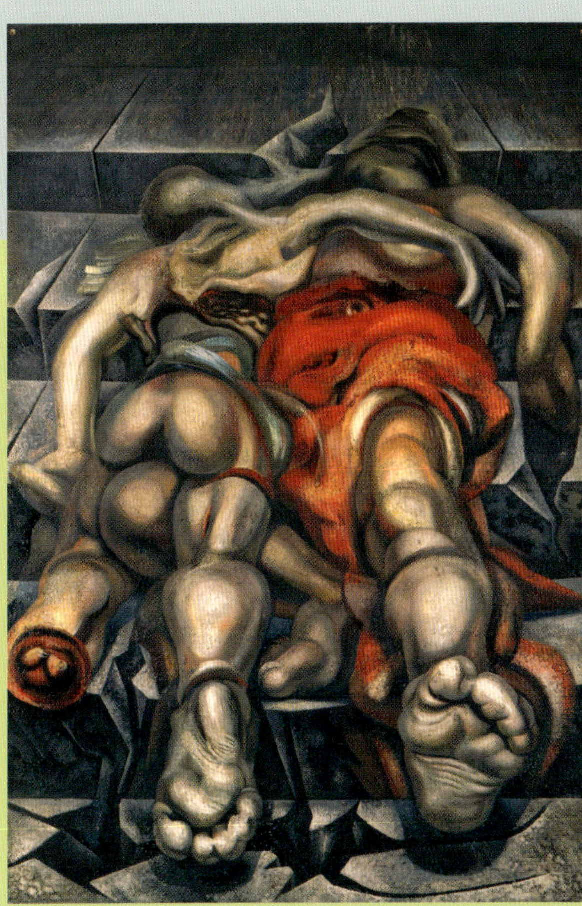

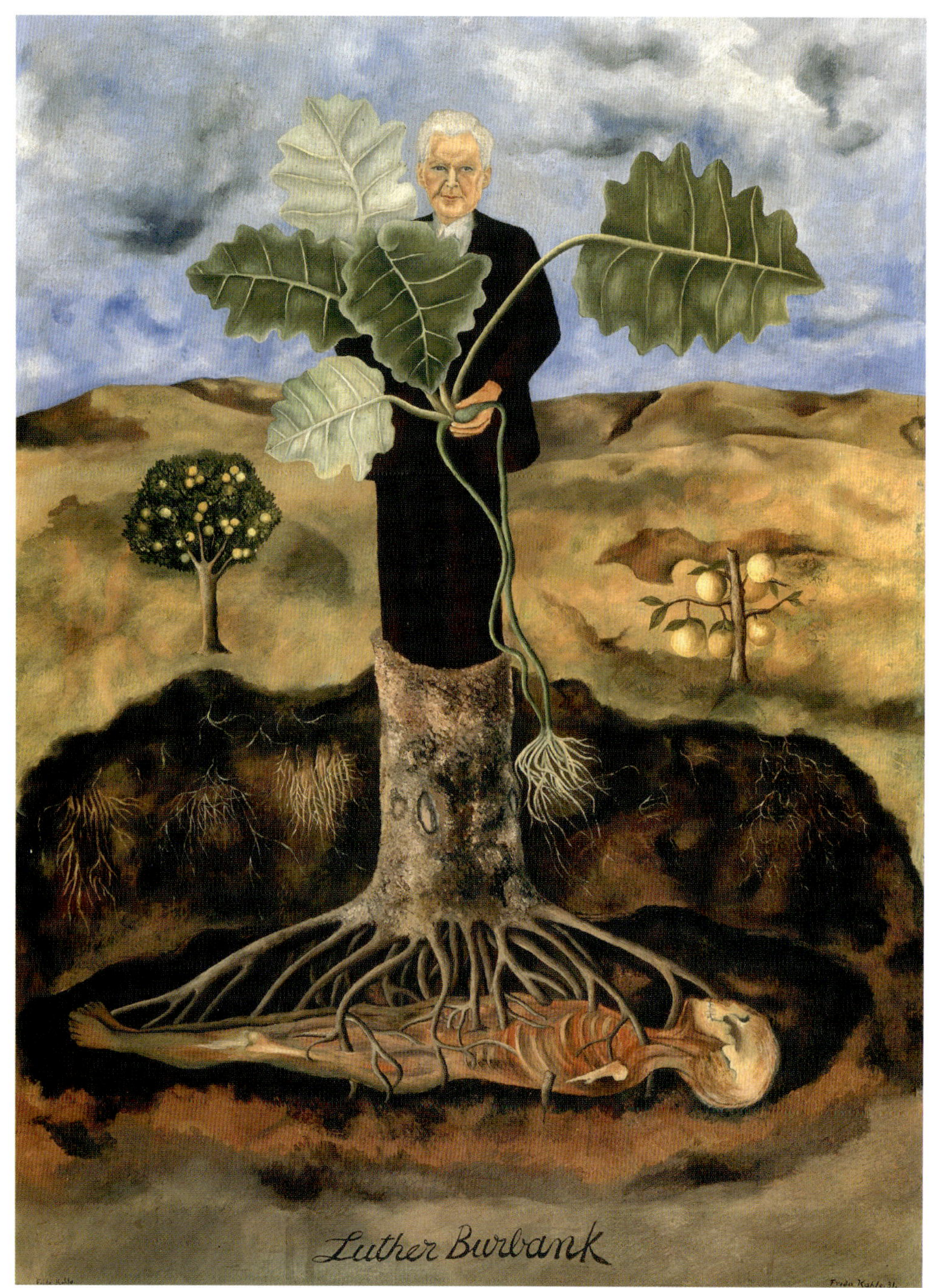

Frida Kahlo
(Coyoacán 1907 - 1954)

Portrait of Luther Burbank
Bildnis des Luther Burbank
Portret van Luther Burbank
Retrato de Luther Burbank

●

1931
88 x 62 cm / 34.6 x 24,4 in.
Museo Dolores Olmedo,
Ciudad de México

oil on masonite
Öl auf Holzfaserplatte
olieverf op masoniet
óleo sobre masonita

▶ **Frida Kahlo**
(Coyoacán 1907 - 1954)

The Two Fridas
Die zwei Fridas
De twee Frida's
Las dos Fridas

●●●

1939
172 x 172 cm / 68.1 x 68.1
Museo Nacional de Arte
Moderno, Ciudad de México

oil on canvas
Öl auf Leinwand
olieverf op doek
óleo sobre lienzo

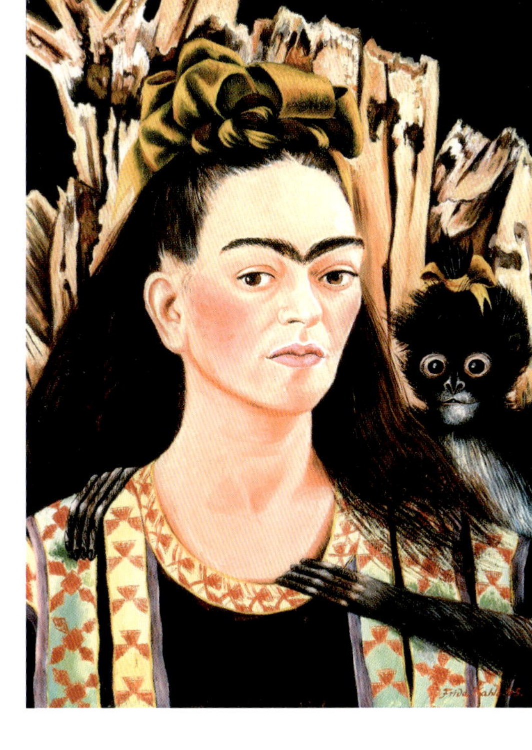

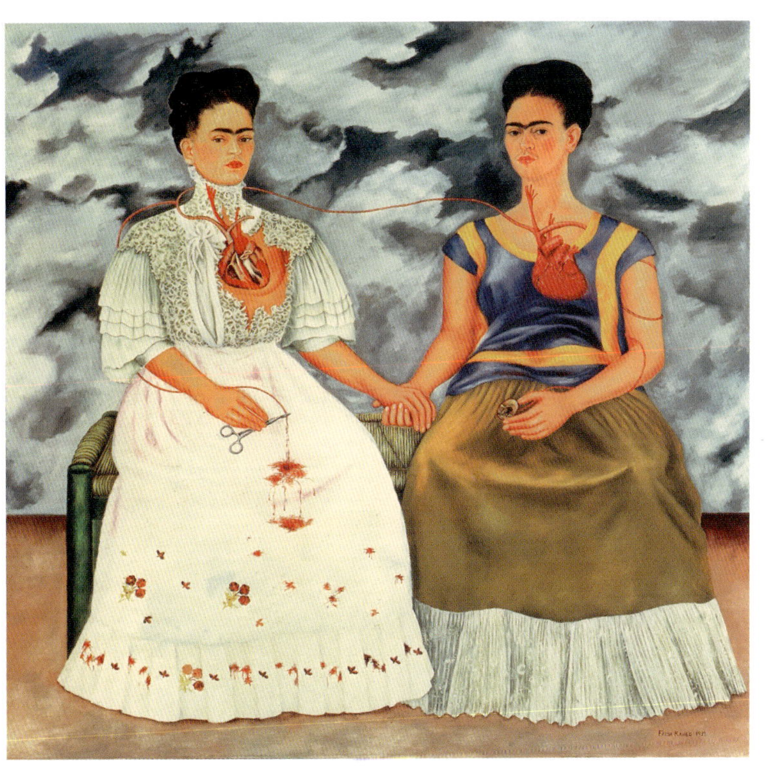

Frida Kahlo, in this painful, double self-portrait painted after her divorce from Rivera shows the two faces of her personality: the Mexican and the European.

Frida Kahlo zeigt in diesem schmerzhaften Doppelporträt, das sie nach der Scheidung von Rivera malte, die zwei Gesichter ihrer Persönlichkeit: das der Mexikanerin und der Europäerin.

Frida Kahlo toont in dit pijnlijke dubbele zelfportret vlak na haar scheiding met Rivera de twee gezichten van haar karakter: het Mexicaanse en het Europese.

Frida Kahlo, en este doloroso doble autorretrato pintado después de su divorcio con Rivera muestra las dos caras de su personalidad: la mejicana y la europea.

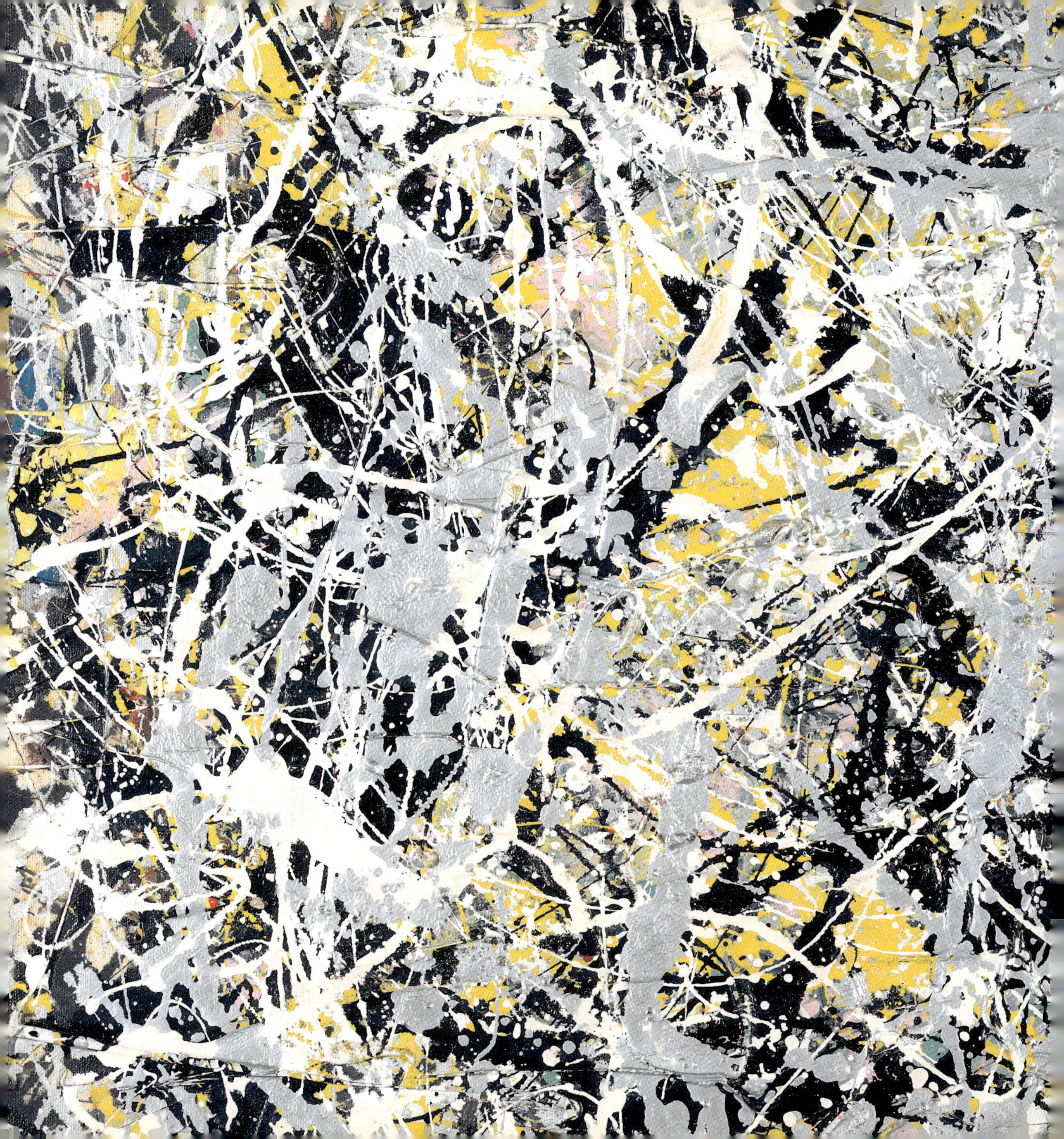

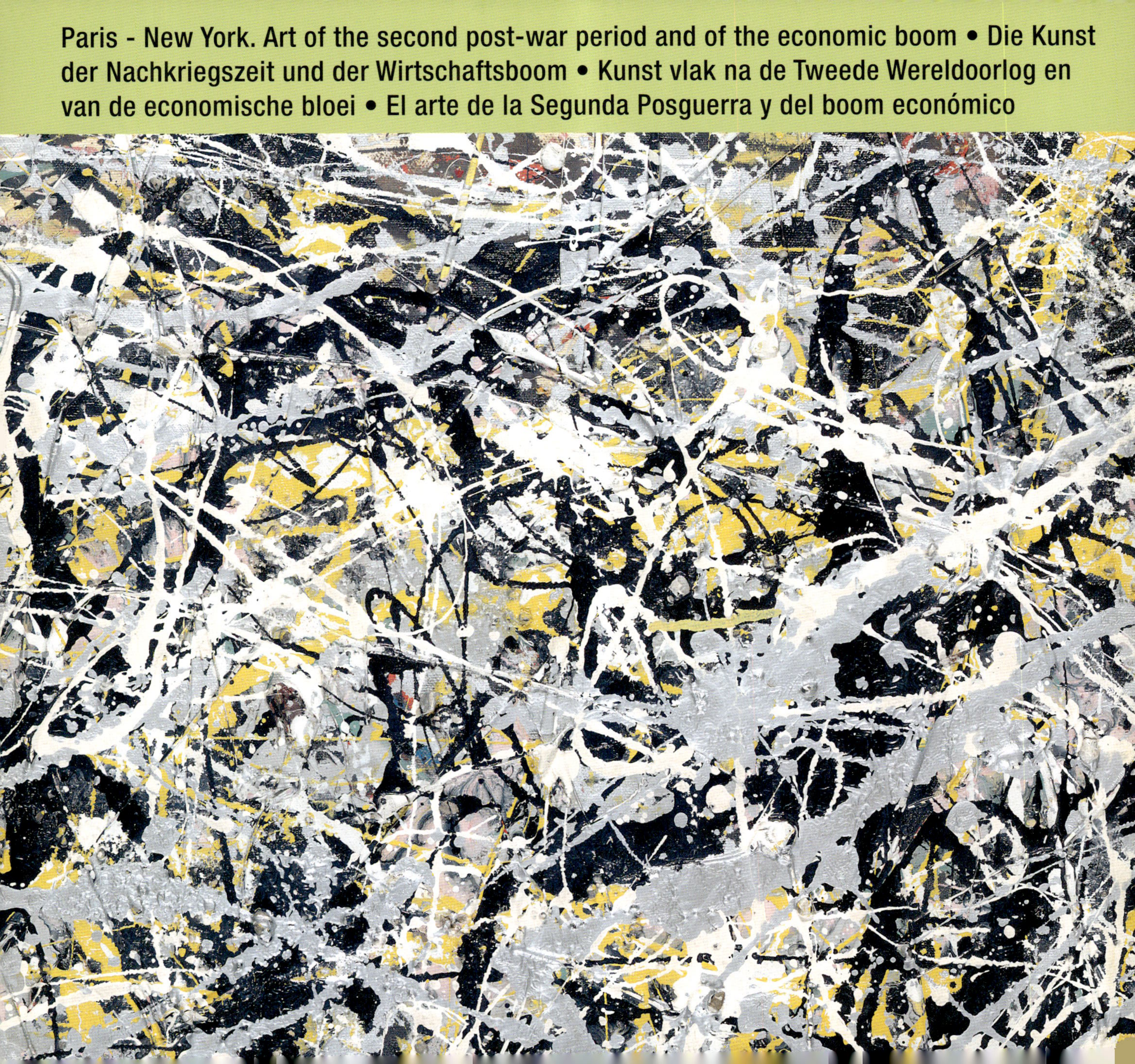

Paris - New York. Art of the second post-war period and of the economic boom ● Die Kunst der Nachkriegszeit und der Wirtschaftsboom ● Kunst vlak na de Tweede Wereldoorlog en van de economische bloei ● El arte de la Segunda Posguerra y del boom económico

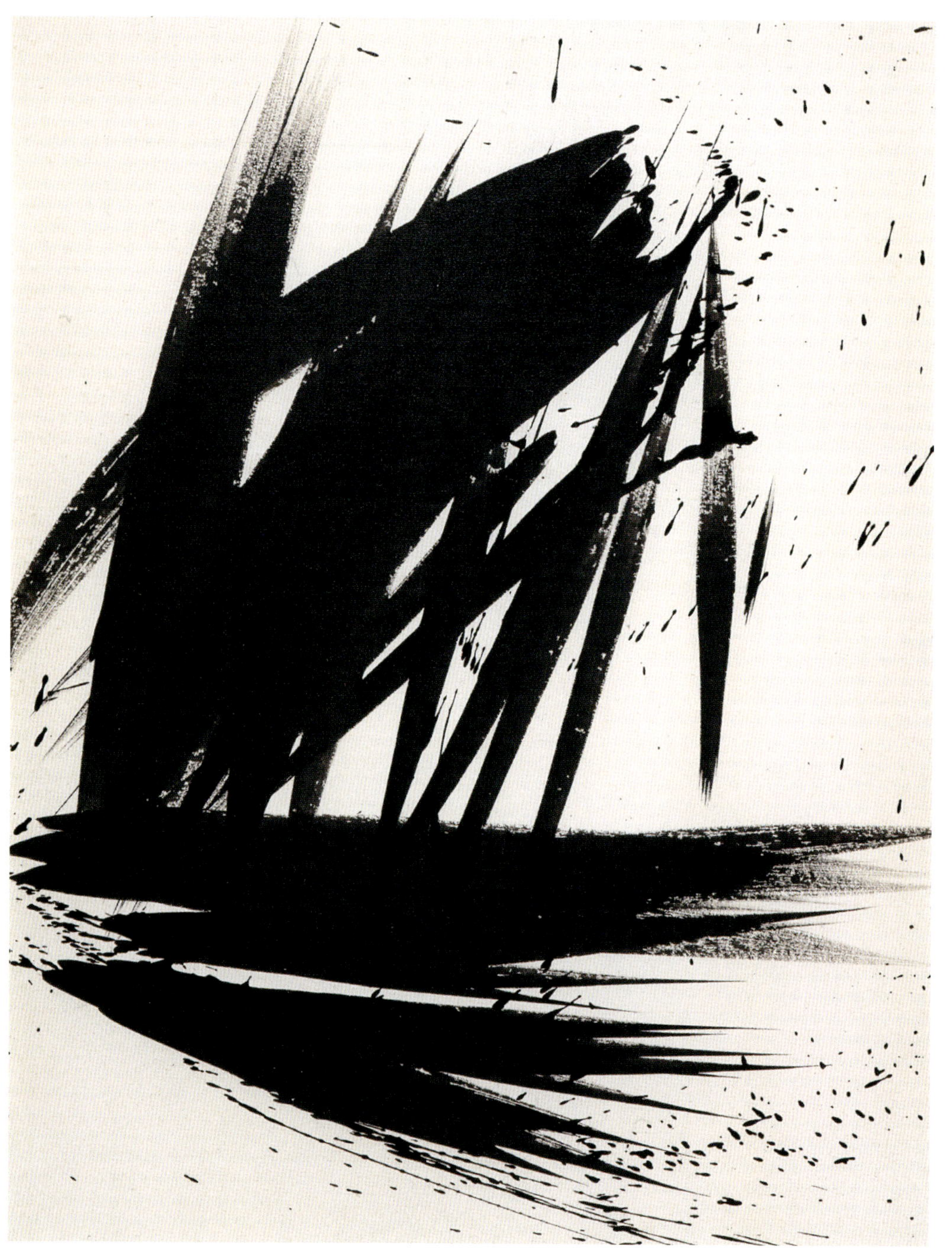

Hans Hartung
(Leipzig 1904 - Antibes 1989)

Untitled
Ohne Titel
Zonder titel
Sin título

●●●

1956
27,3 x 20,8 cm / 10.7 x 7.9 in
Private collection
Private Sammlung
Privécollectie
Colección privada

indian ink on paper
Tuschentinte auf Papier
encre de Chine sur papier oos
indische inkt op papier
tinta china sobre papel

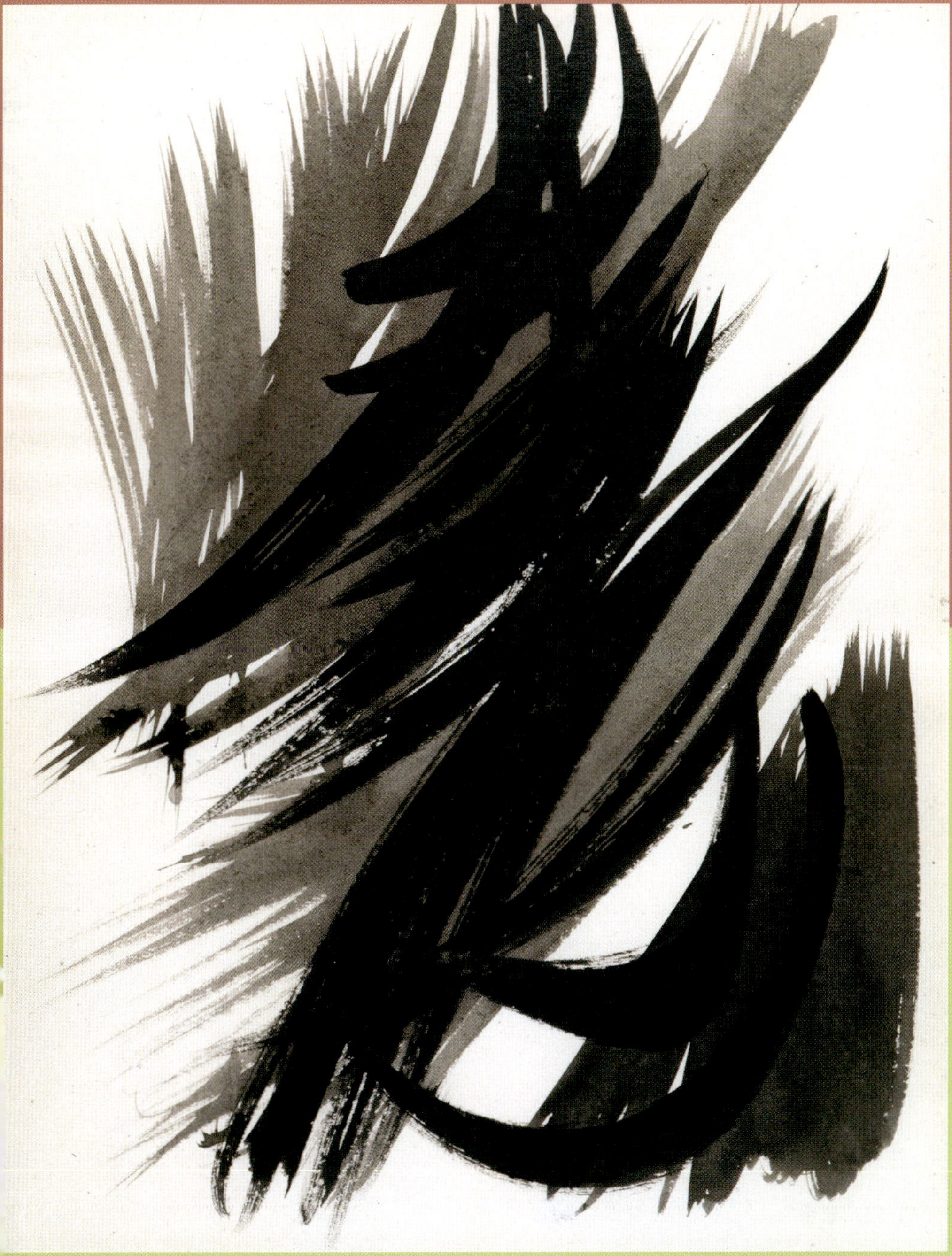

Hans Hartung
(Leipzig 1904 - Antibes 1989)

Untitled
Ohne Titel
Zonder titel
Sin título

●●●

1956
27,3 x 20,8 cm / 10.7 x 7.9 in.
Private collection
Private Sammlung
Privécollectie
Colección privada

ink on paper
Tinte auf Papier
inkt op papier
tinta sobre papel

An abstract, lyrical painting that also expresses the suffering of the experience of war.

Ein abstraktes, lyrisches Bild, das aber auch das Leiden der Kriegserfahrungen ausdrückt.

Een abstract en lyrisch schilderij, dat ook het leed van de oorlog uitdrukt.

Un cuadro abstracto, lírico, pero que expresa también el sufrimiento de la experiencia de la guerra.

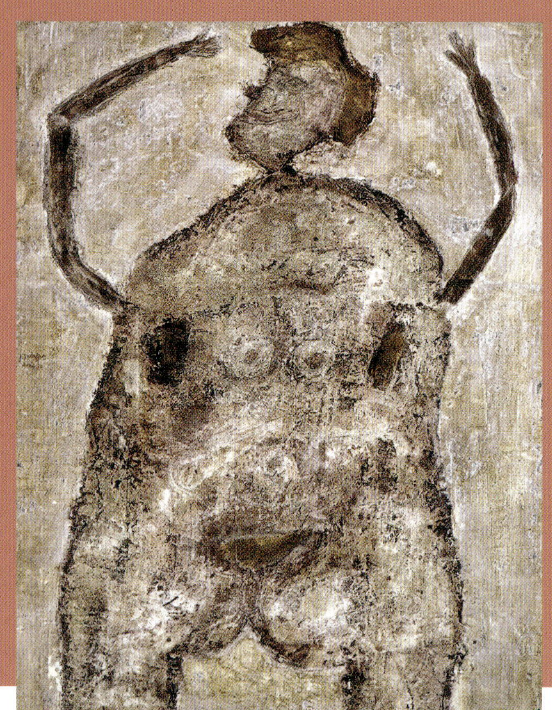

Jean Dubuffet
(Le Havre 1901 - Paris 1985)

The Bear
Die Bärin
Berin
La osa

● ● ●

1951
116 x 89 cm / 45.6 x 35 in.
Nationalgalerie, Staatliche Museen, Berlin

oil on canvas / Öl auf Leinwand
olieverf op doek / óleo sobre lienzo

Jean Dubuffet
(Le Havre 1901 - Paris 1985)

Olympia

● ●

1950
81 x 100 cm / 31.9 x 39.3 in.
Hamburger Kunsthalle, Hamburg

oil on canvas / Öl auf Leinwand
olieverf op doek / óleo sobre lienzo

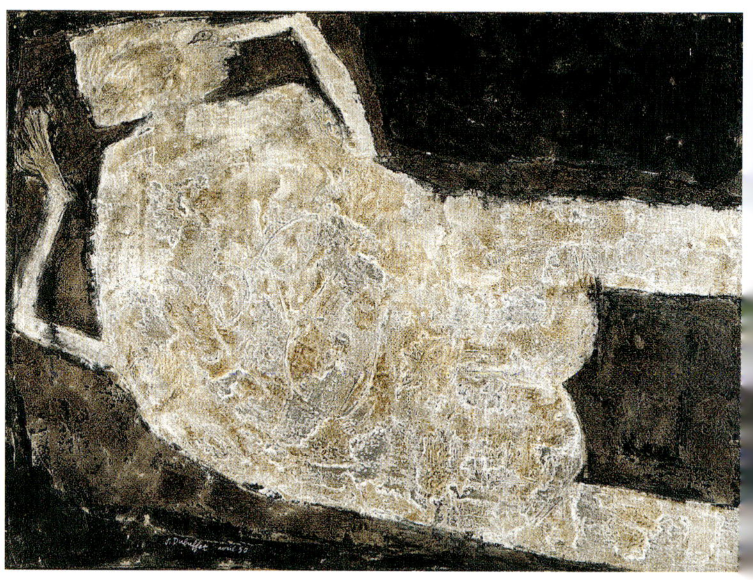

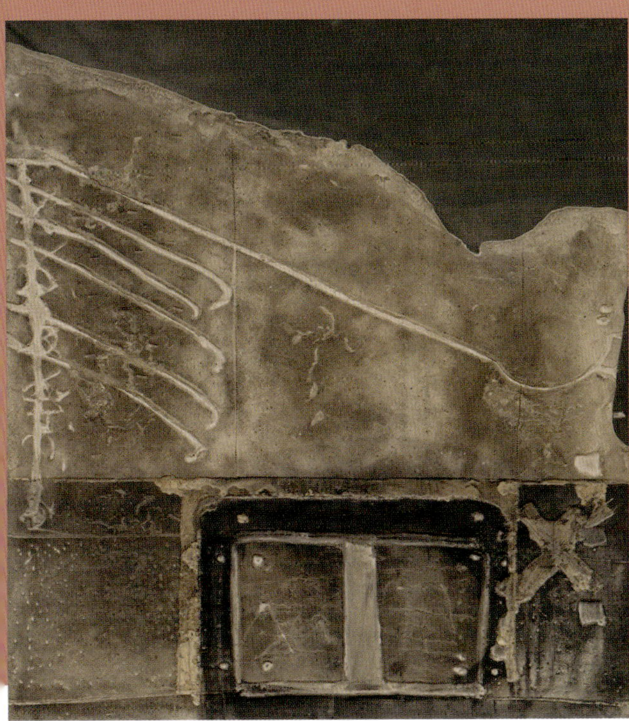

Antoni Tápies
(Barcelona 1923)

Grey relief on black
Graues Relief auf schwarz
Grijs op zwart reliëf
Relieve gris sobre negro

●

1959
194,6 x 170 cm / 76.6 x 66.9 in.
Hamburger Kunsthalle, Hamburg

latex and marble dust on canvas
Latex und Marmorpulver auf Leinwand
latex en marmerpoeder op doek
látex y polvo de mármol sobre lienzo

Jean Fautrier
(Paris 1898 - Chatenay-Malabry 1964)

Untitled
Ohne Titel
Zonder titel
Sin título

●

1954
17,5 x 25 cm / 6.8 x 8.8 in.
Private collection / Private Sammlung
Privécollectie / Colección privada

mixed media on paper mounted on canvas
Mischtechnik auf Papier, auf Leinwand montiert
gemengde techniek op papier op doek
técnica mixta sobre papel montado sobre lienzo

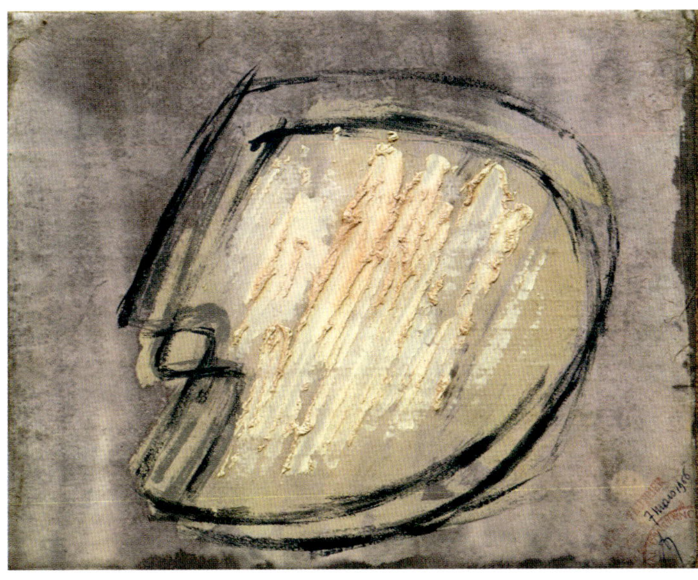

Pierre Soulages
(Rodez 1919)

Painting 26
Gemälde 26
Schilderij 26
Pintura 26

● ●

1955
161,5 x 113,5 cm / 63.6 x 44.7 in.
Hamburger Kunsthalle, Hamburg

oil on canvas / Öl auf Leinwand
olieverf op doek / óleo sobre lienzo

Pierre Soulages
(Rodez 1919)

Untitled
Ohne Titel
Zonder titel
Sin título

●

1973
153 x 108 cm / 60.3 x 42.5 in.
Musée Cantini, Marseille

vinyl / Vinyl
vinilo

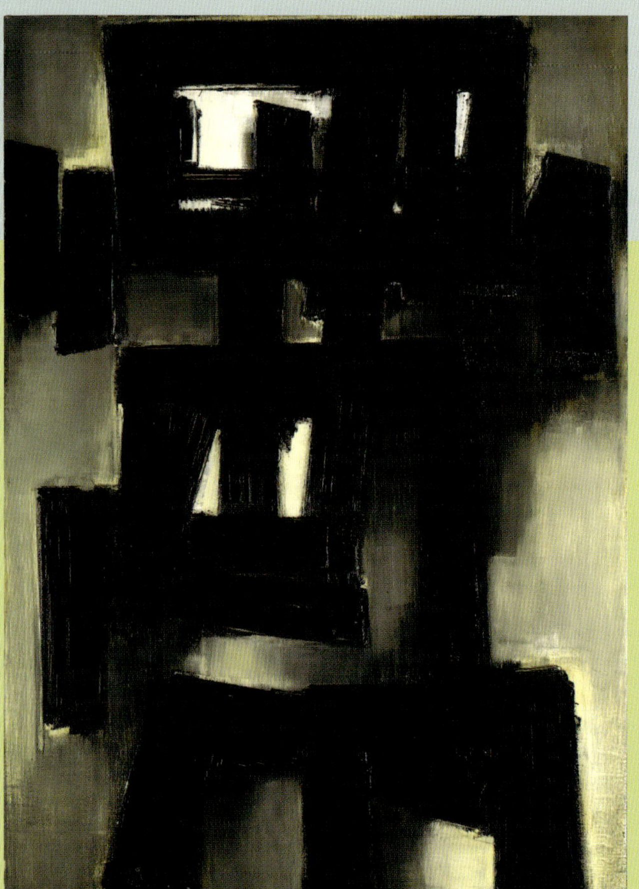

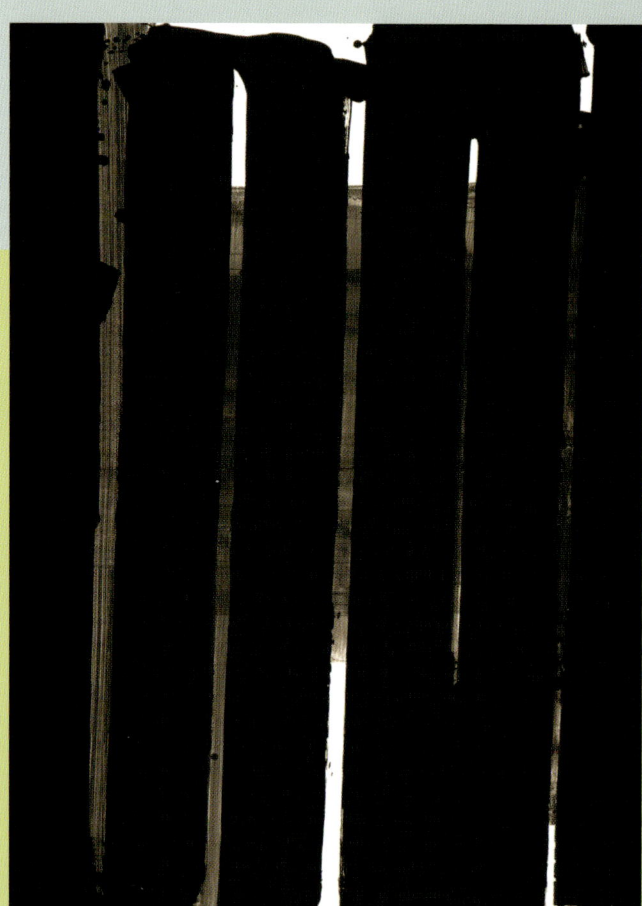

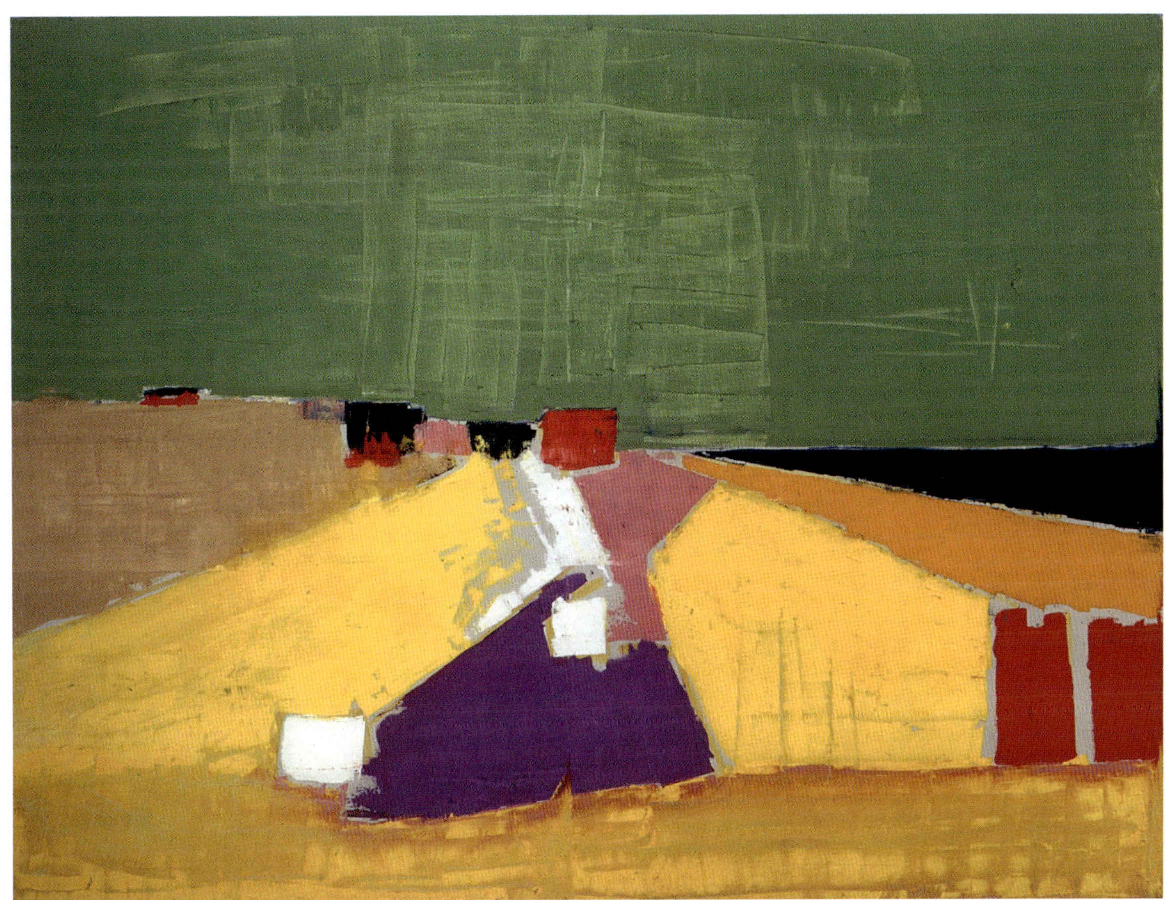

Nicolas de Staël
(St. Petersburg 1914 - Antibes 1955)

Sicily
Sizilien
Sicilië
Sicilia

●

1954
114 x 146 cm / 44.8 x 57.4 in.
Musée de Grenoble, Grenoble
oil on canvas / Öl auf Leinwand
olieverf op doek / óleo sobre lienzo

Nicolas de Staël, who was also an architect, never wanted to choose between abstraction and depiction.

Nicolas de Staël, der auch Architekt war, wollte sich nie zwischen Abstraktion und Darstellung entscheiden.

Nicolas de Staël die ook architect was, heeft nooit willen kiezen tussen abstractie of symbolische voorstellingen.

Nicolas de Staël, que era también arquitecto, no ha querido nunca elegir entre abstracción o figuración.

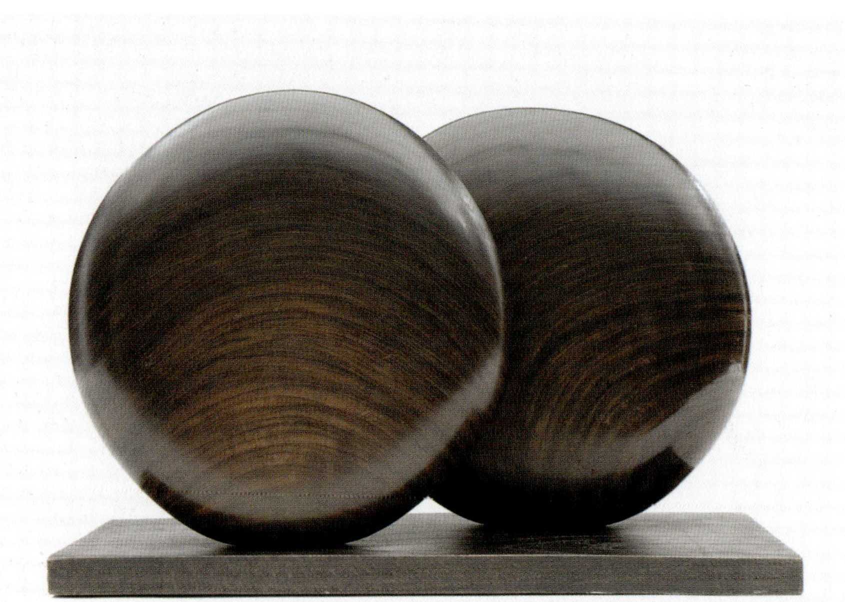

Barbara Hepworth
(Wakefield 1903 - St. Ives 1975)

Staggered Disks
Scheiben in Echelon
Schuin opgestelde schijven
Discos escalonados

●●

1935
31,1 x 49,1 x 22,5 cm / 12.2 x 19.3 x 8.8 in.
Museum of Modern Art (MoMA),
New York

Padauk wood / Padouk-Holz
Padouk-hout / madera Padouk

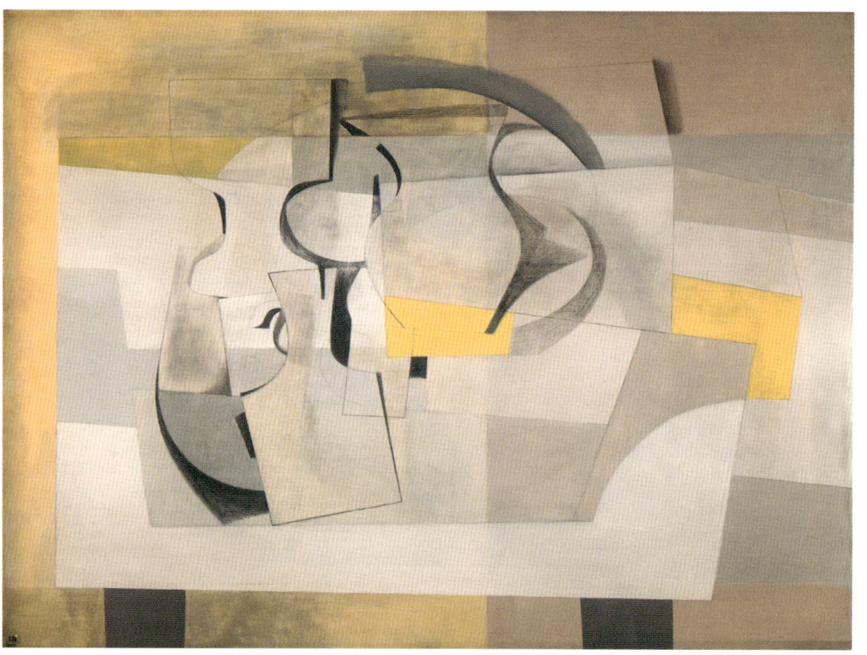

Ben Nicholson
(Denham 1894 - London 1976)

Poisonous Yellow
Giftgelb
Gifgeel
Amarillo venenoso

●●

1949
124 x 163 cm / 48.8 x 64.2 in.
Ca' Pesaro Galleria d'Arte Moderna, Venezia

oil on canvas / Öl auf Leinwand
olieverf op doek / óleo sobre lienzo

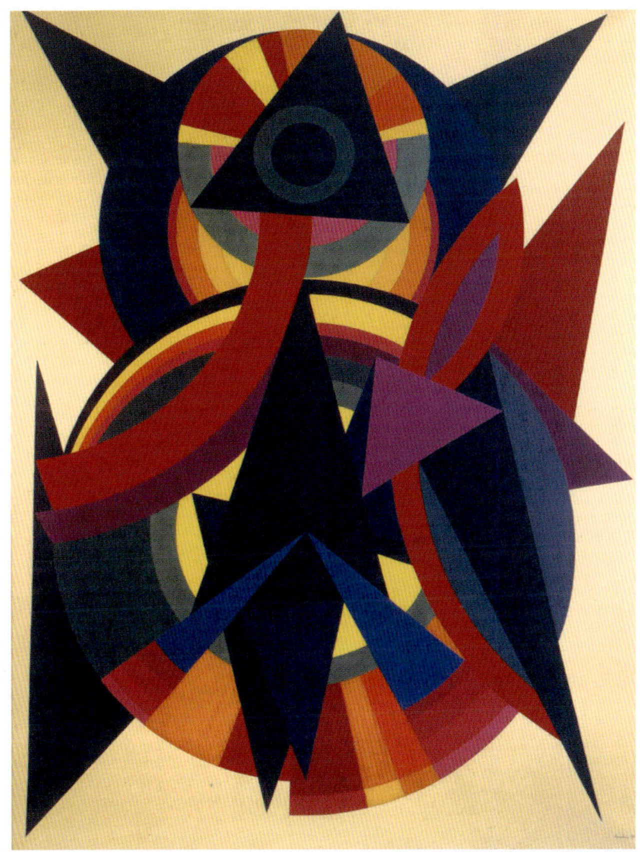

Auguste Herbin
(Quiévy 1882 - Paris 1960)

Composition on yellow background
Komposition auf gelbem Grund
Compositie op een gele achtergrond
Composición sobre fondo amarillo

●

1940
Private collection / Private Sammlung
Privécollectie / Colección privada

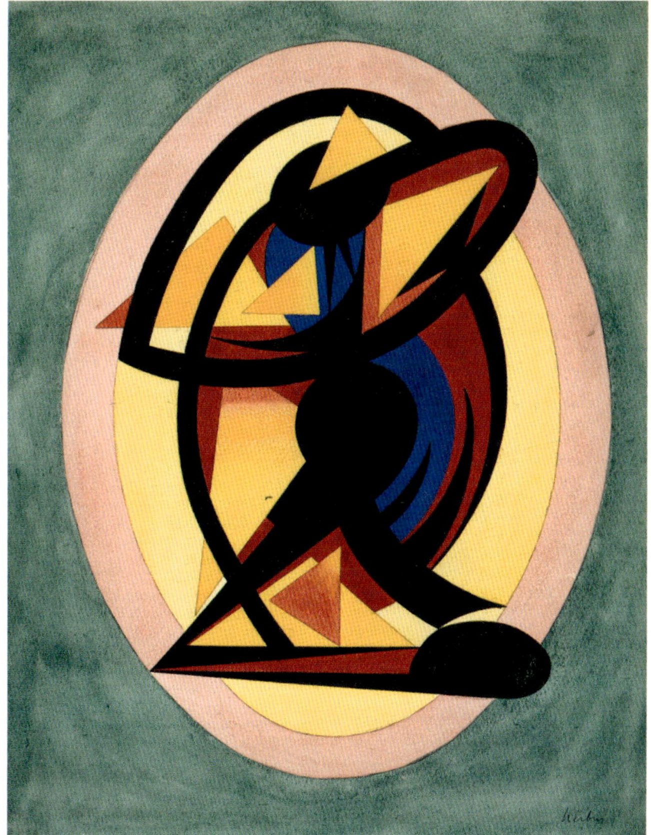

Auguste Herbin
(Quiévy 1882 - Paris 1960)

Composition
Komposition
Compositie
Composición

●

1932
32 x 24,5 cm / 12.6 x 9.6 in.
Musée Cantini, Marseille

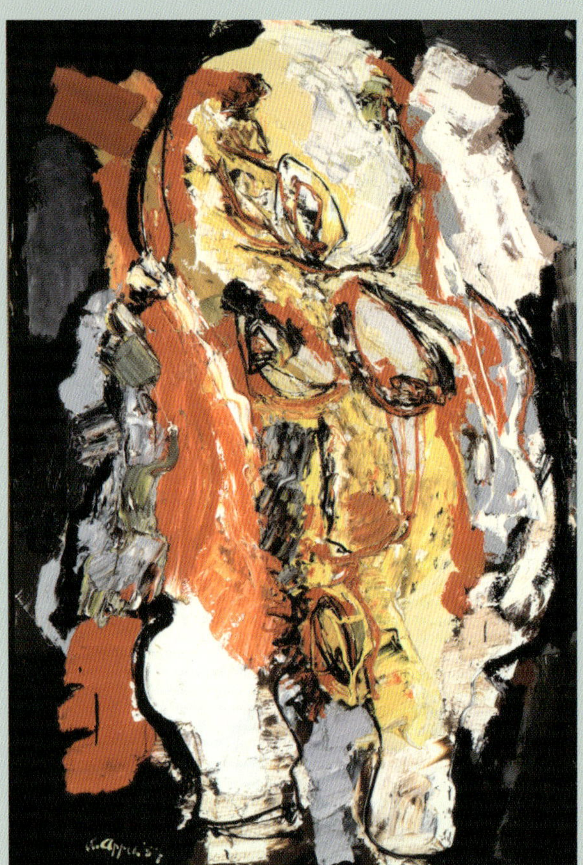

Karel Appel
(Amsterdam 1921- Zurich 2006)

Red Nude
Roter Akt (Roode naakt)
Barbaars naakt
Desnudo rojo
●●

Museum voor Schone Kunsten, Gent

434

Karel Appel
(Amsterdam 1921 - Zurich 2006)

Woman and dog on the road
Frau und Hund auf der Straße
Vrouw en hond op straat
Mujer y perro por la calle
●●●

1953
143,5 x 110,2 cm / 56.5 x 43.4 in.
Nationalgalerie, Staatliche Museen, Berlin

oil on jute / Öl auf Jute
olieverf op jute / óleo sobre yute

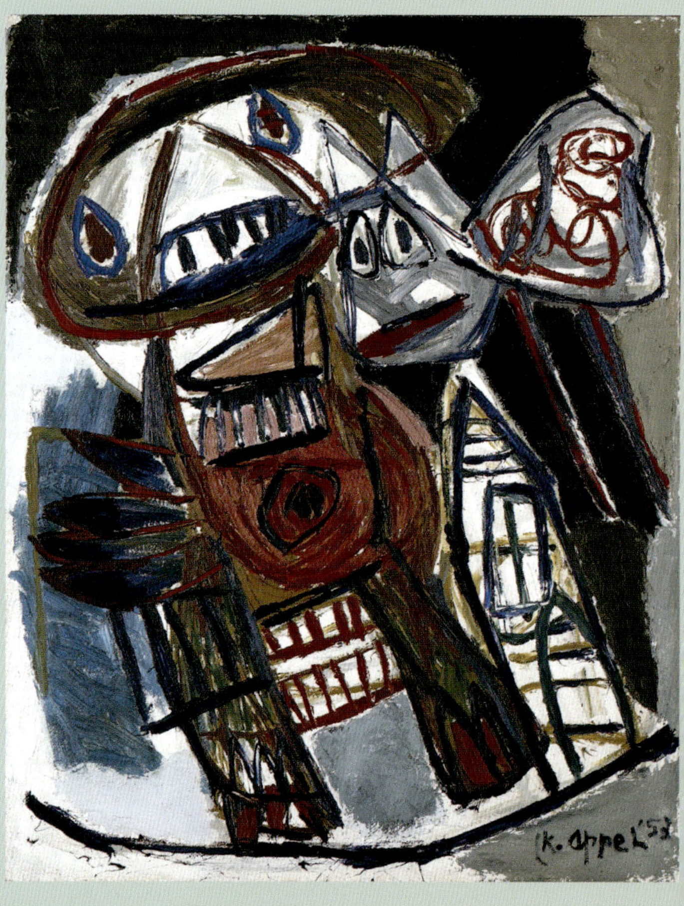

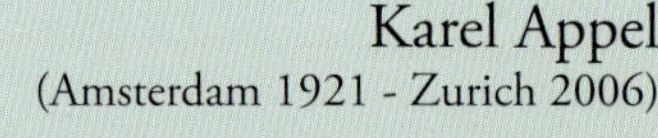

Serge Poliakoff
(Moscow 1900 - Paris 1969)

Composition in grey and red
Komposition in Grau und Rot
Grijs met rode compositie
Composición en gris y rojo

●

1964
160 x 130 cm / 63 x 51.2 in.
Musée Fabre, Montpellier

acrylic on canvas
Akryl auf Tafel
acrylverf op paneel
acrílico sobre tabla

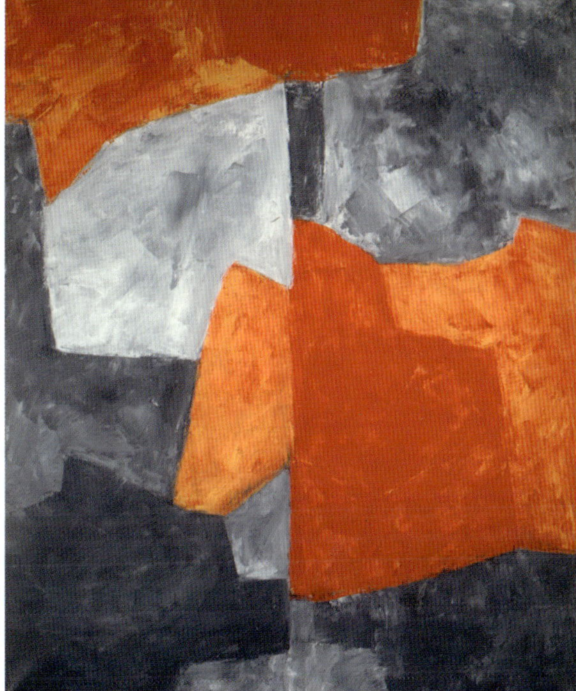

Jean-Paul Riopelle
(Montreal 1923 - Île-aux-Grues 2002)

A la plante des pieds

●

1958
88 x 115 cm / 34.6 x 45.3 in.
Galerie Gianna Sistu, Paris

oil on canvas / Öl auf Leinwand olieverf
op doek / óleo sobre lienzo

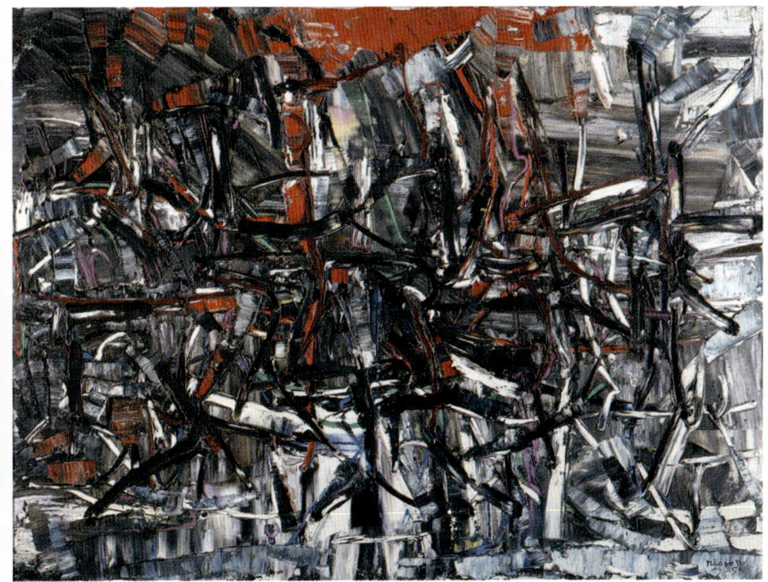

An abstract painting made of embedded surfaces, neither geometric nor lyrical, rendered through rich pictorial brushstrokes.

Eine abstrakte Malerei aus ineinander gesteckten Oberflächen, die weder geometrisch noch lyrisch sind und durch einen reichhaltigen Farbauftrag zum Vorschein kommen.

Een abstract schilderij met verstrikte oppervlakken die noch geometrisch noch lyrisch zijn en rijkelijk met verf uitgestreken zijn.

Una pintura abstracta construida a partir de superficies encastradas, ni geométricas ni líricas, expresadas a través de ricas pinceladas.

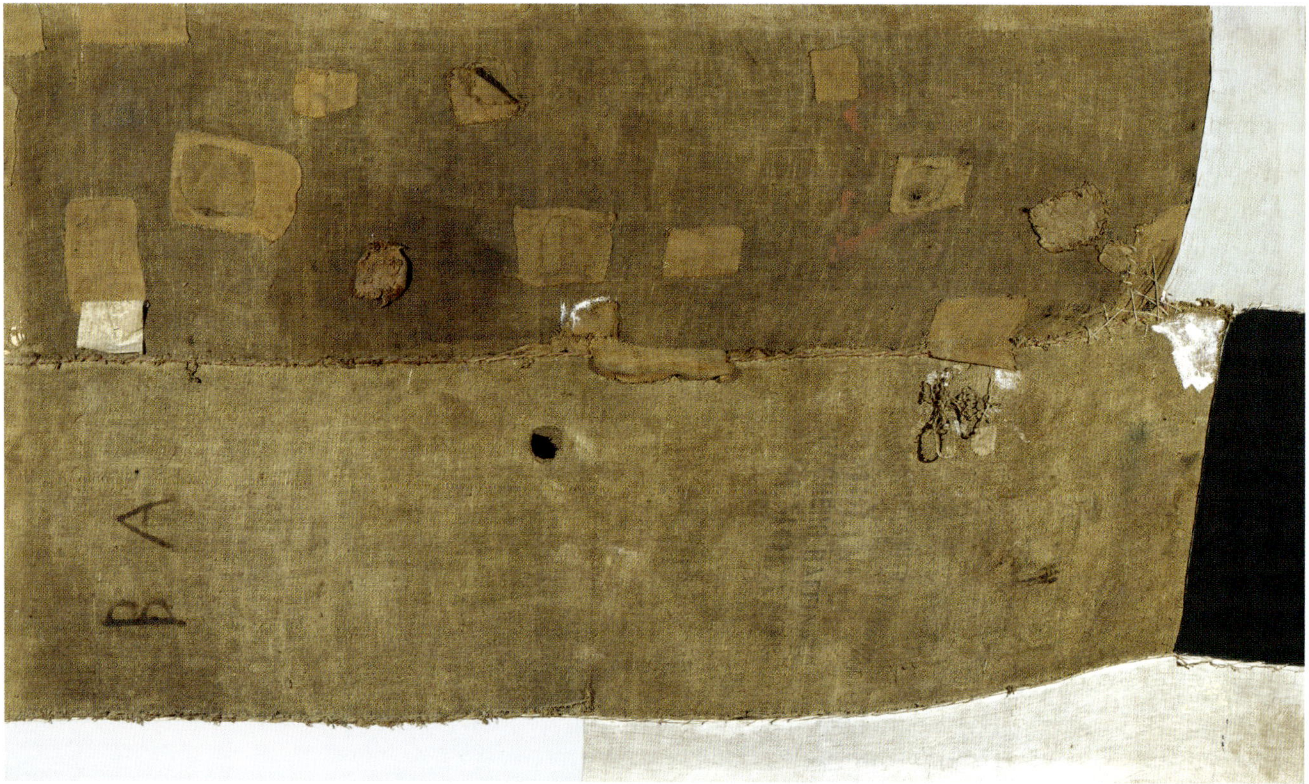

436

Alberto Burri
(Città di Castello 1915 - Nice 1995)

Large sack
Großer Sack
Grote zak
Bolsa grande

●●●

1952
150 x 250 cm / 50 x 48.4 in.
Galleria Nazionale d'Arte Moderna, Roma

sack cloth, string, acrylic color on frame / Sackleinwand, Schnur, Akrylfarbe auf Leinwand
jute, touw, acrylverf op spieraam / lienzo de costal, hilo bramante, color acrílico sobre lienzo

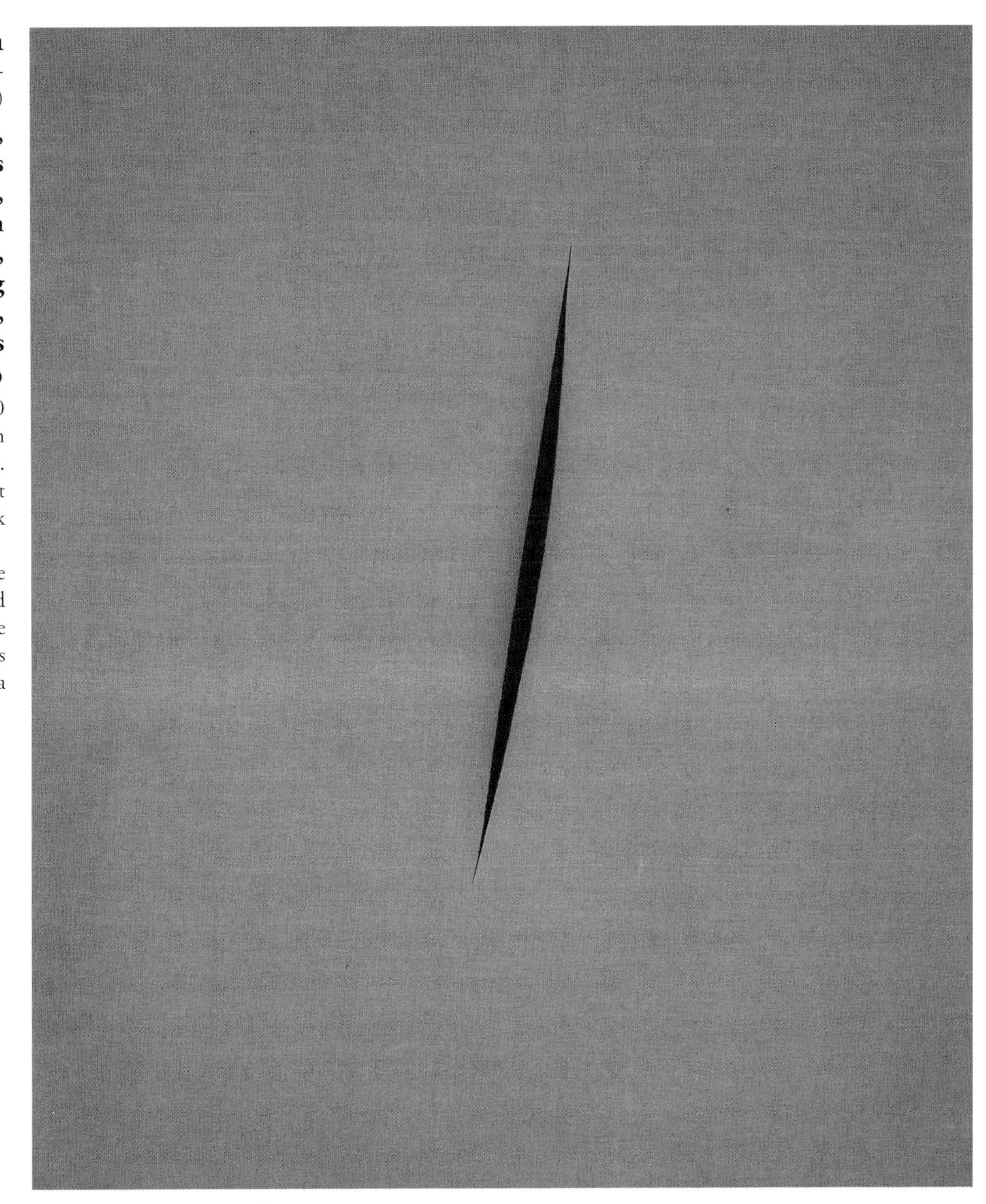

Lucio Fontana
(Rosario 1899 -
Comabbio 1968)

**Spatial Concept,
Expectations
Räumliches Konzept,
Erwartungen
Ruimtelijk concept,
verwachting
Concepto Espacial,
Esperas**
●●●
1960
100,3 x 80,3 cm
39.5 x 31.6 in.
Museum of Modern Art
(MoMA), New York

slashed canvas and gauze
zerschnittene Leinwand
und Gaze
verknipt doek en gaas
lienzo cortado y gasa

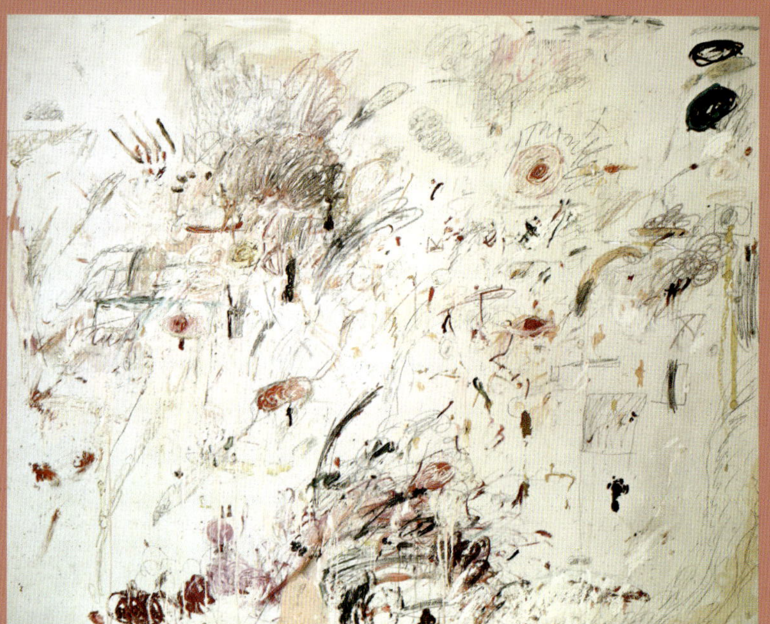

The Empire of Flora
Das Reich der Flora
Het rijk van Flora
El triunfo de Flora

●●

1961
200 x 242 cm / 78.7 x 95.2 in.
Nationalgalerie im Hamburger Bahnhof, Staatliche
Museen, Berlin
oil, grease pens, pencil, colored pencils on canvas
Öl, Wachsstifte, Bleistift, Farbstifte auf Leinwand
olie, waskrijt, potlood, kleurpotloden op doek
óleo, crayones, lápiz, lápices de colores sobre lienzo

Twombly's paintings are made of marks traced
on the canvas quickly, of indecipherable writing,
neither illustrative nor totally abstract.

Die Bilder von Twobly bestehen aus Zeichen,
die schnell in unleserlicher Schrift auf Leinwand
gezeichnet sind und weder illustrativ noch
vollkommen abstrakt sind.

De schilderijen van Twombly zijn gemaakt met
snel getrokkcn tekens en onleesbare teksten die
noch illustratief noch geheel abstract zijn.

Los cuadros de Twobly están realizados a partir
de marcas trazadas sobre el lienzo velozmente,
de escrituras indescifrables, que no son ni
ilustrativas ni totalmente abstractas.

► Jackson Pollock
(Cody 1912 - Long Island 1956)

Enchanted Forest
Verzauberter Wald
Betoverd bos
Bosque encantado

● ● ●

1947
221,3 x 114,6 cm / 87.1 x 45.1 in.
Collezione Peggy Guggenheim, Venezia

oil on canvas / Öl auf Leinwand
olieverf op doek / óleo sobre lienzo

◄ Cy Twombly
(Lexington 1925)

The Four Seasons: Spring
Die vier Jahreszeiten: Frühling
De vier seizoenen: Lente
Las cuatro estaciones: Primavera

● ●

1993-1994
312,5 x 190 cm / 123 x 74.8 in.
Museum of Modern Art (MoMA),
New York

synthetic paints, oil, lead and crayon
on canvas
Synthetische Lacke, Öl, Blei und
Wachspastell auf Leinwand
synthetische vernis, olieverf, lood en
waskrijt op doek
pinturas sintéticas, óleo, plomo
y crayones sobre lienzo

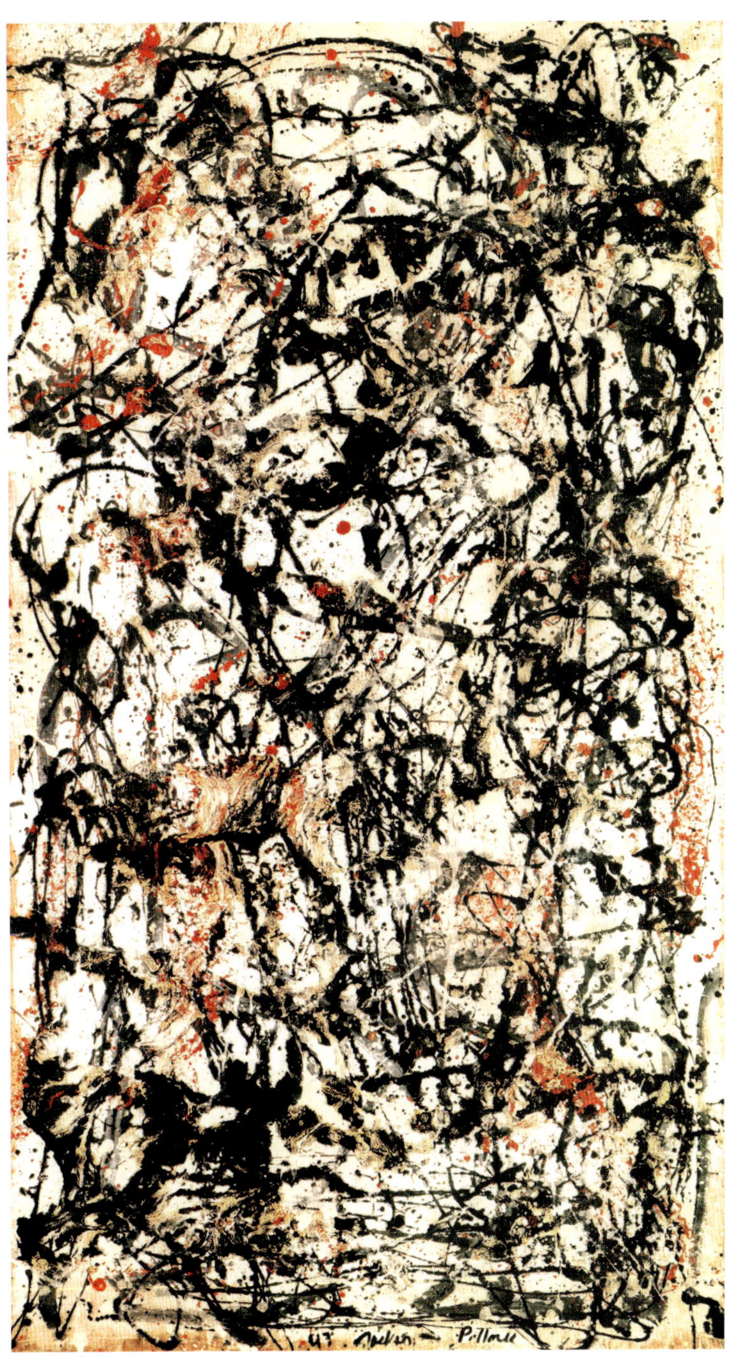

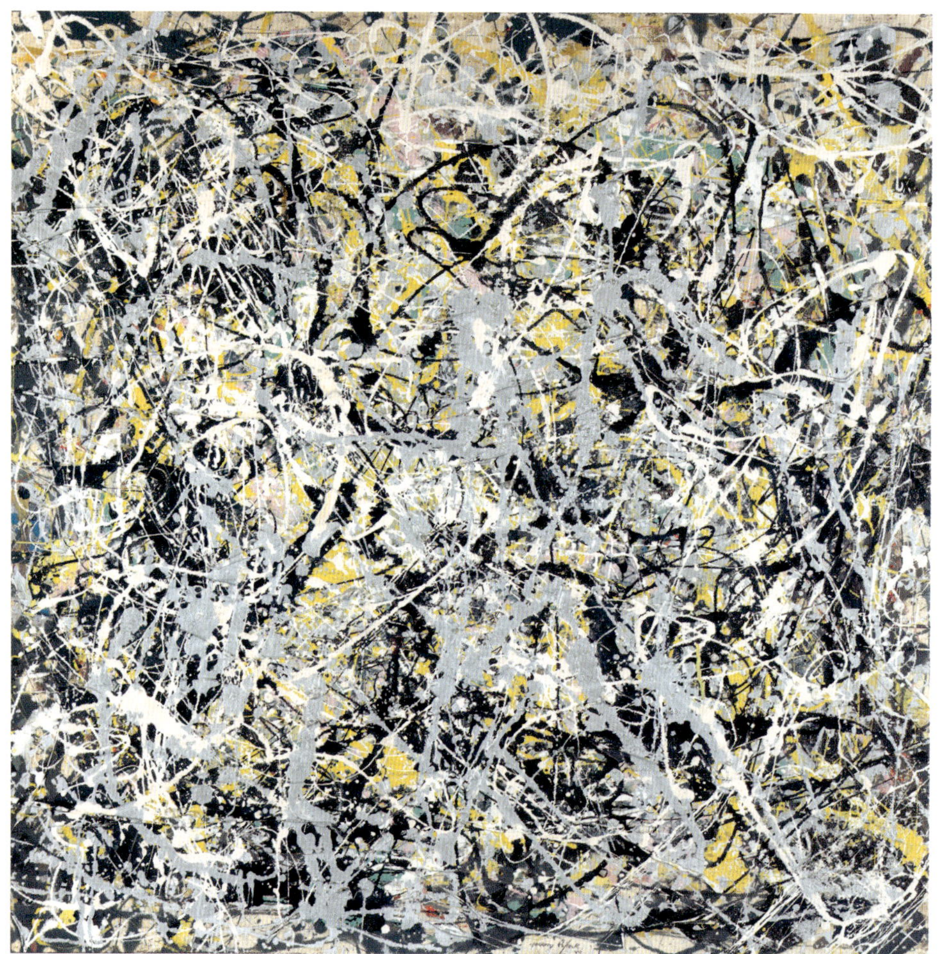

Jackson Pollock
(Cody 1912 - Long Island 1956)

Number 4
Nummer 4
Número 4

●●●

1949
90,2 x 87,3 cm / 35.5 x 34.3 in.
Yale University Art Gallery, New Haven (CT)

oil, enamel and aluminium paint on canvas
Öl, Email und Aluminiumlack auf Leinwand
olieverf, emailverf en aluminiumverni op doek
óleo, esmalte y pintura de aluminio sobre lienzo

Stretching the canvas on the floor, Pollock goes around it making the paint drip and creating a pictorial improvisation rich in vital energy.

Pollock legte die Leinwand auf den Boden, umkreiste diese und tropfte dabei die Farbe auf das Bild. So schuf er eine malerische Improvisation voller Lebensenergie.

Pollock loopt om het op de grond gelegde doek heen en laat de verf erop druipen waardoor hij een energierijke beeldende improvisatie creëert.

Con el lienzo extendido sobre el suelo, Pollock gira a su alrededor, haciendo gotear la pintura y creando así una improvisación pictórica cargada de energía vital.

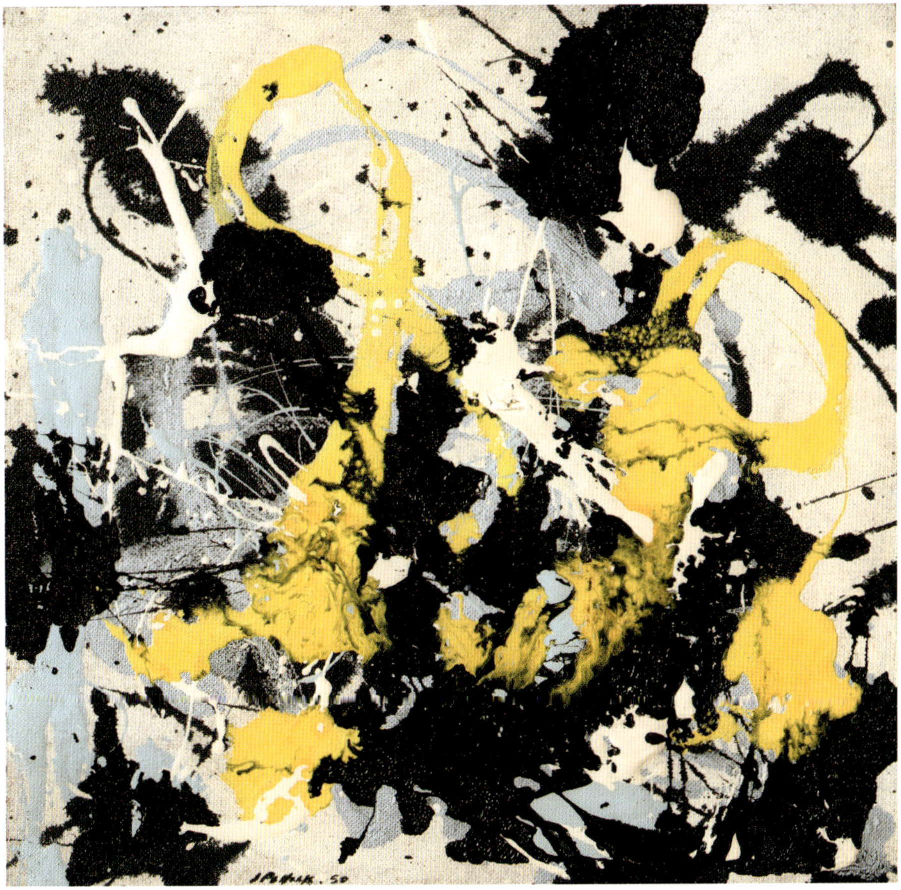

Jackson Pollock
(Cody 1912 - Long Island 1956)

Number 22
Nummer 22
Número 22

●●

1950
56,4 x 56,4 cm / 22.2 x 22.2 in.
Philadelphia Museum of Art, Philadelphia

enamel on masonite / Email auf Holzfaserplatte
email op masoniet / esmalte sobre masonita

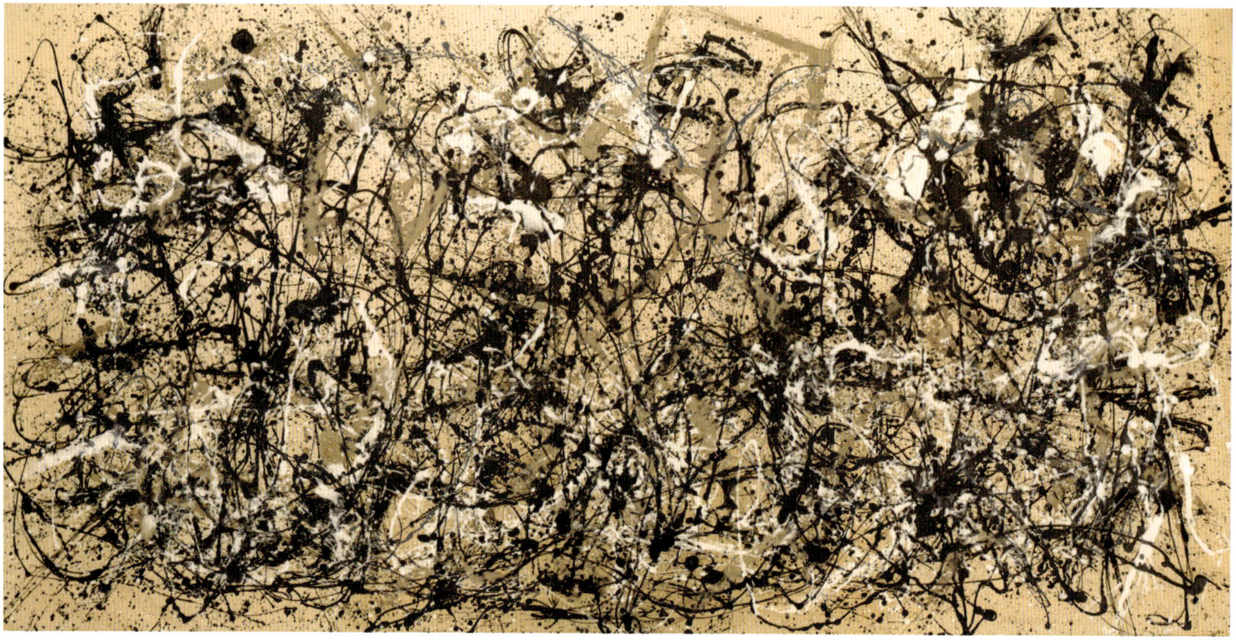

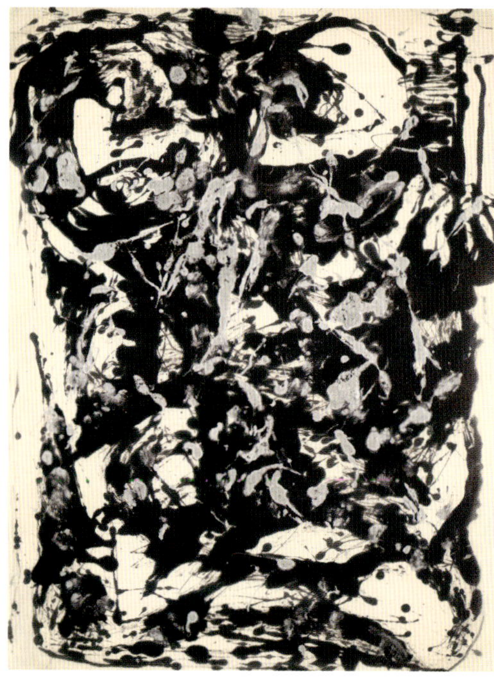

Jackson Pollock
(Cody 1912 -
Long Island 1956)

Black and Silver I
Braun und Silber I
Zwart en silver I
Marrón y plata I

●●●

ca. 1951
145 x 101 cm
57.1 x 39.7 in.
Museo Thyssen-Bornemisza,
Madrid

silver paint and enamel on canvas
Lack, Silber und Email auf
Leinwand
zilververnis en email op doek
pintura plateada y esmalte sobre
lienzo

Jackson Pollock
(Cody 1912 - Long Island 1956)

Autumn Rhythm (Number 30)
Herbstrhythmus (Nummer 30)
Ritme van de herfst (nummer 30)
Ritmo de otoño (Número 30)

●●●

1950
266,7 x 525,8 cm / 105 x 207 in.
The Metropolitan Museum of Art, New
York

enamel on canvas
Email auf Holzfaserplatte
email op doek
esmalte sobre lienzo

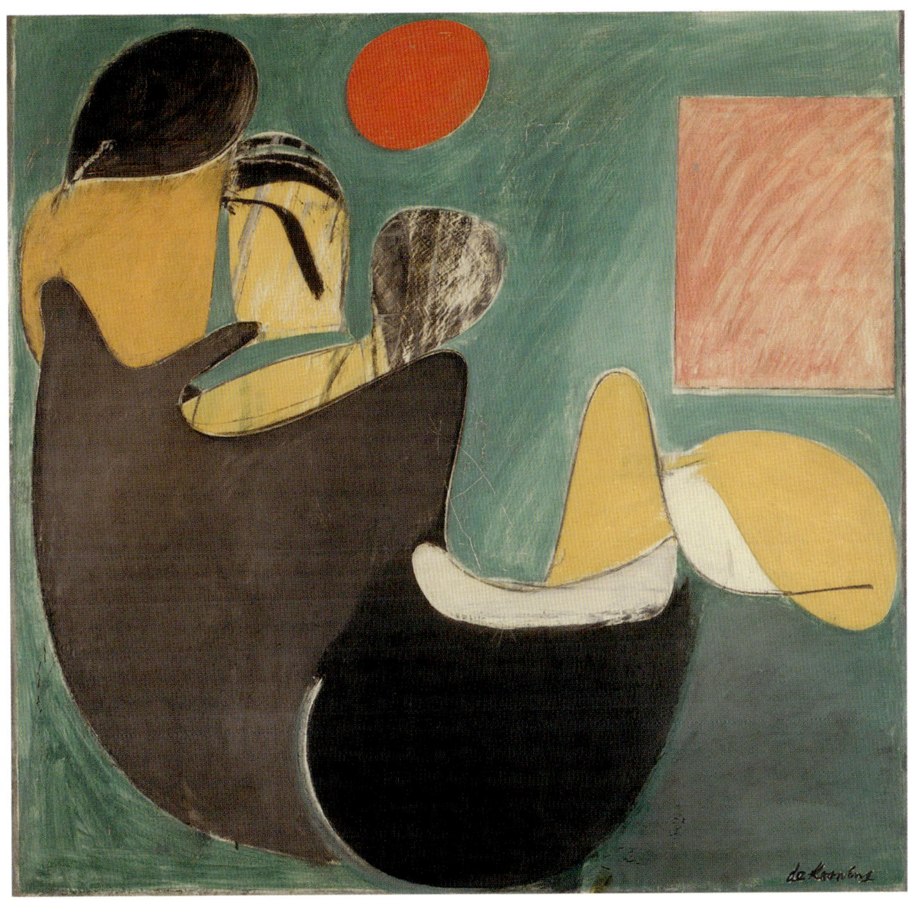

Willem de Kooning
(Rotterdam 1904 - New York 1997)

The Wave
Die Welle
De golf
La ola

●●

ca. 1942-1944
121,9 x 121,9 cm / 48 x 48 in.
Smithsonian American Art Museum, Washington DC

oil on fibre panel / Öl auf Faserbrett
olieverf op vezeldoek / óleo sobre panel de fibras

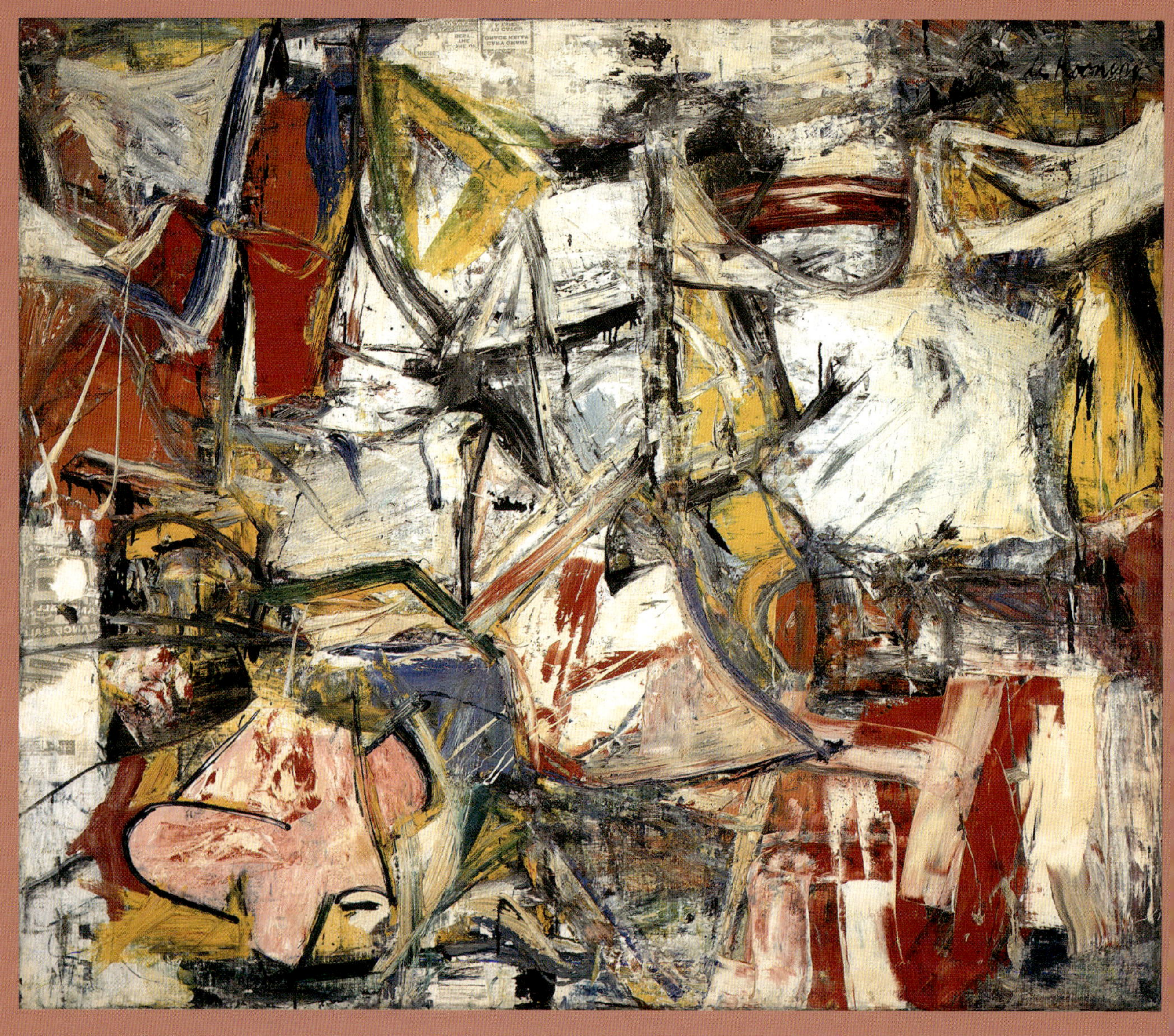

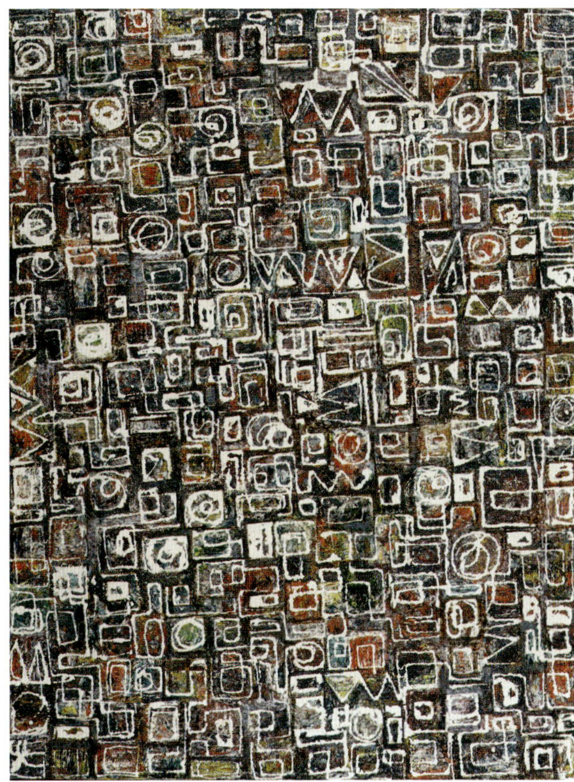

Lee Krasner
(New York 1908 - 1984)

Composition
Compositie
Composición

● ●

1949
96,7 x 70,6 cm / 38.1 x 27.8 in.
Philadelphia Museum of Art,
Philadelphia

oil on canvas / Öl auf Leinwand
olieverf op doek / óleo sobre lienzo

Lee Krasner
(New York 1908 - 1984)

Creatures of the Night
Nachtgestalten
Schepsels van de nacht
Criaturas de la noche

●

1965
76,2 x 108 cm / 30 x 42.5 in.
The Metropolitan Museum of Art, New
York

acrylic on paper / Akryl auf Papier
acrylverf op papier / acrílico sobre papel

 Willem de Kooning
(Rotterdam 1904 - New York 1997)

Gotham News

● ●

1955
181,6 x 208,2 x 6,9 cm / 71.4 x 82 x 2.7 in.
Albright-Knox Art Gallery, Buffalo

oil on canvas / Öl auf Leinwand
olieverf op doek / óleo sobre lienzo

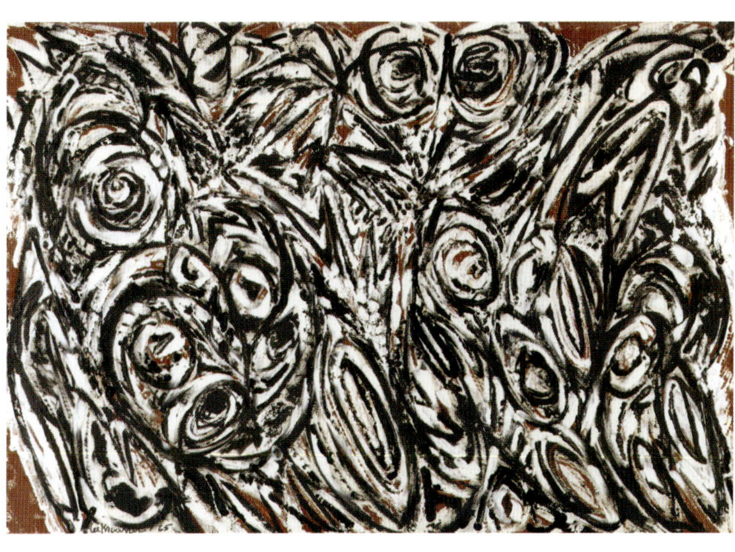

Franz Kline
(Wilkes-Barres 1910 - New York 1962)

Torches Mauve
Torches Mauves (Malvenfarbige Fackeln)
Zachtpaarse zaklamp
Antorchas malva

●●●

1960
305,1 x 206,1 cm / 120.1 x 81.1 in.
Philadelphia Museum of Art, Philadelphia

oil on canvas / Öl auf Leinwand
olieverf op doek / óleo sobre lienzo

Franz Kline
(Wilkes-Barres 1910 - New York 1962)

Blueberry eyes
Blaubeeraugen
Bosbessen ogen
Ojos de arándano

●●

1959-1960
101,9 x 75,5 cm / 40.1 x 29.7 in.
Smithsonian American Art Museum, Washington DC

oil on cardboard / Öl auf Karton
olieverf op karton / óleo sobre cartón

446

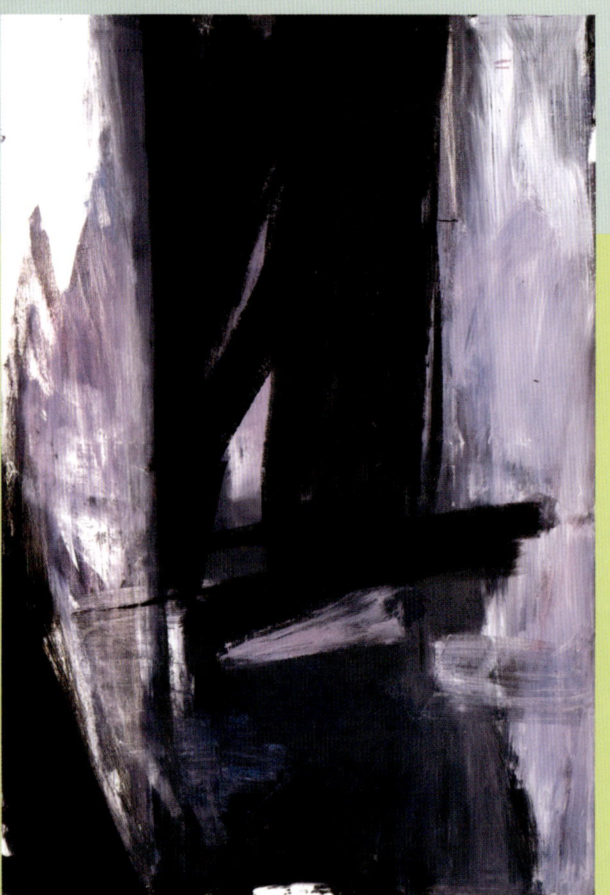

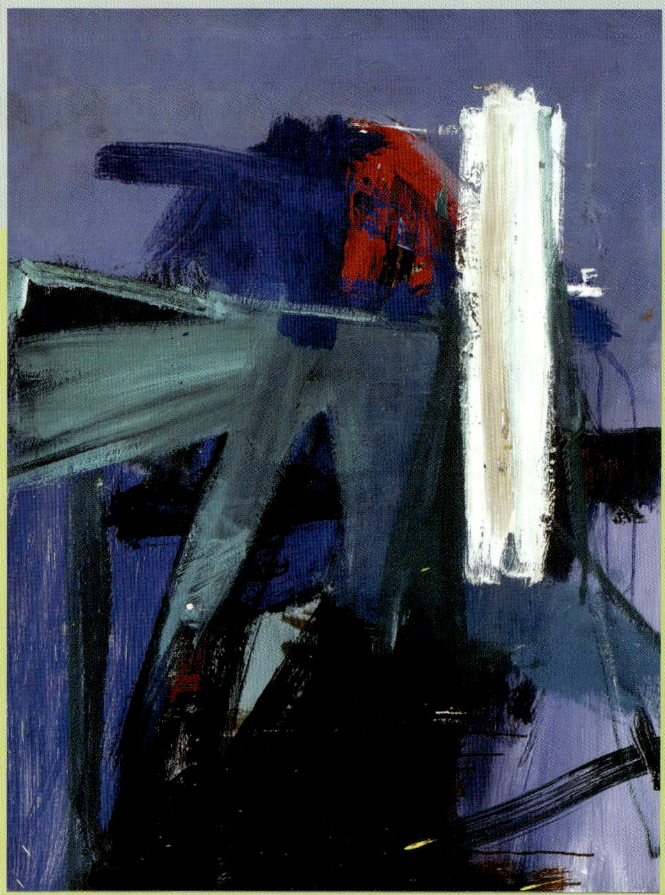

Franz Kline
(Wilkes-Barres 1910 -
New York 1962)

**Black Reflections
Schwarze
Reflektionen
Zwarte
weerspiegelingen
Reflexiones en
negro**

●

1959
48,3 x 49,2 cm
19 x 19.4 in.
The Metropolitan
Museum of Art, New
York

oil and paper glued
on paper, mounted on
masonite
Öl und geleimtes
Papier auf Papier, auf
Holzfaserplatte montiert
olieverf en papier
op papier geplakt,
gemonteerd op masoniet
óleo y papel encolado
sobre papel, montado
sobre masonita

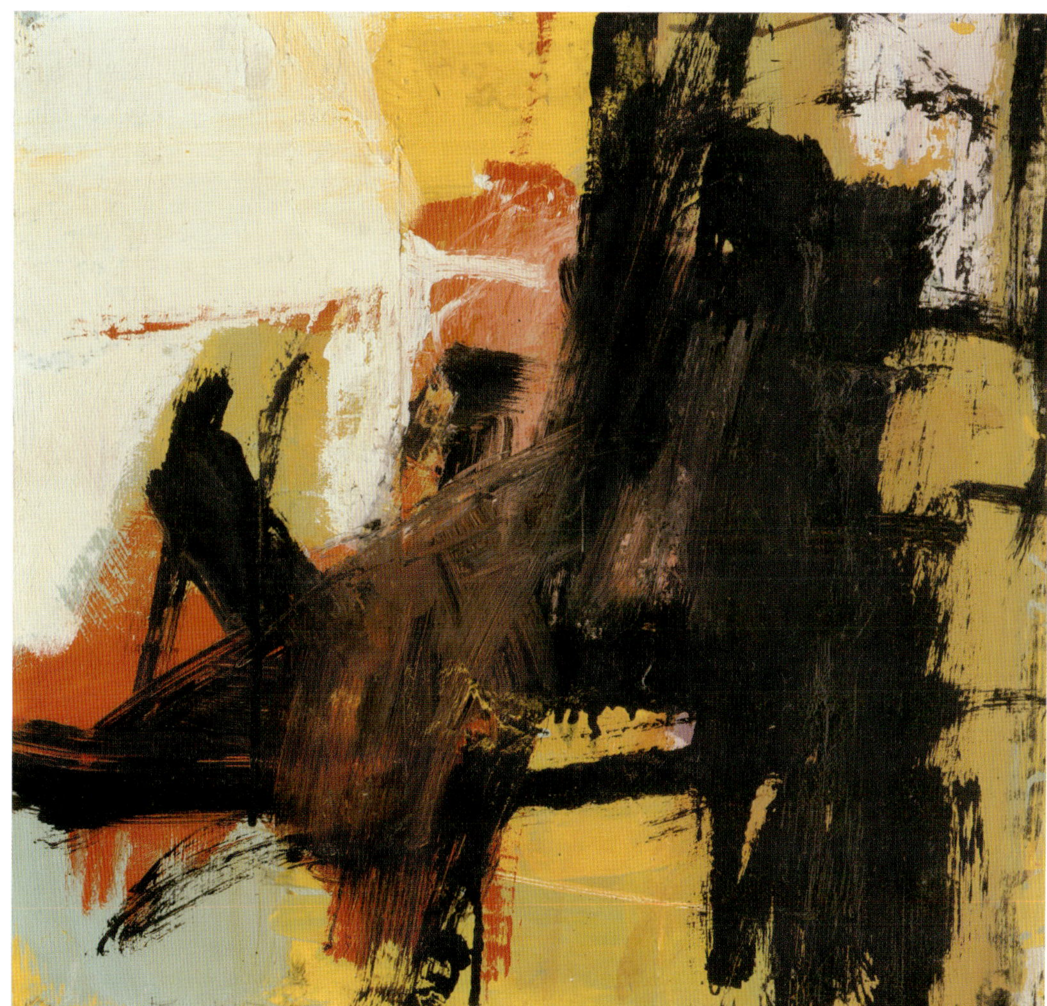

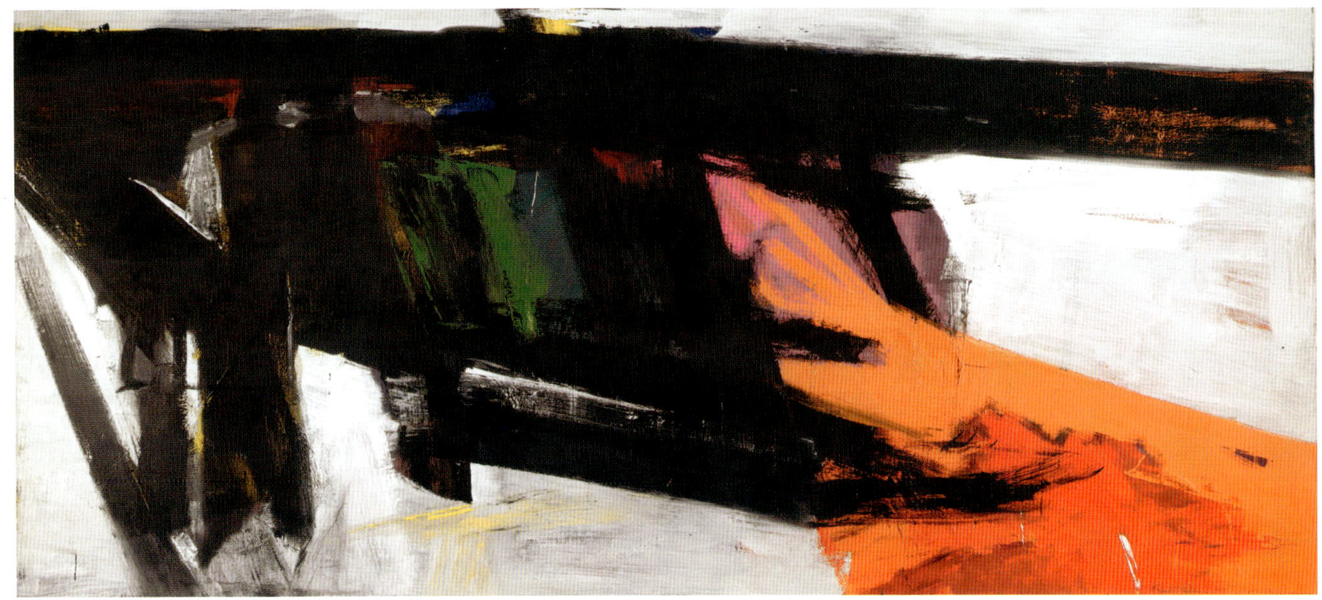

448 Franz Kline
(Wilkes-Barres 1910 - New York 1962)

Orange and Black Wall
Orangefarbene und schwarze Wand
Zwart met oranje muur
Pared naranja y negra

●

Thyssen-Bornemisza Collection

Abstract and gestural, Kline's painting expresses relationships of force and tension between space and surfaces.

Abstrakt und gestisch: Die Malerei von Kline drückt starke und spannungsreiche Beziehungen zwischen Raum und Oberfläche aus.

Het schilderij van Kline is abstract en vol gebaren en drukt de sterke en gespannen relatie uit tussen ruimte en oppervlak.

Abstracta y gestual, la pintura de Kline expresa relaciones de fuerza y tensión entre el espacio y las superficies.

Mark Rothko

(Daugavpils 1903 -
New York 1970)

Number 18
Nummer 18
Número 18

●●●

1951
207 x 177,4 cm
81.5 x 69.8 in.
Munson-Williams-Proctor
Arts Institute, Utica (NY)

oil on canvas
Öl auf Leinwand
olieverf op doek
óleo sobre lienzo

**Brushstrokes of color
floating, fluctuating, with
undefined contours but
extremely vibrant.**

**Fließende, fluktuierende
Pinselstriche mit
unbestimmten, stark
vibrierenden Umrissen.**

**Drijvende,
schommelende
penseelstreken met vage
randen die tegelijkertijd
zeer vibrerend zijn.**

**Pinceladas de color
flotantes, fluctuantes, de
bordes indefinidos, pero
fuertemente vibrantes.**

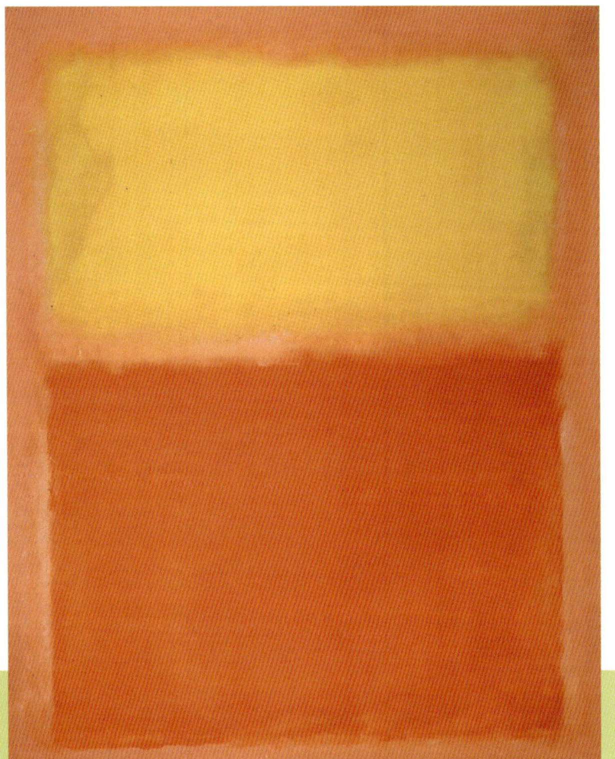

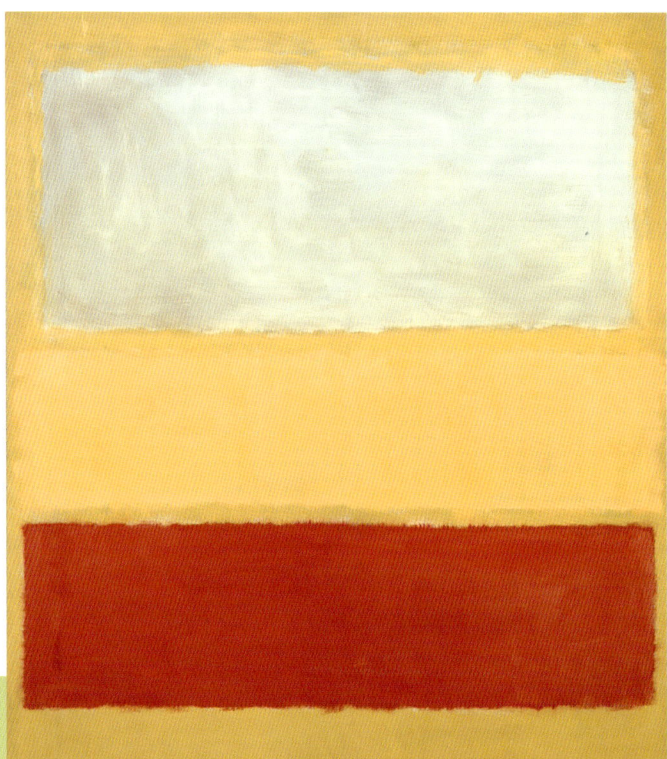

Mark Rothko
(Daugavpils 1903 - New York 1970)

Orange and Yellow
Orange und Gelb
Oranje en geel
Naranja y amarillo
●●●
1956
231,1 x 180,3 cm / 91 x 71 in.
Albright-Knox Art Gallery, Buffalo

oil on canvas
Öl auf Leinwand
olieverf op doek
óleo sobre lienzo

Mark Rothko
(Daugavpils 1903 - New York 1970)

No. 13 (White, red on yellow)
Nr. 13 (Weiß, Rot auf Gelb)
N. 13 (Wit, rood op geel)
N. 13 (Blanco, rojo sobre amarillo)
●●●
1958
242,3 x 206,7 cm / 95.4 x 81.4 in.
The Metropolitan Museum of Art, New York

oil and acrylic with pigments dusted on canvas
Öl und Akryl mit Pulverpigmenten auf Leinwand
olieverf en acrylverf met poederpigment op doek
óleo y acrílico con pigmentos espolvoreados sobre lienzo

Adolph Gottlieb
(New York 1903 -1974)

Blue
Blau
Blauw
Azul

●●●

1962
122,3 x 91,4 cm / 48.1 x 36 in.
Smithsonian American Art Museum,
Washington DC

oil on canvas / Öl auf Leinwand
olieverf op doek / óleo sobre lienzo

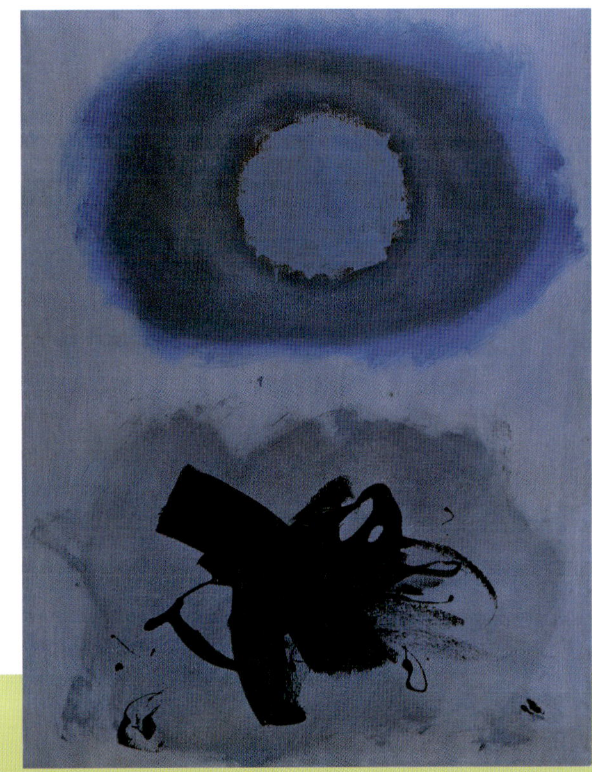

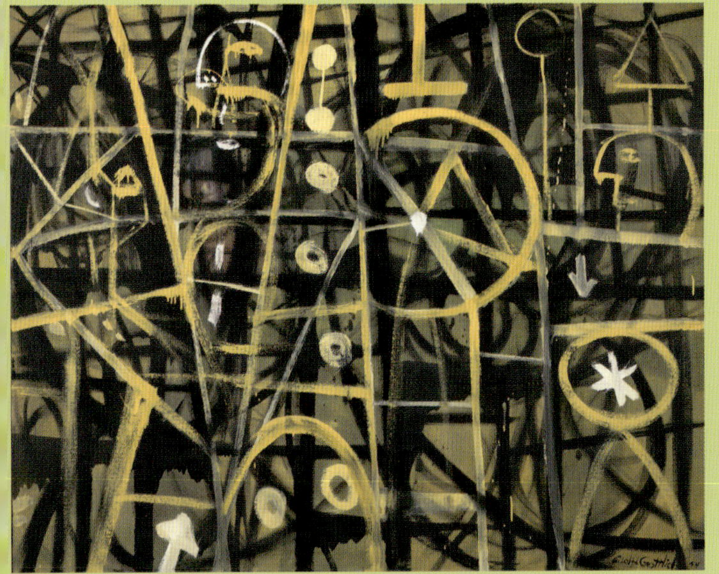

Adolph Gottlieb
(New York 1903 -1974)

The Cadmium Sound
Der Klang von Kadmium
Het geluid van cadmium
El sonido del cadmio

●●●

1954
152,6 x 183,5 cm / 60.1 x 72.2 in.
Philadelphia Museum of Art, Philadelphia

oil on canvas / Öl auf Leinwand
olieverf op doek / óleo sobre lienzo

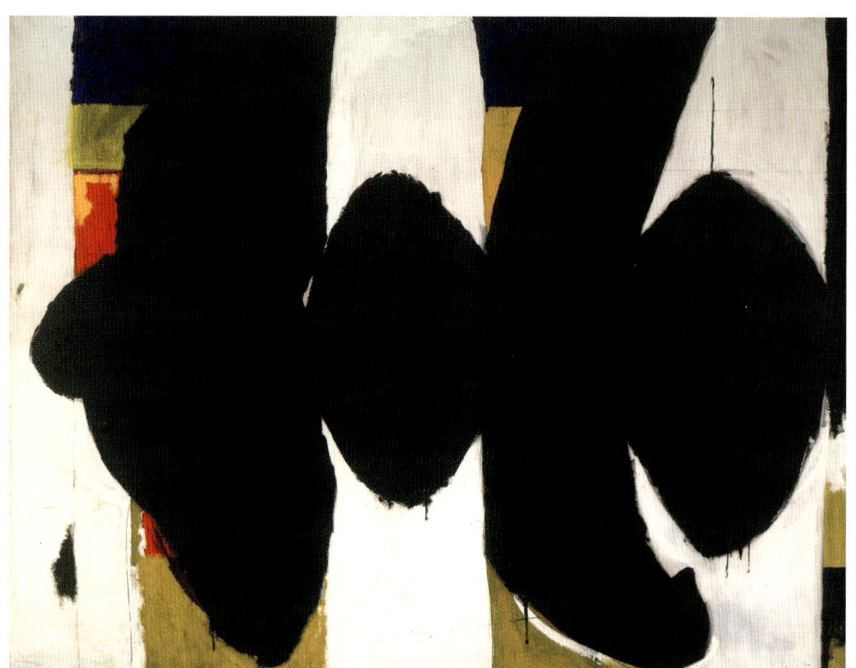

Robert Motherwell
(Aberdeen 1915 - Provincetown 1991)

**Elegy to the Spanish
Republic No. 34
Elegie auf die Spanische
Republik Nr. 34
Elegie aan de Spaanse
Republiek n. 34
Elegía a la República
Española n. 34**

●●●

1953-1954
203,2 x 254 cm / 80 x 100 in.
Albright-Knox Art Gallery, Buffalo

oil on canvas / Öl auf Leinwand
olieverf op doek / óleo sobre lienzo

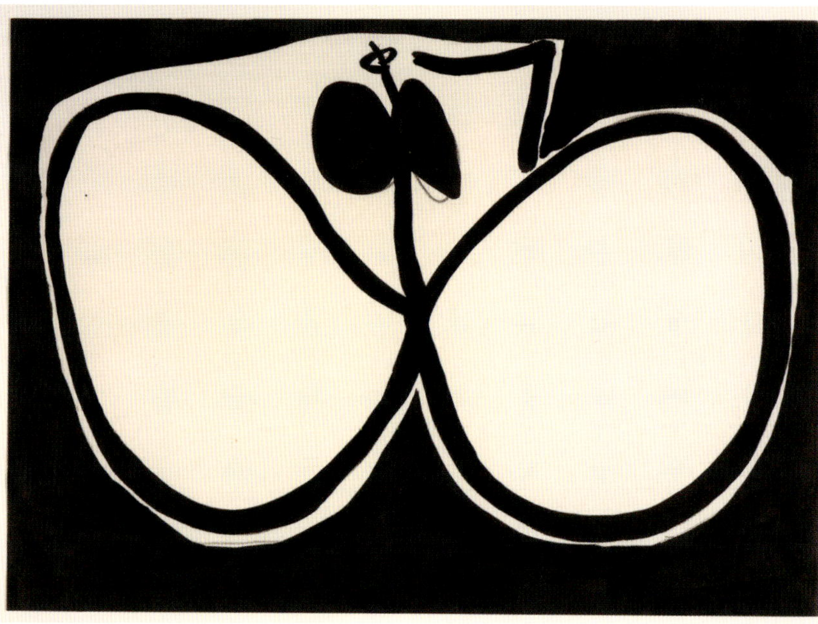

Robert Motherwell
(Aberdeen 1915 - Provincetown 1991)

**Nude
Akt
Naakt
Desnudo**

●●●

1952
54,6 x 74,6 cm / 21.5 x 29.3 in.
Munson-Williams-Proctor Arts Institute,
Utica (NY)
brush-applied black ink over graphite on wove
paper mounted on illustration board / Schwarze
Tinte mit Pinsel über Graphit auf geharztes
Papier aufgetragen und auf eine Illustrationstafel
montiert / zwarte inkt met penseel op grafiet op
rasterpapier aangebracht, gemonteerd op een
illustratiepaneel / tinta negra aplicada con pincel
sobre grafito sobre papel tramado montado
sobre una tabla de dibujo

William Baziotes
(Pittsburgh 1912 -
New York 1963)

**Toy
Spielzeug
Speelgoed
Juguete**

●●
1949
45,7 x 35,8 cm
18 x 14.1 in.
Munson-Williams-Proctor
Arts Institute, Utica (NY)

oil on canvas
Öl auf Leinwand
olieverf op doek
óleo sobre lienzo

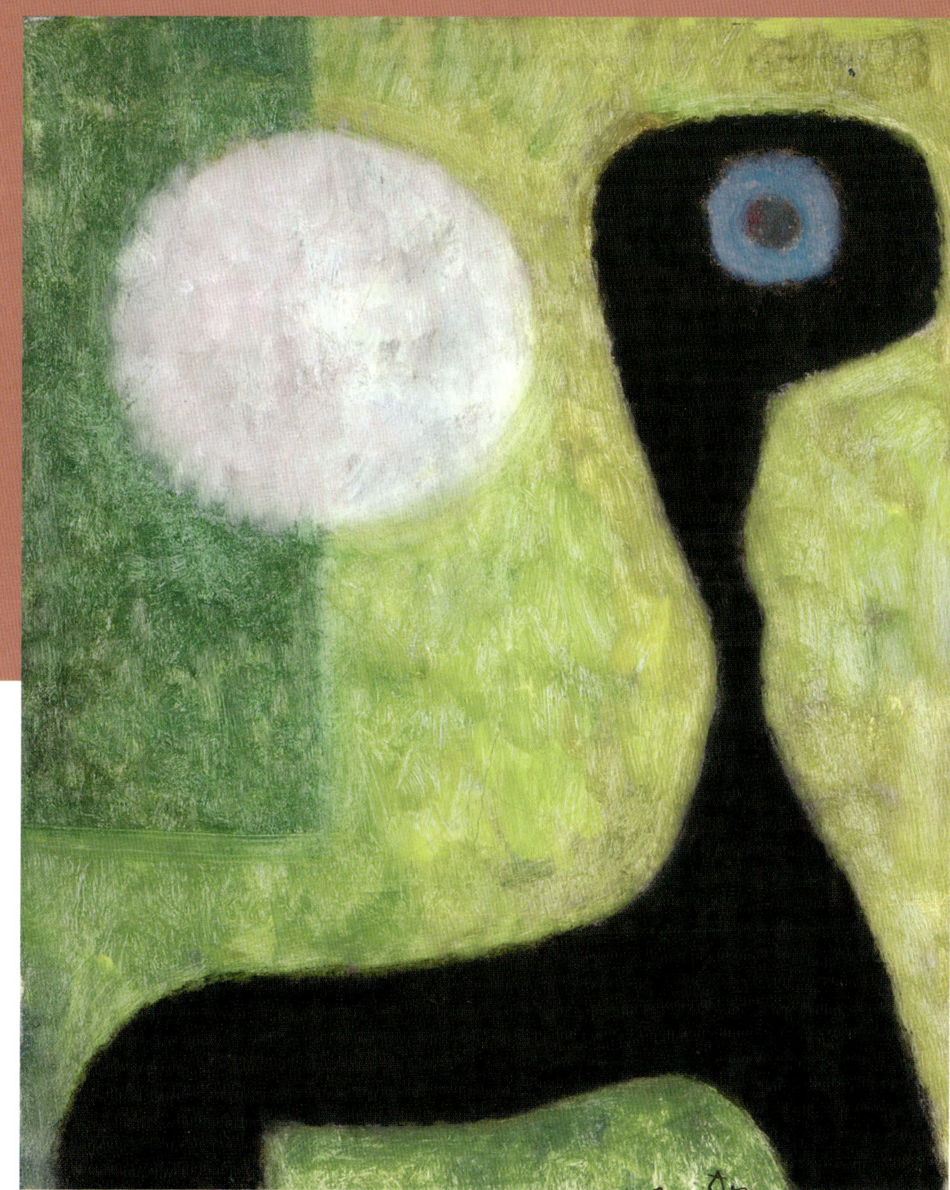

For Motherwell, it is a question of finding a pictorial equivalent to a funeral song and to convey the emotion.

Für Motherwell geht es darum, ein malerisches Gegenstück zu einem Trauerlied zu finden und das Gefühl umzusetzen.

Het gaat Motherwell om het vinden van een beeldend equivalent voor begrafeniszang en om het uitdrukken van emotie.

Para Motherwell, se trata de encontrar un equivalente pictórico a un canto fúnebre y de transmitir la emoción que éste genera.

Philip Guston
(Montreal 1913 - Woodstock 1980)

Painter III
Maler III
Schilder III
Pintor III

●

1960
154,1 x 172,8 cm / 60.6 x 68 in.
Smithsonian American Art Museum,
Washington DC

oil on canvas / Öl auf Leinwand
olieverf op doek / óleo sobre lienzo

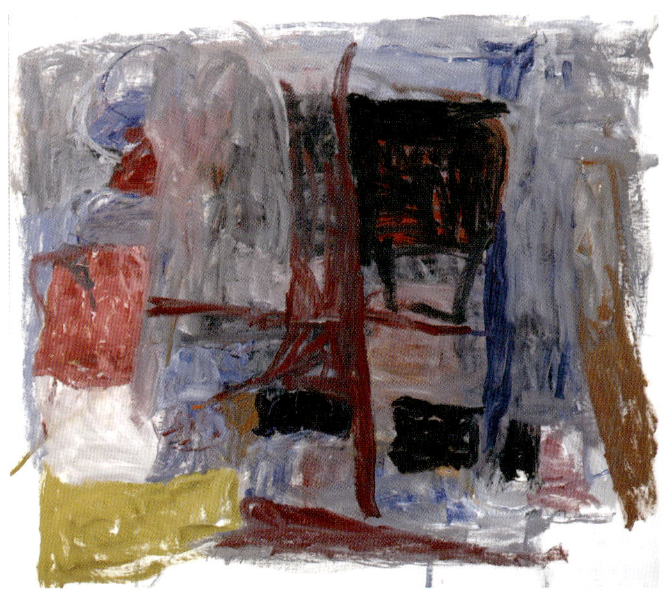

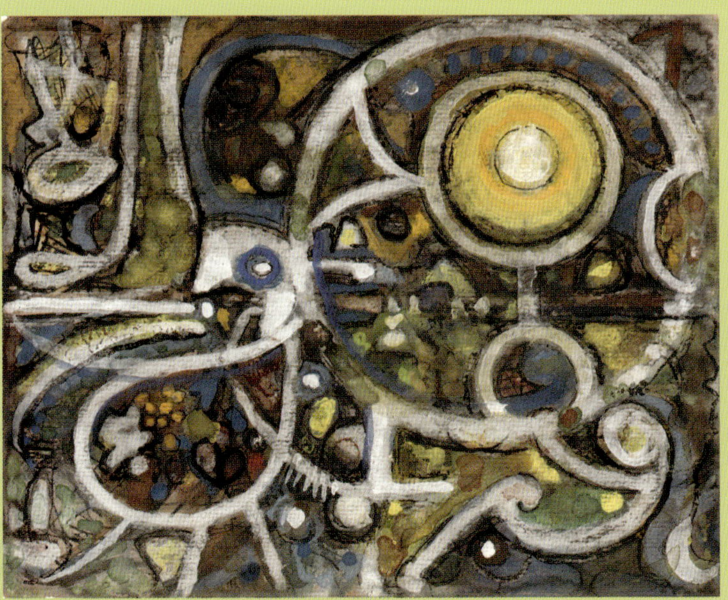

Richard Pousette-Dart
(Saint Paul, Minnesota 1916 - Rockland County,
New York 1992)

Composition
Compositie
Composición

●●●

1949
16,5 x 20,3 cm / 6.5 x 8 in.
Munson-Williams-Proctor Arts Institute, Utica (NY)
transparent and opaque watercolor, black crayon,
and black ink on machine-made paper with a laid
texture / Opakes und transparentes Aquarell, schwarze
Zeichenkohle und schwarze Tinte auf grobkörnigem
Druckpapier / opake en transparante aquarel, houtskool
en zwarte inkt op gevergeerd printpapier / acuarela opaca
ý transparente, carboncillo negro y tinta negra sobre papel
de impresión con filigrana vergueteado

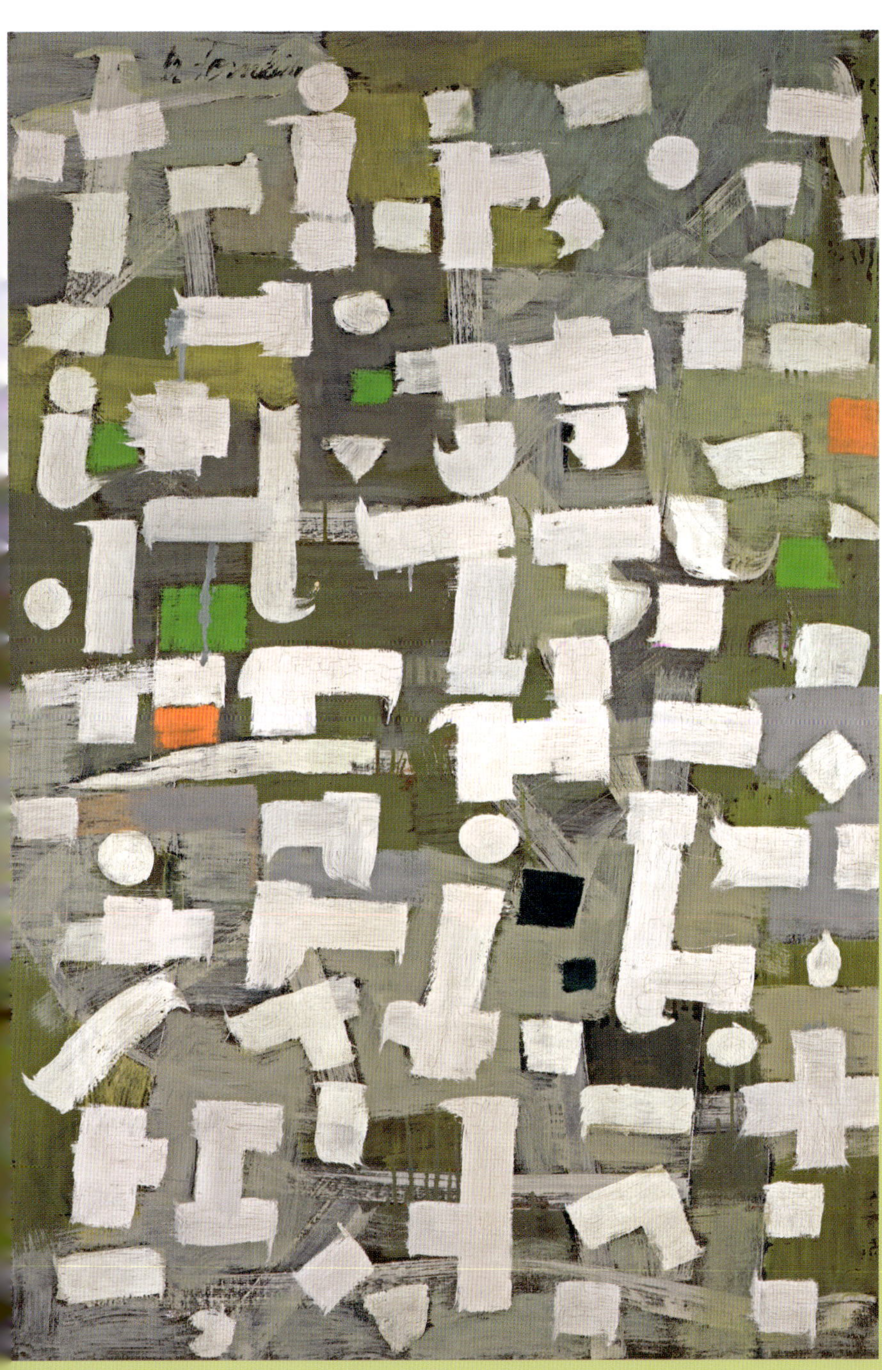

Bradley Walker Tomlin
(Syracuse 1899 - New York 1953)

No. 11
Nr. 11
N. 11

●

1949
112 x 73,6 cm / 44.1 x 28.9 in.
Munson-Williams-Proctor Arts Institute,
Utica (NY)

oil on canvas / Öl auf Leinwand
olieverf op doek / óleo sobre lienzo

Sam Francis
(San Mateo, California
1923 - Santa Monica,
California 1994)

**Towards the
Disappearance II
Im Verschwinden
begriffen II
Richting de
verdwijning II
Hacia la
desaparición II**

● ● ●

1958
275,6 x 319,7 cm
108.5 x 125.9 in.
Metropolitan Museum
of Art, New York

oil on canvas
Öl auf Leinwand
olieverf op doek
óleo sobre lienzo

456

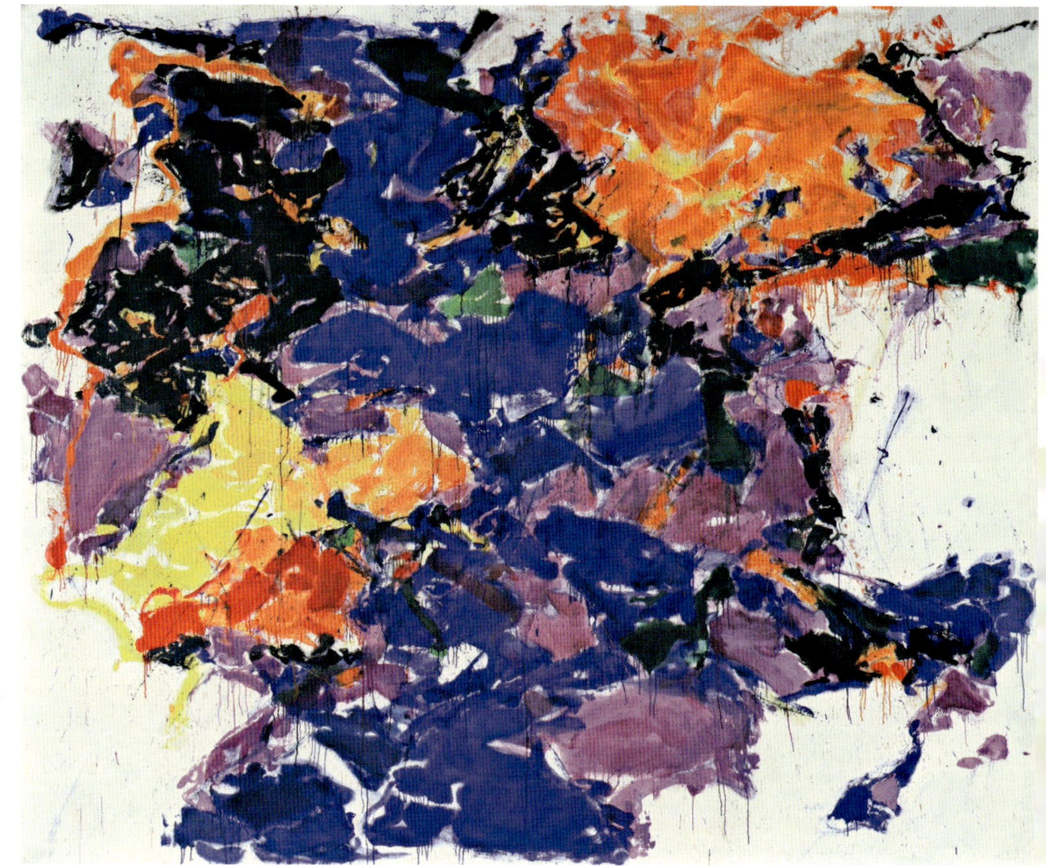

There have been many American artists "marked" by Monet's *Water Lilies* exhibited at the time of a large retrospective in New York in 1945.

Es gibt viele amerikanische Künstler, die von Monets *Seerosen* "geprägt" sind. Diese wurden 1945 in New York auf einer großen Retrospektive ausgestellt.

Veel Amerikaanse kunstenaars zijn "getekend" door de waterlelies van Monet die in 1945 tentoongesteld werden bij een groot retrospectief in New York.

Muchos son los artistas estadounidenses "marcados" por las *Ninfeas* de Monet expuestas en ocasión de una gran retrospectiva realizada en Nueva York en 1945.

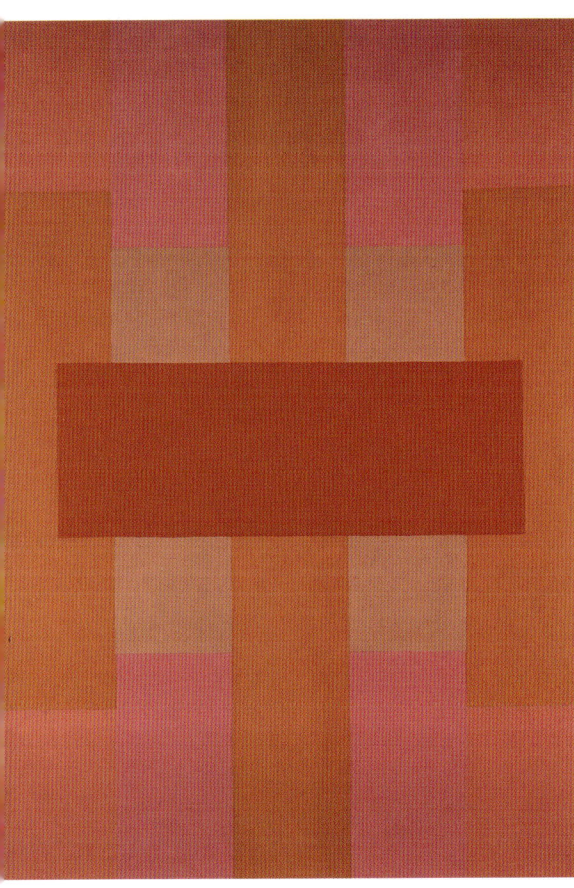

Ad Reinhardt
(Buffalo 1933 - New York 1967)

Red Abstract
Rot Abstrakt
Rood Abstract
Abstracto rojo

●●●

1952
152,4 x 101,3 cm / 60 x 39.9 in.
Yale University Art Gallery, New Haven (CT)

oil on canvas / Öl auf Leinwand
olieverf op doek / óleo sobre lienzo

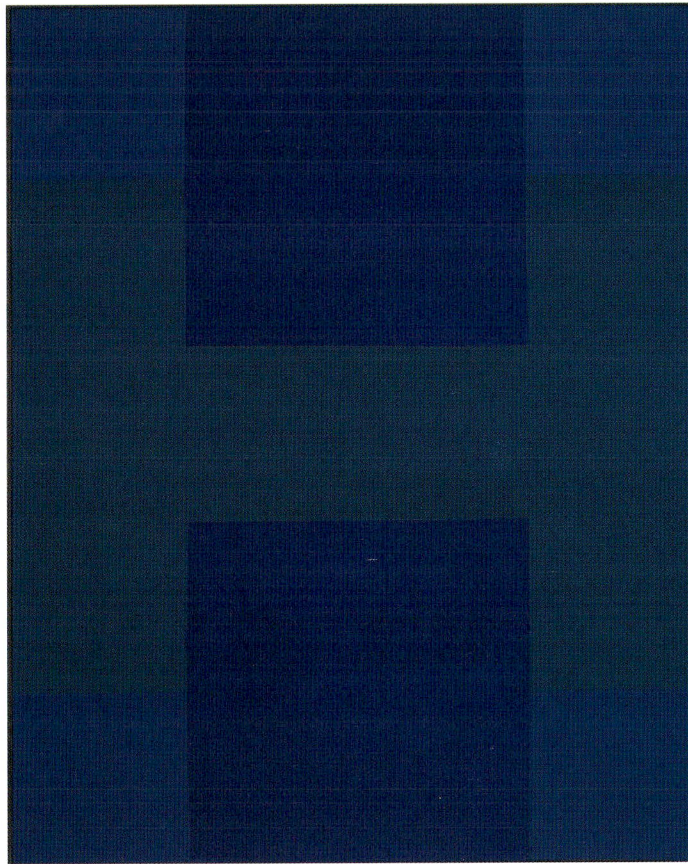

Ad Reinhardt
(Buffalo 1933 - New York 1967)

Blue Abstract Painting
Blaues, abstraktes Gemälde
Blauw abstract schilderij
Pintura abstracta azul

●●●

ca. 1953
50,8 x 40,6 cm / 20 x 16 in.
Yale University Art Gallery, New Haven (CT)

oil on canvas / Öl auf Leinwand
olieverf op doek / óleo sobre lienzo

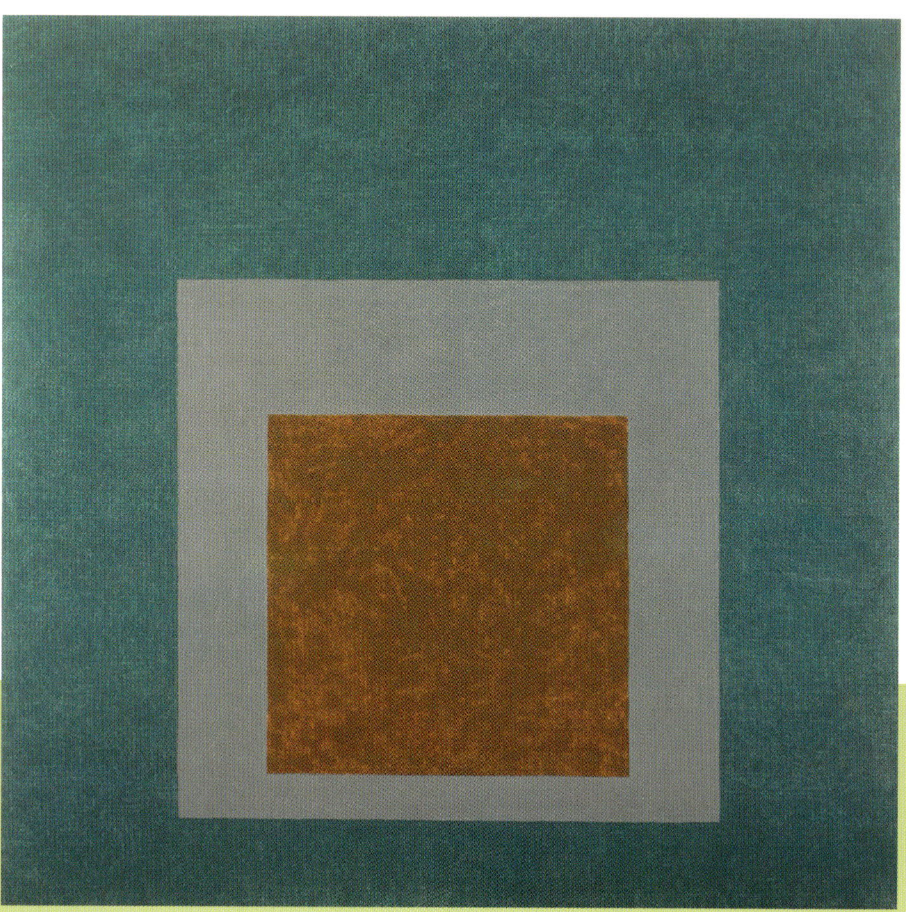

Josef Albers
(Bottrop 1888 - New Haven 1976)

Tribute to the Square: Solitary
Huldigung an das Quadrat: Einsam
Hulde aan het vierkant: alleen
Homenaje al cuadrado: Solitario

●●●

1963
121,9 x 121,9 cm / 48 x 48 in.
The Newark Museum, Newark

oil on wood / Öl auf Holz / olieverf op hout / óleo sobre madera

In the series, *Tribute to the Square*, Albers explores the shape/light interactions that influence color.

In der Serie *Huldigung an das Quadrat* erforscht Albers die Wechselwirkungen von Form und Licht in ihrer Wirkung auf die Farbe.

Josef Albers
(Bottrop 1888 - New Haven 1976)

**Tribute to the Square: Untitled
Huldigung an das Quadrat: Ohne Titel
Hulde aan het vierkant: zonder titel
Homenaje al cuadrado: Sin título**

● ● ●

1965
101,6 x 101,6 cm / 40 x 40 in.
Nationalgalerie, Staatliche Museen, Berlin

oil on wood / Öl auf Holz / olieverf op hout / óleo sobre madera

In de serie *Hulde aan het vierkant* onderzoekt Albers de interacties tussen vorm en licht die de kleur beïnvloeden.

En la serie *Homenaje al cuadrado*, Albers explora las interacciones forma/luz que influencian en el color.

Ellsworth Kelly
(Newburgh, New York 1923)

**Blue on White
Blau auf Weiß
Blauw op wit
Azul sobre blanco**

●

1961
217,5 x 172,1 cm
85.6 x 67.7 in.
Smithsonian American Art
Museum, Washington DC

oil on canvas
Öl auf Leinwand
olieverf op doek
óleo sobre lienzo

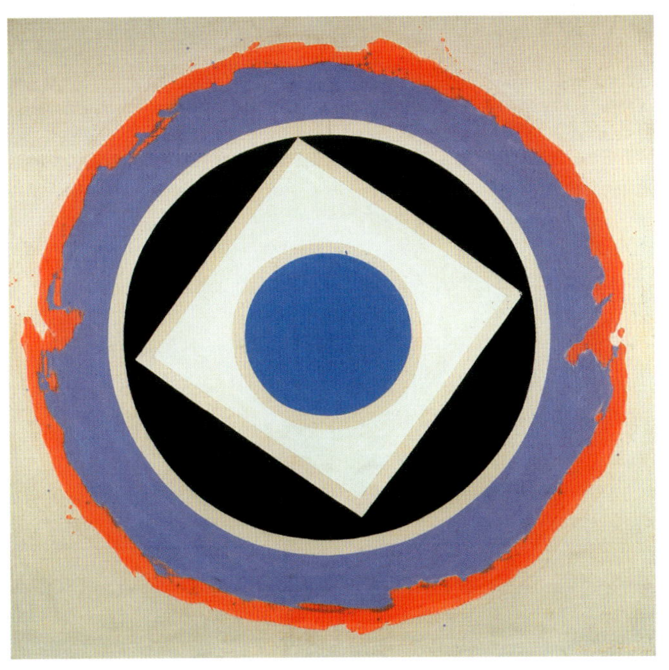

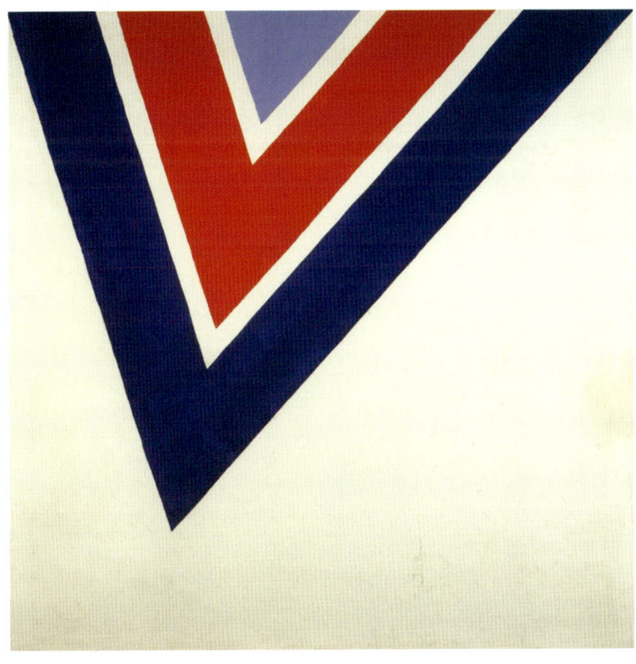

Kenneth Noland
(Asheville, North Carolina 1924)

**Chasm
Spaltung
Scheur
División**
●●●
1959
237,8 x 238,5 cm / 93.7 x 93.7 in.
Smithsonian American Art Museum,
Washington DC

acrylic on canvas
Akryl auf Leinwand
acrylverf op doek
acrílico sobre lienzo

Kenneth Noland
(Asheville, North Carolina 1924)

Sarah's reach
●●
1964
238,2 x 232,8 cm / 93.7 x 91.6 in.
Smithsonian American Art Museum,
Washington DC

acrylic on canvas
Akryl auf Leinwand
acrylverf op doek
acrílico sobre lienzo

Clyfford Still
(Grandin 1904 - Baltimore 1980)

1946-H
(Indian red and black)
(Indisch rot und schwarz)
(kastanjerood en zwart)
(Rojo índigo y negro)
●●●

1946
198,8 x 173,7 cm / 78.2 x 68.3 in.
Smithsonian American Art Museum,
Washington DC

oil on canvas
Öl auf Leinwand
olieverf op doek
óleo sobre lienzo

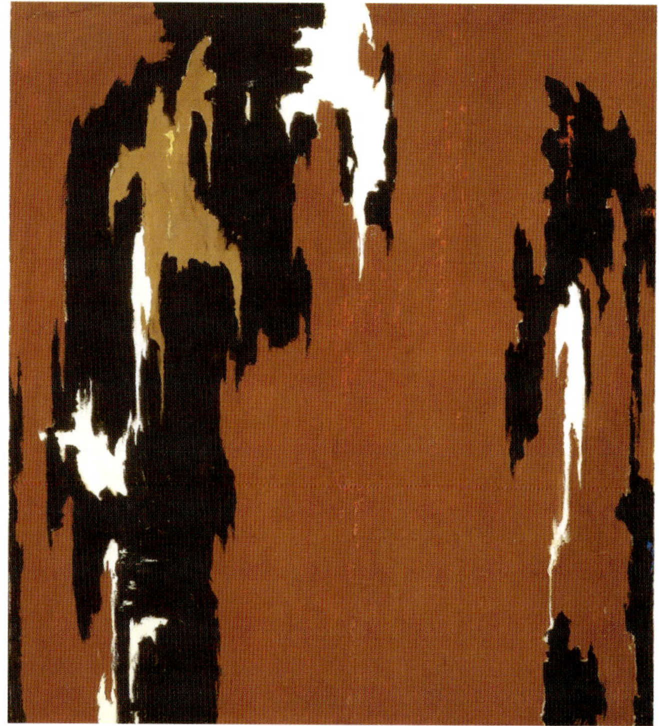

Clyfford Still
(Grandin 1904 - Baltimore 1980)

1954
●●

1954
288,3 x 396,2 cm / 113.5 x 156 in.
Albright-Knox Art Gallery, Buffalo

oil on canvas
Öl auf Leinwand
olieverf op doek
óleo sobre lienzo

Mark Tobey
(Centerville 1890 - Basel 1976)

**Washington
(United States Series)
(Serie Vereinigte Staaten)
(Serie Verenigde Staten)
(Serie Estados Unidos)**

●●

1946
60,9 x 55,7 cm / 23.9 x 21.9 in.
Smithsonian American Art
Museum, Washington DC

gouache on paper
Gouache auf Papier
gouache op papier
gouache sobre papel

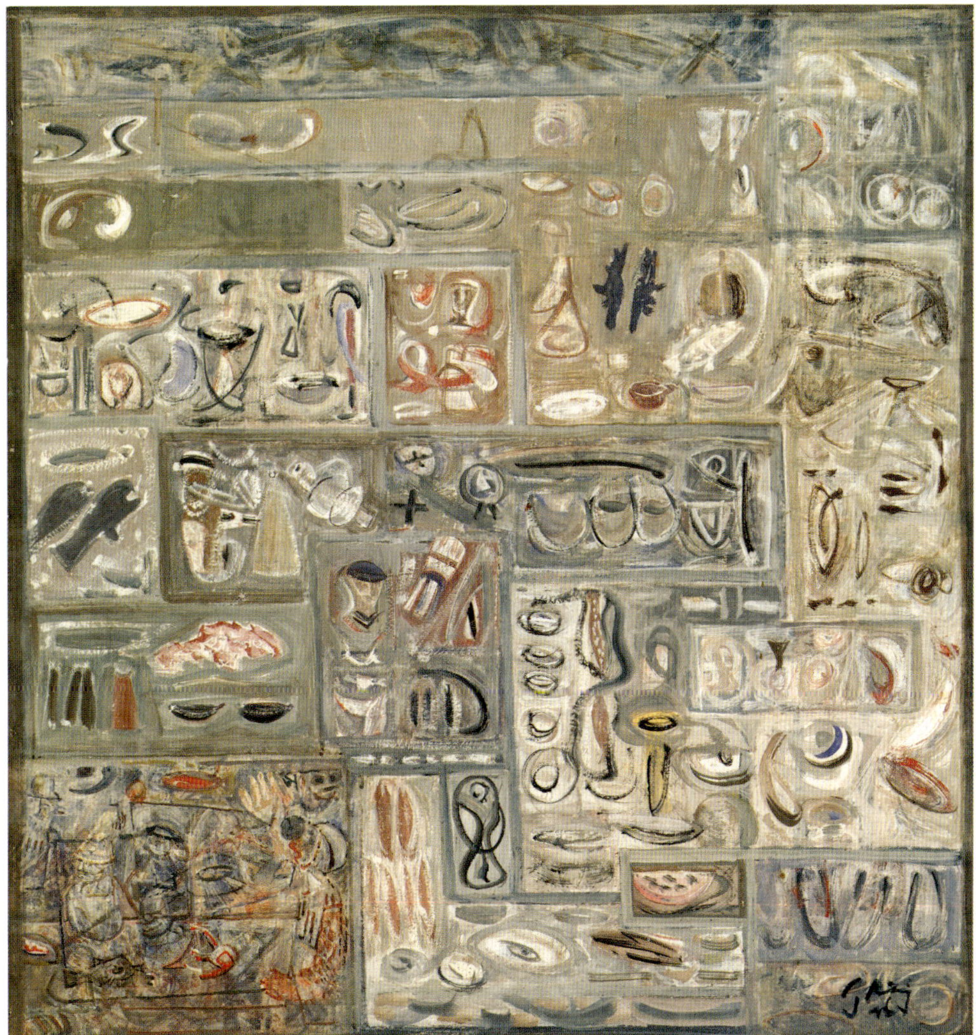

Barnett Newman
(New York 1905 - 1970)

Abraham

1949
210,2 x 87,7 cm
82.7 x 34.5 in.
Museum of Modern Art (MoMA),
New York

oil on canvas
Öl auf Leinwand
olieverf op doek
óleo sobre lienzo

▶ Barnett Newman
(New York 1905 - 1970)

**Who is Afraid of Red,
Yellow and Blue IV
Wer hat Angst vor Rot,
Gelb und Blau IV
Wie is bang voor Rood,
Geel en Blauw IV
¿Quién teme al rojo, al
amarillo y al azul?**

1969-1970
274 x 603 cm / 107.8 x 237.4 in.
Nationalgalerie, Staatliche
Museen, Berlin

oil on canvas
Öl auf Leinwand
olieverf op doek
óleo sobre lienzo

▶ Yves Klein
(Nice 1928 - Paris 1962)

**Anthropometry without title (ANT 100)
Anthropometrie ohne Titel (ANT 100)
Antropometrie zonder titel (ANT 100)
Antropometría sin título (ANT 100)**

1960
145 x 298 cm / 57.1 x 117.3 in.
Hirshhorn Museum, Washington DC

paint and synthetic resin on paper mounted on canvas
Lack und Kunstharz auf Papier, auf Leinwand angebracht
vernis en kunsthars op papier gemonteerd op doek
pintura y resina sintética sobre papel montado sobre lienzo

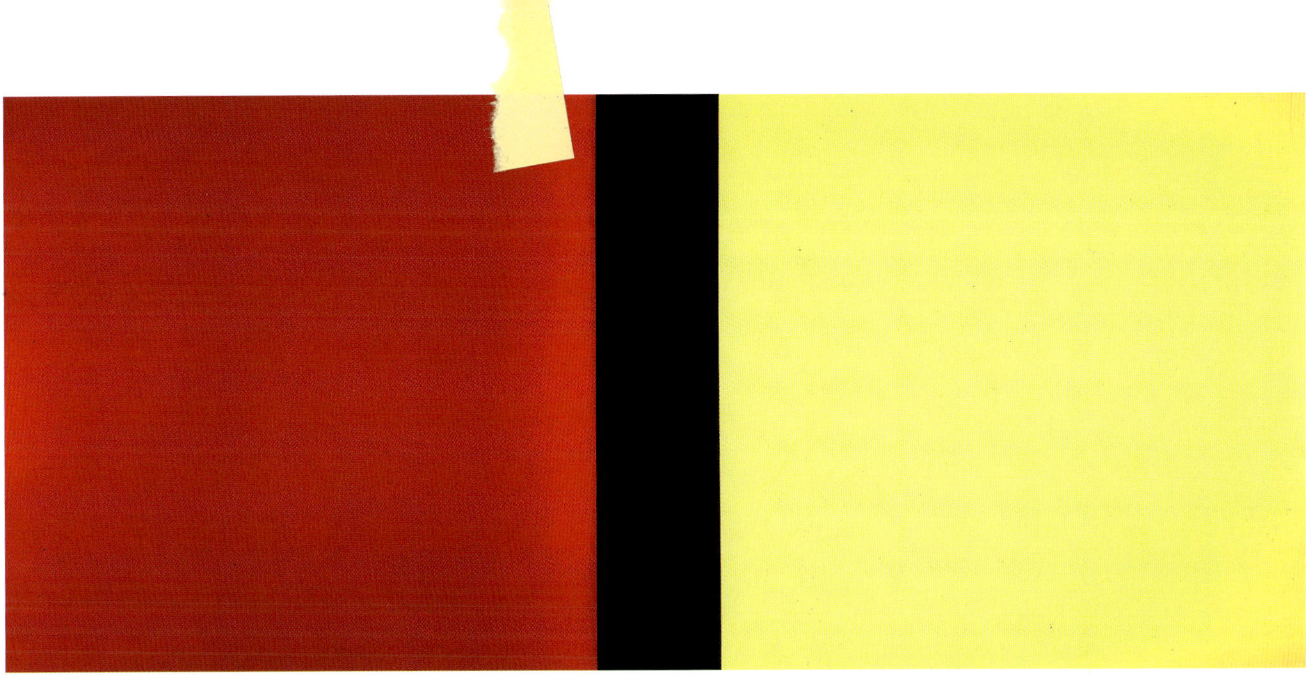

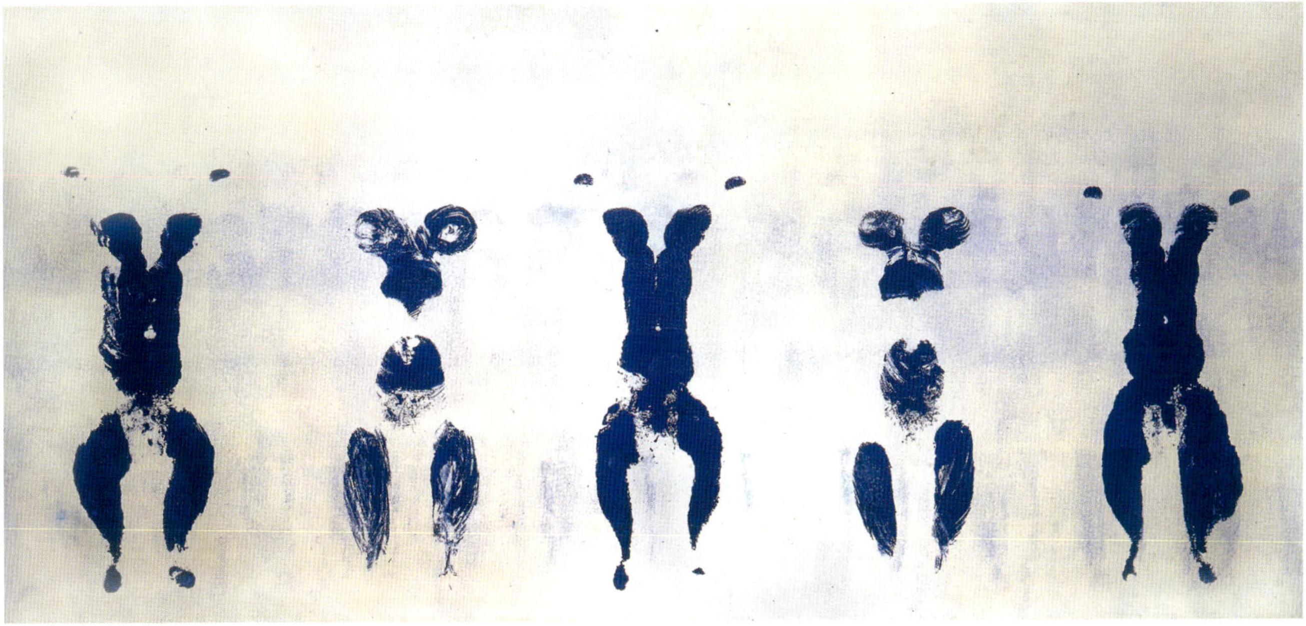

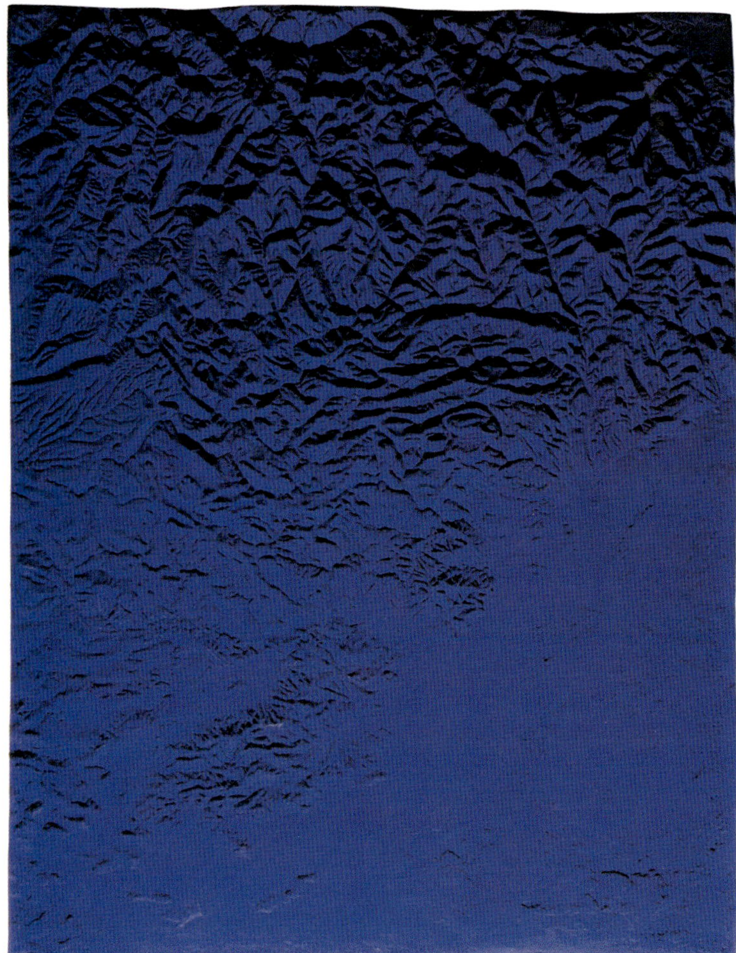

◀ Yves Klein
(Nice 1928 - Paris 1962)

RP 10 Region of Grenoble
RP 10 Region von Grenoble
RP 10 Regio van Grenoble
RP 10 Región de Grenoble

●●●

1961
86 x 65 cm / 33.8 x 25.6 in.
Private collection / Private Sammlung
Privécollectie / Colección privada

paint and synthetic resin on bronze / Lack und
Kunstharz auf Bronze / vernis en kunsthars
op brons / pintura y resina sintética sobre bronce

▶ Yves Klein
(Nice 1928 - Paris 1962)

Victory of Samothrace
Nike von Samothrake
Overwinning van Samothrake
Victoria de Samotracia

●●

1962
49,5 x 25,5 x 36 cm / 19.5 x 10 x 14.2 in.
Private collection / Private Sammlung
Privécollectie / Colección privada

pure pigment and synthetic resin on plaster mounted
on stone base / Reines Pigment und Kunstharz auf
Kreide, auf einer Steinbasis angebracht / puur pigment
en kunsthars op gips gemonteerd op een stenen basis
/ pigmento puro y resina sintética sobre yeso montado
sobre base en piedra

Klein patented the chemical formula of his blue with the name IKB (International Klein Blue).

Klein hat die chemische Formel seines Blaus mit dem Namen IKB (International Klein Blue) patentiert.

Klein heeft patent gekregen op de chemische formule van zijn blauw waar hij de naam I.K.B. (International Klein Blue) aan gaf.

Klein ha patentado la fórmula química de su color azul con la denominación IKB (International Klein Blue, *Azul Klein
Internacional*).

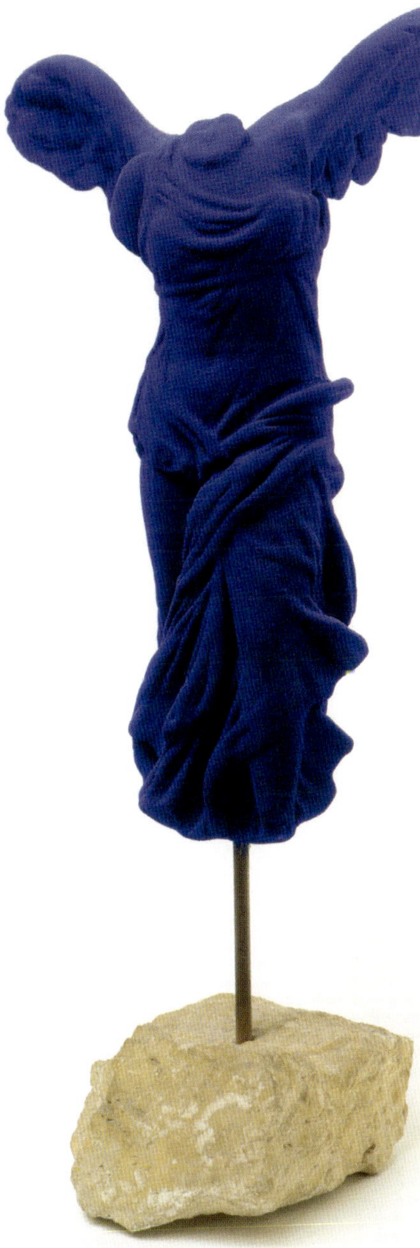

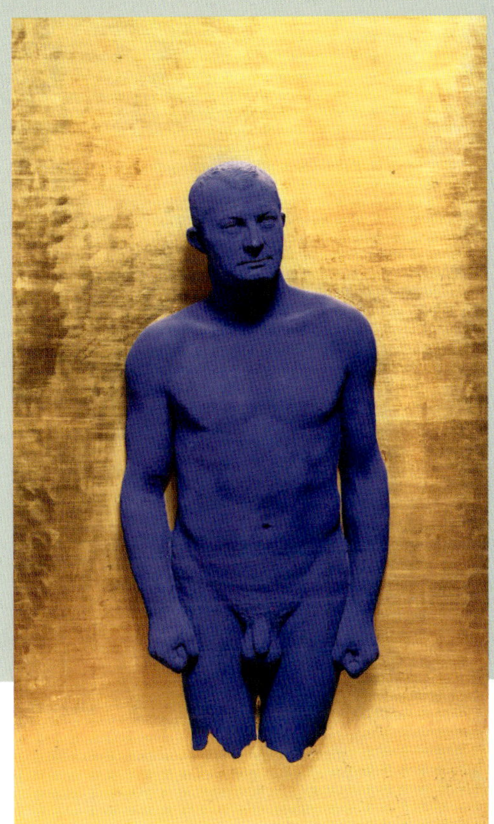

Yves Klein
(Nice 1928 - Paris 1962)

Relief Portrait I: Arman
Reliefporträt I: Arman
Reliëfportret I: Arman
Retrato en relieve I: Arman

●●

1962
175.3 x 94 cm / 69 x 37 in.
Philadelphia Museum of Art, Philadelphia

bronze painted on gilt panel
Bemalte Bronze auf vergoldetem Brett.
brons op verguld paneel geverfd
bronce pintado sobre panel dorado

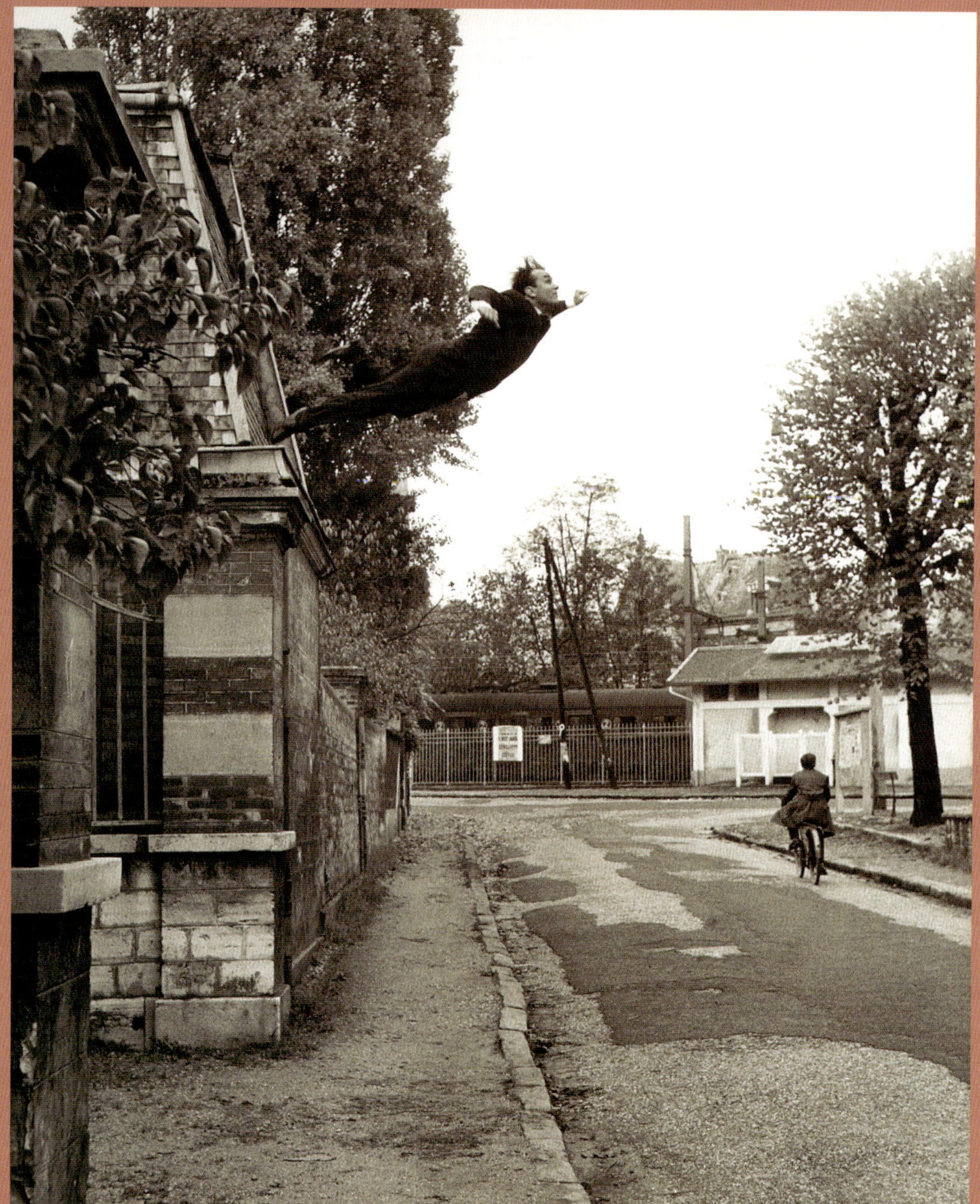

Yves Klein
(1928 - 1962)
Harry Shunk
(1924 - 2006)
John Kender
(1937 - 1983)
**Leap into the void
Der Sprung in die
Leere
Sprong in de leegte
Salto al vacío**
● ●
1960
25,9 x 20 cm / 10.2 x 7.9 in.
Metropolitan Museum
of Art, New York

silver gelatin print
Silbergelatinedruck
gelatine-zilverprint
impresión en gelatina
de plata

468

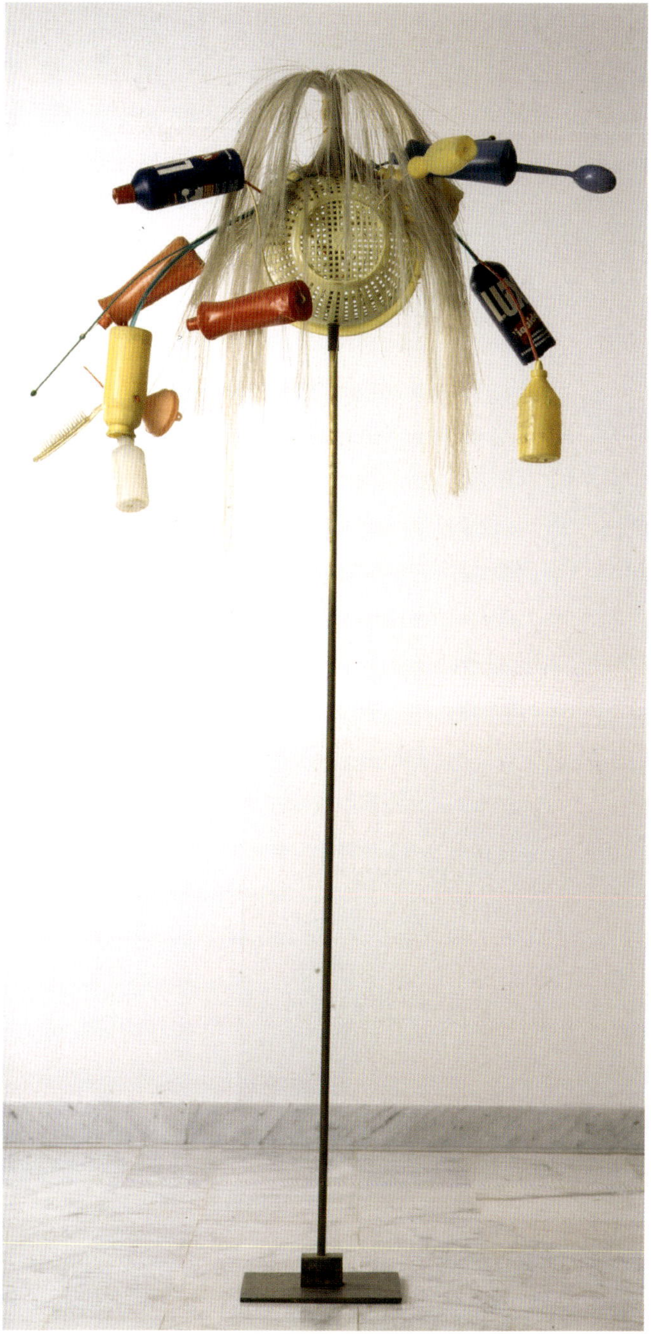

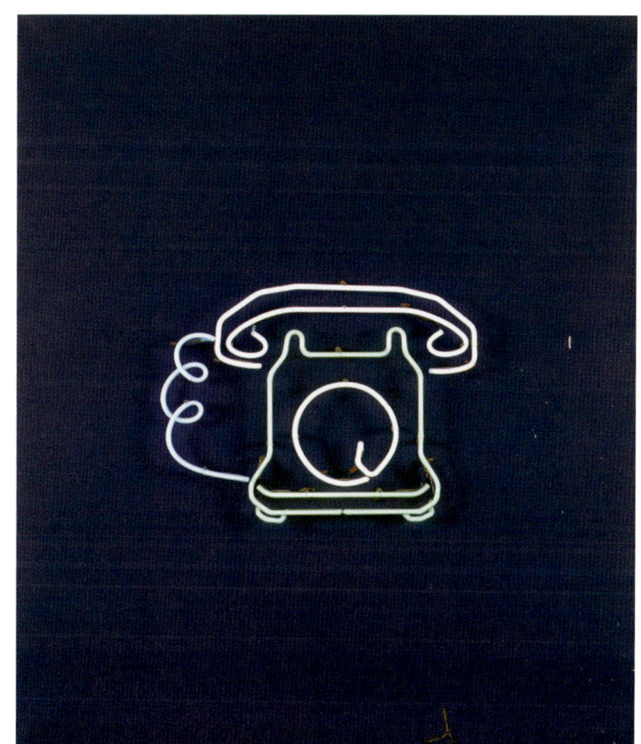

Martial Raysse
(Golfe-Juan 1936)

**High Tension
Hochspannung
Hoogspanning
Alta tensión**

●

1964

Martial Raysse
(Golfe-Juan 1936)

**Bird
Vogel
Pájaro**

●●●

Musée d'Art Contemporain,
Marseille

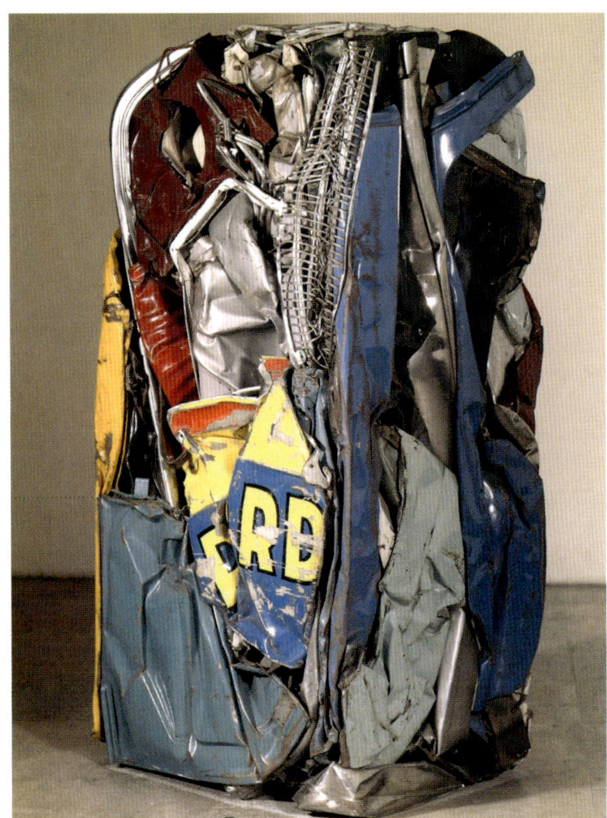

César
(Marseille 1921 - Paris 1998)
Compression
Kompression
Compressie
Compresión
●●●
1962
153 x 73 x 65 cm / 60.3 x 28.7 x 25.6 in.
Centre Georges Pompidou, Musée National d'Art Moderne, Paris

compressed automobile. Painted metal sheet
Komprimiertes Auto. Bemaltes Metallblatt
platgewalste auto. Beschilderd metaalblad
coche comprimido. Hoja metálica pintada

César
(Marseille 1921 - Paris 1998)
Yellow naxos met - FI594A
Gelb naxos met - FI594A
Gele naxos met - FI594A
Amarillo naxos met - FI594A
●●
1998
161 x 81 x 80 cm / 63.4 x 31.9 x 31.5 in.
Private collection / Private Sammlung
Privécollectie / Colección privada

Fiat Marea compressed / Fiat Marea gepresst
platgewalste Fiat Marea / Fiat Marea comprimido

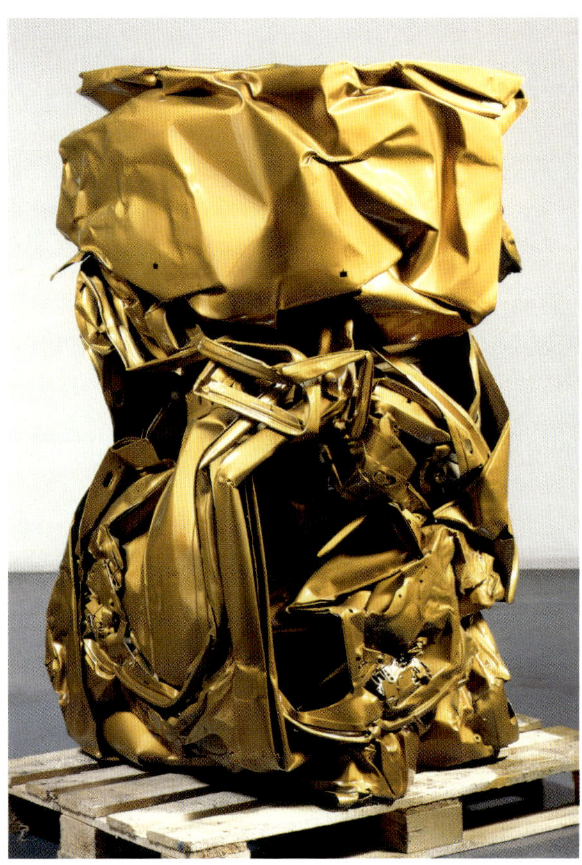

Raymond Hains
(Dinard 1926 - Paris 2005)

Seita

●

1970
98 x 80 x 25 cm
38.6 x 31.5 x 9.8 in.
Musée d'Art Moderne
et d'Art Contemporain, Nice

painted wood
Bemaltes Holz
beschilderd hout
madera pintada

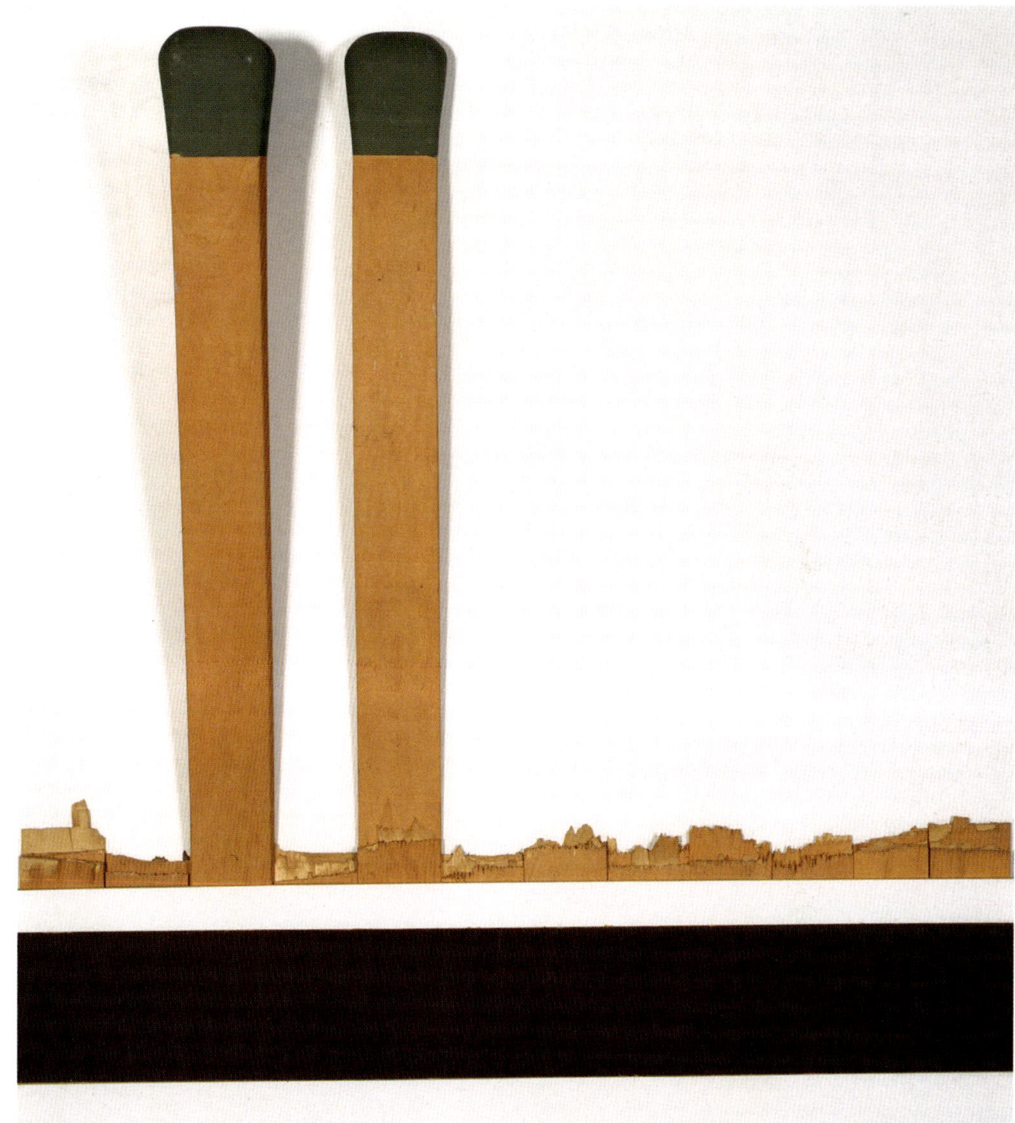

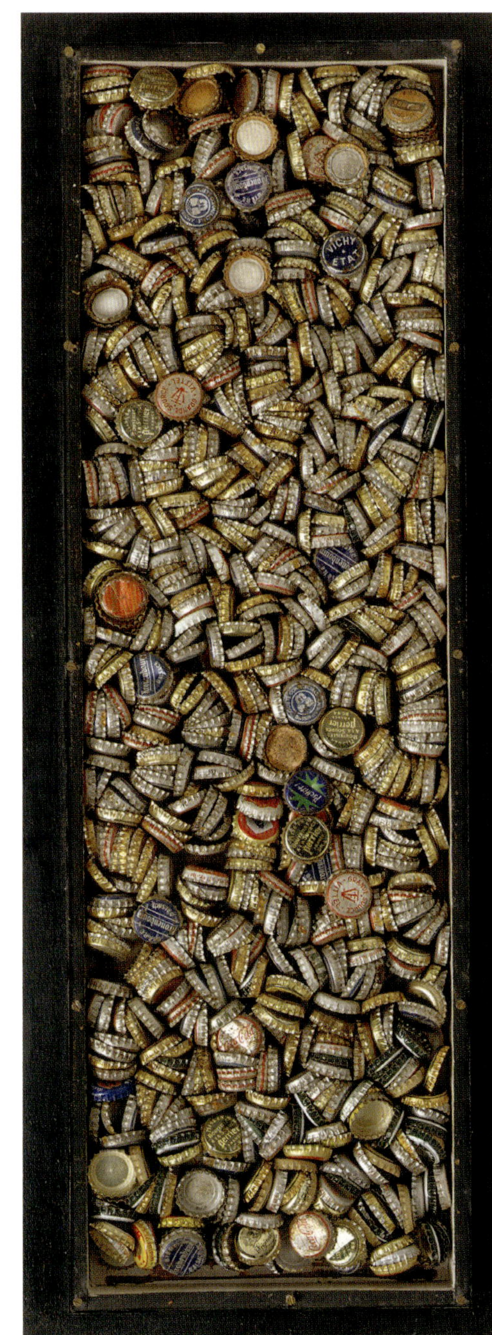

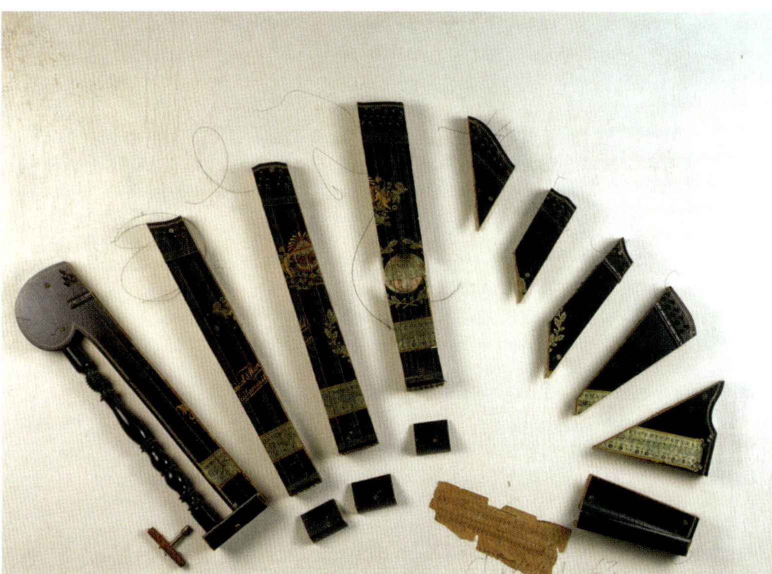

Arman
(Nice 1928 - Paris 2005)

O Tannenbaum

●

1963
Musée d'art, Toulon

Arman
(Nice 1928 - Paris 2005)

Bebida Loca

● ●

1960
80 x 30 x 6 cm / 31.5 x 11.8 x 2.3 in.
Private collection / Private Sammlung
Privécollectie / Colección privada

accumulation of bottle caps in a
wood and plexiglas container
Ansammlung von Kronkorken in
einem Behälter aus Holz und Plexigas
verzameling flessendoppen in een
doos van hout en plexiglas
acumulación de tapitas de botellas en
un contenedor de madera y plexiglás

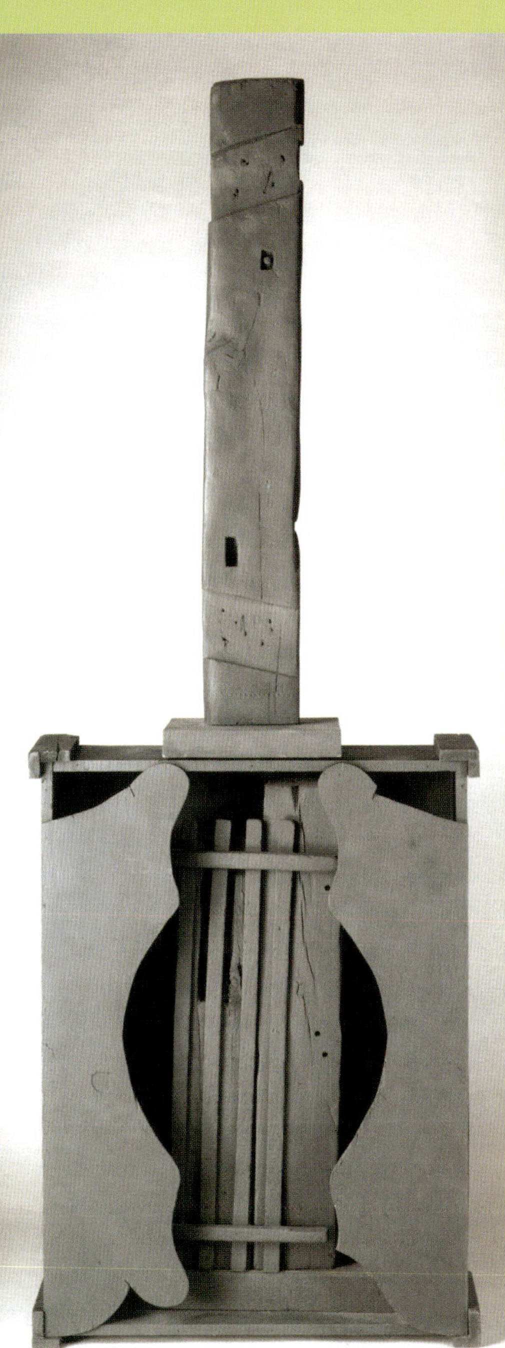

Louise Nevelson
(Kiev 1899 - New York 1988)

Classic column
Klassische Säule
Klassieke zuil
Columna clásica

●

1967
106,7 x 76,2 x 22,9 cm / 42 x 30 x 9 in.
The Jewish Museum, New York

painted wood / Bemaltes Holz
beschilderd hout / madera pintada

Louise Nevelson
(Kiev 1899 - New York 1988)

Constructing a Legend
Konstruktion einer Legende
Een legende bouwen
Construyendo una leyenda

●●●

1959
The Jewish Museum, New York

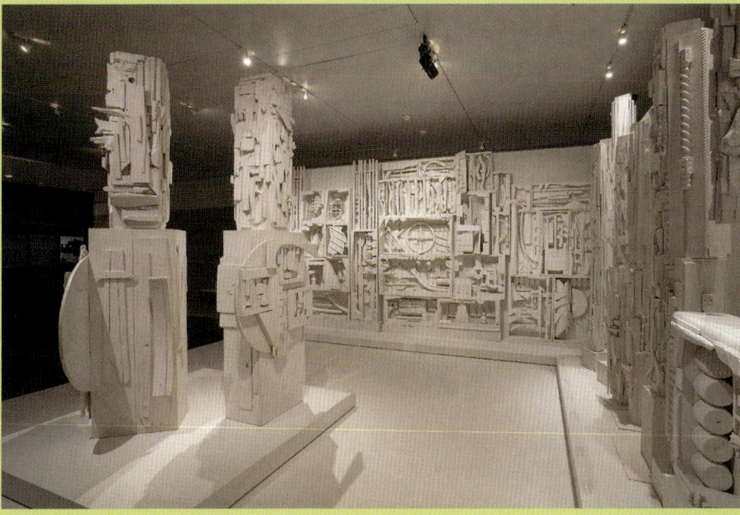

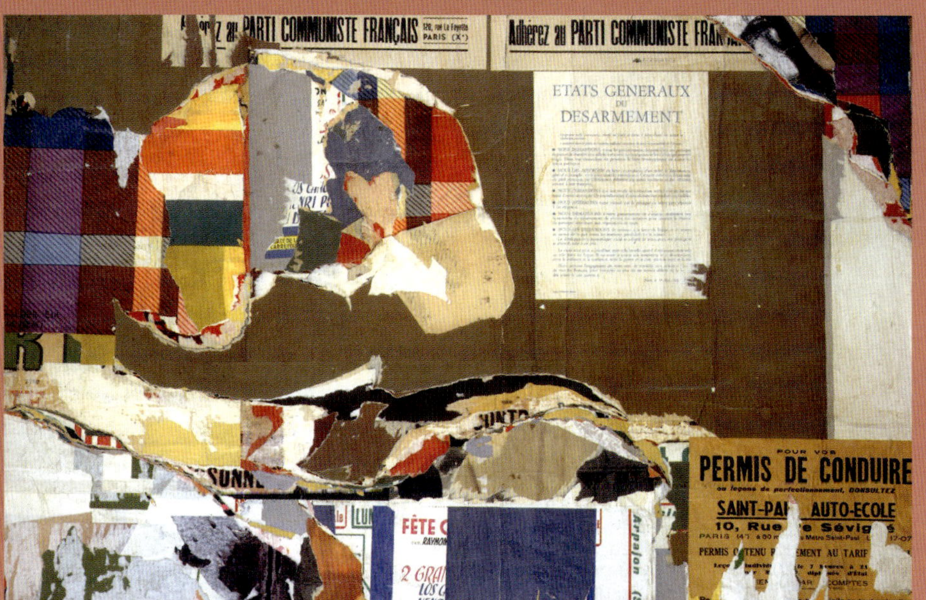

Jacques Mahe de la Villeglé
(Quimper, Brittany 1926)

Rue des Etuves Saint-Martin

●●●

1963
104 x 154 cm / 40.9 x 60.6 in.

collage of slashed posters rolled
on to canvas
Collage von Posterfragmenten
auf Leinwand
collage gescheurde en
gemaroufleerde affiches op doek
collage de carteles rasgados encolados
sobre lienzo

Jacques Mahe de la Villeglé
(Quimper, Brittany 1926)

**Accademia bridge, Venice
Accademia-Brücke Venedig
Ponte dell'Accademia Venetië
Puente de la Academia, Venecia**

●●●

1970
16 x 26 cm / 6.3 x 10.2 in.

collage of slashed posters
Collage aus Posterfragmenten
collage gescheurde affiches
collage de carteles rasgados

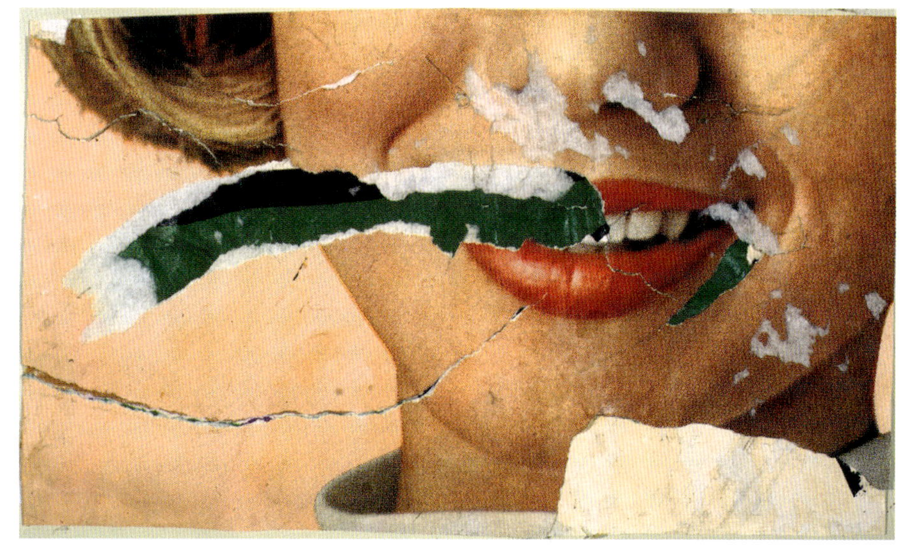

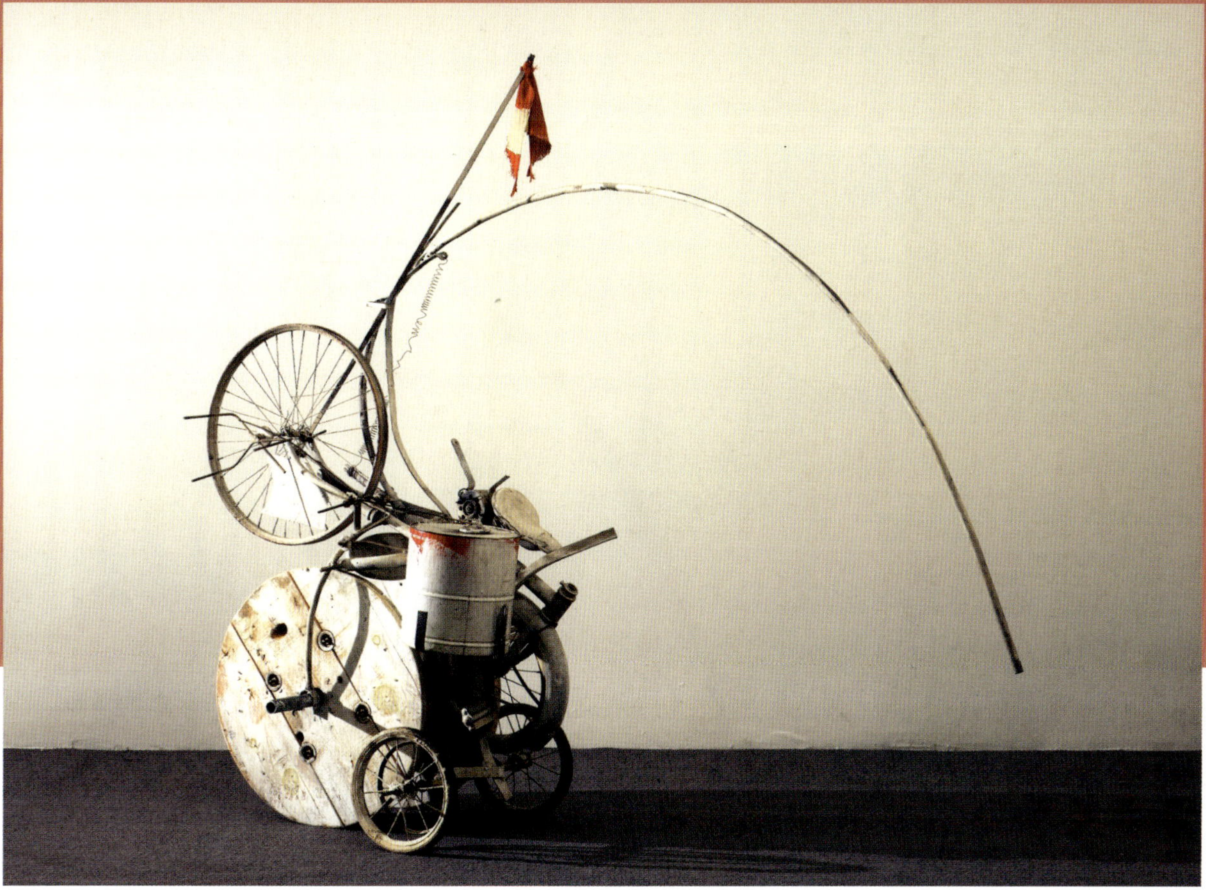

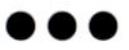

Jean Tinguely
(Fribourg 1925 - Bern 1991)

Fragment from "Tribute to New York"
Fragment der "Homage à New York"
Fragment uit "Hulde aan New York"
Fragmento de "Homenaje a Nueva York"

●●●

1960
203,7 x 75,1 x 223,2 cm / 80.2 x 29.5 x 87.8 in.
Museum of Modern Art (MoMA), New York

painted metal, wood, and cloth / Bemaltes Metall, Holz, Kleidung
geschilderd metaal, hout, stof / metal, madera y tela pintados

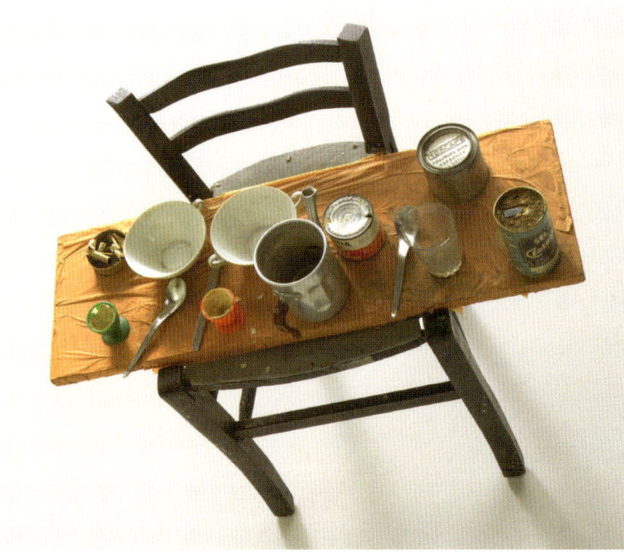

◀ Daniel Spoerri
(Galati 1930)

**Kichka's Breakfast I
Kichkas-Frühstück I
Kichka's ontbijt I
Desayuno de Kichka I**

●

1960
36,6 x 69,5 x 65,4 cm
14.4 x 27.3 x 25.7 in.
Museum of Modern Art (MoMA),
New York

assemblage
Montage
assemblage
ensamblaje

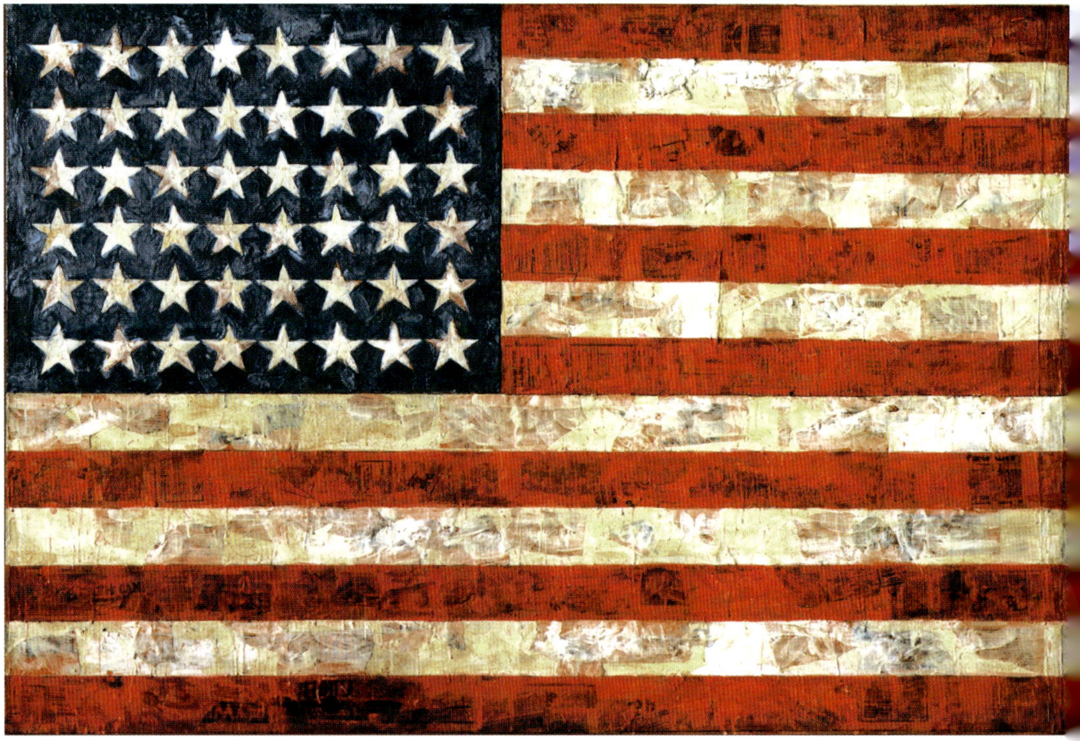

► **Robert Rauschenberg**
(Port Arthur 1925 - Captiva Island 2008)

Bed
Bett
Cama

●●●

1955
191,1 x 80 x 20,3 cm / 75.2 x 31.5 x 8 in.
Museum of Modern Art (MoMA),
New York

oil and pencil on cushion, quilt and sheet on
wooden support
Öl und Bleistift auf Kissen, Steppdecke und
Betttuch auf Holzunterlage
olieverf en potlood op kussen, deken en laken
op houten support
óleo y lápiz sobre almohada, colcha y sábanas
sobre soporte de madera

◄ **Jasper Johns**
(Augusta, Georgia 1930)

Flag
Flagge
Vlag
Bandera

●●●

1954
107,3 x 153,8 cm / 42.2 x 60.5 in.
Museum of Modern Art (MoMA),
New York

encaustic, oil and collage on fabric mounted
on plywood
Wachsmalerei, Öl und Collage auf Stoff, auf
Sperrholz angebracht
encaustiek, olieverf en collage op stof
gemonteerd op multiplex
encáustica, óleo y collage sobre tela montada
sobre aglomerado

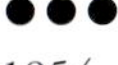

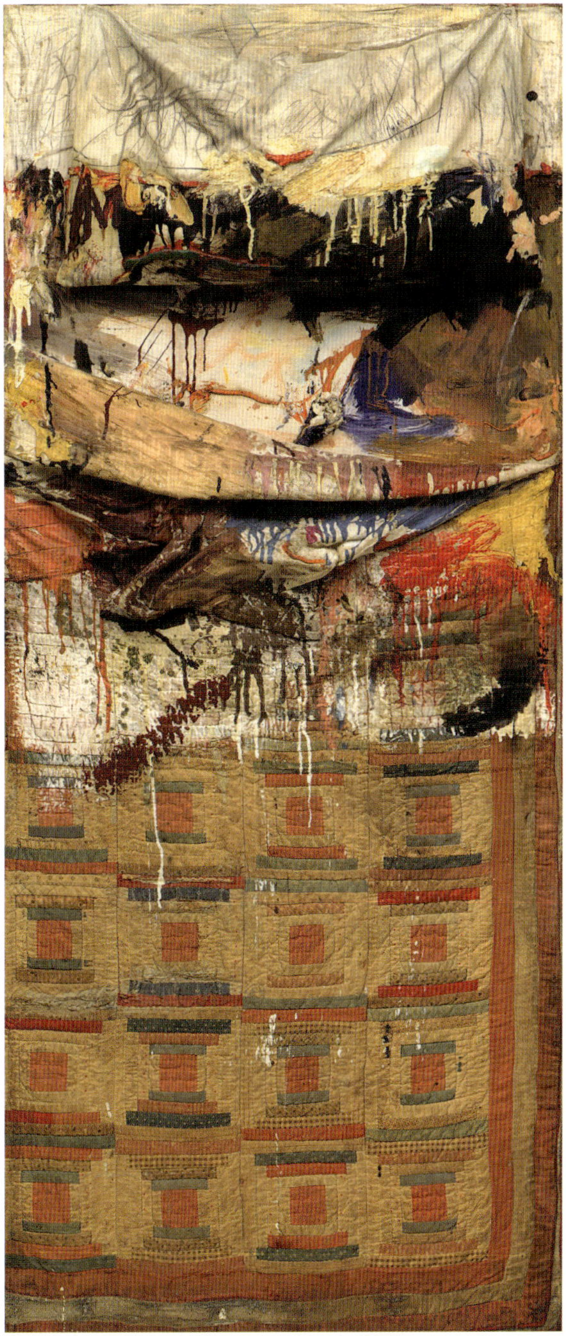

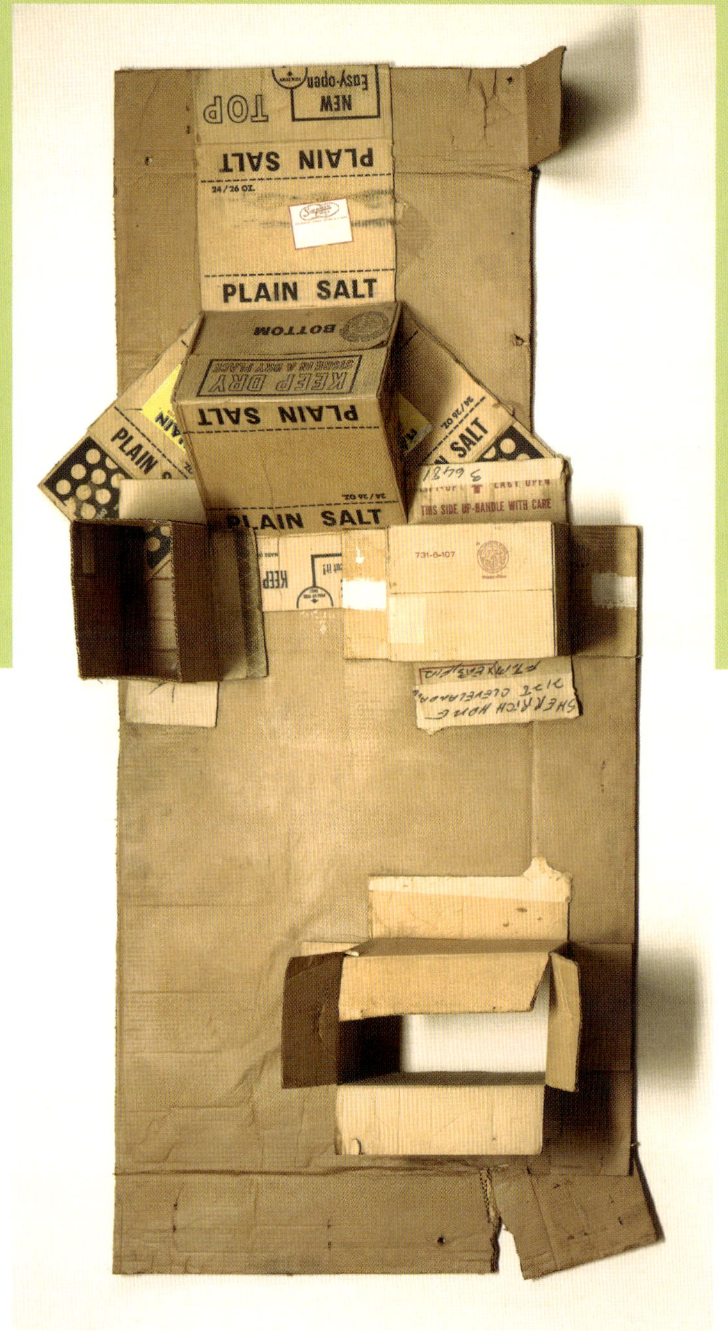

Robert Rauschenberg
(Port Arthur 1925 - Captiva Island 2008)

Plain Salt (Cardboards)
Feines Salz (Karton)
Fijn zout (karton)
Sal común (cartones)
●●

1971
204,5 x 94 x 26,7 cm
80.5 x 37 x 10.5 in.
Museum of Fine Arts, Boston

cardboard and plywoo
Karton und Sperrholz
karton en multiplex
cartón y madera aglomerada

▶ Richard Hamilton
(London 1922)

Interior
Interieur
Interior
●●

1964
56 x 69,7 cm / 22 x 27.4 in.
Museum of Modern Art
(MoMA), New York

serigraphy
Siebdruck
zeefdruk
serigrafía

Jim Dine
(Cincinnati 1935)

Five Feet of Colored Equipment
Fünf Füße aus gefärbten Geräten
Vijf voet gekleurd gereedschap
Cinco pies de herramientas coloreadas

●

1962
141,2 x 152,9 x11 cm / 55.6 x 60.2 x 4.3 in.
Museum of Modern Art (MoMA), New York

oil on unprimed canvas surmounted by a board on which painted tools hang from hooks / Öl auf nicht grundierter Leinwand mit einer Tafel, an der bemalte Geräte hängen / olieverf op een niet-gegrondverfd doek overdekt met een paneel waaraan geverfd gereedschap aan haken hangt / óleo sobre lienzo no imprimado, sobre el cual se encuentra una tabla con ganchos de los que cuelgan distintas herramientas pintadas

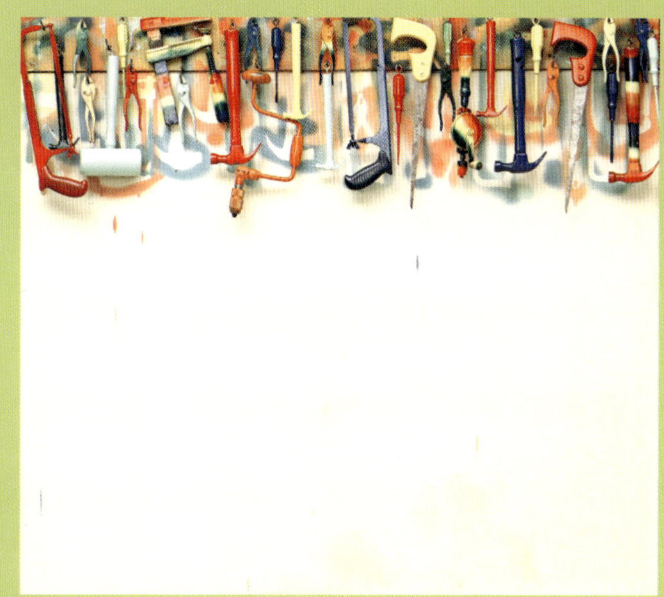

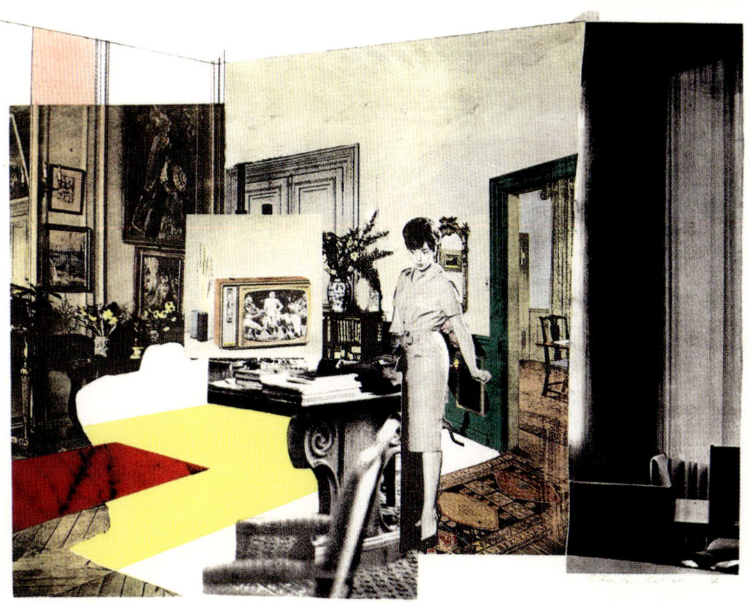

A new source of inspiration for artists: mass culture with its stereotyped magazine-type photos.

Eine neue Inspirationsquelle für Künstler: die Massenkultur mit ihren stereotypen Zeitschriftenfotografien.

Een nieuwe inspiratiebron voor kunstenaars: de massacultuur met stereotype foto's uit een tijdschrift.

Una nueva fuente de inspiración para los artistas: la cultura de masas con sus fotografías estereotipadas de revista.

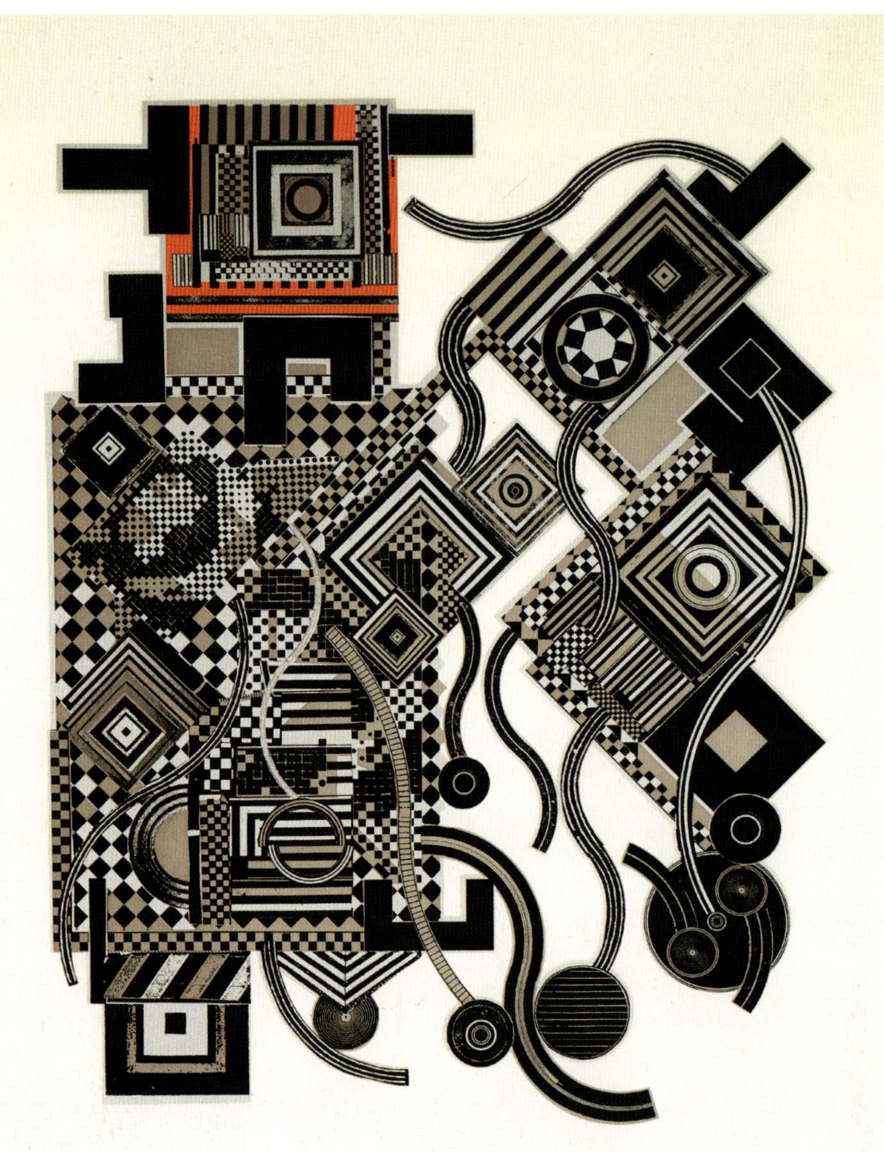

Eduardo Paolozzi
(Leith 1924 - London 2005)

Tormented Life (panel, sheet 5) from the illustrated book 'As Is When'
Geplagtes Leben (Tafel, Blatt 5) aus dem illustrierten Buch 'As Is When'
Bewogen leven (paneel, blad 5) uit het geïllustreerde boek 'As is When'
Vida atormentada (tabla, hoja 5) del libro ilustrado 'As Is When'

●●

1965
96,3 x 65,8 cm / 37.9 x 25.9 in.
Museum of Modern Art (MoMA),
New York

color serigraphy
Farbsiebdruck.
kleurenzeefdruk
serigrafía a color

Ronald B. Kitaj
(Chagrin Falls 1932 - Los Angeles 2007)

**The Band of the Ohio
Die Ohio Gang
De Ohio gang
La banda de Ohio**

•

1964
183,1 x 183,5 cm / 72.1 x 72.3 in.
Museum of Modern Art (MoMA),
New York

oil and graphite on canvas
Öl und Graphit auf Leinwand
olieverf en grafiet op doek
óleo y grafito sobre lienzo

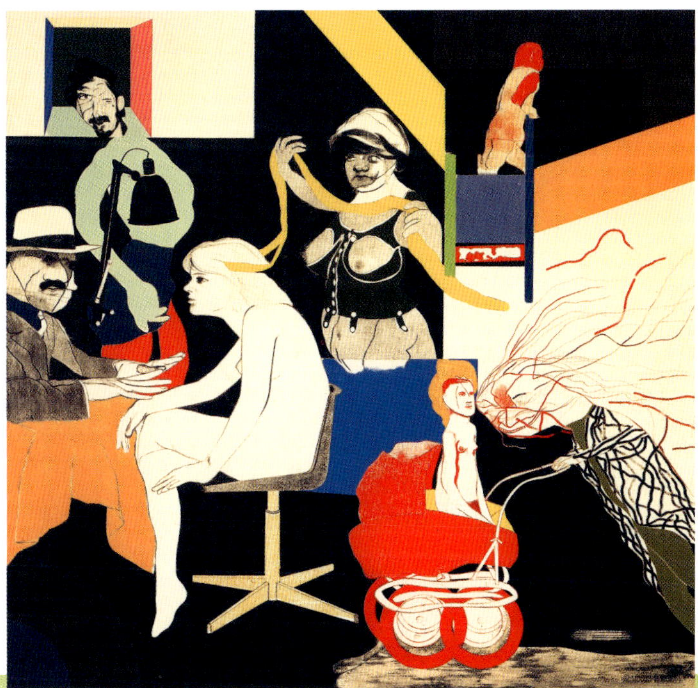

David Hockney
(Bradford 1937)

**Hollywood Garden
Hollywood Garten
Tuin in Hollywood
Jardín de Hollywood**

••

1966
183 x 183 cm / 72.1 x 72.1 in.
Hamburger Kunsthalle, Hamburg

acrylic on canvas
Akryl auf Leinwand
acrylverf op doek
acrílico sobre lienzo

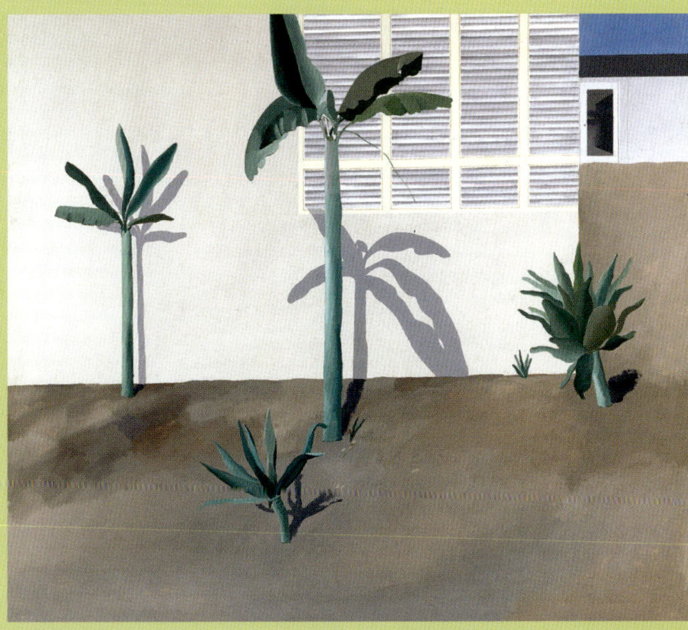

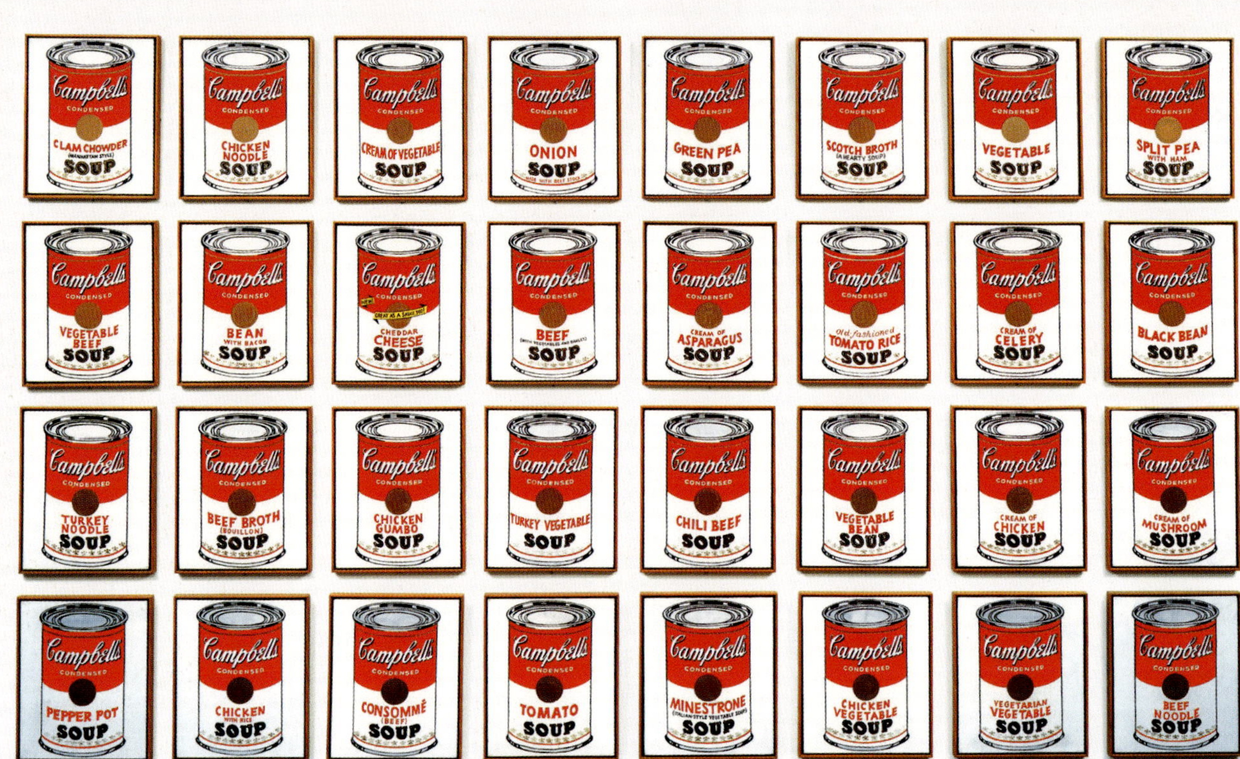

Andy Warhol
(Pittsburgh 1928 - New York 1987)

"Campbell's Soup" Tins
Dosen der "Campbell's Soup"
Blikken "Cambell's Soep"
Latas de Sopa Campbell's

●●●

1962
50,8 x 40,6 cm / 20 x 16 in.
Museum of Modern Art (MoMA), New York

acrylic on 32 canvases / Akryl auf 32 Leinwänden
acrylverf op 32 doeken / acrílico sobre 32 telas

Warhol confuses the tracks: serigraphy or *manual* painting? Sacredness of the consumer society or its critic?

Warhol bringt bewusst die Reihen durcheinander: Siebdruck oder *manuelle* Malerei? Entweihung der Konsumgesellschaft oder Kritik?

Warhol verwart de lijnen: zeefdruk of *handmatig* gemaakt schilderij? Heiligmaking van de consumptiemaatschappij of kritiek?

Warhol confunde los trazos: ¿serigrafía o pintura *manual*? ¿Sacralización de la sociedad de consumo o crítica de ésta?

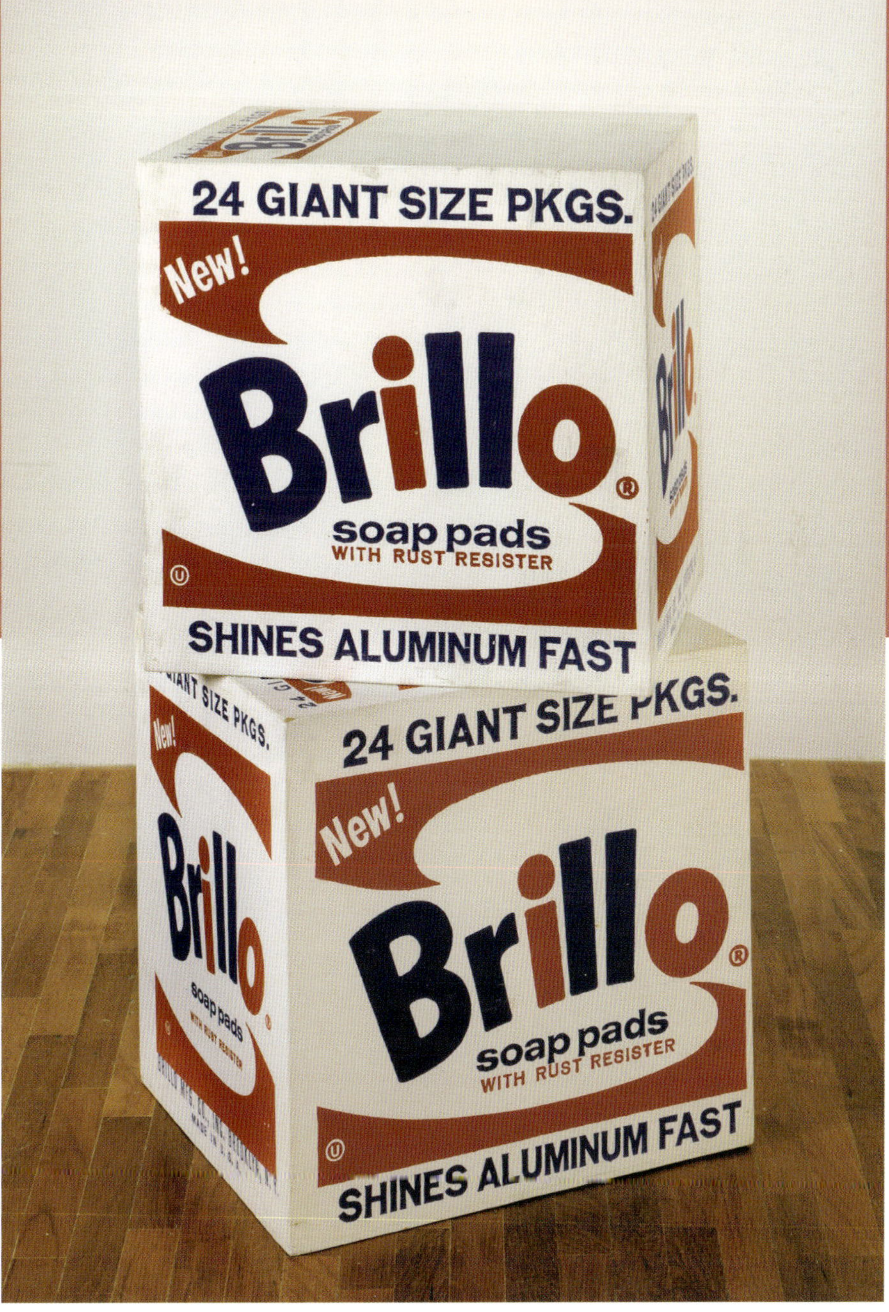

Andy Warhol
(Pittsburgh 1928 - New York 1987)
"Brillo" boxes
"Brillo"-Schachteln
"Brillo" dozen
Cajas "Brillo"
● ● ●
1964
43,5 x 43,2 x 36,5 cm
17.1 x 17 x 14.3 in.
Museum of Modern Art (MoMA),
New York

serigraphy on wood box
Siebdruck auf Holzschachtel
zeefdruk op houten doos
serigrafía sobre caja de madera

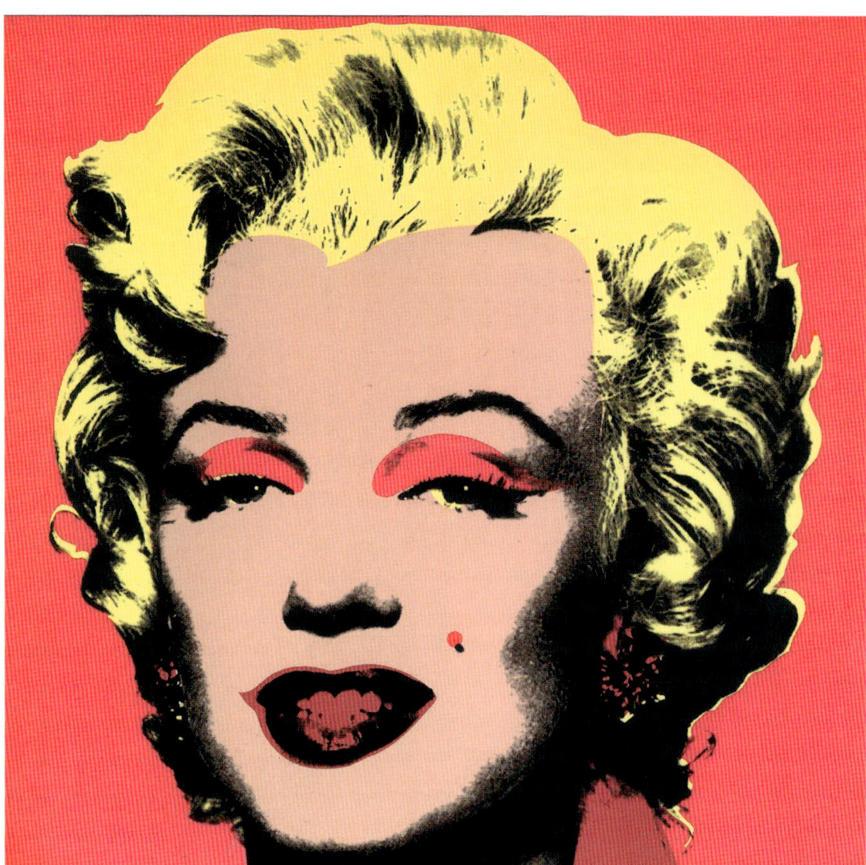

Andy Warhol
(Pittsburgh 1928 - New York 1987)

Marilyn
(pink, yellow)
(rosa, gelb)
(roze, geel)
(rosa, amarillo)

●●●

1964
91,4 x 91,4 cm / 36 x 36 in.
Kupferstichkabinett, Staatliche Museen, Berlin

color serigraphy / Farbsiebdruck
kleurenzeefdruk / serigrafía a color

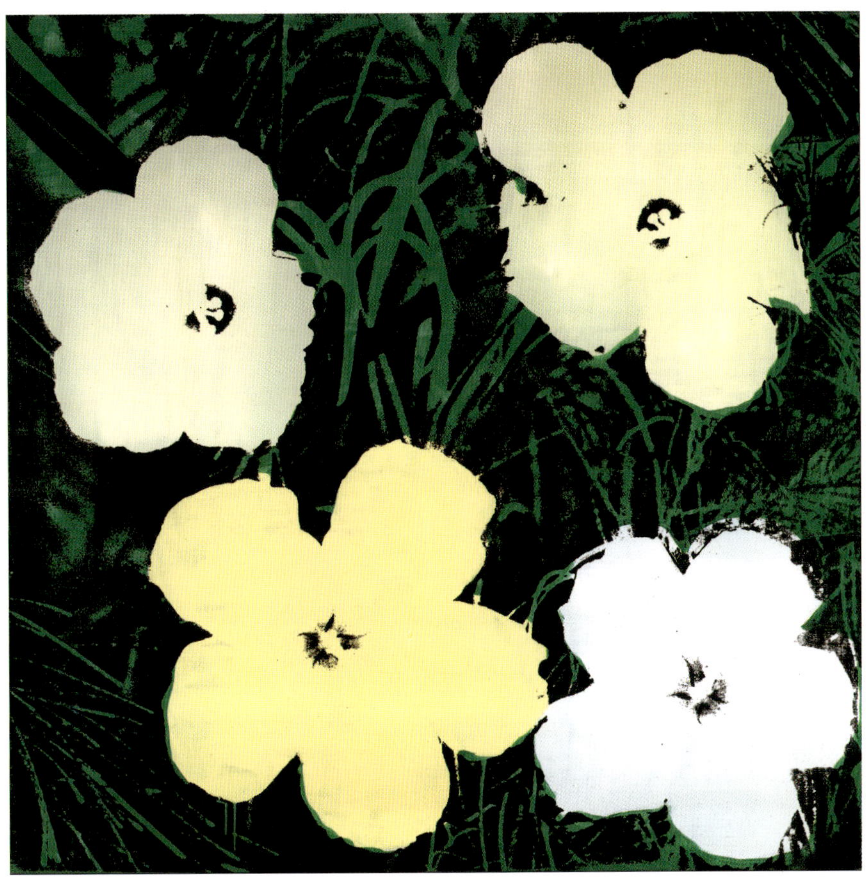

Andy Warhol
(Pittsburgh 1928 - New York 1987)

Flowers
Bloemen
Flores

●●●

1964
119,7 x 117,2 x 2,5 cm / 47.1 x 46.1 x 1 in.
Yale University Art Gallery, New Haven (CT)

serigraphy on canvas
Siebdruck auf Leinwand
zeefdruk op doek
serigrafía sobre lienzo

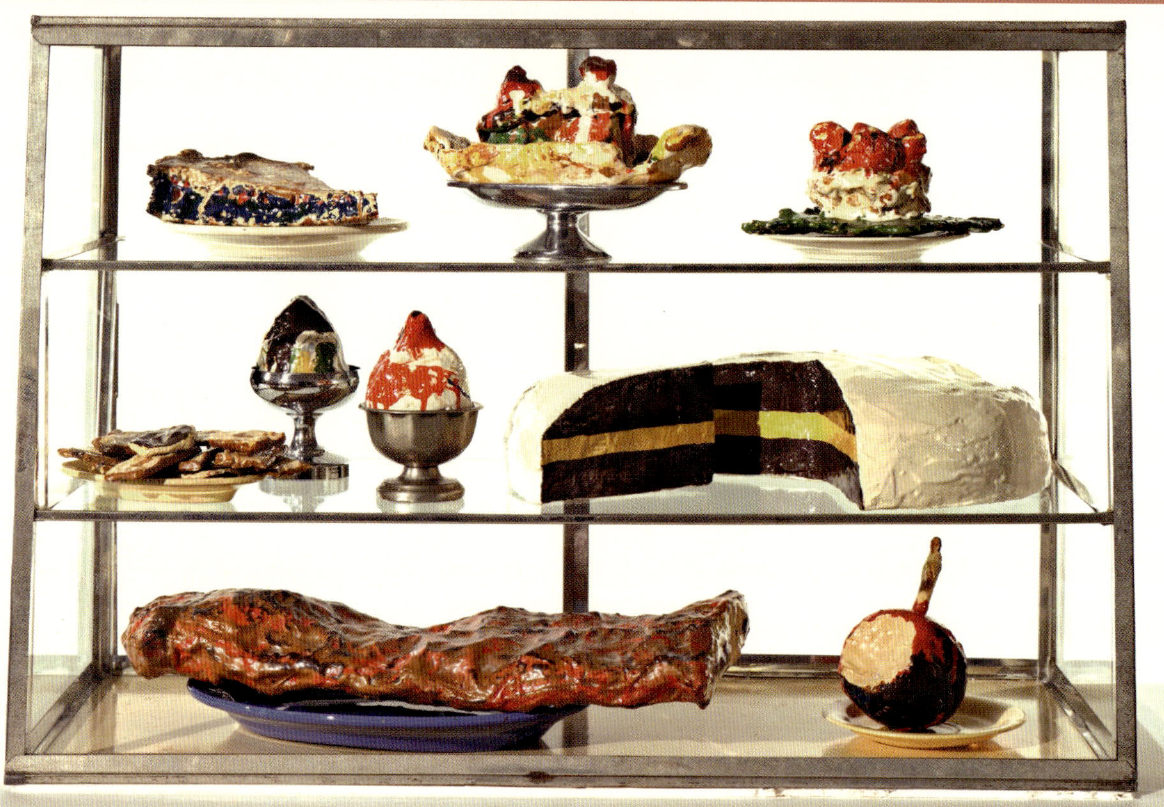

Claes Oldenburg
(Stockholm 1929)

Pastry Shop window I
Konditorei-Schaufenster I
Banketbakkersvitrine
Vitrina de pastelería I

●●

1961-1962
52,7 x 76,5 x 37,3 cm / 20.7 x 30.1 x 14.7 in.
Museum of Modern Art (MoMA), New York

cabinet of glass and wood, with nine scultpures in glazed plaster
Vitrine aus Glas und Holz, mit neun lackierten Skulpturen aus Kreide
glazen en houten vitrine, met negen sculpturen van geëmailleerd gips
vitrina de vidrio y madera, con nueve esculturas en yeso esmaltado

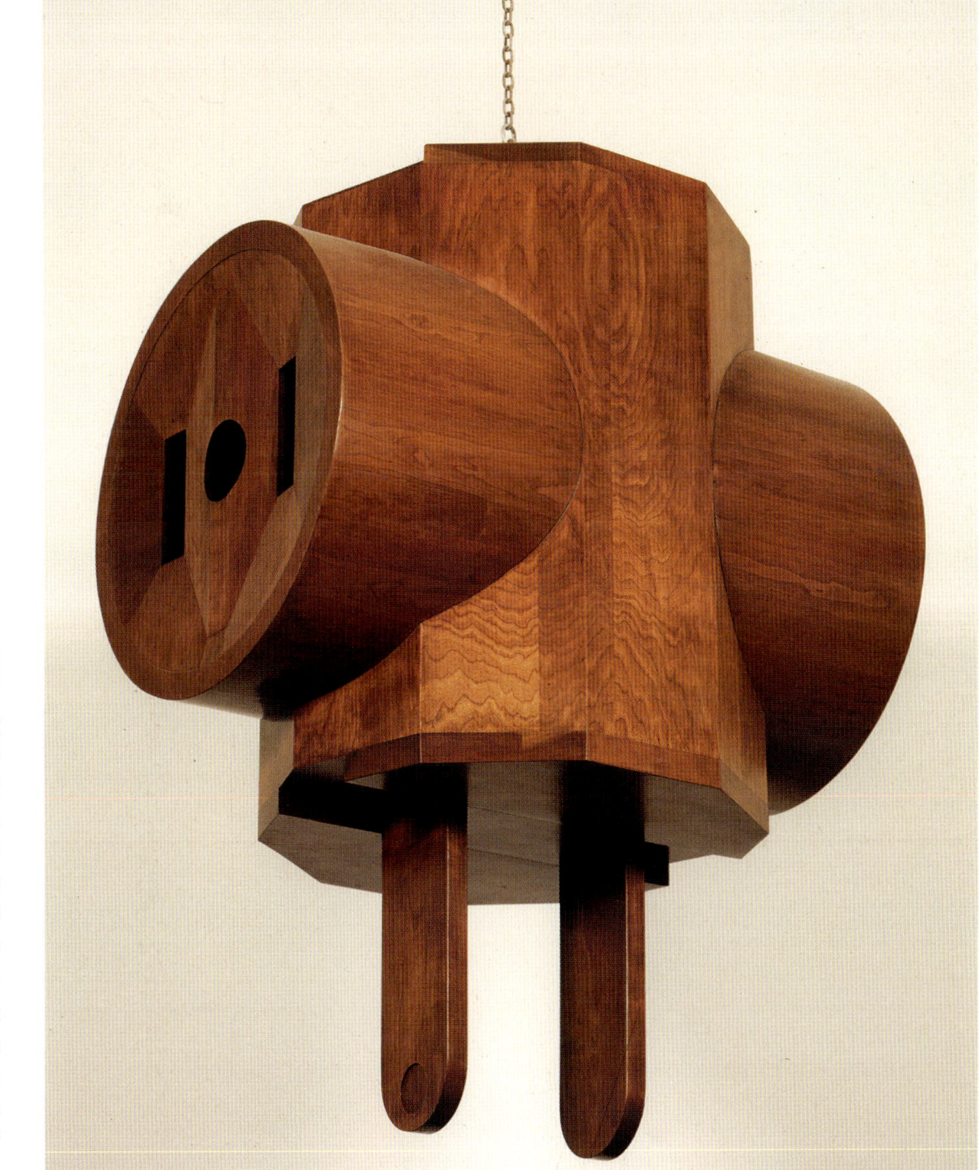

Claes Oldenburg
(Stockholm 1929)

**Giant electric Plug
with Three Holes
Elektrischer Riesenstecker
mit drei Löchern
Enorme stekker
met drie gaten
Enchufe eléctrico gigante
de tres agujeros**

●

1970
147,3 x 99,1 x 72,4 cm
58 x 39 x 28.5 in.
Philadelphia Museum of Art,
Philadelphia

wood of cherry tree / Kirschholz
kersenhout / madera de cerezo

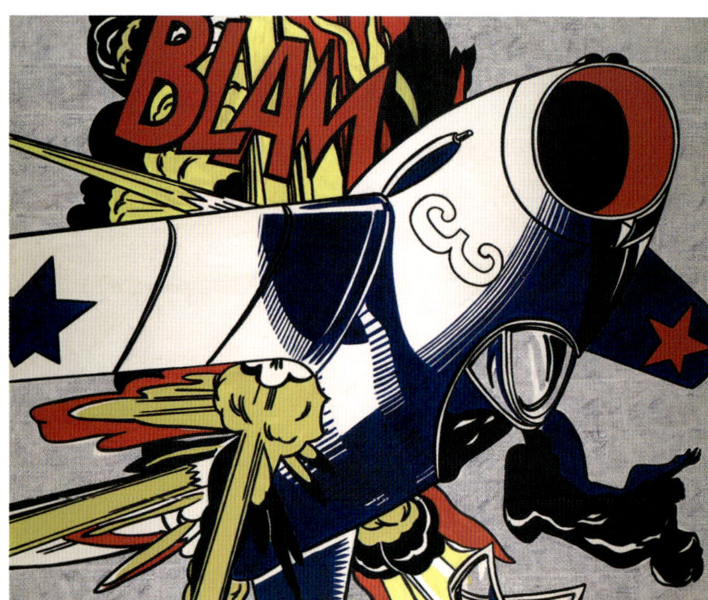

Roy Lichtenstein
(New York 1923 - 1997)

Blam

1962
172,7 x 203,2 cm / 68 x 80 in.
Yale University Art Gallery,
New Haven (CT)

oil on canvas / Öl auf Leinwand
olieverf op doek / óleo sobre lienzo

Roy Lichtenstein
(New York 1923 - 1997)

**Thinking of Him
Denken an ihn
Denkend aan hem
Pensando en él**

1963
172,7 x 173 cm / 68 x 68.1 in.
Yale University Art Gallery, New Haven (CT)

magna on canvas / Magna auf Leinwand
magnaverf op doek / acrílico sobre lienzo

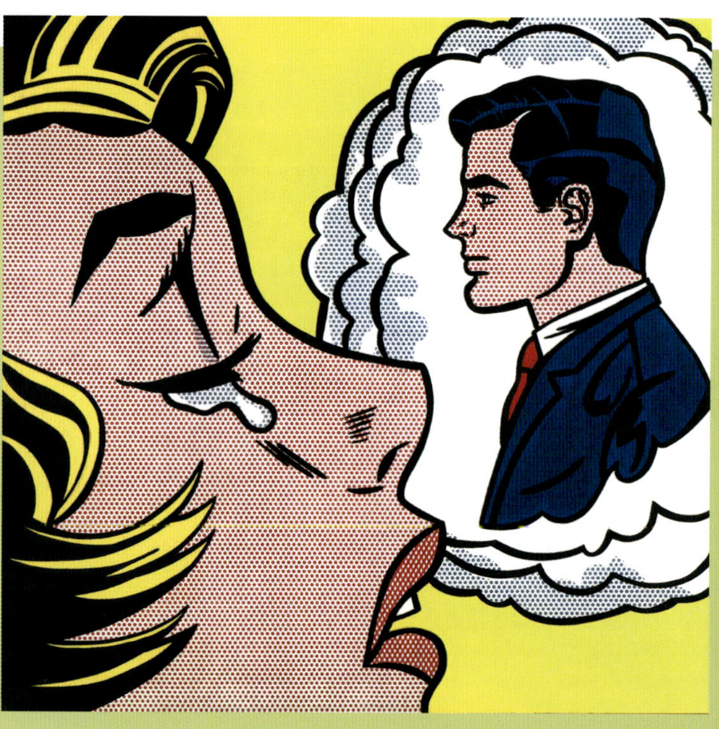

Robert Indiana
(New Castle, Indiana 1928)

**The Number Five
Die Ziffer fünf
Het cijfer vijf
El número 5**

●●●

1963
152,4 x 127 cm / 60 x 50 in.
Smithsonian American Art Museum,
Washington DC

oil on canvas
Öl auf Leinwand
olieverf op doek
óleo sobre lienzo

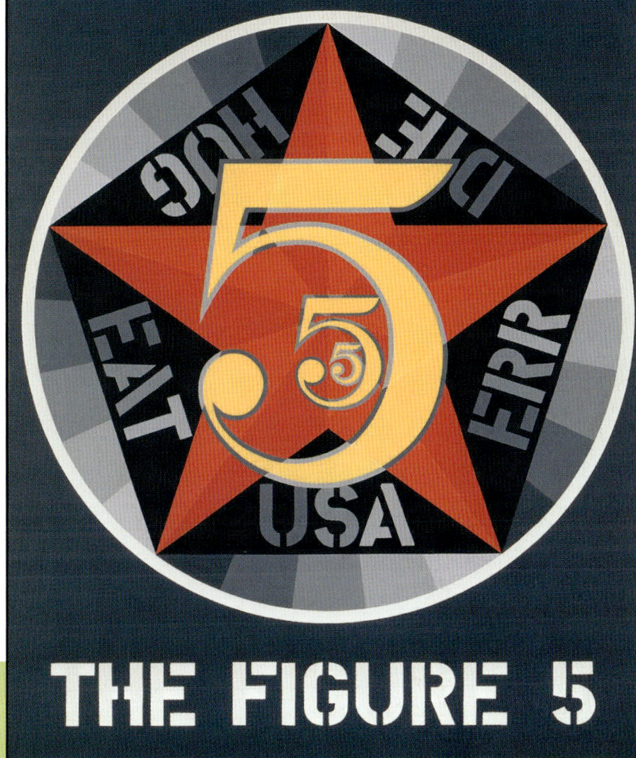

THE FIGURE 5

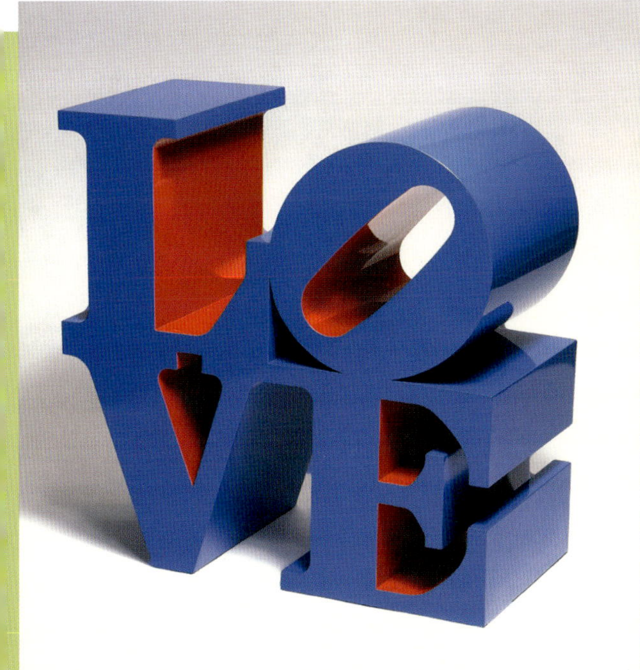

Robert Indiana
(New Castle, Indiana 1928)

LOVE

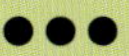
●●●

1966-1996
91,4 x 91,4 x 45,7 cm / 36 x 36 x 18 in.
Private collection / Private Sammlung
Privécollectie / Colección privada

colored aluminium
Farbiges Aluminium
gekleurd aluminium
aluminio pintado

James Rosenquist
(Green Forks, North Dakota, 1933)

Zone
Zona
●●
1961
241,3 x 242,6 cm / 95 x 95.5 in.
Philadelphia Museum of Art, Philadelphia

oil on two panels / Öl auf zwei Tafeln
olieverf op twee panelen / óleo sobre dos tablas

James Rosenquist
(Green Forks, North Dakota, 1933)

The friction disappears
Die Kupplung verschwindet
Die frictie verdwijnt
El embrague desaparece
●●●
1965
122,2 x 112,4 cm / 48.1 x 44.2 in.
Smithsonian American Art Museum, Washington DC

oil on canvas / Öl auf Leinwand
olieverf op doek / óleo sobre lienzo

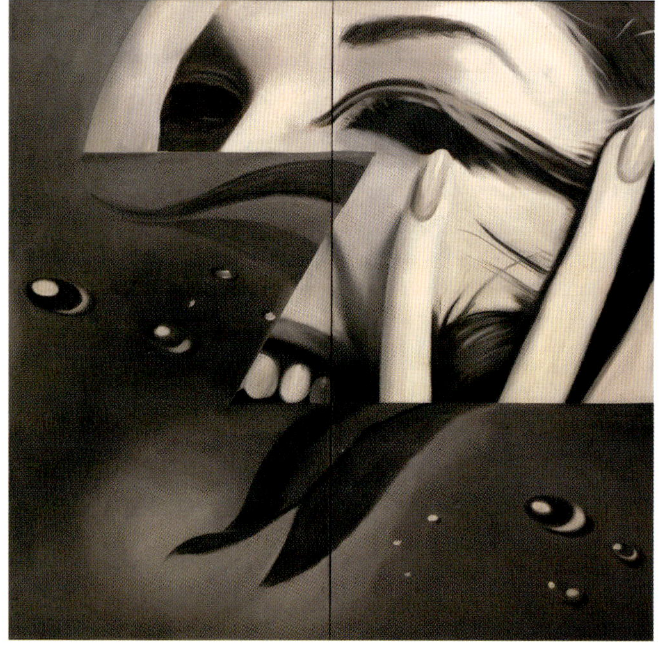

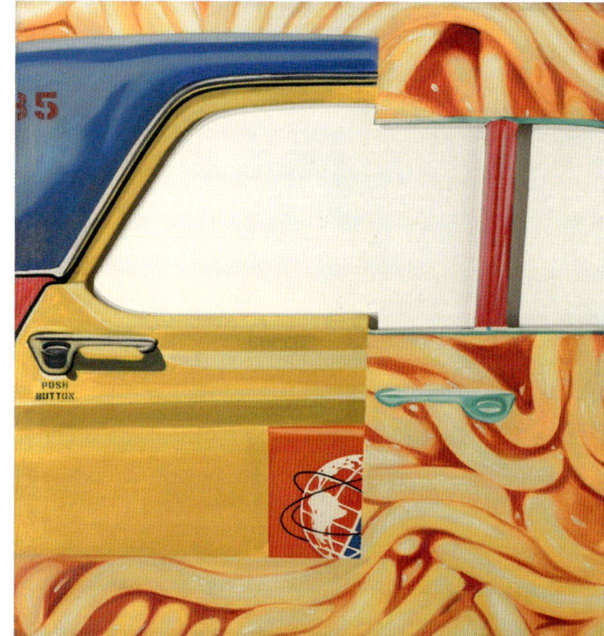

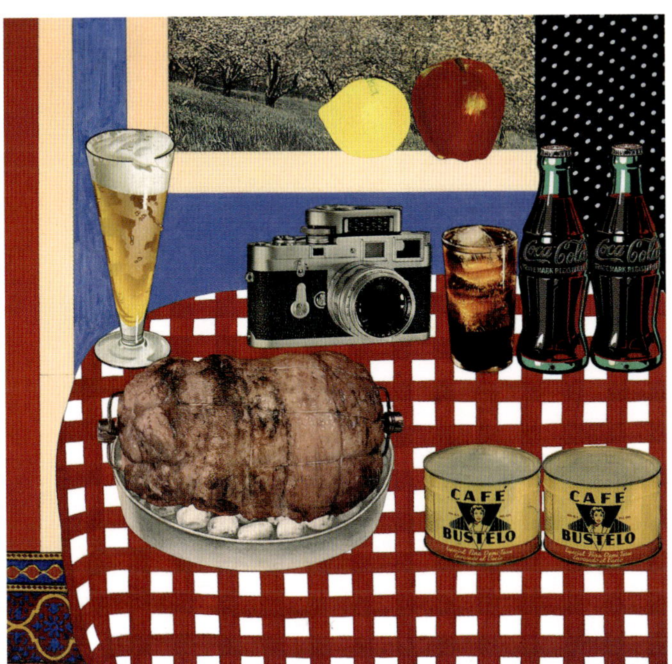

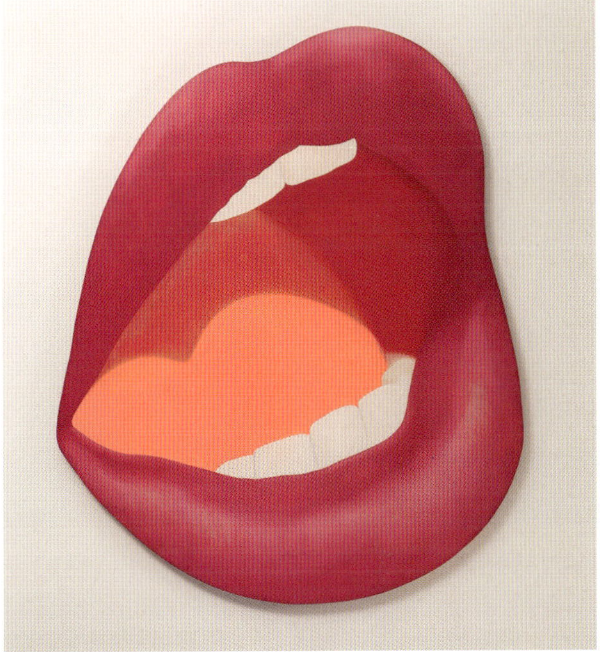

Tom Wesselmann
(Cincinnati 1931 - New York 2004)

Still Life #12
Stillleben #12
Stilleven #12
Naturaleza muerta #12

●●●

1962
121,9 x 121,9 cm / 48 x 48 in.
Smithsonian American Art Museum, Washington DC

acrylic and collage of fabric, photo copperplate
engraving, metal, etc., on fibre panel
Akryl und Stoffcollage, Fotocalcographie, Metall, etc.,
auf Faserbrett
acrylverf en collage op stof, fotogravure, metaal, etc,
op vezeldoek
acrílico y collage de tela, fotocalcografía, metal, etc.,
sobre panel de fibras

Tom Wesselmann
(Cincinnati 1931 - New York 2004)

Mouth, 7
Mund, 7
Mond, 7
Boca, 7

●●●

1966
206,3 x 165,1 cm / 81.2 x 65 in.
Museum of Modern Art (MoMA), New York

oil on shaped canvas
Öl auf profilierter Tafel
olieverf op geprofileerd paneel
óleo sobre tabla recortada siguiendo una forma

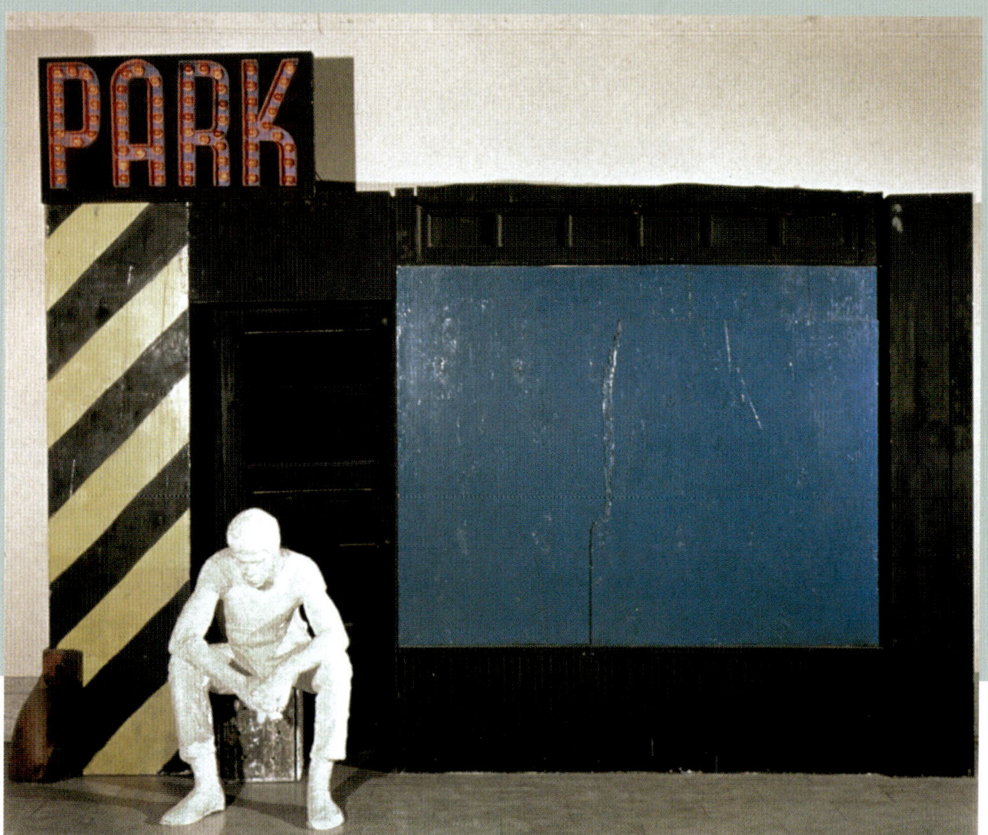

George Segal
(New York 1924 - New Jersey 2000)

The Garage
Die Garage
De garage
El garaje

●●●

1968
299 x 393,7 cm / 117.7 x 155 in.
The Newark Museum, Newark

stucco, wood, electric parts and light bulbs
Stuck, Holz, elektrische Teile und Glühbirnen
plamuur, hout, elektrisch deel en lampjes
estuco, madera, parte eléctrica y bombillas

Segal's sculptures, created from casts
of living beings, staging, evoke the
tragedy of the human condition.

**Segals Skulpturen entstehen aus
Abgüssen vom lebenden Modell,
die er in Szene setzt, um damit die
Tragik der menschlichen Verfassung
zu beschwören.**

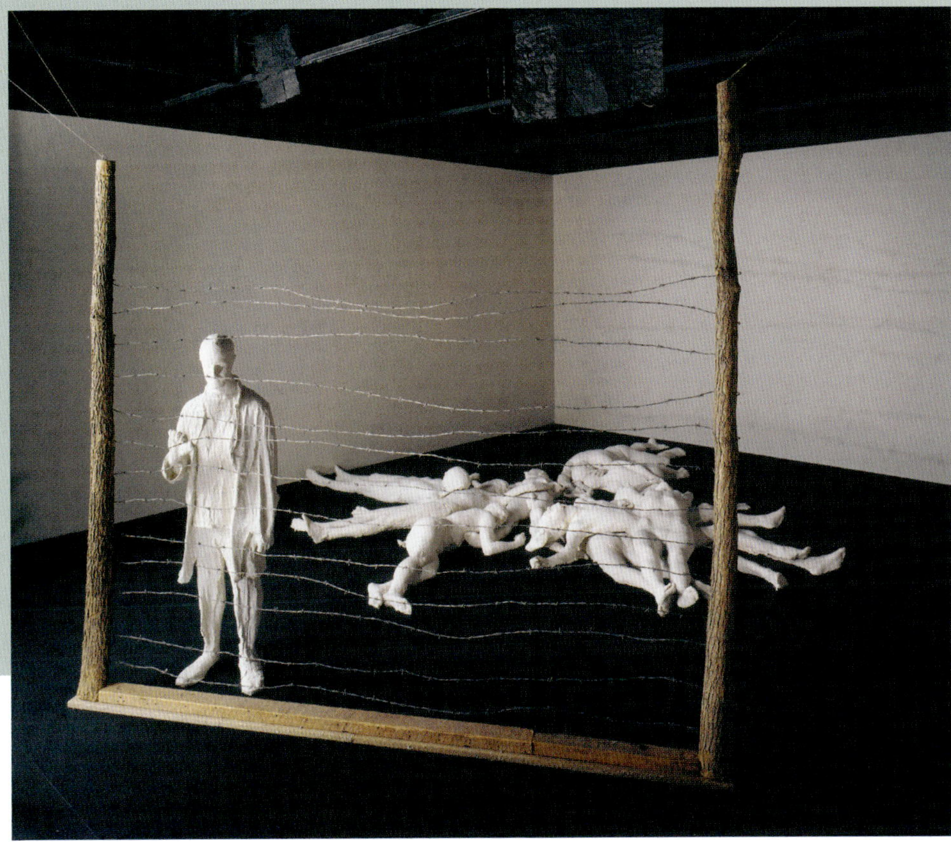

George Segal
(New York 1924 - New Jersey 2000)

The Holocaust
Der Holocaust
De holocaust
El holocausto

●●●

1982
300 x 610 x 610 cm / 118.1 x 240.1 x 240.1 in.
The Newark Museum, Newark

plaster, wood and metal cable
Kreide, Holz und Metallseil
gips, hout en metaaldraad
yeso, madera y cable metálico

De sculpturen van Ségal die gemaakt
zijn van mensenafdrukken, beelden
de tragiek van de menselijke
omstandigheden uit.

Realizadas a partir de moldes de seres
vivos, las esculturas de Ségal, puestas
en escenas, evocan el carácter trágico
de la condición humana.

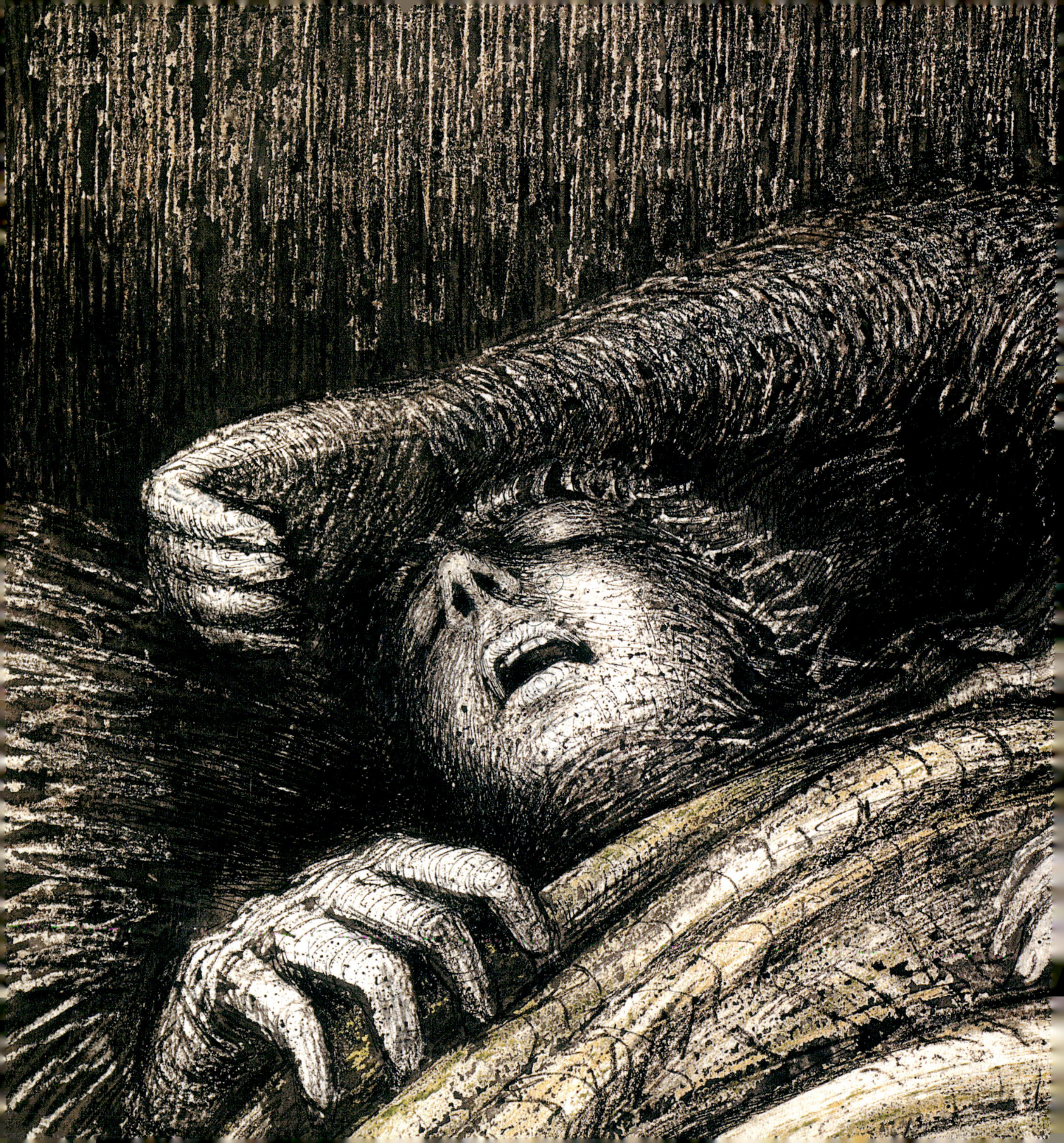

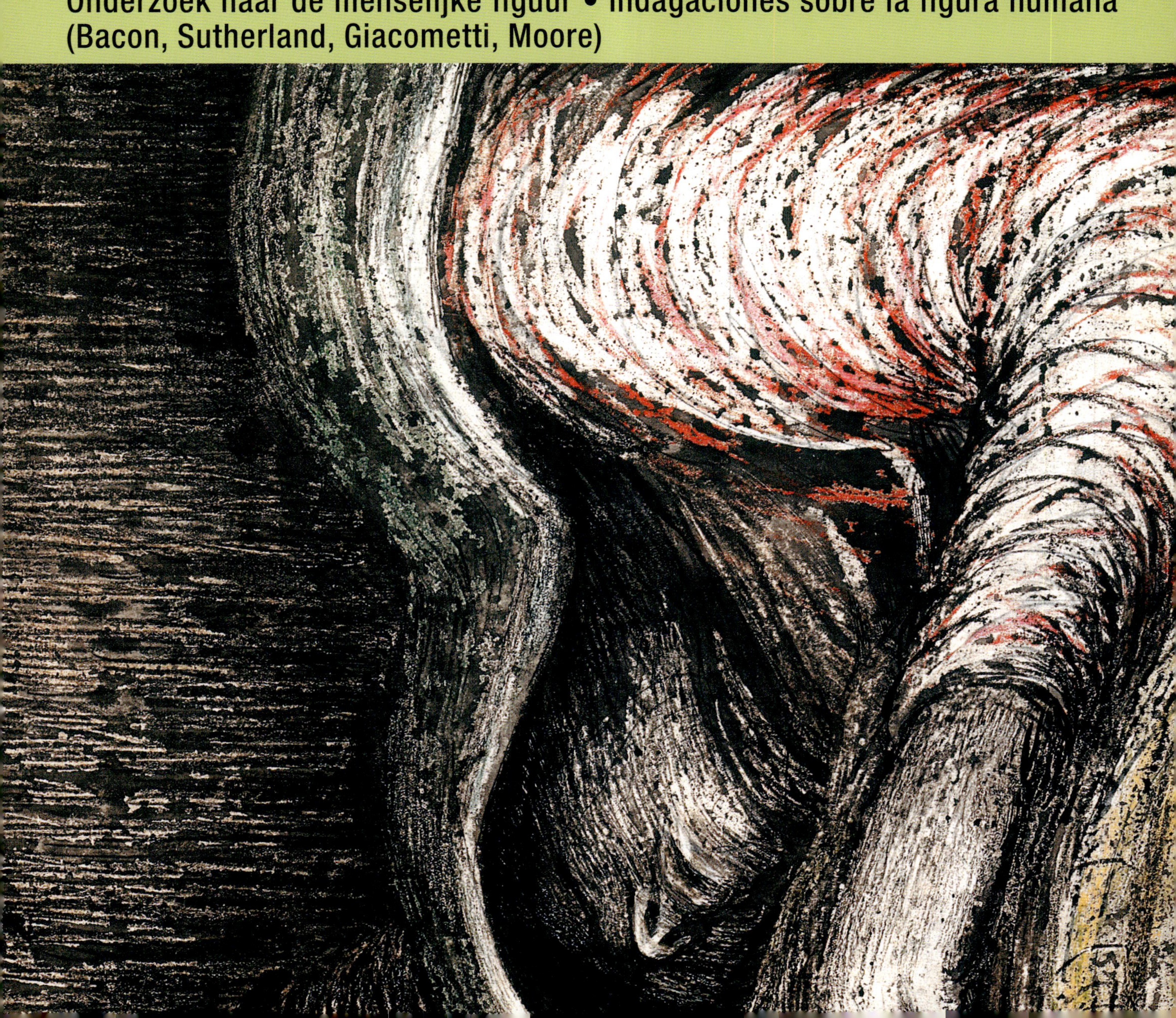

Research on the human figure • Forschungen zur menschlichen Figur
Onderzoek naar de menselijke figuur • Indagaciones sobre la figura humana
(Bacon, Sutherland, Giacometti, Moore)

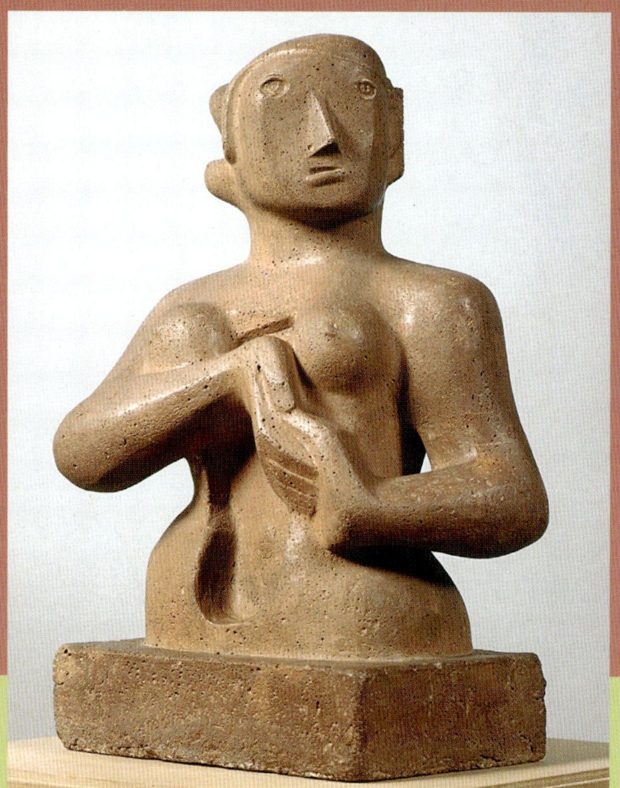

► Henry Moore
(Castleford 1898 - Much Hadham 1986)

**King and Queen
König und Königin
Koning en Koningin
Rey y reina**

●●●

1952-1953
h. 164 cm / 64.6 in.
Henry Moore Foundation, Much Hadham

bronze / Bronze / brons / bronce

Henry Moore
(Castleford 1898 -
Much Hadham 1986)

**Half bust of figure
Figur mit halber Büste
Figuur met half
bovenlichaam
Figura de medio cuerpo**

●

1929
42,5 x 25,5 x 18,5 cm
16.7 x 10 x 7.3 in.
British Council, London

cast concrete / Zementguss
cement / hormigón moldeado

Henry Moore
(Castleford 1898 -
Much Hadham 1986)

**Family group
Familiengruppe
Familiegroep
Grupo familiar**

●●●

1949
12 x 9 x 6 cm
4.7 x 3.5 x 2.3 in.
Tate Gallery, London

bronze / Bronze
brons / bronce

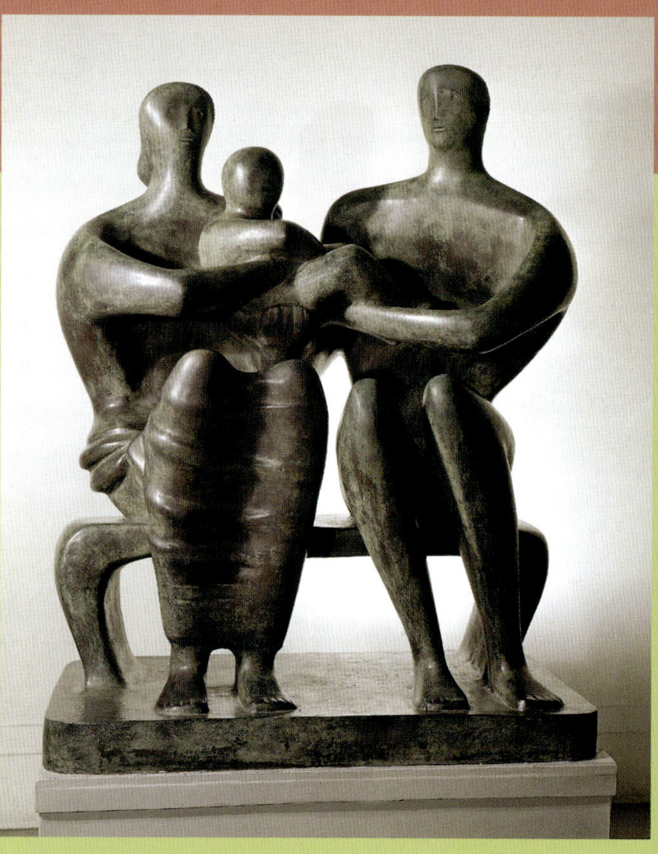

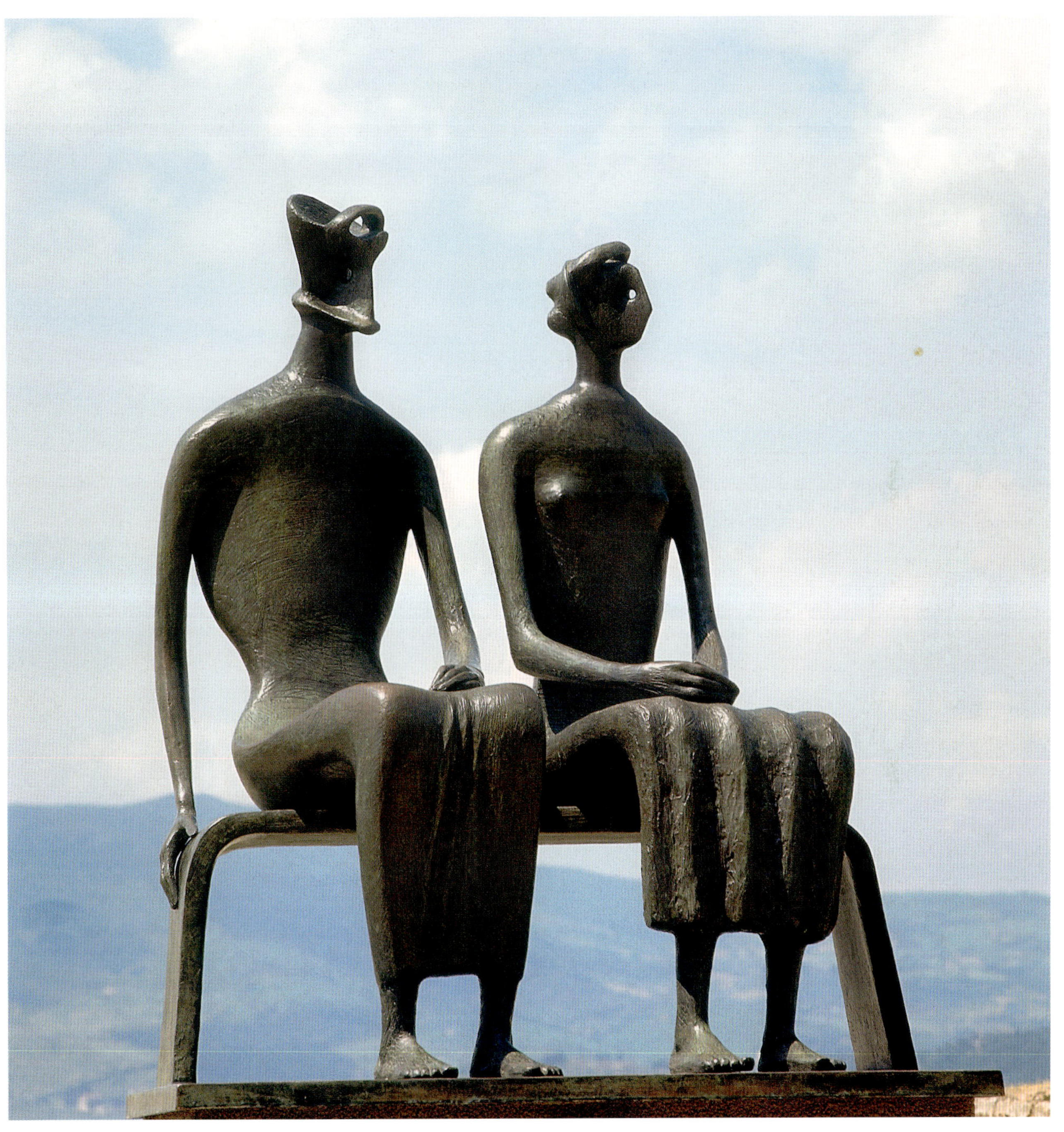

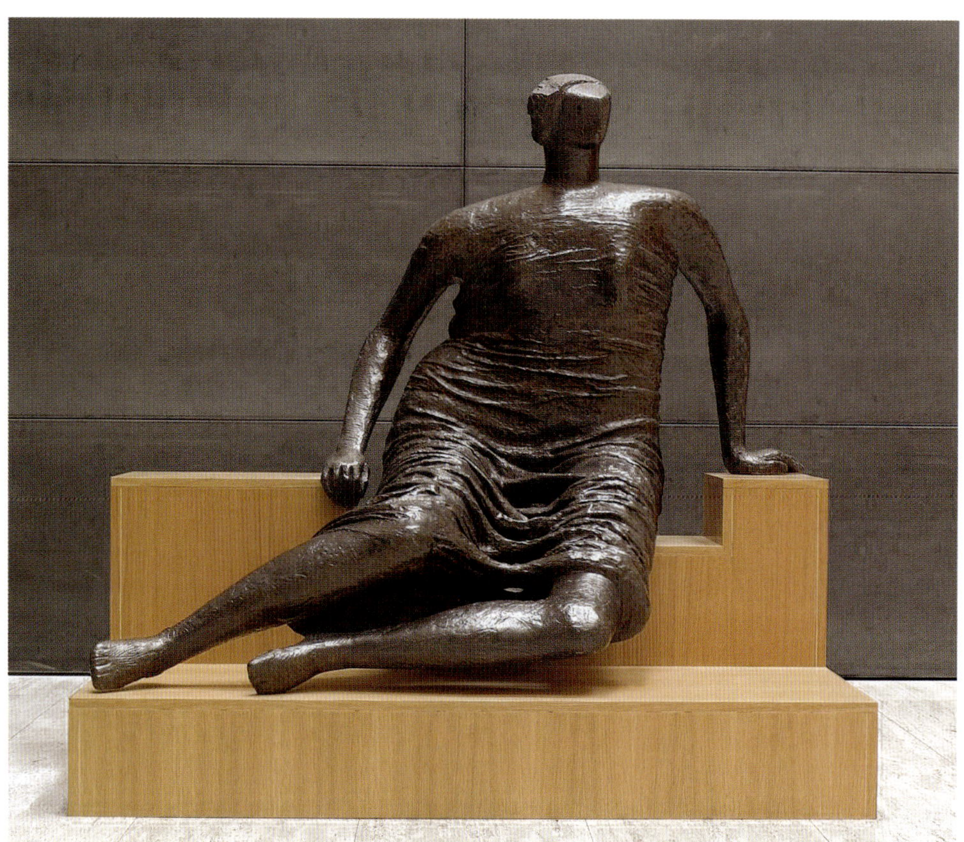

Henry Moore
(Castleford 1898 - Much Hadham 1986)

Draped woman seated
Drapierte, sitzende Frau
Gedrapeerde zittende vrouw
Mujer sentada con drapeado

● ● ●

1957-1958
184,2 x 215,9 x 145,7 cm / 72.5 x 85 x 57.3 in.
Yale University Art Gallery, New Haven (CT)

bronze / Bronze / brons / bronce

Important exponent of English sculpture, inspired by Egyptian and Pre-Colombian art, Moore preferred the subjects of the woman and the family.

Als bedeutender Vertreter der englischen Bildhauerei und inspiriert von der ägyptischen und präkolumbianischen Kunst bevorzugte Moore die Themen Frau und Familie.

Moore was een belangrijke vertegenwoordiger van de Engelse beeldhouwkunst, en geïnspireerd door de Egyptische en Pre-Columbiaanse kunst geeft hij de voorkeur aan thema's waar vrouwen en de familie centraal staan.

Importante exponente de la escultura inglesa, inspirado en el arte egipcio y precolombino, Moore privilegiaba los temas relacionados con la mujer y la familia.

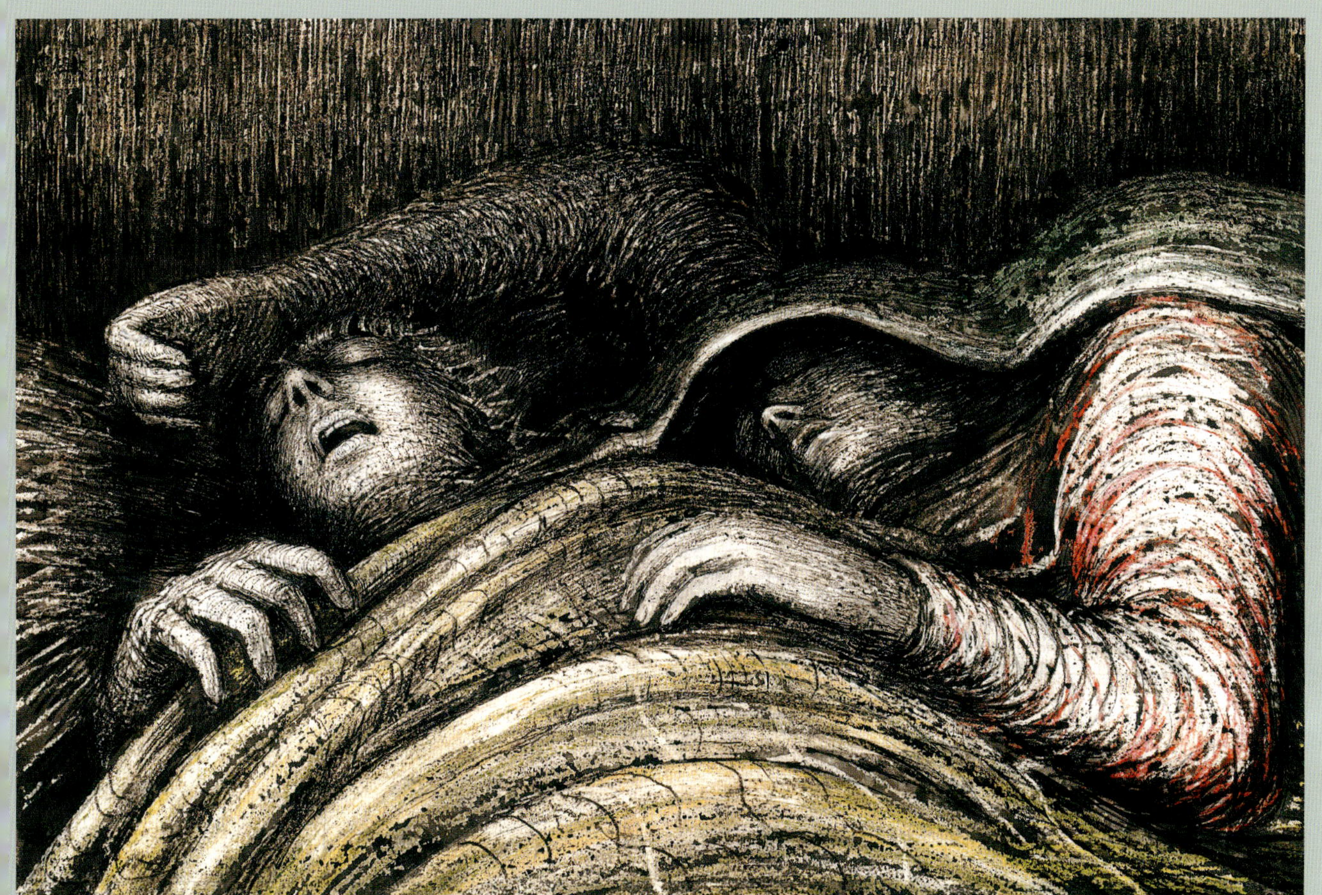

Henry Moore
(Castleford 1898 - Much Hadham 1986)

Sleepers in pink and green
Schlafende in Rosa und Grün
Slapers in roze en groen
Durmientes en rosa y verde

●

1941
38 x 55 cm / 14.9 x 21.6 in.
Tate Gallery, London

pencil, ink, gouache and wax on paper / Bleistift, Tinte, Gouache und Wachs auf Papier
potlood, inkt, gouache en was op papier / lápiz, tinta, gouache y cera sobre papel

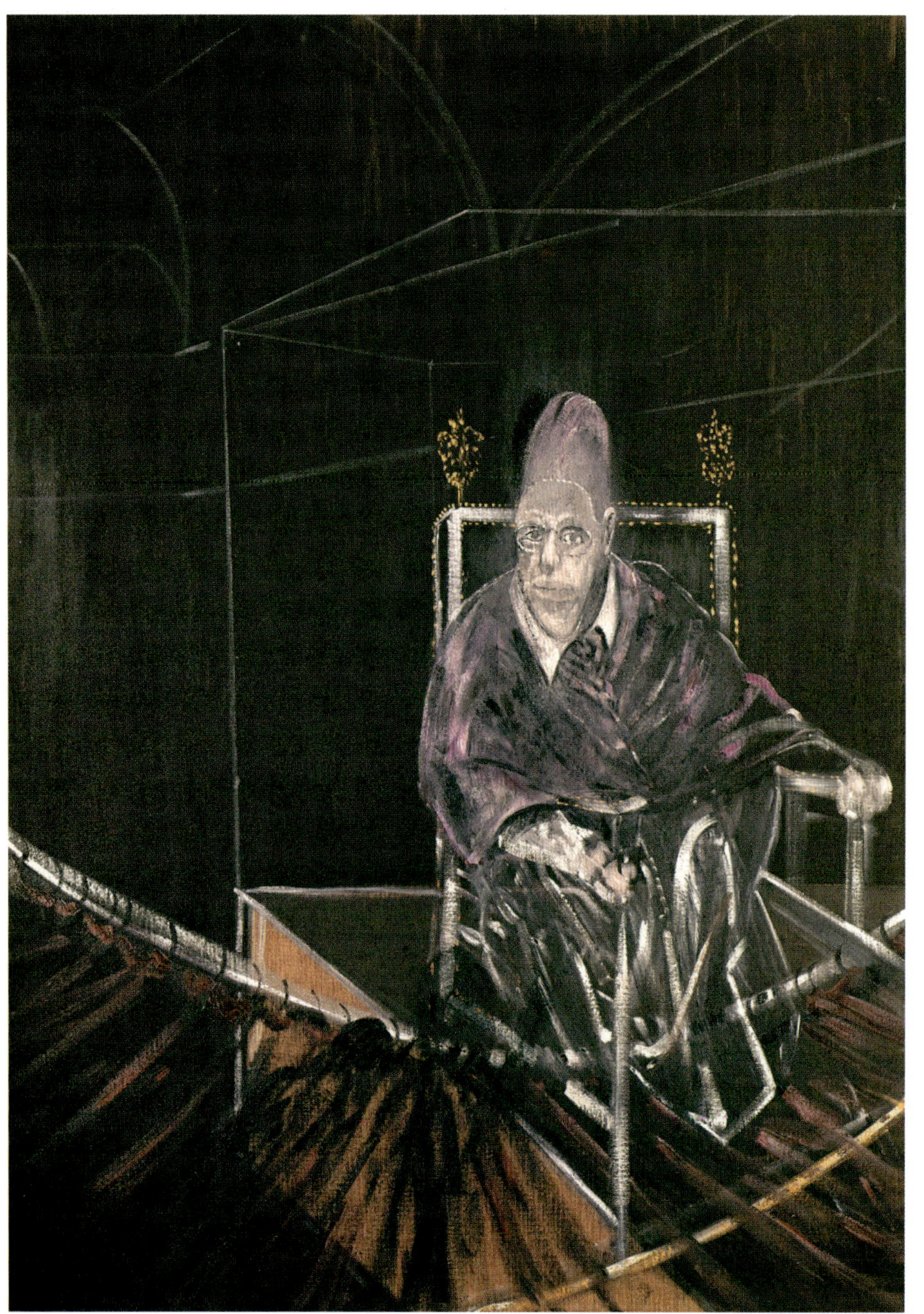

500

Francis Bacon
(Dublin 1909 - Madrid 1992)

Pope I 1951
Papst I 1951
Paus I 1951
Papa I 1951

●●●

1951
197,8 x 137,4 cm / 77.8 x 54.1 in.
Art Gallery and Museum, Aberdeen

oil on canvas / Öl auf Leinwand
olieverf op doek / óleo sobre lienzo

Fiercely atheist, the painting by Velázquez of Pope Innocent X tormented Bacon who never wanted to see the original displayed in Rome.

Velázquez' Bild des Papstes Innozenz X. hat den Atheisten Bacon beeindruckt, der allerdings nie das Original in Rom sehen wollte.

De onvermoeibare atheïst Bacon was door het schilderij van Velázquez van Paus Innocentus X erg gekweld en hij heeft nooit het origineel in Rome willen zien.

Valiente y tenazmente ateo, el cuadro de Velázquez del Papa Inocencio X ha atormentado a Bacon, que nunca ha querido ver el original expuesto en Roma.

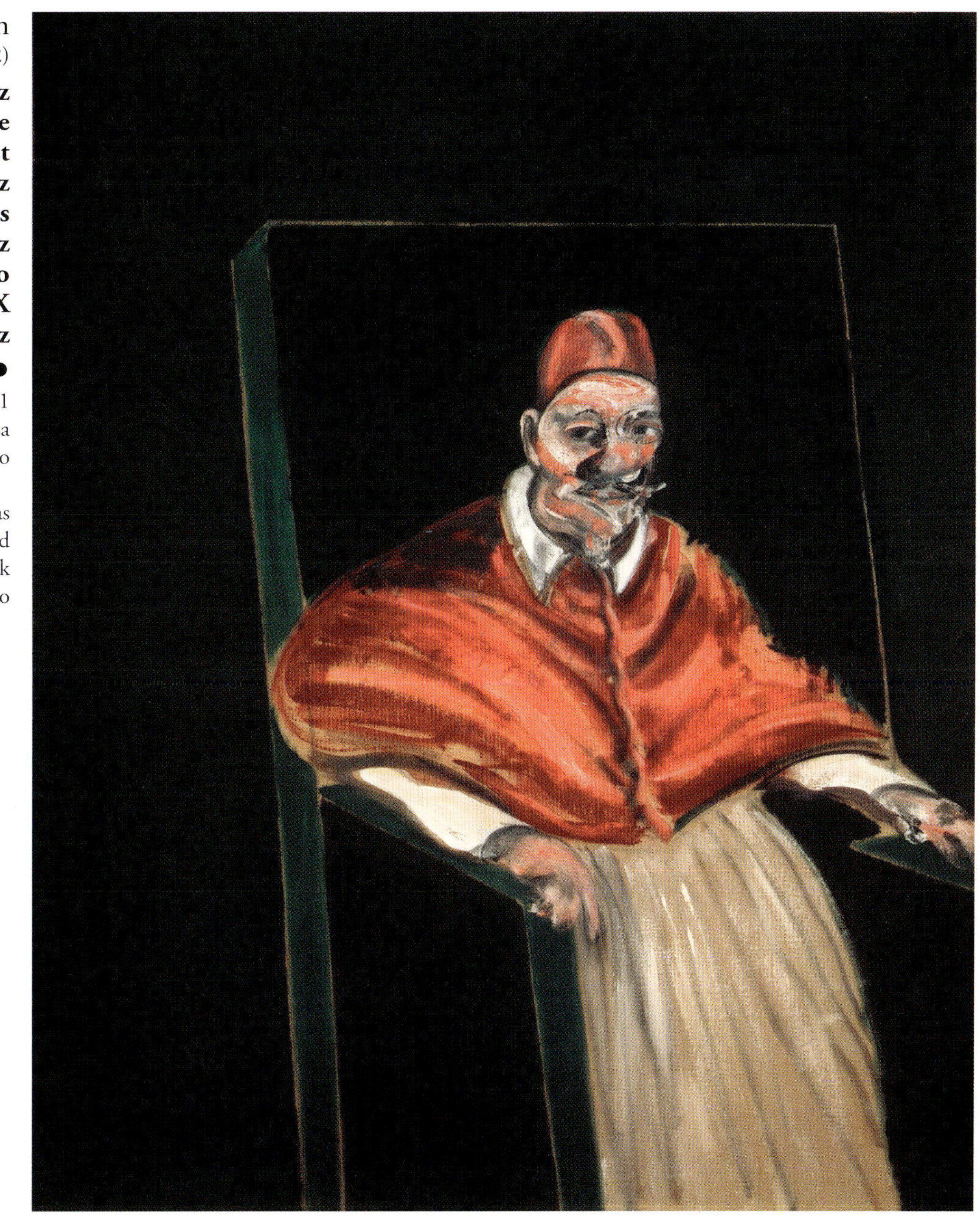

Francis Bacon
(Dublin 1909 - Madrid 1992)
**Study for Velázquez
Pope
Studie für den Papst
von Velázquez
Studie voor de Paus
van Velázquez
Estudio del retrato
de Papa Inocencio X
de Velázquez**
● ● ●
1961
Collezione d'Arte Religiosa
Moderna, Città del Vaticano

oil on canvas
Öl auf Leinwand
olieverf op doek
óleo sobre lienzo

501

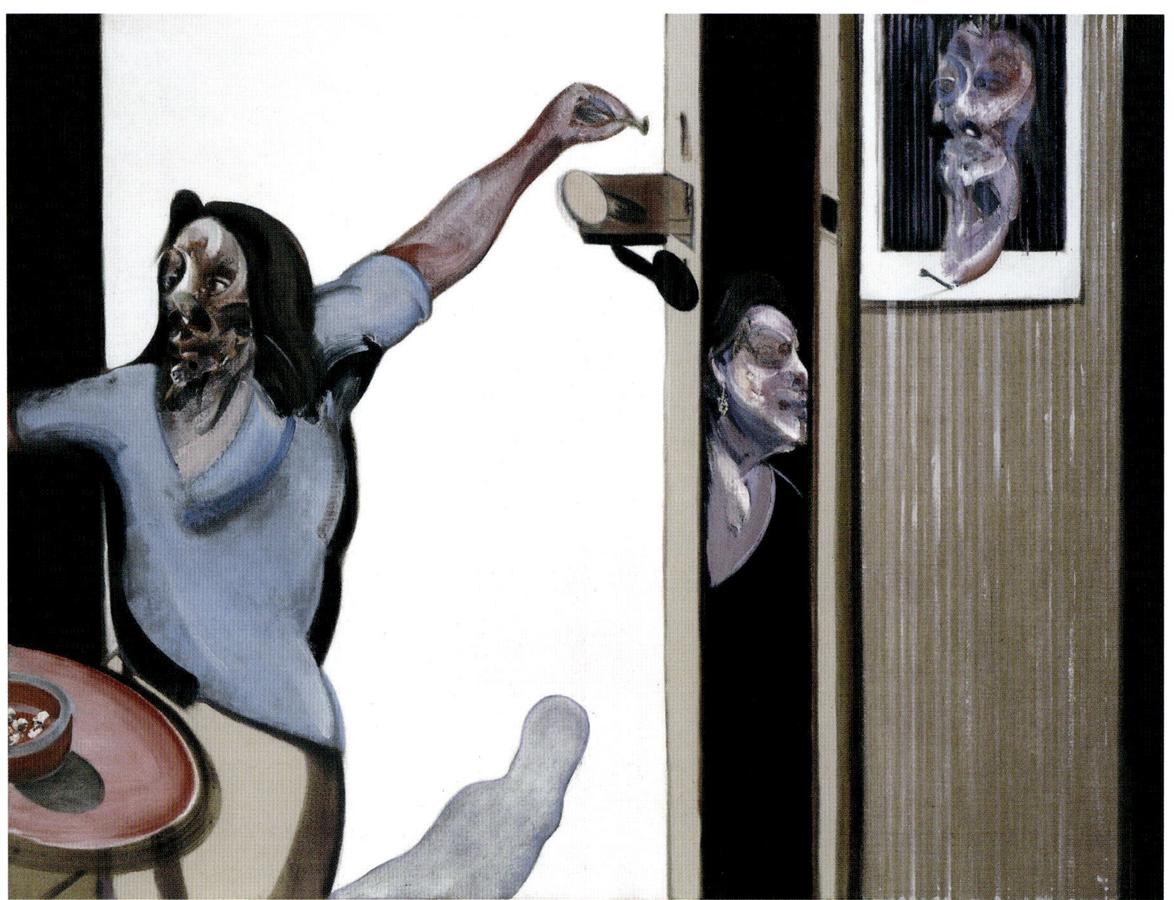

Francis Bacon
(Dublin 1909 - Madrid 1992)

Three studies of Isabel Rawsthorne
Drei Studien von Isabel Rawsthorne
Drie studies van Isabel Rawsthorne
Tres estudios de Isabel Rawsthorne

●●

1967
119,5 x 152,5 cm / 47 x 60 in.
Nationalgalerie, Staatliche Museen, Berlin

oil on canvas / Öl auf Leinwand
olieverf op doek / óleo sobre lienzo

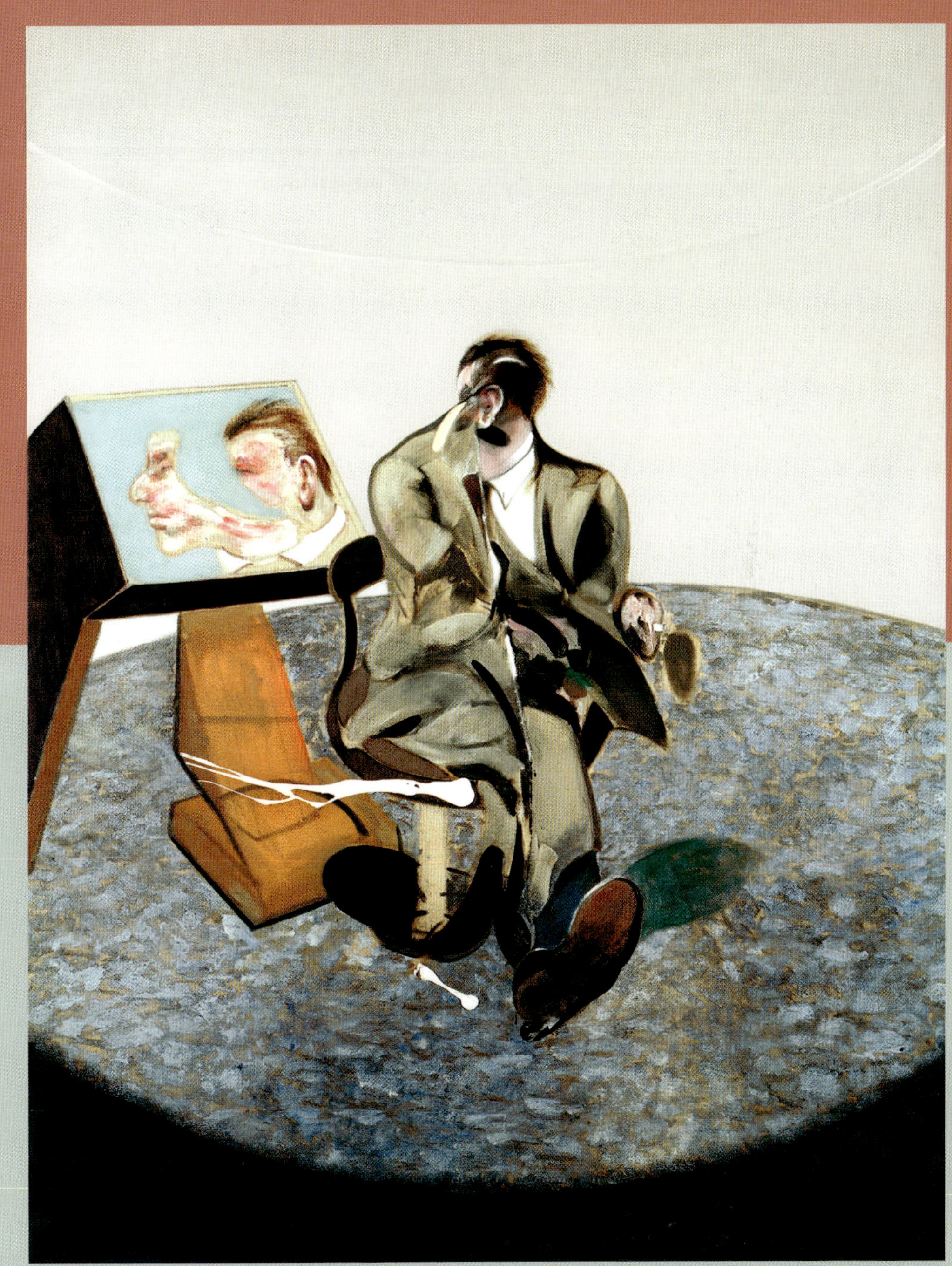

Francis Bacon
(Dublin 1909 - Madrid 1992)

**Portrait of George Dyer
in a mirror**
**Porträt von George Dyer
im Spiegel**
**Portret van George Dyer
in een spiegel**
**Retrato de George Dyer
en un espejo**

●●●

1968
198 x 147 cm / 77.9 x 57.8 in.
Museo Thyssen-Bornemisza,
Madrid

oil on canvas
Öl auf Leinwand
olieverf op doek
óleo sobre lienzo

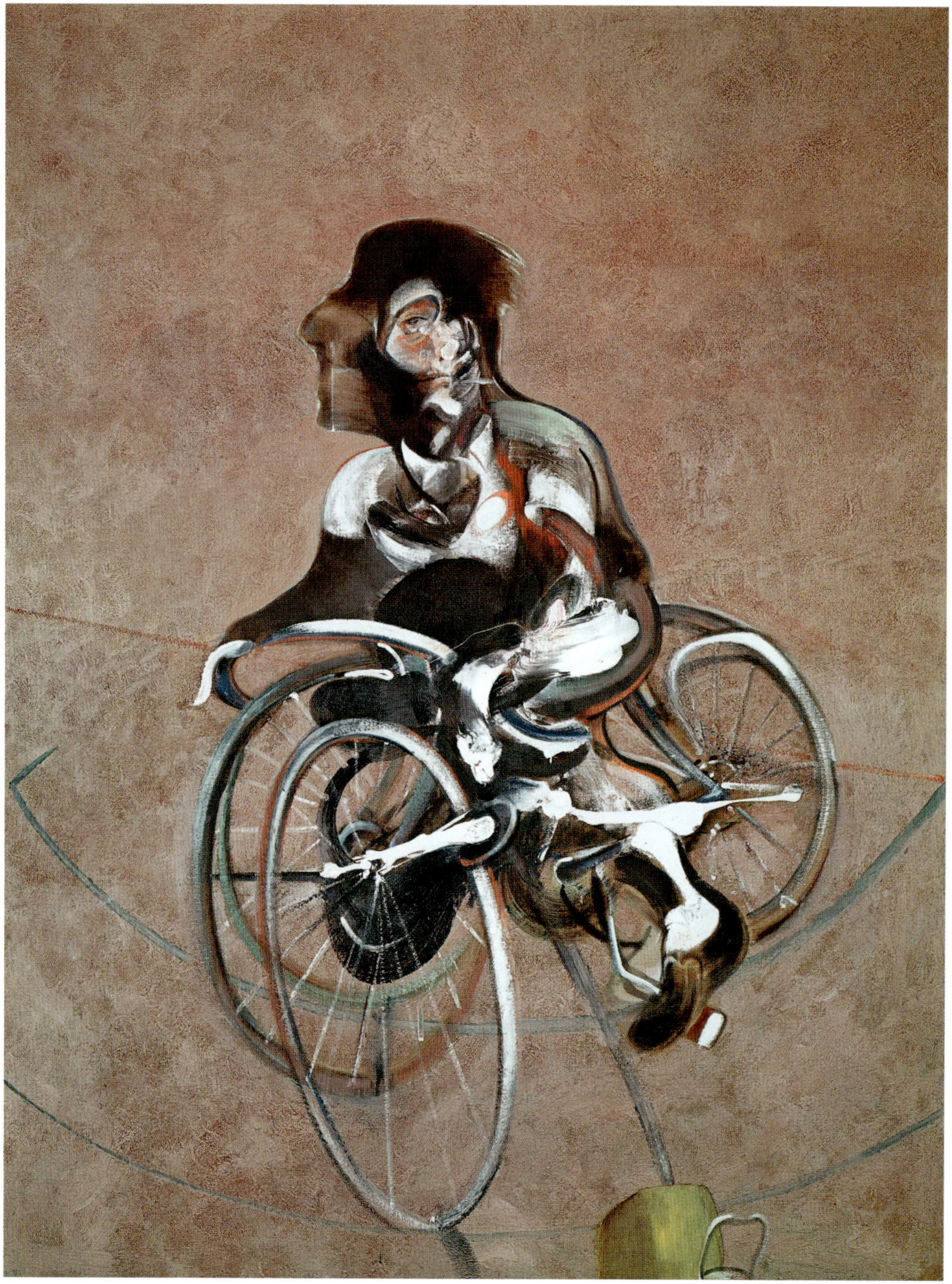

Francis Bacon
(Dublin 1909 - Madrid 1992)

**George Dyer
on bicycle
Porträt von George Dyer
auf einem Fahrrad fahrend
George Dyer op de fiets
George Dyer en bicicleta**

●●

1966
198 x 147,5 / 77.9 x 58 in.
Fondation Beyeler, Basel

oil on canvas
Öl auf Leinwand
olieverf op doek
óleo sobre lienzo

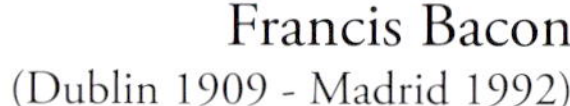

Francis Bacon
(Dublin 1909 - Madrid 1992)

Self-portrait
Selbstporträt
Zelfportret
Autorretrato

●●●

1970
152 x 147,5 cm / 59.8 x 58 in.
Marlborough Gallery,
London

oil on canvas
Öl auf Leinwand
olieverf op doek
óleo sobre lienzo

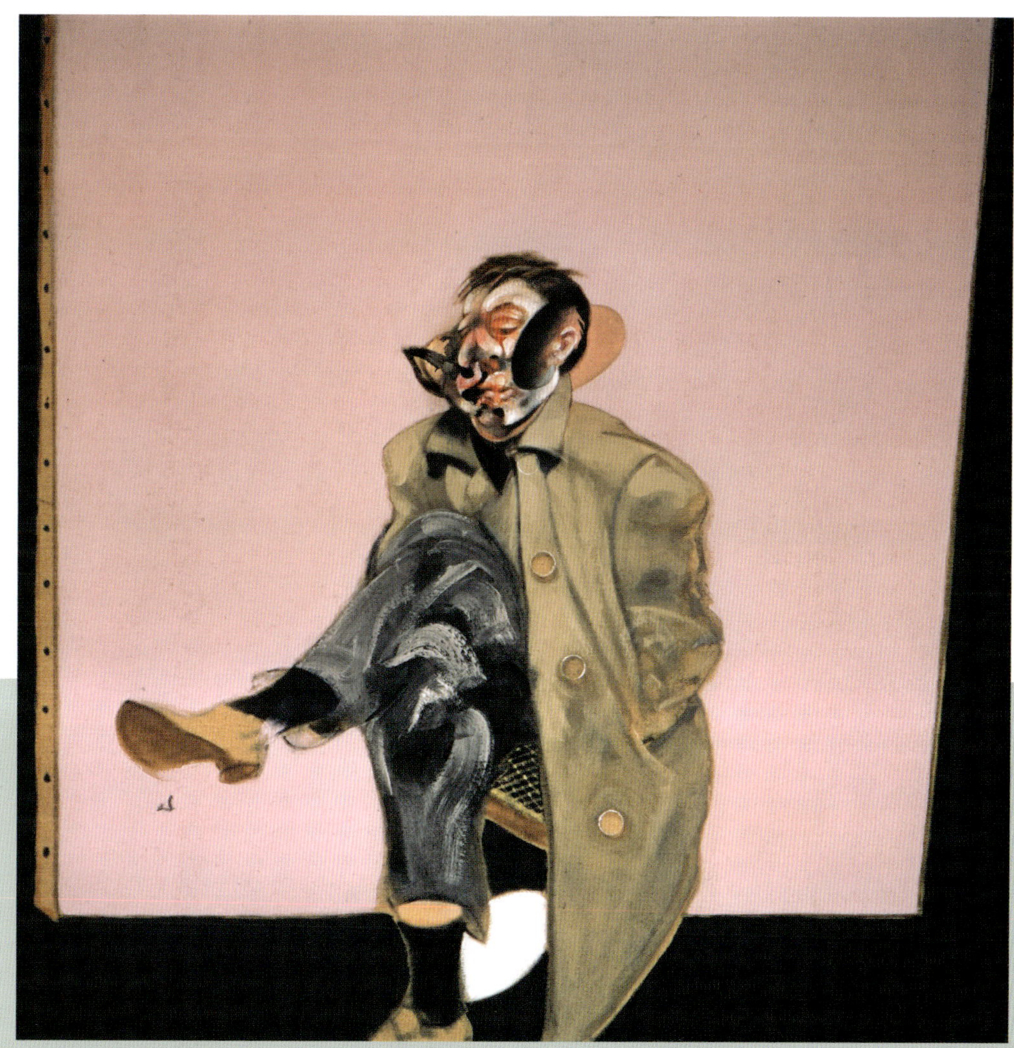

Bacon worked from photographs and was always influenced by the movie image.

Bacon arbeitete nach Fotografien und war stets von Bildern des Films beeinflusst.

Bacon werkte op basis van foto's en werd steeds meer door de film beïnvloed.

Bacon trabajaba a partir de fotografías y estaba siempre influenciado por la imagen cinematográfica.

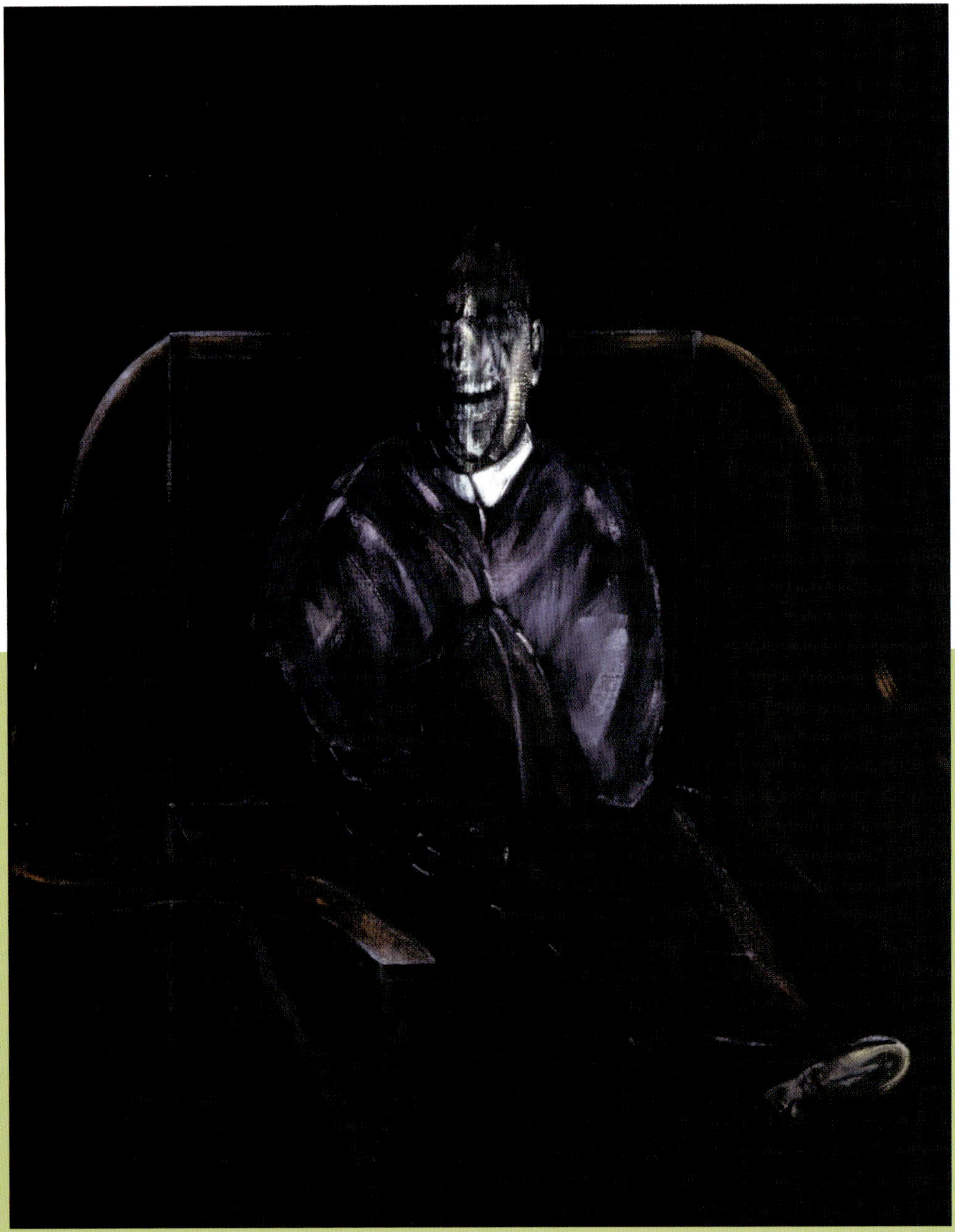

◀ **Francis Bacon**
(Dublin 1909 - Madrid 1992)

Person seated
Sitzende Person
Zittend persoon
Persona sentada

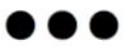

Museum voor Schone Kunsten,
Gent

▶ **Graham Sutherland**
(London 1903 - 1980)

Crucifixion
Kreuzigung
Kruisiging
Crucifixión

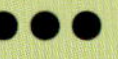

1947
Collezione d'Arte Religiosa
Moderna, Città del Vaticano

oil on canvas
Öl auf Leinwand
olieverf op doek
óleo sobre lienzo

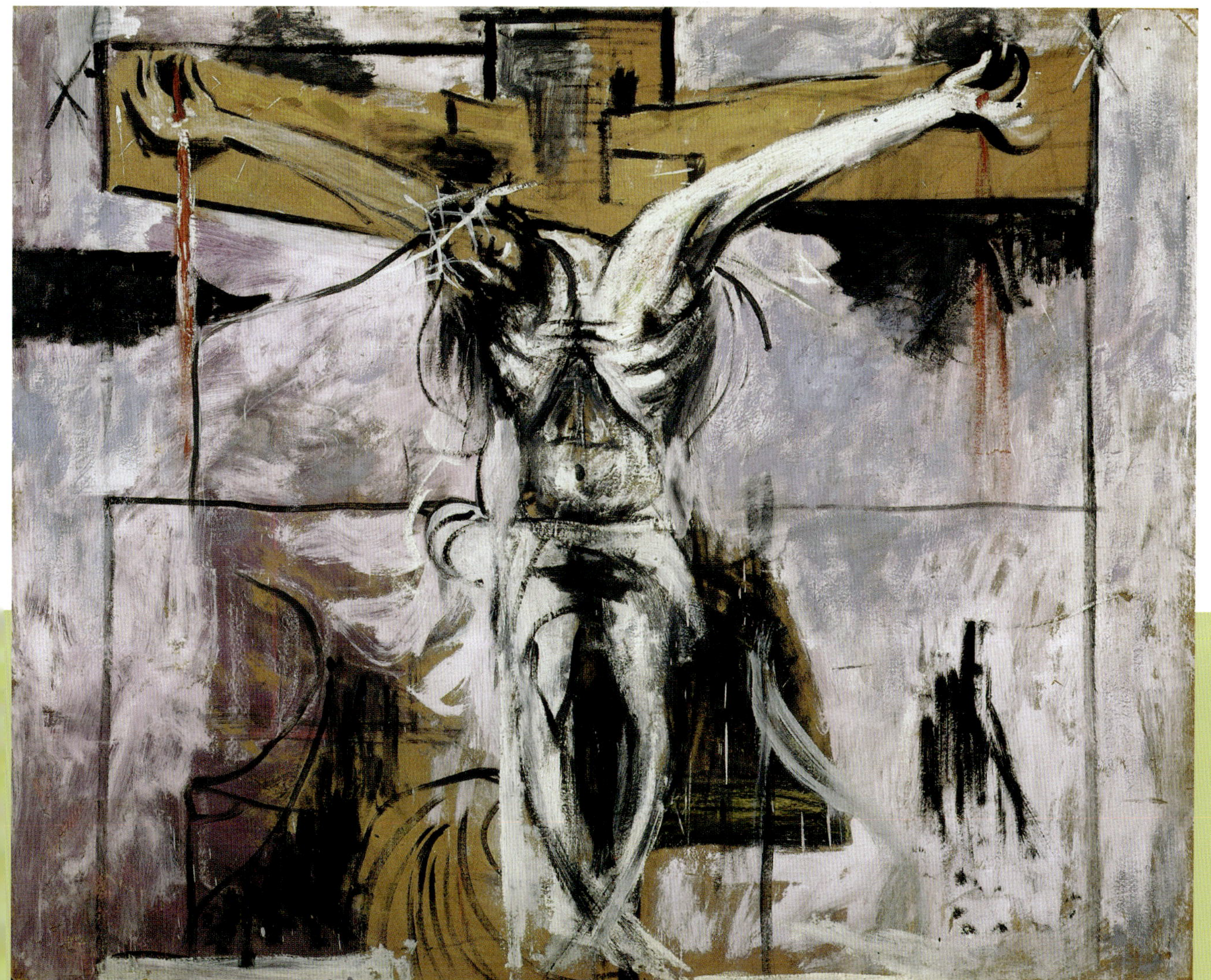

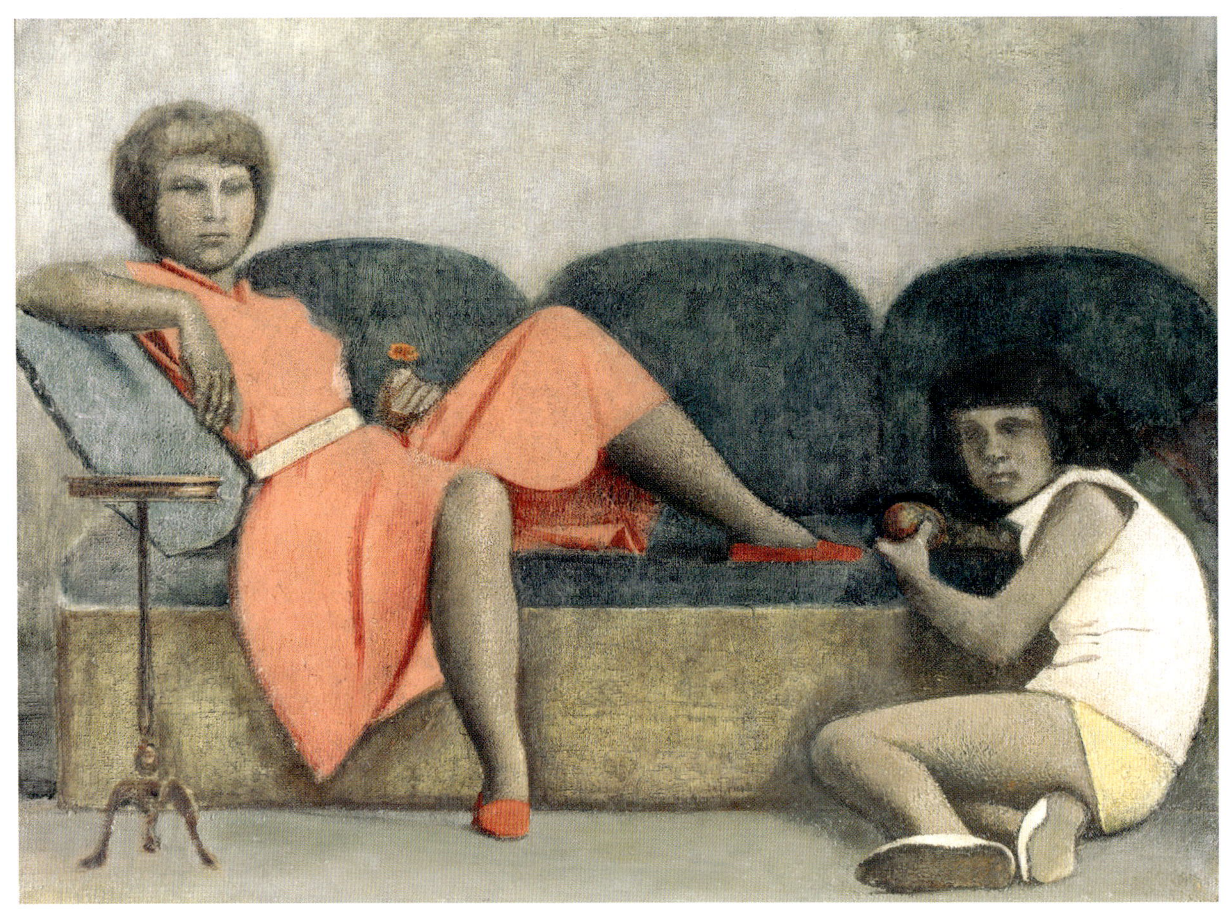

Balthus
(Paris 1908 - Rossinière 2001)

Girls on sofa
Mädchen auf dem Sofa
Meisjes op de bank
Niñas sobre el sillón

●

Collezione Tazzoli, Torino

Balthus loved to say that he did not paint dreams just dreamers.

Balthus behauptete stets, dass er keine Träume, sondern Träumerinnen malte.

Balthus hield ervan te zeggen dat hij geen dromen schilderde maar droomsters.

A Balthus le gustaba decir que no pintaba sueños, sino soñadores.

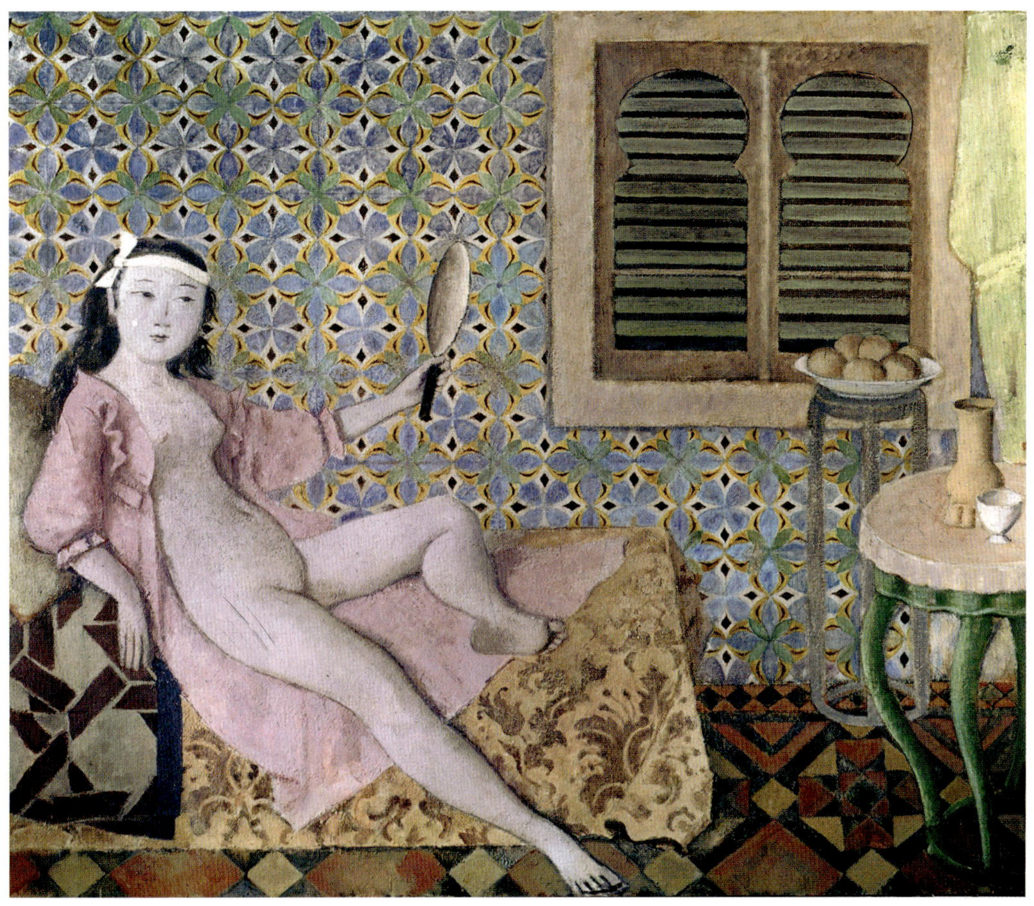

Balthus
(Paris 1908 - Rossinière 2001)

Turkish Room
Das türkische Zimmer
De Turkse kamer
La habitación turca

●●●

1963
180 x 210 cm / 70.9 x 82.7 in.
Centre Georges Pompidou, Musée National d'Art Moderne, Paris

casein and tempera on canvas / Kaseinfarbe und Tempera auf Leinwand
caseïne en tempera op doek / caseína y temple sobre lienzo

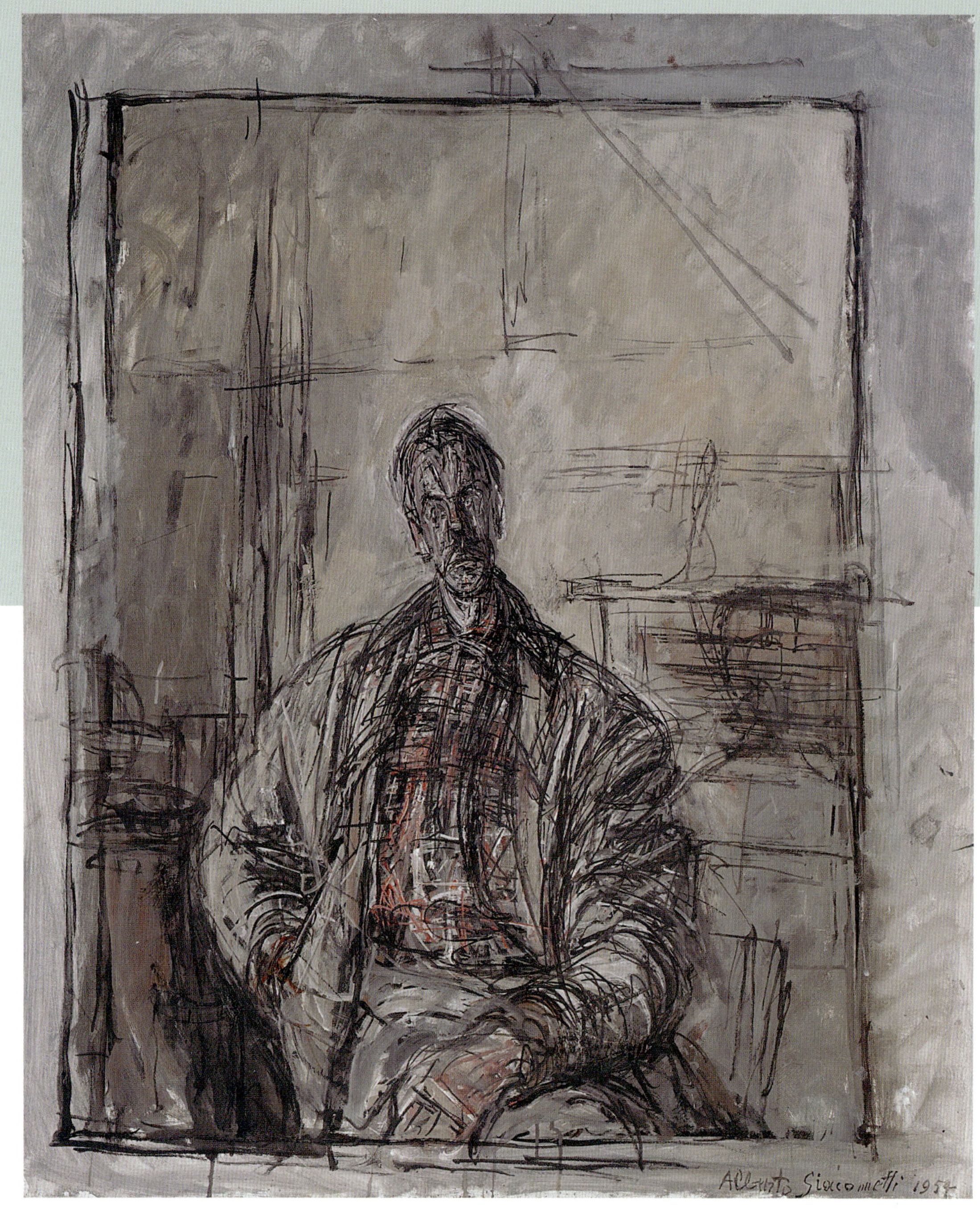

◀ **Alberto Giacometti**
(Borgonovo di Stampa 1901 - Chur 1966)

Portrait of Diego seated
Porträt des sitzenden Diego
Portret van een zittende Diego
Retrato de Diego sentado
●●●
Galerie Maeght, Paris

Alberto Giacometti
(Borgonovo di Stampa 1901 - Chur 1966)

The Square II
Der Platz II
Het plein II
La plaza II
●●●
1948-1949
23 x 63,5 x 43,5 cm / 9 x 25 x 17.1 in.
Museum Berggruen, Staatliche Museen, Berlin

bronze / Bronze / brons / bronce

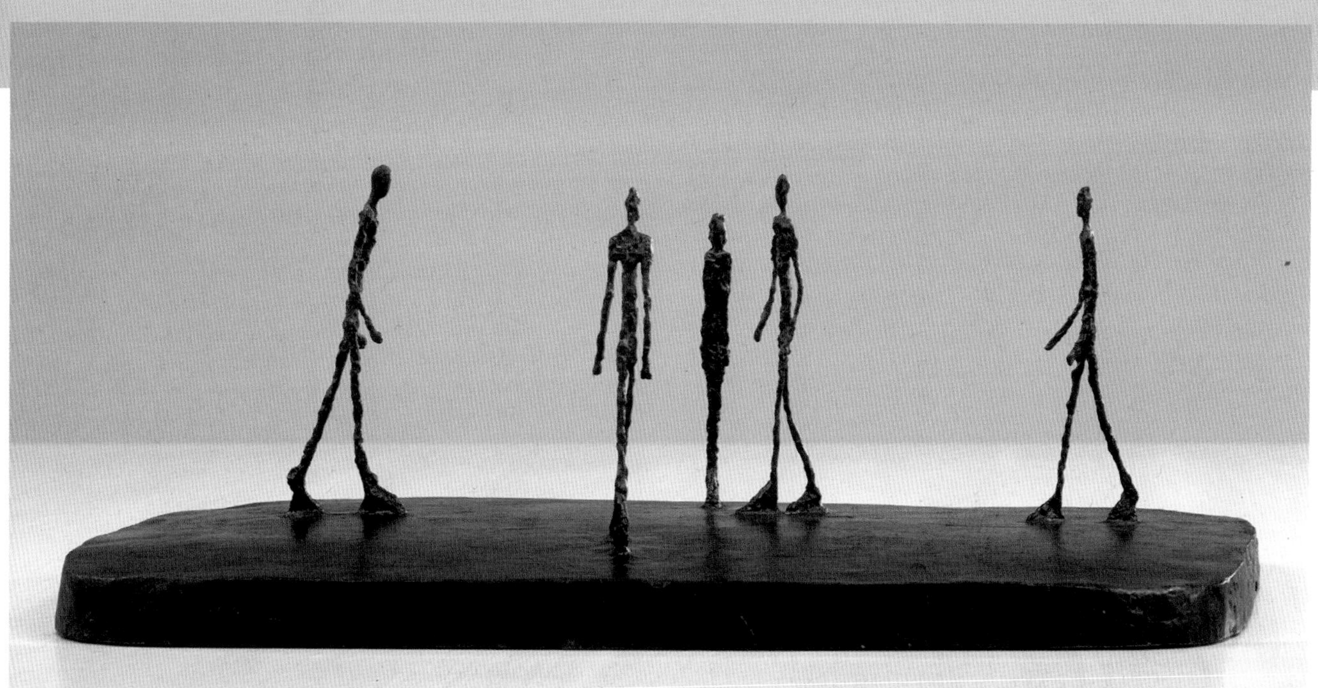

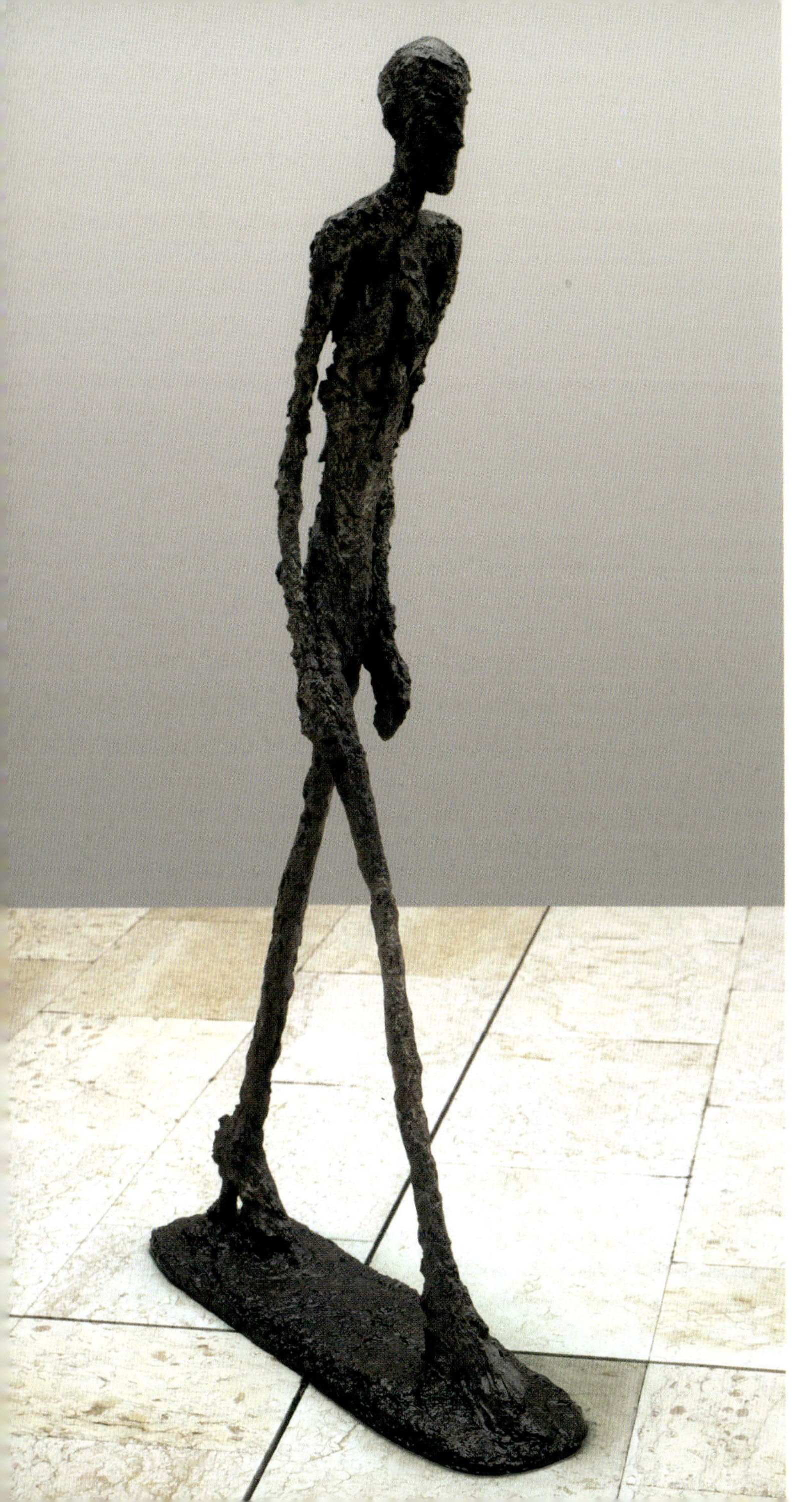

The man is walking while the woman is static, solemn, like in Egyptian statues.

Der Mann bewegt sich während die Frau statisch und streng wie eine ägyptische Statue ist.

De man loopt terwijl de vrouw statisch is, verheven, zoals bij de Egyptische beelden.

El hombre está en movimiento, mientras la mujer está estática, hierática, como en las estatuas egipcias.

Alberto Giacometti
(Borgonovo di Stampa 1901 - Chur 1966)
Man Walking
Schreitender Mann
De lopende man
El hombre que camina
●●

1960
h. 120 cm / 47.2 in.
Private collection / Private Sammlung
Privécollectie / Colección privada

bronze / Bronze / brons / bronce

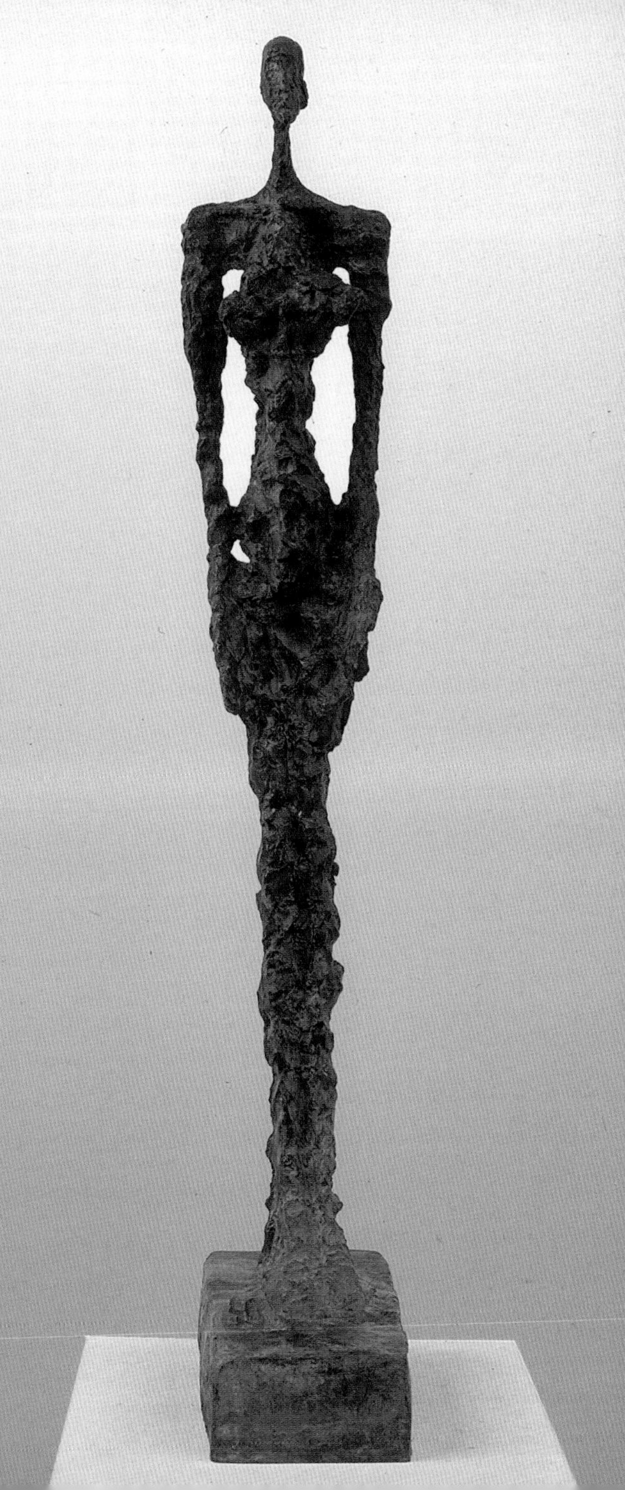

Alberto Giacometti
(Borgonovo di Stampa 1901 - Coira 1966)

Woman for Venice IV
Frau für Venedig IV
Vrouw voor Venetië IV
Mujer de Venecia IV

●●

1956
h. 116 cm / 45.7 in.
Museum Berggruen, Staatliche Museen, Berlin

bronze / Bronze / brons / bronce

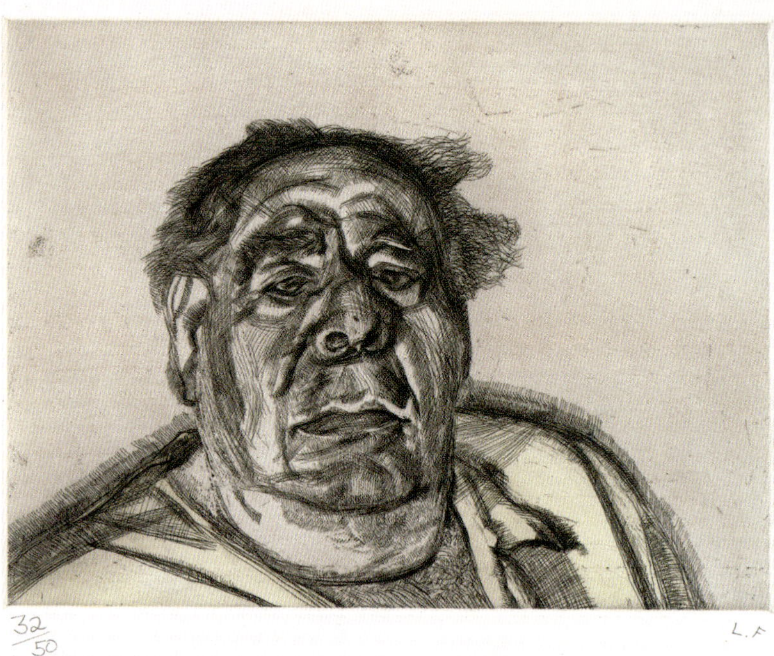

Lucien Freud
(Berlin 1922)

Lord Goodman in His Yellow Pyjamas
Lord Goodman in seinem gelben Pyjama
Lord Goodman in zijn gele pyjama
Lord Goodman en su pijama amarillo

●●

1987
48,3 x 55,6 cm / 19 x 21.9 in.
Museum of Modern Art, New York

engraving in black with details in watercolor
Radierung in Schwarz mit Details in Aquarell
zwarte gravure met details in aquarel
grabado en negro con detalles en acuarela

▶ Lucien Freud
(Berlin 1922)

Naked man, back view
Männlicher Akt - Rückenansicht
Naakte man, van achteren gezien
Hombre desnudo, vista posterior

●●●

1991-1992
183,5 x 137,4 cm
72.2 x 54.1 in.
The Metropolitan Museum of Art, New York

oil on canvas / Öl auf Leinwand
olieverf op doek / óleo sobre lienzo

Nephew of the famous
psychoanalyst, Freud
is the painter without
embellishments of
human flesh, which
appears on his canvases
as minced into the color
spread with strokes of
spatula.

Freud, der Engel
des berühmten
Psychoanalytikers,
ist ein Maler, der das
menschliche Fleisch nicht
verschönert.
Es erscheint wie durch
den Fleischwolf gedreht
und mit dem Spatel
auf seine Leinwände
aufgetragen.

Freud is als neef
van de beroemde
psychoanalyticus,
een schilder van het
menselijk vlees zonder
verfraaiingen, dat door
de kleuren die met
de spatel op het doek
geklopt zijn net gehakt
lijkt .

Nieto del célebre
psicoanalista, Freud es
el pintor de la carne
humana sin ornamentos,
que en sus lienzos se
muestra como triturada
en el color aplicado con
golpes de espátula.

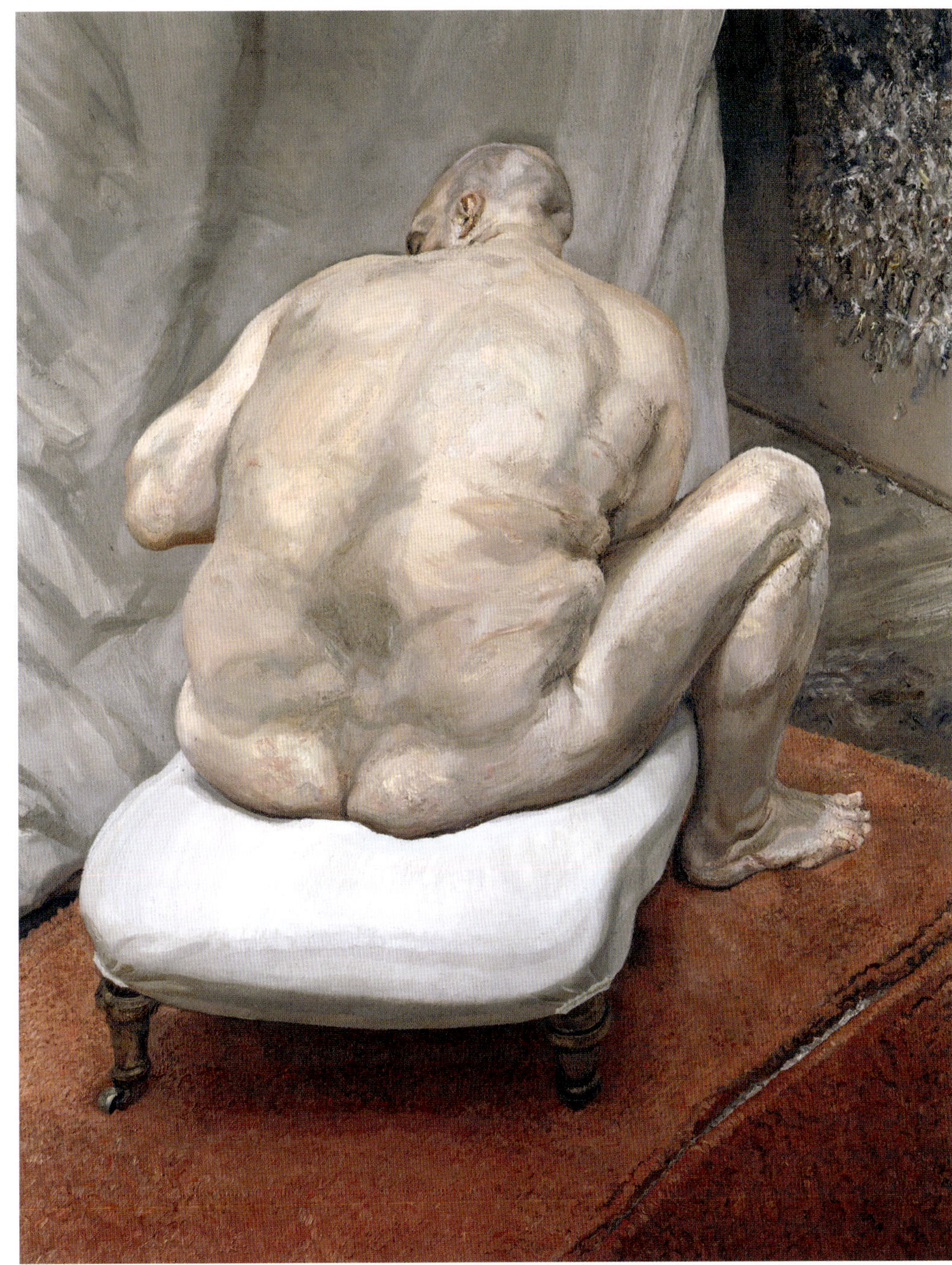

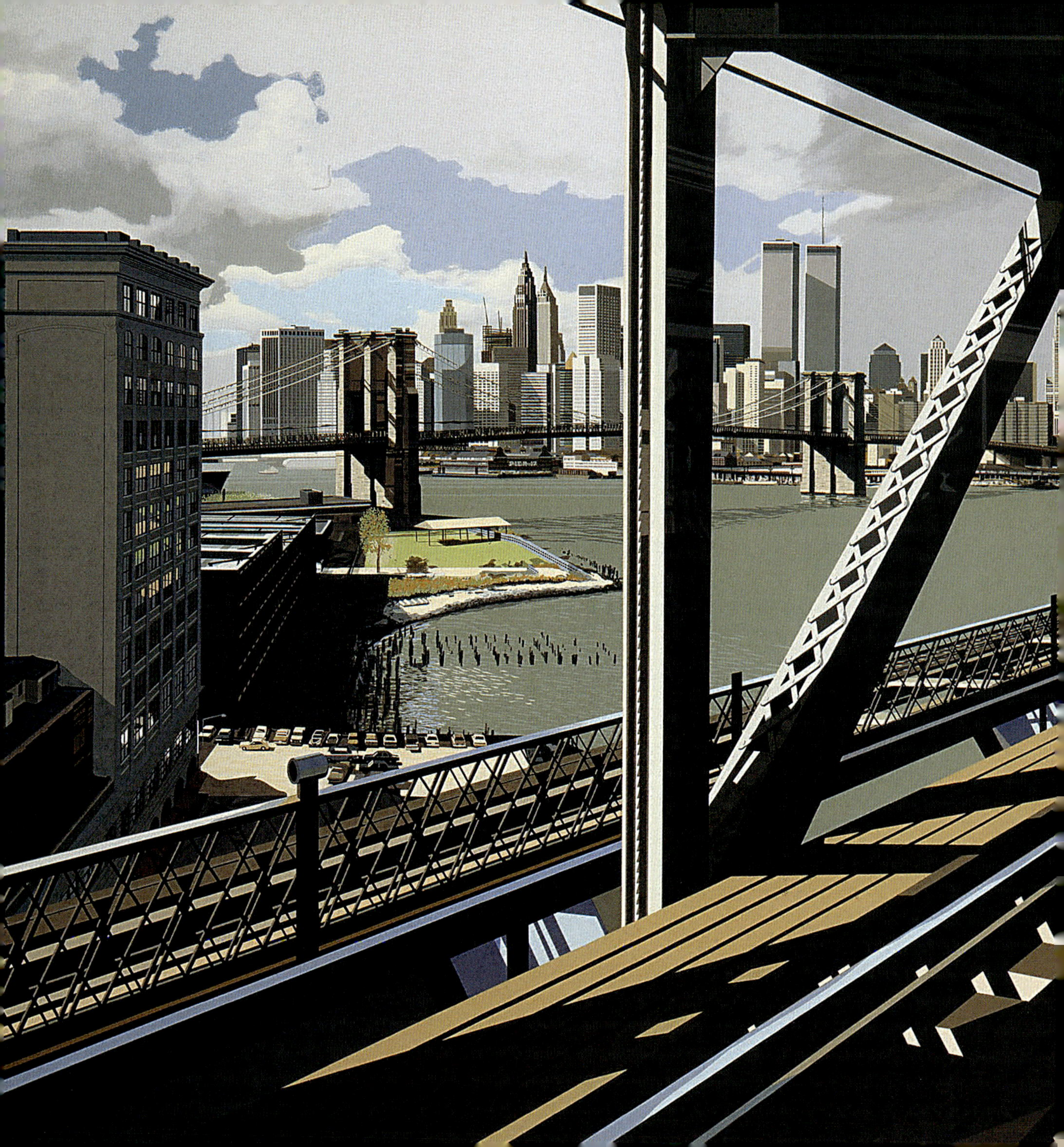

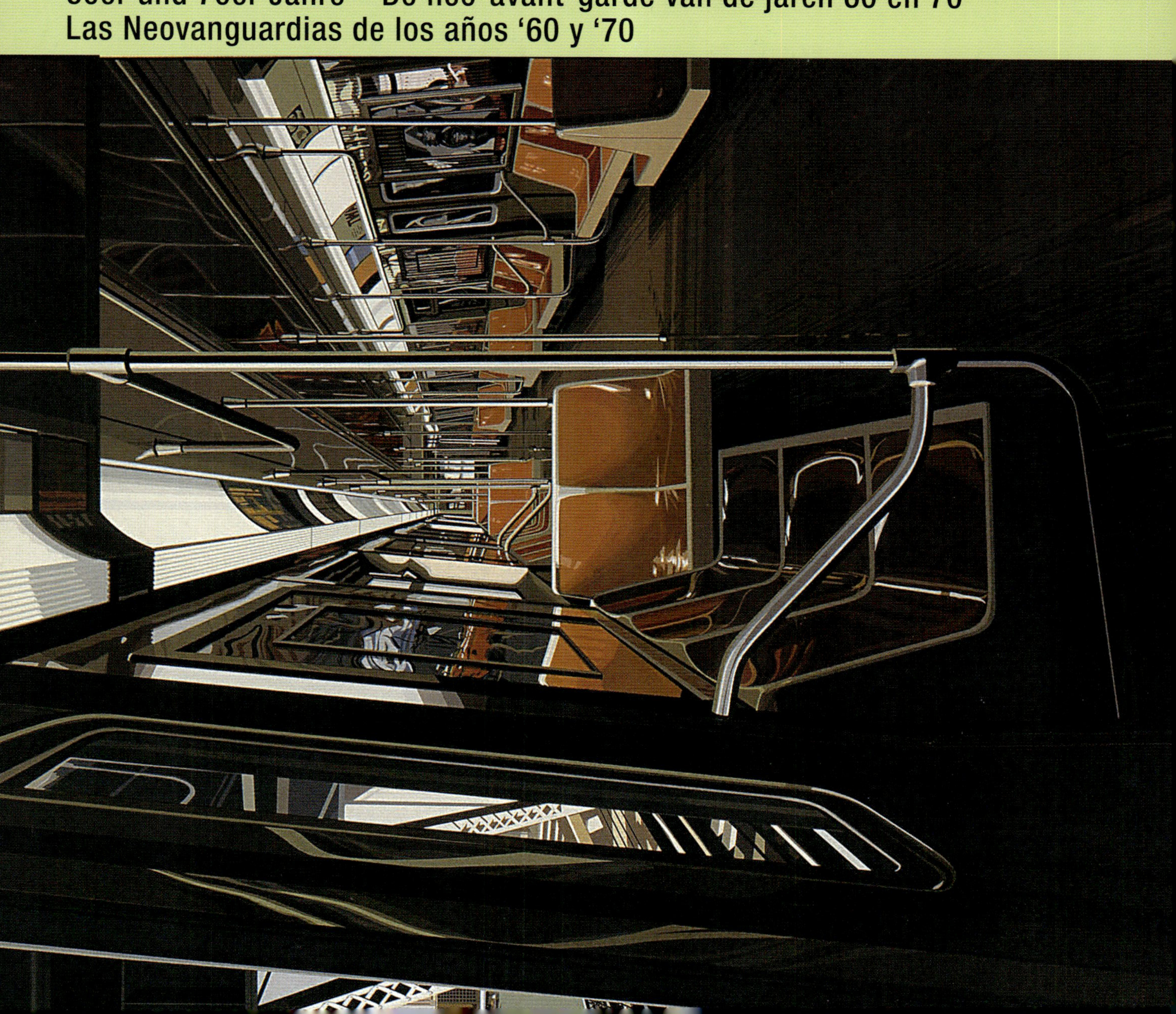

The Neoavanguardia of the 1960s and 1970s • Die Neo-Avantgarde der 60er und 70er Jahre • De neo-avant-garde van de jaren 60 en 70 Las Neovanguardias de los años '60 y '70

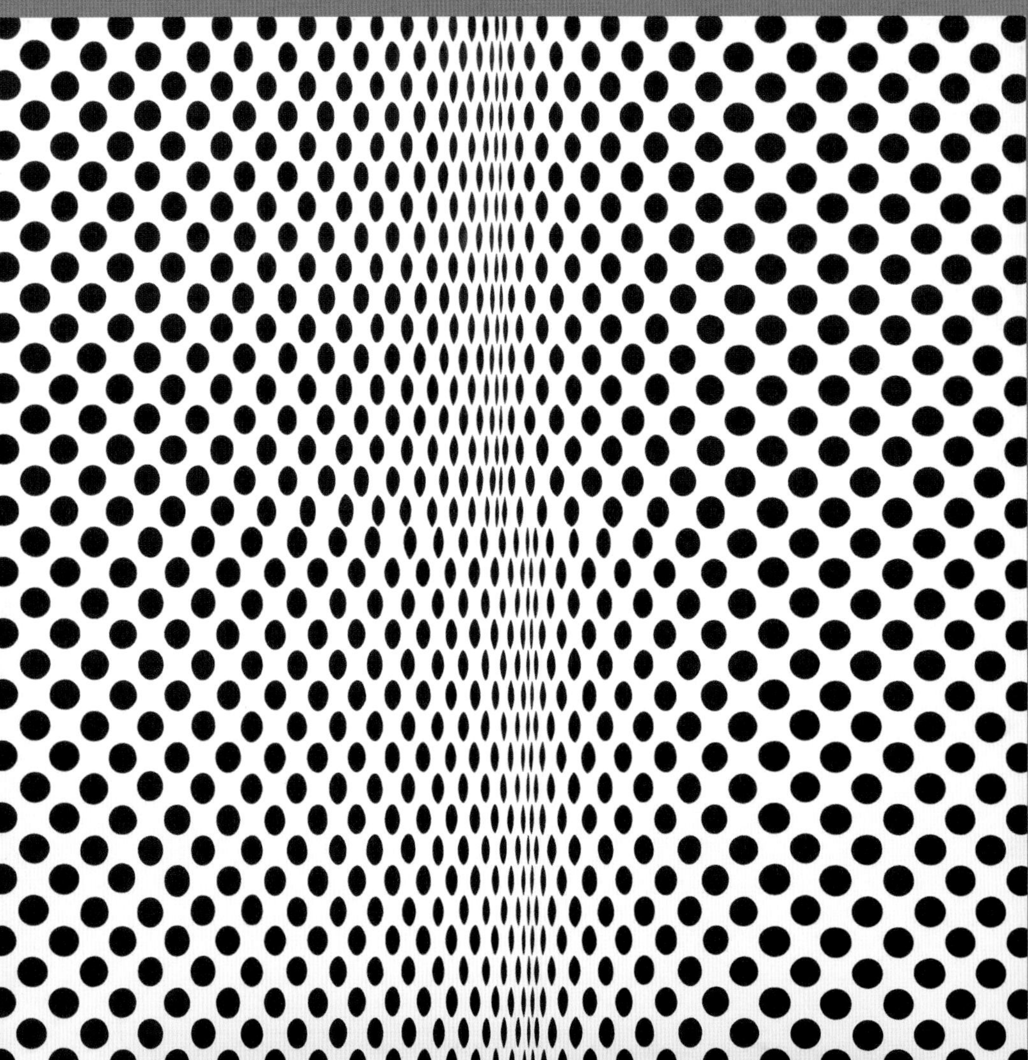

Bridget Riley
(London 1931)

**Fission
Spaltung
Splijting
Fisión**

●●

1963
88,8 x 86,2 cm
34.9 x 33.9 in.
Museum of Modern Art
(MoMA), New York

tempera on wood
Tempera auf Holz
tempera op hout
temple sobre madera

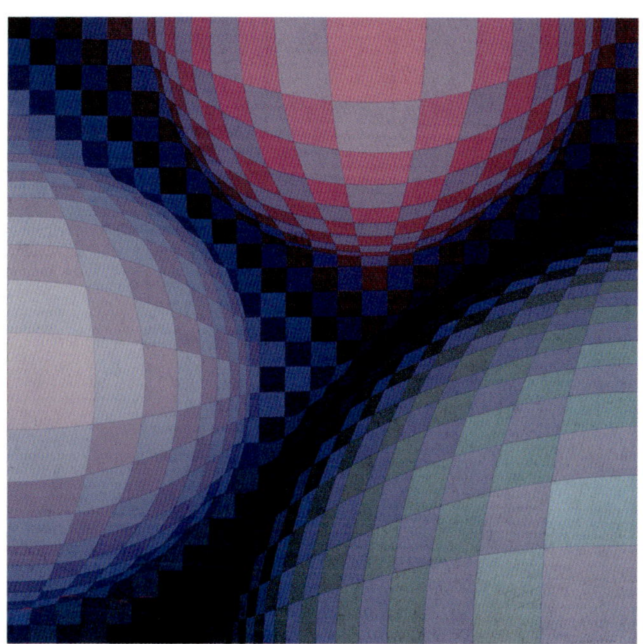

Victor Vasarely
(Pécs 1906 - Paris 1997)

Triond

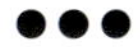

1973
Private collection / Private Sammlung
Privécollectie / Colección privada

acrylic on canvas / Akryl auf Leinwand
acrylverf op doek / acrílico sobre lienzo

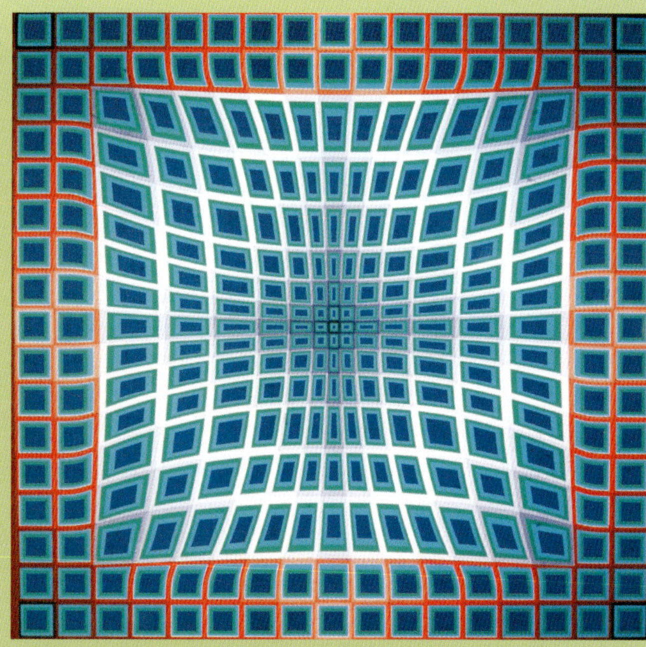

Victor Vasarely
(Pécs 1906 - Paris 1997)

V.P 102

1979
60 x 60 cm / 23.6 x 23.6 in.

oil on plywood / Öl auf Sperrholz
olieverf op multiplex / óleo sobre aglomerado

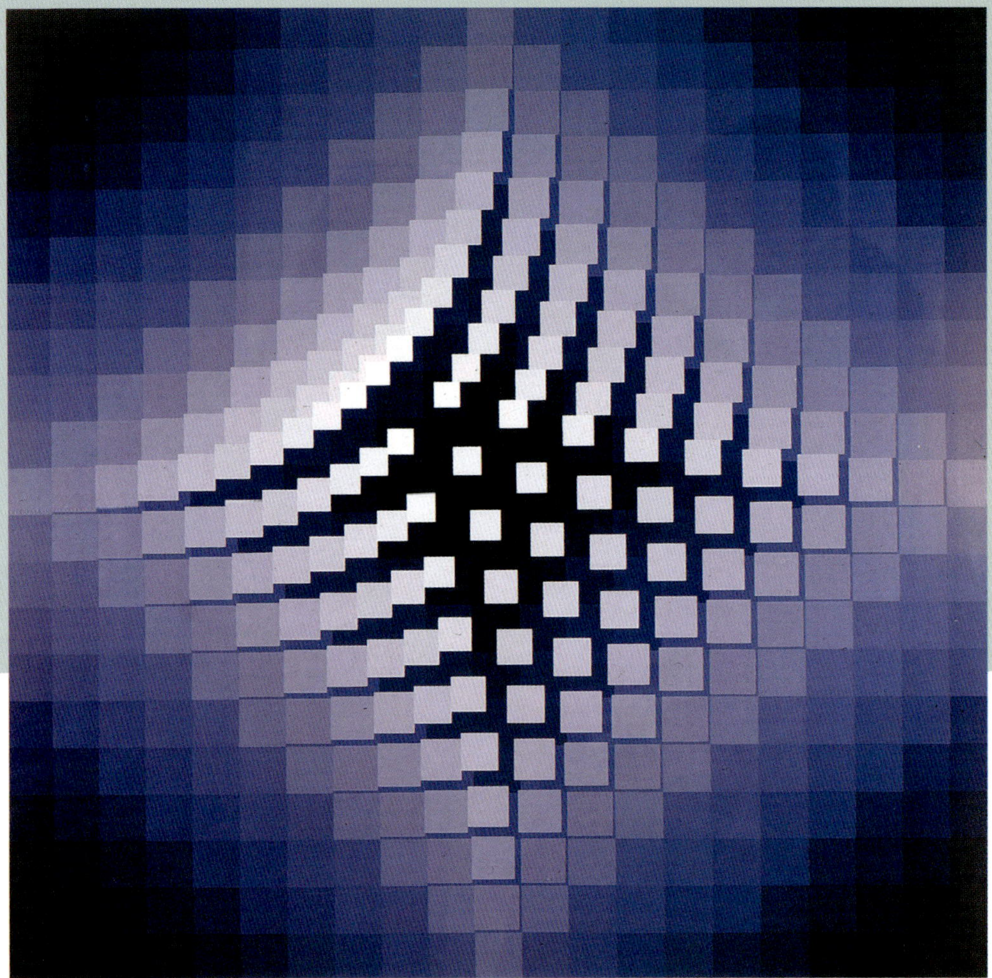

Yvaral
(Jean Pierre Vasarely)
(Paris 1934 - 2002)
Cubic structure
Kubische Struktur
Kubusvormige
structuur
Estructura cúbica

●

Private collection
Private Sammlung
Privécollectie
Colección privada

Vasarely, master of optical illusion, bases his vocabulary on the combination
of circles/squares associated to color scales.

Vasarely, der Meister der optischen Illusionen, basiert sein Vokabular auf der Kombination
aus Kreisen/Quadraten, die mit Farbskalen verbunden sind.

Vasarely, meester van het gezichtsbedrog, baseert zijn stijlvormen op de combinaties
van cirkels/vierkanten verbonden met kleurgradaties.

Vasarely, maestro de las ilusiones ópticas, basa su lenguaje expresivo en las combinaciones
de círculos/cuadrados asociados a escalas de color.

Vera Molnar
(Budapest 1924)

Computer Icon / I
Computer Icone / I
Computericoon / I
Íconos de ordenador / I

●

1973
110 x 110 cm / 43.3 x 43.3 in.
Private collection / Private Sammlung
Privécollectie / Colección privada

acrylic on canvas / Akryl auf Leinwand
acrylverf op doek / acrílico sobre lienzo

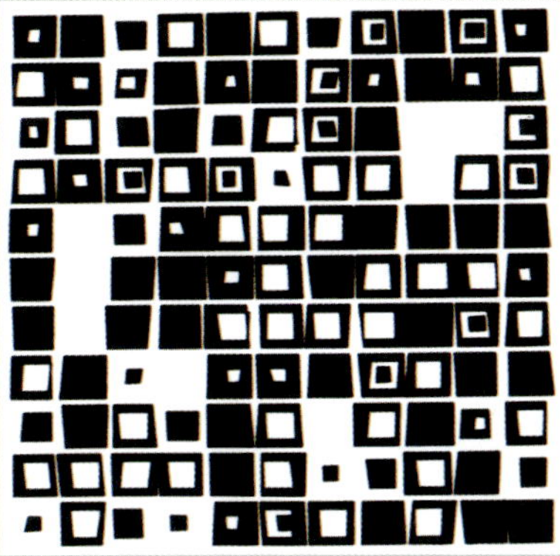

Pol Bury
(Haine-Saint-Pierre 1922 - Paris 2005)

17 horizontal lines and their
cylinders
17 horizontale Schnüren
und ihre Zylinder
17 horizontale koorden
en diens cilinders
17 cuerdas horizontales
y sus cilindros

●●●

1973
125 x 49 x 18,5 cm
49.2 x 19.3 x 7.3 in.
Private collection, Los Angeles

wood, nylon / Holz, Nylon
hout, nylon / madera, nailon

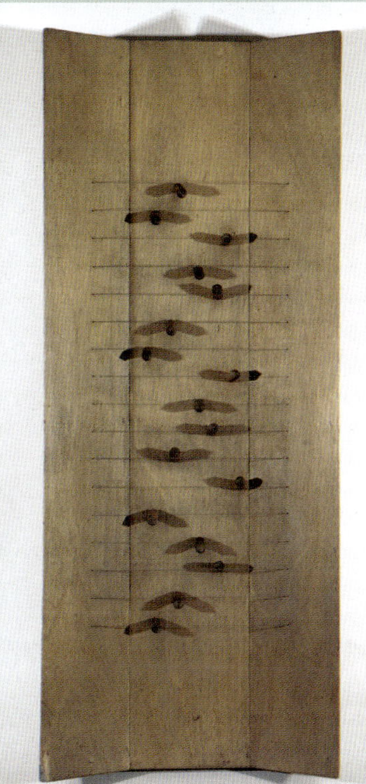

Yaakov Agam
(Rishon LeZion 1928)

Double Metamorphosis II
Doppelte Metamorphose II
Dubbele metamorfose II
Doble metamorfosis II

●

1964
269,2 x 401,8 cm / 106 x 158.3 in.
Museum of Modern Art (MoMA), New York

oil on corrugated aluminium, in 11 parts
Öl auf gewelltem Aluminium, in 11 Teilen
olieverf op golfaluminium
óleo sobre aluminio corrugado, en 11 partes

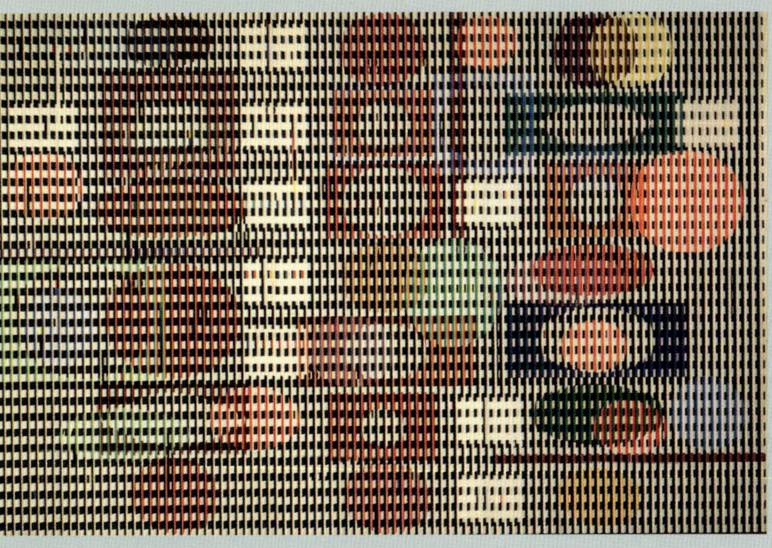

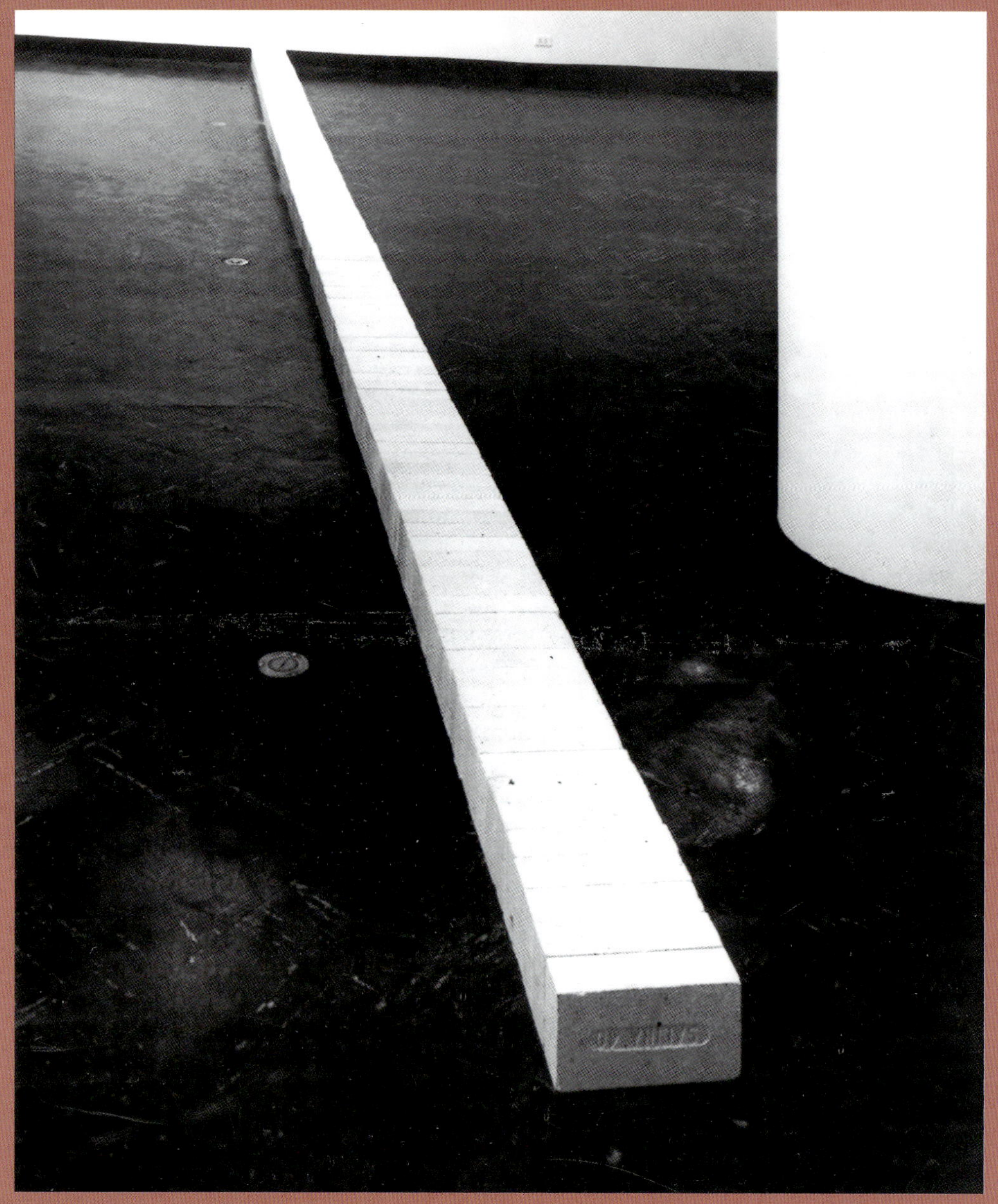

Carl Andre
(Quincy 1935)

Lever, 137
Hefboom, 137
Palanca, 137

● ●

1966
The Jewish Museum, New York

refractory bricks
feuerfeste Backsteine
137 brandstenen
ladrillos refractarios

Andre debunks sculpture: without base, resting on the ground – you can walk on them – they are elementary structures made with industrial materials.

Andre entweiht die Skulptur: ohne Sockel, auf dem Boden liegend, sodass man darüber gehen kann, handelt es sich um elementare Strukturen, die aus industriellen Materialien gefertigt werden.

Andre ontheiligt de sculptuur: de elementaire structuren zijn zonder voetstuk op de grond gezet – men kan er overheen lopen – en zijn gemaakt van industriële materialen.

Andre desacraliza la escultura: sin base, apoyadas en el suelo – se puede caminar sobre ellas – son estructuras elementares realizadas con materiales industriales.

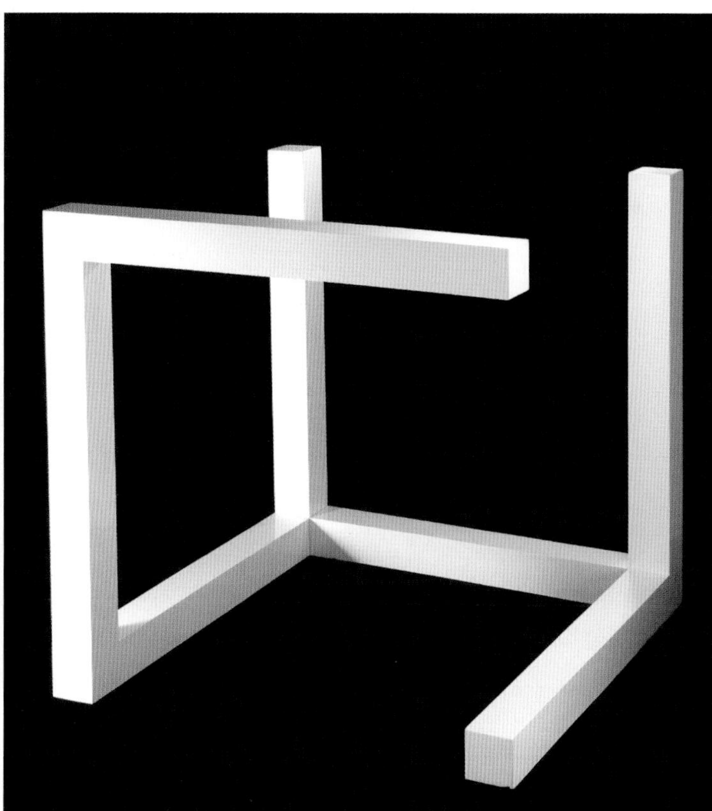

Sol LeWitt
(Hartfotd 1928 - New York 2007)

**Open Cube
Offener Kubus
Open kubus
Cubo abierto**

●●●

1968
105 x 105 x 10 cm / 41.3 x 41.3 x 3.9 in.
Nationalgalerie, Staatliche Museen, Berlin

lacquered akynubuyn / Lackiertes Aluminium
gelakt aluminium / aluminio lacado

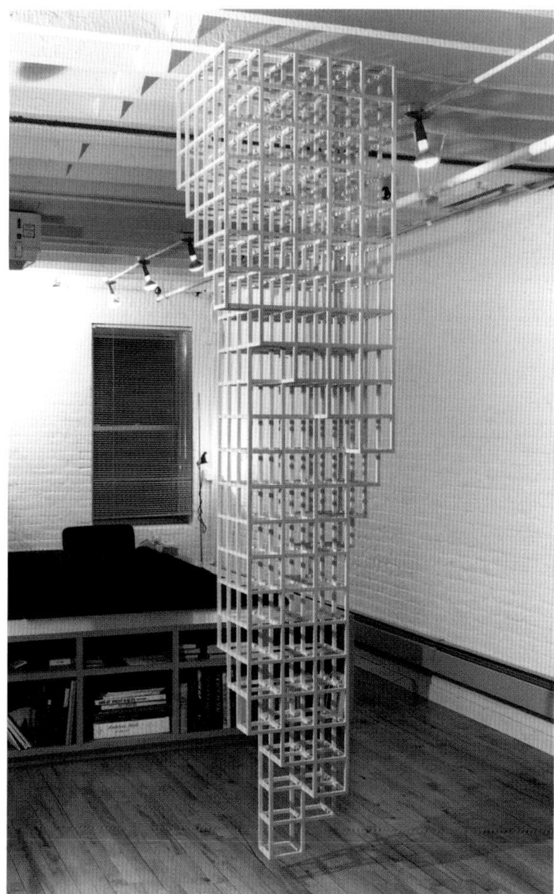

Sol LeWitt
(Hartfotd 1928 - New York 2007)

**Untitled
Ohne Titel
Zonder titel
Sin título**

●

1989
279,4 x 61,6 x 61,6 cm / 110 x 24.2 x 24.2 in.
Wadsworth Atheneum Museum of Art, Hartford (CT)

wood and paint / Holz und Malerei / hout en verf / madera y pintura

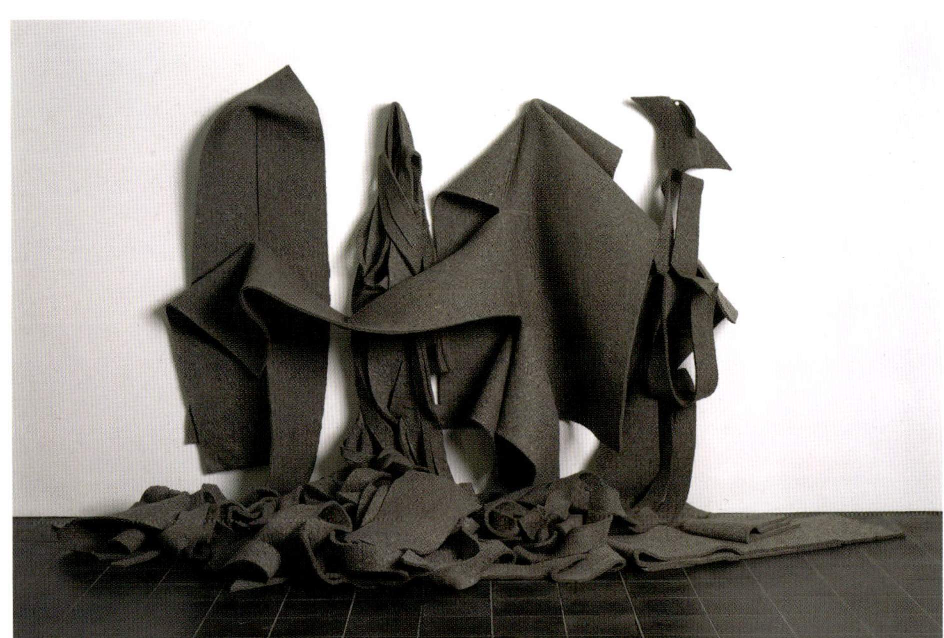

Robert Morris
(Kansas City 1931)

Untitled
Ohne Titel
Zonder titel
Sin título

● ● ●

1967
190 x 400 x 220 cm
74.8 x 157.5 x 86.6 in.
Hamburger Kunsthalle, Hamburg

grey felt, metal
Grauer Filz, Metall
grijs vilt, metaal
fieltro gris, metal

524

Robert Morris
(Kansas City 1931)

Red Felt
Roter Filz
Rood vilt
Fieltro rojo

●

1970
280 x 400 cm / 110.2 x 157.5 in.
Nationalgalerie,
Staatliche Museen, Berlin

felt / Filz / vilt / fieltro

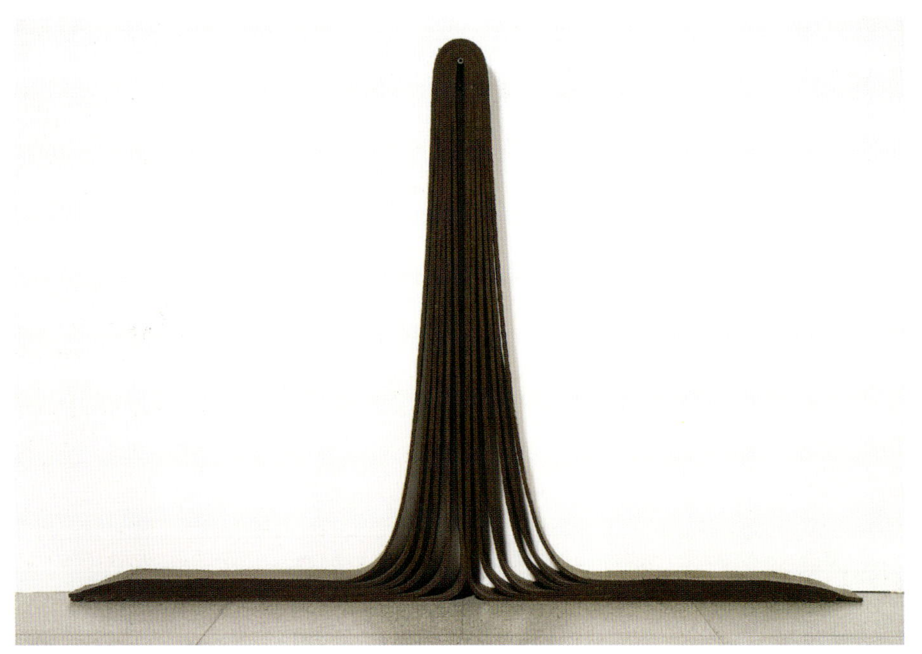

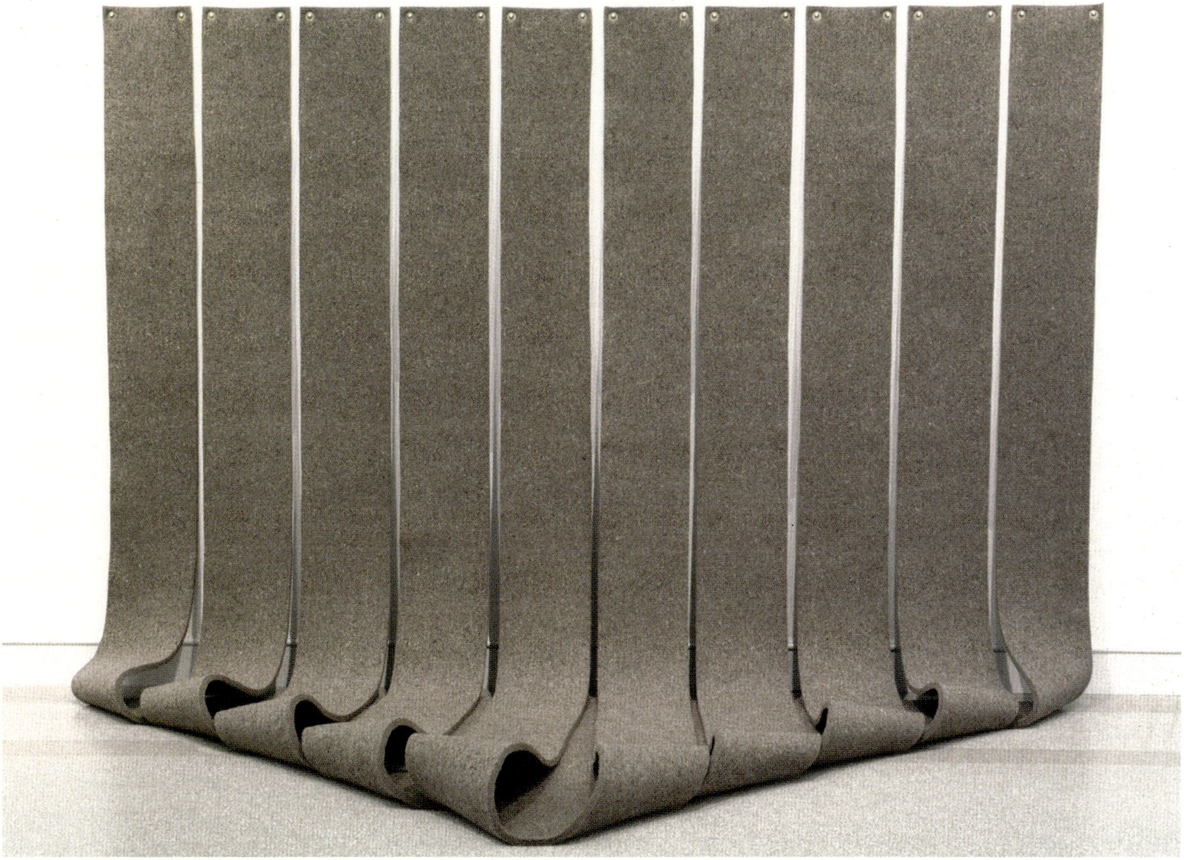

Robert Morris
(Kansas City 1931)

Untitled / Ohne Titel
Zonder titel / Sin título

●

1978
274,3 x 396,2 x 182,8 cm
108 x 156 x 72 in.
Wadsworth Atheneum Museum of Art,
Hartford (CT)

felt / Filz / vilt / fieltro

Robert Morris intervention in this work is minimal: it is the quality
of the material used and its weight that determine its shapes.

Robert Morris' Eingriff in diesem Werk ist geringfügig: Es geht vielmehr um
die Qualität der verwendeten Materialien und die Schwere, die die Formen
bestimmen.

De bijdrage van Robert Morris aan dit werk is miniem: de kwaliteit
en de zwaarte van het gebruikte materiaal bepalen de vormen.

La intervención de Robert Morris en esta obra es mínima: es la calidad
del material utilizado y su peso lo que determina las formas.

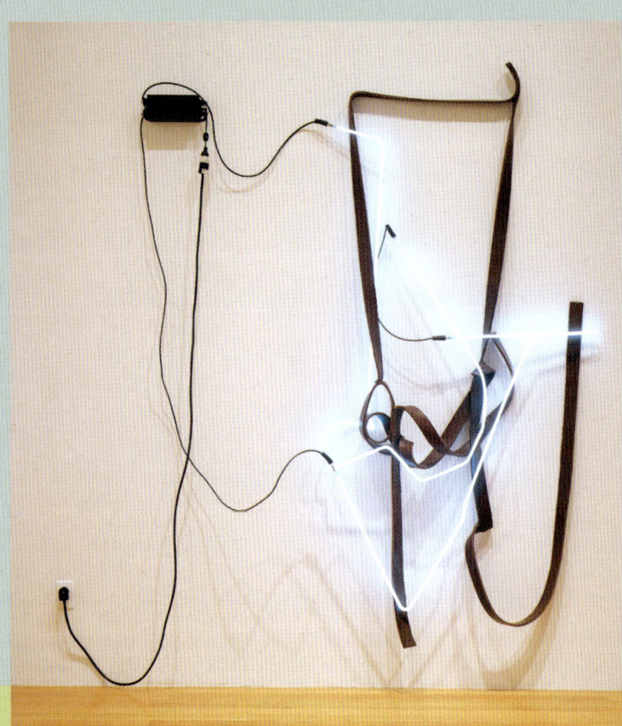

Richard Serra
(San Francisco 1939)

Untitled
Ohne Titel
Zonder titel
Sin título

●●●

1967
244,5 x 186,7 x 17,2 cm / 96.2 x 73.5 x 6.7 in.
Museum of Modern Art (MoMA), New York

vulcanized rubber, neon tubes, transformer and wires
Vulkanisiertes Gummi, Neonröhren, Trasformator und Fäden
gevulkaniseerd rubber, neonbuizen, transformator en draden
goma vulcanizada, tubos de neón, transformadores y cables

Richard Serra
(San Francisco 1939)

One ton support (House of Cards)
Stütze einer Tonne (Schloss aus Papier)
Een stut van een ton (kaartenhuis)
Apeo de una tonelada (Castillo de naipes)

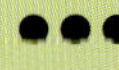

●●●

1969
122 x 122 x 2,5 cm / 48 x 48 x 1 in.
Museum of Modern Art (MoMA), New York

lead-antimony, four plates / Blei-Antimon, vier Platten
lood-antimoon, vier platen / plomo-antimonio, cuatro planchas

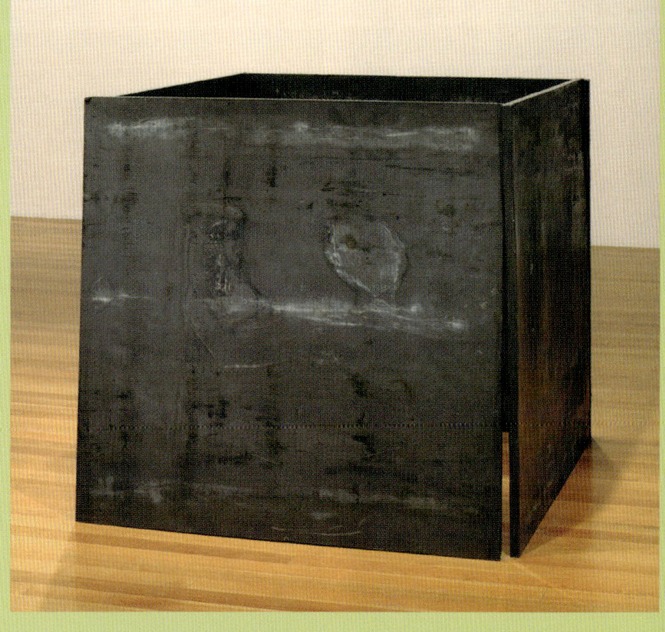

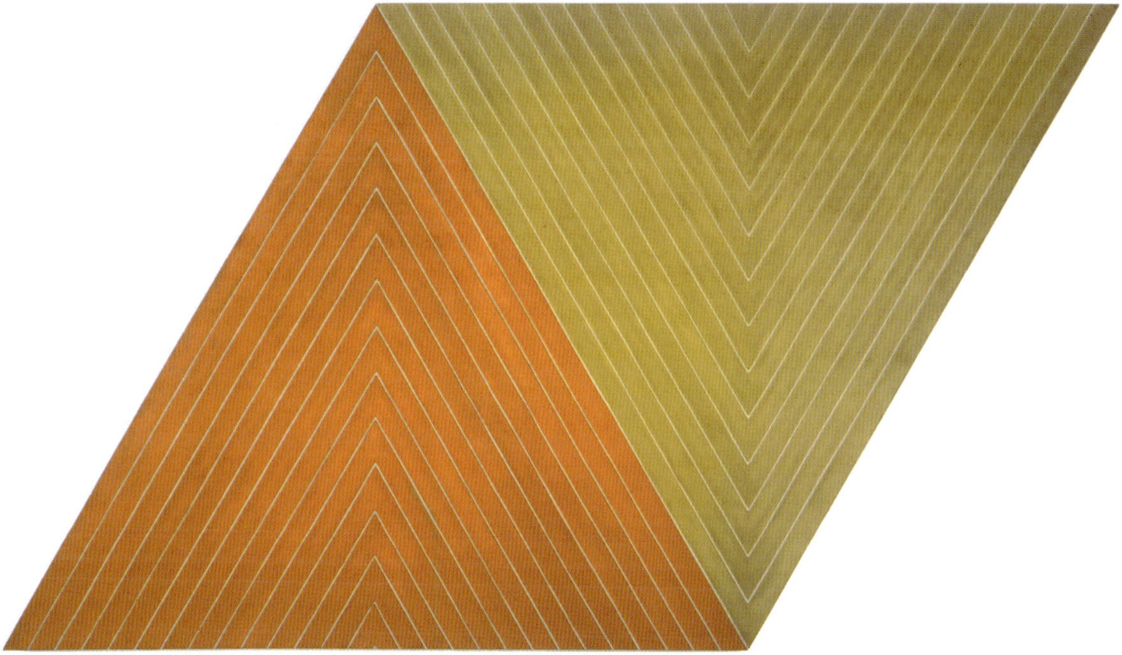

Frank Stella
(Malden 1936)

Valparaiso meat and green
Valparaiso fleischfarben und grün
Valparaiso vleeskleur en groen
Valparaíso carne y verde

●●●

1963
198,1 x 343 x 7,6 cm / 78 x 135 x 3 in.
The Archive of Frank Stella, New York

metal painting on canvas
Metallische Farbe auf Leinwand
metaalverf op doek
pintura metálica sobre lienzo

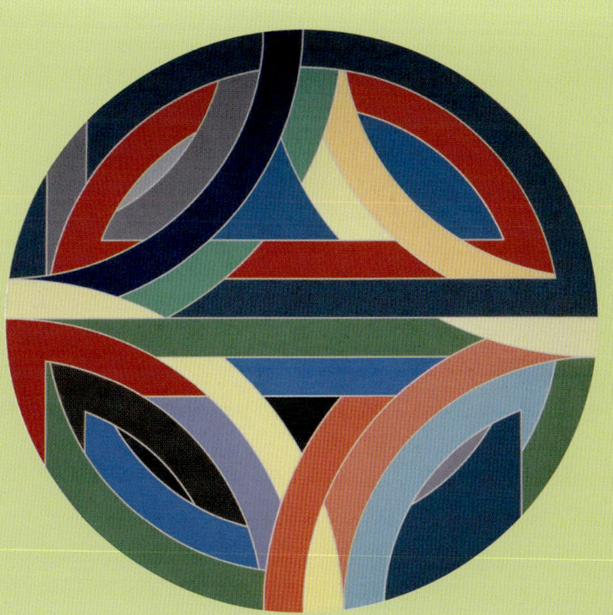

Frank Stella
(Malden 1936)

Sinjerli Variation IV

●

1968
ø 304,8 cm / 120 in.
Wadsworth Atheneum Museum of Art,
Hartford (CT)

acrylic on canvas / Akryl auf Leinwand
acrylverf op doek / acrílico sobre lienzo

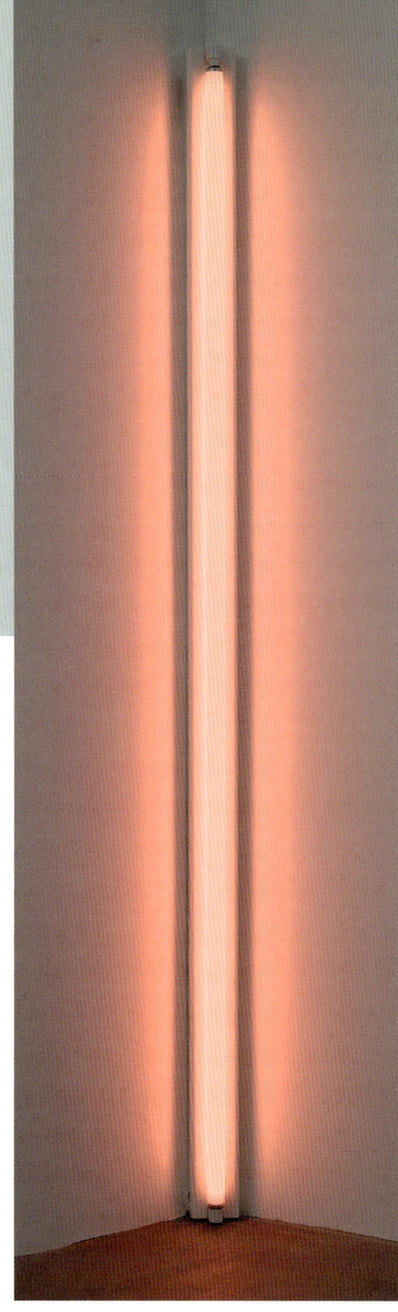

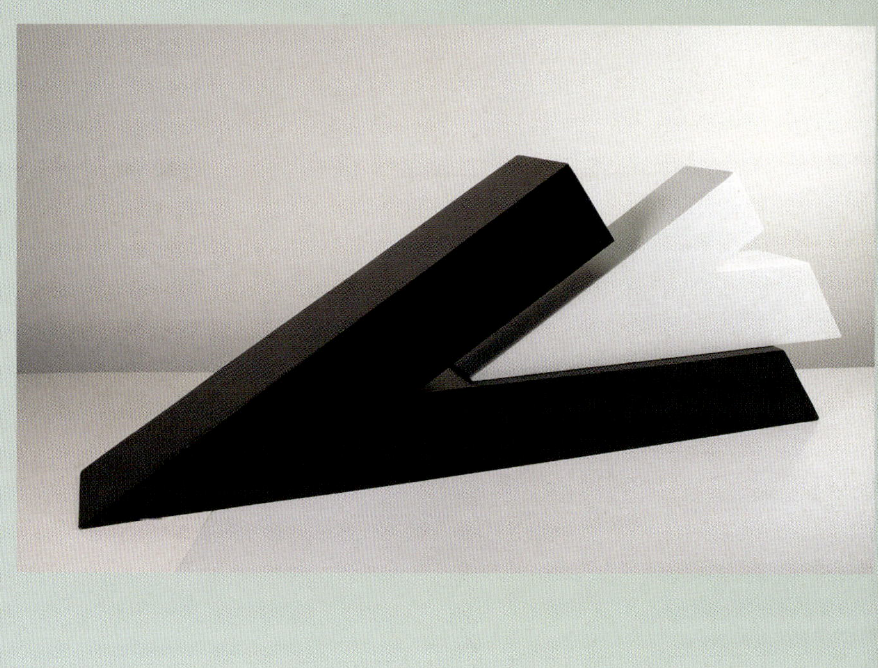

Dan Flavin
(Jamaica, New York 1933 -
Riverhead, New York 1996)

Rose from an corner - A Jasper Johns
Pink aus einer Ecke - Für Jasper Johns
Roze uit een hoek - Voor Jasper Johns
Rosa desde una esquina - A Jasper Johns

●●
1963
243,8 x 13,6 cm / 96 x 5.3 in.
Museum of Modern Art (MoMA),
New York

neon light and metal fastener
Neonlicht und Metallbefestigung
neonlicht op metaal bevestigd
luz de neón y fijación en metal

Ronald Bladen
(Vancouver 1918 - New York 1988)

RAIKO (Modell)

●
1973
51 x 136 x 21 cm
20.1 x 53.6 x 8.2 in.
Nationalgalerie im Hamburger
Bahnhof, Staatliche Museen, Berlin

painted wood / Bemaltes Holz /
beschilderd hout / madera pintada

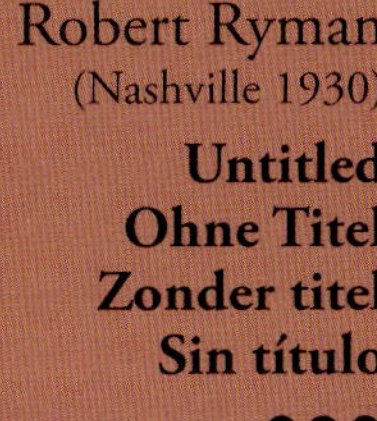

Robert Ryman
(Nashville 1930)

Untitled
Ohne Titel
Zonder titel
Sin título

●●●

1965
28,4 x 28,2 cm / 11.2 x 11.2 in.
Museum of Modern Art
(MoMA), New York

oil on linen canvas
Öl auf Leinenleinwand
olieverf op linnen doek
óleo sobre lienzo de lino

A purified painting that concentrates on the gesture and the matter thanks to the neutral format and the use of white as
detector.

Eine gereinigte Malerei, die sich dank des neutralen Formats und der Verwendung von Weiß als Entwickler
auf die Geste und die Materie konzentriert.

Een zuivere schilderstijl waarbij hij zich door de neutrale vorm en het gebruik van onthullend
wit concentreert op het gebaar en het materiaal.

Una pintura depurada que se concentra en el gesto y en la materia gracias al formato neutro
y a la utilización del blanco como revelador.

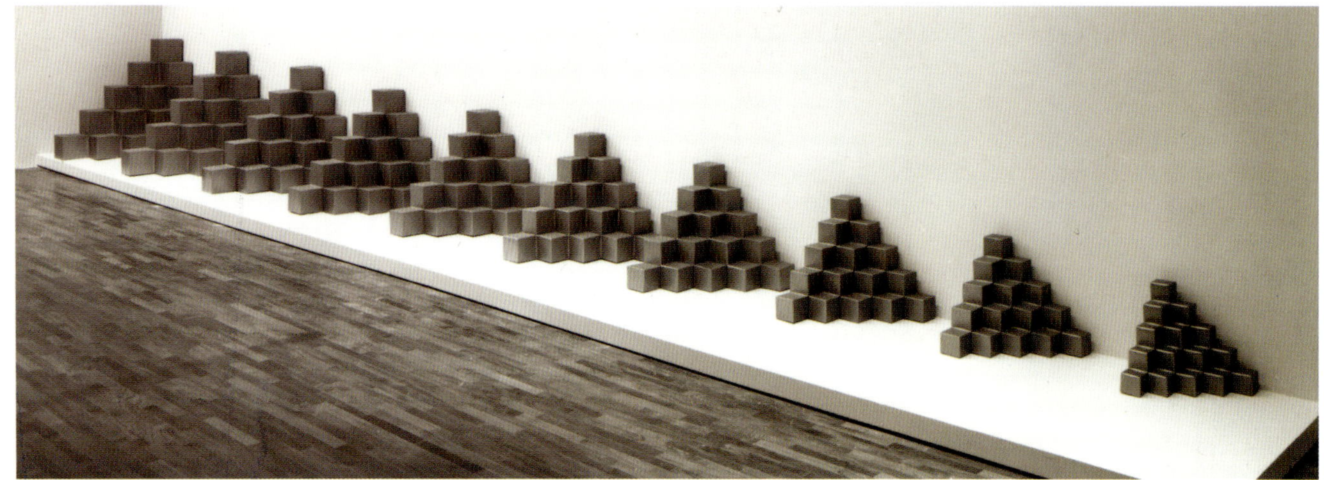

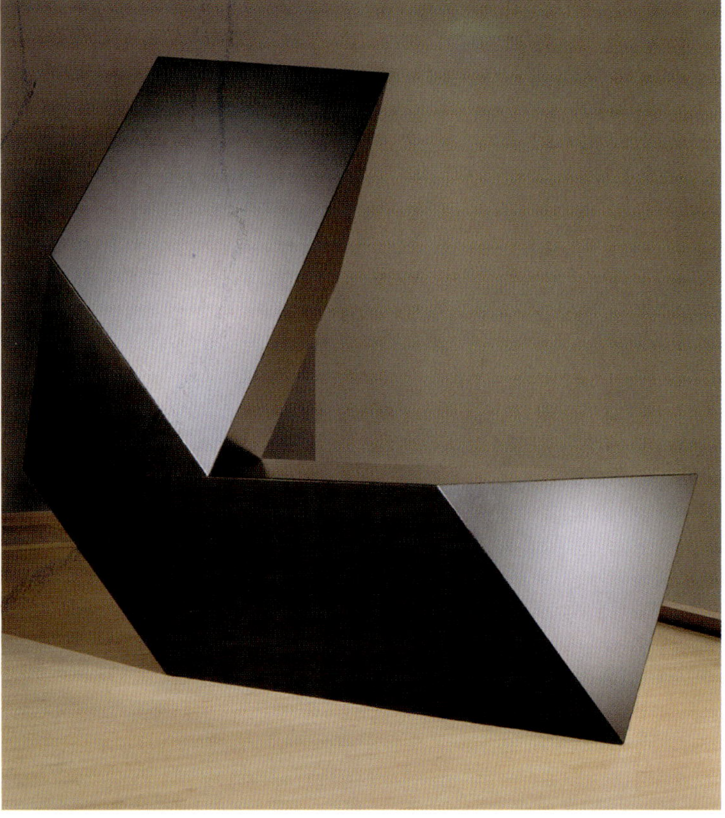

Robert Smithson
(Passaic 1938 - Amarillo 1973)

Alogon #2

1966
Museum of Modern Art (MoMA), New York

◄ Tony Smith
(South Orange 1912 - New York 1980)

Amaryllis

●●

1965
342,9 x 325,1 x 228,6 cm / 135 x 128 x 90 in.
The Metropolitan Museum of Art, New York

painted stee / Bemaltes Stahl
beschilderd staal / acero pintado

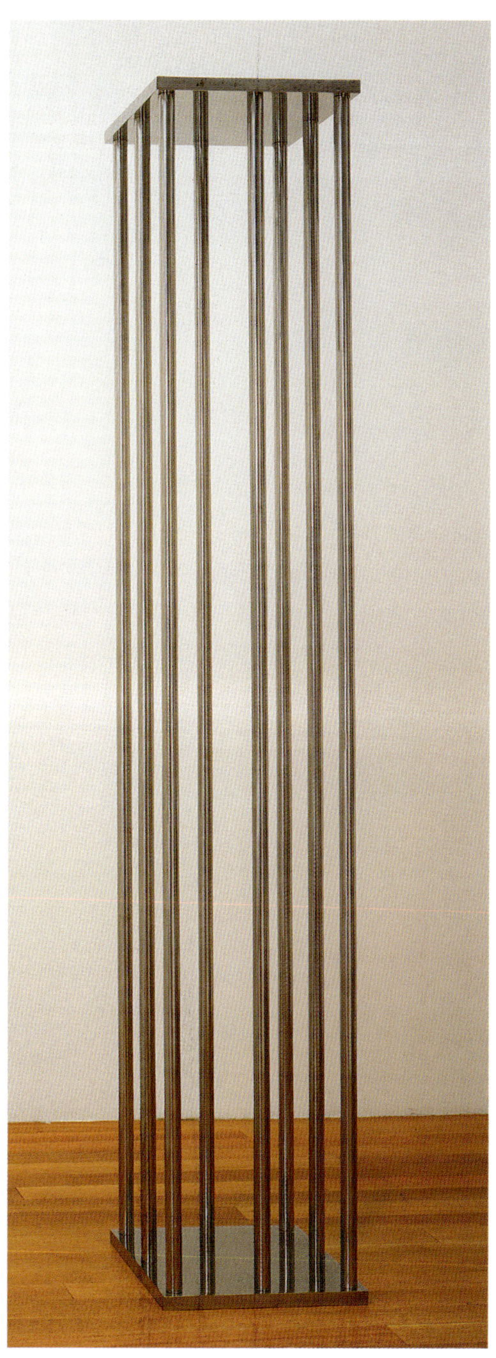

Walter De Maria
(Albany, California 1935)

Cage II
Käfig II
Kooi II
Jaula II

●

1965
216,5 x 36,2 x 36,2 cm / 85.3 x 14.2 x 14.2 in.
Museum of Modern Art (MoMA), New York

stainless steel / Edelstahl / roestvrij staal / acero inoxidable

Joseph Kosuth
(Toledo, Ohio 1945)

It was it No. 5
Es war es Nr. 5
Het was het n. 5

●●●

1986
81 x 214 cm / 31.9 x 84.2 in.
Nationalgalerie, Staatliche Museen, Berlin

photo of text, tubes of white and red neon light
Foto eines Kopfes, Neonlichtröhren in weiß und rot
foto van tekst, witte en rode neonbuizen
foto de texto, tubos de luz de neón blanco y rojo

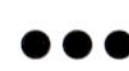

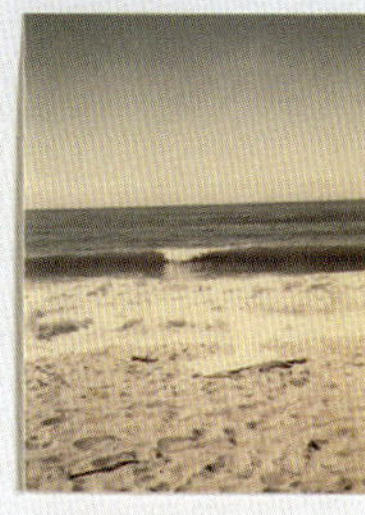

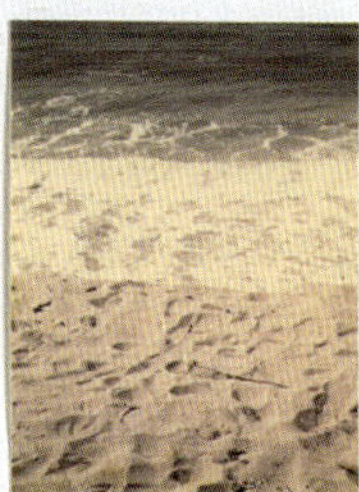

Robert Barry
(New York 1936 - 1989)

Series of the inert gas, Argon (AR) / Inert Gas Series, Argon (AR)
Serie inert gas, Argon (AR) / Serie del gas inerte, Argón (AR)

●

1969
50 x 50 cm / 19.7 x 19.7 in.
Hamburger Kunsthalle, Hamburg

page of photograph catalogue, slides / Seite eines Fotokatalogs, Diapositive
pagina uit een fotocatalogus, dia's / página de catálogo de fotografía, diapositivas

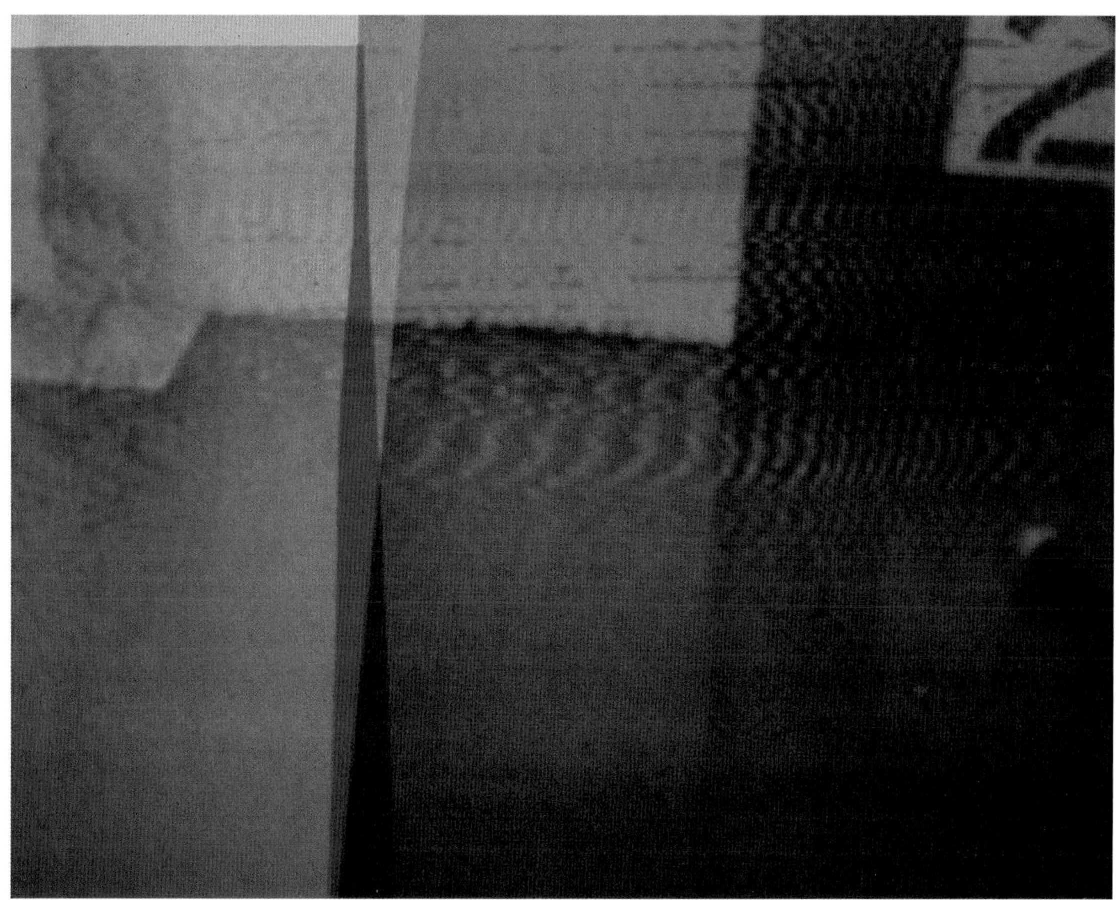

Keith Sonnier
(Momou 1941)

Photogram
Photogramm
Fotogram
Fotograma

●●●

1970
50 x 60 cm / 19.7 x 23.6 in.
Nationalgalerie, Staatliche Museen, Berlin

color photo / Farbfoto / kleurenfoto / foto a color

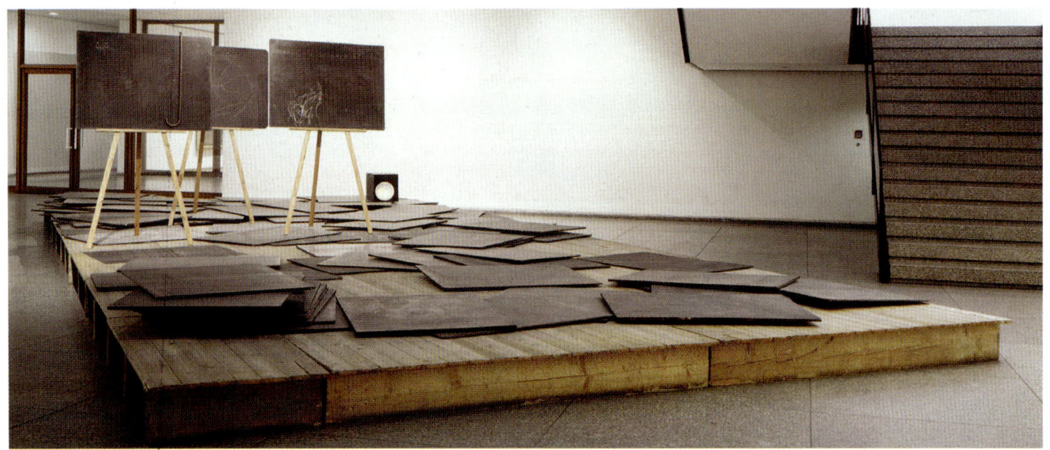

534

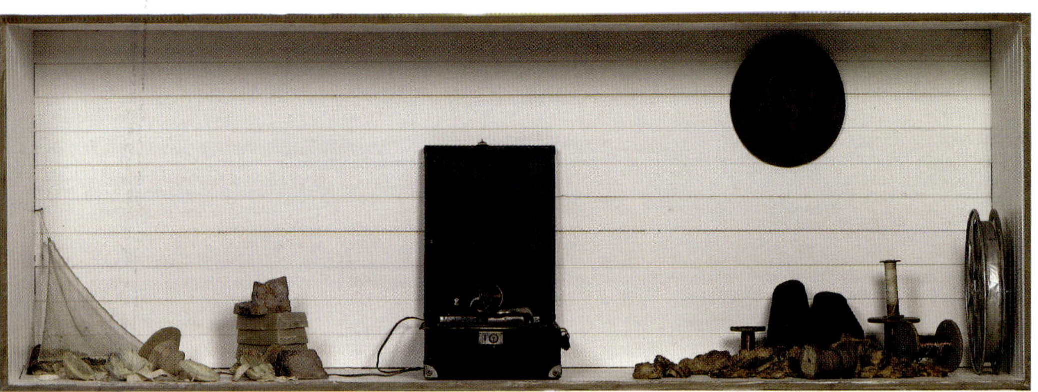

Joseph Beuys
(Krefeld 1921 - Düsseldorf 1986)

Shop window / Vitrine / Vitrina

●●

1981
Hamburger Kunsthalle, Hamburg

case in wood and glass, objects in fat and various materials, some edible
Vitrine aus Holz und Glas, Objekte aus Fett und verschiedene Materialien, darunter Lebensmittel
houten en glazen vitrine, vette objecten en andere materialen, waaronder voedsel
vitrina de madera y vidrio, objetos en grasa y materiales varios, entre ellos, productos alimentarios

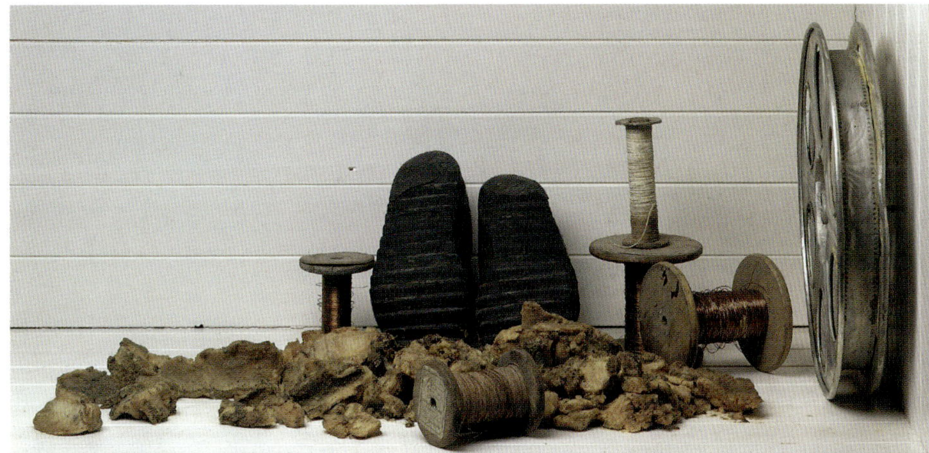

Joseph Beuys
(Krefeld 1921 - Düsseldorf 1986)

Shop window, detail / Vitrine, Detail
Vitrina, detalle

●   535

1981
Hamburger Kunsthalle, Hamburg

case in wood and glass, objects in fat and various materials, some edible
Vitrine aus Holz und Glas, Objekte aus Fett und verschiedene Materialien, darunter Lebensmittel
Houten en glazen vitrine, vette objecten en andere materialen, waaronder voedsel
vitrina de madera y vidrio, objetos de grasa y materiales varios, entre ellos, productos alimentarios

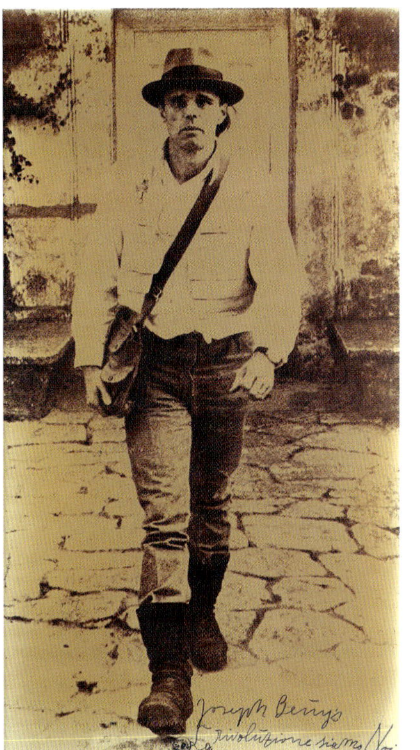

Joseph Beuys
(Krefeld 1921 - Düsseldorf 1986)

The Revolution is us / Die Revolution sind wir
De revolutie zijn wij / La revolución somos nosotros

●●●

1972
191 x 102 cm / 75.2 x 40.2 in.
Hamburger Kunsthalle, Hamburg

transparency (print on polyester sheet) / Transparent (Druck auf Polyesterfolie)
transparantie (print op polyesterblad) / transparencia (impresión sobre hoja de poliéster)

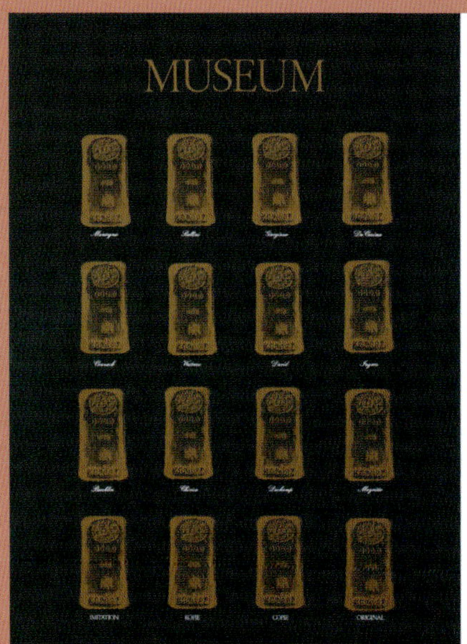
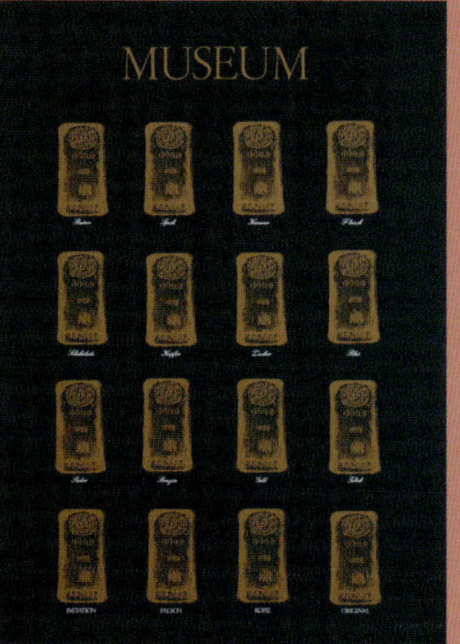

Marcel Broodthaers
(Bruxelles 1924 - Köln 1976)

Museum-Museum

● ●

1972
83 x 59,1 cm / 32.6 x 23.2 in.
Museum of Modern Art
(MoMA), New York

serigraphy / Siebdruck
zeefdruk / serigrafía

Hans Haacke
(Köln 1936)

Oil Painting: Tribute to Marcel Broodthaers
Ölgemälde: Hommage an Marcel Broodthaers
Olieverfschilderij: hulde aan Marcel Broodthaers
Pintura en óleo: Homenaje a Marcel Broodthaers

● ●

1982
518,16 x 883,92 cm x 204 x 348 in.
Los Angeles County Museum of Art, Los Angeles

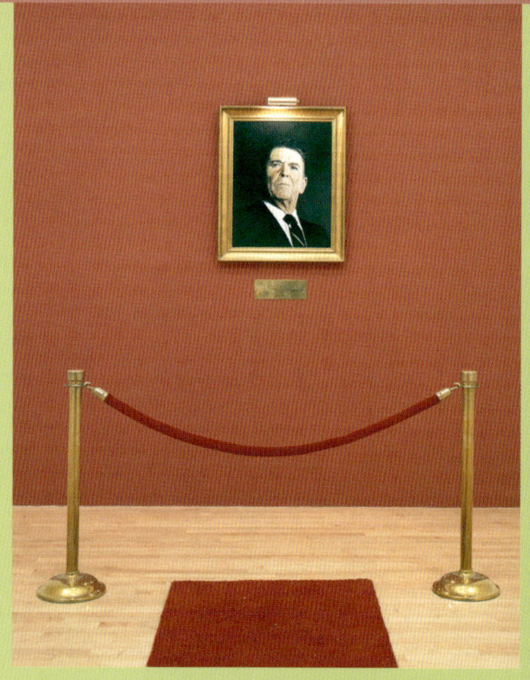

Bruce Nauman
(Fort Wayne 1941)

Human / Need / Desire
Menschlich / Bedürfnis / Sehnsucht
Menselijk / Behoefte / Wens
Humano / Necesidad / Deseo

●●●

1983
239,8 x 179 x 65,4 cm
94.4 x 70.4 x 25.7 in.
The Museum of Modern Art
(MoMA), New York

neon tubes and glass tubes
Neonröhren und Glasröhren
neonbuizen en glazen buizen
tubos de neón y tubos de vidrio

Fascinated by the hypnotic neon
lights of commercial signs,
and using writing as matter,
Nauman questions the viewer on life.

Naumann ist von der hypnotischen
Wirkung der Neonfarben in
Werbeschriftzügen fasziniert. Durch
Verwendung der Schrift als Materie regt
er den Betrachter zum Nachdenken
über das Leben an.

Nauman die gefascineerd is door
de neonlichten van de commerciële
uithangborden en die het schrift
als materie gebruikt, zet de
toeschouwer ertoe aan over het
bestaan na te denken.

Fascinado por los neones hipnóticos
de los carteles comerciales, y
utilizando la escritura como materia,
Nauman interroga al espectador
sobre la existencia.

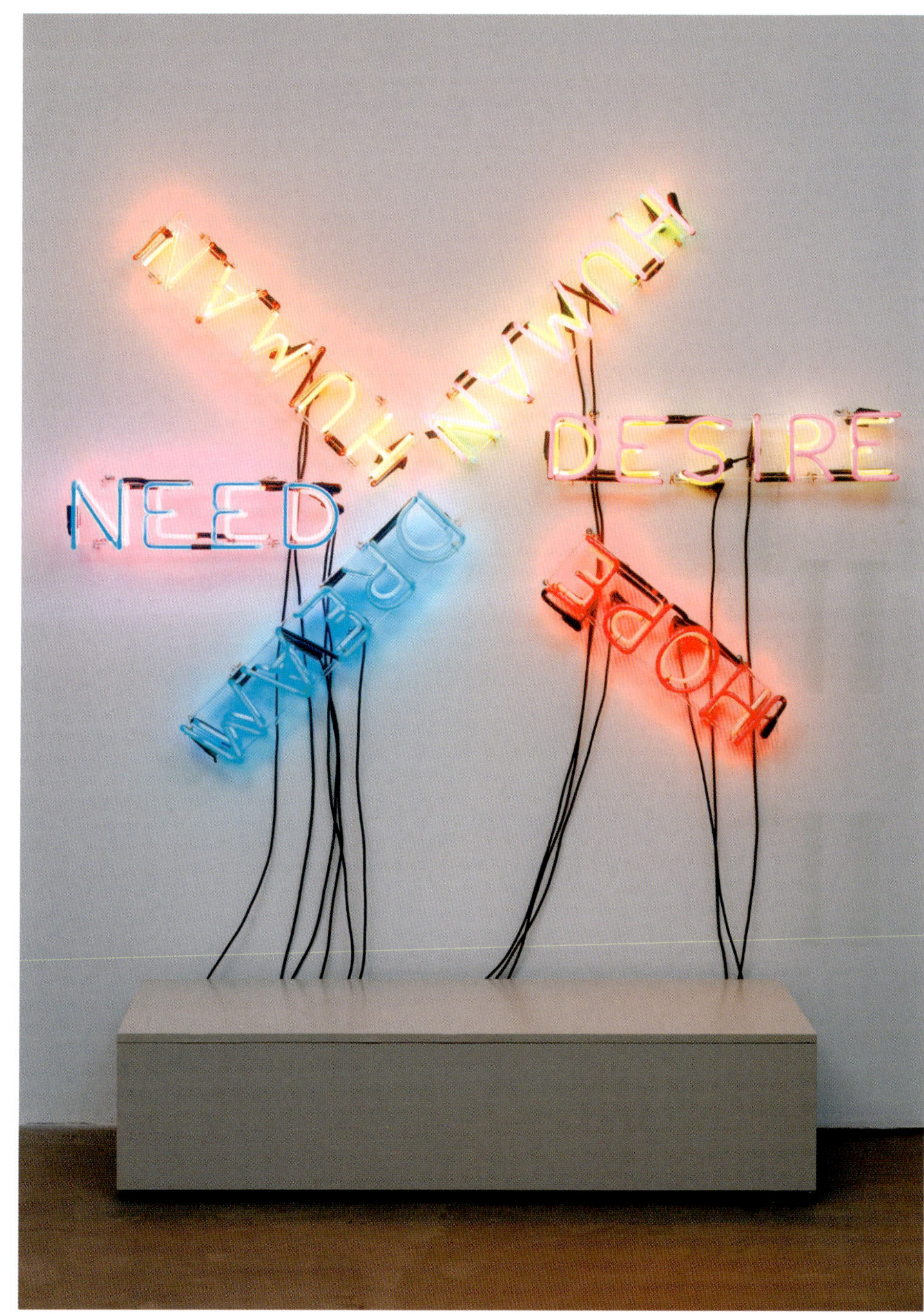

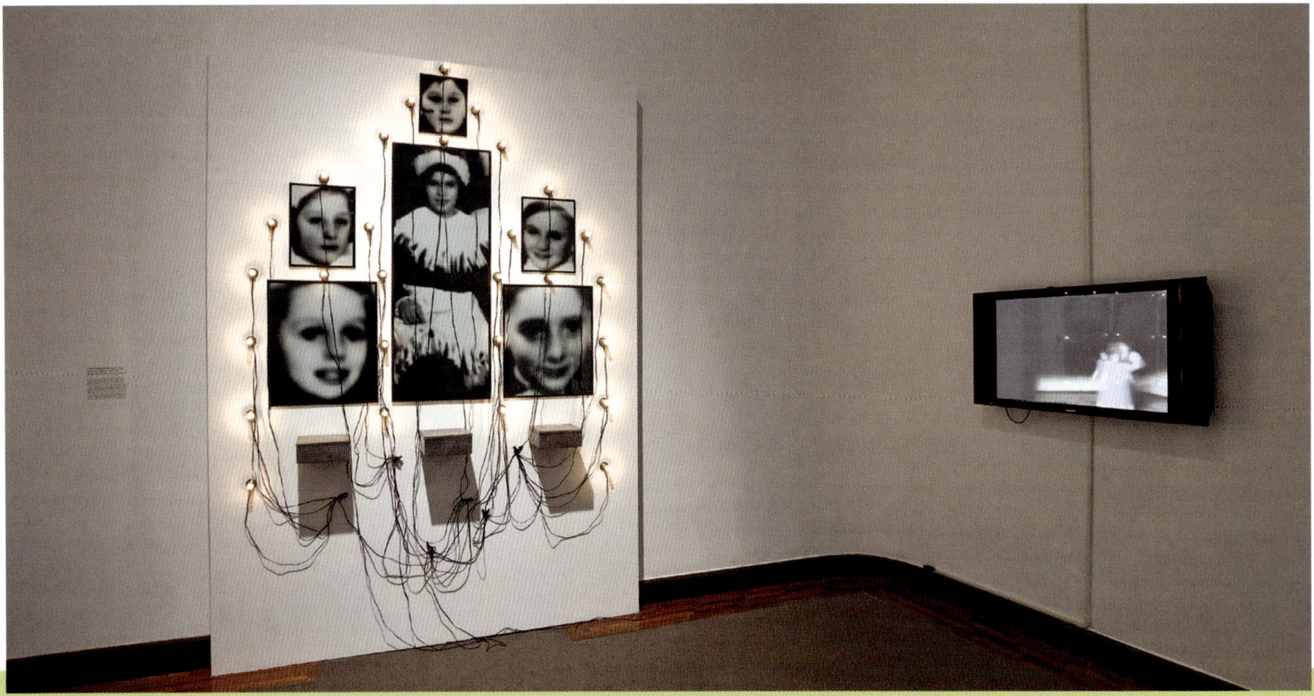

Christian Boltanski
(Paris 1944)

Shop window of reference
Refertenvitrine
Referentievitrine
Vitrina de referencia
● ●

1970
ca. 70 x 120 x 13 cm / 27.6 x 47.2 x 5.1 in.
Hamburger Kunsthalle, Hamburg

shop window in wood and glass with objects in
cardboard, paper, photo paper, fabric, hair, steel, soil
Vitrine aus Holz und Glas mit Objekten aus Karton,
Papier, Fotopapier, Stoff, Haaren, Stahl, Erde
houten en glazen vitrine met objecten gemaakt van
karton, papier, fotopapier, stof, haar, staal, aarde
vitrina de madera y vidrio con objetos de cartón,
papel, papel fotográfico, tela, cabellos, acero, barro

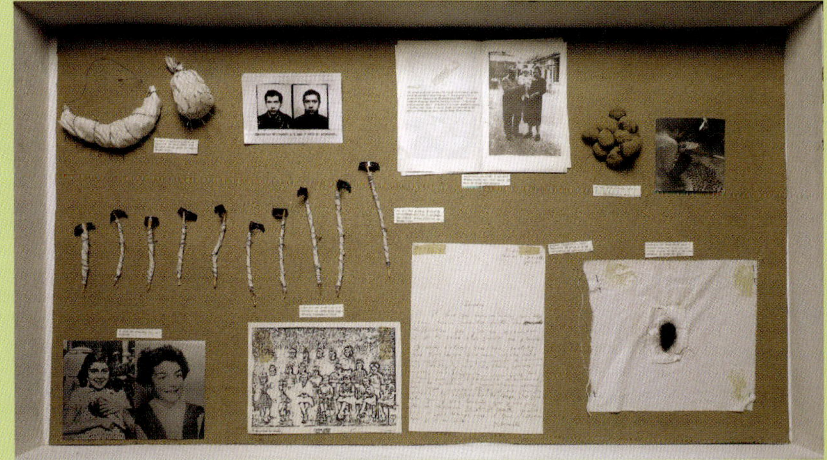

◀ Christian Boltanski
(Paris 1944)

Monument (Odessa)

●

1989-2003
The Jewish Museum, New York

On Kawara
(Kariya 1932)

I am still alive
Ich lebe noch
Ik leef nog
Todavía estoy vivo

●●

1973
14,9 x 21 cm / 5.8 x 8.2 in.
Museum of Modern Art (MoMA), New York

ballpoint pen on 4 telegrams / Kugelfeder auf 4 Telegrammen
balpen op 4 telegrammen / bolígrafo sobre cuatro telegramas

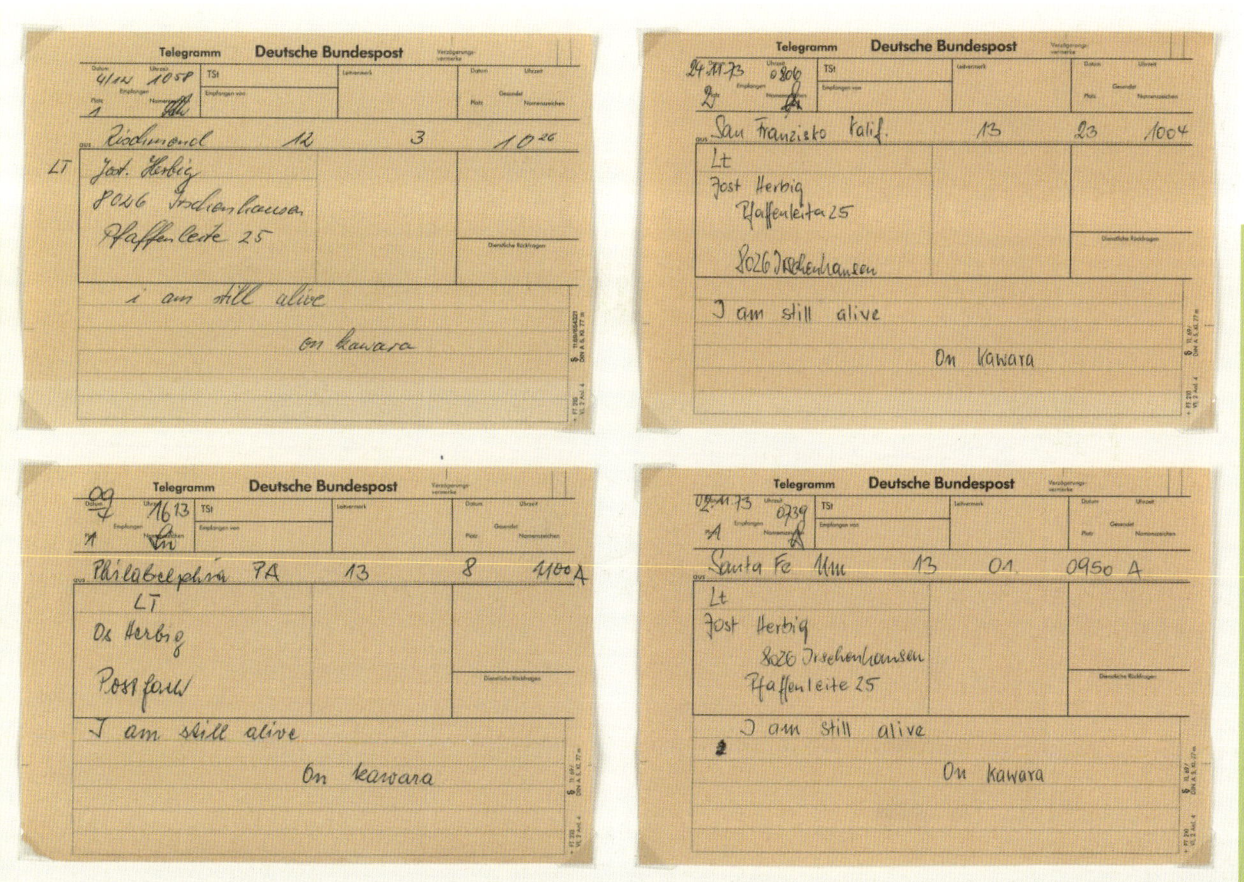

Hanne Darboven
(München 1941 - Hamburg 2009)

Milieu 80, Posthumous
Milieu 80, Posthum
Milieu 80, Postuum
Milieu 80, Póstumo

● ● ●

1987
42 x 30 cm / 16.5 x 11.8 in.
Nationalgalerie im Hamburger Bahnhof, Staatliche Museen,
Berlin

collage and ink on paper, 56 sheets
Collage und Tinte auf Papier, 56 Blätter
collage en inkt op papier, 56 vellen
collage y tinta sobre papel, 56 hojas

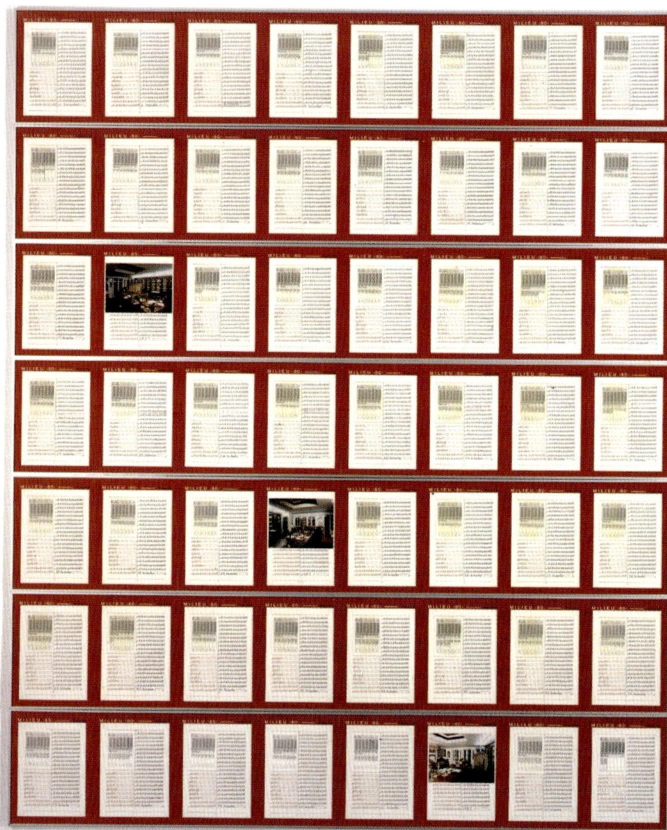

Roman Opalka
(Abbeville 1931)

OPALKA 1965 / 1 - oo Detail 1 - 35327

●

1965
196 x 135 cm / 77.2 x 53.2 in.
Musée Sztuki, Lodz

tempera on canvas / Tempera auf Leinwand
tempera op doek / temple sobre lienzo

John Baldessari
(National City 1931)

**Solving Each Problem
as it Arises**
●●●
1966-1968
150 x 117 cm
59 x 46 in.
Yale University Art Gallery, New
Haven (CT)

acrylic on canvas
Akryl auf Leinwand
acrylverf op doek
acrílico sobre lienzo

Hermann Nitsch
(Wien 1938)

**Stretcher
Trage
Brancard
Camilla**
●●●
1978
240 x 50 x 16 cm / 94.5 x 19.7 x 6.3 in.
Hamburger Kunsthalle, Hamburg

wood and canvas / Holz und Leinwand
hout en doek / madera y lienzo

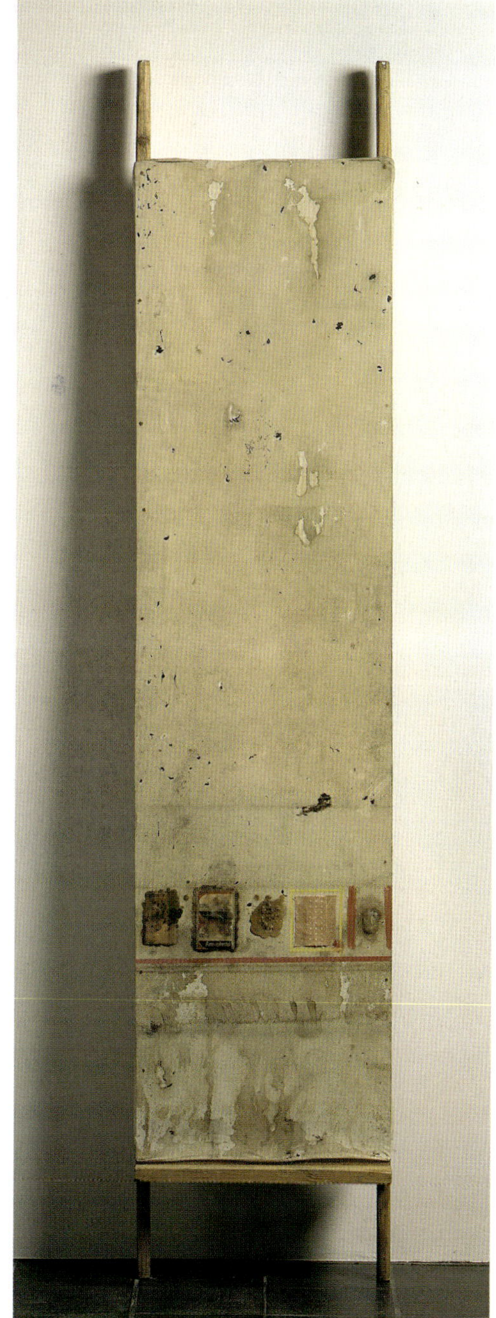

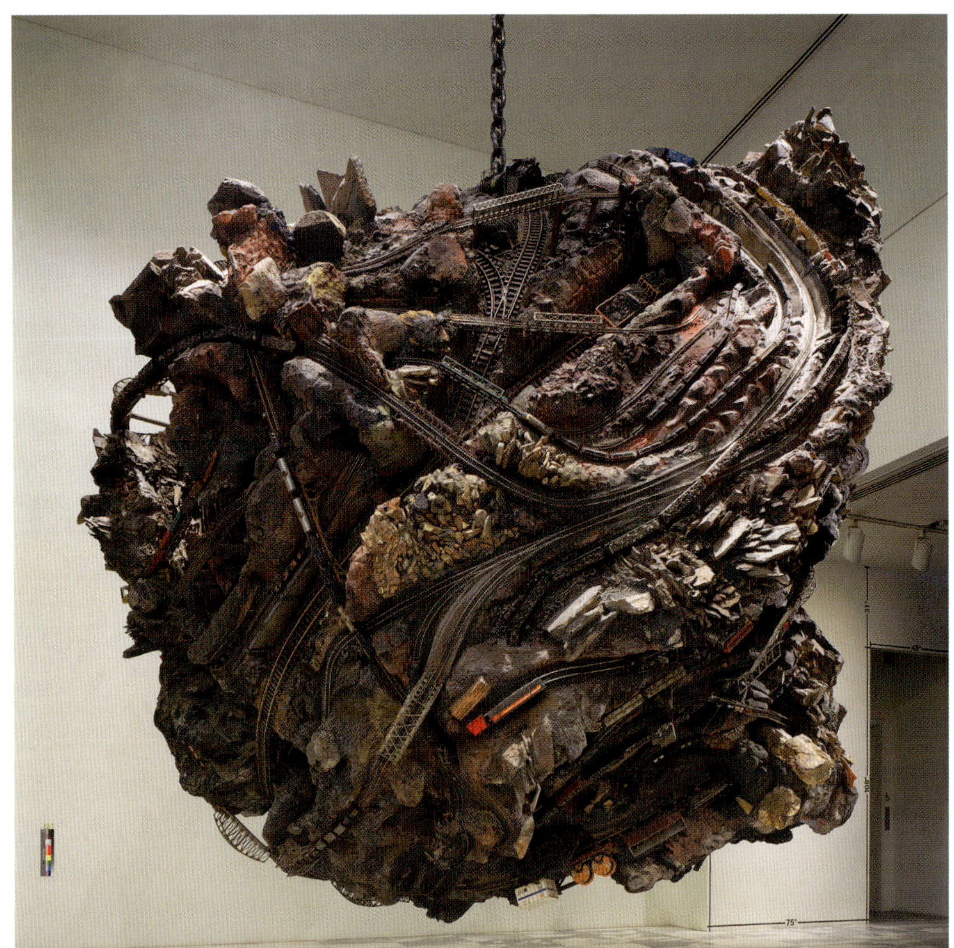

Chris Burden
(Boston 1946)

**Head of Medusa
Kopf der Medusa
Medusahoofd
Cabeza de Medusa**

●●●

1990
ø 426,7 cm / 168.1 in.
The Museum of Modern Art
(MoMA), New York

plywood, steel, cement, rock,
5 tracks and 7 toy trains
Sperrholz, Stahl, Zement, Felsgestein,
5 Spielzeuggleise und 7 Züge
multiplex, staal, cement, rots,
5 spoorlijnen en 7 speelgoedtreintjes
aglomerado, acero, cemento, roca,
cinco vías y siete trenes de juguete

An object that resembles a planet, massive, menacing, but the danger comes from within since this work,
according to Burden, is talking about AIDS.

Ein Objekt, das einem Planeten ähnelt, massiv, bedrohlich, allerdings kommt die Gefahr von innen,
denn dieses Werk, so Burden, handelt von AIDS.

Een op een planeet lijkend object, massief, dreigend; maar het gevaar komt van binnenuit,
daar dit werk naar Burdens eigen zeggen over AIDS gaat.

Un objeto que se asemeja a un planeta, macizo, amenazante, pero el peligro proviene del interior,
dado que esta obra, según Burden, habla del SIDA.

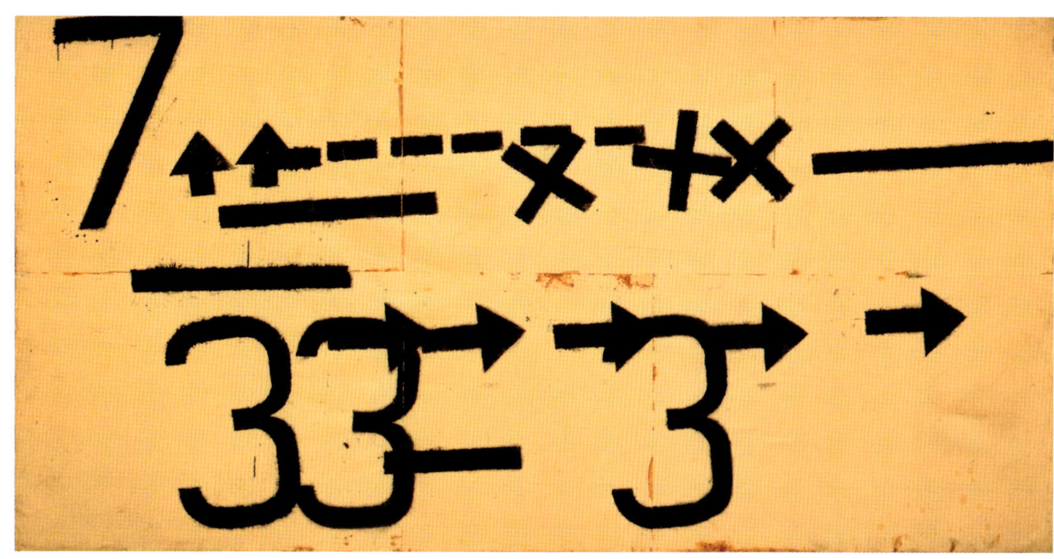

Jannis Kounellis
(Piraeus 1936)

Untitled (7x33)
Ohne Titel (7x33)
Zonder titel (7x33)
Sin título (7x33)

●●●

1959
135 x 255 cm
53.1 x 100.4 in.
Museum of Modern Art
(MoMA), New York

tempera and glue on
paper
Tempera und Leim auf
Papier
tempera en lijm op
papier
temple y cola sobre papel

543

Vito Acconci
(New York 1940)

Adjustable Wall Brassiere
Verstellbarer Wand-BH
Verstelbare wandbeha
Sostén de pared ajustable

●

1990
424,1 x 530,8 x 416,5 cm / 166.9 x 209 x 164 in.
Museum of Modern Art (MoMA), New York

plaster, steel, canvas, electrical light bulbs,
and audio equipment
Kreide, Stahl, Leinwand, Glühbirmen
und Audio-Ausrüstung
gips, staal, doek, lichtpeertjes
en audio-apparatuur
yeso, acero, lienzo, bombillas y equipos de audio

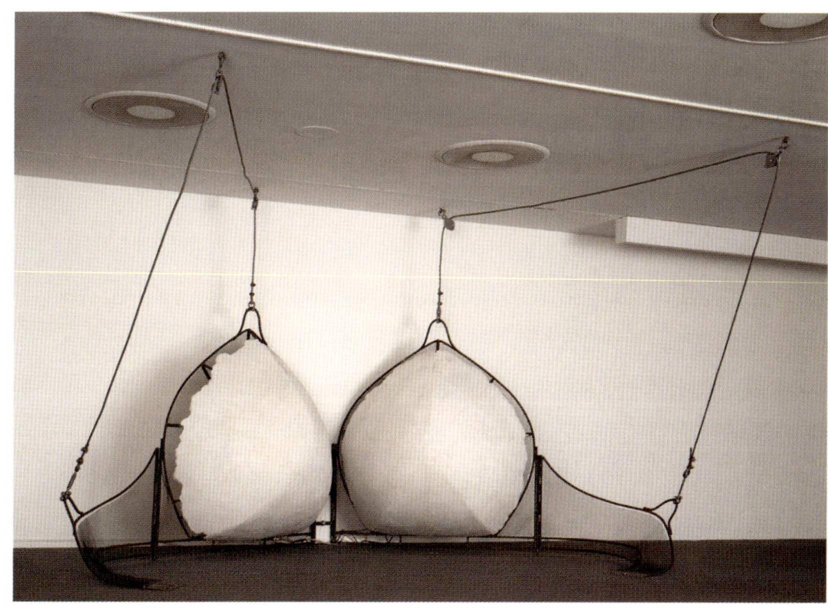

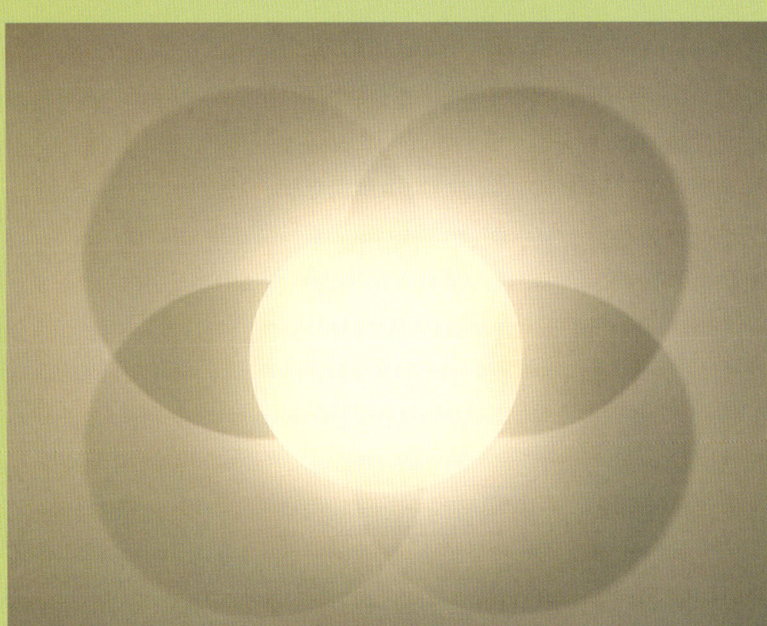

Robert Irwin
(Long Beach 1928)

Untitled
Ohne Titel
Zonder titel
Sin título

1968
Museum of Modern Art (MoMA), New York

synthetic polymer paint on aluminum
Farbe aus synthetischem Polymer auf Aluminium
synthetische polymeerverf op aluminium
color en polímero sintético sobre aluminio

544

James Turrell
(Los Angeles 1943)

A Frontal Passage
Frontaler Durchgang
Frontale doorgang
Un pasaje frontal

1994
391,2 x 685,8 x 1036,3 cm / 154 x 270 x 408 in.
Museum of Modern Art (MoMA), New York

fluorescent light installation
Installation aus fluoriszierenden Lichtern
fluorescerende lichtinstallatie
instalación de luces fluorescentes

Gordon Matta-Clark
(New York 1943 - 1978)

Chasm
Splitting
Scheur
Grieta

●

1974
101,6 x 76,2 cm
40 x 30 in.
The Metropolitan Museum
of Art, New York

prints mounted on panel
Drucke, auf Tafel angebracht
printen op paneel gemonteerd
impresiones montadas sobre
tabla

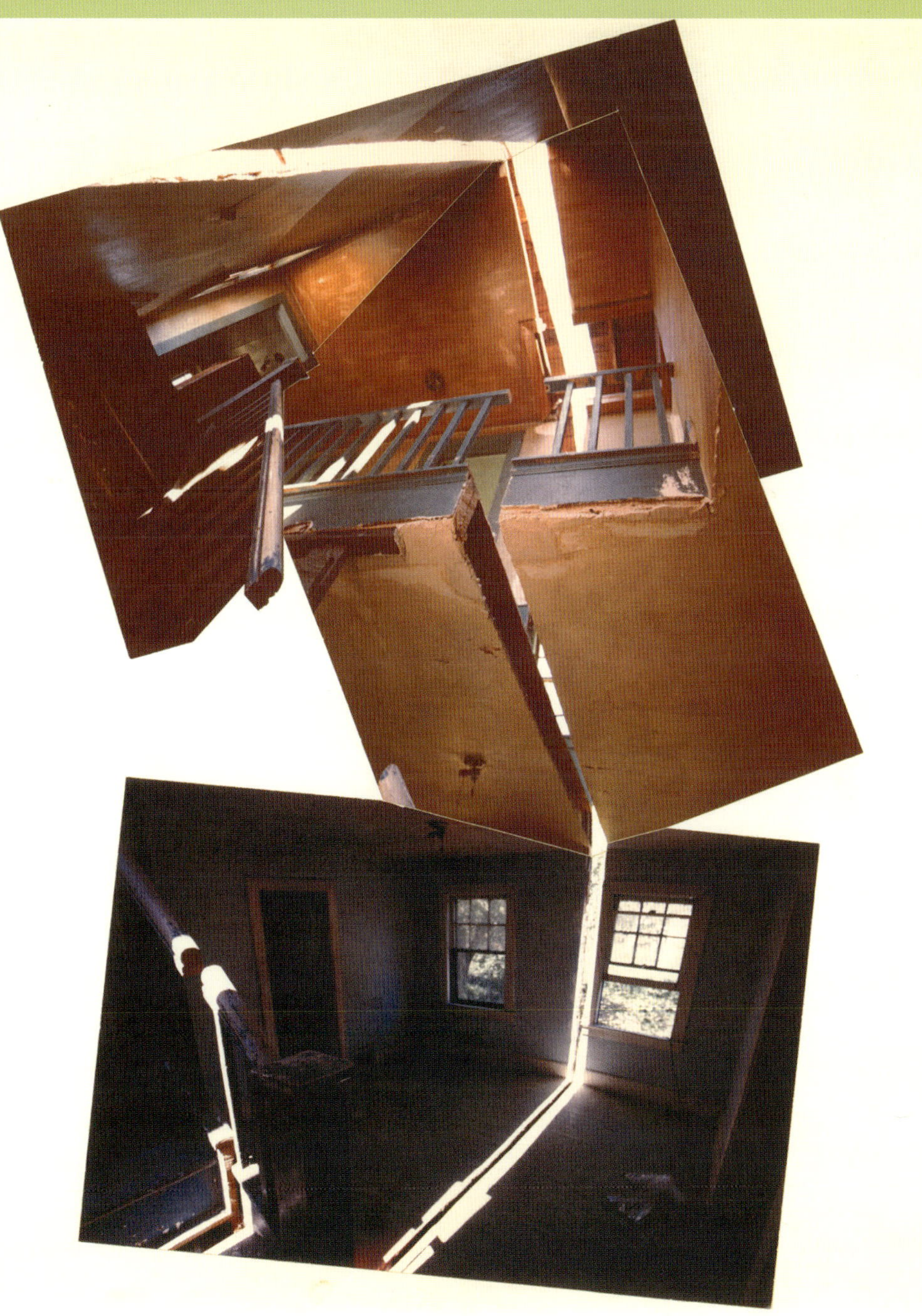

Richard Long
(Bristol 1945)

Circle of Stone in Cornwall
Steinkreis in Cornwall
Stenencirkel in Cornwall
Círculo de piedras en
Cornwall

●●●

1978
ø 600 cm / 236.2 in.
Museum of Modern Art
(MoMA), New York

52 paving stones
52 Steinplatten
52 stenen platen
52 losas de piedra

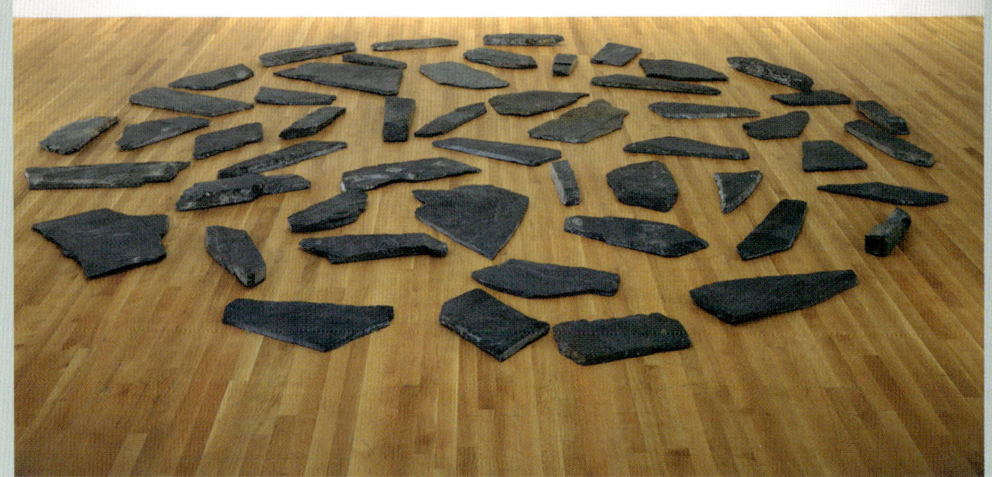

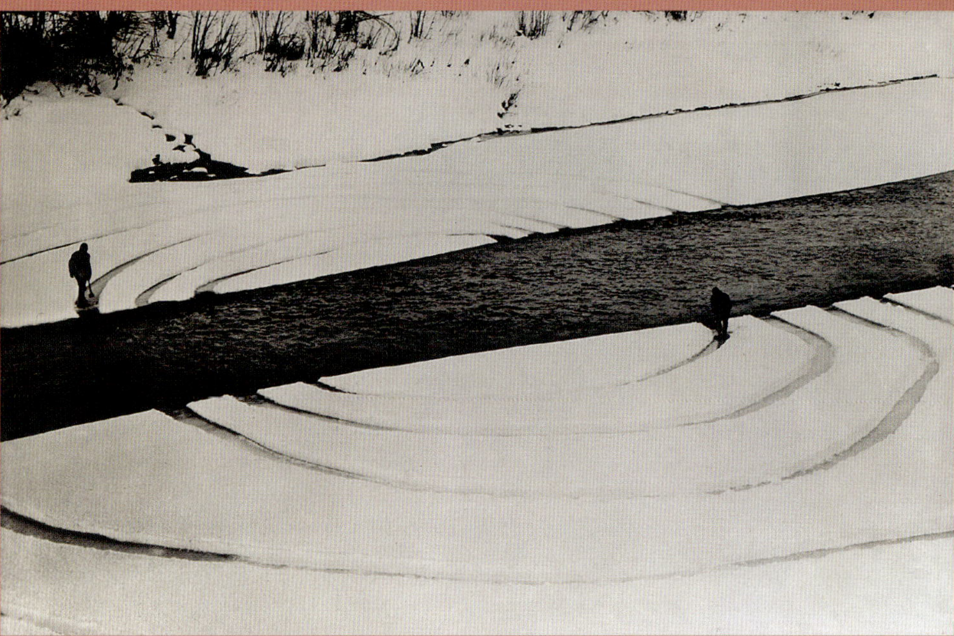

Dennis Oppenheim
(Electric City 1938)

Annual Rings
Jahresringe
Jaarringen
Anillos anuales

●

1968
Hamburger Kunsthalle, Hamburg

Christo
(Gabrovo 1935)

Jeanne-Claude
(Casablanca 1935 - New York 2009)

**The Museum of Modern Art
wrapped (model)
Verhülltes Museum of Modern Art
(Modell)
Ingepakt musem
van de moderne kunsten (model)
El Museo de Arte Moderno
empaquetado (modelo)**

●●

1968
40,3 x 122 x 61 cm / 16 x 48 x 24 in.
Museum of Modern Art (MoMA), New York

painted wood, cloth, twine and polyethylene
Bemaltes Holz, Stoff, Schnur und Polyethylene
beschilderd hout, stof, garen en polyethyleen
madera pintada, tela, hilo bramante y polietileno

▶ Christo
(Gabrovo 1935)

Jeanne-Claude
(Casablanca 1935 - New York 2009)

**Christo in front of a crushed
Volkswagen Beetle
Christo vor einem
verpackten VW Käfer
Christus voor een ingepakte
Volkswagen Kever
Cristo frente a un Volkswagen
escarabajo empaquetado**

●●●

1962

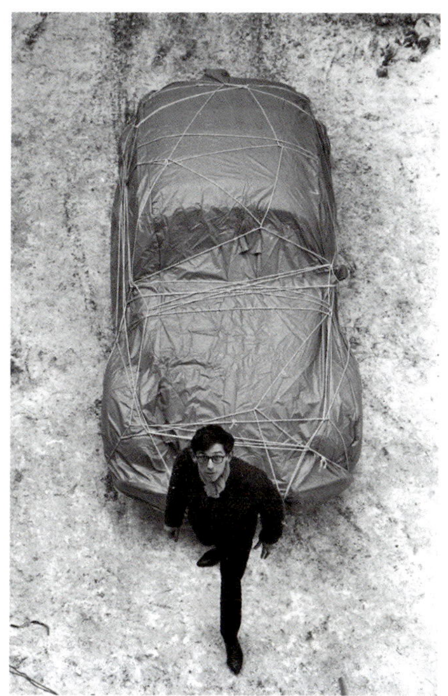

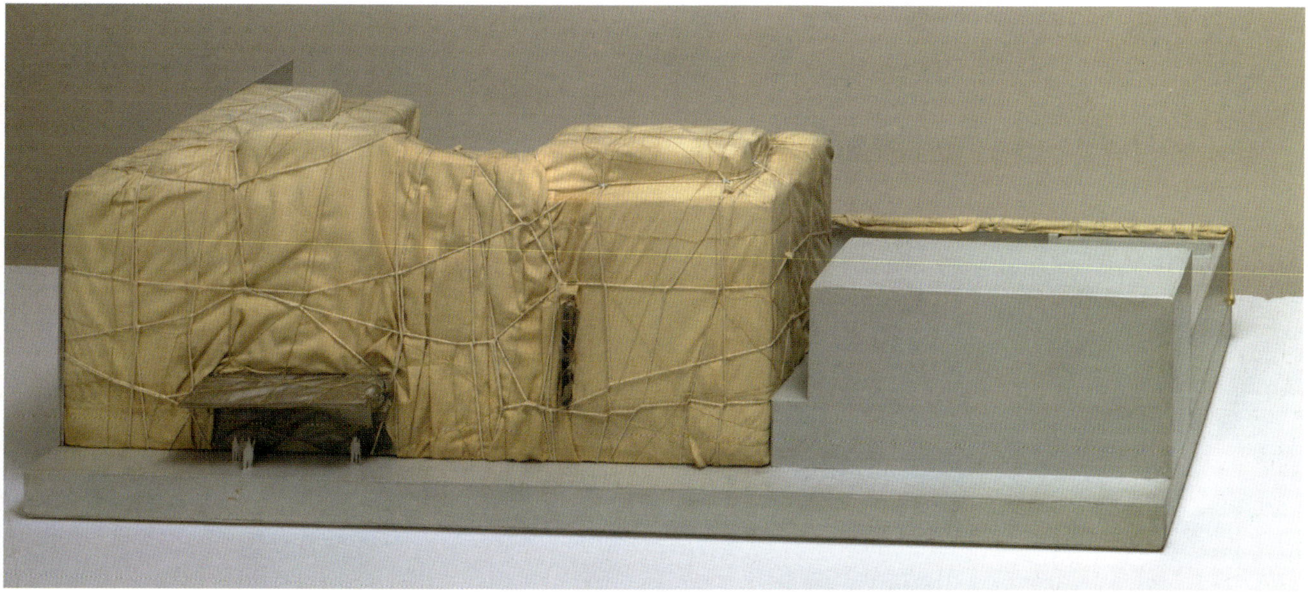

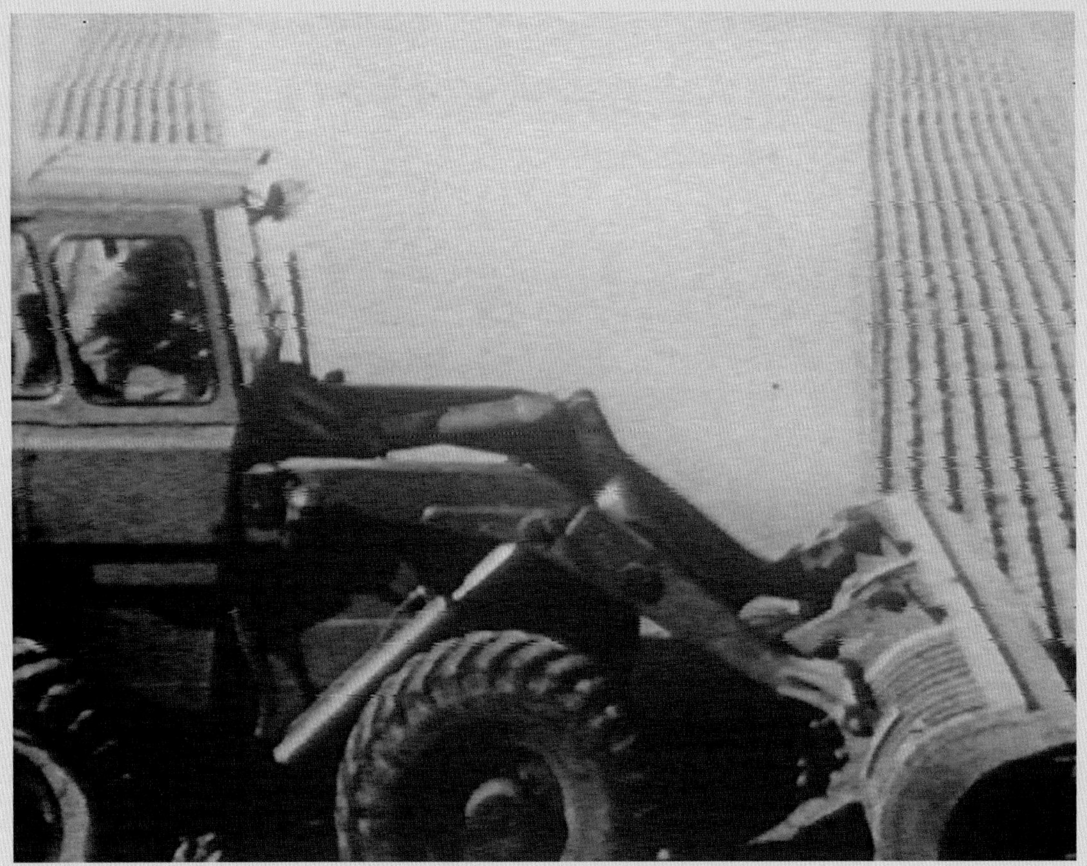

Gerry Schum
(Köln 1938 - Düsseldorf 1973)

Land Art. Television recording n.1 of the Fernsehgalerie of Düsseldorf
Land Art. Fernsehaufzeichnung Nr.1 der Fernsehgalerie in Düsseldorf
Land Art. Televisieopname n. 1 van de Fernsehgalerie van Düsseldorf
Land Art. Transmisión televisiva n.1 de la Fernsehgalerie de Düsseldorf

●●

1968-1969
Hamburger Kunsthalle, Hamburg

B / W, Audio, U-Matic, PAL, 35 Min. 16 mm film transferred to video
B / W, Audio, U-Matic, PAL, 35 Min. Film 16 mm, auf Video übertragen
B / W, Audio, U-Matic, PAL, 35 Min. 16 mm film op video overgezet
B / W, Audio, U-Matic, PAL, 35 Min. Película de 16 mm pasada a vídeo

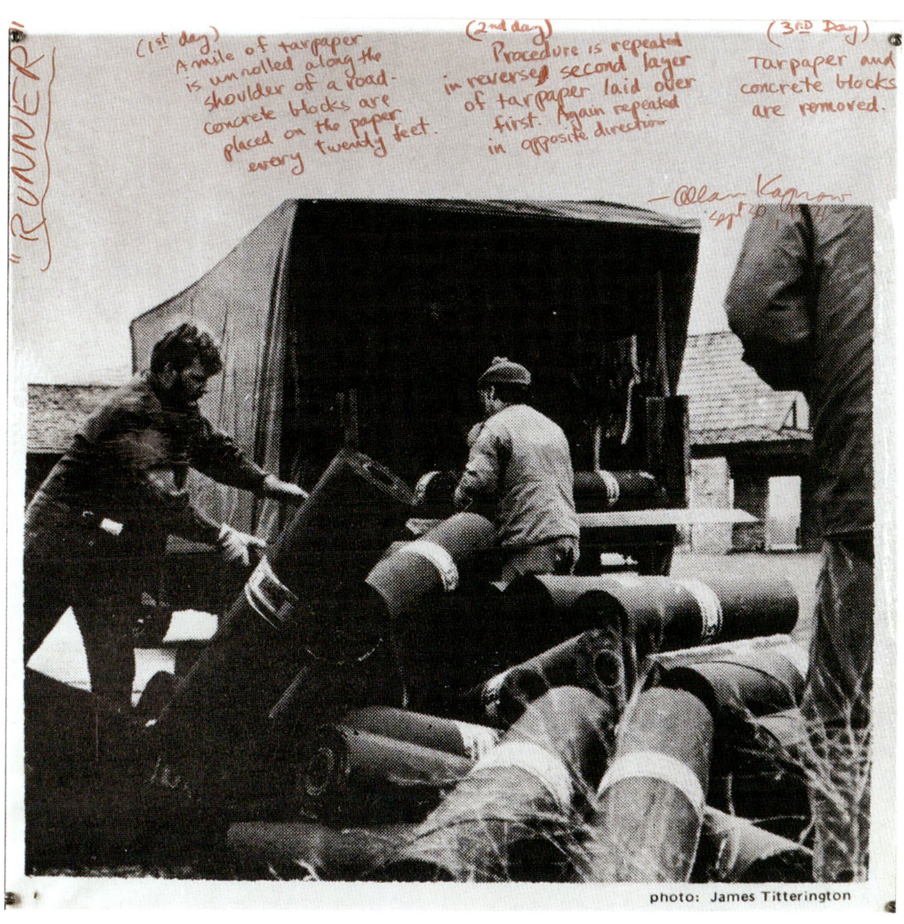

Allan Kaprow
(Atlantic City 1927 - San Diego 2006)

Corridor
Corredor

●

1968-1971
114 x 115 cm / 44.9 x 45.3 in.
Hamburger Kunsthalle, Hamburg

photographic print with the artist's notations / Fotodruck mit Anmerkungen des Künstlers
fotoprint met aantekeningen van de artiest / impresión fotográfica con anotaciones del artista

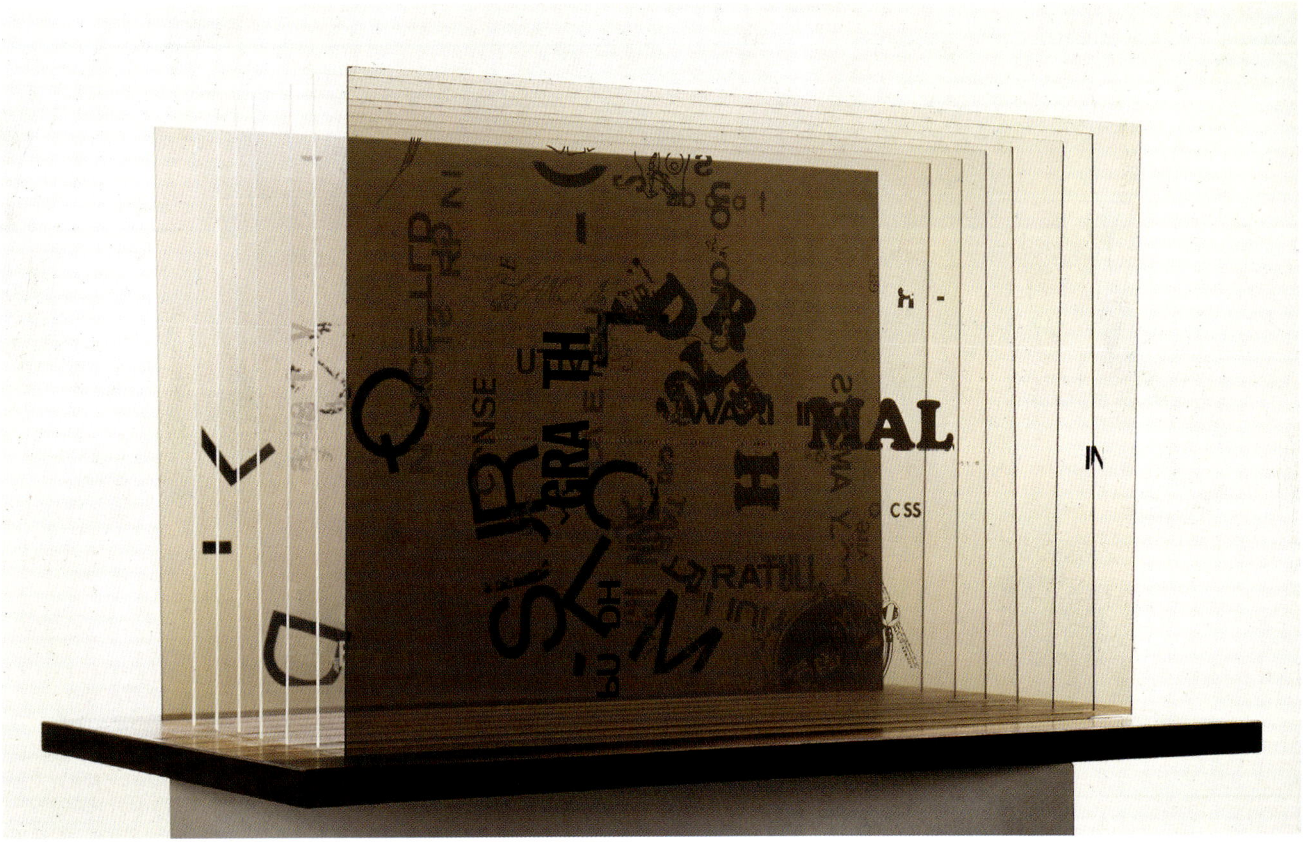

550

John Cage
(Los Angeles 1912 - New York 1992)

I don't want to say anything about Marcel
Ich will nicht über Marcel sprechen
Ik wil niets over Marcel zeggen
No quiero decir nada sobre Marcel

●●

1969
36,5 x 60,8 x 36,8 cm / 14.3 x 23.9 x 14.5 in.
Nationalgalerie, Staatliche Museen, Berlin

one of eight serigraphs on plexiglas on walnut support
Eine von acht Siebdrucken auf Plexiglas auf Nussholzstützen
één van acht zeefdrukken op plexiglas op basis van notenhout
una de ocho serigrafías sobre plexiglás montado en soportes de madera de nogal

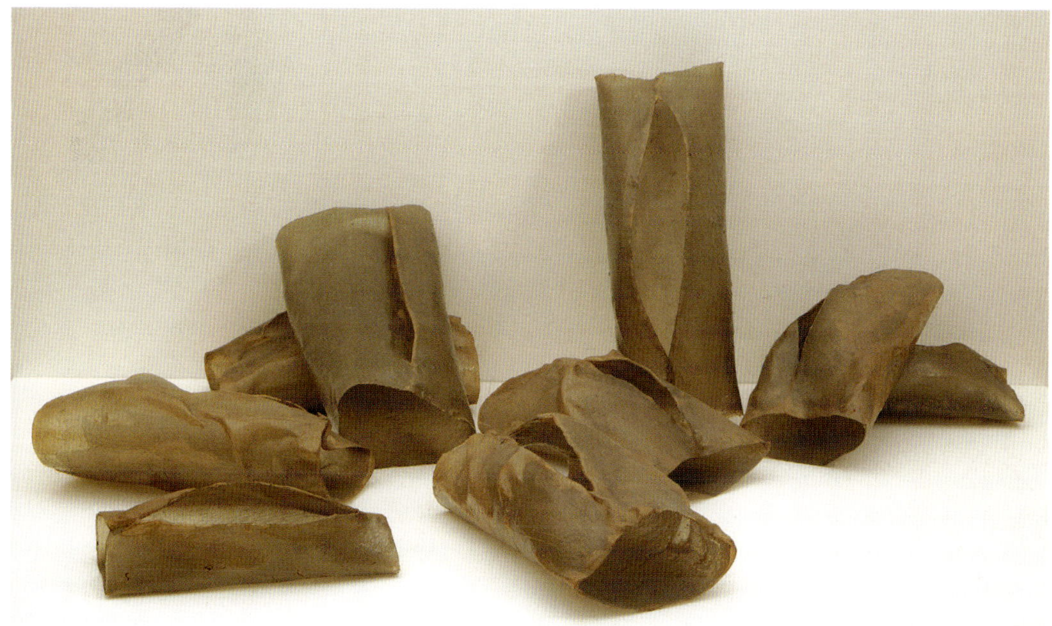

Eva Hesse
(Hamburg 1936 - New York 1970)

Tori

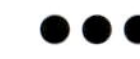

1969
119,3 x 43,1 x 38,1 cm
47 x 17 x 15 in.
Philadelphia Museum of Art,
Philadelphia

glass fibre on metal mesh
Glasfasern auf Metallmaschen
glasvezel op metaalgaas
fibra de vidrio sobre malla metálica

Lynda Benglis
(Lake Charles 1941)

Victor

● ● ●

1974
169,8 x 52 x 33,3 cm
66.8 x 20.4 x 13.1 in.
Museum of Modern Art (MoMA),
New York

aluminum screen, cotton bunting, plaster,
sprayed zinc, steel and tin
Aluminiumbildschirm, Stamina
aus Baumwolle, Kreide, bespritztes Zink,
Stahl und Zinn
aluminiumscherm, katoenen dundoek,
gips, gespoten zink, staal en tin
pantalla de aluminio, estameña de algodón,
yeso, zinc pulverizado, acero y estaño

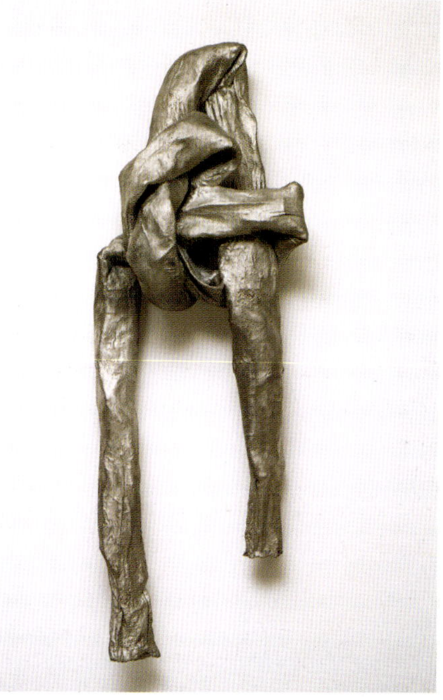

Ana Mendieta
(Havana 1948 -
New York 1985)

**Untitled (Cosmetic
facial variations)**
**Ohne Titel (Kosmetische
Gesichtsveränderungen)**
**Zonder titel (cosmetische
gezichtsvariaties)**
**Sin título (Variaciones
faciales cosméticas)**
●●
1972 (1997)
48,9 x 32,4 cm / 19.2 x 12.7 in.
Museum of Modern Art
(MoMA), New York

four chromogenic color prints
Vier chromogenische
Farbdrucke
vier chromoprinten
cuatro impresiones
cromogénicas a color

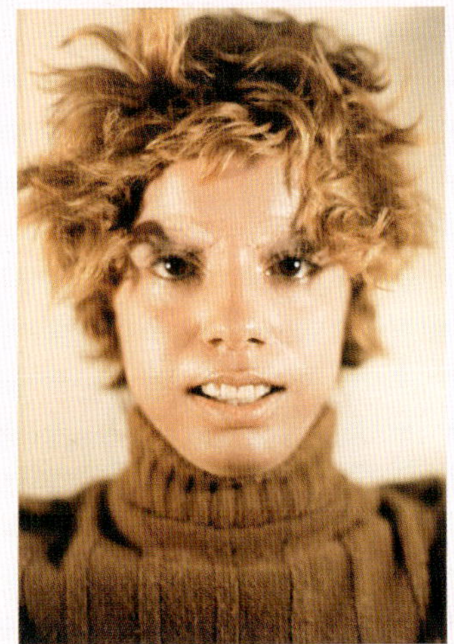
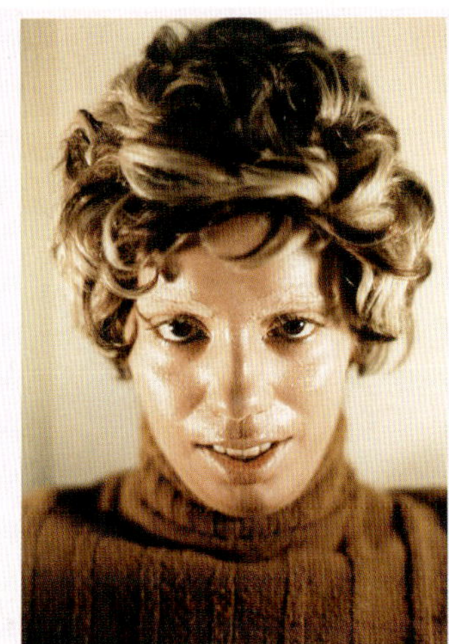
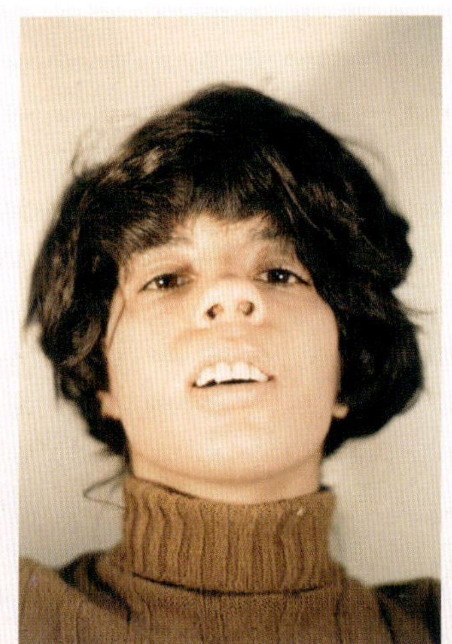
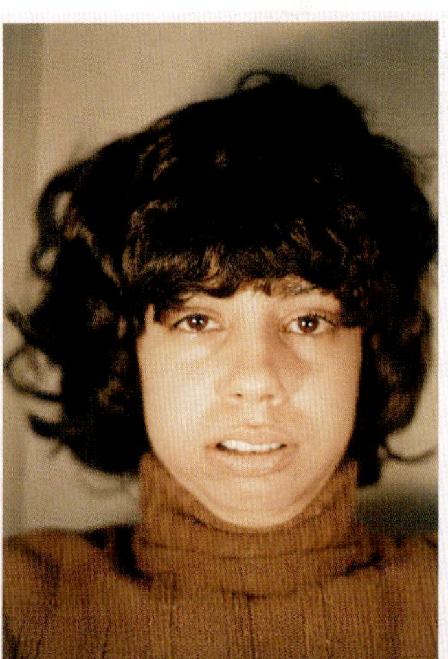

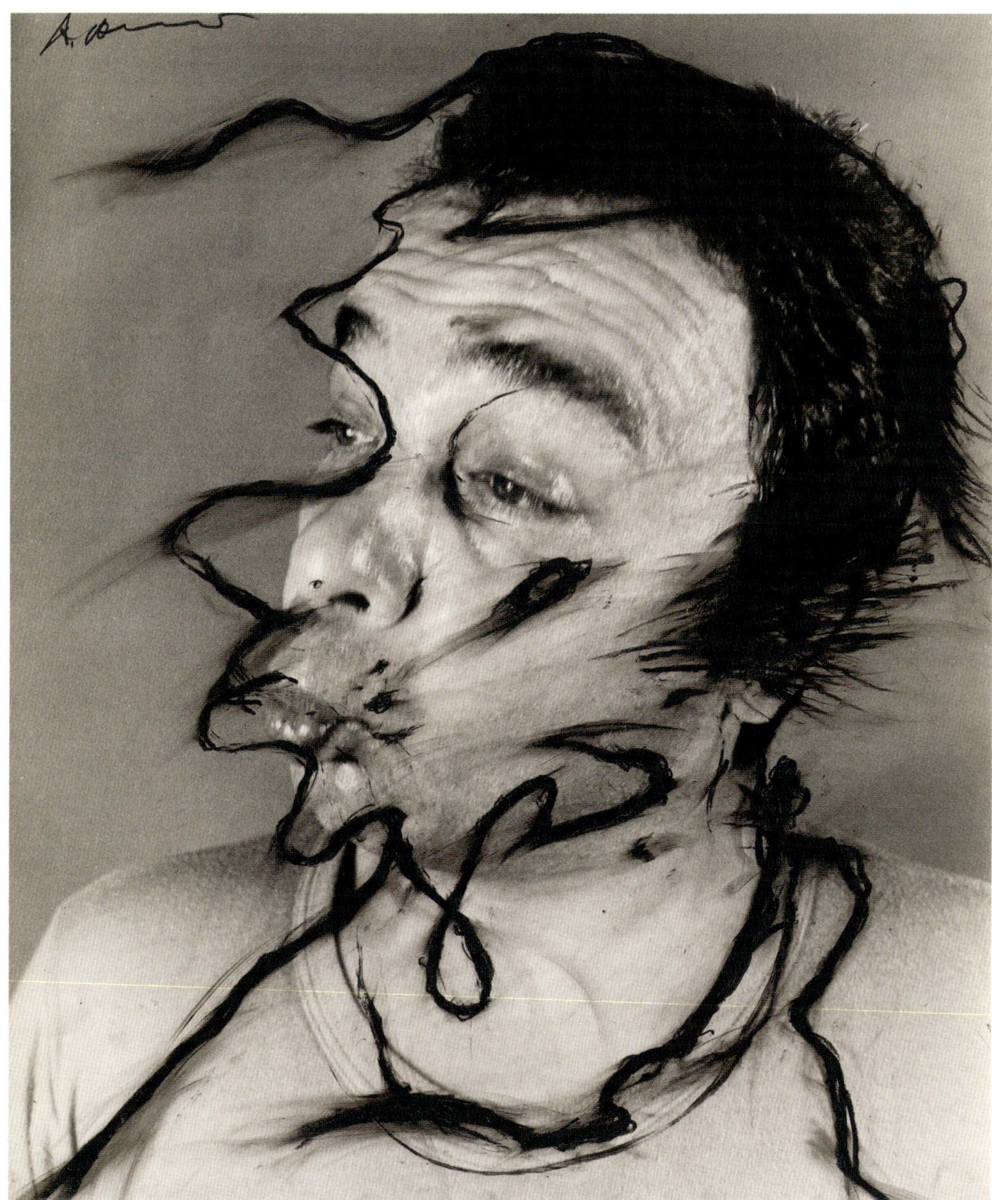

Arnulf Rainer
(Baden bei Wien 1929)

Untitled
Ohne Titel
Zonder titel
Sin título

●

1969-1974
58,4 x 48,4 cm / 23 x 19 in.
Museum of Modern Art
(MoMA), New York
crayon on silver gelatin print
Ölpastell auf Silbergelatinedruck
oliepastel op gelatine-zilverprint
pastel al óleo sobre impresión
en gelatina de plata

**Rainer's twisted self-portraits
testify to an interest pointed
both on the expression of the
faces and on the Art Brut.**

**Rainers krüppelartige
Selbstporträts bezeugen
sein Interesse sowohl an
Gesichtsausdrücken, als auch an
der Art Brut.**

**De verwrongen zelfportretten
van Rainer getuigen van
een interesse zowel in de
uitdrukking op gezichten als in
de art brut.**

**Los autorretratos retorcidos
de Rainer testimonian un
interés dirigido tanto a la
expresión de los rostros como
al art brut.**

553

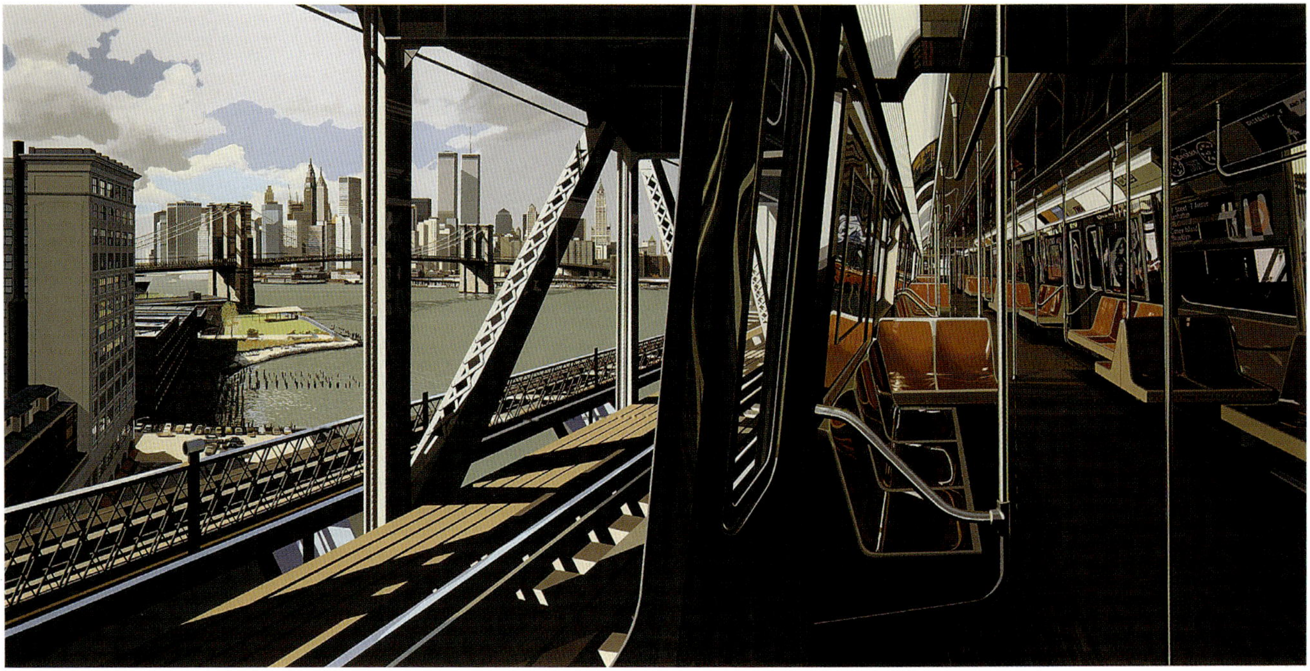

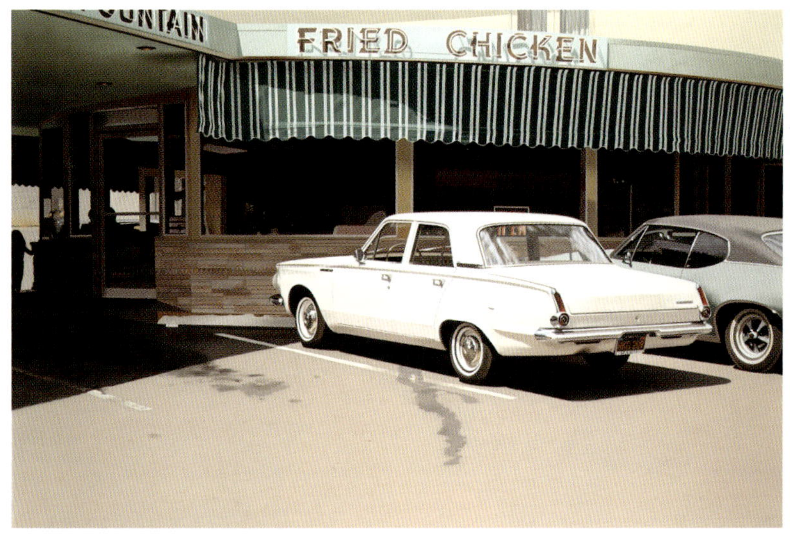

Richard Estes
(Kewanee 1932)

Line D / Linie D / Lijn D / Línea D

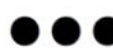

1988
90,8 x 177,2 cm / 35.7 x 69.7 in.
Smithsonian American Art Museum,
Washington DC

segraphy on paper
Siebdruck auf Papier
zeefdruk op papier
serigrafía sobre papel

Robert Bechtle
(San Francisco 1932)

64 Valiant

●●●

1971
122,2 x 176,8 cm / 48.1 x 69.6 in.
Yale University Art Gallery, New Haven (CT)

oil on canvas / Öl auf Leinwand
olieverf op doek / óleo sobre lienzo

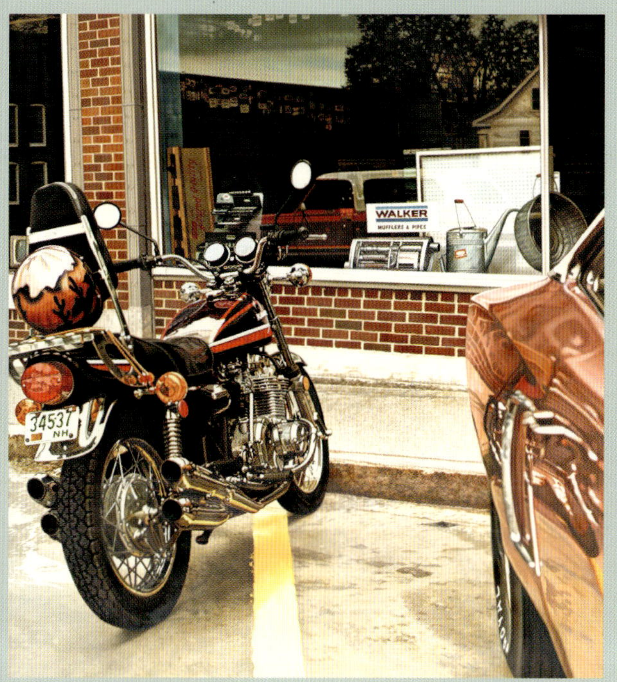

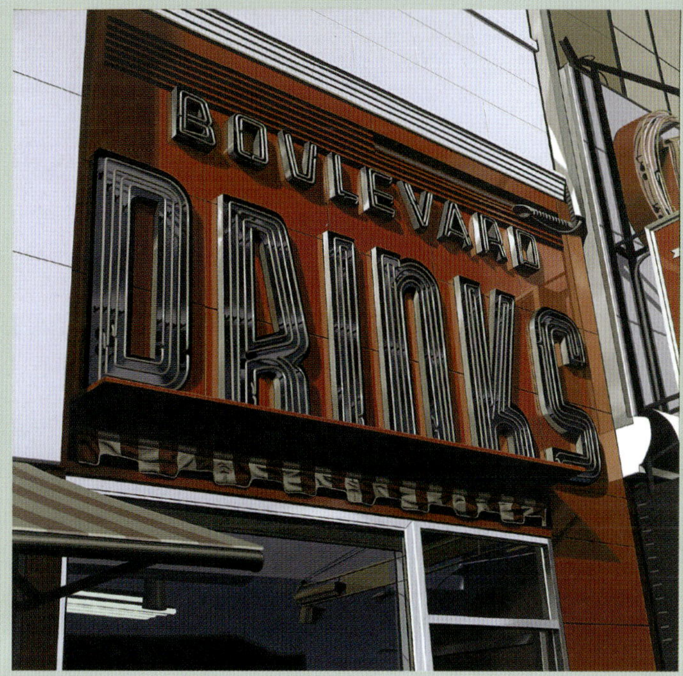

555

Tom Blackwell
(Chicago 1938)

Jaffrey

1976
212,8 x 187,3 cm / 83.8 x 73.8 in.
Museum of Modern Art (MoMA), New York

oil on canvas / Öl auf Leinwand
olieverf op doek / óleo sobre lienzo

Robert Cottingham
(New York 1935)

Boulevard Drinks

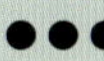

1976
198 x 198 cm / 78 x 78 in.
Hamburger Kunsthalle, Hamburg

acrylic on canvas / Akryl auf Leinwand
acrylverf op doek / acrílico sobre lienzo

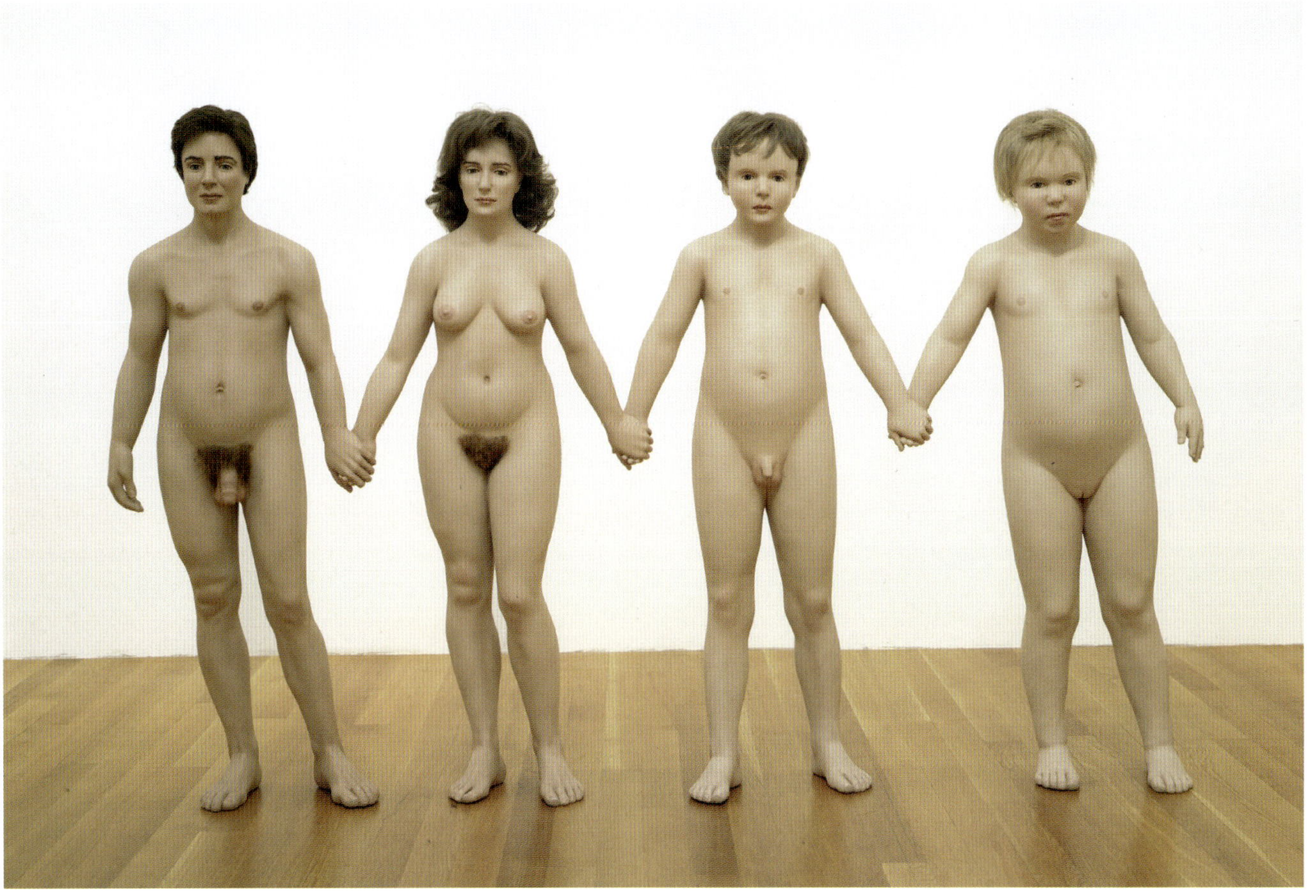

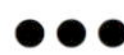

Charles Ray
(Chicago 1953)

Familiar novel
Familienidylle
Familieromance
Novela familiar

●●●

1993
134,6 x 215,9 x 27,9 cm / 53 x 85 x 11 in.
Museum of Modern Art (MoMA), New York

mixed media / Mischtechnik / gemengde techniek / técnica mixta

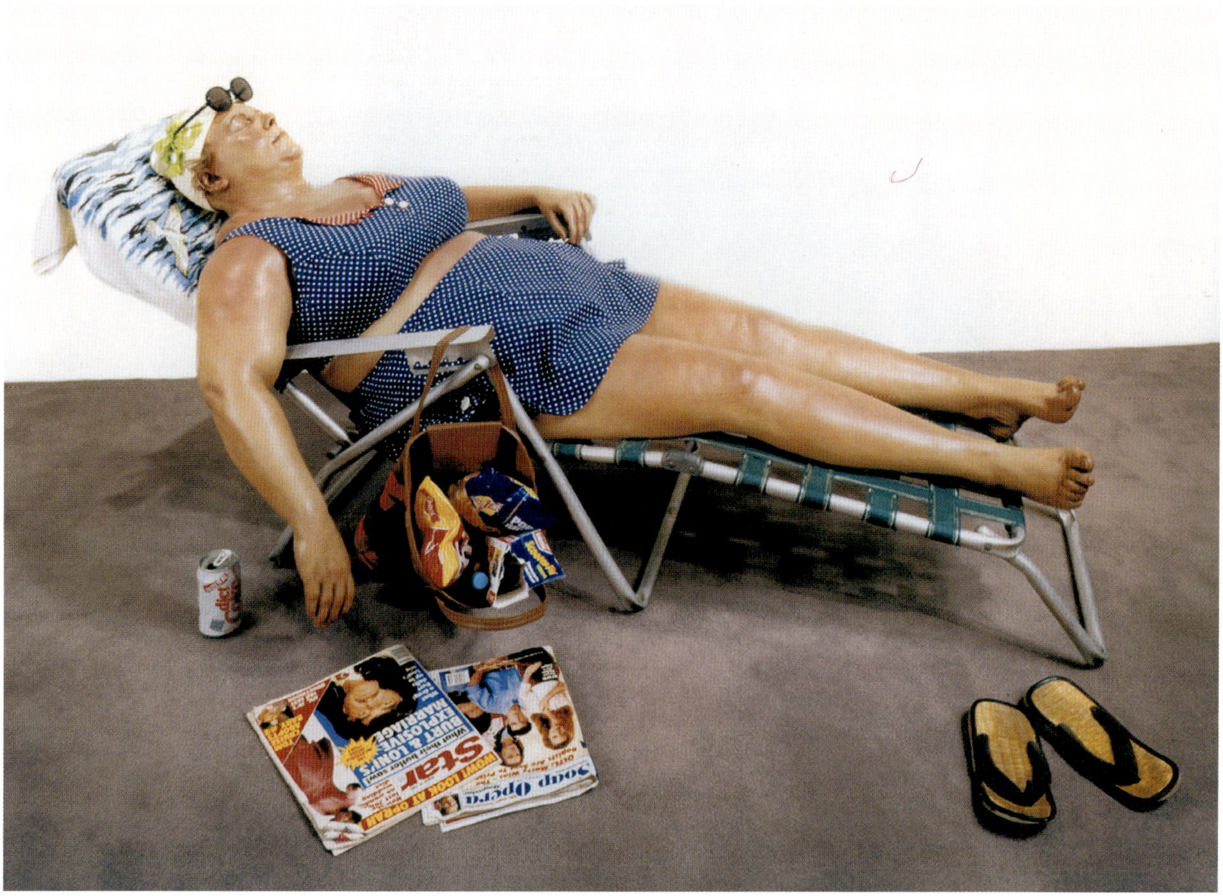

Duane Hanson
(Alexandria 1925 - Boca Raton 1996)

Sunbather

●●

1971
l. 180,3 cm / 71 in.
Wadsworth Atheneum Museum of Art,
Hartford (CT)

polyester, fiberglass, polychromatic and oil
Polyester, Glasfasern, Polychromatie und Öl
polyester, glasvezel, polychroom en olieverf
poliéster, fibra de vidrio, policromático y óleo

Conceived starting from casts of living models, the hyper-realistic sculptures of Hanson provide a sociological and ironic portrait of American society.

Hansons hyperrealistische Skulpturen sind eigentlich Abgüsse von lebenden Modellen. Sie bieten ein gleichsam soziologisches, aber ausgesprochen ironisches Porträt der amerikanischen Gesellschaft.

De hyperrealistische sculpturen van Hanson zijn gemaakt van levende modellen en geven een sociologisch en ironisch beeld van de Amerikaanse maatschappij.

Concebidas a partir de moldes sobre modelos vivientes, las esculturas hiperrealistas de Hanson brindan un retrato sociológico e irónico de la sociedad estadounidense.

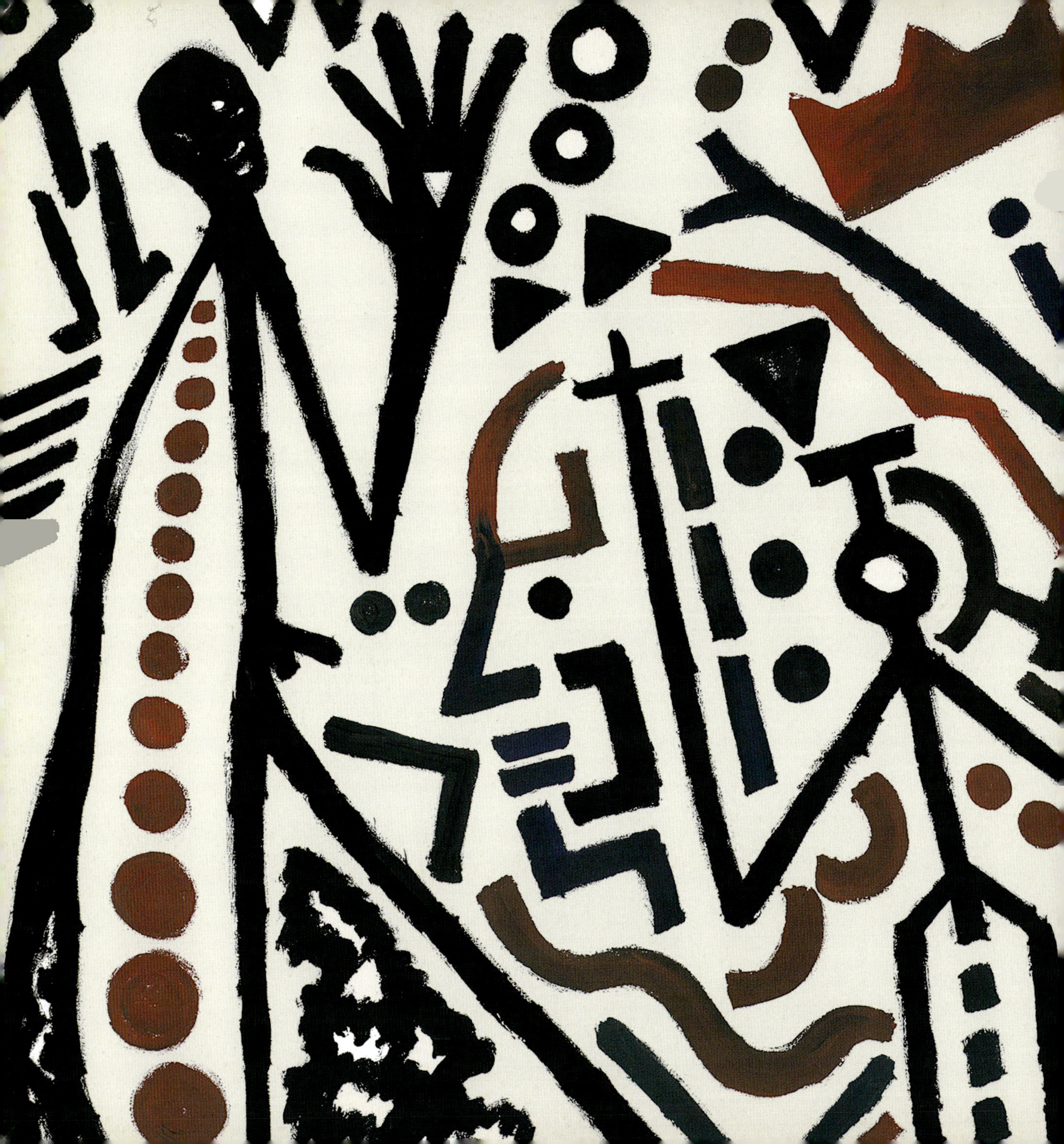

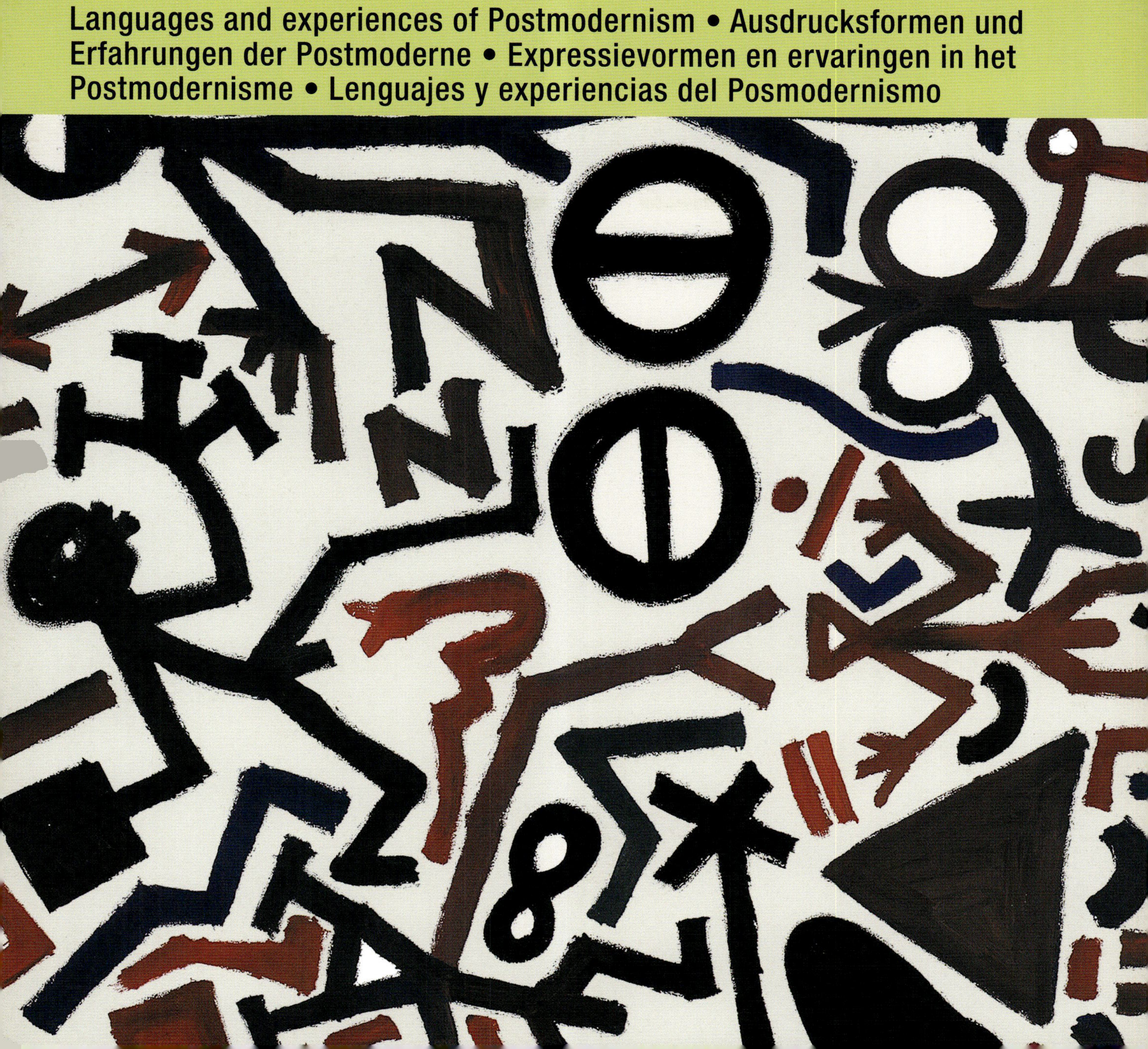

Languages and experiences of Postmodernism • Ausdrucksformen und Erfahrungen der Postmoderne • Expressievormen en ervaringen in het Postmodernisme • Lenguajes y experiencias del Posmodernismo

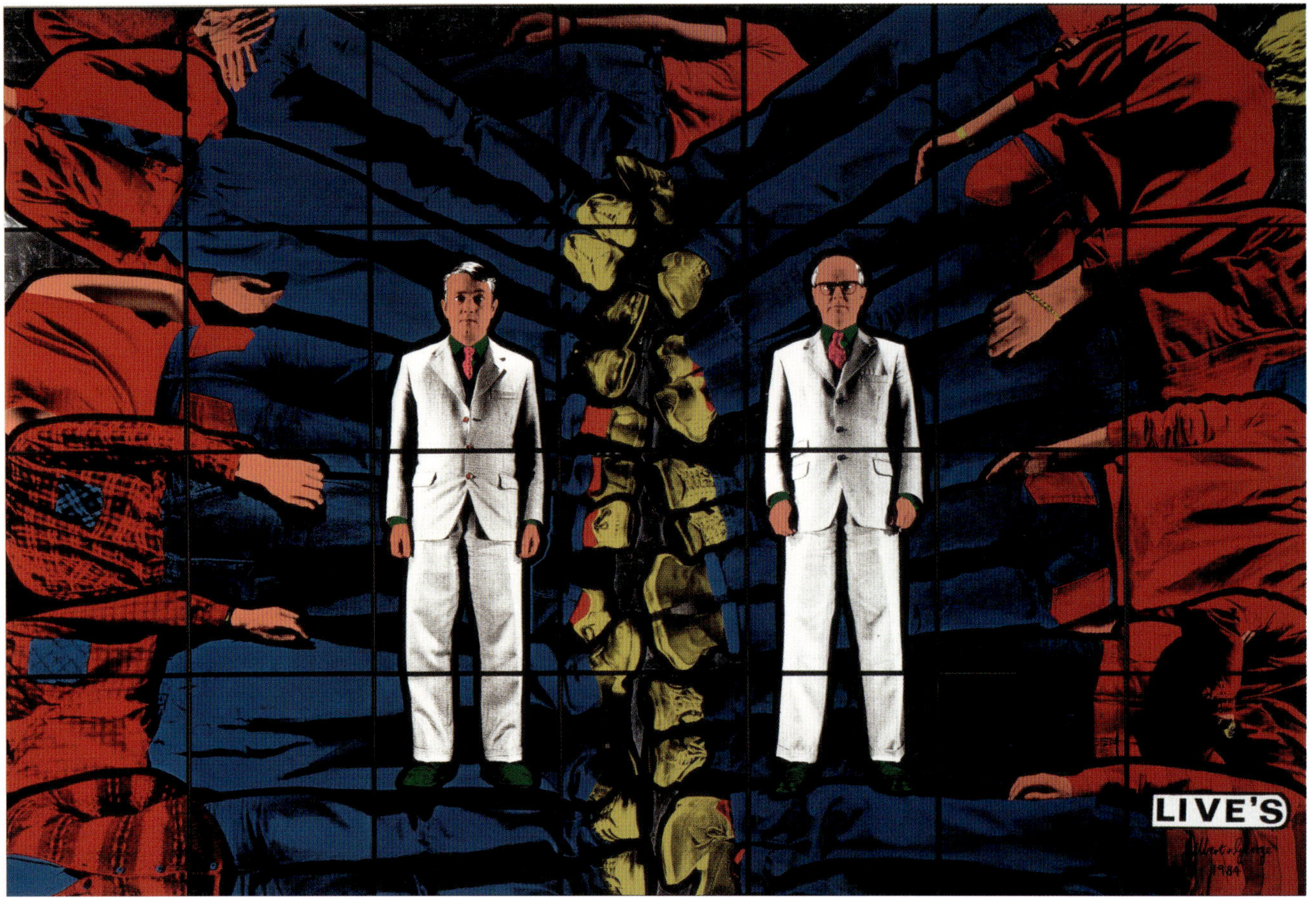

Gilbert & George
(San Martino in Badia 1943) / (Devon 1942)

Live's

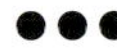

1984
242,7 x 353 cm / 95.5 x 138.9 in.
Museum of Modern Art (MoMA), New York

black and white photographs, colored by hand with ink and colors, applied on aluminium sheet and framed
Schwarz-Weiß-Fotografien, manuell mit Tinte gefärbt, auf eine Aluminiumfolie aufgebracht und eingerahmt
zwart-wit foto's, met de hand ingekleurd met inkt en kleurtinten, op aluminiumfolie geplakt en ingelijst
fotografías en blanco y negro, pintadas a mano con tinta y tinturas, aplicadas sobre hoja de aluminio y enmarcadas

Georg Baselitz
(Deutschbaselitz 1938)

Head with hands
Kopf mit Händen
Hoofd met handen
Cabeza con manos

•

1985
Kupferstichkabinett, Staatliche Museen, Berlin

xylography / Holzschnitt
houtsnede / xilografía

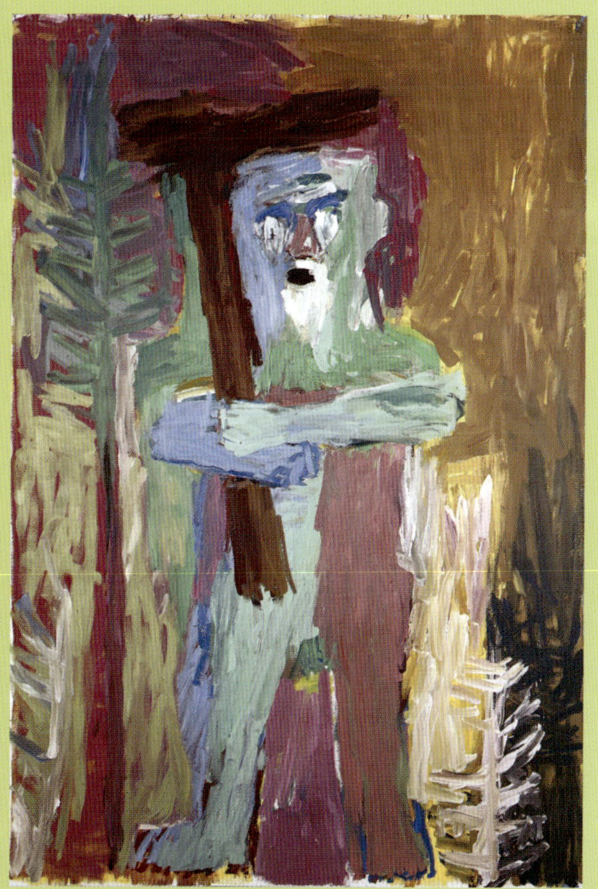

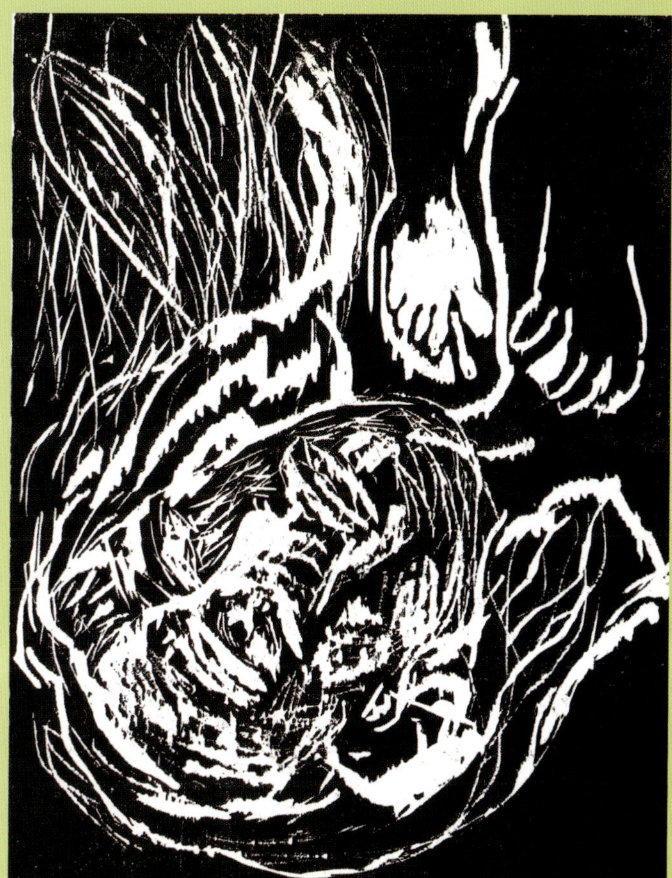

561

Georg Baselitz
(Deutschbaselitz 1938)

Carrying Cross
Kreuztragung
Kruisdrager
Cargando la cruz

•

1983
314 x 210 cm / 123.6 x 82.6 in.
Nationalgalerie, Staatliche Museen, Berlin

oil on canvas / Öl auf Leinwand
olieverf op doek / óleo sobre lienzo

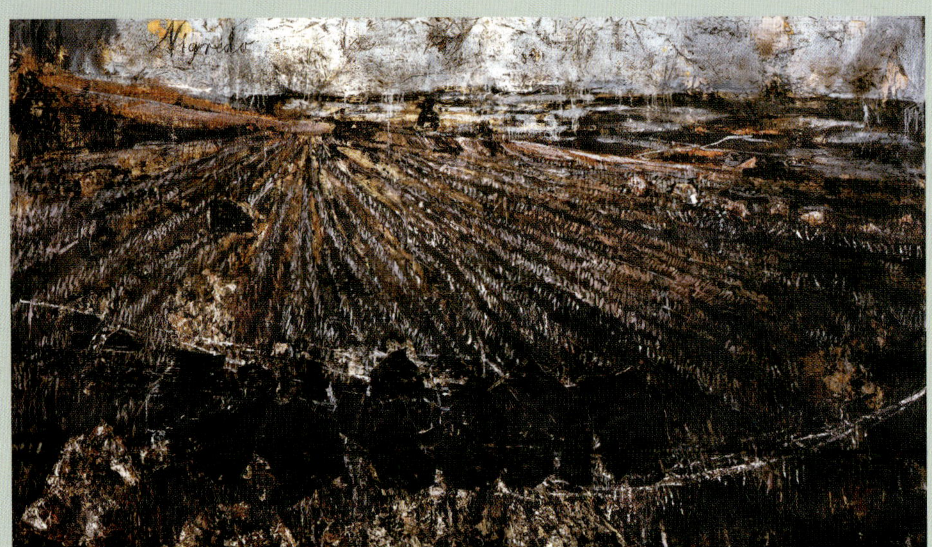

Anselm Kiefer
(Donaueschingen 1945)

Nigredo

●●

1984
330,2 x 555 cm / 130 x 218.5 in.
Philadelphia Museum of Art,
Philadelphia

oil, acrylic, emulsion, rubber
lacquer and straw on photograph,
on canvas with xylography / Öl,
Akryl, Emulsion, Schellack und
Stroh auf Fotografie, auf Leinwand
mit Holzschnitt / olieverf, acrylverf,
emulsie, schellak en riet op foto, op
doek door middel van houtsnede /
óleo, acrílico, emulsión, goma laca
y paja sobre fotografía, sobre lienzo
con xilografía

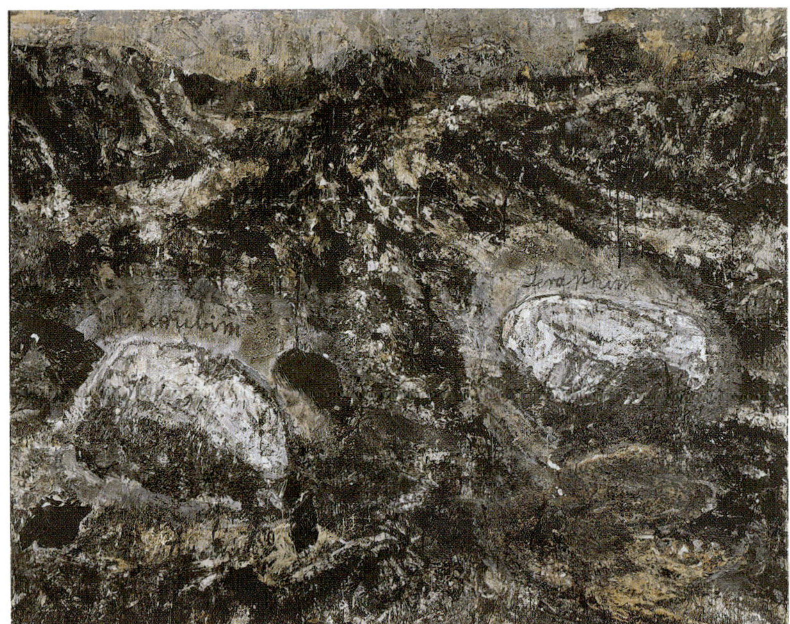

Anselm Kiefer
(Donaueschingen 1945)

**Cherub-Seraph
Cherubim-Seraphim
Cherubino-Serafino
Querubín-Serafín**

●

1983
260 x 320 cm / 102.4 x 126.1 in.
Nationalgalerie, Staatliche Museen,
Berlin

mixed media on canvas
Mischtechniken auf Leinwand
gemengde technieken op doek
técnica mixta sobre lienzo

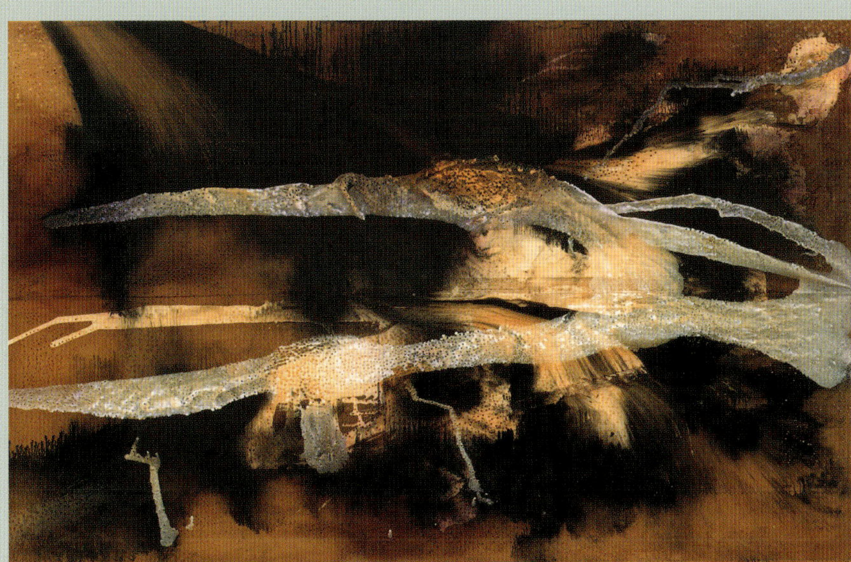

Sigmar Polke
(Oleśnica 1941)

Ginkgo

●●

1989
259,1 x 406,4 cm
102.1 x 160.1 in.
Philadelphia Museum of Art,
Philadelphia

gold, graphite, natural colors,
synthetic resin on woven polyester
Gold, Graphit, Naturfarben,
Kunstharz auf geflochtenem Polyester
goud, grafiet, natuurlijke kleuren,
kunsthars op gevlochten polyester
oro, grafito, colores naturales, resina
sintética sobre tejido de poliéster

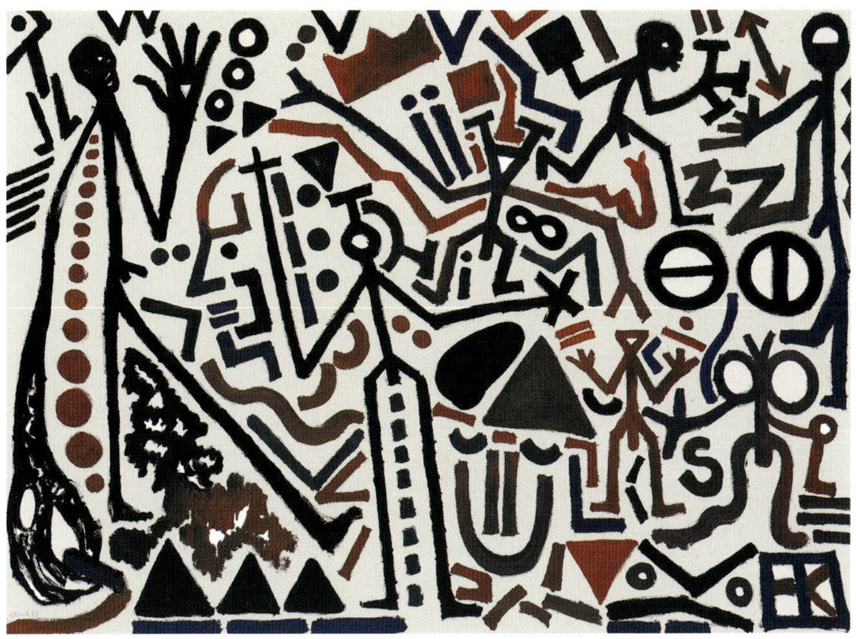

A. R. Penck (Ralf Winkler)
(Dresden 1939)

**The Future of the Emigrants
Die Zukunft des
Emigranten
De toekomst van de
emigranten
El futuro de la inmigración**

●●●

1983
260 x 350 cm / 102.4 x 137.9 in.
Nationalgalerie, Staatliche Museen,
Berlin

acrylic resin on canvas
Akrylharz auf Leinwand
acrylhars op doek
resina acrílica sobre lienzo

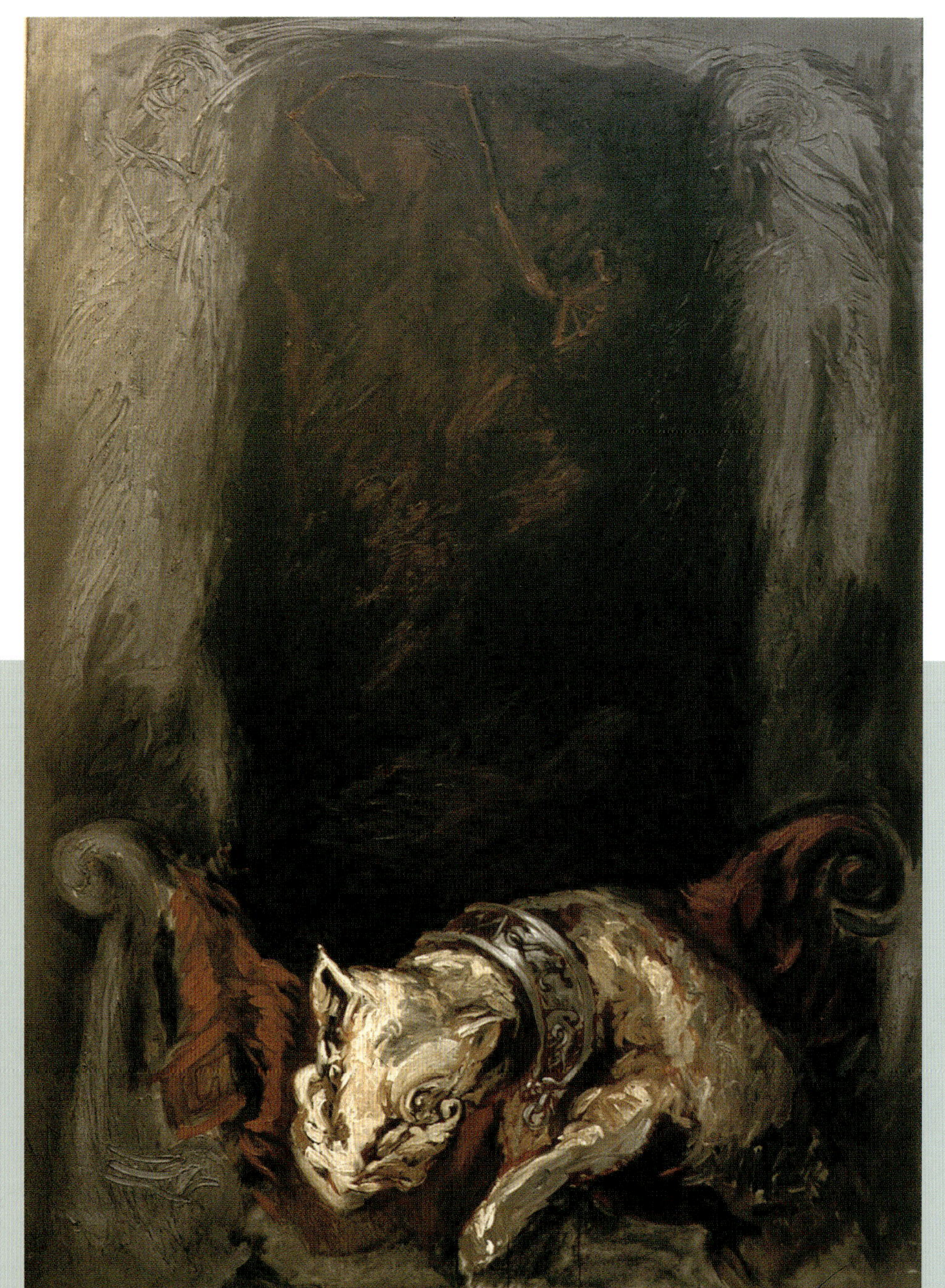

Gerard Garouste
(Paris 1946)

Orion, Maera et le miroir
●

564

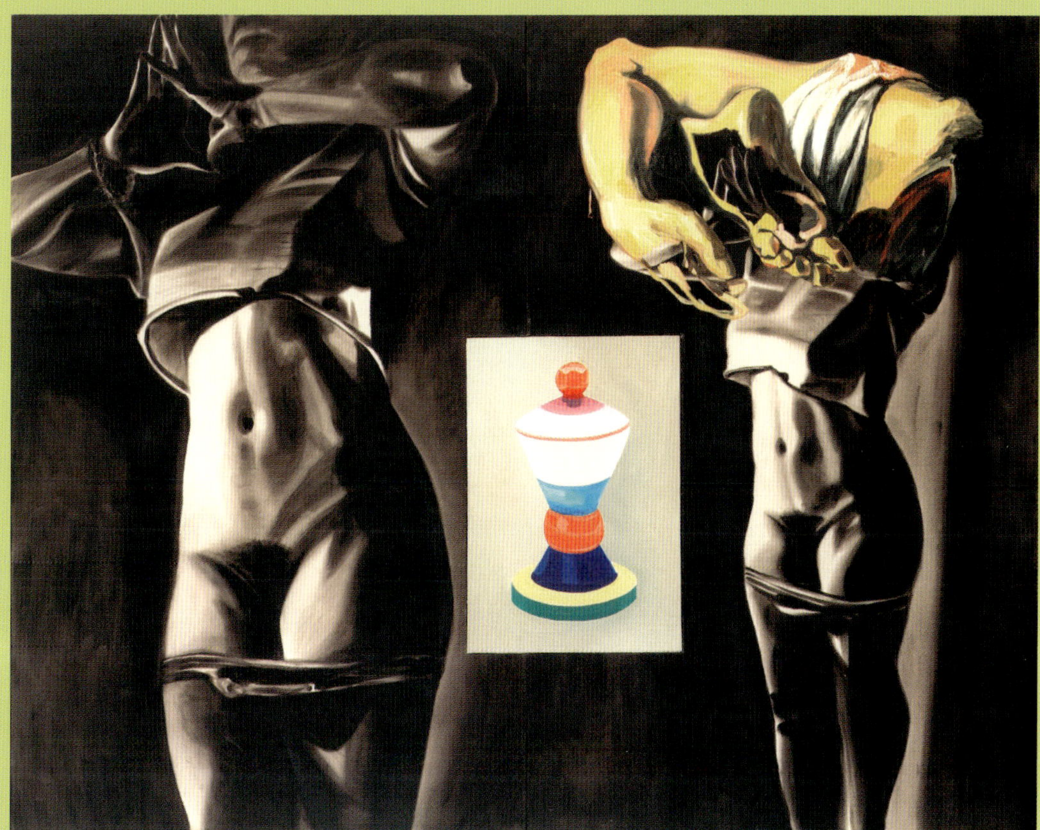

David Salle
(Norman 1952)

The Arm of Géricault
Der Arm von Géricault
De arm van Géricault
El brazo de Géricault

●●●

1985
197,8 x 244,5 cm / 77.8 x 96.2 in.
Museum of Modern Art (MoMA), New York

oil and synthetic paints on canvas
Öl und synthetische Lacke auf Leinwand
olieverf en synthetische vernissen op doek
óleo y pinturas sintéticas sobre lienzo

Salle juxtaposes in his paintings styles and sources, abstraction and depiction.

Salle stellt in seinen Bildern Stile und Quellen, Abstraktion und Darstellung gegenüber.

Salle zet in zijn schilderijen stijl en font, abstractie en symbolische voorstelling naast elkaar.

Salle yuxtapone en sus cuadros los estilos y las fuentes, la abstracción y la figuración.

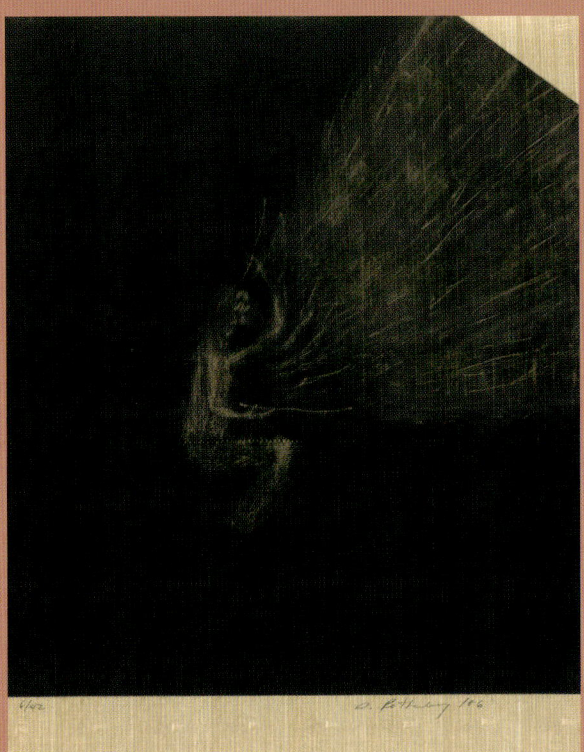

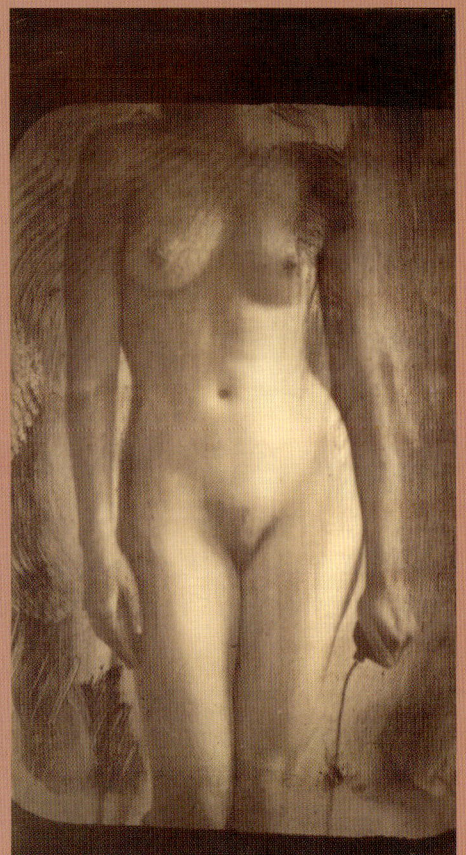

Susan Rothenberg
(Buffalo 1945)

Man of bones
Knochenmann
Bottenman
El hombre de huesos

1986
76,2 x 51,2 cm / 30 x 20,2 in.
Museum of Modern Art (MoMA), New York

etching on grained paper / Radierung auf Papier
mit Maserung / ets op generfd papier / aguafuerte
sobre papel veteado

Francesca Woodman
(Denver 1958 - New York 1981)

Untitled
Ohne Titel
Zonder titel
Sin título

ca. 1980
187 x 93,4 cm / 73.6 x 36.8 in.
The Metropolitan Museum of Art, New York

sepia print
Druck mit Tintenfischtinte
print in sepia / impresión en sepia

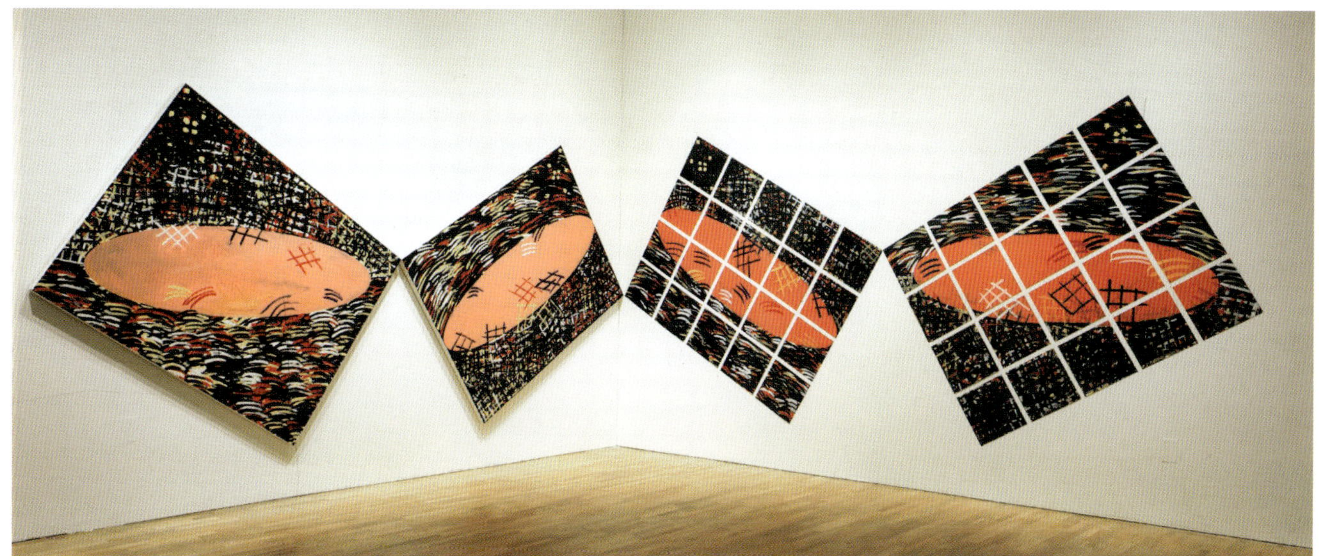

Jennifer Bartlett
(Long Beach 1941)

**Swimmer lost at night
(For Tom Hess)
Bei Nacht verirrter Schwimmer
(Für Tom Hess)
Verdwaalde nachtelijke
zwemmer (Voor Tom Hess)
Nadador perdido de noche
(Para Tom Hess)**

●●

1978
Museum of Modern Art (MoMA),
New York

Ross Bleckner
(New York 1949)

**Double Portrait (Gay Flag)
Doppelporträt (Gay Flag)
Dubbelportret (Gay Flag)
Doble retrato (Bandera Gay)**

●●●

1993
274,6 x 183,5 cm / 108.1 x 72.2 in.
The Jewish Museum, New York

oil on canvas
Öl auf Leinwand
olieverf op doek
óleo sobre lienzo

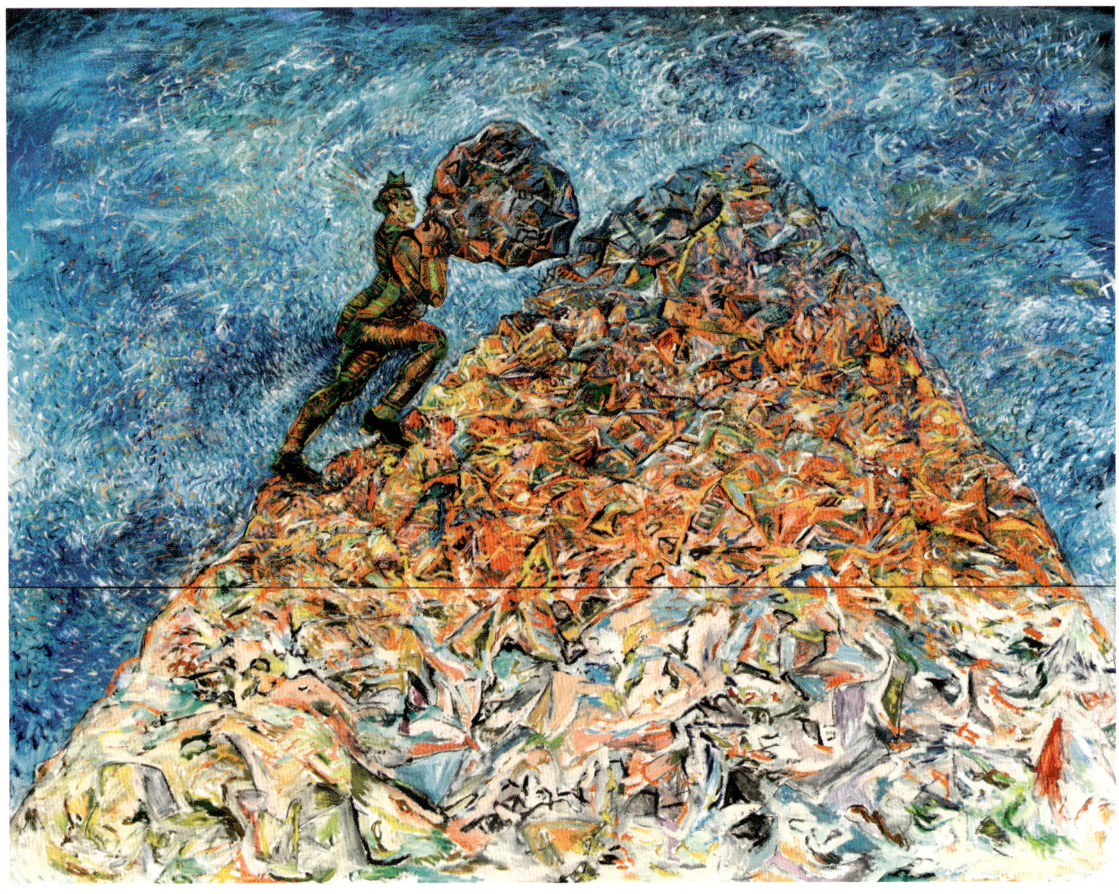

Sandro Chia
(Firenze 1946)

The Idleness of Sisyphus
Der Müßiggang des Sysiphus
Sisyphusarbeid
El ocio de Sísifo

●●●

1981
309,9 x 386,7 cm / 122 x 152.2 in.
Museum of Modern Art (MoMA), New York

oil on canvas / Öl auf Leinwand
olieverf op doek / óleo sobre lienzo

In reaction to conceptual art and its aridity, Chia returns to figurative painting which draws on mythology.

Als Reaktion auf die Konzeptkunst und auf deren Nüchternheit kehrt Chia zu einer figürlichen Malerei zurück, die aus der Mythologie schöpft.

Als reactie op de conceptuele kunst en de ongevoeligheid ervan, keert Chia terug naar een figuratieve schilderkunst ontleend uit de mythologie.

En reacción al arte conceptual y a su aridez, Chia regresa a una pintura figurativa que se inspira en la mitología.

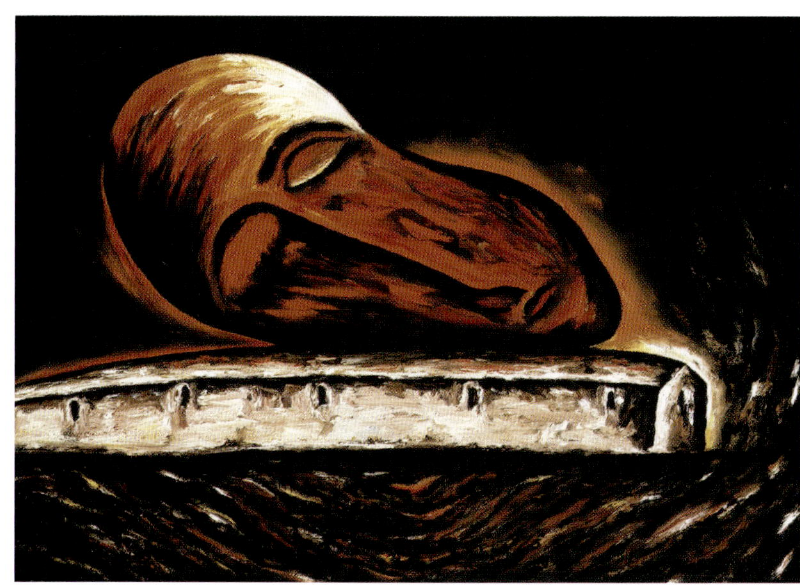

Enzo Cucchi
(Morro d'Alba 1949)

Quadro Tonto

●

post 1945
280 x 360 cm / 110.2 x 141.7 in.
Nationalgalerie, Staatliche Museen, Berlin

oil on canvas / Öl auf Leinwand
olieverf op doek / óleo sobre lienzo

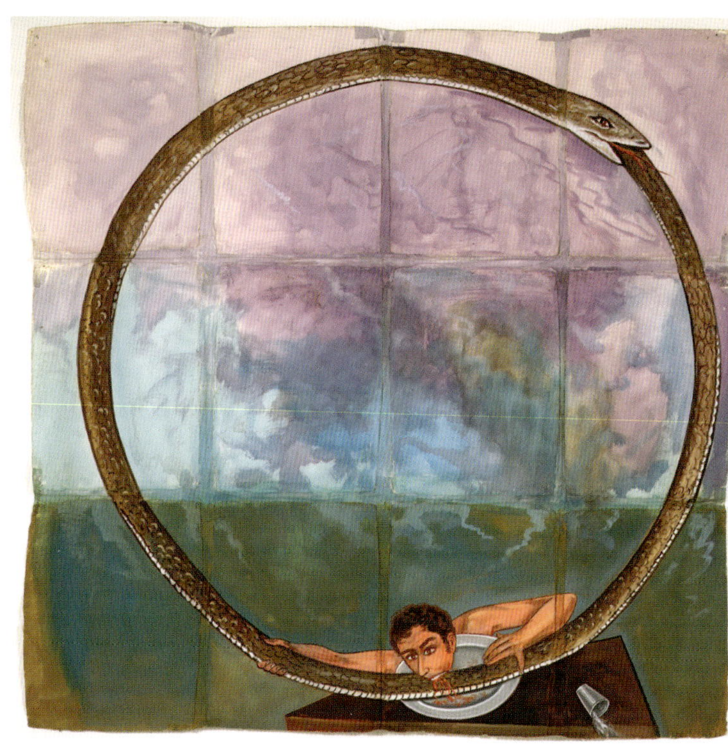

Francesco Clemente
(Napoli 1952)

**Hunger
Honger
Hambre**

●●

1980
237,5 x 245,1 cm / 93.5 x 96.5 in.
Philadelphia Museum of Art, Philadelphia

gouache on Pondicherry paper, joined by cotton
strips / Gouache auf Pondicherry-Papier, vereint mit
Baumwollstreifen / gouache op Pondicherry papier, bij
elkaar gehouden door katoenen strippen / gouache sobre
papel de Pondicherry, unido con tiras de algodón

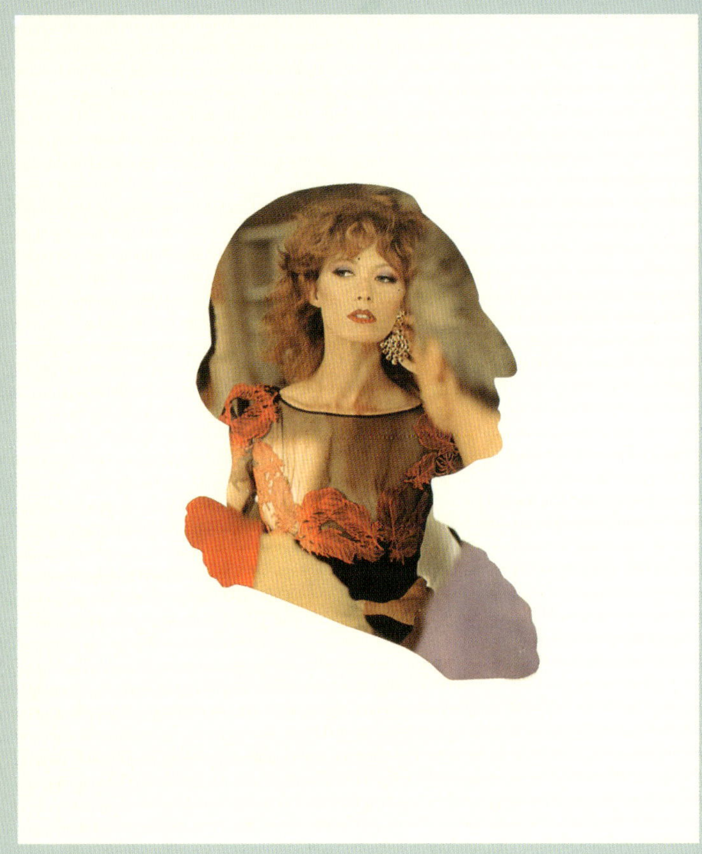

570

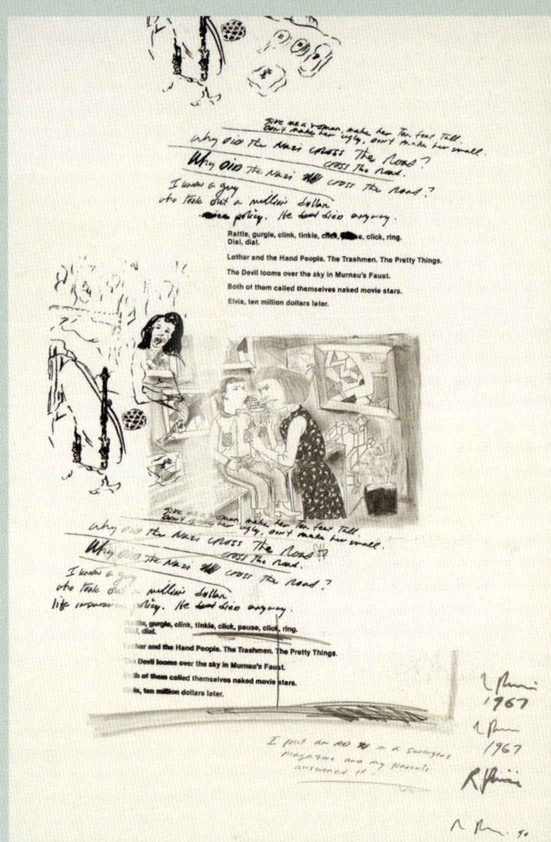

Sherrie Levine
(Hazleton 1947)

President Collage: 1
●●
1979
61 x 45,7 cm / 24 x 18 in.
Museum of Modern Art (MoMA), New York

printed paper recut and glued on paper
zerschnittenes, bedrucktes Papier, auf Papier aufgeklebt
geprint papier uitgeknipt en op papier geplakt
papel impreso recortado y encolado sobre papel

Richard Prince
(Panama Canal zone 1949)

Untitled
Ohne Titel
Zonder titel
Sin título
●
1984 / 1990
101,5 x 66 cm / 40 x 26 in.
Museum of Modern Art (MoMA), New York

pencil and spray paint on printed paper / Bleistift und
Lackspray auf bedrucktem Papier / potlood en vernisspray
op geprint papier / lápiz y pintura en aerosol sobre papel
impreso

Cindy Sherman
(Glen Ridge 1954)

Photogram without title No. 21
Photogramm ohne Titel Nr. 21
Fotogram zonder titel n. 21
Fotograma sin título n. 21

●●●

1978
19,1 x 24,2cm / 7.5 x 9.5 in.

silver bromide print
Silberbromiddruck
zilverbromide print
impresión al bromuro de plata

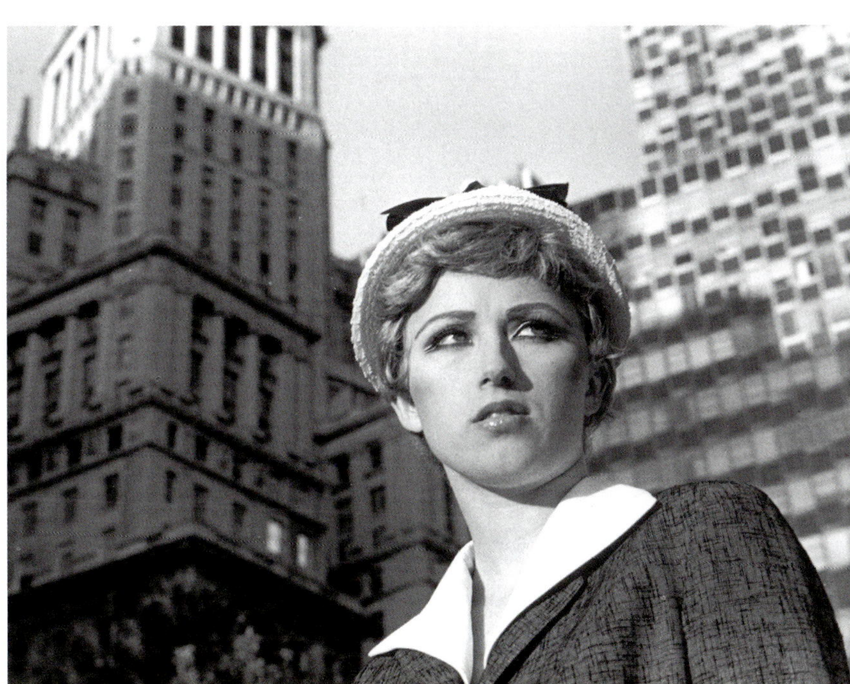

Barbara Kruger
(Newark 1945)

Untitled (Will Be)
Ohne Titel (will)
Zonder titel (zullen)
Sin título (Será)

●

1985
52 x 52 cm / 20.4 x 20.4 in.
Smithsonian American Art Museum,
Washington DC

offset photolithography and serigraphy on paper
Fotolithographie Offset und Siebdruck auf Papier
fotolithografie Offset en zeefdruk op papier
fotolitografía Offset y serigrafía sobre papel

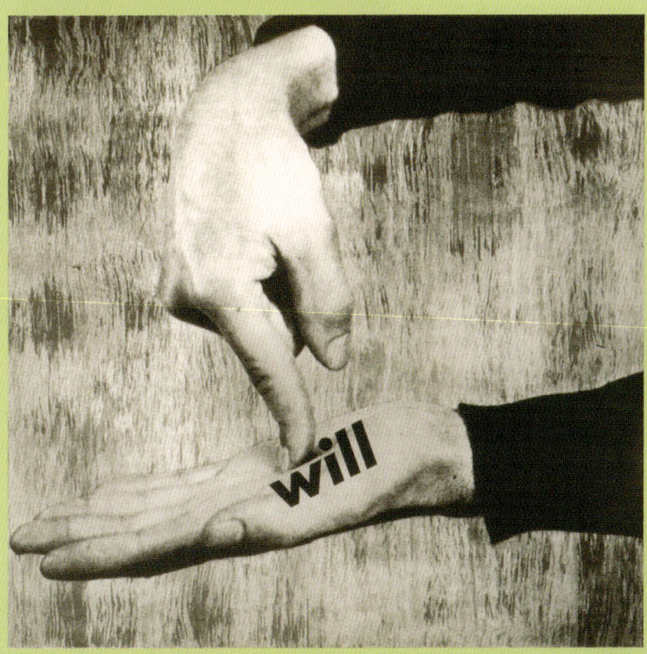

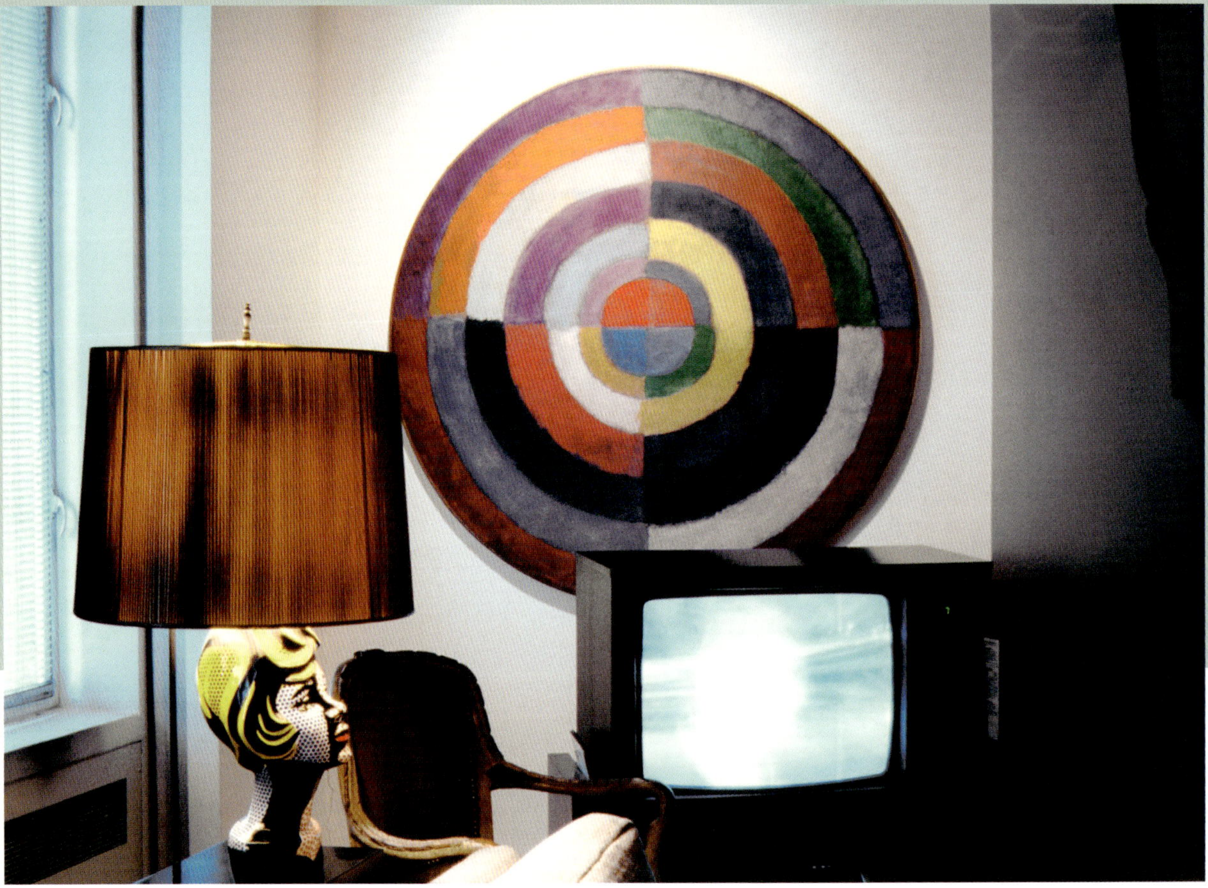

Louise Lawler
(Bronxville 1947)

Living Room Corner
Wohnzimmerecke
Huiskamerhoek
Esquina del salón

1983
73,3 x 99,8 cm / 28.8 x 39.3 in.
Wadsworth Atheneum Museum of Art, Hartford (CT)

color photograph / Farbfotografie
kleurenfoto / fotografía a color

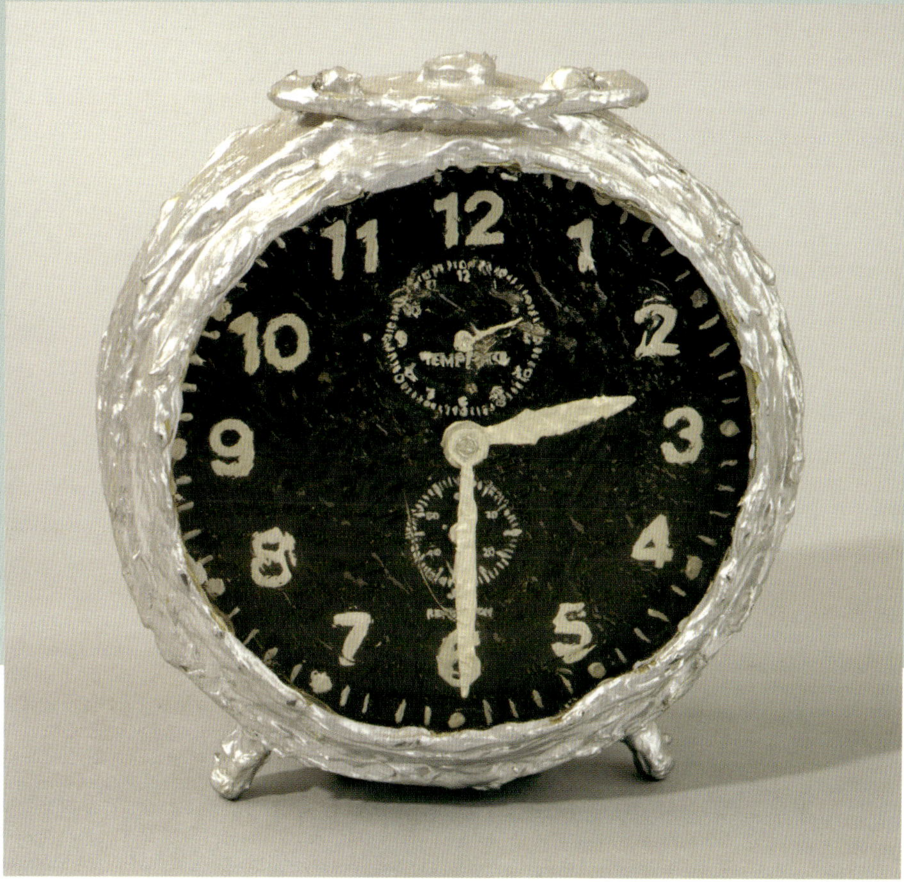

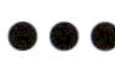

Bertrand Lavier
(Châtillon-sur-Seine 1949)

Jaz
●●●
1980
ø 15 cm / 5.9 in.

acrylic, alarm clock
Akryl, Wecker
acrylverf, wekker
acrílico, despertador

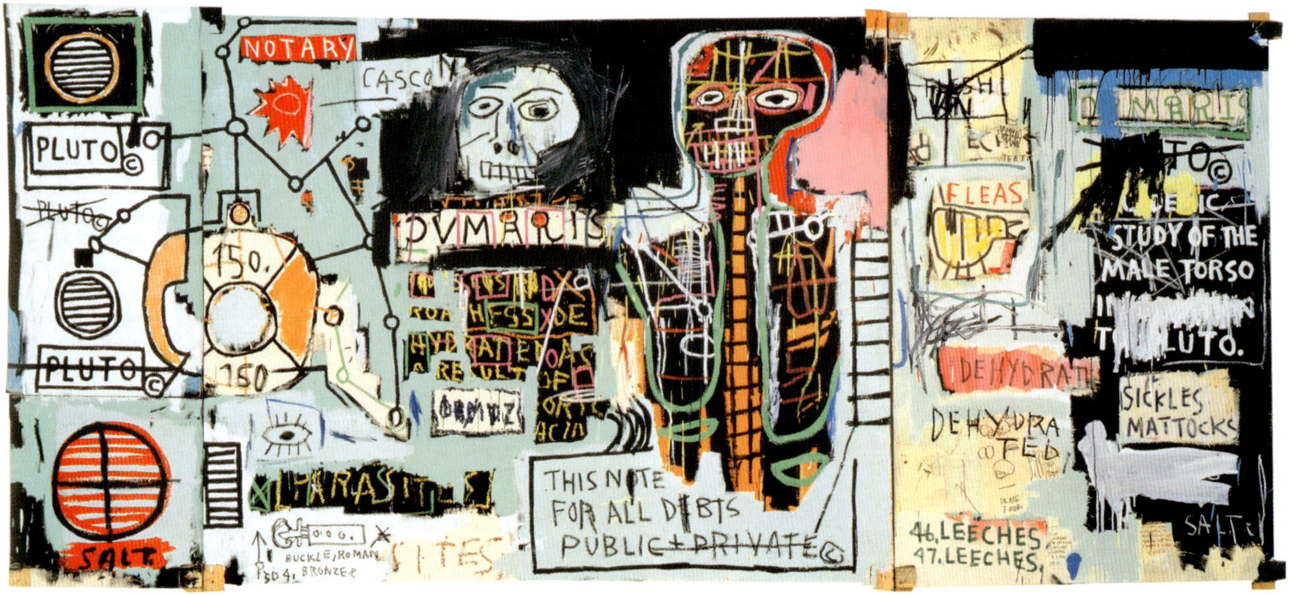

574

First African-American artist to be recognized on the
international art scene, Basquiat's painting, by mixing cultural
references, expresses his rage towards the world.

Basquiat ist der erste afroamerikanische Künstler, der in der
internationalen Kunstwelt Anerkennung findet. Indem sie
verschiedene kulturelle Einflüsse vermischt, bringt seine Malerei
die Wut gegenüber der Welt zum Ausdruck.

De schilderijen van Basquiat die de eerste erkende Afro-
Amerikaanse kunstenaar op internationaal niveau is, mengen
culturele verwijzingen waarmee hij zijn woede tegenover de
wereld uitdrukt.

Primer artista afroamericano en ser reconocido en el panorama
artístico internacional, la pintura de Basquiat, mezclando las
referencias culturales, expresa su ira contra el mundo.

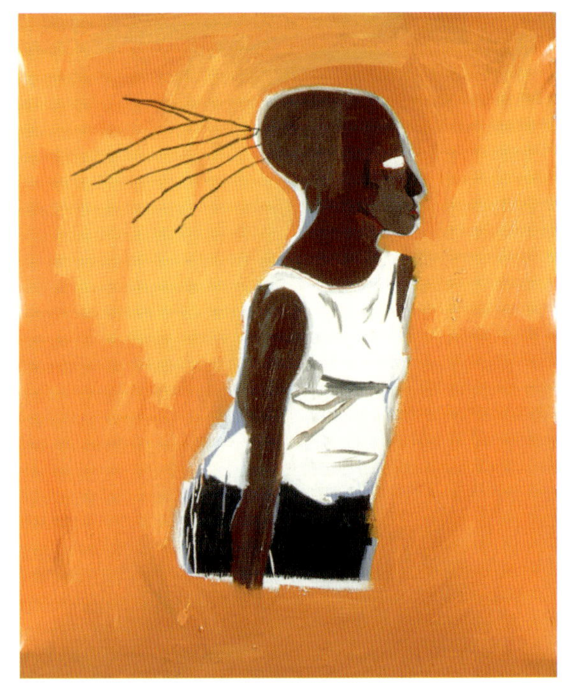

◀ Jean-Michel Basquiat
(Brooklyn 1960 - New York 1988)

Note
Notar
Notaris
Notario
●●●

1983
180,5 x 401,5 cm / 71 x 158 in.
Private collection
Private Sammlung
Privécollectie
Colección privada

collage, acrylic and crayon
Collage, Akryl und fettes Pastell
collage, acrylverf en vette pastelcollage,
acrílico y pastel graso

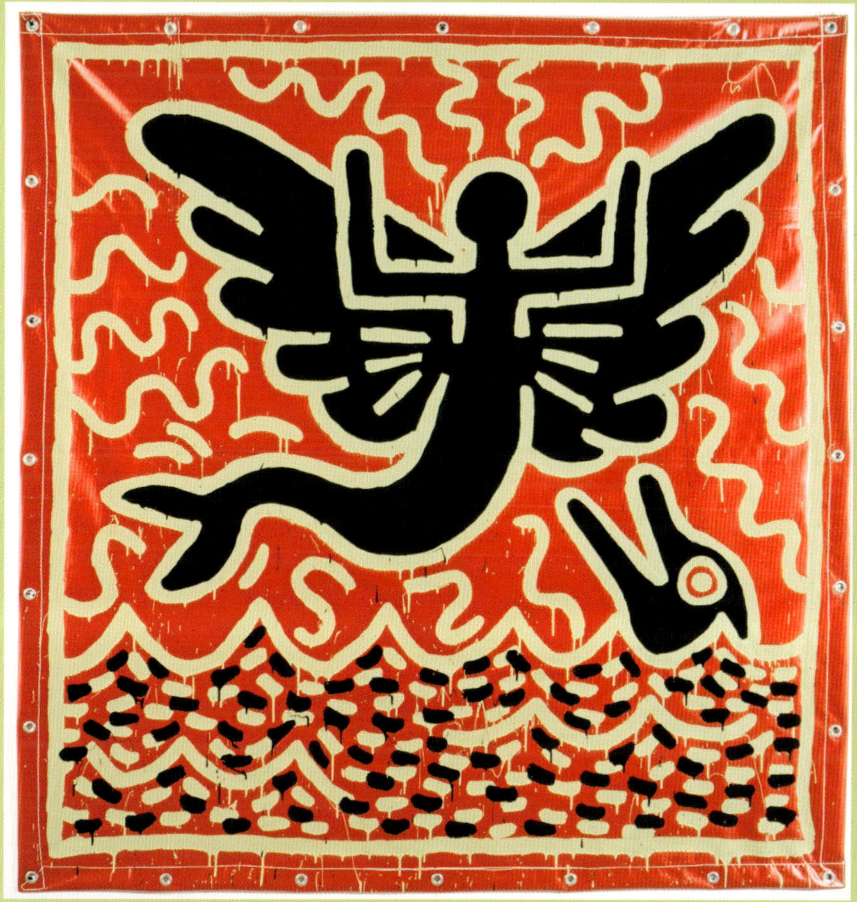

◀ Jean-Michel Basquiat
(Brooklyn 1960 - New York 1988)

Untitled
Ohne Titel
Zonder titel
Sin título
●●●

1985
213,5 x 152,5 cm / 84 x 60 in.
Private collection / Private Sammlung
Privécollectie / Colección privada

acrylic and crayon on canvas
Akryl und fetter Bleistift auf Leinwand
acrylverf en vet potlood op doek
acrílico y lápiz graso sobre lienzo

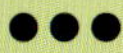

575

Keith Haring
(Reading 1958 -
New York 1990)

Untitled (Angel)
●●●

1982
182,8 x 182,8 cm / 72 x 72 in.
Nationalgalerie im Hamburger Bahnhof,
Staatliche Museen, Sammlung Marx, Berlin

vinyl paint on canvas / Vinylfarbe auf Vinylgewebe
vinylverf op vinyldoek / pintura vinílica sobre lienzo

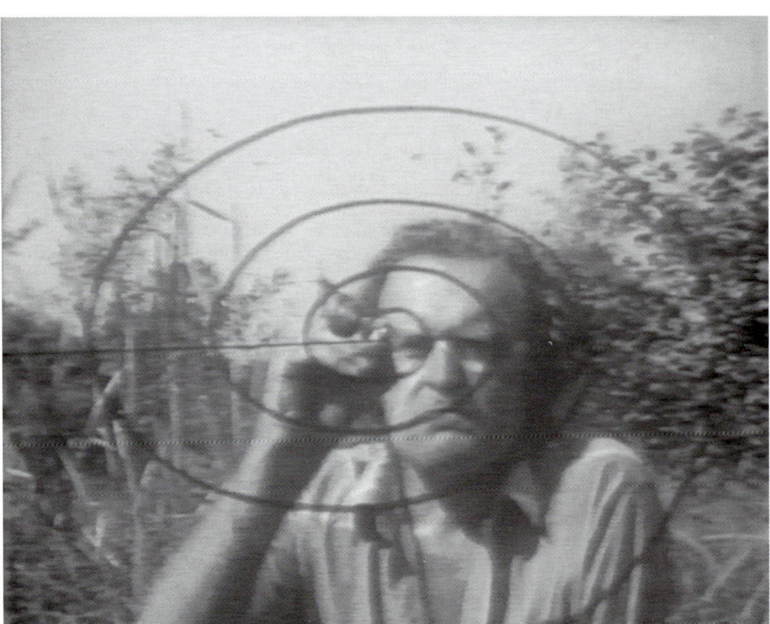

Gerry Schum
(Köln 1938 - Düsseldorf 1973)

**Identifications. Television recording No. 2
of the Fernsehgalerie at Düsseldorf
Identifikationen. Fernsehaufzeichnung
Nr. 2 der Fernsehgalerie in Düsseldorf
Identificatie. Televisieopname n. 2 van de
Fernsehgalerie van Düsseldorf
Identificaciones. Programa televisivo n. 2
de la Fernsehgalerie en Düsseldorf**

••

1970
Hamburger Kunsthalle, Hamburg

B / N, Audio, U-Matic, PAL, 42 Min. 16 mm. film
transferred to video / B / N, Audio, U-Matic, PAL,
42 Min. Film 16 mm. Auf Video übertragen / B / W,
Audio, U-Matic, PAL, 42 Min. 16 mm film op video
overgezet / B / N, Audio, U-Matic, PAL, 42 Min.
Película 16 mm. pasada a vídeo

Douglas Aitken
(Redondo Beach 1968)
Sleepwalkers
•••
2007
Museum of Modern Art (MoMA),
New York

installation for the exhibition
Installation für die Ausstellung
installatie voor de tentoonstelling
Instalación para la muestra

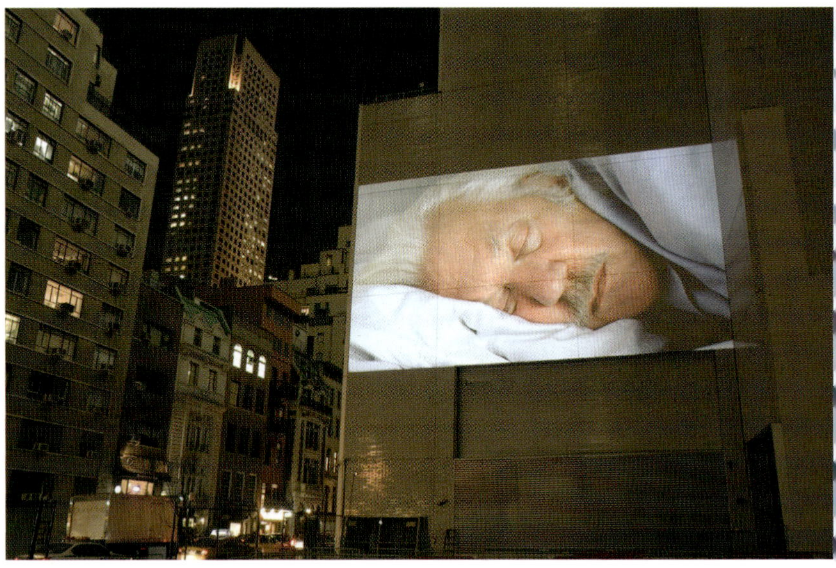

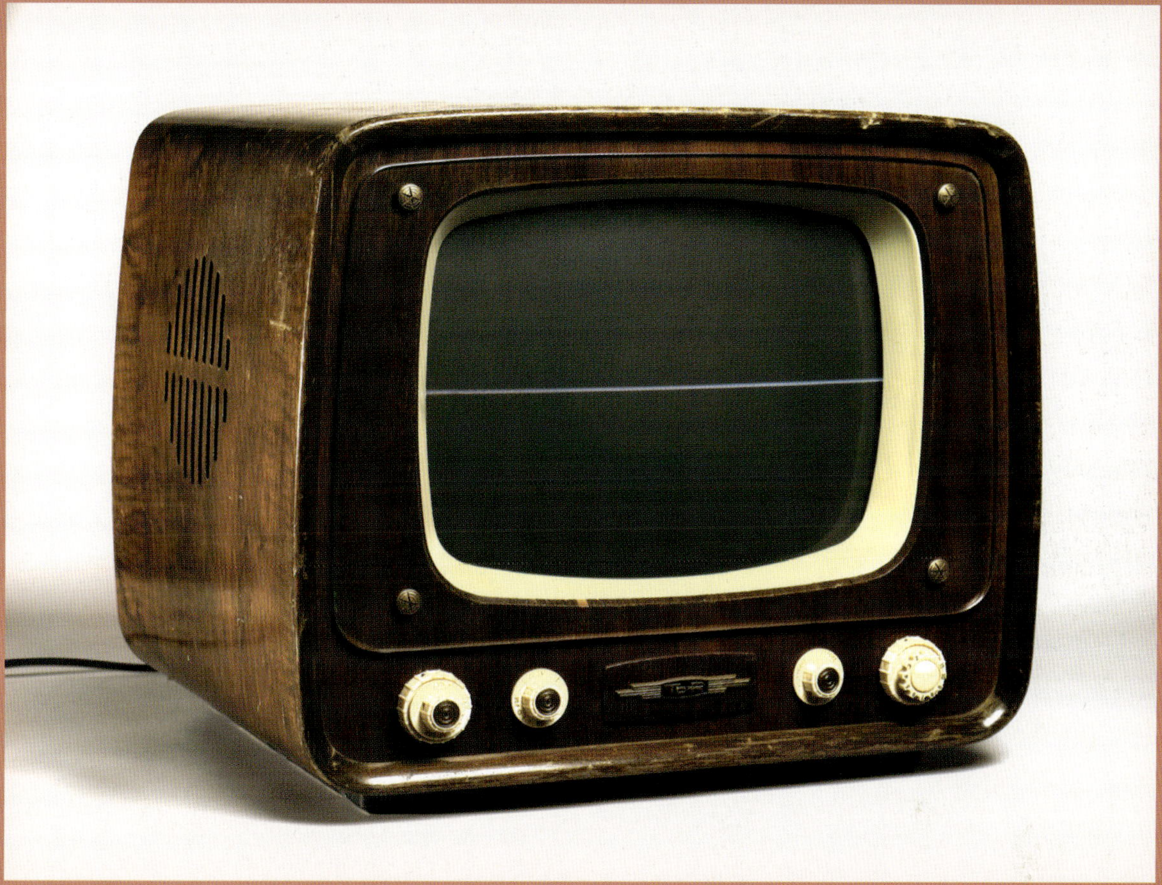

Nam June Paik
(Seoul 1932 - Miami 2006)

Zen for TV
Zen fürs Fernsehen
Zen voor TV
Zen para TV

●

1963 (1976)
48,3 x 57,2 x 45,7 cm / 19 x 22.5 x 18 in.
Smithsonian American Art Museum, Washington DC

period television and modified components / Alter Fernseher mit veränderten Komponenten
oude televisie en gewijzigde onderdelen / televisor antiguo y componentes modificados

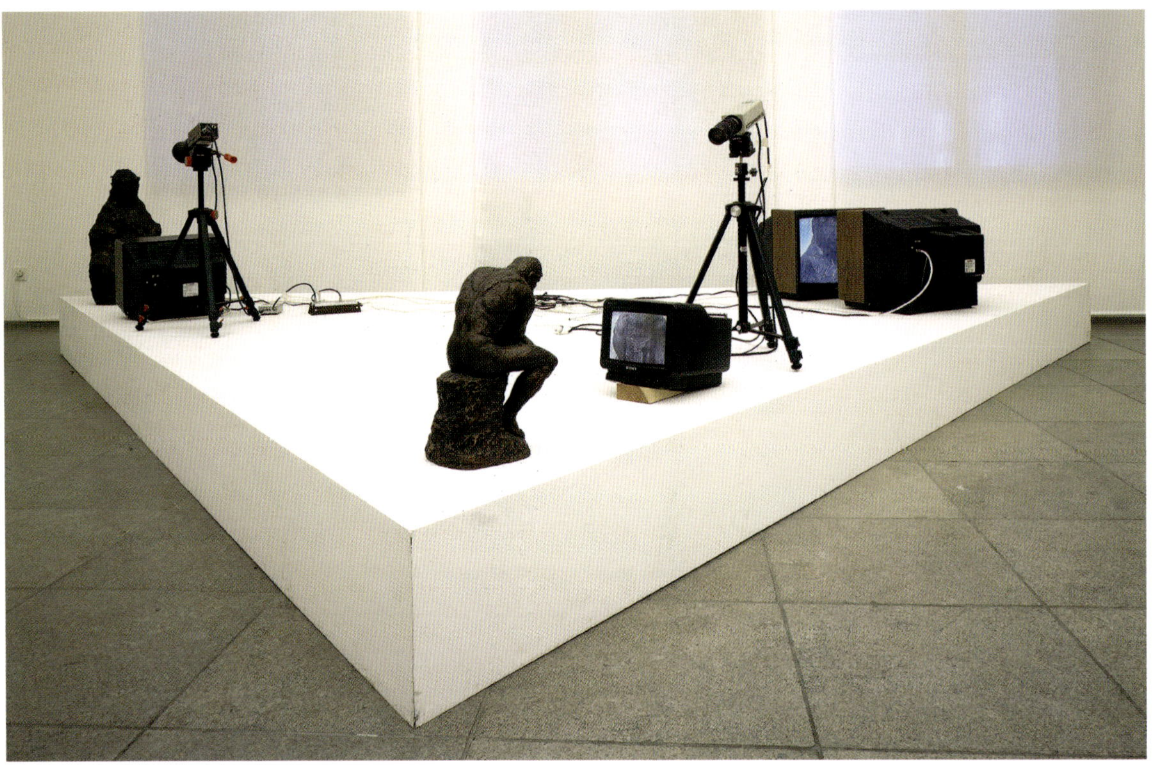

Nam June Paik
(Seoul 1932 - Miami 2006)

Triangle: Video-Buddha and Video-Thinker
Dreieck: TV-Buddha und TV-Denker
Driehoek: Video Boeddha en Videodenker
Triángulo: Vídeo-Budha y Vídeo-pensador

●●●

1976 (1991)
Nationalgalerie, Staatliche Museen, Berlin

installation of 4 monitors, 2 videocameras, 2 sculptures and 2 tripods / Installation mit 4 Monitoren, 2 Videokameras, 2 Skulpturen und 2 Stativen / installatie van 4 monitoren, 2 videocamera's, 2 sculpturen en 2 drievoeten / instalación de cuatro monitores, dos cámaras de vídeo, dos esculturas y dos trípodes

Paik saw in the cathode a medium that would replace the canvas and in his installations or sculptures he uses video to amuse.

Paik hat in der Kathodenstrahlröhre ein Medium gesehen, das die Leinwand ersetzen sollte. Er verwendete das Video in seinen Installationen oder Skulpturen um zu unterhalten.

Paik heeft in de beeldbuis een medium gezien dat het doek zou hebben vervangen en in zijn installaties of sculpturen gebruikt hij video's om de toeschouwers te vermaken.

Paik ha visto en el tubo catódico un medio que habría reemplazado el lienzo, y en sus instalaciones o esculturas utiliza el vídeo para divertir.

Nam June Paik
(Seoul 1932 - Miami 2006)

Technology
Technologie
Tecnología

●●

1991
Smithsonian American Art
Museum, Washington DC

25 video monitors, 3 laser disc
players with unique 3 discs in
cabinet / 25 Video-Monitore,
3 Laserdisc-Lektoren mit drei
einzelnen CDs im Fach / 25
videomonitoren, 3 laserdiskspelers
met drie unieke schijven in kast /
25 monitores de vídeo, tres lectores
de discos láser con tres unidades de
disco en gabinete

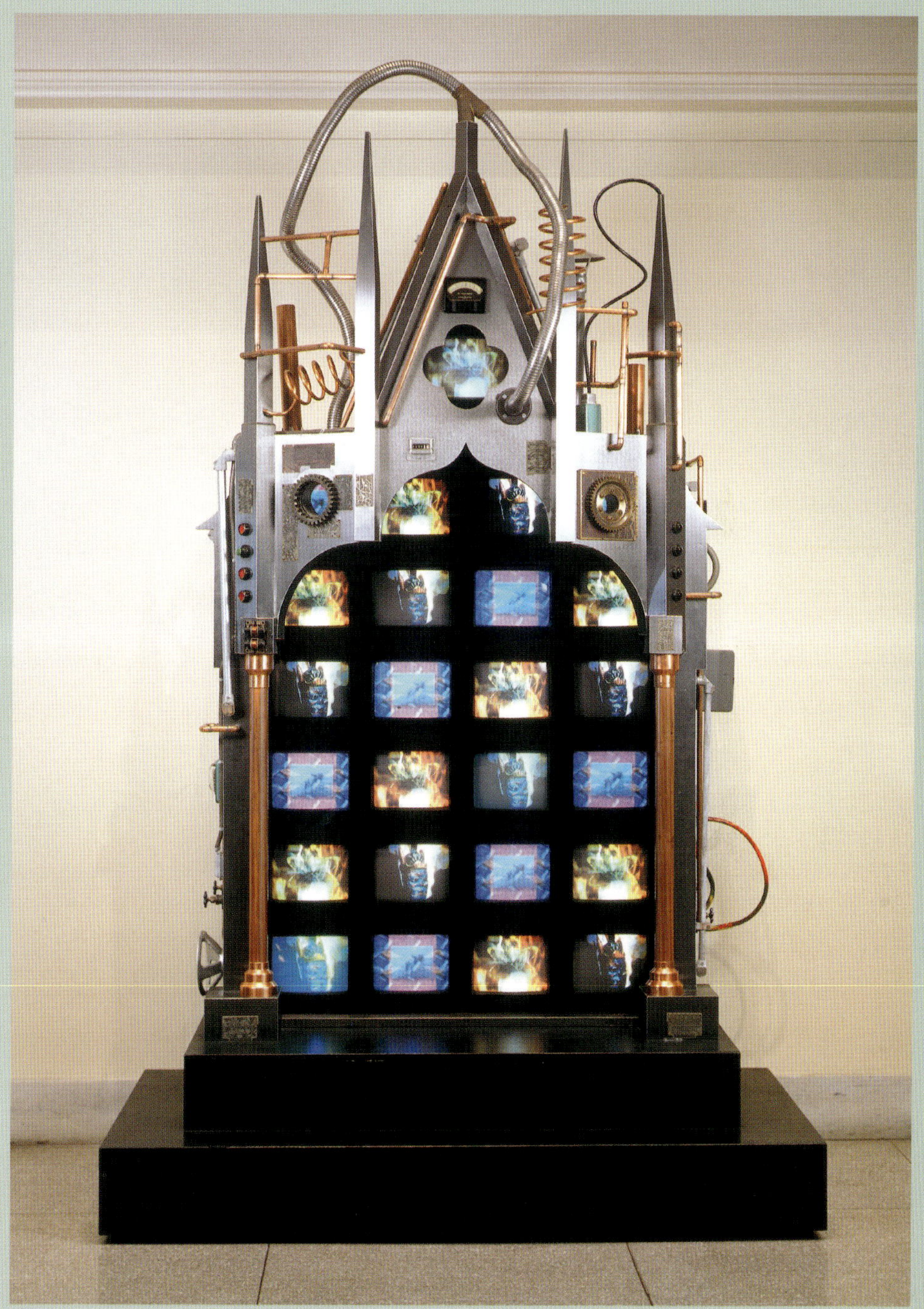

Gerhard Richter
(Dresden 1932)

Hofkirche, Dresden

●●●

2000
80 x 93 cm / 31.5 x 36.6 in.
Museum of Modern Art (MoMA),
New York

oil on canvas / Öl auf Leinwand
olieverf op doek / óleo sobre lienzo

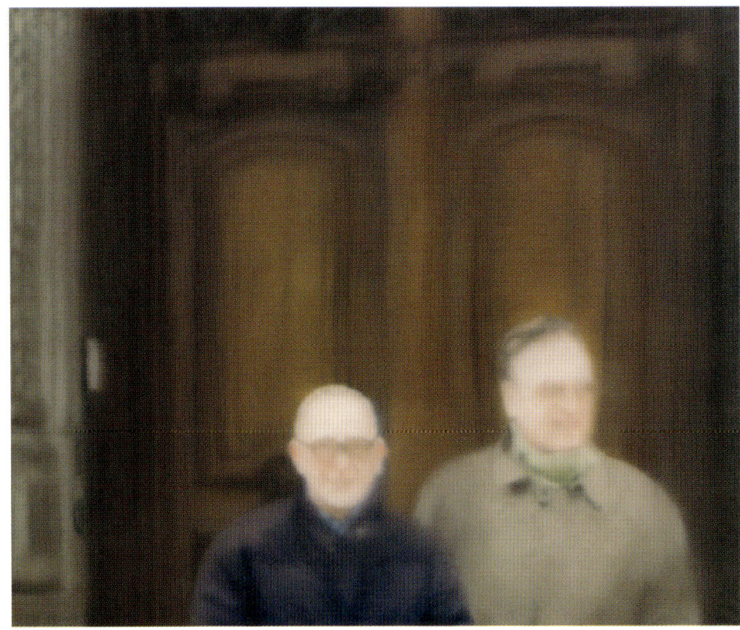

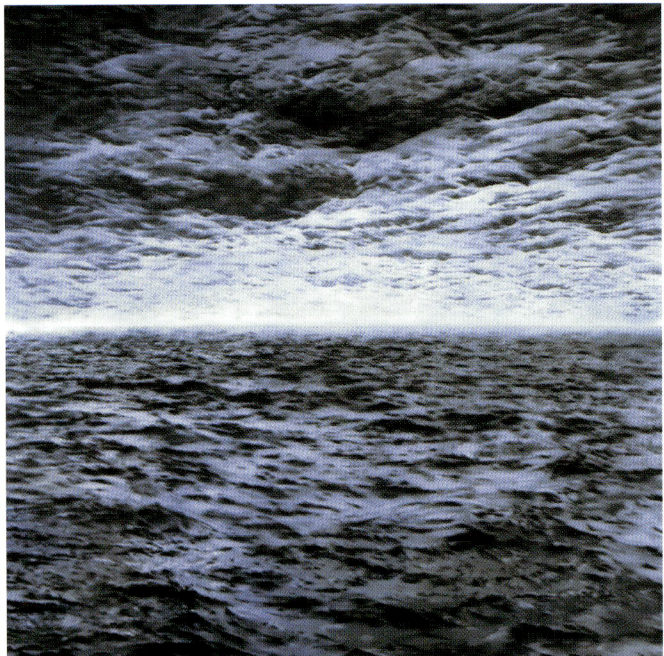

Gerhard Richter
(Dresden 1932)

Seascape (Sea / Sea)
Seestück (See / See)
Zeegezicht (Zee / Zee)
Marina (Mar / Mar)

●●●

1970
200 x 200 cm / 78.7 x 78.7 in.
Nationalgalerie, Staatliche Museen,
Berlin

oil on canvas / Öl auf Leinwand
olieverf op doek / óleo sobre lienzo

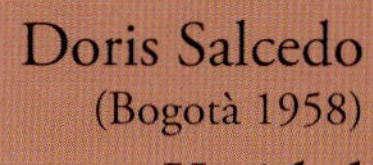

Doris Salcedo
(Bogotà 1958)

Untitled
Ohne Titel
Zonder titel
Sin título

●

1995
236,2 x 104,1 x 48,2 cm
93 x 41 x 18.9 in.
Museum of Modern Art (MoMA), New
York

wood, cement, steel, fabric and leather
Holz, Zement, Stahl, Stoff und Pelz
hout, cement, staal, stof en leer
madera, cemento, acero, tela y piel

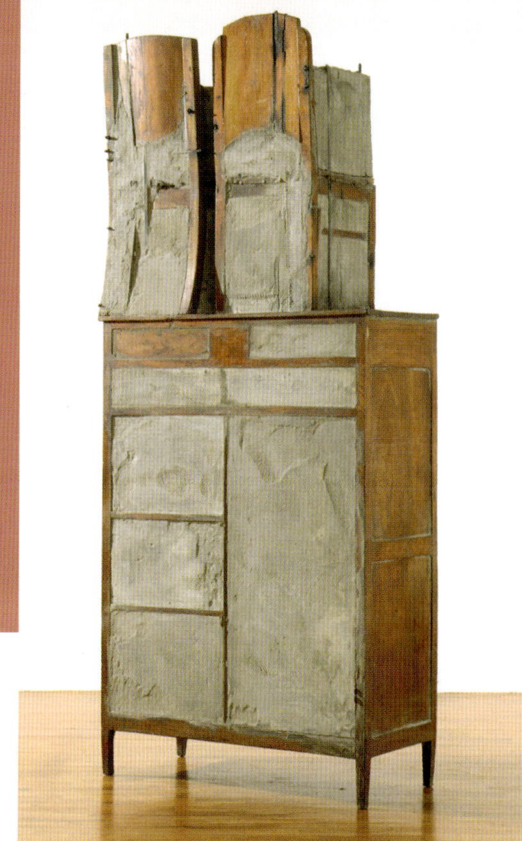

581

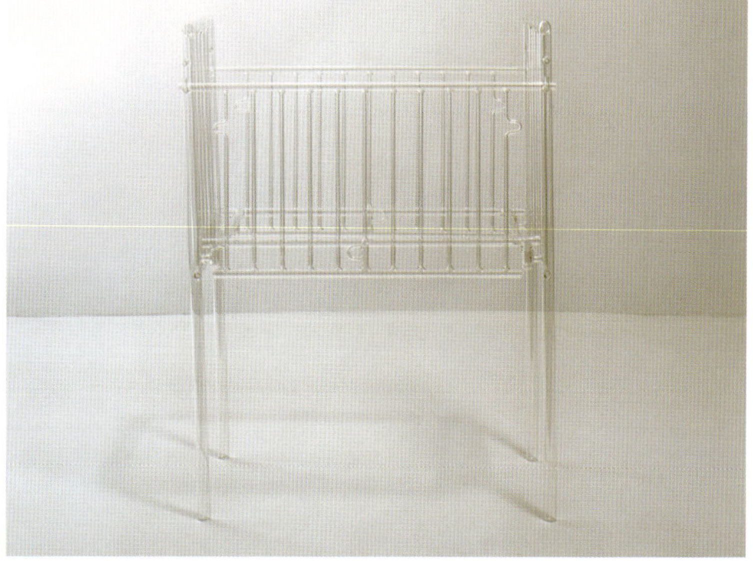

Mona Hatoum
(Beirut 1952)

Silence
Stille
Stilte
Silencio

●

1994
126,6 x 93.7 x 58.7 cm / 49.8 x 36.9 x 23.1 in.
Museum of Modern Art (MoMA), New York

glass / Glas / glas / vidrio

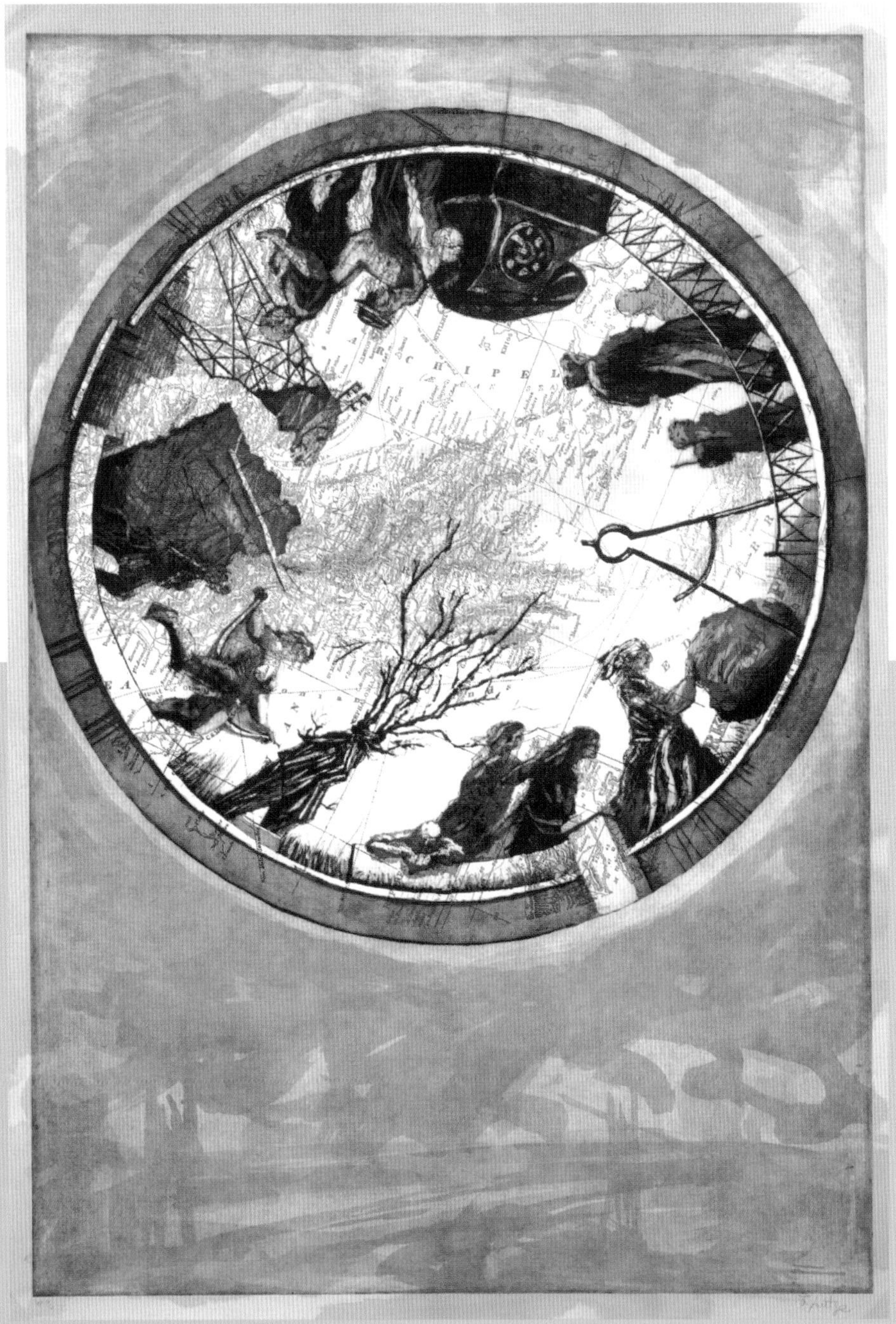

William Kentridge
(Johannesburg 1955)

Atlas Procession I

2000
157,5 x 106,7 cm
62 x 42 in.
The Jewish Museum, New York

etching, aquatint, drypoint, letterpress,
and hand painting / Radierung,
Aquatinta, Kaltnadel, Hochdruck,
Malerei mit den Händen / ets,
aquatint, droge naald, boekdruk,
handschildering / aguafuerte, aguatinta,
punta seca, impresión tipográfica,
pintura con las manos

**Photos of Barney films, shot with
his wife Bjork in Japan, where
beauty and cruelty collide without
respite.**

**Foto aus einem Film , den Barney
mit seiner Frau Björk in Japan
gedreht hat und in dem Schönheit
und Grausamkeit sich ständig
begegnen.**

**Foto van Barneys film, die hij
met zijn vrouw Bjork in Japan
gedraaid heeft, waar schoonheid en
wreedheid zonder oponthoud met
elkaar in conflict zijn.**

**Fotografía de la película de Barney,
filmada junto a su mujer, Björk,
en Japón, donde la belleza y la
crueldad se enfrentan sin tregua.**

Cai Guo-Qiang
(Quanzhou City 1957)

Borrow Your Enemy's Arrows
Borrow Your Enemy's Arrows (Leihe die Pfeile deines Feindes)
De pijlen van de vijand lenen
Pidiendo prestadas las flechas a tu enemigo
●●●
1998
152,4 x 720 x 230 cm / 60 x 283.4 x 90.5 in.
Museum of Modern Art (MoMA), New York

wood boat, sails, arrows, metal, rope, Chinese flag and fan / Holzschiff, Segel, Pfeile, Metall, Strick, chinesische Flage und Ventilator / houten boot, zeilen, pijlen, metaal, kabel, Chinese vlag en ventilator / barco de madera, velas, flechas, metal, cuerda, bandera china y ventilador

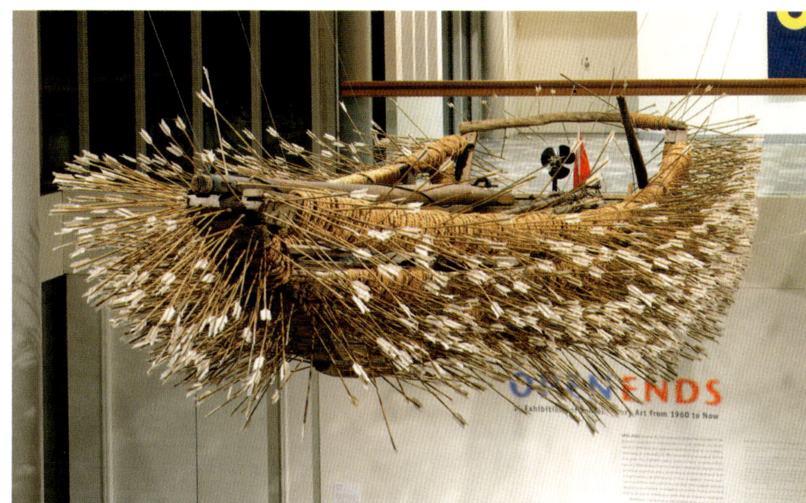

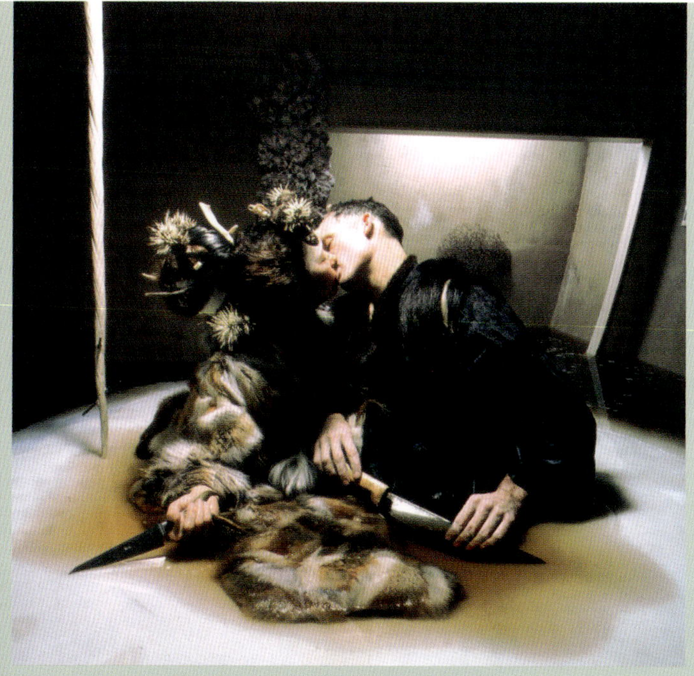

Matthew Barney
(San Francisco 1967)

Drawing Restraint 9: Shimenawa
●●●
2005
109,2 x 109,2 cm / 43 x 43 in.
Museum of Modern Art (MoMA),
New York

chromogenic color print in frame of self-lubricating plastic / Chromogenischer Farbdruck in selbstschmierenden Plastikrahmen / chromogene kleurenprint in een zelf invettende plastieken lijst / impresión cromogénica a color en marco de plástico autolubricante

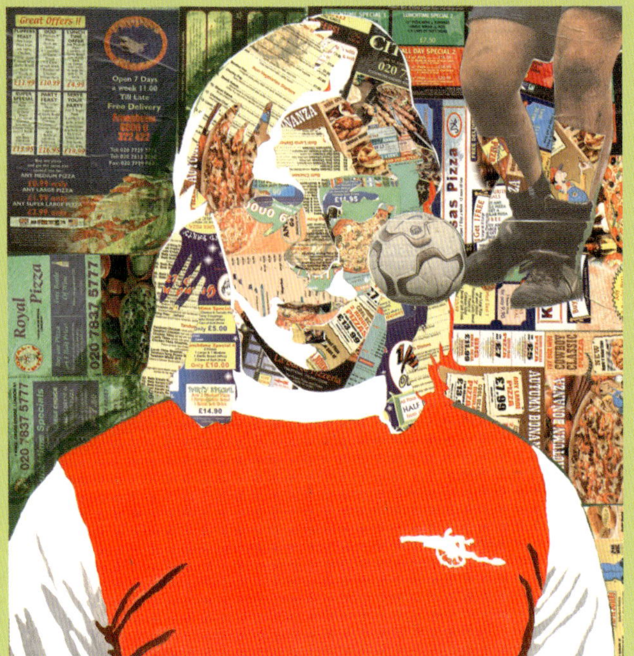

584

Sarah Lucas
(Holloway 1962)

Geezer

● ●

2002
81 x 74,9 cm / 31.9 x 29.5 in.
Museum of Modern Art (MoMA), New York

oil, cut-and-pasted printed paper, and pencil on wood
Öl, zerschnittenes und geklebtes Papier, Bleistift auf Holz
olieverf, uitgeknipt en opgeplakt papier, potlood op hout
óleo, papel cortado y encolado, lápiz sobre madera

Felix Gonzalez-Torres
(Guaimaro 1957 - New York 1996)

Untitled (Petit Palais)
Ohne Titel (Petit Palais)
Zonder titel (Petit Palais)
Sin título (Petit Palais)

● ●

1992
h. 1889,8 cm / 744 in.
Philadelphia Museum of Art, Philadelphia

lightbulbs, electrical wire, porcelain sockets
Glühbirnen, Elektrokabel, Henkel
lichtpeertjes, elektrische bedrading, contactdozen
bombillas, cables de electricidad, enchufes

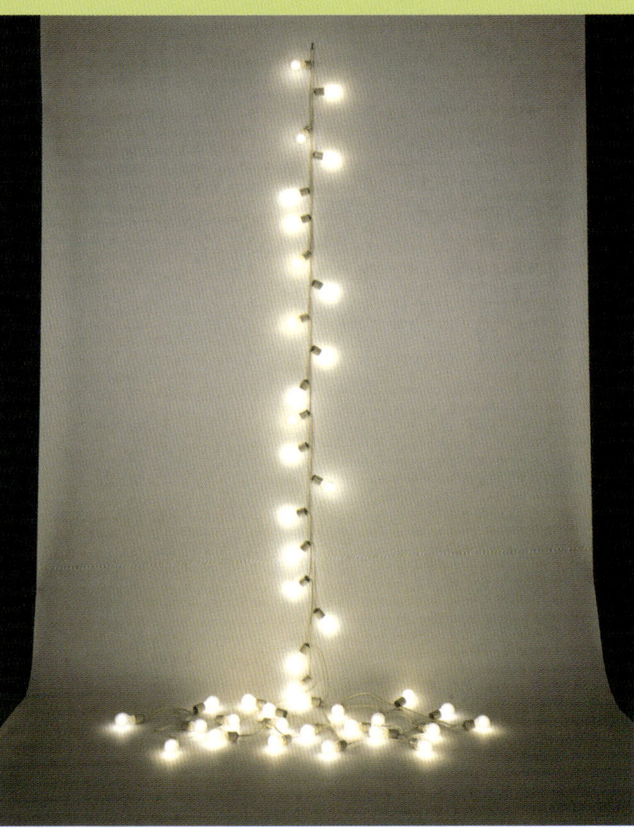

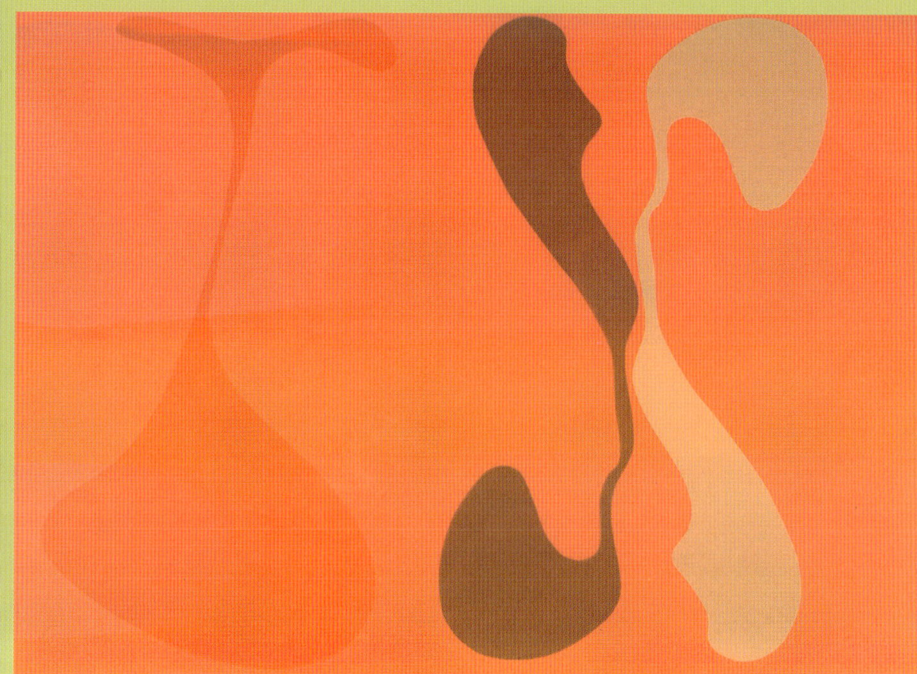

Jorge Pardo
(L'Avana 1963)

Untitled
Ohne Titel
Zonder titel
Sin título

●

2001
55,2 x 75,6 cm / 21.7 x 29.8 in.
Museum of Modern Art (MoMA),
New York

serigraphs / Siebdrucke
zeefdrukken / serigrafías

Andrea Zittel
(Escondido, California 1965)

Escape Vehicle A-Z: personalized by Andrea Zittel
Fluchtfahrzeug A-Z: Personalisiert von Andrea Zittel
**Vluchtvervoermiddel A-Z: verpersoonlijkt
door Andrea Zittel**
Vehículo de fuga A-Z: personalizado por Andrea Zittel

●●

1996
157,5 x 213,3 x 101,6 cm / 62 x 84 x 40 in.
Museum of Modern Art (MoMA), New York

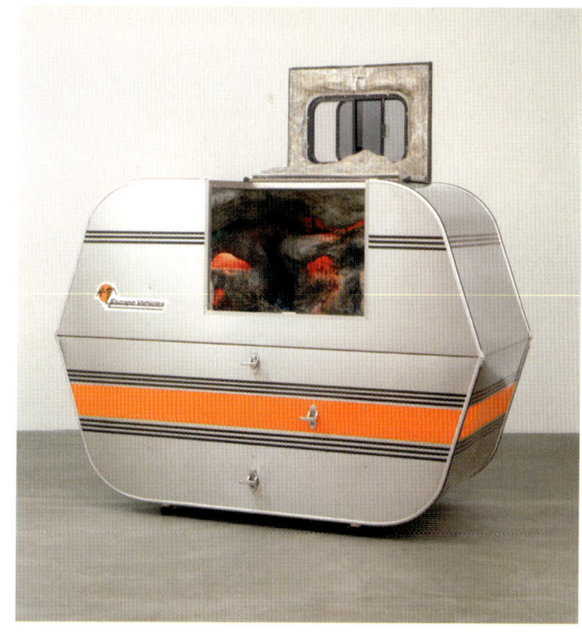

exterior: steel, insulation,wood and glass; interior: colored lights, water, fiberglass, wood, papier mâché, pebbles and paint / Äußeres: Stahl, Isolierstoff, Holz und Glas; Inneres: Farblichter, Wasser, Fiberglas, Holz, Pappmaché, Kieselsteine und Lack / buiten: staal, isoleermiddel, hout en glas; binnen: gekleurde lichten, water, vezelglas, hout, papier-maché, kommen en vernis / exterior: acero, aislante, madera y vidrio; interior: luces de colores, agua, fibra de vidrio, madera, cartapesta, guijarros y pintura

Lucas Samaras
(Kastoria 1936)

**Panorama,
11 / 26 / 84**
● ● ●
1984
27,6 x 91,6 cm
10.8 x 36 in.
Smithsonian American Art
Museum, Washington DC

Polaroid print assemblage
Montage von
Polaroiddrucken
assemblage van
Polaroidprinten / montaje
de impresiones Polaroid

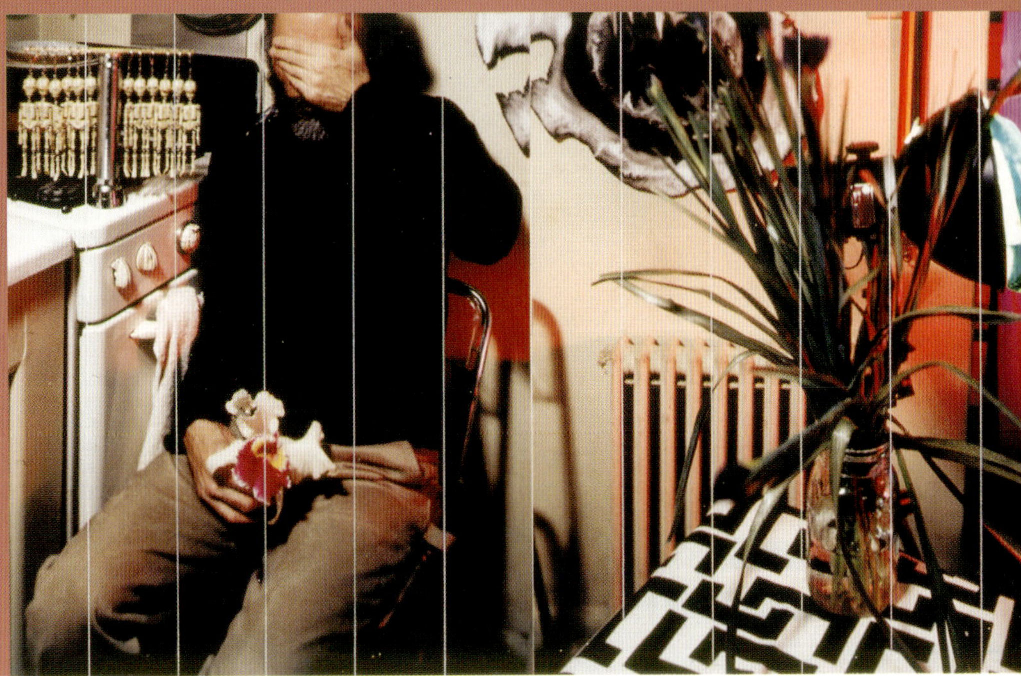

Vanessa Beecroft
(Genova 1969)

VB 43008 TE
● ● ●
2000
Nationalgalerie, Staatliche
Museen, Berlin

photo, digital print on
C-type paper / Digital-
Foto, Druck auf C-type
Papier / foto, digitale print
op papier C-type / foto,
impresión digital sobre
papel C-type

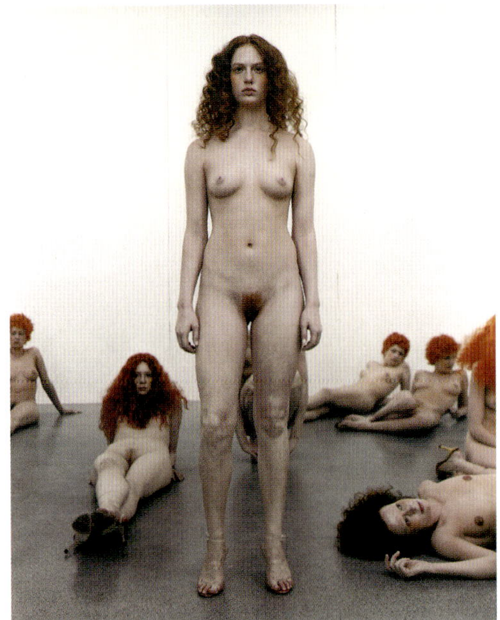

Nude women in high heels, who do
not speak, move very slowly, are barely
distinguishable one from the other, as if in
a mysterious living painting.

Nackte Frauengestalten mit hohen
Absätzen, die nicht sprechen, sich
sehr langsam bewegen und sich kaum
voneinander unterscheiden, wie in einem
mysteriösen lebendenden Bild.

Naakte, stilzwijgende vrouwen op hoge
hakken, bewegen zich langzaam voort en
zijn niet uit elkaar te houden, net zoals in
een levend mysterieus schilderij.

Mujeres desnudas pero con tacones altos,
que no hablan, se mueven muy lentamente,
apenas se distinguen las unas de las otras,
como en un misterioso cuadro viviente.

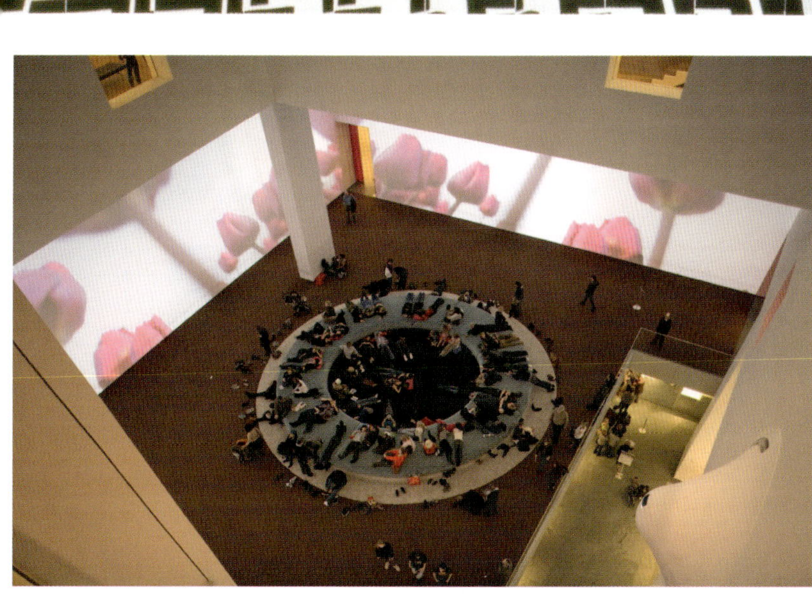

Pipilotti Rist
(Grabs 1962)

**Pour Your Body Out,
(7354 Cubic Metres)
Ström deinen Körper aus
(7354 Kubikmeter)
Giet je lichaam uit
(7354 kubieke meter)
Revierte tu cuerpo hacia afuera,
(7354 metros cúbicos)**

●●●

2008
Installation view at Museum of Modern Art
(MoMA), New York

multichannel video (color, sound), projection,
circular seating carpet / Mulitkanal-Video (Farbe,
Ton), Projektion, Rundsessel, Teppich
multikanaalvideo (kleur, geluitd), projector,
ronde bank, tapijt / vídeo multicanal (color,

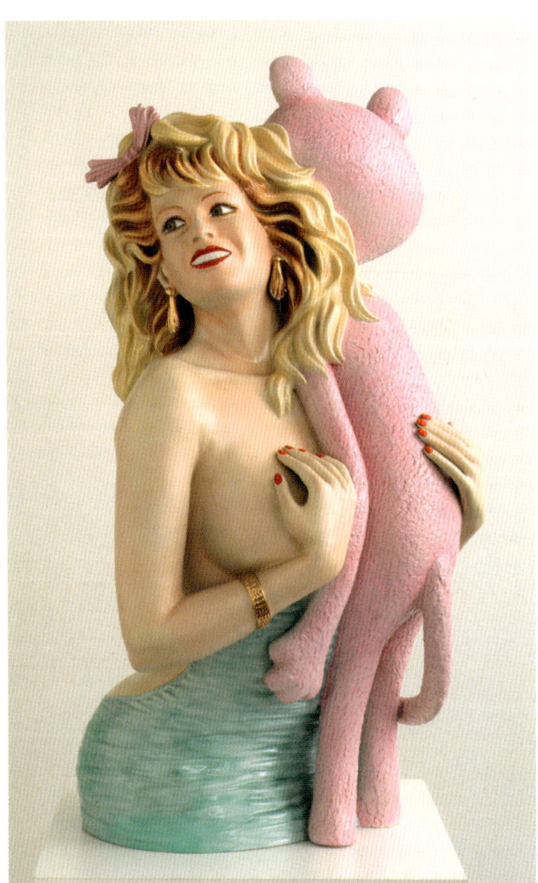

▲ Jeff Koons
(York 1955)

Pink Panther
Rosaroter Panther
Roze panter
Pantera Rosa

● ● ●

1988
104,1 x 52 x 48,2 cm / 41 x 20.5 x 18.9 in.
Museum of Modern Art (MoMA),
New York

porcelain / Porzellan / porcelein / porcelana

▼ Robert Gober
(Wallingford, Connecticut 1954)

Untitled (Leg)
Ohne Titel (Bein)
Zonder titel (Been)
Sin título (Pierna)

● ●

1989-1990
28,9 x 19,7 x 50,8 cm / 11.4 x 7.7 x 20 in.
Museum of Modern Art (MoMA),
New York

beeswax, cotton, wood, leather, human hair
Bienenwachs, Baumwolle, Holz, Leder, menschliche Haare
bijenwas, katoen, hout, leer, mensenharen
cera de abeja, algodón, madera, cuero, cabellos humanos

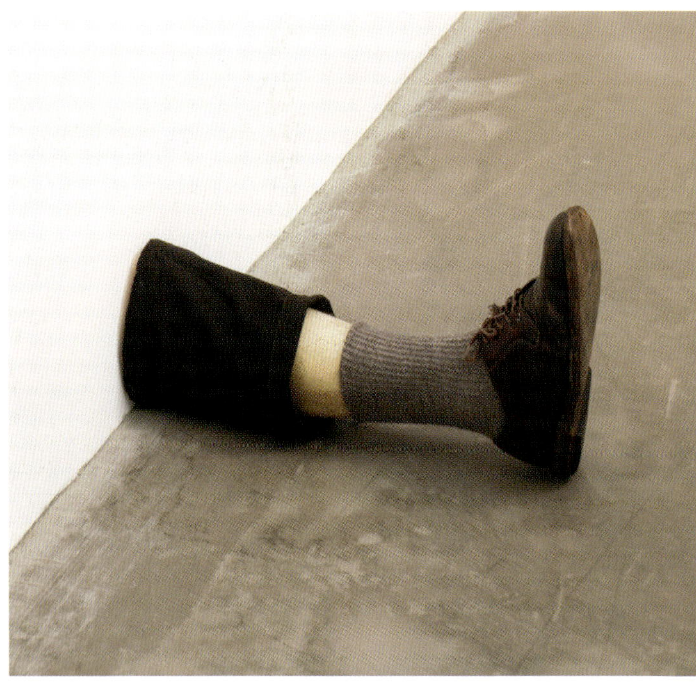

▼ Katharina Fritsch
(Essen 1956)

**Black table with crockery
Schwarzer Tisch mit Geschirr
Zwarte tafel met keukengerei
Mesa negra con vajilla**

●●●

1985
h. 93,3 cm / 36.7 in.; ø 150 cm / 59 in.
Museum of Modern Art (MoMA), New York

wood, paint and plastic / Holz, Malerei, Plastik
hout, verf, plastic / madera, pintura, plástico

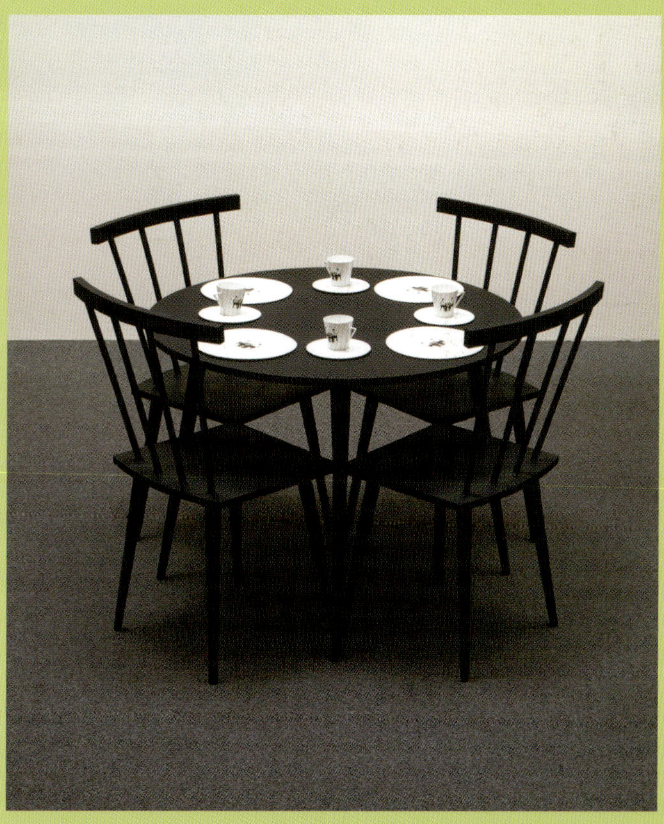

A LITTLE KNOWLEDGE CAN GO A LONG WAY
A LOT OF PROFESSIONALS ARE CRACKPOTS
A MAN CAN'T KNOW WHAT IT'S LIKE TO BE A MOTHER
A NAME MEANS A LOT JUST BY ITSELF
A POSITIVE ATTITUDE MAKES ALL THE DIFFERENCE IN THE WORLD
A RELAXED MAN IS NOT NECESSARILY A BETTER MAN
A SENSE OF TIMING IS THE MARK OF GENIUS
A SINCERE EFFORT IS ALL YOU CAN ASK
A SINGLE EVENT CAN HAVE INFINITELY MANY INTERPRETATIONS
A SOLID HOME BASE BUILDS A SENSE OF SELF
A STRONG SENSE OF DUTY IMPRISONS YOU
ABSOLUTE SUBMISSION CAN BE A FORM OF FREEDOM
ABSTRACTION IS A TYPE OF DECADENCE
ABUSE OF POWER SHOULD COME AS NO SURPRISE
ACTION CAUSES MORE TROUBLE THAN THOUGHT
ALIENATION PRODUCES ECCENTRICS OR REVOLUTIONARIES
ALL THINGS ARE DELICATELY INTERCONNECTED
AMBITION IS JUST AS DANGEROUS AS COMPLACENCY
AMBIVALENCE CAN RUIN YOUR LIFE
AN ELITE IS INEVITABLE
ANGER OR HATE CAN BE A USEFUL MOTIVATING FORCE
ANIMALISM IS PERFECTLY HEALTHY
ANY SURPLUS IS IMMORAL
ANYTHING IS A LEGITIMATE AREA OF INVESTIGATION
ARTIFICIAL DESIRES ARE DESPOILING THE EARTH
AT TIMES INACTIVITY IS PREFERABLE TO MINDLESS FUNCTIONING
AT TIMES YOUR UNCONSCIOUS IS TRUER THAN YOUR CONSCIOUS MIND
AUTOMATION IS DEADLY
AWFUL PUNISHMENT AWAITS REALLY BAD PEOPLE
BAD INTENTIONS CAN YIELD GOOD RESULTS
BEING ALONE WITH YOURSELF IS INCREASINGLY UNPOPULAR
BEING HAPPY IS MORE IMPORTANT THAN ANYTHING ELSE
BEING HONEST IS NOT ALWAYS THE KINDEST WAY
BEING JUDGMENTAL IS A SIGN OF LIFE
BEING SURE OF YOURSELF MEANS YOU'RE A FOOL
BELIEVING IN REBIRTH IS THE SAME AS ADMITTING DEFEAT
BOREDOM MAKES YOU DO CRAZY THINGS
CALM IS MORE CONDUCIVE TO CREATIVITY THAN IS ANXIETY
CATEGORIZING FEAR IS CALMING
CHANGE IS VALUABLE BECAUSE IT LETS THE OPPRESSED BE TYRANTS
CHASING THE NEW IS DANGEROUS TO SOCIETY
CHILDREN ARE THE CRUELEST OF ALL
CHILDREN ARE THE HOPE OF THE FUTURE
CLASS ACTION IS A NICE IDEA WITH NO SUBSTANCE
CLASS STRUCTURE IS AS ARTIFICIAL AS PLASTIC
CONFUSING YOURSELF IS A WAY TO STAY HONEST
CRIME AGAINST PROPERTY IS RELATIVELY UNIMPORTANT
DECADENCE CAN BE AN END IN ITSELF
DECENCY IS A RELATIVE THING
DEPENDENCE CAN BE A MEAL TICKET
DESCRIPTION IS MORE VALUABLE THAN METAPHOR
DEVIANTS ARE SACRIFICED TO INCREASE GROUP SOLIDARITY
DISGUST IS THE APPROPRIATE RESPONSE TO MOST SITUATIONS
DISORGANIZATION IS A KIND OF ANESTHESIA
DON'T PLACE TOO MUCH TRUST IN EXPERTS
DON'T RUN PEOPLE'S LIVES FOR THEM
DRAMA OFTEN OBSCURES THE REAL ISSUES
DREAMING WHILE AWAKE IS A FRIGHTENING CONTRADICTION
DYING AND COMING BACK GIVES YOU CONSIDERABLE PERSPECTIVE
DYING SHOULD BE AS EASY AS FALLING OFF A LOG
EATING TOO MUCH IS CRIMINAL
ELABORATION IS A FORM OF POLLUTION
EMOTIONAL RESPONSES ARE AS VALUABLE AS INTELLECTUAL RESPONSES
ENJOY YOURSELF BECAUSE YOU CAN'T CHANGE ANYTHING ANYWAY
EVEN YOUR FAMILY CAN BETRAY YOU
EVERY ACHIEVEMENT REQUIRES A SACRIFICE
EVERYONE'S WORK IS EQUALLY IMPORTANT
EVERYTHING THAT'S INTERESTING IS NEW
EXCEPTIONAL PEOPLE DESERVE SPECIAL CONCESSIONS
EXPIRING FOR LOVE IS BEAUTIFUL BUT STUPID
EXPRESSING ANGER IS NECESSARY
EXTREME BEHAVIOR HAS ITS BASIS IN PATHOLOGICAL PSYCHOLOGY
EXTREME SELF-CONSCIOUSNESS LEADS TO PERVERSION
FAITHFULNESS IS A SOCIAL NOT A BIOLOGICAL LAW
FAKE OR REAL INDIFFERENCE IS A POWERFUL PERSONAL WEAPON
FATHERS OFTEN USE TOO MUCH FORCE
FEAR IS THE GREATEST INCAPACITATOR
FREEDOM IS A LUXURY NOT A NECESSITY
GIVING FREE REIN TO YOUR EMOTIONS IS AN HONEST WAY TO LIVE
GOING WITH THE FLOW IS SOOTHING BUT RISKY
GOOD DEEDS EVENTUALLY ARE REWARDED
GOVERNMENT IS A BURDEN ON THE PEOPLE
GRASS ROOTS AGITATION IS THE ONLY HOPE
GUILT AND SELF-LACERATION ARE INDULGENCES
HABITUAL CONTEMPT DOESN'T REFLECT A FINER SENSIBILITY
HIDING YOUR MOTIVES IS DESPICABLE

▲ Jenny Holzer
(Gallipolis 1950)

Truismi

●

1978-1987
243,9 x 101,6 cm / 96.1 x 40 in.
Museum of Modern Art (MoMA), New York

photostat, composition
Fotokopie, Komposition
fotokopie, compositie
copia fotostática, composición

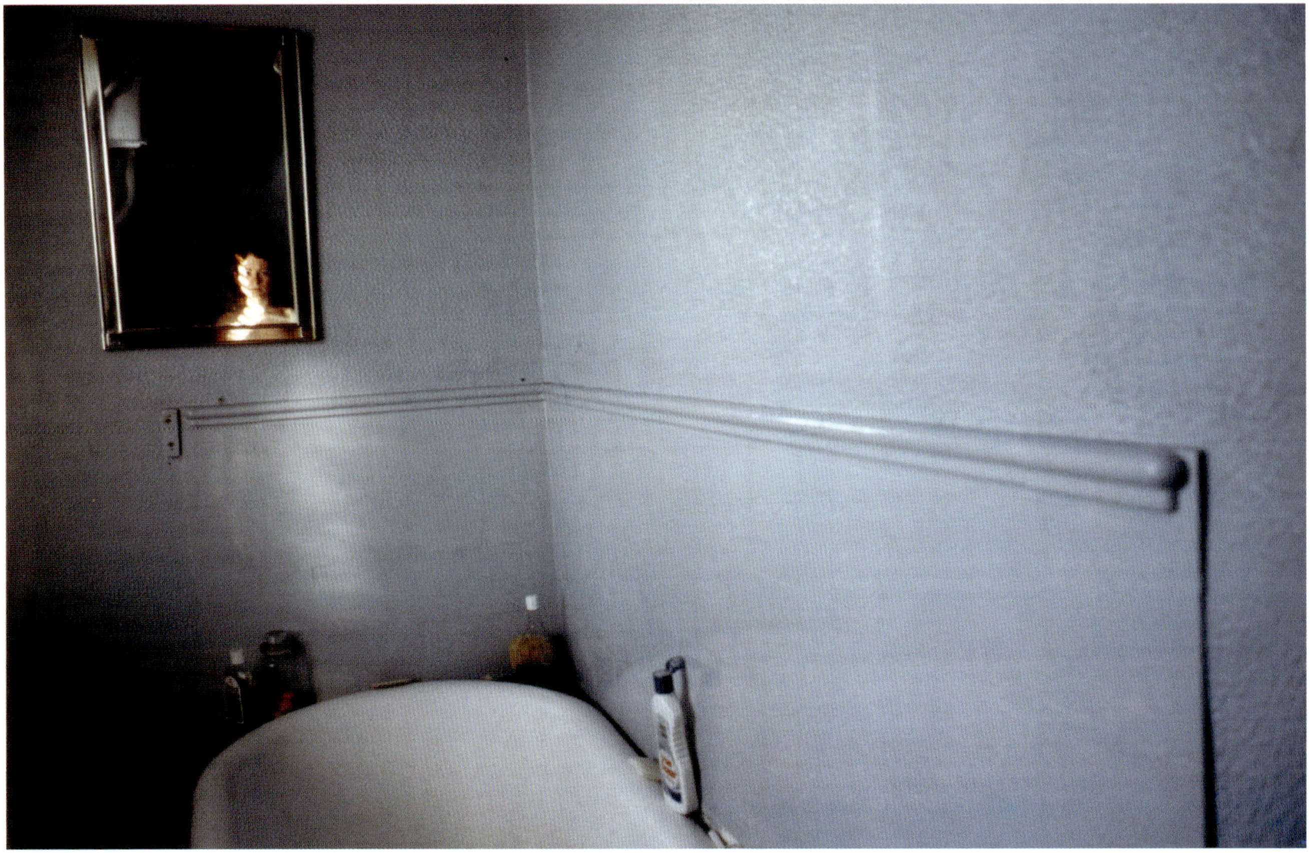

590

Nan Goldin
(Washington 1953)

Self-portrait in blue bathroom, London
Selbstporträt in blauem Badezimmer, London
Zelfportret in blauwe badkamer, Londen
Autorretrato en baño azul, Londres

●●●

1980
70,5 x 102,1 cm / 27.7 x 40.2 in.
The Jewish Museum, New York

silver dye bleach print / Mit Silbertinte gebleichter Druck
zilverkleurige gebleekte print / impresión desteñida con tintura plateada

▶ Thomas Ruff
(Zell am Harmersbach 1958)

Portrait (Anna Giese)
Porträt (Anna Giese)
Portret (Anna Giese)
Retrato (Anna Giese)

●●

1989
205 x 160 cm / 80.7 x 63 in.
Hamburger Kunsthalle, Hamburg

color photo, print n° 2/2 / Farbfoto, Druck Nr. 2/2
kleurenfoto, print n. 2/2 / foto a color, impresión n° 2/2

Candida Hoefer
(Eberswalde 1944)

The Kunsthalle of Hamburg III
Die Hamburger Kunsthalle III
De Kunsthalle van Hamburg III
La Kunsthalle de Hamburgo III

● ● ●

2000
Hamburger Kunsthalle, Hamburg

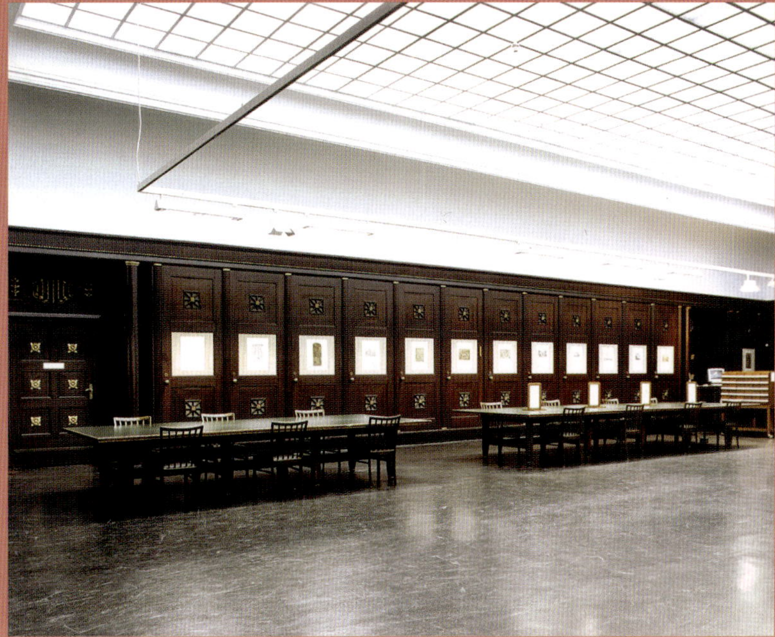

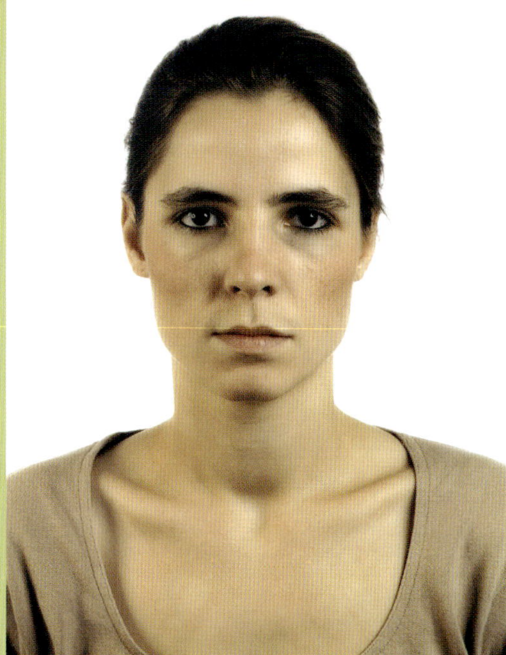

A portrait without emotions, without expressions, as if it were an administrative document: Ruff emphasizes the paradox of the photo in its relationship with reality.

Ein emotionsloses Porträt, ohne Expressionen, ähnlich wie ein Passdokument: Ruff betont das Paradoxe des Fotos in seiner Beziehung zur Realität.

In het portret, even emotieloos en uitdrukkingloos als administratieve documenten, benadrukt Ruff het paradox van de foto in zijn relatie met de werkelijkheid.

Un retrato sin emociones, sin expresiones, como un documento administrativo: Ruff destaca la paradoja de la fotografía en su relación con lo real.

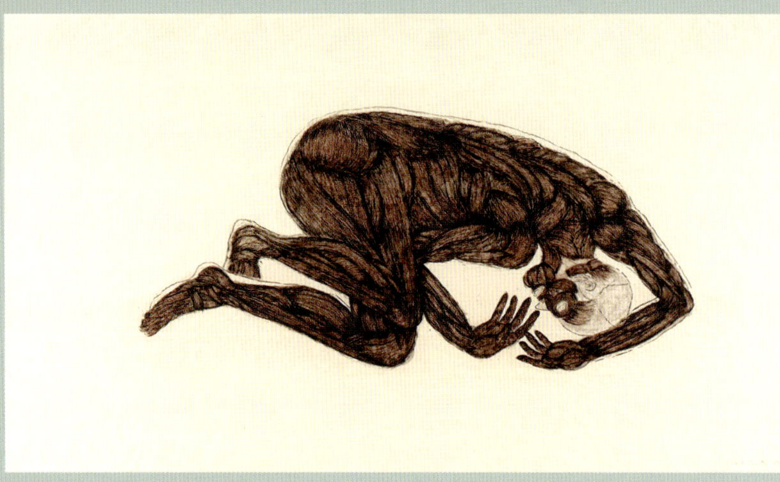

Kiki Smith
(Nuremberg 1954)

Dream
Traum
Droom
Sueño

●

1992
59,5 x 125,1 cm / 23.4 x 49.2 in.
Museum of Modern Art (MoMA),
New York

etching and aquatint on handmade Japanes paper
Radierung, Aquatinta auf handgeschöpftem
japanischen Papier
ets, aquatint op handgemaakt Japans papier
aguafuerte, aguatinta sobre papel japonés hecho
a mano

Anish Kapoor
(Bombay 1954)

Wounds and absent objects
Wunden und fehlende Gegenstände
Wonden en ontbrekende objecten
Heridas y objetos ausentes

● ● ●

1998
44,7 x 53,5 cm / 17.6 x 21 in.
Museum of Modern Art (MoMA), New York

nine color decal / Neunfarbiges Abziehbild
9-kleurige transferprint / calcomanía a nueve colores

Marlene Dumas
(Capetown 1953)
Chlorosis (Love sick)
Chlorose (Liebeskummer)
Chlorose. Liefdesziek
Clorosis. Mal de amores
●
1994
66,2 x 49,5 cm / each 26 x 19.5 in.
Museum of Modern Art (MoMA),
New York

Ink, gouache and synthetic polymer
paint on paper
Tinte, Gouache, synthetische
Polymerfarbe auf Papier
inkt, gouache, synthetische
polymeerverf op papier
tinta, gouache, color en polímero
sintético sobre papel

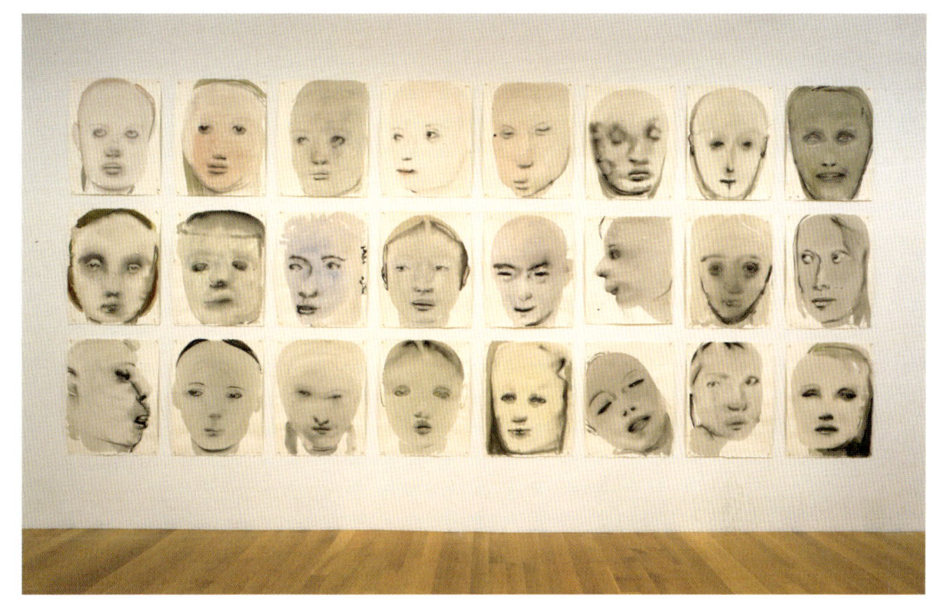

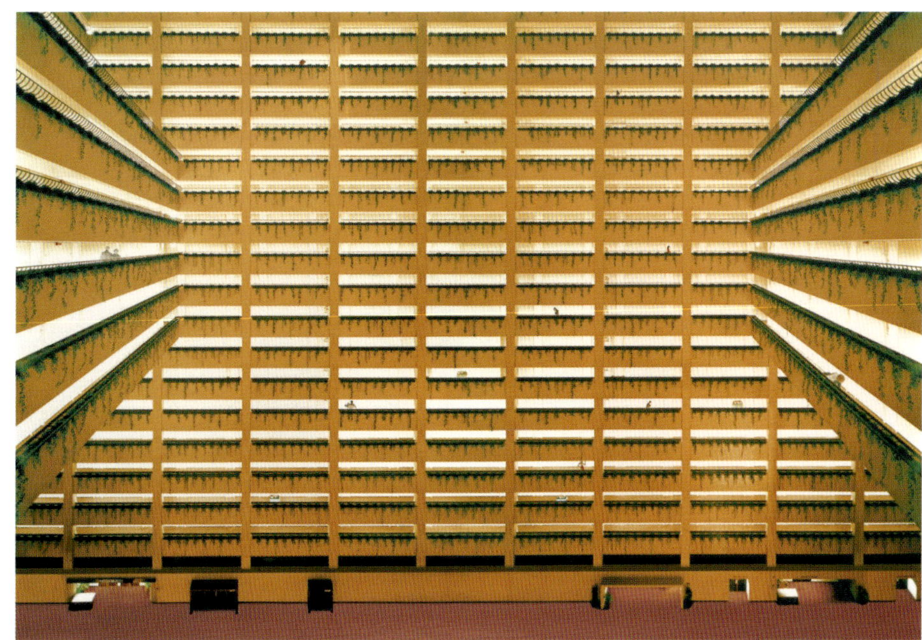

Andreas Gursky
(Lipsia 1955)
Times Square, New York
●●
1997
185,4 x 248,9 cm / 73 x 98 in.
Museum of Modern Art (MoMA),
New York

chromogenic color print
Chromogenischer Farbdruck
chromoprint
impresión a color cromogénica

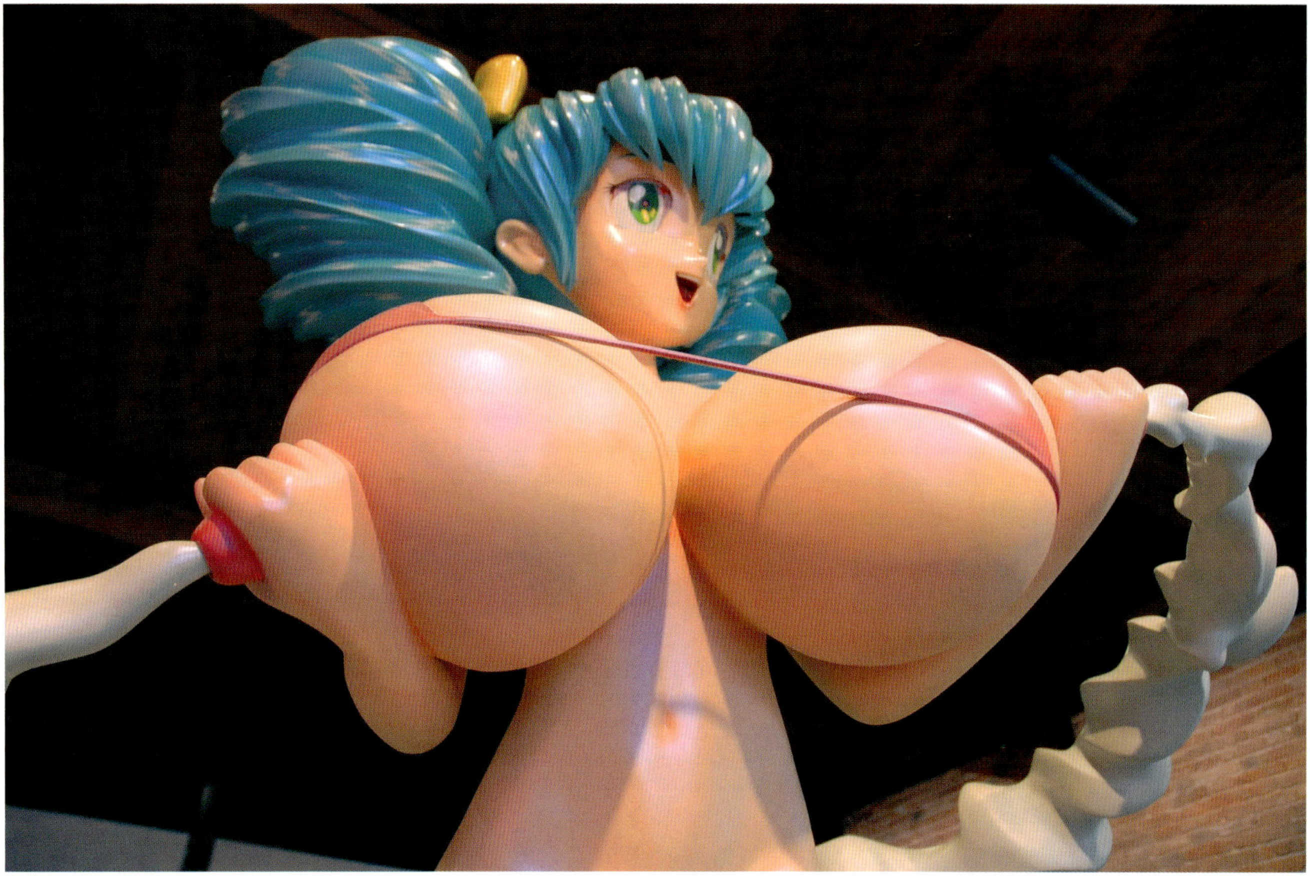

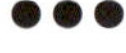

594

Takashi Murakami
(Tokyo 1962)

Hiropon

●●●

1997
Private collection / Private Sammlung
Privecollectie / Coleccion privada

Fan of manga and science fiction, Murakami's art also draws on the *Kavai* culture of Japan: an obsession with the "pretty" that turns here to the grotesque.

Die Kunst von Murakami, einem Manga- und Science Fiction-Fan, greift auch auf die japanische *kavai*-Kultur zurück: eine Besessenheit von dem *Hübschen*, die zum Grotesken neigt.

De kunst van Murakami die groot fan van manga en sciencefiction is, wordt ook uit de Japanse *kavai*-cultuur ontleend: een obsessie voor het mooie dat hier neigt naar het groteske.

Aficionado del manga y de la ciencia ficción, el arte de Murakami se inspira también en la cultura *kavai* de Japón: una obsesión por lo bello que gira aquí hacia lo grotesco.

Mariko Mori
(Tokyo 1967)

Star Doll n. 54 for Parkett
Starpuppe Nr. 54 auf dem Parkett
Star Doll n. 54 voor Parkett
Star Doll n. 54 para Parkett

●●●

1998
26 x 8 x 4 cm / 10.2 x 3.1 x 1.5 in.
Museum of Modern Art (MoMA), New York

series of dolls / Reihe von Puppen
poppenreeks / serie de muñecas

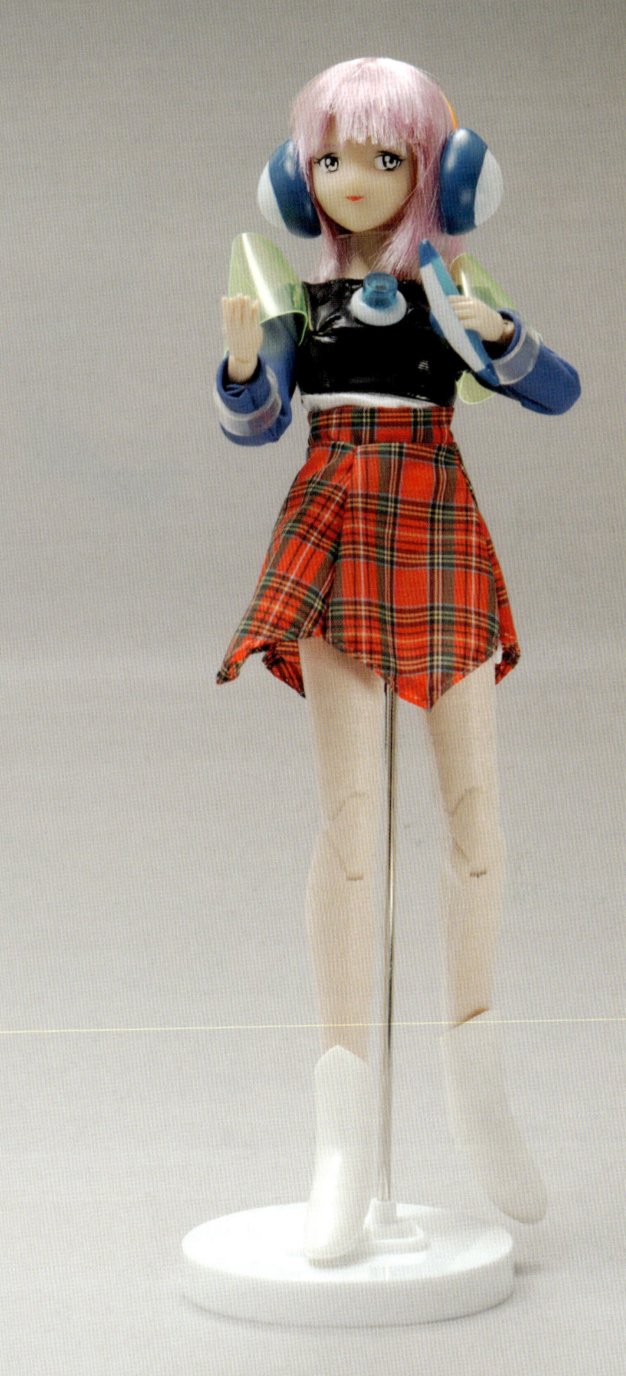

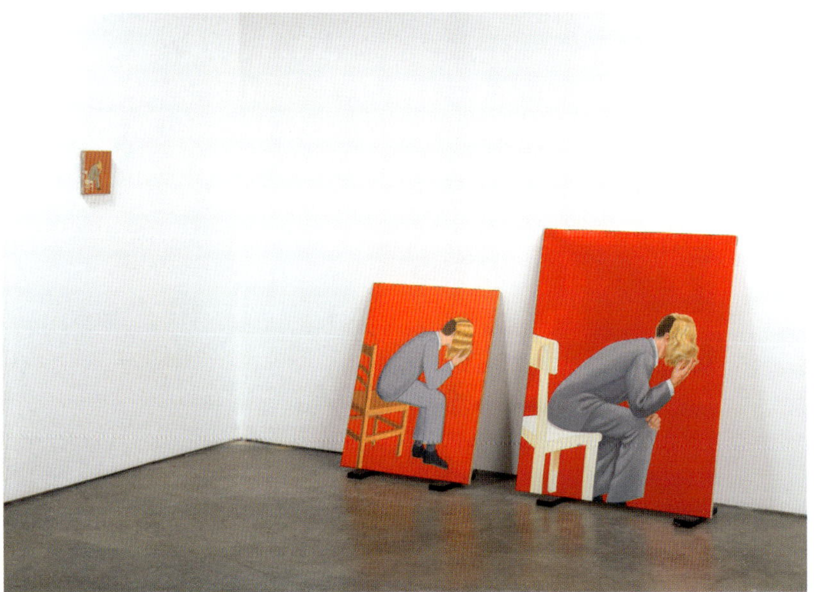

They are always young, beautiful, rich and famous personages, the *beautiful people* who attract the elegant pen of Peyton and determine his success.

Es sind immer junge, schöne, reiche und berühmte Personen, das sogenannte *schöne Volk*, das Peytons elegante Feder anzieht und ihren Erfolg ausmacht.

Het zijn altijd jonge, mooie, rijke en beroemde personages die de elegante pen van Peyton aantrekken en die zijn succes bepalen.

Son siempre personajes jóvenes, hermosos, ricos y célebres, la *gente bella* que atrae la pluma elegante de Peyton y determinan su éxito.

 Francis Alÿs
(Antwerp 1959)

Untitled
Ohne Titel
Zonder titel
Sin título

●●

1994
Museum of Modern Art (MoMA), New York

oil on canvas and acrylic on metal foil, 3 panels
Öl auf Leinwand und Akryl auf Metallplatte, 3 Tafeln
olieverf op doek en acrylverf op metaalplaat, 3 panelen
óleo sobre lienzo y acrílico sobre lámina metálica, tres paneles

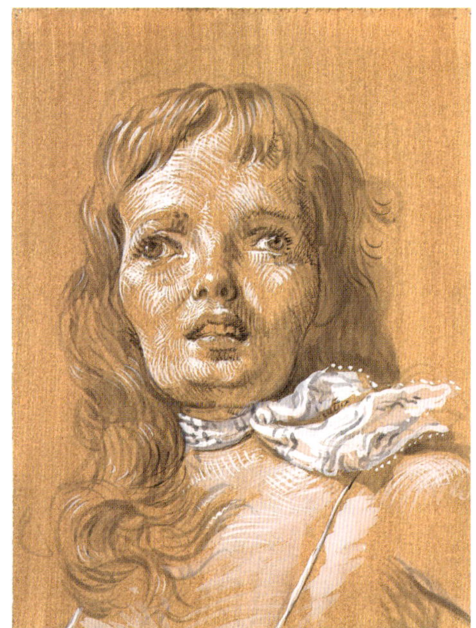

▶ Elizabeth Peyton
(Danbury, Connecticut
1965)

**Hockney at the RCA
Hockney bij de RCA
Hockney en la RCA**
●●●
1997
35,2 x 27,9 cm
13.8 x 11 in.
Museum of Modern Art
(MoMA), New York

pencil on notebook paper
Bleistift auf Blockseite,
Notizen
potlood op blocnotevel
lápiz sobre página de bloc
de notas

◀ John Currin
(Boulder 1962)

**The Clairvoyant
Die Hellseherin
De helderziende
La clarividente**
●
2001
29,5 x 21,3 cm
11.6 x 8.4 in.
Museum of Modern Art
(MoMA), New York

gouache on prepared
paper
Gouache auf
präpariertem Papier
gouache op geprepareerd
papier
gouache sobre papel
preparado

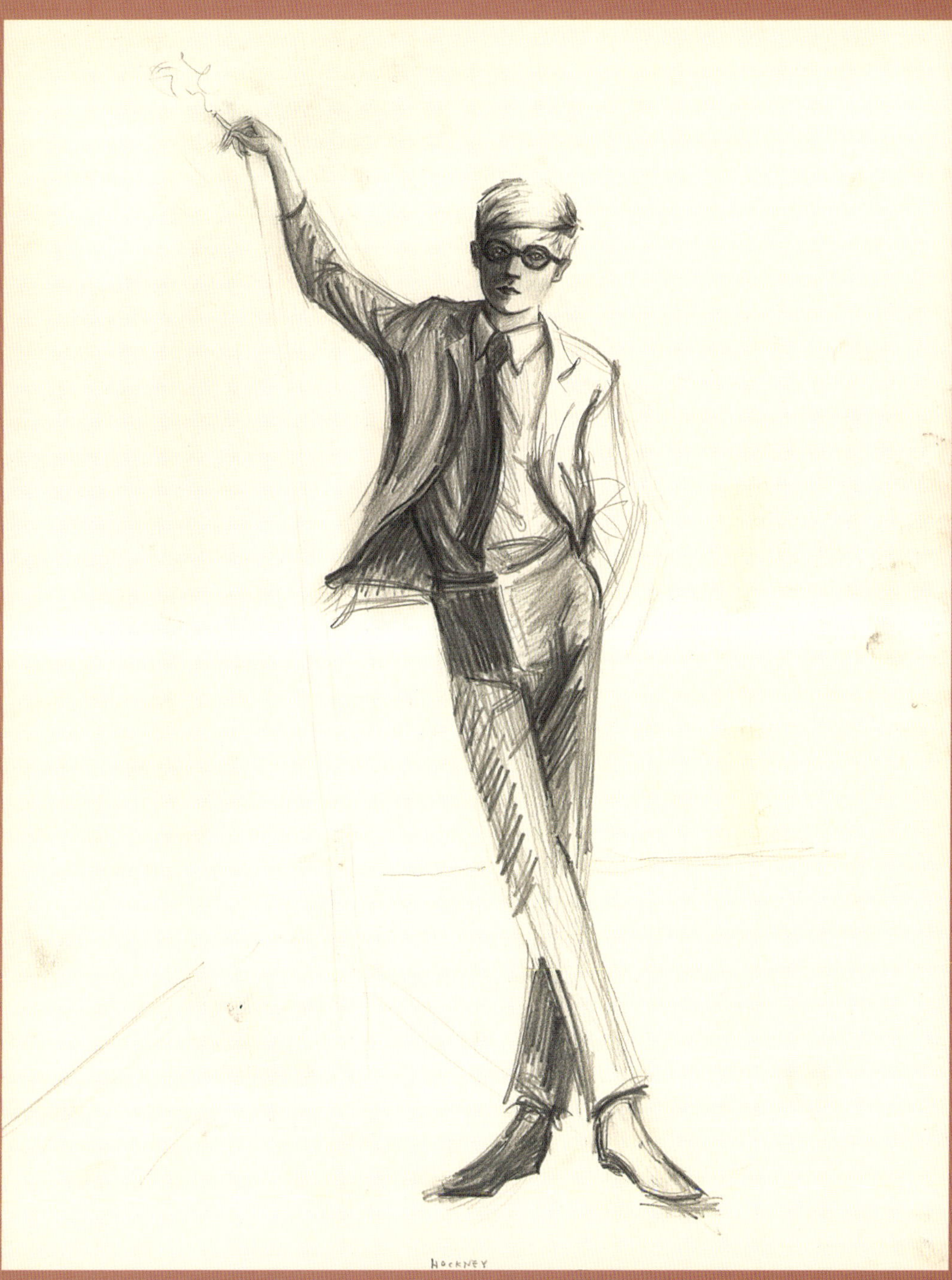

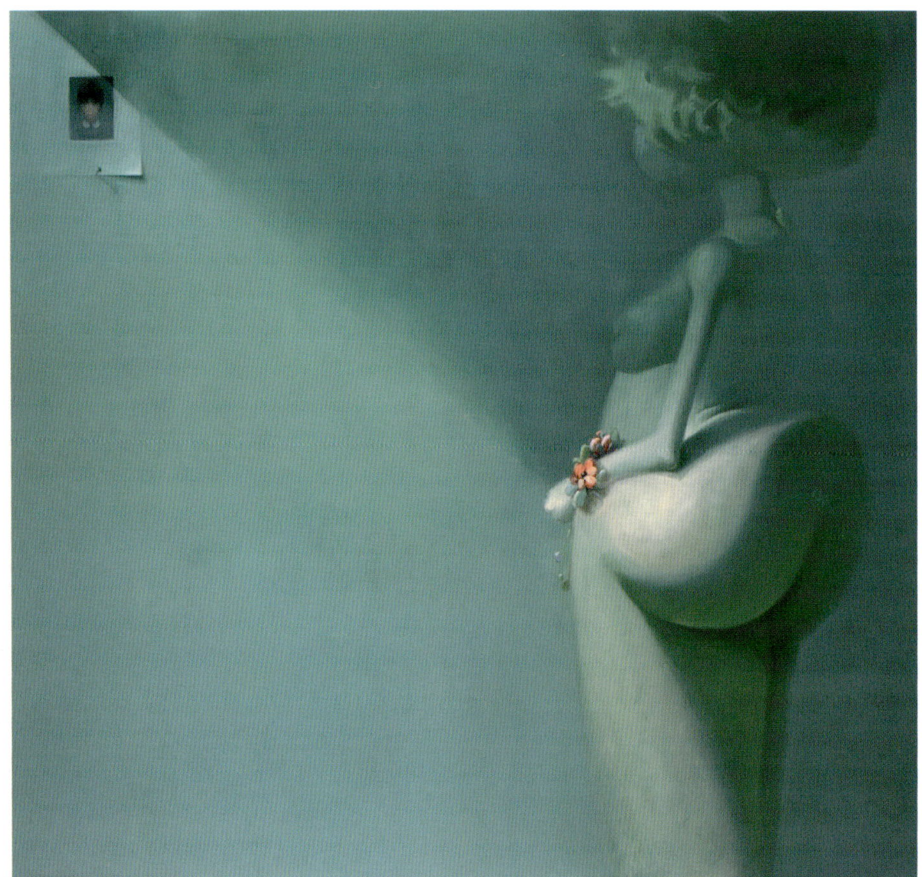

Lisa Yuskavage
(Philadelphia 1962)

Wrist corsage
Handgelenkskorsage
Polscorsage
Ramillete de muñeca

●●●

1996
182,9 x 213,3 cm / 72 x 84 in.
Museum of Modern Art (MoMA), New York

oil on linen canvas / Öl auf Leinenleinwand
olieverf op linnen doek / óleo sobre lienzo de lino

Luc Tuymans
(Morstel 1958)

Lumumba

●

2000
62 x 46 cm / 24.5 x 18 in.
Museum of Modern Art (MoMA),
New York

oil on canvas / Öl auf Leinwand
olieverf op doek / óleo sobre lienzo

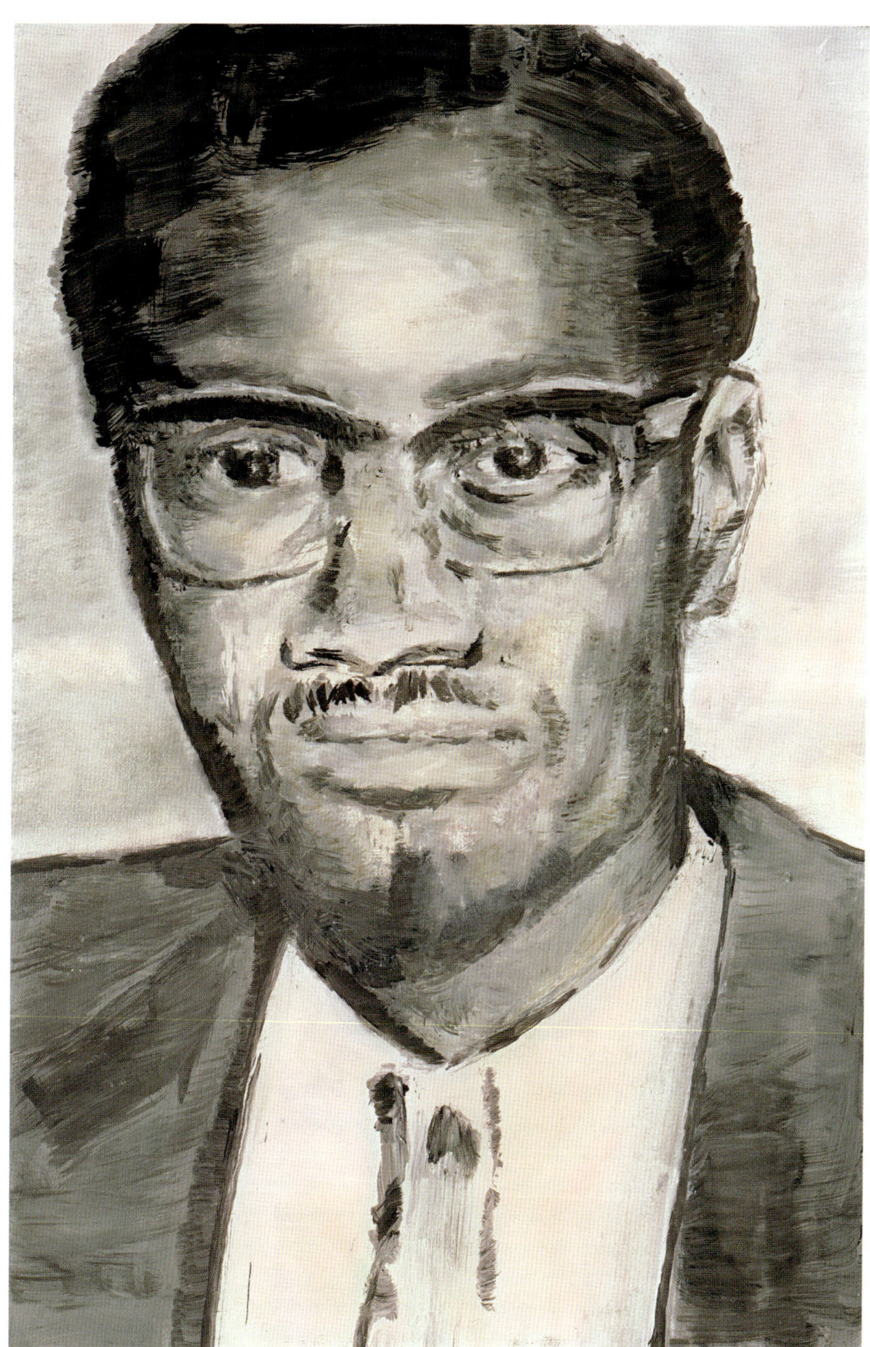

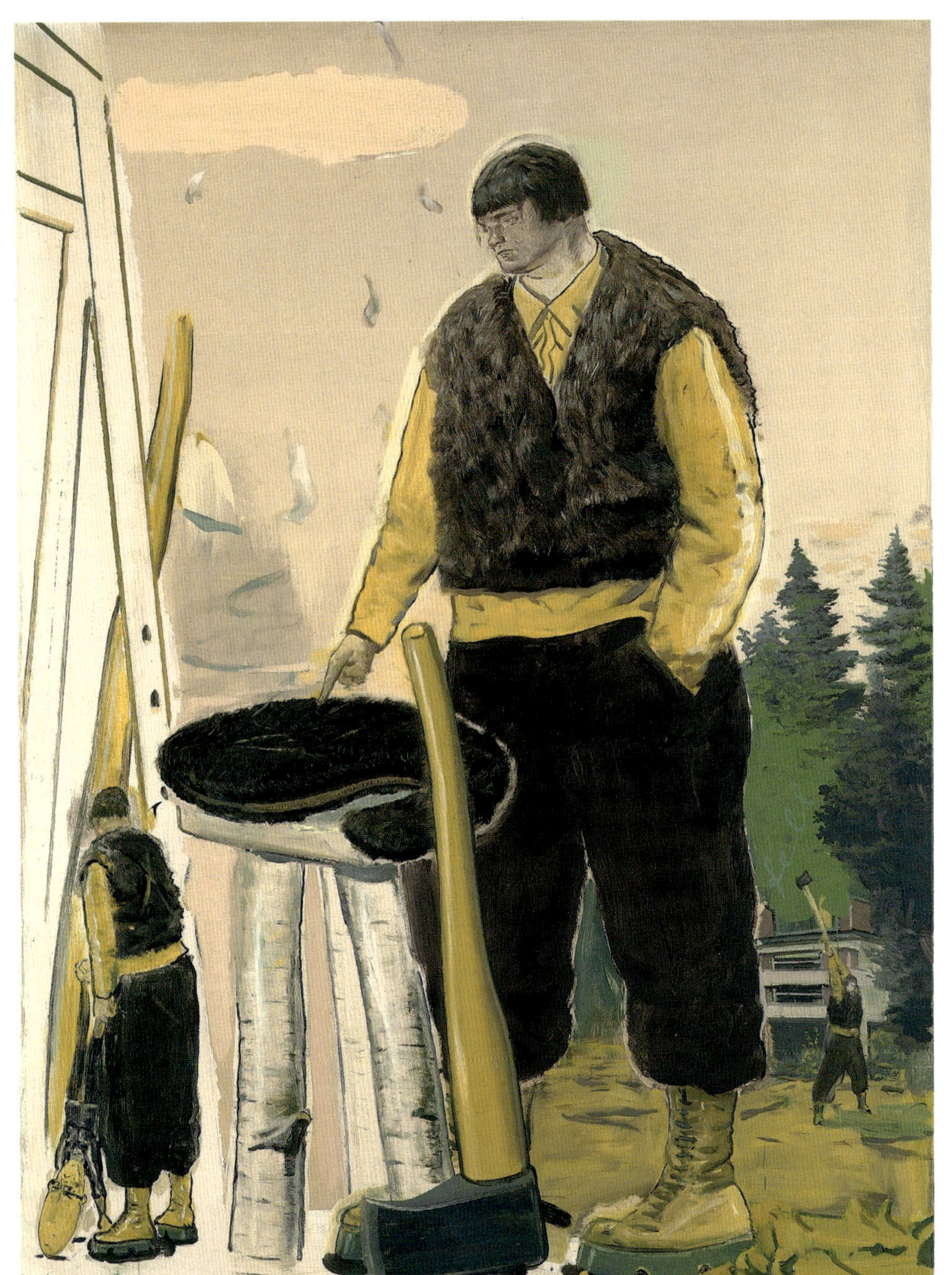

◄ Neo Rauch
(Leipzig 1960)

Fur
Fell
Bont
Piel
●
2000
190 x 135,2 cm / 74.8 x 53.2 in.
Museum der bildenden Künste,
Leipzig

oil on mixed fabrics
Öl auf gemischten Stoffen
olieverf op gemixte stoffen
óleo sobre telas mixtas

► Martin Kippenberger
(Dortmund 1953 - Vienna
1997)

Martin, stay in the
corner, shame on you
Martin, ab in die Ecke
und schäm dich!
Martin, ga in de hoek
staan en schaam je
Martin, al rincón,
deberías avergonzarte
● ●
1990
181,6 x 74,9 x 34,3 cm
71.5 x 29.5 x 13.5 in.
Museum of Modern Art
(MoMA), New York

aluminium, fabric, iron slab
Aluminium, Stoff, Eisentafel
aluminium, stof, ijzeren plaat
aluminio, tejidos, losa de hierro

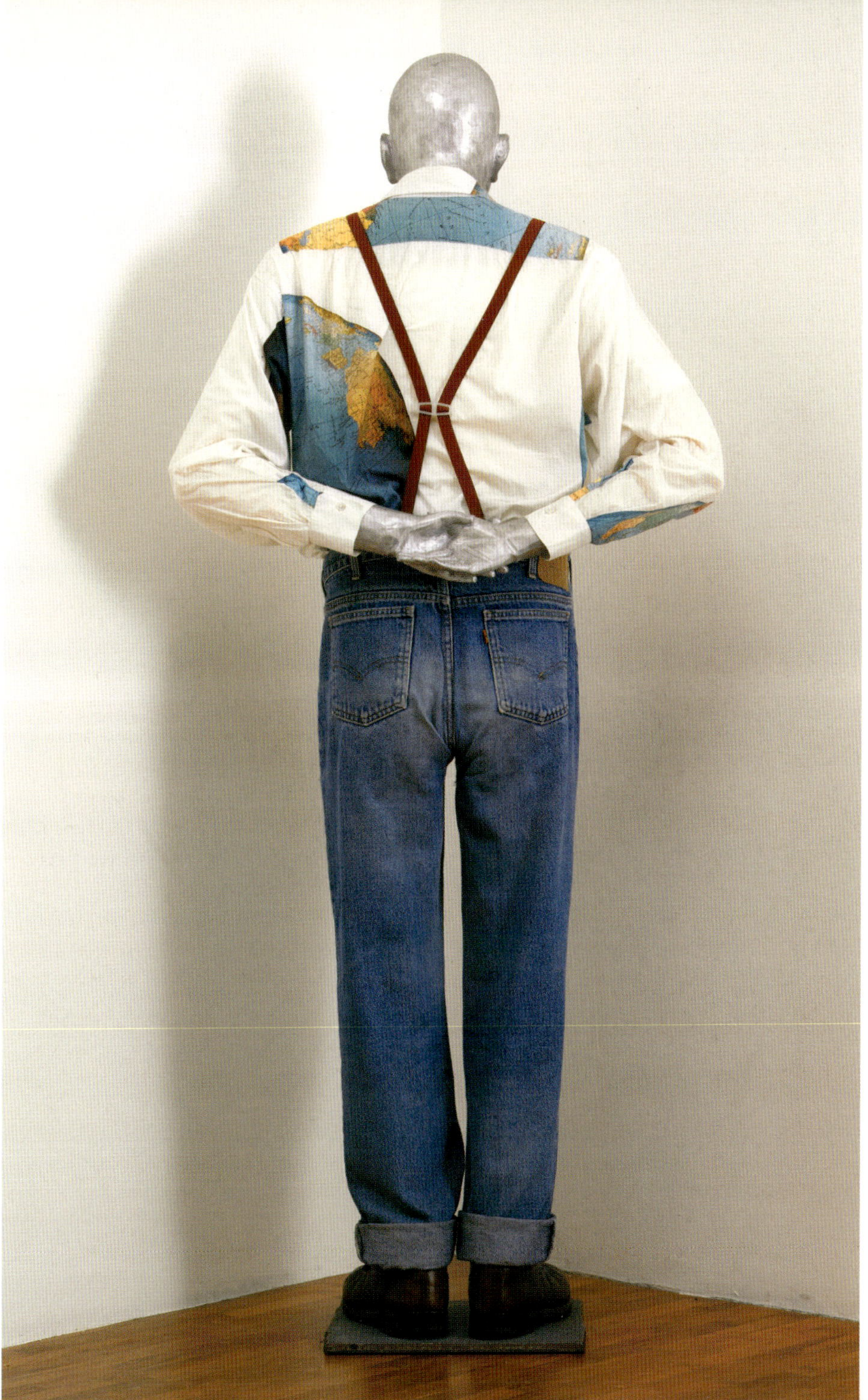

Ironic self-portrait of
Kippenberger unfairly punished
by critics and put in a corner
like a child to reflect on his
evil-doing.

Ein ironisches Selbstporträt
Kippenbergers,
der ungerechterweise
von der Kritik gestraft und
wie ein Kind in die Ecke
gestellt wurde, um über seine
Missetaten nachzudenken.

Ironisch zelfportret van
Kippenberger die onterecht
door de critici werd gestraft
en als een klein kind in een
hoek werd gezet om over zijn
wandaden na te denken.

Autorretrato irónico de
Kippenberger injustamente
castigado por la crítica, y
colocado como un niño en un
rincón para reflexionar por las
travesuras cometidas.

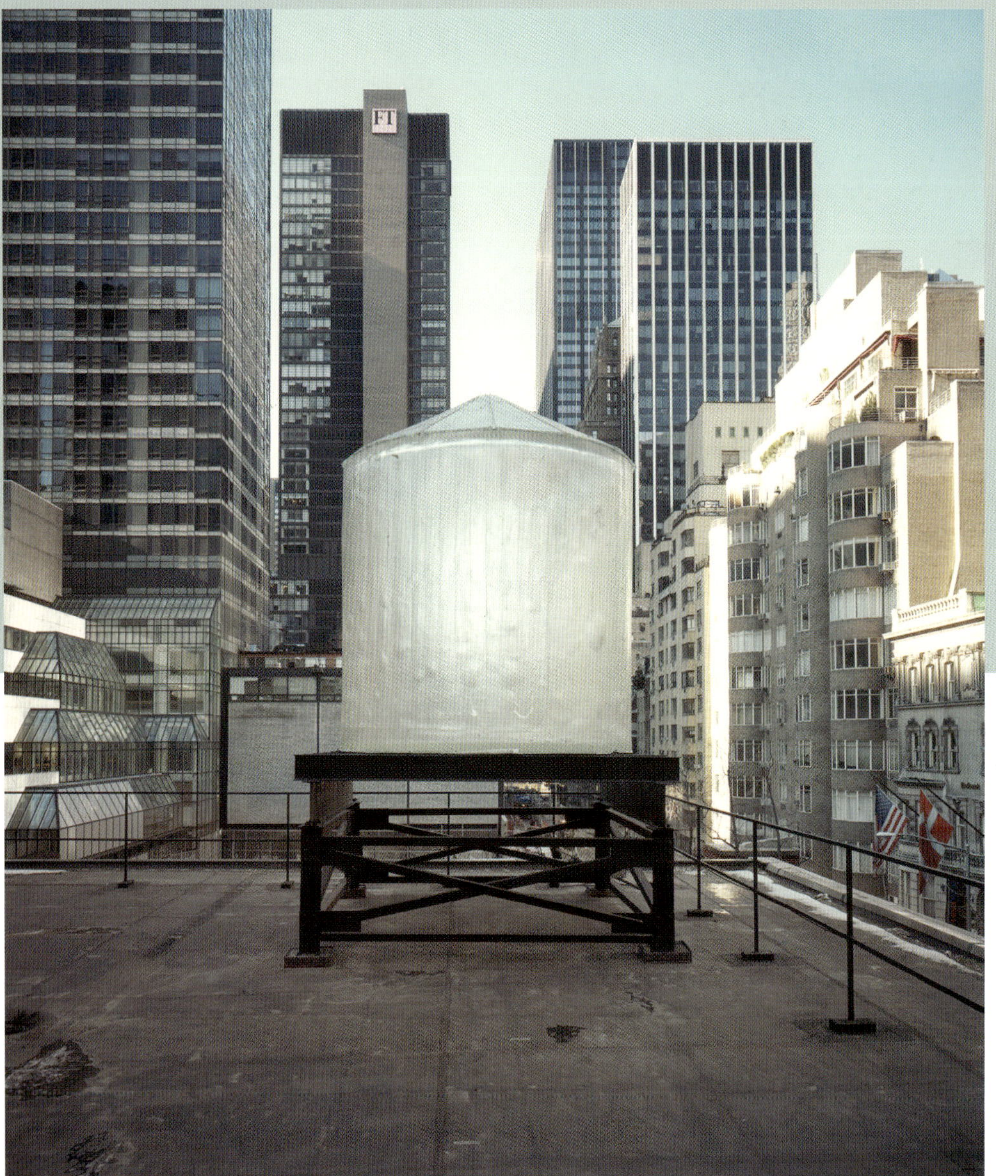

◀ Rachel Whiteread
(London 1963)

Water Tower
Wasserturm
Watertoren
Torre de agua
●

1998
370,8 x 274,3 cm
146.1 x 108 in. diameter
Museum of Modern Art
(MoMA), New York

translucent resin
Transparentes Harz
doorzichtige hars
resina traslúcida

▶ Gabriel Orozco
(Jalapa 1962)

Kytes Tree
●●
2005
200 x 200 cm / 78.8 x 78.8 in.
Museum of Modern Art
(MoMA), New York

acrylic on canvas
Akryl auf Leinwand
acrylverf op doek
acrílico sobre lienzo

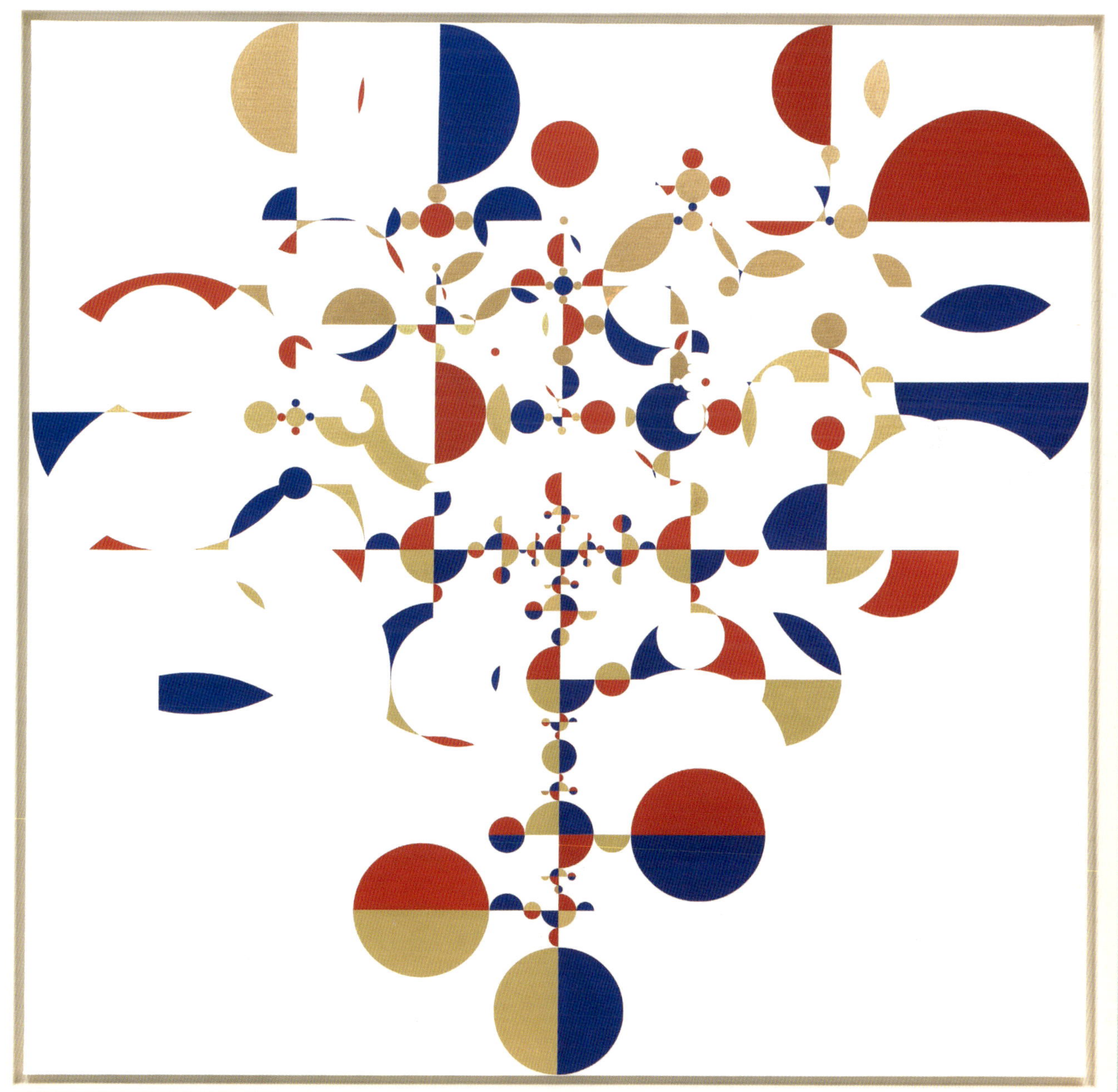

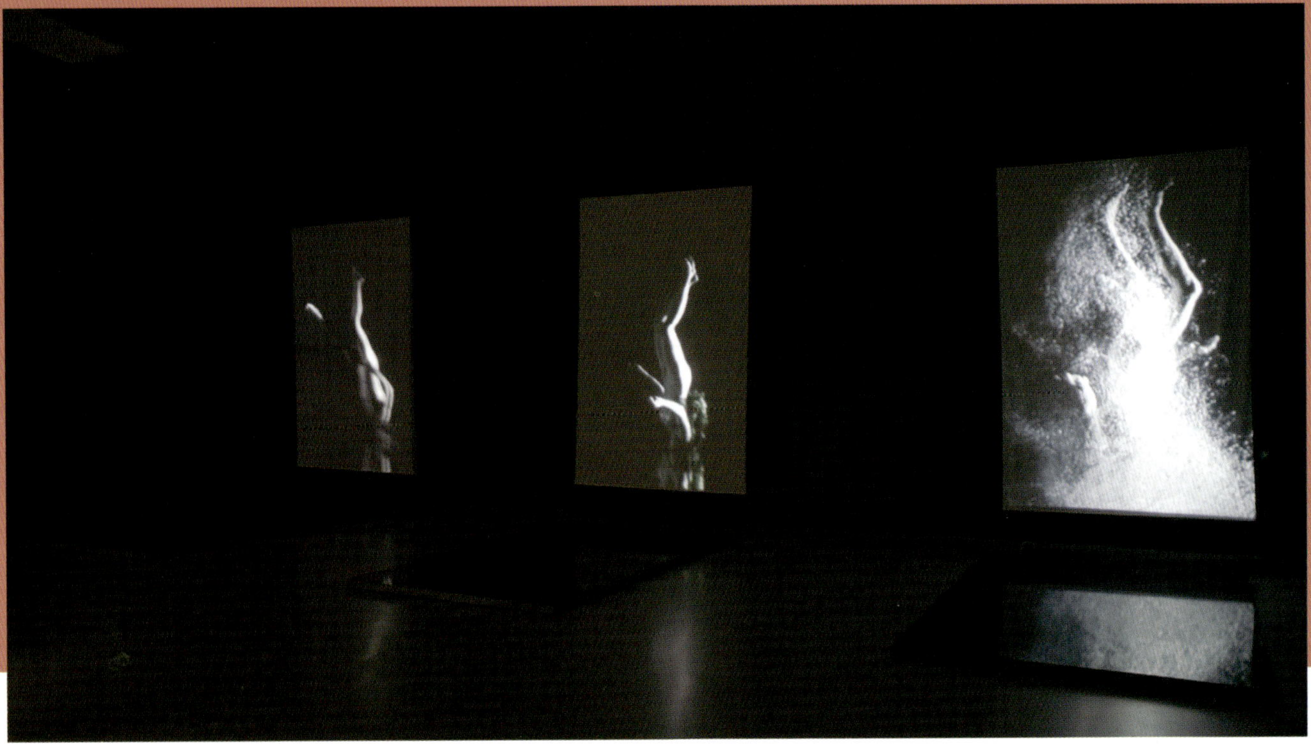

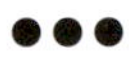

Bill Viola
(New York 1951)

Stations

● ● ●

1994
610 x 1525 x 1525 cm / 240.3 x 600.8 x 600.8 in.
Museum of Modern Art (MoMA), New York

five video channels (color, sound), five granite slabs and five projection screens / Fünfkanal-Video (Farbe, Ton), fünf Granitplatten und fünf Projektionsbildschirme / vijf videokanalen (kleur, geluid), vijf granietplaten en vijf projectieschermen / cinco canales de vídeo (color, sonido), cinco losas de granito y cinco pantallas de proyección

Men move in an aquatic setting, as during an hypnotic ballet that evokes the eternal cycle of life, death and rebirth.

Männer bewegen sich in einem Raum mit Wasser, wie ein hypnotisches Ballett, das den ewigen Kreislauf von Leben, Tod und Wiedergeburt darstellt.

In water voortbewegende mannen, net zoals tijdens een hypnotisch ballet dat aan de levenscirkel, van de dood en de wedergeboorte, doet denken.

Hombres que se mueven en un contexto acuático, como durante una danza hipnótica que evoca el ciclo eterno de la vida, de la muerte y del renacimiento.

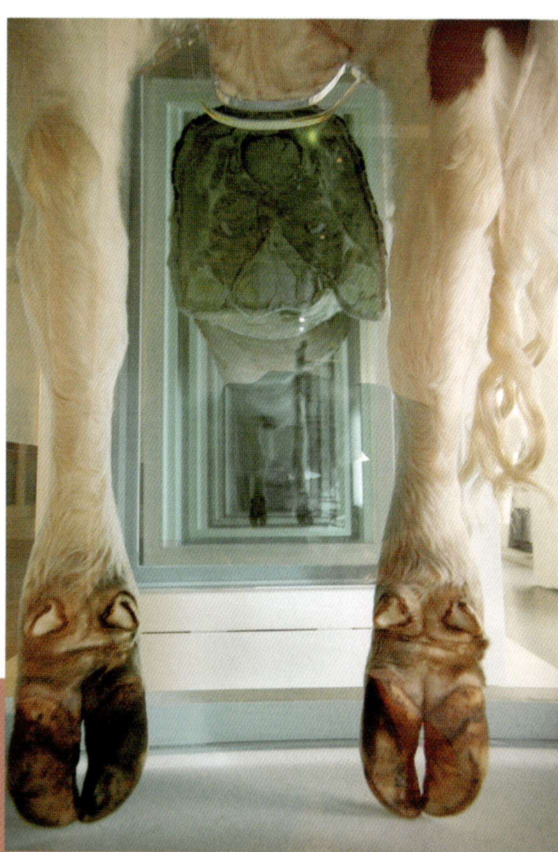

Damien Hirst
(Bristol 1965)

Vivisection
Leichenschau
Vivisectie
Vivisección

●

2004

Private collection / Private Sammlung
Privécollectie / Colección privada

Damien Hirst
(Bristol 1965)

Anatomy of an Angel?
Anatomie eines Engels?
Anatomie van een engel?
¿Anatomía de un ángel?

●●

2008
187 x 98 x 78,5 cm / 73.6 x 38.6 x 30.9 in.

Private collection / Private Sammlung
Privécollectie / Colección privada

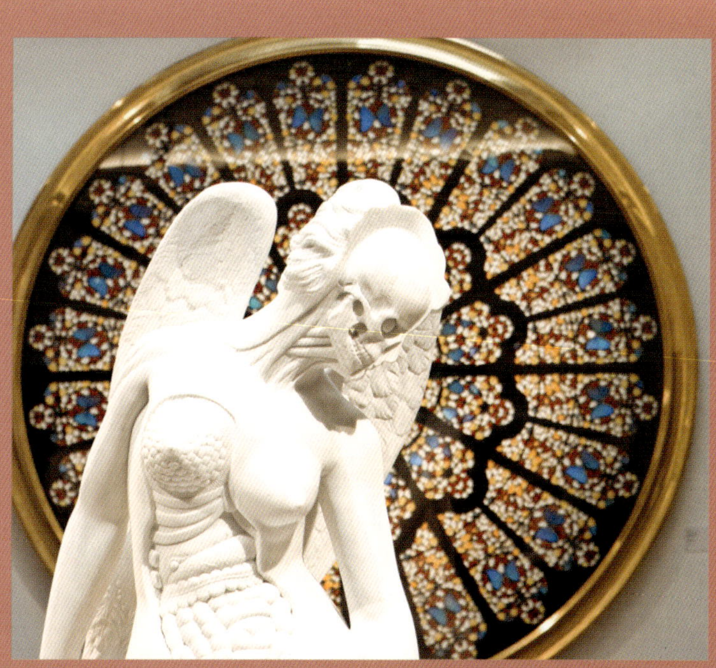

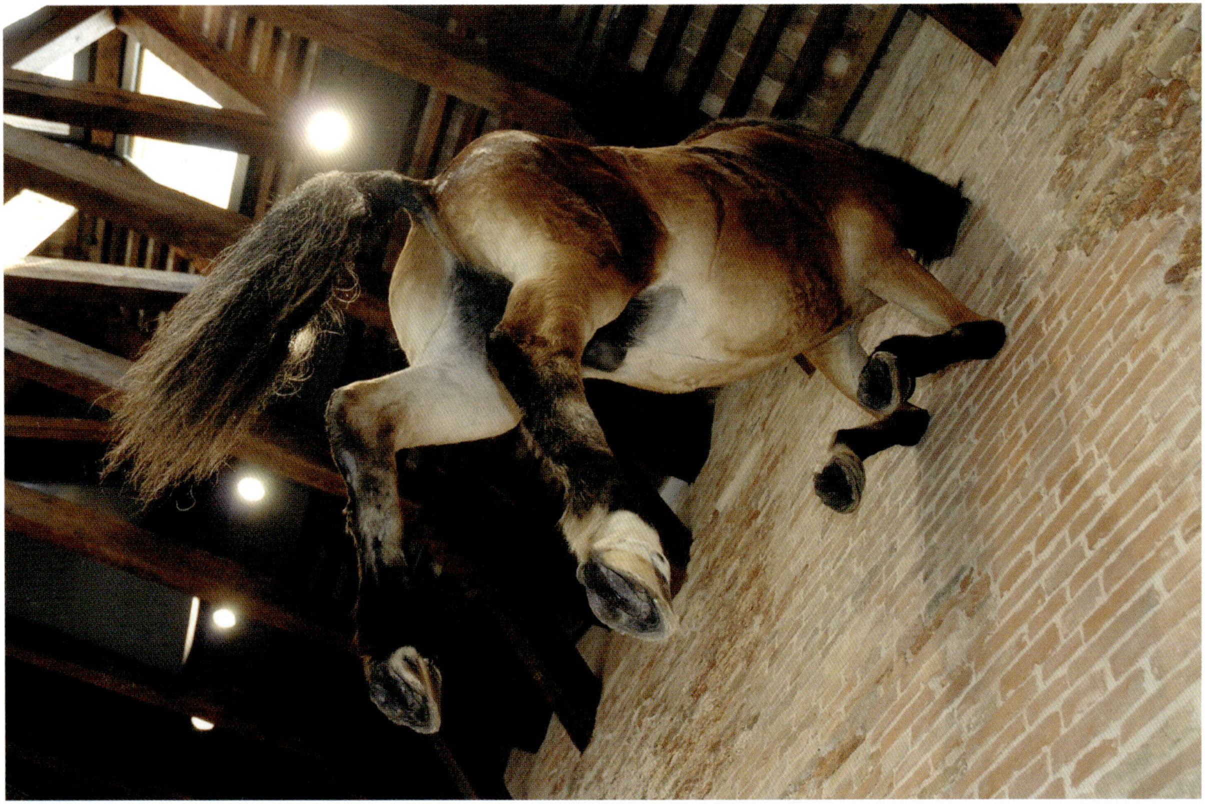

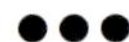

Maurizio Cattelan
(Padova 1960)

Untitled
Ohne Titel
Zonder titel
Sin título

●●●

2007
300 x 170 x 80 cm / 118.2 x 66.9 x 31.5 in.
Private collection / Private Sammlung
Privécollectie / Colección privada

stuffed horse: horse hair, glass fibre, resin taxidermied horse: horse hide, fiberglass, resin
Ausgestopftes Pferd: Pferdefell, Glasfasern
opgezet paard: paardenhuid, glasvezel, hars
caballo de paja: piel de caballo, fibra de vidrio, caballo taxidermizado en resina: piel de caballo, fibra de vidrio, resina

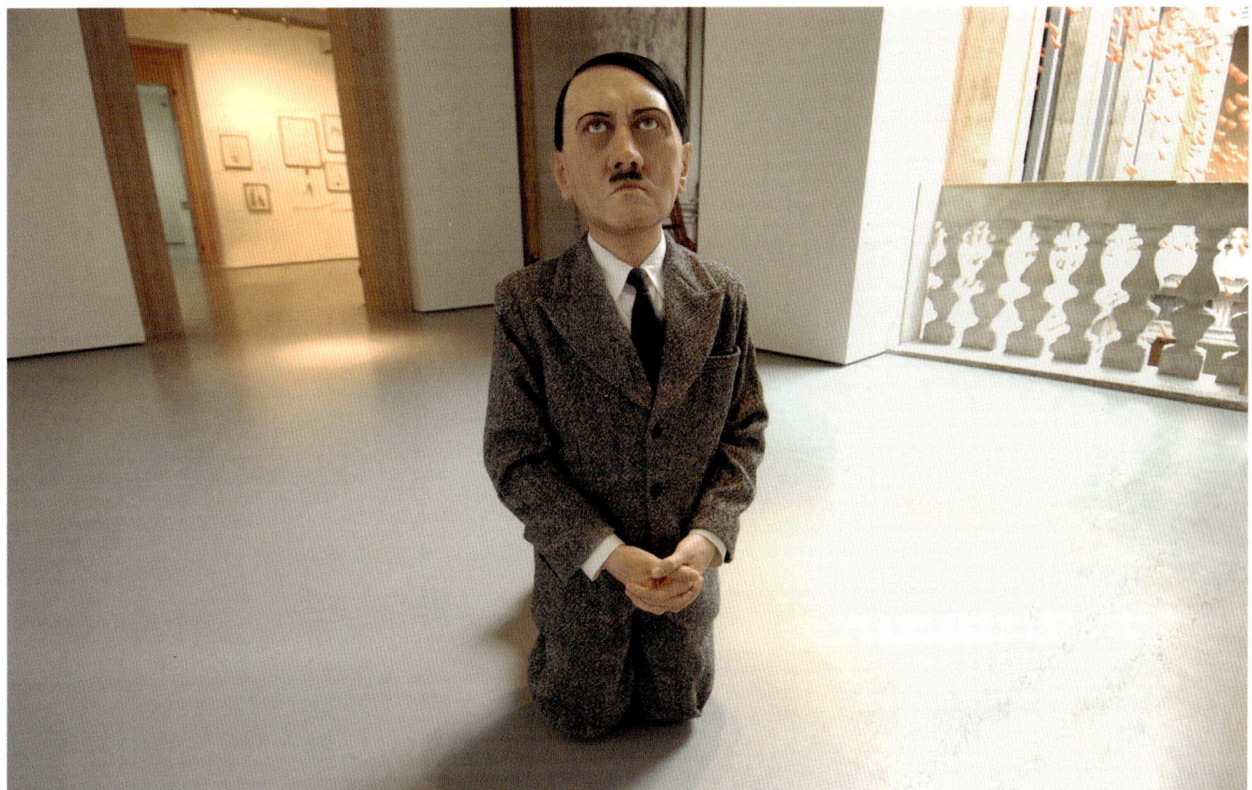

Maurizio Cattelan
(Padova 1960)

"Him"...Adolf Hitler praying
"Ihm"... Adolf Hitler beim Beten
"Hem" ... Biddende Adolf Hilter
"Él"... Adolf Hitler rezando

●●●

2001
101 x 41 x 53 cm / 39.8 x 16.1 x 20.9 in.
Private collection / Private Sammlung
Privécollectie / Colección privada

wax, human hair, suit, polyester resin
Wachs, menschliche Haare, Kleidung,
Polyesterharz
was, mensenharen, pak, polyesterhars
cera, cabellos humanos, traje, resina de poliéster

Cattelan likes visual blows, dramatic situations – consider cruel –
that question the viewer.

Cattalan liebt die sichtbaren Zusammenstöße, die dramatischen -
ja grausamen - Situationen, die den Betrachter prüfen.

Cattelan houdt ervan visueel te schokkeren, van dramatische,
of beter wrede situaties, die de toeschouwer aan het denken zetten.

Cattelan ama los contrastes visuales, las situaciones dramáticas
– ver crueles – que interrogan al observador.

David Hockney © David Hockney "Hollywood garden" 1966 Acrylic on canvas - 72 x 72" © David Hockney
Keith Haring © Ohne Titel (Engel), 1982 © Keith Haring Foundation Used by permission
Henry Moore © Reproduction by permission of The Henry Moore Foundation
Cindy Sherman © Cindy Sherman, Untitled Film Still #21, 1978 © Courtesy of the artist and Metro Pictures
Piet Mondrian © 2010 Mondrian/Holtzman Trust c/o HCR International Virginia
Edward Weston © Edward Weston
Anish Kapoor © Wounds and absent Objects, 1998 © Anish Kapoor
Pipilotti Rist © Pour Your Body Out (7354 Cubic Meters), 2008, Multichannel audio video installation by Pipilotti Rist (installation view at MoMA Museum of Modern Art, New York) Commissioned through the generosity of UBS, the Wallis Annenberg Fund for Innovation in Contemporary Art, Marie-Josée and Henry Kravis, Maja Oeri and Hans Bodenmann, Jerry I. Speyer and Katherine G. Farley, Franz Wassmer, Monique Barbier-Mueller and by Pro Helvetia, Arts Council of Switzerland. © 2009 The Museum of Modern Art, New York, Photography by Thomas Griesel Courtesy the artist, Luhring Augustine, New York and Hauser & Wirth
Ellsworth Kelly © Ellsworth Kelly
Lucas Samaras © Lucas Samaras, courtesy PaceWildenstein, New York
Bill Viola © Bill Viola Studio Permission To Use Photographs
Cai Guo-Qiang © Borrowing Your Enemy's Arrows, 1998 © by Cai Guo-Qiang
Ross Bleckner © Ross Bleckner
Eric Fishel © Eric Fishel
Barbara Hepworth © Bowness, Hepworth Estate
Tom Blackwell © Blackwell Tom, 2010
Emile Nolde © Nolde Stiftung Seebüll
Maurice Utrillo © Maurice Utrillo
Edward Steichen © Edward Steichen

The SCALA images reproducing artworks that belong to the Italian State are published with the permission of the Ministry for Cultural Heritage and Activities.

Every effort has been made to trace all copyright owners, but if any have been inadvertently overlooked, the Publishers will be pleased to make the necessary arrangements at the first opportunity.

Appendix to image credits:
THE MUSEUM OF MODERN ART
Matisse, Henri (1869-1954) Goldfish and Sculpture. Issy-les Moulineaux, 1912 Oil on canvas, 46 x 39 5/8' (116.2 x 100.5 cm). Gift of Mr. and Mrs. John Hay Whitney. 199.1955. Balla, Giacomo (1871-1958) Street Light, 1909 Oil on canvas, 68 3/4 x 45 1/4' (174.7 x 114.5 cm). Hillman Periodicals Fund. Acc. n.: 7.1954. Balla, Giacomo (1871-1958) Swifts: Paths of Movement + Dynamic Sequences, 1913 Oil on canvas, 38 1/8 x 47 1/4' (96.8 x 120 cm). Purchase. Acc. n.: 272.1949.Boccioni, Umberto (1882-1916) Unique Forms of Continuity in Space, 1913 Bronze (cast 1931), 43 7/8 x 34 7/8 x 15 3/4' (111.2 x 88.5 x 40 cm). Acquired through the Lillie P. Bliss Bequest. 231.1948.Calder, Alexander (1898-1976) Lobster Trap and Fish Tail, 1939 Hanging mobile: painted steel wire and sheet aluminum, about 8' 6' h. x 9' 6' diameter (260 x 290 cm). Commissioned by the Advisory Committee for the stairwell of the Museum. 590.1939.a-d.De Chirico, Giorgio (1888-1978) The Enigma of a Day, 1914 Oil on canvas, 6' 1 1/4' x 55' (185.5 x 139.7 cm). James Thrall Soby Bequest. 1211.1979. Dali', Salvador (1904-1989) Illumined Pleasures, 1929 Oil and collage on composition board, 9 3/8 x 13 3/4' (23.8 x 34.7 cm). The Sidney and Harriet Janis Collection. 584.1967. Dali', Salvador (1904-1989) The Persistence of Memory (Persistance de la memoire), 1931 Oil on canvas, 9 1/2 x 13' (24.1 x 33 cm). Given anonymously. 162.1934. Duchamp, Marcel (1887-1968) Fresh Widow, 1920 Miniature French window, painted wood frame, and eight panes of glass covered with black leather, 30 1/2 x 17 5/8' (77.5 x 44.8 cm), on wood sill 3/4 x 21 x 4' (1.9 x 53.4 x 10.2 cm). Katherine S. Dreier Bequest. 151.1953. Duchamp, Marcel (1887-1968) The Passage from Virgin to Bride, 1912 Oil on canvas, 23 3/8 x 21 1/4' (59.4 x 54 cm). Purchase. 174.1945. Hopper, Edward (1882-1967) Gas, 1940 Oil on canvas, 26 1/4 x 40 1/4' (66.7 x 102.2 cm). Mrs. Simon Guggenheim Fund. 577.1943. Johns, Jasper (b. 1930) Flag, 1954 (dated on the reverse) Encaustic, oil and collage on fabric mounted on plywood, 42 1/4 x 60 5/8' (107.3 x 153.8 cm). Gift of Philip Johnson in honor of Alfred H. Barr, Jr. 106.1973. Dix, Otto (1891-1969) Dr. Mayer-Hermann, 1926 Oil and tempera on wood, 58 3/4 x 39' (149.2 x 99.1 cm). Gift of Philip Johnson. 3.1932. Lange, Dorothea (1895-1965) Migrant Mother, Nipomo, California, 1936 Gelatin-silver print, 11 1/8 x 8 9/16' (28.3 x 21.8 cm). Purchase. 331.1995. Picasso, Pablo (1881-1973) Les Demoiselles d'Avignon (Paris, June-July 1907) Oil on canvas, 8' x 7' 8' (243.9 x 233.7 cm). Acquired through the Lillie P. Bliss Bequest. 333.1939. Rauschenberg, Robert (1925-2008) Bed, 1955 Combine painting: oil and pencil on pillow, quilt, and sheet on wood supports, 6' 3 3/4' x 31 1/2' x 8' (191.1 x 80 x 20.3 cm). Gift of Leo Castelli in honor of Alfred H. Barr, Jr. 79.1989. Hatoum, Mona (b. 1952) Silence, 1994 Glass, 49 7/8 x 36 7/8 x 23 1/8' (126.6 x 59.2 x 93.7 cm). Robert B. and Emilie W. Betts Foundation Fund. 126.1995. Man Ray (1890-1976) Noire et Blanche (Black and White), 1926 Gelatin silver print, 6 3/4 x 8 7/8' (17.1 x 22.4 cm). Gift of James Thrall Soby. Acc. n.: 132.1941. Oppenheim, Meret (1913-1985) Object (Le dejeuner en fourrure), 1936 Fur-covered cup, saucer and spoon; cup, 4 3/8' (10.9 cm) diameter; saucer, 9 3/8' (23.7 cm) diameter; spoon, 8' (20.2 cm) long; overall height 2 7/8' (7.3 cm). Purchase. Acc. n.: 130.1946.a-c. Pevsner, Antoine (1885-1962) Torso, 1924-26 Construction in plastic and copper, 29 1/2 x 11 5/8 x 15 1/4' (74.9 x 29.4 x 38.7 cm). Katherine S. Dreier Bequest. 185.1953. Malevic, Kasimir (1878-1935) Suprematist Composition: White on White, 1918 Oil on canvas, 31 1/4 x 31 1/4' (79.4 x 79.4 cm). Acquisition confirmed in 1999 by agreement with the Estate of Kazimir Malevich and made possible with funds from the Mrs. John Hay Whitney Bequest (by exchange). 817.1935. Man Ray (1890-1976) Indestructible Object (or Object to Be Destroyed), 1964 (replica of 1923 original) Metronome with cutout photograph of eye on pendulum, 8 7/8 x 4 3/8 x 4 5/8' (22.5 x 11 x 11.6 cm). James Thrall Soby Fund. 248.1966.a.el. Picasso, Pablo (1881-1973) Guitar (Ceret, after March 31, 1913) Pasted paper, charcoal, ink, and chalk on blue paper, mounted on ragboard, 26 1/8 x 19 1/2' (66.4 x 49.6 cm). Nelson A. Rockefeller Bequest. 967.1979. Twombly, Cy (b. 1928) The Four Seasons: Spring, Summer, Autumn, and Winter, 1993-94 Synthetic polymer paint, oil, house paint, pencil and crayon on four canvases; Spring: 10' 3 1/8" x 6' 2 7/8" (312.5 x 190 cm); Summer: 10' 3 3/4" x 6' 7 1/8" (314.15 x 201 cm); Autumn: 10' 3 1/2" x 6' 2 3/4" (313.7 x 189.9 cm); Winter: 10' 3 1/4" x 6' 2 7/8" (313 x 190.1 cm). Gift of the artist. Acc. N.: 613.1994.a-d. Christo, Javacheff (b. 1935) The Museum of Modern Art Packaged (model), 1968 Scale model: painted wood, cloth, twine, and polyethylene, 16' (40.3 cm) high, including painted wood base, 2 x 48 1/8 x 24 1/8' (5 x 122 x 61 cm). Gift of D. and J. de Menil. 868.1968. Masson, Andre' (1896-1987) Meditation on an Oak Leaf, 1942 Tempera, pastel and sand on canvas, 40 x 33' (101.6 x 83.8 cm). Given anonymously. 1950. Oldenburg, Claes (b. 1929) Pastry Case I, 1961-62 Enamel paint on nine plaster sculptures in glass showcase, 20 3/4 x 30 1/8 x 14 3/4' (52.7 x 76.5 x 37.3 cm). The Sidney and Harriet Janis Collection. 639.1967.a-dd. Picabia, Francis (Martinez Picabia, Francois, 1879-1953) Take Me There (M'Amenez-y), 1919-20 Oil on cardboard, 50 7/8 x 35 3/8' (129,2x89,8 cm). Helena Rubinstein Fund. 68. Shahn, Ben (1898-1969) Bartolomeo Vanzetti and Nicola Sacco, from the 'Sacco-Vanzetti' series of 23 paintings (1931-32) Tempera on paper over composition board, 10 1/2 x 14 1/2' (26.7 x 36.8 cm). Gift of Abby Aldrich Rockefeller. 144.1935. Ray Charles (b. 1953) Family Romance, 1993 Mixed media, 53' x 7' 1' x 11' (134.6 x 215.9 x 27.9 cm). Gift of The Norton Family Foundation. 281.1993. Salle, David (b. 1952) Gericault's Arm, 1985 Oil and synthetic polymer paint on canvas, 6' 5 7/8' x 8' 1/4' (197.8 x 244.5 cm). Gift of the Louis and Bessie Adler Foundation, Inc., Seymour M. Klein, President; Agnes Gund; Jerry I. Speyer Fund; and purchase. 1988. Serra Richard (b. 1939) Untitled, 1967 Vulcanized rubber, neon tubing, transformer, and wires, overall 8' 1/4' x 6' 1/2' x 6 3/4' (244.5 x 186.7 x 17.2 cm). Gift of Mr. and Mrs. Arthur C. Workstel and purchase. 234.1988. Vantongerloo, Georges (1886-1965) Construction within a Sphere, 1917 Silvered plaster, 7 x 5 1/2 x 6 3/4' (17.8 x 14 x 17.2 cm). Purchase. 265.1937. Spoerri, Daniel (b. 1930) Kichka's Breakfast I, 1960 Assemblage: wood chair hung on wall with board across seat, coffee pot, tumbler, china, egg cups, eggshells, cigarette butts, spoons, tin cans, etc. 14 3/8 x 27 3/8 x 25 3/4' (36.6 x 69.5 x 65.4 cm). Philip Johnson Fund. 391.1961 Warhol, Andy (1928-1987) Brillo Boxes, 1964 Synthetic polymer paint and silkscreen on wood, each 17 1/8 x 17 x 14' (43.5 x 43.2 x 36.5 cm). Gift of Doris and

Donald Fisher. Acc. nn.: 357.1997 and 358.1997.Hopper, Edward (1882-1967) Night Windows. (1928) Oil on canvas, 29 x 34" (73,7 x 86,4 cm). Gift of John Hay Whitney. 248.1940. Schwitters, Kurt (1887-1948) Merz Picture 32A. Cherry Picture (Merzbild 32A. Das Kirschbild), 1921 Collage of cloth, wood, metal, gouache, oil, cut and pasted papers, and ink on cardboard, 36 1/8 x 27 3/4' (91.8 x 70.5 cm). Mr. and Mrs. A. Atwater Kent, Jr. Fund. 27.1954. Schwitters, Kurt (1887-1948) Picture with Basket Ring (Bild mit Korbring), 1938 Assemblage: wood, rattan ring, paper, iron and steel nails on wood, 15 x 11 3/4' (38.1 x 29.8 cm). The Riklis Collection of McCrory Corporation. 1070.1983 Tanguy, Yves (1900-1955) Extinction of Useless Lights (Extinction des lumieres inutiles), 1927 Oil on canvas, 36 1/4 x 25 3/4' (92.1 x 65.4 cm). Purchase. 220.1936. Warhol, Andy (1928-1987) Campbell's Soup Cans, 1962 Synthetic polymer paint on thirty-two canvases, each 20 x 16' (50.8 x 40.6 cm). Gift of Irving Blum; Nelson A. Rockefeller Bequest, gift of Mr. and Mrs. William A.M. Burden, Abby Aldrich Rockefeller Fund, gift of Nina and Gordon Bunshaft in honor of Henry Moore, Lillie P. Bliss Bequest, Philip Johnson Fund, Frances Keech Bequest. Acc. n.: 476.1996.1-32. Steichen, Edward (1879-1973) Self-Portrait with Photographic Paraphernalia (New York, 1929) Gelatin silver print, 9 9/16 x 6 7/8' (24.3 x 17.4 cm). Gift of the photographer. 362.1994.Rietveld, Gerrit (1888-1964) Red and Blue Chair, c. 1918 Wood, painted, height, 34 1/8'; width, 26'; depth, 26 1/2' (86.5 x 66 x 83.8 cm); Seat height: 13' (33 cm). Gift of Philip Johnson. 487.1953 Magritte, Rene' (1898-1967) Portrait (Le portrait), 1935 Oil on canvas, 28 7/8 x 19 7/8' (73,3x50,2 cm.). Gift of Kay Sage Tanguy. 574.1956.Man Ray (1890-1976) Gift (Cadeau), c. 1958 (replica of 1921 original) Painted flatiron with row of thirteen tacks, heads glued to the bottom, 6 1/8 x 3 5/8 x 4 1/2 ' (15,3x9x11,4 cm.). James Thrall Soby Fund. 1966.Picabia, Francis (Martinez Picabia, Francois, 1879-1953) Dada Movement, 1919 Pen and ink on paper, 20 1/8 x 14 1/4 ' (51,1x36,2 cm). Purchase. 285.1937.Duchamp, Marcel (1887-1968) Bicycle Wheel (1951 after lost original of 1913) Assemblage: metal wheel, 25 1/2 " (63,8 cm.) diameter, mounted on painted wood stool 23 3/4 " (60,2 cm) high; overall 50 1/2 x 25 1/2 x 16 5/8" (128,3x63,8x42 cm). The Sidney and Harriet Janis Collection. 595.1967 a-b Ensor, James (1860-1949) Tribulations of St. Anthony (Les tribulations de St. Antoine), 1887 Oil on canvas, 46 3/8 x 66" (117,8x167,6 cm.). Purchase. Acc. n.: 1642.1940.Balla, Giacomo (1871-1958) Speeding Automobile (1912) Oil on wood, 21 7/8 x 27 1/8' (55.6 x 68.9 cm). Purchase. Acc. n.: 271.1949. Picasso, Pablo (1881-1973) The Architect's Table (Paris, early 1912) Oil on canvas, mounted on oval panel, 28 5/8 x 23 1/2 ' (72,6x59,7 cm). The William S. Paley Collection. 697.1971 Picasso, Pablo (1881-1973) Pierrot (Paris, 1918) Oil on canvas, 36 1/2 x 28 3/4' (92.7 x 73 cm). Sam A. Lewisohn Bequest. 12.1952. Mies van der Rohe, Ludwig (1886-1969) Glass Skyscraper. Berlin, 1922. Model (no longer extant). The Mies van der Rohe Archive, gift of the architect. Acc. n.: MI2.Newman, Barnett (1905-1970) Abraham, 1949 Oil on canvas, 6' 10 3/4' x 34 1/2' (210.2 x 87.7 cm). Philip Johnson Fund. 651.1959 Tinguely, Jean (1925-1991) Fragment from 'Homage to New York', 1960 Painted metal, wood, and cloth, 6' 8 1/4' x 29 5/8' x 7' 3 7/8' (203.7 x 75.1 x 223.2 cm). Gift of the artist. 227.1968.Boccioni, Umberto (1882-1916) The Laugh (La risata), 1911 Oil on canvas, 43 3/8 x 57 1/4' (110.2 x 145.4 cm). Gift of Herbert and Nannette Rothschild. Acc. N.: 656.1959.Moholy Nagy, Laszlo (1895-1946) Telephone Picture EM 2 (Telefonbild), 1922 Porcelain enamel on steel, 18 3/4 x 11 7/8' (47.5 x 30.1 cm). Gift of Philip Johnson in Memory of Sibyl Moholy Nagy. 91.1971 . Steichen, Edward (1879-1973) Willa Cather, 1926 Gelatin silver print, 16 3/4 x 13 3/8' (42.5 x 34 cm). Gift of the photographer. 209.1961.Larionov, Michel (1881-1964) Rayonist Composition: Domination of red (1912-13; dated on the painting 1911) Oil on canvas, 20 3/4 x 28 1/2' (52.7 x 72.4 cm). Gift of the artist. 36.1936. Balthus (Klossowski de Rola, Balthasar, 1908-2001) The Street. 1933. Oil on canvas, 6' 4 3/4' x 7' 10 1/2' (195 x 240 cm). James Thrall Soby Bequest. 1200.1979. Siqueiros, David Alfaro (1896-1974) Echo of a Scream, 1937 Enamel on wood, 48 x 36' (121.9 x 91.4 cm). Gift of Edward M. M. Warburg. 633.1939.Riley, Bridget (b. 1931) Fission, 1963 Tempera on composition board, 35 x 34" (88.8 x 86.2 cm). Gift of Philip Johnson. 793.1969. Dove, Arthur G. (1880-1946) Grandmother, 1925 Collage of shingles, needlepoint, page from the Concordance, pressed flowers, and ferns, mounted on cloth-covered wood, 20 x 21 1/4' (50.8 x 54 cm). Gift of Philip L. Goodwin (by exchange). 636.1939.Breton, Andre' (1896-1966) Poem-Object, 1941 Assemblage mounted on wood drawing board: carved wood bust of man, oil lantern, framed photograph, toy boxing gloves, 18 x 21 x 4 3/8' (45.8 x 53.2x 10.9 cm). Kay Sage Tanguy Bequest. Acc. n.: 197.1963.Gabo, Naum (1890-1977) Head of a Woman. (c. 1917-20, after a work of 1916) Construction in celluloid and metal, 24 1/2 x 19 1/4 x 14' (62.2 x 48.9 x 35.4 cm). Purchase. Acc. n.: 397.1938.Duchamp, Marcel (1887-1968) Rotary Demisphere (Precision Optics), Paris, 1925 Motor-driven construction: painted wood demisphere, fitted on black velvet disk, copper collar with plexiglass dome, motor, pulley, and metal stand, 58 1/2 x 25 1/4 x 24' (148.6 x 64.2 x 60.9 cm). Gif. Turrell, James (b. 1943) A Frontal Passage, 1994 Fluorescent light installation, dimensions variable: Museum installation 12' 10' 22' 6' x 34' (391.2 x 685.8 x 1036.3 cm). Douglas S. Cramer, David Geffen, Robert and Meryl Meltzer, Michael and JudyOv. Acconci, Vito (b. 1940) Adjustable Wall Bra, 1990 Plaster, steel, canvas, electrical light bulbs, and audio equipment, overall installation variable: 13' 9' x 17' 4' x 13' 6' (424.1 x 530.8 x 416.5 cm); each cup: 7' 3' x 7' 10 1/2' x 37' (221x240x94 cm). Sid R. Bass Fund and purchase. Acc. n.: 91.1991.Dumas, Marlene (b. 1953) Chlorosis (Love Sick), 1994 Ink, gouache and synthetic polymer paint on paper, each 26 x 19 1/2' (66.2 x 49.5 cm). The Herbert and Nannette Rothschild Memorial Fund in memory of Judith Rothschild. Acc. n.: 720.1996.a-x.. Francis, Sam (1923-1994) Towards Disappearance II, 1958 Oil on canvas, 9' 1/2' x 10' 5 7/8' (275.6 x 319.7 cm). Blanchette Rockefeller Fund. Acc. n.: 100.1976. Holzer, Jenny(b. 1950) Truisms, 1978-87 Photostat, composition: 8' x 40' (243.9 x 101.6 cm). Gift of the artist. Acc. n.: 177.1988. Irwin, Robert (b. 1928) Untitled, 1968 Synthetic polymer paint on aluminum, 60 3/8 (153.2 cm) diameter. Mrs. Sam A. Lewisohn Fund. Acc. n.: 235.1969. Kounellis, Jannis (b. 1936) Untitled (7 x 33), 1959 Tempera and glue on graph paper on canvas, 53 1/8' x 8' 4 1/4' (135 x 255 cm). Purchase. Acc. n.: 134.1984. Long, Richard (b. 1945) Cornish Stone Circle, 1978 Fifty-two stone slabs (Delabole slate). overall diameter: 19' 8 3/8' (600 cm). Gift of Barbara Jakobson and John R. Jakobson, Junior Council and Anonymous Funds. 460.1978.a-zz. Baader, Johannes (1876-1955) The Author of the Book 'Fourteen Letters by Christ' in his Home, c. 1920 Collage of pasted photographs on book page, 8 1/2 x 5 3/4' (21.6 x 14.6 cm). Purchase. Acc. n.: 275.1937. Benglis, Lynda (b. 1941) Victor, 1974 Aluminum screen, cotton bunting, plaster, sprayed zinc, steel and tin, 66 7/8 x 20 1/2 x 13 1/8' (169.8 x 52 x 33.3 cm). Purchased with the aid of funds from the National Endowment for the Arts and anonymous donor. Acc. n.: 372.1975 Sherman, Cindy (b. 1954) Untitled Film Still #21, 1978 Gelatin silver print. 7 1/2 X 9 1/2 (19.1 X 24.2cm). Purchase. Acc. num. 830.1995. Pardo, Jorge (b. 1963) Untitled, 2001 Three screenprints. 21 3/4 X 29 3/4 (55.2 X 75.6cm). Lily Auchincloss Fund. Acc. num. 2512.2001.1-3. Kapoor, Anish (b. 1954) Wounds and Absent Objects, 1998 9 pigment transfer prints. comp: 17 5/8 X 21 1/16 (44.7 X 53.5cm). Jacqueline Brody Fund and Harry Kahn Fund. Acc. num. 343.1998.1-9 Freud, Lucian (1922-) Lord Goodman in his Yellow Pijamas, 1987 Etching, printed in black, with watercolor additions. plate: 12 5/16 X 15 3/4; sheet: 19 X 21 7/8. Miranda Kaiser Fund, Lee and Ann Fensterstock Fund. Acc. num. 220.2002. Paolozzi, Eduardo (1924-2005) Tortured Life (plate, folio 5) from the Illustrated Book'As Is When', 1965 Screenprint, printed in color. comp.: 30 11/16 X 22 1/2; sheet: 37 15/16 X 25 15/16. . Acc. num. 503.1967.3. Rothenberg, Susan (b. 1945) Bone Man, 1986 Mezzotint on wood veneer paper, sheet: 30 x 20 1/8' (76.2 x 51.2 cm); plate: 23 7/8 x 20 1/8'. Publisher & printer: Gemini G.E.L., Los Angeles. Edition: 42. John B. Turner Fund. Acc. n.: 336.1986. Serra Richard (b. 1939) One Ton Prop (House of Cards), 1969 Lead antimony, four plates. each: 48 X 48 X 1(122 X 122 X 2.5cm). Gift of the Grinstein Family. Acc. num. 286.1986.a-d Bartlett, Jennifer (b. 1941) Swimmer Lost at Night (For Tom Hess), 1978 2 silkscreen on baked-enamel-on-steel units, each composed of 20 steel plates 12x12' (30.5x30.5 cm), placed 1' apart, hung diagonally; and 2 oil on canvas panels, each 48 1/2 x 60 1/8' (122.2x152.7 cm Baargeld, J.T. (Alfred Gruenewald, 1892-1927) Beetles, 1920 Pen and ink on tissue paper, 11 1/2 x 9 1/8' (29.2 x 23.2 cm). Purchase. Acc. n.: 276.1937. Scan n.: M0216-7 Agam, Yaakov (b. 1928) Double Metamorphosis II, 1964 Oil on corrugated aluminium, in 11 parts, 8' 10' x 13' 2 1/4' (269.2 x 401.8 cm). Gift of Mr. and Mrs. George M. Jaffin. Acc. n.: 104.1965.a-k. Mies van der Rohe, Ludwig (1886-1969) German Pavillion. Barcelona, International Exhibition, 1928-29 Berliner Bild-Bericht. Acc. n.: MMA_1437_CC. De Maria, Walter (b. 1935) Cage II, 1965 Stainless steel, 7' 1/4' x 14 1/4' x 14 1/4' (216.5 x 36.2 x 36.2 cm). Edition 2/2. Gift of Agnes Gund and Lily Auchincloss. Acc. n.: 210.1993 Lucas, Sarah (b. 1962) Geezer, 2002 Oil, cut-and-pasted printed paper, and pencil on wood, 31 7/8 x 29 1/2' (81 x 74.9 cm). Purchased with funds provided by The Buddy Taub Foundation, Dennis A. Roach, Director. Acc. n.: 8.2003. Tuymans, Luc (b. 1958) Lumumba, 2000 Oil on canvas, 24 1/2 x 18' (62 x 46 cm). Fractional and promised gift of Donald L. Bryant, Jr. Acc. n.: 6.2002 - PERMISSION REQUIRED. Gursky, Andreas (b. 1955) Times Square, New York, 1997 Chromogenic color print, 6' 1' x 8' 2' (185.4 x 248.9 cm). The Family of Man Fund. Fritsch, Katharina (1956-) Black Table with Table Ware, 1985 Wood, paint and plastic, overall 36 3/4 (93.3 cm) high x 59 1/8' (150 cm) diameter. Acquisition from Werner and Elaine Dannheisser. Acc. n.: 881.1996.a-q. Archipenko, Alexander (1887-1964) Gondolier, 1914 Bronze 33 x 11 7/8 x 10 1/8' (83.8 x 30.1 x 25.5 cm) including bronze base. Gift of Frances Archipenko in honor of Alfred H. Barr, Jr. Acc. n.: 1052.1969. Dine, Jim (b. 1935) Five Feet of Colorful Tools, 1962 Oil on unprimed canvas surmounted by a board on which painted tools hang from hooks, 55 5/8 x 60 1/4 x 4 3/8' (141.2 x 152.9 x 11 cm). The Sidney and Harriet Janis Collection. Acc. n.: 587.1967. a-g. Wesselmann, Tom (1931-2004) Mouth, 7 (1966) Oil on shaped canvas, 6' 8 1/4 x 65'. The Sidney and Harriet Janis Collection. Acc. n.: 663.1967. Ernst, Max (1891-1976) The King Playing with the Queen, 1944 (cast 1945) Bronze, 38 1/2' high, 18 3/4 x 20 1/2' at base. Gift of D. and J. de Menil. Acc. n.: 330.1955. Smith, Kiki (b. 1954) Dream (Sueno), 1992 Etching and aquatint on handmade Japanes paper, composition: 23 7/16 x 49 1/4'; sheet: 41 13/16 x 6' 5 1/2'. Publisher and printer: Universal Limited Art Editions, West Islip, NY. Editions: 33. Gift of Emily Fisher Landau. Acc. n.: 21.1993. Mendieta, Ana (1948-1985) Untitled (Facial Cosmetic Variations), January-February, 1972 Four chromogenic color prints, printed 1997, each 19 1/4 x 12 3/4' (48.9 x 32.4 cm). Acquired through the generosity of The Contemporary Arts Council of The Museum of Modern Art, in honor of Barbara Foshay-Miller. Acc. n.: 628.1997.a-dx1-x2. Whiteread, Rachel (b. 1963) Watertower, 1998 Translucent resin, 12' 2' x 9' diameter (370.8 x 274.3 cm). Gift of the Freedman Family in memory of Doris C. and Alan J. Freedman. Acc. n.: 1260.1999.a-b. Koons (20th cent.) Pink Panther, 1988 Porcelain, 41 x 20 1/2 x 19' (104.1 x 52 x 48.2 cm). Gift of Werner and Elaine Dannheisser. Acc. n.: 187.1996. Archipenko, Alexander (1887-1964) Glass on a Table, 1920 Painted wood and plaster, 16 1/8 x 13 x 1 1/4' (41 x 33 x 3.2 cm). Katherine S. Dreier Bequest. Acc. n.:141.1953. Nauman Bruce (b. 1941) Human/ Need/Desire, 1983 Neon tubing and wire with glass tubing suspension frames, 7' 10 3/8' x 70 1/2' x 25 3/4' (239.8 x 179 x 65.4 cm). Gift of Emily and Jerry Spiegel. Acc. n.: 228.1991.a-g. Tatlin, Vladimir (1885-1953) Pamiatnik III Internatsionala (Monument to the Third International) by Nikolaj Punin, 1920 Cover with letterpress illustration on front; 1 letterpress illustration. Page: 11 x 8 5/8' (28 x 21.9 cm). Publisher: Izo NKP, Petersburg. Edition: unknown. Gift of the Judith Rothschild Foundation. Acc. n.: 215.2001.1-2. Bataille Georges (1897-1962) Untitled drawing for 'Soleil Vitre', n.d. Conté crayon and graphite on buff paper, 11 1/2 x 8 3/4' (29.2 x 22.2 cm). Transferred to the Drawings Collection from the Eluard Dausse Collection, The Museum of Modern Art Library. Acc. n.: SC608.1966.1. Bataille Georges (1897-1962) Untitled drawing for Soleil Vitre', n.d. Conté crayon and graphite on buff paper, 11 1/2 x 8 3/4' (29.2 x 22.2 cm). Transferred to the Drawings Collection from the Eluard Dausse Collection, The Museum of Modern Art Library. Acc. n.: SC608.1966.3. Rozanova, Olga (1886-1918) Vzorval' (Explodity), second edition by Aleksei Kruchenykh, 1913 Illustrated book with 17 litographed illustrations by various artists (Natan Altman, Natalia Goncarova, Nikolai Kulbin, Kazimir Malevic and Olga Rozanova), litographed manuscript and rubber stamped text. Page (irreg.): 6 7/8 x 4 5/8' (17.4 x 11.7 cm). Publisher and printer: unknown, St. Petersburg. Edition: 450. Gift of The Judith Rothschild Foundation. Acc. n.: 54.2001.9. Taeuber-Arp, Sophie (1889-1943) Echelonnement desaxe', 1934 Gouache on paper, 13 7/8 x 10 5/8' (35.2 x 27 cm). The Riklis Collection of McCrory Corporation. Acc. n.: 967.1983. Gonzalez, Julio (1876-1942) Standing Figure, c. 1941 Watercolor and ink on paper, 12 1/2 x 9 5/8' (31.8 x 24.3 cm). Gift of the James S. and Marvelle W. Adams Foundation. Acc. n.: 235.1956. Albers, Anni (1899-1994) Design for Wall Hanging, 1926 Gouache and pencil on paper, 13 3/4 x 9 3/8' (34.9 x 23.8 cm). Gift of the designer. Acc. n.: 399.1951. Hamilton, Richard (b. 1922) Interior, 1964 Screenprint, composition: 19 5/16 x 25 1/8' (49.1 x 63.8 cm); sheet: 22 1/4 x 27 7/16' (56 x 69.7 cm). Publisher: Editions Alecto, London. Printer: Kelpra Studio, London. Edition: 4. Dorothy Braude Edinburg Fund. Acc. n.: 168.1965. Kitaj, Ronald B. (1932-2007) The Ohio Gang, 1964 Oil and graphite on canvas, 6' 1/8' x 6' 1/4' (183.1 x 183.5 cm). Philip Johnson Fund. Acc. n.: 109.1965. Ryman, Robert (b. 1930) Untitled, 1965 Oil on linen, 11 1/4 x 11 1/8' (cm 28.4 x 28.2). Gift of Werner and Eliane Dannheisser. Acc.n.: 201.1996. Maar, Dora (Markovitch, Henriette Theodora, 1907-1997) Untitled (man with his head in a manhole cover), c. 1935 Gelatin silver print, 11 3/4 x 9 3/16' (29.8 x 23.4 cm). Robert and Joyce Menschel Fund. Acc. n.: 315.1993. Maar, Dora (Markovitch, Henriette Theodora, 1907-1997) Untitled (woman with coat uplifted by wind), 1930's Gelatin silver print, 10 3/8 x 9 3/8' (26.4 x 23.9 cm). Anonymous Purchase Fund. Acc. n.: 779.1998. Calder, Alexander (1898-1976) Spider, 1939 Painted sheet aluminum, steel rod, and steel wire, 6' 8 1/2' x 7' 4 1/2' x 36 1/2' (203.5 x 224.5 x 92.6 cm). Gift of the artist. Acc. n.: 391.1966.a-c. Blackwell, Tom (b. 1938) Jaffrey, 1976 Oil on canvas, 7'7/8 x 6'1 7/8' (212.8 x

187.3 cm). Mr. and Mrs. Stuart M. Speiser Fund. Acc. n.: 590.1976. Rainer Arnulf (b. 1929) Untitled, 1969-74 Oilstick on gelatin silver print, 23 x 19' (58.4 x 48.4 cm). Gift of Joan and Lester Avnet (by exchange). Acc. n.: 214.1988. Kokoschka, Oskar (1886-1980) Kokoschka, Drama-Komeoedie, 1907 Lithograph 46 1/2 x 30' (118.1 x 76.2 cm) Purchase 343.1966 Moholy Nagy, Laszlo (1895-1946) Bauhausbucher 11, 1931 Gelatin silver print 5 1/4 x 4 1/16' (13.3 x 10.3 cm) Jan Tschichold Collection, Gift of Philip Johnson 775.1999 Tapies, Antoni (b. 1923) Relleu gris sobre negre (Gray Relief on Black), 1959 Latex paint with marble dust on canvas, 6' 4 5/8' x 67' (194.6 x 170 cm). Gift of G. David Thompson. Acc. n.: 13.1961. Mies van der Rohe, Ludwig (1886-1969) MR Armchair, 1927 Chrome-plated steel tubing and leather 31 x 20 7/16 x 32 1/4' (78.7 x 51.9 x 81.9 cm). Gift of Edgar Kaufmann, Jr. Acc.n.: 20.1949. Burden, Chris (b. 1946) Medusa's Head, 1990 Plywood, steel, cement, rock, five gauges model railroad track, and seven scale model trains, 14' (426.7 cm) in diameter. Gift of Sid and Mercedes Bass. Acc. n.: 214.2000.a-iii. Guo-Qiang, Cai (b. 1957) Borrowing Your Enemy's Arrows, 1998 Wood boat, canvas sail, arrows, metal, rope, Chinese flag, and electric fan. Boat approximately 60' x 23' 7' x 7' 6' (152.4 x 720 x 230 cm), arrows approximately 24' (62 cm). Gift of Patricia Phelps de Cisneros in honor of Glenn D. Lowry. Acc. n.: 318.1999. Doesburg, Theo van (1883-1931) Simultaneous Counter-Composition, 1929-30 Oil on canvas, 19 3/4 x 19 5/8' (50.1 x 49.8 cm). The Sidney and Harriet Janis Collection. Acc. n.: 588.1967. Arp, Jean (Arp, Hans, 1888-1966) Arabische Acht (Arabic Eight). Plate 7 from '7 Arpaden von Hans Arp', 1923 One from a portfolio of seven lithographs. Composition: 6 1/8 x 3 7/8' (15,5 x 9,8 cm); sheet: 17 3/4 x 13 3/4' (45.1 x 34.9 cm). Publisher: Merzverlag (Kurt Schwitters), Hannover, Germany. Printer: unknown. Edition: 50. Gift of J. B. Neumann. Acc. n.: 578.1939.2. Calder, Alexander (1898-1976) Untitled, 1939. Painted sheet aluminum and steel wire, 14 5/8 x 9 x 10 7/8' (37.1 x 22.8 x 27.5 cm). Kay Sage Tanguy Bequest. Acc. n.: 1122.1964. Fontana, Lucio (1899-1968) Concetto Spaziale, Attese (Spatial Concept: Expectations), 1960. Slashed canvas and gauze, 39 1/2 x 31 5/8' (100.3 x 80.3 cm). Gift of Philip Johnson. Acc. n.: 508.1970. Salcedo, Doris (b. 1958) Untitled, 1995. Wood, cement, steel, cloth, and leather, 7' 9' x 41' x 19' (236.2 x 104.1 x 48.2 cm). The Norman and Rosita Winston Foundation, Inc. Fund and purchase. Acc. n.: 4.1996. Kippenberger, Martin (1953-1997) Martin, Stand in the Corner and Be Ashamed of Yourself, 1990. Cast aluminum, clothing, and iron plate, 71 1/2 x 29 1/2 x 13 1/2' (181.6 x 74.9 x 34.3 cm). Blanchette Hooker Rockefeller Fund Bequest, Anna Marie and Robert F. Shapiro, Jerry I. Speyer, and Michael and Judy Ovitz Funds. Acc. n.: 525.1992. Hepworth, Barbara (1903-1975) Disks in Echelon, 1935. Padouk wood, 12 1/4 x 19 1/4 x 8 7/8' (31.1 x 49.1 x 22.5 cm). Gift of W. B. Bennet. Acc. n.: 80.1936. Richter, Gerhard (b. 1932) Court Chapel, Dresden (Hofkirche, Dresden), 2000. Oil on canvas, 31 1/2 x 36 5/8' (80 x 93 cm). Promised gift of Donald L. Bryant, Jr. Acc. n.: 2478.2001. Albers, Josef (1888-1976) Lettering Set, 1926-31. Milk glass and painted wood, 24 1/8 x 23 7/8' (61.3 x 60.6 cm). Gift of the designer. Acc. n.: 216.1957. Zittel, Andrea (b. 1965) A-Z Escape Vehicle: Customized by Andrea Zittel, 1996. Exterior: steel, insulation, wood and glass. Interior: colored lights, water, fiberglass, wood, papier-mâché, pebbles and paint, 62' x 7' x 40' (157.5 x 213.3 x 101.6 cm). The Norman and Rosita Winston Foundation, Inc. Fund and an anonymous fund. Acc. n.: 46.1997. Man Ray (1890-1976) Rayograph (spirals of film), 1923. Gelatin silver print, 11 9/16 x 9 1/4' (29.4 x 23.5 cm). Gift of James Thrall Soby. Acc. n.: 116.1941. Mori, Mariko (b. 1967) Star Doll for Parkett No. 54, 1998 Multiple of doll, overall (doll) 10 1/4 x 3 1/8 x 1 9/16' (26 x 8 x 4 cm). Publisher: Parkett, Zuerich. Fabricator: Marmitte, Tokyo. Edition: 99. Linda Barth Goldstein Fund. Acc. n.: 431.1999. Smithson, Robert (1938-1973) Alogon #2, 1966 Acc. n.: 184.1994.a-j (The Museum of Modern Art Archives, IN2030.01). Prince, Richard (b. 1949) Untitled, 1984 and 1990 Pencil and spray paint on printed paper, 40 x 26' (101.5 x 66 cm). Gift of the Robert Lehman Foundation, Inc. Acc. n.: 148.1991. Gilbert & George (Proesch, Gilbert, b. 1943; Passmore, George, b. 1942) Live's, 1984 Black and white photographs, hand-colored with ink and dyes, and aluminum foil, mounted and framed, overall 7' 11 1/2' x 11' 7' (242.7 x 353 cm); each panel frame 23 7/8 x 19 7/8' (60.5 x 50.5 cm). Given anonymously. Acc. n.: 130.1985.a-bb. Installation view of the exhibition 'Douglas Aitken: Sleepwalkers', MoMA, NY, January 16 through February 12, 2007 The Museum of Modern Art Archives, NY. Acc. n.: IN1991.37. Alys, Francis (b. 1959) Untitled, 1994 Oil on canvas and synthetic polymer paint on sheet metal, three panels: small panel by Francis Alys 12 1/2 x 10' (31.8 x 25.4 cm), medium panel by Emilio Rivera 36 x 28 1/8' (91.4 x 71.4 cm), large panel by Juan Garcia 47

1/4 x 36' (120 x 91.4 cm). Gift of Eileen and Peter Norton. Acc. n.: 14.2000.a-c. Gober, Robert (b. 1954) Untitled Leg, 1989-90 Beeswax, cotton, wood, leather, and human hair, 11 3/8 x 7 3/4 x 20' (28.9 x 19.7 x 50.8 cm). Gift of the Dannheisser Foundation. Acc. n.: 172.1996 Flavin, Dan (1933-1996) Pink out of a Corner - To Jasper Johns, 1963 Fluorescent light and metal fixture, 8' x 6' x 5 3/8' (243.8 x 15.2 x 13.6 cm). Gift of Philip Johnson. Acc. n.: 67.1979. Broodthaers, Marcel (1924-1976) Museum-Museum, 1972 Screenprint on two sheets, composition: 33 x 46 1/2' (83.9 x 118.2 cm); sheet (each): 33 x 23 1/4' (83 x 59.1 cm). Publisher: Edition Staeck, Heidelberg, Germany. Printer: Gerhard Steidl, Goettingen, Germany. The Associates Fund. Acc. n.: 240.1991.a-b Man Ray (1890-1976) Untitled (Hand), 1929 Gelatin silver print, 11 5/8 x 8 7/8' (29.7 x 22.6 cm). Gift of James Thrall Soby. Acc. n.: 147.1941 Yuskavage, Lisa (b. 1962) Wrist Corsage, 1996 Oil on linen, 6 x 7' (182.9 x 213.3 cm). Fractional and promised gift of David Teiger. Acc. n.: 332.2004 Barney Matthew (b. 1967) Drawing Restraint 9: Shimenawa, 2005 Chromogenic color print in self-lubricating plastic frame, 43 x 43' (109.2 x 109.2 cm). Gift of Barbara Gladstone. Acc. n.: 580.2007 Orozco, Gabriel (b. 1962) Kytes Tree, 2005 Synthetic polymer paint on canvas, 6' 6 3/4' x 6' 6 3/4' (200 x 200 cm). Purchase and gift of Anna Marie and Robert F. Shapiro and Donald B. Marron. Acc. n.: 981.2005. Rist Pipilotti (b. 1962) Pour Your Body Out (7354 Cubic Meters), 2008 Multichannel video (color, sound), projector enclosures, circular seating element, carpet. Commissioned through the generosity of UBS, the Wallis Annenberg Fund for Innovation in Contemporary Art, Marie-Josee and Henry Kravis, Maja Oeri and Hans Bodenmann, Jerry I. Speyer and Katherine G. Farley, Franz Wassmer, Monique Barbier-Mueller and by Pro Helvetia, Arts Council of Switzerland. Acc. n.: 1180.2008Levine, Sherrie (b. 1947) President Collage: 1, 1979 Cut-and-pasted printed paper on paper, 24 x 18' (61 x 45.7 cm). The Judith Rothschild Foundation Contemporary Drawings Collection Gift. Acc. n.: TR12112.1161. Peyton, Elizabeth (b. 1965) Hockney at the RCA, 1997 Pencil on notebook paper, 13 7/8 x 11' (35.2 x 27.9 cm). The Judith Rothschild Foundation Contemporary Drawings Collection Gift. Acc. n.: TR12112.1695. Kawara, On (b. 1933) I am still alive, 1973 Ballpoint pen on four telegrams, each: 5 7/8 x 8 1/4' (14.9 x 21 cm). The Judith Rothschild Foundation Contemporary Drawings Collection Gift (Purchase, and gift, in part, of The Eileen and Michael Cohen Collection). Acc. n.: TR12112.982.a-d. Currin, John (b. 1962) The Clairvoyant, 2001 Gouache on prepared paper, 11 5/8 x 8 3/8' (29.5 x 21.3 cm). Gift of Frank and Nina Moore in memory of Elaine Dannheisser. Acc. n.: 1356.2001. Viola, Bill (b. 1951) Stations, 1994 Five-channel video (color, sound), five granite slabs, and five projection screens, overall 20' x 50' x 50' (610 x 1525 x 1525 cm). Gift of the Bohen Foundation in honor of Richard E. Oldenburg. Acc. n.: IN1978.3

THE METROPOLITAN MUSEUM OF ART, NEW YORK
Benton, Thomas Hart (1889-1975) July Hay, 1943 Egg tempera, methyl cellulose, and oil on Masonite, 38 x 26 3/4 in. (96.5 x 67.9 cm).George A. Hearn Fund, 1943. Acc.n.: 43.159.1 Brauner Victor (1903-1966) Prelude to a Civilization, 1954 Encaustic, and pen and ink on Masonite, H. 51, W. 79-3/4 inches (129.5 x 202.5 cm.).Jacques and Natasha Gelman Collection, 1998. Acc.n.: 1999.363.13.Photo: Malcom Varon .Dali', Salvador (1904-1989) The Accommodations of Desire, 1929 Oil and cut-and-pasted printed paper on cardboard, 8 3/4 x 13 3/4 in. (22.2 x 34.9 cm).Jacques and Natasha Gelman Collection, 1998. Acc.n.: 1999.363.16.Photo: Malcolm Varon .Galle, Emile (1846-1904) Autumn Crocus Vase, c. 1900 Glass, H. 17-3/8, W. 3-3/4 inches (44.1 x 9.5 cm.) base W. 4-1/2 inches (11.4 cm). Gift of Lloyd and Barbara Macklowe, 1984. Acc.n.: 1984.553 Klee, Paul (1879-1940) Hammamet with Its Mosque, 1914 Watercolor and pencil on paper, H. 8-1/8, W. 7-5/8 inches (20.6 x 19.4 cm.).The Berggruen Klee Collection, 1984. Acc.n.: 1984.315.4. Klee, Paul (1879-1940) Static-Dynamic Gradation, 1923 Oil and gouache on paper, bordered with gouache, watercolor, and ink, H. 15, W. 10-1/4 inches (38.1 x 26.1 cm.).The Berggruen Klee Collection, 1987. Acc.n.: 1987.455.12 Kline, Franz (1910-1962) Black Reflections, 1959 Oil and pasted paper on paper, mounted on Masonite, H. 19, W. 19-3/8 inches (48.3 x 49.2 cm.). Gift of Mr. and Mrs. Norman Schneider, 1964. Acc.n.: 64.146 Leger, Fernand (1881-1955) Woman with a Cat, 1921 Oil on canvas, H. 51-3/8, W. 35-1/4 in. (130.5 x 89.5 cm.). Gift of Florene M. Schoenborn, 1994. Acc.n.: 1994.486 Pollock, Jackson (1912-1956) Autumn Rhythm

(Number 30), 1950 Enamel on canvas, H. 105, W. 207 in. (266.7 x 525.8 cm).George A. Hearn Fund, 1957. Acc.n.: 57.92 Soutine, Chaim (1893-1943) Madeleine Castaing, c. 1929 Oil on canvas, H. 39-3/8, W. 28-7/8 inches (100 x 73.3 cm.).Bequest of Miss Adelaide Milton de Groot (1876-1967), 1967. Acc.n.: 67.187.107 Woodman, Francesca (1958-1981) Untitled, c. 1980 Sepia print 187 x 93.4 cm (73 5/8 x 36 3/4 in.). Purchase, The Herbert and Nannette Rothschild Fund Gift, in memory of Judith Rothschild, 1996. Acc.n.: 1996.322 Balthus (Klossowski de Rola, Balthasar 1908-2001) The Mountain, 1937 Oil on canvas, H. 98, W. 144 in. (248.9 x 365.8 cm). Purchase, Gifts of Mr. and Mrs. Nate B. Spingold and Nathan Cummings, Rogers Fund and The Alfred N. Punnett Endowment Fund, by exchange, and Harris Brisbane Dick Fund, 1982. Acc.n.: 1982.530 Delvaux, Paul (1897-1994) The Great Sirens, 1947 Oil on Masonite, H. 79-1/2, W. 112-1/2 inches (305 x 203 cm.). Gift of Julian J. Aberbach, 1979. Acc.n.: 1979.356 Dix, Otto (1891-1969) The Businessman Max Roesberg, Dresden, 1922 Oil on canvas, 37 x 25 in. (94 x 63.5 cm). Purchase, Lila Acheson Wallace Gift, 1992. Acc.n.: 1992.146 Krasner, Lee (1908-1984) Night Creatures, 1965 Acrylic on paper, 30 x 42 1/2 in. (76.2 x 108 cm). Inscribed: (L.L.): Lee Krasner 1 65. Gift of Robert and Sarah W. Miller, in honor of Lee Krasner, 1995. Acc.n.: 1995.595 Lalique, Rene' (1860-1945) Necklace, c. 1900 Gold, enamel, Australian opal, Siberian amethysts, Overall diam. 9-1/2 in. (24.1 cm) 9 large pendants: H. 2-3/4, W. 2-1/4 in. (7 x 5.7 cm) 9 small pendants: H. 1-3/8, W. 1-1/4 in (3.5 x 3.2 cm). Gift of Lillian Nassau, 1985. Acc.n.: 1985.114 Matta-Clark Gordon (1943-1978) Splitting, 1974 Chromogenic prints mounted on board, 101.6 x 76.2 cm (40 x 30 in.). Purchase, The Horace W. Goldsmith Foundation Gift, 1992. Acc.n.: 1992.5067. Rothko, Mark (1903-1970) No. 13 (White, Red on Yellow), 1958 Oil and acrylic with powdered pigments on canvas, 95 3/8 x 81 3/8 in. (242.3 x 206.7 cm). Gift of The Mark Rothko Foundation Inc. 1985. Acc.n.: 1985.63.5.Photo Lynton Gardiner. Smith, Tony (1912-1980) Amaryllis, 1965 Painted steel, 135 x 128 x 90 in. (342.9 x 325.1 x 228.6 cm). Anonymous Gift, 1986. Acc.n.: 1986.432ab Tanguy, Yves (1900-1955) The Satin Tuning Fork, 1940 Oil on canvas, H. 39, W. 32 inches (99 x 81.3 cm.).Jacques and Natasha Gelman Collection, 1998. Acc.n.: 1999.363.80.Photo: Malcom Varon .Pascin, Jules (1885-1930) Pierre Mac Orlan, 1924 Oil on canvas, H. 36-1/4, W. 28-3/4 inches (92.1 x 73 cm.) . The Mr. and Mrs. Klaus G. Perls Collection, 1997. Inv. 1997.149.8 Miro', Joan (1893-1983) Women, Birds, and a Star 1949 Oil on canvas, 1949. Jacques and Natasha Gelman Collection, 1998. Inv.1999.363.55Tiffany Louis Comfort (1848-1933) Vase, ca. 1903. (Manufacturer: Tiffany Furnaces) Favrile glass, H. 11 3/16 in. (28.4 cm). Gift of Louis Comfort Tiffany Foundation, 1951. Acc.n. 51.121.8 Klein, Yves (1928-1962); Shunk, Harry (1924-2006); Kender Janos (1937-1983) Leap into the Void, 1960 Gelatin silver print, 10 3/16 x 7 7/8' (25.9 x 20 cm). Purchase, The Horace W. Goldsmith Foundation Gift, through Joyce and Robert Menschel, 1992 (1992.5112) Freud, Lucian (1922-) Naked Man Back View. 1991-92 Oil on canvas. H. 72-1/4, W. 54-1/8 inches (183.5 x 137.5 cm.). Purchase, Lila Acheson Wallace Gift, 1993.